2007 AT-A-GLANCE

General Income T...

D1234170

Tax Rates	
Ordinary Income Top Rate	
Regular Capital Gain Top Rate	

Standard Deduction	
Joint Returns and Surviving Spouse	$10,700
Heads of Households	$7,850
Single Individuals	$5,350
Married Filing Separate	$5,350
Dependent	$850, or
	$300 plus earned income, if greater
Aged and Blind - Unmarried and not Surviving Spouse	$1,300 each
Aged and Blind - Other	$1,050 each

Overall Limitation on Itemized Deductions	
Married Filing Separate	$78,200
Other	$156,400

Personal Exemption ($3,400) Phaseout	
Joint Returns and Surviving Spouse	$234,600 - $357,100
Heads of Households	$195,500 - $318,000
Single Individuals	$156,400 - $278,900
Married Filing Separate	$117,300 - $178,550

Kiddie Tax	
Amount	$850
Alternative Minimum Tax Exemption	$6,300 plus earned income

Child Tax Credit	
Amount	$1,000
Refundable Limit	$11,750

Hope Scholarship Credit	
100% Amount	$1,100
50% Amount	$1,100

Hope and Lifetime Learning Credit Phaseout	
Joint return	$94,000
Other	$47,000

U.S. Savings Bond Income Exclusion for Qualified Higher Education Expenses Phaseout	
Joint return	$98,400 - $128,400
Other	$65,600 - $80,600

The A Unit of Highline Media
National Underwriter Company
The Leader in Insurance and Financial Services Information

©2007, The National Underwriter Company

Eligible Long-Term Care

Attained Age in Year	Limitation on Premiums
40 or Less	$290
41 to 50	$550
51 to 60	$1,110
61 to 70	$2,950
More than 70	$3,680
Per Diem Limitation For LTC Benefits	$260

Health/Archer Medical Savings Accounts

Coverage	Minimum Deductible	Maximum Deduction	Out-of-Pocket
Self-only	$1,100/$1,900	$2,850/$2,850	$5,500/$3,750
Family	$2,200/$3,750	$5,650/$5,650	$11,000/$6,900

Employee Benefit Limits

Defined Benefit Plans	$180,000
Defined Contribution Plans	$45,000 or 100% of pay
Elective Deferral Limit for 401(k) Plans, SAR-SEPs, and TSAs	$15,500
Catch-up for 401(k) Plans, SAR-SEPs, and TSAs	$5,000
Elective Deferral Limit for SIMPLE IRAs and SIMPLE 401(k) Plans	$10,500
Catch-up for SIMPLE IRAs and SIMPLE 401(k) Plans	$2,500
Elective Deferral Limit for 457 Plans	$15,500
Minimum Compensation Amount for SEPs	$500
Maximum Compensation for VEBAs, SEPs, TSAs, Qualified Plans	$225,000
Highly Compensated Employee Definition Limit	$100,000
ESOP Payout Limits	$180,000, $915,000
Contribution Limit for Traditional & Roth IRAs	$4,000
Catch-up for Traditional & Roth IRAs	$1,000

Estate Planning Amounts

Top Gift and Estate (and GST) Tax Rate	45%
Gift (and GST) Tax Annual Exclusion	$12,000
Annual Exclusion: Non-U.S. Spouse	$125,000
Gift Tax Unified Credit (shelters)	$345,800 ($1,000,000)
Estate Tax Unified Credit (shelters)	$780,800 ($2,000,000)
State Death Tax	Deduction
Estate Tax Deferral: Closely Held Business	$562,500
Special Use Valuation Limitation	$940,000
Qualified Conservation Easement Exclusion	$500,000
GST Exemption	$2,000,000

Social Security Amounts

OASDI - Earnings Base	$97,500
Rate	6.20%
Employer and Employee - Max Tax (each)	$6,045
Self-Employed - Max Tax	$12,090
HI (Medicare) Rate	1.45%
Cost of Living Benefit Increase	3.3%
Quarter of Coverage Earnings	$1,000
Earnings Test - Under NRA (normal retirement age) All of 2007	$12,960
Reach NRA During 2007	$34,440

Year After Year, Rules Change.
Strategies Change.
Even Solar Systems Change.

Do You Know What You're Missing?

See reverse for details

QTY	ITEM DESCRIPTION	PRODUCT #	RETAIL 1-9	SALE PRICE 10 OR MORE	TOTAL PRICE
	2007 Tax Facts Complete Power Combo[2]	TFBPC07	$164.90	CALL	
	2007 Tax Facts on Insurance & Employee Benefits	2920007	$47.95	$43.16 (10+)	
	2007 Field Guide to Estate Planning, Business Planning, & EB	1790007	$44.95	$40.46 (10+)	
	2007 Tax Facts on Investments	2930007	$47.95	$43.16 (10+)	
	2007 Field Guide to Financial Planning	1780007	$44.95	$40.46 (10+)	
	2007 Benefits Facts	6030007	$59.95	$53.96 (10+)	
	2007 ERISA Facts	1170007	$44.95	$40.46 (10+)	
	2007 Social Security & Medicare Kit	5860007	$49.90	$44.91 (10+)	
	2007 Social Security Source Book	2860007	$27.95	$25.16 (10+)	
	2007 All About Medicare	1460007	$21.95	$19.76 (10+)	
	2007 Social Security Slide-O-Scope & Planner Set (set consists of 5)	2810007	$27.95	$25.16 (10+)	
	2007 Medicare Planner Set (set consists of 5)	1710007	$13.95	$12.56 (10+)	

Sales Tax: Residents of CA, CT, DC, FL, GA, IL, KS, KY, MI, NJ, NY, OH, PA, TX and WA must add appropriate sales tax

SUBTOTAL $ _____

Shipping & Handling (see chart) $ _____

ORDER TOTAL $ _____

Promo Code: BCARD

Offer Ends 10/30/07.

Discounts are based on a minimum purchase of the same
title/product number. If you do not meet the minimum quantity to
qualify for the printed discount, you will be invoiced the retail price.

☐ Invoice Me   ☐ Call Me

Company _____

Name _____ Title _____

Phone ( ) _____ E-mail _____

Fax ( ) _____

Address _____

City _____ State _____ Zip _____

TAX FACTS
Series

2007

TAX FACTS
On Investments

www.TaxFactsOnline.com

Stocks

Bonds

Options

Futures

Mutual Funds

Exchange-Traded Funds

Hedge Funds

Real Estate

Oil & Gas

Gold

Deborah A. Miner, J.D., CLU, ChFC, Editorial Director

William J. Wagner, J.D., LL.M., CLU, Associate Editor

Joseph F. Stenken, J.D., CLU, ChFC, Assistant Editor

Sonya E. King, J.D., LL.M., Assistant Editor

John H. Fenton, J.D., M.S.B.A., Staff Writer

Connie L. Jump, Supervisor, Editorial Services

Patti O'Leary, Editorial Assistant

Always Something NU to Discover

1-800-543-0874
www.NUCOstore.com

2007 Edition

Tax Facts on Investments (formerly *Tax Facts 2*) is published annually by the Professional Publishing Division of The National Underwriter Company. This edition reflects selected pertinent legislation, regulations, rulings and court decisions as of January 1, 2007. For the latest developments throughout the year, check out www.TaxFactsOnline.com.

Circular 230 Notice – The content in this publication is not intended or written to be used, and it cannot be used, for the purposes of avoiding U.S. tax penalties.

ISBN 978-0-87218-901-0
ISSN 0739-6619

The National Underwriter Company
P.O. Box 14367, Cincinnati, Ohio 45250-0367

Printed in U.S.A.

TABLE OF CONTENTS

Page

Introduction vii
Finding Aids vii
About the Citations.. vii
Planning Point Contributors viii
Abbreviations ix
Tax Facts Navigator.. xi

Part I: Federal Income Tax on Investments

	Q	Q	Q
Stocks			**1001-1041**
Dividends		1001-1016	
General	1001		
Dividends Paid In Cash or Property..........................	1002-1007		
Stock Dividends	1008-1012		
Stock Splits	1013		
Return of Capital Distributions................................	1014		
Dividend Reinvestment Plans	1015-1016		
Sale or Exchange	1017-1031		
General...	1017-1020		
Short Sales..	1021-1028		
Wash Sales..	1029-1031		
Worthless Securities	1032		
Stock Warrants	1033-1035		
Incentive Stock Options....................................	1036-1041		
Options..			**1042-1071**
Generally...	1042-1045		
Equity Options..	1046-1067		
Stock Options...	1047-1066		
Other Equity Options	1067		
Nonequity Options...	1068-1069		
Option Spread Transactions	1070-1071		
Futures			**1072-1076**
Securities Futures Contracts....................................	1072-1073		
Section 1256 Contracts	1074-1076		
Straddles...			**1077-1084**
Conversion Transactions			**1085-1086**
Constructive Sales Of Appreciated Financial Positions			**1087-1089**
Gains From Constructive Ownership Transactions........................			**1090-1091**
Bonds			**1092-1153**
Short-Term Taxable Obligations (Maturities One Year or Less).........	1092-1097		
Treasury Bills...	1092-1094		
Short-Term Corporate Obligations.................	1095-1097		
Treasury Bonds and Notes......................................	1098-1101		
Corporate Bonds	1102-1106		
Inflation-Indexed Bonds	1107-1108		
Market Discount	1109-1115		
Disposition	1111-1115		
Original Issue Discount...	1116-1119		
Bond Premium	1120-1122		
Municipal Bonds	1123-1132		

	Q	Q	Q
Bonds Traded "Flat"			1133
Zero Coupon Bonds			1134
Stripped Bonds			1135-1138
United States Savings Bonds			1139-1144
Mortgage Backed Securities			1145-1148
Asset Backed Securities			1149-1150
Registration Requirement			1151-1152
Structured Products			1153
Financial Institutions			**1154-1160**
General			1154-1160
Mutual Funds, Unit Trusts, Reits			**1161-1181**
Mutual Funds			1161-1177
Generally		1161-1172	
Money Market Funds		1173-1174	
Closed-End Funds		1175	
Exchange-Traded Funds		1176	
Hedge Funds		1177	
Unit Trusts			1178
Real Estate Investment Trusts			1179-1181
Precious Metals And Collectibles			**1182-1188**
Precious Metals			1182-1184
Collectibles			1185-1188
Limited Partnerships			**1189-1217**
Publicly Traded Limited Partnerships			1189
Limited Partnerships Not Taxed as Corporations			1190-1197
Deductions			1198-1200
Cash Distributions			1201
Self-employment Tax			1202
Sale, Exchange or Liquidation of Partnership Interest			1203-1208
Allocation of Distributive Share		1203	
Sale Proceeds		1204-1205	
Purchaser		1206-1207	
Cash Liquidation of Partnership Interest		1208	
Gift of Partnership Interest			1209-1212
Donor		1209-1211	
Donee		1212	
Death of a Partner			1213-1215
Adjustment of Partnership Basis			1216
Partnership Anti-abuse Rule			1217
S Corporations			**1218**
Real Estate			**1219-1239**
At Risk Limitation			1221
Passive Loss Rule			1222
Vacant Land			1223-1224
Generally		1223	
Development and Subdivision		1224	
Vacation Home			1225
Low-Income Housing			1226-1227
Old Buildings and Certified Historic Structures			1228-1229
Deferred Rent			1230
Demolition			1231
Sale			1232-1236
Seller Financing		1236	
Exchange			1237-1238
Sale of Personal Residence			1239

	Q	Q	Q
Oil And Gas			**1240-1263**
Generally	1240-1247		
Intangible Drilling Costs...........................	1248-1251		
Depletion..	1252-1261		
Enhanced Oil Recovery Credit	1262		
Tax Preferences..................................	1263		
Equipment Leasing..			**1264-1278**
General..	1264-1267		
Investment Tax Credit............................	1268		
Deductions	1269-1275		
Depreciation	1269-1271		
Interest............................	1272		
Expense s...........................	1273		
At Risk Limitation	1274		
Passive Loss Rule...................	1275		
Deferred Rent....................................	1276		
Disposition of Equipment	1277		
Alternative Minimum Tax..........................	1278		
Cattle			**1279-1284**
Cattle Feeding	1279		
Breeding Cattle	1280-1284		
Generally	1280		
Deductions	1281-1282		
Sale Or Disposition Of Cattle.......	1283		
Alternative Minimum Tax...........	1284		
Limitation On Loss Deductions			**1285-1300**
At Risk	1285-1291		
Passive Loss Rule	1292-1299		
Hobby Loss Rule..................................	1300		
Deduction Of Interest And Expenses			**1301-1314**
Interest	1301-1309		
Generally	1301		
Personal Interest	1302		
Qualified Residence Interest........	1303		
Investment Interest.................	1304-1308		
Interest on Education Loans	1309		
Expenses...	1310-1314		
Charitable Gifts			**1315-1341**
General..	1315-1319		
Deduction Limits	1320-1324		
Bargain Sales	1325		
Property Subject To A Liability.....................	1326		
Partial Interests..................................	1327-1339		
General............................	1327		
Charitable Remainder Trusts........	1328-1336		
Charitable Lead Trusts	1337-1338		
Conservation and Facade Easements...	1339		
Partnership Interest	1340		
Charitable IRA Rollover	1341		

Part II: General Federal Income Taxation of Individuals

General Rules..			**1400-1442**
Filing Requirements	1400-1401		
Tax Year...	1402		
Calculating the Tax...............................	1403		

	Q	Q	Q

Gross Income 1404-1422
Adjusted Gross Income 1423-1424
Exemptions and Deductions from Adjusted Gross Income 1425-1430
   Deductions 1427-1430
Standard Deduction 1431
Rates 1432-1435
Credits 1436-1439
Alternative Minimum Tax 1440
Social Security Taxes 1441-1442
Community Property **1443-1446**
Divorce **1447-1448**
Property Settlement 1447-1448
Trusts And Estates **1449-1450**

Part III: Federal Transfer Taxes on Investments

Estate Tax **1500-1508**
General 1500
Gross Estate 1501-1504
Exclusion 1505
Deductions 1506
Credits 1507
Filing and Payment 1508
Generation-Skipping Transfer Tax **1509-1516**
Gift Tax **1517-1534**
General 1517-1518
Complete Gift 1519
Disclaimers 1520
Interest-free and Bargain Rate Loans 1521
Forgiveness of Debt 1522
Income Tax Exempt Obligations 1523
Joint Ownership 1524
Net Gifts 1525
Uniform Gifts to Minors Act 1526
Education Savings Account 1527
Qualified Tuition Program 1528
Split Gifts 1529
Exclusions 1530
Deductions 1531-1532
Unified Credit 1533
Filing and Payment 1534
Valuation **1535-1553**
General 1535-1548
Chapter 14 Special Valuation Rules 1549-1553

Appendices and Tables

Income Tax Tables .... Appendix A
Transfer Tax Tables ....Appendix B
Valuation Tables .... Appendix C
Property That Can Be Given Under Uniform Gifts to Minors Act (by state) ....Appendix D
Donee's Age When Custodianship Established Under UGMA or UTMA Ends.. Appendix D
States Authorizing Durable Power of Attorney .... Appendix E
Ages of Majority in the Various States ....Appendix F
Tax Exempt Equivalents ....Appendix G
Table of Cases .... Page 731
Numerical Finding List .... Page 737
Table of IRC Sections Cited .... Page 745
Index .... **Page 763**

INTRODUCTION

It is the primary purpose of this book to answer federal tax questions individual investors ask themselves and their advisers about their investments. The answers have been limited to individual investors who are resident United States citizens, who pay taxes on a cash basis, and who use a calendar tax year. Anyone using the book should understand that stocks, bonds, etc., held, not as investments but for other purposes, such as for sale to others, will be subject to very different rules in many situations. It is not the purpose of this book to tell a reader how to evaluate any specific investment opportunity or how to make investment decisions. Nor is it the purpose of this book to give legal advice.

FINDING AIDS

To help you locate specific tax information quickly, a subject matter index, "Numerical Finding List," "Table of Cases," and "Table of IRC Sections Cited" are included in the back of the book. All references are to Q numbers.

ABOUT THE CITATIONS

Many sources are cited as authority for statements in this book. Knowing something about some of these sources helps one evaluate the significance of a statement. The *Internal Revenue Code* and *valid uncodified tax legislation* are law. *Final Treasury regulations* state the interpretation the IRS will use in enforcing the law and have the effect of law if they are not inconsistent with the statutes. *Temporary regulations* are strong authority. *Proposed regulations* are generally considered to be the partisan opinions of the IRS and not to bind the IRS or anyone else. *Revenue Rulings* state the interpretation the IRS will use in applying the law to a particular set of facts. They can be revoked without prior notice but generally revocation is not retroactive. The weight given to *Revenue Rulings* by courts varies. While it is not clear, it seems that *Notices* and *Announcements* bind the IRS to the same extent *Revenue Rulings* do. *Letter Rulings* (including *TAMs*) and *Special Rulings* are only uncertain indications of one line of reasoning at IRS. IRS is not bound to follow them with respect to third parties or future events in a continuing transaction. *Letter Rulings* are not precedent, but courts have considered them in reaching decisions. The IRS believes that *GCMs* cannot be used as precedent. *IRs* and *TIRs* are intended to state an official IRS position. All courts and the IRS follow *Supreme Court decisions*. District courts within a circuit must follow a decision of a court of appeals if the *Tax Court's* decision in a particular case would be appealable to that circuit. Neither the IRS nor any court other than the issuing court is bound to follow a *district court, Tax Court,* or *Court of Federal Claims decision*, although federal courts are strongly influenced by decisions of other federal courts. Tax Court summary opinions are issued in matters involving $50,000 or less and have no precedential value, but may indicate the line of reasoning the Tax Court would follow in a particular situation.

TAX FACTS ON INSURANCE & EMPLOYEE BENEFITS (FORMERLY TAX FACTS 1)

Tax Facts on Insurance & Employee Benefits covers the federal income, estate and gift taxation of annuities, life insurance, health insurance, individual retirement accounts (IRAs), pension and profit sharing plans (including 401(k) plans), ESOPs, nonqualified deferred compensation plans, tax sheltered annuities for teachers and employees of certain tax exempt organizations, rollovers, cafeteria plans, VEBAs, and business continuation arrangements. It includes actuarial tables for valuing annuities, remainder interests and life estates, and tables reflecting income tax and estate and gift tax rates. *Tax Facts on Insurance & Employee Benefits* rounds out the total financial planning picture. To order, call toll-free 1-800-543-0874 or visit www.NUCOStore.com.

PLANNING POINT CONTRIBUTORS

Gregory W. Baker, J.D., CFP®, CAP, is Senior Vice President of Legal Services for Renaissance, the nation's leading third-party administrator of charitable gifts. For the past 18 years, he has provided trust, tax and philanthropic financial planning advice to over 4,000 attorneys and 7,000 financial planners in all 50 states regarding more than 14,000 charitable remainder trusts, more than 800 charitable lead trusts, and numerous foundations, charitable gift annuities and donor-advised funds. Baker's advice has helped advisors close cases for their high net worth clients in the areas of charitable, investment, retirement, gift, estate and tax planning. Baker is currently an Advisory Board Member of the Chartered Advisor in Philanthropy designation at the American College, member of the Financial Planning Association, National Committee on Planned Giving and the Indiana Bar. Baker was previously VP, Charitable Fiduciary Risk Manager for the Merrill Lynch Center for Philanthropy & Nonprofit Management in Princeton, NJ. Baker speaks at national and local conferences for professional advisors, high net worth clients and charities regarding charitable gift planning, asset-allocation, investment modeling and tax issues.

Ted R. Batson, Jr., MBA, CPA, is Senior Vice President of Professional Services for Renaissance, the nation's leading third-party administrator of charitable gifts. Since his employment in 1993, Batson has developed a wealth of practical, hands-on experience in dealing with complex issues related to the creative use of unmarketable and unusual assets to fund charitable gifts. He routinely consults with the more than 2,000 attorneys, CPAs and financial service professionals who look to Renaissance for case assistance. Batson has spoken to numerous groups regarding charitable planning and has been published in several professional publications. Batson is a member of the American Institute of Certified Public Accountants (AICPA) and the Indiana CPA Society. He is a graduate of Asbury College (BA in computer science) and Indiana University (MBA in accounting).

Robert S. Keebler, CPA, MST, is a partner with Virchow, Krause & Company, LLP and chair of the Virchow, Krause Estate and Financial Planning Group. His practice includes family wealth transfer and preservation planning, charitable giving, retirement distribution planning, taxation of securities and investments, and estate administration. Mr. Keebler is nationally recognized as an expert in retirement planning and works collaboratively with other experts on academic reviews and papers, and client matters. He is also a frequent speaker for legal, accounting, insurance and financial planning groups throughout the United States at seminars and conferences on advanced IRA distribution strategies, estate planning and trust administration topics.

ABBREVIATIONS

Acq. (Nonacq.)	Commissioner's acquiescence (nonacquiescence) in decision
AFTR	American Federal Tax Reports (Prentice-Hall, early decisions)
AFTR2d	American Federal Tax Reports (Prentice-Hall, second series)
AJCA 2004	American Jobs Creation Act of 2004
AOD	Action on Decision
BTA	Board of Tax Appeals decisions (now Tax Court)
BTA Memo	Board of Tax Appeals memorandum decisions
CA or Cir.	United States Court of Appeals
CB	Cumulative Bulletin of Internal Revenue Service
CCA	Chief Counsel Advice
CFR	Code of Federal Regulations
Cl. Ct.	U.S. Claims Court (designated U.S. Court of Federal Claims in 1992)
CRTRA 2000	Community Renewal Tax Relief Act of 2000
Ct. Cl.	Court of Claims (designated U.S. Claims Court in 1982)
EGTRRA 2001	Economic Growth and Tax Relief Reconciliation Act of 2001
ERTA	Economic Recovery Tax Act of 1981
EUCA '91	Emergency Unemployment Compensation Act of 1991
Fed.	Federal Reporter (early decisions)
Fed. Cl.	U.S. Court of Federal Claims
Fed. Reg.	Federal Register
F.2d	Federal Reporter, second series (later decisions of U.S. Court of Appeals to Mid-1993)
F.3rd	Federal Reporter, third series (decisions of U.S. Court of Appeals since Mid-1993)
F. Supp.	Federal Supplement (decisions of U.S. District Court)
FS	Fact Sheet
FSA	Field Service Advice
GCM	General Counsel Memorandum (IRS)
General Explanation	General Explanation of the revenue provisions (of a particular Act) by the Joint Committee on Taxation
GOZA 2005	Gulf Opportunity Zone Act of 2005
HIPAA '96	Health Insurance Portability and Accountability Act
INFO	IRS Information Letter
IR	Internal Revenue News Release
IRB	Internal Revenue Bulletin of Internal Revenue Service
IRC	Internal Revenue Code
IRS	Internal Revenue Service
IRSRRA '98	IRS Restructuring and Reform Act of 1998
ITCA	Installment Tax Correction Act of 2000
JCWAA	Job Creation and Worker Assistance Act of 2002
JGTRRA 2003	Jobs and Growth Tax Relief Reconciliation Act of 2003
Let. Rul.	Letter Ruling (issued by IRS)
MFTRA	Military Family Tax Relief Act of 2003
OBRA	Omnibus Budget Reconciliation Act of (year of enactment)
P.L.	Public Law
PPA 2006	Pension Protection Act of 2006

Prop. Reg.	Proposed Regulation
RA '87	Revenue Act of 1987
Rev. Proc.	Revenue Procedure (issued by IRS)
Rev. Rul.	Revenue Ruling (issued by IRS)
SBJPA '96	Small Business Job Protection Act of 1996
SCA	Service Center Advice
TAM	Technical Advice Memorandum (IRS)
TAMRA '88	Technical and Miscellaneous Revenue Act of 1988
TC	Tax Court (official reports)
TC Memo	Tax Court memorandum decisions (official reports)
TC Supp.	Tax Court Summary Opinion (unofficial)
T.D.	Treasury Decision
TEFRA	Tax Equity and Fiscal Responsibility Act of 1982
TIPRA 2005	Tax Increase Prevention and Reconciliation Act of 2005
TIR	Technical Information Release (from the IRS)
TRA	Tax Reform Act of (year of enactment)
TRA '97	Taxpayer Relief Act of 1997
TRHCA 2006	Tax Relief and Health Care Act of 2006
TTCA 2005	Tax Technical Corrections Act of 2005
TTREA '98	Tax and Trade Relief Extension Act of 1998
US	United States Supreme Court decisions
USTC	United States Tax Cases (Commerce Clearing House)
VTTRA 2001	Victims of Terrorism Tax Relief Act of 2001
WFTRA 2004	Working Families Tax Relief Act of 2004

TAX FACTS NAVIGATORS

AMT NAVIGATOR

- The alternative minimum tax (AMT) is discussed generally in [Q 1440].

- How mutual fund dividends are treated for purposes of the AMT is covered in [Q 1169].

- How incentive stock options are treated for purposes of the AMT is discussed at the end of [Q 1037] and [Q 1039].

- How tax-exempt interest of municipal bonds is treated for purposes of the AMT is discussed in [Q 1124].

- Whether the dividends of real estate investment trusts are a preference item for purposes of the AMT is covered in [Q 1180].

- The tax preferences that apply to investments in oil and gas properties are covered in [Q 1263].

- How an equipment leasing program is treated for purposes of the AMT is discussed in [Q 1278].

- The adjustments and preferences of a cattle breeding program are covered in [Q 1284].

CHARITABLE NAVIGATOR

- What documentation is required to deduct a gift? [Q 1318]

- What percentage limits generally apply to deductions for charitable contributions? [Q 1320]

- What documentation is required to claim a deduction for a car donation? [Q 1317]

- What is "fair market value"? How is fair market value determined? [Q 1316]

- What planning goals can be achieved with charitable remainder trusts? [Q 1328]

- What rules must a charitable remainder annuity trust (CRAT) follow? [Q 1330]

- What rules must a charitable remainder unitrust (CRUT) follow? [Q 1331]

- How are distributions from charitable remainder trusts taxed? [Q 1335]

- How does a charitable lead trust differ from a charitable remainder trust? [Q 1337]

- What are donor advised funds? How are they currently viewed by the IRS? [Q 1333]

- Are gifts to private foundations subject to any special deduction limits? [Q 1324]

- What special rules apply to conservation easement donations? [Q 1339]

- Are donations of art subject to any special deduction limits? [Q 1323]

CONSTRUCTIVE SALE NAVIGATOR

- Taxpayers must recognize gain (but may not recognize losses) upon any "constructive sale" of an "appreciated financial position" in any stock, debt instrument, or partnership interest. See, generally, [Q 1087] to [Q 1089].

- An "appreciated financial position" is any interest in a stock, debt instrument, or partnership on which there would a gain if the interest were sold, assigned, or otherwise terminated at its fair market value. [Q 1087].

- A "constructive sale" occurs where a taxpayer has an "appreciated financial position" and enters into a "short sale" [Q 1021], a "futures contract" or "forward contract" [Q 1074], or an "offsetting notional principal contract" [Q 1089] with respect to the "appreciated financial position" or "substantially identical property" [Q 1023].

- In a "short sale" an individual contracts to borrow and then sell stock or other securities belonging to someone else. In a short sale "against the box," the seller already owns the same or substantially identical securities, but chooses to borrow the necessary shares rather than deliver his own. If the seller's own shares are an "appreciated financial position," a sale short against the box will constitute a constructive sale. [Q 1021].

- "Futures contracts" or "forward contracts" are contracts to purchase or sell a particular commodity at a specified time for a specified price. Futures contracts generally require delivery of the property. Forward contracts are settled only in cash. Entering into a future or forward contract to sell property that is the same as or substantially identical to an appreciated financial position will constitute a constructive sale. [Q 1074].

DIVORCE NAVIGATOR

Basics:

- In general, the spouse paying *alimony* (spousal support) gets to claim the deduction for the payments, and the spouse receiving alimony has to include the payments in his or her income. [Q 1448]

- *Property transfers* between former spouses are generally not a taxable event (i.e., these transactions generally do not result in recognition of gain or loss). The primary exception is when the timing rule is not met. The basis of the transferring spouse is ordinarily "carried over" to the recipient spouse. With respect to home sales, a special holding period rule applies to property owned by former spouses. [Q 1447], [Q 1239]

- *Child support payments* are taxed differently from alimony. Child support payments generally are not taxed to the spouse receiving the payments, nor are they deductible by the spouse making the payments. [Q 1448]

- If divorced parents both provide more than one-half of a child's support, and both have custody for over one-half of the year, the custodial parent generally gets to claim the *dependency exemption*. But the non-custodial parent may be able to claim the exemption if certain requirements are met. [Q 1426]

Details:

- If the divorce (or separation) instrument granting *alimony* does not meet certain requirements, the deduction may be lost. Most importantly, there should not be any obligation of the spouse making the alimony payments to do so after the recipient spouse dies. [Q 1448]

- If a *property transfer* between former spouses is not made "incident to divorce," the transfer may result in taxable income to the transferring spouse. To avoid this unfavorable treatment, the transfer generally should be made within one year after the date the marriage ends (a six month rule may apply under limited circumstances). [Q 1447]

Planning Considerations:

- Generally, alimony payments made *during* the divorce proceedings ("pendent lite") are also deductible. "Unallocated" family support payments (i.e., a combination of alimony and child support payments) may be beneficial when there is a disparity between the incomes and tax brackets of the divorced parties. The spouse paying alimony can claim a larger deduction and the recipient spouse can receive more money, and at a lower tax rate. But there is a split among the federal appeals courts regarding whether unallocated family support payments made during divorce proceedings are deductible (Third Circuit – yes; Tenth Circuit - no). [Q 1448]

- The dependency exemption should be analyzed closely so that it goes to whichever parent can derive the most tax benefit from claiming it. The economic benefit of the exemption should be examined periodically because the tax situations of the divorced parties may change. [Q 1426]

EDUCATION NAVIGATOR

- What are some different savings vehicles for funding education costs on a tax deferred basis?

    - Coverdell Education Savings Account (ESA) [Q 1412]

    - Qualified Tuition Program (QTP) [Q 1413], [Q 1414]

- What tax credits are available for education costs?

    - Hope Scholarship Credit [Q 1438]

    - Lifetime Learning Credit [Q 1438]

- What deductions are available for college costs?

    - Student loan interest [Q 1309]

    - Tuition expense (limited time) [Q 1314]

- Is an "Education IRA" the same thing as a "Cordell Education Savings Account? [Q 1412]

- Is a "529 plan" the same thing as a "qualified tuition program" (QTP)? [Q 1413]

- What types of expenses may be paid for using distributions from an ESA? [Q 1412]

- What types of expenses may be paid for using distributions from a QTP? [Q 1413], [Q 1414]

- What penalties apply if withdrawn funds are used for non-educational expenses? [Q 1412], [Q 1414]

- Can private high school tuition is paid using funds from an ESA? [Q 1412]

- What is the maximum amount of student loan interest that is deductible? [Q 1309]

- Do U.S. Savings Bonds provide any special tax treatment if the funds are used for education? [Q 1141]

- How can a grandparents pay for college tuition on a tax preferred basis?

- Gifts to UGMA (Uniform Gift to Minors Account) or UTMA (Uniform Transfer to Minor) accounts [Q 1526]

- Gifts to Education Savings Accounts (ESAs) [Q 1527]

- Gifts to Qualified Tuition Programs (QTPs) [Q 1528]

PART I

FEDERAL INCOME TAX

on
INVESTMENTS

STOCKS

DIVIDENDS

General

1001. What is a dividend?

A dividend is a distribution in the ordinary course of business of cash or property, made by a corporation to its shareholders out of accumulated or current earnings and profits.[1] It is a distribution made "with respect to" a corporation's common or preferred stock; that is, it is made because of stock ownership, not because of some other reason—such as compensation for services rendered or goods provided or in payment of a debt—even though it is made to a stockholder. While distribution by a company of its own stock or of stock rights is commonly called a stock dividend, it is not considered a dividend for tax purposes, because it is not made from earnings and profits.[2]

Concerning "stock dividends" and distributions of stock rights, see Q 1008 and Q 1009.

The amount received from a short-seller to reimburse the lender of stock in a short sale (see Q 1021) for dividends paid during the loan period is not a dividend to the lender.[3] For the treatment of such payments made to shareholders in lieu of dividends ("i.e., substitute payments") under JGTRRA 2003, see Q 1420.

Dividends Paid In Cash or Property

1002. How is a shareholder taxed on cash dividends he receives?

Ordinary cash dividends, whether paid on common or preferred stock, are generally included in the shareholder's gross income for the year in which they are actually received, regardless of the period for which they are paid; however, if there is an earlier constructive receipt, the shareholder will be taxed in the year in which the constructive receipt occurs.[4] Thus, dividends that have accumulated prior to an individual's purchase of cumulative preferred stock are taxed to the purchaser as dividends when actually

---

1. IRC Sec. 316(a); Treas. Reg. §1.316-1(a).
2. IRC Sec. 317(a); Treas. Reg. §1.317-1.
3. Rev. Rul. 60-177, 1960-1 CB 9.
4. IRC Secs. 61, 301(c); Treas. Regs. §§1.61-9, 1.301-1(b). See *Avery v. Comm.*, 292 U.S. 210 (1934).

or constructively received; accumulated dividends are not a return of a portion of his purchase price and, thus, do not reduce his tax basis.[1]

Under JGTRRA 2003, "qualified dividend income" (generally, dividends paid by domestic corporations and certain foreign corporations to shareholders – see Q 1420) is treated as net capital gain subject to new lower tax rates, while nonqualifying dividends continue to be treated as ordinary income subject to ordinary income tax rates. For taxpayers in the 25% income tax bracket and higher (see Q 1432), the maximum rate on qualified dividend income is 15% in 2003 through 2010. For taxpayers in the 15% and 10% income tax brackets, the tax rate on qualified dividend income is reduced to 5% in 2003 through 2007, and all the way down to 0% in 2008 through 2010.[2] The preferential treatment of qualified dividends being treated as net capital gains will "sunset" (expire) on December 31, 2010, after which time the prior tax treatment for dividends will, once again, apply to all dividends across the board. In other words, all dividends will, once again, be taxed at ordinary income tax rates.[3]

If stock is sold (or otherwise assigned) and a dividend is both declared and paid after the sale, the dividend is included in the purchaser's, not the seller's, income. When stock is sold (or assigned) after the dividend is declared but before payment: it is ordinarily taxed to the purchaser if the sale occurred *before* the record date or the date the stock begins selling ex-dividend; however, it is ordinarily taxed to the seller if the sale occurred *after* the record date. The fact that the dividend is reflected in the sale price does not change these results.[4]

1003. How is a dividend paid in property taxed?

A dividend paid in property other than stock or stock rights of the distributing corporation is taxed in the same manner as a cash dividend (see Q 1002).[5] A dividend paid in property other than cash is often referred to as a dividend "in kind." For tax purposes, the amount of a dividend paid in kind is generally the fair market value of the property on the date of the distribution.[6] See also Rev. Rul. 80-292,[7] where the distribution by a wholly owned subsidiary of rights to acquire its stock to the shareholders of its parent was deemed for tax purposes to be a distribution *by the parent corporation* of a dividend "in kind" to its shareholders.

A dividend paid in rights to acquire stock in another corporation (i.e., not the distributing corporation) is a dividend in kind.[8]

The shareholder's tax basis in property (including stock or stock rights) distributed in a taxable dividend is generally equal to the fair market value of that property on the date of the dividend distribution.[9]

---

1. Rev. Rul. 56-211, 1956-1 CB 155.
2. IRC Sec. 1(h)(11), as amended by TIPRA 2005.
3. Sec. 102, TIPRA 2005, *amending*, Sec. 303, JGTRRA 2003.
4. See Treas. Reg. §1.61-9(c); Rev. Rul. 74-562, 1974-2 CB 28.
5. IRC Secs. 301(a), 317(a).
6. IRC Sec. 301(b); Treas. Reg. §1.301-1(b).
7. 1980-2 CB 104.
8. See Rev. Rul. 70-521, 1970-2 CB 72.
9. IRC Sec. 301(d); Treas. Reg. §1.301-1(a).

If a dividend is paid in numismatic or bullion-type coins or currencies that have a fair market value in excess of their face values, the amount of the dividend is their aggregate fair market value.[1]

1004. How is a shareholder taxed if the corporation pays a dividend by distributing its own bonds, notes or other obligations?

A dividend paid in bonds, notes or other obligations of the distributing corporation is treated as a dividend "in kind" and the obligations are treated as property received in a dividend distribution.[2] See Q 1003 for the taxation of dividends "in kind."

1005. How should a shareholder report ordinary dividends on stocks held for him in street name by his broker?

He should report, *without itemization*, the total amount of dividends received on securities held in the broker's name for the taxpayer (i.e., held in "street name"), as shown on each statement furnished by his broker(s) on Schedule B of Form 1040.[3]

1006. Can a shareholder reduce his taxable income by assigning or making a gift of future dividends to another individual?

No; without the transfer of the underlying stock, a gift or gratuitous assignment of future dividends will not shift the taxability of the dividends away from the owner of the stock.[4]

The bona fide sale of future dividends for good and sufficient consideration will result in the dividends being taxed to the purchaser and not the shareholder; however, this will accelerate rather than reduce the shareholder's tax since the net sales proceeds must be reported by the shareholder-seller as ordinary income in the year of the sale.[5]

1007. What is "stripped preferred stock?" How is "stripped preferred stock" taxed?

Stripped preferred stock is stock with respect to which there has been a separation of ownership between the stock and any dividend on it that has not become payable, if the stock: (1) is limited and preferred as to dividends and does not participate in corporate growth to any significant extent, and (2) has a fixed redemption price.[6]

An individual who purchases stripped preferred stock generally must (while he holds the stock) treat the stock as though it were a bond issued on the purchase date with an original issue discount equal to the excess, if any, of the redemption price over the price at which he purchased the stock. This tax treatment also applies with respect to any holder of the stock whose basis is determined by reference to the basis in the hands of the purchaser (such as a donee or legatee).[7] (See Q 1116 for an explanation of the treatment of original issue discount.)

---

1. See *Cordner v. U.S.*, 671 F.2d 367 (9th Cir. 1982).
2. See IRC Sec. 317(a); Treas. Reg. §1.317-1.
3. Rev. Rul. 64-324, 1964-2 CB 463.
4. See *Van Brunt v. Comm.*, 11 BTA 406 (1928); *Lucas v. Earl*, 281 U.S. 111 (1930).
5. *Est. of Stranahan v. Comm.*, 472 F.2d 867 (6th Cir. 1973).
6. IRC Sec. 305(e)(5).
7. IRC Sec. 305(e)(1).

An individual who strips the rights to one or more dividends from stock described above (i.e., stock that is limited and preferred as to dividends, does not participate in corporate growth to any significant extent and has a fixed redemption price) and disposes of those dividend rights generally will be treated as having purchased the stripped preferred stock on the date of the disposition, for a purchase price equal to his adjusted basis in the stripped preferred stock.[1]

The amounts includable in gross income under these provisions are treated as ordinary income, and the basis of the stock will be adjusted accordingly.[2]

"Purchase," for purposes of this provision, is defined as an acquisition of stock where the basis of such stock is not determined in whole or in part by reference to the adjusted basis of the stock in the hands of the person from whom the stock was acquired.[3]

Stock Dividends

1008. What is a "stock dividend"?

A *stock dividend* is a dividend paid in shares of stock of the distributing corporation to its shareholders with respect to its outstanding stock. A distribution of stock to compensate the recipient for services rendered, goods provided, or in payment of a debt is not made with respect to the distributing corporation's outstanding stock and, therefore, is not a stock dividend.[4]

A distribution of stock warrants (or other rights to acquire stock of the distributing corporation) is treated in the same manner as a stock dividend so long as the distribution of such warrants is made with respect to the corporation's outstanding stock (and not as compensation for services, etc.).[5]

A distribution of stock of the distributing corporation made with respect to outstanding stock rights or convertible securities of that corporation to the owners thereof will also qualify as a stock dividend.[6]

1009. Is a stock dividend taxable?

Generally, no.[7] However, in the following cases a stock dividend will be taxed under the rules applicable to dividends paid in cash or other property (see Q 1001 to Q 1003).[8]

(1) If *any* shareholder has any election or option to choose to receive the dividend (partly or completely) in cash or property other than stock or stock rights of the distributing corporation, then the dividend is taxable with respect to *all* shareholders.[9] The Tax Court has held that such an "election or option" did not exist where certain shareholders had the right to *request* redemption of a portion of their stock for cash subsequent to the

---

1. IRC Sec. 305(e)(3).
2. IRC Secs. 305(e)(2), 305(e)(4).
3. IRC Sec. 305(e)(6).
4. IRC Sec. 305(a); Treas. Reg. §1.305-1.
5. See IRC Sec. 305(d); Treas. Reg. §1.305-1(d).
6. IRC Sec. 305(d).
7. IRC Sec. 305(a).
8. IRC Sec. 305(b).
9. Treas. Reg. §1.305-2.

distribution, and where the issuer retained complete discretion as to whether it would redeem the shares; however, the court noted that "under different factual circumstances, a discretionary act of the board of directors of a shareholder corporation to redeem stock dividends might constitute an 'option' that arises after the distribution."[1]

(2) A stock dividend or dividend paid in stock rights is taxable if the dividend distribution (or series of distributions of which such dividend is a part) results in the receipt by some shareholders of cash or property other than stock or stock rights of the corporation and in an increase for other shareholders in their proportionate interests in the assets or earnings and profits of the corporation (i.e., a disproportionate distribution).[2] This, however, does not apply to the distribution of cash or scrip in lieu of fractional shares if the purpose of the cash or scrip is to save the expense and inconvenience of transferring fractional shares. (The treatment of cash or scrip received in lieu of a fractional share is explained in Q 1012.)[3]

(3) A stock dividend or dividend paid in stock rights of the distributing corporation is taxable if the dividend distribution (or series of distributions of which such dividend is a part) results in the receipt of preferred stock by some common stock shareholders and the receipt of common stock by other common stock shareholders.[4]

(4) Any dividend or dividend paid in stock rights of the distributing corporation paid with respect to the corporation's preferred stock is taxable unless it is a "deemed" (rather than actual) distribution made with respect to convertible preferred stock to take into account a stock dividend, stock split, or similar event that would otherwise result in dilution of the conversion right.[5]

(5) Any dividend paid in convertible preferred stock of the distributing corporation or in rights to acquire such convertible preferred is taxable unless the corporation establishes that the distribution will not result in a disproportionate distribution as described in (2), above.[6]

If a stock dividend or dividend paid in stock rights of the distributing corporation is taxable under (1) through (5), the dividend is treated as a dividend in kind so that the amount that generally must be included in the recipient-shareholder's income is the fair market value of such stock or rights on the date of distribution (see Q 1003).[7]

The IRS ruled that shareholders who received all or part of a REIT's special stock dividend would be treated as having received a distribution to which IRC Section 301 through IRC Section 305 applied. The amount of the distribution paid in stock would be equal to the value of the stock on the valuation date rather than on the date of the distribution.[8] The Service also determined that a distribution of earnings and profits from a newly established REIT (arising from earnings and profits accumulated during the pre-REIT years), in which shareholders could elect to receive cash, stock, or a combination of both, should be treated as a distribution of property to which IRC Section 301 applies.[9]

---

1. *Western Fed. Sav. & Loan Ass'n v. Comm.*, TC Memo 1988-107, *aff'd*, 880 F.2d 1005 (8th Cir. 1989).
2. Treas. Reg. §1.305-3.
3. Treas. Reg. §1.305-3(c); Rev. Rul. 69-202, 1969-1 CB 95.
4. Treas. Reg. §1.305-4.
5. Treas. Reg. §1.305-5; Rev. Rul. 83-42, 1983-1 CB 76.
6. Treas. Reg. §1.305-6.
7. Treas. Reg. §1.305-1(b).
8. Let. Rul. 200122001.
9. Let. Rul. 200348020.

1010. What is the tax basis of stock acquired in a stock dividend? When does the holding period of the stock begin?

If a shareholder acquires stock in a *nontaxable* stock dividend (see Q 1008), his present tax basis in his "old" stock, with respect to which the stock dividend was paid, is reallocated between the old and the new shares in proportion to the fair market value of each on the date of distribution (not the declaration or record date).[1] If the stock with respect to which the dividend was paid was purchased at different times and for different prices, the shareholder may *not* use his overall average basis for purposes of this allocation. If he can adequately identify the various purchases, he may allocate the proportionate amount of the dividend stock to each lot and, with respect to each lot separately, reallocate his tax basis between the "old" and "new" shares according to the fair market value of each. If he cannot adequately identify the stock in each lot, the dividend stock is matched to the "old" stock in the order in which the "old" stock was acquired (i.e., a FIFO tracing approach), and the tax basis of those "old" shares is reallocated between the old and new matched shares according to their fair market values.[2]

The holding period of the "new" stock received in a nontaxable stock dividend includes the holding period of the stock with respect to which the stock dividend was paid (i.e., the holding period of the "old" stock is "tacked" (i.e., added) onto the holding period of the new stock).[3] If the "old" stock was purchased at different times, the "new" shares must be allocated to the individual lots of the "old" stock by adequate identification or a FIFO tracing approach as discussed above.

1011. What is the tax basis of warrants or other stock rights received in a nontaxable stock dividend distribution from the issuing corporation?

If a shareholder acquires stock warrants or other stock rights of the distributing corporation in a nontaxable stock dividend distribution (see Q 1009) and either exercises or sells the warrants or rights, his tax basis in his "old" shares with respect to which the distribution of warrants or rights was made is generally reallocated (in the same manner as discussed in Q 1010 for stock dividends) between the old shares and the warrants or rights, in proportion to the fair market value of each on the date of distribution (not the declaration or record date). However, if the fair market value of the warrants or rights is less than 15% of the fair market value of the "old" stock, the tax basis of the warrants will automatically be zero, unless the shareholder makes an irrevocable election to reallocate the basis of his old stock with respect to which the warrants or rights were distributed to *all* warrants or other rights received in the distribution.[4] It has been held, however, that where the subscription rights became valueless and the subscriptions received were refunded, no adjustment to the shareholders' basis was required.[5]

Apparently, if the warrants or rights are allowed to expire without exercise or sale, the tax basis of the warrants or rights is zero.

1012. How is a shareholder taxed when, as part of a stock dividend, he receives cash or scrip in lieu of fractional shares?

1. IRC Sec. 307; Treas. Regs. §§1.307-1, 1.307-2.
2. Rev. Rul. 71-350, 1971-2 CB 176; Rev. Rul. 56-653, 1956-2 CB 185; I.T. 2417, VII CB 59.
3. IRC Sec. 1223(5); Treas. Reg. §1.1223-1(e).
4. Treas. Regs. §§1.307-1, 1.307-2.
5. See Rev. Rul. 74-501, 1974-2 CB 98.

The distribution of cash or scrip in lieu of fractional shares in a stock dividend will generally not, in and of itself, cause the entire stock dividend to be taxable (see Q 1009).

If a shareholder receives cash in lieu of a fractional share, the regulations state that the shareholder will be taxed as though he had actually received that fractional share and then redeemed it with the corporation.[1] Unfortunately, it is not clear whether all the redemption rules of IRC Section 302 apply for the purpose of determining whether the cash is ordinary income or gives rise to capital gain.

It is clear, however, that if the corporation, with the approval of the shareholders, combines into whole shares the fractional shares due the shareholders, sells them in the market, and distributes the proceeds of the sale, the shareholders who receive the proceeds in lieu of a fractional share are treated as though they had received the fraction and made the sale themselves. Each such shareholder thus has a gain or loss to the extent of the difference between the cash received by him and his tax basis in his fractional share.[2] (See the example on p. 22 of Publication 550 (2005)). Similarly, if a shareholder is allowed to elect to have the corporation sell scrip certificates that would otherwise be distributed to him in lieu of a fractional share and pay him the proceeds, he is treated as having sold the scrip himself for a capital gain or loss to the extent of the difference between the cash received and his tax basis in the scrip certificate.[3]

If a shareholder does receive scrip certificates in lieu of a fractional share, he realizes no taxable income on the receipt.[4] He will, however, be taxed when he sells or exchanges the scrip in the same manner as when he sells the whole shares of stock received in the stock dividend (see Q 1009).

The tax basis and holding period of fractional shares or scrip received in a nontaxable stock dividend are determined in the same manner as the whole shares received in that dividend (see Q 1010).

See Q 1420 for an explanation of the treatment of capital gain.

Stock Splits

1013. How is a shareholder taxed on a stock split?

A stock split is treated in the same manner as a stock dividend.[5] Therefore, a stock split is generally a nontaxable event for the shareholder (see Q 1009). The tax basis and holding period of the "new" stock received in a stock split is determined as discussed in Q 1010.

Return of Capital Distributions

1014. How is a shareholder taxed if the corporation makes a distribution in excess of its accumulated earnings and profits? How is a "return of capital" taxed?

---

1. Treas. Reg. §1.305-3(c).
2. Rev. Rul. 69-15, 1969-1 CB 95.
3. Rev. Rul. 69-202, 1969-1 CB 95; IRS Pub. 550 (2005), p. 22.
4. See Rev. Rul. 69-202, above.
5. IRC Sec. 305(a).

To the extent that a distribution paid with respect to its stock exceeds the corporation's accumulated earnings and profits, the shareholders will be deemed to have received a "return of capital."[1]

When a shareholder receives a "return of capital" distribution he reduces his tax basis (but not below zero) in his stock by the amount of the distribution. He is not taxed to the extent that his basis is reduced. Any excess of "return of capital" over the shareholder's tax basis in his stock is generally treated as capital gain.[2]

Dividend Reinvestment Plans

1015. How is a shareholder taxed if he participates in a dividend reinvestment plan?

Although dividends received or credited under a dividend reinvestment plan will be taxed as dividend income, the specifics depend on which of the two basic types of plans is involved.

(1) If, under the plan, the corporation pays the cash dividends (that would otherwise be paid to the plan participants) to an independent agent who purchases shares of the distributing corporation's stock in the open market and credits them to the plan accounts of the individual shareholders, each participating shareholder is treated as though the cash had been distributed directly to him in a cash dividend.[3] Thus, the total amount of the cash dividend paid on the shareholder's behalf to the agent must be included by the shareholder in his ordinary income as discussed in Q 1002. The value of brokerage commissions paid by a corporation to an agent under a dividend reinvestment plan is a constructive dividend to each shareholder in the amount of each shareholder's pro rata share of the brokerage fees actually paid.[4] The shares credited to a shareholder under the plan are treated as though the shareholder himself had made the purchase. Where the corporation does not pay the brokerage commissions to an agent purchasing the shares, commissions paid by the agent are treated as if paid by the individual shareholder (i.e., added to the shareholder's tax basis in the new shares) (see Q 1310).[5]

(2) If, under the plan, the corporation (a) manages the plan itself and credits the accounts of participating shareholders with shares, or (b) pays the cash dividends to an independent agent who purchases shares (often at a discount) from the distributing corporation, each participating shareholder is treated as if he had received a *taxable* stock dividend (see Q 1009). As a result, each participating shareholder must include as dividend income the fair market value (on the dividend payment date) of the shares credited to his account in the plan *plus* any service charge paid to the agent (if one is used) out of the shareholder's portion of the cash dividend paid. Apparently, any service and administrative charges paid *by the corporation* need not be included in income by shareholders participating in the plan.[6] The shareholder's tax basis in the shares credited to his account is the fair market value of those shares on the dividend payment date, even though the shares may have been purchased at a discount or premium.[7] The holding

---

1. IRC Sec. 301(c).
2. IRC Secs. 301(c), 316.
3. Rev. Rul. 77-149, 1977-1 CB 82.
4. GCM 39482 (5-5-86).
5. Rev. Rul. 75-548, 1975-2 CB 331; Rev. Rul. 70-627, 1970-2 CB 159.
6. See Let. Rul. 7928066.
7. Rev. Rul. 79-42, 1979-1 CB 130; Rev. Rul. 78-375, 1978-2 CB 130; Rev. Rul. 76-53, 1976-1 CB 87.

period of the shares credited to a participating shareholder's account begins on the day following the dividend payment date.[1]

If a service charge is paid to an independent agent out of the cash dividend under either type of plan, that service charge may be deductible by the participating shareholder.[2] See Q 1310 regarding the deduction of expenses paid in connection with the production of investment income.

A participating shareholder realizes no taxable income when he eventually receives certificates representing whole shares credited to his account in the plan.[3] Upon withdrawal from or termination of the plan, if cash is distributed to a participating shareholder in lieu of fractional share interests, the shareholder is treated as though he received the fractional shares and redeemed them (see Q 1012).[4] If on withdrawal from or termination of the plan, fractional shares and/or whole shares are sold or exchanged on behalf of the participating shareholders, each shareholder recognizes capital gain or loss as though he had received and sold the shares himself.[5]

1016. If a dividend reinvestment plan allows a participating shareholder to make additional purchases of stock at a discount, how is the purchase taxed?

Many dividend reinvestment plans offer participating shareholders an option to invest additional cash to purchase *at a discount* limited quantities of the distributing corporation's stock. If a shareholder elects to do so, he must include as dividend income on his federal income tax return the difference between the fair market value of the stock on the dividend payment date and the optional payment. (Apparently, this would normally be the amount of the discount.) A shareholder's tax basis in the shares purchased under this type of option is generally their fair market value on the dividend payment date.[6]

The holding period of stock purchased under the optional aspect of a dividend reinvestment plan begins on the day following the date the shares are purchased.[7]

SALE OR EXCHANGE

General

1017. How is a shareholder taxed on the sale or exchange of his stock?

Generally, a shareholder who sells or exchanges his stock (other than IRC Section 1202 stock, see Q 1020) for other property realizes a *capital* gain or loss.[8] Whether such gain or loss is short-term or long-term usually depends on how long the shareholder held the stock before selling (or exchanging) it.[9] For an explanation of how the holding

---

1. Rev. Rul. 76-53, above.
2. Rev. Ruls. 78-375, 70-627, above.
3. See Rev. Ruls. 76-53, 78-375, above.
4. Rev. Ruls. 78-375, 76-53, above.
5. Rev. Rul. 78-375, above.
6. Rev. Rul. 78-375, 1978-2 CB 130.
7. Rev. Rul. 76-53, 1976-1 CB 87.
8. See IRC Secs. 1221, 1222.
9. See IRC Secs. 1222, 1223.

period is calculated, see Q 1417; for the treatment of capital gains and losses, including the new lower rates for capital gains incurred on or after May 6, 2003, see Q 1420.

Specific circumstances may result in the conversion of what appears to be a long-term capital gain to short-term, short-term capital loss to long-term, capital gain to ordinary income, or in the disallowance of a loss. See Q 1007 concerning stripped preferred stock, Q 1086 concerning conversion transactions, and Q 1419 concerning sales between related individuals. Also, certain derivative securities transactions may result in a *constructive sale* (see Q 1087 to Q 1089) with respect to an appreciated stock position, which may result in immediate recognition of gain, and the start of a new holding period. See Q 1022 concerning short sales and Q 1074 concerning futures and forward contracts.

For an explanation of the rollover of gain into specialized small business investment company stock, see Q 1018. For an explanation of the 50% exclusion for gain from the sale of qualified small business stock, see Q 1020.

Assuming none of the special rules described above apply, when shares of stock are sold, the amount of gain (or loss) is the difference between the selling price and the shareholder's tax basis in the shares at the time of sale. If the shares are exchanged for property, or for property and cash, the amount of gain (or loss) is the difference between the fair market value of the property plus the cash received in the exchange and the shareholder's tax basis.[1] However, if common stock in a corporation is exchanged for common stock in the same corporation, or if preferred stock is exchanged for preferred stock in the same corporation, gain or loss is generally not recognized unless cash or other property is also received; that is, the exchange is taxed in substantially the same manner as a "like-kind" exchange. The exchange of stocks of different corporations and exchanges of common for preferred do *not* qualify for the general "like-kind" exchange rules, even if the stocks are similar in all respects.[2] The nonrecognition rules of IRC Section 1036 apply to exchanges of common stock for common stock in the same corporation, even though the stocks are of a different class and have different voting, preemptive, or dividend rights.[3] For an explanation of "like-kind" exchanges, see Q 1422.

Special rules apply to stock exchanges made pursuant to a plan of corporate reorganization.[4] The IRS has released final regulations under IRC Section 358 providing guidance regarding the determination of the basis of stock or securities received in exchange for, or with respect to, stock or securities in certain transactions (see Q 1415).[5]

Demutualization. For guidance on determining the (1) holding period and (2) capital gain treatment of stock received by a policyholder in a demutualization transaction that does (or does not) qualify as a tax-free reorganization, see CCA 200131028. The IRS has provided guidance on how to determine the cost basis of stock received in a demutualization.[6] In a tax refund suit concerning the gain from a sale of stock received in a demutualization, the Federal Court of Claims denied both the taxpayer's and the government's motions for summary judgment. The court determined that contrary

---

1. See IRC Sec. 1001.
2. IRC Sec. 1036; Treas. Reg. §1.1036-1. See IRC Sec. 1031(a).
3. Rev. Rul. 72-199, 1972-1 CB 228. See Treas. Reg. §1.1036-1.
4. See IRC Sec. 354.
5. See Treas. Regs. §§1.358-1. 1.358-2; TD 9244, 71 Fed. Reg. 4264 (1-26-2006). See also TD 9244, 71 Fed. Reg. 62556 (10-26-2006); Ann. 2006-91, 2006-47 IRB 953; Ann. 2006-31, 2006-20 IRB 912.
6. See Information Letter INFO 2002-0057 (3-14-2002).

to the government's argument that the voting and liquidation rights were worthless, there was some indication that the voting and liquidation rights may have had some value—not only because the insurance company had a surplus of nearly $5.7 billion, but also because the insurance company stock exchanged (at least in part) for those rights apparently had some value. To the extent that the voting and liquidation rights had some value, that would diminish the amount of income that would be taxable. In short, the court viewed the amount of the premiums that should be attributed to the liquidation and voting rights as a material question of fact that could not be resolved on the record presented and, thus, required a trial.[1]

If a shareholder's holdings in a stock were all acquired on the same day and at the same price, he will have little difficulty in establishing his tax basis and holding period of the shares he sells or exchanges. However, where his shares were acquired at different times or prices and he sells less than his entire holdings in the stock, the process becomes more difficult while also becoming more significant; unless the shareholder can "adequately identify" the lot from which the shares being sold originated, the shares sold will be deemed to have come from the earliest of such lots purchased or acquired (i.e., under a first-in, first-out (FIFO) method).[2] For an explanation of how lots can be "adequately identified," see Q 1418 and Treas. Reg. §1.1012-1.

If the stock sold was acquired on the conversion of a market discount bond, a portion of the sales proceeds may have to be treated as interest income (see Q 1114).

1018. Under what circumstances may a taxpayer roll over and, thus, defer gain from the sale of publicly traded securities?

Individual taxpayers and C corporations may elect to roll over certain capital gain from the sale of publicly traded securities if the taxpayer or corporation uses the amount realized from the sale to purchase common stock or a partnership interest in a *specialized small business investment company* within 60 days of the sale.[3] A specialized small business investment company (SSBIC) is any corporation or partnership that is licensed by the Small Business Administration under Section 301(d) of the Small Business Investment Act of 1958.[4] (Note that due to budget cutbacks, the SBIC did not license any new SBICs in fiscal year 2005.) "Publicly traded securities" means securities traded on an established securities market.[5]

If the election is made, gain from the sale of the publicly traded securities is currently taxable only to the extent that the amount realized from the sale exceeds the cost of the SSBIC stock or interest.[6] IRC Section 1044(a)(2) states that the cost of the SSBIC stock or interest is to be reduced by any portion of such cost previously taken into account under IRC Section 1044.

The amount of gain that may be rolled over by an individual in a taxable year is generally limited to $50,000. However, the aggregate amount of gain that may be rolled over during a taxpayer's lifetime is $500,000.[7] Thus, a taxpayer who had previously

---

1. *Fisher v. U.S.*, ___ F.Supp.2d ___ (No. 04-1726T) (Cl. Ct. 2006).
2. Treas. Reg. §1.1012-1(c).
3. IRC Sec. 1044.
4. IRC Sec. 1044(c)(3).
5. IRC Sec. 1044(c)(1).
6. IRC Sec. 1044(a).
7. IRC Sec. 1044(b)(1).

rolled over a total of $475,000 in gain in prior tax years, but who has $50,000 in gain in the current year, would be limited in his current year rollover to $25,000 of otherwise eligible gain. The $50,000 and $500,000 limits are reduced to $25,000 and $250,000, respectively, for married taxpayers filing separately. In the case of a C corporation, the gain that may be deferred in a taxable year may not exceed $250,000; the total amount of gain that may be rolled over during the corporation's existence is $1,000,000.[1]

A taxpayer's basis in the SSBIC stock or partnership interest is generally reduced by the amount of gain that is rolled over into the stock or interest. However, the basis of any SSBIC common stock is not reduced for purposes of calculating the gain eligible for the 50% exclusion for qualified small business stock provided by IRC Section 1202 (see Q 1020).[2]

The election under IRC Section 1044 must be made on or before the due date (including extensions) for the income tax return for the year in which the publicly traded securities are sold.[3]

Estates, trusts, partnerships, and S corporations are ineligible to roll over gain under this section.[4]

1019. What is qualified small business stock?

IRC Section 1202 provides for special treatment of *qualified small business stock*, which generally means stock (a) in a C corporation that is a "qualified small business," (b) that meets the *active business* requirement (explained below), and (c) that was originally issued after August 10, 1993, and (except as otherwise provided) acquired by the taxpayer at its original issue in exchange for money or other property (not including stock), or as compensation for services to the corporation.[5] For the tax treatment of qualified small business stock, see Q 1020.

An issuing corporation is a *qualified small business* if it is a domestic corporation with *aggregate gross assets* of $50,000,000 or less at all times after August 10, 1993. Generally, "aggregate gross assets" means the amount of cash and the aggregate adjusted bases of other property held by the corporation. Under certain circumstances, a parent corporation and its subsidiary corporations may be treated as one corporation for purposes of determining a corporation's aggregate gross assets.[6]

As a general rule, stock acquired by the taxpayer will not be treated as "qualified small business stock" if the issuing corporation has directly or indirectly purchased any of its stock from the taxpayer (or a related person) within two years before or after the date of issuance.[7] However, an issuing corporation may redeem *de minimis* amounts of stock without the loss of qualified small business stock treatment. Stock redeemed from a taxpayer (or related person) exceeds a de minimis amount of stock only if the aggregate amount paid for the stock exceeds $10,000 and more than 2% of the stock held by the taxpayer and related persons is acquired.[8]

---

1. IRC Sec. 1044(b)(2).
2. IRC Sec. 1044(d).
3. Treas. Reg. §1.1044(a)-1.
4. IRC Sec. 1044(c)(4).
5. IRC Sec. 1202(c)(1).
6. IRC Sec. 1202(d).
7. IRC Sec. 1202(c)(3)(A).
8. Treas. Reg. §1.1202-2(a)(2).

Similarly, stock issued by a corporation will generally not be treated as qualified small business stock if the issuing corporation makes a *significant redemption* of stock or, in other words, redeems stock with an aggregate value of more than 5% of the value of all of its stock within one year before or after the date of issuance.[1] However, an issuing corporation may redeem *de minimis* amounts of stock without the loss of qualified small business stock treatment. Stock redeemed by an issuing corporation exceeds a de minimis amount only if the aggregate amount paid exceeds $10,000 and more than 2% of all outstanding stock is purchased.[2]

In addition, the following stock redemptions are disregarded in determining whether redemptions exceed de minimis amounts and will not result in the loss of qualified small business stock treatment: (1) a redemption of stock acquired in connection with the performance of services as an employer or director (or an option to acquire it) incident to the seller's retirement or other bona fide termination of such services; (2) a purchase from a deceased shareholder's estate, beneficiary, heir, surviving joint tenant, surviving spouse or a trust established by the decedent or decedent's spouse and the purchase is within three years and nine months of the decedent's death, provided that prior to the decedent's death, the stock (or an option to acquire the stock) was held by the decedent or decedent's spouse (or by both), by the decedent and joint tenant, or by a trust revocable by the decedent or decedent's spouse (or by both); (3) a purchase incident to the disability or mental incompetence of the selling shareholder; *or* (4) a purchase incident to the divorce (within the meaning of IRC Section 1041(c)) of the selling shareholder (see Q 1447). Also, transfers by shareholders to an employee or independent contractor (or beneficiary thereof) in connection with the performance of services are generally not treated as redemptions.[3]

Stock acquired through the conversion of qualified small business stock of the same corporation will be considered qualified small business stock held for the same period that the converted stock was held by the taxpayer.[4]

In order to satisfy the *active business* requirement, at least 80% of the issuing corporation's assets must be committed to the active conduct of one or more "qualified trades or businesses," and the corporation must be an "eligible corporation."[5] (A specialized small business investment company is not subject to this requirement.[6] See Q 1018.) The term "qualified trade or business" is a trade or business *other than* one that involves (a) the performance of services in a field where the principal asset of the trade or business is the reputation or skill of one or more employees, such as the fields of law, accounting, performing arts, or athletics, (b) any insurance, banking, financing, leasing, investing, or similar business, (c) any farming business, (d) any mining business for which a percentage depletion deduction is allowed under the IRC, or (e) any business operating a hotel, motel, restaurant, or similar business.[7]

Regardless of whether the *active business* requirement is met, stock will not be treated as qualified small business stock unless the issuing corporation is an *eligible corporation*. An "eligible corporation" is a domestic corporation *other than* (a) a DISC or former

---

1. IRC Sec. 1202(c)(3)(B).
2. Treas. Reg. §1.1202-2(b)(2).
3. Treas. Regs. §§1.1202-2(c), 1.1202(d).
4. IRC Sec. 1202(f).
5. IRC Sec. 1202(e)(1).
6. IRC Sec. 1202(c)(2)(B).
7. IRC Sec. 1202(e)(3).

DISC, (b) a regulated investment company, a real estate investment trust, or a real estate mortgage investment conduit, (c) a cooperative, or (d) a corporation that has made an election under IRC Section 936 (relating to the U.S. possession tax credit).[1]

1020. How is qualified small business stock treated for tax purposes?

If certain requirements are met, a noncorporate taxpayer (including certain partnerships and S corporations) may exclude from gross income 50% of any gain from the sale or exchange of *qualified small business stock* held for more than five years.[2] For an explanation of what constitutes "qualified small business stock," see Q 1019. For the treatment of capital gains and losses, including IRC Section 1202 gain, see Q 1420. Special rules provide an increased exlusion of gain from the sale of qualifying empowerment zone stock.[3]

The aggregate amount of eligible gain from the disposition of qualified small business stock issued by one corporation that may be taken into account in a tax year may not exceed the greater of (a) $10,000,000 ($5,000,000 in the case of married taxpayers filing separately) reduced by the aggregate amount of such gain taken into account in prior years, *or* (b) 10 times the aggregate bases of qualified stock of the issuer disposed of during the tax year. For purposes of the limitation in (b), the adjusted basis of any qualified stock will not include any additions to basis occurring after the stock was issued.[4]

Gain realized by a partner, shareholder, or other participant that is attributable to a disposition of qualified small business stock held by a pass-through entity (i.e., a partnership, S corporation, regulated investment company, or common trust fund) is eligible for the exclusion if the entity held the stock for more than five years, and if the taxpayer held an interest in the pass-through entity at the time of acquisition and at all times since the acquisition of the stock.[5]

IRC Section 1202 provides that if the taxpayer has an *offsetting short position* with respect to any qualified small business stock, the exclusion is unavailable unless (a) the stock was held for more than five years as of the date of entering into the short position, *and* (b) the taxpayer elects to recognize gain as if the stock were sold at its fair market value on the first day the offsetting position was held.[6]

A taxpayer has an "offsetting short position" with respect to any qualified small business stock if he (or a related party) has (a) made a short sale of substantially identical property, (b) acquired an option to sell substantially identical property at a fixed price, or (c) to the extent provided in future regulations, entered into any other transaction that substantially reduces the risk of loss from holding the qualified small business stock.[7] (See Q 1021 for an explanation of short sales, Q 1023 for an explanation of "substantially identical property" for purposes of the short sale rules, and Q 1042 for a definition of options.)

---

1. IRC Sec. 1202(e)(4).
2. IRC Sec. 1202. See also IRC Sec. 1(h)(7).
3. See IRC Sec. 1202(a)(2).
4. IRC Sec. 1202(b).
5. IRC Sec. 1202(g).
6. IRC Sec. 1202(j)(1).
7. IRC Sec. 1202(j)(2).

Obviously, some offsetting short positions (e.g., a short sale) may also result in constructive sale treatment under the rules of IRC Section 1259 (see Q 1087 to Q 1089). While the IRC does not specify the effect of IRC Section 1259 on IRC Section 1202, it would appear that if the requirements of IRC Section 1202(j) are otherwise met, the exclusion provided under IRC Section 1202 would not be lost merely because immediate gain recognition may be required under IRC Section 1259.

Any gain excluded under IRC Section 1202 by a married couple filing jointly must be allocated equally between the spouses for purposes of claiming the exclusion in subsequent tax years.[1]

Special rules apply to IRC Section 1202 stock for alternative minimum tax purposes. Under JGTRRA 2003, an amount equal to 7% of the amount excluded from gross income for the taxable year under IRC Section 1202 will be treated as a preference item.[2]

Individual taxpayers may not exclude any gain under IRC Section 1202 in determining net operating loss for the year.[3]

Rollover of Gain

Generally, a noncorporate taxpayer, including certain partnerships and S corporations, may elect to roll over gain from the sale or exchange of qualified small business stock held more than six months to the extent that the taxpayer purchases other qualifying small business stock within 60 days of the sale of the original stock.[4]

If the rollover election is made, gain will be recognized only to the extent that the amount realized on the sale exceeds: (1) the cost of any qualified small business stock purchased by the taxpayer during the 60-day period beginning on the date of the sale, reduced by, (2) any portion of such cost previously taken into account under this rollover provision. The rollover provisions of IRC Section 1045 will not apply to any gain that is treated as ordinary income.[5]

Rules similar to those applicable to rollovers of gain by an individual from certain small business stock[6] will apply to the rollover of such gain by a partnership or S corporation.[7] Thus, for example, the benefit of a tax-free rollover with respect to the sale of small business stock by a partnership will flow through to a partner who is not a corporation provided the partner held his partnership interest at all times during which the partnership held the small business stock.[8] (A similar rule applies to S corporations.)[9] For the proposed rules regarding (1) the deferral of gain on a partnership's sale of qualified small business stock, and (2) the deferral of gain on a partner's sale of qualified small business stock distributed by a partnership, see Prop. Reg. §1.1045-1; REG-150562-03.[10]

---

1. IRC Sec. 1202(b)(3)(B).
2. IRC Sec. 57(a)(7), as amended by JGTRRA 2003.
3. IRC Sec. 172(d)(2).
4. See IRC Sec. 1045(a).
5. IRC Sec. 1045(a).
6. IRC Sec. 1202.
7. IRC Sec. 1045(b)(5).
8. See Prop. Treas. Reg. §1.1045-1(a)(2).
9. General Explanation of Tax Legislation Enacted in 1998 (JCS-6-98), p. 167 (the 1998 Blue Book).
10. 69 Fed. Reg. 42370 (7-15-2004).

The amount of gain not recognized because of a rollover of qualified small business stock will be applied to reduce (in the order acquired) the basis for determining gain or loss of any qualified small business stock purchased by the taxpayer during the 60-day rollover period.[1]

Ordinarily, the holding period of qualified small business stock purchased in a rollover transaction will include the holding period of the stock sold; however, for purposes of determining whether the nonrecognition of gain applies to the stock that is sold, the holding period for the replacement stock begins on the date of purchase. In addition, only the first six months of the taxpayer's holding period for the replacement stock will be taken into account for purposes of determining whether the active business requirement is met (see Q 1019).[2]

An IRC Section 1045 election must be made by the due date (including extensions) for filing the income tax return for the taxable year in which the qualified small business stock is sold.[3] The election is made by: (1) reporting the entire gain from the sale of qualified small business stock on Schedule D; (2) writing "IRC Section 1045 rollover" directly below the line on which the gain is reported; *and* (3) entering the amount of the gain deferred under IRC Section 1045 on the same line as (2), above, as a loss, in accordance with the instructions for Schedule D.[4] If a taxpayer has more than one sale of qualified small business stock in a taxable year that qualifies for the IRC Section 1045 election, the election can be made for any one or more of those sales. An IRC Section 1045 election is revocable only with the Commissioner's consent.[5]

The Service has stated that in order to be granted approval to make a late Section 1045 election (when the requirements for an automatic extension are not met), the requesting taxpayer must provide evidence to establish that he acted reasonably and in good faith and that granting of the relief would not prejudice the interests of the government. A taxpayer is deemed to have not acted reasonably and in good faith if the taxpayer either uses hindsight in requesting relief, or was informed in all material respects of the required election and related tax consequences but chose not to file the election. Furthermore, the taxpayer must provide a detailed affidavit from the individuals having knowledge or information about the events leading to the failure to make a valid regulatory election. The affidavit must describe the engagement and responsibilities of the individual as well as the advice that the individual provided to the taxpayer.[6]

Short Sales

1021. What is a "short sale"? What is meant by the expression "short against the box"?

In a "short sale" an individual contracts to sell stock (or other securities) that he "does not own or the certificates for which are not within his control so as to be available for delivery when, under the rules of the Exchange, delivery must be made."[7] Thus, in a short sale, the seller usually borrows the stock (or security) for delivery to the buyer.

---

1. IRC Sec. 1045(b)(3).
2. IRC Secs. 1045(b)(4), 1223(15).
3. Rev. Proc. 98-48, 1998-2 CB 367.
4. Rev. Proc. 98-48, above.
5. Rev. Proc. 98-48, above.
6. Let. Rul. 200604004.
7. *Provost v. U.S.*, 269 U.S. 443 (1926).

(He must generally pay a premium for the privilege of borrowing such stock and will usually be required to reimburse the lender for any dividends paid during the loan period.) At a later date, the short seller will repay the borrowed stock to the lender with shares he held (but that were not available) at the time of the short sale or with shares he purchases in the market, whichever he chooses.[1]

The act of delivering stock (or securities) to the lender in repayment for the borrowed shares is referred to as "closing" the short sale. The date the sales agreement is made is considered to be the "date of the short sale."

In a sale "short against the box" the short seller already owns (on the date of the short sale) shares of stock (or securities) that are identical to those sold short, but chooses to borrow the necessary shares rather than deliver his own.

A contract to sell stock or securities on a "when issued" basis is considered a short sale; the performance of the contract is considered to be the "closing" of that short sale.[2]

A transaction in which a taxpayer purchases convertible bonds and as nearly simultaneously as possible sells the stock into which the bonds are convertible at a price relatively higher than the price of the bonds, then converts the bonds and uses the stock received to close the stock sale is a short sale.[3] (Such a transaction is also an arbitrage operation. See Q 1026.) See Q 1022 regarding the tax treatment of short sales.

The purchase of a put option—see Q 1047, Q 1049—is treated as a short sale for some purposes.[4] It is unclear whether such treatment will be applied for purposes of the constructive sales rules of IRC Section 1259. See Q 1087 to Q 1089.

In applying the short sale rules, a *securities futures contract*—see Q 1072—to *acquire* property will be treated in a manner similar to the property itself.[5] Thus, for example, the holding of a securities futures contract to acquire property and the short sale of property that is substantially identical to the property under the contract will result in the application of the rules under IRC Section 1233(b) (regarding short-term gains and holding periods). (Because securities futures contracts are not treated as commodity futures contracts under IRC Section 1234B(d), the rule providing that commodity futures are not substantially identical if they call for delivery in different months does not apply.) In addition, a securities futures contract to *sell* is treated as a short sale of the property.[6]

1022. When and how is a short sale taxed?

The timing of the taxable event depends on when the short sale occurs and whether it constitutes a *constructive sale of an appreciated financial position*. See Q 1087 to Q 1089. Special rules also govern the determination of the holding period of property subject to a short sale (and thus its tax treatment) as explained below.

---

1. See also Rev. Rul. 72-478, 1972-2 CB 487.
2. See S. Rep. No. 2375 (Rev. Act of 1950), 1950-2 CB 545; Treas. Reg. §1.1233-1(c)(6), Ex. (6).
3. Rev. Rul. 154, 1953-2 CB 173.
4. See, e.g., IRC Sec. 1233(b).
5. H.R. Conf. Rep. No. 106-1033 (CRTRA 2000). See IRC Sec. 1233(e)(2)(D).
6. IRC Sec. 1233(e)(2)(E); H.R. Conf. Rep. No. 106-1033 (CRTRA 2000). See IRC Sec. 1234B(b).

Transactions Subject to Constructive Sale Treatment

Generally, if a taxpayer holds an appreciated financial position—see Q 1087—that is the same as or substantially identical to the property sold short, the short sale will be treated as a constructive sale of that position, unless certain requirements are met for closing out the short position.[1] Furthermore, if a taxpayer holds a short sale position that has appreciated, the acquisition of the same or substantially identical property (e.g., to cover the short sale) constitutes a constructive sale of the short sale position, which is subject to the same rules.[2]

Unless certain exceptions apply, a constructive sale results in immediate recognition of gain as if the position were sold, assigned, or otherwise terminated at its fair market value on the date of the constructive sale.[3] For an explanation of the constructive sale rules for appreciated financial positions under IRC Section 1259, see Q 1087 to Q 1089.

A sale of appreciated stock "short against the box" constitutes a constructive sale of an appreciated financial position. See Q 1087 to Q 1089.[4] (Under earlier law, short sales against the box were taxed as a short sale.[5])

The nature of capital gain recognized as a result of a constructive sale of an appreciated financial position may be subject to the rules of IRC Section 1233 and regulations thereunder, which generally govern the determination of a taxpayer's holding period for gain or loss on short sale transactions. (Those rules are described below under the heading "Short-Term or Long-Term.") The treatment of capital gains and losses is explained in Q 1420.

Transactions Not Subject to Constructive Sale Treatment

In the case of a short sale that, if terminated, would result in a loss, the taxable event following a short sale does not occur until the seller delivers stock to the lender to "close" the sale, not when the sales agreement was made, nor when the borrowed stock was delivered to the purchaser. See Q 1021.[6] If the seller's tax basis exceeds the sale proceeds, he will realize a capital loss.[7]

If the seller does not hold the same or substantially identical property, a short sale alone will not result in constructive sale treatment; but at such time as he acquires the same or substantially identical property to close the sale, a constructive sale takes place, under the rules described above, if the short position has appreciated.[8]

Short-Term or Long-Term

Ordinarily, whether capital gain or loss on a short sale is long-term or short-term will generally be determined by how long the seller held the stock he uses to close the sale.[9] For most purposes, the holding period requirement is "more than one year." (See Q 1420 for the treatment of capital gains and losses.)

---

1. See IRC Secs. 1259(c)(1)(A), 1259(c)(3).
2. IRC Sec. 1259(c)(1)(D).
3. See IRC Sec. 1259(a).
4. IRC Secs. 1259(b)(1), 1259(c)(1)(A).
5. *DuPont v. Comm.*, 110 F.2d 641 (3d Cir. 1940), *cert. den.*, 311 U.S. 657.
6. See Rev. Rul. 2002-44, 2002-28 IRB 84.
7. Treas. Reg. §1.1233-1(a).
8. See IRC Sec. 1259(c)(1)(D).
9. Treas. Reg. §1.1233-1(a)(3). See *Bingham*, 27 BTA 186 (1932), *acq.* 1933-1 CB 2.

Under provisions predating the constructive sale rules—see Q 1087 to Q 1089—to prevent individuals from using short sales to convert short-term gains to long-term gains or long-term losses to short-term losses, and to prevent the creation of artificial losses the IRC and regulations provide special rules as follows:

(1) If on the date the short sale is closed (see below), any "substantially identical property"—see Q 1023—has been held by the seller for a period of one year or less, any *gain* realized on property used to close the sale will, to the extent of the quantity of such substantially identical property, be *short-term* capital gain.[1] This is true even though the stock actually used to close the short sale has been held by the seller for more than one year. This rule does not apply to *losses* realized on the property used to close the sale.

(2) If *any* substantially identical property is acquired by the seller after the short sale and on or before the date the sale is closed, any *gain* realized on property used to close the sale will, to the extent of the quantity of such substantially identical property, be *short-term* capital gain.[2] This is true regardless of how long the substantially identical property has been held, how long the stock used to close the short sale has been held, and how much time has elapsed between the short sale and the date the sale is closed. This rule does not apply to *losses* realized on the property used to close the sale.

(3) The holding period of any substantially identical property held one year or less, or acquired after the short sale and on or before the date the short sale is closed will, to the extent of the quantity of stock sold short, be deemed to have begun on the date the sale is closed or the date such property is sold or otherwise disposed of, whichever is earlier. If the quantity of such substantially identical property held for one year or less or so acquired exceeds the quantity of stock sold short, the "renewed" holding period will normally be applied to individual units of such property in the order in which they were acquired (beginning with earliest acquisition), but only to so much of the property as does not exceed the quantity sold short. Any excess retains its original holding period.[3] But where the short sale is entered into as part of an *arbitrage operation* in stocks or securities (see Q 1026) this order of application is altered so that the "renewed" holding period will be applied first to substantially identical property acquired for arbitrage operations and held at the close of business on the day of the short sale and then in the order of acquisition as described in the previous sentence. The holding period of substantially identical property *not* acquired for arbitrage operations will be affected only to the extent that the quantity sold short exceeds the amount of substantially identical property acquired for arbitrage operations.[4]

If substantially identical property acquired for arbitrage operations is disposed of without closing the short sale, see Q 1027.

(4) If on the date of a short sale *any* substantially identical property has been held by the seller for more than one year, any *loss* realized on property used to close the sale will, to the extent of the quantity of such substantially identical property, be *long-term* capital loss.[5] This is true even though the stock actually used to close the short sale has been held by the seller for a year or less. This rule does not apply to *gains* realized on the property used to close the sale.

1.   IRC Sec. 1233(b)(1); Treas. Reg. §1.1233-1(c).
2.   IRC Sec. 1233(b)(1); Treas. Reg. §1.1233-1(c).
3.   IRC Sec. 1233(b)(2); Treas. Reg. §1.1233-1(c)(2).
4.   IRC Sec. 1233(f); Treas. Reg. §1.1233-1(f).
5.   IRC Sec. 1233(d); Treas. Reg. §1.1233-1(c)(4).

Short Sales of Property That Becomes Substantially Worthless

If a taxpayer enters into a short sale of property and the property becomes substantially worthless, a special rule requires that the taxpayer recognize gain in the same manner as if the short sale were closed when the property became substantially worthless.[1] (To the extent provided in future regulations, this rule will also apply with respect to options and offsetting notional principal contracts with respect to property, any future or forward contract to deliver property, and any similar transaction.)

Special rules are provided regarding the statute of limitations for assessing a deficiency if property becomes substantially worthless during a taxable year and any short sale of property remains open at the time the property becomes substantially worthless.[2] For an explanation of the taxation of stock or other securities that become worthless, see Q 1032.

Miscellaneous Rules

For the tax treatment of the "premium" paid by the short seller to borrow the stock for delivery to the buyer, see Q 1024. The treatment of capital gain or loss on sales is subject to the rules set forth in Q 1420.

Special rules are provided where a taxpayer holds an offsetting short position with respect to qualified small business stock (see Q 1020).

If a short sale is deemed to be part of a conversion transaction, a portion of the gain recognized upon the sale of stock sold short may be treated as ordinary income.[3] See Q 1085 to Q 1086 for an explanation of conversion transactions and the tax treatment of them.

No deduction is allowed for a loss incurred in a short sale if, within the 61-day period that begins 30 days before the date the short sale was closed and ends 30 days after such date, the short seller entered into a wash sale.[4]

The definition of "substantially identical stock or securities" for purposes of the short sale rules is the same as that used for purposes of the wash sale rule, see Q 1023, Q 1031. It would appear that the same definition would be used for purposes of constructive sales of appreciated financial positions, see Q 1087 to Q 1089.

Capital gain or loss from the sale or exchange of a *securities futures contract*—see Q 1072—to sell property (i.e., the short side of a futures contract) will generally be short-term capital gain or loss unless the position is part of a straddle. See Q 1079. In other words, a securities futures contract to sell property is treated as equivalent to a short sale of the underlying property.[5]

1023. What is "substantially identical property"?

In the case of stocks and securities, "substantially identical property," for purposes of the short sale rules, has the meaning given to "substantially identical stock or securi-

---

1. IRC Sec. 1233(h)(1).
2. IRC Sec. 1233(h)(2).
3. IRC Sec. 1258(a).
4. See IRC Sec. 1091(e); AOD 1985-019.
5. H.R. Conf. Rep. No. 106-1033 (CRTRA 2000). See IRC Sec. 1234B(b).

ties" for purposes of the wash sale rule.[1] See Q 1031 for details. It would appear that the same definition should apply for purposes of constructive sales of appreciated financial positions under IRC Section 1259.

A *securities futures contract*—see Q 1072—to acquire substantially identical property will be treated as substantially identical property.[2]

In addition, for purposes of short sales entered into as part of an *arbitrage operation*—see Q 1026—a taxpayer will be deemed to hold substantially identical property for arbitrage operations at the close of any business day if he owns any other property acquired for arbitrage operations (whether or not substantially identical) or has entered any contract in an arbitrage operation which in either case, at the close of that day, gives him the right to receive or acquire substantially identical property.[3]

1024. May an investor deduct the premium he pays to borrow stock in connection with a short sale?

The premium paid by an investor to borrow the stock he delivers to the buyer in a short sale is an expense incurred for the production of income.[4] But the amount is generally treated as interest expense (subject to the limitation on the deduction of investment interest), and not treated as a miscellaneous itemized deduction.[5] As a result, a short seller may find that only a portion (or none) of his premium is deductible for income tax purposes.[6] See Q 1304 regarding the deduction of investment interest.

Furthermore, if the proceeds of a short sale are used to purchase or carry tax-exempt obligations, the amount of the premium is treated as interest for purposes of the general rule that prohibits the deduction of interest expense incurred or continued to purchase or carry tax-exempt obligations. (But this does not apply if the short seller provided cash as collateral for the short sale and does not receive material earnings on such cash.)[7] See Q 1306 and Q 1311 for an explanation of this rule.

If the proceeds of a short sale are used to purchase or carry short-term obligations or market discount bonds, an otherwise allowable deduction of the short sale premium may have to be deferred under the rules discussed in Q 1307 and Q 1308. (A short-term obligation is one which has a fixed maturity date not more than one year from the date of issue.)[8]

1025. May an investor deduct his expenses incurred in reimbursing the lender of stock in a short sale for dividends paid on the borrowed stock?

Cash Dividends

The answer generally depends on the period the short sale is open. If a short sale is held open less than 46 days, any amount paid by the short seller to reimburse the

---

1. Treas. Reg. §1.1233-1(d).
2. IRC Sec. 1233(e)(2)(D).
3. IRC Sec. 1233(f)(3); Treas. Reg. §1.1233-1(f)(2).
4. Rev. Rul. 72-521, 1972-2 CB 128.
5. IRC Sec. 67(b)(8).
6. IRC Sec. 163(d).
7. IRC Secs. 265(a)(2), 265(a)(5).
8. IRC Secs. 1277, 1282, 1283.

lender of stock for *cash* dividends paid on the borrowed stock during the period of the loan will not be deductible by the seller. Instead, the seller will be required to add such amount to his tax basis in the stock he uses to close the short sale (i.e., he will be required to capitalize the expenditure).[1]

But if the amount of the *cash* dividends being reimbursed equals or exceeds 10% (5% in the case of a short sale of stock that is preferred as to dividends) of the amount realized by the short seller in the short sale, the expenditure must be capitalized (i.e., added to the basis of the stock used to close the short sale) *unless* the short sale is open for at least 366 days. For this purpose, all dividends paid on the short sale stock that have ex-dividend dates within the same 85 consecutive day period must be treated as a single dividend. (Dividends that equal or exceed the 10% (or 5%) threshold are referred to as "extraordinary dividends.")[2]

Assuming the short sale is open for a period of 46 days—366 days in the case of an extraordinary dividend—or more, the amount paid by the short seller to reimburse the lender for *cash* dividends is usually deductible as an expense incurred in the production of income.[3] But when it has appeared that the sole motive for the short sale was the reduction of income taxes (through the deduction or offset of capital losses), the Service has taken the position that such amounts are not deductible.[4]

If the short seller must report ordinary income as a result of receiving compensation for the use of collateral he provided in connection with borrowing stock for the short sale, he will generally be permitted to deduct, to the extent of such income, the amounts paid to reimburse the lender for dividends even though the sale was not open more than 45 days. (This exception does not apply in the case of "extraordinary dividends.")[5]

For purposes of determining whether a short sale has been open for at least 46 (or 366) days, the running of such period must be suspended during any period in which (1) the seller holds, has an option to buy, or is under a contractual obligation to buy, stock or securities that are substantially identical to those sold short, or (2) as set forth in regulations, the seller has diminished his risk of loss by holding one or more other positions in substantially similar or related property.[6]

Even though an amount is deductible under the foregoing rules, a short seller may still find that his deduction is limited or must be deferred as follows:

(1) If the proceeds of the short sale are used to purchase or carry tax-exempt obligations, the deduction may be disallowed under the general rule prohibiting the deduction of interest expense incurred or continued to purchase or carry tax-exempts. (But this does not apply if the seller provided cash as collateral for the short sale and does not receive material earnings on such cash.) See Q 1306, Q 1311.[7]

(2) If the proceeds of the short sale are used to purchase or carry market discount bonds or short-term obligations, an otherwise allowable deduction of amounts incurred

---

1. IRC Sec. 263(h)(1).
2. IRC Sec. 263(h).
3. See Rev. Rul. 72-521, 1972-2 CB 128.
4. See *Hart v. Comm.*, 338 F.2d 410 (2d Cir. 1964), wherein the Second Circuit agreed with the Service.
5. IRC Sec. 263(h)(5).
6. IRC Sec. 263(h)(4).
7. IRC Sec. 265(a)(5).

to reimburse the lender of stock for cash dividends may have to be deferred under the rules discussed in Q 1307 and Q 1308. (A short-term obligation is a bond, note, debenture, certificate, or other evidence of indebtedness that has a fixed maturity date not more than one year from the date of issue.)[1]

(3) In any event, the amount of the otherwise deductible reimbursement must be treated as investment interest expense and thus is subject (along with any other investment interest expense) to the general limitation on the deduction of investment interest (see Q 1304).[2]

The amount received by the lender of stock as a reimbursement for a cash dividend from the borrower is *not* a dividend,[3] but is nevertheless treated as ordinary income.

Stock Dividends and Liquidating Dividends

The cost of purchasing additional shares of stock to reimburse the lender for non-taxable *stock* dividends and any amount paid to reimburse the lender for a liquidating dividend are always capital expenditures and not tax deductible.[4] As such, these amounts should be added to the investor's basis in the stock he uses to close the short sale.

1026. For purposes of the short sale rules, what are "arbitrage operations"?

"Arbitrage operations" are transactions involving the purchase and sale of stock or securities (or the right to acquire stock or securities) entered into for the purpose of profiting from a current difference between the price of the property purchased and the price of the property sold. The property purchased must either be identical to the property sold (e.g., stock X trading for different prices on different exchanges) or must entitle the owner to acquire property that is identical to the property sold (e.g., bonds convertible into stock X). To qualify as an arbitrage operation for purposes of the short sale rules, the taxpayer *must* properly identify the transaction as an arbitrage operation on his records as soon as he is able to do so; ordinarily, this must be done on the day of the transaction. Only property properly identified as such will be treated as property acquired for arbitrage operations.[5]

Property that has been properly identified as acquired for arbitrage operations will continue to be treated as such even though, because of subsequent events, the taxpayer sells the property outright rather than using it to complete the arbitrage operation.[6] But see Q 1027 as to the effects of disposing of such property without closing a short sale that was entered into as part of the arbitrage operation.

It is unclear whether an arbitrage operation may be subject to treatment as a conversion transaction—see Q 1085, Q 1086—or whether it may constitute a constructive sale of an appreciated financial position. See Q 1087 to Q 1089.

1. IRC Secs. 1277, 1282, 1283.
2. IRC Sec. 163(d)(3)(C).
3. See Rev. Rul. 60-177, 1960-1 CB 9.
4. Rev. Rul. 72-521, above.
5. IRC Sec. 1233(f); Treas. Reg. §1.1233-1(f)(3).
6. Treas. Reg. §1.1233-1(f)(3).

1027. What are the effects on the short sale rules if substantially identical property acquired for an arbitrage operation is disposed of without closing a short sale that was part of arbitrage operations?

If substantially identical property acquired for arbitrage operations is sold or otherwise disposed of without closing the short sale that was entered into as part of the arbitrage operations so that a net short position in assets acquired for arbitrage is created, a short sale in the amount of the net short position will be deemed to have been made on the date that short position is created. The holding period of any substantially identical property *not* acquired for arbitrage operations will then be determined under the rules discussed in Q 1022 as though the "deemed" short sale was not entered into as part of an arbitrage operation.[1]

> *Example.* On August 13, Mr. Copeland buys 100 bonds of X corporation for purposes other than arbitrage operations. The bonds are convertible (one bond for one share) at Mr. Copeland's option into common stock of X corporation. On November 1, Mr. Copeland sells short 100 shares of X common stock, buys an additional 100 bonds of X corporation, and identifies both transactions as part of arbitrage operations. The bonds acquired on August 13 and November 1 are, on the basis of all the facts, substantially identical to the X common stock. On December 1, Mr. Copeland sells the bonds acquired on November 1, but does not close the short sale. Since a net short position in assets acquired for arbitrage operations is thus created, a short sale is deemed to have been made on December 1. Accordingly, the holding period of the bonds acquired on August 13 will, by application of the rule discussed in Q 1022, begin on the date that the "deemed" short sale is closed (or, if earlier, the date such bonds are disposed of or sold).[2]

It is unclear whether certain arbitrage operations may be subject to treatment as a constructive sale of an appreciated financial position (see Q 1087 to Q 1089).

1028. How is a short sale taxed if the seller dies shortly after making the short sale and his estate or a trust "closes" the sale?

If the short sale constitutes a constructive sale of an appreciated financial position, it will be subject to special transition rules explained in Q 1089. Otherwise, a short sale closed by a seller's estate will be taxed under the earlier rules for short sales. See Q 1022. But for purposes of determining gain or loss, if the sale is closed with stock owned by the seller at his death, the tax basis in that stock will be its value for federal estate tax purposes—generally, fair market value on the date of the seller's death.[3]

It has been determined (under a ruling pre-dating the constructive sales rules of IRC Section 1259) that where a trust established by a seller closed a short sale after the death of the seller with stock it held for the seller's benefit, the basis of such stock generally would be its fair market value either on the date of the seller's death or on an alternate valuation date determined under IRC Section 2032.[4]

For short sales that are not subject to the constructive sales rules of IRC Section 1259—see Q 1022—the taxable event of the short sale occurred when the estate or trust "closed" the sale—see Rev. Rul. 73-524 and Let. Rul. 9319005, above. Thus, any gain recognized on the short sale would *not* constitute "income in respect of a decedent." See Q 1430. But special rules may apply to decedents who held an open short sale position within three years of death. See Q 1089.

1. Treas. Reg. §1.1233-1(f)(1)(ii).
2. See Treas. Reg. §1.1233-1(f)(1)(iii).
3. Rev. Rul. 73-524, 1973-2 CB 307.
4. Let. Rul. 9319005.

Wash Sales

1029. What is a "wash sale"?

A "wash sale" is a sale or other disposition of stock or securities in which the seller, within a 61-day period (that begins 30 days before and ends 30 days after the date of such sale or disposition), replaces the stock or securities by acquiring (by way of a purchase or an exchange on which the full gain or loss is recognized for tax purposes) or entering a contract or option to acquire substantially identical stock or securities.[1] Typically, the objective of a wash sale—were it not subject to the special rules of IRC Section 1091(a) explained in Q 1030—would be to take advantage of the deduction for any capital losses, and then repurchase the shares immediately thereafter.

The replacement of stock or securities by way of gift, inheritance, or tax-free exchange will not result in a wash sale.[2] For the definition of "substantially identical stock or securities," see Q 1031. Except as provided in regulations, the term "stock or securities" includes "contracts or options to acquire or sell stock or securities." For an explanation, see Q 1045.

Where there is no substantial likelihood that a put option (see Q 1047) will *not* be exercised, its sale will be treated as a contract to acquire the stock.[3]

For purposes of the wash sale rule, a stock warrant is considered to be an option to acquire stock of the issuing corporation.[4] Preferred stock that is convertible into common stock of the same corporation *without restriction* is considered to be an option to acquire such common stock.[5]

A seller of stock who agrees at the time of the sale to repurchase that same stock after a minimum of 30 days has entered into a contract, and the sale is a wash sale. It is irrelevant whether the contract is enforceable under state law.[6]

A bona fide sale of a portion of the shares of stock purchased in a single lot for purposes of reducing the purchaser's holdings in that stock is *not* a wash sale even though the sale occurs within 30 days after the lot was acquired.[7]

A disposition of stock or securities may not be taken out of the definition of a "wash sale" by merely postponing delivery until more than 30 days after the date the shares of stock or securities are replaced.[8] A purchase of substantially identical stock or securities during the 61-day period will trigger the wash sale rule even though the purchase is made on margin or pursuant to subscription rights acquired prior to the beginning of the 61-day period.[9]

Where a taxpayer received 10 shares of stock as a bonus from his employer, sold them at a loss, and then within the 61-day period received another bonus of 10 shares of the same stock, the Service ruled that a wash sale had occurred; the tax basis of

---

1. IRC Sec. 1091(a); Treas. Reg. §1.1091-1(a).
2. See Treas. Reg. §1.1091-1(f).
3. Rev. Rul. 85-87, 1985-1 CB 268.
4. Rev. Rul. 56-406, 1956-2 CB 523.
5. Rev. Rul. 77-201, 1977-1 CB 250.
6. *Est. of Estroff v. Comm.*, TC Memo 1983-666.
7. Rev. Rul. 56-602, 1956-2 CB 527.
8. Rev. Rul. 59-418, 1959-2 CB 184.
9. See respectively, Rev. Rul. 71-316, 1971-2 CB 311; Rev. Rul. 71-520, 1971-2 CB 311.

shares received as a bonus is their fair market value at the time of payment.[1] It appears that the sale or purchase of "when-issued" securities is deemed to occur on the date the final settlement is made.[2]

An employee who, under an employer-employee restricted stock option plan, was granted an option to purchase stock of his employer was deemed for purposes of the wash sale rule to have entered into an option to acquire that stock on the date the option is granted; the stock purchased pursuant to such option is deemed to have been acquired on the date the certificates are issued.[3] See Q 1037 to Q 1041 for the tax treatment of incentive stock options.

Securities futures contracts. "The wash sale rules apply to any loss from the sale, exchange, or termination of a securities futures contract (other than a dealer securities futures contract) if within a period beginning 30 days before the date of such sale, exchange, or termination and ending 30 days after such date: (1) stock that is substantially identical to the stock to which the contract relates is sold; (2) a short sale of substantially identical stock is entered into; or (3) another securities futures contract to sell substantially identical stock is entered into."[4]

The taxation of a wash sale is explained in Q 1030. For the application of the wash sale rule in the context of a short sale, see Q 1022.

1030. How is the sale or disposition of stock or securities in a wash sale taxed? What effect does a wash sale have on the replacement stock or securities?

Stock or Securities Sold

No special tax rules apply if an investor realizes a *gain* in a wash sale of stock or other securities; rather, the sale will be taxed under the rules peculiar to both the type of disposition and to the particular stock or security sold. For the taxation of gain on treasury bills, bonds and notes, and municipal bonds, see respectively Q 1094, Q 1100, and Q 1125. For taxation of gain on corporate obligations, see Q 1096 and Q 1103. For taxation of stocks, see Q 1017 to Q 1020.

On the other hand, to the extent that shares of stock or securities sold are replaced in a wash sale (as defined in Q 1029), any *loss* realized on the stock or securities sold may *not* be recognized for income tax purposes and, therefore, may not be used to offset capital gains or otherwise deducted; however, if the quantity of the stock or securities sold at a loss exceeds the quantity replaced, the loss realized on the excess shares or securities may be recognized as a capital loss for income tax purposes.[5]

Replacement Stock or Securities

As part of a scheme to postpone the recognition of an economic wash sale loss, rather than disallow it permanently, the IRC provides that both the tax basis and hold-

---

1. Rev. Rul. 73-329, 1973-2 CB 202.
2. See I.T. 3858, 1947-2 CB 71.
3. Rev. Rul. 56-452, 1956-2 CB 525.
4. See IRC Sec. 1091(e); Joint Committee on Taxation, Technical Explanation of the "Job Creation and Worker Assistance Act of 2002" (JCX-12-02), March 6, 2002.
5. IRC Sec. 1091(b); Treas. Reg. §1.1091-1(c); Rev. Rul. 70-231, 1970-1 CB 171.

ing period of the replacement stock or securities are to be adjusted. Specifically, the tax basis of the replacement stock or securities is deemed to be equal to the tax basis of the stock or securities disposed of in the wash sale increased or decreased, as the case may be, by the difference (if any) between the price at which the property was acquired and the price at which the substantially identical stock or securities were sold or otherwise disposed of. (This generally has the effect of adding the amount of the unrecognized loss to the cost basis of the replacement stock or securities.)[1]

Furthermore, the investor's holding period in the stock or securities disposed of in the wash sale is "tacked" (i.e., added) onto his holding period in the replacement stock or securities.[2]

Matching

Where identical quantities of stock or securities are sold and replaced in a wash sale, there is little problem in applying the rules discussed above. But where unequal quantities are sold and replaced or where sales and/or replacements are made in multiple lots (or transactions), the stock or securities sold and the replacement stock or securities must be matched on a chronological basis (beginning with the earliest loss and earliest replacement) before the rules can be properly applied.[3]

> *Example.* On March 1, Ms. Whalen sells 1000 shares of X stock (lot A) at a loss of $10,000 and a second lot of 1000 (lot B) on March 2 at a loss of $25,000. On March 10, Ms. Whalen purchases 1000 shares of X stock (lot C). This purchase will result in the nonrecognition for income tax purposes of the $10,000 loss on lot A and an increase of $10,000 in the tax basis of the replacement stock (lot C). In addition, the holding period of lot C will include the holding period of lot A (i.e., the holding period of lot A will be "tacked" onto the holding period of lot C).

> If, on March 20, Ms. Whalen purchases another lot (lot D) of 1000 shares of stock X, the $25,000 loss on the sale of lot B will not be recognized for income tax purposes. The tax basis of lot D will be increased by $25,000, and the holding period of lot B will be tacked onto the holding period of lot D.

1031. When are stocks or securities "substantially identical" for purposes of the wash sale rule?

Whether stocks or securities are substantially identical depends on the facts and circumstances of each case.[4] Beyond that, unfortunately, the IRC and regulations offer little guidance as to when stocks or securities are substantially identical; but it is clear that "something less than precise correspondence will suffice."[5]

Ordinarily, stocks or securities of one corporation are not substantially identical to stocks or securities of another corporation; however, a different result may occur as, for example, in a reorganization, where facts and circumstances indicate that the stocks and securities of predecessor and successor corporations are substantially identical.[6] Where voting trust certificates eventually could be exchanged for common stock held by the trust, the certificates were held to be substantially identical to the common stock of the same corporation.[7]

---

1. IRC Sec. 1091(d); Treas. Reg. §1.1091-2.
2. IRC Sec. 1223(4).
3. IRC Secs. 1091(b), 1091(c); Treas. Reg. §1.1091-1.
4. Treas. Reg. §1.1233-1(d)(1).
5. *Hanlin v. Comm.*, 108 F.2d 429 (3d Cir. 1939).
6. Treas. Reg. §1.1233-1(d)(1).
7. See *Kidder v. Comm.*, 30 BTA 59 (1934).

When preferred stock is convertible into common stock of the same corporation, the relative values, price changes and other circumstances may make the preferred and common stocks substantially identical.[1] Also, when a sale of a stock warrant is followed within 30 days by a purchase of stock of the same corporation, the warrant and the newly acquired stock are substantially identical only if the relative values and price changes are similar.[2]

For purposes of the wash sale rule, options to buy stock or securities apparently can be considered substantially identical not only to the underlying stock, but to other options or contracts to buy stocks or securities.[3]

Under the wash sale rule, a contract or option to acquire or sell stock or securities will include options and contracts that are (or may be) settled in cash or property other than the stock or securities to which the contract relates.[4] Thus, for example, the acquisition within the period set forth in IRC Section 1091 of a *securities futures contract*—see Q 1072—to acquire stock of a corporation could cause the taxpayer's loss on the sale of stock in that corporation to be disallowed under the wash sale rule, notwithstanding that the contract may be settled in cash.[5]

Generally, *bonds* are substantially identical if they are not substantially different in any material feature and are not substantially different in several material features considered together (each of which, if considered alone, would not be regarded as substantial).[6] Although very few concrete criteria exist to aid in determining which features are material and when such material features alone or in conjunction will result in a substantial difference, the following may be of guidance:

…The interest rate of a bond is considered a material feature.[7]

…In determining whether bonds purchased are substantially identical to bonds sold, the bonds purchased must be compared as they existed when purchased with the bonds sold as they existed when sold.[8]

…Issue dates of bonds are not material features unless some material features are dependent on such dates.[9]

…Whether a difference in maturity dates is substantial or not is directly affected by the total time period to maturity (i.e., "6 months added to the duration of one year is vital—added to a duration of twenty years, negligible").[10]

WORTHLESS SECURITIES

1032. How is a shareholder taxed when his stock or other security becomes worthless?

1. Treas. Reg. §1.1233-1(d)(1); Rev. Rul. 77-201, 1977-1 CB 250.
2. GCM 39036 (9-22-83).
3. See IRC Sec. 1091(a).
4. H.R. Conf. Rep. No. 106-1033 (CRTRA 2000).
5. H.R. Conf. Rep. No. 106-1033 (CRTRA 2000). See IRC Sec. 1091(f).
6. Rev. Rul. 58-211, 1958-1 CB 529.
7. Rev. Rul. 60-195, 1960-1 CB 300.
8. Rev. Rul. 58-211, 1958-1 CB 529.
9. Rev. Rul. 58-210, 1958-1 CB 523.
10. *Hanlin v. Comm.*, 108 F.2d 429 (3d Cir. 1939).

If an investor's security (whether it be stock in a corporation or some other security) becomes worthless at any time during the year, his loss is treated as a capital loss realized in a sale or exchange of the worthless security on the last day of that year.[1] (Special rules, however, apply to certain small business and small business investment company stocks.[2])

The determination as to when a security becomes worthless is often very difficult and has been the subject of an extensive amount of litigation. The investor must be able to show that an identifiable event (or events) resulting in the worthlessness occurred in the year in which he claims the loss occurred.[3] He must also be able to show that the security had some intrinsic or potential value at the close of the prior year.[4] In fact, the determination is often so difficult that the Second Circuit Court of Appeals has said that the "only safe practice … is to claim a loss for the earliest year when it may possibly be allowed and to renew the claim in subsequent years if there is any reasonable chance of its being applicable … in those years."[5]

In determining whether a security is, in fact, worthless, any potential future value as well as any present value must be considered.[6] The security must be totally worthless; a "paper" loss on a security that is partially worthless or that has declined in value is not realized and may not be recognized until the security is actually sold or exchanged.[7]

In Field Service Advice released in 2002, the IRS discussed at length several issues relating to worthless stock including: (1) the factual nature of the inquiry into the worthlessness of stock; (2) the 2-part test for the worthlessness of stock, and the application of the test; (3) identifiable events in general; (4) determining worthlessness without an identifiable event; (5) timing of the loss using identifiable events; (6) liquidation as an identifiable event, and liquidation as destroying potential worth; (7) the fact that stock is not worthless simply because nothing is received for it; (8) the potential worth of (a) stock disposed of by sale, (b) the investment after the election, (c) canceled stock, and (d) surrendered stock; and (9) the potential worth because of claims for reimbursement.[8]

According to the Tax Court, the principles for establishing the worthlessness of stock in a particular taxable year are virtually identical to the principles for establishing a worthless debt. Thus, as in the case of a bad debt deduction due to the worthlessness of a debt, to sustain a worthless stock loss the taxpayer must show an absence of potential as well as liquid value by year-end.[9]

Generally, the amount of the capital loss resulting from a security's becoming worthless is the shareholder's tax basis in the security as of the last day of the year in

---

1.   IRC Secs. 165(g), 165(f); Treas. Reg. §1.165-5(c).
2.   See IRC Secs. 1243, 1244; see also *Crigler v. Comm.*, TC Memo 2003-93, aff'd per curiam, No. 03-1861 (4th Cir. 2004).
3.   Treas. Reg. §1.165-1(b); *Boehm v. Comm.*, 326 U.S. 287 (1945); see also *In re Steffen*, 294 BR 388 (Bankr. M.D. FL. 2003).
4.   *Dunbar v. Comm.*, 119 F.2d 367 (8th Cir. 1941).
5.   *Young v. Comm.*, 123 F.2d 597 (2d Cir. 1941).
6.   See Rev. Rul. 77-17, 1977-1 CB 44.
7.   Treas. Regs. §§1.165-1(b), 1.165-5(c).
8.   See FSA 200226004.
9.   See *Rendall v. Comm.*, TC Memo 2006-174, citing *Morton v. Comm.*, 38 BTA 1260, 1278 – 1279 (1938), aff'd, 112 F.2d 320 (7th Circ. 1940).

which it becomes worthless.[1] However, capital loss treatment will be allowed only to the extent that the loss is not compensated for by insurance or otherwise.[2]

The loss from a capital asset that becomes worthless during a taxable year is determined as if the asset were sold or exchanged on the last day of the year; thus, the taxpayer's holding period would apparently be determined as of that date.[3]

Because of the difficulties in proving the "if" and "when" of worthlessness, it is often suggested that a security nearing worthlessness be sold to establish the loss; however, a loss on such sale may be disallowed if it can be shown that the security became worthless in a prior year.[4]

In the case of a capital loss claimed to have been sustained as a result of a security becoming worthless, the normal 3-year statute of limitations for amending federal income tax returns is extended to seven years.[5] In *Georgeff v. United States*,[6] the taxpayers filed their 1997 tax return on September 25, 2002, identifying an alleged worthless security loss and also claiming entitlement to a refund for that loss on the same return. The taxpayers argued that the special seven-year statute of limitations should apply. Rejecting the taxpayers' argument, the United States Court of Federal Claims stated that IRC Section 6511(d) was designed to protect against freshly discovered or newly increased bad debt deductions after the filing of an original tax return, not those identified before the tax return was filed. The court concluded that the taxpayers were not entitled to the benefit of an enlarged statute of limitations from three to seven years because the alleged loss based on the worthless security was known well in advance of the time that their 1997 tax return was due on April 15, 1998 and filed on September 25, 2002. Accordingly, the court dismissed the taxpayers' complaint and entered the United States' motion for summary judgment.

Special rules apply in the case of a short sale of property that becomes substantially worthless.[7] See Q 1022. See Q 1420 regarding the tax treatment of capital gains and losses.

STOCK WARRANTS

1033. What is a stock warrant?

A stock warrant is an instrument issued by a corporation granting the owner thereof the right to buy a certain amount of stock at a specified price, usually for a limited time. In the case of the holder, a stock warrant is generally treated like an option.[8]

1034. How is the acquisition of a stock warrant taxed? What is its tax basis?

If a warrant to acquire stock in the distributing corporation is acquired in a dividend distribution, taxation to the recipient-shareholder depends on whether the dividend is

---

1. IRC Sec. 165(b); Treas. Reg. §1.165-1(c).
2. IRC Sec. 165(a).
3. See IRC Sec. 165(g)(1).
4. See *DeLoss v. Comm.*, 28 F.2d 803 (2d Cir. 1928), *cert. den.*, 279 U.S. 840 (1929); *Rand v. Helvering*, 116 F.2d 929 (8th Cir. 1941), *cert. den.*, 313 U.S. 594 (1941); *Heiss v. Comm.*, 36 BTA 833 (1937), *acq.*
5. IRC Sec. 6511(d)(1).
6. No. 05-385T (Fed. Cl. 2005).
7. IRC Sec. 1233(h)(1).
8. See IRC Sec. 1234; Rev. Rul. 56-406, 1956-2 CB 523.

taxable or not (see Q 1009). If it is a nontaxable stock dividend, there is no immediate income taxation. See Q 1011 to determine the tax basis of a warrant acquired in a nontaxable stock dividend. If the dividend is taxable, it is treated as a dividend "in kind," so that the amount that generally must be included in the recipient-shareholder's income is the fair market value of the warrant on the date of distribution.[1] This is also the warrant's tax basis (see Q 1003).

If a corporation distributes a warrant to acquire stock in another corporation, it is also taxed as a dividend in kind. The basis of the warrant to an individual shareholder is its fair market value (see Q 1003).

If a warrant is acquired through purchase, gift, or inheritance, there are no immediate income tax consequences. The tax basis of a warrant acquired in this manner is determined under general rules discussed in Q 1415.

1035. How is the owner of a warrant taxed when the warrant is sold, exercised, or allowed to lapse?

The sale, exercise, or lapse of a stock warrant is taxed in the same general manner as an unlisted call option.[2]

Sale. If a warrant distributed in a nontaxable stock dividend is sold, the owner realizes a capital gain or loss to the extent of the difference between his tax basis in the warrant and the proceeds of the sale. (For the tax basis of a warrant acquired in a nontaxable stock dividend, see Q 1011.)[3] In determining the owner's holding period with respect to the warrant, the holding period of the stock with respect to which the dividend was paid is included.[4] See Q 1420 for the tax treatment of capital gain or loss.

If a warrant distributed in a taxable dividend, or acquired by purchase, gift, or inheritance is sold, the owner realizes a capital gain or loss to the extent of the difference between his tax basis in the warrant and the proceeds of the sale. (For the tax basis of a warrant distributed in a taxable dividend, see Q 1003. For the tax basis of a warrant acquired by purchase, gift, or inheritance, see Q 1415.)

Exercise. The owner of a warrant will realize no capital gain or loss when he exercises his warrant and purchases the stock. However, for purposes of determining gain or loss on a subsequent sale or exchange of that stock, the tax basis of the warrant is added to the subscription price paid for the stock.[5]

Lapse. If allowed to expire without exercise (i.e., lapse), a warrant is deemed to have been sold on the date of lapse.[6] The owner of the warrant will realize a loss only if he has a tax basis in the warrant. This occurs only when the owner acquired the warrant in a taxable stock dividend, or through purchase, gift, or inheritance; the basis of a warrant received in a nontaxable stock dividend is zero unless it is actually sold or exercised (see Q 1011).

---

1. Treas. Reg. §1.305-1(b).
2. See IRC Sec. 1234.
3. See IRC Sec. 1234(a).
4. IRC Sec. 1223(5).
5. See Treas. Reg. §1.307-1(b).
6. See IRC Sec. 1234(a)(2).

INCENTIVE STOCK OPTIONS

1036. What is an incentive stock option?

An incentive stock option is an option granted to an individual in connection with his employment by the employer corporation (or its parent or subsidiary corporation) to purchase stock of the corporation, if all of the following requirements are met:

(1) The option is granted pursuant to a plan that specifies the number of shares to be issued and the employees or class of employees to receive the option. The plan must be approved by the stockholders of the corporation within 12 months before or after the date the plan is adopted.

(2) The option is granted within 10 years of the date the plan is adopted or approved by the shareholders, whichever occurs first.

(3) The option must, by its terms, be exercisable within not more than 10 years of the date it is granted.

(4) The exercise price of the option is not less than the fair market value of the stock at the time it is granted.

(5) The option is nontransferable and exercisable only by the transferee (except that it may be transferred by will or the laws of descent and distribution).

(6) The grantee of the option may not own stock representing more than 10% of the voting power of all classes of stock of the employer corporation, or its parent or subsidiary corporation. There is an exception to this rule where (i) the option price is at least 110% of the fair market value of the stock subject to the option, and (ii) the option is exercisable only within five years after it is granted.[1]

In determining the extent of an individual's ownership of stock for purposes of the 10% limitation, an individual will be considered to own stock of the employer corporation or of a related corporation that is owned (directly or indirectly) by the individual's brothers, sisters, spouse, ancestors, and lineal descendants.[2]

If the stock covered by options that *may be exercised* by any individual employee for the first time in a calendar year (under all plans of the employer corporation, and its parent and subsidiary corporations) has an aggregate fair market value that exceeds $100,000, the excess options may not be treated as incentive stock options. For purposes of the $100,000 limitation, the options are taken into account in the order in which they were granted, and their fair market value is determined as of the date the option was granted.[3]

An employee exercising an ISO may pay for the stock with stock of the corporation granting the option.[4] In determining whether the exercise price of the option is not less than the fair market value of the shares at the time the option is granted, a down payment required prior to exercise may be aggregated with the price to be paid at the time of exercise.[5]

---

1. IRC Secs. 422(b), 422(c)(5); Treas. Reg. §1.422-2.
2. Treas. Reg. §1.424-1(d).
3. IRC Sec. 422(d).
4. IRC Sec. 422(c)(4)(A).
5. Let. Rul. 9109026.

1037. How is the grant of an incentive stock option taxed? How is the exercise of the option taxed?

No income is realized by the employee upon granting of an incentive stock option. If the transfer of stock pursuant to his exercise of an incentive stock option is a *qualifying transfer*, no income will be realized by the employee at the time the option is exercised.[1] The transfer will be a qualifying transfer if both of the following requirements are met:

(1) *Holding period requirement:* no *disposition* (defined below) of the stock may be made by the employee within two years of the date the option was granted to him, nor within one year of the date the stock was transferred to him pursuant to the option;

(2) *Employment requirement:* the transferee must be employed by the corporation granting the option (or its parent or subsidiary) at all times from the date the option was granted until three months before the date of exercise.[2]

If an employee becomes permanently and totally disabled, the 3-month employment period is extended to 12 months.[3] In the case of the death of an employee, the employment and holding requirements are waived.[4]

If an incentive stock option is exercised by an individual who does not meet the employment requirement described above (except in the event of the employee's death), there will *not* be a qualifying transfer and the individual will recognize compensation income in the year the option is exercised. The amount of compensation income realized will be the excess, if any, of the fair market value of the stock over the exercise price of the option.[5] (See Q 1039 regarding disqualifying transfers.)

In other words, if the employment requirement is met, the question of whether a transfer is a *qualifying transfer* can be answered with certainty only after the holding periods have been satisfied. If the holding periods (and employment requirement) are met, the taxpayer's subsequent disposition of the stock will be taxed as explained in Q 1038. If the 1-year and 2-year holding periods are not eventually satisfied, ordinary income is realized as of the date the option is exercised, which is *recognized*, (i.e., taxed) in the year of the disposition, as explained in Q 1039.

For purposes of the holding period requirement, "disposition" includes sales, exchanges, gifts, and transfers of legal title. But the following will not constitute a disposition: (i) a transfer from a decedent to an estate or a transfer by bequest or inheritance; (ii) certain exchanges pursuant to a corporate reorganization or exchanges of stock for stock of the same corporation or a controlled corporation; or (iii) the making of a mere pledge or hypothecation. Additionally, the acquisition of stock as a joint tenant with right of survivorship or transfer of stock to joint ownership will not constitute a disposition until the joint tenancy is terminated.[6] A transfer between spouses or former spouses incident to divorce also will not be considered a disposition, and the transferee

---

1.   IRC Sec. 421(a); Treas. Reg. §1.422-1(a)(1).
2.   IRC Sec. 422(a).
3.   IRC Sec. 422(c)(6).
4.   IRC Sec. 421(c)(1).
5.   Treas. Reg. §1.422-1(c); IRC Sec. 83(a).
6.   IRC Sec. 424(c).

spouse will receive the same tax treatment that would have applied to the transferor.[1] The IRS determined that a transfer to a grantor trust, resulting in ownership of stock by a husband and wife with right of survivorship, did not constitute a disposition.[2]

For purposes of the 1-year and 2-year holding period requirements, a transfer resulting from bankruptcy proceedings will not be considered a disposition.[3] But such a transfer will be considered a disposition for purposes of the recognition of capital gain or loss.[4]

Generally, an individual's basis in stock acquired in a qualifying transfer upon exercise of an incentive stock option is the amount he paid to exercise the option. (If there is a *disqualifying disposition*, the individual's basis is increased by amounts includable as compensation income. See Q 1039.)

In informational guidance released in 2002, the IRS analyzed whether the "deemed sale" election under Section 311(e) of TRA '97 (see Q 1420) is a "disposition" within the meaning of IRC Section 424(c) under two circumstances: (1) where employees are holding incentive stock options that were granted to them prior to 2001, but that were not exercised as of January 1, 2001; (2) where employees were granted incentive stock options and exercised those options during November 2000. In the first situation, the IRS stated that there is no provision in Section 311(e) or the incentive stock option rules providing for a "deemed exercise" of the option in order to have the holding period start in 2001. In the second situation, the Service stated it appeared that any deemed sale of the stock acquired upon exercise of an incentive stock option would be treated as a disqualifying disposition for purposes of the incentive stock option rules, thus triggering the application of IRC Section 83. The Service concluded by stating that the informational guidance did not constitute a ruling on any issue. The Service also recognized that the interaction of the incentive stock option rules with the Section 311(e) election is a novel issue that the Service has not yet addressed.[5]

FICA and FUTA taxes. Proposed regulations would provide that at the time an incentive stock option is exercised, the individual exercising the option would receive wages for FICA and FUTA purposes.[6] *But* the IRS has announced that until further guidance is issued, the Service will not assess the FICA or FUTA tax, or apply federal income tax withholding obligations, upon either the exercise of the option or the disposition of the stock acquired by an employee pursuant to the exercise of an option. Furthermore, the Service and the Treasury Department anticipate that any final guidance that would apply employment taxes to incentive stock options will not apply to any exercise of an incentive stock option that at occurs at least two years after the date the final regulations are published.[7]

For guidance concerning an employer's income tax withholding and reporting obligations upon the sale or disposition of stock pursuant to the exercise of an incentive stock option, see Notice 2001-72.[8] For details on the rules of administrative conve-

---

1. IRC Sec. 424(c)(4).
2. Let Rul. 9021046.
3. IRC Sec. 422(c)(3).
4. Treas. Reg. §1.422-1(a)(2)(ii).
5. INFO 2002-0137 (7-5-2002).
6. Prop. Treas. Regs. §§31.3121(a)-1(k)(1)(ii), 31.3306(b)-1(l)(1)(ii).
7. See Notice 2002-47, 2002-28 IRB 97.
8. 2001-2 CB 548. See also CCA 200114001.

nience relating to the application of FICA and FUTA tax to incentive stock options, see Notice 2001-73.[1]

Alternative Minimum Tax. For purposes of the alternative minimum tax, the excess of the fair market value of the stock on the date of exercise of the option over the exercise price will be added to alternative minimum taxable income in the year the option is exercised, provided the taxpayer's rights are not subject to a substantial risk of forfeiture. But if the taxpayer is subject to the alternative minimum tax, his basis in the stock for alternative minimum tax purposes will be increased by the amount included in income.[2] A taxpayer with unvested stock may wish to make a special election under IRC Section 83(b) to include in his gross income for the taxable year an amount equal to the excess of the fair market value of the property at the time it was transferred over the amount (if any) paid for such property. By making the special election, the adjustment for AMT purposes will be reported in the year the election is made instead of the year the stock actually vests. This may be beneficial if the stock price is expected to significantly appreciate before the stock vests.

1038. How is a disposition of stock acquired pursuant to the exercise of an incentive stock option taxed if the transfer of the stock to the individual was a qualifying transfer?

If the transfer of stock to an individual upon his exercise of an incentive stock option was a *qualifying transfer* (see Q 1037), then no taxable event occurs until the stock is disposed of.[3] At the time of disposition, the general rules for treatment of a sale of stock will apply; thus, the taxpayer will recognize capital gain or loss to the extent of the difference between the sale price of the stock and his adjusted basis. See Q 1017 regarding the sale of stock, and Q 1420 for an explanation of the treatment of capital gains and losses.

1039. What is the tax on disposition of stock acquired pursuant to the exercise of an incentive stock option if the requisite holding periods are not met?

If exercise of an incentive stock option would otherwise qualify as a nontaxable event except that the 1-year or 2-year holding requirement is not met (i.e., there is a *disqualifying disposition*), the employee's gain (if any) on the disposition will be treated as follows:

(i) any gain that is *compensation attributable to the exercise of the option* will be taxed as ordinary income (and the employer will have a corresponding deduction) in the year the disposition occurs. "Compensation attributable to the exercise of the option" means the excess of the fair market value of the stock on the date the option was exercised over the amount paid for the share at the time of exercise. The employee's basis in the stock is then increased by the amount he included as income.[4]

(ii) Any gain in excess of compensation attributable to the exercise of the option will be treated as capital gain. See Q 1420 for the treatment of capital gains and losses.[5]

---

1. 2001-2 CB 549.
2. IRC Sec. 56(b)(3).
3. IRC Sec. 421(a).
4. IRC Sec. 421(b); Treas. Reg. §1.421-2(b)(1).
5. Treas. Reg. §1.421-2(b)(1)(ii), Example (2).

If, in a disqualifying disposition, the employee recognizes a loss, then the compensation income attributable to exercise of the option will be limited to the excess of the amount realized on disposition over the adjusted basis of the stock (i.e., generally the amount paid to exercise the option). This rule applies only to transactions in which loss would otherwise be allowable; it does not apply, for example, to losses on related party sales or wash sales. Thus, in the event that the disqualifying disposition is a related party sale, wash sale, or other transaction on which loss would be disallowed, the transferor will be required to recognize gain in the amount of the excess of the fair market value of the stock at the time the option was exercised *over* the option price. The income includable as a result of such a disposition will generally be treated as compensation.[1] It has been determined that where stock acquired through the exercise of an incentive stock option is transferred to a charitable remainder trust before the 1-year holding period is up, the transfer will be treated as if a loss on a related party sale occurred. Thus, the transferor must include in gross income in the year of transfer the difference between the fair market value of the stock at the date the option was exercised *over* the option price.[2] In 2002, the Service announced an exception from reporting on Form 1099-B for transactions involving an employee, former employee or other service provider who has obtained a stock option. Where the employee purchases stock through the exercise of the stock option, and then sells that stock on the same day through a broker, the broker executing such a sale is not required to report the sale on Form 1099-B provided certain conditions are met.[3]

Example 1: On June 1, 2006, CB Corporation grants an incentive stock option to Mr. Stephens, an employee of CB Corporation, entitling him to purchase one share of CB stock for $100, its fair market value on that date. Mr. Stephens exercises the option on August 1, 2006, and the stock is transferred to him the same day. Its fair market value on the date of exercise is $125. In order to meet the holding period requirements of IRC Section 422(a)(1), Mr. Stephens must not dispose of the stock before June 1, 2008. But Mr. Stephens transfers the stock on September 1, 2006 for $150 (the stock is transferable and not subject to a substantial risk of forfeiture). The amount of compensation attributable to Mr. Stephens' exercise of the option will be $25 (the excess of the fair market value on the date of exercise over the exercise price). On his 2006 return, as a result of the disposition of the stock, Mr. Stephens' will include $25 as compensation income and $25 as capital gain income. CB Corporation will be permitted a deduction of $25 for compensation attributable to Mr. Stephens' exercise of the option. If Mr. Stephens sold the stock in 2007 instead of 2006, he would include the $25 compensation income and the $25 capital gain as income on his 2007 return.

Example 2: Assume the same facts as example (1), except that instead of selling the stock on September 1, 2006 for $150, Mr. Stephens sells it for $75. The rule in IRC Section 422(c)(2) applies to limit the amount of income attributable to the exercise of the option to the excess (if any) of the sale price ($75) over the adjusted basis of the stock ($100). Mr. Stephens will not be required to recognize any compensation income, and he will be permitted a capital loss of $25 (the adjusted basis of the share minus the amount realized on the sale). CB Corporation will not be permitted any deduction for compensation attributable to Mr. Stephens' exercise of the option. If Mr. Stephens had, instead, sold the stock for $115, he would realize compensation income of $15 (the sale price minus his adjusted basis), but he would realize no capital gain income since the sale price was less than the amount that was the fair market value of the stock on the date he exercised the option.

Example 3: Assume the same facts as example (2), except that the sale on September 1, 2006 is to Mr. Stephens' daughter, Janice. Under the related party sale rules of IRC Section 267, no loss sustained on such a sale may be recognized. Thus, Mr. Stephens must recognize compensation income of $25 (the excess of the fair market value on the date of exercise over the exercise price) and will not recognize a capital gain or loss on the transaction. CB Corporation will be permitted a deduction of $25 for compensation attributable to Mr. Stephens' exercise of the option, provided certain withholding requirements are met.

---

1. IRC Sec. 422(c)(2); Treas. Reg. §1.422-1(b)(2).
2. Let. Rul. 9308021.
3. See Rev. Proc. 2002-50, 2002-2 CB 173.

Alternative Minimum Tax

If there is a recognizable loss on a disqualifying disposition in the same year as the exercise of the option, the taxpayer's alternative minimum taxable income will be increased only by the excess of the amount realized on disposition over the adjusted basis of the stock.[1] For a definition of "disposition" see Q 1037.

1040. What is the tax effect of modification, renewal, or extension of an incentive stock option?

The modification, renewal or extension of an incentive stock option is, for tax purposes, the equivalent of the granting of a new option; therefore, the requirements explained in Q 1036 will apply.[2] Thus a new option price is required if the fair market value of the stock is greater than the price of the original option, since the option price must equal at least 100% of the fair market value of the stock at the time the option is granted.

"Modification" generally means any change in the terms of the option that gives the employee additional benefits under the option. For example, a change that shortens the period during which the option is exercisable is not a modification. But a change that provides more favorable terms for the payment for the stock purchased under the option *is* a modification. A change in the number of shares subject to the option will not be considered a modification of the existing option, but it will constitute the grant of a new option with respect to the additional shares. But a change in the number or price of shares of stock subject to an option merely to reflect a stock dividend or stock split-up is not a modification of the option.[3]

The IRC states that the following changes in the terms of an option will not be considered a "modification": (i) changes attributable to certain corporate reorganizations and liquidations; and (ii) in the case of an option not immediately exercisable in full, changes that accelerate the time at which the option may be exercised.[4] For examples of reorganizations that did not result in modifications of options, see Let. Ruls. 9810024, 9849002.

The Service has privately ruled that a downward adjustment to the exercise price of a company's outstanding stock options, to reflect a return of capital to the company's shareholders, was a "corporate transaction," and not a modification, extension, or renewal of those options.[5] A company's failure to adjust options to reflect a reverse stock split did not result in a modification.[6]

The IRS has determined that modification did not take place where the exercise of incentive stock options was conditioned on the achievement of performance-related goals which changed from time to time.[7]

The Service has also determined that an amendment to a plan, which would allow payment for option stock through constructive delivery (rather than physical delivery)

1. IRC Sec. 56(b)(3).
2. IRC Sec. 424(h).
3. IRC Sec. 424(h)(1); Treas. Reg. §1.424-1(e)(4).
4. IRC Sec. 424(h)(3).
5. Let. Rul. 9801030.
6. Let. Rul. 200007033.
7. Let. Rul. 8444071.

of previously owned shares of company stock, would not result in modification of the options.[1]

1041. Is the special tax treatment for incentive stock options available if an incentive stock option and a stock appreciation right are granted together?

Under long-standing rules, the tax treatment provided for incentive stock options has been available for the combination of an incentive stock option (ISO) and a stock appreciation right (SAR) even though the right to exercise one affects the right to exercise the other, provided the SAR, by its terms, meets certain requirements:

(1) The SAR will expire no later than the expiration of the underlying ISO.

(2) The SAR may be for no more than 100% of the spread (i.e., the difference) between the exercise price of the underlying option and the market price of the stock subject to the underlying option at the time the SAR is exercised.

(3) The SAR is transferable only when the underlying ISO is transferable, and under the same conditions.

(4) The SAR may be exercised only when the underlying ISO is eligible to be exercised.

(5) The SAR may be exercised only when there is a positive spread, (i.e., when the market price of the stock subject to the option exceeds the exercise price of the option).

The SAR could be paid in either cash or property or a combination thereof, so long as any amounts paid are includable in income under IRC Section 83.[2]

When the IRS issued final ISO regulations in August 2004, it removed the previous rule, apparently without comment. It is unclear whether the pre-existing rules are still valid.

A SAR granted after an ISO as a matter of right upon satisfaction of a condition and pursuant to a common plan or plans will be considered to have been granted at the same time as the ISO for purposes of IRC Section 422 so long as the SAR otherwise meets the above requirements.[3]

OPTIONS

GENERALLY

1042. What is an option?

An *option* is a contract in which an individual or entity, in return for consideration, grants for a specified time to the purchaser of the option the privilege of purchasing

---

1. See Let. Ruls. 9809025, 200207005.
2. Temp. Treas. Reg. §14a.422A-1, A-39, removed by T.D. 9144, 69 Fed. Reg. 46401 (August 3, 2004).
3. Let. Rul. 9032016.

from the grantor (or selling to the grantor) certain specified property at a fixed price. Under an option contract, only the grantor (or writer) is obligated to perform; the purchaser (including any subsequent purchasers) may choose to exercise the option or may allow it to lapse. (An option differs from a futures contract which, although similar to an option in that it provides for a purchase and sale of property at a fixed price some time in the future, obligates both parties (or their successors) to perform. See Q 1074.) The property specified in the option is referred to as the "underlying property" or "underlying security."

1043. What is a "cash settlement option"?

A *cash settlement option* is an option that on exercise settles in, or could be settled in, cash or property other than the underlying property.[1] For example, an option on a stock index that contemplates that cash rather than stock be transferred if the option holder elects to exercise the option is a cash settlement option.

1044. How are options classified for purposes of the federal income tax?

For federal income tax purposes, options are categorized as *listed* or *unlisted* options, and as *equity* or *nonequity* options.

An option is "listed" if it is traded on, or subject to the rules of, one of the following: a national securities exchange registered with the SEC (as, for example, in the case of a stock option trading on the AMEX); a domestic board of trade that has been designated as a contract market by the Commodities Futures Trading Commission (as in the case of certain options on regulated futures contracts); or, another exchange, board of trade, or market designated by the Secretary of the Treasury. All other options are considered "unlisted."[2]

A listed option covers 100 shares of a particular stock, specifies a fixed ("striking") price per share for exercise and has a fixed expiration date. Only the premium (i.e., the price to be paid by the purchaser of the option) and the transaction costs are not fixed. The Options Clearing Corporation (OCC) assumes certain rights and obligations of the purchaser and writer of listed options; the writer is contractually bound only to the OCC and the owner may look to the OCC for performance if he elects to exercise the option.

Unlisted options are traded over the counter and have no fixed elements; the number of shares covered, striking price, premium, and expiration are all negotiable between the writer and purchaser. There is no intermediary organization (such as the OCC); therefore, the writer and purchaser remain tied together in a contractual relationship.

For the definitions of *equity* and *nonequity* options, see Q 1046 and Q 1068 respectively.

1045. How does the wash sale rule apply to transactions involving options?

---

1.   IRC Sec. 1234(c)(2)(B).
2.   IRC Sec. 1256(g)(5).

A "wash sale"—see Q 1029—is a sale or other disposition of *stock or securities* in which the seller, within a 61-day period (which begins 30 days before and ends 30 days after the date of such sale or disposition), replaces those shares of stock or securities by acquiring (by way of a purchase or an exchange on which the full gain or loss is recognized for tax purposes), or entering into a contract or option to acquire substantially identical *stock or securities*.[1] For the tax effect of a wash sale involving a sale of stock at a loss followed by a purchase of an option, see Q 1029.

Options to acquire or sell stock or securities are generally included in the definition of stock or securities for purposes of the wash sale rule—see Q 1031—consequently, the sale (at a loss) and reacquisition of options, with or without ownership of the underlying stock, would trigger the wash sale rule. Similarly, it would appear that "substantially identical stock or securities" would include "substantially identical options or contracts to acquire or sell stock or securities" as well.[2]

EQUITY OPTIONS

1046. What option contracts are classified as "equity" options?

The term "equity option" means any option (A) to buy or sell stock, *or* (B) whose value is determined directly or indirectly by reference to any stock or any *narrow-based security index* (see below).[3] Thus, single stock futures and narrow-based stock index futures are classified as equity options. See Q 1072 and Q 1073 for the treatment of securities futures contracts. For example, an option on IBM common stock trading on the Chicago Board is an equity option. Likewise, a futures contract on IBM common stock is an equity option. In addition, an option on a narrow-based index of stock will generally be an equity option. Alternatively, "broad-based security index" means a group or index of securities that does *not* constitute a narrow-based security index.[4]

Single stock futures and narrow-based stock index futures are subject to the joint jurisdiction of the Commodity Futures Trading Commission (CFTC) and the Securities Exchange Commission (SEC). (Prior to December 21, 2000, if the Commodity Futures Trading Commission had designated a contract market for trading an option whose value was determined directly or indirectly by reference to a particular stock, or if the Treasury had determined that the requirements for CFTC designation had been met, then the option was a nonequity option.[5]) Broad-based stock index futures, however, remain under the exclusive jurisdiction of the CFTC.

An option may be an "equity" option regardless of whether it is listed or unlisted (see Q 1044). The term "equity option" includes an option on a group of stocks *only if* that group meets the requirements for a *narrow-based security index* (as defined in Section 3(a)(55)(A) of the Securities Exchange Act of 1934).[6] According to securities law provisions, the term "narrow-based security index" means an index:

(1) that has nine or fewer component securities;

---

1. IRC Sec. 1091(a); Treas. Reg. §1.1091-1(a).
2. See IRC Sec. 1091(a).
3. IRC Sec. 1256(g)(6). See also Section 3(a)(55)(A) of the Securities Exchange Act of 1934.
4. Commodities Exchange Act Rule 41.1(c).
5. IRC Sec. 1256(g)(6)(B), prior to amendment by CRTRA 2000.
6. IRC Sec. 1256(g)(6).

(2) in which a component security comprises more than 30% of the index's weighting;

(3) in which the five highest weighted component securities in the aggregate comprise more than 60% of the index's weighting; *or*

(4) in which the lowest weighted component securities comprising, in the aggregate, 25% of the index's weighting have an aggregate dollar value of average daily trading volume of less than $50,000,000 (or in the case of an index with 15 or more component securities, $30,000,000), except that if there are two or more securities with equal weighting that could be included in the calculation of the lowest weighted component securities comprising, in the aggregate, 25% of the index's weighting such securities will be ranked from lowest to highest dollar value of average daily trading volume and will be included based on their ranking starting with the lowest ranked security.[1]

Any security index that does *not* have any of the four characteristics set forth in (1), (2), (3), or (4) is, in effect, a broad-based security index. For example, the Standard and Poor's 500 (S&P 500) would be a broad-based security index. Proposed rules state that indices that satisfy certain criteria are specifically *excluded* from the definition of narrow-based security index.[2]

Stock Options

1047. In the stock market, what is a "call" option? What is a "put" option?

In the case of options on individual stocks, a "call" option (or simply, a "call") is an option contract giving the owner thereof the right to *purchase* from the writer of the call, at any time before a specified future date and time, a stated number of shares of a particular stock at a specified price.[3] See Q 1048 through Q 1071 for the tax treatment of various transactions involving the purchase, holding and disposition of puts, calls, nonequity options, and combinations thereof.

A "put," on the other hand, is an option contract giving the owner thereof the right to *sell* to the writer of the put (i.e., to "put it to him"), at any time before a specified future date and time, a stated number of shares of a particular stock at a specified price.[4]

In any case, only the grantor of an option is obligated to perform on it; the purchaser or subsequent owner of a "call" or "put" may choose to dispose of it or allow it to expire. The owner of an option (whether it is a put or a call) is referred to as holding a "long" position; the writer (i.e., grantor or seller) of an option is referred to as holding a "short" position. Thus, it is always the holder of the short position who is obligated to perform on the contract and the holder of the long position who may choose to exercise the contract or permit it to lapse.

The price a purchaser pays to the writer of an option as consideration for the writer's obligation under the option is referred to as the "premium" or "option premium."

---

1. Sec. 3(a)(55)(B) of the Securities Exchange Act of 1934. See also Commodities Exchange Act Rule 41.1(e).
2. See Commodities Exchange Act Rule §§41.1.(c), 41.1(e), 41.12, 41.13, 41.14, "Background and Overview of New Rules." See also Securities and Exchange Act §§240.3a55-2, 240.3a55-3.
3. Rev. Rul. 78-182, 1978-1 CB 265; Rev. Rul. 58-234, 1958-1 CB 279.
4. Rev. Ruls. 78-182, 58-234, 1978-1 CB 265.

1048. How are puts and calls held by an investor treated for income tax purposes?

"Puts" and "calls" (whether listed or unlisted) are capital assets in the hands of an investor.[1] Furthermore, puts and calls on individual stocks are "equity options" and, thus, are not subject to the mark-to-market tax rules as are "nonequity options."[2] The tax treatment of equity options depends on the circumstances of their exercise, lapse, or termination. See Q 1049 through Q 1067. See Q 1068 and Q 1069 for the treatment of nonequity options.

The contemporaneous holding of a call option and granting of a put option with respect to an equity interest in a pass-through entity may constitute a "constructive ownership transaction" under IRC Section 1260. See Q 1090 to Q 1091.

1049. How is an investor taxed when he purchases a put or call?

An investor realizes no taxable gain or loss on the purchase of a listed or unlisted put or call; neither does he incur any deductible expense; but the purchase may trigger adverse tax consequences, as described below, depending on other positions held by the taxpayer.

Future regulations will provide that if a taxpayer enters into certain option transactions (e.g., purchases a put) and the underlying property becomes substantially worthless, the taxpayer will recognize gain in the same manner as if the contract were closed when the property became substantially worthless.[3]

Option Premium

The premium paid to purchase a put or call (generally referred to as the "option premium") represents the cost of the option and is a nondeductible capital expenditure.[4] As such, the premium is carried in a deferred account as a capital expenditure made in an uncompleted transaction until the option is exercised—see Q 1053, Q 1058—allowed to expire without exercise—see Q 1052, Q 1057—or otherwise terminated. See Q 1050, Q 1051, Q 1055, Q 1056.[5]

Commissions

Commissions paid in connection with the purchase of a put or call are aggregated with, and treated for tax purposes as part of, the total "option premium" paid by the investor to purchase the option; commissions are *not* tax deductible.[6]

Effect of Purchase on Other Transactions

Depending on the taxpayer's other holdings, the purchase of a put may trigger any of several provisions that may affect the holding period or tax treatment of the put and the other holdings.

---

1. See IRC Sec. 1234(a); Treas. Reg. §1.1234-1(a).
2. IRC Secs. 1256(g), 1256(b).
3. See IRC Sec. 1233(h)(1).
4. Rev. Rul. 78-182, 1978-1 CB 265.
5. Rev. Rul. 71-521, 1971-2 CB 313.
6. Rev. Rul. 58-234, 1958-1 CB 279.

Certain combinations of options, or options held contemporaneously with off-setting positions that have the effect of reducing both the taxpayer's risk of loss and opportunity for gain, may trigger constructive sales treatment under IRC Section 1259. See Q 1087 to Q 1089.

The contemporaneous holding of a call option and granting of a put option with respect to an equity interest in a pass-through entity may constitute a "constructive ownership transaction" under IRC Section 1260. See Q 1090 and Q 1091.

The purchase of a put is treated under IRC Section 1233(b) in the same manner as a short sale and may result in the creation of a tax straddle with respect to the underlying stock.[1] Each may adversely affect the taxation of the stock which is subject to the put option. For details, see Q 1054, Q 1055, and Q 1058.

The purchase of an option may trigger the wash sale rule if it occurs within 30 days before or after the sale of "substantially identical stock or securities."[2] The purchase of a put option may also create a conversion transaction if the purchase of the put and the acquisition of the underlying stock occurred contemporaneously. For an explanation of the conversion transaction rules, see Q 1085 to Q 1086.

For an explanation of the short sale rules, see Q 1021 to Q 1023. For an explanation of the tax straddle rules, see Q 1077 to Q 1084. For an explanation of the wash sale rule, see Q 1029 to Q 1031.

1050. If the owner of an unlisted call sells it prior to exercise or expiration, how is the sale taxed?

The sale is taxed to the seller as the sale of a capital asset.[3] The seller realizes capital gain to the extent that the selling price exceeds his tax basis in the call option; if his tax basis exceeds the selling price, the seller realizes a capital loss. (See Q 1420 for the treatment of capital gains and losses.) An investor's tax basis in a call option is the total option premium (including commissions) paid by him to acquire the call.[4] The nature of capital gain or loss realized on the sale of a call option will ordinarily depend on the length of the taxpayer's holding period. See Q 1417 and Q 1420.[5]

For an explanation of the effect of the wash sale rule on transactions involving options, see Q 1029 and Q 1045.

Certain combinations of options, or options held contemporaneously with off-setting positions that have the effect of reducing both the taxpayer's risk of loss and opportunity for gain, may trigger constructive sale treatment under IRC Section 1259. See Q 1087 to Q 1089.

The contemporaneous holding of a call option and granting of a put option with respect to an equity interest in a pass-through entity may constitute a "constructive ownership transaction" under IRC Section 1260. See Q 1090 and Q 1091.

1. IRC Sec. 1233(b).
2. IRC Sec. 1091(a).
3. IRC Sec. 1234(a).
4. See IRC Sec. 1234(a); Rev. Rul. 78-182, 1978-1 CB 265.
5. Treas. Reg. §1.1234-1(a).

If a call option was part of a tax straddle in the hands of the investor, the tax straddle rules may result in a deferral of the recognition of a loss realized on a sale of the call option and, furthermore, may have unfavorable effects on the characterization of gains and losses realized on positions making up the straddle. See Q 1077 to Q 1084 for details.

1051. If the owner of a listed call terminates his position by making a closing sale in the market, how is the transaction taxed?

A "closing sale" (i.e., the "sale" in the market of an option identical to the one held) is taxed as the sale of a capital asset. To the extent that the premium received in the closing sale (less any commission paid by the seller) exceeds the owner's tax basis in the call option, he realizes a capital gain; if the premium he receives in the closing sale is less than his tax basis, the difference is a capital loss. (See Q 1420 for the treatment of capital gains and losses.) An investor's tax basis in a call option is the total option premium (including commissions) paid by him to acquire the call.[1] The nature of capital gain or loss realized on the sale of a call option will ordinarily depend on the length of the taxpayer's holding period. See Q 1417 and Q 1420.[2]

For an explanation of the effect of the wash sale rule on transactions involving options, see Q 1029 and Q 1045.

Certain combinations of options, or options held contemporaneously with off-setting positions that have the effect of reducing both the taxpayer's risk of loss and opportunity for gain, may trigger constructive sales treatment under IRC Section 1259. See Q 1087 to Q 1089.

The contemporaneous holding of a call option and granting of a put option with respect to an equity interest in a pass-through entity may constitute a "constructive ownership transaction" under IRC Section 1260. See Q 1090 and Q 1091.

If a call option was part of a tax straddle in the hands of the investor, the tax straddle rules may result in a deferral of the recognition of a loss realized on a closing sale of the call option and, furthermore, may have unfavorable effects on the characterization of gains and losses realized on positions making up the straddle. See Q 1077 to Q 1084 for details.

1052. How is the owner of a call taxed if he allows it to expire without exercising it?

If allowed to expire without exercise (i.e., lapse), a listed or unlisted call is deemed to have been sold or exchanged on the expiration date.[3] Thus, the amount of the option "premium" paid by the owner to acquire the call will be treated as a capital loss, the treatment of which will depend on the holding period of the call (see Q 1417). (See Q 1420 for the treatment of capital gains and losses.)[4]

Certain combinations of options, or options held contemporaneously with off-setting positions that have the effect of reducing both the taxpayer's risk of loss and

---

1. IRC Sec. 1234(a); Rev. Rul. 78-182, 1978-1 CB 265.
2. Treas. Reg. §1.1234-1(a).
3. IRC Sec. 1234(a)(2).
4. Treas. Reg. §1.1234-1(b); Rev. Rul. 78-182, 1978-1 CB 265.

opportunity for gain, may trigger constructive sales treatment under IRC Section 1259. See Q 1087 to Q 1089.

The contemporaneous holding of a call option and granting of a put option with respect to an equity interest in a pass-through entity may constitute a "constructive ownership transaction" under IRC Section 1260. See Q 1090 and Q 1091.

If a call option was part of a tax straddle in the hands of the investor, the tax straddle rules may result in a deferral of the recognition of the loss realized on the expiration of a call option and, furthermore, may have unfavorable effects on the characterization of gains and losses realized on positions making up the straddle. See Q 1077 to Q 1084 for details.

1053. How is an owner taxed if he exercises a call?

The owner of a call (whether listed or unlisted) will realize no taxable gain or loss when he exercises his call option and purchases the underlying stock. But for purposes of determining gain or loss in a subsequent sale or exchange of that stock, the option premium paid by the owner to acquire the call is added to his tax basis in the stock.[1]

Certain combinations of options, or options held contemporaneously with off-setting positions that have the effect of reducing both the taxpayer's risk of loss and opportunity for gain, may trigger constructive sales treatment under IRC Section 1259. See Q 1087 to Q 1089.

The contemporaneous holding of a call option and granting of a put option with respect to an equity interest in a pass-through entity may constitute a "constructive ownership transaction" under IRC Section 1260. See Q 1090 and Q 1091.

1054. What effect does the purchase of a put have on the underlying stock?

Because the acquisition of a listed or unlisted put—other than a "married" put (see Q 1059)—is treated as a short sale for the purposes of IRC Section 1233(b) (i.e., the treatment of gains and losses from short sales), the purchase of a put by a taxpayer who holds substantially identical property (e.g., such as the underlying stock) will, at the very least, generally have the effect of cancelling the holding period of the underlying stock, as explained below. In addition, it is possible that the purchase of a put could constitute a constructive sale (i.e., a short sale) of an appreciated financial position if the underlying stock has appreciated.[2] See Q 1087 to Q 1089.

In its provisions governing the treatment of short sales,[3] the IRC states that if (1) on the date the put is acquired the purchaser of the put has held the underlying stock for a period of time that is less than the long-term capital gain (or loss) holding period for that stock—see Q 1417 and Q 1420—or (2) the underlying stock is acquired after the acquisition of the put and on or before the date the put is exercised, sold, or expires, then the holding period of the underlying stock will be deemed to begin on the date the purchaser of the put disposes of the underlying stock, exercises the put, sells the

---

1.   Rev. Rul. 78-182, 1978-1 CB 265.
2.   See IRC Secs. 1259(b)(1), 1259(c)(1)(A).
3.   IRC Section 1233.

put, or allows the put to lapse, whichever occurs first. Any previous holding period is lost.[1] For this purpose, the exercise or failure to exercise the option will be considered a closing of the short sale.[2]

The holding period of underlying stock held for more than the long-term capital gain (or loss) holding period before the put is acquired is not affected by the rules of IRC Section 1233, but if the transaction is construed as a constructive sale of an appreciated financial position (and assuming no exceptions apply), underlying stock will be subject to being treated as sold and reacquired on the date the put is purchased; thus a new holding period would begin.[3]

If an investor owns (1) the stock that underlies the put option, (2) stock or securities that are substantially identical to the underlying stock, or (3) other positions that are offsetting with respect to the put option, the purchase of a put may trigger the loss deferral, wash sale, and short sale rules which apply to tax straddles. See Q 1077 to Q 1084 for details. Such a combination of holdings may also trigger a series of constructive sales under IRC Section 1259.[4]

For the tax treatment of capital gains and losses, see Q 1420. For an explanation of the effect of the wash sale rule on transactions involving options, see Q 1029 and Q 1045. For an explanation of the conversion transaction rules with respect to transactions involving the contemporaneous acquisition of a put option and the underlying (or substantially identical) stock, see Q 1086.

1055. How is the owner of an unlisted put taxed if he sells the put instead of exercising it?

The sale is taxed as the sale of a capital asset.[5] Thus, the seller realizes capital gain to the extent that the selling price exceeds his tax basis in the put; if his tax basis is greater than the selling price, he realizes a capital loss. (See Q 1420 for the treatment of capital gains and losses.) The seller's tax basis in a put is the total option premium he paid to acquire the put.[6]

The length of the taxpayer's holding period will ordinarily determine the nature of the gain or loss. See Q 1417 and Q 1420. But a capital gain realized on the sale of a put (other than a "married" put) is, under the short sale rules, automatically a short-term capital gain if (1) as of the date the put was acquired the underlying stock had been held by the put holder for a period that is less than the long-term capital gain (or loss) holding period for that stock—see Q 1417—or (2) the underlying stock was acquired after the put was purchased but on or before the date the put was sold.[7] For the tax treatment of "married" puts, see Q 1059.

Certain combinations of options, or options held contemporaneously with offsetting positions that have the effect of reducing both the taxpayer's risk of loss and opportunity for gain, may trigger constructive sales treatment under IRC Section 1259. See Q 1087 to Q 1089.

---

1. Rev. Rul. 78-182, 1978-1 CB 265.
2. IRC Sec. 1233(b).
3. See IRC Sec. 1259(a).
4. See IRC Secs. 1259(e)(1), 1259(e)(3).
5. IRC Sec. 1234(a).
6. Rev. Rul. 78-182, 1978-1 CB 265.
7. IRC Sec. 1233(b); Rev. Rul. 78-182, above.

If a put option was part of a tax straddle in the hands of the investor, the tax straddle rules may result in a deferral of the recognition of a loss realized on the sale of a put option, and may have additional unfavorable effects on the characterization of gains and losses realized on positions making up the straddle. See Q 1077 to Q 1084 for details.

For an explanation of the effect of the wash sale rule on transactions involving options, see Q 1029 and Q 1045. For the effect that the acquisition and subsequent sale of a put has on the underlying stock, see Q 1054. For an explanation of the effect of the conversion transaction rules on transactions involving the contemporaneous acquisition of a put option and the underlying (or substantially identical) stock, see Q 1086.

1056. How is the owner of a listed put taxed if he liquidates his position by making a "closing sale" in the market?

Any gain or loss realized by the owner of a listed put in a closing sale (i.e., the "sale" in the market of a put identical to the one held) is capital gain or loss.[1] (See Q 1420 for the treatment of capital gains and losses.) The amount of capital gain or loss realized is the difference between the premium the owner receives in the closing sale and the premium the owner paid to acquire the put in the first place.

The length of the taxpayer's holding period will ordinarily determine the nature of the gain or loss. See Q 1417 and Q 1420. But apparently a *capital gain* realized in a closing sale of a put (other than a "married" put) is, under the short sale rules, automatically a short-term capital gain if (1) as of the date the put was acquired the underlying stock had been held by the put holder for a period that is less than the long-term capital gain (or loss) holding period for that stock—see Q 1417—or (2) the underlying stock was acquired after the put was purchased, but on or before the closing sale of the put.[2] For the tax treatment of "married" puts, see Q 1059.

Certain combinations of options, or options held contemporaneously with offsetting positions that have the effect of reducing both the taxpayer's risk of loss and opportunity for gain, may trigger constructive sales treatment under IRC Section 1259. See Q 1087 to Q 1089.

If a put option was part of a tax straddle in the hands of the investor, the tax straddle rules may result in a deferral of the recognition of a loss realized on the closing sale, and may have additional unfavorable effects on the characterization of gains and losses realized on positions making up the straddle. See Q 1077 to Q 1084 for details.

For an explanation of the effect of the wash sale rule on transactions involving options, see Q 1029 and Q 1045. For the effects that the acquisition and subsequent liquidation of a put has on the underlying stock, see Q 1054. For an explanation of the effect of the conversion transaction rules on transactions involving the contemporaneous acquisition of a put option and the underlying (or substantially identical) stock, see Q 1086.

1057. How is an owner of a put taxed if he allows the put to expire without exercising it?

---

1. IRC Sec. 1234(a).
2. IRC Sec. 1233(b); Rev. Rul. 78-182, 1978-1 CB 265.

Except in the case of a "married" put—see Q 1059—any put allowed to expire without exercise (i.e., lapse) is deemed to have been sold or exchanged on the expiration date, and the owner realizes capital loss in the amount of the total option premium he paid to acquire the put.[1] (See Q 1420 regarding the treatment of capital losses.) The length of the taxpayer's holding period will ordinarily determine the nature of the gain or loss. See Q 1417 and Q 1420.[2]

Future regulations will provide that if a taxpayer enters into certain option transactions (e.g., the purchase of a put) and the underlying property becomes substantially worthless, the taxpayer will recognize gain in the same manner as if the contract were closed when the property became substantially worthless.[3]

Certain combinations of options, or options held contemporaneously with offsetting positions that have the effect of reducing both the taxpayer's risk of loss and opportunity for gain, may trigger constructive sales treatment under IRC Section 1259. See Q 1087 to Q 1089.

If a put option was part of a tax straddle in the hands of the investor, the tax straddle rules may result in a deferral of the recognition of the loss realized on the expiration of the put and, in addition, may have unfavorable effects on the characterization of gains and losses realized on positions making up the straddle. See Q 1077 to Q 1084 for details.

For the effect that the acquisition and subsequent lapse of a put has on the underlying stock, see Q 1054. The tax effects of allowing "married" puts to lapse are discussed in Q 1059.

1058. How is the owner of a put taxed if he exercises it?

When a put (listed or unlisted) is exercised the owner sells the underlying stock to the writer of the put; it is that sale, not the put, which is taxed.

To determine his gain or loss on a sale made pursuant to the exercise of a put, the owner offsets the total option premium he paid for the put against the price received for the stock (i.e., the striking price) to arrive at the total amount realized in the sale. If the total amount realized exceeds his tax basis in the stock sold, the excess is capital gain; if the amount realized is less than his tax basis, the difference is capital loss.[4] See Q 1420 for the treatment of capital gains and losses.

The nature of a capital *loss* realized on a sale made pursuant to the exercise of a put will generally depend on how long the stock has been held by the put holder. Similarly, the character of a capital *gain* realized on the exercise of a put *generally* depends on how long the put holder has owned the stock he sells. But a capital gain realized on the exercise of a put—other than a "married" put (see Q 1059) —is, under the short sale rules, a *short-term* capital gain if: (1) as of the date the put was acquired the underlying stock had been held by the put holder for a period of time that is less than the long-term capital gain (or loss) holding period for that stock—see Q 1417—or (2) the underlying stock was acquired after the put was purchased but on or before the date the put was exercised.[5]

1. IRC Sec. 1234(a)(2); Treas. Reg. §1.1234-1(b); Rev. Rul. 78-182, 1978-1 CB 265.
2. Treas. Reg. §1.1234-1(a).
3. See IRC Sec. 1233(h)(1).
4. Rev. Rul. 78-182, 1978-1 CB 265; Rev. Rul. 71-521, 1971-2 CB 313.
5. IRC Sec. 1233(b); Rev. Rul. 78-182, above.

Certain combinations of options, or options held contemporaneously with off-setting positions that have the effect of reducing both the taxpayer's risk of loss and opportunity for gain, may trigger constructive sales treatment under IRC Section 1259. It is unclear whether the acquisition of a put will be treated as a short sale under IRC Section 1259 (as it is under IRC Section 1233(b)). See Q 1054. If so, the constructive sales rules explained in Q 1087 to Q 1089 may affect the treatment of the put option, upon acquisition, upon exercise, or both.

If the put option was part of a tax straddle in the hands of the investor, the tax straddle rules may result in a deferral of the recognition of a loss realized on the exercise of the put and, in addition, may have unfavorable effects on the characterization of gains and losses realized on positions making up the straddle. See Q 1077 to Q 1084 for details.

If the put option was part of a conversion transaction in the hands of the investor, the conversion transaction rules may result in a portion of any gain being treated as ordinary income. See Q 1085 and Q 1086.

1059. What is a "married" put? How does the taxation of a "married" put differ from that of an ordinary put?

"Married" puts are a special exception to the treatment under IRC Section 1233 of the purchase of a put as a short sale. There are three requirements for a put to be treated as a "married" (or "identified") put: (1) it must be purchased *on the same day* as stock the investor intends to use in exercising the put; (2) the option must specify that such stock is to be used in exercising it, *or* the investor's records must identify within 15 days after the acquisition of the property the stock that is to be so used; and (3) if the put is exercised, it must be exercised through the sale of the property so identified.[1]

In other words, the stock is "married" to the put. A married put may be listed or unlisted. Unlike ordinary put options, the acquisition of a married put is *not* treated as a short sale for federal income tax purposes.[2] If a married put is exercised by delivering stock other than the identified stock, the short sale rules will apply as explained in Q 1058.

In the event the put expires without being exercised, its cost will be added to the taxpayer's basis in the stock with which the option was identified; it will not be a capital loss in the year of expiration as would an ordinary put option.[3]

It is not clear whether a married put that falls within the definition of a tax straddle will be subject to the straddle rules—see Q 1077 to Q 1084—nor whether one that falls within the definition of a conversion transaction will be subject to the conversion transaction rules. See Q 1085 and Q 1086. It also is unclear how the sale of an unlisted married put or the liquidation of a married listed put in a closing sale is treated for income tax purposes; however, it would seem that the short sale rules would not be triggered and a gain or loss would be realized on the sale as discussed in Q 1055 and Q 1056.

1060. How is the "premium" received by the writer of a "put" or "call" taxed?

---

1. IRC Sec. 1233(c); Treas. Reg. §1.1233-1(c)(3).
2. IRC Sec. 1233(c); Rev. Rul. 78-182, 1978-1 CB 265; Rev. Rul. 71-521, 1971-2 CB 313.
3. IRC Secs. 1233(c), 1234(a)(3)(C); Rev. Rul. 78-182, above.

Regardless of whether the option is listed or unlisted, there is no federal income tax incident on account of the receipt by the writer of an option premium. It is not included in income at the time of receipt, but is carried in a deferred account as part of an uncompleted transaction until such time as the option is exercised, sold, or lapses, or until the writer's obligation is terminated in a closing transaction.[1] Under future regulations, if the underlying property on which the option is written becomes worthless, the taxpayer will recognize gain or loss in the same manner as if the contract were closed when the property became substantially worthless.[2]

1061. Are the commissions a writer of a put or call pays in connection with the sale of that option tax deductible?

No. Commissions paid by a writer to sell his put or call (whether listed or unlisted) merely reduce the total "option premium" he receives in consideration for his obligations under the option.[3]

1062. If a put or call expires without exercise, how is the writer taxed?

When a put or call (whether listed or unlisted) expires without exercise (i.e., lapses), the premium that has been carried by the writer in a deferred account since the option was sold—see Q 1060—is recognized as short-term capital gain and included in the writer's gross income for the tax year in which the option expired.[4] See Q 1420 for the treatment of capital gains and losses.

Under future regulations, if the underlying property on which the option is written becomes worthless, the taxpayer will recognize gain or loss in the same manner as if the contract were closed when the property became substantially worthless.[5]

1063. How is the writer of a call taxed when the option is exercised by the owner?

When a listed or unlisted call is exercised and the writer thereof is called on to sell the underlying stock, the writer adds the amount of the option "premium" he received for writing the call to the total striking price to determine the total amount realized in the sale. Then, to the extent that the total amount realized exceeds the writer's tax basis in the stock sold, he realizes a capital gain; if his tax basis exceeds the total amount realized he has a capital loss. (See Q 1420 for the treatment of capital gains and losses.) The nature of such gain or loss generally depends on the holding period of the stock sold—see Q 1417 and Q 1420—irrespective of the time the "call" was outstanding.[6]

If an investor writes a call option as part of an overall tax straddle, the tax straddle rules may result in a deferral of the recognition of a loss realized on the exercise of the call option and, in addition, may have unfavorable effects on the characterization of gains and losses realized on positions making up the straddle. See Q 1077 to Q 1084 for details.

1. Rev. Rul. 78-182, 1978-1 CB 265; Rev. Rul. 58-234, 1958-1 CB 279.
2. See IRC Sec. 1233(h)(1).
3. Rev. Rul. 58-234, 1958-1 CB 279.
4. IRC Sec. 1234(b)(1); Rev. Rul. 78-182, 1978-1 CB 265.
5. See IRC Sec. 1233(h)(1).
6. Rev. Rul. 78-182, 1978-1 CB 265.

It is unclear whether the writer of a call will be deemed to have entered into a contract to sell the underlying property, within the meaning of IRC Section 1258(c)(2). For more on conversion transactions, see Q 1085 and Q 1086. See Q 1078 for an explanation of the rules governing covered call options.

1064. How is the writer of a put taxed when the option is exercised by the owner?

The writer of a put (listed or unlisted) realizes no taxable gain or loss when he purchases the underlying stock pursuant to the exercise of a put. But for purposes of determining the writer's gain or loss on a subsequent sale of the underlying stock, the writer's tax basis in that stock is reduced by the amount of the option "premium" he received in the original sale of the put. Furthermore, the holding period of the underlying stock begins on the date of its purchase, not on the date the put was written.[1]

1065. How is the writer of an unlisted put or unlisted call taxed if he repurchases his option from the holder?

If the writer of an unlisted option repurchases his option from its holder, he will realize *short-term* capital gain or loss to the extent of the difference between the premium paid to repurchase the option and the premium originally received by the writer.[2] See Q 1420 for the treatment of capital gains and losses.

Certain combinations of options, or options held contemporaneously with offsetting positions that have the effect of reducing both the taxpayer's risk of loss and opportunity for gain, may trigger constructive sales treatment under IRC Section 1259. The operation of these rules is explained at Q 1087 to Q 1089, and the effect of closing out or reopening certain transactions that are subject to constructive sale treatment is explained at Q 1088.

The contemporaneous holding of a call option and granting of a put option with respect to an equity interest in a pass-through entity may constitute a "constructive ownership transaction" under IRC Section 1260. See Q 1090 and Q 1091.

1066. How is the writer of a listed call or listed put taxed if he terminates his obligation by making a closing purchase in the market?

Any gain or loss realized by the writer of a listed option in a closing purchase (i.e., the "purchase" in the market of an option identical to the one written) is short-term capital gain or loss.[3] The amount of such gain or loss will be the difference between the premium paid by the writer in the closing purchase and the premium previously received by him in his original sale of the option.[4] See Q 1420 for the treatment of capital gains and losses.

Certain combinations of options, or options held contemporaneously with offsetting positions that have the effect of reducing both the taxpayer's risk of loss and opportunity for gain, may trigger constructive sales treatment under IRC Section 1259. The operation of these rules is explained at Q 1087 to Q 1089, and the effect of closing

1. Rev. Rul. 78-182, 1978-1 CB 265.
2. IRC Sec. 1234(b); Rev. Rul. 78-181, 1978-1 CB 261.
3. IRC Sec. 1234(b); Rev. Rul. 78-182, 1978-1 CB 265.
4. Rev. Rul. 78-182, 1978-1 CB 265.

out or reopening certain transactions that are subject to constructive sale treatment is explained at Q 1088.

The contemporaneous holding of a call option and granting of a put option with respect to an equity interest in a pass-through entity may constitute a "constructive ownership transaction" under IRC Section 1260. See Q 1090 and Q 1091.

It is unclear whether the writer of a call will be deemed to have entered into a contract to sell the underlying property, within the meaning of IRC Section 1258(c)(2). For more on conversion transactions, see Q 1085 and Q 1086.

Other Equity Options

1067. Other than stock options, what kinds of options are classified as "equity" options? How are these options taxed?

For taxable years beginning after 2001, the term "equity option" includes an option on a group of stocks *only if* that group meets the requirements for a *narrow-based security index* (as defined in Section 3(a)(55)(A) of the Securities Exchange Act of 1934). See Q 1046.[1] For taxable year beginning before 2000, options *other than stock options* could be classified as "equity" options for purposes of the federal income tax, if their value was determined by reference to a *group* of stocks or stock index, but they were of a type that was ineligible to be traded on a commodity futures exchange. (An example of such an option would have been an option contract on a sub-index based on the price of nine hotel-casino stocks.) An equity option could be either a *listed option* or an *unlisted option* (i.e., traded over-the-counter, or otherwise).[2]

These "other" equity options were generally taxed under the same rules that apply to stock options. See Q 1042 to Q 1066 for details. For the application of the straddle rules to such options, see Q 1077 to Q 1084.

NONEQUITY OPTIONS

1068. What is a "nonequity" option?

For federal income tax purposes, a *nonequity option* is any option traded on a national securities exchange or commodity futures exchange (or other exchange, board of trade, or market designated by Treasury) that is not an "equity" option.[3] Thus, options on regulated futures contracts are nonequity options. In addition, the term "nonequity option" includes any option traded on a national securities exchange (or other market designated by Treasury) whose value is determined directly or indirectly by reference to *broad-based* groups of stocks and *broad-based* stock indexes.[4] See Q 1046 for the definition of "broad-based security index."

The IRS has ruled that options to buy or sell stock based on a stock index that are traded on (or subject to the rules of) a qualified board or exchange meet the requirements for contract market designation and are nonequity options if (a) the options provide for cash settlement, and (b) the Securities Exchange Commission has determined that the

1. IRC Sec. 1256(g)(6).
2. See IRC Sec. 1256(g)(6), prior to amendment by CRTRA 2000.
3. IRC Secs. 1256(g)(3), 1256(g)(7).
4. See H.R. Conf. Rep. No. 106-1033 (CRTRA 2000); IRC Sec. 1256(g)(6).

stock index is a "broad-based" index. These options are considered "IRC Section 1256 contracts." See Q 1076. Furthermore, warrants that are based on a stock index and that are economically, substantively identical in all material respects to options based on a stock index are treated as options based on a stock index.[1]

As one of several types of "IRC Section 1256 contracts," a nonequity option is taxed under the "mark to market" requirements. See Q 1076. Such a position is excluded from the definition of an *appreciated financial position* under IRC Section 1259(b)(2)(B), see Q 1087. But depending on the taxpayer's other holdings, it would appear possible that a constructive sale could result from the acquisition of a nonequity option. See Q 1087 to Q 1089.[2]

For an explanation of the application of the conversion transaction rules to transactions involving the contemporaneous acquisition of a put option and the underlying (or substantially identical) stock, see Q 1086.

1069. How are nonequity options taxed?

Nonequity options are taxed under the mark-to-market rules that apply to regulated futures contracts and other IRC Section 1256 contracts. See Q 1076.

Like any other position taxed under the "mark to market" requirements, a nonequity option is excluded from the definition of an *appreciated financial position* under IRC Section 1259(b)(2)(B). See Q 1087. But it appears to be possible that depending on the taxpayer's other holdings, the acquisition of a nonequity option could be construed as a constructive sale of a position that is substantially identical to the nonequity option or the property underlying it.[3] Future regulations may clarify this and other issues with respect to the application of IRC Section 1259 to options transactions.

For the tax treatment of a nonequity option that is part of a tax straddle, see Q 1077 to Q 1084. For the tax treatment of a nonequity option that is considered part of a conversion transaction, see Q 1085 and Q 1086.

OPTION SPREAD TRANSACTIONS

1070. What is a "spread" transaction?

A "spread" is a position consisting of both long (purchased) and short (sold) options of the same type (i.e., put or call). The options may have different exercise prices and exercise dates. The basic purpose of the various types of spread transactions is to limit or define the risks of the options transaction. The "spread" is the actual dollar difference between the buy premium and sell premium.[4]

> *Example:* ILM corporation's stock is trading at $91 in November, but Ms. Noel expects it to decline. She writes a ILM January 80 call and collects a premium of $1300 for it. Since she does not own ILM stock and does not wish to assume the risks of writing an uncovered call, Ms. Noel also buys a ILM January 90 call at a cost of $600. If the price of ILM drops to $79, Ms. Noel will have

---

1. Rev. Rul. 94-63, 1994-2 CB 188.
2. IRC Sec. 1259(c)(1)(E).
3. See IRC Sec. 1259(c)(1)(E).
4. See *Resser v. Comm.*, TC Memo 1991-423; *Laureys v. Comm.*, 92 TC 101 (1989), *acq. in part, nonacq. in part*, 1990-1 CB 1, footnotes 5 and 11.

made a profit of $700 (the difference between the premium she paid and the premium she collected). If the price does not drop, she has limited her loss to $300 (the $1000 difference between the strike prices of the two options minus the $700 net premium).

The three basic types of spreads are vertical (or price), horizontal (or time) and diagonal (combination of vertical and horizontal). Spreads are also (regardless of their type) referred to either as credit, debit, or even. In a debit spread, the costs of the long (purchased) position exceed the proceeds of the short (sold) position. In a credit spread, the proceeds of the short position exceed the cost of the long position. If the costs and proceeds are equal, the spread is even.

Vertical Spreads. A vertical spread (also referred to as a price, money or perpendicular spread) is the simultaneous purchase and sale of puts or calls with the same underlying security and expiration date, but with different strike prices. An investment in a vertical spread is based upon the expectation that the option purchased is undervalued relative to the option sold.

Horizontal Spreads. A horizontal spread (also referred to as a time or calendar spread) is the simultaneous purchase and sale of puts or calls with the same underlying security and strike price, but with different expiration dates. Horizontal spreads are purchased in anticipation that over time the spread will widen.

Diagonal Spreads. A diagonal spread is a combination of a vertical spread and a horizontal spread; thus, it is the simultaneous purchase and sale of puts and calls with the same underlying security but with different strike prices and expiration dates.

Within each of the categories described above (vertical, horizontal, diagonal), a spread can also be characterized as a bull spread, bear spread, or butterfly spread. A *bull spread* is the combination of a long position at a lower strike price and a short position at a higher strike price. It is so named because it will generally be profitable if the underlying security goes up in value. In a *bear spread* the opposite is true: the strike price of the long position is higher than the strike price of the short position, and the investor will generally profit if the trading price of the underlying security goes down. A *butterfly spread* is a combination in which the investor holds three put or call positions in the same underlying security at three different strike prices. The expiration dates may be the same or the spread may be "diagonalized" by having different expiration dates.

Butterfly spreads are so named because the respective "sizes" of the positions invoke the image of a butterfly. The Tax Court has described butterfly spreads as follows: "The highest and lowest strike positions are one-half the size of the middle position, and the middle position (the body) is long (or short) and the highest and lowest positions (the wings) are short (or long). The highest and lowest positions are equidistant from the middle position."[1]

See Q 1071 for an explanation of the tax treatment of spread transactions.

1071. How are spread transactions taxed?

Generally, spread transactions are subject to the tax straddle rules to the extent that the positions in the spread are offsetting (see below). Consequently, certain spreads

---

1. See *Laureys v. Comm.*, 92 TC 101 (1989), *acq. in part, nonacq. in part*, 1990-1 CB 1, footnotes 5 and 11. See also Andrea S. Kramer, *Financial Products: Taxation, Regulation and Design* (New York: John Wiley & Sons, Inc. 1991, Supp. 1993), §5.4(c).

will apparently be subject to the constructive sale treatment of IRC Section 1259, see Q 1087 to Q 1089.[1]

Generally, positions are offsetting if the taxpayer substantially reduces his risk of holding one position with respect to personal property by holding another position with respect to personal property, whether or not it is of the same type. IRC Sec. 1092(c). See Q 1077 for an explanation of the IRC definition of "offsetting" and Q 1079 for an explanation of the treatment of tax straddles.

The Tax Court has taken the position that spread transactions are not "similar arrangements" within the meaning of IRC Section 465(b)(4), and that losses on stock option spreads are thus not limited by the "at risk" rule.[2] But the IRS, issuing a very limited partial acquiescence to the *Laureys* decision, noted its nonacquiescence as to whether offsetting positions in stock options are subject to the limitations of IRC Section 465(b)(4). See Q 1286 and Q 1287 for an explanation of the "at risk" rule.

To the extent that one position of a spread is offset by only a portion of the other position, only those portions of the spread that offset one another will be treated as offsetting (and subject to the tax straddle rules) unless the position is part of a larger tax straddle.[3] Apparently, any options positions that are not offset by other positions will be taxed under the general rules governing equity options. See Q 1046 to Q 1067.

Positions consisting entirely of options that are IRC Section 1256 contracts (i.e., dealer equity options and nonequity options) are exempt from the tax straddle rules and, instead, taxed under the mark-to-market rules in IRC Section 1256. Such positions will not constitute an "appreciated financial position"—see Q 1087—but may constitute a constructive sale of another position. See Q 1088. See Q 1076 for an explanation of IRC Section 1256 treatment. Spreads consisting of at least one, but not all, IRC Section 1256 contracts are subject to the rules for "mixed straddles." For an explanation, see Q 1081.

Aside from the special rules for IRC Section 1256 contracts (see above), it is clear that certain combinations of options (to be specified in future regulations) or options held contemporaneously with offsetting positions that have the effect of reducing both the taxpayer's risk of loss and opportunity for gain, will trigger constructive sales treatment under IRC Section 1259, unless certain exceptions apply, see Q 1087 to Q 1089.[4]

A spread transaction that is a straddle under IRC Section 1092(c) may also constitute a conversion transaction. See Q 1085 and Q 1086 for the definition and tax treatment of conversion transactions.

FUTURES

Securities Futures Contracts

1072. What are securities futures contracts?

1. See IRC Sec. 1259(c)(1)(E); Conference Committee Report for TRA '97.
2. See *Resser v. Comm.*, TC Memo 1991-423; *Laureys v. Comm.*, 92 TC 101 (1989), *acq. in part, nonacq. in part*, 1990-1 CB 1, footnotes 5 and 11.
3. IRC Sec. 1092(c)(2)(B).
4. IRC Sec. 1259(c)(1)(E).

Under 2000 legislation, the definition of "equity option"—see Q 1046—was amended to include *securities futures contracts* (i.e., single stock futures and narrow-based stock index futures).[1] For purposes of the income tax rules, the term "securities futures contract" means a contract of sale for future delivery of a single security *or* a narrow-based security index.[2]

A securities futures contract will generally *not* be treated as a commodity futures contract for purposes of the Internal Revenue Code (an exception exists for dealer securities futures contracts).[3] Thus, holders of these contracts generally are *not* subject to the mark-to-market rules of IRC Section 1256—see Q 1076—and are not eligible for 60% long-term capital gain treatment. Instead, gain or loss on these contracts will be recognized under the general rules relating to the disposition of property.[4] For the tax treatment of securities futures contracts, generally, and the treatment of such contracts under the rules governing short sales, wash sales, and straddles, see Q 1073.

1073. How are securities futures contracts taxed?

Generally, gain or loss on *securities futures contracts*—see Q 1072—will be treated under the rules relating to the disposition of the underlying property.[5] IRC Section 1234B provides that gain or loss from the sale, exchange, or termination of a securities futures contract (other than a dealer securities futures contract) will be considered as gain or loss from the sale, exchange, or termination of property that has the same character as the property to which the contract relates has (or would have) in the hands of the taxpayer.[6] Thus, if the underlying security would be a capital asset in the taxpayer's hands, then gain or loss from the sale or exchange of the securities futures contract would be capital gain or loss.[7]

Holding period. If property is delivered in satisfaction of a securities futures contract to acquire property, the holding period for the property will include the period the taxpayer held the contract, provided that the contract was a capital asset in the hands of the taxpayer.[8]

Short sale treatment. In applying the short sale rules—see Q 1021 to Q 1028—a securities futures contract to *acquire* property will be treated in a manner similar to the property itself.[9] Thus, for example, the holding of a securities futures contract to acquire property and the short sale of property which is substantially identical to the property under the contract will result in the application of the rules under IRC Section 1233(b) (regarding short-term gains and holding periods). (Because securities futures contracts are not treated as commodities futures contracts under IRC Section 1234B(d), the rule providing that commodity futures are not substantially identical if they call for delivery in different months does not apply.) In addition, a securities futures contract to *sell* property is treated as a short sale, and the settlement of the contract is treated as the closing of the short sale.[10]

---

1. See the Commodity Futures Modernization Act of 2000 and Section 401 of the Community Renewal Tax Relief Act of 2000 (CRTRA 2000), both incorporated by reference in the Consolidated Appropriations Act of 2001.
2. See IRC Sec. 1234B(c); Sec. 3(a)(55)(A) of the Securities Exchange Act of 1934.
3. H.R. Conf. Rep. No. 106-1033 (CRTRA 2000). See IRC Sec. 1234B(d).
4. H.R. Conf. Rep. No. 106-1033 (CRTRA 2000). See IRC Sec. 1256(b).
5. H.R. Conf. Rep. No. 106-1033 (CRTRA 2000).
6. IRC Sec. 1234B(a).
7. H.R. Conf. Rep. No. 106-1033 (CRTRA 2000).
8. See IRC Sec. 1223(16); H.R. Conf. Rep. No. 106-1033 (CRTRA 2000).
9. H.R. Conf. Rep. No. 106-1033 (CRTRA 2000). See IRC Sec. 1233(e)(2)(D).
10. IRC Sec. 1233(e)(2)(E).

Except as otherwise provided in the straddle regulations under IRC Section 1092(b)—which treats certain losses from a straddle as long-term capital losses (see Q 1079)—or in IRC Section 1233 (gains and losses from short sales, special holding period rules), capital gain or loss from the sale, exchange, or termination of a securities futures contract to sell property (i.e., the short side of a futures contract) will be short-term capital gain or loss.[1]

Wash sale treatment. "The wash sale rules apply to any loss from the sale, exchange, or termination of a securities futures contract (other than a dealer securities futures contract) if, within a period beginning 30 days before the date of such sale, exchange, or termination and ending 30 days after such date: (1) stock that is substantially identical to the stock to which the contract relates is sold; (2) a short sale of substantially identical stock is entered into; or (3) another securities futures contract to sell substantially identical stock is entered into."[2]

Straddle treatment. Stock that is part of a straddle, at least one of the offsetting positions of which is a securities futures contract with respect to the stock or substantially identical stock, will be subject to the straddle rules. See Q 1077 to Q 1084.[3] The regulations under IRC Section 1092(b) applying the principles of IRC Sections 1233(b) and 1233(d) (regarding the determination of short-term and long-term losses) to positions in a straddle will also apply.[4] See Q 1079 for the treatment of a tax straddle. These rules are demonstrated in the following example from H.R. Conf. Rep. No. 106-1033 (CRTRA 2000):

> *Example*: Assume a taxpayer holds a long-term position in actively traded stock (which is a capital asset in the taxpayer's hands) and enters into a securities futures contract to sell substantially identical stock (at a time when the position in the stock has *not* appreciated in value so that the constructive sale rules of IRC Section 1259 do not apply). The taxpayer has a straddle. Any loss on closing the securities futures contract will be a long-term capital loss.

Constructive sale of an appreciated financial position. As indicated in the example, above, if a taxpayer holds a long-term position in actively traded stock (which is a capital asset in the taxpayer's hands) and enters into a securities futures contract to sell substantially identical stock at a time when the position in the stock has appreciated in value, the constructive sale rules apparently will apply. See Q 1087 to Q 1089.[5]

Mark-to-market treatment not applicable. Securities futures contracts (or options on such contracts) generally are *not* treated as IRC Section 1256 contracts (an exception to the general rule exists for dealer securities futures contracts).[6] Thus, holders of these contracts are *not* subject to the mark-to-market rules of IRC Section 1256. See Q 1076. Consequently, gains and losses from securities futures contracts are not eligible for 60% long-term gain and 40% short-term gain treatment.[7] Although a narrow-based security index is not subject to mark-to-market treatment, a broad-based security index remains subject to such tax treatment.[8]

---

1. See IRC Sec. 1234B(b).
2. Joint Committee on Taxation, Technical Explanation of the "Job Creation and Worker Assistance Act of 2002" (JCX-12-02), March 6, 2002; see IRC Sec. 1091(e).
3. H.R. Conf. Rep. No. 106-1033 (CRTRA 2000). See IRC Sec. 1092(d)(3)(B)(i)(II).
4. H.R. Conf. Rep. No. 106-1033 (CRTRA 2000).
5. See H.R. Conf. Rep. No. 106-1033 (CRTRA 2000), "Straddle Rules," p. 1035.
6. See IRC Sec. 1256(b)(5).
7. H.R. Conf. Rep. No. 106-1033 (CRTRA 2000).
8. See IRC Sec. 1256(g)(6); H.R. Conf. Rep. No. 106-1033 (CRTRA 2000).

SECTION 1256 CONTRACTS

1074. What are futures? What is a regulated futures contract?

Generally speaking, a future is an executory contract (i.e., a contract which requires performance in the future) to purchase or sell a particular commodity for delivery in the future; a future may be either a "futures contract" or a "forward contract."

Futures Contracts

Futures contracts are bought and sold (i.e., traded) on at least one of the various commodities or futures exchanges. All terms and provisions of a futures contract, except price and delivery month, are fixed by the bylaws and rules of the exchange; price and delivery month are agreed to when the trade is made on the floor of the exchange. Although all futures contracts originate between a buyer and seller, the exchange's clearing organization, at the end of each business day, substitutes itself as the "other party" of each contract written that day. (That is, the clearing organization creates two new futures contracts by becoming the buyer to each seller and the seller to each buyer.) Once written, futures contracts traded on a domestic exchange are subject to a "variations margin" under which they are marked to market daily. See Q 1075.

Until the date trading in futures contracts for a particular commodity and delivery month stops, an owner of a contract for that commodity and delivery month may close out his contract by making an offsetting purchase or sale (as the case may be) on the exchange of another futures contract. Once trading stops, the owners of "short" futures contracts (i.e., contracts to sell) are required to make delivery of the underlying commodity to the owners of the "long" futures contracts (i.e., contracts to buy) for that commodity and month on the basis of match-ups established by the clearing organization. Futures contracts traded on a domestic exchange are subject to regulation by the Commodity Futures Trading Commission (CFTC).

A taxpayer who enters into a futures contract to deliver property that is the same as or substantially identical to an appreciated financial position that he holds—see Q 1087—will generally be treated as having made a constructive sale of that position, unless certain requirements are met for closing out the futures contract.[1] See Q 1087 to Q 1089.

A taxpayer who enters into a futures contract to acquire an equity interest in a pass-through entity may be subject to the "constructive ownership" rules under IRC Section 1260. See Q 1090 to Q 1091.

Special rules apply to *securities futures contracts*. See Q 1072 and Q 1073.

Forward Contracts

Forward contracts (or "forwards"), in contrast to futures, exist only in the cash market, are not subject to CFTC regulation, are not standardized as to terms and provisions, and do not involve a variations margin. All terms and provisions of a "forward" are subject to negotiation between the buyer and seller.

A taxpayer who enters into a forward contract to deliver property that is the same as or substantially identical to an appreciated financial position that he holds—see Q

---

1. IRC Sec. 1259(c)(1)(C).

1087—will generally be treated as having made a constructive sale of that position.[1] But not all forward contracts will be subject to constructive sale treatment.[2] According to the Blue Book, a forward contract results in a constructive sale *only* if it provides for delivery, or for cash settlement, of a substantially fixed amount of property and a substantially fixed price. If the amount of property provided for by the forward contract is subject to significant variation under the terms of the contract, it will not constitute a forward contract.[3] Furthermore, an agreement that is not a "contract" under applicable contract law, or that is subject to "very substantial contingencies" was not intended to be treated as a forward contract.[4]

But the Service distinguished a case in which in addition to entering into a forward contract pledging to deliver property that is the same as or substantially identical to an appreciated financial position that he holds, a taxpayer loaned and delivered the shares to the other party at the time of the contract. In that case, the IRS found a constructive sale.[5]

For those forwards that do result in a constructive sale under IRC Section 1259, unless certain requirements are met for closing out the forward contract, the constructive sale generally will result in immediate recognition of gain by the taxpayer as if the appreciated financial position were sold and repurchased on the date of the deemed sale.[6] See Q 1087 to Q 1089.

A taxpayer who enters into a forward contract to acquire an equity interest in a pass-through entity may be subject to the "constructive ownership" rules under IRC Section 1260. See Q 1090 to Q 1091.

Regulated Futures Contracts

For income tax purposes, a "regulated futures contract" is a "futures contract" (as described above) that is traded on a domestic exchange *or* on a foreign exchange that employs a cash flow system similar to the "variations margin" system and is designated by the Secretary of the Treasury.[7] Besides calling for the delivery of many types of property (including agricultural commodities, T-bills, foreign currencies, and financial instruments), regulated futures contracts may cover things not generally thought of as property and call for settlement in cash rather than delivery (e.g., stock index or interest rate futures).

For income tax purposes, a regulated futures contract is one of several types of "IRC Section 1256 contracts" (see Q 1076).[8] Consequently, such a position is excluded from the definition of an *appreciated financial position* under IRC Section 1259(b)(2)(B), see Q 1087. But depending on the taxpayer's other holdings, it would appear that a constructive sale could result from entering into a regulated futures contract to deliver property that is the same as or substantially identical to an appreciated financial position held by the taxpayer, see Q 1087 to Q 1089.[9]

1. IRC Sec. 1259(c)(1)(C).
2. See General Explanation of Tax Legislation Enacted in 1997 (JCS-23-97), p. 176 (the 1997 Blue Book).
3. See Rev. Rul. 2003-7, 2003-5 IRB 363.
4. 1997 Blue Book, p. 176.
5. TAM 200604033.
6. IRC Sec. 1259(a).
7. IRC Sec. 1256(g).
8. IRC Sec. 1256(b).
9. IRC Sec. 1259(c)(1)(C).

For an explanation of when a foreign currency contract will be considered a regulated futures contract or listed option and, thus, require mark-to-market treatment under IRC Section 1256, see FSA 200041006.

1075. What is a variations margin?

A *variations margin* is a daily cash flow system under which each owner of a "futures contract" (including a regulated futures contract) declining in value during a trading day must provide additional cash margin (i.e., cash payment to his margin account) equal to the decline in value; an owner of a contract which gained in value during the day is permitted to withdraw margin money from his account equal to his "profit" for that day. Profit or loss (i.e., an increase or decline in value) for any trading day is measured by comparing the closing price of the "futures contract" on that day with the closing price on the previous day.

In other words, in a variations margin system each "futures contract" or regulated futures contract is "marked to the market" at the end of each trading day. See Q 1076.

1076. How are regulated futures contracts and other Section 1256 contracts taxed?

Regulated futures contracts are generally taxed under a mark-to-market tax rule that closely corresponds to the daily cash settlement system used for futures contracts on domestic exchanges (see Q 1075). Regulated futures contracts are one of the types of "IRC Section 1256 contracts" that are subject to those rules. Other types of instruments that are taxed in the same manner are foreign currency contracts and nonequity options. See Q 1068.[1] The term "IRC Section 1256 contract" generally does *not* include any "securities futures contract" or option on such a contract (an exception exists for dealer securities futures contracts).[2] For the definition of securities futures contract, see Q 1072.

Regulated futures contracts and IRC Section 1256 contracts, like other positions that are subject to the mark-to-market requirements, are excluded from the definition of an *appreciated financial position* under IRC Section 1259(b)(2)(B). See Q 1087. But depending on the taxpayer's other holdings, it would appear possible that a constructive sale could result from the taxpayer entering into a regulated futures contract (or another IRC Section 1256 contract) to deliver property that is the same as or substantially identical to an appreciated financial position held by the taxpayer.[3] See Q 1087 to Q 1089.

The owner of a regulated futures contract that is part of a tax straddle or a conversion transaction may be subject to different tax rules. See Q 1077 to Q 1086.[4]

Gains and losses on IRC Section 1256 contracts held for investment are capital gains and losses regardless of the nature of the underlying property.[5]

IRC Section 1256 contracts—other than those subject to the special rules for tax straddles (see Q 1080)—must be "marked to the market." Under the mark-to-market

---

1. IRC Sec. 1256(b).
2. IRC Sec. 1256(b).
3. IRC Sec. 1259(c)(1)(C).
4. IRC Sec. 1256.
5. IRC Sec. 1234A(2); *Moody v. Comm.*, TC Memo 1985-20.

tax rules, gains and losses inherent in IRC Section 1256 contracts owned by an investor at the end of the year or at any time during the year must be reported annually, even if those gains or losses have not been realized by the investor. To accomplish this, any IRC Section 1256 contract that has not been terminated or transferred before the end of the tax year is treated as if it was sold for its fair market value on the last business day of that year.[1] Any gain or loss on such a "deemed" sale must be reported and taxed as discussed below. Any IRC Section 1256 contract terminated or transferred during the year is deemed to have been sold for its fair market value on the date it was terminated or transferred. (Termination or transfer may include offset, taking or making delivery, exercise, assignment, lapse, or any other transaction that terminates or transfers the taxpayer's rights or obligations under the contract.)[2] If the IRC Section 1256 contract was closed out during the year in an arm's-length transaction, its fair market value is considered to be the actual price paid or received in the closing transaction, and the amount of gain or loss required to be reported equals the amount actually realized. In all other cases, including where the IRC Section 1256 contract remains open at year-end, fair market value is ordinarily the settlement price on the exchange as of the appropriate date.[3]

Any gain or loss required to be reported by an investor on an IRC Section 1256 contract under the mark-to-market rules is treated as if 40% of the gain or loss is *short-term* capital gain or loss and 60% is *long-term* capital gain or loss.[4] The usual holding period rule for determining whether a gain or loss is short-term or long-term is ignored.[5] For the taxation of capital gains and losses, see Q 1420.

IRC Section 1091 (relating to losses from wash sales of stock and securities) does not apply to any loss taken into account under the general rule governing losses for Section 1256 contracts.[6]

The mark-to-market tax rules do not apply to hedging transactions entered into as part of the taxpayer's trade or business.[7] According to the General Explanation of Tax Legislation Enacted in 1997 (JCS-23-97; i.e., the 1997 Blue Book), it was the intent of Congress that the constructive sale provisions—see Q 1087 to Q 1089—would apply to such transactions.

An investor who has a "net IRC Section 1256 contracts loss" for a year may elect to carry such loss back three years and then, to the extent not depleted, carry it forward to succeeding years under the rules provided in IRC Section 1212(c). A United States District Court determined that IRC Section 1256 contract losses could be carried back to offset gains in a previous year even though the losses were attributable in part to contracts subject to a mixed straddle account election. See Q 1083.[8]

If an investor reports gain or loss on an IRC Section 1256 contract that was taxed to him in a prior year under the mark-to-market rules, that gain or loss is adjusted to reflect the gain or loss reported in that prior year (or years).[9]

1. IRC Sec. 1256(a).
2. IRC Sec. 1256(c).
3. See General Explanation—ERTA, pp. 296-297.
4. IRC Sec. 1256(a)(3).
5. See IRC Sec. 1222.
6. IRC Sec. 1256(f).
7. IRC Sec. 1256(e).
8. *Roberts v. U.S.*, 734 F.Supp. 314 (D.C. Ill. 1990).
9. IRC Sec. 1256(a)(2).

STRADDLES

1077. What is a "tax straddle"?

A "tax straddle" is the simultaneous ownership of offsetting interests (i.e., "positions") in actively traded personal property. For this purpose, an "interest" may be ownership of the property itself or may be a regulated futures contract, a futures contract other than a regulated futures contract, a forward contract, or an option. Interests owned by an investor's spouse, partnership, S corporation, or trust of which the investor is a deemed owner are treated as owned by the investor for purposes of determining whether a tax straddle exists.[1]

Interests (i.e., positions) are offsetting if the risk of loss from owning any particular interest is substantially reduced by reason of the ownership of such other interest (or interests). But risk reduction through mere diversification is not considered to be substantial if the positions are not balanced. Interests may be treated as offsetting even though they or the underlying personal properties are not the same kind (e.g., ownership of silver and a futures contract to sell the same amount of silver; or a long futures contract for silver and a short futures contract for silver coins). If positions are not equally offsetting, the tax straddle rules will apply, under regulations yet to be issued, only to the extent the positions are balanced.[2]

Under the following circumstances, two or more positions will be *presumed* to be offsetting, unless the investor is able to show to the contrary:[3] (1) the positions are in the same personal property and the value of one or more such positions ordinarily varies inversely with the value of one or more of other such positions; (2) the positions are in debt instruments of similar maturity (or other debt instruments described in future regulations) *and* the value of one or more such positions ordinarily varies inversely with the value of one or more of other such positions; (3) the positions are marketed as offsetting positions, or (4) the aggregate margin requirement for such positions is lower than the sum of the margin requirements for each such position if each position were held separately.

Direct ownership of stock may be exempted from the straddle rules. See Q 1078 for an explanation of when the rules will apply.

PROPERTY SUBJECT TO STRADDLE RULES

Section 1256 Contracts	Non-Section 1256 Property
Regulated futures contracts	Stock options
Nonequity option contracts — see Q 1068	Other equity options — see Q 1067
Foreign currency contracts	Direct ownership of stock—but
Dealer equity options	only when at least one offsetting position is:
	1) an option (other than a qualified covered call option) on such stock or on substantially similar stock or securities;
	2) substantially similar property; or

---

1. IRC Secs. 1092(c), 1092(d)(4).
2. IRC Sec. 1092(c); General Explanation—ERTA, p. 288.
3. See IRC Sec. 1092(c)(3).

3) stock of certain corporations which take positions that offset positions held by shareholders — see Q 1078

Forward contracts

Other *actively traded personal property* which is not a Section 1256 contract

Securities futures contracts — see Q 1072

1078. When will direct ownership of stock be subject to the tax straddle rules? What is a "qualified covered call option"?

Direct ownership of stock (i.e., ownership of the stock certificates) is considered to be ownership of personal property for purposes of the tax straddle rules if such stock is of a type that is actively traded and at least one of the positions offsetting such stock is a position with respect to such stock or substantially similar or related property.[1] (This limited definition does not apply for purposes of determining whether a straddle constitutes a conversion transaction. See Q 1085 and Q 1086).[2]

In the American Jobs Creation Act of 2004, Congress repealed the pre-existing exclusion for most direct ownership of stock from the tax straddle rules. The new statutory rule expands on previously proposed regulations that limited the scope of the statutory exclusion. Under the proposed regulations, personal property included any stock of a type that is actively traded and that is part of a straddle at least one of the offsetting positions of which is a position with respect to substantially similar or related property other than stock. A position with respect to substantially similar or related property other than stock did not include direct ownership of stock or a short sale of stock, but included any other position with respect to substantially similar or related property. Thus, under the proposed regulations, stock and an equity swap with respect to property that is substantially similar or related to that stock could constitute a straddle for purposes of IRC Section 1092.[3]

The IRS has not yet issued any guidance on the new rules, but the new provision eliminates the ability to hold offsetting positions in a target and an acquiring corporation's stock without being subject to the tax straddle rules, including termination of holding periods.

Stock in a corporation that was formed or availed of to take positions in personal property that offset positions taken by shareholders of such corporation will also be subject to the straddle rules regardless of whether it is actively traded.[4]

Stock that is part of a straddle at least one of the offsetting positions of which is a *securities futures contract* (see Q 1072) with respect to the stock or substantially identical stock will be subject to the straddle rules.[5] The regulations under IRC Section 1092(b) applying the principles of IRC Section 1233(b) and IRC Section 1233(d) (regarding the determination of short-term and long-term losses) to positions in a straddle will also apply (see Q 1079).[6] These rules are demonstrated in the following example from H.R. Conf. Rep. No. 106-1033 (CRTRA 2000):

---

1. IRC Sec. 1092(d)(3)(A).
2. IRC Secs. 1258(c)(2)(B), 1258(d)(1).
3. Prop. Treas. Reg. §1.1092(d)-2.
4. IRC Sec. 1092(d)(3)(B)(ii); Prop. Treas. Reg. §1.1092(d)-2(a)(2).
5. H.R. Conf. Rep. No. 106-1033 (CRTRA 2000). See IRC Sec. 1092(d)(3)(B)(i)(II).
6. H.R. Conf. Rep. No. 106-1033 (CRTRA 2000).

Example: Assume a taxpayer holds a long-term position in actively traded stock (that is a capital asset in the taxpayer's hands) and enters into a securities futures contract to sell substantially identical stock (at a time when the position in the stock has not appreciated in value so that the constructive sale rules of IRC Section 1259 do not apply). The taxpayer has a straddle. Any loss on closing the securities futures contract will be a long-term capital loss.

The IRS has determined that investment "units" consisting of stock and a future payment right (that varied inversely with the value of the stock and that was found to be a "cash settlement put option") constituted a straddle when both positions were held simultaneously.[1] The Service has also privately ruled that two positions consisting of (1) a put option that was part of a "costless collar" (i.e., the purchase of a cash-settlement put option and the sale of a cash-settlement call option), and (2) shares of the underlying stock, constituted a straddle under IRC Section 1092(c). Similarly, the call option, which was part of the same costless collar, and the shares of the underlying stock also constituted a straddle.[2] See also FSA 200150012 (a straddle existed where the corporate taxpayer directly owned shares of a company (i.e., the long position) and had also issued purported debt instruments in which the value of the instruments was linked to the price of the underlying stock).

How a straddle that includes a position (or positions) in stock will be taxed depends on the overall make-up of the straddle and whether the straddle constitutes a conversion transaction. For details, see Q 1079, Q 1085, and Q 1086.

Qualified Covered Call Options

A covered call option is a call option (see Q 1047) written (i.e., granted) by an investor on stock that is owned by the investor or acquired by the investor in connection with the writing of the call option. Because the writing of a covered call option will not substantially reduce the investor's risk of loss with respect to the underlying stock unless the option is deep-in-the-money, the IRC provides that writing at-the-money and non-deep-in-the-money call options on stock owned or acquired by the investor (i.e., "qualified covered call options") is generally excluded from straddle treatment.[3] (A call option is "in-the-money" when the striking price of the option is below the market price of the underlying stock.) A qualified covered call option also will generally not be subject to the capitalization requirements of IRC Section 263(g).[4]

But where the underlying stock and one or more qualified covered call options are part of a larger straddle the overall straddle does receive straddle treatment.[5] For example, the IRS ruled that buying a put on the same underlying stock on which the taxpayer wrote a qualified covered call option did create a larger straddle subject to straddle treatment.[6]

The holding period of any stock underlying a qualified covered call option written by an investor where the strike price is less than the applicable stock price will be tolled during the period that such option is open. Furthermore, any loss realized by an investor on a qualified covered call option that has a striking price less than the applicable stock price (as defined below) will be treated as *long-term* capital loss if, at the time the loss is

---

1. Rev. Rul. 88-31, 1988-1 CB 302.
2. Let. Rul. 199925044.
3. IRC Sec. 1092(c)(4).
4. See General Explanation—TRA '84, pp. 309-310.
5. IRC Sec. 1092(c)(4)(A)(ii).
6. Rev. Rul. 2002-66, 2002-45 IRB 812.

realized, a sale of the underlying stock would have resulted in a long-term capital gain.[1] For most purposes, the holding period requirement for long-term capital gain treatment is "more than one year."[2] (See Q 1420 for the treatment of capital gains and losses.)

A call option is a "qualified covered call option" if: (1) it is an exchange-traded (i.e., listed) option *or* under the regulations, an over-the-counter option meeting certain requirements (see *Over-the-counter options*, below); (2) it is written by the investor on stock held by him or acquired by him in connection with writing the call; (3) the term of the call is longer than 30 days but no longer than 33 months; (4) gain or loss with respect to such call option is not ordinary income or loss; and (5) the call's striking price is not lower than the *lowest qualified bench mark* for that option (i.e., the option is not deep-in-the-money). (If the investor is an options dealer, the call must not be written in the ordinary course of his business.)[3]

For purposes of determining if an option is a qualified covered call option, the "lowest qualified bench mark" is generally the highest available striking price for such option which is less than the *applicable stock price* of the underlying stock. But several special rules apply as follows:

1. If the term of the call option is more than 90 days and its striking price is greater than $50, then the "lowest qualified bench mark" is the *second highest* available striking price that is less than the applicable stock price.

2. If the applicable stock price is $25 or less and the lowest qualified bench mark would otherwise be less than 85% of the applicable stock price, the "lowest qualified bench mark" will be treated as equal to the amount which is 85% of the applicable stock price.

3. If the applicable stock price is $150 or less, and the lowest qualified bench mark would otherwise be more than $10 less than the applicable stock price, then the "lowest qualified bench mark" is the applicable stock price *reduced by* $10.[4]

4. If the term of the call option is more than 12 months, the applicable stock price is multiplied by an adjustment factor found in Treasury Regulation Section 1.1092(c)-4(e).

Under the usual circumstances, the "applicable stock price" is the closing price of the optioned stock on the most recent day such stock was traded *before* the date on which the option was written. But if the opening price of the optioned stock on the day the option was written is greater than 110% of the closing price on the last previous trading day, the "applicable stock price" is such opening price.[5]

Flex options are customized options that allow investors to customize key contract terms, including strike prices. But the determination of the "lowest qualified bench mark" for standardized options is based upon the striking prices for standardized options, not for equity options with flexible terms (i.e., flex options).[6] Thus, certain taxpayers (primarily

---

1. IRC Sec. 1092(f).
2. IRC Sec. 1222(3).
3. IRC Secs. 1092(c)(4)(B), 1092(c)(4)(C); Treas. Reg. §1.1092(c)-1.
4. IRC Sec. 1092(c)(4)(D).
5. IRC Sec. 1092(c)(4)(G).
6. See Treas. Reg. §1.1092(c)-2(b).

institutional and other large investors) can engage in transactions that would otherwise be unavailable to them, and other investors can continue to do business without regard to the existence of the institutional product.

Currently, exchange rules provide for $2.50 bench marks (i.e., strike prices at $2.50 intervals) for standardized options on stocks trading between $5 and $25, $5 bench marks for options on stocks trading between $25 and $200 per share, and $10 bench marks for options on stocks trading at more than $200. Apparently, if these bench marks are modified by the exchanges or the exchanges otherwise change their practices, the IRS has broad authority to revise the foregoing rules.[1]

Regardless of the foregoing rules, a covered call option is *not* treated as qualified (and a tax straddle does exist) *if* the gain from the disposition of the underlying stock is includable in the investor's gross income for a tax year subsequent to the tax year in which either the call option was closed or the stock was disposed of at a loss *and* the stock or option was not held for 30 days or longer following the date the call was closed or the stock was disposed of; but the rules discussed above, which require the tolling of the holding period of the underlying stock and that treat loss as long-term loss if there would have been long-term gain on a sale of the underlying stock, continue to apply.[2]

It is unclear whether a qualified covered call option can constitute a conversion transaction (see Q 1085). If so, it may be subject to the additional rules set forth in Q 1086.

Equity options with flexible terms. Unlike equity options with standardized terms, equity options with flexible terms can have strike prices at other than fixed intervals and can have expiration dates other than standardized expiration dates. Under the regulations, equity options with flexible terms may be qualified covered call options if they satisfy certain requirements. Specifically, an equity option with flexible terms is a qualified covered call option *only if* (1) the option meets the requirements of IRC Section 1092(c)(4)(B) (as stated above); (2) the only payments permitted with respect to the option are a single fixed premium paid no later than five business days after the day on which the option is granted, and a single fixed strike price stated as a dollar amount that is payable entirely at (or within five business days of) exercise; (3) an equity option with standardized terms is outstanding for the underlying equity; and (4) the underlying security is stock in a single corporation.[3] An equity option with standardized terms means an equity option that is traded on a national securities exchanges (i.e., a listed option) and that is not an equity option with flexible terms.[4]

For purposes of applying the general rules, the bench mark for an equity option with flexible terms will be the same as the bench mark for an equity option with standardized terms on the same stock having the same applicable stock price.[5]

Over-the-counter options. Under the regulations, certain over-the-counter options may also qualify as qualified covered call options. A *qualifying over-the-counter option* is an equity option that is not traded on a national securities exchange registered with the Securities and Exchange Commission *and* is entered into with a person registered with the Securities and Exchange Commission as a broker-dealer or alternative trad-

1. See IRC Sec. 1092(c)(4)(H); General Explanation–TRA '84, p. 310.
2. IRC Sec. 1092(c)(4)(E).
3. Treas. Reg. §1.1092(c)-2(c)(1).
4. Treas. Reg. §1.1091(c)-4(b).
5. See Treas. Reg. §1.1092(c)-2(c)(2).

ing system.[1] A qualifying over-the-counter option must meet the same requirements outlined above for equity options with flexible terms.[2]

1079. How is a tax straddle taxed?

The tax treatment applicable to a tax straddle depends on the types of property that make up the positions in the straddle. It will also depend on whether substantially all of the taxpayer's expected return from the investment is attributable to the time value of the taxpayer's net investment in the transaction (see the discussion of conversion transactions, below). If the straddle is made up solely of IRC Section 1256 contracts—see Q 1077—it will be taxed as explained in Q 1080. If the straddle is a "mixed" straddle, it will be taxed according to the rules explained in Q 1081. If the straddle qualifies as an "identified tax straddle," it is subject to the rules explained in Q 1082.

If none of the foregoing exceptions or elections applies or have been made, the straddle will generally be taxed under the *loss deferral, wash sale,* and *short sale* rules explained below. Straddles are also subject to the requirement that interest and carrying charges allocable to property that is part of the straddle be capitalized.[3] See the proposed regulations, below.

The Service stated that it may be permissible for a taxpayer to identify which shares of stock are part of a straddle and which shares are used as collateral for a loan using appropriately modified versions of Treasury Regulation §1.1012-1(c)(2) or Temporary Treasury Regulation §1.1092(b)-3T(d)(4) in order to establish that the shares that are part of the collar are not used as collateral for the loan.[4]

These rules apply to all "dispositions" of positions in a straddle regardless of whether such disposition is by sale, exchange, cancellation, lapse, expiration, or any other termination of interest with respect to a position.[5] (Apparently, "other terminations" would include exercise, delivery, assignment, offset, etc.)

Loss deferral and wash sale rules. If the owner of a straddle disposes of less than all the positions making up the straddle, any loss realized with respect to the position (or positions) disposed of may be recognized for tax purposes only to the extent that the loss exceeds the aggregate amount of *unrecognized gain,* if any, on (1) positions in the straddle that offset the position(s) disposed of at a loss, (2) successor positions (if any), or (3) any positions that are offsetting to such successor position(s). *Unrecognized gain,* for this purpose, is (a) the amount of gain that would result from the sale of the position at fair market value on the last business day of the year, if the position is still held at the close of the year, or (b) the amount of realized but unrecognized gain, if gain was realized on that position during the tax year, but for some reason was not recognized for tax purposes in that year.[6]

Basically, a "successor position" is a new straddle position that is acquired within 30 days before, or 30 days after, the original position was disposed of at a loss and that replaces that original position in the straddle. More specifically, a "successor position"

---

1. Treas. Reg. §1.1092(c)-3(a).
2. Treas. Reg. §1.1092(c)-3(b).
3. IRC Sec. 263(g).
4. See Let. Rul. 199925044.
5. Temp. Treas. Reg. §1.1092(b)-5T(a).
6. IRC Secs. 1092(a)(1), 1092(b)(1); Temp. Treas. Reg. §1.1092(b)-1T(a).

is a position (call it "P1") that is offsetting to another position ("P2") (or would have been offsetting to P2 had P2 been held at the time P1 was entered into) if (i) P2 was offsetting to the loss position disposed of, (ii) P1 is entered into during a period which begins 30 days before, and ends 30 days after, the disposition of the loss position, and (iii) P1 is entered into no later than 30 days after the loss position is no longer included in the straddle.[1] (The effect of establishing a successor position to a loss position disposed of is analogous to the general wash sale rule explained in Q 1029.)

Any loss in excess of the amount allowed to be recognized under these rules (i.e., the amount of loss disallowed as a deduction) is carried forward and treated as if sustained in the succeeding tax year (in which it will again be subject to these deferral rules). A capital loss deferred under these rules will retain its character as a capital loss in the carryover year (even if loss with respect to a successor position would give rise to an ordinary loss).[2] See Q 1420 for the treatment of capital gains and losses.

Losses were denied to an investor who participated in a stock forwards program in which he incurred significant tax losses in one year while deferring the corresponding gain into future taxable years by holding instruments in the form of a purported "straddle." The appeals court upheld the Tax Court, stating that the purported "straddle" trades lacked economic substance and did not have any "practical economic effects other than the creation of income tax losses." Accordingly, the losses were properly disallowed.[3]

Short sale rules. For purposes of determining whether a gain or loss on the disposition of a straddle position is long-term or short-term, two rules similar to the general short sale rules (see Q 1022) apply. First, unless a position was held by the taxpayer for a period of time at least equal to the long-term capital gain holding period before a straddle including that position was established, the holding period of that position will be treated as beginning no earlier than the date on which the taxpayer no longer holds, directly or indirectly, an offsetting position with respect to that position. Second, the loss on the disposition of a straddle position (or positions) will, regardless of the holding period of such position, be treated as *long-term* capital loss *if* on the date such loss position was entered into the taxpayer held, directly or indirectly, one or more offsetting positions *and* all gain or loss on one or more positions in the straddle would have been treated as long-term capital gain or loss had such position(s) been disposed of on the day the loss position was entered into.[4]

Conversion transaction rules. A portion of any gain recognized upon disposition or other termination of a straddle that is part of a *conversion transaction* (see Q 1085), may be treated as ordinary income. A straddle will be subject to these rules if substantially all of the taxpayer's expected return from the investment is attributable to the time value of the taxpayer's net investment in the transaction.[5] See Q 1085 and Q 1086 for the definition and tax treatment of conversion transactions.

Capitalization of Interest and Carrying Charges

Interest and carrying charges properly allocable to personal property that is part of a straddle must be capitalized.[6] The purpose of this rule is to coordinate the character

---

1. Temp. Treas. Reg. §1.1092(b)-5T(n) (as amended by Ann. 85-91, 1985-26 IRB 39).
2. IRC Sec. 1092(a)(1)(B). Temp. Treas. Regs. §§1.1092(b)-1T(b), 1.1092(b)-1T(c).
3. *Keeler v. Comm.*, 87 AFTR 2d ¶2001-634 (10th Cir. 2001) (concerning pre-DEFRA law).
4. IRC Sec. 1092(b)(1); Temp. Treas. Reg. §1.1092(b)-2T.
5. IRC Sec. 1258(c).
6. IRC Sec. 263(g)(1).

and timing of items of income and loss attributable to a taxpayer's positions that are part of a straddle.[1]

According to proposed regulations, for purposes of the straddle interest and carrying charges rules "personal property" means property, whether or not actively traded, that is not real property; for this purpose a position in personal property may itself be property. But in general a position in personal property is not property of a taxpayer unless the position confers substantial rights on the taxpayer.[2]

Personal property includes (1) a stockholder's ownership of common stock, (2) a holder's ownership of a debt instrument, and (3) either party's position in a forward contract or conventional swap agreement. Personal property does *not* include a position that imposes obligations but does not confer substantial rights on the taxpayer. Thus, the obligor's position in a debt instrument generally is not personal property even though the obligor may have the typical rights of a debtor. But the obligor on a debt instrument has a position in any personal property underlying the debt instrument.[3]

A put or call option imposes obligations but does not confer substantial rights on the grantor, whether or not the option is cash-settled.[4]

Interest and carrying charges properly allocable to personal property that is part of a straddle means the excess of interest and carrying charges (as defined below) over the allowable income offsets (as defined below).[5] "Interest and carrying charges" are: (1) otherwise deductible amounts paid or accrued with respect to *indebtedness or other financing incurred or continued to purchase or carry personal property that is part of a straddle* (see below); (2) indebtedness or other financing incurred or continued to purchase or carry personal property that is part of a straddle; and (3) otherwise deductible amounts paid or incurred to carry personal property that is part of a straddle. "Interest" includes any amount paid or incurred in connection with personal property used in a short sale. Interest and carrying charges include otherwise deductible payments or accruals on debt or other financing issued or continued to purchase or carry personal property that is part of a straddle, or financial instruments that are part of a straddle or that carry part of a straddle. Interest and carrying charges subject to capitalization also include fees or expenses paid or incurred in connection with acquiring or holding personal property that is part of a straddle including, but not limited to, fees or expenses incurred to purchase, insure, store, maintain, or transport the personal property.[6]

Indebtedness or other financing incurred or continued to purchase or carry personal property that is part of a straddle includes indebtedness or other financing (1) the proceeds of which are used directly or indirectly to purchase or carry personal property that is part of the straddle, (2) that is secured directly or indirectly by personal property that is part of the straddle, and (3) the payments on which are determined by reference to payments with respect to the personal property or the value of, or change in value of, the personal property.[7]

Financial instruments that are part of a straddle or that carry part of a straddle include:

1. Prop. Treas. Reg. §1.263(g)-1(a).
2. Prop. Treas. Reg. §1.263(g)-2(a).
3. Prop. Treas. Reg. §1.263(g)-2(a)(1).
4. Prop. Treas. Reg. §1.263(g)-2(a)(2).
5. Prop. Treas. Reg. §1.263(g)-3(a).
6. IRC Sec. 263(g)(2); Prop. Treas. Reg. §1.263(g)-3(b).
7. Prop. Treas. Reg. §1.263(g)-3(c).

(1) a financial instrument that is part of the straddle;

(2) a financial instrument that is issued in connection with the creation or acquisition of a position in personal property if that position is part of the straddle;

(3) a financial instrument that is sold or marketed as part of an arrangement that involves a taxpayer's position in personal property that is part of the straddle *and* that is purported to result in either economic realization of all or part of the appreciation in an asset without simultaneous recognition of taxable income or a current tax deduction (for interest, carrying charges, payments on a notional principal contract, or otherwise) reflecting a payment or expense that is economically offset by an increase in value that is not concurrently recognized for tax purposes or has a different tax character (e.g., an interest payment that is economically offset by an increase in value that may result in a capital gain in a later tax period).

Any other financial instrument may also be included if the totality of the facts and circumstances support a reasonable inference that the issuance, purchase, or continuation of the financial instrument by the taxpayer was intended to purchase or carry personal property that is part of the straddle.[1]

Allowable income offsets. The allowable income offsets are: (1) the amount of interest (including original issue discount) includable in gross income for the taxable year with respect to such personal property; (2) any amount treated as ordinary income with respect to such personal property for the taxable year; (3) the excess of any dividends includable in gross income with respect to such personal property for the taxable year over the amount of any deductions allowable with respect to such dividends; (4) any amount that is a payment with respect to a security loan includable in income with respect to the personal property for the taxable year; and (5) any amount that is a receipt or accrual includable in income for the taxable year with respect to a financial instrument to the extent the financial instrument is entered into to purchase or carry the personal property.[2]

Allocation Rules. Interest and carrying charges paid or accrued on debt or other financing issued or continued to purchase or carry personal property that is part of a straddle are allocated in the following order:

(1) to personal property that is part of the straddle purchased, directly or indirectly, with the proceeds of the debt or other financing;

(2) to personal property that is part of the straddle and directly or indirectly secures the debt or other financing; *or*

(3) if all or a portion of such interest and carrying charges are determined by reference to the value or change in value of personal property, to such personal property.[3]

"Fees and expenses" (described above) are allocated to the personal property, the acquisition or holding of which resulted in the fees and expenses being paid or incurred. But in all other cases, interest and carrying charges are allocated to personal property that is part of a straddle in the manner that under all the facts and circumstances is most appropriate.[4]

---

1. Prop. Treas. Reg. §1.263(g)-3(d).
2. Prop. Treas. Reg. §1.263(g)-3(e).
3. Prop. Treas. Reg. §1.263(g)-4(a).
4. Prop. Treas. Reg. §1.263(g)-4(a).

Coordination with other provisions. In the case of a short sale, IRC Section 263(g) applies after IRC Section 263(h) (dealing with payments in lieu of dividends in connection with short sales).[1] In addition, IRC Section 263(g) applies after IRC Section 1227 (dealing with the deferral of interest deduction allocable to accrued market discount) and also applies after IRC Section 1282 (dealing with the deferral of interest deduction allocable to certain accruals on short-term indebtedness). Furthermore, capitalization under IRC Section 263(g) applies before loss deferral under IRC Section 1092.[2]

1080. How is a tax straddle taxed if it is made up solely of Section 1256 contracts?

If a tax straddle is made up solely of regulated futures contracts, foreign currency contracts, and nonequity option contracts (i.e., "IRC Section 1256 contracts"), each contract is generally taxed independently under the mark-to-market tax rules explained in Q 1076, except that if the investor takes delivery under, or exercises, any of the contracts making up the straddle, all the contracts in the straddle are deemed to have been terminated on the day of the delivery or exercise. That is, all contracts will be deemed to have been sold or otherwise terminated on that day.[3]

A tax straddle made up solely of IRC Section 1256 contracts is excepted from the loss deferral, wash sale, and short sale rules of IRC Section 1092 and the capitalization provisions of IRC Section 263(g). (See Q 1079 for an explanation of those rules.)[4]

A portion of any gain recognized upon disposition or other termination of a straddle that is part of a *conversion transaction*—see Q 1085—may be treated as ordinary income. A straddle will be subject to these rules if substantially all of the taxpayer's expected return from the investment is attributable to the time value of the taxpayer's net investment in the transaction.[5] See Q 1085 and Q 1086 for the definition and tax treatment of conversion transactions.

Although IRC Section 1256 contracts are excluded from the definition of an *appreciated financial position* under IRC Section 1259(b)(2)(B)—see Q 1087—depending on the taxpayer's other holdings, it would appear that a constructive sale could result from entering into an IRC Section 1256 contract to deliver property that is the same as or substantially identical to an appreciated financial position held by the taxpayer. See Q 1087 to Q 1089.[6]

1081. What is a "mixed" straddle? What tax choices are available to the owner of a "mixed" straddle?

A "mixed" straddle is a tax straddle—see Q 1077—made up of one or more IRC Section 1256 contracts (i.e., regulated futures contracts, foreign currency contracts and nonequity options) and at least one other position which is not an IRC Section 1256 contract, *but only if* each position making up the straddle is clearly identified in the investor's records as being part of a mixed straddle within the time period prescribed by the IRC and regulations.[7]

1. See IRC Secs. 263(g)(4)(A) and 263(h)(6).
2. Prop. Treas. Reg. §1.263(g)-4(b).
3. IRC Secs. 1256(a), 1256(c)(2).
4. IRC Sec. 1256(a)(4).
5. IRC Sec. 1258(c).
6. See IRC Secs. 1259(c)(1)(C), 1259(c)(1)(E).
7. IRC Sec. 1256(d); Temp. Treas. Reg. §1.1092(b)-5T(e).

Basically, an owner of a mixed straddle has three initial choices to make:

(1) He may elect to exclude the IRC Section 1256 contract (or contracts) from the mark-to-market tax rules explained in Q 1076 and have all the positions in the straddle taxed under the loss deferral, wash sale, and short sale rules of IRC Section 1092 (see Q 1079). But this election is available only where the investor has identified in his records all the positions in the mixed straddle before the close of the day on which the first IRC Section 1256 contract forming part of the straddle is acquired.[1]

(2) If the mixed straddle also qualifies as an "identified tax straddle," he may elect (subject to the conditions described in (1), above) to exclude the IRC Section 1256 contract (or contracts) from the mark-to-market tax rules and further elect to have all positions in the straddle (including the IRC Section 1256 contracts) taxed under the rules that apply to "identified tax straddles." See Q 1082.

(3) He may choose not to make either election described in (1) or (2), above, in which case he will be taxed as discussed in Q 1083.

A portion of any gain recognized upon disposition or other termination of a straddle that is part of a *conversion transaction*—see Q 1085—may be treated as ordinary income. A straddle will be subject to these rules if substantially all of the taxpayer's expected return from the investment is attributable to the time value of the taxpayer's net investment in the transaction.[2] See Q 1085 and Q 1086 for the definition and tax treatment of conversion transactions.

1082. How is a mixed straddle taxed if it qualifies and is designated as an "identified tax straddle"?

Assuming the straddle qualifies—see Q 1084—the owner of a mixed straddle who has elected to have the IRC Section 1256 contract positions in the straddle excluded from the mark-to-market tax rules may also elect to have the tax straddle taxed as an "identified straddle."[3] (Note that this election does *not* create what the regulations refer to as a "IRC Section 1092(b)(2) identified mixed straddle." These are discussed in Q 1083 under the heading "Straddle-by-Straddle Identification.")

If this election is made, the straddle will not be subject to the loss deferral and wash sale rules discussed in Q 1079. Instead, any loss with respect to a position in the straddle (including the IRC Section 1256 contract positions) will be treated as sustained no earlier than the day on which all positions making up the straddle are disposed of.[4] The tax straddle short sale rules continue to apply. For details, see Q 1079 and Q 1084. The application of the constructive sale rules of IRC Section 1259 to identified straddles is discussed in Q 1084.

An election to remove the IRC Section 1256 contracts from the mark-to-market tax rules is necessary in order for a mixed straddle to be taxed as an identified straddle because without this election the mixed straddle rules discussed in Q 1083 will control.

---

1. IRC Sec. 1256(d). See General Explanation—TRA '84, p. 317.
2. IRC Sec. 1258(c).
3. IRC Sec. 1092(a)(2)(B).
4. IRC Sec. 1092(a)(2)(A)(ii).

1083. How is a mixed straddle taxed if there is no election to remove the regulated futures contracts from the mark-to-market tax rules?

If the owner of a mixed straddle does not elect to remove the IRC Section 1256 contract positions from the mark-to-market tax rules, gain or loss on each IRC Section 1256 contract in the straddle is determined under the mark-to-market tax rules. See Q 1069 and Q 1076. Gain or loss on each of the other positions of the straddle is determined under the general tax rules. But whenever a straddle position is disposed of (or deemed disposed of, as in the case of an IRC Section 1256 contract), the loss deferral, wash sale, and short sale rules of IRC Section 1092 (see Q 1079) are applied to determine whether and in what manner that gain or loss may be recognized for income tax purposes.

The short sale rules that apply to mixed straddles will generally have the effect of recharacterizing short-term losses on non-IRC Section 1256 positions of the mixed straddle as 60% long-term and 40% short-term.[1] Although the owner of a mixed straddle may avoid this result by making the election to exclude the IRC Section 1256 contracts from the mark-to-market rules, doing so will forfeit the 60%/40% treatment of gains on the IRC Section 1256 contract positions. See Q 1081. But if desirable, it is possible to avoid the loss recharacterization rule while retaining 60%/40% treatment for mixed straddle net gains derived from IRC Section 1256 contracts by electing to be taxed under the "straddle-by-straddle identification" rules or the "mixed straddle account" rules prescribed by the IRC and defined by regulation. (Remember, making either of these elections will not avoid the loss deferral and wash sale rules that apply to tax straddles generally.)

A portion of any gain recognized upon disposition, or other termination of a straddle that is part of a *conversion transaction*—see Q 1086—may be treated as ordinary income. A straddle will be subject to these rules if substantially all of the taxpayer's expected return from the investment is attributable to the time value of the taxpayer's net investment in the transaction.[2] See Q 1085 and Q 1086 for the definition and tax treatment of conversion transactions.

While the Internal Revenue Code does not plainly specify the application of the constructive sale rules of IRC Section 1259 to mixed straddles, it apparently is the intent of Congress that mixed straddles under IRC Section 1092(b)(2) will be subject to the rules for constructive sales of an appreciated financial position under IRC Section 1259, generally resulting in immediate gain recognition, the start of a new holding period, and an adjustment to basis (unless certain requirements are met for closing out the constructive sale transaction).[3] See Q 1087 to Q 1089.

The 1997 Blue Book states that where either position in such an identified transaction is an appreciated financial position and a constructive sale of that position results from acquiring the second position, Congress intended that the constructive sale would be treated as having occurred immediately before the identified transaction. It adds that the constructive sale will not prevent qualification of the transaction as an identified straddle transaction. It is also the intent of Congress that future regulations will clarify the extent to which straddle transactions will be subject to or excepted from

1. Temp. Treas. Reg. §1.1092(b)-2T(b)(2). See General Explanation–TRA '84, p. 317.
2. IRC Sec. 1258(c).
3. General Explanation of Tax Legislation Enacted in 1997 (JCS-23-97), p. 176-177 (the 1997 Blue Book).

the constructive sale provisions.[1] Future regulations may clarify the manner in which these rules may be applied to mixed straddles.

Straddle-by-Straddle Identification
"Identified Mixed Straddles"

Regulations use the term "identified mixed straddle" to refer to those straddles for which the taxpayer has elected "straddle-by-straddle identification." To avoid confusion, this discussion will refer to straddles for which this election has been made as "mixed straddles." In order to make a straddle-by-straddle identification election, the taxpayer must clearly identify each position that is part of the mixed straddle before the close (i.e., midnight, local time) of the day on which the straddle is established.[2] No election is permitted for any straddle composed of one or more positions that are included in a mixed straddle account (see discussion under "Mixed Straddle Accounts" below), and no election is permitted if the taxpayer has made the election to exclude the IRC Section 1256 contract positions in the straddle from the mark-to-market tax rules. See Q 1081.[3]

If one or more positions included in a mixed straddle for which this election is made were held by the taxpayer on the day prior to the day the straddle was established, then such position (or positions) is deemed to have been sold for its fair market value as of the close of the last business day preceding the day the straddle was established; but an adjustment for any gain or loss recognized on such deemed sale will be made (through adjustment to basis or otherwise) to any subsequent gain or loss realized with respect to such position.[4]

Gains or losses from positions that are part of a mixed straddle for which a straddle-by-straddle identification election has been made are determined and treated according to the rules discussed in the following paragraphs. These rules apply prior to the application of the loss deferral and wash sale rules described in Q 1079.[5] The only portion of the tax straddle short sale rules that applies under these circumstances is that which provides that the holding period of any position that is part of the straddle is deemed not to begin before the date that the taxpayer no longer holds an offsetting position to that position.[6]

1. *All positions disposed of on the same day.* If all positions of the mixed straddle are disposed of on the same day, gains and losses from the IRC Section 1256 contracts in the straddle are netted. Gains and losses from non-IRC Section 1256 contract positions are also netted. Net gain or loss from the IRC Section 1256 contracts is then offset against the net gain or loss from non-IRC Section 1256 positions. If total net gain or loss from the straddle is attributable to IRC Section 1256 positions, then the capital gain or loss will be treated as 60% long-term and 40% short-term. If the total net gain or loss from the straddle is attributable to non-IRC Section 1256 positions, then the gain or loss will be *short-term* capital gain or loss.[7]

---

1. See 1997 Blue Book, p. 177.
2. Temp. Treas. Reg. §1.1092(b)-3T(d).
3. Temp. Treas. Reg. §1.1092(b)-3T(a).
4. Temp. Treas. Reg. §1.1092(b)-3T(b)(6).
5. Temp. Treas. Reg. §1.1092(b)-3T(c).
6. Temp. Treas. Regs. §§1.1092(b)-2T, 1.1092(b)-3T.
7. Temp. Treas. Reg. §1.1092-3T(b)(2).

Example. On March 1, Nathan enters into a non-IRC Section 1256 position and an offsetting IRC Section 1256 contract and makes a valid election to use the straddle-by-straddle identification rules. On March 10, Nathan disposes of the non-IRC Section 1256 position at a $600 loss and the IRC Section 1256 contract at a $800 gain. The total net gain of $200 on the straddle is attributable to the IRC Section 1256 position. Thus, 60% of the net gain ($120) will be long-term capital gain and 40% ($80) will be short-term capital gain.

2. *All non–IRC Section 1256 positions disposed of on the same day.* If all of the non-IRC Section 1256 positions of the mixed straddle are disposed of on the same day, gains and losses realized from the non-IRC Section 1256 positions in the straddle are netted. Also, *realized and unrealized* gains and losses with respect to IRC Section 1256 contract positions are netted *as of that day* (see Q 1076). Net gain or loss realized from the non-IRC Section 1256 positions is then offset against the gain or loss from the IRC Section 1256 contracts. Any total net gain or loss from the straddle that is attributable to the non-IRC Section 1256 positions must be realized and treated as *short-term* capital gain or loss on that day. Any total net gain or loss that is attributable to *realized* gain or loss with respect to IRC Section 1256 positions must be realized and treated as 60% long-term and 40% short-term. Any gain or loss subsequently realized on the IRC Section 1256 contracts will be adjusted (through a basis adjustment or otherwise) to take into account the extent to which gain or loss was offset by unrealized gain or loss on the IRC Section 1256 contracts on that day.[1]

Example. On June 20, Matthew enters into an IRC Section 1256 contract and an offsetting non-IRC Section 1256 position and makes a valid election to use the straddle-by-straddle identification rules. On June 27, Matthew realizes a $1,700 loss on the non-IRC Section 1256 position. As of June 27, there is $1,500 of unrealized gain in the IRC Section 1256 contract. On June 27, Matthew offsets the $1,700 loss on the non-IRC Section 1256 position against the $1,500 unrealized gain on the IRC Section 1256 contract. Because the resulting $200 loss on the straddle (realized on June 27th) is attributable to the non-IRC Section 1256 position, it is treated as a $200 *short-term* capital loss. Furthermore, assuming that Matthew still holds the IRC Section 1256 contract at year end, and assuming that there is $1,800 of unrealized gain in it at that time, then Matthew will also realize a gain of $300 ($1,800 minus $1,500 adjustment for unrealized gain offset against the non-IRC Section 1256 position in June) in that year because the IRC Section 1256 contract will be deemed to have been disposed of at year end (see Q 1076).

3. *All IRC Section 1256 positions disposed of on the same day.* If all of the IRC Section 1256 contract positions in the mixed straddle are disposed of (or deemed disposed of) on the same day, gains and losses realized on the IRC Section 1256 positions are netted. Also, realized *and unrealized* gains and losses with respect to non-IRC Section 1256 positions of the straddle are netted on that day. Net gain or loss realized from the IRC Section 1256 positions is then treated as *short-term* capital gain or loss to the extent of the net gain or loss on the non-IRC Section 1256 positions on the day. Net gain or loss with respect to the IRC Section 1256 positions that exceeds the net gain or loss on the non-IRC Section 1256 positions is treated as 60% long-term and 40% short-term.[2]

Example. On December 30, Joshua enters into an IRC Section 1256 contract and an offsetting non-IRC Section 1256 position and makes a valid election to use the straddle-by-straddle identification rules. On December 31, Joshua disposes of the IRC Section 1256 contract at a gain of $1,500. As of December 31, there is $1,000 of unrealized loss in the non-IRC Section 1256 position. Under these circumstances, $1,000 of the gain realized on the IRC Section 1256 contract is short-term capital gain (i.e., to the extent of the unrealized loss on the non-IRC Section 1256 position). The other $500 of gain from the straddle is treated as 60% long-term capital gain ($300) and 40% short-term capital gain ($200).

1.   Temp. Treas. Reg. §1.1092(b)-3T(b)(3).
2.   Temp. Treas. Reg. §1.1092(b)-3T(b)(4).

4. *Disposition of one or more, but not all, positions on the same day.* If one or more, but not all, of the positions of the mixed straddle are disposed of on the same day, but neither all IRC Section 1256 positions, nor all non-IRC Section 1256 positions are disposed of on that day (i.e., neither (2) nor (3), above applies), then the straddle is taxed as follows: Gains and losses from the non-IRC Section 1256 positions that are disposed of on that day are netted. Gains and losses from the IRC Section 1256 positions that are disposed of on that day are netted. Then net gain or loss from the IRC Section 1256 positions disposed of is offset against the net gain or loss from the non-IRC Section 1256 positions disposed of. If the total net gain or loss from the dispositions on that day is attributable to the non-IRC Section 1256 positions disposed of, the rules described above in (2) are applied. If the total net gain or loss from the dispositions is attributable to the IRC Section 1256 positions disposed of, the rules described above in (3) are applied. If the net gain or loss from IRC Section 1256 positions disposed of and the net gain or loss from non-IRC Section 1256 positions disposed are either both net gains or both net losses, then the rules described in (2) are applied to the net gain or loss from the non-IRC Section 1256 positions and the rules described in (3) are applied to the net gain or loss from the IRC Section 1256 positions. For purposes of taxing the gain or loss subsequently realized on another position in such straddle, to the extent that unrealized gain or loss on a position was used to offset realized gain or loss on a non-IRC Section 1256 position under (2) above, or resulted in the gain or loss on an IRC Section 1256 position being treated as short-term capital gain or loss under (3) above, such amount may not be used for such purpose again.[1]

> *Example.* On June 15, Allison enters into a straddle consisting of four non-IRC Section 1256 positions and four IRC Section 1256 contracts and makes a valid election to use the straddle-by-straddle identification rules. On June 20, Allison disposes of one non-IRC Section 1256 position at a gain of $800 and one IRC Section 1256 contract at a loss of $300. On the same day, there is $400 of unrealized net loss on the IRC Section 1256 contracts retained by Allison and $100 of unrealized net loss on the non-IRC Section 1256 positions retained by Allison. The loss of $300 on the IRC Section 1256 contract disposed of is offset against the gain of $800 on the non-IRC Section 1256 position disposed of. The resulting net gain of $500 is attributable to the non-IRC Section 1256 position. Therefore, the rules discussed above in (2) apply. Under those rules, the net loss of $700 ($300 + $400) on the IRC Section 1256 contracts is offset against the net gain of $800 attributable to the non-IRC Section 1256 position disposed of. As a result, the total net gain of $100 is treated as short-term capital gain (because it is attributable to the non-IRC Section 1256 position disposed of). Gain or loss subsequently realized on the IRC Section 1256 contracts will be adjusted to take into account the unrealized loss of $400 that was offset against the $800 gain attributable to the non-IRC Section 1256 position disposed of.

5. *Gain or loss from non-IRC Section 1256 positions after disposition of all IRC Section 1256 contracts.* If one or more non-IRC Section 1256 positions are held after all the IRC Section 1256 contract positions in the straddle have been disposed of, any gain or loss realized on those non-IRC Section 1256 positions will be *short-term* capital gain or loss to the extent that such gain or loss is attributable to the period when such positions were part of the straddle.[2] See Temp. Treas. Reg. §1.1092(b)-2T for the rules for determining the holding period with respect to such positions.

Mixed Straddle Accounts

A taxpayer who owns mixed straddles may elect to establish one or more mixed straddle accounts for the purpose of determining gains and losses on positions includ-

---

1. Temp. Treas. Reg. §1.1092(b)-3T(b)(5).
2. Temp. Treas. Reg. §1.1092(b)-3T(b)(7).

able in such account.[1] Because the mixed straddle account rules are designed to accommodate taxpayers who have such a large volume of transactions that identification of specific mixed straddles is impractical, the rules are beyond the scope of this book. For details on the mixed straddle account rules, see Temp. Treas. Reg. §1.1092(b)-4T.[2] The carryback rules of IRC Section 1212(c) were held applicable to the IRC Section 1256 contract leg of a mixed straddle account.[3]

1084. What is an "identified straddle"? How is it taxed?

An "identified straddle" is a straddle in which (1) all the original positions are acquired on the same day, (2) all positions are clearly identified in the investor's records as being part of an identified straddle before the close of that day (or other time prescribed by future regulations), (3) no position is part of a larger straddle, and (4) all positions remain open at the close of the year, or were closed out on the same day during the year.[4] Apparently, if a successor or substitute position replaces an original position of the straddle, the straddle ceases to be an identified straddle.[5]

In the case of an identified straddle, the loss deferral and wash sale rules discussed in Q 1079 do not apply. Instead, any loss realized with respect to a position in an identified straddle is treated as sustained no earlier than the day on which all positions making up the straddle are disposed of.[6]

The tax straddle short sale rules discussed in Q 1079 do apply to identified straddles.[7]

While the IRC does not plainly set forth the application of the constructive sales rules of IRC Section 1259 to identified straddles, it apparently is the intent of Congress that a straddle designated as an identified tax straddle under IRC Section 1092(a)(2) will be treated as a constructive sale of an appreciated financial position under IRC Section 1259, resulting generally in immediate gain recognition, the start of a new holding period, and an adjustment to basis (unless certain requirements are met for closing out the position constituting the constructive sale).[8] See Q 1087 to Q 1089.

The 1997 Blue Book states that where either position in such an identified transaction is an appreciated financial position and a constructive sale of that position results from acquiring the second position, Congress intended that the constructive sale would be treated as having occurred immediately before the identified transaction. It adds that the constructive sale will not prevent qualification of the transaction as an identified straddle transaction. It is also the intent of Congress that future regulations will clarify the extent to which straddle transactions will be subject to or excepted from the constructive sale provisions.[9] Future regulations may clarify the manner in which these rules may be applied to identified straddles.

---

1. IRC Sec. 1092(b)(2); Temp. Treas. Reg. §1.1092(b)-4T.
2. See also General Explanation–TRA '84, pp. 319-321.
3. See *Roberts v. U.S.*, 734 F.Supp. 314 (D.C. Ill. 1990).
4. IRC Sec. 1092(a)(2)(B).
5. See General Explanation–ERTA, p. 284.
6. IRC Sec. 1092(a)(2)(A).
7. See Temp. Treas. Reg. §1.1092(b)-2T.
8. General Explanation of Tax Legislation Enacted in 1997 (JCS-23-97), p. 176-177 (the 1997 Blue Book).
9. See 1997 Blue Book, p. 177.

A portion of any gain recognized upon disposition or other termination of a straddle that is part of a *conversion transaction*—see Q 1085—may be treated as ordinary income. According to the IRC, these rules are applicable where substantially all of the taxpayer's expected return from the investment is attributable to the time value of the taxpayer's net investment in the transaction.[1] See Q 1085 and Q 1086 for the definition and tax treatment of conversion transactions.

Note: Do not confuse "identified straddles" discussed above with what the temporary regulations refer to as a "IRC Section 1092(b)(2) identified mixed straddle." The latter is discussed in Q 1083 under the heading "Straddle-by-Straddle Identification."

CONVERSION TRANSACTIONS

1085. What is a "conversion transaction"?

A "conversion transaction" is a transaction from which substantially all of the taxpayer's expected return is attributable to the time value of the taxpayer's net investment in the transaction, and that is (1) a transaction that encompasses an acquisition of any property and a substantially contemporaneous agreement to sell such property (or substantially identical property) at a price determined in accordance with the agreement, (2) an applicable straddle, (3) any transaction that is marketed or sold as producing capital gains from a transaction from which substantially all of the taxpayer's expected return is attributable to the time value of the net investment in the transaction, *or* (4) any transaction specified in future regulations.[2] In short, a conversion transaction is a financial arrangement that resembles a loan in an economic sense.

An "applicable straddle" means any straddle within the meaning of IRC Section 1092(c), except that the term personal property includes stock.[3]

The income tax consequences of conversion transactions are explained in Q 1086.

1086. How is a "conversion transaction" treated for income tax purposes?

In general, any gain that would otherwise be treated as gain from the sale or exchange of a capital asset, and that is recognized on the disposition or other termination of any position held as part of a *conversion transaction*—see Q 1085—will be treated as ordinary income to the extent that such gain does not exceed an "applicable imputed income amount," as defined below.[4] The purpose of IRC Section 1258 is to prevent the use of conversion transactions to transform ordinary income into capital gain.

"Applicable imputed income amount" (for purposes of a disposition or termination of a conversion transaction) means the amount of interest that would have accrued on the taxpayer's net investment in the conversion transaction for the period ending on the date of such disposition (or on the date the transaction ceased to be a conversion transaction, if earlier) at a rate equal to 120% of the *applicable rate* (see below) reduced by any amounts previously treated as ordinary income under IRC Section 1258.[5] Fu-

---

1. IRC Sec. 1258(c).
2. IRC Sec. 1258(c).
3. IRC Sec. 1258(d)(1).
4. IRC Sec. 1258(a).
5. IRC Sec. 1258(b).

ture regulations will provide for reduction of the applicable imputed income amount for amounts capitalized under IRC Section 263(g). A taxpayer's net investment in a conversion transaction includes the fair market value of any position that becomes part of the transaction.[1]

The term "applicable rate" refers to the applicable federal rate as determined under IRC Section 1274(d) (compounded semiannually) as if the conversion transaction were a debt instrument, or, if the term of the conversion transaction is indefinite, the federal short-term rates in effect under IRC Section 6621(b) (relating to the determination of interest rates for overpayments and underpayments of tax) during the period of the conversion transaction (compounded daily).[2]

Regulations provide taxpayers with a method to net certain gains and losses from positions of the same conversion transaction before determining the amount of gain treated as ordinary income.[3] If a taxpayer disposes of or terminates all the positions of an "identified netting transaction" within a 14 day period in a single taxable year, all gains and losses on those positions realized within that period (other than built-in losses, see below) are netted solely for purposes of determining the amount of gain treated as ordinary income. An "identified netting transaction" is a conversion transaction that the taxpayer identifies as an identified netting transaction on its books and records. Identification of each position of the conversion transaction must be made before the close of the business day on which the position becomes part of the conversion transaction.[4]

A position with a "built-in" loss that becomes part of a conversion transaction is taken into account at its fair market value, determined as of the date the position becomes part of the conversion transaction; but upon disposition or other termination of the position (in a transaction in which gain or loss is realized), the built-in loss will be recognized and its character will be determined without regard to IRC Section 1258.[5] Thus, if a position with a built-in capital loss becomes part of a conversion transaction, upon a disposition of the position the built-in loss will retain its character as a capital loss for purposes of IRC Section 1258. "Built-in loss" means any loss that would have been realized if the position had been disposed of or otherwise terminated at its fair market value as of the time the position became a part of the conversion transaction.[6] A "built-in loss" can also arise if a taxpayer realizes a gain or loss on any one position of a conversion transaction and, as of the date that gain or loss is realized, there is unrealized loss in any other position of the conversion transaction that is not disposed of, terminated, or treated as sold under any provision of the IRC or regulations within 14 days of and within the same taxable year as the realization event.[7]

Although built-in loss is not recharacterized for purposes of IRC Section 1258, it appears that property with a built-in gain will not be afforded the same treatment. IRC Section 1258(a) states that *any* capital gain that is recognized on the disposition of a position held as part of a conversion transaction will be recharacterized as ordinary income to the extent the gain does not exceed the applicable imputed income amount.

---

1. IRC Sec. 1258(d)(4).
2. IRC Sec. 1258(d)(2).
3. Treas. Reg. §1.1258-1(a).
4. Treas. Reg. §1.1258-1(b).
5. IRC Sec. 1258(d)(3).
6. IRC Sec. 1258(d)(3)(B).
7. Treas. Reg. §1.1258-1(c).

Thus, it would seem that gain generated prior to property's inclusion in a conversion transaction is subject to recharacterization.

The conversion transaction rules do not apply to the transactions of an options or commodities dealer entered into in the normal course of business; but limited partners and certain investors who have an interest in an enterprise other than as a limited partner will generally be subject to the conversion transaction rules.[1]

CONSTRUCTIVE SALES OF APPRECIATED FINANCIAL POSITIONS

1087. What is an "appreciated financial position"?

IRC Section 1259 generally provides special treatment for "constructive sales of appreciated financial positions." Very generally, unless certain exceptions apply, such transactions result in a deemed sale with immediate recognition of gain (and a corresponding increase in basis in the property deemed sold), as well as the start of a new holding period. See Q 1089. The definition of "constructive sale" is explained in Q 1088.

For purposes of the constructive sales rules of IRC Section 1259, an *appreciated financial position* is any *position* with respect to any stock, debt instrument, or partnership interest if there would be a gain were the position sold, assigned, or otherwise terminated at its fair market value.[2] The term "position" is further defined as an interest, including a futures or forward contract—see Q 1074 to Q 1076—short sale—see Q 1021 to Q 1028—or option—see Q 1042 to Q 1067.[3] Furthermore, it was the intent of Congress that *offsetting notional principal contracts*—see Q 1089—also be included in the definition of "appreciated financial position," and such a definition is supported by the language of IRC Section 1259(c)(1)(D).[4]

An interest in a trust that is actively traded will be treated as stock, for purposes of determining whether it is an appreciated financial position, unless substantially all (by value) of the property held by the trust is debt that qualifies for the debt interest exception described below.[5]

Debt instrument exception. The term "appreciated financial position" does *not* include any position with respect to debt (e.g., bonds) if: (1) the *position* unconditionally entitles the holder to receive a specified principal amount, (2) the interest payments (or other similar amounts) with respect to such *position* are payable based on a fixed rate or, to the extent provided in regulations, at a variable rate, and (3) such *position* is not convertible (directly or indirectly) into stock of the issuer or any *related person* (see Q 1088).[6] Furthermore, the term "appreciated financial position" does not include any *hedge* of a position satisfying all three of the foregoing requirements.[7]

Consequently, to qualify for the exception for a position with respect to debt instruments, the position *itself* would have to *either* meet the requirements as to unconditional

---

1. IRC Sec. 1258(d)(5).
2. IRC Sec. 1259(b)(1).
3. IRC Sec. 1259(b)(3).
4. General Explanation of Tax Legislation Enacted in 1997 (JCS-23-97), p. 175 (the 1997 Blue Book).
5. IRC Sec. 1259(e)(2).
6. IRC Sec. 1259(b)(2)(A).
7. IRC Sec. 1259(b)(2)(B).

principal amount, nonconvertibility and interest terms *or*, alternatively, be a hedge of a position meeting these requirements. A hedge for purposes of the provision includes any position that reduces the taxpayer's risk of interest rate or price changes or currency fluctuations with respect to another position.[1]

Mark to market exception. The term "appreciated financial position" does not include any position which is marked to the market. See Q 1076.[2]

1088. What constitutes a "constructive sale" of an appreciated financial position"?

A taxpayer is generally treated as having made a constructive sale of an appreciated financial position (see Q 1087) if the taxpayer or a *related person*: (1) enters into a short sale—see Q 1021—of the same or substantially identical property, (2) enters into an *offsetting notional principal contract* (defined below) with respect to the same or substantially identical property, or (3) enters into a futures contract (see Q 1074) or *forward contract* (defined below) to deliver the same or substantially identical property.[3]

In addition, if the appreciated financial position is a short sale, a futures contract—see Q 1074—a forward contract (see below), or an offsetting notional principal contract (see below), *with respect to any property*, a taxpayer who acquires the same or substantially identical property is generally treated as having made a constructive sale of the position.[4]

It appears that if a taxpayer holds a long-term position in actively traded stock (which is a capital asset in the taxpayer's hands) and enters into a securities futures contract to sell substantially identical stock at a time when the position in the stock has appreciated in value, the constructive sale rules will apply.[5]

The Secretary of the Treasury is authorized to issue regulations providing that certain other positions or transactions having substantially the same effect as those described above will also constitute a constructive sale.[6] The types of transactions intended to be targeted by such regulations are those that result in the reduction of both risk of loss and opportunity for gain; transactions that reduce only one or the other would not be affected.[7]

Nonpublicly traded property. A constructive sale does not include any contract for sale of any stock, debt instrument, or partnership interest that is not a *marketable security* if the contract settles within one year after the date the contract is entered into.[8] For this purpose, a *marketable security* means any security for which, as of the date of disposition, there was a market on an established securities market or otherwise.[9]

---

1. General Explanation of Tax Legislation Enacted in 1998 (JCS-6-98), p. 184 (the 1998 Blue Book).
2. IRC Sec. 1259(b)(2)(C).
3. IRC Sec. 1259(c)(1)(A)-(C).
4. IRC Sec. 1259(c)(1)(D).
5. See H.R. Conf. Rep. No. 106-1033 (CRTRA 2000), "Straddle Rules," p. 1035.
6. IRC Sec. 1259(c)(1)(E).
7. See General Explanation of Tax Legislation Enacted in 1997 (JCS-23-97), p. 177 (the 1997 Blue Book).
8. IRC Sec. 1259(c)(2).
9. IRC Secs. 1259(c)(2), 453(f).

Closed Transactions

If a transaction that would otherwise be a constructive sale is closed within certain time limits, it will be disregarded. The IRC states that constructive sales treatment will not apply to any transaction (that would otherwise be treated as a constructive sale) during the taxable year if

(1) the transaction is closed before the end of the 30th day after the close of the taxable year (i.e., the "extended taxable year");

(2) the taxpayer holds the appreciated financial position throughout the 60-day period beginning on the date the transaction is closed; *and*

(3) at no time during the 60-day period is the taxpayer's risk of loss with respect to the position reduced by reason of a transaction such as holding an option to sell, an obligation to sell, or a short sale, being the grantor of a call option, or certain other transactions diminishing the risk of loss.[1]

A closed transaction that is, in essence, reestablished (or replaced with a substantially similar transaction) before the 60-day period described above elapses, then closed again within the extended taxable year, may also be disregarded. The Internal Revenue Code states that if

(a) a transaction, which would otherwise be treated as a constructive sale of an appreciated financial position, is closed during the taxable year or during the 30 days thereafter (the extended taxable year), *and*

(b) another substantially similar transaction is entered into during the 60-day period beginning on the date that the original transaction is closed, that (i) also would otherwise be treated as a constructive sale of the position, and (ii) is closed before the end of the extended taxable year in which the original transaction occurs, and the transaction meets requirements (2) and (3), above,

then the substantially similar transaction will be disregarded for purposes of determining whether the original transaction met requirement (3), above, (relating to the reduction of the taxpayer's risk of loss during the 60-day period following the closed transaction).[2]

Constructive Sales of Multiple
Appreciated Financial Positions

The Internal Revenue Code states that if there is a constructive sale of any appreciated financial position, such position is subsequently disposed of, and at the time of the disposition, the transaction resulting in the constructive sale of the position is still open with respect to the taxpayer or any related person (defined below), then solely for purposes of determining whether the taxpayer has entered into a constructive sale of any other appreciated financial position held by the taxpayer, the taxpayer will be treated as entering into the transaction immediately after the disposition. For purposes of this rule, an assignment or other termination will be treated as a disposition.[3]

---

1. See IRC Secs. 1259(c)(3), 246(c)(4).
2. IRC Sec. 1259(c)(3)(B).
3. IRC Sec. 1259(e)(1).

The 1997 Blue Book explains the preceding paragraph (and provides an example) as follows: "A transaction that has resulted in a constructive sale of an appreciated financial position (e.g., a short sale) is not treated as resulting in a constructive sale of *another* appreciated financial position as long as the taxpayer holds the position that was treated as constructively sold. But when that position is assigned, terminated or disposed of by the taxpayer, the taxpayer immediately thereafter is treated as entering into the transaction that resulted in the constructive sale (e.g., the short sale) if it remains open at that time. Thus, the transaction can cause a constructive sale of another appreciated financial position at any time thereafter."[1]

> *Example*: Assume a taxpayer holds two appreciated stock positions and one offsetting short sale, and the taxpayer identifies the short sale as offsetting one of the stock positions. If the taxpayer then sells the stock position that was identified, the identified short position would cause a constructive sale of the taxpayer's other stock position at that time.[2]

The Internal Revenue Code also provides that if a taxpayer holds multiple positions in property, the determination of whether a specific transaction is a constructive sale and, if so, which appreciated financial position is deemed sold will be made in the same manner as actual sales.[3]

Identified Pre-TRA '97 Positions

Under Section 1001(d)(2) of the Taxpayer Relief Act of 1997, if a taxpayer entered into a transaction which was a constructive sale of any appreciated financial position before June 9, 1997, and so-identified the offsetting positions to the IRS by August 5, 1997, the rules of IRC Section 1259 shall not apply to determine whether a constructive sale occurred.

Where a taxpayer with identified pre-TRA '97 offsetting positions transferred the short position from the original broker to a second broker, the grandfather provision continued to apply.[4]

Definitions

A *forward contract* is a contract to deliver a substantially fixed amount of property, including cash, for a substantially fixed price.[5] The amended provision clarifies that the definition of a forward contract includes a contract that provides for cash settlement with respect to a substantially fixed amount of property at a substantially fixed price.[6] According to the 1997 Blue Book, a forward contract results in a constructive sale *only* if it provides for delivery, or for cash settlement, of a substantially fixed amount of property and a substantially fixed price. If the amount of property provided for by the forward contract is subject to significant variation under the terms of the contract, it will not constitute a forward contract.[7] Furthermore, an agreement that is not a "contract" for purposes of applicable contract law or that is subject to "very substantial contingencies" was not intended to be treated as a forward contract.[8]

---

1. 1997 Blue Book, pp. 174-175 (emphasis added).
2. 1997 Blue Book, p. 175.
3. IRC Sec. 1259(e)(3).
4. Rev. Rul. 2004-15, 2004-8 IRB 515.
5. IRC Sec. 1259(d)(1).
6. General Explanation of Tax Legislation Enacted in 1998 (JCS-6-98), p. 185 (the 1998 Blue Book).
7. See Rev. Rul. 2003-7, 2003-5 IRB 363.
8. 1997 Blue Book, p. 176.

But the Service distinguished a case in which in addition to entering into a forward contract pledging to deliver property that is the same as or substantially identical to an appreciated financial position that he holds, a taxpayer loaned and delivered the shares to the other party at the time of the contract. In that case, the IRS found a constructive sale.[1]

The term *offsetting notional principal contract* means, with respect to any property, an agreement that includes (1) a requirement to pay (or provide credit for) all or substantially all of the investment yield (including appreciation) on such property for a specified period and (2) a right to be reimbursed for (or receive credit for) all or substantially all of any decline in the value of such property.[2] (A "swap" is one type of offsetting notional principal contract.)

For purposes of the constructive sales rules, a person is *related* to another person with respect to a transaction if (a) the relationship is described in IRC Section 267(b) (which includes persons related by family as well as related entities) or IRC Section 707(b) (related partnerships)—see Q 1419—for details of both definitions *and* (b) the transaction is entered into with a view toward avoiding the purposes of the constructive sales rules.[3]

"Substantially identical stock or securities" is not defined in IRC Section 1259. Under earlier law, the meaning of the term as used for purposes of the short sale rules is the same as that used for the wash sale rule. See Q 1023, Q 1031. It would seem logical that the same definition would be used for purposes of constructive sales of appreciated financial positions.

Note: Do not confuse a "constructive sale of an appreciated financial position" with a "constructive ownership transaction." See Q 1090 and Q 1091. The former applies to certain hedging positions held by a taxpayer and results in deemed sale treatment and immediate recognition of gain. The latter applies to a taxpayer's purchase of a derivative whose investment return is tied to the performance of a pass-through entity, instead of purchasing a direct interest in the pass-through entity itself, and results in the conversion of long-term capital gain into ordinary income. In other words, the former represents a deemed sale and the latter represents deemed (i.e., constructive) ownership.

1089. How is a constructive sale of an appreciated financial position treated for tax purposes?

If there is a constructive sale of an appreciated financial position, the taxpayer generally recognizes *gain* as if the position were sold, assigned, or otherwise terminated at its fair market value on the date of the constructive sale (and any gain is taken into account for the taxable year that includes the date of the constructive sale).[4]

For purposes of the tax treatment of the position after a constructive sale has been taxed under IRC Section 1259, the IRC states that "proper adjustment shall be made in the amount of any gain or loss subsequently realized with respect to such position for any gain taken into account" under the constructive sale treatment described above.[5] Since

1. TAM 200604033.
2. IRC Sec. 1259(d)(2).
3. IRC Sec. 1259(c)(4).
4. IRC Sec. 1259(a)(1).
5. IRC Sec. 1259(a)(2)(A).

constructive sale treatment by definition applies only to *appreciated* financial positions, this provision should have the effect of increasing the taxpayer's basis for purposes of any future disposition.[1]

The taxpayer must also begin a new holding period, as if the appreciated financial position were originally acquired on the date of the constructive sale.[2] But except as provided in future regulations, a constructive sale generally is not treated as a sale for other Internal Revenue Code purposes.[3]

Part of the complexity of IRC Section 1259 treatment lies in the fact that some positions constitute an appreciated financial position, some transactions result in a constructive sale, and some (depending on the taxpayer's other holdings) can do either. For example, a short sale can constitute either an appreciated financial position *or* a constructive sale, depending on the taxpayer's other holdings. The same is true of certain futures or forward contracts and offsetting notional principal contracts.[4]

Under the plain wording of IRC Section 1259, the holding of an option constitutes an appreciated financial position, but *not* a constructive sale.[5] But as authorized by IRC Section 1259(c)(1)(E), future regulations may clarify the definition of "constructive sale" to include certain combinations of options.[6] Furthermore, under the rules of IRC Section 1233 governing short sales, the acquisition of a put option is treated as a short sale; obviously, such an application in the context of IRC Section 1259 would have broad consequences.

According to the 1997 Blue Book, the intent of Congress was to treat as a constructive sale any transaction that reduces *both* the risk of loss *and* the opportunity for gain. Thus, for example, the holding of a stock position and the purchase of an at-the-money put option would not constitute a constructive sale since the option reduces only the taxpayer's risk of loss, not his opportunity for gain.[7] Future regulations should offer clarification of the interaction of IRC Section 1259 and the treatment of options.

GAINS FROM CONSTRUCTIVE OWNERSHIP TRANSACTIONS

1090. What is a "constructive ownership transaction"?

IRC Section 1260 generally provides special treatment for "constructive ownership transactions" occurring after July 11, 1999.[8] In general, IRC Section 1260 targets the use of certain derivative contracts by taxpayers in arrangements that are primarily designed to convert what otherwise would be ordinary income and short-term capital gain into long-term capital gain. Congress was particularly concerned about derivative contracts with respect to partnerships and other pass-through entities. The use of such contracts would otherwise result in the taxpayer being taxed in a more favorable manner than

---

1. See also, General Explanation of Tax Legislation Enacted in 1997 (JCS-23-97), p. 174 (the 1997 Blue Book).
2. IRC Sec. 1259(a)(2)(B).
3. 1997 Blue Book, pp. 173-174.
4. See IRC Secs. 1259(b)(3), 1259(c)(1).
5. See IRC Secs. 1259(b)(3), 1259(c).
6. 1997 Blue Book, pp. 177-178.
7. See 1997 Blue Book, p. 177.
8. TREA '99, Secs. 534(a), 534(c).

if the taxpayer had actually acquired an ownership interest in the pass-through entity (i.e., being taxed at the 15% capital gains rate rather than at the top marginal rate of 35% on ordinary income).[1]

Generally, a taxpayer is generally treated as having entered into a *constructive ownership transaction* with respect to any *financial asset* if the taxpayer

(1) holds a *long position under a notional principal contract* (defined below) with respect to the financial asset;

(2) enters into a *forward contract* (defined below) or futures contract (see Q 1074) to acquire the financial asset;

(3) is the holder of a call option and the grantor (i.e., writer) of a put option (see Q 1047) on a financial asset, and the options have substantially equal strike prices and substantially contemporaneous maturity dates; or

(4) to the extent provided in future regulations, enters into one or more other transactions (or acquires one or more positions) that have substantially the same effect as those described above.[2]

The types of transactions intended to be targeted by the regulations are those that replicate the economic benefits of direct ownership of a financial asset without a significant change in the risk-reward profile with respect to the underlying transaction.[3] The Secretary may also issue regulations that permit taxpayers to mark constructive ownership transactions to the market instead of applying these rules, and to exclude certain forward contracts that do not convey substantially all of the economic return with respect to a financial asset.[4]

Mark to market exception. A constructive ownership transaction will not be subject to these rules if all of the positions are marked to the market. See Q 1076.[5]

For the tax treatment of gain from a constructive ownership transaction, see Q 1091.

One example of a conversion transaction involving a derivative contract is set forth in the Senate Report for TREA '99. The transaction involves an arrangement between a taxpayer and a securities dealer whereby the dealer agrees to pay the taxpayer any appreciation with respect to a notional investment in a hedge fund. In return, the taxpayer agrees to pay the securities dealer any depreciation in the value of the notional investment. The arrangement lasts for more than one year. The taxpayer is substantially in the same economic position as if he owned the interest in the hedge fund directly, yet the taxpayer may treat any appreciation resulting from the contractual arrangement as long-term capital gain. Moreover, any tax attributable to such gain is deferred until the arrangement is terminated.[6]

---

1. S. Rep. No. 106-201 (TREA '99).
2. IRC Sec. 1260(d)(1).
3. S. Rep. No. 106-201 (TREA '99).
4. IRC Sec. 1260(g).
5. IRC Sec. 1260(d)(2).
6. S. Rep. No. 106-201 (TREA '99).

Definitions

Financial asset means any equity interest in any pass-through entity and, to the extent provided in regulations, any debt instrument and any stock in a corporation that is not a pass-through entity.[1]

Pass-through entity is defined as: (1) a regulated investment company (i.e., mutual fund) (see Q 1161); (2) a real estate investment trust (REIT) (see Q 1179); (3) an S corporation (see Q 1218); (4) a partnership (see Q 1184 to Q 1186); (5) a trust (see Q 1140 to Q 1141); (6) a common trust fund; (7) a passive foreign investment company; (8) a foreign personal holding company; (9) a foreign investment company; and (10) a REMIC (see Q 1147 and Q 1148).[2]

A taxpayer will be treated as holding a *long position under a notional principal contract* with respect to any financial asset if the taxpayer has the right to be paid (or receive credit for) all or substantially all of the investment yield (including appreciation) on that financial asset for a specified period, *and* is obligated to reimburse (or provide credit for) all or substantially all of any decline in the value of that financial asset.[3]

The term *forward contract* means any contract to acquire in the future (or provide or receive credit for the future value of) any financial asset.[4]

Note: Do not confuse a "constructive sale of an appreciated financial position"—see Q 1087 to Q 1089—with a "constructive ownership transaction." The former applies to certain hedging positions held by a taxpayer and results in deemed sale treatment and immediate recognition of gain. The latter applies to a taxpayer's purchase of a derivative contract whose investment return is tied to the performance of a pass-through entity, instead of purchasing a direct interest in the pass-through entity itself, and results in the conversion of long-term capital gain into ordinary income. In other words, the former represents a deemed sale, and the latter represents deemed (i.e., constructive) ownership.

1091. How is a "constructive ownership transaction" treated for tax purposes?

If a taxpayer has gain from a "constructive ownership transaction"—see Q 1090—with respect to any "financial asset"—see Q 1090—and that gain would ordinarily be treated as a long-term capital gain, such gain will instead be treated as ordinary income to the extent that the gain exceeds the *net underlying long-term capital gain*.[5]

For purposes of the constructive ownership transaction rules, *net underlying long-term capital gain* means the aggregate net capital gain that the taxpayer would have had if (1) the financial asset had been acquired for fair market value on the date the transaction was opened and sold for fair market value on the date the transaction was closed; *and* (2) only gains and losses that would have resulted from the deemed ownership under (1) were taken into account. If the taxpayer does not establish the amount

---

1. IRC Sec. 1260(c)(1).
2. IRC Sec. 1260(c)(2).
3. IRC Sec. 1260(d)(3).
4. IRC Sec. 1260(d)(4).
5. IRC Sec. 1260(a).

of the net underlying long-term capital gain with respect to any financial asset by clear and convincing evidence, the amount of such gain will be treated as zero.[1]

If any gain is treated as ordinary income for any taxable year on account of these rules, the tax imposed for that year is increased by imposing interest at the underpayment rate for every prior tax year in which any portion of the constructive ownership transaction was open.[2] The calculation of the interest is explained in IRC Section 1260(b)(2). No credits are allowed against the increase in tax.[3]

To the extent that gain is treated as long-term capital gain after the application of IRC Section 1260(a)(1) (i.e., instead of being recharacterized as ordinary income), it will be subject to the capital gain tax in the same manner as is the net underlying long-term capital gain.[4] See Q 1420 for the treatment of capital gains and losses.

Special rule where taxpayer takes delivery. Except as provided in regulations, if a constructive ownership transaction is closed by reason of taking delivery, the constructive ownership rules will be applied as if the taxpayer had sold all the contracts, options, or other positions that are part of the transaction for fair market value on the closing date. The amount of gain recognized under the preceding sentence will not exceed the amount of gain treated as ordinary income under IRC Section 1260(a). The IRC states that proper adjustments will be made in the amount of any gain or loss subsequently realized for gain recognized and treated as ordinary income under this special rule.[5]

The intended effect of IRC Section 1260 is to limit the amount of long-term capital gain a taxpayer can recognize from derivative transactions with respect to certain pass-through entities. The amount that may be treated as long-term capital gain is limited to the amount of such gain the taxpayer would have had if the taxpayer owned a direct interest in the pass-through entity during the term of the derivative contract. Any gain in excess of this amount is treated as ordinary income. In addition, an interest charge is imposed on the amount of gain that is treated as ordinary income. The provision does not alter the amount of gain that is not treated as ordinary income.[6]

---

1. IRC Sec. 1260(e).
2. See IRC Sec. 1260(b)(1).
3. IRC Sec. 1260(b)(4).
4. IRC Sec. 1260(a)(2).
5. IRC Sec. 1260(f).
6. Joint Committee on Taxation, *Summary of Conference Agreement on H.R. 1180 Relating to Expiring Tax Provisions and Other Revenue Provisions* (JCX-85-99), November 17, 1999.

BONDS

SHORT-TERM TAXABLE OBLIGATIONS (MATURITIES ONE YEAR OR LESS)

Treasury Bills

1092. What is a Treasury bill?

Treasury bills (T-bills) are obligations of the United States government, generally issued with 4-week, 13-week and 26-week maturity periods. Treasury bills are issued in minimum denominations of $1,000 with $1,000 increments thereafter. Treasury bills are issued without interest and on a discount basis (that is, they are issued at a price which is less than the amount for which they will be redeemed at maturity). The price is determined at auction (generally on Monday of each week for 13- and 26-week bills; 4-week bills are generally auctioned on Tuesday of each week).

1093. Is an investor who holds a T-bill required to include interest in income prior to sale or maturity of the bill?

No. The amount of interest, represented by the discount (at issue or on the market) from face value, is not required to be included in income by a cash basis investor until the date on which the obligation is paid at maturity, sold or otherwise disposed of as discussed in Q 1094.[1]

However, a cash basis investor may elect to include in income as it accrues prior to sale or redemption the difference between the stated redemption price at maturity and his basis in the obligation (this difference is called "acquisition discount"). Such an election may not be limited to a particular bill, but applies to all short-term taxable obligations acquired on or after the first day of the first taxable year for which the election is made, and it continues to apply until the Service consents to revocation of the election.[2] (Short-term obligations are those having a fixed maturity date of one year or less after issue.[3]) The election affects short-term taxable corporate obligations, as well; however, in the case of corporate obligations, original issue discount is included unless the investor chooses to include "acquisition discount" with respect to all of them.[4] With respect to interest-paying, short-term corporate obligations, elections to include discount as it accrues will also have the effect of requiring the taxpayer to include stated interest payments (not otherwise includable in income until paid) in income as they accrue.[5] See also Q 1095.

Under the election, acquisition discount is considered to accrue daily on a ratable basis. That is, the amount of discount is divided by the number of days after the day the taxpayer acquired the obligation up to and including the day of its maturity.[6] He must include an amount equal to the sum of the daily portions for each day in the tax year he held the obligation.[7] However, a taxpayer electing to include acquisition discount as it accrues may elect, under regulations, with respect to particular obligations, a constant

1. IRC Secs. 454(b), 1272(a)(2).
2. IRC Sec. 1282(b)(2).
3. IRC Sec. 1283(a).
4. IRC Sec. 1283(c).
5. IRC Sec. 1281(a)(2).
6. IRC Sec. 1283(b)(1).
7. IRC Sec. 1281(a).

interest rate (using yield to maturity based on the cost of the bill and daily compounding) and use ratable accrual on other short-term obligations. Once made, this election is irrevocable with respect to the obligations to which it applies.[1]

This election may, under some circumstances, be advantageous where leveraging is used by a cash basis investor to purchase or carry Treasury bills, since deduction of the interest expense up to the amount of discount accruing during the year must be deferred unless discount is currently included (see Q 1307).

While a cash basis investor is not usually required to include discount in income prior to sale or other disposition, certain taxpayers must include acquisition discount in income. The mandatory accrual rules apply to bills (1) held by accrual basis taxpayers, (2) held by a bank, (3) held by a regulated investment company or common trust fund, (4) held as inventory, (5) identified[2] as part of a hedging transaction, or (6) held by a pass-through entity (e.g., a trust, partnership or S corporation) formed or availed of to avoid the mandatory inclusion rule, or a pass-through entity in any year in which 20% or more of the value of the interests in the entity are owned for 90 days or more in a year by taxpayers who would be subject to the rule.[3] A taxpayer subject to these mandatory accrual rules may, under regulations, elect irrevocably to accrue discount with respect to any obligation on a constant rate (compounded daily) instead of ratably.[4]

The basis of a T-bill is increased by amounts of accrued discount and interest included in income prior to disposition or redemption.[5]

1094. How is an investor taxed on the gain or loss on the sale or maturity of a Treasury bill?

T-bills are capital assets.[6] On sale or maturity of the bill, the seller recovers his tax basis (generally his cost plus broker's fees on acquisition) tax free. Any gain realized over his tax basis must be treated as ordinary income to the extent it represents recovery of discount. Any excess over that is capital gain.[7] (Generally, the gain is short-term because the holding period for short-term gain is one year or less.[8] See Q 1420 for the treatment of capital gains and losses.)

The amount of discount treated as ordinary income is determined in the following manner. Any individual holding the bill at maturity includes as ordinary income the difference between his tax basis and the bill's face value. (The difference between an individual's basis and the bill's face value is called "acquisition discount.") Any individual who sells the bill prior to maturity includes as ordinary income only a portion of his acquisition discount based on the total time he held the bill; the amount included is his acquisition discount multiplied by a fraction having as numerator the number of days he held the obligation and as denominator the number of days after he acquired the bill up to and including the maturity date.[9] This formula enables each holder to

---

1. IRC Sec. 1283(b)(2).
2. Under IRC Sec. 1256(e).
3. IRC Sec. 1281(b).
4. IRC Sec. 1283(b)(2).
5. IRC Sec. 1283(d).
6. IRC Sec. 1221.
7. IRC Sec. 1271(a)(3).
8. IRC Sec. 1222.
9. IRC Sec. 1271(a)(3).

determine the portion of any gain to be treated as interest income without reference to the original discount or the treatment applicable to any other holder.

An owner may elect irrevocably on a bill-by-bill basis to compute the amount of discount on a daily compounding basis instead of in equal daily portions.[1]

If the investor has elected to include discount in income as it accrues prior to sale, his basis is increased by the amount included, and the entire gain is capital gain (see Q 1093).[2]

If instead of a gain, loss is realized on sale or maturity, it is capital loss.

The installment method for recognizing and taxing gain is not available for securities traded on an established securities market. As a result, gain from sale is included in income for the year in which the trade date occurs even if one or more payments are received in the subsequent tax year.[3]

The interest is exempt from all state and local income taxes.[4]

If a Treasury bill was held as part of a tax straddle, the additional rules and qualifications explained in Q 1077 to Q 1084 apply; if a Treasury bill was held as part of a conversion transaction, the additional rules explained in Q 1085 and Q 1086 apply.

If the transfer is between spouses, or between former spouses incident to divorce, see Q 1447.[5]

Short-Term Corporate Obligations

1095. Is an investor who holds a short-term taxable corporate obligation required to include discount in income prior to sale or maturity? Is he required to include interest as it accrues?

Original issue discount (the difference between the issue price and the stated redemption price) on a taxable corporate debt instrument having a maturity date of one year or less is generally not included in income by a cash basis investor prior to sale or redemption.[6] Interest payable on such bonds is generally not included in income by a cash basis taxpayer until it is received. However, a cash basis investor may elect to include original issue discount as it accrues. Such an election may not be limited to a particular obligation but applies to all short-term taxable corporate obligations (and to Treasury bills with respect to acquisition discount) acquired on or after the first day of the first taxable year for which the election is made, and it continues to apply until the Service consents to revocation of the election.[7] If a taxpayer elects to include discount as it accrues, he must also include stated interest (not otherwise included in income until it is paid) as it accrues.[8]

---

1. IRC Sec. 1271(a)(3)(E); Treas. Reg. §1.1271-1(b)(2).
2. IRC Sec. 1283(d).
3. IRC Sec. 453(k). See Rev. Rul. 93-84, 1993-2 CB 225.
4. 31 USC 3124.
5. IRC Sec. 1041.
6. IRC Sec. 1272(a)(2).
7. IRC Secs. 1282(b), 1283(c).
8. IRC Sec. 1281(a)(2).

The taxpayer making the election must include as income an amount equal to the sum of the daily portions of original issue discount (in the case of T-bills, daily portions of acquisition discount) for each day that he held the obligation in the tax year.

An irrevocable election may be made, on an obligation-by-obligation basis, to determine the amount of original issue discount by using daily compounding at a constant interest rate.[1]

Rather than electing to include original issue discount as it accrues, a taxpayer may elect to include "acquisition discount" (the difference between the stated redemption price at maturity and his basis in the obligation) as it accrues.[2] The manner in which acquisition discount accrues is discussed in Q 1093. The election to accrue acquisition discount applies to all such obligations (and Treasury bills) acquired by the taxpayer on or after the first day of the first taxable year to which the election applies and thereafter until the Service consents to a revocation.

Certain investors *must* include original issue discount (or, by election, acquisition discount) in income prior to sale or other disposition of corporate short-term taxable obligations. They must also include interest payable on the obligation as it accrues.[3] The mandatory inclusion rules apply to obligations: (1) held by accrual basis taxpayers; (2) held by a bank; (3) held by a regulated investment company or common trust fund; (4) held as inventory; (5) identified[4] as part of a hedging transaction; or (6) held by a pass-through entity (e.g., a trust, partnership or S corporation) formed or availed of to avoid the mandatory inclusion rule, or a pass-through entity in any year in which 20% or more of the value of the interests in the entity are owned for 90 days or more in a year by taxpayers who would be subject to the rule.[5] Discount must also be included in income as it accrues on a stripped bond or stripped coupon held by the person who stripped the bond or coupon or by a person whose basis is determined by reference to the basis in the hands of the person who stripped the bond or coupon (e.g., a person who receives it as a gift) (see Q 1136).[6]

The basis of a short-term taxable corporate obligation is increased by amounts of accrued discount included in income prior to disposition or redemption.[7] As to how gain or loss is treated upon disposition of corporate short-term taxable obligations with original issue discount when the taxpayer has not made an election to include discount as it accrues, see Q 1096.

1096. How is an investor taxed on gain or loss on the sale or maturity of a short-term taxable corporate obligation?

As a general rule, gain or loss is a capital gain or loss. However, gain on the sale or redemption of short-term corporate obligations is ordinary income up to the portion of the original issue discount allocable to the time the obligation was held by the taxpayer (and not included in income as it accrued).[8] Original issue discount is the difference between the stated redemption price and the issue price.[9]

---

1. IRC Sec. 1271(a)(4); Treas. Reg. §1.1271-1(b)(2).
2. IRC Sec. 1283(c)(2).
3. IRC Sec. 1281(a).
4. Under IRC Sec. 1256(e).
5. IRC Sec. 1281(b).
6. IRC Sec. 1281(b)(1)(F).
7. IRC Sec. 1283(d).
8. IRC Sec. 1271(a)(4).
9. IRC Sec. 1273(a).

The share of original issue discount allocable to the taxpayer is the amount that bears the same ratio to the total discount as the number of days he held the obligation bears to the number of days after the issue date up to and including the date of maturity of the obligation. An irrevocable election may be made, on an obligation-by-obligation basis, to determine the amount using daily compounding at a constant interest rate.[1]

Short-term corporate obligations are not subject to the market discount rules that require market discount to be treated as ordinary income on disposition.[2] Therefore, any excess amount realized on sale after recovery of basis and original issue discount not previously included in income (see Q 1095) is treated as capital gain.[3] See Q 1417 regarding holding periods and Q 1420 for the treatment of capital gains and losses.

If the taxpayer has a loss resulting from a sale to a related person (see Q 1419), the loss may not be deducted or used to offset other capital gains.[4]

If "substantially identical" securities are acquired within 30 days before or 30 days after a sale that results in a loss, the loss deduction will be disallowed under the wash sale rule (see Q 1030), but the amount of loss disallowed is added to the basis of the new property.[5]

The installment method for reporting gain is not available for securities traded on an established securities market. As a result, gain from sale is included in income for the year in which the trade date occurs even if one or more payments are received in the subsequent tax year.[6]

Generally, neither gain nor loss is recognized on a transfer between spouses, or between former spouses if incident to divorce (see Q 1447).[7]

Interest expense and short sale expense that were not deductible in the previous year because of the deferred taxability of the discount or interest (see Q 1307) are deductible in the year the obligation is sold or redeemed, whether at a gain or loss.[8]

If a corporate obligation was held as part of a tax straddle, the additional rules and qualifications explained in Q 1077 to Q 1084 apply; if a corporate obligation was held as part of a conversion transaction, the additional rules discussed in Q 1085 and Q 1086 apply.

1097. Are interest expenses deductible if Treasury bills or short-term taxable corporate obligations are purchased or carried with borrowed funds?

Deduction of interest paid on amounts borrowed by the taxpayer to purchase or carry Treasury bills or short-term taxable corporate obligations may be subject to limitation and deferral. See Q 1307 for details.[9] Certain short sale expenses (see Q 1024, Q

---

1. IRC Sec. 1271(a)(4); Treas. Reg. §1.1271-1(b)(2).
2. IRC Sec. 1278(a)(1)(B)(i).
3. IRC Sec. 1271(a)(3)(A).
4. IRC Sec. 267(a).
5. IRC Sec. 1091.
6. IRC Sec. 453(k). See Rev. Rul. 93-84, 1993-2 CB 225.
7. IRC Sec. 1041.
8. IRC Sec. 1282(c).
9. IRC Sec. 1282(a).

1025) may be treated as interest within this rule.[1] Any deductible interest expense will also be subject to the general limit on otherwise allowable investment interest expense deductions—see Q 1304.

TREASURY BONDS AND NOTES

1098. What are Treasury bonds and Treasury notes?

Treasury bonds and notes are obligations of the federal government. They are essentially similar, except that bonds mature in more than 10 years while Treasury notes have maturity dates ranging from one to 10 years. (The Treasury Department reintroduced regular auctions of the 30-year bond in February 2006, beginning with a bond that will mature on February 15, 2036. Beginning in 2007, 30-year bonds are auctioned quarterly in February, May, August, and November.) They are issued in denominations ranging from $1,000 to $5,000,000. Bonds issued after September 3, 1982 and notes issued after 1982 must be in registered form (see Q 1151); however, bearer bonds and notes issued before the registration requirement date may continue to be bought and sold in bearer form. Bearer notes and bonds have coupons attached that are cut off and redeemed, generally through a commercial bank or the Federal Reserve bank (or a branch). In the case of registered obligations, interest payments are paid to the registered owner by the Treasury Department. Interest is generally payable on these obligations every six months. They are redeemable at maturity for face value.

1099. What does the holder of a Treasury note or bond include in annual income?

(1) Unless the note or bond was issued before March 1, 1941 (in which case it may be only partly taxable), stated interest that accrues after the date of purchase is included as ordinary income in the year in which it is received or made available (i.e., as a general rule, the date the coupon becomes due or the interest check is received).[2] If an individual purchased the bond between interest dates and paid the seller interest accrued but not yet due at the date of purchase, he does not deduct the amount or include it in his basis; instead, he recovers that amount tax free out of the first interest payment he receives and includes in income only the balance.[3]

(2) If the bond or note was originally issued at a discount (that is, at a price below the stated maturity, or face amount) after July 1, 1982, any holder who did not pay more than the face value of the obligation must include in income each year a daily share of the "original issue discount" as discussed in Q 1116. (A discount of less than ¼ of 1% (.0025) times the number of years from issue to maturity may be disregarded. This is normally the case with Treasury notes and bonds.)[4] The holder's basis is increased by the amount of original issue discount he actually includes in income each year.[5]

However, if the obligation was originally issued before July 2, 1982 the amount of discount is not includable in income until it is received on sale or maturity of the obligation (see Q 1100).[6]

---

1. IRC Sec. 1282(c).
2. Treas. Regs. §§1.61-7, 1.451-2(b); *Lavery v. Comm.*, 158 F.2d 859 (7th Cir. 1946); *Obland v. U.S.*, 67-2 USTC ¶9751 (E.D. Mo. 1967).
3. *L.A. Thompson Scenic Ry. Co. v. Comm.*, 9 BTA 1203 (1928); Rev. Rul. 69-263, 1969-1 CB 197.
4. IRC Sec. 1273(a).
5. IRC Sec. 1272(d).
6. IRC Sec. 1271(b); Treas. Reg. §1.67-7(c).

(3) Market discount accrued during the year on notes and bonds (acquired in tax years ending after July 18, 1984) must be included in income if an election to include market discount is in effect (see Q 1110).

(4) If the holder purchased the bond at a premium, he may elect to amortize the premium and reduce his basis accordingly (see Q 1120).

For tax on the sale or exchange of a Treasury bond or note, see Q 1100.

1100. How are the proceeds taxed on sale or redemption of Treasury notes and bonds?

On sale or on redemption at maturity, the proceeds must be separated into identifiable components for tax purposes.

(1) If the sale occurs between interest dates, as it generally does, the seller usually receives from the buyer an amount stated separately from the purchase price representing stated interest accrued to the date of sale, but not yet due. This is reported by the seller as interest income, not gain.[1]

(2) Out of the proceeds (other than interest, discussed above) an amount equal to the taxpayer's adjusted basis in the note or bond and expenses of sale are recovered tax free.[2] His basis is generally his cost of acquisition adjusted by (i) adding any original issue discount and market discount included in income as it accrued,[3] or (ii) subtracting the amount of premium deductible or applied to reduce interest payments over the period he held the bond if he elected to amortize the premium (see Q 1110, Q 1116, Q 1120).[4]

(3) As a general rule amounts in excess of (1) and (2) are treated as capital gain—long-term or short-term—depending on the holding period and the date of acquisition (see Q 1417 and Q 1420). However, in special circumstances part or all of the gain must be treated as ordinary income:

(a) If the note or bond was issued after July 18, 1984, or if the note or bond was issued on or before July 18, 1984 and was purchased on the market after April 30, 1993, gain equal to market discount accrued up to the date of disposition and not previously included in income is treated as interest income, not capital gain (see Q 1111, Q 1113).[5] If a bond was issued on or before July 18, 1984, but acquired after that date at a market discount using *borrowed funds*, a part or all of the gain must be treated as ordinary income to the extent that a deferred interest expense deduction is taken (see Q 1308).

(b) If a note or bond originally issued on or before July 1, 1982 and after December 31, 1954 was originally issued at a discount of ¼ of 1% (.0025) or more of the stated redemption price multiplied by the number of full years from issue to maturity and the holder did not pay a premium for it, any *gain* realized must be treated as ordinary

---

1. Treas. Reg. §1.61-7(d).
2. IRC Sec. 1001(a).
3. IRC Secs. 1272(d), 1276(d)(2), 1278(b)(4); General Explanation–TRA '84, p. 99
4. IRC Sec. 1016(a)(5).
5. IRC Sec. 1276.

income up to a prorated portion of the original issue discount.[1] (The prorated portion is explained in Q 1117.)

If the seller purchased the note or bond at a premium (i.e., at a price in excess of the face amount of the obligation), none of the gain is original issue discount.[2] The holder is considered to have purchased at a premium if his basis is the same, in whole or in part, for purposes of determining gain or loss from a sale or exchange as the basis in the hands of another person who purchased at a premium. Thus, for example, the donee is considered to have purchased at a premium if the donor did.[3]

(c) With respect to bonds issued before January 1, 1955, the IRC did not deal with the problem of original issue discount; nonetheless, the Supreme Court ruled that under the pre-1954 Code original issue discount "serves the same function as stated interest" and "earned original issue discount, like stated interest, should be taxed … as ordinary income" when realized.[4] However, gain or loss from *retirement* of a bond is capital gain or loss only if the bond was issued with coupons attached or in registered form or was in such form on March 1, 1954.[5]

(4) If there was no gain, the loss is treated as a capital loss—long-term or short-term—depending on the length of the holding period (see Q 1417). If "substantially identical" obligations were acquired (or a contract to acquire them was made) within 30 days before or 30 days after the sale, the loss will be subject to the "wash sale" rule discussed in Q 1030. If the sale is made to a related person, the loss deduction may be disallowed (see Q 1419).

If a Treasury bond or note was held as part of a tax straddle, the additional rules and qualifications explained in Q 1077 to Q 1084 apply; if the bond or note was held as part of a conversion transaction, the additional rules discussed in Q 1085 and Q 1086 will apply.

For the rules governing the substitution of newly issued bonds for outstanding bonds, see Rev. Proc. 2001-21.[6]

1101. When does the holding period begin if Treasury notes and bonds were bought at auction or on a subscription basis?

The holding period of United States Treasury notes and bonds sold at auction on the basis of yield generally starts the day after the Secretary of the Treasury, through news releases, gives notification of his acceptance of successful competitive and non-competitive bids. The holding period of Treasury bonds and notes sold through an offering on a subscription basis at an established yield generally starts the day after the subscription is submitted.[7] (Under some circumstances, a holding period may be tolled or be deemed to have begun at a later date. See, for example, the rules for tax straddles (Q 1077 to Q 1084).)

---

1. IRC Sec. 1271(c)(2).
2. IRC Sec. 1271(a)(2)(B).
3. Treas. Reg. §1.1232-3(d)(2).
4. *U.S. v. Midland-Ross Corp.*, 381 U.S. 54 (1965).
5. IRC Sec. 1271(c).
6. 2001-9 CB 742.
7. Rev. Rul. 78-5, 1978-1 CB 263.

The donee of a bond can include in his holding period the time the bond was held by the donor.[1]

CORPORATE BONDS

1102. What amounts are included in income currently by an investor who holds a taxable corporate bond?

(1) Interest that accrues after the date of purchase is included as ordinary income in the year in which it is received or made available.[2] As a general rule, interest is considered received on the date the interest check is received, if the bond is registered, or on the date the coupon matures, in the case of a bearer coupon bond.[3] (See Q 1405 for an explanation of the doctrine of constructive receipt.) If the investor purchased the bond between interest dates and he paid the seller interest accrued but not yet due at that time, he receives that amount as a tax-free return of capital out of the first interest payment he receives. He includes in income only the balance of the interest.[4] If principal or interest was in default at the time of purchase and the bond traded without allocation of price between principal and accrued interest, see Q 1133.

(2) If the holder purchased the bond at a premium, he may elect to amortize a part of the premium each year and reduce his basis by the amount deductible (or applied to reduce interest payments) (see Q 1120).

(3) Unless the bondholder purchased the bond at a premium (i.e., at an amount in excess of the face value of the bond), the holder of a bond originally issued at a discount after May 27, 1969 must include in income a portion of the original issue discount. However, if the discount at issue was less than ¼ of 1% (.0025) of the stated redemption price multiplied by the number of full years from the date of original issue to maturity, the bond is treated as if it were not issued at a discount and no part of the discount is included in income as it accrues.[5] Original issue discount on bonds issued after May 27, 1969 and on or before July 1, 1982 accrues as discussed in Q 1118. Original issue discount on bonds issued after July 1, 1982 accrues as discussed in Q 1116.

(4) If the bond was issued after July 18, 1984, or if the bond was issued on or before July 18, 1984 and was purchased after April 30, 1993, and the purchase occurred on the market at a discount of ¼ of 1% (.0025) or more of the stated redemption price at maturity times the number of years until maturity, a cash basis investor must include the market discount in income as it accrues *if* he has made an election to include accrued market discount with respect to that bond or other market discount obligations, as discussed in Q 1110.[6]

(5) Any partial payment of principal on a market discount bond acquired after October 22, 1986, is treated as a payment of market discount and included in income to the extent that market discount has accrued up to that time.[7] Where principal is

---

1. IRC Sec. 1223(2).
2. Treas. Reg. §1.61-7.
3. Treas. Reg. §1.451-2(b); *Lavery v. Comm.*, 158 F.2d 859 (7th Cir. 1946); *Obland v. U.S.*, 67-2 USTC ¶9751 (E.D. Mo. 1967).
4. *L.A. Thompson Scenic Ry. Co. v. Comm.*, 9 BTA 1203 (1928); Rev. Rul. 69-263, 1969-1 CB 197.
5. IRC Secs. 1272(a), 1272(b), 1273(a)(3); see Treas. Reg. §1.1232-3.
6. See IRC Sec. 1278(b).
7. IRC Sec. 1276(a)(3).

to be paid in two or more payments, the amount of accrued market discount will be determined under regulations.[1]

1103. How are proceeds on the sale or retirement of a corporate bond taxed?

(1) If the sale occurs between interest due dates, as it generally does, stated interest accrued to the date of sale but not yet due is customarily added to the purchase price. This must be included in the seller's income as interest.[2]

(2) Proceeds in excess of item (1), above, are recovered tax free to the extent of the investor's adjusted basis in the bond.[3] As a general rule, his adjusted basis is his cost of acquisition adjusted by (a) adding any original issue discount included in income as it accrued (see Q 1116, Q 1118) and market discount included in income prior to the sale (see Q 1110, Q 1112, Q 1113), or (b) subtracting amounts of premium deductible or applied to reduce interest payments if an election was made to amortize bond premium (see Q 1120).

(3) Ordinarily, amounts in excess of interest and basis are treated as capital gain – long-term or short-term – depending on the investor's holding period (see Q 1417 regarding holding periods and Q 1420 for the treatment of capital gains and losses). However, if the bond was originally issued at a discount or was purchased on the market at a discount, part or all of the gain must be treated as interest instead of capital gain, if the discount was not included in income as it accrued. (Discount that is less than ¼ of 1% (.0025) of face value multiplied by the number of complete years to maturity is considered no discount.)

(a) If the bond was issued after July 18, 1984, or if the bond was issued on or before July 18, 1984 and purchased on the market after April 30, 1993, gain to the extent it does not exceed market discount must be treated as interest income, not capital gain (see Q 1109, Q 1111, Q 1113). If a bond issued on or before July 18, 1984 was acquired after July 18, 1984 but before May 1, 1993 at a market discount using borrowed funds, a part of the gain must be treated as ordinary income if a deferred interest expense deduction is taken (see Q 1308).

(b) If the bond was originally issued at a discount of ¼ of 1% (.0025) or more of the face amount multiplied by the number of full years from issue to maturity and the seller had not purchased the bond at a premium, a part of any *gain* realized is treated as ordinary income in the following cases:

If the bond was issued after May 27, 1969, original issue discount is includable in income annually (see Q 1116, Q 1118) and basis is adjusted for amounts included;[4] however, if at the time of original issue there was an intention to call the bond in for redemption before maturity, gain on sale or redemption is ordinary income up to the entire amount of the original issue discount reduced by the portions of original issue discount previously includable in income by any holder.[5] An intention to call is discussed in Q 1119. The amount of original issue discount allocable to each day, in the case of

---

1. IRC Sec. 1276(b)(3).
2. Treas. Reg. §1.61-7(d).
3. IRC Sec. 1001(a).
4. IRC Sec. 1272(d)(2).
5. IRC Sec. 1271(a)(2).

bonds issued after July 1, 1982, is discussed in Q 1116; the amount allocable to each month in the case of bonds issued on or before July 1, 1982 and after May 27, 1969, is discussed in Q 1118.

If the bond was issued on or before May 27, 1969 and after December 31, 1954, any gain realized on sale or redemption is taxed as ordinary income to the extent of an amount that bears the same ratio to the total original issue discount as the number of full months the bond was held by the taxpayer bears to the number of full months from issue date to maturity date. Days amounting to less than a full month are not counted. The period the taxpayer held the bond must include any period it was held by another person if the bond has the same basis, in whole or in part, in the taxpayer's hands as it would have in the hands of the other person.[1] However, if there was an intention at the time of issue to call the bond before maturity, gain up to the entire original issue discount is included as ordinary income.[2]

If the obligation was issued before 1955, the Supreme Court has ruled that original issue discount serves the same purpose as interest and should be taxed as ordinary income rather than capital gain.[3]

(4) If there was a *loss* on the sale or redemption, no original issue discount or market discount is recovered. Loss will be treated as a capital loss. However, if "substantially identical" obligations were acquired (or a contract for their acquisition was made) within 30 days before or 30 days after the sale, the loss will be subject to the "wash sale" rule discussed in Q 1030. If the sale is made to a related party, the loss deduction may be disallowed (see Q 1419).

(5) Amounts received on retirement are treated as amounts received on sale (but for obligations issued before 1955, only if the obligation was in coupon or registered form on March 1, 1954).[4]

The installment method for reporting gain is not available for securities traded on an established securities market. As a result, gain from sale is included in income for the year in which the trade date occurs even if one or more payments are received in the subsequent tax year.[5]

If a corporate bond was held as part of a tax straddle, the additional rules and qualifications explained in Q 1077 to Q 1084 apply; if a bond was held as part of a conversion transaction, the additional rules discussed in Q 1085 and Q 1086 will apply.

If principal or interest was in default and the bond was bought or sold "flat", see Q 1133.

Generally, neither gain nor loss is recognized on a transfer between spouses, or between former spouses if incident to divorce (see Q 1447).[6]

1104. How is the donor of a corporate bond taxed on interest that has accrued prior to the date of the gift?

---

1. See Treas. Reg. §1.1232-3(c).
2. IRC Sec. 1271(c).
3. *U.S. v. Midland-Ross Corp.*, 381 U.S. 54 (1965).
4. IRC Secs. 1271(a), 1271(c).
5. IRC Sec. 453(k). See Rev. Rul. 93-84, 1993-2 CB 225.
6. IRC Sec. 1041.

Interest accrued, but not yet due, on corporate bonds (and Treasury bonds and notes) before the date of a gift is includable as ordinary income in the donor's income for the taxable year during which the bond interest is actually or constructively received by the donee. Therefore, the donor will not necessarily be taxed on such income in the year in which the gift is made. Amounts received from interest accruing after the transfer date are includable in the gross income of the donee.[1]

For treatment of accrued market discount in a disposition by gift, see Q 1112. See Q 1139 regarding gifts of Series E and EE bonds.

1105. How is a convertible bond taxed on conversion?

Ordinarily, a convertible bond is one exchangeable, at the holder's option, into a specified number of the company's common shares at a fixed price within a certain time period—usually up to the maturity of the bond. A bond may also be issued in such a form as to grant to the holder a right to convert the bond into another debt instrument of the issuing company.

Gain or loss is not recognized when, under the terms of a bond convertible into stock of the issuing corporation, the bond is exchanged for (converted into) that stock. This is true whether or not the fair market value of the stock exceeds the holder's adjusted basis in the bond and any additional amount paid on exercise of the conversion right. The holder's basis in the stock is his adjusted basis in the bond plus any amount he paid on conversion.[2] It is unclear whether the same tax treatment would apply upon the conversion of a bond convertible into another bond of the issuer.

The conversion of a bond (in accordance with its terms) into stock of a different corporation is a taxable event (see Q 1103).[3]

For the treatment of original issue discount in the case of a convertible bond, see Q 1106.

For the treatment of the sale of stock acquired on conversion of a market discount bond, see Q 1114.

For the treatment of a convertible bond that is part of a *conversion transaction* (as defined in IRC Section 1258), see Q 1085 and Q 1086.

1106. How is original issue discount determined in the case of a convertible bond?

No adjustment is made for the value of the conversion feature of a bond convertible into stock or another debt instrument of the issuer or a related party in calculating the bond's issue price for purposes of determining whether the bond was issued at an original issue discount.[4] Under final regulations, the issue price of a bond convertible into stock or another debt instrument of the issuer includes any amount paid for the conversion privilege, even if the privilege may be satisfied for the cash value of the

---

1. Rev. Rul. 72-312, 1972-1 CB 22.
2. Rev. Rul. 72-265, 1972-2 CB 222.
3. Rev. Rul. 69-135, 1969-1 CB 198.
4. See Treas. Regs. §§1.1232-3(b)(2)(i); 1.1273-2(j).

stock or other debt instrument.[1] Although the final regulations are effective for bonds issued after April 3, 1994, taxpayers may rely on the final regulations for bonds issued after December 21, 1992. (However, under amendments (issued February 28, 1991) to the 1986 proposed regulations, a portion of the bond's issue price was allocable to the conversion feature if the conversion feature could have been satisfied in cash. This amendment was modified by further proposed regulations (issued December 22, 1992) and is not mentioned in the final regulations (adopted January 27, 1994)).

Bonds that are convertible into stock or a debt instrument of a corporation *other than the issuer* are valued under the noncontingent bond method.[2] This method provides for a projected payment schedule consisting of all noncontingent payments and a projected amount for each contingent payment.[3] Except in the case of a contingent payment that is fixed more than six months before it is due, the projected payment schedule generally remains fixed throughout the term of the debt instrument and any income, deductions, gain, or loss attributable to the debt instrument are based on this schedule.[4] (Proposed regulations formerly provided for valuing the bond and conversion feature separately and allocating the issue price to the separate components.) The Service has ruled that the noncontingent bond method applied to a debt instrument that was convertible into stock of the issuer and that also provided for one or more contingent cash payments.[5]

INFLATION-INDEXED BONDS

1107. What are Treasury Inflation-Protection Securities?

Treasury Inflation-Protection Securities (TIPS) are obligations of the federal government whose principal value is adjusted for inflation and deflation based on monthly changes in the nonseasonally adjusted U.S. City Average All Items Consumer Price Index for All Urban Consumers (CPI-U). Treasury Inflation-Protection Securities are issued in minimum denominations of $1,000 with $1,000 increments thereafter. They provide for semiannual payments of interest and a payment of principal at maturity. The interest rate of Treasury Inflation-Protection Securities is fixed although the amount of each interest payment will vary with changes in the value of the principal of the security as adjusted for inflation and deflation. Each semiannual interest payment is determined by multiplying the single fixed rate of interest by the inflation-adjusted principal amount (determined as explained below) of the security for the date of the interest payment.[6]

The inflation-adjusted principal amount of the security for the first day of any month is an amount equal to the principal amount at issuance multiplied by a ratio, the numerator of which is the value of the index for the adjustment date and the denominator of which is the value of the index for the issue date. The inflation-adjusted principal amount of the security for a day other than the first day of a month will be determined based on a straight-line interpolation between the inflation-adjusted principal amount for the first day of the month and the inflation-adjusted principal amount for the first day of the next month. The value of the index used to determine the adjustment for the first day of a particular month will be the value of the index reported for the third preceding month.[7]

1. Treas. Reg. §1.1273-2(j).
2. Treas. Reg. §1.1275-4(b)(1).
3. Treas. Reg. §1.1275-4(b)(2).
4. Treas. Reg. §1.1275-4(b).
5. See Rev. Rul. 2002-42, 2002-2 CB 76.
6. Notice 96-51, 1996-2 CB 216.
7. Notice 96-51, 1996-2 CB 216.

A Treasury Inflation-Protection Security also provides for an additional payment at maturity if the security's inflation-adjusted principal amount for the maturity date is less than the security's principal amount at issuance. The additional amount payable will equal the excess of the security's principal amount at issuance over the security's inflation-adjusted principal amount for the maturity date.[1] This type of payment is referred to in regulations (see Q 1108) as a *minimum guarantee payment*.

Treasury Inflation-Protection Securities were first issued in January 1997 and are currently available in the form of 5-year, 10-year, and 20-year inflation-indexed notes. The Treasury Department is authorized to offer notes with maturities as short as one year.[2]

Treasury Inflation-Protection Securities are taxed under the general rules applicable to inflation-indexed bonds (see Q 1108).

For the treatment of inflation-indexed *savings* bonds, see Q 1144.

1108. How are inflation-indexed bonds treated for tax purposes?

A bond is considered inflation-indexed for federal income tax purposes if: (1) it was issued for U.S. dollars and all payments on the instrument are denominated in U.S. dollars, (2) each payment on the debt instrument is indexed for inflation and deflation except for a *minimum guarantee payment* (defined below), and (3) no payment on the debt instrument is subject to a contingency other than the inflation contingency, a minimum guarantee payment, or certain inflation-indexed payments under one or more alternate schedules.[3] A minimum guarantee payment is an additional payment that is made at maturity if the total amount of the inflation-adjusted principal paid on the bond is less than the bond's stated principal amount.[4]

Holders and issuers of inflation-indexed debt instruments, including Treasury Inflation-Protection Securities (see Q 1107), are required to account for interest and original issue discount (inflation adjustments) with constant yield principles using either the coupon or discount bond methods described below.

Coupon Bond Method

The coupon bond method is a simplified version of the discount method (see below) that will apply if two conditions are satisfied: (1) the bond must be issued at par and (2) all stated interest must be *qualified stated interest*.[5] A bond is issued at par if there is less than a de minimis difference between the bond's issue price and its principal amount at issuance.[6] An amount is de minimis if it is equal to .0025 multiplied by the product of the stated redemption price at maturity and the number of complete years to maturity from the issue date.[7] *Qualified stated interest* is stated interest that is unconditionally payable in cash, or is constructively received at least annually at a fixed rate.[8] Any qualified

---

1. Notice 96-51, above.
2. See 31 U.S.C. §3103(a).
3. Treas. Reg. §1.1275-7(c); see Notice 96-51, 1996-2 CB 216.
4. Treas. Reg. §1.1275-7(c)(5).
5. Treas. Reg. §1.1275-7(d)(2).
6. Treas. Reg. §1.1275-7(d)(2)(i).
7. Treas. Reg. §1.1273-1(d).
8. Treas. Reg. §1.1275-7(d)(2)(ii).

stated interest is taken into account under the taxpayer's regular method of accounting.[1] Because Treasury Inflation-Protection Securities that are not stripped satisfy both of the above conditions, the coupon bond method applies to such securities.[2]

Under the coupon bond method, an inflation adjustment is taken into account for each taxable year in which the bond is outstanding in an amount equal to the sum of the inflation-adjusted principal amount at the end of the period and the principal payments made during the period minus the inflation-adjusted principal amount at the beginning of the period. A positive inflation adjustment will result in original issue discount while a negative inflation adjustment will be accounted for under the deflation adjustment rules (see below).[3]

Discount Bond Method

An inflation-indexed bond that does not qualify for the coupon bond method (e.g., it is issued at a discount) is subject to the more complex discount bond method. In general, the discount bond method requires holders and issuers to make current adjustments to their original issue discount accruals for inflation and deflation. A taxpayer determines the amount of original issue discount allocable to an accrual period using steps similar to those for original issue discount bonds that are not inflation-indexed (see Q 1116).[4] First, the taxpayer determines the yield to maturity of the debt instrument as if there were no inflation or deflation over the term of the instrument. Second, the taxpayer determines the length of the accrual period, provided that accrual period is no longer than one month. Third, the percentage change in the reference index during the accrual period is determined by comparing the value at the beginning of the period to the value at the end of the period.[5] Fourth, the taxpayer determines the original issue discount allocable to the accrual period and, fifth, allocates a ratable portion of the original issue discount for the accrual period to each day in the period.[6]

Holders of stripped Treasury Inflation-Protection Securities must use the discount bond method to account for the original issue discount on the principal and coupon components of the bond.[7]

Deflation Adjustments

Under the coupon and discount bond methods, a deflation adjustment reduces the amount of interest otherwise includable in a bondholder's income with respect to the bond for the taxable year. "Interest," for this purpose, includes original issue discount, qualified stated interest, and market discount.[8] If the amount of the deflation adjustment exceeds the amount of interest otherwise includable in income by the holder for the taxable year with respect to the bond, the excess is treated as an ordinary loss for the taxable year. However, the amount treated as an ordinary loss is limited to the amount by which the holder's total interest inclusions on the bond in prior taxable years exceed the total amount treated by the holder as an ordinary loss on the bond in prior taxable years. If the deflation adjustment exceeds the interest otherwise includable in income

1. Treas. Reg. §1.1275-7(d)(3).
2. Treas. Reg. §1.1275-7(d)(2).
3. Treas. Reg. §1.1275-7(d)(4).
4. See Treas. Reg. §1.1272-1(b)(1).
5. See Treas. Reg. §1.1275-7(e)(3)(iii).
6. Treas. Regs. §§1.1275-7(e)(3)(iv) and 1.1275-7(e)(3)(v).
7. Treas. Reg. §1.1286-2.
8. Treas. Reg. §1.1275-7(f)(1).

by the holder with respect to the bond for the taxable year and the amount treated as an ordinary loss for the taxable year, this excess is carried forward to reduce the amount of interest otherwise includable in income with respect to the bond for subsequent taxable years.[1]

Miscellaneous Rules

If a bond features a minimum guarantee payment, the payment is treated as interest on the date it is paid. However, under both the coupon and discount bond methods, the minimum guarantee payment is ignored until such a payment is made.[2]

A subsequent holder determines the amount of acquisition premium or market discount by reference to the adjusted issue price of the instrument on the date the holder acquires the instrument. The amount of bond premium is determined by assuming the amount payable at maturity on the instrument is equal to the instrument's inflation-adjusted principal amount for the day the holder acquires the instrument. Furthermore, any premium or market discount is taken into account over the remaining term of the bond as if there were no further inflation or deflation.[3] For the treatment of market discount bonds, see Q 1109 to Q 1115. The treatment of bond premium is explained in Q 1120 to Q 1122.

A bondholder's adjusted basis is determined under the rules for original issue discount bonds that are not inflation-indexed (see Q 1116).[4] However, the adjusted basis is decreased by the amount of any deflation adjustment the bondholder takes into account to reduce the amount of interest otherwise includable in income or treats as an ordinary loss with respect to the bond during the taxable year.[5]

In the event of the temporary unavailability of a qualified inflation index, special rules apply.[6]

Special rules apply in determining bond premium on inflation-indexed bonds.[7] Bond premium is explained in Q 1120 to Q 1121.

For the treatment of qualified tuition programs, see Q 1413. For the treatment of inflation-indexed *savings* bonds, see Q 1144.

MARKET DISCOUNT

1109. What is market discount? What is a "market discount bond"?

Bond prices on the market fluctuate as interest rates change and as the borrower's credit rating changes. Therefore, bonds may be bought at a discount because of a decline in value of the obligation after issue. A bond acquired at a discount on the market is called a "market discount bond." For tax purposes the term "market discount bond" does not include tax-exempt municipal obligations purchased before May 1, 1993, short-term

---

1. Treas. Reg. §1.1275-7(f)(1)(i).
2. Treas. Reg. §1.1275-7(f)(4).
3. Treas. Reg. §1.1275-7(f)(3).
4. See Treas. Reg. §1.1272-1(g).
5. Treas. Reg. §1.1275-7(f)(2).
6. See Treas. Reg. §1.1275-7(f)(5).
7. See Treas. Reg. §1.171-3(b).

obligations, or U.S. Savings Bonds.[1] With certain exceptions (e.g., bonds acquired at issue for less than issue price–usually by large institutional investors)–bonds acquired at the time of original issue are not "market discount" bonds.[2]

Market discount is the amount by which the stated redemption price exceeds the taxpayer's basis in the bond immediately after its acquisition, if the bond was originally issued at par.[3] If the bond was originally issued at a discount and purchased on the market for less than the original issue price increased by the amount of original issue discount accruing since issue up to the date of purchase, the difference is market discount.[4] If the total market discount is less than ¼ of 1% (.0025) of the stated redemption price at maturity (or, if the bond was issued at a discount of the issue price increased by original issue discount accruing since issue to the date of purchase) multiplied by the number of complete years until maturity, it is treated as if there is no market discount.[5]

1110. Is market discount on a taxable bond included annually in gross income as it accrues?

As a rule, market discount is not includable in income by a cash basis investor before sale or disposition of the bond or note. However, an election may be made to include market discount as it accrues on bonds and notes other than tax-exempt obligations purchased before May 1, 1993, short-term obligations, U.S. Savings Bonds, or certain obligations arising from installment sales of property.[6] (Such an election may be necessary to permit current deduction of interest paid on amounts borrowed to acquire bonds issued after July 18, 1984, or issued on or before July 18, 1984 and purchased on the market after April 30, 1993. See Q 1308.) Once the election is made, it applies to *all* obligations having market discount (other than tax-exempt obligations purchased before May 1, 1993, short-term obligations, certain obligations arising from installment sales of property, or U.S. Savings Bonds) *acquired* by the taxpayer in the tax year of the election and any future years (whether or not using borrowed funds) unless he receives permission from the IRS to revoke the election.[7] Amounts includable under the election are treated as interest (except for purposes of the tax on non-business income of nonresident aliens and foreign corporations and, apparently, for withholding generally). Thus, for example, includable market discount is counted as investment income for purposes of determining the limit on deductible interest expense (see Q 1304).

Any partial payment of principal on a market discount bond acquired after October 22, 1986, is includable as ordinary income to the extent it does not exceed the market discount on the bond that has accrued up to that time. The amount of accrued market discount is reduced accordingly (see Q 1111).[8] If the principal of a bond acquired after October 22, 1986, is to be paid in two or more payments, the amount of accrued market discount is to be determined under regulations.[9]

Under the election to include market discount in income as it accrues, market discount is accrued on a ratable basis, but the taxpayer may elect to use instead a constant

---

1. IRC Sec. 1278(a)(1).
2. IRC Sec. 1278(a)(1)(D).
3. IRC Sec. 1278(a)(2).
4. IRC Sec. 1278(a)(2)(B).
5. IRC Sec. 1278(a)(2)(C).
6. IRC Sec. 1278(b).
7. IRC Sec. 1278(b)(3).
8. IRC Sec. 1276(a)(3).
9. IRC Sec. 1276(b)(3).

interest rate with respect to particular bonds and notes. Under the ratable accrual method, the amount of market discount is determined by dividing the total market discount on the bond by the number of days after the date of acquisition up to and including the date of maturity. This method will accrue market discount in equal daily installments during the period between acquisition and maturity. Alternately, the taxpayer may elect to accrue market discount on a constant interest rate method (the method used in determining daily portions of original issue discount on bonds issued after July 1, 1982–see Q 1116.) The constant interest rate election is irrevocable as to the bond for which the election is made, but the ratable method will apply to other obligations for which the constant interest rate election was not made.[1]

The Service has established procedures for taxpayers to use in making the elections described above. Specific procedures are required to be followed under the following circumstances: (1) the taxpayer wishes to make an election under IRC Section 1278(b) for a taxable year ending after July 18, 1984, and his income tax return is filed (on time) on or after September 23, 1992, (2) the taxpayer wishes to make an election under IRC Section 1276(b) to have apply a constant interest rate to a market discount bond acquired in a taxable year ending after July 18, 1984, and his income tax return is filed (on time) on or after September 23, 1992, or (3) the taxpayer wishes to request consent to revoke an election under IRC Section 1278(b). If the procedures detailed by the Service are followed with respect to elections made under IRC Sections 1278(b) and 1276(b), the Service's consent to such elections will be automatic.[2]

The taxpayer who elects to include market discount as it accrues increases his basis by the amounts included in gross income each year.[3]

The rules applicable to market discount on tax-exempt municipal bonds are discussed in Q 1125.

Disposition

1111. How is gain or loss treated when a market discount bond is sold?

When a cash basis taxpayer sells a market discount bond (as defined in Q 1109) issued after July 18, 1984, or issued on or before July 18, 1984 and purchased after April 30, 1993, or if the taxpayer sells a tax-exempt bond purchased on the market after April 30, 1993 at a discount, his gain is generally treated as interest income to the extent of market discount accrued up to the date of disposition.[4] Only gain in excess of the amount of accrued market discount may be treated as capital gain. (See Q 1420 for the treatment of capital gains and losses.) However, if the taxpayer elected to include market discount in his income annually as it accrued, and to increase his basis, his gain would not include previously included market discount.[5] The rule reflects recognition that market discount is a substitute for stated interest.

In determining how much market discount has accrued up to the time of sale, the discount is treated as accruing in equal amounts each day after the date of acquisition

---

1. IRC Sec. 1276(b)(2).
2. Rev. Proc. 92-67, 1992-2 CB 429; *as modified by* Rev. Proc. 99-49, 1999-2 CB 725; *modified, amplified, and superseded by* Rev. Proc. 2002-9, 2002-1 CB 327.
3. IRC Sec. 1278(b)(4).
4. IRC Secs. 1276, 1278.
5. IRC Sec. 1278(b).

up to and including the date of maturity. But the taxpayer may elect (irrevocably) on a bond by bond basis to accrue using a constant rate of interest compounded at least annually as used in determining daily portions of original issue discount accruing on bonds issued after December 31, 1984 (see Q 1116).[1] Under the constant rate method, the daily portions will accrue more slowly than under the ratable method in early years and more rapidly in later years, but the total amount accrued will always be less until maturity.

An adjustment must be made in determining the amount of accrued market discount on obligations issued after October 22, 1986, if a partial payment of principal was previously made, or if principal is paid in two or more payments (see Q 1110).

Gain treated as interest income will generally be treated as interest for all purposes of federal taxation. Thus, for example, it is investment income for purposes of the limitation on the deduction of interest expense—see Q 1304. However, accrued market discount will presumably not be treated as interest for withholding.[2]

For taxable bonds issued on or before July 18, 1984 and acquired on the market after that date but before May 1, 1993, and for tax-exempt bonds purchased on the market before May 1, 1993, recovery of market discount on sale or disposition is generally treated as capital gain, rather than as interest income. However, gain on such *taxable* bonds acquired with borrowing (or the proceeds of a short sale) must be recognized as ordinary income to the extent of any deferred disallowed interest (or short sale) expense (discussed in Q 1308) that is deductible in the year of disposition.[3]

Loss on sale or disposition of a market discount bond is capital loss (see Q 1420).[4] For the revised rules governing the treatment of market discount when there is a substitution of newly issued bonds for outstanding bonds, see Rev. Proc. 2001-21.[5]

The installment method for reporting gain is not available for securities traded on an established securities market (see Q 1408). As a result, gain from sale is included in income for the year in which the trade date occurs even if one or more payments are received in the subsequent tax year.[6]

If the disposition is by gift, see Q 1112; by conversion of a convertible bond into stock, see Q 1105 and Q 1114; if the bond sold was acquired by gift, see Q 1113.

If a market discount bond was held as part of a tax straddle, the additional rules and qualifications explained in Q 1077 to Q 1084 apply; if a market discount bond was held as part of a conversion transaction, the additional rules discussed in Q 1085 and Q 1086 will apply.

Generally, neither gain nor loss is recognized on a transfer between spouses, or between former spouses if incident to divorce (see Q 1447).[7]

---

1. IRC Sec. 1276(b)(2).
2. General Explanation–TRA '84, p. 94.
3. IRC Sec. 1277(d), prior to repeal by OBRA '93.
4. Rev. Rul. 60-210, 1960-1 CB 38.
5. 2001-1 CB 742.
6. IRC Sec. 453(k). See Rev. Rul. 93-84, 1993-2 CB 225.
7. IRC Sec. 1041.

1112. Does a donor include accrued market discount in income when he makes a gift of a market discount bond?

When a taxpayer makes a gift of a taxable bond issued after July 18, 1984, or a taxable bond issued on or before July 18, 1984 and purchased after April 30, 1993, or a tax-exempt bond purchased after April 30, 1993, any of which he acquired at a market discount and that has appreciated in value at the time of the gift, he must include in his gross income an amount equal to the market discount accrued to the date of the gift, but limited to the amount of gain he would have realized had he received fair market value on making the gift.[1] The amount is treated as interest income (but not for withholding at the source).[2] Discount is considered to have accrued on a ratable basis, or, if the taxpayer elects (irrevocably), at a constant interest rate, just as if he had sold the bond—see Q 1111. Had he previously elected to include market discount in his gross income as it accrued (see Q 1110), no accrued discount would be includable as a result of the gift.[3]

If a bond was issued on or before July 18, 1984 and purchased before May 1, 1993, or if the bond is a tax-exempt issue purchased before May 1, 1993, no accrued market discount is included in income.[4]

1113. How is market discount treated on sale of a market discount bond received as a gift?

If gain is realized by a donee on disposition of a taxable bond issued after July 18, 1984, or a taxable bond issued on or before July 18, 1984 and purchased after April 30, 1993, or a tax-exempt bond purchased after April 30, 1993, any of which were previously received as a gift but acquired at a market discount by the donor, the gain is reported as interest up to the amount of market discount accrued prior to the time of sale and not previously included in income by the donor or donee (see Q 1111).[5] An adjustment to basis is made for any amount of accrued market discount recognized by the donor at the time of the gift and for any market discount included in the gross income of the donor and donee as it accrued.[6]

If the donor used borrowed funds (or the proceeds of a short sale) to acquire or carry a *taxable* bond described above, and as a result there was disallowed interest expense (or short sale expense) with respect to the bond at the time of the gift that was not entirely deductible by the donor at the time the donor made the gift, the donee may take the excess disallowed expense deduction as his own when he sells the bond (see Q 1308).[7]

Even if the taxable bond was issued on or before July 18, 1984 but acquired by the donor before May 1, 1993, the donee may deduct the disallowed expense.[8]

---

1. IRC Sec. 1276.
2. General Explanation–TRA '84, p. 94.
3. IRC Sec. 1278(b).
4. TRA '84, Sec. 44(c)(1). See IRC Secs. 1276, 1277, and 1278.
5. IRC Sec. 1276(c).
6. IRC Secs. 1276(c), 1278(b).
7. IRC Secs. 1277(b)(2)(B), 1278(a)(1)(C).
8. IRC Sec. 1277(b)(2). However, if there is a gain on the sale of such a bond, he must treat an amount equal to the interest (or short sale) expense deduction as ordinary income instead of capital gain (see Q 1308). <IRC Sec. 1277(d), prior to repeal by OBRA '93.

1114. How is market discount treated on the sale of stock received on conversion of a market discount bond?

If, on conversion of a market discount bond issued after July 18, 1984, or issued on or before July 18, 1984 and purchased after April 30, 1993, a taxpayer receives stock in the issuer of the bond, the amount of market discount accrued to the date of exchange must be treated as ordinary interest income upon sale or disposition of the stock, unless the taxpayer had elected to include in income market discount on the bond as it accrued.[1]

1115. Are interest expenses deductible if market discount bonds are purchased or carried with borrowed funds?

If interest is paid on borrowing incurred or continued by the taxpayer in order to purchase or carry *taxable* market discount bonds, deduction of the interest expense may be subject to limitation and deferral.[2] Certain short sale expenses (see Q 1024, Q 1025) may be treated as interest within this rule.[3] See Q 1308 for details. Any amount deductible under these rules will also be subject to the general limit on the otherwise allowable deduction of investment interest (see Q 1304).

ORIGINAL ISSUE DISCOUNT

1116. How is original issue discount on corporate and Treasury obligations issued after July 1, 1982 included in income?

If a bond is originally issued at a price that is less than its stated redemption price at maturity, the difference is original issue discount (OID). However, if the discount at which a bond was issued is less than ¼ of 1% (.0025) of the stated redemption price multiplied by the number of complete years to maturity, the bond is treated (for tax purposes) as if it were issued without a discount.[4]

If a bond is issued for property (stock or securities, or to the extent provided for in regulations, for other property in tax years ending after July 18, 1984) and either the bond or the property is traded on an established market, the issue price of the bond is considered to be the fair market value of the property.[5]

The amount of original issue discount is included in income as it accrues over the life of the bond. For bonds issued after April 4, 1994, OID must be accrued at a constant rate. The holder of a bond may use accrual periods of different lengths provided that no accrual period is longer than one year. Payments may occur either on the first day or final day of an accrual period.[6]

The amount of original issue discount accruing each period is ratably allocated to each day in the period. These "daily portions" must be included in gross income by each owner for each day he holds the bond during his tax year.[7] (More often than not, the

---

1. IRC Secs. 1276(c), 1278(b).
2. IRC Secs. 1277(a), 1278(a)(1)(C).
3. IRC Sec. 1282(c). See General Explanation–TRA '84, p. 98.
4. IRC Sec. 1273(a).
5. IRC Sec. 1273(b)(3).
6. Treas. Reg. §1.1272-1(b)(1).
7. IRC Sec. 1272(a)(1).

individual's tax year will overlap two periods. If so, the owner simply totals the appropriate daily portions for the parts of each period that fall in his tax year.) Taxpayers who use the cash receipts and disbursement method of accounting and maintain a brokerage account that includes original issue discount debt instruments and stripped bonds must include in gross income for the taxable year the amount of accrued discount allocable to the portion of the taxable year in which they held the debt instrument. The taxpayers cannot defer the inclusion of original issue discount until it is actually received.[1]

Gain on the sale, exchange, or retirement of a bond is treated as ordinary income to the extent of unaccrued original issue discount if at the time of original issue there existed an intention to call the bond prior to maturity. According to final regulations, an intention to call exists only if there is an agreement not provided for in the debt instrument that the issuer will redeem the instrument prior to maturity.[2] This rule is not applicable to publicly offered bonds.[3] The rules of this paragraph are effective for bonds issued on or after April 4, 1994 and may be relied upon by taxpayers with bonds issued after December 21, 1992.

If the holder purchased the debt instrument at a premium or an acquisition premium or made an election to treat all interest as original interest discount, the amount of original issue discount must be adjusted.[4] Furthermore, for bonds held on or after March 2, 1998, a holder making an election to treat all interest on a bond as original issue discount is deemed to have elected to amortize any existing bond premium (see Q 1120).[5]

The owner's basis is increased by the amount of discount included in income and decreased by the amount of any payment from the issuer to the holder under the debt instrument other than a payment of qualified stated interest.[6]

The application of these rules to bonds acquired in a debt-for-debt exchange in a corporate reorganization is covered in Treasury Regulation Section 1.1272-2.

The Service ruled that a taxpayer who acquired two debt instruments that were structured so that it was expected that the value of one would increase significantly at the same time that the value of the other debt instrument would decrease significantly was not allowed to claim a current loss on the sale of the debt instrument that decreased in value while not recognizing the gain on the other debt instrument. The loss deductions for each set of debt instruments were denied under IRC Section 165(a) and Treas. Regs. §§1.1275-6(c)(2) (the integration rule) and 1.1275-2(g) (the anti-abuse rule), respectively.[7]

Special rules apply to determine the inclusion in income of original issue discount on debt instruments issued after 1986 that have a maturity that is initially fixed, but that is accelerated based on prepayments on other debt obligations securing the debt instrument.[8] For rules applying to variable rate debt instruments and debt instruments

---

1. *Gaffney v. Comm.*, TC Memo 1997-249.
2. Treas. Reg. §1.1271-1(a)(1).
3. Treas. Reg. §1.1271-1(a)(2)(i).
4. Treas. Reg. §1.1272-1(b)(3).
5. Treas. Reg. §1.171-4(a)(2).
6. IRC Sec. 1272(d)(2); Treas. Reg. §1.1272-1(g).
7. Rev. Rul. 2000-12, 2000-1 CB 744.
8. See IRC Sec. 1272(a)(6).

that provide for contingent payments, see Treas. Reg. §1.1272-1(b)(2). The sale of additional Treasury or corporate debt instruments that are issued after the original issue but that are treated as part of the original issue is referred to as a "qualified reopening." For rules governing the treatment of original issue discount with respect to such sales, see Treas. Regs. §§1.163-7(e), 1.1275-1(f), 1.1275-2(d); 1.1275-2(k), 1.1275-7(g). See also Rev. Proc. 2001-21,[1] (providing an election that will facilitate the substitution of newly issued bonds for outstanding bonds).

These rules do not apply to tax-exempt bonds, to short-term government (federal or state) obligations (such as T-bills), to savings bonds (e.g., EE bonds), or to short-term corporate obligations.[2]

The treatment of Treasury bills is discussed in Q 1093 and Q 1094, and short-term corporate obligations in Q 1095 and Q 1096.

1117. How is original issue discount treated in the case of Treasury notes and bonds issued before July 2, 1982 and after December 31, 1954?

Any original issue discount on Treasury notes and bonds issued between January 1, 1955 and July 1, 1982 (inclusive) is not included in income until the bond is sold or redeemed.[3] (If the discount at issue was less than ¼ of 1% (.0025) of the stated redemption price, multiplied by the number of full years from the date of original issue to maturity, the bond is not considered issued at a discount.[4])

If the owner purchased the bond at a premium (i.e., at a price above the stated redemption price) no original issue discount is included in income on the sale or maturity of the obligation.[5]

If the obligation is sold or redeemed by a seller who did not buy at a premium and *gain* is realized, a part of the proceeds must be treated by the seller as ordinary income attributable to the original issue discount. The amount of discount treated as ordinary income is based on the proportionate part of the time from issue to the date of maturity that the seller held the obligation; it is computed by multiplying the original issue discount by a fraction having as numerator the number of full months the obligation was held by the seller and as denominator the number of full months from the date of original issue to the stated date of maturity.[6] Any days amounting to less than a full month are not counted.[7]

In determining how many months the seller held the obligation, he must include any period it was held by another person if his tax basis for determining gain or loss is the same, in whole or in part, as it would be in the hands of the other person.[8]

> *Example:* Mr. Wolfram purchases a 10-year bond for $900 at original issue on February 1. He sells it to Mr. Mueller on February 20 five years later for $940. The redemption price is $1,000. Mr. Wolfram has held the bond 60 complete months. The number of complete months from issue to

---

1. 2001-1 CB 742.
2. IRC Sec. 1272(a).
3. IRC Sec. 1271(c)(2).
4. IRC Sec. 1273(a)(3).
5. IRC Sec. 1271(a)(2)(B). See Treas. Reg. §1.1232-3(d). See also Treas. Reg. §1.1272-2.
6. IRC Sec. 1271(c).
7. See Treas. Reg. §1.1232-3(c), Ex.(1).
8. Treas. Reg. §1.1232-3(c).

maturity is 120. The proportionate part of the original issue discount attributable to Mr. Wolfram's period of ownership is $50 ($100 × 60/120). Thus, Mr. Wolfram's $40 gain is all ordinary income. If Mr. Wolfram had sold the bond for $800 instead of $940, he would have a long-term capital loss of $100. If Mr. Mueller had bought it on February 1 for $800 and held it until maturity he would have $50 ($100 x 60/120) ordinary income and $150 in long-term capital gain.

U.S. Savings Bonds are discussed at Q 1139 to Q 1143. Treasury Bills are discussed in Q 1093 and Q 1094.

1118. How is original issue discount on corporate bonds issued before July 2, 1982 and after May 27, 1969 treated?

A prorated part of the original issue discount is included in income as interest each year, even though it is not actually received, unless the owner paid a premium (i.e., more than the stated redemption price) when he purchased the bond, or the obligation matured in one year or less. The amount is determined as follows:

By the original owner. The original issue discount is divided by the number of complete months plus any fractional part of a month (as explained below) from the date of original issue through the day before the stated maturity date. (This is called the "ratable monthly portion.")[1] The ratable monthly portion is multiplied by the number of complete months plus any fractional part of a month the taxpayer held the bond during the year.[2]

By a subsequent owner. Like the original owner, a subsequent owner includes in income each year a "ratable monthly portion" of original issue discount multiplied by the number of months plus fractional parts of a month he held the bond. However, he may determine the ratable monthly portion in a different way if it results in a lower amount. Instead of dividing the original issue discount by the term of the bond, he may divide the amount by which the bond's stated redemption price at maturity exceeds the bond's cost to him by the number of complete months plus any fractional part of a month beginning on the day he *purchased* the obligation and ending on the day before the stated maturity date of the obligation.[3] An individual is not considered to have "purchased" the bond if his basis is determined, in whole or in part, by reference to the basis of the obligation in the hands of the person from whom it was acquired, or by reference to the estate tax valuation.[4]

Thus, if the amount paid by the subsequent owner is not more than the original issue price plus all amounts of original issue discount previously includable (whether or not included) in income by previous holders, his ratable monthly portion of the original issue discount is calculated like the original holder's. But, if he paid more than the original issue price plus the amount of original issue discount includable in the income of any previous holder, he may reduce the original issue discount remaining by the excess amount before determining his monthly portion. This excess amount is called an "acquisition premium." (In computing the amount of original issue discount includable by previous holders, one does not take into consideration any acquisition premium paid by previous holders or that a holder may, in fact, have purchased at a premium.[5])

---

1. Treas. Reg. §1.1232-3A(a)(2)(i); IRC Sec. 1272(b)(2).
2. IRC Sec. 1272(b)(1); Treas. Reg. §1.1232-3A(a)(1).
3. IRC Sec. 1272(b)(4); Treas. Regs. §§1.1232-3A(a)(2)(ii), 1.1232-3A(a)(3)(i).
4. IRC Sec. 1272(d); Treas. Reg. §1.1232-3A(a)(4).
5. IRC Sec. 1272(b); Treas. Reg. §1.1232-3A(a)(2)(ii).

For either an original or subsequent holder, a complete or fractional month begins with the date of original issue and the corresponding day of each following calendar month (or the last day of a calendar month in which there is no corresponding day). If a holder sells the bond on any other day in the month, a part of the ratable monthly portion for that month is allocated between the seller and buyer based on the number of days in the month each held the bond. (Seller and buyer may allocate on the basis of a 30-day month.) The transferee is deemed to hold the obligations the entire day of acquisition, but not on the day of redemption.[1]

The original or any subsequent holder increases his basis by amounts of includable original issue discount he actually included in his income.[2]

1119. How is original issue discount on corporate bonds issued before May 28, 1969 and after December 31, 1954 taxed?

Original issue discount is included in income in the same manner as Treasury securities issued before July 2, 1982 (see Q 1117).[3]

However, if at the time of original issue there was an intention to call the obligation before maturity, the gain up to the entire original issue discount is treated as ordinary income.[4]

There is an intention to call before maturity if there is an understanding between the issuing corporation and the original purchaser that the issuer will redeem the obligation before maturity. The understanding need not be communicated directly to the purchaser by the issuer and the understanding may be conditional (e.g., it may be dependent on the issuer's financial condition on the proposed call date). Whether there is an understanding depends on all the facts and circumstances. That the obligation on its face gives the issuer the privilege of redeeming the obligation before maturity is not determinative of an intention, and if the obligation was part of an issue registered with the SEC and sold to the public without representation that the obligor intends to call, it is presumed that there was no intention at issue to call.[5]

BOND PREMIUM

1120. Must premium paid on taxable bonds be amortized annually? Must basis be reduced by the amount of amortizable premium?

An individual who purchased a taxable bond at a premium (that is, at an amount in excess of its face value), whether or not on original issue, may *elect* to amortize the premium over the remaining life of the bond (or in some cases, until an earlier call date).[6] If the election to amortize bond premium is not made, the premium is recovered as part of the owner's basis in the bond, if the bond is sold for as much as or more than it cost, or is deducted as a capital loss if the bond is redeemed at face value or sold for less than the basis. See Q 1121 for an explanation of how the amount of amortizable bond premium is determined.

1.   Treas. Reg. §1.1232-3A(a)(3).
2.   IRC Sec. 1272(d)(2); Treas. Reg. §1.1232-3A(c).
3.   IRC Sec. 1271(c)(2).
4.   IRC Sec. 1271(c).
5.   See Treas. Reg. §1.1232-3(b)(4).
6.   IRC Sec. 171.

The election to amortize applies to all taxable bonds that are owned at the beginning of the first year to which the election applies and all bonds acquired thereafter, and may be revoked only with the consent of the Service.[1] Under final regulations generally in effect for bonds acquired on or after March 2, 1998, a revocation of the election applies to all taxable bonds held during or after the taxable year for which the revocation is effective, and the holder may not amortize any remaining bond premium on bonds held at the beginning of the taxable year for which the revocation is effective.[2] See below for the effective date of the final regulations.

The term "bond" to which the election applies includes any taxable bond, debenture, certificate or other evidence of indebtedness issued by any corporation, government or political subdivision.[3] The taxpayer is not required to amortize premium on taxable bonds just because he has *tax-exempt* bonds that he is amortizing.

For bonds acquired after December 31, 1987, an electing taxpayer applies the part of the premium attributable to the year as an offset to interest payments (that is, in direct reduction of interest income) received on the bond to which the premium is attributable.[4]

Taxpayers who elected to amortize premium on bonds acquired after October 22, 1986 and before January 1, 1988 could elect to use either the deduction or the offset method.[5] These taxpayers treat the deduction as investment interest expense subject to the investment interest deduction limitations.[6]

With respect to bonds acquired before October 23, 1986, a taxpayer who elected to amortize takes an annual itemized interest expense deduction.[7] The deduction is not subject to the 2% floor on miscellaneous deductions.[8] Such an election to amortize in effect on October 22, 1986, does not apply to bonds acquired after October 22, 1986 unless the taxpayer so elected.[9]

Under final regulations generally in effect for bonds acquired on or after March 2, 1998, a holder makes the election to amortize by offsetting interest income with bond premium in the holder's timely filed federal income tax return for the first taxable year to which the holder desires the election to apply. A holder should also attach a statement to the return that he is making the election. See below for the effective date of final regulations. Regulations reflecting the law in effect prior to October 23, 1986 provided that the election was made by deducting the premium attributable to the year as an interest expense for the first year to which the election was to apply. The election to amortize could not be made in a refund claim.[10]

A bondholder making an election to treat all interest on a bond as original issue discount is deemed to have elected to amortize any existing bond premium (see Q 1116).[11]

1. IRC Sec. 171(c)(2); Treas. Reg. §1.171-4.
2. Treas. Reg. §1.171-4(d).
3. IRC Sec. 171(d).
4. IRC Sec. 171(e).
5. TAMRA '88, Sec. 1803(a)(11)(B).
6. IRC Sec. 171(e), as in effect prior to amendment by TAMRA '88, Sec. 1006(j)(1).
7. IRC Sec. 171(a).
8. IRC Sec. 67(b)(11); see Conf. Report 99-841, Vol. II at page 34, 1986-3 CB Vol. 4.
9. TAMRA '88, Act Sec. 1006(j)(2).
10. *Woodward Est. v. Comm.*, 24 TC 883 (1955) *aff'd sub. nom. Barnhill v. Comm.*, 241 F.2d 496 (5th Cir. 1957), *acq.*, 1956-2 CB 4, 1956-2 CB 9.
11. Treas. Reg. §1.171-4(a)(2).

If a bondholder elects to amortize bond premium and holds a taxable bond acquired before the taxable year for which the election is made, the holder may not amortize amounts that would have been amortized in prior taxable years had an election been in effect for those prior years.[1]

A taxpayer electing to amortize must also reduce his basis in the bond by the amount of premium that is an allowable deduction or that was applied in reduction of interest payments each year.[2]

A bond with interest that is partially excludable from gross income is treated as two instruments, a tax-exempt obligation and a taxable bond. The holder's basis in the bond and each payment on the bond are allocated between the two instruments based on a reasonable method.[3] See Q 1126 and Q 1127 regarding the amortization of premium on tax-exempt bonds.

Regulations provide special rules that apply to certain variable rate debt instruments, bonds subject to certain contingencies, and inflation-indexed debt instruments.[4]

The final regulations under IRC Section 171 do not apply to (1) a bond described in IRC Section 1272(a)(6)(C) (relating to regular interests in a REMIC, qualified mortgages held by a REMIC, and certain other debt instruments, or pools of debt instruments, with payments subject to acceleration); (2) a bond to which Treasury Regulation Section 1.1275-4 applies (relating to certain contingent pay debt instruments); (3) a bond held by a holder that elected to treat all interest on a debt instrument as original issue discount; (4) a bond that is stock in trade of the holder, a bond of a kind that would properly be included in the inventory of the holder if on hand at the close of the taxable year, or a bond held primarily for sale to customers in the ordinary course of the holder's trade or business; or (5) a bond issued before September 28, 1985, unless the bond bears interest and was issued by a corporation or by a government or political subdivision thereof.[5]

Regulations generally in effect for bonds acquired before March 2, 1998 (or held before a taxable year containing March 2, 1998 in which an election to amortize is made) provided that, if in any year an individual who amortizes bond premium by deducting it as an interest expense does not itemize his deductions, but takes a standard deduction, the deduction is deemed to have been allowed and reduces his basis.[6] Regulations also provided that an individual may, but need not, amortize premium in a year in which no interest is received.[7] The additional final regulations, amended December 30, 1997, do not include the above rules.

Amortization of premium on tax-exempt bonds is discussed in Q 1126.

Effective date of regulations. The final regulations under IRC Section 171 (as amended December 30, 1997) apply to bonds acquired on or after March 2, 1998. However, if a bondholder elected to amortize bond premium for the taxable year containing March

---

1. Treas. Reg. §1.171-4(c).
2. IRC Sec. 1016(a)(5); Treas. Reg. §1.1016-5(b).
3. Treas. Reg. §1.171-1(c)(3).
4. See Treas. Reg. §1.171-3.
5. Treas. Reg. §1.171-1(b)(2).
6. Treas. Reg. §1.171-1(b)(5).
7. Treas. Reg. §1.171-2(e).

2, 1998, or any subsequent taxable year, the final regulations under IRC Section 171 apply to bonds held on or after the first day of the taxable year in which the election is made.[1]

Furthermore, a holder is deemed to have made the election under regulations for the taxable year containing March 2, 1998, if the holder elected to amortize bond premium under IRC Section 171 and that election was effective on March 2, 1998. If the holder is deemed to have made such an election, the final regulations under IRC Section 171 will apply to bonds acquired on or after the first day of the taxable year containing March 2, 1998.[2]

Substitution of debt instruments. For the revised rules governing the treatment of bond premium when there is a substitution of newly issued bonds for outstanding bonds, see Rev. Proc. 2001-21.[3]

1121. How is the amount of amortizable bond premium determined?

The amortizable premium on taxable bonds acquired on or after January 1, 1958 is the excess of the individual's tax basis for determining *loss* on sale or exchange of the bond (determined at the start of the year) over the amount payable at maturity, or in the case of a callable bond, the earlier call date if using the earlier call date would result in a smaller amortizable amount being allocated to the year.[4] It makes no difference whether the premium is original issue premium or "market" premium (generally reflecting a higher coupon interest rate on the bond than the market interest rate for bonds of similar quality). See Q 1122 in the case of a convertible bond with amortizable bond premium.

Under final regulations generally in effect for bonds acquired on or after March 2, 1998, a holder acquires a bond at premium if the holder's basis in the bond immediately after its acquisition by the holder exceeds the sum of all amounts payable on the bond after the acquisition date (other than payments of qualified stated interest); the excess is bond premium, which a holder amortizes.[5] Bond premium is allocable to an accrual period based on a constant yield that is used to conform the treatment of bond premium to the treatment of original issue discount (see Q 1116).[6] Under a transition rule, the use of a constant yield to amortize premium does not apply to a bond issued before September 28, 1985.[7] See Q 1120 for an explanation of the effective date of the final regulations.

In general, the holder's basis in the bond is the holder's basis for purposes of determining loss on the sale or exchange of the bond. This determination of basis applies only for purposes of amortizing premium; a holder's basis in the bond for purposes of amortizing premium may differ from the holder's basis for purposes of determining gain or loss on the sale or exchange of the bond.[8]

---

1. Treas. Reg. §1.171-5(a).
2. Treas. Reg. §1.171-5(b).
3. 2001-1 CB 742.
4. IRC Sec. 171(b).
5. Treas. Reg. §1.171-1(d).
6. Treas. Reg. §1.171-1(a).
7. Treas. Reg. §1.171-5(a)(2).
8. Treas. Reg. §1.171-1(e).

For purposes of determining the amount amortizable, if the bond is acquired in an exchange for other property and the bond's basis is determined (in whole or in part) by the basis of the property, the basis of the bond is not more than its fair market value immediately after the exchange.[1] This rule applies to exchanges occurring after May 6, 1986.[2] A special rule applies to a bond acquired in a bond-for-bond exchange in a corporate reorganization.[3]

If the bond is *transferred basis property* and the transferor had acquired the bond at a premium, the holder's basis in the bond is the holder's basis for determining loss on the sale or exchange of the bond reduced by any amounts that the transferor could not have amortized (under the basis rules or because of an election to amortize in a subsequent taxable year), except to the extent that the holder's basis already reflects a reduction attributable to the nonamortizable amounts.[4] *Transferred basis property* is property having a basis determined in whole or in part by the basis of the transferor.[5]

For a detailed explanation of the effective dates for the final regulations under IRC Section 171 (as amended December 30, 1997), see Q 1120.

Calculation of Annual Deduction or Offset

Bonds Issued After September 27, 1985

Except as provided in regulations (see below), the determination of the amount of the deduction or offset in any year is computed on the basis of the taxpayer's yield to maturity by using the taxpayer's basis in the bond (for purposes of determining loss) and by compounding at the close of each accrual period. Generally, an accrual period is the same as used in determining original issue discount (see Q 1116). If the amount payable on a call date that is earlier than maturity is used for purposes of determining the yield to maturity, the bond is treated as maturing on the call date and then as reissued on that call date for the amount payable on the call date.[6] If a taxpayer had an election to amortize bond premium in effect on October 22, 1986, the election applies to bonds issued after September 27, 1985 only if the taxpayer so chooses (as may be prescribed in regulations).[7]

Under final regulations generally in effect for bonds acquired on or after March 2, 1998, a holder amortizes bond premium by offsetting the qualified stated interest allocable to an accrual period with the bond premium allocable to the accrual period. This offset occurs when the holder takes the qualified stated interest into account under the holder's regular method of accounting.[8] The accrual period to which qualified stated interest is allocable is determined under the regulations to IRC Section 446 (relating to the general rule for methods of accounting).[9] For a detailed explanation of the effective date of the final regulations, see Q 1120.

The bond premium allocable to an accrual period is calculated using the following three steps.

---

1. IRC Sec. 171(b)(4); Treas. Reg. §1.171-1(e)(1)(ii).
2. TRA '86, Sec. 1803(a)(12)(A).
3. IRC Sec. 171(b)(4)(B).
4. Treas. Reg. §1.171-(1)(e)(2).
5. IRC Sec. 7701(a)(43).
6. IRC Sec. 171(b)(3).
7. TRA '86, Sec. 1803(a)(11)(A).
8. Treas. Reg. §1.171-2(a)(1).
9. Treas. Reg. §1.171-2(a)(2).

Step one: Determine the holder's yield. The holder's yield is the discount rate that, when used in computing the present value of all remaining payments to be made on the bond (including payments of qualified stated interest), produces an amount equal to the holder's basis in the bond. The remaining payments include only payments to be made after the date the holder acquires the bond. The yield calculated as of the date the holder acquires the bond must be constant over the term of the bond, and must be calculated to at least two decimal places when expressed as a percentage.[1]

Step two: Determine the accrual periods. An accrual period is an interval of time over which the accrual of bond premium is measured. Accrual periods may be of any length over the term of the debt instrument, provided that each accrual period is no longer than one year and each scheduled payment occurs on the final day of an accrual period or on the first day of an accrual period.[2]

Step three: Determine the bond premium allocable to the accrual period. The bond premium allocable to an accrual period is the excess of the qualified stated interest allocable to the accrual period over the product of the holder's *adjusted acquisition price* at the beginning of the accrual period and the holder's yield. In performing this calculation, the yield must be stated appropriately taking into account the length of the particular accrual period.[3] The *adjusted acquisition price* of a bond at the beginning of the first accrual period is the holder's basis (see below). Thereafter, the adjusted acquisition price is the holder's basis in the bond decreased by (1) the amount of bond premium previously allocable (as calculated above), and (2) the amount of any payment previously made on the bond other than the payment of qualified stated interest.

If the bond premium allocable to an accrual period exceeds the qualified stated interest allocable to the accrual period, the excess is treated by the holder as a bond premium deduction for the accrual period. However, the amount treated as a bond premium deduction is limited to the amount by which the holder's total interest inclusions on the bond in prior accrual periods exceeds the total amount treated by the holder as a bond premium deduction on the bond in prior accrual periods. A deduction determined under this rule is not subject to the 2% floor on miscellaneous itemized deductions.[4] If the bond premium allocable to an accrual period exceeds the sum of the qualified stated interest allocable to the accrual period and the amount treated as a deduction for the accrual period, the excess is carried forward to the next accrual period and is treated as bond premium allocable to that period.[5]

Additional rules apply to determine the amortization of bond premium on a variable rate debt instrument, an inflation-indexed debt instrument, a bond that provides for certain alternative payment schedules, and a bond that provides for remote or incidental contingencies.[6]

The final regulations are generally effective for bonds acquired after March 2, 1998; but certain transition rules may apply. See Q 1120.

---

1. Treas. Reg. §1.171-2(a)(3)(i).
2. Treas. Regs. §§1.171-2(a)(3)(ii), 1.1272-1(b)(1)(ii).
3. Treas. Reg. §1.171-2(a)(3)(iii).
4. Treas. Reg. §1.171-2(a)(4)(i)(A).
5. Treas. Reg. §1.171-2(a)(4)(i)(B).
6. See Treas. Reg. §1.171-3.

Bonds Issued On Or Before September 27, 1985

The amount of the deduction or offset each year may be determined under any reasonable method of amortization, but once an individual has used a method, he must consistently use the same method. (The Service has approved use of the "yield" method of amortizing bond premium.[1]) Instead of any other method, he may use the straight line method set forth in regulations (in effect for bonds acquired before March 2, 1998, or held before a taxable year containing March 2, 1998). Under that method, the amount of premium that is deductible or offset each year is an amount that bears the same ratio to the bond premium as the number of months in the tax year the bond was held by the individual bears to the number of months from the beginning of the tax year (or, if the bond was acquired in the tax year, from the date of acquisition) to the date of maturity or to an earlier call date if appropriate. A fractional part of a month is counted only if it is more than one-half of a month and then it is counted as a month.[2] The additional final regulations, amended December 30, 1997, do not include the above rules.

Under regulations in effect for bonds acquired before March 2, 1998 (or held before a taxable year containing March 2, 1998), if the premium is solely a result of capitalized expenses (such as buying commissions), an individual using the straight line method provided in the regulations may amortize the capital expenses; if such expenses are a part of a larger premium, he must treat them as part of the premium, if he uses the straight line method.[3] The additional final regulations, amended December 30, 1997, do not include the above rule.

Earlier Call Date

If the bond is called before maturity, the amount of premium amortizable in that year is the excess of adjusted basis for determining loss over the greater of the amount received on call or the amount payable on maturity.[4]

Under regulations in effect for bonds acquired before March 2, 1998 (or held before a taxable year containing March 2, 1998), the earlier call date (if it is used to determine amortizable premium) may be the earliest call date specified in the bond as a day certain, the earliest interest payment date if the bond is callable at such date, the earliest date at which the bond is callable at par, or such other call date, prior to maturity, specified in the bond as may be selected by the taxpayer.[5] Where amortization is determined with respect to one of alternative call dates, if in fact the bond is not called on that date, the premium must be amortized to a succeeding date or to maturity. The additional final regulations, amended December 30, 1997, do not include the above rules.

Basis Adjustment

Regulations in effect for bonds acquired before March 2, 1998 (or held before a taxable year containing March 2, 1998) provided that, in determining each year the amount of premium to be amortized, the basis was adjusted for amortizable premium previously deducted or offset.[6] Also, an adjustment had to be made for premium not amortized in years the individual held the bond before he elected to amortize. However,

1. Rev. Rul. 82-10, 1982-1 CB 46.
2. Treas. Reg. §1.171-2(f).
3. Treas. Reg. §1.171-2(d).
4. IRC Sec. 171(b)(2).
5. Treas. Reg. §1.171-2(b).
6. Treas. Reg. §1.171-2(f)(2)(ii).

this adjustment was made only for the purpose of determining the amortizable amount; the amount not amortized before the election did not affect basis for determining gain or loss on sale or exchange.[1] If the bond was acquired by gift (or the individual's basis is for some other reason determined by reference to the basis in the hands of another), the same adjustment must include the period the bond was held by the other person. The additional final regulations, amended December 30, 1997, do not include the above rules.

Amortization Disallowed

The Service will disallow amortization in situations that lack economic substance.[2] A deduction for amortization was disallowed where sales were not bona fide sales;[3] and where an individual who put up no margin, signed no note and intended to sell the bonds to cover his liability, was ruled not to be the owner of the bonds for purposes of deducting a part of the premium.[4]

Amortization of premium on tax-exempt bonds is discussed in Q 1126.

1122. How is amortizable bond premium determined in the case of a convertible bond?

The amount of amortizable bond premium on a convertible bond may not include any amount attributable to the bond's conversion features.[5] Under final regulations generally in effect for bonds acquired on or after March 2, 1998 (see Q 1120), the holder's basis in the bond is reduced by an amount equal to the value of the conversion option. The value of the conversion option may be determined under any reasonable method. For example, the holder may determine the value of the conversion option by comparing the market price of the convertible bond to the market prices of similar bonds that do not have conversion options.[6]

On January 1, 2005, John Smith purchases for $1,100 a convertible bond maturing on January 1, 2008, with a stated principal amount of $1,000, payable at maturity. The bond provides for unconditional payments of interest of $20.00 on January 1 and July 1 of each year. In addition, the bond is convertible into 15 shares of the corporation's stock at the option of the holder. On January 1, 2005, the corporation's nonconvertible, publicly-traded, 3-year debt with a similar credit rating trades at a price that reflects a yield of 4.50%, compounded semiannually.

Mr. Smith's basis for determining loss on the sale or exchange of the bond is $1,100. As of January 1, 2005, discounting the remaining payments on the bond at the yield at which the corporation's similar nonconvertible bonds trade (4.50%, compounded semiannually) results in a present value of $985. Thus, the value of the conversion option is $115. Mr. Smith's basis is $985 ($1,100 - $115) for purposes of the rules and regulations of IRC Section 171. The sum of all amounts payable on the bond other than qualified stated interest is $1,000. Because Mr. Smith's basis (under IRC Section 171) does not exceed $1,000, he does not acquire the bond at a premium.

Regulations in effect for bonds acquired before March 2, 1998 (or held before a taxable year containing March 2, 1998) provided that the value of the conversion features is determined as of the date of acquisition by adjusting the price of the bond to a yield

---

1. Treas. Reg. §1.171-2(a)(4).
2. Rev. Rul. 62-127, 1962-2 CB 84.
3. *Lieb v. Comm.*, 40 TC 161 (1963).
4. *Starr v. Comm.*, 46 TC 450 (1966), *acq.* 1967-2 CB 3.
5. IRC Sec. 171(b)(1).
6. Treas. Reg. §1.171-1(e)(1)(iii).

determined by comparison with the yields of bonds of similar character without conversion features that are sold on the open market.[1] The above language is not included in the additional final regulations, amended December 31, 1997.

Under final regulations, if a convertible bond is acquired in exchange for other property and the holder's basis in the bond is determined in whole or in part by reference to the holder's basis in the other property, the holder's basis in the bond may not exceed its fair market value immediately after the exchange reduced by the value of the conversion option.[2]

The amount of premium amortizable in a year is discussed in Q 1121. The tax treatment of the amount is explained in Q 1120.

MUNICIPAL BONDS

1123. Is interest on obligations issued by state and local governments taxable?

Interest paid on certain bonds issued by or on behalf of state or local governments is *not* tax-exempt. These are generally private purpose bonds (such as industrial development bonds and "private activity" bonds) and arbitrage bonds. For tax purposes, such non-exempt issues are government bonds taxed like Treasury bonds (see Q 1098 to Q 1101).

Interest on certain categories of private purpose bonds *is* tax-exempt, although tax-exempt interest on some private activity bonds is a tax preference item for both the individual and corporate alternative minimum tax (see Q 1124, Q 1440).[3]

Interest on general purpose obligations of states and local governments (i.e., states, territories, possessions of the United States, or political subdivisions of any of them, or the District of Columbia) issued to finance operations of the state, local government, or instrumentality is generally tax-exempt. In addition, some obligations are tax-exempt under special legislation.

In a case of first impression, the Kentucky Court of Appeals concluded that Kentucky's tax on the income derived from bonds issued outside Kentucky violates the Commerce Clause of the United States Constitution. Accordingly, the court held that the trial court's decision to grant summary judgment to the Department of Revenue was erroneous.[4]

Whether a particular issue meets the requirements for tax exemption can involve complex legal and factual questions. Law firms specializing in municipal debt offerings, often called "bond counsel," provide legal opinions concerning the validity of bond issues that generally include the exemption of interest from federal income tax. (For the proposed regulations applicable to practitioners rendering opinions concerning the tax treatment of municipal bonds, see Prop. Treas. Reg. §10.35(b)(9); REG-159824-04.[5])

---

1. Treas. Reg. §1.171-2(c)(2).
2. Treas. Reg. §1.171-1(e)(iii)(B).
3. IRC Sec. 57(a)(5).
4. See *Davis v. Department of Revenue*, ___ S.W.3d ___ (Ky. App. 2006), *cert. denied*, *Department of Revenue v. Davis*, No. 2006-SC-000105-D (8-17-2006).
5. 69 Fed. Reg. 75887 (12-20-2004).

These opinions are customarily printed on the bonds. It has been held that where bonds issued by a city as tax-exempt were later found invalid under state law, the interest on them was not excludable from gross income under IRC Section 103(a).[1] Where a county housing authority refused to pay a rebate to the federal government relating to bonds that were ruled to be arbitrage bonds by the Service and not tax-exempt, the interest was not excludable from the gross income of bondholders under IRC Section 103(a).[2]

Where tax-exempt bonds trade "flat" because interest is in default, see Q 1133.

Bonds issued after June 30, 1983, must be in registered form in order to be tax-exempt (see Q 1151 and Q 1152).

Tax-exempt interest is included in the calculation made to determine whether Social Security payments are includable in gross income.[3] It has been determined that although this provision may result in the indirect taxation of tax-exempt interest, it is not unconstitutional (see Q 1410).[4]

Every person who receives tax-exempt interest (and who is required to file an income tax return) must report for informational purposes the amount of tax-exempt interest received during the tax year on that return.[5] The Code requires the reporting of tax-exempt interest paid after December 31, 2005.[6] The Service has released transitional guidance regarding the new information reporting requirements for payments of tax-exempt interest on state or local bonds.[7]

1124. Is tax-exempt interest treated as an item of tax preference for purposes of the alternative minimum tax?

Tax-exempt interest on private activity bonds other than qualified 501(c)(3) bonds is a tax preference item for both the individual and corporate alternative minimum tax (see Q 1440). The interest may be reduced by any deduction not allowable in computing regular tax that would have been allowable if the interest were includable in gross income (e.g., amortizable bond premium).[8] The preference item includes exempt-interest dividends paid by a mutual fund to the extent attributable to such interest.[9]

The alternative minimum tax applies to such bonds issued after August 7, 1986 (or on or after September 1, 1986 in the case of bonds covered by the "Joint Statement on Effective Dates of March 14, 1986"). Interest on bonds issued to refund immediately pre-August 8, 1986 bonds is not an item of tax preference.[10]

1125. How is gain or loss taxed on sale or redemption of tax-exempt bonds issued by a state or local government?

---

1. Rev. Rul. 87-116, 1987-2 CB 44.
2. *Harbor Bancorp & Subsidiaries v. Comm.*, 115 F.3d 722 (9th Cir. 1997), *cert. den.*, 118 S.Ct. 1035 (1998).
3. IRC Sec. 86(b)(2)(B).
4. *Goldin v. Baker*, 809 F.2d 187 (2nd Cir. 1987), *cert. denied*, 108 S.Ct. 69 (1988).
5. IRC Sec. 6012(d).
6. See IRC Sec. 6049(b), as amended by TIPRA 2005.
7. See Notice 2006-93, 2006-44 IRB 798.
8. IRC Sec. 57(a)(5)(A).
9. IRC Sec. 57(a)(5)(B).
10. See the Conference Report, TRA '86, page 333). IRC Sec. 57(a)(5)(C).

The seller may recover an amount equal to his adjusted basis tax free. If the bond was purchased at a premium, the seller's basis for determining gain or loss is adjusted to reflect the amortization of the premium. (see Q 1126).

With respect to a bond both issued after September 3, 1982 and acquired after March 1, 1984, the owner's basis is increased by the amount of tax-exempt original issue discount that accrued while he owned the bond (subject to an adjustment if he purchased the bond at a price in excess of the issue price plus original issue discount accrued up to the time he acquired it).[1] Original issue discount accrues daily at a constant rate as it does generally for taxable original issue discount bonds issued after July 1, 1982 (see Q 1116), except that discounts of less than ¼ of 1% (.0025) times the number of years to maturity are accounted for.[2] For obligations with a maturity of one year or less, discount will accrue daily on a ratable basis, as it does for taxable short-term government obligations (that is, by dividing discount by the number of days after the day the taxpayer acquired the bond up to and including the day of its maturity); however, the taxpayer apparently may make an irrevocable election to use a constant rate (under regulations) with respect to individual short-term obligations.[3]

With respect to any bond acquired on or before March 1, 1984 or any bond issued on or before September 3, 1982, whenever acquired, the seller's basis is not adjusted to reflect annual accrual of original issue discount. Consequently, loss on sale is determined without regard to original issue discount accrued up to the date of sale.[4] Nonetheless, to the extent there is gain on sale or redemption, an amount equal to original issue discount allocable to the period the investor held the bond is excludable as tax-exempt interest that accrued over the period it was held. The amount of tax-free discount apportioned to any holder is the amount that bears the same ratio to the original issue discount as the number of days he held the bond bears to the number of days from the date of original issue to the date of maturity, assuming there was no intention at issue to call the obligation before maturity.[5] If the bond is redeemed before maturity, any unaccrued original issue discount realized is taxable as capital gain, not excludable interest, except that in the case of a bond issued before June 9, 1980, it is recovered tax free as tax-exempt interest.[6]

Stated interest that is unconditionally payable at maturity on short-term tax-exempt bonds may be treated as includable in the stated redemption price at maturity *or* as qualified stated interest at the choice of the taxpayer, provided all short-term tax-exempt bonds are treated in a consistent manner. This guidance is effective for tax-exempt bonds issued after April 4, 1994, and until the Service provides further guidance.[7] Scheduled instrument payments are not unconditionally payable when, under the terms of a debt instrument, the failure to make interest payments when due requires that the issuer forgo paying dividends, or that interest accrue on the past-due payments at a rate that is two percentage points greater than the stated yield.[8]

---

1. IRC Sec. 1288(a)(2).
2. IRC Sec. 1288(b)(1).
3. IRC Sec. 1288(b).
4. TAM 8541003.
5. Rev. Rul. 73-112, 1973-1 CB 47.
6. Rev. Rul. 80-143, 1980-1 CB 19; Rev. Rul. 72-587, 1972-2 CB 74.
7. Notice 94-84, 1994-2 CB 559.
8. See Rev. Rul. 95-70, 1995-2 CB 124.

If the buyer paid the seller any stated interest accrued, but not yet due at the date of the sale, that amount is recovered tax free as return of capital.[1]

Gain in excess of tax-exempt interest will generally be capital gain, including gain from any premium paid on call (see Q 1128). See Q 1420 regarding the treatment of capital gains and losses.

If the bond was bought on the market at a discount reflecting a decline in value of the obligation after issue, this market discount does not represent tax-exempt interest paid by the issuer.[2] Market discount is the amount by which the purchase price is less than the face value of the bond (or, in the case of a bond originally issued at a discount, less than the issue price plus the amount of original issue discount apportioned, as above, to the previous holders).

With respect to tax-exempt bonds purchased *after* April 30, 1993, market discount recovered on sale is treated as taxable interest instead of capital gain.[3] For tax-exempt bonds purchased *before* May 1, 1993, gain attributable to market discount has generally been treated by the Service as capital gain.[4] Capital gain is not exempt from federal income tax.[5]

If a loss is realized on the sale or redemption, it is a capital loss. However, if "substantially identical" obligations were acquired (or a contract to acquire them was made) within 30 days before or 30 days after the sale, the loss will be subject to the "wash sale" rule discussed in Q 1030.

The IRS concluded that a modification of tax-exempt revenue bonds constituted a deemed exchange under IRC Section 1001 because the modified bonds, which had been issued in an exchange, were materially different from the original bonds; thus, the modified bonds would be treated as newly issued securities for federal income tax purposes.[6]

The installment method for recognizing and taxing gain is not available for securities traded on an established securities market. As a result, gain from sale is included in income for the year in which the trade date occurs even if one or more payments are received in the subsequent tax year.[7]

If the bond traded "flat" because interest was in default, see Q 1133.

Bonds issued after June 30, 1983 must be in registered form in order to deduct loss on sale or to treat gain as capital (as opposed to ordinary) gain (see Q 1151, Q 1152).

If the bond was held as part of a tax straddle, see Q 1077 to Q 1084. If the bond was held as part of a conversion transaction, the additional rules discussed in Q 1085 and Q 1086 will apply.

---

1. See Rev. Rul. 69-263, 1969-1 CB 197.
2. Rev. Rul. 73-112, above; Rev. Rul. 60-210, 1960-1 CB 38; Rev. Rul. 57-49, 1957-1 CB 62.
3. IRC Secs. 1276(a), 1278(a)(1).
4. Rev. Rul. 60-210, above; Rev. Rul. 57-49, above.
5. *Willcuts v. Bunn*, 282 U.S. 216 (1931); *U.S. v. Stewart*, 311 U.S. 60 (1940); Rev. Rul. 81-63, 1981-1 CB 455.
6. FSA 200116012.
7. IRC Sec. 453(k). See Rev. Rul. 93-84, 1993-2 CB 225.

If the transfer is between spouses, or between former spouses and incident to divorce, see Q 1447.

1126. Is premium paid for a tax-exempt bond deductible? Must basis in a tax-exempt bond be reduced by bond premium?

An individual who owns any fully tax-exempt interest bearing bond (or debenture, note, certificate or other evidence of indebtedness) *must* amortize any premium he paid for the bond, but the part of the premium allocable to the year is not deductible.[1] (The premium paid, in effect, reduces the annual interest; therefore, because the tax-free interest received each year represents in part a tax-free return of premium, premium is not deductible.) Regulations in effect for bonds acquired before March 2, 1998 (or held before a taxable year containing March 2, 1998) provided substantially similar rules. See Q 1127 for an explanation of the effective date for final regulations under IRC Section 171. The individual *must* reduce his basis each year by the amount of premium allocable to the year.[2]

For an explanation of how the annual amount of amortization is calculated, see Q 1127.

1127. How is premium on tax-exempt bonds amortized?

Bond premium that must be amortized is the amount by which an individual's tax basis for determining *loss* (adjusted for prior years' amortization) exceeds the face amount of the bond at maturity (or earlier call date in the case of a callable bond).[3] (A taxpayer's basis for determining loss can be lower than his basis for determining gain, as in the case of a gift. See Q 1415.)

Under final regulations generally effective for bonds acquired on or after March 2, 1998 (see Q 1120), a holder amortizes bond premium by offsetting qualified stated interest allocable to an accrual period with the bond premium allocable to the accrual period.[4] Bond premium is allocable to an accrual period based on a constant yield that is used to conform the treatment of bond premium to the treatment of original issue discount (see Q 1116).[5]

For the purpose of determining the amount amortizable, if the bond is acquired in an exchange for other property and the bond's basis is determined (in whole or in part) by the basis of the property, the basis of the bond is not more than its fair market value immediately after the exchange.[6] This rule applies to exchanges occurring after May 6, 1986.

Calculation of Amount Amortized

Bonds Issued After September 27, 1985

Except as provided in regulations (see below), the determination of the annual amortizable amount is computed on the basis of the taxpayer's yield to maturity by using

---

1. IRC Sec. 171; Treas. Reg. §1.171-1(c).
2. IRC Sec. 1016(a)(5).
3. IRC Sec. 171(b)(1).
4. Treas. Reg. §1.171-2.
5. Treas. Reg. § 1.171-1. See also Treas. Reg. §1.171-2(c), Ex. 4.
6. IRC Sec. 171(b)(4).

the taxpayer's basis in the bond (for purposes of determining loss) and by compounding at the close of each accrual period. (The accrual period is determined as discussed in Q 1116.) If the amount payable on a call date that is earlier than maturity is used for purposes of determining the yield to maturity, the bond is treated as maturing on the call date and then as reissued on that call date for the amount payable on the call date.[1]

Under final regulations generally in effect for bonds acquired on or after March 2, 1998, a holder amortizes bond premium under the same rules that apply to taxable bonds (see Q 1121); however, in the case of tax-exempt bonds, bond premium in excess of qualified stated interest is treated under a separate rule. If the bond premium allocable to an accrual period exceeds the qualified stated interest allocable to the accrual period, the excess is a nondeductible loss.[2]

See Q 1120 for an explanation of the effective date of final regulations under IRC Section 171.

Bonds Issued on or Before September 27, 1985

The amount of the premium allocable to each year may be determined under any reasonable method of amortization, but once an individual has used a method, he must consistently use the same method. (The Service has approved use of the "yield" method of amortizing bond premium.[3]) Instead of any other method, a taxpayer may use the straight line method set forth in the regulations. Under that method, the amount of premium that is allocable to each year is an amount that bears the same ratio to the bond premium as the number of months in the tax year the bond was held by the individual bears to the number of months from the beginning of the tax year (or, if the bond was acquired in the tax year, from the date of acquisition) to the date of maturity or to an earlier call date if appropriate. A fractional part of a month is counted only if it is more than one-half of a month and then it is counted as a month.[4] The additional final regulations, amended December 30, 1997, do not include the above rules.

If the premium is solely a result of capitalized expenses (such as buying commissions), an individual using the straight line method provided in the regulations may amortize the capital expenses; if such expenses are a part of a larger premium, he must treat them as part of the premium, if he uses the straight line method.[5] The additional final regulations, amended December 30, 1997, do not include the above rules.

Where there is more than one call date, the premium paid for a tax-exempt bond must be amortized to the *earliest* call date.[6] If the bond is not called at that date, the premium is then amortized down to the next lower call price, and so on to maturity.[7] The Service apparently reasons that because amortization is mandatory in the case of tax-exempt bonds, the entire premium must be subject to amortization.

> *Example:* A $100 bond is acquired at the time of issue for $125. The bond is callable in five years at $115 and in 10 years at $110. The individual may amortize $10 of the premium during the first five years and, if the bond is not then called, an additional $5 of premium during the next five

---

1. IRC Sec. 171(b)(3).
2. Treas. Reg. §1.171-2(a)(4)(ii).
3. Rev. Rul. 82-10, 1982-1 CB 46.
4. Treas. Reg. §1.171-2(f).
5. Treas. Reg. §1.171-2(d).
6. *Pacific Affiliate, Inc. v. Comm.*, 18 TC 1175 (1952), *aff'd*, 224 F.2d 578, *cert. den.*, 350 U.S. 967.
7. Rev. Rul. 60-17, 1960-1 CB 124.

years. If the bond is not called at the end of 10 years, the remaining $10 of premium must be amortized to maturity.

1128. Is premium paid on call of a tax-exempt bond before maturity tax-exempt interest?

No, it is a capital payment taxable as capital gain.[1] See Q 1125, if the bond was originally issued at a discount. For the treatment of capital gains and losses, see Q 1420.

1129. Is interest on a tax-exempt municipal bond paid by a private insurer because of default by the state or political subdivision tax-exempt?

Yes, interest that would have been tax-exempt if paid by the issuer will be tax-exempt if paid by a private insurer on the issuer's default.[2] It makes no difference whether the issuer or the underwriter pays the premium on insurance obtained by the issuer covering payment of the principal and interest or whether the individual investors obtain their own insurance.[3]

A bondholder, however, may *not* exclude from gross income interest paid or accrued under an agreement for defaulted interest if the agreement is not incidental to the bonds or is in substance a separate debt instrument or similar investment when purchased. If, at the time the contract is purchased, the premium is reasonable, customary, and consistent with the reasonable expectation that the issuer of the bonds, rather than the insurer will pay debt service on the bonds, then the agreement will be considered both incidental to the bonds and not a separate debt instrument or similar investment. Under these circumstances, a bondholder may exclude interest paid or accrued under an agreement for defaulted interest.[4]

If the interest or principal is guaranteed by the federal government, see Q 1130.

1130. Is interest on municipal bonds tax-exempt if payment is guaranteed by the United States or corporations established under federal law?

Interest on bonds issued by states, territories and possessions or their political subdivisions, which would otherwise be exempt from federal income tax, may not be exempt if payment of interest or principal is federally guaranteed.[5]

Generally, an obligation issued after 1983 is federally guaranteed if payment of principal or interest (in whole or in part, directly or indirectly) is guaranteed by: (1) the United States; (2) any U.S. agency; (3) under regulations to be prescribed; any entity with authority to borrow from the United States (the District of Columbia and U.S. possessions are usually excepted); or (4) if proceeds of the issue are to be used in making loans so guaranteed.[6]

---

1. Rev. Rul. 72-587, 1972-2 CB 74; GCM 39309 (11-28-84); see also Rev. Rul. 74-172, 1974-1 CB 178; *District Bond Co. v. Comm.*, 1 TC 837 (1943); *Bryant v. Comm.*, 2 TC 789 (1943), *acq.* 1944 CB 4.
2. Rev. Rul. 72-134, 1972-1 CB 29.
3. Rev. Rul. 72-575, 1972-2 CB 74; Rev. Rul. 76-78, 1976-1 CB 25.
4. Rev. Rul. 94-42, 1994-2 CB 15.
5. IRC Sec. 149(b)(1); Treas. Reg. §1.149(b)-1.
6. IRC Sec. 149(b).

Exceptions to this rule include certain bonds guaranteed by the Federal Housing Administration, the Veterans' Administration, the Federal National Mortgage Association, the Federal Home Loan Mortgage Corporation, the Government National Mortgage Association, and the Student Loan Marketing Association. Some housing program obligations and qualified mortgage bonds and veterans' mortgage bonds are also excepted, provided proceeds are not invested in federally insured deposits or accounts. Bonds issued or guaranteed by Connie Lee Insurance Company are not considered "federally guaranteed."[1]

Some state and local obligations are secured by certificates of deposit federally insured by the Savings Association Insurance Fund (SAIF–formerly the Federal Savings and Loan Insurance Corporation (FSLIC)) or the Federal Deposit Insurance Corporation (FDIC) up to $100,000 per bondholder. Bonds issued after April 14, 1983, other than any obligations issued pursuant to a binding contract in effect on March 4, 1983, are denied tax-exempt status if 5% or more of the proceeds of the issue are to be invested in federally insured deposits or accounts.[2]

The IRS ruled that interest on refunding bonds that were issued in an advance refunding of previously issued private activity bonds would be excludable from gross income under IRC Section 103(a).[3]

1131. Are interest and expense deductions limited because of ownership of municipal bonds?

If interest is paid on loans by an individual who owns tax-exempt municipal bonds, deduction of the interest may be partly or entirely denied (see Q 1306). In addition, some expense deductions may be denied to individuals holding obligations the interest on which is tax-exempt (see Q 1311).

1132. If the interest on an obligation issued by a state or local government is not tax-exempt, how is it taxed?

Short-term obligations issued on a discount basis and payable without interest at a fixed maturity date of one year or less are treated like U.S. Treasury bills (see Q 1092 to Q 1094).[4] Other bonds are treated like U.S. Treasury notes and bonds (see Q 1098 to Q 1101).[5]

BONDS TRADED "FLAT"

1133. How are buyer and seller taxed on a bond bought or sold "flat"?

Bonds on which interest or principal payments are in default may be quoted "flat", that is, without any allocation in the quoted price between accrued but unpaid interest and principal.

---

1. Notice 88-114, 1988-2 CB 449.
2. IRC Sec. 149(b)(2)(B).
3. Let. Rul. 200139007.
4. IRC Sec. 1271(a)(3); IRC Sec. 454(b).
5. IRC Secs. 1271 and 1272.

The purchaser of a bond quoted flat treats any payment he receives attributable to interest that accrued before he purchased the bond as a return of capital that reduces his basis. Amounts received in excess of his tax basis in the bond are capital gain.[1] They are not treated as interest.[2] Thus, if the bond is a tax-exempt municipal bond, return of interest accrued prior to acquisition reduces the owner's basis and any excess is taxable as capital gain; it is not tax-free interest.[3]

The owner of a bond, whether or not purchased flat, treats any payment of interest attributable to defaulted interest that accrued after he purchased the bond as interest when it is received. It does not make any difference whether the amounts are received from the obligor or from a purchaser, or whether or not the obligation is held to maturity.[4]

Thus, where the face amount and all interest accrued before and after purchase is paid in full on redemption of the bonds by the obligor, the amount of interest accrued after purchase is interest and the balance of the proceeds is return of capital, which is tax free to the extent of the purchaser's basis, and capital gain to the extent it exceeds basis.[5] See Q 1420 for the treatment of capital gains and losses.

But where the amount received on a flat sale or on redemption is less than the entire amount due (principal and interest), the amount recovered is allocated between principal and interest accruing while the seller held the bond under this formula:[6]

$$\frac{\text{purchase price allocable to interest accrued while seller owned bond}}{\text{amount received on sale}} = \frac{\text{face amount of interest accrued while seller owned bond}}{\text{face amount of principal and interest due at sale}}$$

However, the appeals court in *Jaglom* suggested (but did not decide because the question was not appealed) that where sale occurred in anticipation of imminent payment by the debtor, fair market value of principal and interest would be more appropriate in the formula than face value.

If a bond was held as part of a tax straddle, the additional rules and qualifications explained in Q 1077 to Q 1084 apply. If a bond was held as part of a conversion transaction, the rules as explained in Q 1085 and Q 1086 will apply.

ZERO COUPON BONDS

1134. What is a zero coupon bond? How is the owner taxed?

Zero coupon bonds are obligations payable without interest at a fixed maturity date and issued at a deep discount. Maturities can range from short-term to long-term.

1. *Rickaby v. Comm.*, 27 TC 886 (1957), *acq.* 1960-2 CB 6; Rev. Rul. 60-284, 1960-2 CB 464.
2. *First Ky. Co. v. Gray*, 190 F. Supp. 824 (W.D. Ky. 1960), *aff'd*, 309 F.2d 845 (6th Cir. 1962).
3. *R.O. Holton & Co. v. Comm.*, 44 BTA 202 (1941); *Noll v. Comm.*, 43 BTA 496 (1941).
4. *Fisher v. Comm.*, 209 F.2d 513 (6th Cir. 1954), *cert. den.*, 374 U.S. 1014; *Jaglom v. Comm.*, 36 TC 126 (1961), *aff'd*, 303 F.2d 847 (2d. Cir. 1961); *Tobey v. Comm.*, 26 TC 610 (1956), *acq.* 1956-2 CB 8; *Shattuck v. Comm.*, 25 TC 416 (1955); *First Ky. Co. v. Gray*, above; Rev. Rul. 60-284, above.
5. *Tobey v. Comm.*, above.
6. *Jaglom v. Comm.*, above. See also *First Ky. Co. v. Gray*, above, and *Shattuck v. Comm.*, above.

For tax purposes, they are considered original issue discount bonds, and the original issue discount is included in ordinary income depending on when issued, as explained in Q 1103 and Q 1116 to Q 1119.[1] In the case of a tax-exempt zero-coupon bond, the original issue discount is apportioned among holders as explained in Q 1117, but not included in income.[2]

STRIPPED BONDS

1135. What is a stripped bond?

It is a bond issued with interest coupons where the ownership of any unmatured coupon is separated from the ownership of the rest of the bond.[3] It may be a Treasury, corporate or municipal obligation. With respect to purchases after July 1, 1982, a coupon includes any right to interest.[4] In 2002, the Service released guidance on the application of the coupon stripping rules to certain fees payable out of mortgage payments received by mortgage pool trusts.[5]

1136. How is an individual taxed who sells separately the corpus or coupons of a taxable bond he originally acquired as a unit?

After July 1, 1982

If an individual strips one or more unmatured coupons (or rights to interest) from a taxable bond and, after July 1, 1982, disposes of the bonds or the coupon(s), the tax treatment is as follows:

(1) he must include in his income (a) any interest accrued but not yet due on the bond at the time of sale (and not already included in income), and (b) with respect to obligations acquired after October 22, 1986, any accrued market discount on the bond (not already included in income);

(2) he must then increase his tax basis in the bond and coupon(s) by the amount of accrued interest and market discount included in income ((1) above);

(3) he must allocate the tax basis immediately before disposition (as increased in (2) above) among the items retained and those disposed of in proportion to their respective fair market values;

(4) the individual is then treated as if he purchased on the date of disposition any part he retains for an amount equal to the basis allocated to the item. He is taxed on the part retained as if it were an original issue discount obligation issued on the date of purchase. The amount of OID is the excess of the amount payable at maturity of the bond or the due date of the coupon, whichever is applicable, over the purchase price. Under regulations effective after August 7, 1991, the discount is disregarded if it is less than ¼ of 1% (.0025) of the amount so payable multiplied by the full number of years from the date the stripped bond or coupon was purchased to final maturity.[6] A person who strips a taxable bond or coupon must include in income original issue discount on

---

1. Rev. Rul. 75-112, 1975-1 CB 274.
2. Rev. Rul. 73-112, 1973-1 CB 47.
3. IRC Sec. 1286(e)(2).
4. IRC Sec. 1286(e)(5).
5. See Chief Counsel Notice CC-2002-016 (January 24,2002).
6. Treas. Reg. §1.1286-1(a).

the part retained as it accrues without regard to whether it is considered a short-term or long-term obligation; and

(5) he recognizes gain or loss on the part he sells to the extent the amount realized exceeds or is less than the basis allocated to the part sold; the part he sells is treated by the buyer as an original issue discount bond issued on the date of purchase, as discussed in Q 1137.[1]

Transfers between spouses, or between former spouses if incident to divorce are discussed in Q 1447.[2]

Before July 2, 1982

A taxpayer who stripped bonds and then sold the bonds and retained the detached coupon properly allocated his entire basis to the stripped bonds and was not required, for purposes of determining loss, to allocate basis between the coupons he detached and retained and the stripped bonds he sold (as is required for transactions occurring after July 1, 1982).[3] However, he must treat the coupon as a right to interest, so that on sale or redemption of the coupons, the entire proceeds are interest.[4]

1137. How is an individual taxed if he buys a stripped taxable bond corpus or coupons?

After July 1, 1982

A stripped taxable bond or coupon is considered, for tax purposes, as an original issue discount bond issued at the time of purchase. The discount is the amount by which the stated redemption price at maturity of the bond, or the amount payable on the due date of the coupon, exceeds its ratable share of the purchase price.[5] Under regulations effective after August 7, 1991, the discount is disregarded if it is less than ¼ of 1% (.0025) of the amount so payable multiplied by the full number of years from the date the stripped bond or coupon was purchased to final maturity.[6]

The owner must include in income each year a portion of the discount and increase his tax basis each year by the amount included (see Q 1116). (Ratable shares of the purchase price are determined on the basis of respective fair market values on the date of purchase.) The amount of discount that accrues each day is determined the same way as the amount of original issue discount on an OID bond that has not been stripped, using the acquisition price instead of issue price in the formula and increasing the acquisition price each accrual period by the amount accrued in the previous period. A stripped coupon has no stated interest for purposes of the formula (see Q 1116). On sale or redemption, any gain or loss is generally capital gain or loss. Where leveraging is used to purchase or carry stripped coupons or bonds (acquired after July 18, 1984) that are payable not more than one year from the date of purchase, it is possible, but not at all clear, that the rules deferring the deductibility of interest expense on short-term obligations may apply (see Q 1307).[7]

1. IRC Sec. 1286.
2. IRC Sec. 1041.
3. TAM 8602006.
4. Rev. Rul. 58-275, 1958-1 CB 22.
5. IRC Sec. 1286(a).
6. Treas. Reg. §1.1286-1(a).
7. See General Explanation–TRA '84, pp. 92, 102.

On or Before July 1, 1982

On sale of a *bond* that was bought without all unmatured coupons before July 2, 1982 and after December 31, 1957 (or purchased on or before December 31, 1957 but after August 16, 1954 without all coupons maturing more than 12 months after the date of purchase), any gain recognized must be treated as ordinary income up to the amount by which the fair market value the obligation would have had at the time of purchase *with* the coupons was greater than the actual price the individual paid for the bond without the coupons.[1] Gain in excess of that amount may generally be treated as capital gain;[2] however, the bond, if originally issued at a discount, may also be subject to the rules discussed in Q 1118.

On sale of *coupons* bought separately from the bond corpus, any interest accrued but not due at the time an individual purchased a detached coupon and that he paid the seller is recovered tax free. Any additional gain *on sale* of coupons bought separately prior to maturity is capital gain, but the same gain *on redemption* at maturity is ordinary income.[3] Where a series of coupons is purchased in a block, the cost is allocated among the individual coupons by taking their maturity dates into account.[4]

1138. If tax-exempt bonds are stripped, how are the purchaser and seller of the stripped bond or coupons taxed?

If an individual strips one or more unmatured coupons from a tax-exempt bond and, after July 1, 1982, disposes of the bond or the coupon(s), he must increase the tax basis of the bond by any interest accrued but not paid up to the time of disposition and allocate this tax basis between the items disposed of and the items retained, in proportion to their respective fair market values. (He does not include the interest in income.) If he strips coupons after October 22, 1986, he must also increase his basis by accrued original issue discount prior to allocation of basis among the items retained and the items disposed of. The calculation of this original issue discount is explained below. If an individual strips coupons after June 10, 1987, he must also calculate the amount of original issue discount that is allocable to the "tax-exempt portion" of the stripped bond or coupon. Any excess over this amount will be treated as original issue discount attributable to a taxable obligation.[5]

After June 10, 1987

In the case of a tax-exempt bond stripped after June 10, 1987, a portion of the original issue discount may be treated as if it comes from a taxable obligation. The "tax-exempt portion" of the original issue discount is the excess of the obligation's stated redemption price at maturity (or the amount payable on a coupon's due date) over an issue price that would produce a yield to maturity as of the purchase date of the stripped bond or coupon equal to the lower of (1) the coupon rate of interest on the obligation from which the coupons were stripped, or (2) the yield to maturity (on the basis of the purchase price) of the stripped coupon or bond. Alternatively, the purchaser may use the original yield to maturity in (1), above, rather than the coupon rate of interest.[6]

---

1. IRC Sec. 1286(c); Treas. Reg. §1.1232-4.
2. *Hood v. Comm.*, TC Memo 1961-231.
3. Rev. Rul. 58-536, 1958-2 CB 21; Rev. Rul. 54-251, 1954-2 CB 172.
4. Rev. Rul. 54-251, above.
5. IRC Sec. 1286(d).
6. IRC Sec. 1286(d).

Any original issue discount in excess of the "tax-exempt portion" will be treated as discount on an obligation that is not tax-exempt.[1] The person who strips the bond increases his basis by any interest and market discount accrued on the bond but not yet paid before the disposition, to the extent that such amounts have not previously been reflected in his basis.[2]

October 23, 1986 through June 10, 1987

In the case of a tax-exempt bond stripped after October 22, 1986 and before June 11, 1987, the amount of original issue discount that is added to the basis of the person who strips the bond is the amount that produces a yield to maturity (as of the purchase date) equal to the lower of (1) the coupon rate before the separation or (2) the yield to maturity (on the basis of purchase price) of the stripped obligation or coupon. The holder increases his basis by this amount (prior to allocating his basis between the parts retained and disposed of) and is then treated as having purchased on the date of disposition any part he retains for an amount equal to the tax basis allocated to the retained item.[3]

An individual who purchased a stripped tax-exempt bond or coupon after October 22, 1986 but before June 11, 1987 (except as provided below) is treated as if he bought a tax-exempt obligation issued on the purchase date having an original issue discount equal to an amount that produces a yield to maturity of the lower of: (a) the coupon rate of interest before separation, or (b) the yield to maturity, on the basis of purchase price, of the obligation or coupon.[4] The holder's basis is adjusted to reflect the discount so determined as it accrues at a constant interest rate, but the accruing discount is not included in income.[5] This rule also applies to obligations purchased after June 10, 1987 if such bond or coupon was held in stripped form by the dealer on June 10, 1987.

Before October 23, 1986

An individual who purchased after December 31, 1957 and before October 23, 1986, a stripped tax-exempt bond without *all* unmatured coupons (or after August 16, 1954 but before January 1, 1958 without all coupons maturing more than 12 months after purchase) treats, on his subsequent disposition of the bond, any gain as *ordinary income* to the extent the fair market value with coupons attached exceeds the actual purchase price.[6] The IRC does not clarify, for purposes of these pre-October 23, 1986 purchases, whether "ordinary income" is to be treated as tax-exempt interest.

UNITED STATES SAVINGS BONDS

1139. When is the interest on United States Savings Bonds Series E or EE taxed?

United States savings bonds (Series E before 1980 and Series EE after), including Patriot Bonds (see below) are issued on a noninterest bearing discount basis. Interest accrues at stated intervals and becomes part of the redemption value paid when the bond is cashed or finally matures. The difference between the price paid and the larger

---

1. IRC Sec. 1286(d)(1)(A)(ii).
2. IRC Sec. 1286(d)(1)(C).
3. IRC Sec. 1286(d), prior to amendment by TAMRA '88.
4. IRC Sec. 1286(d).
5. IRC Sec. 1286(d)(2), prior to amendment by TAMRA '88.
6. IRC Sec. 1286(d) (prior to amendment by TRA '86).

redemption value is interest. Savings bonds continue to accrue interest after the stated maturity until the Treasury announces discontinuance of payments, generally after 30 years. For the new method of calculating interest, see "New fixed interest rates," below. This interest is subject to all federal taxes (unless it qualifies for the exclusion described in Q 1141), and the bonds are subject to federal and state estate, inheritance, gift or other excise taxes, but not state or local taxes on principal or interest.[1] Bonds held less than five years from issue date are subject to a 3-month interest penalty.

Minimum holding period. In 2003, the Treasury Department extended the minimum holding period applicable to United States savings bonds from 6 to 12 months, effective with issues dated on and after February 1, 2003. The minimum holding period is the length of time from issue date that a bond must be held before it is eligible for redemption. Both Series EE and Series I savings bonds are affected. Series EE and Series I savings bonds bearing issue dates prior to February 1, 2003 retain the 6-month holding period in effect when they were issued.[2]

New fixed interest rates. The Treasury Department has announced that Series EE savings bonds issued on and after May 1, 2005, will earn fixed, instead of variable, rates of interest.[3] Previously, a new variable rate was announced each May 1 and November 1, and applied to bonds during the first semiannual rate period beginning on or after the effective date of the rate. Consequently, a Series EE bond purchased prior to May 1, 2005, earned a new rate of interest every six months. However, a Series EE bond purchased on or after May 1, 2005, will have one rate of interest that will continue for the life of the bond (although a different rate or method of determining the rate may be used for any extended maturity period).

The interest rate for a Series EE bond issued on or after May 1, 2005, will be a fixed rate of interest as determined by the Secretary of the Treasury and announced each May 1 and November 1. The most recently announced fixed rate will apply to Series EE bonds purchased during the six months following the announcement (or for any other period of time announced by the Secretary). The fixed rate will be established for the life of the bond, including the extended maturity period, unless the Secretary announces a different fixed rate or amends the terms and conditions prior to the beginning of the extended maturity period. All other Series EE terms and conditions remain unchanged. These changes do not affect bonds that were purchased before May 1, 2005.[4]

Deferred reporting of interest. An owner of E, EE or Series I savings bonds (see Q 1144) who reports on a cash basis may treat the increase in redemption value, for federal income tax purposes, either of two ways:

(1) he may defer reporting the increase to the year of maturity, redemption, or other disposition, whichever is earlier; or

(2) he may elect to treat the increase as income each year as it accrues.[5]

Ordinarily, an election made by the owner of an E, EE or I bond to report interest annually applies to all E, EE and I bonds he then owns or subsequently acquires.[6]

---

1. 31 CFR §351.8(a).
2. See News Release (1-15-2003) at: http://publicdebt.treas.gov/.
3. See News Release (4-4-2005), at: http://www.publicdebt.treas.gov/com/comeefixedrate.htm.
4. See Final Rule, Offering of United States Savings Bonds, Series EE, 31 CFR Part 351, 70 Fed. Reg. 17288 (4-5-2005).
5. IRC Sec. 454(a).
6. See IRS Pub. 550.

However, a taxpayer who reports interest annually may elect to change to deferred reporting with automatic consent of the IRS, provided certain requirements are met. To obtain *automatic consent* for the taxable year for which the change is requested, the taxpayer may file a *statement* in lieu of Form 3115.[1] The statement must be identified at the top as follows: "CHANGE IN METHOD OF ACCOUNTING UNDER SECTION 6.01 OF THE APPENDIX OF REV. PROC. 2002-9." The statement must set forth:

(i) the Series E, EE, or I savings bonds for which the change in accounting method is requested;

(ii) an agreement to report all interest on any bonds acquired during or after the year of change when the interest is realized upon disposition, redemption, or final maturity, whichever is earliest; and

(iii) an agreement to report all interest on the bonds acquired before the year of change when the interest is realized upon disposition, redemption, or final maturity, whichever is earliest, with the exception of any interest income previously reported in prior taxable years.

The statement must include the name and Social Security number of the taxpayer underneath the heading.[2] The change is effective for any increase in redemption price occurring after the beginning of the year of change for all Series E, EE, and I savings bonds held by the taxpayer on or after the beginning of the year of change.[3] The taxpayer must attach the signed statement to his tax return for the year of the change, which must be filed by the due date (including extensions).[4] (Alternatively, instead of filing the statement, the taxpayer can request permission to change from deferred reporting to annual reporting by filing Form 3115 and following the form instructions for an automatic change.) If the taxpayer is precluded from using the automatic consent procedure under Rev. Proc. 2002-9, above, the taxpayer must file Form 3115 in accordance with the regulations.[5]

Taxpayers may switch from deferred reporting to annual reporting in any year without permission; however, an election under Revenue Procedure 2002-9 may not be made more than once in any 5-year period.[6] The year of change is *included* within the 5-year prohibition regarding prior changes.[7]

The election to treat accruing interest as income annually is made by including the interest in gross income on the owner's tax return for the year he makes the election.[8] It may not be made by amended return.[9] He must include (in the year he elects to report interest annually) the increase in the redemption price of all his E, EE, and I bonds that has occurred since the date of acquisition. If he owns any bond (such as H or HH) that retains interest deferred on an E or EE bond, that interest must also be reported.[10] After making the election, he must include the actual increase in redemption value that occurs on the stated intervals in each year. (This is not necessarily the amount that would accrue ratably.)[11]

1.   Rev. Proc. 2002-9, 2002-1 CB 327, Appendix 6.01.
2.   See IRS Pub. 550.
3.   Rev. Proc. 2002-9, above, Appendix Sec. 6.01.
4.   IRS Pub. 550.
5.   Rev. Proc. 2002-9, above, Sec. 4.03.
6.   See Rev. Proc. 2002-9, above, Sec. 4.02(6); IRC Sec. 454; 31 CFR §351.8(b).
7.   Rev. Proc. 2002-9, above, Sec. 4.02(6).
8.   IRC Sec. 454(a).
9.   Rev. Rul. 55-655, 1955-2 CB 253.
10. IRC Sec. 454(a).
11. Treas. Reg. §1.454-1(a)(2).

A bond owner whose income is not sufficient to require filing a return is not deemed to have automatically elected to treat accruing interest as income; however, the election may be made by filing a return reporting the interest, even though no return is otherwise required.[1]

A previous election to report annual increases in redemption value does not bind anyone to whom the bond is transferred.[2] For example, an executor who elects to include deferred interest in an estate's income is not bound by the election to report annually when the bond is transferred to him in his capacity as trustee of a trust created under a will.[3]

To the extent the increase in redemption value (interest) has not been includable in gross income previously by the taxpayer or any other taxpayer, it is included by a cash basis taxpayer for the tax year in which the obligation is redeemed or disposed of.[4] (For an explanation of the exclusion for interest on certain Series EE and Series I bonds used for educational expenses, see Q 1141.) If the obligation is partially redeemed or partially disposed of by being partially reissued to another person, the increase is included in income by the taxpayer in proportion to the total denominations redeemed or disposed of.[5]

Similarly, where Series E and EE bonds were transferred incident to a divorce, the transferor was required to include unrecognized interest as income in the year of transfer. The transferee's basis in such bonds was adjusted by adding the amount of interest includable by the transferor.[6]

Previously, an individual could, at maturity or before, exchange a Series E or EE bond for a Series HH bond (or Series H bond before 1980–but see *Editor's Note*, Q 1143) without recognizing the unreported interest, except that he must report the interest to the extent he receives cash in the exchange.[7]

Transfer of an E/EE bond to a revocable personal trust does not require inclusion of unreported interest in income because the grantor continues to be considered the owner of the bonds.[8] Reissuance of a Series H bond (received in exchange of a Series E bond on which reporting of interest has been deferred) to a trustee of a trust where the trust corpus will revert to the grantor and any previously unreported interest is allocable to corpus, will not result in inclusion of the previously unreported interest in the grantor's income. He will include the interest in his gross income in the year the bond is redeemed, disposed of, or reaches final maturity.[9]

Surrender of an E bond, bought entirely with his own funds, by one co-owner for reissue in the sole name of the other co-owner causes recognition of unreported appreciation to the date of reissue in the purchasing co-owner's name (see also Q 1540

---

1. *Apkin v. Comm.*, 86 TC 692 (1986).
2. Treas. Reg. §1.454-1(a).
3. Rev. Rul. 58-435, 1958-2 CB 370.
4. See, e.g., *Landers v. Comm.*, TC Memo 2003.
5. Treas. Reg. §1.454-1(c).
6. Rev. Rul. 87-112, 1987-2 CB 207.
7. IRC Sec. 1037(a); TD Circular, Pub. Debt Series No. 1-80, 1980-1 CB 715; 31 CFR §352.7(g)(3).
8. Rev. Rul. 58-2, 1958-1 CB 236; Let. Rul. 9009053.
9. Rev. Rul. 64-302, 1964-2 CB 170.

regarding the gift).[1] However, if the bond is reissued in the sole name of the co-owner who originally purchased the bond with his own funds there is no taxable transaction.[2]

Patriot Bonds. Patriot Bonds are regular Series EE Savings Bonds specially inscribed with the legend "Patriot Bond." As with regular Series EE Savings Bonds, Patriot Bonds are sold at one-half of face value ($50, $75, $100, $200, $500, $1,000, $5,000, and $10,000). Patriot Bonds earn 90% of 5-year Treasury security yields. Patriot Bonds increase in value monthly, but interest is compounded semiannually. Interest on Patriot Bonds is exempt from state and local income taxes; federal tax can be deferred until the bond is redeemed or it stops earning interest (in 30 years). Patriot bonds can be redeemed anytime after six months for issue dates of January 2003 and earlier; bonds with issue dates on or after February 1, 2003 can be cashed anytime after 12 months. Depending on interest rates, bonds may actually reach face value anywhere between 12 and 17 years. However, a 3-month interest penalty is applied to bonds redeemed before five years. Patriot Bonds can be purchased in person at banks or credit unions, or on the Internet at: http:www.savingsbonds.gov.[3]

1140. Can a child owning Series E or EE bonds elect to include interest?

According to IRS Publication 550 (2004), if a child is the owner of an E, EE, or I bond, the election to report interest annually may be made by the child or by the parent. The choice is made by filing a return showing all the interest earned through the year and stating that the child is electing to report interest each year. The child then does not have to file another return until he or she has enough gross income during a year to require filing.

A child could elect to change from annual to deferred reporting under Revenue Procedure 89-46. This provision is not included in the current revenue procedure governing such elections.[4] However, Publication 550 states that neither the parent nor the child can change the way that interest is reported unless permission from the IRS is requested (in accordance with the procedures outlined in Q 1139). Thus, it appears that a child may make such election. If the election is available, the parent of a child making such an election may sign Form 3115 on behalf of the child. See Q 1411 for an explanation of the taxation and filing requirements of children under age 14.

1141. May the interest on Series EE or Series I bonds used to meet education expenses be excluded from income?

Subject to certain limitations and phaseout rules, interest on *qualified United States savings bonds* may be excluded from gross income to the extent that the proceeds are used to pay *qualified higher education expenses* during the taxable year in which the redemption occurs. The exclusion is available only to taxpayers whose *modified adjusted gross income* falls within certain ranges.[5]

---

1. Rev. Rul. 55-278, 1955-1 CB 471.
2. Rev. Rul. 68-61, 1968-1 CB 346.
3. See Treasury Press Release, *Treasury Department Unveils Patriot Bond on 3-Month Anniversary of September 11 Attacks* (December 22, 2001).
4. See Rev. Proc. 2002-9, 2002-1 CB 327.
5. IRC Sec. 135.

The special tax benefits available for education savings with Series EE bonds also apply to Series I (inflation-indexed) savings bonds, provided the requirements set forth below are satisfied.[1] For the treatment of inflation-indexed savings bonds, see Q 1144.

Definitions

Qualified United States savings bonds are any United States savings bonds issued (i) after 1989, (ii) to an individual who has attained age 24 before the date of issuance.[2] The "date of issuance" is the first day of the month the bonds are purchased; therefore, a purchaser who has just reached the age of 24 and wishes to take advantage of the exclusion should purchase the bonds in the month following his birthday.[3]

Qualified higher education expenses are tuition and fees required for enrollment or attendance at an eligible educational institution or certain vocational education schools. Qualified higher education expenses do not include amounts by which educational fees are reduced by items such as scholarships, grants, employer provided educational assistance, or other amounts that reduce tuition. The term also does not include expenses with respect to any course or other education involving sports, games, or hobbies other than as part of a degree program. The IRC specifies "tuition and fees required for enrollment or attendance ... at an eligible educational institution"; the term does not include expenses incurred for room and board or travel expenses to and from college.[4]

Qualified higher education expenses include any contribution to a qualified tuition program (formerly known as a qualified *state* tuition program – see Q 1413) on behalf of a designated beneficiary or to a Coverdell Education Savings Account (formerly known as an Education Individual Retirement Account – see Q 1412) on behalf of an account beneficiary, who is the taxpayer, the taxpayer's spouse, or any dependent with respect to whom the taxpayer is allowed a dependency exemption (see Q 1426).[5] For purposes of applying the rules applicable to qualified tuition programs under IRC Section 529, the investment in the contract is not increased because of any portion of the contribution to the program that is not includable in gross income as a qualified higher education expense.[6]

The rules allowing the exclusion of interest on qualified United States savings bonds are coordinated with the Hope and Lifetime Learning Credits (see Q 1438). Generally, the amount of the qualified higher education expenses otherwise taken into account under IRC Section 135(a) with respect to the education of an individual is reduced by the amount of the qualified higher education expenses taken into account in determining the credit allowable to the taxpayer or any other person under the rules for the Hope and Lifetime Learning credits with respect to qualified higher education expenses. Likewise, the rules allowing the exclusion of interest on qualified United States savings bonds are also coordinated with the amounts taken into account in determining the exclusions for qualified tuition programs (see Q 1413) and Coverdell Education Savings Account distributions (see Q 1412).[7] The above amounts are reduced before the application of the interest limitation and phaseout rules (see below).

1. See 31 CFR §359.10.
2. IRC Sec. 135(c)(1).
3. Notice 90-7, 1990-1 CB 304.
4. IRC Secs. 135(c), 135(d); See Instructions to Form 8815.
5. IRC Sec. 135(c)(2)(C).
6. IRC Sec. 135(c)(2)(C).
7. IRC Sec. 135(d)(2).

Modified adjusted gross income refers to adjusted gross income (AGI) determined without regard to this exclusion and without regard to IRC Sections 137 (exclusions for qualified adoption expenses), 221 (deduction for student loan interest), 222 (deduction for higher education expenses, which expires 12-31-2007), 911, 931, or 933, (exclusions of foreign earned income or income earned in certain possessions of the United States) but determined *after* application of IRC Sections 86, (partial inclusion of Social Security and railroad retirement benefits), 469 (adjustments with respect to limitations of passive activity losses and credits) and 219 (adjustments for contributions to IRAs and SEPs).[1]

Limitations and Phaseout

If the aggregate proceeds of the bond exceed the amount of expenses paid, the amount of the exclusion is limited to an "applicable fraction" of the interest otherwise excludable. Essentially, this calculation simply reduces the amount of excludable interest pro rata, based on the proportion of educational expenses to redemption amounts. The numerator of the "applicable fraction" is the amount of expenses paid; the denominator is the aggregate proceeds redeemed. For example, a taxpayer whose Series EE bonds have reached maturity may exclude the amount of redemption, up to the amount of fees paid; generally, half of any excess bond proceeds will be treated as taxable interest and the other half as a return of principal. If the qualified education expenses equal or exceed the proceeds of the redemption, this limitation does not apply.[2]

An additional limitation is imposed by means of a phase-out rule, designed to confine the tax benefit to lower and middle income taxpayers. The exclusion is phased out beginning at the following levels of modified adjusted gross income in the 2007 tax year; single or head of household – $65,600; married filing jointly – $98,400. The range over which the phaseout occurs is $15,000 (single) or $30,000 (joint return); thus the exclusion is fully phased out at $80,600 for single filers, or $128,400 for married individuals filing jointly.[3] (The exclusion is not available to married taxpayers filing separately.) The income levels at which the phase-out begins are indexed for inflation and rounded to the nearest $50.[4]

The phaseout amount for tax years beginning in 2007 is calculated as follows:

1. A fraction is determined as follows: (a) the numerator is the excess of the taxpayer's modified adjusted gross income for 2007 over $65,600 (single or head of household) or $98,400 (married filing jointly; (b) the denominator is $15,000 (single or head of household), or $30,000 (joint return). For example, for a single or head of household taxpayer with modified adjusted gross income of $70,600 the ratio would be $5,000 to $15,000, or one-third.

2. The amount otherwise excludable is reduced by that proportion. In the example above, an otherwise permitted exclusion of $12,000 would be reduced by one-third, to $8,000.

---

1. IRC Sec. 135(c)(4).
2. IRC Sec. 135(b)(1).
3. Rev. Proc. 2006-53, 2006-48 IRB 996.
4. IRC Sec. 135 (b)(2)(B).

The operation of both limitations may be seen in the following example:

> *Example*: Mr. and Mrs. Mabry pay $18,000 in tuition expenses and redeem savings bonds of $20,000 in 2007. They file jointly and their modified adjusted gross income is $108,400.

> *Exclusion limitation:* Of the $20,000 redemption amount, assume that $10,000 is return of principal and $10,000 is interest. Since less than $20,000 was spent on tuition, the exclusion is limited to the amount that represents the proportion of tuition payments to redemption proceeds. The applicable fraction is $18,000/$20,000. Thus, $9,000 of the $10,000 interest is *potentially* excludable and $1,000 would be taxed as ordinary income.

> *Phaseout amount:* The threshold amount in 2007 for the phase-out of the exclusion is $98,400 (joint return), and their $108,400 modified adjusted gross income is $10,000 over that amount. The ratio of $10,000 to $30,000 is one-third, therefore their *otherwise excludable* interest ($9,000) is reduced by one-third, leaving $6,000 that may be excluded from income.

There are several additional rules governing the savings bond exclusion and limiting the potential for abuse of it. The taxpayer must be the original and sole owner of the bond (or own it jointly with his spouse).[1] A bond purchased from another individual will not qualify for the exclusion. The taxpayer purchasing the bond must have attained the age of 24 by the date of issuance. (This rule prevents savings bonds that are purchased in a child's name to avoid the "kiddie tax" from obtaining preferred treatment when redeemed.) The tuition expenses must be for the taxpayer, the taxpayer's spouse, or a dependent of the taxpayer (with respect to whom he can claim a dependency exemption). The exclusion is not available for bonds obtained as part of a tax-free rollover of Series E savings bonds into Series EE bonds.[2]

1142. How is interest on a Series E or EE bond taxed after the death of the owner?

An executor or administrator may make an election on behalf of a decedent (who has not previously elected) to include all interest in the decedent's final income tax return.[3] If the decedent or his representative had not elected to include interest in the decedent's gross income annually, all interest earned before and after death is income to the estate or other beneficiary receiving the bond, either on his election to include interest annually or on redemption, final maturity or disposal of the bond. Either may defer reporting or elect to report just as any owner (see Q 1139).

Unreported interest earned on E and EE bonds up to the date of death and unreported interest that was part of the consideration for H and HH bonds held at death, are income in respect of a decedent.[4] The person who eventually includes the deferred interest in income may take a deduction in the year he reports the interest for any estate tax attributable to the income in respect of a decedent (see Q 1430).[5] The Service has ruled that in determining the fair market value of Series E savings bonds for estate tax purposes, the estate should not calculate a discount for lack of marketability for the income taxes due on the interest that accrued on the bonds from the date of purchase to the date of maturity.[6]

---

1. Conference Committee Report, TAMRA '88.
2. Conference Committee Report, TAMRA '88.
3. Rev. Rul. 68-145, 1968-1 CB 203; Rev. Rul. 79-409, 1979-2 CB 208.
4. See Let. Rul. 9024016.
5. See Treas. Regs. §§1.691(a)-2(b) Ex. 3, 1.691(b)-1(a); Rev. Rul. 64-104, 1964-1 CB 223.
6. See TAM 200303010.

Like the owner of any other E or EE bond, the owner of E and EE bonds acquired from a decedent could exchange them for Series HH bonds (or H bonds before 1980 – but see *Editor's Note*, below) without recognition of unreported interest.[1] However, the interest must be included in income on disposal, redemption or final maturity of the H or HH bonds received in the exchange, or on the election of the owner to report annually interest on E and EE bonds. (*Editor's Note*: The Bureau of the Public Debt stopped offering Series HH Savings Bonds to the public after August 31, 2004. HH bonds issued through August 2004 will continue to earn interest until they reach final maturity 20 years after issue. HH bonds, issued since 1980, are available in exchange for Series E or EE bonds.[2])

The Service privately ruled that: (1) the distribution of Series E and Series HH savings bonds from a decedent's estate to several tax-exempt organizations did not result in the recognition of income by the estate; (2) the accrued interest attributable to the bonds would be includable in the gross income of the exempt organizations in the year in which the bonds were disposed of, redeemed, or reached maturity; and (3) assuming that the organizations continued their exempt status, the accrued interest would be exempt when recognized by the organizations.[3]

1143. How is the owner of Series H or HH bonds taxed?

Editor's Note: The Bureau of the Public Debt stopped offering Series HH Savings Bonds to the public after August 31, 2004. HH bonds issued through August 2004 will continue to earn interest until they reach final maturity 20 years after issue. HH bonds, issued since 1980, are available in exchange for Series E or EE bonds.[4]

Series H and HH bonds are interest-paying United States savings bonds. Interest is paid by check semiannually, and the amounts paid in a year are included in gross income.[5] The bonds are nontransferable. Interest received on H/HH bonds is subject to all federal taxes, and the bonds are subject to federal and state estate, gift, inheritance, or other excise taxes but not to state or local taxes on principal or interest.[6]

If H or HH bonds were received in exchange for E or EE bonds on which reporting of interest was deferred, the owner may continue to defer reporting the interest accrued on the E or EE bonds exchanged until the year in which the H or HH bonds received in the exchange reach final maturity, are redeemed, or are otherwise disposed of. At that time, the amount of unreported interest on the E or EE bonds that was not recognized at the time of the exchange must be reported as interest.[7] HH bonds bear a legend showing how much of the issue price represents interest on the securities exchanged. The owner of Series H or HH bonds received in exchange for E or EE bonds on which reporting was deferred, may elect to report the past increases in redemption value of the E or EE bonds. The election would also apply to any other E or EE bonds or H or HH bonds he owns or thereafter acquires in any subsequent years, unless the Service permits him to change his method of reporting.[8]

---

1. Rev. Rul. 64-104, above.
2. See Press Release (2-18-2004), at: www.publicdebt.treas.gov/com/comtdhhw.htm.
3. Let. Rul 9845026.
4. See Press Release (2-18-2004), at: www.publicdebt.treas.gov/com/comtdhhw.htm.
5. 31 CFR §352.2(e)(1)(i).
6. 31 CFR §352.10.
7. 31 CFR §352.7(g).
8. Rev. Rul. 64-89, 1964-1 (part 1) CB 172.

The Service privately ruled that: (1) the distribution of Series E and Series HH savings bonds from a decedent's estate to several tax-exempt organizations did not result in the recognition of income by the estate; (2) the accrued interest attributable to the bonds would be includable in the gross income of the exempt organizations in the year in which the bonds were disposed of, redeemed, or reached maturity; and (3) assuming that the organizations continued their exempt status, the accrued interest would be exempt when recognized by the organizations.[1]

1144. How is the owner of Series I bonds taxed?

In 1998, the Treasury Department began offering a type of savings bonds whose rates are adjusted for inflation. Series I (inflation-indexed) savings bonds are sold at par value (face amount) in denominations ranging from $50 to $10,000.[2] An individual can purchase no more than $30,000 in Series I bonds during any calendar year.[3] The difference between the purchase price and the redemption value is taxable interest, which is payable when the bond is redeemed or finally matures.[4] Series I savings bonds mature in 30 years.[5]

Series I savings bonds accrue earnings based on *both* a fixed rate of return *and* the semiannual inflation rate.[6] A single rate is constructed to reflect the combined effects of the two rates.[7] The following example demonstrates how the *composite earnings rate* is determined:

> *Example*: The 4.52% composite earnings rate for Series I savings bonds bought from November 2006 through April 2007, applies for the first six months after their issue. The earnings rate combines the 1.40% fixed rate with the 1.55% semiannual inflation rate (as measured by the Consumer Price Index for all Urban Consumers (CPI-CU)).[8]
>
> The formula for computing the composite rate is:
>
> Composite rate = [Fixed rate + (2 x semiannual inflation rate) + (fixed rate x semiannual inflation rate)]
>
> For 2007, the composite rate is calculated as follows:
>
> Composite rate = [0.0140 + (2 x 0.0155) + (0.0140 x 0.0155)]
>
> Composite rate = [0.0140 + 0.0310 + 0.0002170]
>
> Composite rate = [0.045217]
>
> Composite rate = 0.0452
>
> Composite rate = 4.52%

The fixed rate of return, applicable at the time a Series I savings bond is issued, will apply to the bond throughout its 30-year life.[9] The semiannual inflation rate, an-

---

1. Let. Rul 9845026.
2. 31 CFR §359.2(b).
3. 31 CFR §359.5.
4. 31 CFR §359.9(a), 31 CFR §359.2(e)(4).
5. 31 CFR §359.2(c), 31 CFR §359.2(e)(1)(xi).
6. 31 CFR §359.2(e)(1)(v).
7. 31 CFR §359.2(e)(1)(v).
8. See 31 CFR §359.2(e)(v).
9. 31 CFR §359.2(e)(1)(ii).

nounced each May and November, will be reflected in a Series I savings bond's value beginning on that bond's next semiannual interest period following the announcement.[1] In general, a bond's composite rate will be higher than its fixed rate if the semiannual inflation rate reflects any inflation. In other words, inflation will cause a bond to earn additional interest. Likewise, a bond's composite rate will be lower than its fixed rate if the semiannual inflation rate reflects any deflation. Deflation will cause a bond to increase in value slowly, or not increase in value at all. However, even if deflation becomes so great that it would reduce the composite rate to below zero, the Treasury will not allow the value of a bond to decrease from its most recent redemption value.[2]

A Series I savings bond may be redeemed anytime after six months for issue dates of January 2003 and earlier. Bonds with issue dates on or after February 1, 2003 can be cashed anytime after 12 months. A bond redeemed less than five years from the date of issue will be subject to a 3-month interest penalty.[3] Tables of redemption values are made available in various formats and media, including the Internet.[4] The bonds have an interest paying life of 30 years after the date of issue, and cease to increase in value as of that date.[5]

Interest earned on Series I savings bonds is subject to all federal taxes (unless it qualifies for the exclusion described in Q 1141), and the bonds are subject to federal and state estate, inheritance, gift or other excise taxes, but not state or local taxes on principal or interest.[6]

Interest earned on Series I savings bonds is includable on federal income tax returns in the same way as Series EE bonds (see Q 1139).[7] In general, owners may defer reporting the increment for federal income tax purposes until: (i) they redeem the bonds, (ii) the bonds cease earning interest after 30 years, or (iii) the bonds are otherwise disposed of, whichever is earlier.[8] However, an owner may elect to accrue the increment each year it is earned.[9] If an investor takes no action, the gain is deferred until the first of the three events described above occurs.[10] The increase in value will be includable in income annually *only* if an investor affirmatively acts by making such an election.[11]

The special tax benefits available for education savings with Series EE bonds also apply to Series I savings bonds.[12] (See Q 1141.) Essentially, a taxpayer who otherwise satisfies the requirements set forth in IRC Section 135 (see Q 1141) may be able to exclude all or part of the interest earned on Series I savings bonds from income for that tax year.[13]

Series I savings bonds are nontransferable.[14] Although these bonds can be exchanged for Series EE savings bond, they can no longer be exchanged for Series HH savings

1. 31 CFR §359.2(e)(1)(iii).
2. U.S. Treasury Department, *Series I Bonds: Information Statement*, p. 6.
3. 31 CFR §359.2(d), 31 CFR §359.2(e)(3).
4. 31 CFR §359.2(e)(6).
5. 31 CFR §359.2(e)(1)(xi).
6. 31 CFR §359.9(a).
7. 31 CFR §359.9(a).
8. 31 CFR §359.9(b)(1)(i).
9. 31 CFR §359.9(b)(1)(ii).
10. See 31 CFR §359.9(b).
11. 31 CFR §359.9(b)(1)(ii).
12. 31 CFR §359.10.
13. 31 CFR §359.10.
14. 31 CFR §360.15.

bonds because the Bureau of Public Debt stopped offering Series HH bonds to the public effective August 31, 2004.

MORTGAGE BACKED SECURITIES

1145. What is a "Ginnie Mae" mortgage backed pass-through certificate?

A Ginnie Mae pass-through certificate represents ownership of a proportionate interest in a fixed pool of mortgages insured or guaranteed by the Federal Housing Administration (FHA), the Department of Veteran's Affairs (VA), the Department of Agriculture's Rural Housing Service (RHS), and the Department of Housing and Urban Development's Office of Public and Indian Housing (PIH). The mortgages in the pool have the same interest rate, term to maturity and type of dwelling. The certificates are generally issued by a mortgage banker or savings and loan association and are secured by the pool of mortgages that have been placed by the issuer with a bank custodian. They call for payment by the issuer of specified monthly installments based on the amortization schedules of the mortgages in the pool. In addition, the certificates provide for payment of a proportionate share of prepayments or other early recoveries of principal. An amount is withheld each month by the issuer to discharge the certificate holder's obligation to pay servicing, custodian and guarantee fees. Pass-through certificates may be either "fully modified" or "straight."

Timely payment of the principal and interest, *whether or not collected*, is guaranteed to the fully modified pass-through certificate holder by the Government National Mortgage Association (GNMA, or "Ginnie Mae"). Straight pass-through certificates provide for the payment by the issuer of a proportionate share of proceeds, *as collected*, on the pool of mortgages, less servicing fees and other costs. Straight pass-through certificates are guaranteed by GNMA only as to proper servicing of the mortgages by the issuer (i.e., payment of interest and principal actually collected or collectible through due diligence).

The full faith and credit of the United States is pledged to the payment of all amounts guaranteed by GNMA.[1] Certificates are issued in registered form and are fully transferable and assignable. They are marketable in the secondary market. They are available in minimum denominations of $25,000 ($1 thereafter) and may be available for less in the secondary market. The maximum maturity is 30 years; however, experience has shown that the average life is shorter. If all certificate holders and the issuer agree, the pool arrangement may be terminated at any time prior to the final maturity date.

Similar mortgage backed pass-through certificates are issued by "Fannie Mae" (Federal National Mortgage Association or FNMA), guaranteed by FNMA but are not backed by the full faith and credit of the United States.

1146. How is the monthly payment on Ginnie Mae mortgage backed pass-through certificates taxed?

Payments on pass-through certificates to certificate holders are made monthly. Each payment represents part interest and part principal (i.e., payments on the underlying portfolio of mortgages passed through to certificate holders). The issuer

---

1. 8 USC §306(g).

provides each certificate holder with a monthly statement indicating which part of the distribution represents scheduled principal amortization, which part is interest, and which part represents unscheduled collection of principal. Interest and other items of income, including prepayment penalties, assumption fees, and late payment charges, must be included in gross income in the year received. Principal payments are tax free to the extent they represent recovery of capital.[1] To the extent they represent discount on purchase of the mortgages, they must be included as ordinary income; as owners of undivided interests in the entire pool, pass-through certificate owners must include as ordinary income their ratable shares of any discount income realized on purchase of each of the mortgages in the pool. Discount on mortgages that are taxable obligations of corporations or governments or their political subdivisions, is included in income as original issue discount under the rules discussed in Q 1116 to Q 1119.[2]

Income from Ginnie Mae certificates is not exempt from state taxation despite the pledging of the full faith and credit of the United States on all amounts guaranteed by the GNMA because the government is a guarantor, not an obligor, of the instruments.[3]

Amounts withheld by the issuer of the certificate to pay servicing, custodian and guarantee fees are expenses incurred for the production of income. (See Q 1310 for an explanation of the rules governing deduction of such expenses by pass-through entities.) Certificate holders may amortize their proportionate share of any premium paid to acquire mortgages under rules applicable to corporate interest-bearing bonds—see Q 1120.[4]

1147. What is a "REMIC?"

A REMIC is a "real estate mortgage investment conduit." In general, a REMIC is a fixed pool of real estate mortgages that issues multiple classes of securities backed by the mortgages and that has elected to be taxed as a REMIC. It can issue several different classes of "regular interests" and must issue one (and only one) class of "residual interests." IRC Sec. 860D. A regular interest is a debt obligation (or is treated as one) and a "residual interest" participates in the income or loss of the REMIC.[5] A REMIC is not treated as a separate taxable entity (unless it engages in certain prohibited transactions); instead, the income is taxable to the interest holders as explained in Q 1148.[6]

Generally, entities that do not qualify as REMICs, but that issue multiple maturity debt obligations, the payments on which are related to payments on the mortgages and other obligations held by the entity, are classified as Taxable Mortgage Pools (TMPs).[7] (Domestic building and loan associations are not considered TMPs.) TMPs are taxed as corporations.[8]

1148. How is the owner of a REMIC interest taxed?

As a general rule, REMICs issue several classes of "regular" interests and a single class of "residual interests." Interests are subject to federal income tax under the following rules.

---

1. Rev. Rul. 84-10, 1984-1 CB 155; Rev. Rul. 70-545, 1970-2 CB 7.
2. Rev. Rul. 84-10, above; Rev. Rul. 74-169, 1974-1 CB 147; Rev. Rul. 70-544, 1970-2 CB 6.
3. *Rockford Life Ins. v. Illinois Department of Revenue*, 107 S.Ct. 2312 (1987).
4. Rev. Rul. 84-10, above.
5. IRC Secs. 860B, 860C.
6. IRC Secs. 860A, 860F(a)(1).
7. IRC Sec. 7701(i)(2); Treas. Reg. §301.7701(i)-1(b).
8. IRC Sec. 7701(i)(1).

Regular Interests

An interest in a REMIC is a regular interest if it (1) was issued as a designated regular interest on the "startup day" selected by the REMIC, (2) unconditionally entitles the holder to a specified principal amount, and (3) provides for interest payments (if any) that (a) are based on a fixed rate, or, to the extent provided in regulations, at a variable rate, or (b) consist of a specified, unvarying portion of the interest payments on qualified mortgages.[1] See Notice 93-11[2] (for the Service's acceptance of a floating rate as a variable rate);[3]

Under final regulations effective for most obligations issued on or after April 4, 1994, a variable rate includes a qualified floating rate as defined in Treas. Reg. §1.1275-5(b)(1).[4] In addition, a rate equal to the highest, lowest, or average of two or more qualified floating rates is a variable rate for purposes of IRC Section 860G.

A REMIC may issue a regular interest that bears interest that can be expressed as a percentage of the interest payable on a specified portion of a regular interest acquired from another REMIC (sometimes called a specified portion regular interest or an "Interest Only" interest or "IO").[5] The Treasury Department and the Service are considering whether to issue regulations with respect to the tax treatment of REMIC IOs for issuers and initial- and secondary-market purchasers. An advance notice of proposed rulemaking has been released regarding the proper timing of income or deduction attributable to an "interest only" regular interest in a REMIC. The advance notice provides additional background information and sets forth summary descriptions of possible approaches to the pertinent issues.[6]

The timing (but not the amount) of the principal payment may be contingent on the extent of prepayment on mortgages and the amount of income from permitted investments.[7] No minimum specified principal amount is required; it may be zero.[8]

Similar requirements apply if the interest is in the form of stock, a partnership interest, interest in a trust, or other form permitted under state law. If an interest is not in the form of debt, it must entitle the holder to a specified amount (even if it is zero) that would, if it were issued in debt form, be identified as the principal amount of the debt.[9]

A REMIC may issue regular interests that are subordinated to other classes of regular interests, which bear all or a disproportionate share of losses or expenses from cash flow shortfalls such as, for example, losses from defaults or delinquencies on mortgages or other permitted investments.[10]

The Service has ruled that in the event that payments received from certain preexisting interests were insufficient to distribute interest at the applicable stated rate on

---

1. IRC Sec. 860G(a).
2. 1993-1 CB 298.
3. Notice 87-67, 1987-2 CB 377; Notice 87-41, 1987-1 CB 500.
4. Treas. Reg. §1.860G-1(a)(3).
5. Treas. Reg. §1.860G-1(a)(2)(v) (effective for entities whose startup day is on or after November 12, 1991).
6. See REG-106679-04, 69 Fed. Reg. 52212 (8-25-2004).
7. IRC Sec. 860G(a)(1). See Treas. Reg. §1.860G-1(a)(5).
8. Treas. Reg. §1.860G-1(a)(2)(iv).
9. Treas. Reg. §1.860G-1(b)(4).
10. Treas. Reg. §1.860G-1(b)(3)(iii).

interests in a newly formed REMIC, a "funds-available" cap would not prevent the new interests from qualifying as regular interests under IRC Section 860G.[1]

Generally, holders of regular interests are taxed as if the interest were a debt instrument, except that holders must account for income from the interest on the accrual basis method (regardless of the accounting method otherwise used by the holder). IRC Sec. 860B. Periodic payments of interest (or similar amounts) are treated as accruing pro rata between interest payment dates. Original issue discount on regular interests is includable as it accrues. Special rules apply to the determination of original issue discount on regular interests.[2] For the proposed regulations addressing the special rule for accruing original issue discount on certain REMIC regular interests, which provide for delayed payment periods of fewer than 32 days, see Prop. Treas. Reg. §1.1275-2(m); REG-108637-03.[3]

The IRC prohibits (with some exceptions) the indirect deduction through pass-through entities of amounts that would not be allowable as a deduction if paid or incurred directly by an individual.[4] Under some circumstances (e.g., if the REMIC is substantially similar to an investment trust) holders of regular interests may be required under IRC Section 67(c) and regulations thereunder, to include in income as interest an allocable share of certain investment expenses of the REMIC. The amount may be deducted as a miscellaneous itemized deduction if the holder itemizes deductions; however, aggregate miscellaneous deductions are subject to a 2% floor.[5] No increase in basis is allowed for the amount passed through as miscellaneous expense even though it is included in income.[6] See Q 1428 regarding the treatment of miscellaneous itemized deductions.

The REMIC is required to report to regular interest holders amounts includable as interest, original discount and miscellaneous expenses.[7] However, under final regulations effective June 16, 2000, the requirement that REMIC issuers set forth certain "legending" information on the face of certificates when issued (i.e., the total amount of original issue discount on the instruments, the issue date, the rate at which interest is payable as of the issue date, and the yield to maturity) has been eliminated.[8]

On disposition, gain is ordinary income to the extent that it does not exceed the excess (if any) of (1) the interest the holder would have included in gross income if the yield on the regular interest were calculated at a rate of 110% of the applicable federal rate as of the beginning of the taxpayer's holding period, over (2) the amount of interest actually includable in gross income by the taxpayer prior to disposition.[9]

Regular interests may be treated as market discount bonds (see Q 1109) if the revised issue price (within the meaning of IRC Section 1278) exceeds the holder's basis in the interest. Market premium on a regular interest can be amortized currently (see Q 1120).

1.   Let. Rul. 199920030.
2.   IRC Sec. 1272(a)(6).
3.   69 Fed. Reg. 52217 (8-25-2004).
4.   IRC Sec. 67(c).
5.   Temp. Treas. Reg. §1.67-3T(b)(3).
6.   Temp. Treas. Reg. §1.67-3T(b)(5).
7.   Treas. Reg. §1.67-3(f); Treas. Reg. §1.6049-7(f).
8.   TD 8888, 65 Fed. Reg. 37701 (6-16-2000); Treas. Reg. §1.6049-7(g), withdrawn.
9.   IRC Sec. 860B(c).

FASIT transfers to REMICS. The FASIT rules have been repealed.[1] (See Q 1149.) The amendments are generally effective on January 1, 2005.[2] The definitions of REMIC regular interests, qualified mortgages, and permitted investments have been modified so that certain types of real estate loans and loan pools can be transferred to, or purchased by, a REMIC. According to the Conference Committee Report, modifications to the present-law REMIC rules are intended to permit the use of REMICS by taxpayers that have relied on FASITs to securitize certain obligations secured by interests in real property.[3]

Residual Interests

In general, a residual interest is any interest in the REMIC, other than a regular interest, that is issued on the startup day and is designated as a residual interest.[4] However, there may be only one class of such interests and any distributions with respect to such interests must be pro rata.[5]

The holder of a residual interest takes into account his daily portion of the taxable income or net loss of the REMIC for each day that he held the interest during his taxable year.[6] Any reasonable convention may be used to determine the holder's daily portion of income or loss.[7] This amount is treated as ordinary income or loss. IRC Sec. 860C(e). Such income in excess of daily accruals of income on the issue price at 120% of the long term federal rate are called "excess inclusions," and a holder of a residual interest can in no event have a taxable income of less than his excess inclusions. In other words, they cannot be offset by any deductions.[8]

In addition, a REMIC must allocate to certain residual interest holders each calendar quarter a proportionate share of investment expenses paid or accrued for the quarter for which a deduction is allowed under IRC Section 212 to the REMIC: these holders are individuals, any other persons (such as a trust or estate) that compute taxable income in the same manner as an individual, and certain pass-through entities (such as partnerships, S corporations and grantor trusts) having as a partner, shareholder, beneficiary, participant or interest holder an individual, a person who computes taxable income in the same manner as an individual, or a pass-through entity. Such a residual interest holder must include in income his allocable share of these expenses and may deduct them as miscellaneous itemized expenses subject to the 2% floor.[9]

Distributions from the REMIC are not included in gross income by the holder unless they exceed his adjusted basis in the interest. To the extent distributions exceed his basis, the excess is treated as gain from sale of the residual interest.[10] The amount of net loss that may be taken into account by the holder with respect to any calendar quarter is limited to the adjusted basis of his interest as of the close of the quarter; disallowed loss may be carried over indefinitely in succeeding quarters.[11]

1. IRC Secs. 860H, 860I, 860J, 860K, 860L, as repealed by Act. Sec. 835(a), AJCA 2004.
2. Act. Sec. 835(c)(1), AJCA 2004.
3. H.R. Conf. Rep. No. 108-755 (AJCA 2004). See IRC Secs. 860G(a)(1), 860G(a)(3), 860G(a)(7), as amended by AJCA 2004.
4. IRC Sec. 860G(a)(2).
5. IRC Sec. 860D(a).
6. IRC Sec. 860C(a).
7. Treas. Reg. §1.860C-1(c).
8. IRC Sec. 860E(a); Treas. Reg. §1.860E-1(a).
9. IRC Sec. 67(c); Temp. Treas. Reg. §1.67-3T(a).
10. IRC Sec. 860C(c).
11. IRC Sec. 860C(e)(2).

The adjusted basis of a residual interest is increased by the amount of taxable income of the REMIC taken into account by the holder; it is decreased (not below zero) by the amount of distributions and by any net loss taken into account.[1] However, no increase in the holder's basis is allowed for the amount of miscellaneous expenses allocated to him and included in his income.[2]

With certain exceptions, the REMIC's taxable income, for purposes of determining the amount includable by holders of residual interests, is determined in the same manner as for individuals, using a calendar year and using the accrual method of accounting.[3]

The Service privately ruled that whether a holder is liable for taxes associated with a noneconomic REMIC residual interest depends on the facts and circumstances associated with the transfer of the interest.[4]

The REMIC is required to provide information quarterly (on Schedule Q) to holders of residual interests regarding their share of income or loss, the amount of excess inclusion, and allocable investment expenses.[5]

For purposes of the wash sale rule (see Q 1030), a residual interest in a REMIC is treated as a security and, except as provided in regulations, such a residual interest and an interest in a "taxable mortgage pool" are treated as substantially identical stock or securities. Furthermore, the 30-day period in the wash sale rule is enlarged to six months in applying it to such interests. (For this purpose, the definition of a taxable mortgage pool is treated as if in effect in tax years beginning after 1986.)[6]

The Service has released final regulations relating to safe harbor transfers of noneconomic REMIC residual interests in REMICs. The final regulations provide additional limitations on the circumstances under which transferors may claim safe harbor treatment.[7]

The Service has issued temporary regulations relating to income associated with a residual interest in a REMIC and that is allocated through certain entities to foreign persons who have invested in those entities.[8]

If a charitable remainder trust (CRT—see Q 1328, Q 1330, and Q 1331) is a partner in a partnership or a shareholder in a real estate investment trust (REIT—see Q 1179), and if the partnership or the REIT has excess inclusion income from holding a residual interest in a REMIC, the Service has ruled that: (1) the excess inclusion income allocated to a CRT is not UBTI to the CRT and, thus, does not affect the CRT's tax exemption for the taxable year; (2) a CRT is a disqualified organization for purposes of IRC Section 860E; and (3) a pass-through entity that has excess inclusion income allocable to a CRT is subject to the pass-through entity tax under IRC Section 860E(e)(6)(A).[9]

---

1. IRC Sec. 860C(d).
2. Temp. Treas. Reg. §1.67-3T(b)(5).
3. IRC Sec. 860C(b). See Treas. Reg. §1.860C-2.
4. Let. Rul. 200032001.
5. Treas. Reg. §1.67-3(f); Treas. Reg. §1.860F-4(e)(1).
6. IRC Sec. 860F(d).
7. See Treas. Regs. §§1.860E-1(c)(4), 1.860E-1(c)(5) through 1.860E-1(c)(10), 67 Fed. Reg. 47451 (7-19-2002), *superseding*, Rev. Proc. 2001-12, 2001-3 CB 335.
8. See TD 9272, 71 Fed. Reg. 43363 (8-1-2006); see also Ann. 2006-68, 2006-38 IRB 510.
9. See Rev. Rul. 2006-58, 2006-46 IRB 876.

The Service has provided interim guidance relating to excess inclusion income of pass-through entities, particularly real estate investment trusts (see Q 1179). The interim guidance applies to excess inclusion income from REMIC residual interests (and REIT taxable mortgage pools), whether received directly or allocated from another pass-through entity.[1]

Rules for coordinating excess inclusions with net operating losses: Any "excess inclusion" (see above) for any taxable year is not to be taken into account in determining the amount of any net operating loss (NOL) for the taxable year (i.e., in determining the loss for a "loss year").[2] Any excess inclusion for a taxable year is not to be taken into account in determining taxable income for the taxable year for purposes of the second sentence of IRC Section 172(b)(2).[3] The Service has ruled that in computing an NOL for the taxable year, no excess inclusion is taken into account. If, during the same taxable year, a taxpayer both recognizes an excess inclusion and incurs an NOL, the excess inclusion may not be offset by the NOL and is not taken into account in determining the amount of the NOL that may be carried to another taxable year. The Service has further ruled that if an NOL is carried back or carried over to a taxable year in which an excess inclusion is recognized, the excess inclusion cannot be offset by the NOL carryback or carryover, and is not included in the calculation of taxable income for NOL absorption purposes.[4]

REMIC Inducement Fees. In 2004, the IRS released final regulations relating to the proper timing and source of income from fees received to induce the acquisition of noneconomic residual interests in REMICS. The final regulations provide that an inducement fee must be included in income over a period reasonably related to the period during which the applicable REMIC is expected to generate taxable income (or net loss) allocable to the holder of the noneconomic residual interest. Under a special rule applicable upon disposition of a residual interest, if any portion of an inducement fee received with respect to becoming the holder of a noneconomic residual interest has not been recognized in full by the holder as of the time the holder transfers (or otherwise ceases to be the holder for federal income tax purposes) of that residual interest in the applicable REMIC, the holder must include the unrecognized portion of the inducement fee in income at that time. The final regulations set forth two safe harbor methods of accounting for inducement fees, and also contain a rule that an inducement fee is income from sources within the United States.[5] The Service also released the procedures by which taxpayers can obtain automatic consent to change from any method of accounting for inducement fees to one of the two safe harbor methods.[6] The Service reached a settlement with two entities that purportedly brokered noneconomic residual interests in a manner based on what the IRS perceived to be an overly aggressive interpretation of the tax laws.[7]

ASSET BACKED SECURITIES

1149. What is a "FASIT"?

1. See Notice 2006-97, 2006-46 IRB 904.
2. See IRC Section 860E(a)(3)(A).
3. See Section 860E(a)(3)(B).
4. Rev. Rul. 2005-68, 2005-44 IRB 853.
5. See Treas. Regs. §§1.446-6, 1.860C-1(d), 1.863-1(e), 1.863-1(f), 69 Fed. Reg. 26040 (5-11-2004).
6. See Rev. Proc. 2004-30, 2004-21 IRB 950.
7. See IR-2004-97 (7-26-2004).

Editor's Note: The FASIT rules have been repealed.[1] (For the underlying reasons triggering the repeal, see H.R. Conf. Rep. No. 108-755 (AJCA 2004).) The amendments are generally effective on January 1, 2005.[2] However, the repeal provision also provides a transition period for existing FASITS, under which the repeal of the FASIT rules generally does not apply to any FASIT in existence on the date of the enactment to the extent that regular interests issued by the FASIT prior to such date continue to remain outstanding in accordance with their original terms of issuance.[3] See Q 1148 for modifications to the present-law REMIC rules that permit the use of REMICs by taxpayers that have relied upon FASITs to securitize certain obligations secured by interests in real property.

A *financial asset securitization investment trust* (FASIT) is any entity (1) for which an election to be treated as a FASIT applies for the taxable year, (2) all of the interests in which are regular interests or the ownership interest (as defined in Q 1150), (3) that has only one ownership interest and such ownership interest is held directly by an eligible corporation, (4) "substantially all" (see "substantiality test" below) of the assets of which consist of *permitted assets* as of the close of the third month beginning after the day of its formation and at all times thereafter (except during liquidation), and (5) is not a regulated investment company (see Q 1161).[4] Transition rules apply to securitization trusts in existence before September 1, 1997 that elected FASIT treatment.[5]

FASITs are a type of investment instrument that are designed to facilitate the securitization of debt obligations such as credit card receivables, home equity loans, and automobile loans.[6] A *regular interest* in a FASIT may be held by any person; however, if the interest constitutes a *high-yield interest*, it may be held only by another FASIT or an eligible corporation.[7] An *ownership interest* may be held only by an eligible corporation.[8] An *eligible corporation* is any non-exempt domestic C corporation other than a RIC, REIT, REMIC, or subchapter T cooperative.[9] See Q 1150 for the definitions of regular interest, high-yield interest, and ownership interest.

For purposes of IRC Section 860L(a)(1)(D), a FASIT meets the "substantiality test" if the aggregate adjusted basis of its assets other than *permitted assets* is less then 1% of the aggregate adjusted basis of all its assets.[10] *Permitted assets* that may be held by a FASIT are: (1) cash or cash equivalents;[11] (2) any debt instrument (as defined in IRC Section 1275(a)(1)) under which interest payments (or other similar amounts), if any, at or before maturity meet certain requirements applicable to regular interests in a REMIC (see Q 1148); (3) foreclosure property (as defined in IRC Section 860L(c)(3)[12]); (4) any asset (i) that is an interest rate or foreign currency notional principal contract, letter of credit, insurance, guarantee against payment defaults, or other similar instrument permitted by the Secretary, and (ii) that is reasonably required to guarantee or hedge against the FASIT's risks associated with being the obligor on interests issued by the

---

1. IRC Secs. 860H, 860I, 860J, 860K, 860L, as repealed by Act. Sec. 835(a), AJCA 2004.
2. Act. Sec. 835(c)(1), AJCA 2004.
3. See Act. Sec. 835(c)(2), AJCA 2004.
4. IRC Sec. 860L(a)(1).
5. See Prop. Treas. Reg. §1.860L-3; Ann. 96-121, 1996-47 IRB 12.
6. Ann. 96-121, 1996-47 IRB 12.
7. Ann. 96-121.
8. Prop. Treas. Reg. §1.860H-1(a)(1); Ann. 96-121, above.
9. IRC Sec. 860L(a)(2); Prop. Treas. Reg. §1.860H-1(a); Ann. 96-121, above.
10. See Prop. Treas. Reg. §1.860H-2(a).
11. See Prop. Treas. Reg. §1.860H-2(c).
12. See Prop. Treas. Reg. §1.860H-2(f).

FASIT[1]); (5) contract rights to acquire debt instruments described under (2) above, or assets described under (4) above[2]; (6) any regular interest in another FASIT; and (7) any regular interest in a REMIC.[3] Special rules apply for contracts or agreements in the nature of a line of credit.[4] *Permitted assets* do not include any debt instrument issued by the holder of the ownership interest or a related person other than a cash equivalent, or any direct or indirect interest in such a debt instrument.[5]

A *permitted debt instrument* is: (1) a fixed rate debt instrument, including a debt instrument having more than one payment schedule for which a single yield can be determined under Treas. Regs. §§1.1272-1(c) or 1.1272-1(d); (2) a variable rate debt instrument within the meaning of Treas. Reg. §1.1272-5 if the debt instrument provides for interest at a qualified floating rate within the meaning of Treas. Reg. §1.1275-5(b); (3) a REMIC regular interest; (4) a FASIT regular interest (including a FASIT regular interest issued by another FASIT in which the owner (or a related person) holds an ownership interest; (5) an inflation-indexed debt instrument as defined in Treas. Reg. §1.1275-7; (6) any receivable generated through an extension of credit under a revolving credit agreement (such as a credit card account; (7) a stripped bond or stripped coupon (as defined in IRC Sections 1286(e)(2) and 1286(e)(3)), if the debt instrument from which the stripped bond or stripped coupon is created is described in (1) - (6), above; and (8) a certificate of trust representing a beneficial ownership interest in a debt instrument described in items (1) - (7), above.[6] Special rules apply to short-term instruments issued by the owner or a related person.[7] Debt instruments that are not permitted assets include: (1) an equity-linked debt instrument (e.g., a debt instrument convertible into stock); (2) a defaulted debt instrument; (3) owner debt; (4) certain owner-guaranteed debt; (5) a debt instrument linked to the owner's credit; (6) partial interests in non-permitted debt instruments; and (7) certain foreign debt subject to withholding tax.[8]

Once an entity elects to be treated as a FASIT, the election applies for all subsequent taxable years unless revoked with the consent of the Service. In the event the entity ceases to be a FASIT, it will not be treated as a FASIT after the date of cessation unless the termination is inadvertent and adjustments are made to restore the entity to FASIT status.[9]

Under the proposed regulations, in the event of cessation, the FASIT owner is treated as disposing of the FASIT's assets for their fair market value in a prohibited transaction. Gain on this deemed distribution is subject to the prohibited transactions tax. Any loss is disallowed.[10] The owner must recognize cancellation of indebtedness income in an amount equal to the adjusted issue price of the regular interests outstanding immediately before the cessation over the fair market value of those interests immediately before the cessation.[11] Holders of the regular interests are treated as exchanging their FASIT regular interests for interests in the underlying arrangement. Gain must be recognized if a regular interest is exchanged either for an interest not classified as

1. See Prop. Treas. Regs. §§1.860H-2(d) and 1.860H-2(e).
2. See Prop. Treas. Reg. §1.860H-2(h).
3. IRC Sec. 860L(c).
4. Prop. Treas. Reg. §1.860H-2(g).
5. IRC Sec. 860L(c).
6. Prop. Treas. Regs. §§1.860H-2(b)(1)(i)-(viii).
7. See Prop. Treas. Reg. §1.860H-2(b)(2).
8. Prop. Treas. Regs. §§1.860H-2(b)(3)(i)-(vii).
9. IRC Sec. 860L(a); Prop. Treas. Reg. §1.860H-3(a).
10. See Prop. Treas. Reg. §1.860H-3(c)(2)(i).
11. Prop. Treas. Reg. §1.860H-3(c)(2)(ii).

debt or for an interest classified as debt that differs materially either in kind or extent. No loss may be recognized on the exchange.[1] The underlying arrangement is no longer treated as a FASIT and generally is prohibited from being the subject of a new FASIT election. In addition, the underlying arrangement is treated as holding the assets of the terminated FASIT and is classified under general tax principles (e.g., as a corporation or partnership).[2]

A FASIT is not treated as a taxable entity (however, a penalty is imposed on the holder of the ownership interest if the FASIT engages in certain prohibited transactions); instead, the income is taxable to the interest holders as explained in Q 1150.[3]

1150. How is the holder of a FASIT interest taxed?

Editor's Note: The FASIT rules have been repealed. IRC Secs. 860H, 860I, 860J, 860K, 860L, as repealed by Act. Sec. 835(a), AJCA 2004. (For the underlying reasons triggering the repeal, see H.R. Conf. Rep. No. 108-755 (AJCA 2004).) The amendments are generally effective on January 1, 2005.[4] However, the provision provides a transition period for existing FASITS under which the repeal of the FASIT rules generally does not apply to any FASIT in existence on the date of the enactment to the extent that regular interests issued by the FASIT prior to such date continue to remain outstanding in accordance with their original terms of issuance.[5] See Q 1148 for modifications to the present-law REMIC rules that permit the use of REMICs by taxpayers that have relied upon FASITs to securitize certain obligations secured by interests in real property.

A *financial asset securitization investment trust* (FASIT - see Q 1149) may issue one or more classes of "regular interests" and a single "ownership" interest.[6] Transition rules apply to securitization trusts in existence before September 1, 1997 that elected FASIT treatment.[7]

Regular Interests

A *regular interest* is any interest that is issued by a FASIT on or after the *startup day* with fixed terms and that is designated as a regular interest if it, (1) unconditionally entitles the holder to receive a specified principal amount (or other similar amounts) as described below, (2) provides that interest payments, if any, are based on a fixed rate or, to the extent provided in regulations, at a variable rate, (3) does not have a stated maturity (including options to renew) greater than 30 years, although a longer period may by permitted by regulations, (4) has an *issue price* that does not exceed 125% of its stated principal amount, and (5) has a yield to maturity less than the sum of the applicable federal rate for the calendar month in which the obligation is issued plus five percentage points.[8]

A regular interest will not fail to meet the first requirement merely because the timing (but not the amount) of the principal payments (or similar amounts) may be contingent on (a) the extent to which payments on debt instruments held by a FASIT

---

1. See Prop. Treas. Reg. §1.860H-3(c)(3).
2. See Prop. Treas. Reg. §1.860H-3(c)(1).
3. IRC Secs. 860H(a), 860L(e).
4. Act. Sec. 835(c)(1), AJCA 2004.
5. See Act. Sec. 835(c)(2), AJCA 2004.
6. IRC Sec. 860L(a)(1); see Prop. Treas. Reg. §1.860L-1(a).
7. See Prop. Treas. Reg. §1.860L-3; Ann. 96-121, 1996-47 IRB 12.
8. IRC Secs. 860L(b)(1), 163(i)(1)(B).

are made in advance of anticipated payments and on (b) the amount of income from permitted assets.[1] The term *startup day* means the date designated in the FASIT election as the startup day of the FASIT.[2] The *issue price* of a FASIT regular interest not issued for property is determined under IRC Section 1273(b).[3] Notwithstanding IRC Sections 1273 and 1274, the issue price of a FASIT regular interest issued for property is the fair market value of the regular interest determined as of the issue date.[4]

Generally, a holder of a regular interest is taxed as if the regular interest were a debt instrument, except that a holder must account for income from the interest on an accrual basis (regardless of the accounting method otherwise used by the holder).[5] The holder of a regular interest will not be subject to special rules under IRC Section 163(e)(5) for original issue discount on certain high-yield obligations.[6]

High-Yield Interests

The term *regular interest* may also include any *high-yield interest*. A high-yield interest is one that would meet the definition of a regular interest except that it does not meet one or more of the clauses of requirements (1), (4), or (5) in the definition of regular interests above. Furthermore, an interest that fails to meet requirement (2), above, may constitute a high-yield interest if interest payments (or similar amounts), if any, consist of a specified portion of the interest payments on permitted assets (see Q 1149 for a definition of *permitted assets*) and such portion does not vary during the period such interest is outstanding. A high-yield interest can be held only by another FASIT or an *eligible corporation* (defined in Q 1149).[7]

The taxable income of a holder of a high-yield interest may not be less than the sum of (1) the holder's taxable income determined solely with respect to such interests and (2) any excess inclusion (if any) imposed on the holder of a residual interest of a REMIC.[8] Any increase in taxable income for any taxable year that results from the application of the above rule is disregarded in determining the amount of any net operating loss for the taxable year and determining taxable income for purposes of carrybacks and carryforwards of a net operating loss.[9] Similar rules apply to the holders of high-yield interests subject to the alternative minimum tax.[10]

Special rules apply to high-yield interests that are held by *disqualified holders*.[11] A disqualified holder is any holder other than a FASIT or an eligible corporation (as defined in Q 1149).[12]

Ownership Interest

An *ownership interest* is defined as any interest issued by the FASIT after the *startup day* (defined above) that is designated as an ownership interest and is not a regular

---

1. IRC Sec. 860L(b)(1).
2. IRC Sec. 860L(d).
3. Prop. Treas. Reg. §1.860H-4(a)(1).
4. Prop. Treas. Reg. §1.860H-4(a)(2).
5. IRC Sec. 860H(c).
6. IRC Secs. 860H(c)(2), 163(e)(5).
7. IRC Sec. 860L(b)(1)(B)(ii); Ann. 96-121, 1996-47 IRB 12.
8. IRC Secs. 860J(a), 860E(a)(1).
9. IRC Sec. 860J(b).
10. IRC Sec. 860J(c).
11. See IRC Sec. 860K(a); see also Prop. Treas. Reg. §1.860H-4(b)(1).
12. See IRC Secs. 860K(c), 860L(a)(2).

interest.[1] A FASIT may have only one ownership interest, which must be directly held by an eligible corporation (see Q 1149).[2]

The following rules are applied in determining the taxable income of the holder of an ownership interest in a FASIT: (1) all assets, liabilities, and items of income, gain, deduction, loss, and credit of a FASIT are treated as those of the ownership interest holder; (2) a constant yield method (including the special rules under IRC Section 1272(a)(6) for accelerated payments) under the accrual method of accounting must be used to determine all interest, acquisition discount, original issue discount, market discount, and premium deductions or adjustments with respect to each debt instrument of the FASIT; (3) no items of income, gain or deduction allocable to a *prohibited transaction* are taken into account, and (4) any tax-exempt interest accrued by the FASIT is treated as ordinary income of the holder.[3]

For the owner's annual reporting requirements, including the manner in which the items of income, gain, loss, deduction, and credit from permitted transactions and prohibited transactions are to be taken into account separately, see Prop. Treas. Reg. §1.860H-6(e). The method of accounting for permitted hedges, and the character of such hedges, are set forth in Prop. Treas. Reg. §1.860H-6(c). Rules coordinating the FASIT owner rules with the mark to market provisions are stated in Prop. Treas. Reg. §1.860H-6(d). For the rule governing the transfer of an ownership interest, see Prop. Treas. Reg. §1.860H-6(g). In early 2001, the Service announced an alternative safe harbor under which the transfer of a FASIT ownership interest is presumed to be accomplished without an intention to impede the assessment or collection of tax.[4]

A *prohibited transaction* means (1) the receipt of any income derived from any asset that is not a permitted asset (as defined in Q 1149) (with certain exceptions), (2) the disposition of any permitted asset other than foreclosure property (with certain exceptions), (3) the receipt of any income derived from any loan originated by the FASIT,[5] and (4) the receipt of any income representing a fee or other compensation for services (other than any fee received as compensation for a waiver, amendment, or consent under permitted assets not acquired through foreclosure).[6] The receipt of any income derived from any asset that is not a permitted asset will not constitute a prohibited transaction where income is derived from the disposition of certain former hedge assets or contracts to acquire such assets.[7] Additionally, dispositions of permitted assets that will not constitute a prohibited transaction include certain substitutions of debt instruments to reduce over-collateralization, certain transactions that are excepted from the prohibited transactions penalty under the REMIC rules (see Q 1148), and the complete liquidation of any class of regular interests.[8]

Whether an activity will or will not be presumed to be loan orgination is determined under Proposed Treasury Regulation Sections 860L-1(a)(2) and 1.860L-1(a)(3). The proposed regulations provide five safe harbors to limit the scope of the prohibited transaction rules as they relate to loan orgination.[9] The distribution to the owner of a

---

1. IRC Sec. 860L(b)(2).
2. IRC Secs. 860L(a)(C); Prop. Treas. Reg. §1.860H-1(a)(1).
3. IRC Sec. 860H(b); Prop. Treas. Regs. §§1.860H-6(a) and 1.860H-6(b); Ann 96-121, 1996-47 IRB 12.
4. See Rev. Proc. 2001-12, 2001-1 CB 335.
5. See Prop. Treas. Reg. §1.860L-1(a)(1).
6. IRC Sec. 860L(e)(2).
7. IRC Sec. 860L(e)(3)(D); Prop. Treas. Reg. §1.860L-1(d).
8. IRC Sec. 860L(e)(3).
9. See Prop. Treas. Regs. §§1.860L-1(a)(2) and 1.860L-1(a)(4).

debt instrument contributed by the owner, and the transfer to the owner of one debt instrument in exchange for another, are prohibited transactions *if* within 180 days of receiving the debt instrument the owner realizes a gain on the disposition of the instrument to any person regardless of whether the realized gain is recognized.[1] To clarify the application of the distribution rule, the proposed regulations deem a distribution of a debt instrument to be carried out principally to recognize gain if the owner (or a related person) sells the substituted or distributed debt instrument at a gain within 180 days of the substitution or distribution.[2]

The taxable income of a holder of an ownership interest may not be less than the sum of (1) the holder's taxable income determined solely with respect to such interests and (2) any excess inclusion (if any) of a holder of a residual interest of a REMIC.[3] Any increase in taxable income for any taxable year that results from the application of the above rule is disregarded in determining the amount of any net operating loss for the taxable year and determining taxable income for purposes of carrybacks and carryforwards of a net operating loss.[4] Similar rules apply to the holders of an ownership interest subject to the alternative minimum tax.[5]

Gain recognition on property transferred to FASIT. If property is sold or contributed to a FASIT by the holder of the ownership interest (or a related person), gain (but not loss) is recognized by the holder (or related person) in an amount equal to the excess (if any) of the property's value (determined under IRC Section 860I(d)) on the date of sale or contribution over its adjusted basis on such date.[6] If the FASIT acquires property other than from a holder of an ownership interest or related person, the property is treated as having been acquired by the holder of the ownership interest for an amount equal to the FASIT's cost of acquiring such property, and then as having been sold to the FASIT at the value determined under IRC Section 860I(d).[7] An owner (or a related person) does not have to recognize gain under IRC Section 860I on a transfer or pledge of property to a regular interest holder if the owner (or related person) makes the transfer or pledge in a capacity other than as owner (or related person) and the regular interest holder receives the transfer or pledge in a capacity other than regular interest holder.[8]

Determination of value for gain recognition purposes. The value of property, for purposes of the FASIT provisions, is determined under special rules set forth in IRC Section 860I(d). In the case of a nonpublicly traded debt instrument, the value is equal to the sum of the present values of the reasonably expected payments under such instrument determined (in the manner provided by regulations prescribed by the Secretary) (1) as of the date of the event resulting in the gain recognition under IRC Section 860I and (2) by using a discount equal to 120% of the applicable federal rate (see Q 1409), or such other discount rate specified in the regulations, compounded semiannually.[9] Reasonably expected payments on an instrument must be determined in a commercially reasonable manner and may take into account reasonable assumptions concerning early repayments, late payments, non-payments, and loan servicing costs. No other assumptions may be

---

1. Prop. Treas. Reg. §1.860L-1(c).
2. See Prop. Treas. Reg. §1.860L-1(c).
3. IRC Secs. 860J(a), 860E(a)(1).
4. IRC Sec. 860J(b).
5. IRC Sec. 860J(c).
6. IRC Sec. 860I(a)(1); Prop. Treas. Reg. §1.860I-1(a)(1); Ann. 96-121, 1996-47 IRB 12.
7. IRC Sec. 860I(a)(2); Prop. Treas. Reg. §1.860I-1(g).
8. Prop. Treas. Reg. §1.860I-1(a)(2).
9. IRC Sec. 860I(d)(1)(A); see Prop. Treas. Reg. §1.860I-2(a).

considered.[1] Any assumption used in determining the reasonably expected payments on an instrument must satisfy the consistency test.[2] In addition to the consistency test, the proposed regulations place a ceiling on projected loan servicing costs.[3]

The proposed regulations provide exceptions from the special valuation rules (discussed above) for certain beneficial and stripped interests.[4] The proposed regulations also provide an exception for certain debt instruments that are contemporaneously purchased and transferred to the FASIT (i.e., the spot purchase rule). Under this provision, the value of a debt instrument is its cost to the owner if four conditions are met.[5] The special valuation rule for guarantees is set forth in Prop. Treas. Reg. §1.860I-2(d)(4).

In the case of any other property (i.e., debt traded on an established securities market), the value is its fair market value.[6] A debt instrument is traded on an established securities market if it is traded on a market described in Treasury Regulation Sections 1.1273-2(f)(2), 1.1273-2(f)(3), or 1.1273-2(f)(4).[7] In the case of revolving loan accounts, each extension of credit (other than the accrual of interest) will be treated as a separate debt instrument, and payments on such extensions of credit having substantially the same terms will be applied to such extensions beginning with the earliest extension.[8]

Gain is determined and recognized immediately before the property is transferred to the FASIT or becomes support property, or in the case of foreclosure property, on the day immediately following the termination of the grace period allowed for foreclosure property.[9]

If property held by the holder of the ownership interest in a FASIT (or by a person related to such holder) supports any regular interest in the FASIT, gain is recognized to the holder or related person in the same manner as if the holder had sold the property (at the value determined under IRC Section 860I(d)) on the earliest date that the property supports such an interest. In addition, the property is treated as held by the FASIT.[10] Support property is defined in Prop. Treas. Reg. §1.860I-1(b).

Future regulations were authorized that would have provided for the deferral of gain that would otherwise have been recognized under IRC Section 860I(a) or IRC Section 860I(b) above (but see *Editor's Note*, above).[11]

The basis of any property on which gain is recognized under the FASIT rules is increased by the amount of such gain.[12] Furthermore, the rules governing recognition of gain by FASITs supersede any other nonrecognition provisions (e.g. like-kind exchanges) that might otherwise apply.[13]

---

1. Prop. Treas. Reg. §1.860I-2(c)(1).
2. See Prop. Treas. Reg. §1.860I-2(c)(2).
3. See Prop. Treas. Reg. §1.860I-2(c)(3).
4. See Prop. Treas. Regs. §§1.860I-2(d)(1) and 1.860I-2(d)(2).
5. See Prop. Treas. Reg. §1.860I-2(d)(3).
6. IRC Sec. 860I(d)(1)(B).
7. Prop. Treas. Reg. §1.860I-2(b).
8. IRC Sec. 860I(d)(2).
9. Prop. Treas. Reg. §1.860I-1(c).
10. IRC Sec. 860I(b).
11. IRC Sec. 860I(c). See Prop. Treas. Reg. §1.860I-1(d).
12. IRC Sec. 860I(e).
13. IRC Sec. 860I(e).

For purposes of the FASIT rules, persons are *related* if they meet the definition with respect to individuals described in IRC Section 267(b) or controlled partnerships under IRC Section 707(b), except that in applying IRC Sections 267(b) or 707(b)(1), "20 percent" will be substituted for "50 percent" where applicable (see Q 1419).[1] A related person also includes certain persons engaged in trades or businesses under common control.[2]

For purposes of the wash sale rule (see Q 1030), an ownership interest is subject to rules similar to those applicable to REMICS (see Q 1148). Under those rules, an ownership interest is treated as a security, and an ownership interest and any interest in a taxable mortgage pool comparable to a residual interest in an ownership interest are treated as substantially identical stock or securities. Furthermore, the 30-day period in the wash sale rule is enlarged to six months in applying it to such interests.[3]

The FASIT anti-abuse rule evaluates transactions against the underlying purpose of the FASIT provisions, which is to promote the spreading of credit risk on debt instruments by facilitating the securitization of debt instruments. If a FASIT is formed or used to achieve a tax result inconsistent with this purpose, the Commissioner may take remedial action including disregarding the FASIT election, reallocating items of income, deductions and credits, recharacterizing regular interests, and redesignating the holder of the ownership interest.[4]

REGISTRATION REQUIREMENT

1151. Must bonds be in registered form? What are "registration required" bonds?

Any obligation of a type offered to the public that has a maturity of more than one year must be in registered form (a "registration required" bond). This includes obligations of federal, state and local governments as well as corporations and partnerships. An exception is made for certain obligations reasonably designed to be sold only outside the United States to non-United States persons and payable outside the United States and its possessions. However, if they are in bearer form, these obligations must carry a statement that any United States person holding the obligation will be subject to tax limitations.[5] A "United States person" is a United States citizen or resident, a domestic partnership or corporation, or an estate or certain trusts (other than a foreign estate or trust).[6]

Bonds that are "not of a type offered to the public" do not have to meet the registration requirement.[7] Temporary regulations state that a bond is "of a type offered to the public" if similar obligations are publicly offered or traded.[8] Even if a bond is not publicly traded, it may be considered "of a type offered to the public" if: (a) the bond would be treated as readily tradable in an established securities market under the installment sales rules; (2) the bond is comparable to a bond described in (1); or (3) similar obligations are publicly offered or traded.[9]

1. IRC Sec. 860L(g).
2. IRC Secs. 860L(g), 52(a), 52(b).
3. IRC Secs. 860L(f)(1), 860F(d)(1).
4. See Prop. Treas. Reg. §1.860L-2.
5. IRC Secs. 103(b), 149, 163(f).
6. IRC Sec. 7701(a)(30).
7. IRC Sec. 163(f)(2)(A)(ii).
8. Temp. Treas. Reg. §5f.163-1(b)(2).
9. Prop. Treas. Reg. §5f.163-1(b)(2) (effective for bonds issued after January 21, 1993 unless substantially all of the terms of the obligation were agreed upon in writing on or before that date).

The Treasury also has authority to require registration of other obligations if they are used frequently for tax avoidance.[1]

A book entry obligation is considered registered if the right to principal of, and stated interest on, the obligation may be transferred only through a book entry system that identifies the owner of an interest in the obligation. Regulations may permit book entries in the case of a nominee or a chain of nominees.[2]

Registration is required for some U.S. Treasury issues after September 3, 1982 and other Treasury issues and issues of U.S. agencies and instrumentalities issued after 1982.[3] Obligations issued by other than the United States and its agencies and instrumentalities must be in registered form in order for the issuer (or holder, in some cases) to qualify for certain tax benefits (see Q 1152). This requirement generally applies to municipal bonds issued after June 30, 1983 (although some previously had to be in registered form in order to qualify for tax-exemption). Other bonds must be in registered form after 1982.

The constitutionality of the registration requirement was unsuccessfully challenged in *South Carolina v. Baker*,[4] in which the Supreme Court upheld the constitutionality of both the registration requirement and the tax consequences imposed on most unregistered bonds.

Issuers of registration required obligations not in registered form are denied a deduction for interest paid or accrued on the obligation, and their earnings and profits may not be decreased by such nondeductible interest (except for certain foreign issuers).[5] In addition, they are subject to an excise tax of 1% of the principal times the number of years to maturity, except in the case of obligations that would be tax-exempt if issued in registered form.[6]

Generally, then, the tax limitations apply to the issuer rather than the holder. However, in the case of obligations the issuance of which would not be subject to the 1% excise tax, and obligations that would be tax-exempt if issued in registered form, limitations are imposed directly on the holder (see Q 1152).

An obligation, the terms of which are fixed and for which full consideration is received before December 31, 1982, is not required to be registered even if smaller denomination certificates in that obligation are not distributed to ultimate investors until after that date, according to the General Explanation of TEFRA by the Joint Committee on Taxation.

The Service has provided clarification on whether bonds held through certain book-entry systems are treated as registered or in bearer form under Treasury Regulation Section 5f.103-1(c) and Section 1.871-14.[7]

---

1. IRC Sec. 163(f)(2)(C).
2. IRC Secs. 149(a)(3), 163(f)(3), 4701(b), 165(j); Temp. Treas. Reg. §5f.103-1.
3. TEFRA Sec. 310(d).
4. 108 S.Ct. 1355 (1988).
5. IRC Sec. 163(f); IRC Sec. 312(m).
6. IRC Sec. 4701.
7. See Notice 2006-99, 2006-46 IRB 907.

1152. What tax limitations apply to the holder of registration required bonds that are not in registered form?

Income from otherwise tax-exempt bonds that do not meet the registration requirement (see Q 1151) is not exempt from federal income tax in the hands of a U.S. person. However, this limitation does not apply to interest exempt from tax by the United States under a treaty.[1]

Loss on the sale, exchange, theft, loss, etc., of a registration required obligation that would be tax-exempt if registered is not deductible if not in registered form.[2] Gain on sale or exchange of a registration required bond that would otherwise be tax-exempt but that is not registered must be treated as ordinary income. It is denied capital gain treatment.[3] These sanctions also apply to U.S. persons holding unregistered bonds that are not required to be registered because they were designed for distribution outside the United States.[4]

Regulations allow the loss deduction and capital gains treatment by a holder who, within 30 days of the date when the seller or other transferor is reasonably able to make the bearer obligation available to the holder, surrenders the obligation to a transfer agent or to the issuer for conversion into registered form.[5]

STRUCTURED PRODUCTS

1153. What is a structured product? How are structured products taxed?

"Structured products are not specifically defined in the securities laws. They have been described as securities that may be derived from or based on a particular security or commodity, a basket of securities, an index, a debt issuance, or a foreign currency. Many involve innovative financing techniques creating customized financing and investment products to suit specific financial needs of customers. They may involve complex "tranched" (i.e., segmented) liabilities and transfers through special purpose vehicles. Such transactions may be structured for any number of reasons — for example, for principal protection, tax minimization, accounting cosmetics, monetization, or other specific purposes."[6] Some of the more popular types of structured products sold to retail investors include principal-protected notes, equity-linked notes, and indexed-linked notes.

The taxation of a structured product will depend on the tax treatment of its individual components. See Q 1017 – stock; Q 1042 through Q 1071 – options; Q 1102 through Q 1106 – corporate bonds; Q 1109 through Q 1115 – market discount; and Q 1116 through Q 1120 – original issue discount.

---

1. IRC Secs. 103(b), 149; Temp. Treas. Reg. §5f.103-1.
2. IRC Sec. 165(j)(1).
3. IRC Sec. 1287.
4. IRC Secs. 165(j), 1287(a).
5. IRC Sec. 165(j)(3); Treas. Reg. §1.165-12(c)(4).
6. "Speech by SEC Staff: Structured Finance Activities: The Regulatory Viewpoint," given by Mary Ann Gadziala, Associate Director, Office of Compliance Inspections and Examinations, U.S. Securities and Exchange Commission to the International Bar Association Conference — Financial Services Section, Chicago, Illinois, September 20, 2006, at: www.sec.gov/news/speech/2006/spch092006mag.htm.

FINANCIAL INSTITUTIONS

GENERAL

1154. What forms of deposits or other services are available in banks and other financial institutions?

Although the varieties of savings vehicles and services available through banks and other financial institutions seem endless, they may generally be grouped into one of four categories–demand deposits, time deposits, savings deposits, or life insurance and annuities.

A *demand deposit* is a deposit of funds that is payable on demand and generally includes all deposits that are not "time deposits" or "savings deposits." With some exceptions, demand deposits do not pay interest.

A *time deposit* is a deposit of funds that the depositor does not have a right to withdraw for a specified period following the date of the deposit. Time deposits include deposits payable on a specified future date, after the expiration of a specified period of time, on written notice given a specified number of days prior to payment, or, as in the case of Christmas clubs and similar clubs, after a certain number of periodic deposits have been made during a specified minimum period of time. Time deposits may be evidenced by certificates of deposit (CDs), passbooks, statements, or otherwise. Time deposits evidenced by certificates of deposit are usually payable only on presentation of the certificate.

A *savings deposit* is generally any deposit of funds that is not payable on a specified date or at the expiration of a specified period of time. Money in a savings deposit may usually be withdrawn at any time; however, a financial institution may require that an advance written notice be given prior to a withdrawal. A savings deposit may be subject to "negotiable orders of withdrawal" (i.e., a NOW account).

In addition, banks and other financial institutions may make *life insurance* and *annuities* available to individual investors, subject to certain restrictions.[1]

1155. How is interest earned on a time or savings deposit taxed? In what year should the interest be reported?

Generally, any interest earned on time or savings deposits is ordinary income that must be included in the account owner's gross income.[2] Because "interest" in this sense includes any compensation paid by the financial institution for the use of its depositors' money, many distributions commonly referred to as "dividends" are actually payments of interest and will be taxed as such.[3] These include "dividends" on deposits or share accounts in cooperative banks, credit unions, domestic building and loan associations, federal savings and loan associations, and mutual savings banks. On the other hand, dividends on the capital stock of such organizations should be reported as dividends

---

1. *NationsBank v. Variable Annuity Life Ins. Co.*, 115 S.Ct. 810 (1995).
2. Treas. Reg. §1.61-7(a).
3. See *Deputy v. duPont*, 308 U.S. 488 (1940).

and not as interest.[1] Although "interest" and "dividends" are taxed in the same manner, the distinction is still made for reporting purposes.

"Dividends" received from a mutual savings bank that received a deduction under IRC Section 591 are *not* eligible for the 15% (5%) rates applicable to "qualified dividend income" (see Q 1420).[2]

Generally, interest must be included in gross income for the year in which (1) it is actually received by the taxpayer or, if earlier, (2) it is constructively received by the taxpayer.[3] Interest is constructively received by a taxpayer in the year during which it is credited to his account, set apart for him, or otherwise made available so that he might draw upon it at any time, or so that he could have drawn upon it during the year if notice of intention to withdraw had been given.[4] Interest may be constructively received even though the taxpayer was never notified that the interest was available to him.[5] On the other hand, interest is not constructively received if the taxpayer's control of its receipt is subject to substantial limitations or restrictions (see Q 1405).[6]

If certificates of deposit (and certain other time deposits) with a term in excess of one year are issued at a price less than the "stated redemption price" that will be paid on maturity (i.e., it is issued at a discount), the depositor must treat the "original issue discount" as interest received over the term of the certificate. Thus, the amount of original issue discount deemed to have been received during the calendar year must be included in the depositor's ordinary income on his tax return for that year (see Q 1116).[7]

Original issue discount on certificates of deposit with a term of one year or less does not have to be reported until the year of disposition.[8] However, for short-term obligations a taxpayer may elect to include original issue discount (or "acquisition discount" under an alternative election) as it accrues.[9] Such an election applies to all short-term taxable corporate obligations (and Treasury bills with respect to acquisition discount) acquired on or after the first day of the first taxable year for which the election is made, and it continues to apply until the Service consents to revocation of the election. Thus, an election with respect to a certificate of deposit will apply to such other taxable short-term obligations (including Treasury bills), and vice versa. See Q 1095 regarding these elections.

If the certificate has a stated interest feature, any interest actually or constructively received during the calendar year under that feature must also be included in ordinary income for that year.

It is unclear how "indexed" certificates of deposit will be treated for income tax purposes. A certificate of deposit is considered "indexed" if the payment of principal at maturity corresponds to increases or decreases in a market standard, such as the S&P 500 or the NASDAQ 100. In many cases, no interest is paid on the investment. Instead, the payment of principal at maturity is determined in proportion to any increase in

---

1. See IRS Pub. 17; IRS Pub. 550.
2. See, generally, IRC Sec. 1(h)(11).
3. Treas. Reg. §1.451-1(a).
4. Treas. Reg. §1.451-2(a).
5. See *Gajewski v. Comm.*, 67 TC 181 (1976), *aff'd without opinion*, 578 F.2d 1383 (8th Cir. 1978).
6. Treas. Reg. §1.451-2(a). See Rev. Rul. 73-220, 1973-1 CB 297.
7. IRC Sec. 1272; Treas. Regs. §§1.1232-1(d), 1.1232-3A(e).
8. IRC Sec. 1272(a)(2)(C); see Rev. Rul. 73-221, 1973-1 CB 298; Rev. Rul. 80-157, 1980-1 CB 186.
9. IRC Sec. 1283(c).

the underlying index. It is possible that the owner of an indexed certificate of deposit may be required to report all or a portion of any accrued interest annually, even though no payments are received prior to maturity. Whether the interest expense on amounts borrowed to purchase an indexed certificate of deposit will be deductible only in the year of maturity is even more unclear (see Q 1158).

Banks and other financial institutions must supply their depositors who earn original issue discount with a statement (Form 1099-OID) setting forth the amount of original issue discount deemed to have been received by them during the year.[1]

1156. If deposits are made to a joint savings account, who should report the interest income?

For federal income tax purposes, if two or more persons own a joint savings account the interest earned is owned and must be reported by each person to the extent that each is entitled *under local law* to share in such income.[2]

1157. Are "gifts" received from a financial institution for opening a savings account or making a time deposit taxed?

Generally, yes. The fair market value of any gift (or premium) received by a depositor from a financial institution as an incentive for opening a savings account or making a time deposit is interest income that must be reported for the year in which it is received. Typically such amounts will be shown on the individual's Form 1099-INT from the institution, along with interest paid on the account.[3] This is true whether the "gift" is a household appliance, automobile, cash or other merchandise.

However, certain non-cash inducements provided by a financial institution to a depositor to open, or add to, an account will be treated as *de minimis premiums*. A non-cash inducement that does not have a value in excess of (1) $10 for a deposit of less than $5,000, or (2) $20 for a deposit of $5,000 or more will be treated as a de minimis premium. The cost to the financial institution of the premium is used in determining whether the dollar limitations are met. For administrative convenience, the Service will not require a depositor who receives a de minimis premium to treat the value of the premium as includible in gross income. In addition, the Service will not require the depositor to reduce the basis in the account by the de minimis premium. Furthermore, the Service will not require a financial institution that provides a de minimis premium to treat it as interest for purposes of reporting interest income.[4]

If the financial institution gives merchandise to an individual, other than an employee, who induces another person to open a savings account or make a time deposit, the fair market value of the "gift" is includable in gross income of that individual rather than that of the depositor.[5] Presumably, such income is not "interest" since it is not paid as compensation for the use of the recipient's money.

---

1. See Treas. Reg. §1.6049-4.
2. Rev. Rul. 76-97, 1976-1 CB 15. See e.g., *Royster v. Comm.*, TC Memo 1985-258, *aff'd*, 820 F.2d 1156 (11th Cir. 1987).
3. See IRS Pub. 17; IRS Pub. 550; IR-1032 (4-14-70).
4. Rev. Proc. 2000-30, 2000-1 CB 113.
5. See Rev. Rul. 80-61, 1980-1 CB 287.

1158. If an individual borrows the minimum required deposit on a certificate of deposit, is his interest expense on the loan deductible?

Generally, yes (if the taxpayer itemizes his deductions); however, the total amount of investment interest expense otherwise deductible by a taxpayer is subject to the limitation explained in Q 1304.

If the loan and certificates are from the same bank, the loan and deposit will, regardless of the structure of the transaction, be treated as two separate transactions for tax purposes: the interest earned on the full face value of the certificate will be reported by the bank on Form 1099-INT and must be included by the individual in his gross income for the year in which the certificate matures.[1] The interest paid on the loan will be subject to the limitations explained in Q 1304, (as well as the general rules for interest deductions – see Q 1301 through Q 1308) and may be deducted only if the individual itemizes his deductions on his income tax return for the year.

> *Example.* Dr. Gasik deposits $5,000 and borrows $5,000 from Last National Bank to purchase a $10,000 6-month money market certificate. At maturity, the certificate will pay interest of $793, but Dr. Gasik will receive only $372 (the interest earned minus $421 of interest due on the $5,000 loan from Last National). Dr. Gasik must report $793 as interest income on his income tax return for the year in which the certificate matures. If Dr. Gasik itemizes his deductions, he may include the $421 interest expense in the computation of his investment interest deduction. However, if he does not itemize, any deduction will be lost. Neither Dr. Gasik nor the bank may offset the interest expense against the interest income for purposes of income tax reporting requirements.

If a short-term (i.e., with a term of one year or less) certificate of deposit is issued at a discount, any interest expense paid or incurred on amounts borrowed to purchase or carry such certificate is usually deductible only in the year the certificate matures (or is disposed of); however, if there is an election to include the original issue discount on the certificate in income as it accrues, the current deduction of the interest expense will be limited only by the investment interest limitation explained in Q 1304 (see Q 1307).

1159. May an individual deduct the fees charged by his bank with respect to an interest bearing account on which checks may be drawn?

It depends. Fees charged by a bank for the privilege of writing checks rather than for maintaining the interest-bearing account are personal in nature and are not deductible.[2] However, fees charged by a bank for the management of a money market deposit account, which requires a minimum balance and limits check writing and pre-authorized transfers, are treated as a "miscellaneous itemized deduction" because they are paid or incurred by the individual for the management, conservation, or maintenance of investments held for the production of income.[3]

"Miscellaneous itemized deductions" are deductible only to the extent that the aggregate of all such deductions exceeds 2% of adjusted gross income (see Q 1428).

1160. Is the penalty paid for early withdrawal of funds in a time deposit tax deductible?

---

1. See Rev. Rul. 81-148, 1981-1 CB 574; Let. Rul. 8051033.
2. Rev. Rul. 82-59, 1982-1 CB 47.
3. Let. Ruls. 8345067, 8423008.

Yes. Interest and principal forfeited to a bank or other financial institution as a penalty for premature withdrawal of funds from a certificate of deposit or other time deposit are deductible "above-the-line" (i.e., in calculating adjusted gross income and not as an itemized deduction) for income tax purposes.[1]

MUTUAL FUNDS, UNIT TRUSTS, REITS

MUTUAL FUNDS

Generally

1161. What are mutual funds?

A mutual fund is a company that offers investors an interest in a portfolio of professionally managed investment assets. Mutual funds are "open-ended" in the sense that they maintain a continuous market and a constantly changing number of outstanding shares. The term "mutual fund" is sometimes used (incorrectly) to refer to closed-end investment companies, which have a fixed number of outstanding shares and are actively traded on the secondary market (see Q 1175).

Mutual funds are managed, in the sense that the underlying portfolio is changing as assets are bought and sold. Funds are generally designed to accomplish some primary investment objective, such as growth, income, capital appreciation, tax-exempt interest, international investing, etc., and therefore emphasize investments they consider appropriate to this purpose. Many funds (e.g., asset allocation funds, balanced funds, equity-income funds, hybrid funds) combine two or more investment objectives in an effort to maintain a more diversified portfolio. "Tax-managed" funds (i.e., tax-sensitive, tax-efficient funds) employ investment strategies designed to minimize current income taxes by keeping taxable gains and income as low as possible and emphasizing long-term growth. Although the specific methods vary from one fund to another, they generally include: (1) keeping turnover low; (2) offsetting capital gains with capital losses; and (3) keeping dividends and interest at a minimum. "Life cycle" funds (or "target date" funds) invest in stocks, bonds, and cash in a ratio considered appropriate for investors with a particular age and risk tolerance.[2]

The Securities and Exchange Commission requires mutual fund companies to disclose standardized after-tax returns for 1-, 5-, and 10-year periods to help investors understand the magnitude of tax costs and compare the impact of taxes on the performance of different funds. After-tax returns must accompany before-tax returns in a fund's prospectus and must be presented in two ways: (1) returns after taxes on fund distributions only; and (2) returns after taxes on fund distributions and redemption of fund shares. The SEC also requires that funds include standardized after-tax returns in certain advertisements and other sales material.[3]

Portfolio investment programs provide investors with the opportunity to use a sponsoring broker-dealer's web site to "create and manage portfolios of securities ("baskets") based on each investor's individual needs and objectives." (Portfolio investment programs

---

1. IRC Sec. 62(a)(9); Temp. Treas. Reg. §1.62-1T(c)(10); Rev. Rul. 82-27, 1982-1 CB 32; Rev. Rul. 75-20, 1975-1 CB 29; Rev. Rul. 75-21, 1975-1 CB 367.
2. See United States Securities and Exchange Commission, Frequently Asked Questions about Rule 35d-1 (Investment Company Names), at: http://www.sec.gov/divisions/investment/guidance/rule35d-1faq.htm.
3. See 17 CFR Parts 230, 239, and 270.

are frequently referred to as "folios," the name of the initial sponsor's product.) However, unlike a mutual fund, "the investor does not hold an undivided interest in a pool of securities; rather the investor is the direct beneficial owner of each of the securities included in the portfolio. Each investor has all of the rights of ownership with respect to such securities."[1] In 2001, the Securities and Exchange Commission denied a request from the Investment Company Institute (ICI) to adopt a rule that would deem portfolio investment programs to be regulated as mutual funds. See Letter in Response to Petition for Rulemaking from Investment Company Institute, above.

Because investors in investment portfolio programs own the stocks directly, they are taxed on distributions and the sale of their shares in the same manner as stockholders. For the treatment of cash dividends, see Q 1002. For the treatment of capital gain on the sale or exchange of stock, see Q 1017. For the treatment of capital gains and losses, see Q 1420.

1162. How are dividends received from a mutual fund taxed?

Mutual funds may pay three kinds of dividends to their shareholders; generally, taxable dividends will be reported to the shareholder on Form 1099-DIV.

(1) *Ordinary income dividends.* Ordinary income dividends are derived from the mutual fund's net investment income (i.e., interest and dividends on its holdings) and short-term capital gains. A shareholder generally includes ordinary income dividends in his income for the year in which they are received by reporting them as "dividend income" on his income tax return.[2]

However, under JGTRRA 2003, *qualified dividend income* (see Q 1420) is treated as *net capital gain* and is, therefore, eligible for the 15%/5% tax rates instead of the higher ordinary income tax rates. As a result of JGTRRA 2003, mutual funds are required to report on Form 1099-DIV the nature of the ordinary dividend being distributed to shareholders—that is, whether the ordinary dividend is a "qualified dividend" subject to the 15%/5% rates (Box 1b), or a nonqualifying dividend subject to ordinary income tax rates (Box 1a). Unless otherwise designated by the mutual fund, all distributions to shareholders are to be treated as ordinary income dividends.

Ordinary income dividends paid by mutual funds are eligible for the 15% (or 5%) rate *if* the income being passed from the fund to shareholders is qualified dividend income in the hands of the fund and *not* short-term capital gains or interest from bonds (both of which continue to be taxed at ordinary income tax rates).[3]

The Service has stated that mutual funds that pass through dividend income to their shareholders must meet the holding period test (see Q 1420) for the dividend-paying stocks that they pay out to be reported as qualified dividends on Form 1099-DIV. Investors must also meet the holding period test relative to the shares they hold directly, from which they received the qualified dividends that were reported to them.[4] In summary,

---

1. U.S. Securities and Exchange Commission, Letter in Response to Petition for Rulemaking from Investment Company Institute, (August 23, 2001); Speech by Paul F. Roye (Director of Investment Management, U.S. Securities and Exchange Commission) to the American Law Institute - American Bar Association Conference on Investment Management Regulation, (October 11, 2001).
2. Reg. §1.852-4(a).
3. See IRC Secs. 854(b)(1), 854(b)(2), 854(b)(5).
4. IRS News Release IR-2004-22 (2-19-2004).

the holding period test (see Q 1420) must be satisfied by both the mutual fund and the shareholder in order for the dividend to be eligible for the 15% (or 5%) rate.[1]

The Service has ruled that in making dividend designations (under IRC Sections 852(b)(3)(C), 852(b)(5)(A), 854(b)(1), 854(b)(2), 871(k)(1)(C), and 871(k)(2)(C)), a mutual fund may designate the maximum amount permitted under each provision even if the aggregate of all the amounts so designated exceeds the total amount of the mutual fund's dividend distributions. (IRC Section 852(b)(3) provides rules for determining the amount distributed by a mutual fund to its shareholders that may be treated by the shareholders as a capital gain dividend (see below). IRC Section 854 provides rules for determining the amount distributed that may be treated as qualified dividend income. IRC Section 871(k) provides rules for determining the amount distributed that may be treated as interest-related dividends or short-term capital gain dividends.) The Service further ruled that individual U.S. shareholders may apply designations to the dividends they receive from the mutual fund that differ from designations applied by shareholders who are nonresident alien individuals.[2]

Varying distributions paid by a mutual fund to shareholders in different "qualified groups" (shares in the same portfolio of securities that have different arrangements for shareholder services or the distribution of shares, or based on investment performance) constitute deductible dividends for the mutual fund.[3]

An award of points to a shareholder under an airline awards program, in which one point is awarded for each new dollar invested in the mutual fund, will not result in the payment of a preferential dividend by the fund; instead, the investor will be informed of the fair market value of the points and informed that his basis in the shares giving rise to the award of points should be adjusted downward by the fair market value of the points as a purchase price adjustment.[4]

Certain pass-through entities are required, in addition to ordinary income dividends actually paid to a shareholder, to report as part of a shareholder's ordinary income dividends the shareholder's allocated share of certain investment expenses (i.e., those which would be classified as *miscellaneous itemized deductions* if incurred by an individual). The shareholder then must include such additional amount in income and treat the amount as a miscellaneous itemized deduction (subject to the 2% floor) in the same year. However, publicly offered regulated investment companies (i.e., generally mutual funds) are excluded from the application of this provision.[5]

See Q 1166 regarding dividends declared for a year prior to the year of receipt.

(2) *Exempt interest dividends.* Some mutual funds invest in securities that pay interest exempt from federal income tax. This interest may be passed through to the fund's shareholders, retaining its tax-exempt status, provided at least 50% of the fund's assets consist of such tax-exempt securities. Thus, a shareholder does not include exempt-interest dividends in his income. The mutual fund will send written notice to its shareholders advising them of the amount of any exempt-interest dividends.[6] Any person

---

1. See also IRS Pub. 564, p. 2 (2005).
2. Rev. Rul. 2005-31, 2005-21 IRB 1084.
3. Rev. Proc. 99-40, 1999-46 IRB 565.
4. Let. Rul. 199920031.
5. IRC Sec. 67(c).
6. IRC Sec. 852(b)(5).

required to file a tax return must report the amount of tax-exempt interest received or accrued during the taxable year on that return.[1] Under JGTRRA 2003, exempt-interest dividends do *not* count as *qualified dividend income* (see Q 1420) for purposes of the 15%/5% tax rates.[2]

(3) *Capital gain dividends.* Capital gain dividends result from sales by the mutual fund of stocks and securities that result in long-term capital gains. The mutual fund will notify shareholders in writing of the amount of any capital gain dividend. The shareholder reports a capital gain dividend on his federal income tax return for the year in which it is received as a long-term capital gain regardless of how long he has owned shares in the mutual fund.[3] As such, a capital gain dividend may be partially or totally offset by the shareholder's capital losses (if any); if not totally offset by capital losses, the excess (i.e., *net capital gain*) will be taxed at the applicable capital gains rate.[4] For additional guidance on designations of capital gain dividends, see Rev. Rul. 2005-31, above.

The Service issued guidance clarifying that capital gain dividends received from a mutual fund in 2004 would be taxed at the new, lower capital gain rates enacted under JGTRRA 2003. Concern had been expressed that the existing rules for dividend designation and the transition to the new, lower capital gain rates, might cause some 2004 capital gain dividends to be taxed to mutual fund shareholders at the old, higher rates. However, the guidance clarified that this would not occur.[5]

See Q 1420 for the treatment of capital gains and losses, including the new lower rates (15%/5%) for long-term capital gains incurred on or after May 6, 2003 under JGTRRA 2003. See Q 1165 for the taxation of undistributed capital gains. See Q 1165 for the taxation of undistributed capital gains.

Generally, a shareholder may elect to treat all or a portion of *net capital gain* (i.e., the excess of long-term capital gain over short-term capital loss) as investment income.[6] If the election is made, the amount of any gain so included is taxed as investment income. This election may be advantageous if the shareholder's investment interest expense would otherwise exceed his investment income for the year. If the shareholder makes the election, he must also reduce his net capital gain by the amount treated as investment income (see Q 1420).

Detailed instructions for reporting mutual fund distributions on Form 1040 or Form 1040A are set forth in Publication 564, *Mutual Fund Distributions* (2005), which can be viewed or downloaded at: http://www.irs.gov.

1163. How is the shareholder taxed if the mutual fund pays a dividend in its portfolio stocks or securities rather than in cash?

The taxability of a dividend distribution is the same whether the distribution is in cash or portfolio stocks or securities; thus, the distribution will be treated as an ordinary income dividend, exempt-interest dividend, or capital gains dividend, as the case may be (see Q 1162). The amount (if any) that the shareholder reports on his income

---

1. IRC Sec. 6012(d).
2. See IRC Sec. 1(h)(11)(B).
3. IRC Sec. 852(b)(3)(B); Treas. Reg. §1.852-4(b)(1).
4. IRC Sec. 1(h).
5. See Notice 2004-39, 2004-22 IRB 982.
6. IRC Sec. 163(d)(4); Temp. Treas. Reg. §1.163(d)-1T.

tax return is the fair market value of the stocks or securities received as of the date of distribution.[1]

1164. How are dividends that are automatically reinvested taxed?

Some mutual funds automatically reinvest shareholder dividends under a plan that credits the shareholder with additional shares, but gives him the right to withdraw the dividends at any time. Even though the dividend is not distributed directly to the shareholder, it is credited to his account. Such dividends are considered "constructively" received by the shareholder and are included in his income for the year in which they are credited to his account.[2] The basis of the new shares is the net asset value used to determine the dividend (i.e., the amount of the dividend used to purchase the new shares).[3]

1165. How is a mutual fund shareholder taxed on undistributed capital gains?

A mutual fund may declare, but retain a capital gain dividend. If it does so, the mutual fund will notify its shareholders of the amount of the undistributed dividend and will pay federal income tax on the undistributed amount at the corporate alternative capital gains rate, which is currently 35%.[4]

A shareholder who is notified of an undistributed capital gain dividend includes the amount of the dividend in income in the same manner as a normal capital gain dividend (see Q 1162). However, the shareholder is also credited with having paid his share of the tax paid by the mutual fund on the undistributed amount; thus, on his income tax return he is treated as though he has made an advance payment of tax equal to 35% of the amount of the undistributed dividend he reported. The shareholder reports the undistributed dividend and is credited with the payment of tax for the calendar year that includes the last day of the mutual fund's taxable year during which the dividend was declared.[5]

Generally, a shareholder who reports an undistributed capital gain dividend increases his tax basis in his shares of the mutual fund by the difference between the amount of the undistributed capital gain dividend and the tax deemed paid by the shareholder in respect of such shares.[6]

See Q 1420 for the treatment of capital gains and losses.

1166. How is a mutual fund dividend taxed if it is declared for a prior year?

In some cases, a mutual fund may declare a dividend after the close of its taxable year and treat the dividend as having been paid in the prior year. This is often done in order for the fund to retain its status as a regulated investment company (because it must distribute a certain percentage of its income).

---

1. IRC Sec. 301(b); see Rev. Rul. 57-421, 1957-2 CB 367.
2. Rev. Rul. 72-410, 1972-2 CB 412.
3. See IRS Pub. 564; Treas. Reg. §1.305-2.
4. See IRC Sec. 1201(a); IRC Sec. 852(b)(3)(A).
5. IRC Sec. 852(b)(3)(D).
6. IRC Sec. 852(b)(3)(D)(iii); Treas. Reg. §1.852-4(b)(2).

As a general rule, ordinary income dividends and capital gains dividends declared for a prior mutual fund tax year are treated as received and included in income (as discussed in Q 1162) by the shareholder in the year in which the distribution is made. Similarly, exempt-interest dividends for a prior mutual fund tax year are treated as received in the year when the distribution is made, but are not included in the shareholder's income (see Q 1162).[1]

However, if a mutual fund declares a dividend in October, November or December of a calendar year, which is payable to the shareholders on a specified date in such a month, the dividend is treated as having been received by the shareholders on December 31 of that year (so long as the dividend is actually paid during January of the subsequent calendar year).[2] This rule applies to ordinary income dividends, capital gain dividends, and exempt-interest dividends.

1167. How is a return of capital taxed?

A distribution from a mutual fund that does not come from its earnings is a return of capital distribution (sometimes incorrectly referred to as a "nontaxable dividend" or "tax-free dividend"). These often occur when the fund is liquidating. The shareholder treats the return of capital as nontaxable to the extent of his tax basis in his shares. Any excess over the shareholder's basis is treated as a capital gain, which will be long-term or short-term depending on how long the shareholder held the mutual fund shares with respect to which the distribution was made. The shareholder must also reduce his tax basis (but not below zero) in those shares by the amount of the return of capital distribution.[3] See Q 1420 for the treatment of capital gain.

1168. How is a shareholder taxed when his mutual fund passes through a foreign tax credit?

Mutual funds with more than 50% of the value of their total assets invested in stocks or securities of foreign corporations may elect to give the benefit of the foreign tax credit to their shareholders.[4]

When a mutual fund makes this election, each shareholder, in addition to reporting any ordinary income and capital gains dividends, includes in income his proportionate share of foreign taxes paid by the fund. Each shareholder then treats his proportionate share of foreign taxes paid by the mutual fund as if paid by him for which he may take a tax credit or an itemized deduction. (In calculating the credit or deduction, each shareholder treats his share of the foreign taxes and the amount of any dividends paid to him with respect to the foreign income of the fund as foreign income.)[5] The shareholder may take the deduction or the credit; he may not take both.[6]

A mutual fund that makes this election must notify each shareholder of his share of the foreign taxes paid by the fund and the portion of the dividend that represents foreign income.[7] The Service has released proposed regulations that would generally

---

1. IRC Sec. 855; Treas. Reg. §1.855-1.
2. IRC Sec. 852(b)(7).
3. IRC Sec. 301(c); See Rev. Rul. 57-421, 1957-2 CB 367; IRS Pub. 564.
4. IRC Sec. 853.
5. IRC Sec. 853(b); Treas. Reg. §1.853-2(b).
6. IRC Sec. 275.
7. IRC Sec. 853(c); Treas. Reg. §1.853-3(a).

eliminate country-by-country reporting by a mutual fund to its shareholder of foreign source income that the mutual fund takes into account and foreign taxes that it pays. The proposed regulations would require that only summary foreign income and foreign tax amounts be reported to the fund's shareholders. The mutual fund would be required to provide aggregate per-country information on a statement filed with its tax return. [1]

1169. Do mutual fund dividends give rise to tax preference items for purposes of the alternative minimum tax?

The receipt of an exempt-interest dividend creates a tax preference to the extent that the dividend is derived from interest paid on certain private activity bonds issued after August 7, 1986 (see Q 1440).[2] (The receipt of capital gain and ordinary income mutual fund dividends generally do not create tax preferences.) Also, mutual funds do pass through, and each shareholder must report a proportionate share of, the fund's own tax preference items.[3]

For an explanation of the alternative minimum tax, see Q 1440.

1170. Can a shareholder deduct the interest he pays on a loan used to purchase mutual fund shares?

Yes, subject to the general limitation applicable to the deduction for investment interest (see Q 1304) and subject to total or partial disallowance if the company pays an exempt-interest dividend.[4]

Under JGTRRA 2003, "qualified dividend income" is taxable at 15% (5% for taxpayers in the 10% and 15% brackets) rather than at ordinary income tax rates. See Q 1420. However, qualified dividend income does not include any amount that the taxpayer takes into account as investment income under IRC Section 163(d)(4)(B).[5]

A shareholder may not deduct interest on indebtedness incurred or continued to purchase or carry shares of a mutual fund to the extent that the company distributed exempt-interest dividends to the shareholder during the year.[6] The amount of interest disallowed is the amount that bears the same ratio to total interest paid on the indebtedness for the year as the exempt-interest dividends bear to exempt interest and taxable dividends received by the shareholder (excluding capital gains dividends).[7]

In determining whether the indebtedness was "incurred or continued to purchase or carry" shares, one should be able to look to interpretations of comparable language with respect to deductions for interest on "indebtedness incurred or continued to purchase or carry" certain other property. See, for example, Q 1306.[8] For purposes of determining whether interest is investment interest, temporary regulations provide complex rules under which interest expense is allocated on the basis of the use of the proceeds of the underlying debt–see Q 1305.

1. See REG-105248-04, 71 Fed. Reg. 54598 (9-18-2006).
2. IRC Sec. 57(a)(5)(B).
3. IRC Sec. 59(d).
4. IRC Sec. 163(d); IRC Sec. 265(a)(4).
5. IRC 1(h)(11)(D)(i).
6. IRC Sec. 265(a)(4); Treas. Reg. §1.265-3.
7. Treas. Reg. §1.265-3(b)(2).
8. Rev. Rul. 95-53, 1995-2 CB 30; Rev. Rul. 82-163, 1982-2 CB 57.

1171. How is a shareholder taxed when he sells, exchanges, or redeems his mutual fund shares?

When a shareholder sells, exchanges, or redeems his mutual fund shares, he will generally have a capital gain or loss. Whether such gain or loss is short-term or long-term usually depends on how long the shareholder held the shares before selling (or exchanging) them.[1] If the shares were held for one year or less, the capital gain or loss will generally be short-term; the capital gain will generally be long-term if the shares were held for more than one year. See Q 1417 for an explanation of the holding period calculation, and Q 1420 for the treatment of capital gains and losses, including the new lower rates for capital gains incurred on or after May 6, 2003.

The gain or loss is the difference between the shareholder's adjusted tax basis in his shares (see below) and the amount realized from the sale, exchange, or redemption (which includes money plus the fair market value of any property received). IRC Sec. 1001. For the taxation of a wash sale of mutual fund shares, see Q 1172. For the treatment of mutual fund shares that were held as part of a conversion transaction, see Q 1085 and Q 1086.

In some cases, a company that manages mutual funds will allow shareholders in one mutual fund to exchange their shares for shares in another mutual fund managed by the same company without payment of an additional sales charge. Nevertheless, the exchange is treated as a taxable transaction; any gain or loss on the original shares must be reported as a capital gain or loss in the year the exchange occurs. (The exchange does not qualify as a "like-kind" exchange, nor as a tax-free exchange of common stock for common stock, or preferred for preferred, in the same corporation. Because stock in each fund is "backed" by a different set of assets (i.e., the portfolio securities held by each fund), shares in the funds are neither common nor preferred stock in the managing company.[2] Furthermore, such an exchange may be subject to special rules delaying an adjustment to basis for load charges if the exchanged shares were held for less than 90 days (see below).

In *Paradiso v. Comm.*,[3] the Tax Court stated that IRC Section 1031(a)(1), which provides for nonrecognition of gain or loss from like-kind exchanges, expressly does not apply to the sale of stock or other securities (citing IRC Sections 1031(a)(2)(B) and 1031(a)(2)(C)). Accordingly, the court held that the taxpayer realized taxable income from sales of mutual fund shares.

The Service has privately ruled that a mutual fund's redemption of stock pursuant to a tender offer would constitute a single and isolated transaction that was not part of a periodic redemption plan; thus, the transaction would not result in an IRC Section 305 deemed distribution to any of the fund's shareholders.[4] The Service has also stated that no gain or loss was required to be recognized by shareholders on the conversion of institutional class shares to Class A shares of the same mutual fund. Each shareholder's basis in the Class A shares would equal the shareholder's basis in the converted institutional class shares immediately before the conversion, and each shareholder's holding period for the Class A shares would include the shareholder's holding period for the

---

1. See IRC Secs. 1222, 1223.
2. Rev. Rul. 54-65, 1954-1 CB 101. See IRS Pub. 564.
3. TC Memo 2005-187.
4. Let. Rul. 200025046.

converted institutional class shares, provided that the shareholder held those converted shares as capital assets immediately before the conversion.[1] In addition, the Service privately ruled that the conversion of two classes of mutual fund shares into a single class of shares, based on the relative net asset value of the respective shares, did not result in gain or loss to the shareholders.[2]

If a shareholder purchases mutual fund shares, receives a capital gain dividend (or is credited with an undistributed capital gain) and then sells the shares *at a loss* within six months after purchasing the shares, the loss is treated as a *long-term* capital loss to the extent of the capital gain dividend (or undistributed capital gain).[3] Similarly, if a shareholder purchases mutual fund shares, receives an exempt-interest dividend, and then sells the shares at a loss within six months after purchasing the shares, the loss (to the extent of the amount of the dividend) will be *disallowed.*[4] In the case of a fund that regularly distributes at least 90% of its net tax-exempt interest, regulations may prescribe that the holding period for application of the loss disallowance rule is less than six months (but not less than the longer of 31 days or the period between the regular distributions of exempt-interest dividends).[5] For purposes of calculating the 6-month period, periods during which the shareholder's risk of loss is diminished as a result of holding other positions in substantially similar or related property, or through certain options or short sales, are not counted.[6] Regulations will provide a limited exception to these rules for shares sold pursuant to a periodic redemption plan.[7]

Generally a shareholder's tax basis in mutual fund shares is his cost of acquiring them, including any load charges (i.e., sales or similar charges incurred to acquire mutual fund shares). (See Q 1415 regarding the determination of basis.) However, a shareholder who exercises a *reinvestment right*, which was acquired as a result of the load charge, is subject to a 90-day holding period during which the load charge will not be fully included in his basis. ("Reinvestment right" is defined to mean the right to acquire stock of one or more regulated investment companies without a load charge or at a reduced load charge.) If such a shareholder (1) disposes of the shares before the 91st day after the date of acquisition, and (2) subsequently acquires other shares (in the same or another mutual fund) and the otherwise applicable load charge is reduced as a result of the reinvestment right, then the initial load charge will not be included in his basis for purposes of determining the gain or loss on the disposition (except to the extent that it exceeds the reduction applicable to the second load charge). Instead, it will be includable in his basis in the newly acquired shares. If the original shares are transferred by gift, the donee succeeds to the treatment of the donor.[8]

If all of a shareholder's shares in a mutual fund were acquired on the same day and for the same price (or, if by gift or inheritance, at the same tax basis), he will have little difficulty in establishing his tax basis and holding period of the shares he sells or redeems. However, if his shares were acquired at different times or prices (or bases), the process is more difficult; unless the shareholder can "adequately identify" (see Q 1418) the lot from which the shares being sold or redeemed originated, he must either treat the sale or redemption as disposing of shares from the earliest acquired lots (i.e.,

1. Let. Rul. 199941016.
2. Let. Rul. 9807026.
3. IRC Sec. 852(b)(4).
4. IRC Sec. 852(b)(4)(B).
5. IRC Sec. 852(b)(4)(E).
6. IRC Secs. 852(b)(4)(C), 246(c).
7. IRC Sec. 852(b)(4)(D).
8. IRC Sec. 852(f).

by a first-in, first-out (FIFO) method) or, if he qualifies, elect to use one of two *average basis* methods for determining his adjusted basis and holding period of shares sold or redeemed.[1]

A shareholder may elect to use an "average basis" for his shares if (1) the shares are held in a custodial account maintained for the acquisition or redemption of shares in the fund, and (2) the shareholder purchased or acquired the shares at different prices or bases.[2]

Under the *double-category method* of determining average basis, all shares in the mutual fund account are divided into two categories–those with a holding period of more than one year and those with a holding period of one year or less. The basis for each share in either category is the total cost (or other basis) of all the shares in that category, divided by the number of shares in that category. The shareholder can then elect to have the shares being sold to come from either the "more than one year" category (thus recognizing long-term gain or loss), or the "one year or less" category (thus recognizing short-term gain or loss). If the shareholder does not designate the category from which the shares are to be sold, the shares are deemed to come from the "more than one year" category first.[3]

When shares in the "one year or less" category have been held for more than one year, they are transferred to the "more than one year" category. If some of the shares in the "one year or less" category have been sold or transferred, they are deemed to have been the earliest acquired shares (i.e., by a FIFO method). The basis of unsold shares transferred to the "more than one year" category is the average basis of the shares in the "one year or less" category at the time of the most recent sale, determined as discussed above. If no shares have been sold from the "one year or less" category, the basis of the shares transferred to the "more than one year" category is their cost or other basis (not the average basis).[4]

Under the *single category method* of determining average basis, all shares in the mutual fund account are added together. The basis of each share in the account is the total cost or other basis of all the shares in the account, divided by the total number of shares. Any shares sold or redeemed are deemed to be those acquired first. The single category method may not be used for the purpose of converting short-term gain or loss to long-term gain or loss, or vice versa.[5]

The election to use either of the "average basis" methods is made on the shareholder's tax return for the first year for which he wishes the election to apply and will apply to all shares in the same mutual fund held by the shareholder, even if in different accounts. In reporting gain or loss, the taxpayer reports on the return for each year to which the election applies that an average basis is being used, and which method has been selected. An election may not be revoked without the consent of the IRS.[6]

In the case of shares acquired by gift, the basis in the hands of a donee is the same as it was in the hands of the donor; however, this rule applies only for purposes of deter-

---

1. Treas. Regs. §§1.1012-1(c), 1.1012-1(e). See IRS Pub. 564.
2. Treas. Reg. §1.1012-1(e).
3. Treas. Reg. §1.1012-1(e)(3).
4. Treas. Reg. §1.1012-1(e)(3)(iii).
5. Treas. Reg. §1.1012-1(e)(4).
6. Treas. Reg. §1.1012-1(e)(6).

mining gain. In the event that the shares' adjusted basis exceeds their fair market value at the time of the gift, the basis in the hands of the donee for purposes of determining loss is their fair market value at the time the gift was made. Ordinarily, an average basis method may not be used on such shares; however, a donee shareholder can elect to apply an average basis method to accounts containing shares acquired by gift if he includes a statement with his tax return indicating that he will use the fair market value of the shares at the time of the gift in computing the average bases. The statement applies to all shares acquired either before or after the statement is filed, for as long as the election to use average basis remains in effect.[1]

A unit trust unit holder (see Q 1178) may not use either of the average basis methods discussed above unless the unit trust invests primarily in the securities of one management company, or one other corporation, and unless the trust has no power to invest in any other securities except those issued by a single other management company.[2]

1172. How is a wash sale of mutual fund shares taxed?

A wash sale of mutual fund shares is taxed in the same manner as a wash sale of regular corporation stock or other securities (see Q 1029 to Q 1031).

However, when the double category method is used for determining basis and holding period, a wash sale of mutual fund shares from the "one year or less" category *after* acquisition of the replacement shares will result in the aggregate basis of the shares remaining in the "one year or less" category being increased by the amount of the loss that is disallowed.[3] When the single category method is used for determining basis, or when an average basis method is not used, the general wash sale tax basis rules apply.[4]

Money Market Funds

1173. What is a "money market fund"?

A money market fund is a mutual fund generally seeking maximum current income and liquidity through investment in short-term money market instruments, such as Treasury bills, certificates of deposit, or commercial paper. Dividends are customarily declared daily, and automatically reinvested in additional shares, unless a distribution option is elected. Shares may be redeemed at any time.

1174. How is a money market fund shareholder taxed?

Because a money market fund is a mutual fund, its shareholders are taxed in the manner discussed in Q 1162 through Q 1172. Money market funds ordinarily do not have capital gain dividends because of the policy to invest in short-term securities. Note that money market fund dividends are not qualified dividends and, thus, do not qualify for the lower tax rates (15%/5%) under JGTRRA 2003. See Q 1420.

Closed-End Funds

1175. What is a closed-end fund? How are shareholders in a closed-end fund taxed?

---

1. Treas. Reg. §1.1012-1(e)(1)(ii).
2. Treas. Reg. §1.1012-1(e)(5)(ii).
3. Treas. Reg. §1.1012-1(e)(3)(iii)(d); IRC Sec. 1091(d).
4. See Treas. Reg. §1.1012-1(e)(4)(iv).

A closed-end fund holds a portfolio of investment assets, but does not ordinarily redeem shares at net asset value or sell new shares. Shares of the fund itself are actively traded on the secondary market.

Although a closed-end fund is not actually a mutual fund, if the fund qualifies and makes the necessary election to be taxed as a regulated investment company, its shareholders will be taxed like shareholders of a mutual fund. See Q 1162 through Q 1172 for details. If, on the other hand, the closed-end fund is established as a regular corporation, its shareholders will be taxed accordingly (see Q 1001 to Q 1032).

Because closed-end fund shares are traded in the open market or on an exchange and are not redeemed by the company, capital gain or loss on sale is based on the sale price and not on redemption price.

Exchange-Traded Funds

1176. What is an exchange-traded fund? How are shareholders in an exchange-traded fund taxed?

The term "exchange-traded fund share" includes securities representing interests in unit investment trusts (see Q 1178) or open-end management investment companies that hold securities based on an index or portfolio of securities.[1] "Unlike typical open-end funds or unit investment trusts, exchange-traded funds do not sell or redeem their individual shares at net asset value. Instead, exchange-traded funds sell and redeem shares at NAV only in large blocks (such as 50,000 exchange traded shares). In addition, national securities exchanges list exchange-traded funds shares for trading, which allows investors to purchase and sell individual such shares among themselves at market prices throughout the day. Exchange-traded funds, therefore, possess characteristics of traditional open-end funds and unit investment trusts (both of which issue redeemable shares), and of closed-end funds (which generally issue shares that trade at negotiated prices on national securities exchanges and are not redeemable). A fundamental characteristic of exchange-traded funds in the United States is that they are based on specific domestic and foreign market indices."[2]

Exchange-traded fund shares can be sold short (see Q 1021 to 28), and bought on margin. Thus, exchange-traded funds are promoted as offering the benefits of index investing at a lower cost, and with greater trading flexibility in comparison to some mutual funds.

Exchange-traded funds are also promoted as being more tax-efficient than mutual funds. For example, "[w]hen a mutual fund sells portfolio securities to pursue its investment strategies or to generate cash for shareholder redemptions, the mutual fund may realize capital gains if the value of the securities increased while they were in the fund portfolio. A mutual fund distributes accumulated capital gains to its shareholders, and shareholders generally must pay taxes on those distributions. An exchange-traded fund may also accumulate and distribute capital gains to its investors. However, like index funds, an exchange-traded fund may be more tax efficient than many mutual funds because of the low turnover in its portfolio securities. In addition, the exchange-traded fund structure may allow an exchange-traded fund to avoid capital gains to a greater

---

1. Securities and Exchange Commission Release No. 34-40985, fn 3.
2. *Concept Release: Actively Managed Exchange-Traded Funds*, 66 Fed. Reg. 57514 (11-15-2001).

extent than some index funds. Because an exchange-traded fund typically redeems creation units of exchange-traded shares by delivering securities in the "redemption basket," an exchange-traded fund generally does not have to sell securities (and thus possibly realize capital gains) in order to pay redemptions in cash."[1] It is important to note that although exchange-traded funds may produce fewer, and smaller, capital gain distributions than some mutual funds, that does not mean that such funds never make capital gain distributions, or that the amount of a distribution will always be smaller than a capital gain distribution from a mutual fund.

Exchange-traded funds organized as unit investment trusts (see Q 1178) generally qualify for tax treatment as regulated investment companies for tax purposes. For the treatment of dividends, see Q 1162. For the treatment of capital gain on the sale or exchange of exchange-traded shares, see Q 1171. For the treatment of capital gains and losses, see Q 1420.

Hedge Funds

1177. What is a hedge fund? How are shareholders in a hedge fund taxed?

There is no statutory or regulatory definition of *hedge fund*, a type of pooled investment vehicle, but such funds have several characteristics in common. "Hedge funds are organized by professional investment managers who frequently have a significant stake in the funds they manage and receive a management fee that includes a substantial share of the performance of the fund."[2]

"Hedge funds were originally designed to invest in equity securities and short selling to 'hedge' the portfolio's exposure to movements of the equity markets. Today, however, advisers to hedge funds utilize a wide variety of investment strategies and techniques designed to maximize the returns for investors in the hedge funds they sponsor."[3]

"Hedge funds utilize a number of different investment styles and strategies and invest in a wide variety of financial instruments. Hedge funds invest in equity and fixed income securities, currencies, over-the-counter derivatives, futures contracts, and other assets. Some hedge funds may take on leverage, sell securities short, or use hedging and arbitrage strategies. *** Hedge funds offer investors an important risk management tool by providing valuable portfolio diversification because hedge fund returns in many cases are not correlated to the broader debt and equity markets."[4] A *fund of funds* is a fund that invests in several hedge funds.

Traditionally, hedge fund investors were limited to the very wealthy. Beginning in the mid-to-late 1990s, the SEC was increasingly faced with a number of important policy concerns, including: (1) the growing number of hedge funds; (2) the accompanying growth of hedge fund fraud; and (3) the growing exposure of smaller investors, pensioners, and other market participants to hedge funds (due, in part, to the lowering

---

1. *Concept Release: Actively Managed Exchange-Traded Funds*, 66 Fed. Reg. 57514 (11-15-2001).
2. SEC Final Rule Release No. IA-2333, Registration Under the Act of Certain Hedge Fund Advisers, at: www.sec. gov/rules/final/ia-2333.htm.
3. SEC Final Rule Release No. IA-2333, Registration Under the Act of Certain Hedge Fund Advisers, at: www.sec. gov/rules/final/ia-2333.htm.
4. United States Securities and Exchange Commission, *Implications of the Growth of Hedge Funds, Staff Report to the United States Securities and Exchange Commission* (September 2003), at: http://www.sec.gov/spotlight/hedgefunds.htm.

of minimum investment requirements by some hedge funds).[1] To address these concerns, in 2004 the SEC adopted a final rule requiring certain hedge funds to register with the SEC and be subject to that agency's oversight.[2] But a federal court rejected the rule.

Domestic hedge funds are generally set up as limited partnerships. Thus, holders of interests in hedge funds are taxed on their distributions as limited partners. For the treatment of cash distributions, see Q 1201. For the treatment of capital gain on the sale or exchange of interests, see Q 1204 and Q 1205.

UNIT TRUSTS

1178. What is a unit trust? How are unit holders taxed?

A unit trust (unit investment trust) holds a fixed portfolio of specified assets, such as tax-exempt bonds, Ginnie Maes, corporate bonds, or certificates of deposit. The trust issues redeemable securities, each of which represents an undivided interest in the assets held by the trust.[3] The assets in the trust are not traded, but are monitored instead. When the assets mature, the trust ends. A contractual or periodic payment plan mutual fund is a type of unit trust.

If the trust is established as a "grantor" trust (that is, a trust under subpart E, subchapter J of Chapter 1 of the Internal Revenue Code, as the prospectus may say), the unit holder is treated as the owner of a part of the trust assets in proportion to his investment. In a grantor trust, income, deductions, and credits against tax of the trust are attributed to the investor as if he owned directly a share of the securities themselves.[4] (Expenses of the trust that would have been "miscellaneous itemized deductions" had they been incurred by an individual are included with the investor's miscellaneous itemized deductions for purposes of calculating the investor's taxation. See Q 1428.) Thus, gain on any sale of trust assets by the trust is taxable to the unit holders. What is passed through by the trust depends on the character of its assets. For example, the unit holder may have to reduce his basis in his unit to reflect amortization of bond premium, especially in exempt-interest trusts (see Q 1126). The unit holder may also have to reduce basis for accrued interest received, if any, on bonds delivered after payment is made for the unit.

Gain on the sale of a unit by the unit holder is capital gain, to the extent it does not include accrued interest or earned original issue discount (see Q 1116 to Q 1119). For the treatment of capital gain, see Q 1420.

If the trust qualifies and makes the election to be taxed as a regulated investment company, unit holders will be taxed like shareholders in a mutual fund (see Q 1162 to Q 1172).

Interest on indebtedness incurred or continued to purchase or carry exempt-interest units is not deductible (see Q 1170, Q 1306).[5]

---

1. SEC Final Rule Release No. IA-2333, Registration Under the Act of Certain Hedge Fund Advisers, at: www.sec.gov/rules/final/ia-2333.htm.
2. See SEC Rule 203(b)(3)-2, 17 CFR 275.203(b)(3)-2.
3. 15 USC §80a-4.
4. IRC Sec. 671.
5. IRC Sec. 265(a)(2).

In 2006, the IRS released final regulations clarifying the reporting obligations for trustees and middlemen of widely-held fixed investment trusts (WHFITs).[1]

REAL ESTATE INVESTMENT TRUSTS

1179. How is a shareholder (or beneficiary) in a real estate investment trust taxed?

A real estate investment trust (REIT) invests principally in real estate and mortgages. Shareholders (or holders of beneficial interests) in real estate investment trusts are taxed like shareholders in regular corporations (Q 1001 to Q 1032) unless the REIT distributes at least a certain percentage of its real estate investment trust taxable income. IRC Sec. 857(a). A REIT is required to distribute 90% of its taxable income. If the required distribution is made, the taxation is similar to that of mutual fund shareholders.

(1) *Ordinary income dividends.* Under JGTRRA 2003, *qualified dividend income* is treated as *net capital gain* (see Q 1420) and is, therefore, eligible for the 15%/5% tax rates instead of the higher ordinary income tax rates. Because REITS generally do not pay corporate income taxes, most ordinary income dividends paid by REITS do *not* constitute qualified dividend income, and, consequently, are not eligible for the 15%/5% rates.[2] However, a small portion of dividends paid by REITS may constitute qualified dividend income – for example, if the: (1) dividend is attributable to dividends received by the REIT from non-REIT corporations, such as taxable REIT subsidiaries; or (2) income was subject to tax by the REIT at the corporate level, such as built-in gains, or when a REIT distributes less than 100% of its taxable income. Earnings and profits, which were accumulated prior to becoming a REIT, and distributed by a REIT in order to qualify as such, may also count as qualified dividend income.[3]

REITs that pass through dividend income to their shareholders must meet the holding period test (see Q 1420) for the dividend-paying stocks that they pay out to be reported as qualified dividends on Form 1099-DIV. Investors must *also* meet the holding period test relative to the shares they hold directly, from which they received the qualified dividends that were reported to them.[4]

Unless designated by the REIT as qualified dividend income, all distributions are ordinary income dividends.[5] Ordinary income dividends are included in the shareholder's (or beneficiary's) income for the taxable year in which they are received. (Shareholders do not include a share of a REIT's investment expenses in income, nor with the shareholder's miscellaneous itemized deductions, as in the case of certain other pass-through entities. See Q 1428.)

(2) *Capital gain dividends.* Capital gain dividends are designated as such by the REIT in a written notice to the shareholder (beneficiary).[6] The shareholder (beneficiary) reports capital gain dividends as long-term capital gain in the year received, regardless of how long he has owned an interest in the REIT.[7] See Q 1420 for the treatment of

---

1. See TD 9308, 71 Fed. Reg. 78351 (12-29-2006). See also TD 9241, 71 Fed. Reg. 4002 (1-24-2006); Notice 2006-30, 2006-24 IRB 1044, Notice 2006-29, 2006-12 IRB 644.
2. See IRC Sec. 857(c); see also National Association of Real Estate Investment Trusts, *Policy Bulletin*, (5-28-2003).
3. See IRC Sec. 857(c). See also IRS News Release IR-2004-22 (2-19-2004).
4. IRS News Release IR-2004-22 (2-19-2004).
5. Treas. Reg. §1.857-6(a).
6. IRC Sec. 857(b)(3)(C).
7. IRC Sec. 857(b)(3)(B); Treas. Reg. §1.857-6(b).

capital gains and losses, including the new lower rates under JGTRRA 2003 (15%/5%) for long-term capital gains incurred on or after May 6, 2003, and the availability of the election to include *net capital gain* in investment income.

Generally, ordinary income dividends and capital gain dividends declared for the prior REIT tax year are included in income by the shareholder in the year they are received.[1] However, any dividend declared by a REIT in October, November, or December of any calendar year and payable to shareholders on a specified date in such a month are treated as received by the shareholder on December 31 of that calendar year so long as the dividend is actually paid during January of the following calendar year.[2]

A REIT may declare, but retain a capital gain dividend. If it does so, the REIT must notify its shareholders of the amount of the undistributed dividend and pay federal income tax on the undistributed amount at the corporate alternative capital gains rate, which is currently 35%.[3]

A shareholder who is notified of an undistributed capital gain dividend is required to include the dividend in computing his long-term capital gains for the taxable year that includes the last day of the REIT's taxable year. However, the shareholder is credited or allowed a refund for his share of the tax paid by the REIT on the undistributed amount; thus, on his income tax return he is treated as though he has made an advance payment of tax equal to 35% of the amount of the undistributed dividend he reported.[4] The adjusted basis of a shareholder's shares in a REIT is increased by the difference between the amount of the undistributed capital gain dividend and the tax deemed paid by the shareholder in respect of such shares.[5]

The IRS ruled that shareholders who received all or part of a REIT's special stock dividend would be treated as having received a distribution to which IRC Section 301 through IRC Section 305 applied. The amount of the stock distribution would be equal to the value of the stock on the valuation date, rather than on the date of the distribution.[6] The Service also determined that a distribution of earnings and profits from a newly established REIT (arising from earnings and profits accumulated during the pre-REIT years), in which shareholders could elect to receive cash, stock, or a combination of both, should be treated as a distribution of property to which IRC Section 301 applies.[7]

1180. Do REIT dividends give rise to tax preference items for purposes of the alternative minimum tax?

REIT dividends ordinarily do not create tax preferences. However, real estate investment trusts do pass through, and each shareholder must report a proportionate share of, the REIT's own tax preference items. IRC Sec. 59(d).

For an explanation of the alternative minimum tax, see Q 1440.

---

1. IRC Sec. 858(b); Treas. Reg. §1.858-1(c).
2. IRC Sec. 857(b)(8).
3. IRC Sec. 857(b)(3)(A). See IRC Sec. 1201(a).
4. IRC Sec. 857(b)(3)(D).
5. IRC Sec. 857(b)(3)(D)(iii).
6. Let. Rul. 200122001.
7. Let. Rul. 200348020.

1181. How is a REIT shareholder taxed when he sells, exchanges, or redeems his shares?

When a shareholder (or owner of a beneficial interest) sells, exchanges, or redeems his shares, he will generally have a capital gain or loss. The capital gain or loss will be short-term if the shares were held for one year or less; it will be long-term if the shares were held for more than one year (see Q 1417; see Q 1420 for the treatment of capital gains and losses, including the new lower rates for capital gains incurred on or after May 6, 2003). However, if a loss is realized on the sale of shares held less than six months, such loss must be treated as long-term loss to the extent of any capital gains dividend received on those shares during such period. (This 6-month period is tolled during any time that the shareholder's risk of loss with respect to the shares is reduced through certain option contracts, short sales, or offsetting positions in substantially similar property.) A limited exception will, however, be provided by regulation for sales pursuant to a periodic liquidation plan.[1]

The gain or loss is the difference between the shareholder's adjusted tax basis in his shares and the amount realized from the sale, exchange, or redemption (which includes money plus the fair market value of any property received – see Q 1415).[2]

If a shareholder's shares in the REIT were acquired on the same day and for the same price, he will have little difficulty in establishing his tax basis and holding period of the shares he sells, exchanges, or redeems. However, if his shares were acquired at different times or prices, the process is more difficult; unless the shareholder can "adequately identify" the lot from which the shares being sold or exchanged originated, he must treat the sale or exchange as disposing of the shares from the earliest acquired lots (i.e., by a first-in, first-out (FIFO) method).[3] The "average basis" methods discussed in Q 1171 for mutual fund shares are *not* available to REIT shareholders. For an explanation of how shares may be "adequately identified," see Q 1418.

See Q 1085 and Q 1086 for the income tax consequences upon the disposition of a position that is held as part of a conversion transaction.

PRECIOUS METALS AND COLLECTIBLES

PRECIOUS METALS

1182. How may an individual invest in precious metals?

Depending on the metal, investments may be made in two or three ways. In the case of gold or silver, an investor may purchase gold or silver *bullion-type* coins (e.g., the Canadian Maple Leaf), bars, or certificates that certify that a specific amount of the metal is housed in a specific warehouse for the investor. In the case of other metals, such as platinum or palladium, investments are made by the purchase of bars or certificates.

Each method of investing in precious metals has its own advantages and disadvantages.

---

1. IRC Sec. 857(b)(7).
2. IRC Sec. 1001.
3. Treas. Reg. §1.1012-1(c).

If an investor acquires *bullion-type* coins in a taxable transaction (such as in a nonlike-kind exchange or as payment of a stock dividend or for services rendered), the coins will be valued at fair market value, not face value, for purposes of that transaction (see Q 1188).

For the distinction between bullion-type coins and other valuable coins, see Q 1185.

1183. When a precious metal is sold, how is the transaction taxed?

Unless a precious metal is part of a tax straddle owned by the investor, or is part of a conversion transaction, no special tax rules apply to its sale. Therefore, to the extent that the selling price received exceeds the individual's tax basis (see Q 1415) in the metal, he must report a taxable gain; if the individual's tax basis in the metal exceeds the selling price, he may report a loss from the transaction. Metal held as an investment is considered a capital asset, and gain or loss on the sale will be considered a capital gain or loss (see Q 1416). IRC Sec. 1221. Whether the capital gain or loss will be long-term or short-term depends on how long the investor owned the metal prior to sale (see Q 1417). For the treatment of capital gains and losses, see Q 1420.

When bullion-type coins are acquired in the ordinary course of a taxpayer's trade or business, the taxpayer's purpose for holding the coins at the time of their disposition (even if different from his purpose in acquiring them) apparently controls for purposes of determining whether their sale results in capital gain (or loss) or ordinary income (or loss).[1]

The sale of a precious metal that is part of a tax straddle is subject to special tax rules (see Q 1077 to Q 1084), as is the sale of a precious metal that was held as part of a conversion transaction (see Q 1085 and Q 1086).

1184. How is an individual taxed if, instead of selling a precious metal, he exchanges it for other property?

Like-Kind Exchanges

If a precious metal is exchanged solely for another precious metal of the *same nature and character* (e.g., gold for gold, or silver for silver), the transaction will generally receive nonrecognition treatment, subject to the rules for like-kind exchanges in IRC Section 1031 (see Q 1422). Thus, the exchange of *bullion-type* gold coins minted by one country for *bullion-type* gold coins minted by another country will qualify as a like-kind exchange.[2] Similarly, the exchange of gold bullion for Canadian Maple Leaf gold coins (i.e., bullion-type coins) is a like-kind exchange.[3]

However, the exchange of a *numismatic* coin for a *bullion-type* coin is not a like-kind exchange.[4] Likewise, the exchange of gold bullion for silver bullion does not qualify as a like-kind exchange, since silver and gold are intrinsically different metals and are used in different ways.[5] (This reasoning would appear to apply to an exchange of any two different metals.)

---

1. See TAM 8413001.
2. Rev. Rul. 76-214, 1976-1 CB 218.
3. Rev. Rul. 82-96, 1982-1 CB 113.
4. Rev. Rul. 79-143, 1979-1 CB 264.
5. Rev. Rul. 82-166, 1982-2 CB 190.

For an explanation of like-kind exchanges and the effect of giving or receiving money or other property in connection with an otherwise like-kind exchange, see Q 1422. For the distinction between *bullion-type* coins and other valuable coins, see Q 1185.

Other Exchanges

If an individual exchanges a precious metal he holds as an investment for (1) another precious metal of a different kind or class, or (2) other property that is not a precious metal, he will recognize a taxable gain (or loss) to the extent that the sum of the fair market value of the property and money (if any) received in the transaction is greater (or less) than his tax basis in the precious metal he transferred.[1] Normally, these will be capital gains and losses (see Q 1416). Whether the capital gain or loss will be long-term or short-term depends on how long the metal had been owned (see Q 1417). For the treatment of capital gains and losses, see Q 1420.

COLLECTIBLES

1185. What is a collectible?

In the broad sense, a "collectible" is any item of property that derives its value directly from its rarity and popularity. An item's history, condition, composition, artistic and aesthetic qualities, and the number of similar items in existence may each play a part in determining the value of a particular collectible. However, the presence or absence of a ready market where the item may be traded will have a great deal to do with whether a particular class of property is an investment quality collectible.

Common investment quality collectibles include rare coins and currencies, works of art, gems, and stamps. Oriental rugs, antiques, and certain alcoholic beverages are also often held as investments.

Coins

There are two types of coins held for investment purposes. *Numismatic* coins (such as the United States $20 gold piece) derive their value from qualities, such as condition and number minted, which make it rare; metal content is only one of many elements contributing to the value of a numismatic (or rare) coin. On the other hand, *bullion-type* coins (such as the Canadian Maple Leaf, the Mexican Peso, and the Austrian Corona) derive their value solely from their metal content (although a striking premium may also be added into the market value); they represent investments in the world gold or silver markets rather than in the coins themselves.[2]

For tax purposes, numismatic coins should be considered collectibles, but a bullion-type coin should not be unless it has a numismatic value in excess of its bullion value—as, for example, in the case of a "proof" of a bullion-type coin. (Since the value of such a "proof" depends not only on its metal content, but also on factors such as the number and date minted, a "proof" of an otherwise bullion-type coin should be treated as a numismatic coin.)

1186. When a collectible is sold, how is the transaction taxed?

---

1. IRC Sec. 1001.
2. See Rev. Rul. 79-143, 1979-1 CB 264.

No special tax rules apply to sales of collectibles held for investment; therefore, to the extent that the selling price received exceeds the individual's tax basis (see Q 1415) in the collectible, he must report a taxable gain; if the individual's basis in the collectible exceeds the selling price, he may report a loss from the transaction.[1] *Collectibles gain* (i.e., gain on the sale or exchange of a collectible that is a capital asset held for more than one year – see Q 1420) is subject to separate treatment from other capital gains and losses, which generally results in it being subject to a capital gain rate of 28%.[2] (See Q 1416 for the definition of capital asset.) See Q 1420 for the tax treatment of capital gains and losses.

If the entire purchase price for the collectible is received in the taxable year of sale, the gain (or loss) must be reported on that year's income tax return; otherwise, the installment sales rules will apply (see Q 1408).

1187. How is an individual taxed if, instead of selling the collectible, he exchanges it for other property?

Like-Kind Exchanges

If the collectible is exchanged solely for another collectible (or collectibles) of the same nature or character, the transaction will generally receive nonrecognition treatment, subject to the rules for like-kind exchanges in IRC Section 1031. Thus, the exchange of numismatic coins for other numismatic coins or stamps for stamps should qualify as a like-kind exchange. For an explanation of like-kind exchanges and the effect of giving or receiving money or other property in connection with an otherwise like-kind exchange, see Q 1422.

The exchange of a numismatic coin for a bullion-type coin (see Q 1185) is not a like-kind exchange.[3]

Other Exchanges

If an individual exchanges a collectible he holds as an investment for (1) another collectible of a different kind or class, or (2) other property that is not a collectible, he will recognize a taxable gain (or loss) to the extent that the sum of the fair market value of the property and money (if any) received in the transaction is greater (or less) than his tax basis in the collectible he transferred.[4] Normally, these will be capital gains and losses (see Q 1416). Capital gains or losses will be short-term or long-term depending on how long the transferred collectible had been owned. (see Q 1417).

Collectibles gain (i.e., gain on the sale or exchange of a collectible that is a capital asset held for more than one year) is subject to separate treatment from other capital gains and losses, which generally results in it being subject to a capital gain rate of 28%.[5] For the tax treatment of capital gains and losses, see Q 1420.

1188. Is a "rare" coin or currency money or "property"? How will it be valued when it is used in a taxable transaction?

1. IRC Sec. 1001.
2. IRC Sec. 1(h).
3. Rev. Rul. 79-143, 1979-1 CB 264.
4. IRC Sec. 1001.
5. See IRC Sec. 1(h).

Rare (numismatic) coins or currencies that have been removed from circulation and coins or currencies in circulation that have a numismatic value in excess of face value are "property other than money" for purposes of the federal income tax.[1]

As "property other than money" a rare coin or currency will be valued at its fair market value rather than face value when it is used in a taxable transaction. Thus, where a taxpayer "sold" real property with a tax basis of $2,000 for silver coins having a face value of $2,000 and a fair market value of $6,000, the taxpayer realized a $4,000 taxable gain in the transaction.[2] Similarly, a dividend paid to a taxpayer in U.S. Double Eagle $20 gold coins having a total face value of $5,500 had to be reported as $70,396 of dividend income.[3] Also, an individual who receives compensation for services rendered in the form of rare but circulating coins or currencies that have a fair market value in excess of their face value must include the higher fair market value in his income.[4]

---

1. See *California Fed. Life Ins. Co. v. Comm.*, 76 TC 107 (1981), *aff'd*, 680 F.2d 85 (9th Cir. 1982); *Joslin v. U.S.*, 81-2 USTC 88,710 (10th Cir. 1981); *Lary v. Comm.*, TC Memo 1987-169, *aff'd*, 842 F.2d 296 (11th Cir. 1988).
2. Rev. Rul. 76-249, 1976-2 CB 21.
3. *Cordner v. U.S.*, 671 F.2d 367 (9th Cir. 1981).
4. *Joslin v. U.S.*, above.

LIMITED PARTNERSHIPS

PUBLICLY TRADED LIMITED PARTNERSHIPS

1189. How is a publicly traded partnership taxed?

A *publicly traded partnership* is taxed as a corporation unless 90% of the partnership's income is passive-type income and has been passive-type income for all taxable years beginning after 1987 during which the partnership (or any predecessor) was in existence. For this purpose, a partnership (or a predecessor) is not treated as being in existence until the taxable year in which it is first publicly traded.[1] On the first day that a publicly traded partnership is treated as a corporation under these rules, the partnership is treated as having transferred all of its assets (subject to its liabilities) to a new corporation in exchange for stock of the corporation, followed by a distribution of the stock to its partners in liquidation of their partnership interests.[2] A publicly traded partnership is a partnership that is (1) traded on an established securities market, or (2) is readily tradable on a secondary market or the substantial equivalent thereof (discussed below).[3] In general, "passive-type income" for this purpose includes interest, dividends, real property rents, gain from the sale of real property, income and gain from certain mineral or natural resource activities, and gain from sale of a capital or IRC Section 1231 asset.[4]

The passive-type income exception is not available to a publicly traded partnership that would be treated as a regulated investment company as described in IRC Section 851(a) if the partnership were a domestic corporation. Regulations may provide otherwise if the principal activity of the partnership involves certain commodity transactions.[5]

A partnership that fails to meet the passive-type income requirement may be treated as continuing to meet the requirement if: (1) the Service determines that the failure was inadvertent; (2) no later than a reasonable time after the discovery of the failure, steps are taken so that the partnership once more meets the passive-type income requirement; and (3) the partnership and each individual holder agree to make whatever adjustments or pay whatever amounts as may be required by the Service with respect to the period in which the partnership inadvertently failed to meet the requirement.[6]

A grandfather rule provides that partnerships that were publicly traded, or for which registrations were filed with certain regulatory agencies, on December 17, 1987 ("existing partnerships"), are exempt from treatment as a corporation until taxable years beginning after 1997. (See below for treatment of electing 1987 partnerships after 1997.) However, the addition of a substantial line of business to an existing partnership after December 17, 1987 will terminate such an exemption. For purposes of the 90% passive-type income requirement above, an existing partnership is not treated as being in existence before the earlier of (1) the first taxable year beginning after 1997 or (2) such a termination of exemption due to the addition of a substantial new line of business. In other words, an existing partnership need not meet the 90% requirement while it

---

1. IRC Sec. 7704(c)(1).
2. IRC Sec. 7704(f).
3. IRC Sec. 7704(b).
4. IRC Sec. 7704(d)(1).
5. IRC Sec. 7704(c)(3).
6. IRC Sec. 7704(e).

is exempt under the transitional rules in order to meet the 90% requirement when its exemption has expired.[1]

A partnership will be treated as an existing partnership if: (1) it was a publicly traded partnership on December 17, 1987, (2) a registration statement indicating that the partnership was to be a publicly traded partnership was filed with the Securities and Exchange Commission (SEC) on or before December 17, 1987, or (3) an application was filed with a state regulatory commission on or before December 17, 1987, seeking permission to restructure a portion of a corporation as a publicly traded partnership.[2]

An existing partnership's exemption terminates if it adds a substantial new line of business after December 17, 1987. A new line of business is any business activity of the partnership not closely related to a pre-existing business of the partnership. All of the facts and circumstances will determine whether a new business activity is closely related to a pre-existing business of the partnership. However, a new line of business will not be classified as substantial if the partnership derives no more than 15% of its gross income from the new line of business and no more than 15% of the value of partnership assets are used in the new line of business. A new activity of a partnership is not considered a new line of business to the extent the activity generates passive-type income, as described above. An activity of a corporation controlled by a publicly traded partnership may be treated as an activity of the partnership if the facts and circumstances indicate that the effect of the arrangement is to permit the partnership to engage in an activity the income from which is not subject to a corporate-level tax and which would be a new line of business if conducted directly by the partnership. A safe harbor provides that an activity conducted by a corporation controlled by an existing partnership will not be treated as an activity of the partnership if no more than 10% of the gross income the partnership derives from the corporation during the taxable year is income *other than* passive-type income.[3] An additional safe harbor provides that certain listed business activities will not be treated as substantial new lines of business if the pre-existing and new business activities are assigned the same four-digit industry number standard identification code (Industry SIC Code) set forth in the *Standard Industrial Classification Manual*.[4]

A publicly traded partnership taxed as a corporation under the above rules is treated, in general, as a taxable entity and tax benefits are taken at the partnership level. Individual investors are unable to take tax benefits such as depreciation deductions and tax credits on their own tax returns. A publicly traded partnership that is taxed as a corporation should not be subject to the "at risk" rules (see Q 1285) or the "passive loss" rules (see Q 1292). Also, a publicly traded partnership would not generally qualify to make an election to be treated as an *S corporation* (see Q 1218).

A publicly traded partnership that is not taxed as a corporation under the above rules is treated, in general, as a flow-through entity, whose partners are taxed under the partnership rules contained in Q 1190 through Q 1217. Partners in such a partnership are subject to the "at risk" rules (see Q 1285) and the "passive loss" rules (see Q 1292). As noted above, an electing 1987 partnership is also subject to tax at the partnership level.

---

1. RA '87, Sec. 10211(c), as amended by TAMRA '88, Sec. 2004(f)(2).
2. Treas. Reg. §1.7704-2(b).
3. Treas. Reg. §1.7704-2.
4. Rev. Proc. 92-101, 1992-2 CB 579.

Electing 1987 Partnerships

The Taxpayer Relief Act of 1997 added a new exception to corporate taxation for a publicly traded partnership. This exception is available if the publicly traded partnership is an electing 1987 partnership. An electing 1987 partnership is (1) an existing partnership (as described above), (2) that has not been taxed as a corporation (and would not have been taxed as a corporation without regard to the passive income exception) for all prior taxable years beginning after 1987 and before 1998, and (3) that elects to be exempt from corporate taxation. An electing 1987 partnership is taxed at a rate of 3.5% on its gross income from the active conduct of its trades and businesses. No credits are allowed to be applied against this tax. If a partnership is a partner in another partnership, its gross income will include its distributive share of the gross income from the active conduct of trades or businesses of the other partnership. A similar rule applies in the case of lower-tiered partnerships. The election may be revoked by the partnership without the consent of the IRS; but once revoked, it may not be reinstated. If a partnership adds a substantial new line of business it will no longer be considered an electing 1987 partnership. The 3.5% tax is an exception to the general rule that a partnership does not pay taxes (see Q 1190).[1]

Readily Tradable on a Secondary Market or the Substantial Equivalent Thereof Post-1995 Partnerships

The rules set out in this section apply to the taxable years of a partnership beginning after December 31, 1995, except if the partnership was actively engaged in an activity before December 4, 1995. In that case, these rules apply to taxable years beginning after December 31, 2005, unless the partnership added a substantial new line of business (as defined in Treas. Reg. §1.7704-2, see above, but substituting December 4, 1995 for December 17, 1987) after December 4, 1995, in which case these rules apply to taxable years beginning on or after the addition of the new line of business.[2]

Generally, a partnership, that is not traded on an established securities market, will be treated as readily tradable on a secondary market or the substantial equivalent thereof if, taking into account all of the facts and circumstances, the partners are readily able to buy, sell, or exchange their partnership interests in a manner that is comparable, economically, to trading on an established securities market. This occurs if: (1) partnership interests are regularly quoted by any person making a market in the interests; (2) any person regularly makes bid or offer quotes pertaining to the interests available to the public and stands ready to effect buy or sell transactions regarding same for itself or on behalf of others; (3) a partnership interest holder has a readily available, regular, and ongoing opportunity to sell or exchange the interest through a public means of obtaining or providing information of offers to buy, sell, or exchange interests in the partnership; or (4) prospective buyers and sellers have the opportunity to buy, sell or exchange partnership interests in a time frame and with the regularity and continuity that is comparable to that described in (1)-(3) above. The fact that a partnership fails to satisfy the safe harbors set out below does not create a presumption that the partnership is publicly traded.[3]

---

1. IRC Sec. 7704(g).
2. Treas. Reg. §1.7704-1(l). Notice 88-75, 1988-2 CB 386, (see below) generally applies to partnerships exempted from the rules in this section.
3. Treas. Reg. §1.7704-1(c).

However, interests in a partnership will not be treated as readily tradable on a secondary market or the substantial equivalent thereof unless (1) the partnership participates in the establishment of the market or the inclusion of its interests thereon, or (2) the partnership recognizes transfers made on that market.[1]

Generally, percentage of partnership interest calculations take into account both general and limited partnership interests. However, if at any time during the taxable year, the general partner and persons related in certain ways to the general partner (under IRC Section 267(b) or IRC Section 707(b)(1)) own more than 10% of the outstanding interests in partnership capital and profit, such calculations are made without regard to interests owned by the general partner and the related persons.[2]

The percentage of partnership interests traded in a taxable year is equal to the sum of the monthly percentages. The percentage of partnership interests traded during a month is determined by reference to partnership interests outstanding during the month. Any reasonable and consistently used monthly convention may be used (e.g., first of month, 15th of month, end of month). In the case of "block transfers," see below, the determination of percentage of partnership interests traded during a thirty day period is made with reference to partnership interests outstanding immediately prior to the block transfer.[3]

Private Transfers Safe Harbor. Certain transfers not involving trading (private transfers) are disregarded in determining whether interests in a partnership are readily tradable on a secondary market or the substantial equivalent thereof.[4] These include:

(1) transfers in which the basis of the partnership interest in the hands of the transferee is determined by reference to the transferor's basis or is determined under IRC Section 732;

(2) transfers at death, including transfers from an estate or testamentary trust;

(3) transfers between members of a family as defined in IRC Section 267(c)(4);

(4) the issuance of partnership interests for cash, property, or services;

(5) distributions from a qualified retirement plan or individual retirement account;

(6) transfers by a partner during a 30 day period of interests exceeding 2% of total interests in partnership capital and profit ("block transfers");

(7) transfers under redemption or repurchase agreements that are exercisable only upon (a) death, disability, or mental incompetence of the partner, or (b) retirement or termination of service of a person actively involved in managing the partnership or in providing full time services to the partnership;

(8) transfers of an interest in a closed end partnership pursuant to a redemption agreement if the partnership does not issue any interest after the initial offering (and

---

1. Treas. Reg. §1.7704-1(d).
2. Treas. Reg. §1.7704-1(k)(1).
3. Treas. Regs. §§1.7704-1(k)(2) to 1.7704-1(k)(4).
4. Treas. Reg. §1.7704-1(e).

substantially identical investments are not available through the general partner or a person related in certain ways to the general partner under IRC Section 267(b) and IRC Section 707(b)(1));

(9) transfers of at least 50% of the total interests in partnership capital and profits in one transaction or a series of related transactions; and

(10) transfers not recognized by the partnership.

Redemption and Repurchase Agreements Safe Harbor. Transfers involving redemption and repurchase agreements (other than those described in (7) and (8) of "Private Transfers Safe Harbor," see above) are disregarded in determining whether interests in the partnership are readily tradable on a secondary market or the substantial equivalent thereof only if certain requirements are met: (1) the agreement provides that the partner must give written notice to the partnership at least 60 days prior to the redemption or repurchase date; (2) either (a) the agreement provides that the redemption or repurchase price not be established until at least 60 days after such notification, or (b) the redemption or repurchase price is not established more than four times during the partnership's taxable year; and (3) no more than 10% of partnership interests are traded during a taxable year (disregarding only private transfers, see above).[1]

Qualified Matching Services Safe Harbor. Transfers involving matching services are disregarded in determining whether partnership interests are readily tradable on a secondary market or the substantial equivalent thereof if the following requirements are met: (1) the matching service consists of a computerized or printed listing system of customers' bid/ask quotes and matching occurs by matching the list of buyers and sellers or through appropriate bidding procedure; (2) the selling partner cannot enter into an agreement to sell the interest until the 15th day after the date information regarding the sale is made available to potential buyers and there is written evidence of this time period; (3) the closing of a sale (treated as occurring at the earlier of the passage of title or the payment of the purchase price or when funds are made available for the purchase) involving a matching service does not occur within 45 days after information of the sale is made available; (4) the matching service displays only nonfirm price quotes or nonbinding indications of interest and does not display firm quotes (5) the selling partner's information is removed from the matching service within 120 days after information of the sale is made available; (6) once such information is removed from the matching service (other than by reason of sale), the selling partner does not enter an offer to sell a partnership interest in the matching service during the next 60 days; and (7) no more than 10% of partnership interests are traded during a taxable year (disregarding only private transfers, see above).[2]

Private Placement Safe Harbor. Interests in a partnership will not be treated as publicly traded if: (1) all interests in such partnership were issued in transactions that were not required to be registered under the Securities Act of 1933, and (2) the partnership does not have more than 100 partners at any time during the taxable year. Each person indirectly owning an interest in the partnership through a partnership, S corporation, or grantor trust is treated as a partner if (1) substantially all of the value of the owner's interest in the entity is attributable to its interest in the partnership; and (2) a principal purpose of the tiered arrangement is to satisfy the 100 partner limitation.[3]

---

1. Treas. Reg. §1.7704-1(f).
2. Treas. Reg. §1.7704-1(g).
3. Treas. Reg. §1.7704-1(h).

Two Percent Safe Harbor. Interests are not tradable on a secondary market or the substantial equivalent thereof if less than 2% of the percentage interests in partnership capital or profits are transferred during the taxable year (disregarding certain transfers involving private transfers, those involving qualified matching services and certain redemption and repurchase agreements).[1]

Pre-1996 Partnerships

The rules set out in this section apply to the taxable years of a partnership beginning before December 31, 1995, and, in the case of partnerships engaged in an activity prior to December 4, 1995, to taxable years before the earlier of (1) the first taxable year beginning after December 31, 2005, or (2) the first taxable year beginning on or after the addition of a substantial new line of business after December 4, 1995. Partnerships that qualify for this transition period may continue to rely on the rules set out in Notice 88-75.[2]

A partnership will not be treated as readily tradable on a secondary market or the substantial equivalent thereof if certain safe harbors are met.[3] Thus, interests in a partnership will not be treated as publicly traded if: (1) all interests in the partnership were issued in a private placement, as defined below; (2) no more than 5% of partnership interests are traded during a taxable year (disregarding certain transfers not involving trading); or (3) less than 2% of partnership interests are traded during a taxable year (disregarding certain transfers not involving trading, certain transfers involving matching services, and certain redemption and repurchase agreements). No inference is to be drawn as to the treatment of partnerships which do not satisfy the safe harbor requirements. Even if the safe harbor requirements are not met, the IRS will consider requests for rulings on whether a partnership is readily tradable on a secondary market or the substantial equivalent thereof pending the issuance of regulations.

Generally, percentage of partnership interest calculations take into account both general and limited partnership interests. However, if at any time during the taxable year, the general partner and persons related in certain ways to the general partner (under IRC Section 267(b) or IRC Section 707(b)(1)) own more than 10% of the outstanding interests in partnership capital and profit, such calculations are made without regard to interests owned by the general partner and the related persons.

The percentage of partnership interests traded in a taxable year is equal to the sum of the monthly percentages. The percentage of partnership interests traded during a month is determined by reference to partnership interests outstanding during the month. Any reasonable and consistently used monthly convention may be used (e.g., first of month, 15th of month, end of month). In the case of "block transfers," see below, the determination of percentage of partnership interests traded during a 30 day period is made with reference to partnership interests outstanding immediately prior to the block transfer.

Private Placement Safe Harbor. Interests in a partnership will not be treated as publicly traded if: (1) all interests in such partnership were issued in transactions which were not registered under the Securities Act of 1933, and (2) either (a) the partnership has no more than 500 partners, or (b) the initial offering price of each unit of partner-

---

1. Treas. Reg. §1.7704-1(j).
2. 1988-2 CB 386. Treas. Reg. §1.7704-1(l).
3. Notice 88-75, 1988-2 CB 386.

ship interest is at least $20,000 (and each unit may not be subdivided for resale into a unit the initial offering price of which would have been less than $20,000). Each person indirectly owning an interest through a partnership, S corporation, or grantor trust is treated as a partner for this purpose. Where separate partnerships conduct joint or related operations with the principal purpose of qualifying the multiple partnerships as private placements, such partnerships will be aggregated when determining the number of partners.

Five Percent Safe Harbor. Interests in a partnership will not be treated as publicly traded if no more than 5% of total interests in partnership capital and profit are traded during a taxable year (disregarding certain transfers not involving trading). The transfer of an interest that has been previously transferred during the year is counted as an additional transfer. The following transfers are treated as transfers not involving trading:

(1) transfers in which the basis of the partnership interest in the hands of the transferee is determined by reference to the transferor's basis;

(2) transfers in which the basis of the partnership interest in the hands of the transferee is determined by reference to the basis of property distributed by a partnership to a partner under IRC Section 732;

(3) transfers at death;

(4) transfers between members of a family (an individual's brothers and sisters, spouse, ancestors, and lineal descendants);

(5) the issuance of partnership interests for cash, property, or services;

(6) distributions from a qualified pension, profit-sharing, or stock bonus plan;

(7) transfers by a partner during a 30 day period of interests exceeding 5% of total interests in partnership capital and profit ("block transfers");

(8) transfers of an interest in a closed end partnership pursuant to a redemption agreement if the partnership does not issue any interest after the initial offering (and substantially identical investments are not available through the general partner or a person related in certain ways to the general partner under IRC Section 267(b) and IRC Section 707(b)(1)); and

(9) transfers under redemption or repurchase agreements that are exercisable only upon (a) death, disability, or mental incompetence of the partner, or (b) retirement or termination of service of a person actively involved in managing the partnership or in providing full time services to the partnership.

Two Percent Safe Harbor. Interests in a partnership will not be treated as publicly traded if no more than 2% of partnership interests are traded during a taxable year (disregarding certain transfers not involving trading (described above), certain transfers involving matching services, and certain redemption and repurchase agreements). The transfer of an interest that has been previously transferred during the year is counted as an additional transfer.

Transfers involving matching services, whether provided by the general partner of the partnership itself, the underwriter that handled the issuance of the partnership interests, or an unrelated third party, are not treated as trading for purposes of the 2% safe harbor if all the following requirements are met: (1) a 15 day delay occurs between the date the operator of the matching service receives written confirmation that a partnership interest is available for sale (the "contact date") and the earlier of (a) the day such information is made available to potential buyers, or (b) the day information is made available to listing customers concerning outstanding bids; (2) the closing of a sale (treated as occurring at the earlier of the passage of title or the payment of the purchase price) involving a matching service does not occur within 45 days of the contact date; (3) the listing customer's information is removed from the matching service within 120 days of the contact date; (4) once such information is removed from the matching service (other than by reason of sale), the listing customer does not enter a partnership interest in the matching service during the next 60 days; and (5) no more than 10% of partnership interests are traded during a taxable year (disregarding only certain transfers not involving trading, see above). If prior to November 2, 1988, all necessary steps were taken to ensure that an existing matching service satisfied requirements (1) through (4), transfers before November 2, 1988 involving such matching services are considered to have met those requirements.

Transfers involving certain redemption and repurchase agreements are not treated as trading for purposes of the 2% safe harbor. Transfer of an interest in a closed end partnership pursuant to a redemption agreement is not treated as trading if the partnership does not issue any interest after the initial offering (and substantially identical investments are not available through the general partner or a person related in certain ways to the general partner under IRC Section 267(b) and IRC Section 707(b)(1)). Transfer of an interest in an open end partnership pursuant to a redemption or repurchase agreement is not treated as trading if: (1) the agreement provides that a limited partner must give written notice to the partnership or general partner at least 60 days prior to the redemption or repurchase date; (2) either (a) the agreement provides that the redemption or repurchase price not be established until at least 60 days after such notification, or (b) the redemption or repurchase price is not established more than four times during the partnership's taxable year; and (3) no more than 10% of partnership interests are traded during a taxable year (disregarding only certain transfers not involving trading, see above). If prior to November 2, 1988, all necessary steps were taken to ensure that an existing redemption or repurchase agreement of an open end partnership satisfied requirements (1) and (2), transfers before November 2, 1988 involving such agreements are considered to have met those requirements.

LIMITED PARTNERSHIPS NOT TAXED AS CORPORATIONS

1190. How do limited partners report partnership income, gains, losses, deductions, and credits?

The federal income tax laws recognize a partnership as an entity having its own taxable year (within limits) and having its own income and losses. It computes its income much as an individual does. However, once its income for its tax year is determined, the partnership does not, in general, pay taxes.[1] Certain publicly traded partnerships and electing 1987 partnerships are nonetheless subject to tax at the entity level (see Q 1189).

---

1. IRC Secs. 701, 703.

An electing 1987 partnership is also subject to the "flow through" rules described below. The "flow-through" rules for electing large partnerships (see Q 1191) are somewhat different than those described here. Also, a partnership may be required to make an accelerated tax payment on behalf of the partners, if the partnership elects not to use a required taxable year.[1] See Q 1217 regarding the partnership anti-abuse rule.

The partnership reports its income on an information return (Form 1065). It also reports to each individual partner his share of items of partnership income, gains, losses, deductions and credits (on Schedule K-1, Form 1065). Schedule K-1 identifies separately the partner's share of combined net short-term capital gains and losses, combined net long-term capital gains and losses, combined net gains and losses from sales or exchanges of "IRC Section 1231 property" (see Q 1233), miscellaneous itemized deductions (see Q 1428), each class of charitable contributions, taxes subject to the foreign tax credit, and certain other items required by regulation to be stated separately (including: intangible drilling and development costs; any item subject to special allocation that differs from allocation of taxable partnership income or loss generally; and the partner's share of any partnership items "which if separately taken into account by any partner would result in an income tax liability for that partner different from that which would result if the partner did not take the item into account separately"). Finally, the schedule reports the partner's share of the partnership taxable income or loss exclusive of separately stated items.[2]

A multi-tiered partnership may not be used to avoid the separately stated requirement. Items that might affect the tax liability of a partner owning his interest indirectly through a multi-tiered partnership arrangement, retain their character while flowing through an intermediate partnership. Consequently, such items must be separately stated by each of the different tier partnerships.[3]

A limited partner then reports on his individual income tax return, subject to any limitations applicable to him, his distributive share of the partnership's taxable income or loss, and separately stated items of partnership income, gain, loss, deductions and credits. For example, he includes his share of partnership long-term and short-term capital gains and losses and "IRC Section 1231" gains and losses with his own.[4] A partner's share of partnership miscellaneous itemized deductions is combined with his individual miscellaneous deductions for purposes of the 2% floor on such deductions.[5] A partner's share of the partnership's investment interest expense is combined with his individual investment interest expense to determine the amount deductible as investment interest (explained in Q 1304).[6] A partner's distributive share of income, losses, and credits that are passive to the partner enter into the calculation of the taxpayer's passive income and losses, and tax attributable to passive activities, to determine whether passive credits may be taken and passive losses deducted (see Q 1292 to Q 1299).

As a consequence of this "flow through" system of taxability, distributions he may have received during the year are not the measure of a partner's share of partnership income for a year. A partner may have taxable income without having received a distribution. The existence of conditions upon actual or constructive receipt is irrelevant

1. IRC Sec. 7519.
2. IRC Sec. 702(a); Treas. Reg. §1.702-1(a).
3. Rev. Rul. 86-138, 1986-2 CB 84.
4. IRC Sec. 702(a); Treas. Reg. §1.702-1(a).
5. Temp. Treas. Reg. §1.67-2T(b).
6. Rev. Rul. 84-131, 1984-2 CB 37.

for this purpose.[1] Similarly, he may have a deductible loss even though he received a distribution.

As a general rule, the character of items for tax purposes is determined at the partnership level and they retain that character in the hands of the partner.[2] Whether or not an activity is passive with regard to a partner is determined at the level of the partner (see Q 1292 to Q 1299).

Partnership income is computed using a cash or accrual method of accounting, whichever the partnership uses, regardless of the accounting method used by the individual partners in reporting their own incomes.[3] However, in some cases a partnership may not use the cash method. In general, a partnership that has average gross receipts in excess of $5,000,000 and has a C corporation (other than a personal service corporation) as a partner may not use the cash method.[4] Also, a partnership that is a "tax shelter" may not use the cash method.[5] A limited partnership is a "tax shelter" within this rule if (1) at any time interests in it have been offered for sale in any offering required to be registered with any federal or state agency having the authority to regulate the offering of securities for sale, (2) more than 35% of the losses during the taxable year are allocable to limited partners, and (3) a significant purpose of the partnership is the avoidance or evasion of federal income tax.[6]

Because items of partnership income, gain, loss, deductions, and credits are "passed through" the partnership and taxed as the items of the individual partners, the partnership has typically been the most popular form for tax shelter syndications. It remains to be seen how popular the electing large partnership form (see Q 1191) will be for tax shelter syndications. The limited partnership has been particularly popular because it offers limited liability to limited partners.

1191. What is an electing large partnership, and how is it treated for tax purposes?

Certain partnerships may elect to be treated as electing large partnerships. An electing large partnership generally has fewer separately stated items of income, gain, loss, deduction, and credit than partnerships that are not electing large partnerships (see Q 1190 generally).[7] The electing large partnership provisions were enacted in part to ease the reporting requirements of limited partners.[8] An electing large partnership is subject to the regular partnership rules (see Q 1190 to Q 1217) except to the extent that the regular rules are inconsistent with the electing large partnership rules.[9] It appears that a publicly traded partnership could not be an electing large partnership unless it is an electing 1987 partnership (see Q 1189).

1. *Stonehill v. Comm.*, TC Memo 1987-405.
2. IRC Sec. 702(b); Treas. Reg. §1.702-1(b); *Brannen v. Comm.*, 84-1 USTC ¶9144 (11th Cir. 1984); *Podell v. Comm.*, 55 TC 429 (1970).
3. *Truman v. U.S.*, 4 F.Supp. 447 (N.D. Ill. 1933).
4. IRC Secs. 448(a)(2), 448(b)(3).
5. IRC Sec. 448(a)(3).
6. IRC Sec. 448(d)(3).
7. IRC Secs. 771-777.
8. General Explanation of Tax Legislation Enacted in 1997, p. 354 (the 1997 Blue Book).
9. IRC Sec. 771.

Electing Large Partnership Defined

An electing large partnership is a partnership, which for a taxable year had at least 100 partners in the previous taxable year and elects to be treated as an electing large partnership. To the extent provided in regulations, a partnership shall cease to be treated as an electing large partnership if the number of partners falls below 100 during a taxable year. The election to be treated as an electing large partnership applies to the taxable year for which it is made and all subsequent years. The election may be revoked with the consent of the IRS.

For purposes of determining the number of partners, those partners performing substantial services for the partnership, or individuals who performed services in the past at the time they were partners will not be counted toward the 100 partners needed to elect. Also, an election to be treated as an electing large partnership will not be effective with respect to a partnership if substantially all the partners are performing substantial services for the partnership or are personal service corporations (the owner-employees of which perform such substantial services), are retired partners who performed substantial services in the past, or are spouses of partners who are or were performing substantial services for the partnership. A partnership whose principal activity is the buying and selling of commodities, or options, futures, or forwards with respect to commodities may not elect large partnership status.[1]

Simplified Flow-Through

The following items are separately stated by an electing large partnership: (1) taxable income or loss from passive loss limitation activities (see Q 1293); (2) taxable income or loss from other activities; (3) net capital gain or loss allocable to passive loss limitation activities (see Q 1293, Q 1420); (4) net capital gain or loss allocable to other activities (see Q 1420); (5) tax-exempt interest; (6) a net alternative minimum tax (AMT) adjustment for passive loss limitation activities (see Q 1293, Q 1440); (7) a net AMT adjustment for other activities (see Q 1440); (8) general credits; (9) low income housing credit (see Q 1227); (10) rehabilitation credit (see Q 1228); (11) foreign income taxes; and (12) other items that the IRS determines should be separately stated.[2] The credit for fuel from nonconventional sources is separately stated in tax years ending before 2006.[3] If the electing large partnership has income from the discharge of indebtedness, it is also separately stated.[4]

In the case of a limited partnership interest, a partner's share of taxable income or loss from passive loss limitation activities is considered to be income or loss from the conduct of a trade or business which is a single passive activity. A similar rule applies to net capital gain or loss allocable to passive loss limitation activities and to the AMT adjustment for passive loss limitation activities. However, in the case of a general partnership interest, that partner's distributive share of partnership items allocable to passive loss limitation activities is taken into account separately as necessary to comply with the rules under IRC Section 469. A passive loss limitation activity is any activity that involves the conduct of a trade or business, any rental activity, and any activity involving property held for the production of income. See Q 1292 to Q 1299 regarding the passive loss rule.

---

1. IRC Sec. 775.
2. IRC Sec. 772(a).
3. IRC Sec. 772(a)(10), prior to amendment by ETIA 2005.
4. IRC Sec. 773(c).

A partner's distributive share of income or loss from other activities (item (2) above) is treated as an item of income or expense with respect to property held for investment (see Q 1310), except that any deduction due to such a loss is not treated as a miscellaneous itemized deduction for purposes of the 2% floor on such deductions (see Q 1428). A partner's distributive share of net capital gain or loss (from both passive loss limitation activities and other activities) is treated as a long-term capital gain or loss. A partner's distributive share of general credits is taken into account as a current year business credit (see Q 1436). General credits are any credit except the low-income housing credit (see Q 1227), the rehabilitation credit (see Q 1228), and the foreign tax credit. The credit for producing fuel from a nonconventional source is not a general credit in tax years ending before 2006. Tax-exempt interest is interest on state and local bonds that is excludable from gross income (see Q 1123).

The net AMT adjustment is determined with the adjustments applicable to individuals or corporations, depending on whether the partner is an individual or corporation. It is calculated by determining what adjustments would occur to income from passive or other activities (as the case may be) if these items were determined using the AMT adjustments and preferences (see Q 1440).[1]

Partnership Level Computations

In determining the taxable income of an electing large partnership, miscellaneous itemized deductions are taken at the partnership level, but instead of the 2% floor (see Q 1428), 70% of these deductions are disallowed. Charitable contributions are deducted at the partnership level but this deduction generally may not exceed 10% of the partnership's taxable income. Elections affecting the computation of the taxable income or any credit of the electing large partnership are made by the partnership (except for elections relating to income from the discharge of indebtedness and the foreign tax credit). Most limitations and provisions affecting the computation of the taxable income or any credit of the electing large partnership are applied at the partnership level. However, provisions relating to the overall limitation on itemized deductions (see Q 1427), the at risk limitations, the limitations on passive activity losses and credits, and any other provision specified in regulations are applied at the partner level.[2]

Computations at the partnership level are made without regard to (1) the optional adjustment to basis of partnership property (see Q 1216) and (2) the reduction of certain tax attributes when certain discharges of indebtedness are excluded from gross income. However, items of a partner's distributive share are adjusted (as appropriate) to take into account these rules.

Credit recapture is taken into account at the partnership level and is determined as if the credit with respect to which the recapture is made had been fully utilized to reduce tax. The partnership takes into account credit recapture by reducing the amount of the appropriate current year credit. If the recapture amount exceeds the current year credit, the partnership is liable to pay such excess. Credit recapture means any increase in tax due to low income housing credit recapture (see Q 1227) and investment credit recapture (see Q 1268).

No credit recapture is required due to a transfer of a partnership interest. Also, an electing large partnership is not considered terminated due to the sale or exchange of 50% or more of partnership interests within a 12-month period.

---

1. IRC Sec. 772.
2. IRC Sec. 773.

The interest surcharge rules for certain installment obligations (see Q 1408) are applied at the partnership level, and in determining the amount of interest payable under these rules, the partnership is treated as subject to the highest tax rate under IRC Sections 1 or 11 (35% in 2007).[1]

Oil and Gas Properties

Electing large partnerships with oil and gas properties are subject to special rules. The allowance for depletion (see Q 1252) is computed at the partnership level, except in the case of a disqualified person. Such depletion is determined without regard to the limits of production for which percentage depletion is allowable (see Q 1256), and without regard to the limit of percentage depletion to 65% of taxable income (see Q 1258). Also, a partner's basis in the partnership interest is not reduced by any depletion allowance computed at the partnership level (see Q 1260). Such depletion would generally be treated as from a passive loss limitation activity (see above).

If any partner is a disqualified person, that partner's distributive share of income, gain, loss, deduction or credit attributable to a partnership oil or gas property is determined without regard to the electing large partnership rules. In addition, that partner's distributive share attributable to oil or gas property is excluded for purposes of the simplified flow-through and partnership level computations. A disqualified person is a retailer or refiner of crude oil or natural gas (see Q 1256) or any other person whose average daily production of domestic crude oil and natural gas exceeds 500 barrels. In determining a person's average daily production, all production of domestic crude oil and natural gas is taken into account, including the person's share of any production by the partnership.[2]

1192. In what year does an individual include partnership income and loss on his tax return?

A partner includes on his return for a year his distributive share of partnership items of income, gain, loss, deductions, and credits for the partnership year that ends in or at the same time as his own year. Since most individuals report on a calendar year basis, an individual partner generally includes partnership income for the same calendar year as a partnership that reports on the calendar year basis. If the partnership uses a non-calendar fiscal year, the calendar year partner includes partnership income, gains, losses, deductions, and credits for the partnership year that *ends* in his calendar year.[3]

The amounts included in the year a partnership interest is acquired, or in which a partner sells, liquidates, or gives away his partnership interest or the year a partner dies, are explained in Q 1196, Q 1203, Q 1209, and Q 1213.

1193. What is a limited partner's adjusted basis in his partnership interest?

A partner's "basis" is an account of his interest in the partnership for tax purposes; for example, to determine tax on cash distributions (see Q 1201), gain or loss on sale (see Q 1205), or the limit on loss deduction (see Q 1200). Initially, his basis is the amount of money and the adjusted basis of any property he has contributed to the partnership;

---

1. IRC Sec. 774.
2. IRC Sec. 776.
3. IRC Sec. 706(a); Treas. Reg. §1.706-1(a).

it undergoes a series of adjustments thereafter.[1] His basis is increased by any further contributions and by his distributive share of taxable income, tax-exempt income, and the excess of the deductions for depletion over the basis of the property subject to depletion.[2] His basis is decreased (but not below zero) by current distributions to him by the partnership and by his distributive share of losses, nondeductible expenditures not properly chargeable to capital, and decreased (but not below zero) by the amount of his deduction for depletion with respect to oil and gas wells.[3]

A partner's basis also includes his share of partnership liabilities. See Q 1194. His basis is increased by any increase in his share of partnership liabilities as if he had made a cash contribution.[4] A partner is deemed to receive a cash distribution to the extent his share of partnership liabilities decreases; thus, his basis is decreased if his share of partnership liabilities decreases.[5]

Contribution of a limited partner's personal note to the partnership does not increase the basis of his partnership interest, because it is a contribution of property in which he has no basis.[6] When the note is paid, the amount is an additional contribution that is added to his basis.

If the interest was acquired by purchase, see Q 1207; by gift, see Q 1212; or on death, see Q 1215.

1194. What liabilities are included in a partner's adjusted basis in his partnership interest?

Liabilities Incurred or Assumed by Partnership After January 29, 1989 and Partner Loans and Guarantees After February 29, 1984

A partner's basis includes his share of *partnership* liabilities.[7] Regulations provide an economic risk of loss analysis that is used to determine which liabilities are included in a partner's adjusted basis. A partnership liability is treated as a *recourse* liability to the extent that any partner bears the economic risk of loss for that liability.[8] A partner bears the economic risk of loss for a partnership liability to the extent that the partner (or certain related parties) would be obligated to make a payment to any person or a contribution to the partnership with respect to a partnership liability (and would not be entitled to reimbursement by another partner, certain parties related to another partner, or the partnership) if the partnership were to undergo a "constructive liquidation." A "constructive liquidation" would treat (1) all of the partnership's liabilities as due and payable in full; (2) all of the partnership assets (including money), except those contributed to secure a partnership liability, as worthless; (3) all of the partnership assets as disposed of in a fully taxable transaction for no consideration (other than relief from certain liabilities); (4) all items of partnership income, gain, loss, and deduction for the year as allocated among the partners; and (5) the partner's interests in the enterprise as liquidated.[9] See Q 1217 regarding the partnership anti-abuse rule.

---

1. IRC Secs. 722, 705.
2. IRC Sec. 705(a)(1), Treas. Reg. §1.705-1(a)(2).
3. IRC Secs. 705(a)(2), 705(a)(3).
4. IRC Secs. 752(a), 705(a).
5. IRC Secs. 752(b), 705(a)(2).
6. *Oden v. Comm.*, TC Memo 1981-184; Rev. Rul. 80-235, 1980-2 CB 229.
7. IRC Secs. 752, 705(a).
8. Treas. Reg. §1.752-1(a)(1).
9. Treas. Reg. §1.752-2(b)(1).

If one or more partners or related persons guarantee the payment of more than 25% of the interest that will accrue on a partnership nonrecourse liability over its remaining term and it is reasonable to expect that the guarantor will be required to pay substantially all of the guaranteed interest if the partnership fails to do so, the loan will be deemed to be recourse with respect to the guarantor to the extent of the present value of the future interest payments.[1] An obligation will be considered recourse with respect to a partner to the extent of the value of any property that the partner (or related party in the case of a direct pledge) directly or indirectly pledges as security for the partnership liability.[2] An obligation will be considered recourse to a partner to the extent that the partner or a related party makes (or acquires an interest in) a nonrecourse loan to the partnership and the economic risk of loss for the liability is not borne by another partner.[3]

A recourse liability allocated to a partner under the above rules is included in the partner's basis in the partnership. A limited partner generally will not bear the economic risk of loss for any partnership recourse liability because limited partners are not typically obligated to make additional contributions and do not typically guarantee interest, pledge property, or make loans to the partnership. Otherwise, a limited partner can include a share of a partnership liability in his basis only if it is nonrecourse liability (see below).

A partnership liability is treated as a *nonrecourse* liability if no partner bears the economic risk of loss (see above) for that liability. Generally, partners share nonrecourse liability in the same proportion as they share profits (see Q 1195). However, nonrecourse liabilities are first allocated among partners to reflect the partner's share of (1) any partnership minimum gain or (2) IRC Section 704(c) minimum gain. Partnership minimum gain is the amount of gain that would be realized if the partnership were to sell all of its property that is subject to nonrecourse liabilities in full satisfaction of such liabilities. IRC Section 704(c) minimum gain is the amount of gain that would be allocated under IRC Section 704(c) to property contributed by a partner if the partnership were to sell all of its property that is subject to nonrecourse liabilities in full satisfaction of such liabilities and for no other consideration.[4]

These regulations apply to any liability incurred or assumed on or after December 28, 1991, other than those incurred or assumed pursuant to a written binding contract in effect before that date and at all times thereafter. A partnership may elect to apply the provisions of the regulations to liabilities incurred or assumed prior to December 28, 1991 as of the beginning of the first taxable year ending on or after that date.[5]

Substantially similar temporary regulations apply to liabilities incurred or assumed by a partnership after January 29, 1989 and before December 28, 1991, unless the liability was incurred or assumed by the partnership pursuant to a written binding contract in effect prior to December 29, 1988 and at all times thereafter.[6] They also apply to partner loans and to guarantees of partnership liabilities that were incurred or assumed by a partnership after February 29, 1984, and before December 28, 1991, beginning on the later of March 1, 1984 or the first date on which the partner bore the economic risk of loss with respect to a liability because of his status as a creditor or guarantor of such

1. Treas. Reg. §1.752-2(e).
2. Treas. Reg. §1.752-2(h).
3. Treas. Reg. §1.752-2(c).
4. Treas. Regs. §§1.752-3(a), 1.704-2(d).
5. Treas. Reg. §1.752-5.
6. Temp. Treas. Reg. §1.752-4T(a), prior to removal by TD 8380.

liability.[1] A partnership could elect to extend application of the temporary regulations to all of its liabilities as of the beginning of its first taxable year ending after December 29, 1988, and before December 28, 1991, subject to certain consistency rules.[2]

Liabilities Incurred or Assumed by Partnership Before January 30, 1989 and Partner Loans and Guarantees Before March 1, 1984

For an election to extend application of the final or the temporary regulations discussed above to all of a partnership's liabilities, see above.

A partner's basis includes his share of *partnership* liabilities.[3] However, accrued but unpaid expenses and accounts payable of a cash basis partnership are not treated as partnership liabilities for this purpose.[4] Where none of the partners has any personal liability with respect to a partnership liability (*nonrecourse* debt), all partners (including limited partners) share the liability in the same proportion as they share profits. Prior regulations gave as an example of such a liability a mortgage on real estate acquired by the partnership without the assumption by the partnership or any of the partners of any liability on the mortgage. Partnership *recourse* liabilities are shared by the partners in the same ratio that they share losses, but a limited partner's share of partnership recourse liability may not exceed the difference between his actual contribution and the total contribution to the partnership that he is obligated to make under the partnership agreement.[5]

Because limited partners who are not obligated to make additional contributions can include in basis a share of a partnership liability only if it is nonrecourse (no partner has personal liability with respect to the obligation), the question has come up whether a partner who guarantees an otherwise nonrecourse partnership loan has "personal liability" within the meaning of the regulations. The IRS takes the position that a general partner's guarantee makes him personally liable to the extent the value of the property securing the loan is insufficient to cover the amount due and, as a consequence, the guaranteed loan is one for which a partner is personally liable. Therefore, limited partners not committed to make future contributions are not able to include a share of such an obligation in their bases.[6]

Guaranteeing a partnership recourse obligation does not increase a limited partner's obligation to make additional contributions "under the partnership agreement." Therefore, a limited partner may not increase his share of partnership recourse liability by making such a guarantee.[7] Similarly, a limited partner's agreement to indemnify a general partner for certain recourse liabilities does not increase the limited partner's basis in his partnership interest by a share of partnership recourse liabilities because it does not increase his obligation "to the partnership."[8] Where a partnership obligation is partly nonrecourse and partly recourse, a limited partner may include in his basis his share of the portion that is nonrecourse. (For example, a note provides that to the extent property securing a loan of $350X is inadequate, the general partner is liable

---

1. Temp. Treas. Reg. §1.752-4T(b), prior to removal by TD 8380.
2. Temp. Treas. Reg. §1.752-4T(c), prior to removal by TD 8380.
3. IRC Secs. 752, 705(a).
4. Rev. Rul. 88-77, 1988-2 CB 128.
5. Treas. Reg. §1.752-1(e), prior to removal by TD 8237; Rev. Rul. 69-223, 1969-1 CB 184.
6. Rev. Rul. 83-151, 1983-2 CB 105; *Raphan v. U.S.*, 85-1 USTC ¶9297 (Fed. Cir. 1985). See also P.L. 98-369 (TRA '84), Sec. 79.
7. *Brown v. Comm.*, TC Memo 1980-267; *Block v. Comm.*, TC Memo 1980-554.
8. Rev. Rul. 69-223, 1969-1 CB 184.

up to $150X; a limited partner may share the $200X nonrecourse liability in the same proportion he shares profits.)[1]

If the likelihood the limited partner will have to make additional contributions is contingent or indefinite, he cannot share partnership recourse liabilities. The IRS determined that the obligation to make additional contributions represented by letters of credit contributed by limited partners was too contingent and indefinite where the principal on a partnership loan, which was assumed by limited partners and secured by the letters of credit, was not due for four years. The Service noted that the partnership could have generated sufficient income to pay the loan through income from operations or sale of assets prior to the due date and that the likelihood of a default in the tax year which would cause the loan to be immediately payable was remote since interest payments were not due until the next taxable year.[2] The IRS is reviewing the question of whether a limited partner can increase his basis as a result of a contribution to the partnership of a letter of credit and the assumption of a partnership loan.[3]

To increase basis, the loan must be a bona fide loan. Such an increase has been denied where the "loan" was determined to be an investment or capital contribution to the venture. A nonrecourse loan from a general partner to limited partners or to the partnership is a contribution to the capital of the partnership by the general partner, not a loan; therefore, the amount increases the basis of the partnership interest of the general partner, but not of the limited partners.[4] A nonrecourse loan by an unrelated third party to a partnership engaged in exploring for oil and gas, secured by property of limited value but convertible into an interest in partnership profits, was ruled not a bona fide loan, but capital at risk in the venture.[5]

Increase in basis has been denied where the obligation was so speculative as to be considered a contingent obligation. For example, the IRS ruled that a partnership nonrecourse note payable only out of partnership cash flow was not includable in basis because payment was so speculative that the liability was a contingent liability. The partnership business involved a commercially untested new process and no realistic predictions could be made about the partnership's net cash flow.[6]

A nonrecourse note to be paid only if there was production from oil wells was too uncertain and indefinite an obligation to be treated as a partnership liability.[7]

The Service will not recognize a sham liability entered into for the purpose of increasing the basis of property and, as a result, the allowable depreciation, or enlarging a partner's basis against which he may deduct partnership losses. A nonrecourse note did not represent genuine indebtedness because the principal amount of the note greatly exceeded the value of the property purchased by it and securing it.[8]

1195. How are partnership income, gains, losses, deductions, and credits allocated among partners?

1. Rev. Rul. 84-118, 1984-2 CB 120.
2. TAM 8404012.
3. TAM 8636003.
4. Rev. Rul. 72-135, 1972-1 CB 200.
5. Rev. Rul. 72-350, 1972-2 CB 394.
6. Rev. Rul. 80-235, 1980-2 CB 229.
7. *Brountas v. Comm.*, 82-2 USTC ¶9626 (1st Cir. 1982); *Gibson Products Co.–Kell Blvd. v. U.S.*, 78-2 USTC ¶9836 (N.D. Tex. 1978), aff'd, 81-1 USTC ¶9213 (5th Cir. 1981).
8. *Hager v. Comm.*, 76 TC 759 (1981); *Wildman v. Comm.*, 78 TC 943 (1982); *Narver v. Comm.*, 75 TC 53 (1980), aff'd per curiam, 82-1 USTC ¶9265 (9th Cir. 1982).

The partnership agreement can dictate the allocation of separately stated items of partnership income, gain, loss, deductions, credits, and other bottom line income and loss, even if the allocation is disproportionate to the capital contributions of the partners (a so-called "special allocation"). However, if the method of allocation lacks "substantial economic effect" (or if no allocation is specified in the partnership agreement) the distributive shares will be determined in accordance with the partner's interest in the partnership, based on all the facts and circumstances.[1] See Q 1217 regarding the partnership anti-abuse rule.

The purpose of the substantial economic effect test is to "prevent use of special allocations for tax avoidance purposes, while allowing their use for bona fide business purposes."[2] Regulations provide that generally an allocation will not have economic effect unless the partners' capital accounts are maintained properly, liquidation proceeds are required to be distributed in accordance with the partners' capital account balances and, following distribution of such proceeds, partners are required to restore any deficits in their capital accounts to the partnership. The economic effect will generally not be considered substantial unless the allocation has a reasonable possibility of affecting substantially the dollar amounts received by partners, independent of tax consequences. Allocations are insubstantial if they merely shift tax consequences within a partnership tax year or are likely to be offset by other allocations in subsequent tax years.[3]

Nonrecourse Allocations

Over the last several years, changes in regulations have modified the rules relating to the allocation of losses and deductions attributable to nonrecourse obligations. In addition, if there is no substantial modification to the partnership agreement, various transitional rules permit the use of the earlier regulations under certain circumstances.[4]

Taxable Years Beginning After December 27, 1991

An allocation of a loss or deduction attributable to the nonrecourse liabilities (see Q 1194) of a partnership ("nonrecourse deductions") cannot have economic effect with respect to a partner because the nonrecourse lender and not the partner bears the ultimate risk of economic loss with respect to the deductions.[5] The amount of nonrecourse deductions for a partnership year is equal to the excess, if any, of the net increase in "partnership minimum gain" for the year, over the amount of any distributions of proceeds of nonrecourse liabilities allocable to an increase in "partnership minimum gain."[6] Partnership minimum gain is the amount of gain which would be realized in the aggregate if the partnership were to sell each of its properties which is subject to a nonrecourse liability for an amount equal to the nonrecourse liability.[7]

Generally, for taxable years beginning after December 27, 1991, nonrecourse deductions must be allocated in accordance with the partners' interests in the partnership, unless the following requirements are met:

1. IRC Secs. 704(a), 704(b).
2. Sen. Fin. Comm. Report No. 938, 94th Cong., 2d Sess. 100 (1976).
3. Treas. Reg. §1.704-1(b)(2).
4. See Treas. Reg. §1.704-2(l).
5. Treas. Reg. §1.704-2(b)(1).
6. Treas. Reg. §1.704-2(c).
7. Treas. Reg. §1.704-2(d).

(1) Allocation of nonrecourse deductions are provided for in a manner which is consistent with allocations, which have substantial economic effect, of some other significant partnership item attributable to the property securing the nonrecourse financing.

(2) All other material allocations and basis adjustments either have economic effect or are allocated in accordance with the partners' interests in the partnership.

(3) The partners' capital accounts are maintained properly.

(4) Liquidation proceeds are required to be distributed in accordance with the partners' capital account balances.

(5) Following distribution of liquidation proceeds, partners are required to either (a) restore any deficits in their capital accounts to the partnership or (b) allocate income or gain sufficient to eliminate any deficit.

(6) If there is a net decrease in partnership minimum gain, see above, during a year, each partner must be allocated items of partnership income and gain ("minimum gain chargeback") for that year equal to that partner's share of the net decrease in partnership minimum gain. (This requirement does not apply to the extent that a partner's share of the net decrease in minimum gain is caused by a guarantee, refinancing, or other change in the debt instrument causing it to become partially or wholly recourse debt or partner nonrecourse debt, and the partner bears the risk of economic loss for the liability. Nor does it apply to the extent that a partner contributes capital to the partnership to repay the nonrecourse liability and the partner's share of net decrease in minimum gain results from the repayment.)[1]

A distinction must be made between nonrecourse debt and nonrecourse liabilities. Nonrecourse debt refers to the traditional concept of nonrecourse, for example, where a creditor's right to repayment is limited to one or more assets of the partnership. Nonrecourse liability, on the other hand, means partnership liability with respect to which no partner bears the economic risk of loss (as described in Q 1194). If a partner bears the economic risk of loss with respect to nonrecourse debt, deductions and losses allocable to such nonrecourse debt must be allocated to such partner.[2]

Taxable Years Beginning After December 29, 1988 and Before December 28, 1991

For those partnerships which qualified under the 1989-1991 (generally) rules and choose to remain grandfathered under such rules, former Temporary Treasury Regulation §1.704-1T(b)(4)(iv) generally provides that nonrecourse debt be treated under the rules described above. Nonrecourse deductions will be deemed to be allocated in accordance with the partners' interests in the partnership if the first four and part (a) of the fifth of the current requirements, above, are met, and if the partnership agreement contains a clause complying with the minimum gain chargeback requirements contained in former Temporary Treasury Regulation §1.704-1T(b)(4)(iv). Those requirements provide that if there is a net decrease in partnership minimum gain during a year, each partner must be allocated a minimum gain chargeback equal to the greater of (1) the partner's share of the net decrease in minimum gain attributable to a disposition of property securing nonrecourse liabilities, or (2) the partner's deficit capital account, as specially defined in the former temporary regulations.

---

1. Treas. Regs. §§1.704-2(b)(1); 1.704-2(e); 1.704-2(f).
2. Treas. Reg. §1.704-2(i).

Taxable Years Beginning Before December 30, 1988

For those partnerships which qualified under the pre-December 30, 1988 rules and choose to remain grandfathered under such rules, former Treasury Regulation §1.704-1(b)(4)(iv) generally provides that nonrecourse debt be treated under the rules described in former Temporary Treasury Regulation §1.704-1T(b)(4)(iv) above, except that:

(1)   The amount of nonrecourse deductions for a partnership year is equal to the net increase in partnership minimum gain for the year. There is no reduction for certain distributions as there was under the former temporary regulations.

(2)   Nonrecourse deductions need not be allocated in accordance with the partners' interests in the partnership if current requirements (1) through (4) are met and either: (1) following distribution of liquidation proceeds, partners are required to restore any deficits in their capital accounts to the partnership; or (2) if there is a net decrease in partnership minimum gain during a year, each partner must be allocated items of partnership income and gain for that year equal to that partner's share of the net decrease in partnership minimum gain.

Contributions of Property

If a partner contributes property to a partnership, generally, allocations of income, gain, loss, and deductions must be made to the partner to reflect any variation between the basis of the property to the partnership and its fair market value at the time of contribution. When contributed property is distributed to a partner other than the contributing partner, the contributing partner will recognize gain or loss upon such distribution if it occurs within seven years of the contribution. However, a contributing partner is treated as receiving property which he contributed if the property he contributed is distributed to another partner and like-kind property is distributed to the contributing partner within the earlier of (1) 180 days after the distribution to the other partner, or (2) the partner's tax return due date (including extensions) for the year in which the distribution to the other partner occurs.

For contributions of property made after October 22, 2004, if the property has a built-in loss, the loss is considered only in determining the items allocated to the contributing partner. Also, when determining items allocated to other partners, the basis of the property is considered its fair market value when it was contributed to the partnership.[1]

Distortions of Income

The Service may reallocate income and deductions attributable to distributions of property from a partnership to an individual and his controlled corporation to prevent distortions of income.[2] (See also Q 1217.)

1196. Can a limited partner who enters a partnership late in the year receive a "retroactive" allocation of partnership losses that occurred before he became a partner?

---

1. IRC Sec. 704(c).
2. IRC Sec. 482; *Dolese v. Comm.*, 87-1 USTC ¶9175 (10th Cir. 1987).

Partnership income or loss may not be retroactively allocated to a partner acquiring his interest during the year. The partner's allocable share may be determined according to the portion of the year he was a partner or by an interim closing of the books.[1]

Thus, a partner admitted during the year cannot deduct a full year's depreciation. Losses not shown to have occurred after he became a partner are prorated and a deduction allowed only for the part of the partnership year that he was a partner.[2] However, where an interim closing of the books had been made, it accurately reflected the losses incurred by the partnership after the new partner entered the partnership, with the result that year end total loss could not be prorated according to the portion of the year the new partner was a partner.[3] Losses accrued by an accrual basis partnership prior to cash basis partners' becoming partners were not deductible by the cash basis partners.[4] However, new partners have been permitted to deduct losses incurred by a cash basis partnership prior to their entry where an interim closing of the books established the losses were paid by the partnership after their entry and the interim closing of the books method reflected economic reality because the contributions of the new partners were needed to pay the expenses.[5]

However, the IRC provides for special allocation rules with respect to certain amounts attributable to periods after March 31, 1984, in cash basis partnerships, and with respect to amounts paid or accrued by a lower tiered partnership after March 31, 1984, to prevent avoidance of the retroactive allocation prohibition.[6]

In the case of a cash method partnership, interest, taxes, payments for services or for the use of property, and other items prescribed by regulations, are to be assigned to each day in the period to which it is economically attributable (i.e., to the day or days in such period to which the item would accrue if the partnership were on the accrual method) and allocated among the partners in proportion to their interests in the partnership at the close of each day.[7] If, using this method, any portion of such an item is economically attributable to periods before the beginning of the taxable year, that portion will be assigned to the first day of the year and allocated to the persons who were partners on that day, in proportion to their varying interests in the partnership. (Similarly, any portion economically attributable to periods after the end of the taxable year will be assigned to the last day of the year.) This determination will require allocation of such items in the manner in which the partners would have borne the corresponding economic cost even though the cost is actually borne by another partner (typically, a later-admitted partner) in connection with a change in the partners' interests in the partnership. If persons to whom all or part of such items are allocable are not partners in the partnership on the first day of the partnership taxable year in which the item is taken into account, then their portions must be capitalized by the partnership and allocated to the basis of partnership assets.[8]

In the case of tiered partnerships, if a partnership is a partner (an upper-tier partnership) its share of any item of income, gain, loss, deduction, or credit of the lower-tier

---

1. *Richardson v. Comm.*, 76 TC 512 (1981), *aff'd*, 83-1 USTC ¶9109 (5th Cir. 1982); Sen. Fin. Comm. Rep. No. 938, 94th Cong. 2d Sess. 100 (1976); Treas. Reg. §1.706-1(c)(2)(ii).
2. *Hawkins v. Comm.*, 83-2 USTC ¶9475 (8th Cir. 1983).
3. *Lipke v. Comm.*, 81 TC 689 (1983).
4. *Williams v. U.S.*, 82-2 USTC ¶9467 (5th Cir. 1982).
5. *Richardson v. Comm.*, above.
6. IRC Sec. 706(d).
7. IRC Sec. 706(d)(2).
8. IRC Sec. 706(d)(2)(D).

partnership will, except as otherwise provided in regulations, be allocated among the partners of the upper-tier partnership (1) by assigning the appropriate portion of each item to the appropriate day in the upper-tier partnership's taxable year on which the upper-tier partnership is a partner in the lower-tier partnership, and (2) by allocating the portion assigned to a day among the partners in proportion to their interests in the upper-tier partnership as of the close of the day (determined in a manner consistent with IRC Section 704). For this purpose, items allocable to periods before or after the upper-tier partnership's taxable year will be assigned to the first or last day of that year, respectively. If the persons to whom items are properly allocated are no longer partners in the upper-tier partnership on the first day of the upper-tier partnership taxable year in which the item is taken into account, then such persons' portions of such items are capitalized and allocated to the basis of partnership assets.[1]

1197. What are the tax consequences of a change ("flip-flop") in allocation of profits and losses in a limited partnership after a specified time?

Limited partnerships frequently provide for allocations that give to the limited partners a large share of income, expenses, and losses until their contribution is recovered. For example, the partnership agreement might allocate 95% to limited partners and 5% to general partners. Then after a period of time, or after the limited partners have recovered their contributions, the allocation changes ("flip-flops") so that, for example, 60% is allocated to the limited partners and 40% to the general partners. (Such an allocation was upheld as reflecting economic reality, where limited partners had contributed 95% of the partnership's capital and the general partners had contributed 5%.)[2]

A flip-flop can have unexpected tax results. Under general principles, when a partner's interest in partnership profits changes, his share of partnership liabilities changes (see Q 1194). The IRC provides that any decrease in a partner's share of the liabilities of a partnership is considered a distribution of money to the partner.[3] As a result, commentators have concluded, there can be a taxable gain to the partner if the amount of the reduction in his share of partnership liabilities (that is, the distribution of money) exceeds his adjusted basis in his partnership interest immediately before the flip. (Taxation of a cash distribution in excess of basis is discussed in Q 1201.) Furthermore, a change in a partner's share of liabilities affects his basis in his partnership interest. When the change occurs, each limited partner experiences a decrease in the amount of his share of nonrecourse liabilities and consequently a decrease in his adjusted basis in his partnership interest against which he may deduct partnership losses or offset future distributions.

DEDUCTIONS

1198. Can limited partners deduct the expenses of partnership organization?

A partnership may deduct up to $5,000 of organizational expenses in the year the partnership begins business. The $5,000 amount is reduced (but not below zero) be the amount of organization expenses that exceed $50,000. Remaining organizational expenses may be deducted over a 180-month period beginning with the month that

---

1. IRC Sec. 706(d)(3).
2. *Hamilton v. U.S.*, 82-2 USTC ¶9546 (Ct. Cl. 1982). See also Treas. Reg. §1.704-1(b)(5) Ex. 3, Ex. 5.
3. IRC Sec. 752(b).

the partnership begins business. IRC Sec. 709(b). These expenses include legal fees for services incident to organization, accounting fees for establishment of the partnership accounting system, and necessary filing fees.[1]

The determination of the date the partnership begins business is a question of fact, but ordinarily it begins when it starts the business operations for which it was organized. For example, the acquisition of operating assets that are necessary to the type of business contemplated may constitute beginning business. The mere signing of a partnership agreement is not sufficient to show the beginning of business.[2]

1199. Can limited partners deduct the expenses of selling interests in the partnership and other expenses of syndication?

No. Expenses to promote the sale of (or to sell) an interest in the partnership cannot be deducted and cannot be amortized.[3] They must be capitalized.[4]

Syndication expenses are those connected with issuing and marketing partnership interests. For example, according to the regulations, syndication expenses include brokerage fees, registration fees, legal fees for securities advice and advice pertaining to tax disclosures in the prospectus or placement memorandum, printing costs of prospectus, placement memorandum and other selling and promotional material.[5]

1200. Is there a limit on the deduction of a limited partner's share of partnership losses?

Yes.

Partnership basis. A partner may not deduct his share of partnership losses in excess of his basis in his partnership interest determined as of the end of the partnership year in which the loss occurred (before reduction for the loss). Any excess loss may be deducted in succeeding years, but only to the extent of his basis at the end of the particular partnership year.[6]

In order to apply the limit properly, the partner's basis is first increased, as explained in Q 1193. Then it is decreased, as explained in Q 1193, by any current distributions and nondeductible expenditures not chargeable to capital, but not by losses for the year (and not by any losses previously disallowed and carried over). If the partner's losses exceed his basis, he must allocate his basis among the loss items in order to determine how much of each item may be deducted. He allocates his basis to each loss in the same proportion as that loss bears to the total loss. (In determining this fraction, the total loss must include the partner's share of losses for the current year and any disallowed losses he has carried over from prior years.)[7]

> *Example.* A partner received the following distributive share of partnership items: long-term capital loss of $5,000; short-term capital gain of $1,000; IRC Section 1231 loss of $3,000; and "bottom line" income of $3,000. Prior to adjustment for any of these items, his adjusted basis in his

1. Treas. Reg. §1.709-2(a).
2. Treas. Reg. §1.709-2(c).
3. IRC Sec. 709(a); Rev. Rul. 81-153, 1981-1 CB 387.
4. Treas. Reg. §1.709-2(b); Rev. Rul. 85-32, 1985-1 CB 186.
5. Treas. Reg. §1.709-2(b).
6. IRC Sec. 704(d); Treas. Reg. §1.704-1(d)(1).
7. Treas. Reg. §1.704-1(d)(2).

partnership interest was $2,000. His basis is increased by the short term gain of $1,000 and bottom line income of $3,000 to $6,000. His total loss is $8,000. His $6,000 basis is allocated 5/8 ($3,750) to long-term capital loss and 3/8 ($2,250) to IRC Section 1231 loss. Thus, he may deduct $3,750 of long-term capital loss and $2,250 of IRC Section 1231 loss. He may carry over a long-term capital loss of $1,250 and an IRC Section 1231 loss of $750.[1]

At risk limitation. A partner may not deduct in a year a loss from any activity to the extent the loss exceeds the amount he has "at risk" in the activity.[2] Thus, a limited partner may deduct losses of a limited partnership to the extent of his basis, but the limited partner may not deduct losses in excess of the amount he has "at risk" in the venture if that is less than his basis in his partnership interest. See Q 1285 to Q 1291 on the "at risk" limitation.

Passive loss limitation. Income, losses, and credits from a limited partnership interest will generally be passive. Such items are aggregated with the limited partner's income, losses, and credits from other passive activities. In general, passive losses are deductible only against passive income; passive credits may only be used against tax liability attributable to passive activities. IRC Sec. 469. See Q 1292 to Q 1299 on the "passive loss" rule.

See also Q 1304 on the limitation on deduction of investment interest expense, and Q 1306 on the deduction of interest expense if the partner owns tax exempt obligations.

Cash Distributions

1201. Is a limited partner taxed on a current cash distribution?

Current cash distributions (i.e., not in liquidation of a partner's interest) that are not in excess of the partner's adjusted basis in his partnership interest immediately before the distribution, are a nontaxable return of capital.[3] The partner's adjusted basis in his partnership interest is reduced by the amount of such cash distributions.[4] See Q 1193.

To the extent that a cash distribution to a partner exceeds his basis in his partnership interest immediately before the distribution, the partner realizes a gain that is taxed as if there were a sale of a partnership interest.[5] See Q 1205. This is true of a current cash distribution or a cash distribution in liquidation of a partner's interest.[6]

A decrease in a partner's share of nonrecourse liabilities is considered, for tax purposes, a cash distribution.[7] See Q 1193. Such a decrease can occur when a mortgage is satisfied, a liability is discharged through foreclosure, or the partnership sells property subject to a mortgage. To the extent that such a deemed distribution exceeds the partner's adjusted basis in his partnership interest, he has a taxable gain.[8]

Loss is not recognized on a distribution other than a liquidating distribution.[9]

---

1. See Treas. Reg. §1.704-1(d)(4) Ex.3.
2. IRC Sec. 465.
3. IRC Sec. 731(a).
4. IRC Sec. 733.
5. IRC Sec. 731(a).
6. Treas. Reg. §1.731-1(a)(1)(i).
7. IRC Sec. 752(b).
8. IRC Sec. 731(a).
9. IRC Sec. 731(a)(2).

SELF-EMPLOYMENT TAX

1202. Is a limited partner's distributive share of partnership income subject to the self-employment tax?

Generally, no. A limited partner's distributive share of partnership trade or business income is not treated as earnings from self-employment subject to social security tax on self-employment income. However, guaranteed payments to limited partners for services actually rendered to or on behalf of the partnership are treated as self-employment income.[1]

SALE, EXCHANGE OR LIQUIDATION OF PARTNERSHIP INTEREST

Allocation of Distributive Share

1203. What is a partner's distributive share of partnership income and loss in the year he sells, exchanges, or liquidates his entire partnership interest?

A partner includes the distributive share of partnership items up to the time of sale, exchange, or liquidation. The taxable year of the partnership closes with respect to the partner when he sells or exchanges his entire interest in the partnership, or if his interest is liquidated, but does not close with respect to any other partner.[2] Thus, the distributive share of income or loss for the short partnership year resulting from the disposition is included in the tax year in which the sale is made, because that is the year in which the short partnership year ends as to him. See Q 1192. If the partnership and partner have different years (i.e., the partnership is on a fiscal year and the individual uses a calendar tax year), it is possible that both a regular full partnership year and the short partnership year will end in the same year of the individual. Consequently, there can be a bunching of more than one year's partnership income (or loss) in one year's return of the individual.

The partner's distributive share of partnership income for the part of the partnership year that ends when he sells, exchanges, or liquidates his interest may be determined under the method used to determine a new partner's share, as discussed in Q 1196.

The partnership year does not end as to a partner who disposes of less than his entire interest.[3] A liquidation is a termination of a partner's interest by a distribution or a series of distributions to the partner from the partnership. The entire interest of a partner is not liquidated until the final distribution of a series is made. Thus, the partnership year does not close with respect to a liquidating partner until the final distribution.[4]

Sale Proceeds

1204. What amount does a limited partner realize on sale of his partnership interest?

---

1. IRC Sec. 1402(a)(13).
2. IRC Sec. 706(c).
3. IRC Sec. 706(c)(2)(B).
4. Treas. Reg. §1.706-1(c).

In addition to any money and the value of property received, a limited partner is considered to have received an amount equal to his share (see Q 1194) of any partnership liabilities, both recourse and nonrecourse, of which he has been relieved.[1] This includes his share of the nonrecourse debt even if it exceeds the value of the property securing the debt.[2]

If the sale or exchange of an interest in an upper-tier partnership results in a termination of the upper-tier partnership, the upper-tier partnership is treated as exchanging its entire interest in the lower-tier partnership (with additional amounts realized with respect to the lower-tier partnership).[3]

1205. How does a limited partner treat the amount realized on a sale of his partnership interest?

If the amount the partner realizes (see Q 1204) exceeds his adjusted basis in his partnership interest, the gain is capital gain *except* that if part of the *amount realized* (whether it is more or less than his basis) is attributable to his share of certain ordinary income property (i.e., partnership assets which, if sold, would result in ordinary gain), part of the amount realized (not just part of the gain) will generally have to be treated as ordinary income.[4] The IRC uses the terms "unrealized receivables" and "inventory items of the partnership" to identify the kinds of ordinary income property.[5] These items are also often called "hot assets" or "IRC Section 751 property."

In effect, a sale of a partnership interest is treated as two transactions, a sale of "IRC Section 751 property" and a sale of other property. In order to determine the gain or loss on each sale, the total amount realized by the partner on the sale of his interest and his adjusted basis in his interest must each be allocated between his share of the partnership's IRC Section 751 property and his share of other property.[6]

IRC Section 751 property includes much more than the term "unrealized receivables," on its face, suggests. In order to prevent the conversion of ordinary income on certain items of partnership property to capital gain, Congress has frequently used the term "unrealized receivables" as a catch-all for various items generating ordinary income. Thus, for example, the term includes potential depreciation recapture computed as if the property had been sold by the partnership at its fair market value at the time the partnership interest is sold, and amounts that would be treated as ordinary income attributable to market discount if the partnership had sold market discount bonds (issued after July 18, 1984) or short term obligations it held.[7] (See Q 1111 regarding market discount bonds, Q 1094 and Q 1096 regarding short term obligations.) "Inventory items" include property held primarily for sale to customers and other property that would not be considered a capital asset or "IRC Section 1231" property.[8]

The amount realized by a partner upon the sale or exchange of his interest in IRC Section 751 property is the amount of income or loss from IRC Section 751 property that would have been allocated to the partner if the partnership had sold all of its property

---

1. IRC Sec. 752(d); Treas. Reg. §1.752-1(c); Rev. Rul. 74-40, 1974-1 CB 159. See *Crane v. Comm.*, 331 U.S. 1 (1947).
2. *Comm. v. Tufts*, 83-1 USTC ¶9328 (U.S. 1983).
3. Treas. Reg. §1.708-1(b)(2).
4. IRC Sec. 741.
5. IRC Sec. 751.
6. IRC Secs. 741, 751.
7. IRC Sec. 751(c).
8. IRC Sec. 751(d).

in a taxable transaction in an amount equal to the fair market value of the property immediately before the partner's transfer of his interest in the partnership. Any gain or loss recognized that is attributable to IRC Section 751 property is ordinary gain or loss. The difference between the amount of capital gain or loss that the partner would realize in the absence of these rules and the amount of ordinary income or loss determined under these rules is the partner's capital gain or loss on the sale of his partnership interest.[1] It is possible to have ordinary income on the sale of IRC Section 751 property and a capital loss on sale of the other property.

Example. Partner B sells his one-half interest in partnership AB, when the balance sheet is:

	Assets			Liabilities and Capital	
	basis	market value		book value	market value
Cash	$ 3,000	$ 3,000	Liabilities	$ 2,000	$ 2,000
Capital Assets	17,000	15,000	Capital A	9,000	15,000
Unrealized receivables	0	14,000	B	9,000	15,000
	$20,000	$32,000		$20,000	$32,000

B receives $16,000 for his one-half interest ($15,000 in cash and $1,000 in reduction of partnership liabilities). B's interest in partnership property includes his one-half interest in unrealized receivables worth $7,000. Thus, $7,000 of the $16,000 realized is considered received in exchange for his interest in unrealized receivables and is therefore ordinary income. B's basis for his partnership interest is $10,000. The difference between the amount of capital gain or loss that the partner would realize in the absence of IRC Section 751 ($16,000 - $10,000 = $6,000) and the amount of ordinary income or loss determined above ($7,000) is B's capital gain or loss on the sale of its partnership interest. In this case, B will recognize a $1,000 capital loss.[2]

On sale of an interest in an upper tier partnership, a proportionate share of the lower tier partnership's "unrealized receivables" and "inventory items" will be deemed sold.[3]

Regulations require a statement relating to the sale.[4]

The partner's distributive share of partnership gains and losses are included in his return for the year of sale, and are not part of the sale proceeds. See Q 1203. Such income increases his basis. If he fails to consider this when selling his partnership interest, he may realize ordinary income from operations instead of gain on the sale.

Gain or loss from sale of a partnership interest is generally treated as passive for purposes of the "passive loss" rule (see Q 1292 through Q 1299) if the activity is passive with respect to the partner (see Q 1293).

Partnership interests in different partnerships are not eligible for non-recognition treatment under the like-kind exchange rules.[5] (See Q 1422 regarding the like-kind exchange rules generally, and Q 1237 to Q 1238 regarding like-kind exchanges of real estate.)

---

1. Treas. Reg. §1.751-1(a)(2).
2. Treas. Reg. §1.751-1(g)(Ex. 1).
3. *Madorin v. Comm.*, 84 TC 667 (1985); IRC Sec. 751(f).
4. Treas. Reg. §1.751-1(a)(3).
5. IRC Sec. 1031(a)(2)(D).

The installment sales rules (see Q 1408) are applied to the sale of a partnership interest in the same manner that the rules would be applied to a direct sale of the underlying assets. Thus, for example, the installment method cannot be used to report income from the sale of a partnership interest to the extent that the sales proceeds represent income attributable to the partnership's inventory items, which would not qualify for installment treatment if sold directly.[1]

Purchaser

1206. What is the transferee's distributive share of partnership income in the year he purchases a partnership interest?

Any partner who is a transferee of a partnership interest includes in his taxable income, as his distributive share of partnership items with respect to the transferred interest, the pro rata part of the amount of such items that he would have included had he been a partner from the beginning of the partnership's taxable year. His pro rata share may be determined based on the portion of the year that he holds the interest, or by any other reasonable method, but must be determined by the same method used to determine the transferor's share.[2] See Q 1203. While the regulations use the word "partner," they would apparently apply to an assignee of an interest who is not formally made a partner through agreement by the general partner.[3]

1207. What is an individual's basis in a partnership interest that is purchased from a limited partner?

The initial basis of a purchased interest is its cost basis and thereafter it is adjusted as explained in Q 1193.[4]

Cash Liquidation of Partnership Interest

1208. How is a partner taxed if the partnership liquidates his interest in cash?

Cash payments (including the partner's share of partnership liabilities of which he is relieved–see Q 1201) in liquidation of a partnership interest may represent several items.[5] Part may represent the fair market value of the partner's interest in partnership assets, part may be attributable to his interest in "unrealized receivables," and part may be attributable to goodwill.

In general, the cash liquidation of a partnership interest is treated like a sale. Thus, the difference between the amount of payment allocated to inventory items and the amount of basis allocated to such inventory is ordinary gain or loss. Presumably, the amount of payment allocated to "unrealized receivables" is fully taxable as ordinary income. Also, the difference between the amount of payment allocated to the balance of the partnership property (presumably, including good will) and the amount of basis

---

1. IRC Sec. 453(b)(2)(B); Rev. Rul. 89-108, 1989-2 CB 100.
2. Treas. Reg. §1.706-1(c)(2)(ii).
3. See Rev. Rul. 77-137, 1977-1 CB 178 (assignee of partner's interest treated for tax purposes as substitute limited partner although other partners had not consented to his admission as a partner), and Rev. Rul. 77-332, 1977-2 CB 484 ("principal" who could not be a partner in a CPA firm because he was not a CPA was nonetheless treated as a partner for tax purposes).
4. Treas. Reg. §1.742-1.
5. Treas. Reg. §1.736-1(a).

allocated to such property is capital gain or loss.[1] See Q 1205. The gain or loss is includable in the individual's income for his tax year in which the payment is received without regard to the partnership year in which it is received.[2]

However, with respect to a general partner in a partnership in which capital is not a material income-producing factor, the portion of the payment attributable to the partner's share of "unrealized receivables" (e.g., potential depreciation recapture) (see Q 1205) or goodwill (in the absence of an agreement to the contrary) will be treated as a distributive share (if determined with reference to the partnership's profits) or a guaranteed payment (if not) and taxed as ordinary income.[3] It is includable in the individual's tax year in which or with which the partnership year ends.[4] A transition rule provides that the rules in this paragraph also apply to any partner (without regard to whether the partner is a general partner or whether capital is a material income-producing factor for the partnership) who retires after January 4, 1993 if a written contract to purchase such partner's interest was binding on January 4, 1993 and at all times thereafter.[5]

Example. Assume the ABC partnership's balance sheet is as follows:

	Assets				Capital	
	basis	market value			basis	value
cash	$13,000	$13,000	Liabilities		$ 3,000	$ 3,000
unrealized receivables	0	30,000	Capital A		10,000	21,000
			B		10,000	21,000
capital assets	20,000	23,000	C		10,000	21,000
	$33,000	$66,000			$33,000	$66,000

A, a limited partner, withdraws from the partnership and receives $22,000 ($21,000 in cash and $1,000 in liabilities assumed by the partnership). A's one-third interest in partnership assets other than unrealized receivables is $12,000 (one-third of ($13,000 + $23,000 fair market value of capital assets)). The basis of A's partnership interest is $11,000 ($10,000 + $1,000 partnership liabilities). His gain is $1,000. It is capital gain because there are no inventory items involved. The remaining $10,000 he realized ($22,000 - $12,000) represents his share of unrealized receivables and is ordinary income.[6]

GIFT OF PARTNERSHIP INTEREST

Donor

1209. Does a limited partner report partnership income and losses in the year he makes a gift of his limited partnership interest?

A partner includes the distributive share of partnership items up to the time of the gift of the interest. The taxable year of the partnership closes with respect to the partner when he gives away his entire interest in the partnership, but does not close with respect to any other partner.[7] Thus, the distributive share of income or loss for the short

---

1. IRC Sec. 736(b); Treas. Reg. §1.736-1(a)(2).
2. Treas. Reg. §1.736-1(a)(5).
3. IRC Sec. 736; Treas. Reg. §1.736-1(a)(3).
4. Treas. Reg. §1.736-1(a)(5).
5. OBRA '93 Sec. 13262(c)(2).
6. See Treas. Reg. §1.736-1(b)(7)(Ex. 1).
7. IRC Sec. 706(c).

partnership year resulting from the gift is included in the tax year in which the gift is made, because that is the year in which the short partnership year ends as to him. See Q 1192. If the partnership and partner have different years (i.e., the partnership is on a fiscal year and the individual uses a calendar tax year), it is possible that both a regular full partnership year and the short partnership year will end in the same year of the individual. Consequently, there can be a bunching of more than one year's partnership income (or loss) in one year's return of the individual. The partnership year does not end as to a partner who terminates less than his entire interest.[1]

1210. Will an individual who gives away his interest in a limited partnership realize taxable gain?

As a general rule, there is no gain or loss to the donor on the gift of property. However, where the gift is of an interest in a partnership that has liabilities, there may be taxable gain to the donor. The IRS takes the position that if the amount of an individual's proportionate share of partnership liabilities exceeds the adjusted basis in his partnership interest, he is considered to have received gain and the transfer is deemed, in part, a sale.[2] The Service has found support in court.[3] (The Service takes the same position with regard to a gift to charity. See Q 1340.) The treatment of the amount received on a sale and allocation of basis is explained in Q 1205. Thus, there may be ordinary gain to the extent the partner making the gift has "IRC Section 751 property" (e.g., potential depreciation recapture) and long-term or short-term capital gain.

If his share of liabilities is less than his adjusted basis, there is no deductible loss.[4]

To the extent the fair market value of his partnership interest exceeds the liability (the amount realized on the sale), there is a gift.[5] If the value exceeds the liability by more than $12,000 (in 2007, $24,000 in the case of a gift by husband and wife) there may be a gift tax. See Q 1530.

1211. Does the grantor of a "grantor" trust that owns a partnership interest realize gain when he renounces retained powers and the trust ceases to be treated as a "grantor" trust?

The IRS and the Tax Court take the position that he does. They reason that where a grantor of a trust retains certain powers and as a result is treated as owner of the trust for tax purposes, he is considered, for tax purposes, owner of a partnership interest purchased by the trust. As owner, the grantor reports the distributive share of partnership income, gains, losses, deductions and credits allocable to the trust. When he renounces the retained powers that resulted in the trust's being classified as a grantor trust, the grantor is no longer considered owner of the trust's assets. In effect, he has transferred ownership of the partnership interest to the trust. On the transfer, the grantor is deemed to receive his share of partnership liabilities.[6] The amount realized is taxable as proceeds of a sale, as discussed in Q 1205. The fair market value of his interest in excess of the liability is a gift to the trust. See Q 1210.

---

1. IRC Sec. 706(c)(2)(B).
2. Treas. Reg. §1.1011-2(a); Rev. Rul. 75-194, 1975-1 CB 80.
3. *Guest v. Comm.*, 77 TC 9 (1981); *Est. of Levine v. Comm.*, 72 TC 780 (1979), aff'd, 80-2 USTC ¶9549 (2d Cir. 1980).
4. Treas. Reg. §1.1001-1(e).
5. *Johnson v. Comm.*, 59 TC 791 (1973), aff'd, 74-1 USTC ¶9355 (6th Cir. 1974), cert. den., 419 U.S. 1040 (1974).
6. *Madorin v. Comm.*, 84 TC 667 (1985); Treas. Reg. §1.1001-2(c)(Ex. 5); Rev. Rul. 77-402, 1977-2 CB 222.

Donee

1212. What is the basis of the donee of a limited partnership interest?

The donee's unadjusted basis for determining gain is the greater of the amount of the donee partner's share of liabilities (see Q 1194) or the transferor's adjusted basis (see Q 1193) at the time of the transfer. If the fair market value of the interest is greater than the donor's adjusted basis, the donee's unadjusted basis is increased by the amount of the gift tax paid that is attributable to the appreciation in value, but not increased in excess of the fair market value of the gift. The donee's unadjusted basis for determining loss is the lesser of the unadjusted basis as used in determining gain or the fair market value of the interest at the time of the transfer.[1] Thereafter, the donee's basis is adjusted as any other partner's. See Q 1193.[2]

DEATH OF A PARTNER

1213. Is partnership income and loss included in a deceased partner's final return? In the return of his successor in interest?

The taxable year of a partnership will close with respect to a limited partner whose entire interest in the partnership terminates for any reason, including the death of the limited partner.[3] A decedent's own tax year also ends on the date of death and is ordinarily a short year.[4] Thus, since the partnership tax year and the decedent's tax year will end on the same day, partnership income or loss will be included in the decedent's final return.

If the successor sells or exchanges its entire interest, or its interest is liquidated, the partnership year will end as to the selling successor at the date of sale. See Q 1203.

1214. Does a limited partner realize gain or loss on his partnership interest at death?

No. The death of a taxpayer and the transfer of his assets to his estate is not considered a taxable sale or exchange.

1215. What is the basis of the estate or other successor in interest in a limited partnership?

The estate or other successor in interest has a basis in the partnership interest "stepped up" (or down) to the fair market value of the interest on the date of death, or alternate valuation date used for estate tax purposes, increased by the estate's (or successor's) share of partnership liabilities on that date, and reduced to the extent the value is attributable to items of income in respect of a decedent.[5] A modified carryover basis replaces stepped up basis for property acquired from a decedent dying in 2010. See Q 1415, Q 1430. For partnership tax years beginning after 1997, the partnership tax year ends with respect to a partner who dies (see Q 1213). For partnership tax years

---

1. IRC Secs. 742, 1015; Treas. Reg. §1.1015-4.
2. Treas. Reg. §1.742-1.
3. IRC Sec. 706(c)(2)(A).
4. Treas. Reg. §1.443-1(a)(2).
5. Treas. Reg. §1.742-1.

beginning before 1998, the distributive share attributable to the period ending with the date of death which was taxable to the estate or successor was income in respect of a decedent, not part of the basis.[1]

ADJUSTMENT OF PARTNERSHIP BASIS

1216. What is the effect of a partnership's not electing to adjust the basis of partnership property on the sale or exchange of a partnership interest or on the death of a limited partner?

Large syndicated limited partnerships generally state that they will not elect to adjust the partnership basis in property on the sale or exchange of an interest or on the death of a partner. Failure to make the election can have unfavorable tax consequences for an individual who purchases or succeeds to an interest.

Generally, a partner's adjusted basis in his partnership interest reflects his proportionate share of the partnership's basis in its property. However, this is not necessarily true of a person who buys or succeeds to a partnership interest from another partner. See Q 1207, Q 1215.

Example. A, B, and C are partners in a partnership having $3,000 in cash, and real property with an adjusted basis of $24,000. Each partner's adjusted basis in his partnership interest is $9,000. C sells his ⅓ interest in the partnership to D for $15,000, at a time when the fair market value of the land is $42,000. The balance sheet of the partnership at the date of sale shows the following:

	Assets			Capital	
Assets	adjusted basis	market value		adjusted basis	market value
cash	$ 3,000	$ 3,000	A	$ 9,000	$15,000
land	24,000	42,000	B	9,000	15,000
	$27,000	$45,000	C	9,000	15,000

Following the sale, the partnership's adjusted basis in its property remains at $27,000 and each partner's share of partnership basis remains at $9,000, but D's basis in his partnership interest is $15,000, its cost to him.

If the land is sold in 2006 for $42,000, its fair market value, the partnership will realize a capital gain of $18,000. Each partner must report a capital gain of $6,000 as his distributive share of the partnership gain. In effect, D is now realizing gain and paying tax on $6,000 of appreciation that was already included in the purchase price he paid to C (and that was taxed to C at that time).

Assume the partnership terminates in 2007, distributing $15,000 to each partner in liquidation of his ⅓ interest. D had an adjusted basis of $21,000 in his partnership interest ($15,000 purchase price plus $6,000 distributive share of capital gain) and so has a $6,000 capital loss in 2007 on the liquidation of his interest. However, D's capital loss in 2007 does not make him whole for the capital gain in 2006. His $6,000 loss may be of limited use in 2007 and he has lost use of the amount paid in taxes in 2006.

In acknowledgement of the unfair results, the IRC permits the partnership to elect to adjust the partnership's basis in partnership property with respect to a partner to whom an interest in a partnership is transferred by sale or exchange or on the death

---

1. Treas. Regs. §§1.753-1(b), 1.706-1(c)(3)(v).

of a partner. (Adjustment is not made in the case of a gift.) For transfers after October 22, 2004, a basis adjustment is *required* if the partnership has a built-in loss of more than $250,000 immediately after the transfer. The adjustment decreases or increases the partnership's basis in partnership assets by the amount by which the purchasing or succeeding partner's basis in his interest exceeds or is less than his proportionate share of the adjusted basis of partnership property. The effect of the adjustment is limited to the particular partner.[1] If a partnership is terminated by a sale of an interest in the partnership, an election under IRC Section 743 that is in effect for the year the sale occurs applies to the incoming partner. The bases of property are adjusted before their deemed contribution to the new partnership.[2]

Example. Under the facts in the above example, if the election had been in effect with respect to C's transfer to D, A's share of partnership basis would have continued to be $9,000, B's share of partnership basis would have continued to be $9,000 and D's share would have been adjusted to $15,000. Thus on sale of the property in 2006, D's account would not reflect a share of the gain:

	Partnership	A's share	B's share	D's share
Sale price of land	$42,000	$14,000	$14,000	$14,000
Less adjusted basis				
common basis	24,000	8,000	8,000	8,000
adjustment to partnership basis for D	6,000	0	0	6,000
Total adjusted basis	$30,000	$8,000	$8,000	$14,000
Taxable gain from sale	$12,000	$6,000	$6,000	$ 0

If, instead of selling his interest, C dies in 2007 and D succeeds to C's interest, D's basis would be stepped up to the fair market value on date of death.[3] See Q 1213. Therefore, D would have a problem similar to that of the purchaser of an interest, if the partnership does not make the election.

An incoming partner of an upper-tier partnership (UTP) is entitled to an adjustment in his share of the lower-tier partnership's (LTP) adjusted basis in the LTP's partnership property, if and only if, the election has been made by both the UTP and the LTP.[4]

Regulations require that the election be filed with the partnership return for the taxable year during which the transfer occurs.[5]

In the case of an electing large partnership, see Q 1191.

PARTNERSHIP ANTI-ABUSE RULE

1217. What is the Subchapter K (partnership) anti-abuse rule?

Subchapter K provides for the formation of partnerships to conduct business transactions without incurring an entity-level tax. The partnership must be bona fide and transactions entered into for a substantial business purpose. The transactions must

1. IRC Sec. 743.
2. Treas. Reg. §1.708-1(b)(5).
3. IRC Sec. 1014(a).
4. Rev. Rul. 87-115, 1987-2 CB 163.
5. Treas. Reg. §1.754-1(b)(1).

be respected under substance over form principles and the tax consequences of the transactions must accurately reflect the partners' economic agreement and clearly reflect the partner's income.[1] The anti-abuse rule provides that if a partnership is involved in a transaction with a principal purpose of substantially reducing the present value of the partners' aggregate tax liability in a manner that is inconsistent with the intent of subchapter K, the IRS can recast the transaction for federal tax purposes to achieve tax results that are consistent with subchapter K.[2] The anti-abuse rule applies only to income taxes, which are governed under IRC subtitle A. It does not apply to transfer taxes, such as estate and gift taxes, which are governed under IRC subtitle B.[3]

The determination as to whether a partnership has violated the anti-abuse rule will be based on an analysis of all of the facts and circumstances, including a comparison of the purported business purpose of the transaction and the claimed tax benefits resulting therefrom. Factors to be considered include whether: (1) the present value of the partners' aggregate federal tax liability is substantially less than (a) if the assets were owned and business conducted directly, or (b) if separate transactions were integrated and treated as a single transaction; (2) necessary partners either have a nominal interest in the partnership, are substantially protected from any risk of loss from the partnership's activities or have little or no participation in the profits from the partnership's activities other than a preferred return; (3) substantially all of the partners are related to one another, either directly or indirectly; (4) partnership items are allocated in compliance with Treasury Regulation Section 1.704-1 and Treasury Regulation Section 1.704-2, but the results are inconsistent with the purpose of IRC Section 704(b) and these regulations (see Q 1195); (5) the benefits and burdens of ownership of partnership property are either substantially retained by the contributing partner or substantially shifted to a distributee partner.[4] These regulations generally apply to transactions occurring after May 11, 1994.[5]

Further, the regulations allow the IRS to treat a partnership as an aggregate of its partners, unless IRC provisions prescribe the treatment of a partnership as an entity and that treatment and resulting tax implications are clearly contemplated by those IRC provisions.[6] This provision is effective for transactions occurring after December 28, 1994.[7]

S CORPORATIONS

1218. How is an S corporation taxed?

An S corporation is one that elects to be treated, in general, as a passthrough entity, thus avoiding most tax at the corporate level.[8] To be eligible to make the election, a corporation must meet certain requirements as to the kind and number of shareholders, classes of stock, and sources of income. An S corporation must be a domestic corporation with only a single class of stock and may have up to 100 shareholders (none of whom are nonresident aliens) who are individuals, estates, and certain trusts. An S corporation

---

1. Treas. Reg. §1.701-2(a).
2. Treas. Reg. §1.701-2(b).
3. Treas. Reg. §1.701-2(h).
4. Treas. Reg. §1.701-2(c).
5. Treas. Reg. §1.701-2(g).
6. Treas. Reg. §1.701-2(e).
7. Treas. Reg. §1.701-2(g).
8. See IRC Secs. 1361, 1362, 1363.

may not be an ineligible corporation. An ineligible corporation is one of the following: (1) a financial institution that uses the reserve method of accounting for bad debts; (2) an insurance company; (3) a corporation electing (under IRC Section 936) credits for certain tax attributable to income from Puerto Rico and other U.S. possessions; and (4) a current or former domestic international sales corporation (DISC). Qualified plans and certain charitable organizations may be S corporation shareholders.[1]

Members of a family are treated as one shareholder. "Members of the family" are defined as "the common ancestor, lineal descendants of the common ancestor, and the spouses (or former spouses) of such lineal descendants or common ancestor." Generally, the common ancestor may not be more than six generations removed from the youngest generation of shareholders who would be considered members of the family.[2]

Trusts that may be S corporation shareholders include: (1) a trust all of which is treated as owned by an individual who is a citizen or resident of the United States under the grantor trust rules (see Q 1450); (2) a trust that was described in (1) above immediately prior to the deemed owner's death and continues in existence after such death may continue to be an S corporation shareholder for up to two years after the owner's death; (3) a trust to which stock is transferred pursuant to a will may be an S corporation shareholder for up to two years after the date of the stock transfer; (4) a trust created primarily to exercise the voting power of stock transferred to it; (5) a qualified subchapter S trust (QSST); (6) an electing small business trust (ESBT); and (7) in the case of an S corporation that is a bank, an IRA or Roth IRA.[3]

A QSST is a trust that has only one current income beneficiary (who must be a citizen or resident of the U.S.), all income must be distributed currently, and corpus may not be distributed to anyone else during the life of such beneficiary. The income interest must terminate upon the earlier of the beneficiary's death or termination of the trust, and if the trust terminates during the lifetime of the income beneficiary, all trust assets must be distributed to that beneficiary. The beneficiary must make an election for the trust to be treated as a QSST.[4]

An ESBT is a trust in which all of the beneficiaries are individuals, estates, or charitable organizations.[5] Each potential current beneficiary of an ESBT is treated as a shareholder for purposes of the shareholder limitation.[6] A potential current beneficiary is generally, with respect to any period, someone who is entitled to, or in the discretion of any person may receive, a distribution of principal or interest of the trust. In addition, a person treated as an owner of a trust under the grantor trust rules (see Q 1450) is a potential current beneficiary.[7] If for any period there is no potential current beneficiary of an ESBT, the ESBT itself is treated as an S corporation shareholder.[8] Trusts exempt from income tax, QSSTs, charitable remainder annuity trusts, and charitable remainder unitrusts may not be ESBTs. An interest in an ESBT may not be obtained by purchase. IRC Sec. 1361(e). If any portion of a beneficiary's basis in the beneficiary's interest is

---

1. IRC Sec. 1361.
2. IRC Sec. 1361(c)(1).
3. IRC Secs. 1361(c)(2), 1361(d).
4. IRC Sec. 1361(d).
5. IRC Sec. 1361(e).
6. IRC Sec. 1361(c)(2)(B)(v).
7. Treas. Reg. §1.1361-1(m)(4).
8. Treas. Reg. §1.1361-1(h)(3)(i)(F).

determined under the cost basis rules, the interest was acquired by purchase.[1] An ESBT is taxed at the highest income tax rate under IRC Section 1(e) (35% in 2007).[2]

An S corporation may own a qualified subchapter S subsidiary (QSSS). A QSSS is a domestic corporation that is not an ineligible corporation, if 100% of its stock is owned by the parent S corporation and the parent S corporation elects to treat it as a QSSS. Except as provided in regulations, a QSSS is not treated as a separate corporation and its assets, liabilities, and items of income, deduction, and credit are treated as those of the parent S corporation.[3] Regulations provide special rules regarding the recognition of a QSSS as a separate entity for tax purposes if an S corporation or its QSSS is a bank.[4]

If a QSSS ceases to meet the above requirements, it will be treated as a new corporation acquiring all assets and liabilities from the parent S corporation in exchange for its stock. If the corporation's status as a QSSS terminates, the corporation is generally prohibited from being a QSSS or an S corporation for five years.[5] Regulations provide that in certain cases following a termination of a corporation's QSSS election, the corporation may be allowed to elect QSSS or S corporation status without waiting five years if, immediately following the termination, the corporation is otherwise eligible to make an S corporation election or QSSS election, and the election is effective immediately following the termination of the QSSS election. Examples where this rule would apply include an S corporation selling all of its QSSS stock to another S corporation, or an S corporation distributing all of its QSSS stock to its shareholders and the former QSSS making an S election.[6]

A corporation will be treated as having one class of stock if all of its outstanding shares confer identical rights to distribution and liquidation proceeds.[7] However, "bona fide agreements to redeem or purchase stock at the time of death, disability or termination of employment" will be disregarded for purposes of the one-class rule unless a principal purpose of the arrangement is to circumvent the one-class rule. Similarly, bona fide buy-sell agreements will be disregarded unless a principal purpose of the arrangement is to circumvent the one-class rule and they establish a purchase price that is not substantially above or below the fair market value of the stock. Agreements that provide for a purchase price or redemption of stock at book value or a price between book value and fair market value will not be considered to establish a price that is substantially above or below fair market value.[8] Regulations provide that agreements triggered by divorce and forfeiture provisions that cause a share of stock to be substantially nonvested will be disregarded in determining whether a corporation's shares confer identical rights to distribution and liquidation proceeds.[9]

An S corporation is generally not subject to tax at the corporate level.[10] However, a tax is imposed at the corporate level under certain circumstances described below. When an S corporation disposes of property within 10 years after an election has been

---

1. Treas. Reg. §1.1361-1(m)(1)(iii).
2. IRC Sec. 641(c).
3. IRC Sec. 1361(b)(3).
4. Treas. Reg. §1.1361-4(a)(3).
5. IRC Sec. 1361(b)(3).
6. Treas. Reg. §1.1361-5(c).
7. Treas. Reg. §1.1361-1(l)(1).
8. Treas. Reg. §1.1361-1(l)(2)(iii). See IRC Secs. 1361, 1362.
9. Treas. Reg. §1.1361-1(l)(2)(iii)(B).
10. IRC Sec. 1363(a).

made, gain attributable to pre-election appreciation of the property (built in gain) is taxed at the corporate level to the extent such gain does not exceed the amount of taxable income imposed on the corporation if it were not an S corporation.[1]

For S elections made after December 17, 1987, a corporation switching from a C corporation to an S corporation may also be required to recapture certain amounts at the corporate level in connection with goods previously inventoried under a LIFO method.[2]

In addition, a tax is imposed at the corporate level on *excess* "net passive income" of an S corporation (passive investment income reduced by certain expenses connected with the production of such income) but only if the corporation, at the end of the tax year, has accumulated earnings and profits (either carried over from a year in which it was a nonelecting corporation or due to an acquisition of a C corporation), and if passive investment income exceeds 25% of gross receipts. The rate is the highest corporate rate (currently 35%).[3] "Passive investment income" for this purpose is rents, royalties, dividends, interest, annuities, and gains from sales or exchanges of stock or securities.[4] However, passive investment income does not include rents for the use of corporate property if the corporation also provides substantial services or incurs substantial cost in the rental business, or interest on obligations acquired from the sale of a capital asset or the performance of services in the ordinary course of a trade or business of selling the property or performing the services. Also, passive investment income does not include gross receipts derived in the ordinary course of a trade or business of lending or financing; dealing in property; purchasing or discounting accounts receivable, notes, or installment obligations; or servicing mortgages.[5] Regulations provide that if an S corporation owns 80% or more of a C corporation, passive investment income does not include dividends from the C corporation to the extent the dividends are attributable to the earnings and profits of the C corporation derived from the active conduct of a trade or business.[6] If amounts are subject to tax both as built-in gain and as excess net passive income, an adjustment will be made in the amount taxed as passive income.[7] For rulings on passive income involving S corporations involved in real estate rentals, equipment rentals and/or farming, see Let. Ruls. 9837003, 9611009, 9610016, 9548012, 9534024, 9514005.

Also, tax is imposed at the corporate level if investment credit attributable to years for which the corporation was not an S corporation is required to be recaptured.[8]

Furthermore, an S corporation may be required to make an accelerated tax payment on behalf of its shareholders, if the S corporation elects not to use a required taxable year.[9] The corporation is also subject to estimated tax requirements with respect to the tax on built in gain, the tax on excess net passive income and any tax attributable to recapture of investment credit.[10]

---

1. IRC Sec. 1374.
2. IRC Sec. 1363(d).
3. IRC Sec. 1375(a).
4. IRC Secs. 1362(d)(3), 1375(b)(3).
5. Treas. Reg. §1.1362-2(c)(5).
6. Treas. Reg. §1.1362-8(a).
7. IRC Sec. 1375(b)(4).
8. IRC Sec. 1371(d).
9. IRC Sec. 7519.
10. IRC Sec. 6655(g)(4).

Like a partnership, an S corporation computes its taxable income similarly to an individual, except that certain personal and other deductions are allowed to a shareholder but not to the S corporation, and the corporation may elect to amortize organizational expenses.[1] Each shareholder then reports on his individual return his proportionate share of the corporation's items of income, loss, deductions and credits; these items retain their character on pass through.[2] Certain items of income, loss, deduction or credit must be passed through as separate items because they may have an individual effect on each shareholder's tax liability. For example, net capital gains and losses pass through as such to be included with the shareholder's own net capital gain or loss. Any gains and losses on certain property used in a trade or business are passed through separately to be aggregated with the shareholder's other IRC Section 1231 gains and losses. (Gains passed through are reduced by any tax at the corporate level on gains.) Miscellaneous itemized deductions pass through to be combined with the individual's miscellaneous deductions for purposes of the 2% floor on such deductions. Charitable contributions pass through to shareholders separately subject to the individual shareholder's percentage limitations on deductibility. Tax exempt income passes through as such. Items involving determination of credits pass through separately.[3] Before passthrough, each item of passive investment income is reduced by its proportionate share of the tax at the corporate level on excess net passive investment income.[4] Items that do not need to be passed through separately are aggregated on the corporation's tax return and each shareholder reports his share of such nonseparately computed net income or loss on his individual return.[5] Items of income, deductions, and credits (whether or not separately stated) that flow through to the shareholder are subject to the "passive loss" rule (see Q 1292 through Q 1299) if the activity is passive with respect to the shareholder (see Q 1293). Apparently, items taxed at the corporate level are not subject to the passive loss rule unless the corporation is either closely held or a personal service corporation (see Q 1292).

Thus, whether amounts are distributed to them or not, shareholders are taxed on the corporation's taxable income. Shareholders take into account their shares of income, loss, deduction and credit on a per-share, per-day basis.[6] The S corporation income must also be included on a current basis by shareholders for purposes of the estimated tax provisions (see Q 1401).[7]

The Tax Court determined that when an S corporation shareholder files for bankruptcy, all the gains and losses for that year flowed through to the bankruptcy estate. The gains and losses should not be divided based on the time before the bankruptcy was filed.[8]

The basis of each shareholder's stock is *increased* by his share of items of separately stated income (including tax-exempt income), by his share of any nonseparately computed income, and by any excess of deductions for depletion over basis in property subject to depletion.[9] An S corporation shareholder may *not* increase his basis due to excluded discharge of indebtedness income.[10] The basis of each shareholder's stock is *decreased* (not below zero)

---

1. IRC Sec. 1363(b).
2. IRC Secs. 1366(a), 1366(b).
3. IRC Sec. 1366(a)(1).
4. IRC Sec. 1366(f)(3).
5. IRC Sec. 1366(a).
6. IRC Sec. 1377(a).
7. Let. Rul. 8542034.
8. *Williams v. Comm.*, 123 TC 144 (2004).
9. IRC Sec. 1367(a)(1).
10. IRC Sec. 108(d)(7)(A).

by items of distributions from the corporation that are not includable in the income of the shareholder, separately stated loss and deductions and nonseparately computed loss, any expense of the corporation not deductible in computing taxable income and not properly chargeable to capital account, and any depletion deduction with respect to oil and gas property to the extent that the deduction does not exceed the shareholder's proportionate share of the property's adjusted basis. For tax years beginning after 2005 and before 2008, if an S corporation makes a charitable contribution of property, each shareholder's basis is reduced by the pro-rata share of their basis in the property.[1] If the aggregate of these amounts exceeds his basis in his stock, the excess reduces the shareholder's basis in any indebtedness of the corporation to him.[2] A shareholder may not take deductions and losses of the S corporation that, aggregated, exceed his basis in his S corporation stock plus his basis in any indebtedness of the corporation to him.[3] Such disallowed deductions and losses may be carried over.[4] In other words, he may not deduct in any tax year more than he has "at risk" in the corporation.

Generally, earnings of an S corporation are not treated as earnings and profits. A corporation may have accumulated earnings and profits for any year in which a valid election was not in effect or as the result of a corporate acquisition in which there is a carryover of earnings and profits under IRC Section 381.[5]

A distribution from an S corporation that does not have accumulated earnings and profits lowers the shareholder's basis in the corporation's stock.[6] Any excess is generally treated as gain.[7]

If the S corporation does have earnings and profits, distributions are treated as distributions by a corporation without earnings and profits, to the extent of the shareholder's share of an accumulated adjustment account (i.e., post-1982 gross receipts less deductible expenses, which have not been distributed). Any excess distribution is treated under the usual corporate rules. That is, it is a dividend up to the amount of the accumulated earnings and profits. Any excess is applied to reduce the shareholder's basis. Finally, any remainder is treated as a gain.[8] However, in any tax year, shareholders receiving the distribution may, if all agree, elect to have all distributions in the year treated first as dividends to the extent of earnings and profits and then as return of investment to the extent of adjusted basis and any excess as capital gain.[9] If the IRC Section 1368(e)(3) election is made, it will apply to all distributions made in the tax year.[10]

Certain distributions from an S corporation in redemption of stock receive sale/exchange treatment. (Generally, only gain or loss, if any, is recognized in a sale.) In general, redemptions that qualify for "exchange" treatment include redemptions not essentially equivalent to a dividend, substantially disproportionate redemptions of stock, complete redemptions of stock, certain partial liquidations, and redemptions of stock to pay estate taxes.[11]

---

1. IRC Sec. 1367(a)(2), as amended by PPA 2006.
2. IRC. Sec. 1367(b)(2)(A).
3. IRC Sec. 1366(d)(1).
4. IRC Sec. 1366(d)(2).
5. IRC Sec. 1371(c).
6. IRC Sec. 1367(a)(2)(A).
7. IRC Sec. 1368(b).
8. IRC Sec. 1368(c).
9. IRC Sec. 1368(e)(3).
10. Let. Rul. 8935013.
11. See IRC Secs. 302, 303.

If the S corporation distributes appreciated property to a shareholder, gain will be recognized to the corporation as if the property were sold at fair market value; the gain will pass through to shareholders like any other gain.[1]

The rules discussed above generally apply in tax years beginning after 1982. Nonetheless, certain casualty insurance companies and certain corporations with oil and gas production will continue to be taxed under the rules applicable to Subchapter S corporations prior to these rules.[2]

REAL ESTATE

1219. How does real estate shelter income?

Real estate investments can provide "shelter" from taxes through (1) deferral of payment of tax from one year to another and (2) absolute tax savings.

Tax Deferral

When depreciation deductions and any other noncash deductions are large enough, the taxable income from the property can be substantially less than its positive "cash flow" (the amount of cash receipts remaining after subtracting from gross cash receipts all cash expenses and payments on mortgage principal). Often, the noncash deductions produce a loss that partly or totally "shelters" the net cash flow. In many instances, deductions for depreciation and other expenses can produce a tax loss that offsets other taxable income. Because investment in real estate will generally be a passive activity, such losses may normally offset only other passive income of the taxpayer, although passive losses and the deduction-equivalent of credits with respect to certain rental real estate activities may offset up to $25,000 of nonpassive income of an individual. (The passive loss rules are discussed in Q 1222 and Q 1292 through Q 1299).

However, when mortgage amortization payments exceed the depreciation on the property, taxable income and even the tax itself can exceed the investor's share of cash flow or tax savings. This taxable but noncash income is often referred to as "phantom income" and, assuming constant rental income and constant mortgage amortization, phantom income can increase each year. The carryover of disallowed passive losses from earlier years may reduce or even eliminate the phantom income in later years. If the individual has not prepared for phantom income, he may want to unburden himself of the investment. The tax consequences of disposition of property, including a partnership interest, are discussed in Q 1203 to Q 1216 and Q 1232 to Q 1235.

Absolute Savings

Some types of real estate investment (e.g., low-income housing and rehabilitation of old or historic structures) provide tax credits that directly reduce the tax on an individual's income. See Q 1227 and Q 1228. Because investment in real estate will generally be a passive activity, such credits may normally offset only taxes from passive activities of the taxpayer, although passive losses and the deduction-equivalent of credits with respect to certain rental real estate activities may offset up to $25,000 of nonpassive income of an individual. (The passive loss rules are explained in Q 1292 to Q 1299). Investment

---

1. IRC Secs. 1371(a), 311(b).
2. Subchapter S Revision Act of 1982, Sec. 6.

tax credits can offer absolute shelter of income that would otherwise be spent for taxes, provided the property is held long enough. If not, there is some recapture. Even so, there has been the benefit of deferral.

Use of Limited Partnership

Because a limited partnership "passes through" the income, gain, losses, deductions, and credits of its real estate operations, the partnership provides virtually the same tax benefits offered by direct individual ownership. Passthrough of items may differ somewhat for electing large partnerships (see Q 1191), as compared to other partnerships (see Q 1190), because of the different requirements for separately stated items for the two types of partnerships. In addition, a limited partnership permits passive investment by providing management, permits participation for less capital investment, has some flexibility in allocating gains and losses among partners, and offers individual investors limited liability. While real estate investment can utilize forms other than partnership, partnership is the most common form. See Q 1190 to Q 1216 on limited partnerships.

A *publicly traded partnership* is taxed as a corporation unless 90% of the partnership's income is passive-type income. A publicly traded partnership is a partnership that is traded on an established securities market or is readily tradable on a secondary market or a substantial equivalent. In general, "passive-type income" for this purpose includes interest, dividends, *real property rents, gain from the sale of real property*, income and gain from certain mineral or natural resource activities, and gain from sale of a capital or IRC Section 1231 asset. A grandfather rule treats electing 1987 partnerships (see Q 1189) as not subject to corporate taxation if they elect to be taxed at a rate of 3.5% on gross income; such a partnership otherwise operates as a passthrough entity. Taxation as a corporation would defeat the "passthrough" feature of a limited partnership. See Q 1189 on publicly traded partnerships.

Particular programs vary in their tax sheltering goals and methods. Some emphasize tax free cash flow, some losses that offset other income, and some appreciation and equity build up. Real estate investments combine these elements in varying proportions—more of one element generally means less of another.

Another form of real estate investment, the real estate investment trust (REIT), is discussed at Q 1179 to Q 1181.

1220. In general, what are the tax benefits of real estate investment? What limitations may restrict enjoyment of those benefits?

The rental and management of real property is generally considered a trade or business even if the owner owns only one property,[1] is actively engaged in another profession or business and carries on all management activities through an agent,[2] or, continuously, over a period of several years, experiences losses from the operation of the business.[3] However, it has been held that where activities were minimal, rental of a single residence was not a trade or business.[4]

---

1. *Lagreide v. Comm.*, 23 TC 508 (1954).
2. *Fackler v. Comm.*, 45 BTA 708 (1941), aff'd, 133 F.2d 509 (6th Cir. 1943).
3. *Allen v. Comm.*, 72 TC 28 (1979).
4. *Grier v. U.S.*, 120 F. Supp. 395 (D. Conn. 1954), aff'd, 218 F.2d 603 (2d Cir. 1955). See also *Bauer v. U.S.*, 168 F.Supp. 539 (Ct. Cl. 1959); *Union Nat'l Bank of Troy v. U.S.*, 195 F.Supp. 382 (N.D.N.Y. 1961); GCM 39126 (2-7-84); TAM 8350008.

Credits

Credits against tax liability may be taken for certain investments in low-income housing (see Q 1227) or rehabilitation of old or historic structures (see Q 1228). Use of these credits may be subject to certain limitations (see heading "Limitations," below).

Depreciation

An owner of residential or nonresidential improved real property (either used in a trade or business or held for the production of income) may deduct each year amounts for depreciation of the buildings, but not the land itself, even though no cash expenditure is made. Furthermore, the depreciable amount is not limited to the owner's equity in the property.[1] See Q 1424. However, the deductions may be subject to certain limitations (see heading "Limitations," below). Also, where accelerated depreciation is used, part or all of the amount deducted is subject to "recapture" on sale of the property. See Q 1235.

Interest

An investor in improved or unimproved real estate may generally deduct each year amounts paid for mortgage interest (subject to certain limitations, see heading "Limitations," below). However, prepaid interest must be deducted over the period to which the prepayment relates.[2] A further limitation on deduction of interest is that construction period interest must be capitalized.[3] The interest subject to capitalization may not be reduced by interest income earned from temporarily investing unexpended debt proceeds.[4]

Taxes

The investor in real property is permitted to deduct amounts paid for real property taxes (subject to certain limitations, see heading "Limitations," below).[5] In the year of acquisition the buyer may deduct the real estate taxes allocable to the number of days he owns the property.[6] "Taxes" that are actually assessments for improvements (e.g., sidewalks, sewers, etc.) and that enhance the value of the property cannot be currently deducted, but must be added to the investor's basis in the property (i.e., capitalized) and deducted through depreciation allowances over the recovery period.[7] A further limitation on deduction of real estate taxes is that construction period taxes must be capitalized.[8]

Expenses

An investor in real estate may deduct each year "all the ordinary and necessary expenses paid or incurred during the taxable year in carrying on any trade or business…"[9] and all ordinary and necessary expenses paid or incurred during the taxable year (1) for the production and collection of income; (2) for the management, conservation, or maintenance of property held for the production of income; or (3) in connection with

---

1. IRC Secs. 167, 168.
2. IRC Sec. 461(g)(1).
3. IRC Sec. 263A(f).
4. Rev. Rul. 90-40, 1990-1 CB 52.
5. IRC Sec. 164(a).
6. IRC Sec. 164(d).
7. IRC Sec. 164(c).
8. IRC Sec. 263A.
9. IRC Sec. 162(a).

the determination, collection, or refund of any tax.[1] See also Q 1310, Q 1312. Routine repair and maintenance expenses are deductible in the year paid as business expenses or expenses incurred in connection with property held for the production of income, but the cost of improvements must be capitalized (added to the owner's basis in the property) and recovered through depreciation deductions.[2] Repairs are those "which neither materially add to the value of the property nor appreciably prolong its life, but keep it in an ordinary, efficient operating condition…"[3] Capital improvements increase the value, prolong the life or alter the use for which the property is suitable.[4]

The first $5,000 of "start-up" expenses are deductible, but the rest must be amortized over a 180-month period, beginning with the month the business begins. The $5,000 figure is reduced by the amount that start-up expenses exceed $50,000. Expenses included in this category are those (other than interest and taxes) incurred in connection with investigating the creation or acquisition of a new business, creating an active trade or business, and "any activity engaged in for profit and for the production of income before the day on which active trade or business begins." The expenses must be expenses that would be deductible if incurred in connection with an existing active business.[5]

Generally, accrual basis taxpayers may not deduct expenses payable to related cash basis taxpayers before the amount is includable in the income of the cash basis taxpayer. The rule applies to amounts accrued by a partnership to its partners, by partners to their partnership, by an S corporation to its shareholders and by shareholders to their S corporation. Related parties also include those discussed in Q 1419.[6]

Disposition

On disposition of the property, the owner may generally defer tax on gain by exchanging it for "like kind" property (see Q 1237, Q 1238, Q 1422). Alternatively, he may be able to spread out his gain by using the installment method of reporting; however, an interest surcharge applies to certain installment sales of property with a sales price exceeding $150,000. See Q 1408. Furthermore, the installment method of reporting is unavailable for sales of real property held by the taxpayer for sale to customers in the ordinary course of the taxpayer's trade or business.[7]

Generally, losses on disposition may be treated as ordinary losses instead of capital losses, unlimited by the $3,000 cap on the ordinary income offset by capital losses. See Q 1233 for discussion of gain or loss on sale.

Special Benefits and Limitations

Special benefits or limitations may apply to certain kinds of real estate investment: low-income housing (see Q 1226), "rehabs" (see Q 1228), vacation homes (see Q 1225). In addition, an investor can develop vacant land within limits without being classified as a "dealer" (see Q 1223).

---

1. IRC Sec. 212.
2. IRC Sec. 263(a).
3. Treas. Reg. §1.162-4.
4. Treas. Regs. §§1.263(a)-1(a), 1.263(a)-1(b); *Illinois Merchants Trust Co. v. Comm.*, 4 BTA 103 (1926).
5. IRC Sec. 195.
6. IRC Secs. 267(a)(2), 267(e).
7. IRC Secs. 453(b)(2)(A), 453(l)(1)(B).

As a general rule, an investor takes the same deductions, credits and recognizes income whether he owns the property directly or has an interest in a limited partnership that "passes through" the deductions, credits and income. See Q 1190 regarding regular partnerships and Q 1191 regarding electing large partnerships. However, if a publicly traded partnership is taxed as a corporation (see Q 1189), investors are unable to take partnership deductions, credits, and income on their own tax returns.

Limitations

If the property is used in an activity in which the investor does not materially participate, deductions and credits are subject to the passive loss rule; however, if the property is used in a rental real estate activity in which an individual actively participates, a special exemption for up to $25,000 of passive losses and the deduction-equivalents of credits with respect to rental real estate activities may apply. Active participation is not required with respect to the low-income housing or rehabilitation tax credits. See Q 1222.

Losses incurred after 1986 with respect to real estate activities are subject to the "at risk" limitation (see Q 1221).

AT RISK LIMITATION

1221. Does the "at risk" limitation on losses apply to an investor in real estate? If so, what effect will it have?

Generally, the "at risk" rule applies to losses incurred after 1986 with respect to real estate placed in service after 1986.[1] However, in the case of an interest in an S corporation, a partnership, or other pass-through entity acquired after 1986, the "at risk" rule will apply to losses incurred after 1986 no matter when the real estate is placed in service.[2]

In general, the "at risk" rule limits the deduction an investor may claim for his share of net losses generated by the real estate activity to the amount he has at risk in that activity. The rule does not prohibit an investor from offsetting his share of the deductions generated by the activity against the income he receives from the activity. For a detailed explanation of the operation of the "at risk" limitation, see Q 1288 to Q 1291.

Put as simply as possible, an investor is initially "at risk" to the extent that he is not protected against the loss of money or other property he contributes to the program. An investor is considered at risk with respect to certain qualified nonrecourse financing incurred in the holding of real property. For the specifics as to how an investor's "amount at risk" is calculated, see Q 1287.

PASSIVE LOSS RULE

1222. Are investments in real estate subject to the passive loss rule? If so, what is the effect to an investor in real estate?

Rental real estate activities will generally be considered passive activities subject to the passive loss rule.[3] However, if the personal use of a residence that is also rented out

---

1. IRC Sec. 465(c); TRA '86 Sec. 503(c)(1).
2. TRA '86 Sec. 503(c)(2).
3. IRC Sec. 469(c)(2).

exceeds 14 days or, if greater, 10% of the rental days (see Q 1225), the rental activity is not treated as a passive activity.[1] A real property business of a taxpayer is not automatically considered a rental activity subject to the passive loss rules for a year, but only if during the year (1) more than one-half of the personal services performed by the taxpayer in trades or businesses during the year is in real property trades or businesses in which the taxpayer materially participates, and (2) the taxpayer performs more than 750 hours of service during the year in such real property trades or businesses.[2] See Q 1293. Few investors in real estate syndications will qualify for this exception.

In general, the passive loss rule limits the amount of the taxpayer's aggregate deductions from all passive activities to the amount of his aggregate income from all passive activities; credits attributable to passive activities can be taken only against tax attributable to passive activities.[3] The rule is intended to prevent taxpayers from off-setting income in the form of salaries, interest, and dividends with losses from passive activities. However, the benefit of the disallowed passive losses and credits is generally not lost, but rather is postponed until such time as the taxpayer has additional passive income or disposes of the activity. If an individual *actively participates* in a rental real estate activity subject to the passive activity rules, the individual may use up to $25,000 of losses and the deduction-equivalent of credits to offset nonpassive income. An individual need not actively participate in a rental real estate activity to obtain the $25,000 rental real estate exemption with respect to taking the low-income housing or rehabilitation tax credits. See Q 1292 through Q 1299 for a more detailed explanation of the rule and, in particular, Q 1299 with respect to the $25,000 exclusion applicable to rental real estate activities.

If the investment is in real estate that is not rental property, the real estate activity will generally be considered a passive activity subject to the passive loss rule unless the taxpayer *materially participates* in the activity. The $25,000 rental real estate exemption is not available with respect to nonrental property. See Q 1292 through Q 1299. As to whether an investment in vacant land is a "passive activity," see Q 1223.

If the investment in real estate is made through a publicly traded partnership subject to the passive loss rule, further restrictions may apply. See Q 1292.

See Q 1191 regarding investment in an electing large partnership.

VACANT LAND

Generally

1223. What deductions are available to the owner of vacant land? How is gain or loss on sale treated?

An investor in vacant land may take various deductions, including real estate taxes, interest charges on indebtedness incurred to buy the land, and other expenses paid or incurred in connection with holding the land (possibly subject to the "passive loss" rule or the "investment" interest limitation, see below).[4] Land is not depreciable, but expenses incurred in managing, conserving, or maintaining property held for the production of

---

1. IRC Sec. 469(j)(10).
2. IRC Sec. 469(c)(7).
3. IRC Sec. 469.
4. IRC Secs. 163, 164.

income (see Q 1310) and in connection with any business use of the land are deductible.[1] If the vacant land is held by the taxpayer primarily for sale to customers in the ordinary course of his trade or business, taxes, interest, and other expenses paid or incurred in connection with the land must be included in inventory costs.[2]

Apparently, investment in vacant land is treated as a passive activity if the activity is (1) a rental activity (as defined below and in Q 1293 and Q 1294), or (2) a trade or business in which the investor does not materially participate.[3] The rental of property used in a trade or business is treated as incidental to a trade or business activity (rather than a rental activity) during any year if (1) the taxpayer owns an interest in the trade or business activity during the year, (2) the property was predominantly used in the trade or business activity either during the year or in two out of the five preceding years, and (3) the gross rental from the property for the year is less than 2% of the lesser of (a) the unadjusted basis of the property, or (b) the fair market value of the property.[4]

It also appears that investment in vacant land is treated as an investment activity (rather than a passive activity) during any year in which the principal purpose for holding the property during such year is to realize gain from the appreciation of the property. The rental of investment property is treated as incidental to an investment activity (rather than a rental activity) if the gross rental from the property for the year is less than 2% of the lesser of (1) the unadjusted basis of the property, or (2) the fair market value of the property.[5]

> *Example 1.* Mrs. Martin holds 1,000 acres of unimproved land with a fair market value of $350,000 and an unadjusted basis of $210,000. She holds the land for the principle purpose of realizing gain from appreciation. In order to defray the cost of carrying the land, she rents the land to a rancher who uses the land to graze cattle and who pays rent of $4,000 per year. The rental of the land is treated as incidental to an investment activity rather than a rental activity. This is determined as follows: (1) The lesser of the unadjusted basis ($210,000) or the fair market value ($350,000) is $210,000. (2) Two percent of $210,000 equals $4,200. (3) Gross rental of $4,000 is less than $4,200.[6]

> *Example 2.* In 2006, Mrs. Vickers acquired vacant land for the purpose of constructing a shopping mall. Before commencing construction, she leases the land under a 1-year lease to a car dealer, who uses the land to park cars held in his inventory. In 2007, Mrs. Vickers begins construction of a shopping mall on the land. Since the land was acquired principally for purpose of development rather than held for appreciation, the rental of the land in 2006 cannot be treated as incidental to an investment activity. Also, the rental of the land cannot be treated as incidental to a trade or business activity because the land has never been used in a trade or business. The rental of the land is thus treated as a rental activity subject to the passive loss rule.[7]

In general, a taxpayer's aggregate losses from passive activities may offset only his aggregate income from passive activities.[8] See Q 1292 to Q 1299. Interest allocable to property held for investment purposes is generally deductible only up to the aggregate amount of the taxpayer's "investment" income.[9] See Q 1304.

---

1. IRC Secs. 212, 162.
2. IRC Sec. 263A.
3. IRC Sec. 469(c); Temp. Treas. Reg. §1.469-1T(e)(1).
4. Temp. Treas. Regs. §§1.469-1T(e)(3)(ii)(D), 1.469-1T(e)(3)(vi)(A), 1.469-1T(e)(3)(vi)(C).
5. Temp. Treas. Regs. §§1.469-1T(e)(3)(ii)(D), 1.469-1T(e)(3)(vi)(A), 1.469-1T(e)(3)(vi)(B).
6. Temp. Treas. Reg. §1.469-1T(e)(3)(viii)(Ex. 5).
7. Temp. Treas. Reg. §1.469-1T(e)(3)(viii)(Ex. 7).
8. IRC Sec. 469.
9. IRC Sec. 163.

Gain or loss on sale will be treated as capital gain or loss unless the property is (1) used in the taxpayer's trade or business, in which case it will be "IRC Section 1231" property subject to rules discussed in Q 1233, or (2) held by the taxpayer primarily for sale to customers in the ordinary course of his trade or business in which case it will be ordinary gain.[1] A special rule applies to gain of a person who is not a dealer but develops land and sells parcels—see Q 1224. If the investment in vacant land is treated as a passive activity, gain or loss from sale of the property is generally gain or loss from a passive activity, see above.

Development and Subdivision

1224. If an individual develops vacant land and sells parcels will he be considered a "dealer"?

An individual's gain on the sale of real property will be taxed as ordinary income if he is a "dealer," that is, if he holds the property "primarily for sale to customers in the ordinary course of trade or business."[2] Where an individual has bought and sold several parcels of land, subdivided land or participated actively in its sale, he may be treated as a dealer. The following are some of the factors considered in determining whether an individual is a dealer with respect to property:[3]

(1) the purpose and use for which the property was acquired and thereafter held;

(2) the length of time between purchase and sale;

(3) the number and frequency of sales made over a period of time;

(4) the activities of the taxpayer and his agents and the developments and improvements made to put the property in a saleable condition;

(5) the activity of the taxpayer and his agents in advertising and promoting sales;

(6) the extent and substantiality of the above transactions;

(7) miscellaneous factors, such as membership in a dealer organization, newspaper publicity, the nature of the taxpayer's business as shown in directory listings and tax returns, documents, and the use of a business office to sell the property;

(8) the amount of gain derived from sales as compared with other income of the taxpayer, and whether the gain is attributable to appreciation or development and promotion;

(9) prior and subsequent activities of the taxpayer in selling real estate;

(10) replacement of the property sold with additional real estate.

There are special rules that permit an individual owning a tract of real property to subdivide it; to actively promote its sale; to erect a temporary field office, survey, fill, drain, level, clear and construct a minimum all-weather access road on the property

---

1. IRC Secs. 64, 1221(a), 1231.
2. IRC Secs. 64, 1221(a)(1).
3. *Brandenburger v. U.S.*, 31 AFTR 2d ¶73-498 (E.D. Cal. 1973).

without being considered a "dealer" *solely* because of those activities. He is within these rules only if: (1) he did not hold the land primarily for sale to customers in the ordinary course of business in a previous year and he did not hold other land primarily for sale to customers in the ordinary course of business during the same taxable year, (2) the land, unless inherited, has been held for five years by the investor, and (3) no "substantial" improvements that substantially increase the value of the land are made to the land. (He may be deemed to have made improvements made by certain related parties.)[1] Under very limited circumstances, the individual is permitted to install water and sewer lines, drainage facilities and to build hard surface roads, gutters and curbs on the property without being classified as a "dealer."[2]

Gain from the sale of such property is treated under special rules. If the individual has sold fewer than six lots or parcels from the same tract up to the end of his taxable year, the entire gain will be capital gain, or, if the property is real property used in a trade or business, "IRC Section 1231" gain as explained in Q 1233.[3] In computing the number of lots or parcels sold, two or more contiguous lots sold to a single buyer in a single sale will be counted as only one parcel.[4]

In the taxable year the sixth lot or parcel is sold from the same tract, the taxpayer will be required to recognize ordinary income as follows: the amount, if any, by which 5% of the selling price of each lot sold in the taxable year exceeds the expenses incurred in connection with its sale or exchange will (to the extent that it represents gain) be ordinary income. Any part of the gain not treated as ordinary income will be treated as capital gain, or, if the property is used in a trade or business, as "IRC Section 1231" gain. All expenses of sale of the lot are to be deducted first from the 5% of the gain that would otherwise be considered ordinary income, and any remainder of such expenses will reduce the gain upon the sale or exchange that would otherwise be considered capital gain or "IRC Section 1231" gain. Such expenses cannot be deducted as ordinary business expenses from other income. The 5% rule applies to all lots sold from the tract in the year the sixth lot or parcel is sold. Thus, if the taxpayer sells the first six lots of a single tract in one year, 5% of the selling price of each lot sold is treated as ordinary income and reduced by the selling expenses. On the other hand, if the taxpayer sells the first three lots of a single tract in 2007, and the next three lots in 2008, only the gain realized from the sales made in 2008 will be so treated.[5]

If the taxpayer sells or exchanges no lots from the tract for a period of five years after the sale or exchange of at least one lot in the tract, then the remainder of the tract will be deemed a new tract for the purpose of counting the number of lots sold from the same tract. The pieces in the new tract need not be contiguous. The five-year period is measured between the dates of the sales or exchanges.[6]

VACATION HOME

1225. Are the expenses of a vacation rental home deductible?

1. IRC Sec. 1237(a).
2. IRC Sec. 1237(b)(3).
3. Treas. Regs. §§1.1237-1(e)(2)(i), 1.1237-1(f).
4. Treas. Reg. §1.1237-1(e)(2)(i).
5. Treas. Reg. §1.1237-1(e)(2)(ii).
6. Treas. Reg. §1.1237-1(g)(2).

IRC Section 280A provides rules for the disallowance of certain expenses in connection with the rental of a vacation home. Different rules apply depending on the amount of personal use and rental use (see below).

Personal Use Not Exceeding 14 Days or 10% of Rental Days

An individual who makes part time use of a dwelling and rents it other parts of the year may take deductions for depreciation and expenses, but subject to some limitations. If his personal use (discussed below) does not exceed the longer of 14 days per year or 10% of the number of days the unit is rented at fair rental, he may deduct all ordinary and necessary expenses allocable to rental use even if they show a loss (provided the activity is engaged in for profit and subject to the passive loss rule).[1] In determining expenses allocable to rental use, the IRS applies the following formula:[2]

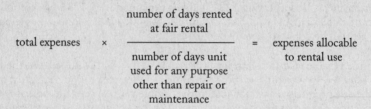

Interest, taxes and casualty losses not allocable to rental use can be deducted as personal expenses (to the extent otherwise allowable) if the individual itemizes deductions.[3] The Service uses the same ratio for allocating interest and taxes between personal and rental use as it does in allocating other expenses.

However, if it is determined that the activity is one "not engaged in for profit," the amount of deductions is limited to the amount of gross rental income.[4] (If deductions are limited to gross rental income, the order in which deductions are allowed is the same as that applicable where personal use exceeds the longer of 14 days or 10% of the rental days, discussed below. See also Q 1300.) Whether the activity is engaged in for profit depends on all the facts and circumstances involved.[5] If the gross income exceeds the deductions attributable to the rental use for at least three of the five consecutive tax years ending with the current tax year, the rental use is presumed to be for profit.[6] (The individual may elect to defer the determination as to whether the presumption applies until the end of the fourth taxable year following the first tax year he began rental use. If he makes this election, the period for determining a tax deficiency for the period remains open for two years after his return is due (without extensions) for the last year in the five year period.[7])

If the personal use does not exceed the greater of 14 days or 10% of rental days, the rental activity will generally be subject to the passive loss rule (see Q 1222). However, if the individual actively participates in the rental real estate activity, as much as $25,000

1. IRC Sec. 280A(e).
2. Prop. Treas. Reg. §1.280A-3(c).
3. IRC Sec. 280A(b).
4. IRC Sec. 183(b).
5. Treas. Reg. §1.183-2(a).
6. IRC Sec. 183(d).
7. IRC Sec. 183(e).

of losses (and the credit-equivalents of such losses) from the rental activity could be used to offset nonpassive income of the taxpayer.[1]

Personal Use Exceeding 14 Days or 10% of Rental Days

If the owner uses the dwelling unit for more than the longer of 14 days or 10% of the days the unit is rented at fair rental, the owner's deductions allocable to rental use (using the above ratio) are limited to gross rental income (as reduced by expenditures to obtain tenants).[2] The Service's position is that mortgage interest and real estate taxes must be allocated to rental use in the ratio that the number of days rented bears to the number of days of use.[3] This position with respect to interest and taxes has been ruled unreasonable.[4] *Bolton* and *McKinney* held that interest and taxes, unlike maintenance expenses, are allocable to the rental period in the ratio that the number of days the property was rented bears to the number of days in the year. Whether the IRS and other courts will accept this position and whether it can be extended to the situation where personal use does not exceed 14 days or 10% of rental days is still not settled.

Where, because of the limit, not all deductions are allowed, deductions are allowable in the following order: (1) allocable amounts of expenses that are deductible without regard to rental use (such as mortgage interest and real estate taxes); (2) allocable amounts of deductions allowable because of rental use but that do not result in adjustment to basis; (3) allocable amounts of deductions that would result in an adjustment to basis (such as depreciation).[5]

Example: Mr. Jones owns a summer home that he uses for 30 days and rents to Mr. Green for 60 days for $2,000; it is vacant for the remainder of the year. Advertising and realtor's fees total $100; taxes, $600; interest, $900; utilities, $300; maintenance, $600; insurance, $150; depreciation, $2,400. He calculates his deduction as follows:

	IRS rule	*Bolton* rule
gross receipts from rental	$2,000	$2,000
less: unallocated expenses to procure tenant	(100)	(100)
limitation on deductions	$1,900	$1,900
less: taxes and interest for rental period		
(2/3 × ($600 + $900))	(1,000)	
(2/12 × ($600 + $900))		(250)
	$900	$1,650
less: maintenance, insurance and utilities ($1,050) portion allocable to rental period (2/3 × $1,050)	(700)	(700)
	$ 200	$ 950
depreciation $2,400 portion allocable to rental period (2/3 × $2,400)	$1,600	$1,600

Using the IRS rule, Mr. Jones may deduct all allocable expenses except $1,400 of depreciation. Using the *Bolton* rule, Mr. Jones may deduct all allocable expenses except $650 of depreciation.

---

1. IRC Sec. 469(i).
2. IRC Sec. 280A; Prop. Treas. Reg. §1.280A-3(d)(2).
3. Prop. Treas. Reg. §1.280A-3(d).
4. *Bolton v. Comm.*, 82-2 USTC ¶9699 (9th Cir. 1982); *McKinney v. Comm.*, 83-2 USTC ¶9655 (10th Cir. 1983). See also *Buchholz v. Comm.*, TC Memo 1983-378.
5. Prop. Treas. Reg. §1.280A-3(d)(3).

In determining whether personal use exceeds 10% of the number of days a unit in a rental pool is rented at fair rental, only the days the units are actually rented are counted; days when the units are merely held out for rent or are used rent-free for business purposes cannot be included.[1]

If the personal use of a residence that is also rented out exceeds the greater of 14 days or 10% of the rental days, the rental activity is not treated as a passive activity for such year (see Q 1222). Deductions from such a residence are subject to limitation under the rules above, and any income, gain, loss, or deduction from the residence is not taken into account under the passive loss rule for the year.[2] However, such a residence may constitute a "qualified residence" for purposes of the deduction of mortgage interest. See Q 1303.

"Personal Use" Defined

"Personal use" includes: (1) use, for personal purposes, by the owner or by anyone who has an interest in the unit or by a brother, sister, spouse, ancestor or lineal descendent of the owner or other person having an interest in the unit; (2) use by a person under an arrangement that enables the owner to use some other unit whether or not the taxpayer pays rent to use the other unit and regardless of the length of time he uses it; and (3) use by any individual at less than fair rental value. Fair rental is determined by taking into account factors such as comparable rents in the area. This third requirement does not apply to an employee to whom the premises are furnished for the convenience of the employer, under IRC Section 119.[3] Nonetheless, it has been held that days of rent-free use of units in a rental pool by prospective renters are not personal use days, where unit owners have no control over such use and the use was an ordinary and necessary business use.[4] Where the owner of a vacation home donated a week's use of the home to a charitable auction, the use of the home by the successful bidder was treated as personal use.[5]

Use by the owner on any day on which the principal purpose of the use is to perform repair or maintenance work on the unit does not constitute personal use. Whether the principal purpose is to perform repair or maintenance work depends on all the facts and circumstances, including the amount of time devoted to repair and maintenance, the frequency of the use for repair and maintenance purposes during the tax year, and the presence and activities of companions. A day on which the taxpayer engages in repair or maintenance on a substantially full time basis will not be considered a day of personal use by the taxpayer.[6] The IRC authorizes the Secretary to prescribe regulations on use by the owner while performing maintenance or repairs, but if the taxpayer is engaged in repairs and maintenance on a substantially full-time basis for a particular day "such authority shall not allow the Secretary to treat a dwelling unit as being used for personal use by the taxpayer on such day merely because other individuals who are on the premises on such day are not so engaged."[7]

If a family member makes the unit rented to him his principal residence, it is not personal use by the owner. However, the preceding exception does not apply if the

1. *Byers v. Comm.*, 82 TC 919 (1984).
2. IRC Sec. 469(j)(10).
3. IRC Sec. 280A(d)(2).
4. *Byers v. Comm.*, above.
5. Rev. Rul. 89-51, 1989-1 CB 89.
6. Prop. Treas. Reg. §1.280A-1(e)(6).
7. IRC Sec. 280A(d)(2).

family member also has an interest in the dwelling unit unless the rental is pursuant to a "shared equity financing agreement." A shared equity financing agreement is an agreement under which two or more persons acquire "qualified ownership interests" in a dwelling unit, and the person(s) holding one or more of such interests is entitled to occupy the dwelling unit for use as a principal residence, and is required to pay rent to one or more other persons holding qualified ownership interests in the dwelling unit. A qualified ownership interest is an undivided interest for more than 50 years in the dwelling unit and appurtenant land being acquired in the transaction to which the shared equity financing agreement relates.[1]

A dwelling unit subject to these rules includes a house, apartment, condominium, mobile home, boat or similar property that provides basic living accommodations such as sleeping space, toilet and cooking facilities and all structures and other property appurtenant thereto.[2]

Fewer Than 15 Days Rental

If an individual rents a dwelling unit (as defined above) for fewer than 15 days during the year, and he has used it as a residence during the taxable year, the income received from such a rental is excluded from gross income and no deductions for rental are allowed.[3]

Low-Income Housing

1226. What special tax benefits are available for investment in low-income housing?

A low-income housing tax credit is available with respect to property placed in service after 1986. In general, the credit may be taken annually over a 10-year period and can be substantial.[4] The credit is discussed in detail in Q 1227.

Construction period interest and taxes must be capitalized. Rehabilitation expenditures must also be capitalized.[5] Low-income housing will generally be depreciated using a straight line method over 27.5 years.[6] However, the straight line depreciation is not subject to the recapture rule or to the alternative minimum tax.[7] Additionally, low-income housing is generally a residential rental activity subject to the "passive loss" rule (see Q 1299).

The Service will not disallow losses on the theory that low-income housing is an activity entered into "not for profit" simply because of legal restrictions on rents, charges, rates of return and methods of low income housing operations.[8] In addition, the hobby loss provisions of IRC Section 183 (see Q 1300) will not apply to disallow losses, deductions, or credits attributable to the ownership and operation of qualified low-income housing credit activities, for buildings placed in service after 1986.[9]

---

1. IRC Sec. 280A(d)(3).
2. Prop. Treas. Reg. §1.280A-1(c)(1).
3. IRC Sec. 280A(g).
4. IRC Sec. 42.
5. IRC Sec. 263A.
6. IRC Secs. 168(b)(3)(B), 168(c).
7. See IRC Secs. 1250, 56(a)(1).
8. Rev. Rul. 79-300, 1979-2 CB 112.
9. Treas. Reg. §1.42-4.

For housing placed in service before 1987, substantially different rules applied.

1227. What is the low-income housing tax credit?

The low-income housing tax credit is an income tax credit based on a percentage of the qualified basis of certain low-income housing placed in service after 1986. Generally, the credit is determined in the year in which the property is placed in service and may be taken annually for 10 years. Subject to certain limitations, the adjusted basis qualifying for the credit consists of expenditures for certain new housing or substantially rehabilitated housing.[1]

Taxpayers seeking the credit make application to the local housing agency in order to obtain a building identification number.[2] All taxpayers, except those who finance the project through certain tax-exempt bonds described in IRC Section 42(h)(4), must receive an allocation of the credit for the building.[3] All taxpayers, however, must comply with IRS certification requirements in order to obtain the credit.[4] If, during the 15-year compliance period, there is a change in the portion of housing that is low-income housing or the property ceases to qualify as low-income housing, there is a recapture of all or part of the credit.[5]

Amount of Credit

The amount of credit depends on when the property was first placed in service. A letter ruling treated a project as placed in service in the year that a temporary certificate of occupancy was issued for the project and the taxpayer advertised the property as available for occupancy.[6]

For property placed in service in 1987, the credit percentage was 9% annually for 10 years for new buildings that are not federally subsidized for the taxable year. The credit was 4% annually for 10 years for (1) existing buildings or (2) new buildings that are federally subsidized.[7]

For property placed in service after 1987, the credit percentage is the amount prescribed by the Service for the earlier of (1) the month in which the building is placed in service, or (2) at the election of the taxpayer, (a) the month in which the taxpayer and the housing credit agency enter into an agreement allocating the tax credit to the project, or (b) the month in which certain tax-exempt obligations (described in IRC Section 42(h)(4)(B)) that finance the project are issued. The election described in (2) above is irrevocable and must be made no later than five days after the close of the month elected. The amount that will be prescribed by the Service is a percentage that will yield over a 10-year period an amount of credit that has the present value of 70% of the qualified basis of new buildings that are not federally subsidized for the year, and 30% of the qualified basis of existing buildings and new buildings that are federally subsidized for the year.[8]

---

1. IRC Sec. 42.
2. Notice 88-91, 1988-2 CB 414.
3. IRC Sec. 42(h)(1).
4. IRC Sec. 42(l).
5. IRC Sec. 42(j).
6. Let. Rul. 8844062.
7. IRC Sec. 42(b)(1).
8. IRC Sec. 42(b)(2).

However, the rules in the preceding paragraph are modified with respect to credits allocated from state housing credit ceilings after 1989 so that a credit is not allowed with respect to the acquisition of an existing building unless substantial rehabilitations are made to the building.[1] Generally, rehabilitation expenditures within a 24 month period must exceed the greater of (1) $3,000 per low-income housing unit, or (2) 10% of the building's adjusted basis. If such an existing building is substantially rehabilitated, the 70% present value credit is available for the rehabilitation portion and the 30% present value credit is available for the balance.[2] Furthermore, the credit for an existing building may not begin before the credit for the rehabilitations are allowed.[3]

The minimum expenditures requirement of IRC Section 42(e)(3) may be met in less than 24 months, and treated as placed in service at the close of the period in which the requirement is met, but the aggregation period for such expenses may not exceed 24 months.[4]

When the Credit May be Claimed

The *10-year credit period* generally begins in the taxable year in which the building is placed in service, or upon the irrevocable election of the taxpayer, in the succeeding taxable year, but only if the building is a qualified low-income building at the close of the first year of the credit period.[5] However, for post-1987 credit allocations, the taxpayer may begin claiming the credit in either of the next two years, so long as the taxpayer has incurred at least 10% of the total project costs in that year.[6] The credit stays constant throughout the 10-year period in which the credit may be claimed. Thus, if a 3.51% credit is taken in 2006 for property placed in service in 2006, a 3.51% credit may also be taken in years 2007 through 2015 (assuming the low-income housing remains qualified, see "Qualification of Low-income Housing," below).[7] For details as to how the election is made under IRC Section 42(f)(1) to defer the start of the credit period, see Rev. Rul. 91-38, above. Further, temporary relief may be granted for buildings located in sites that have been declared major disaster areas by the President.[8]

Certain taxpayers who owned an interest in a low-income housing project on or before October 25, 1990 could elect to accelerate the credit with respect to such interest into their first taxable year ending after October 24, 1990. If this election was made, the credit otherwise available under IRC Section 42 was increased by 50% for the first tax year ending after October 24, 1990. The taxpayer's allowable credits in future years are then reduced pro rata by the additional amount claimed in the year for which the election was made. The election is irrevocable and binding on all successors in interest to the taxpayer. The election was to be made on Form 8609 by the due date for filing the return for the year of the election. Under certain circumstances, the election was available to partnerships and S corporations.[9]

---

1. IRC Sec. 42(d)(2)(B)(iv).
2. IRC Sec. 42(e).
3. IRC Sec. 42(f)(5).
4. Rev. Rul. 91-38, 1991-2 CB 3.
5. IRC Sec. 42(f)(1).
6. IRC Sec. 42(h)(1)(E).
7. IRC Sec. 42(b).
8. Rev. Proc. 95-28, 1995-1 CB 704.
9. See OBRA '90, Sec. 11407(c); Rev. Proc. 91-7, 1991-1 CB 416.

Basis

The *eligible basis* of a building is its adjusted basis (normally, cost).[1] With respect to credits allocated from state housing credit ceilings after 1989, the eligible basis of low-income housing located in designated high cost areas will be treated as being 130% of the otherwise eligible basis.[2]

In order for an existing building to qualify for the credit, (1) the existing building must have been acquired from an unrelated person, (2) the basis of the property is not a stepped-up basis from a decedent's estate or determined by reference to the basis of the property in the hands of a transferee, (3) the building was not previously placed in service by the taxpayer or anyone related to the taxpayer at the time the property was previously placed in service, (4) there is a period of at least 10 years between when the building is acquired and the later of (a) the date the building was last placed in service, or (b) the date of the most recent nonqualified substantial improvement of the building, and (5) there have been substantial rehabilitations made to the building (see above).[3] Special rules apply to the 10-year requirement, and under special circumstances it may be waived.[4] For allocations of credit made after 1990, a placement in service of a single-family residence by any individual who owned and used the residence for no other purpose than as his principal residence is not considered a placement for purposes of the 10-year rule.[5]

A nonqualified substantial improvement is a 25% addition, made over a 24-month period, to the adjusted basis (calculated without reduction for depreciation allowances) of property that is subject to depreciation methods in effect prior to 1987.[6] The adjusted basis of an existing building does not include any portion of the basis of the building that is determined by reference to the basis of other property held at any time by the person acquiring the building.[7]

The adjusted basis of property (for purposes of the low-income housing tax credit) is determined as of the close of the first taxable year of the credit period.[8] The eligible basis is reduced by the amount of any federal grant received with respect to the property.[9] The eligible basis must also be reduced by an amount equal to the portion of the adjusted basis of the building that is attributable to residential rental units which are not low-income housing units and which are of a higher quality than the average low-income housing unit in the building, unless an election is made to exclude certain excess costs from the eligible basis.[10]

Nonrecourse financing is included in the cost or other basis of a building (for purposes of the low-income housing tax credit) only if (1) the building is acquired by the investor from an unrelated person, (2) the financing is not convertible debt, and (3) the financing is borrowed from a "qualified person" or represents a loan from any federal, state, or local government or instrumentality thereof, or is guaranteed by any

---

1. IRC Sec. 42(d).
2. IRC Sec. 42(d)(5)(C).
3. IRC Secs. 42(d)(2)(B), 179(d)(2).
4. See Treas. Reg. §1.42-2.
5. IRC Sec. 42(d)(2)(D)(ii)(V); see Rev. Rul. 91-38, above, at Questions 9-11.
6. IRC Sec. 42(d)(2)(D).
7. IRC Sec. 42(d)(2)(C).
8. IRC Secs. 42(d)(1), 42(d)(2)(A).
9. IRC Sec. 42(d)(5)(A).
10. IRC Sec. 42(d)(3).

federal, state, or local government. A "qualified person" is a person who is actively and regularly engaged in the business of lending money and who is not (1) a person from whom the taxpayer acquired the property (or related to such a person), or (2) a person who receives a fee with respect to the investment in the real estate (or related to such a person). In the case of a partnership or an S corporation, the determination of whether nonrecourse financing is qualified for purposes of the low-income housing tax credit is made at the partner or shareholder level, respectively.[1]

If there is a decrease in the amount of nonqualified nonrecourse financing (not including a decrease through the surrender or similar use of the property) in a subsequent year, the amount of decrease is treated as an additional qualified investment in the low-income housing made in the year the property was placed in service. A credit for the applicable percentage of the amount of the increase is taken in the year of the increase. For purposes of determining the amount of the credit or of any subsequent recapture (see heading "Recapture," below), the investment is treated as made in the year the property was placed in service.[2]

An investor may also include certain nonrecourse financing obtained from certain qualified nonprofit organizations in basis for the purpose of determining the low-income housing tax credit.[3]

The eligible basis of a building is allocated to the low-income housing units in the building to determine the *qualified basis* of the qualified low-income building for any tax year. The qualified basis is determined annually by multiplying the eligible basis of the building by the lower of (1) the unit fraction or (2) the floor space fraction. The unit fraction is equal to the number of low-income units in the building divided by the number of residential units (whether or not occupied) in the building. The floor space fraction is equal to the total floor space of low-income units in the building divided by the total floor space of the residential rental units (whether or not occupied) in the building.[4] Vacant apartments, formerly occupied by low-income individuals, continue to be treated as occupied by low-income individuals so long as reasonable attempts are made to rent the apartment and no other units of comparable size or smaller are rented to nonqualified individuals.[5] A unit occupied by a full-time resident manager will be included in the eligible basis of the building; however, that unit will not be included in either the numerator or denominator of the unit fraction or floor space fraction for purposes of determining the qualified basis of the building.[6]

If there is an *increase in the qualified basis* (i.e., the applicable fraction of low-income housing units or floor space, see above, has increased) after the first year of the credit period, an additional credit is allowed with respect to such increase in an amount equal to 2/3 × the applicable credit percentage × the increase in qualified basis. This additional credit may be taken in each of the years remaining in the *15-year compliance period* which begins with the first taxable year of the 10-year credit period.

> *Example.* Nine percent property placed in service in January, 1987 would receive additional credit of 6% (2/3 × 9%) for an increase in the qualified basis in 1989. The 6% credit could be taken annually for years 1989 through 2001.[7]

1. IRC Secs. 42(k), 49(a)(1).
2. IRC Sec. 49(a)(2).
3. IRC Sec. 42(k).
4. IRC Sec. 42(c).
5. H.R. Conf. Rep. No. 99-841 (TRA '86), *reprinted in* 1986-3 CB (vol. 4) 94.
6. Rev. Rul. 92-61, 1992-2 CB 7.
7. IRC Sec. 42(f)(3).

The *first year's credit* (including the year in which there has been an increase in the qualified basis resulting in additional credit being allowed) may be limited under an averaging convention. Under the averaging convention, the sum of the applicable fractions (unit or floor space, see above) as of the close of each full month in the year in which the property is placed in service is divided by 12. The resulting average fraction is multiplied by the eligible basis to determine the qualified basis for the first year only. This qualified basis is in turn multiplied by the credit percentage to determine the first year's credit (as modified under the averaging convention). The part of the first year's credit that is disallowed under this convention may be taken in the year following the credit period (i.e., the eleventh year).[1]

With respect to credits allocated from state housing credit ceilings before 1990, if *rehabilitation expenditures* incurred within a 24-month period with respect to any building increased the qualified basis attributable to such expenditures by an average of $2,000 or more per low-income housing unit, the rehabilitation expenditures were treated as a separate new building for purposes of the low-income housing credit. If such expenditures were paid or incurred before the close of the first credit period with respect to the acquisition of the property to which the rehabilitation expenditures were made, the taxpayer could elect to have the rehabilitation expenditures included in the eligible basis of the acquired property or treated as a separate new building.[2] With respect to credits allocated from state housing credit ceilings after 1989, the low-income housing tax credit is not available with respect to the acquisition of existing housing unless the rehabilitation is substantial (as described under "Amount of Credit," above).

A subsequent owner of a building during its 15-year compliance period is eligible to continue to receive the low-income housing tax credit as if the new owner were the original owner, using the original owner's credit percentage and qualified basis.[3] The prior owner need not have actually claimed the credit for the new owner to claim it.[4]

Qualification of Low-Income Housing

In order to qualify for the low-income housing credit, a low-income housing project must meet certain minimum set-aside requirements and rent restrictions. Either (1) 20% or more of the residential units in the project must be rent-restricted and occupied by individuals (i.e., set aside for such individuals) whose income is 50% or less of area median gross income (AMGI) (the 20-50 test), or (2) 40% or more of the residential units in the project must be rent-restricted and occupied by individuals whose income is 60% or less of AMGI (the 40-60 test). An irrevocable election is made to use either the 20-50 or 40-60 test in the year the credit is first taken.[5] A residential unit is rent-restricted if the gross rent with respect to the unit does not exceed 30% of the set-aside income limitations above. (Income is imputed based on the number of bedrooms in a unit.)[6] Thus, rent may not exceed 15% of AMGI if the 20-50 test is used (30% × 50%) and 18% of AMGI if the 40-60 test is used (30% × 60%). The determination of an individual's income and the AMGI is to be made in accordance with Section 8 of the United States Housing Act of 1937 (and is not based on gross income for federal income

---

1. IRC Sec. 42(f)(2).
2. IRC Sec. 42(e), prior to amendment by OBRA '89.
3. IRC Sec. 42(d)(7); H.R. Conf. Rep. 99-841 (TRA '86), *reprinted in* 1986-3 CB (vol. 4) 102.
4. See Rev. Rul. 91-38, above.
5. IRC Sec. 42(g)(1).
6. IRC Sec. 42(g)(2).

tax purposes).[1] Income limitations fluctuate with changes in AMGI for purposes of initially qualifying an individual under IRC Section 42(g)(1).[2] Rent does not include any Section 8 rental payment, certain fees for supportive services, or payments to the extent the owner pays an equivalent amount to the Farmer's Home Administration under section 515 of the Housing Act of 1949. However, it does include any Section 8 utility allowance.[3] The tenant's gross rent may exceed the 30% limitation if there is compliance with the federal housing law.[4] Whether a unit is rent restricted is determined on the date a housing credit agency initially allocates a housing credit dollar amount to the building under IRC Section 42(h)(1) or on the building's placed in service date, if so designated by the building owner. In the case of a bond-financed building, the determination is made on the date a determination letter is initially issued to the building or on the building's placed in service date, if so designated by the building owner.[5]

Generally, these requirements must be met throughout a 15-year compliance period which begins with the first taxable year of the 10-year credit period. However, if an individual's income met the applicable income limit when he began occupying the residential unit or when the calculations are made for annual qualification of the low-income housing, the individual continues to meet the applicable income limit in subsequent years (so long as the unit continues to be rent restricted) unless the individual's income exceeds 140% of the applicable income limit and a residential unit of comparable or smaller size in the same project is occupied by a new resident whose income exceeds the applicable income limit (the available unit rule).[6] In the case of a low-income housing project for which the 15% of the low-income units are occupied by individuals whose income is 40% or less of AMGI and an irrevocable election is made, this threshold is increased to 170%, but the income limitation for a new resident occupying a unit of comparable or smaller size cannot exceed 40% of AMGI.[7] Income limitations fluctuate with changes in AMGI for purposes of determining whether any available rental unit must be rented to a new low-income tenant under IRC Section 42(g)(2)(D)(ii).[8] Also, vacant apartments, formerly occupied by low-income individuals, continue to be treated as occupied by low-income individuals so long as reasonable attempts are made to rent the apartment and no other units of comparable size or smaller are rented to nonqualified individuals.[9] Once any comparable unit is rented in violation of the available unit rule, all over-income units lose their status as low-income units.[10]

A low-income housing project that has no other building in service at the time it places a building in service must meet these requirements no later than the close of the first year of the credit period for the building.[11] A low-income housing project that has another building already in service at the time it places a later building in service must meet these requirements with regard to the project already in service on the date the later building is placed in service. If these requirements are met, then the first building and the second building are treated as part of the low-income housing project.[12] A tax-

1. Notice 88-80, 1988-2 CB 396.
2. Rev. Rul. 94-57, 1994-2 CB 5.
3. IRC Sec. 42(g)(2)(B).
4. IRC Sec. 42(g)(2)(E).
5. Rev. Proc. 94-57, 1994-2 CB 744.
6. IRC Sec. 42(g)(2)(D).
7. IRC Secs. 42(g)(2)(D)(ii), 142(d)(4)(B).
8. Rev. Rul. 94-57, 1994-2 CB 5.
9. H.R. Conf. Rep. No. 99-841 (TRA '86), *reprinted in* 1986-3 CB (vol. 4) 94.
10. Treas. Reg. §1.42-15(f).
11. IRC Sec. 42(g)(3)(A).
12. IRC Sec. 42(g)(3)(B).

payer may elect to have a building not treated as part of a qualified low-income housing project if the building has completed its 15-year compliance period.[1]

With respect to credits allocated from state housing credit ceilings after 1989, an extended low-income housing commitment is required in order to obtain the low-income housing tax credit. In general, the commitment obligates the taxpayer (and the taxpayer's successors) to maintain the property as low-income housing for a period of 15 years after the 15 year credit compliance period has expired (generally, a 30 year commitment). However, the extended low-income housing commitment terminates if (1) the property is subject to foreclosure (unless the foreclosure was prearranged by the taxpayer to terminate the commitment period), or (2) no buyer willing to maintain the property as low-incoming housing can be found after the 15 year credit compliance period has ended.[2] A taxpayer who receives a low-income housing credit before 1990 must enter into an extended low-income housing credit commitment in order to be eligible for an additional housing credit allocation for the building after December 31, 1989.[3]

Limitations

The amount of low-income housing tax credit that can be taken is limited to the housing credit dollar amount that has been allocated to the building by a state housing credit agency. Once granted, the housing credit dollar amount applies to the building for the remaining years of the 15-year compliance period.[4] To facilitate tracking of credits, each building for which an allocation of the low-income housing credit is made is assigned a building identification code (BIN).[5] Allocation of the credit is made on Form 8609 which should be filed with the taxpayer's income tax return.

The low-income housing tax credit is added with certain other credits into the general business credit calculation, and is subject to the general business credit limitation.[6] See Q 1262 concerning the general business credit limitation.

The passive loss rules generally apply to the low-income housing tax credit. However, the low-income housing tax credit is given special treatment under the rental real estate rules. A taxpayer need not actively participate in the low-income housing rental activity to obtain the $25,000 rental real estate exemption amount with respect to the low-income housing tax credit.[7] Also, for property placed in service after 1989, there is no phase-out of the $25,000 rental real estate exemption with respect to the low-income housing credit.[8] For property placed in service before 1990, the $25,000 exemption amount for rental real estate with respect to the low-income housing credit began to phase-out when a taxpayer had income in excess of $200,000.[9] With respect to an interest in a passthrough entity, this repeal of the phaseout of the $25,000 exemption does not apply unless such interest was acquired after 1989.[10] In addition, the $25,000 rental real estate exemption, which is otherwise unavailable with respect to a publicly traded partnership, is available to the extent that the low-income housing credit and the

---

1. IRC Sec. 42(g)(5).
2. IRC Sec. 42(h)(6).
3. Rev. Rul. 92-79, 1992-3 CB 10.
4. IRC Sec. 42(h).
5. Notice 88-91, 1988-2 CB 414.
6. IRC Sec. 38(b)(5).
7. IRC Sec. 469(i)(6)(B)(i).
8. IRC Sec. 469(i)(3)(D).
9. IRC Sec. 469(i)(3)(B), prior to amendment by OBRA '89.
10. OBRA '89, Sec. 7109(b)(2).

rehabilitation investment credit (see Q 1228) exceed the regular tax liability attributable to income from the partnership.[1] See Q 1299.

The not-for-profit rules of IRC Section 183 do not apply to disallow losses, deductions, or credits attributable to the operation of low-income housing.[2]

Recapture

If, at the close of any taxable year in the 15-year compliance period, the amount of the qualified basis of any building is less than the amount of such basis at the close of the preceding taxable year, part of the low-income housing credit may have to be recaptured and interest paid from the time when the recaptured credit was originally taken at the federal overpayment rate under IRC Section 6621. A decrease in qualified basis is not subject to the recapture rule to the extent the amount of the decrease does not exceed the amount of a previous increase in qualified basis for which an additional credit of ⅔ of the applicable percentage has been taken (see "Amount of Credit," above). The recaptured credit and interest are added to the taxpayer's regularly calculated tax. No deduction may be taken for the interest paid. The amount of low-income housing credit that is recaptured is determined by subtracting from the aggregate amount of credits allowed in prior taxable years the aggregate amount of credits that would have been allowable if the aggregate credits allowable for the entire compliance period were allowed ratably over 15 years.[3] Temporary relief may be granted for buildings located in sites that have been declared major disaster areas by the President.[4]

Generally, the qualified basis will change if the applicable fraction of low-income housing units or floor space changes or if the property ceases to qualify as low-income housing. However, if there is a *de minimis* change to the floor space fraction and the property continues to be low-income housing following the change, no recapture results.[5]

A disposition of the building (or interest therein) beyond the 15-year compliance period does not result in recapture of the low-income housing tax credit. A disposition within the 15-year compliance period will result in recapture, unless the taxpayer posts a bond and the building is reasonably expected to qualify as low-income housing throughout the remainder of the 15-year compliance period.[6]

A partnership that has 35 or more partners may make an irrevocable election to have the partnership treated as the taxpayer to whom the credit was allowable. A husband and wife (and their estates) are treated as one partner for this purpose. If the election is made, recapture is allocated to the partners in the same manner as the partnership's taxable income is allocated for the year in which recapture occurs.[7] No change of ownership will be deemed to have occurred with respect to a partnership that has made the election if within a 12-month period at least 50% (in value) of the original ownership remains unchanged.[8]

---

1. IRC Sec. 469(k).
2. Treas. Reg. §1.42-4.
3. IRC Sec. 42(j).
4. Rev. Proc. 95-28, 1995-1 CB 704.
5. IRC Sec. 42(j)(4)(F).
6. IRC Sec. 42(j)(6).
7. IRC Sec. 42(j)(5).
8. H.R. Conf. Rep. No. 99-841 (TRA 86), *reprinted in* 1986-3 CB (vol. 4) 96.

OLD BUILDINGS AND CERTIFIED HISTORIC STRUCTURES

1228. What is the credit for rehabilitating old buildings and certified historic structures?

Designed as a tax incentive to encourage the preservation of historic buildings and as a means of spurring commercial growth in older cities and neighborhoods, a special investment tax credit is available for certain expenditures incurred in the rehabilitation of qualified buildings. The credit has been available for qualifying expenditures incurred after 1981 but underwent substantial revision in TRA '86.

Amount of Credit

Currently a 20% credit is available for expenditures incurred in rehabilitations of certified historic structures (residential or nonresidential) and a 10% credit is available for expenditures incurred in the rehabilitation of other buildings (nonresidential) that were first placed in service before 1936. These percentages apply to property placed in service (as a result of the rehabilitation) after 1986.[1]

Property Used for Lodging

Unless the building is a certified historic structure, a building will not qualify for the investment tax credit to the extent it is used for lodging purposes.[2] Thus, the use of a building or structure that is not a certified historic structure must be commercial or nonresidential.

> *Example 1.* Expenditures are incurred to rehabilitate a five-story structure. The top three floors are apartments. The bottom two floors are commercial office space. The building is not a certified historic structure. The building and the rehabilitation work otherwise qualify for the tax credit. Expenditures incurred in connection with the rehabilitation of the top three floors do not qualify for the credit. However, the portion of the building's basis that is attributable to qualified rehabilitation expenditures for the commercial part of the building is not considered to be expenditures for property used primarily for lodging. An allocation of expenditures would therefore be made in order to determine the portion of the basis that qualifies for the credit.[3]

> *Example 2.* Expenditures are incurred to rehabilitate a five-story structure. Each of the five floors is an apartment. The building *is* a certified historic structure. The rehabilitation work otherwise qualifies for the tax credit. Because the building is a certified historic structure, the entire portion of the building's basis attributable to qualified rehabilitation expenditures qualifies for the credit.[4]

Qualified Rehabilitated Buildings

The credit is claimed on the portion of the basis of the building that is attributable to qualified rehabilitation expenditures. Four requirements must be met for the building to be a qualified rehabilitated building and be eligible for the credit.

1. *"Placed in service" requirement.* The building must have been placed in service before the beginning of the rehabilitation.[5] "Placed in service" assumes the meaning

---

1. IRC Secs. 47(a), 50(b)(2), 47(c); Treas. Reg. §1.46-1(q).
2. IRC Sec. 50(b)(2).
3. Treas. Reg. §1.48-1(h)(1)(iii).
4. Treas. Reg. §1.48-1(h)(2)(iv).
5. IRC Sec. 47(c)(1)(A)(ii).

given it in Treasury Regulation Section 1.46-3(d). This requirement is met where *anyone* has placed the property in service prior to the rehabilitation of the building.[1]

2. *Structural preservation test.* Unless it is a certified historic structure, the building must meet an existing external wall or internal structural framework retention test. With respect to rehabilitation expenditures incurred after 1986:

> (a)   50% or more of the existing external walls must be retained in place as external walls;

> (b)   75% or more of the existing external walls must be retained in place as internal or external walls; and

> (c)   75% or more of the existing internal structural framework of the building must be retained in place.[2] "Internal structural framework" includes all load-bearing internal walls and any other internal structural supports, including the columns, girders, beams, trusses, spandrels, and all other members that are essential to the stability of the building.[3]

3. *Age requirement test.* Unless it is a certified historic structure, the building must have been located where it is rehabilitated since before 1936 in order to be entitled to the current tax credit. IRC Sec. 47(c)(1)(B); Treas. Reg. §1.48-12(b)(5).

4. *"Substantially rehabilitated" test.* For rehabilitation to be considered "substantial," the expenditures over a 24-month period selected by the taxpayer (but ending in the tax year) must exceed the greater of $5,000 or the owner's adjusted basis in the building and its structural components not including the cost of the land.[4] For purposes of this test, the adjusted basis of the building may not be allocated between a rehabilitated portion and a portion that is not rehabilitated.[5]

The owner's adjusted basis is generally determined at the start of the 24-month period (but if the owner's holding period begins later, the adjusted basis is determined at the beginning of the owner's holding period).[6] If the rehabilitation can be expected to be completed in phases set forth in architectural plans and specifications completed before rehabilitation work begins, a 60-month period may be used instead of a 24-month period.[7] Once it is determined that the rehabilitation is substantial, the amount of qualified rehabilitation expenditures that qualify for the credit includes expenditures incurred before, within, and after the 24-month or 60-month measuring period provided such expenditures are incurred before the end of the taxable year in which the property is placed in service.[8]

Certified Historic Structure

Generally, a certified historic structure is one that is (1) listed on the National Register of Historic Places or (2) located in a registered historic district and certified

---

1. Treas. Reg. §1.48-12(b)(1)(ii).
2. IRC Sec. 47(c)(1)(A)(iii).
3. Treas. Reg. §1.48-12(b)(3)(iii).
4. IRC Sec. 47(c)(1)(C).
5. *Alexander v. Comm.*, 97 TC 244 (1991).
6. IRC Sec. 47(c)(1)(C)(i).
7. IRC Sec. 47(c)(1)(C)(ii); Treas. Reg. §1.48-12(b)(2)(v).
8. Treas. Reg. §1.48-12(c)(6).

by the Secretary of the Interior as being of historic significance to the district.[1] The rehabilitation of such a structure must be certified by the Secretary of the Interior as consistent with the historic character of the property in order to qualify for the 20% credit.[2] These expenditures and the building must otherwise meet the same requirements as expenditures for the rehabilitation of buildings that are not certified historic structures except that there is no age requirement for certified historic structures.[3] Certified historic structures are exempt from the external wall retention requirement after TRA '86.[4] However, the Secretary of the Interior retains jurisdiction over the certification of a certified historic structure and the Secretary may impose an equivalent requirement.[5]

Any expenditure for rehabilitation of a building that is in a registered historic district but that is not a certified historic structure will not qualify for even the credit for the rehabilitation of buildings that are not certified historic structures unless the Secretary of the Interior has certified that the building is *not* of historic significance to the district. If rehabilitation of such a building began without certification by the Secretary of the Interior that the building is not of historic significance to the district, no credit will be allowed unless the Secretary of the Interior does certify that the building is not of historic significance to the district and the taxpayer certifies that when he began the rehabilitation, he in good faith was not aware that such a certification was necessary.[6]

Qualified Rehabilitation Expenditures

For an amount to be a "qualified rehabilitation expenditure," four requirements must be satisfied.

1. *Amount must be chargeable to capital account.* The expenditure must be includable in the basis of real property, so any amount that is deductible as an expense in the year paid or incurred does not qualify.[7]

2. *Amount must be incurred by the taxpayer.* A qualified rehabilitation expenditure is considered incurred by the taxpayer on the date that the amount would be considered incurred under an accrual method of accounting. Under certain conditions a taxpayer acquiring rehabilitated property (*e.g.*, a condominium unit that has been rehabilitated) may be treated as having incurred the expenditure, provided that (a) the building (or portion of the building) was not used after the rehabilitation and prior to its acquisition, and (b) no other person claimed the credit. In such case, the taxpayer's qualified rehabilitation expenditure is the lesser of (i) the amount of the qualified expenditure or (ii) the amount of the purchase price allocable to the expenditure.[8]

3. *Expenditure must be incurred for depreciable real property.* For property placed in service after 1986, the amount must be added to the basis of depreciable property that is (a) nonresidential real property, (b) residential rental property, (c) real property that has a class life of more than 12.5 years, or (d) an addition or improvement to (a), (b) or (c) above.[9]

---

1. IRC Sec. 47(c)(3).
2. IRC Sec. 47(c)(2)(C).
3. Treas. Reg. §1.48-12(b)(4).
4. IRC Sec. 47(c)(1)(A)(iii).
5. See Notice 87-15, 1987-1 CB 446.
6. IRC Sec. 47(c)(2)(B)(iv); Treas. Reg. §1.48-12(d)(5).
7. Treas. Reg. §1.48-12(c)(2).
8. Treas. Reg. §1.48-12(c)(3).
9. IRC Sec. 47(c)(2)(A).

4. *Expenditure must be made in connection with the rehabilitation of a qualified rehabilitated building.* The Service takes the position that amounts expended that are attributable to work done to facilities related to the building – such as a sidewalk, parking lot, or landscaping – do not qualify for the credit.[1]

The original cost of acquiring the building or any interest in it and amounts spent to enlarge the existing building are not eligible for the credit.[2] Furthermore, expenditures do not qualify unless straight line depreciation has been elected with respect to them, or, in the case of expenditures financed by an industrial revenue bond, is required.[3] The straight line depreciation election need be made only for the portion of the basis that is attributable to qualified rehabilitation expenditures.[4] A letter ruling determined that expenditures to repair fire damage, remove toxic substances, retain environmental and other consultants and renovate and reconstruct the damaged building were qualified rehabilitation expenditures within the meaning of IRC Section 47(a)(2), but that the amount of the rehabilitation credit would be reduced by any gain not recognized under IRC Section 1033 (involuntary conversions). The ruling was conditioned upon the premise that the building was "substantially rehabilitated" (as defined in IRC Section 47(c)(1)(C)(i)) and that the expenditures otherwise met the requirements described above.[5]

Nonrecourse Financing of Rehabilitation Expenditures

Rehabilitation expenditures include nonrecourse financing in the cost or other basis of the property (for purposes of the rehabilitation tax credit) only if (1) the property is acquired by the investor from an unrelated person, (2) the amount of the nonrecourse financing with respect to the property does not exceed 80% of the cost or other basis of the property, (3) the financing is not convertible debt, and (4) the financing is borrowed from a "qualified person" or represents a loan from any federal, state, or local government or instrumentality thereof, or is guaranteed by any federal, state, or local government. A "qualified person" is a person who is actively and regularly engaged in the business of lending money and who is not (1) a person related in certain ways to the investor, (2) a person from whom the taxpayer acquired the property (or related to such a person), or (3) a person who receives a fee with respect to the investment in the property (or related to such a person). In the case of a partnership or an S corporation, the determination of whether nonrecourse financing is qualified for purposes of the rehabilitation tax credit is made at the partner or shareholder level, respectively.[6]

If there is a decrease in the amount of nonqualified nonrecourse financing (not including a decrease through the surrender or similar use of the property) in a subsequent year, the amount of decrease is treated as an additional qualified investment in the property made in the year the property was placed in service. A credit of the applicable percentage of the amount of the increase is taken in the year of the increase. For purposes of determining the amount of the credit or of any subsequent recapture, the investment is treated as made in the year the property was placed in service.[7] See below.

---

1. Treas. Reg. §1.48-12(c)(5).
2. IRC Sec. 47(c)(2)(B); Treas. Reg. §1.48-12(c)(7).
3. IRC Sec. 47(c)(2)(B)(i).
4. Treas. Reg. §1.48-12(c)(8).
5. Let. Rul. 9145019.
6. IRC Sec. 49(a)(1).
7. IRC Sec. 49(a)(2).

Claiming the Credit; Other Tax Considerations

The rehabilitation tax credit is added with certain other credits into the general business credit calculation, and is subject to the general business credit limitation.[1] See Q 1262.

The passive loss rules generally apply to the rehabilitation tax credit. However, the rehabilitation tax credit is given special treatment under the rental real estate rules. A taxpayer need not actively participate in the rental activity with respect to which the rehabilitation tax credit is taken to obtain the $25,000 rental real estate exemption amount with respect to the credit.[2] Also, the $25,000 exemption amount for rental real estate with respect to the rehabilitation tax credit does not begin to phase out until a taxpayer has income in excess of $200,000.[3] In addition, the $25,000 rental real estate exemption, which is otherwise unavailable with respect to a publicly traded partnership, is available to the extent that the rehabilitation investment credit and the low-income housing credit (see Q 1227) exceed the regular tax liability attributable to income from the partnership.[4] See Q 1299.

In the case of partnerships (other than certain publicly traded partnerships taxed as corporations, see Q 1189), generally each partner's distributive share of any item of income, gain, loss, deduction or credit of the partnership will take into account a change in any partner's interest occurring during the taxable year. However, this general rule may not be applicable to investment tax credits for rehabilitation expenditures since the investment tax credit is not a tax item that accrues ratably over the taxable year. Investment tax credits accrue at the moment the property is placed in service. Thus, partners may be entitled to an allocation of the credit as determined by their interests in the partnership at the time the property is placed in service.[5]

For *property placed in service after 1986*, the increase in basis resulting from the rehabilitation expenditures must be reduced by 100% of the credit for all rehabilitation credits taken.[6] For *property placed in service prior to 1987*, the increase in basis resulting from the rehabilitation expenditures was reduced by 100% of the credit taken for non-certified historic structures and, generally for property placed in service in years 1983 through 1986, by 50% of the credit taken with respect to a certified historic structure.[7] The reduced basis is used to compute the cost recovery (depreciation) deduction.

Some or all of the investment credit must be recaptured on early disposition of property for which a credit was taken that reduced tax liability.[8] (If the credit did not reduce tax liability, the credit carrybacks and carryforwards are adjusted.) There is no recapture if the property was held at least five years after it was placed in service, or if the early disposition was by reason of death or a transfer to a corporation in which gain or loss was not recognized because it was in exchange for stock and the individual was in control of the corporation immediately after the exchange. Recapture is accomplished by adding to tax a percentage of the credit as indicated in the following table.[9]

---

1. IRC Sec. 38.
2. IRC Sec. 469(i)(6)(B)(ii).
3. IRC Sec. 469(i)(3)(B).
4. IRC Sec. 469(k).
5. Let. Rul. 8519009.
6. IRC Sec. 50(c)(1).
7. IRC Sec. 48(q), prior to amendment by TRA '86.
8. IRC Sec. 50(a)(1)(A).
9. IRC Sec. 50(a)(1)(B).

	if property disposed of
Percentage to be recaptured	*before the end of*
100% of investment credit..	1st year
80% of investment credit...	2nd year
60% of investment credit...	3rd year
40% of investment credit...	4th year
20% of investment credit...	5th year

A portion of the rehabilitation tax credit is recaptured if a taxpayer claims a rehabilitation tax credit with respect to a building, and then sells or donates a facade easement with respect to the same property during the rehabilitation credit recapture period.[1] See Q 1339 with regard to a charitable contribution of a "facade easement."

For property placed in service after 1986, if part or all of the credit is recaptured, the basis in property previously reduced on account of the credit is increased by 100% of the recapture amount.[2]

For purposes of determining the amount of depreciation recaptured under IRC Sections 1245 and 1250 (see Q 1424) the amount of the basis adjustment is treated as a deduction allowed for depreciation except that the determination of how much depreciation would have been taken using the straight line method is made as if no reduction were made in basis for the credits.[3]

1229. Does a lessee qualify for credit for the rehabilitation of old and certified historic buildings?

Yes. Provided all other requirements for the rehabilitation credit are met, a lessee is eligible for the credit for expenditures the lessee makes if the property is depreciable by the lessee, the improvements are not in lieu of rent and, on the date the rehabilitation is completed, the remaining term of the lease is at least as long as the recovery period for depreciation.[4] In addition, the lessor may elect to allow a lessee to take the credit that otherwise would be allowable to the lessor.[5] In order for expenditures to qualify for the credit, the building and its rehabilitation must conform to the requirements explained in Q 1228.

The lessee's adjusted basis of the building is determined as of the date that would have been used had the owner been the taxpayer.[6] To determine whether the rehabilitation is substantial, the lessee aggregates the adjusted basis of the owner in the building, and the adjusted basis of the lessee (or lessees) in the property held by lease (the "leasehold"), and any leasehold improvements that are structural components of the building.[7] A lessee may include the expenditures of the owner and of other lessees in determining whether rehabilitation has been substantial.[8]

The lessee must reduce his basis in the rehabilitation expenditures for credit taken. See Q 1228.

---

1. Rev. Rul. 89-90, 1989-2 CB 3.
2. IRC Sec. 50(c)(2).
3. IRC Sec. 50(c)(4).
4. IRC Sec. 47(c)(2)(B)(vi); Treas. Reg. §1.167(a)-4; Let. Rul. 8441012.
5. IRC Sec. 50(d)(5); Treas. Reg. §1.48-12(f)(1).
6. Treas. Reg. §1.48-12(b)(2)(ii)(B).
7. Treas. Reg. §1.48-12(b)(2)(iii).
8. Treas. Reg. §1.48-12(b)(2)(vi).

A lessor may elect to pass through to the lessee the rehabilitation credit for rehabilitation work performed by or on behalf of the lessor.[1] If he does, the lessor does not adjust his basis in his expenditures. Instead, the lessee must include in income ratably over the applicable recovery period an amount equal to 100% of the credit taken.[2] If the lessor passes the credit through to the lessee, application of the passive loss rule (see Q 1222) is determined by reference to the material participation of the lessee.[3]

DEFERRED RENT

1230. If a real estate lease provides for deferred or stepped rent, when is rental income includable?

Lessors and lessees under certain deferred or stepped payment lease agreements entered into after June 8, 1984, are required to report rental income and expense as they accrue, as well as interest on rent accrued but unpaid at the end of the period.[4] Agreements are subject to this rule if at least one amount allocable to the use of property during a calendar year is to be paid after the close of the calendar year following the calendar year in which the use occurs, or if there are increases in the amount to be paid as rent under the agreement. However, they do not apply unless the aggregate value of the money and other property received for use of the property exceeds $250,000.[5]

As a general rule, rents will accrue in the tax year to which they are allocable under the terms of the lease.[6] Regulations provide that the amount of rent taken into account for a taxable year is the sum of: (1) the fixed rent for any rental period that begins and ends in the taxable year, (2) a ratable portion of the fixed rent for any other rental period beginning or ending in the taxable year, and (3) any contingent rent that accrues during the taxable year.[7]

In either of two situations, rent will be deemed to accrue on a level present value basis ("constant rental amount") instead of under the terms of the agreement:

(1) if the rental agreement is silent as to the allocation of rents over the lease period; or

(2) if the rental agreement is a "disqualified leaseback or long-term agreement." A disqualified leaseback or long-term agreement is an agreement that provides for increasing rents and one of the principal purposes for increasing rents is tax avoidance and the lease is either (a) part of a leaseback transaction, or (b) for a term in excess of 75% of the "statutory recovery period" for the property subject to the lease.[8] The statutory recovery period is essentially the period provided for depreciation under ACRS, except that a 15-year period may be substituted for 20-year property, and a 19-year period may be used for residential rental property and nonresidential real property.[9] A leaseback transaction is one involving a lease to any person who had an interest in the property (or related person) within the two-year period before the lease went into effect.[10]

1. IRC Sec. 50(d)(5); Treas. Reg. §1.48-12(f).
2. IRC Secs. 50(c), 50(d)(5).
3. Let. Rul. 8951072.
4. IRC Sec. 467(a).
5. IRC Sec. 467(d).
6. IRC Sec. 467(b)(1).
7. Treas. Reg. §1.467-1(d).
8. IRC Sec. 467(b).
9. IRC Sec. 467(e)(3).
10. IRC Sec. 467(e)(2).

Under regulations, certain rent increases are not considered made for tax avoidance purposes: for example, increases determined by reference to price indices, rents based on a percentage of lessee receipts, reasonable rent holidays, and changes in amounts paid to unrelated third persons.[1]

A constant rental amount is the amount that, if paid as of the close of each lease period under the agreement, would result in an aggregate present value equal to the present value of the aggregate payments required under the agreement.[2] Regulations provide a formula to facilitate the computation of the constant rental amount.[3]

If property subject to a leaseback or a lease longer than 75% of the recovery period is not subject to rent leveling (i.e., there is no tax avoidance purpose or no stepped rent) and the rent accrues according to the terms of the agreement, any gain realized by the lessor on disposition of the property during the term of the agreement will be treated as recaptured ordinary income to the extent that the amount which would have been taken into account by the lessor if the rents had been reported on a constant rental basis is more than the amounts actually taken into account. Before this calculation is made, gain realized by the lessor on the disposition is reduced by the amount of any gain treated as ordinary income on the disposition under other IRC provisions: for example, depreciation recapture.[4] Regulations provide for certain exceptions from recapture and provide for carryover of the ordinary income "taint" where the property is transferred and the transferor's basis carries over to the transferee.[5]

Regulations provide comparable rules for agreements calling for decreasing rates and rules applicable to contingent payments.[6]

Present value will be determined at the rate of 110% of the applicable federal rate (AFR), compounded semiannually. The AFR used is that in effect at the time the lease is entered into for debt instruments having a maturity equal to the term of the lease.[7] See Q 1409 for an explanation of the applicable federal rate.

While these rules apply generally to leases entered into after June 8, 1984, there are special exceptions. One of these is for an agreement entered into pursuant to a written agreement binding on June 8, 1984 and at all times thereafter. A limited exception applies to certain plans existing on or before March 15, 1984.[8] The regulations apply to disqualified leasebacks and long-term agreements entered into after June 3, 1996, and for other rental agreements entered into after May 18, 1999.[9]

DEMOLITION

1231. Is the cost of demolishing a structure deductible?

No. The cost to the owner or lessee of demolishing a structure (or any loss sustained on account of the demolition) must be capitalized and added to the tax basis in the *land*

1. IRC Sec. 467(b)(5); Treas. Reg. §1.467-1(c)(2).
2. IRC Sec. 467(e)(1).
3. See Treas. Reg. §1.467-3(d).
4. IRC Sec. 467(c).
5. Treas. Reg. §1.467-7(c).
6. Treas. Regs. §§1.467-1(c), 1.467-3(c).
7. IRC Sec. 467(e)(4). See General Explanation–TRA '84, p. 287, fn. 22.
8. P.L. 98-369 (TRA '84) Sec. 92(c)(2).
9. Treas. Reg. §1.467-9(a).

(thus, they are not depreciable).[1] However, a casualty loss may be allowed if it occurs before the demolition.[2] Similarly, a loss may be allowed for the abnormal retirement of a structure due to the unexpected and extraordinary obsolescence of the structure where the loss occurs prior to the demolition.[3]

A modification of a building, other than a certified historical structure (see Q 1228), is not treated as a demolition under IRC Section 280B if (1) 75% or more of the existing external walls of the building are retained in place as external or internal walls, and (2) 75% or more of the existing internal structural framework is retained in place. A modification of a certified historical structure (see Q 1228) is not treated as a demolition under IRC Section 280B if (1) the modification is part of a certified reha-bilitation (see Q 1228), (2) 75% or more of the existing external walls of the building are retained in place as external or internal walls, and (3) 75% or more of the existing internal structural framework is retained in place. Such costs may generally be expensed or capitalized and added to the tax basis of the building (and thus depreciated) as ap-propriate (see Q 1220).[4]

SALE

1232. If real property subject to a nonrecourse mortgage is sold or abandoned must the seller include the unpaid balance of the mortgage in his calculation of gain or loss?

Yes. Gain from sale of property is defined as the excess of the amount realized over the seller's tax basis (as adjusted for items such as depreciation, etc.). Loss is the excess of the tax basis (as adjusted) over the amount realized.[5] The tax basis of prop-erty includes any unpaid nonrecourse mortgage liability, and on sale of the property subject to the mortgage the amount realized by the owner includes the unpaid balance of any nonrecourse mortgage on the property.[6] It does not make any difference that the unpaid balance of the mortgage exceeds the fair market value of the property at the time of sale.[7]

Abandonment of property subject to a non-recourse debt is treated as a sale or exchange and the amount of outstanding debt is an "amount realized" on sale or exchange for purposes of determining and characterizing gain or loss.[8]

1233. How is gain or loss on the sale of rental real estate treated?

Gain or loss on property used in a trade or business, including rental real estate, is not "capital gain or loss"–it is referred to as "IRC Section 1231 gain or loss."[9] If all of the taxpayer's IRC Section 1231 gains in a year exceed his IRC Section 1231 losses, the net gain is treated as long-term capital gain; however, such net gain must be treated as ordinary income to the extent of net IRC Section 1231 losses of the taxpayer in the

---

1. IRC Sec. 280B.
2. Notice 90-21, 1990-1 CB 332.
3. *De Cou v. Comm.*, 103 TC 80 (1994).
4. Rev. Proc. 95-27, 1995-1 CB 704.
5. IRC Sec. 1001.
6. *Crane v. Comm.*, 331 U.S. 1 (1947).
7. IRC Sec. 7701(g); *Comm. v. Tufts*, 83-1 USTC ¶9328 (U.S. 1983).
8. *Yarbro v. Comm.*, 84-2 USTC ¶9691 (5th Cir. 1984); *Middleton v. Comm.*, 77 TC 310 (1981), aff'd, 82-2 USTC ¶9713 (11th Cir. 1982).
9. IRC Sec. 1231(a)(3).

five most recent prior years beginning after 1981 (which have not been thus previously offset by net gains of a later year).[1] If IRC Section 1231 losses exceed IRC Section 1231 gains, the net loss is treated as ordinary loss.[2]

In order to determine whether gains exceed losses, it is necessary to aggregate *recognized* gains (in excess of recaptured accelerated depreciation) and losses in the year on all IRC Section 1231 property. Nondeductible losses and nonrecognized gains are not included: for example, losses not deductible because they involve transactions between related parties (see Q 1419), gains not recognized because they involve exchanges of like-kind property (see Q 1422) or unreported gain on an installment sale (see Q 1408).[3]

There are generally two kinds of gains and losses that must be included in the IRC Section 1231 netting process:

(1) Includable gains and deductible losses on sales or exchanges of depreciable property and real property that have been held for more than one year and used in a trade or business (but not inventory, property held primarily for sale to customers in the ordinary course of business, or a copyright or certain other literary or artistic property), including certain sales involving timber, coal, iron ore, livestock and unharvested crops;[4] and

(2) Includable gain and deductible losses (not compensated for by insurance) resulting from compulsory or involuntary conversion (as a result of destruction in whole or in part, theft, seizure, or an exercise of the power of requisition or condemnation) of property used in trade or business (as defined above) or of any capital asset held for more than one year and held in connection with a trade or business or a transaction entered into for profit. However, gains and losses arising from fire, storm, shipwreck or other casualty, or from theft, are included only if the gains exceed the losses.[5] If losses arising from fire, storm, shipwreck, or other casualty, or theft, exceed gain from such items, then rather than including such items in the IRC Section 1231 netting process: (1) loss from any such item is deductible as a loss under IRC Section 165, and (2) gain from any such item is recognized as gain (generally as capital gain, but see Q 1235) to the extent that the amount realized on the involuntary conversion exceeds the cost of replacement property (if any) purchased within two years of the involuntary conversion.[6]

Where the sale is between related persons, see Q 1234.

1234. How is gain or loss on the sale of rental property to a related person treated?

Gain on the sale of property depreciable by the purchaser is ordinary gain if the sale is between certain related parties. For this purpose, related parties are: (1) a person and a corporation or partnership of which he owns (directly or indirectly) a 50% or more interest; (2) a person and a trust in which he (or his spouse) is a beneficiary having more than a remote interest; (3) generally, an executor and a beneficiary of an

---

1. IRC Secs. 1231(a)(1), 1231(c).
2. IRC Sec. 1231(a)(2).
3. Treas. Reg. §1.1231-1(d).
4. IRC Sec. 1231(b).
5. IRC Sec. 1231(a).
6. Treas. Reg. §1.165-7(a), IRC Secs. 1033, 1001.

estate; and (4) an employer and a welfare benefit fund.[1] In determining 50% ownership, the general rules of constructive ownership under IRC Section 267(c) apply (except paragraph (3) thereof).[2]

If the sale is an installment sale, the installment method of reporting is denied and the proceeds are deemed to be received in the year of sale, unless the Service is satisfied that avoidance of federal income taxes was not one of the principal purposes of the disposition.[3] See Q 1408.

Gain or loss on transfers between spouses or former spouses incident to a divorce is not recognized and the basis of the property generally remains the same in the hands of the transferee as in the hands of the transferor.[4] See Q 1447.

Loss on the sale of property to certain related persons is not recognized. See Q 1419.

1235. If accelerated depreciation is used, is part of the gain on the sale of real estate treated as "recaptured" ordinary income?

Where certain accelerated methods of depreciating real estate have been used, some of the gain on sale of the property must be treated as ordinary income. In effect, some or all of the ordinary income offset by the depreciation must be "recaptured." Only the gain in excess of the recaptured ordinary income may be treated as capital gain or "IRC Section 1231" gain. The amount of gain that must be treated as recaptured ordinary income will depend on whether the property is ACRS "recovery" property (that is, it was placed in service after 1980) or is depreciated under rules in effect prior to 1981. (If there is a loss on sale of the property, no "recapture" is necessary.)[5]

ACRS Recovery Property

If property is not held more than one year, an amount equal to 100% of the depreciation allowable is recaptured to the extent of gain.[6]

Property Placed in Service After 1986

Residential rental real property and nonresidential real property placed in service after 1986 is depreciated under the straight line method and is not subject to the recapture rule if held for more than one year.

Property Placed in Service Before 1987 and After 1980

If residential real property is held more than one year, gain on sale equal to 100% of "additional depreciation" is treated as ordinary income. Additional depreciation is the amount by which allowable depreciation deductions exceed the amount that would have been deducted if the investor had elected the straight line method of depreciation.[7] Thus, if the owner elected the straight line method of cost recovery (depreciation), there will be no recapture.

---

1. IRC Secs. 1239(a), 1239(d).
2. IRC Sec. 1239(c)(2).
3. IRC Sec. 453(g).
4. IRC Sec. 1041.
5. IRC Sec. 1250(a).
6. IRC Sec. 1250(b)(1).
7. IRC Sec. 1250(b)(1).

Nonresidential property held more than one year is subject to much stricter recapture rules. If the property is depreciated by an accelerated method, 100% of the allowable depreciation deductions (not just "additional depreciation") is recaptured (but not in excess of gain).[1] However, if the individual uses the straight line method of depreciation, there is no recapture.[2]

Property Placed in Service Before 1981

Residential and nonresidential rental properties are subject to the same recapture rules that apply to residential property placed in service after 1980; that is, if accelerated depreciation has been used, the amount allowable in excess of the amount allowable under the straight line method is subject to recapture. This amount is called "additional depreciation." The percentage of additional depreciation on property placed in service before 1981 is, in some instances, reduced, or phased out, if property is held over a certain length of time.

The rules for determining the phase-out effect that the owner's holding period will have on the percentage of additional depreciation to be recaptured varies for the periods 1964-1969, 1970-1975, and 1976-1980. Thus, if property was held during more than one period, the holding period must be divided into these periods for the purpose of determining (1) the additional depreciation attributable to the period and (2) what percentage of that additional depreciation is recapturable.

Depreciation for the period from 1976 through 1980. Additional depreciation allowable from 1976 to 1980 is recaptured in full, to the extent of any gain. However, low-income housing and rehabilitation expenditures are no longer subject to recapture. The 200 month total phase-out period (reduction by one percentage point per month after a 100 month holding period) for low-income housing and rehabilitation expenditures has elapsed.

Depreciation for the period from 1970 through 1975. The percentage of additional depreciation for the years after 1969 and before 1976 that must be recaptured is determined by the classification of the property and the holding period. Low-income housing, property sold pursuant to a written contract in effect on July 24, 1964, residential rental property, and rehabilitation expenditures amortized over 60 months are no longer subject to recapture. All other property (i.e., commercial rental property) is subject to 100% recapture of additional depreciation.

Depreciation for the period before 1970. Additional depreciation allowable before 1970 is no longer subject to recapture. The phase-out provisions applied to all types of real property and the 120 month period for total phase-out (reduction by one percentage point per month after a 20 month holding period) has elapsed.

The recapture rules do not apply to dispositions by gift or to transfers at death. In a like-kind exchange, recapture applies to the extent of the boot received. See Q 1422.

Seller Financing

1236. If the seller finances a sale of real estate, when is interest imputed at a higher rate than the stated rate? When is imputed interest included by the seller? Deducted by the buyer?

1. IRC Sec. 1245(a)(5), as in effect prior to TRA '86.
2. IRC Secs. 1245(a)(5)(C), as in effect prior to TRA '86; 1250.

Where a personal debt obligation that matures more than one year from issue is given for the purchase of real estate and any payment is due more than six months after the sale or exchange, the IRC requires that interest expense deductions taken by the buyer and interest income reported by the seller reflect use of an adequate rate of interest. Furthermore, in most cases, it requires that the interest rate not only be adequate but that interest at that rate be included in income and deducted as it accrues over the term of the loan under the original issue discount rules.

Consequently, it is necessary to test the arrangement made by the parties for adequacy of interest. This test calls for comparing the stated principal amount of the debt obligation to the sum of the present values (as of the date of the sale or exchange) of all payments under the obligation (both principal and interest) discounted at 100% of the applicable federal rate (AFR), compounded semiannually. The AFR is explained in Q 1409. (However, a lower rate may be allowed where the stated principal amount of the obligation is not more than $2,800,000 (as indexed) or if a sale of land to a family member is involved. This is discussed below under "Exceptions.")

If the stated principal amount is *less than or equal to* the sum of the present values discounted at 100% of the AFR, compounded semiannually, there is adequate stated interest.[1] If there is adequate stated interest, the stated principal amount is then compared to the amount payable at maturity (other than interest based on a fixed rate and payable unconditionally at fixed periodic intervals of one year or less during the entire term of the debt instrument). If the amount payable at maturity is greater than the stated principal amount, the difference represents deferred interest, or original issue discount, which must be included by the seller and deducted by the buyer as it accrues over the term of the obligation. (The accrual of original issue discount is discussed in Q 1116.)

If the stated principal amount is *greater* than the sum of the present values discounted at 100% of the AFR, compounded semiannually, there is not adequate stated interest. In effect, the principal amount has been overstated. In this case, the sum of the present values of all the payments due discounted at 100% of the AFR compounded semiannually is imputed as the principal amount of the loan (the "imputed principal amount").[2] Then, if the imputed principal amount is less than all amounts payable at maturity (other than interest based on a fixed rate and payable unconditionally at fixed periodic intervals of one year or less during the entire term of the debt instrument), the difference is original issue discount which must be included and deducted as it accrues over the term of the obligation under the original issue discount rules.

If the transaction is a sale-leaseback, 110% of the AFR must be used in testing for adequacy of interest and in determining imputed principal where there is inadequate interest.[3]

One purpose in requiring adequate interest is to prevent overstatement of the principal amount of the obligation and the consequent overstating of the basis of the property for depreciation and gain calculation. On the other hand, to prevent understatement in potentially abusive situations, the principal amount of the obligation will be the fair market value of the property (reduced by any cash down payment and other property involved), without regard to whether the stated interest is adequate. A potentially abusive

---

1. IRC Sec. 1274(c)(2).
2. IRC Sec. 1274(b).
3. IRC Sec. 1274(e).

situation includes any transaction involving a "tax shelter," or a situation that, because of a recent sale, nonrecourse financing, financing with a term in excess of the economic life of the property, or other circumstance, is of a type identified in regulations as having a potential for abuse.[1] For this purpose a tax shelter is defined as an entity or plan, a significant purpose of which is avoidance or evasion of federal income tax.[2]

Exceptions

(1) Where a personal debt instrument is given in connection with certain sales of property, interest is not treated as accruing under the original issue discount rules, but an adequate rate of interest is treated as included in each payment due more than six months after the date of sale (under a contract calling for payments more than one year after the transaction). These transactions are:

(a)   the sale of a farm for $1,000,000 or less by an individual, estate, testamentary trust or small business organization (corporation or partnership);

(b)   the sale by an individual of his principal residence;

(c)   a sale involving a total payment of $250,000 or less (including interest); and

(d)   a land transfer to a family member (brother, sister, spouse, ancestor or lineal descendant), with respect to the first $500,000.[3]

An adequate portion of each payment must be treated as interest and if adequate interest is not called for, a part of the principal must be recharacterized as interest. To determine whether the contract calls for adequate interest, it is necessary to compare the sum of the payments due more than six months after the sale to the sum of the present value of the payments and the present values of any interest payments due under the contract using a discount rate of 100% of the AFR, compounded semiannually. If the sum of the payments exceeds the sum of the present values, the interest rate is not adequate. The excess amount determined above is considered "total unstated interest," which must be allocated among the payments in a manner consistent with the original issue discount rules.[4] In the case of a sale-leaseback, unstated interest is determined using 110% instead of 100% of AFR.[5]

(2) If the stated principal amount of an obligation given for a sale or exchange after June 30, 1985 (other than for new property that qualifies for the investment tax credit) is not more than $4,800,800 (in 2007, $4,630,300 in 2006), it is to be tested for original issue discount or for unstated interest, using a rate of 9%, compounded semiannually, if that is lower than 100% of the AFR, compounded semiannually.[6] This amount is indexed annually for inflation.[7]

(3) A debt instrument for $3,429,100 (in 2007, $3,307,400 in 2006) or less given in a transaction after June 30, 1985 can avoid the original issue discount accrual require-

---

1. IRC Sec. 1274(b)(3)(B).
2. IRC Sec. 6662(d)(2)(C)(ii).
3. IRC Secs. 483(e), 1274(c)(3).
4. IRC Secs. 483(b), 483(a).
5. IRC Sec. 1274(e).
6. IRC Sec. 1274A(b); Rev. Rul. 2007-4, 2007-4 IRB ____.
7. IRC Sec. 1274A(d)(2).

ment if the lender is on the cash basis and buyer and lender jointly elect.[1] This amount is indexed annually for inflation.[2]

(4) On the sale or exchange of land after June 30, 1985 to a family member (as defined above at (1)(d)) unstated interest on the first $500,000 is determined using a discount rate of 6% compounded semiannually, if that is less than 100% of the AFR, compounded semiannually.[3]

(5) Sales of $3,000 or less are not subject to testing for adequacy of unstated interest.[4]

Personal Use Property

Where substantially all of the buyer's use of the property is personal (i.e., not in connection with a trade or business or for the production of income; a matter to be determined at the time the obligation is issued), *a cash basis buyer* deducts only the amount of interest he pays, without regard to any amount of imputed or unstated interest. (Purchase of a vacation home with the intention of making substantial personal use of it would come within the exception.) The *seller* must nonetheless include original issue discount as it accrues or unstated interest as it is allocated to payments according to his method of accounting.[5]

Third Party Loan Assumptions

If a loan is assumed after June 30, 1985 or property acquired after June 30, 1985 subject to a loan, the assumption (or taking subject to) is disregarded in determining whether the original issue discount rules discussed above apply, *provided* the terms and conditions of the debt instrument are not modified or the nature of the transaction changed.[6] Where the loan was assumed before July 1, 1985, it is less clear. Apparently, Congress intended that such loans assumed or taken subject to would come under the imputed and unstated interest requirements.[7] However, several exceptions were made for loans assumed prior to July 1, 1985 by P.L. 98-612.

Effective Date

These imputed and unstated interest rules apply generally to sales and exchanges occurring after 1984, unless there was a binding commitment in writing (including an irrevocable option) on February 29, 1984.[8] However, as noted above, some different rules, particularly the imputed interest rates, apply where the transaction occurs after June 30, 1985.[9] Transitional rules may apply to transactions entered into prior to July 1, 1985.

EXCHANGE

1237. What kinds of real estate may be exchanged for other real estate tax-free?

1. IRC Sec. 1274A(c); Rev. Rul. 2007-4, 2007-4 IRB ____.
2. IRC Sec. 1274A(d)(2).
3. IRC Sec. 483(e).
4. IRC Sec. 483(d)(2).
5. IRC Sec. 1275(b).
6. IRC Sec. 1274(c)(4).
7. H.R. Rep. No. 98-861, 98th Cong., 2d Sess., p. 889.
8. TRA '84, Sec. 44(b).
9. P.L. 98-612 (Oct. 31, 1984).

Neither gain nor loss is recognized in an exchange of real property held for productive use in a trade or business or for investment for property of a like-kind that is also to be held either for productive use in a trade or business or for investment.[1] (Indeed, recognition is not permitted.) However, gain will be recognized to the extent money or other nonlike-kind property, including net relief from debt, is received in the exchange.[2] Also, gain or loss will generally be recognized if either property exchanged in a like-kind exchange between related persons is disposed of within two years thereafter.[3] It is possible for an exchange to be tax free to one party but not to the other. See Q 1422 for an explanation of the general rules applicable to like-kind exchanges.

To be like-kind, the properties must be of the same nature or character, but not necessarily of the same grade or quality. Unproductive real estate held, by one other than a dealer, for future use or future realization of increase in value is considered held for investment. Property held for investment may be exchanged for property held for productive use in a trade or business and *vice versa*. Unimproved land may be exchanged for improved land. City real estate may be exchanged for a ranch.[4] Rental real estate may be exchanged for a farm. Rev. Rul. 72-151, 1972-1 CB 225. An empty lot held as investment property may be exchanged for two townhouses to be constructed and used as rental property.[5]

Even partial interests in real estate have been held like-kind property. Two leasehold interests have been held like-kind property.[6] A lease for thirty years or more may be exchanged for an entire (fee simple) ownership interest.[7] A remainder interest in real property held for investment qualified as like-kind to a fee interest in real property held for investment or use in a trade or business.[8] Undivided interests in three parcels of land held by three tenants in common were exchanged so that each received a 100% interest in one parcel in a non taxable like-kind exchange.[9] Similarly, the fractional tenancy-in-common interests of related parties may be exchanged for a fee simple interest in real estate.[10] Surrender of the interests of tenant-shareholders in a housing cooperative (stock and proprietary leases with 30 or more years to run) in exchange for condominium interests in the same underlying property qualified as a like-kind exchange. (Whether tenant-shareholder rights in a housing cooperative or in a condominium constitute an interest in real estate depends on state law.)[11] Exchange of an agricultural conservation easement for an unencumbered fee-simple interest in another farm qualified as a like-kind exchange.[12]

Mineral interests have been exchanged for other mineral interests.[13] Mineral interests have also been exchanged for entire interests.[14] Timber rights have been exchanged

---

1. IRC Sec. 1031(a).
2. IRC Sec. 1031(b).
3. IRC Sec. 1031(f).
4. Treas. Reg. §1.1031(a)-1.
5. Let. Rul. 9431025.
6. Rev. Rul. 76-301, 1976-2 CB 241.
7. Rev. Rul. 78-72, 1978-1 CB 258; Treas. Reg. §1.1031(a)-1(c)(2).
8. Let. Rul. 9143053.
9. Rev. Rul. 73-476, 1973-2 CB 300.
10. Let. Rul. 9543011.
11. Let. Ruls. 8443054, 8445010.
12. Let. Rul. 9215049.
13. *Fleming v. Campbell*, 205 F.2d 549 (5th Cir. 1953).
14. *Comm. v. Crichton*, 122 F.2d 181 (5th Cir. 1941); Rev. Rul. 55-749, 1955-2 CB 295.

for entire interests in timberland.[1] However, an exchange of the right to cut standing timber for tracts of timberland did not qualify as a like-kind exchange.[2]

Even if the property is like-kind, nonrecognition of gain will be denied unless the property is "held for productive use in a trade or business or for investment" and is exchanged for property to be likewise "held for productive use in a trade or business or for investment." This "holding" requirement is not met where an individual acquires property in the exchange for the purpose of selling it or otherwise liquidating it.[3]

The Internal Revenue Service takes the position that the "holding" requirement is not met unless the property is owned over a period of time with the intention of making money rather than for personal reasons. The Service determined in a letter ruling that where an individual acquired property in an exchange with the intent to hold the property for use in trade or business or as an investment for at least two years but then to sell it, the holding requirement was met.[4] The IRS also takes the position that if an individual acquires the property in order to exchange it, the transfer will not qualify with respect to that individual because the property is not held for business or investment purposes.[5] Property received in the liquidation of a corporation and immediately exchanged did not qualify for tax free exchange because it had not been held for productive use in a trade or business or for investment by the taxpayer.[6]

However, the Tax Court and the Ninth Circuit Court of Appeals have not been quite so strict. Where property held for investment was exchanged for like-kind property with the intent of immediately contributing the property acquired in the exchange to a partnership for a general partnership interest, the exchange was held to meet the requirement that the acquired property be "held" for investment or productive use in a trade or business, where the purpose of the partnership was to hold the property for investment and where the total assets of the partnership were predominantly of a kind like the taxpayer's original property. The court saw a continuity of holding, although it was as a partner instead of as an individual, which distinguished the situation from those involving an intent to sell or liquidate the property.[7] Where an individual acquired property in a corporate liquidation and immediately agreed to exchange it, the court ruled the holding requirement was met, saying that all that is required is that the individual own property that he does not intend to liquidate or use for personal pursuits. An intent to exchange for like-kind property is holding for investment, the court concluded.[8] However, in a case where it was not to the taxpayer's advantage to receive like-kind treatment, another court held that property acquired for the purpose of immediate use in an exchange was not property held for investment.[9]

Property can qualify for tax free exchange even where the owner has sold to the other party an option either to purchase the land or to exchange similar property for it.[10]

---

1. *Everett v. Comm.*, TC Memo 1978-53; Rev. Rul. 72-515, 1972-2 CB 466; *Starker v. U.S.*, 75-1 USTC ¶9443 (D. Ore. 1975).
2. TAM 9525002.
3. *Regals Realty Co. v. Comm.*, 127 F.2d 931 (2d Cir. 1942); *Black v. Comm.*, 35 TC 90 (1960); *Klarkowski v. Comm.*, TC Memo 1965-328, aff'd on other issues, 385 F.2d 398 (7th Cir. 1967); *Bernard v. Comm.*, TC Memo 1967-176; Rev. Rul. 75-292, 1975-2 CB 333.
4. Let. Rul. 8429039.
5. Rev. Rul. 75-291, 1975-2 CB 332; Rev. Rul. 84-121, 1984-2 CB 168.
6. Rev. Rul. 77-337, 1977-2 CB 305.
7. *Magneson v. Comm.*, 85-1 USTC ¶9205 (9th Cir. 1985), affirming 81 TC 767 (1983).
8. *Bolker v. Comm.*, 85-1 USTC ¶9400 (9th Cir. 1985), affirming 81 TC 782 (1983).
9. *Barker v. U.S.*, 87-2 USTC ¶9444 (C.D. Ill. 1987).
10. Rev. Rul. 84-121, above.

However, if the like-kind exchange is between related persons, an option could operate to extend the 2-year period during which nonrecognition is defeated by a disposition of the property (see Q 1422).

Partnership interests are not "like kind" property, regardless of whether they are general or limited, and regardless of whether they are interests in the same or different partnerships.[1] However, the IRC provides that if a partnership that has in effect a valid election under IRC Section 761(a) to be excluded from the application of the IRC partnership provisions (Subchapter K) it is subject to a special rule. Such an interest will be treated, for purposes of IRC Section 1031, as an interest in each of the assets of the partnership, not as an interest in the partnership itself.[2]

Certain types of depreciable tangible personal property held for investment (such as lamps, carpet and other furnishings in a building that is held for investment) may qualify for nonrecognition under IRC Section 1031.[3]

1238. Which transactions qualify as like-kind exchanges of real estate?

Assuming the properties involved qualify for tax-free exchange purposes, that is, they are like-kind and are held for the required business or investment purposes, it is also necessary that the transaction be an "exchange." A sale followed by purchase of similar property is not an exchange.[4] The exchange of nonqualifying property ("boot") does not make the transaction any the less an "exchange," but simply requires recognition of any gain to the extent of the nonqualifying property.[5] See Q 1422 for an explanation of the general rules for like-kind exchanges.

Simultaneous Exchanges

The simplest form of exchange, one in which parties "swap" properties they already own, is not necessarily the most common. Frequently, a person (A) who wishes to make an exchange can find a buyer (B) for his property, but not one who has the property he wants in return. The IRS has permitted a three-cornered solution to this problem as follows: A transfers his property to B, B transfers his property to C and C transfers his property to A.[6] In a 2-party exchange, the IRS determined that the buyer (B) could acquire the property from a third person or construct a building specifically in order to exchange it for A's property and that the resulting exchange could qualify with respect to A, provided B did not act as A's agent.[7] Such a transaction does not qualify as an exchange for B, who did not hold the property for business or investment but acquired it for exchange.[8]

A number of variations on the three cornered exchange have been permitted. The Tax Court has determined that a third party's property may be purchased by a fourth party intermediary who exchanges it for A's property which it transfers to B for cash used to pay the third party. The transaction has been held an exchange even though

---

1. Treas. Reg. §1.1031(a)-1(a)(1).
2. IRC Sec. 1031(a)(2); Treas. Reg. §1.1031(a)-1(a).
3. See Treas. Reg. §1.1031(a)-2.
4. Treas. Reg. §1.1031(k)-1(a); *Von Muff v. Comm.*, TC Memo 1983-514.
5. IRC Sec. 1031(b).
6. Rev. Rul. 57-244, 1957-1 CB 247.
7. Rev. Rul. 75-291, 1975-2 CB 332.
8. Rev. Rul. 75-291, above; Rev. Rul. 77-297, 1977-2 CB 304.

the fourth party's ownership was transitory.[1] Similarly, a valid exchange would occur if several parties transfer their fragmented interests in real estate to an intermediary who then "reassembles" the interests and transfers whole interests back to the individuals where the total value of the replacement property is approximately equal to the total value of the relinquished property.[2]

Even if B, or a fourth party intermediary, is unable for some reason to acquire title to the third party's property, but has only a right to buy it, transactions have been held exchanges where B directed the third party to transfer title to A who simultaneously transferred his property to B.[3] In these cases, cash paid the third party for his property was transferred directly from B or the intermediary and not to or through A.[4] The IRS has held that such a transaction will qualify as a like-kind exchange.[5] However, where the cash was paid to A who paid it to the third party, the transaction was held to be a sale and repurchase.[6]

As the complexity of the transaction increases, so does the difficulty of distinguishing between exchanges and sales; in addition, the likelihood of a challenge by the IRS increases correspondingly. In three or four party exchanges, the IRS has sometimes taken the position that the exchange party is the agent of the taxpayer and that the taxpayer thus exchanged property with himself, not qualifying for like-kind exchange treatment.[7] For transfers of property on or after June 10, 1991, regulations provide a safe harbor designed to prevent such a characterization. The regulations state that in the case of simultaneous transfers of like-kind properties involving a *qualified intermediary* (as defined below), the qualified intermediary will not be considered the agent of the taxpayer for purposes of IRC Section 1031(a).[8] This safe harbor is also available for deferred exchanges, as explained below.

Deferred Exchanges

Where B wishes title to A's property before suitable replacement property has been located, the IRC specifies a limited period of time that may elapse after property is relinquished in a transfer and the replacement property to be received is identified and transferred. For purposes of IRC Section 1031, the regulations and this discussion, a deferred exchange is any exchange in which, pursuant to an agreement, the taxpayer transfers property held for productive use in a trade or business or for investment (i.e., the "relinquished property") and subsequently receives property to be held for productive use in a trade or business or for investment (i.e., the "replacement property").[9]

Transfers in which property is conveyed in return for a promise to acquire and convey acceptable replacement property by a certain future date were permitted under case law predating the 1984 revision of IRC Section 1031.[10]

---

1. *Barker v. Comm.*, 74 TC 555 (1980). See *Garcia v. Comm.*, 80 TC 491 (1983), acq., 1984-1 CB 1.
2. Let. Rul. 9439007.
3. *Biggs v. Comm.*, 69 TC 905 (1978), aff'd, 632 F.2d 1171 (5th Cir. 1980); *Brauer v. Comm.*, 74 TC 1134 (1980).
4. See also *W.D. Haden Co. v. Comm.*, 165 F.2d 588 (5th Cir. 1948).
5. Rev. Rul. 90-34, 1990-1 CB 154.
6. *Carlton v. U.S.*, 385 F.2d 238 (5th Cir. 1967).
7. See *Garcia v. Comm.*, above; *Rutland v. Comm.* TC Memo 1977-8; *Coupe v. Comm.*, 52 TC 394 (1969), acq., 1970-2 CB xix.
8. Treas. Reg. §1.1031(b)-2.
9. Treas. Reg. §1.1031(k)-1(a).
10. See *Starker v. U.S.*, 75-1 USTC ¶9443 (D. Ore.) (Starker I); *Starker v. U.S.*, 79-2 USTC ¶9541 (9th Cir. 1979) (Starker III), rev'g 77-2 USTC ¶9512 (D. Ore. 1977) (Starker II).

The IRC states that to be treated as "like-kind," the replacement property must be (1) *identified* as the property to be received in the exchange on or before the 45th day after the property relinquished in the exchange is transferred (i.e., the "identification period"), *and* (2) *received* within 180 days after the transfer of the property relinquished or, if earlier, the due date (including extensions) of the transferor's income tax return for the tax year in which the transfer of the relinquished property occurred (i.e., the "exchange period").[1] "Identified" and "received," for this purpose, are defined in the regulations as explained below.

Regulations provide that replacement property is "identified" only if it is unambiguously described and designated as such in a written document, signed by the taxpayer and delivered (faxed, mailed, etc.), before the end of the identification period, to the person obligated to transfer the replacement property, or to any other person involved in the exchange (e.g., an escrow agent, a title company), other than the taxpayer or a "disqualified person" (defined below).[2] However, replacement property actually received before the end of the identification period will be treated as identified.[3]

Because it is not always possible for a taxpayer to identify with precision the replacement property that will ultimately be received, the regulations permit identification of alternative properties. The maximum number of properties that may be identified as replacement property in a single deferred exchange is: (1) three properties, without regard to their fair market values; or (2) any number of properties, as long as their aggregate fair market value as of the end of the identification period does not exceed 200% of the fair market value of the relinquished property as of the date of transfer.[4]

If, as of the end of the identification period, the taxpayer has identified more replacement properties than permitted under the above rules, he will be treated as if no replacement had been identified; however, there are two exceptions: First, any replacement property actually received before the end of the identification period will be treated as satisfying the requirements of the preceding paragraph. Second, a special "95% rule" may apply as follows: Any replacement property identified before the end of the identification period and received before the end of the exchange period will be treated as satisfying the requirements of the preceding paragraph if the taxpayer receives, before the end of the exchange period, identified replacement property having a fair market value that is at least 95% of the aggregate fair market value of all identified replacement properties.[5]

In order to meet the receipt requirement, the replacement property must be received before the end of the (180-day) exchange period, and the replacement property received must be substantially the same property as identified. If more than one replacement property was identified, these requirements apply separately to each replacement property.[6] Special rules apply for identification and receipt of replacement property that does not yet exist or is being produced at the time relinquished property is transferred.[7]

For taxpayers implementing a deferred exchange, the necessity of protecting the owner of the relinquished property until the transaction is completed often results in

---

1. IRC Sec. 1031(a)(3).
2. Treas. Reg. §1.1031(k)-1(c).
3. Treas. Reg. §1.1031(k)-1(c)(1).
4. Treas. Reg. §1.1031(k)-1(c)(4)(i).
5. Treas. Reg. §1.1031(k)-1(c)(4)(ii).
6. Treas. Reg. §1.1031(k)-1(d)(1).
7. Treas. Reg. §1.1031(k)-1(e).

the use of an intermediary and some form of guarantee to secure the obligations of the transferee. Two issues that have tended to result in frequent challenges by the IRS to complex deferred like-kind exchanges are: (a) whether an intermediary is an agent of the taxpayer (see discussion above under "Simultaneous Exchanges") and (b) whether the taxpayer who receives cash or other security guaranteeing the transaction has constructively received payment for the transfer, thus having made a sale rather than an exchange.[1] Final regulations address these problems by providing four safe harbors designed to help taxpayers engaging in deferred exchanges avoid such challenges. (Of these four, only one, the qualified intermediary safe harbor, is also applicable to simultaneous exchanges; see the discussion above.)

(1) *Security or guarantee arrangements*: the transferee's obligation to transfer the replacement property may be secured by: (a) a mortgage, deed of trust or other security interest in property (other than cash or a cash equivalent), (b) a standby letter of credit (provided the requirements of Treas. Reg. §15A.453-1(b)(3)(iii) are met), or (c) a guarantee of a third party, without causing the taxpayer to be in actual or constructive receipt of money or other property.[2]

(2) *Qualified escrow accounts and qualified trusts*: the transferee's obligation to transfer the replacement property may be secured by cash or a cash equivalent if the cash or cash equivalent is held in a qualified escrow account or in a qualified trust. Generally, a qualified escrow account or qualified trust is an account (or trust) in which (a) the escrow holder (or trustee) is not the taxpayer or a *disqualified person* (defined below), and (b) the escrow (or trust) agreement expressly limits the taxpayer's rights to receive, pledge, borrow, or otherwise obtain the benefits of the cash or cash equivalent held in the escrow account (or by the trustee).[3] The regulations specify how the escrow agreement or trust is to impose such limitations.[4]

(3) *Qualified intermediary*: A qualified intermediary is a person who is not the taxpayer or a disqualified person (defined below), and who enters into a written agreement (the "exchange agreement") with the taxpayer and, as required by the exchange agreement, acquires the relinquished property from the taxpayer, transfers the relinquished property, acquires the replacement property and transfers it to the taxpayer.[5] So long as the agreement between the taxpayer and the qualified intermediary expressly limits the taxpayer's rights to receive, pledge, borrow, or otherwise obtain the money or other property held by the qualified intermediary, the qualified intermediary will not be considered the agent of the taxpayer.[6] The regulations specify how the agreement is to impose such limitations.[7]

The use of a qualified intermediary in an exchange involving two related parties caused the exchange to fail to qualify as a like-kind exchange when, as part of the transaction, one of the related parties received non-like-kind property for the replacement property.[8]

---

1. See *Garcia v. Comm.*, above; *Barker v. Comm.*, above.
2. Treas. Reg. §1.1031(k)-1(g)(2). See Let. Rul. 9141018.
3. Treas. Reg. §1.1031(k)-1(g)(3).
4. Treas. Reg. §1.1031(k)-1(g)(6).
5. Treas. Reg. §1.1031(k)-1(g)(4)(iii).
6. Treas. Reg. §1.1031(k)-1(g)(4).
7. Treas. Reg. §1.1031(k)-1(g)(6).
8. Rev. Rul. 2002-83, 2002-2 CB 927.

(4) *Interest and growth factors*: The fact that the taxpayer is or may be entitled to receive any interest or growth factor with respect to the deferred exchange will not cause him to be in constructive receipt of money or other property, so long as the agreement expressly limits the taxpayer's rights to receive the interest or growth factor.[1] The regulations specify how the agreement is to impose such limitations.[2] Generally, a taxpayer will be treated as being entitled to receive interest or a growth factor with respect to a deferred exchange if the amount of money or property the taxpayer is entitled to receive depends upon the length of time between transfer of the relinquished property and receipt of the replacement property.[3]

For purposes of the regulations, "disqualified person" generally means one of the following:

(a) An agent of the taxpayer, including any person who acted as the taxpayer's employee, attorney, accountant, investment banker or broker, or real estate agent or broker within the two years preceding the transfer of the first of the relinquished properties. (However, the performance of services with respect to the like-kind exchange, or routine financial, title insurance escrow or trust services furnished by a financial institution, title insurance company, or escrow company are not taken into account for purposes of this paragraph).[4]

(b) A "related person" as defined in Q 1422, but using "10%" in each place that "50%" appears.[5]

(c) Certain persons who are "related" (based on the definition in paragraph (b)) to a person who would be disqualified as described in paragraph (a). Certain banks and bank affiliates are exempt from this rule.[6]

The safe harbors and other provisions under Treasury Regulation Section 1.1031(k)-1 are effective for transfers of property made by taxpayers on or after June 10, 1991.[7]

Coordination with IRC Section 453

Additional safe harbors provide that, generally, transactions involving qualified escrow accounts, qualified trusts, and qualified intermediaries will not be treated as payments for purposes of the installment sales rules (see Q 1408). Thus, in the case of qualified escrow accounts and qualified trusts, the determination of whether or not the taxpayer has received a payment for purposes of IRC Section 453 will be made without regard to the fact that the transferee's obligation to transfer property is secured by cash or a cash equivalent held in a qualified escrow account or qualified trust. Also, in the case of qualified intermediaries, the determination of whether or not the taxpayer has received a payment for purposes of IRC Section 453 will be made as if the qualified intermediary is not the agent of the taxpayer. Both of these safe harbors apply only so long as the taxpayer has a bona fide intent to enter into a deferred exchange at the beginning of the exchange period and the relinquished property is held for productive use in a trade or business. These safe harbors apply to exchanges occurring after April

---

1. Treas. Reg. §1.1031(k)-1(g)(5).
2. Treas. Reg. §1.1031(k)-1(g)(6).
3. Treas. Reg. §1.1031(k)-1(h)(1).
4. Treas. Reg. §1.1031(k)-1(k)(2).
5. Treas. Reg. §1.1031(k)-1(k)(3).
6. Treas. Reg. §1.1031(k)-1(k)(4).
7. Treas. Reg. §1.1031(k)-1(o).

19, 1994. Taxpayers may apply these safe harbors to transfers occurring after June 9, 1991 and before April 20, 1994 so long as they otherwise meet the requirements of Treas. Reg. §1.1031(k)-1, and to exchanges occurring after May 15, 1990 and before June 10, 1991 if they meet the requirements of either Treas. Reg. §1.1031(k)-1 (as adopted by TD 8346) or the regulation as originally proposed (IA-237-84) published at 1990-1 CB 633.[1]

Reverse Exchanges

A reverse exchange is where the replacement property is acquired before the relinquished is transferred. The regulations above do not apply to reverse exchanges. However, the Service will not challenge the qualification of property as either replacement property or relinquished property if the property is held in a qualified exchange accommodation arrangement (QEAA). Property is considered to be held in a QEAA if the following requirements are met: (1) The property is owned by a person (as the "exchange accommodation titleholder") who is not the taxpayer or a disqualified person and that person is subject to the federal income tax or has 90% of its interests owned by S shareholders or partners who are subject to the federal income tax; (2) At the time property is transferred to an exchange accommodation titleholder the taxpayer has a bona fide intent that the property will be either replacement property or relinquished property; (3) A written agreement providing that the property will be treated as held in a QEAA is entered into between the taxpayer and the exchange accommodation titleholder within five days of the transfer of property to the exchange accommodation titleholder; (4) No later than 45 days after the transfer of the replacement property to the exchange accommodation titleholder, the relinquished property is identified; (5) No later than 180 days after the transfer of property to the exchange accommodation titleholder either (a) the property is transferred to the taxpayer as replacement property, or (b) the property is transferred to a person who is not the taxpayer or a disqualified person as relinquished property; and (6) The combined time that the relinquished property and replacement property are held in a QEAA does not exceed 180 days. This safe harbor is available for QEAAs entered into after September 14, 2000. An exchange may still qualify as a like-kind exchange even if it does not meet the requirements of this safe harbor.[2] This safe harbor will not apply to replacement property held in a QEAA if the property is owned by the taxpayer within the 180-day period ending on the date of transfer to an exchange accommodation titleholder.[3]

SALE OF PERSONAL RESIDENCE

1239. What exclusion is available for gain on the sale of a principal residence?

Generally, an individual who sells or exchanges his principal residence may elect to exclude up to $250,000 of gain from his gross income ($500,000 in the case of certain married taxpayers filing jointly).[4] This treatment applies to sales or exchanges occurring after May 6, 1997; for sales occurring prior to May 7, 1997, different rules applied.

---

1. Treas. Reg. §1.1031(k)-1(j)(2).
2. Rev. Proc. 2000-37, 2000-2 CB 308.
3. Rev. Proc. 2004-51, 2004-33 IRB 294.
4. IRC Sec. 121(b); Treas. Reg. §1.121-2(a)(1).

General

Residence and principal residence. Whether property is used by the taxpayer as his "residence" and his "principal residence" (in the case of a taxpayer using more than one property as a residence) depends upon all the facts and circumstances.[1] A property used by the taxpayer as his principal residence may include a houseboat, a house trailer, or the house or apartment that the taxpayer is entitled to occupy as a tenant-stockholder in a cooperative housing corporation if the dwelling that the taxpayer is entitled to occupy as a stockholder is used by the taxpayer as his principal residence. Property used by the taxpayer as his principal residence does not include personal property that is not a fixture under local law.[2]

If a taxpayer alternates between two properties, using each as a residence for successive periods of time, the property that the taxpayer uses a majority of the time during the year will ordinarily be considered the taxpayer's principal residence. In addition to the taxpayer's use of the property, relevant factors in determining a taxpayers' principal residence, include (but are not limited to): (1) the taxpayer's place of employment; (2) the principal place of abode of the taxpayer's family members; (3) the address listed on the taxpayer's federal and state tax returns, driver's license, automobile registration, and voter registration card; (4) the taxpayer's mailing address for bills and correspondence; (5) the location of the taxpayer's banks; and (6) the location of religious organizations and recreational clubs with which the taxpayer is affiliated. Note that the above list of factors is not exclusive.[3]

Vacant land. The final regulations permit the gain from sales or exchanges of vacant land to be excluded under IRC Section 121 if the following requirements are satisfied: (1) the vacant land must be adjacent to the land containing the taxpayer's principal residence; (2) the taxpayer must have owned and used the vacant land as part of his principal residence; (3) the land sale must occur within two years before or after the date of the sale of the residence; and (4) the statutory requirements must have otherwise been met with respect to the vacant land.[4]

The sale or exchange of the residence and the vacant land are treated as one sale or exchange. Therefore, only one maximum limitation amount of $250,000 ($500,000 in the case of certain married taxpayers filing jointly) applies to the combined sales or exchanges of vacant land and the residence.[5] For more information on the rules governing sales or exchanges of vacant land, see Treas Regs. §§121.1(b)(3)(ii)(A) (how to apply the maximum limitation amount to sales or exchanges occurring in different taxable years); 1.121-1(b)(3)(ii)(B) (sale or exchange of more than one principal residence in a 2-year period); 1.121-1(b)(3)(ii)(C) (sale or exchange of vacant land before residence).

Ownership and use requirements. In order to claim the full amount of the exclusion, the taxpayer generally must have owned and used the residence as his principal residence for an aggregate of two years during the five years prior to the sale or exchange.[6] Additionally, the full amount of the exclusion cannot be claimed if the taxpayer took the exclusion for a prior sale during the 2-year period ending on the date of the sale

---

1. Treas. Regs. §§1.121-1(b)(1), 1.121-1(b)(2). See, e.g., *Beall v. Comm.*, TC Memo 1998-82, *aff'd in part, rev'd in part*, 229 F.3d 1156 (9th Cir. 2000); *Guinan v. United States*, 91 AFTR 2d 2174 (D. Ariz. 2003).
2. Treas. Reg. §1.121-1(b)(1).
3. Treas. Reg. §1.121-1(b)(2).
4. Treas. Reg. §1.121-1(b)(3)(i).
5. Treas. Reg. §1.121-1(b)(3)(ii)(A).
6. IRC Sec. 121(a); Treas. Reg. §1.121-1(a).

or exchange. However, sales or exchanges prior to May 7, 1997 are not taken into account for the purposes of this 2-year limitation.[1] For an explanation of the term "use of" property, see *Gummer v. U.S.*[2]

The ownership and use requirements for periods aggregating two years or more may be satisfied by establishing ownership and use for 24 full months or for 730 days (365 x 2). The ownership and use requirements do not have to be satisfied simultaneously so long as both tests are satisfied during the 5-year period ending on the date of the sale.[3] To establish that a taxpayer has satisfied the 2-year use requirement, occupancy of the residence is required. However, short temporary absences, such as for vacation or other seasonal absence (although accompanied with rental of the residence) are counted as periods of use.[4] For example, a 1-year sabbatical leave abroad is not considered to be a short temporary absence; on the other hand, a 2-month summer vacation does count as a short temporary absence.[5]

Determination of use during period of out-of-residence care. If a taxpayer has become mentally or physically incapable of self-care, and the taxpayer sells or exchanges property that he owned and used as a principal residence for periods aggregating at least one year during the 5-year period preceding the date of the sale, an exception to the use requirement applies. Such a taxpayer will be treated as using the property as his principal residence for any period of time during the 5-year period in which the taxpayer owns the property and resides in any facility (including a nursing home) licensed by a state or a political subdivision to care for an individual in the taxpayer's condition.[6]

Ownership by trusts. If a residence is held by a trust for a period in which the taxpayer is treated (under the grantor trust rules) as the owner of the trust (or the portion of the trust that includes the residence), the taxpayer will be treated as owning the residence during that period for purposes of satisfying the 2-year ownership requirement of IRC Section 121. Accordingly, the sale or exchange of the residence by the trust will be treated as if made by the taxpayer.[7] The Service privately ruled that the income beneficiary of a trust, which held her mother's residence as its only asset, was not considered the owner of the residence because she lacked the power to vest the trust corpus or income in herself; thus, the gain on the home was not excludable under IRC Section 121.[8]

Depreciation taken after May 6, 1997. The exclusion does not apply to the portion of the gain from a sale that does not exceed the portion of the depreciation attributable to the property for periods after May 6, 1997.[9]

Property used in part as a principal residence. IRC Section 121 does not apply to the gain allocable to any portion of property that is separate from the "dwelling unit" to which a taxpayer does not satisfy the use requirement. A taxpayer is *not* required to allocate gain if both the residential and business portions of the property are within the *same* dwelling unit. Although the taxpayer must pay tax on the gain equal to the total depreciation taken after May 6, 1997, he may exclude any additional gain on the

---

1. IRC Sec. 121(b)(3); Treas. Reg. §1.121-2(b).
2. 98-1 USTC ¶50,401 (Fed. Cl. 1998).
3. Treas. Reg. §1.121-1(c)(1)(i).
4. Treas. Reg. §1.121-1(c)(2)(i).
5. Treas. Reg. §1.121-1(c)(4), Example 4 and Example 5. See, e.g., *Taylor v. Comm.*, TC Summary Opinion 2001-17.
6. IRC Sec. 121(d)(7); Treas. Reg. §1.121-1(c)(2)(ii).
7. Treas. Reg. §1.121-1(c)(3)(i).
8. Let. Rul. 200018021.
9. IRC 121(d)(6); Treas. Reg. §1.121-1(d)(1).

residence up to the maximum amount. However, if the business portion of the property is *separate* from the dwelling unit, the taxpayer is required to allocate the gain, and is able to exclude only the portion of the gain attributable to the resident unit.[1] The term "dwelling unit" has the same meaning as in IRC Section 280A(f)(1), but does not include appurtenant structures or other property.[2] The method for determining the amount of gain allocable to the residential and nonresidential portions of the property is explained in Treas. Reg. §1.121-1(e)(3).

Limitations

Generally, the amount of gain that may be excluded is $250,000. A taxpayer is eligible for only one maximum exclusion per principal residence.[3]

Married couples may exclude up to $500,000 if: (1) they file a joint return for the taxable year of the sale; (2) either spouse meets the 2-year ownership requirement (described above); (3) both spouses meet the 2-year use requirement (described above); and (4) neither spouse is ineligible to use the exclusion as a result of having taken the exclusion in the 2-year period ending on the date of the sale.[4]

For married taxpayers filing jointly, if either spouse does not meet the requirements described in the preceding paragraph, the maximum dollar limitation is the sum of each spouse's limitation amount, determined on a separate basis as if they had not been married. For this purpose, each spouse is treated as owning the property during the entire period that either spouse owned it.[5] In other words, the full or incremental amounts of gain that would have been allowable as an exclusion to the spouses separately, if each had been single and each had owned the property throughout the period in which one spouse owned it, are added together to obtain a maximum exclusion amount.

For unmarried taxpayers who jointly own a principal residence, but file separate returns, each taxpayer may exclude up to $250,000 of gain that is attributable to each taxpayer's interest in the property (if the requirements of IRC Section 121 have otherwise been met.[6]

Reduced Maximum Exclusion

If the reason that a taxpayer does not meet the ownership and use requirement (see above), or the 2-year limitation on use of the exclusion (see above) is that the sale or exchange resulted from a change in place of employment, health, or unforeseen circumstances, a reduced maximum exclusion may be available. Under such circumstances, the ownership, use, and 2-year limitations will not apply, and the exclusion amount will be computed as described below (see "Computation of reduced maximum exclusion").[7]

According to the final regulations, in order for a taxpayer to claim a reduced maximum exclusion under IRC Section 121, the sale or exchange must be by reason of a change in place of employment, health, or unforeseen circumstances. If a safe harbor applies (see below), a sale or exchange is *deemed* to be by reason of a change in place of

1. Treas. Reg. §1.121-1(e)(1).
2. Treas. Reg. §1.121-1(e)(2).
3. IRC Sec. 121(b); Treas. Reg. §1.121-2(a)(1).
4. IRC Sec. 121(b)(2)(A); Treas. Reg. §1.121-2(a)(3)(i).
5. IRC Sec. 121(b)(2)(B); Treas. Reg. §1.121-2(a)(3)(ii).
6. Treas. Reg. §1.121-2(a)(2).
7. IRC Sec. 121(c)(2).

employment, health, or unforeseen circumstances. However, if a safe harbor does not apply, a sale or exchange is by reason of a change in place of employment, health, or unforeseen circumstances only if the *primary reason* for the sale or exchange is a change in place of employment, health, or unforeseen circumstances. Whether the requirements are satisfied depends upon all the facts and circumstances.[1]

Factors that may be relevant in determining the taxpayer's primary reason for the sale or exchange include (but are not limited to) the extent to which: (1) the sale or exchange and the circumstances giving rise to the sale or exchange are proximate in time; (2) the suitability of the property as the taxpayer's principal residence materially changes; (3) the taxpayer's financial ability to maintain the property is materially impaired; (4) the taxpayer uses the property as the taxpayer's residence during the period of the taxpayer's ownership of the property; (5) the circumstances giving rise to the sale or exchange are not reasonably foreseeable when the taxpayer begins using the property as the taxpayer's principal residence; and (6) the circumstances giving rise to the sale or exchange occur during the period of the taxpayer's ownership and use of the property as the taxpayer's principal residence.[2]

Change in place of employment. According to the final regulations, a sale or exchange is due to a change in place of employment if, in the case of a "qualified individual" (i.e., the taxpayer, the taxpayer's spouse, a co-owner of the house, or a member of the taxpayer's household) the primary reason for the sale or exchange is a change in the location of the individual's employment.[3] Under the *distance safe harbor,* a sale or exchange is deemed to be by reason of a change in place of employment if: (1) the change occurs during the period of the taxpayer's ownership and use of the property as the taxpayer's principal residence; *and* (2) the qualified individual's new place of employment is at least 50 miles farther from the residence sold or exchanged than was the former place of employment (or if there was no former place of employment, the distance between the qualified individual's new place of employment and the residence sold or exchanged is at least 50 miles).[4]

Health reasons. A sale or exchange is by reason of health if the primary reason for the sale or exchange is to obtain, provide, or facilitate the diagnosis, cure, mitigation, or treatment of disease, illness, or injury of a "qualified individual" (described above), or to obtain or provide medical or personal care for a qualified individual suffering from a disease, illness, or injury. A sale or exchange that is merely beneficial to the general health or well-being of the individual is not a sale by reason of health.[5] Under the *physician's recommendation safe harbor,* a sale or exchange is deemed to be by reason of health if a physician recommends a change of residence for reasons of health.[6]

Unforeseen circumstances. A sale or exchange is by reason of unforeseen circumstances if the primary reason for the sale or exchange is the occurrence of an event that the taxpayer could not have reasonably anticipated before purchasing and occupying the residence. A sale or exchange by reason of unforeseen circumstances does not qualify for the reduced maximum exclusion if the primary reason for the sale or exchange is a preference for a different residence or an improvement in financial circumstances.[7]

---

1. Treas. Reg. §1.121-3(b).
2. Treas. Reg. §1.121-3(b).
3. Treas. Regs. §§1.121-3(c)(1), 1.121-3(f).
4. Treas. Reg. §1.121-3(c)(2).
5. Treas. Reg. §1.121-3(d)(1).
6. Treas. Reg. §1.121-3(d)(2).
7. Treas. Reg. §1.121-3(e)(1).

Under the *specific event safe harbor*, a sale or exchange is deemed to be by reason of unforeseen circumstances if any of the events listed below occur during the period of the taxpayer's ownership and use of the residence as his principal residence: (1) the involuntary conversion of the residence; (2) natural or man-made disasters or acts of war or terrorism resulting in a casualty to the residence (without regard to deductibility under IRC Section 165(h)); or (3) in the case of a "qualified individual" described above (a) death, (b) the cessation of employment as a result of which the individual is eligible for unemployment compensation, (c) a change in employment or self-employment status that results in the taxpayer's inability to pay housing costs and reasonable basic living expenses for the taxpayer's household, (d) divorce or legal separation under a decree of divorce or separate maintenance, or (e) multiple births resulting from the same pregnancy.[1]

In addition, the Commissioner may designate other events or situations as unforeseen circumstances in published guidance of general applicability, or in a ruling directed to a specific taxpayer.[2] See e.g., CCA 200630015 (military exception); Let. Ruls. 200630004 (carjacking at taxpayer's residence), 200626024 (to accommodate special needs of the mother-in-law), 200615011 (undercover narcotics investigator whose identity was revealed and family was threatened), 200613009 (accommodations for newly adopted child), 200601023 (grandchild and recently divorced daughter needing a place to live), 200601022 (birth of additional child), 200601009 (assault of family member at taxpayer's residence), 200504012, and 200403049.

Computation of reduced maximum exclusion. The reduced maximum exclusion is computed by multiplying the maximum dollar limitation of $250,000 ($500,000 for certain joint filer) by a fraction. The numerator of the fraction is the shortest of: (1) the period that the taxpayer owned the property during the 5-year period ending on the date of the sale or exchange; (2) the period that the taxpayer used the property as his principal residence during the 5-year period ending on the date of the sale or exchange; or (3) the period between the date of a prior sale of property for which the taxpayer excluded gain under IRC Section 121 and the date of the current sale or exchange. The numerator of the fraction may be expressed in days or months. The denominator of the fraction is 730 days or 24 months (depending on the measure of time used in the numerator).[3] Thus, for example, a single taxpayer who would otherwise be permitted to exclude $250,000 of gain, but who has owned and used the principal residence for only one year and is selling it due to a job transfer, the fraction would be ½ and the maximum excludable amount would be $125,000 [½ x 250,000].[4]

Special Rules

Property of deceased spouse. For purposes of the exclusion, in the case of a surviving spouse, the period in which the deceased spouse owned and used the property as a principal residence will be attributed to the surviving spouse.[5] The final regulations state this rule applies if (1) the taxpayer's spouse is deceased on the date of the sale of the property; and (2) the taxpayer has not remarried at the time of the sale of the

---

1. Treas. Reg. §1.121-3(e)(2).
2. Treas. Reg. §1.121-3(e)(3).
3. Treas. Reg. §1.121-3(g)(1); see also IRC Sec. 121(c)(1).
4. See, e.g., Treas. Reg. §1.121-3(c), Example 1; General Explanation of Tax Legislation Enacted in 1998 (the 1998 Blue Book), p. 166.
5. IRC Sec. 121(d)(2).

property.[1] The Service privately ruled that if a surviving spouse who holds a "5 or 5 power" (see Q 1501) in a trust sells his personal residence, the gain on the residence will be taxable to the trust as the owner of the corpus, and not the surviving spouse, except to the extent the surviving spouse is treated as the owner of a portion of the property pursuant to his "5 or 5" power.[2]

Property owned by former spouse. If property is transferred to the taxpayer by a former spouse pursuant to a divorce decree, the period in which the individual taxpayer owns the property includes the period that the former spouse owned the property. If property is used by a former spouse pursuant to a divorce decree, but is still owned by the taxpayer, the taxpayer is treated, solely for the purposes of this exclusion, as using the property as a principal residence during the use by the former spouse.[3]

Tenant-stockholder in cooperative housing corporation. If a taxpayer is a tenant stockholder in a cooperative housing corporation, the ownership requirement is applied to the holding of the stock, and the use requirement is applied to the house or apartment that the taxpayer is entitled to occupy as a stockholder.[4] In field service advice, the Service determined that tenant-stockholders were allowed to exclude $500,000 of gain from the disposition of their shares of stock in their cooperative apartment which was coordinated with a donation of the same shares to a charitable organization.[5]

Involuntary conversions. For purposes of this exclusion, the destruction, theft, seizure, requisition or condemnation of property is treated as a sale or exchange. For purposes of applying IRC Section 1033 (involuntary conversions), the amount realized from the sale or exchange of the taxpayer's principal residence is equal to the amount of gain (determined without regard to this exclusion), reduced by the exclusion. If the basis of the property acquired as a result on an involuntary conversion is determined, in whole or in part, under the involuntary conversion rules, the holding period and use by the taxpayer of the converted property will be treated as the holding and use by the taxpayer of the property sold or exchanged.[6] *Hurricane Katrina tax relief:* KETRA 2005 extends from two to five years the replacement period in which a taxpayer may replace property located in the Hurricane Katrina disaster area that is either compulsorily or involuntarily converted on or after August 25, 2005, because of Hurricane Katrina. However, the extended replacement period applies only if substantially all of the use of the replacement property is in the disaster area.[7]

Sales of remainder interests. The exclusion applies to gain recognized on the sale or exchange of a remainder interest in a principal residence, provided that the sale or exchange is not to certain related persons; however, the exclusion does not apply to any other interest in such a residence which is sold or exchanged separately.[8] For the explanation of how to make the election to apply the exclusion to gain from the sale or exchange of a remainder interest, see Treas. Reg. §1.121-4(e)(2)(iii). For the rules

---

1. Treas. Reg. §1.121-4(a)(1).
2. Let. Rul. 200104005.
3. IRC Sec. 121(d)(3); Treas. Regs. §§1.121-4(b)(1), 1.121-4(b)(2). See, e.g., IRS INFO 2005-055, at http://www.irs.gov/pub/irs-wd/05-0055.pdf.
4. IRC Sec. 121(d)(4); Treas. Reg. §1.121-4(c).
5. FSA 200149007.
6. IRC Sec. 121(d)(5); see Treas. Reg. §1.121-4(d).
7. See Sec. 405, KETRA 2005; Joint Committee on Taxation, *Technical Explanation of H.R. 3768, the "Katrina Emergency Tax Relief Act of 2005," as Passed by the House and the Senate on September 21, 2005*, (JCX-69-05), September 22, 2005.
8. IRC Sec. 121(d)(8); Treas. Regs. §§1.121-4(e)(2)(ii)(A), 1.121-4(e)(2)(ii)(B).

governing sales or exchanges of partial interests other than remainder interests, see Treas. Reg. §1.121-4(e)(1).

Election to have exclusion not apply. A taxpayer may make an election *not* to have this section apply; if so, the gain from the sale or exchange of a principal residence would not be excluded.[1]

Treatment of exclusion in bankruptcy cases. According to the final regulations and earlier case law (both of which appear to ignore IRC Section 121(f)), the bankruptcy estate of an individual in a Chapter 7 or Chapter 11 bankruptcy case succeeds to and takes into account the individual's IRC Section 121 exclusion with respect to the property transferred into the estate if the individual satisfies the requirements of IRC Section 121.[2] This applies to sales or exchanges on or after December 24, 2002.[3]

Effective dates. Generally, the final regulations are applicable for sales and exchanges on or after December 24, 2002. The final regulations relating to the reduced maximum exclusion apply to sales and exchanges on or after August 13, 2004. For sales or exchanges before August 13, 2004 and on or after May 7, 1997, taxpayers may elect to apply the rules retroactively and will be afforded audit protection.[4] The suspension of the 5-year period for certain members of the uniformed services applies to sales and exchanges on or after May 7, 1997.[5]

Coordination of Exclusion with Like-Kind Exchange Rules

If a taxpayer acquires property in a like-kind exchange under which gain is not recognized (in whole or in part) to the taxpayer under IRC Sections 1031(a) or 1031(b), the exclusion of gain under IRC Section 121(a) does *not* apply to the sale or exchange of such property by the taxpayer (or by any person whose basis in the property is determined, in whole or in part, by reference to the basis in the hands of the taxpayer) during the 5-year period beginning with the date of the acquisition.[6]

The Service and the Treasury Department have released guidance on how to handle a like-kind exchange of a home taking into account IRC Section 121 (home sale gain exclusion) and IRC Section 1031 (like-kind gain deferral).[7] The revenue procedure clarifies that a homeowner who may exclude gain upon a sale or exchange of a home may also benefit from a deferral of gain for a like-kind exchange with respect to the same property.

IRC Section 1031 provides that in the case of business property, a property owner generally would not recognize gain upon the exchange of the business property for replacement property of a like-kind.[8] The property owner would recognize gain to the extent received in cash or property that is *not* of a like-kind ("boot").[9] See Q 1236 and Q 1237. Property used solely as a home would not constitute business property.

---

1. IRC Sec. 121(f); Treas. Reg. §1.121-4(g).
2. Treas. Reg. §1.1398-3.
3. Treas. Reg. §1.1398-3(d). See also *In re Popa*, 98-1 USTC ¶50,276 (Bankr. N.D.Ill. 1998), *In re Godwin*, 99-1 USTC ¶50,287 (Bankr. S.D.OH 1999).
4. Treas. Reg. §1.121-3(h).
5. Treas. Reg. §1.121-5(e).
6. IRC Sec. 121(d)(10), as amended by TTCA 2005.
7. Rev. Proc. 2005-14, 2005-7 IRB 528. See also Treasury Press Release JS-2214 (1-27-2005).
8. IRC Sec. 1031(a).
9. IRC Sec. 1031(b).

The revenue procedure indicates that a homeowner may benefit from both the home sale exclusion *and* the like-kind deferral in cases where the property has been used consecutively or concurrently as a home and a business (e.g., rental residence). The basic rules for applying these statutory provisions are as follows: (1) When computing gain, IRC Section 121 must be applied to the realized gain *before* applying IRC Section 1031. (2) Although IRC Section 121 does not apply to gain attributable to depreciation deductions that have been claimed with respect to the business or investment portion of a residence, IRC Section 1031 may apply to such gain. (3) When "boot" (i.e., cash or other non-like-kind property) is received in exchange for relinquished business property, the boot is taken into account only to the extent that it exceeds the gain excluded under IRC Section 121 with respect to the relinquished business property. (4) When computing the basis of the replacement business property, any gain excluded under IRC Section 121 is treated as gain recognized by the taxpayer. Thus, the basis of the replacement business property is increased by any gain attributable to the relinquished business property excluded under IRC Section 121. Several examples are provided in the revenue procedure, whose effective date is January 27, 2005.[1]

Coordination of Exclusion with Capital Gain Election

Editor's Note: The paragraph below relates to the "deemed sale election," which was *temporarily* repealed under JGTRRA 2003. Note that when the 15% rate for capital gains "sunsets" (expires), the 5-year holding period requirement and 18% rate will, once again, be effective.[2]

A taxpayer who elected to treat his principal residence as having been sold and reacquired on January 1, 2001, to take advantage of the 18% capital gain tax rate for qualified 5-year gain, could *not* exclude from his gross income on his 2001 income tax return any of the gain resulting from the deemed sale-repurchase of the property.[3]

Military Tax Relief

A taxpayer on "qualified official extended duty" in the U.S. Armed Services or the Foreign Service may suspend, for up to 10 years of such duty time, the running of the 5-year ownership-and-use period before the sale of a residence.[4] Qualified official extended duty means any "extended duty" (1) while serving at a duty station that is at least 50 miles from the residence, or (2) while residing under government orders in government housing. "Extended duty" means a period of more than 90 days, or for an indefinite period.[5] This election applies to only one property at a time; furthermore, the taxpayer may exclude gain on only one home sale in any 2-year period. An election may be revoked at any time.[6]

---

1. Rev. Proc. 2005-14, 2005-7 IRB 528. See also Treasury Press Release JS-2214 (1-27-2005).
2. IRC Secs. 1(h)(2), 1(h)(9), as repealed by JGTRRA 2003; Secs. 301, 303, JGTRRA 2003.
3. Rev. Rul. 2001-57, 2001-2 CB 488; see Sec. 414(a), JCWAA 2003; Section 314(c) of CRTRA, amending Sec. 311(e) of TRA '97.
4. IRC Secs. 121(d)(9)(A), 121(d)(9)(B).
5. IRC Sec. 121(d)(9)(C).
6. IRC Sec. 121(d)(9)(D).

OIL AND GAS

GENERALLY

1240. How do individuals invest in oil and natural gas?

Because exploration for, and production of, oil and natural gas requires large amounts of capital and technical expertise and involves a high degree of risk, few individuals are willing to "go it alone" in an oil or gas project. As a result, the normal practice in an oil and gas project is for individuals, groups of individuals, and even corporations to combine efforts and capital in some type of joint organization. The forms of organization commonly used for this purpose are:

...corporations, including S corporations

...trusts

...partnerships

...limited partnerships

...joint ventures

Sometimes a combination of these forms is used, particularly where considerations apart from the actual exploration and production of oil or gas are important to some or all of the investing parties. (For example, an individual may more effectively be able to limit his liability in an oil and gas venture by incorporating his interest and then having the corporation become a member of the oil and gas limited partnership.)

Traditionally, the most commonly used method available to individual investors for investing capital in an oil and gas venture has been the purchase of an interest in an oil and gas limited partnership. Such partnership interests were often tradable, if at all, only on informal secondary markets or to the partnership itself. In recent years there has been a growth in partnerships that are traded on established securities markets or are readily tradable on a secondary market (or the substantial equivalent thereof), referred to in the IRC as publicly traded partnerships. A master limited partnership that is publicly traded would fall within this definition. However, in taxable years beginning after 1987, a publicly traded partnership is taxed as a corporation unless 90% of the partnership's income is passive-type income. In general, "passive-type income" for this purpose includes income and gain from certain mineral or natural resource activities, as well as interest, dividends, real property rents, gain from the sale of real property and gain from the sale of a capital or IRC Section 1231 asset. A grandfather rule is in effect for tax years after 1997 for electing 1987 partnerships (that agree to a 3.5% tax on their gross income); such a partnership otherwise operates as a passthrough entity.[1] Taxation as a corporation would defeat the "passthrough" feature of a limited partnership. (See Q 1189 on publicly traded partnerships.) So long as investors are interested in limiting their liability and do not wish to materially participate in the oil and gas investment, limited partnerships that manage to avoid taxation as a corporation should remain popular. In general, there are now two types of passthrough limited partnerships: regular (see Q 1190) and electing large partnerships (see Q 1191).

---

1. IRC Sec. 7704.

1241. Why are oil and gas limited partnerships attractive to individual investors?

There is no single answer to this question. Because oil and gas programs (i.e., limited partnerships) come in several varieties (see Q 1242) each offering different benefits and risks, an investor may choose a program that suits his needs. In general, however, some of the more common attractions of an oil and gas limited partnership, other than a publicly traded partnership taxed as a corporation (see Q 1240), are as follows:

Small investment. Although the dollar amount needed to purchase a partnership interest in an oil and gas limited partnership would be considered large by many individuals, it is in fact quite modest when compared to the capital required to complete an oil and gas venture.

High front-end deductions. In many oil and gas programs, the investor will be able to take first year income tax deductions for the intangible drilling and development costs associated with drilling the wells. Because a high percentage of his initial investment goes to pay these intangible costs, these deductions are substantial, often exceeding 60% of the initial investment. See Q 1248 to Q 1251. However, for certain limitations on the use of deductions, see Q 1245.

Continuing tax shelter. As most investors will be permitted to take deductions for percentage depletion on producing wells, otherwise taxable income (whether in the form of cash distributions from the oil and gas program or income from other sources of the taxpayer) will be "sheltered" to the extent of those deductions. See Q 1256. For limitations on the use of losses to offset income outside the oil and gas program, see Q 1245.

Striking it rich. Although not always an economic reason for investing in oil and gas, the fact remains that many investors hope to "strike it rich" by hitting a "gusher." And, this may not be too unrealistic, because a successful exploratory well can produce a 10 to 1 (or even greater) profit on the investor's capital investment. Even development wells often produce in the area of a two to one profit.

Liquidity. Although not as liquid as many other investments, an informal secondary market and provisions in many partnership agreements providing for periodic offers from the general partner to purchase interests of the limited partners, or permitting a limited partner to exchange his partnership interest for the stock of the general partner (assuming the general partner is a corporation), creates a small degree of liquidity.

Limited liability. An investor who purchases a limited partnership interest is generally liable for partnership liabilities only to the extent of his capital contributions to the partnership (including contributions he has agreed to make in the future).

Allocations of income, deductions, and credits. Within the limitations imposed by the federal income tax law, the limited partnership form of organization allows the participants (i.e., the general and limited partners) to specially allocate items of income and costs (including corresponding deductions and credits) among the limited and general partners in a manner that is disproportionate to their ownership (capital) interests.

1242. What are the basic types of oil and gas drilling programs?

The four basic types of oil and gas drilling programs are (1) exploratory programs, (2) development programs, (3) income programs, and (4) combination programs.

In *exploratory* drilling programs, wells are drilled far from areas of proven production or, at best, on the periphery of a proven field. As a result, the likelihood of drilling successful wells (versus "dryholes") is reduced and the risk that little or no return on invested capital will be realized is increased. In addition, because exploratory wells are often drilled in remote locations, the drilling and marketing costs are likely to be higher. On the other hand, the return on investment in the case of successful exploratory programs is generally much greater than on successful development or income programs.

In *development* drilling programs, wells are drilled in proven areas. Thus, development programs are less risky than exploratory programs, but because the costs of acquiring drilling rights in a proven area are greater than in an unproven (exploratory) area, the return on investment is likely to be less also.

An *income* purchase program purchases the reserves of proven wells that have already been drilled. As a result, income programs involve the least investment risk. (Previously, income programs were generally not considered to be "tax shelters" because deductions for percentage depletion and intangible drilling and development costs were generally not available. However, percentage depletion may now be available to those who participate in these programs. See Q 1248, Q 1256.)

Combination drilling programs combine the exploratory, development, and income type activities into a single, diversified program. Although the major reason for utilizing a combination program is to offer investors a reduced risk of loss of capital, public programs tend to emphasize exploratory drilling within the combination and participate in income purchase activities to only a very small extent.

1243. Does an individual recognize any gain or loss at the time he purchases a limited interest in an oil or natural gas limited partnership?

No.[1]

1244. What tax deductions and credits are available through an oil or gas limited partnership?

The two deductions that are peculiar to oil and gas programs (and certain other extractive industries) and that provide the major incentives for investing in an oil or gas limited partnership are the deductions for intangible drilling and development costs (see Q 1248 to Q 1251) and depletion (see Q 1252 to Q 1261). Of course, subject to certain limitations (see Q 1245 to Q 1247), deductions for interest, taxes, depreciation, and operating expenses *may* be passed through to the limited partner and deducted by him.

See Q 1191 regarding electing large partnerships.

1245. What limits apply to the deductibility of a limited partner's share of partnership losses in an oil and gas partnership?

---

1. IRC Sec. 721(a); Treas. Reg. §1.721-1.

Three different limitations may result in the total or partial disallowance of a deduction by a limited partner for his share of partnership losses. These limitations *must* be applied separately since they are completely independent of each other. The limitations are as follows:

Partnership basis. A limited partner may deduct his share of partnership losses (including capital loss) only to the extent of his adjusted tax basis in his partnership interest (determined at the end of the tax year, but before reduction for partnership losses for the year). However, any amount disallowed by this rule may be carried forward to succeeding years and deducted to the extent that the partner's adjusted tax basis in his partnership exceeds zero at the end of that tax year.[1]

Where a limited partner's share of partnership losses exceeds that partner's adjusted tax basis of his partnership interest, the amount of the limitation (i.e., the partner's tax basis) must be allocated among several categories (e.g., long-term capital loss, short-term capital loss, IRC Section 1231 loss, etc.) according to the proportion that the loss in each category bears to the total loss. Furthermore, if there is taxable income rather than loss in any category (e.g., short-term gain), the limitation amount (i.e., the partner's tax basis) will be increased by the amount of that income before the limitation is allocated among the categories in which there is a loss.[2]

> *Example.* At the end of the tax year, limited partner C has the following distributive share of partnership items: long-term capital loss, $4,000; short-term capital loss, $2,000; "bottom line" income, $4,000. Partner C's adjusted tax basis in his partnership interest at the end of the year, but before adjustment for any of the foregoing items is $1,000. Adjusted as described in the text above, C's tax basis is increased from $1,000 to $5,000 at the end of the year. C's total distributive share of partnership loss is $6,000. Since without regard to losses, C has a tax basis of only $5,000, C is allowed only 5/6th ($5,000/$6,000) of each loss–$3,333 of his long-term capital loss and $1,667 of his short-term capital loss. C must carry forward $667 as long-term capital loss and $333 as short-term capital loss.[3]

Amount at risk. A limited partner in an oil or natural gas program may deduct his share of partnership losses only to the extent he is "at risk" with respect to his interest in the partnership. For further explanation of this "at risk" limitation, see Q 1246, and Q 1286 to Q 1291.

Passive loss rule. Application of the passive loss rule limitation to an investment in an oil or gas program depends on the form in which the investment is made and the material participation of the investor in the activity, see Q 1247.

1246. How does the "at risk" rule affect a limited partner's interest in an oil and gas program?

In preparing his income tax return for any tax year, a limited partner is permitted to offset his allocated share of tax deductions generated by his partnership against his allocated share of income of the partnership. This is permitted regardless of his "amount at risk" in the partnership. However, should his share of tax deductions (including his share of any partnership loss) exceed his share of partnership income (if any), the limited partner will be permitted to offset the excess of such deductions (i.e., his losses) against the income he receives from other sources only to the extent he is "at risk" in the part-

---

1. IRC Sec. 704(d); Treas. Reg. §1.704-1(d)(1).
2. See Treas. Regs. §§1.704-1(d)(2), 1.704-1(d)(4), Ex. (3).
3. See Treas. Reg. §1.704-1(d)(4), Ex. (3).

nership at the close of the year.[1] See Q 1288. If an individual owns limited interests in more than one oil and gas partnership (or owns limited interests in other types of tax shelters), each partnership interest must be treated separately for purposes of the at risk limitations; no aggregation of "amounts at risk" in different partnerships is permitted.[2] However, until otherwise provided, a partnership is permitted to aggregate its oil and gas properties for purposes of the at risk limitation.[3] See Q 1289.

Basically, a limited partner is "at risk" with respect to his interest in a tax shelter partnership to the extent of the sum of cash or property he has contributed plus the amount of debt incurred in connection with the partnership and for which he is personally liable. An individual is not at risk with respect to amounts that are protected against loss through nonrecourse financing, guarantees, stop loss agreements, repurchase agreements, or other similar arrangements.[4] See Q 1287. Oil and gas limited partners were considered "at risk" at the end of each year to the extent the partners assumed liability for annual accruals of the partnerships' minimum annual royalties and annual license fees.[5]

If a limited partner's "amount at risk" in an oil and gas partnership falls below zero, he will generally be required to recognize income to that extent. See Q 1290 for details.

For a detailed analysis of the "at risk" provisions and their application, see Q 1286 to Q 1291.

Percentage Depletion

It is not completely clear whether the "at risk" rule will ever operate to disallow the deduction of percentage depletion. Some authorities suggest that percentage depletion is deductible regardless of an individual's amount at risk. These authorities point out that the conference committee report and effective date provisions of the Tax Reform Act of 1976 specifically mention depreciation and amortization, but omit any reference to depletion. Furthermore, Proposed Treasury Regulation Section 1.465-45(d) provides that a taxpayer's amount at risk in an oil and gas limited partnership is to be increased by the excess of the deductions for depletion over the basis of the property subject to depletion. As this appears to allow percentage depletion even if the taxpayer has no other amount at risk, the authorities question whether a deduction for percentage depletion should also be allowed in early years when percentage depletion does not exceed the basis of the property and the taxpayer has no other amount at risk in the partnership.[6]

1247. How does the "passive loss" rule affect investment in an oil and gas program?

Application of the passive loss rule to an investment in an oil or gas program depends on the form in which the investment is made and the material participation of the investor in the activity.[7] Investment in an oil or gas activity of a C corporation, other than a personal service corporation or closely held corporation, is not subject to

---

1. IRC Sec. 465; Prop. Treas. Reg. §1.465-45.
2. IRC Sec. 465(c)(2)(A).
3. Notice 89-39, 1989-1 CB 681.
4. IRC Sec. 465(b).
5. *Krause v. Comm.*, 92 TC 1003 (1989).
6. See, e.g., Haft, *1984 Tax Sheltered Investment Handbook* (Clark Boardman Company, Ltd.), at 5-6.
7. IRC Sec. 469.

the passive loss rule. Apparently, a publicly traded partnership taxed as a C corporation is not a taxpayer subject to the passive loss rule also.[1] (However, investment in a C corporation does not permit items of income and deductions to flow through to the shareholder-investor.) Also, a working interest in an oil or gas property that the investor owns directly or through any entity that does not limit the liability of the investor with respect to the interest is not a passive activity (see below).[2] Otherwise, an oil or gas program will be subject to the passive loss rule, unless the investor materially participates in the program.[3] Thus, an investor who wants the tax benefits of an oil or gas investment to flow through to him, but does not wish his oil and gas investment to be passive, must either forgo limited liability or materially participate in the venture. As a result, the typical investor in an oil or gas program will be subject to the passive loss rule. See Q 1292, Q 1293.

For purposes of the working interest exception, an entity is considered to limit liability if the taxpayer's interest is in the form of (1) a limited partnership interest (unless the taxpayer is also a general partner), (2) stock in a corporation, or (3) any other interest in which the potential liability of a holder of such an interest is limited under state law to a determinable fixed amount, such as the taxpayer's capital contribution. However, the following protections against loss are not taken into consideration in determining whether the entity limits liability: (1) an indemnification agreement, (2) a stop loss arrangement, (3) insurance, (4) any similar arrangement, or (5) any combination of (1) through (4).[4] A husband and wife are to be treated as separate taxpayers for purposes of the working interest in an oil or gas property exception.[5]

In general, the passive loss rule limits the amount of the taxpayer's aggregate deductions from all passive activities to the amount of his aggregate income from all passive activities; passive credits can be taken only against tax attributable to passive activities. The rule is applied separately in the case of a publicly traded partnership; aggregation is permitted only within the partnership.[6] The rule is intended to prevent taxpayers from offsetting income in the form of salaries, interest, and dividends with losses from passive activities. However, the benefit of the disallowed passive losses and credits is generally not lost forever, but rather is postponed until such time as the taxpayer has additional passive income or disposes of the activity. See Q 1292 to Q 1299.

With respect to the working interest exception above, gross income from an oil or gas property is not treated as income from a passive activity if any loss from such property in a prior taxable year beginning after 1986 was treated as other than a passive loss solely by reason of the working interest exception, and not by reason of the taxpayer's material participation in the activity.[7]

INTANGIBLE DRILLING COSTS

1248. What are "intangible drilling and development costs"?

Intangible drilling and development costs (more commonly referred to as "intangible drilling costs" or "IDCs") are expenditures made by an operator in the development of an

---

1. IRC Sec. 469(a).
2. IRC Secs. 469(c)(3), 469(c)(4).
3. IRC Sec. 469(c)(1).
4. Temp. Treas. Reg. §1.469-1T(e)(4).
5. Temp. Treas. Reg. §1.469-1T(j)(2)(iii).
6. IRC Sec. 469.
7. Treas. Reg. §1.469-2(c)(6).

oil or natural gas property for wages, fuel, repairs, hauling, supplies, etc. Thus, intangible drilling costs generally include all amounts paid for labor, fuel, repairs, hauling, and supplies that are incurred in drilling, shooting, and cleaning wells, in clearing ground, draining, road making, surveying, and geological work necessary to prepare a site for drilling, and in constructing derricks, tanks, pipelines, and other physical structures necessary for drilling and the production of oil or natural gas.

On the other hand, intangible drilling costs do *not* include expenditures made to acquire tangible property ordinarily considered to have a salvage value. Thus, the costs of the actual materials in structures constructed in the wells or on the property and the cost of drilling tools, pipes, casings, tubings, tanks, engines, boilers, machines, etc. are *not* intangible drilling costs. However, wages, fuel, repairs, hauling, supplies, etc. are not considered to have salvage value even though they are incurred in connection with the installation of physical structures that themselves have salvage values.[1]

Expenditures for wages, fuel, repairs, hauling, supplies, etc. incurred in connection with equipment, facilities, or structures that are *not* incident to or necessary for the drilling of wells (including expenditures for storing and drilling) are *not* intangible drilling costs. (These items must be capitalized and depreciated.)[2] Expenditures for drilling wells solely to obtain geological information and not for the production of oil or natural gas are not intangible drilling costs.[3]

Expenditures for labor, fuel, repairs, hauling, supplies, etc. incurred in connection with the actual operation of wells and other facilities on the property for the production of oil or natural gas are *not* intangible drilling costs, but must be treated as expenses.[4]

Expenditures for labor, fuel, repairs, hauling, supplies, etc. incurred in connection with the drilling of an injection well, or the conversion of a producing or nonproducing well to an injection well, are treated as intangible drilling costs.[5]

If drilling and development work is done by a contractor under an agreement with the operator, intangible drilling and development costs do not include those amounts that are payable to the contractor out of production or proceeds from production if such amounts are depletable income in the hands of the contractor, or amounts that are properly allocable to the cost of depreciable property. Otherwise, any type of contract (including a turnkey contract) between the operator and contractor may be used without jeopardizing the classification of expenditures as intangible drilling costs.[6]

Numerous rulings and cases have considered the eligibility of specific expenditures to be treated as intangible drilling and development costs and the special problems encountered in the case of offshore wells.[7]

---

1. Treas. Reg. §1.612-4(a).
2. Treas. Regs. §1.612-4(c)(1).
3. Rev. Rul. 80-342, 1980-2 CB 99.
4. Treas. Reg. §1.612-4(c)(2).
5. GCM 39619 (3-19-87), TAM 8728004.
6. Treas. Reg. §1.612-4(a).
7. See Rev. Rul. 89-56, 1989-1 CB 83; Rev. Rul. 88-10, 1988-1 CB 112; Rev. Rul. 78-13, 1978-1 CB 63; Rev. Rul. 70-414, 1970-2 CB 132; TAMs 8406006, 8141028; Let. Ruls. 7924101, 7837004, 7834002; *Texaco, Inc. v. U.S.*, 84-2 USTC ¶9866 (S.D. Tex. 1984); *Standard Oil Co. (Ind.) v. Comm.*, 77 TC 349 (1981), acq. in result, 1989-1 CB 1; *Sun Co., Inc. v. Comm.*, 74 TC 1481 (1980), aff'd, 677 F.2d 294 (3d Cir. 1982); *Gates Rubber Co. v. Comm.*, 74 TC 1456 (1980), aff'd per curiam, 82-2 USTC ¶9702 (10th Cir. 1982); *Standard Oil Co. (Ind.) v. Comm.*, 68 TC 325 (1977); *Miller v. U.S.*, 78-1 USTC ¶9127 (C.D. Cal. 1977); *Exxon v. U.S.*, 76-1 USTC ¶9205 (Ct. Cl. 1976); GCM 39085 (12-1-83) (revoking GCM 37359 dated 12-28-77).

1249. How are intangible drilling and development costs treated for purposes of the federal income tax?

Intangible drilling and development costs (IDCs) are capital in nature; however, the IRC and regulations provide a choice of alternatives for treatment of such costs. The individual or entity who holds the working or operating interest in the oil or gas property (i.e., the operator) may elect to (1) capitalize the IDCs or (2) deduct them as expenses for the taxable year in which they are paid or incurred.[1] (With respect to oil or gas property located outside the United States, intangible drilling and development costs paid or incurred after 1986 must be (1) capitalized, or (2) deducted ratably over 10 years. This, however, does not apply to a nonproductive well.[2])

If intangible drilling costs are capitalized, they may be recovered through depreciation or depletion (see Q 1257, Q 1424).

In the case of certain enhanced oil recovery projects (generally referred to as tertiary recovery projects) begun or expanded after 1990, the operator may, instead of expensing or capitalizing IDCs, claim a tax credit generally equal to 15% of qualified enhanced oil recovery costs. See Q 1262.

In the case of the typical oil and gas limited partnership, it is the partnership that holds the working interest in the oil or gas property and undertakes the drilling and development expenditures. Thus, the election to capitalize or expense intangible drilling costs is made at the partnership level by the general partner.[3] The general partner's intent as to this election is normally stated in the prospectus provided to potential investors by the oil and gas program; however, good faith reliance on the prospectus and general partner (or promoter) will not sustain a deduction if there is a failure by the partnership to satisfy the requirements for deduction.[4]

As to how individual limited partners treat their allocated shares of intangible drilling and development costs after the partnership has made its election to capitalize or expense, see Q 1250 and Q 1251.

Nonproductive Wells

If a limited partnership (i.e., the operator) has elected to capitalize intangible drilling and development costs, the regulations provide an additional option with respect to intangible drilling and development costs incurred in drilling a nonproductive well. Intangible drilling costs incurred with respect to individual nonproductive wells may be taken as a deductible loss for the first taxable year in which such nonproductive well is completed. Apparently, once this election is made it is binding for all subsequent years and must be applied to all nonproductive wells completed after the election.[5]

1250. If the limited partnership elects to capitalize intangible drilling costs, how does a limited partner treat his allocated share of such costs?

---

1. IRC Sec. 263(c); Treas. Reg. §1.612-4.
2. IRC Sec. 263(i).
3. Treas. Reg. §1.703-1(b).
4. See, e.g., *Puscas v. Comm.*, TC Memo 1978-73.
5. Treas. Reg. §1.612-4(b)(4).

If the limited partnership has elected to capitalize intangible drilling and development costs, each limited partner must treat his allocated share of such costs as a capital expenditure. Subsequently, each limited partner may recover his share of these capital expenditures on his income tax return through depletion or depreciation.[1] In the case of an electing large partnership, see below.

A limited partner may recover his share of the cost of a particular item of intangible drilling costs that is *not* represented by physical property through the allowance for depletion. See Q 1252. Expenditures for clearing ground, draining, road making, surveying, geological work, excavation, grading, and the drilling, shooting, and cleaning of wells are considered *not* to be represented by physical property and thus may be recovered through depletion.[2]

Amounts of intangible drilling and development costs capitalized and represented by physical property may be recovered by depreciation. See Q 1424. Thus, a limited partner will capitalize and depreciate his allocated share of expenditures paid for wages, fuel, repairs, hauling, supplies, etc. used in the installation of casing and equipment and in the construction on the property of derricks and other physical structures.[3]

If intangible drilling costs are incurred under a drilling contract (e.g., a turnkey contract), the intangible drilling costs under the contract must be allocated between depletable and depreciable classes of costs for purposes of calculating depletion and depreciation at the partner level.[4]

As to how intangible drilling and development costs incurred with respect to a nonproductive well (i.e., a dryhole) are treated by a limited partner, see Q 1249.

Electing Large Partnerships

An electing large partnership generally calculates depletion and depreciation deductions (including those representing capitalized intangible drilling costs) at the partnership level. In the case of a limited partnership interest, these deductions are generally aggregated with other items of income or loss from passive loss limitation activities of the partnership and are considered one passive activity.[5] In the case of a general partnership interest, deductions allocable to passive loss limitation activities are generally taken into account separately to the extent necessary to comply with the passive loss rule.[6] However, in the case of a partner who is a disqualified person, items of income, gain, loss, deduction, or credit from oil and gas property are treated under the regular partnership rules discussed above. A disqualified person is a retailer or refiner of crude oil or natural gas (see Q 1256) or any other person whose average daily production of domestic crude oil and natural gas exceeds 500 barrels.[7] See Q 1191 regarding electing large partnerships; see Q 1292 regarding the passive loss rule.

1251. If the limited partnership elects to expense intangible drilling costs, how does a limited partner treat his allocated shares of such costs?

1. Treas. Reg. §1.612-4(b).
2. Treas. Reg. §1.612-4(b)(1).
3. Treas. Reg. §1.612-4(b)(2).
4. Treas. Reg. §1.612-4(b)(3).
5. IRC Sec. 772(c)(2).
6. IRC Sec. 772(f).
7. IRC Sec. 776(b).

If the limited partnership elects to expense intangible drilling and development costs, each limited partner has a choice as to how to treat his allocated share of intangible drilling costs for federal income tax purposes. The limited partner may (1) deduct his share of intangible drilling costs, or (2) elect to amortize his share of such costs ratably over a 60-month period.[1] In the case of an electing large partnership, see below.

Election to Amortize Costs

If the limited partner makes this election, he may deduct each year on his income tax return a ratable portion of his allocated share of intangible drilling costs over the 60-month period, beginning with the month in which such amounts were expended by the partnership.[2]

If a limited partner elects to amortize intangible drilling costs over the 60-month period, any amount of intangible drilling and development costs covered by the election will *not* be treated as an item of tax preference for purposes of the alternative minimum tax.[3] See Q 1263.

In the case of a disposition of a limited partner's interest in an oil and gas limited partnership, deductions taken under the amortization method may, like expensed intangible drilling costs, be required to be recaptured as ordinary income.[4]

Deduction of Expensed Costs

If a limited partner does not elect to amortize his allocated share of intangible drilling costs, he will deduct (within the limits described in Q 1245) the amount on his federal income tax return.[5]

Assuming the limited partnership has elected cash basis tax accounting (as is usually the case), the limited partner will deduct his allocated share of intangible drilling and development costs with respect to a particular well in the year they are paid by the partnership if (1) the cash basis partnership (or more specifically, the general partner) drills the well and incurs the intangible drilling costs itself, or (2) the drilling is performed by a drilling contractor and the well is drilled in the same (or previous) calendar year that the drilling fees are paid by the partnership.[6] However, where the drilling contractor is paid by the partnership in a year prior to the year in which the drilling services are performed under the contract (i.e., where the intangible drilling costs are "prepaid"), the IRC and the courts have limited the ability to take the deduction in the earlier year.

If intangible drilling costs with respect to a particular well are prepaid and the drilling of that well commences *within 90 days* after the close of the calendar tax year (including where the drilling commenced but had not been completed during the earlier year), the limited partner may deduct his entire allocated share of the intangible drilling costs with respect to that well in the earlier year *if* (1) the expenditure (i.e., the payment of fees under the drilling contract) is a *payment* rather than a refundable deposit, (2) there is an adequate business purpose for prepaying the drilling fees, and

---

1. IRC Secs. 263(c), 59(e); Treas. Reg. §1.612-4.
2. IRC Sec. 59(e).
3. IRC Sec. 59(e)(6).
4. IRC Secs. 59(e)(5), 1254.
5. IRC Sec. 263(c); Treas. Reg. §1.612-4.
6. See IRC Secs. 706(a), 461.

(3) the deduction of such costs in the year of prepayment does not result in a material distortion of income. However, in such case, the portion of the intangible drilling costs attributable to drilling commencing within 90 days after the close of the earlier year is deductible only to the extent of the limited partner's *cash basis* in the partnership.[1] (A limited partner's "cash basis" in his partnership is his adjusted basis in the partnership determined without regard to (1) any liabilities of the partnership, (2) any borrowings of the partner that were arranged by the partnership or an organizer or promoter of the partnership, and (3) any borrowings of the partner that were secured by any assets of the partnership.[2] See Q 1193.)

> *Example 1.* A limited partner purchases an interest in an oil and gas partnership in December, 2006. The partnership hires a drilling contractor to drill the well under a contract that requires payment in December. Drilling is commenced on February 1, 2007. Assuming that the requirements with respect to adequate business purpose, payment rather than deposit, and nondistortion of income are met, the limited partner's entire share of prepaid IDC is deductible for his 2006 taxable year, but only to the extent of his *cash* basis in the partnership.

> *Example 2.* Assume the same facts as in *Example 1*, except that drilling begins in December, 2006 and continues until February 1, 2007. The limited partner's entire share of prepaid IDC is deductible for his 2006 taxable year; however, the limited partner's share of the portion of intangible drilling costs that are attributable to drilling prior to the end of 2006 is not subject to the "cash basis" limitation discussed in the text above. (The limited partner's share of intangible drilling costs attributable to drilling after 2006 is, however, subject to this "cash basis" limitation.)

If the drilling of the well does not commence within 90 days after the close of the calendar tax year in which the intangible drilling costs were prepaid, then the deduction of amounts that constitute intangible drilling costs can be taken only as economic performance occurs with respect to such costs (i.e., only as the drilling services are actually provided to the partnership).[3]

For purposes of determining if an expenditure is a payment rather than a deposit and whether a business purpose exists for a prepayment, the following principles and holdings should be considered: To the extent amounts prepaid pursuant to a footage or daywork contract may be recovered by way of a refund under a work stoppage provision in the contract, the amounts are deposits rather than payments.[4] Turnkey contracts fulfill a substantial business purpose and therefore do not distort income.[5] Where a turnkey drilling contract required payments on completion of each well, the Tax Court found that a valid business purpose existed for payments made after substantial drilling services had been performed but before any wells had been completed.[6] Where prepayments of intangible drilling costs were made to a general contractor who was the parent company of the general partner, the Service ruled that the deductions could *not* be taken for any year before such contractor actually contracted with and paid a drilling contractor.[7] But where prepayments were made under a turnkey-type contract to a corporation related to the general partner, the Tax Court held that limited partners could deduct their shares of intangible drilling costs in the year the fees were prepaid, even though the related

---

1. IRC Sec. 461(i). See General Explanation – TRA '84, pp. 279-282; *Keller v. Comm.*, 79 TC 7 (1982), aff'd, 84-1 USTC ¶9194 (8th Cir. 1984), acq., 1984-1 CB 1.
2. IRC Sec. 461(i)(2). See General Explanation – TRA '84, p. 279.
3. IRC Secs. 461(i), 461(h); See General Explanation – TRA '84, p. 280.
4. *Keller v. Comm.*, above.
5. *Keller v. Comm.*, above.
6. *Levy v. Comm.*, TC Memo 1982-419, aff'd, 84-1 USTC ¶9470 (9th Cir. 1984).
7. Rev. Rul. 80-71, 1980-1 CB 106.

corporation would contract for, rather than perform, the drilling services.[1] In Revenue Ruling 73-211,[2] the Service allowed a deduction for prepaid intangible drilling costs under a turnkey drilling contract with a drilling contractor controlled by the operator, but only to the extent such costs would have been incurred in an arm's length transaction. Where the drilling contract provided that drilling fees were payable when the well reached a predetermined depth, the Service ruled that a voluntary partial prepayment made in a year prior to the year in which the wells were drilled could *not* be deducted in the year paid; instead, the prepayment was deductible in the year the well reached the predetermined depth.[3]

When an interest in an oil or natural gas property (including a limited interest therein) is disposed of, all or part of the intangible drilling costs that were expensed rather than capitalized by the operator must be recaptured as ordinary income.[4]

Electing Large Partnership

An electing large partnership generally calculates intangible drilling and development costs at the partnership level. In the case of a limited partnership interest, these deductions are generally aggregated with other items of income or loss from passive loss limitation activities of the partnership and are considered one passive activity.[5] In the case of a general partnership interest, deductions allocable to passive loss limitation activities are generally taken into account separately to the extent necessary to comply with the passive loss rule.[6] However, in the case of a partner who is a disqualified person, items of income, gain, loss, deduction, or credit from oil and gas property are treated under the regular partnership rules discussed above. A disqualified person is a "retailer" or "refiner" of crude oil or natural gas (see Q 1256), or a person whose average daily production of domestic crude oil and natural gas exceeds 500 barrels.[7] See Q 1191 regarding electing large partnerships; see Q 1292 regarding the passive loss rule.

DEPLETION

1252. What is the depletion allowance?

The depletion allowance is a formula for computing and excluding (i.e., by way of income tax deductions) from the proceeds of mineral operations that part of the proceeds that represents a tax-free return of an investor's capital.[8] In other words, the depletion allowance is an income tax deduction that compensates the owner of wasting mineral assets (e.g., oil or gas) "for the part exhausted in production, so that when the minerals are gone, the owner's capital and his capital assets remain unimpaired."[9] Depletion is similar in concept to depreciation (see Q 1424).

1253. Who is eligible to take deductions for depletion?

---

1. *Jolley v. Comm.*, TC Memo 1984-70.
2. 1973-1 CB 303.
3. Rev. Rul. 71-579, 1971-2 CB 225. See also, *Stradlings Building Materials, Inc. v. Comm.*, 76 TC 84 (1981); *Pauley v. U.S.*, 11 AFTR 2d 955 (S.D. Cal. 1963); Rev. Rul. 71-252, 1971-1 CB 146.
4. IRC Sec. 1254.
5. IRC Sec. 772(c)(2).
6. IRC Sec. 772(f).
7. IRC Sec. 776(b).
8. See *Jefferson Lake Sulphur Co. v. Lambert*, 133 F. Supp. 197 (E.D. La. 1955), aff'd, 236 F.2d 542 (5th Cir. 1956).
9. *Paragon Jewel Coal Co., Inc. v. Comm.*, 380 U.S. 624 (1965).

Depletion allowance deductions are allowed only to individuals or entities that own an "economic interest" in the mineral deposit (i.e., the oil or gas in place).[1] Essentially, an individual or entity has an economic interest in a mineral deposit if (1) he (or it) has acquired by investment any interest in a mineral in place *and* (2) he secures income through the extraction of the mineral.[2] However, it is not required that the taxpayer invest cash or property in acquiring his interest; an economic interest may be acquired by gift, inheritance, personal effort, etc. "The test of the right to depletion is whether the taxpayer has a capital investment in the [mineral] in place which is necessarily reduced as the [mineral] is extracted."[3]

"Economic interests" include working or operating interests, royalties, overriding royalties, net profits interests, and, to the extent not required to be treated as a loan, production payments.[4]

Where a limited partnership owns an economic interest in an oil or gas deposit (or other mineral interest), each individual partner (including any limited partner) is considered as owning an "economic interest" in the deposit.

1254. In the case of a limited partnership, who calculates the depletion allowance?

In the case of a limited partnership, each partner (both general and limited) computes his depletion allowance separately from the partnership and other partners. (The partnership, however, often computes a tentative depletion allowance for its partners which, depending on the circumstances of the individual partner, may or may not need revising.)[5] In the case of an electing large partnership, see below.

So that a partner is able to make these calculations, the partnership is required to allocate to each partner his proportionate share of the tax basis of each partnership domestic oil or gas property. The partner's proportionate share will generally be determined in accordance with the partner's proportionate interest in partnership capital at the time of the allocation, unless (1) the partnership agreement provides for an allocation based upon the partner's proportionate interest in partnership income, and (2) at the time of the allocation it is reasonably expected that such interest will remain unchanged other than to reflect changes in ownership of the partnership. Each partner is charged with maintaining records of his share of the tax basis of each property and is further charged with making and keeping a record of the appropriate adjustments to such bases during the time he is a partner. The basis of each property is generally reduced as depletion is taken. Also, basis is generally reallocated upon a contribution to the partnership by a new or existing partner, or upon the withdrawal of a partner or a decrease in a partner's interest in the partnership.[6]

Electing Large Partnerships

An electing large partnership generally calculates depletion at the partnership level. In the case of a limited partnership interest, these deductions are generally aggregated with other items of income or loss from passive loss limitation activities of the partner-

---

1. Treas. Reg. §1.611-1(b). See *Helvering v. Bankline Oil Co.*, 303 U.S. 362 (1938).
2. Treas. Reg. §1.611-1(b).
3. *Kirby Petroleum Co. v. Comm.*, 326 U.S. 599 (1946). See *Anderson v. Helvering*, 310 U.S. 404 (1940).
4. Treas. Reg. §1.614-1(a)(2).
5. IRC Sec. 613A(c)(7)(D); Treas. Reg. §1.613A-3(e)(1). See IRS Pub. 535 (2005), pp. 40-41.
6. IRC Sec. 613A(c)(7)(D); Treas. Reg. §1.613A-3(e). See Treas. Reg. §1.704-1(b)(4)(v).

ship and are considered one passive activity.[1] In the case of a general partnership interest, deductions allocable to passive loss limitation activities are generally taken into account separately to the extent necessary to comply with the passive loss rule.[2] However, in the case of a partner who is a disqualified person, items of income, gain, loss, deduction, or credit from oil and gas property are treated under the regular partnership rules discussed above. A disqualified person is a retailer or refiner of crude oil or natural gas (see Q 1256) or any other person whose average daily production of domestic crude oil and natural gas exceeds 500 barrels.[3] See Q 1191 regarding electing large partnerships; see Q 1292 regarding the passive loss rule.

1255. How is the depletion allowance calculated?

The IRC provides two different methods for calculating a limited partner's individual depletion allowance. The first method is "cost depletion." Cost depletion essentially involves recovery of a portion of the taxpayer's adjusted basis each year, based on the amount of oil or gas recovered for that year and the total anticipated production. The second method is "percentage depletion." Percentage depletion is determined based on a percentage of the taxpayer's gross income from the property during the year, subject to certain limitations.[4] Assuming that a partnership and partners own a depletable interest in an oil or natural gas property (see Q 1253), there are no further restrictions as to who may use cost depletion. Percentage depletion is available only with respect to domestic oil or natural gas, and only certain individual limited partners are eligible to use the percentage depletion method (see Q 1256).[5]

If a limited partner is not eligible to use the percentage depletion method, he must use cost depletion to determine his total allowable deduction for depletion. If he is eligible to use percentage depletion, the limited partner must each year calculate a depletion allowance for each oil or gas property of the partnership using both the cost and percentage depletion methods, select the greater amount for each property, and deduct the sum of the selected amounts as his total depletion allowance.[6] (Unless an election has been made, interests in a single tract or parcel of land are treated as one property. Interests in different tracts or parcels are treated separately.[7] The election to treat interests in a single tract or parcel is made, if at all, by the partnership; individual partners cannot make this election.[8])

In the case of an electing large partnership (see Q 1191), depletion is generally calculated at the partnership level. See Q 1254.

1256. Who is eligible to use the percentage depletion method?

Percentage depletion is generally available to individuals (including limited partners) who qualify as "independent producers or royalty owners" (i.e., certain "small producers") and to individuals who own a depletable interest in (1) certain domestic regulated natural gas, (2) domestic natural gas sold under certain fixed contracts, and

---

1. IRC Sec. 772(c)(2).
2. IRC Sec. 772(f).
3. IRC Sec. 776(b).
4. See IRS Pub. 535 (2005), p. 39.
5. IRC Secs. 611, 613, 613A.
6. IRC Sec. 613(a); Treas. Regs. §§1.611-1(a), 1.613-1.
7. IRC Sec. 614(a).
8. Rev. Rul. 84-142, 1984-2 CB 117.

(3) certain domestic natural gas produced from geopressured brine.[1] (See Q 1254 regarding calculation of depletion in the case of an electing large partnership.) The IRC formerly prohibited certain transferees of an interest in a "proven" oil or gas property from using the small producer's percentage depletion method; however, for transfers occurring after October 11, 1990, this limitation generally no longer applies.[2] (See Treas. Reg. §1.613A-3(i)(2) regarding "transfers" and "transferees" in the context of "proven" properties and, also, for examples illustrating the effects of the old and new rules on the transfer of such properties.)

Percentage depletion is available under IRC Section 613(b) with respect to certain minerals (other than oil and gas) recovered from an oil or gas well, without regard to the restrictions on oil and gas contained in IRC Sections 613(b)(7) and 613A.[3]

Independent Producers and Royalty Owners

This is currently the most common basis for allowing an individual to claim percentage depletion.

A limited partner is eligible as an "independent producer or royalty owner" (i.e., as a "small producer") to use percentage depletion if: (1) he owns a depletable interest in a domestic oil or natural gas property (see Q 1253); and (2) he is not a "retailer" or a "refiner" of crude oil or natural gas, as described below.[4]

A taxpayer is a "retailer" if (1) he directly or through a related entity sells oil or natural gas (other than certain bulk sales to commercial or industrial users), or any product derived from oil or natural gas (other than certain bulk sales of aviation fuels), through any retail outlet owned, leased, controlled, or operated by him or a related entity, or to any person who has agreed to use the trademark, service mark, etc. owned by him or a related entity, and (2) the combined gross receipts of all retail outlets taken into account exceed $5,000,000 for the tax year.[5]

For tax years ending after August 8, 2005, a taxpayer is a "refiner" if he or one or more related entities has an "average daily refinery run" for the year of more than 75,000 barrels. The average daily refinery run is determined by dividing the aggregate refinery run for the tax year by the number of days in the tax year.[6] For tax years ending before August 9, 2005, a taxpayer is a "refiner" if he and any related entities together refine more than 50,000 barrels of crude oil on any day during the tax year.[7]

For purposes of the above rules, an entity is "related" to the limited partner if the limited partner owns a significant interest in such entity (5% or more in value of the outstanding stock of a corporation; 5% or more interest in the profits or capital of a partnership; 5% or more of the beneficial interests in an estate or trust). In determining such ownership interests, an interest owned by or for a corporation, partnership, trust, or estate is considered to be owned directly both by itself and proportionately by its shareholders, partners, or beneficiaries.[8]

---

1. IRC Secs. 613A(b), 613A(c); Treas. Reg. §1.613A-3.
2. IRC Sec. 613A(c)(9), prior to amendment by OBRA '90.
3. *Louisiana Land and Exploration Co. v. Comm.*, 90 TC 630 (1988).
4. IRC Sec. 613A(d); Treas. Regs. §§1.613A-4(b), 1.613A-4(c), 1.613A-7.
5. IRC Sec. 613A(d)(2).
6. IRC Sec. 613A(d)(4).
7. IRC Sec. 613A(d)(4), prior to amendment by ETIA 2005.
8. IRC Sec. 613A(d)(3).

Transferees of "Proven" Properties

For transfers occurring after October 11, 1990, the "proven property" prohibition for use of percentage depletion is repealed.

For transfers occurring prior to October 12, 1990, the IRC prohibited use of percentage depletion for certain transferees of "proven" properties. Generally, a limited partner who acquired a depletable interest in a "proven" oil or natural gas property after 1974 did not qualify as an independent producer or royalty owner and thus could be prohibited from using the percentage depletion method *unless* his interest was acquired (1) by a transfer at death, (2) from his spouse or minor children, (3) from his parents if he was a minor child at the time of the transfer, (4) as a result of certain changes in the beneficiaries of a trust, or (5) by reversion (in total or in part) of an interest with respect to which he was previously eligible to use the percentage depletion method.[1]

If a partner was eligible to use the percentage depletion method at the time he transferred a proven oil or natural gas property to the partnership, that partner was not treated as a transferee with respect to any retained or reversionary interest he has in the property. A partner who did not have an interest in proven property prior to the time it was transferred to the partnership was not eligible for percentage depletion.[2]

Where an individual transferred his depletable interest in a producing oil and gas property to a Clifford Trust that provided for the maintenance of a depletion reserve, the "proven" property rule did not prohibit the transferor from claiming deductions for percentage depletion either during the period of the trust or after the interest was returned to the transferor.[3]

An oil or natural gas property was considered "proven" if at the time of the transfer the principal value of the property had been demonstrated by prospecting, exploration, or discovery work.[4]

1257. How is cost depletion calculated?

Cost depletion is calculated on each oil or gas property by a unit of production method using the following formula:[5]

$$\text{Cost depletion for tax year} = \frac{\text{Basis of property}}{\text{Units remaining as of tax year}} \times \text{Units sold during year}$$

Basis. For this purpose, "basis" is the adjusted tax basis (including adjustments reflecting prior years' depletion deductions) of the oil or gas property (i.e., excluding the basis of any land or depreciable improvements) that would be used to determine the gain on a sale of the property.[6] If an election has been made to capitalize intangible drilling and development costs some of those costs may be reflected in the individual's adjusted tax basis (see Q 1250).[7] In the case of limited partners in an oil or natural gas

---

1. IRC Sec. 613A(c)(9), prior to amendment by OBRA '90.
2. Let. Rul. 8723073.
3. Rev. Rul. 84-14, 1984-1 CB 147.
4. IRC Sec. 613A(c)(9)(A), prior to amendment by OBRA '90. See Treas. Reg. §1.613A-7(p).
5. Treas. Reg. §1.611-2(a).
6. IRC Sec. 612; Treas. Regs. §§1.611-2, 1.612-1(a).
7. Treas. Reg. §1.612-1(b)(1).

program, the partnership will allocate to each limited partner his proportionate share of the tax basis in each property.[1] See Q 1254. In the case of community property interests, a surviving spouse's basis for calculating cost depletion on property representing the surviving spouse's one-half share of the property will be stepped up or down to reflect the property's estate tax value in the decedent spouse's estate (generally, fair market value at the date of death) (but see Q 1415).[2]

Units. For purposes of the formula, mineral deposits remaining and amounts sold are determined using the unit customarily paid for in the type of mineral sold. In the case of oil, the unit is "barrels"; in the case of natural gas, the unit is "thousands of cubic feet."[3]

Units remaining. The number of units remaining as of the tax year is the number of units of mineral remaining at the end of the year to be recovered from the property (including units recovered but not yet sold) *plus* the number of units sold during the tax year.[4] For this purpose, if the number of recoverable units remaining at the end of the prior year (or years) has been estimated and there have been no known changes that would affect such estimate, the number of recoverable units as of the tax year is the number remaining from the prior estimate.[5]

Units sold. In the case of a cash basis taxpayer, the number of units sold during the tax year includes units for which payments were actually received during the tax year, even if such units were sold or produced in a prior tax year. Units sold but not paid for in the tax year are not counted in that year.[6]

In the case of natural gas, where the annual production is not metered and is not estimable with reasonable accuracy, cost depletion for the tax year may be calculated by multiplying the adjusted tax basis of the property (see "Basis," above) by a fraction, "the numerator of which is equal to the decline in rock pressure during the tax year and the denominator is equal to the expected total decline in rock pressure from the beginning of the tax year to the economic limit of production."[7]

Once an individual's adjusted tax basis for a mineral property has been reduced to zero through reductions for allowable depletion deductions (or otherwise), cost depletion is no longer available with respect to such property; however, if eligible, the individual may continue to use percentage depletion (see Q 1258).[8]

1258. How is percentage depletion calculated on oil or gas properties?

Unlike cost depletion, percentage depletion is not based on the investor's tax basis in each oil or gas property; instead, the percentage method provides for a deduction of a specified percentage of the *gross income* derived from the property (after reduction for rents or royalties paid or incurred by the investor with respect to the property).[9] The

1. Treas. Reg. §1.613A-3(e)(1).
2. Rev. Rul. 92-37, 1992-1 CB 195.
3. Treas. Reg. §1.611-2(a)(1).
4. Treas. Reg. §1.611-2(a)(3).
5. Treas. Reg. §1.611-2(c)(2).
6. Treas. Reg. §1.611-2(a)(2).
7. Treas. Reg. §1.611-2(a)(4).
8. See Treas. Reg. §1.611-2(b)(2).
9. IRC Sec. 613(a); Treas. Reg. §1.613-2(c)(5). See Rev. Rul. 81-266, 1981-2 CB 139; Rev. Rul. 79-73, 1979-1 CB 218. See also *Comm. v. Engle*, 84-1 USTC ¶9134 (U.S. 1984).

applicable percentage rate and various limitations depend on the reason for the investor's eligibility for percentage depletion.[1] See Q 1254 regarding the calculation of depletion in the case of an electing large partnership.

The deduction for percentage depletion for oil and gas properties may offset up to 100% of the taxpayer's taxable income from the property (computed without allowance for depletion).[2] The percentage rate to be used in calculating percentage depletion is to be determined in the year that oil and gas income is reported and not in the year that the oil and gas is extracted.[3]

For purposes of calculating percentage depletion, "gross income" is defined as the amount for which the oil or gas is sold in the immediate vicinity of the well; if the oil or gas is not sold on the premises, but is manufactured or refined prior to sale, or transported from the premises prior to sale, gross income generally is the representative market or field price of the oil or gas prior to conversion or transportation.[4]

Independent Producers and Royalty Owners

In the case of an individual who qualifies as an independent producer or royalty owner (often referred to as a "small producer"–see Q 1256), percentage depletion is available using a rate of 15%. However, in this case, percentage depletion is calculated only on so much of the individual's average daily production of crude oil or natural gas as does not exceed his maximum daily depletable quantity.[5] In the case of crude oil, an individual's "maximum daily depletable quantity" is generally 1,000 barrels.[6] In the case of natural gas, an individual's maximum daily depletable quantity equals the amount determined by multiplying 6,000 cubic feet by the number of barrels by which he has elected to reduce his maximum daily depletable quantity of crude oil. (In other words, one barrel of crude oil is deemed to equal 6,000 cubic feet of natural gas and an individual's maximum daily depletable quantity must be allocated between crude oil and natural gas such that the total daily depletable quantity is the equivalent of 1,000 barrels of crude oil.)[7] If an individual's spouse or minor children own depletable oil or gas interests, the maximum daily depletable quantity must be allocated among such family members in proportion to their respective production of crude oil during the year.[8] An electing large partnership (see Q 1191, Q 1254) calculates its percentage depletion without regard to these production limitations.[9]

An individual's "average daily production" of crude oil or natural gas is determined by dividing his aggregate production from all oil or gas interests, as the case may be, during the tax year by the number of days in that year. A limited partner's annual production of oil or natural gas from specific properties is determined by multiplying the total production of each property by his percentage participation in the revenues from that property.[10] A taxpayer holding a "net profits interest" determines his annual production

---

1. See IRC Secs. 613(b), 613(e).
2. IRC Sec. 613(a).
3. *Potts v. Comm.*, 90 TC 995 (1988).
4. Treas. Reg. §1.613-3.
5. IRC Sec. 613A(c)(1).
6. See IRC Sec. 613A(c)(3).
7. IRC Sec. 613A(c)(4); Treas. Regs. §§1.613A-3, 1.613A-5, 1.613A-7(i).
8. IRC Sec. 613A(c)(8)(C); Treas. Regs. §§1.613A-3(h)(3), 1.613A-3(h)(4)(i).
9. IRC Sec. 776(a)(2).
10. IRC Sec. 613A(c)(2).

by multiplying the total production of the property by his percentage participation in the revenues from the property.[1]

If an individual's average daily production of crude oil exceeds his maximum daily depletable quantity, the amount of percentage depletion allowable with respect to each domestic property is determined using the following formula:

$$\text{Percentage Depletion} = \frac{\text{maximum daily depletable quantity}}{\text{average daily production (all properties)}} \times 15\% \times \text{gross income from property in tax year}$$

This formula may also be used to determine allowable percentage depletion on natural gas production when an individual's average daily production of natural gas exceeds his maximum daily depletable quantity.[2]

Special rules apply to the percentage depletion rate for marginal properties held by small producers. During any year in which the reference price for crude oil for the preceding calendar year drops below $20, the percentage depletion rate of 15% is increased by one percentage point for each whole dollar by which such reference price falls below the $20 level. However, the percentage depletion rate cannot exceed 25%.[3] The applicable percentage for 2006 was 15%.[4] For tax years beginning after 1997 and before 2006, the limit of percentage depletion to 100% of the taxable income from the property (computed without allowance for depletion) did not apply to marginal properties.[5] "Marginal properties" for this purpose refers only to stripper wells or wells that produce heavy oil.[6]

Certain tertiary recovery projects begun or expanded after 1990 may qualify for a special tax credit; see Q 1262.

An additional limitation applies to percentage depletion for small producers. The aggregate deduction for percentage depletion of a small producer's oil and gas properties (i.e., not including percentage depletion on domestic regulated natural gas, etc. – see below) may not exceed 65% of the individual's taxable income; however, for this purpose, taxable income is calculated without regard to (1) certain depletion deductions, (2) any net operating loss carryback, and (3) any capital loss carryback. If this 65% limitation acts to disallow a portion of the percentage depletion deduction, the disallowed amount is allocated among the producing properties in proportion to the percentage depletion otherwise allowable (but for the 65% limitation), and the reduced percentage depletion deduction is compared to the cost depletion allowance on a property-by-property basis to finally determine whether cost or percentage depletion is greater (for each property). Any amount disallowed by reason of the 65% limitation may be carried forward to the following year in which it again will be subject to the 65% limitation.[7] An electing large partnership (see Q 1191) calculates its percentage depletion without regard to the 65% of taxable income limitation.[8]

1. Rev. Rul. 92-25, 1992-1 CB 196.
2. IRC Sec. 613A(c)(7).
3. IRC Sec. 613A(c)(6)(C).
4. Notice 2006-61, 2006-29 IRB 85.
5. IRC Sec. 613A(c)(6)(H).
6. IRC Sec. 613A(c)(6)(D).
7. IRC Sec. 613A(d)(1); Treas. Reg. §1.613A-4.
8. IRC Sec. 776(a)(2).

Regulated Natural Gas and Natural Gas Sold Under Fixed Contract

The applicable percentage in the case of a depletable property that qualifies as "regulated natural gas" or "domestic gas sold under fixed contract" (see Q 1256) is 22%.[1] Thus, 22% of the "gross income" received from the property is the amount allowable as percentage depletion.[2] Remember, however, that the amount which must be deducted as the depletion allowance on a specific property is the *greater of* the percentage depletion or cost depletion (see Q 1255).[3]

Natural Gas from Geopressured Brine

In the case of "natural gas from geopressured brine" (see Q 1256), the applicable percentage rate is 10%.[4]

1259. Is percentage depletion available with respect to advance royalties or lease bonuses?

No. Percentage depletion is not available with respect to advance royalties or lease bonuses.[5] Prior to TRA '86, gross income received in the form of advance royalties or lease bonuses was eligible for percentage depletion by a "small producer" (see Q 1258) even though no oil or natural gas had as yet been extracted from the ground.[6] According-ing to the Service, however, this depletion deduction had to be taken in the year in which the lease bonus or advanced royalty payment was includable in the gross income of the taxpayer.[7]

If the economic interest in the property expires, terminates, or is abandoned be-fore income has been derived from production (in the case of a lease bonus), or before the royalty has been recouped from production (in the case of an advanced royalty), the taxpayer is required to adjust his capital account by restoring any excess depletion deduction taken under the *Engle* rule and to include the excess in income in the year the expiration, termination, or abandonment occurs.[8]

1260. Does depletion affect a limited partner's tax basis in his partnership interest?

Yes, in two ways. First, a limited partner's tax basis in his partnership interest is *increased* by the excess of the deductions for depletion over the basis of the property subject to depletion. (This can occur only when percentage depletion is taken.)[9] How-ever, Treasury Regulation Section 1.705-1(a)(2) provides that the previous rule does not apply in the case of oil and gas property the basis of which is allocated to and computed separately by the partners of the partnership owning such property under IRC Section 613A(c)(7)(D). See Q 1254. Second, his tax basis in his partnership interest is *reduced* (but not below zero) by the amount of his allowable depletion deductions for each tax

---

1. IRC Sec. 613A(b)(1).
2. IRC Sec. 613(a).
3. IRC Sec. 613(a).
4. IRC Sec. 613A(b)(2).
5. IRC Sec. 613A(d)(5).
6. *Comm. v. Engle*, 84-1 USTC ¶9134 (U.S. 1984).
7. Treas. Reg. §1.613A-3(j)(2).
8. Treas. Regs. §§1.612-3(a)(2), 1.612-3(b)(2).
9. IRC Sec. 705(a)(1)(C); Treas. Reg. §1.705-1(a)(2).

year.[1] The basis is not reduced due to depletion deductions calculated at the electing large partnership level (see Q 1191).[2]

1261. How is gain from the disposition of an interest in an oil or natural gas property treated if depletion deductions have been taken?

Gain from the disposition of an interest in an oil or natural gas property is treated as ordinary income ("recaptured") to the extent that depletion deductions reduced the adjusted basis of the oil and natural gas property.[3] Taxation of the recaptured amount may be deferred through use of an installment sale. However, income (other than interest) from an installment sale of an oil or natural gas property is treated as recaptured IRC Section 1254 gain until all such gain is reported, and any remaining income is then treated as other than IRC Section 1254 gain.[4]

ENHANCED OIL RECOVERY CREDIT

1262. What is the enhanced oil recovery credit?

The enhanced oil recovery credit is a credit equal to 15% of a taxpayer's qualified enhanced oil recovery costs in connection with certain certified enhanced oil recovery projects (generally referred to as tertiary recovery projects).[5]

The credit is generally available for projects utilizing one or more qualified tertiary recovery methods located in the United States and begun after December 31, 1990.[6] Qualified enhanced oil recovery costs include amounts paid or incurred for tangible depreciable (or amortizable) property, intangible drilling and development costs, and qualified tertiary injectant costs.[7] Costs paid for acquisition of an existing qualified enhanced oil recovery project are not eligible for the credit.[8]

The credit is phased out as the "reference price" for crude oil (the estimated average annual wellhead price per barrel for domestic crude oil, determined under IRC Section 45K(d)(2)(C)), exceeds $28 (adjusted by an inflation adjustment factor for taxable years beginning after 1991). The phaseout is equal to an amount that bears the same ratio to the amount of the credit as the amount by which the reference price for the calendar year preceding the calendar year in which the taxable year begins exceeds $28 (as adjusted for inflation) bears to $6.[9] Because of the reference price and inflation adjustment factor, the credit was phased out completely in 2006.[10]

> *Example.* In 1993, F, the owner of an operating mineral interest in a property, incurs $100 of qualified enhanced oil recovery costs. The 1992 reference price is $34, and the 1993 inflation adjustment factor is 1.10. F's credit in 1993 determined without regard to the phaseout for crude oil price increases is $15 ($100 × 15%). In determining F's credit, $30.80 (1.10 × $28) is substituted for $28, and the credit is reduced by $8 ($15 × ($34 - $30.80)/6). Accordingly, F's credit is $7.[11]

---

1. IRC Sec. 705(a)(3); Treas. Reg. §1.613A-3(e)(6)(ii).
2. IRC Sec. 776(a)(3).
3. IRC Sec. 1254.
4. Treas. Reg. §1.1254-1(d).
5. IRC Sec. 43.
6. IRC Sec. 43(c)(2).
7. IRC Sec. 43(c)(1).
8. Treas. Reg. §1.43-4(e)(2).
9. IRC Sec. 43(b).
10. Notice 2006-62, 2006-29 IRB 86.
11. Treas. Reg. §1.43-1(c)(3), Ex. 2.

Any deduction otherwise allowable for items such as tangible depreciable property and intangible drilling and development costs taken into account in computing the enhanced oil recovery credit must be reduced by the amount of enhanced oil recovery credit attributable to the expenditure. Also, any increase in basis attributable to qualified enhanced oil recovery costs is reduced by the amount of credit claimed.[1] Partners and S corporation shareholders must reduce the basis of their interest in a partnership or S corporation (but not below zero) to the extent any deduction is disallowed or any basis is reduced under the preceding rules in this paragraph.[2]

General Business Credit

The enhanced oil recovery credit is a component of the general business credit. The amount of the enhanced oil recovery credit is aggregated with other credits, including the low-income housing credit (see Q 1227) and the rehabilitation credit (see Q 1228).[3] The sum of these credits (the general business credit) may not exceed the excess (if any) of the taxpayer's net income tax over the *greater of*:

(1) the taxpayer's tentative minimum tax (as calculated without reduction for the alternative minimum tax foreign tax credit or the taxpayer's regular tax liability), *or*

(2) for most credits, 25 percent of the amount by which the taxpayer's net regular tax liability exceeds $25,000.[4]

"Net income tax" means the *sum of* the taxpayer's regular *and* alternative minimum tax liabilities, *reduced by* the sum of the nonrefundable personal credits, the foreign tax credit, certain energy credits, and the Puerto Rico economic activity credit. "Net regular tax liability" means the taxpayer's regular tax liability reduced by the sum of the nonrefundable personal credits, the foreign tax credit, certain energy credits, and the Puerto Rico economic activity credit.[5] For these purposes the taxpayer's regular tax liability does not include certain specified taxes, such as the alternative minimum tax and certain penalty taxes on premature distributions from qualified plans or ordinary annuity contracts.[6] See Q 1440 on the alternative minimum tax.

The $25,000 amount applies to the individual partners and not to the partnership. Similarly, the $25,000 amount applies to the S corporation shareholder and not to the S corporation. Estates, trusts, and controlled groups of corporations must apportion the $25,000 amount. For married taxpayers filing separately, $12,500 is substituted for $25,000, unless the spouse of the taxpayer has no general business credit for the year. REITs, RICs, and certain banking organizations apply a ratable share of the $25,000 amount.[7]

The amount of the general business credit that exceeds the above limitation (i.e., the unused general business credit) for any taxable year generally may be carried back to the preceding year and carried over to the succeeding 20 years.[8] (For credits arising in tax years beginning before 1998, credits may be carried back to the preceding three

---

1. IRC Sec. 43(d).
2. Treas. Reg. §1.43-1(f).
3. IRC Sec. 38(b).
4. IRC Sec. 38(c).
5. IRC Sec. 38(c)(1).
6. IRC Sec. 26(b).
7. IRC Sec. 38(c)(5).
8. IRC Sec. 39(a).

years and carried over to the succeeding 15 years.) However, there are limitations on certain carrybacks.[1]

Where a portion of the general business credit remains unused at the end of the carryover period, the taxpayer may deduct from adjusted gross income in the first taxable year following the last carryover year available the amount of the unused credit remaining in the case of the qualified business credits, including the enhanced oil recovery credit and the rehabilitation credit (see Q 1228), with respect to which a basis adjustment was required.[2] If a taxpayer dies or ceases to exist before the end of the carryover period, any such allowable deduction is taken in the taxable year in which death or cessation occurs.[3]

The order in which the various general business credits are treated as used, or carried back or forward, is determined by the order in which they are listed in IRC Section 38(b) at the end of the year in which the credits are used.[4]

The allowable general business credit that is attributable to a passive activity may offset tax liability attributable only to passive activities.[5] See Q 1275.

TAX PREFERENCES

1263. What items of tax preference (for purposes of the alternative minimum tax) are peculiar to an oil and gas program?

Two items that are peculiar to oil or gas investments and that may give rise to tax preferences for purposes of the alternative minimum tax are (1) intangible drilling and development costs and (2) percentage depletion.

Intangible drilling costs. The amount (if any) by which "excess intangible drilling costs" exceeds 65% of the limited partner's net income from oil and gas (determined without consideration of such "excess intangible drilling costs") for the tax year is a tax preference item for purposes of calculating the limited partner's alternative minimum tax for the year. "Excess intangible drilling costs" for a tax year is the amount by which the limited partner's allowable deduction for intangible drilling and development costs in the tax year on productive wells exceeds the amount that would have been deducted had the costs been capitalized by the partnership and the limited partner's allocated share amortized over a 120-month period or recovered through cost depletion (i.e., through a straight-line recovery method).[6]

However, only those intangible drilling and development costs (IDCs) that both the partnership and limited partner elect to expense (and deduct) may give rise to a tax preference amount. IDCs that the partnership elects to capitalize and IDCs that the limited partner elects to amortize over 60 months (see Q 1251) will not create tax preferences for purposes of calculating the limited partner's alternative minimum tax.[7]

---

1. IRC Sec. 39(d).
2. IRC Secs. 196(a), 196(c).
3. IRC Sec. 196(b).
4. IRC Sec. 38(d).
5. IRC Secs. 469(d)(2), 469(a).
6. IRC Sec. 57(a)(2).
7. IRC Secs. 57(a)(2), 59(e)(6).

Intangible drilling costs on nonproductive wells are never tax preference items.[1] A well is nonproductive if it was plugged and abandoned without ever having produced oil or natural gas in commercial quantities for any substantial period of time.[2] A well that is merely temporarily shut down is not "nonproductive" for this purpose.[3]

This preference does not apply in the case of taxpayers who are not "retailers" or "refiners" of crude oil or natural gas (see Q 1256). However, this exception is not available to the extent that it reduces the taxpayer's alternative minimum taxable income by more than 40% of the amount of the taxpayer's alternative minimum taxable income calculated without regard to the exception and the alternative tax net operating loss deduction.[4]

For treatment of electing large partnerships, see below.

Percentage Depletion. If a limited partner's deduction for depletion with respect to a specific oil or gas property is greater than his share of the adjusted tax basis of that property (determined at the end of the year and without regard to the depletion deduction for that year), the amount of the difference is a tax preference item for purposes of the partner's alternative minimum tax. This preference does not apply in the case of "independent producers and royalty owners" (see Q 1256).[5] For this purpose, adjusted basis includes intangible drilling and development costs but not unrecovered tangible (depreciable) drilling costs.[6] Thus, once a limited partner's adjusted tax basis in a property has been reduced to zero (on account of previous depletion deductions, etc.), any percentage depletion deductions with respect to the property will generally create a tax preference item.

Of course, as cost depletion may not be taken once a limited partner's adjusted tax basis in a property is reduced to zero, deductions for cost depletion can never result in a tax preference amount (see Q 1257).

Electing Large Partnerships

An electing large partnership generally calculates alternative minimum tax preferences (including those regarding excess IDCs and percentage depletion) at the partnership level. In the case of a limited partnership interest, these preferences are generally aggregated with other items of tax preference from passive loss limitation activities of the partnership and are considered one passive activity.[7] In the case of a general partnership interest, tax preferences allocable to passive loss limitation activities are generally taken into account separately to the extent necessary to comply with the passive loss rule.[8] However, in the case of a partner who is a disqualified person, items of tax preference from oil and gas property are treated under the regular partnership rules discussed above. A disqualified person is a retailer or refiner of crude oil or natural gas (see Q 1256) or any other person whose average daily production of domestic crude oil and natural

1. IRC Sec. 57(a)(2)(B).
2. S. Rep. No. 1236, 94th Cong., 2d Sess. 426 (1976), 1976-3 (Vol. 3) 807, 830.
3. Rev. Rul. 84-128, 1984-2 CB 15 (as modified by Ann. 84-127, 1984-53 IRB 27).
4. IRC Sec. 57(a)(2)(E).
5. IRC Sec. 57(a)(1).
6. *U.S. v. Hill*, 93-1 USTC ¶50,037 (U.S. 1993).
7. IRC Sec. 772(c)(2).
8. IRC Sec. 772(f).

gas exceeds 500 barrels.[1] See Q 1191 regarding electing large partnerships; see Q 1292 regarding the passive loss rule.

For an explanation of the alternative minimum tax, see Q 1440.

EQUIPMENT LEASING

GENERAL

1264. What is equipment leasing?

The equipment leasing business provides equipment to users who want the equipment but, for various reasons, prefer not to purchase it. Ordinarily, the user arranges with an equipment leasing company to have the leasing company buy the equipment from the manufacturer and lease it to the user. The leasing company obtains financing for its purchase and generally secures the loan with a lien against the equipment and an assignment of the flow of rental income to the lender to amortize the loan. The equipment leasing company then sells the equipment (subject to the lease to the user and subject to the rights of the lender) to a limited partnership, a grantor trust, or to individual investors.

In a highly leveraged program, the flow of rental income from the lease is generally used to meet debt service and there is nothing available for cash distributions. These programs anticipate that the debt will be paid off at the expiration of the initial user lease and that the property will have residual value that can be realized through further leasing of the equipment or on the sale of the property. Thus cash distributions are projected for later years. Less highly leveraged programs, or unleveraged programs, are designed to provide for cash distributions to the investors from the start.

1265. What is a "wrap lease"?

An equipment leasing company may enter into a "wrap lease." After entering into the basic arrangement between manufacturer and user and having arranged financing, the equipment leasing company sells the equipment (subject to the user lease and lender's rights) to an unrelated third party who in turn sells the equipment (still subject to the user lease and lender's rights) to a partnership or trust. The partnership or trust then *leases* the equipment (still subject to the user lease and lender's interest) back to the equipment leasing company. This second lease to the equipment leasing company is generally for a longer term than the leasing company's underlying lease to the user. This lease from the investors to the leasing company is termed a wrap lease. (In effect, the second, longer lease to the leasing company is wrapped around the original lease to the user.) In this arrangement, the leasing company both leases from the partnership, trust or directly from the investors and in turn leases to the user. (In other words, the leasing company is a lessor with respect to the user and lessee with respect to the partnership or trust.)

1266. In general, what are the tax effects of equipment leasing programs?

---

1. IRC Sec. 776(b).

The primary tax benefit of equipment leasing programs is tax deferral. Deductions for depreciation, interest, and expenses offset rental income from the program and, depending on the amount of deductions, may offset income from other sources. Because an equipment leasing program will generally be a passive activity, such excess deductions (losses) may normally offset only other passive income of the taxpayer. (See Q 1275.)

Depreciation and interest deductions will decline. Consequently, while there may be tax losses in early years that offset income from sources other than the program, in later years the investor will recognize taxable income that may exceed substantially cash available from the program ("phantom income"). The carryover of disallowed passive losses from earlier years may reduce or even eliminate the phantom income in later years.

Generally, limited partnerships and S corporations act as flow-through entities, and partners and shareholders report their share of the entity's income, deductions, and credits on their own tax returns (see Q 1190). (Electing large partnerships have somewhat different flow-through rules than regular partnerships (see Q 1191).) However, if a publicly traded partnership is taxed as a corporation, the income, deductions, and credits are reported by the partnership and do not flow-through to the partners. Electing 1987 partnerships are subject to both an entity level tax and the flow-through rules. In general, investment in a publicly traded partnership taxed as a corporation will be taxed as an investment in a corporation. See Q 1189 for the treatment of publicly traded partnerships.

1267. Will an equipment leasing arrangement be treated as a lease or a sale?

It is essential that the leasing arrangement be treated, for tax purposes, as a lease rather than a financing arrangement for a sale (or conditional sale) of the equipment, in order for the investor, or partnership, or S corporation to be considered owner of the equipment and eligible to deduct depreciation and other expenses, as well as to claim the investment tax credit, if available. The courts have used various tests that look at facts and circumstances to determine whether the arrangement is a lease or sale. The IRS has published some guidelines as to what it looks for when determining whether a transaction constitutes a lease. The courts have indicated that something less than the guidelines may be acceptable but have provided little guidance as to what is acceptable.

IRS Guidelines

According to the IRS guidelines, the intent of the parties as to the nature of the arrangement is to be determined by examining the agreement in "light of the facts and circumstances existing at the time the agreement was executed."[1] Some factors indicating a conditional sale include:

(1) rentals for a short period of time relative to the life of the equipment, during which time the rent covers the normal purchase price plus interest;

(2) passage of title to the lessee after the payment of a stated amount of rentals;

(3) passage of title to the lessee after a payment at the termination of the agreement which, when added to rental payments, approximates the normal purchase price plus interest;

---

1. Rev. Rul. 55-540, 1955-2 CB 39.

(4) payment of substantial rent over a short period of time relative to the life of the equipment, followed by payment of insignificant rent for use of the equipment over the balance of the useful life;

(5) acquisition of equity by the lessee through "rental" payments;

(6) rental payments that exceed the current fair rental value;

(7) a purchase option that is nominal relative to the value of the property at the time when it may be exercised, as viewed from the time of entering into the agreement;

(8) a purchase option that is nominal when compared to the total payments to be made; and

(9) a portion of the periodic payments that is interest or equivalent to interest.

If even stricter requirements are met, the lessor in a leveraged lease transaction (other than for "limited use" property) can obtain from the IRS an advance ruling recognizing the lease as such unless all the facts and circumstances indicate a contrary intent by the parties. These requirements do not define whether a transaction is a lease or not for income tax purposes, and are not intended to be used for audit purposes. If these requirements are not met, the IRS will consider ruling in appropriate cases on the basis of the facts and circumstances.[1] The requirements are:

(1) A minimum, unconditional, at risk investment must be made by the lessor. At the beginning of and during the term of the lease, this investment must be equal to at least 20% of the cost of the property. The lease term includes all renewal or extension periods except for a renewal or extension at the option of the lessee that is for a fair rental value at the time of renewal or extension.

(2) The lessor must also maintain a minimum unconditional at risk investment at the end of the lease term. This is measured in two ways. First, a reasonable estimate of what will be the fair market value of the property at the end of the lease term must be equal to at least 20% of the cost of the property. Additionally, the remaining useful life of the property at the end of the lease term must be the greater of one year or 20% of the originally estimated useful life. Fair market value must be determined without including adjustments for inflation or deflation, and after subtracting from the fair market value the cost to the lessor for removal and delivery of the property to the lessor at the end of the lease term.

(3) Purchase and sale rights to the property must be restricted to some extent. A member of the "lessee group" (the lessee and others related to the lessee) must have no option to purchase the property at a price that is lower than fair market value at the time the option is exercised. A lessor may not have, at the time the property is first placed in use, a contractual right to require any person to purchase the property. The lessor must also state that he has no intention to acquire such a right. A subsequent acquisition of such a right could require a redetermination of lease characterization. A right to abandon the property to another person is treated as the right to require that person to purchase the property.

---

1.   Rev. Proc. 2001-28, 2001-1 CB 1156.

(4) A member of the lessee group may not furnish any part of the cost of the property or the cost of improvements, modifications or additions to the property ("improvements") with certain exceptions:

(a) A member of the lessee group may pay the cost of an improvement that is owned by the lessee if it is readily removable without causing material damage to the leased property ("severable improvement"). The improvement may not be subject to a contract or option for purchase or sale between the lessor and the lessee at other than fair market value as determined at the time of sale. The improvement must not be necessary to make the property complete for its intended use at the beginning of the lease, unless it is of a kind customarily furnished by lessees of property of the kind leased. For example, a vessel would not be considered complete without a boiler, but would be considered complete without ancillary items such as radar, lines, or readily removable fittings.

(b) A member of lessee group may pay the cost of an improvement that is not readily removable without causing material damage to the property ("nonseverable improvement") only if certain conditions are met:

(i)   The improvement must not be necessary to make the property complete for its intended use by the lessee.

(ii)   A member of the lessee group may not be compensated directly or indirectly for his interest in the improvement. For example, a lessor must not be required to purchase the improvement or to reimburse a member of the lessee group for the improvement; option prices or renewal rental rates must not be adjusted to reflect the improvement; and the lessor must not be required to share with a member of the lessee group proceeds from sale or lease of the property to a third party.

(iii)   The improvement must not cause the property to become limited use property (see heading "Limited Use Property," below).

(iv)   Unless the improvement is furnished to comply with health, safety or environmental standards of a government, it must not increase the productivity or capacity of the property to more than 125% over that when first placed in service, nor "modify the leased property for a materially different use."

(v)   A de minimis rule exists exempting certain improvements totaling not in excess of 10% of the cost of the property. This is calculated with an adjustment for inflation.

(c) Maintenance and repairs required under the lease will not be treated as an improvement furnished by a member of the lessee group.

(d) The lease may provide adjustment for cost overruns.

(5) A member of the lessee group may not lend a lessor funds to acquire the property, nor may he guarantee a lessor's indebtedness incurred in connection with the acquisition of the property. An exception applies to guarantees by a member of the lessee group of

the lessee's obligation to pay rent, to maintain property, to pay insurance premiums or similar obligations of a net lease.

(6) A lessor must demonstrate that it expects to profit from the lease, apart from tax benefits. This must be shown by an overall profit and a positive cash flow. To show an overall profit, rental payments from the property plus the residual investment in the property must exceed the sum of the lessor's disbursements in connection with the property and the lessor's equity investment in the property. Direct costs of financing the equity investment are included in the equity investment. To show positive cash flow, the rental payments from the property over the lease term must exceed by a reasonable amount the disbursements in connection with the property.

The requirements set out in Revenue Procedure 2001-28 were effective May 7, 2001. Prior to May 7, 2001, the requirements for advanced rulings were governed by Revenue Procedure 75-21,[1] whose requirements were similar to those in Revenue Procedure 2001-28.

Limited Use Property

The IRS will not issue rulings concerning whether transactions are leases when the property is limited use property. Limited use property is property that is not expected to have any use to the lessor at the end of the lease term except through continued leasing or sale to a member of the lessee group. The reason given by the Service is that the lessee group will enjoy all the rights of use or ownership for substantially all of the property's useful life.[2]

Court Decisions

The courts have used various tests that look at facts and circumstances to determine whether the arrangement is truly a lease. In general, the tests examine whether the lessor has anything to lose (at risk) at the beginning, during, and at the end of the lease term; whether the lessee will acquire an equity in the property through his rental payments; whether the lessee will feel compelled to exercise an option to purchase the property; whether the lessor can make an economic profit; and whether the lessor is guaranteed a return of his investment. The tests have been variously described: whether there is a "genuine multiple-party transaction with economic substance which is compelled or encouraged by business or regulatory realities, is imbued with tax-independent considerations, and is not shaped solely by tax-avoidance features";[3] totality of facts and circumstances (*Belz Investment Co. v. Comm.*, 72 TC 1209 (1979), aff'd 81-2 USTC ¶9734 (6th Cir. 1981)); whether lessor has an equity in property which he can prudently abandon;[4] "prudent abandonment" test not to be used where lessor paid fair market value for equipment;[5] provisions of lease not viewed independently, does lessor bear benefits and burdens of lease;[6] whether transaction is a sham.[7] An economic analysis of the transaction is often used.[8] A 1986 Tax Court case raised questions as to whether

1. 1975-1 CB 715.
2. Rev. Proc. 2001-28, 2001-1 CB 1156.
3. *Frank Lyon Co. v. U.S.*, 78-1 USTC ¶9370 (U.S. 1978).
4. *Est. of Franklin v. Comm.*, 76-2 USTC ¶9773 (9th Cir. 1976); *Hilton v. Comm.*, 82-1 USTC ¶9263 (9th Cir. 1982); *Rice's Toyota World, Inc. v. Comm.*, 85-1 USTC ¶9123 (4th Cir. 1985).
5. *Est. of Thomas*, 84 TC 412 (1985).
6. *Sun Oil Co. v. Comm.*, 77-2 USTC ¶9641 (3rd Cir. 1977).
7. *Rice's Toyota World, Inc. v. Comm.*, above.
8. *Hilton v. Comm.*, above; *Rice's Toyota World, Inc. v. Comm.*, above.

the investor in a leveraged equipment leasing program can assume the present burdens and benefits necessary for treatment as the owner of equipment which is purchased with nonrecourse debt to be serviced only through rental payments and the equipment is leased under a net lease.[1]

Because the courts have looked at the totality of facts and circumstances, the courts have provided little guidance as to what is acceptable. They indicate that something less than the IRS guidelines is acceptable. A well structured lease meeting the spirit of the guidelines was treated as a lease in *Estate of Thomas*, above, even though the lessor maintained less than the 20% equity the IRS requires for an advance ruling under Revenue Procedure 2001-28, above (requirement one). Treatment as a lease has been allowed for leases with purchase options permitting the lessee to purchase property for as little as 10% of the cost of the property.[2] This would allow a minimum unconditional at risk investment of 10% at the end of the lease term, which is substantially less than the 20% the IRS requires for an advance ruling under Revenue Procedure 2001-28, above (requirement two).

A lessee may have no option to purchase property at a price that is lower than fair market value at the time the option is exercised under requirement three of Revenue Procedure 2001-28 above. However, a fixed price option allowing the lessee to purchase the equipment at fair market value as determined at the lease commencement was permitted in *Lockhart Leasing Co. v. U.S.*[3] Other cases have discussed whether the exercise of an option by a lessee to purchase property was a foregone conclusion,[4] whether it would be imprudent for a lessee to abandon property subject to an option to purchase,[5] and whether there would be an obligation on a lessee to exercise an option to purchase property "by dint of economics".[6] An option to buy leased equipment that is certain to be exercised (e.g., at a nominal price) will defeat lease characterization.[7] An option with a nominal renewal rate is likewise certain to be exercised.[8]

A profit test is required under Revenue Procedure 2001-28, above. However, at least one court has held that no minimum rate of return should be required. "Taxpayers are allowed to make speculative investments without forfeiting the normal tax applications to their actions."[9] But there must be a realistic opportunity of economic profit.[10]

Motor Vehicle Operating Leases–Terminal Rental Adjustment Clause

Terminal rental adjustment clauses will be disregarded for purposes of lease characterization in the case of a qualified motor vehicle operating agreement.[11] A terminal rental adjustment clause is a provision that calls for an additional payment by the lessee if the lessor is not able to obtain a stated amount upon the sale or other disposition of the property at the end of the lease term or a payment by the lessor if the lessor is able to obtain more than the stated amount. Terminal rental adjustment clauses also include

---

1. *Coleman v. Comm.*, 87 TC 178 (1986).
2. *LTV Corp. v. Comm.*, 63 TC 39 (1974), *Northwest Acceptance Corp. v. Comm.*, 74-2 USTC ¶9619 (9th Cir. 1974).
3. 24 AFTR 2d ¶69-5224 (10th Cir. 1971).
4. *Belz Investment Co. v. Comm.*, 72 TC 1209 (1979).
5. *Martin v. Comm.*, 44 TC 731 (1965).
6. *M&W Gear Co. v. Comm.*, 54 TC 385 (1970).
7. *Oesterreich v. Comm.*, 226 F.2d 798 (9th Cir. 1955).
8. *Est. of Starr v. Comm.*, 274 F.2d 294 (9th Cir. 1959).
9. *Hilton v. Comm.*, above.
10. *Rice's Toyota World, Inc. v. Comm.*, above.
11. IRC Sec. 7701(h)(1).

provisions requiring a "lessee who is a dealer in motor vehicles to purchase the motor vehicles at a predetermined price and then resell such vehicle where such provision achieves substantially the same results."[1]

A qualified motor vehicle operating agreement is an agreement with respect to a motor vehicle (including a trailer) that meets the following requirements: (1) the sum of the lessor's recourse liability with regard to the lease and the net fair market value of property pledged as security for the leased property (other than property subject to the lease or financed directly or indirectly by property subject to the lease) must be greater than or equal to the amount borrowed to acquire the property subject to the lease, (2) the lessee must supply a sworn statement that the lessee intends for more than 50% of the use of the property to be in the trade or business of the lessee and that the lessee is aware he will not be treated as owner of the property for federal income tax purposes, and (3) the lessor must not have knowledge that the lessee's sworn statement is false.[2]

INVESTMENT TAX CREDIT

1268. What is the investment tax credit?

The investment tax credit is a direct credit against tax liability. Generally, the regular investment tax credit was repealed for property placed in service after 1985.[3] The basis of property with respect to which the investment tax credit was taken was subject to basis reduction.

For property placed in service after December 31, 1990 the term "investment credit" as used in the IRC, has a substantially different definition. Generally, the term refers to the sum of the rehabilitation credit (see Q 1228), the energy credit,[4] the qualifying advanced coal project credit (see IRC Sec. 48A), and the qualifying gasification project credit.[5] However, the term "investment tax credit"[6] is still applicable for purposes of any transition property for which the credit was available after 1985, or under certain other limited circumstances.[7]

Amount of Credit

The amount of the investment tax credit was generally 6% of the cost of 3-year property (that is, property depreciable over a 3-year period under the accelerated cost recovery system) and 10% for other than 3-year property placed in service during the taxable year.[8] (See Q 1424, as to recovery periods for property.) Different percentages applied to property depreciated under other systems of depreciation. However, the investment tax credit that was available under the transition rules for property placed in service after 1985 or as a carryforward of previously unused credits was generally reduced by 35% for any taxable year beginning after June 30, 1987.[9]

---

1. IRC Sec. 7701(h)(3).
2. IRC Sec. 7701(h)(2).
3. IRC Sec. 49(a) prior to amendment by OBRA '90.
4. See IRC Sec. 48.
5. See IRS Sec. 48B. IRC Sec. 46.
6. As defined in IRC Section 49(a) prior to OBRA '90 amendments.
7. OBRA '90, Sec. 11813(c)(2).
8. IRC Sec. 46, prior to amendment by OBRA '90.
9. IRC Sec. 49(c), prior to amendment by OBRA '90.

The extent to which the credit was available for certain nonrecourse property depended upon the amount for which the taxpayer was at risk with respect to such property.[1]

Noncorporate Lessors

Unless the leased equipment was manufactured or produced by the lessor, a non-corporate lessor (including an S corporation lessor for this purpose) must have met two tests to qualify for the investment tax credit.[2] The first test was that the term of the lease must have been less than 50% of the useful life of the property. The second test was that for the first 12 months following transfer of the equipment to the lessee all the ordinary and necessary expenses incurred by the lessor in carrying on its trade or business with respect to the equipment (other than rents and reimbursed amounts with respect to the equipment) must have exceeded 15% of the rental income produced by the leased equipment. Even if the noncorporate lessor did not qualify for the investment tax credit, it could have elected to pass the credit to the lessee.[3]

Property Used Outside United States

Property used predominantly outside the United States was generally not eligible for the investment tax credit.[4]

Tax-Exempt Use Property

Property that was leased to an organization (other than a farmers' cooperative) exempt from the normal income tax was eligible for the investment tax credit only if the property was used predominantly in an unrelated trade or business which was subject to income tax, or if the property was subject to a lease with a term of less than six months.[5]

Basis Reduction and Recapture

If the investment tax credit was taken with respect to leased equipment placed in service after 1985, the basis of the equipment was reduced by the amount of the credit taken.[6] Thus, the basis of the property for purposes of depreciation was reduced. However, if the lessor elected to pass the investment tax credit to the lessee, the lessor was not required to adjust his basis.[7]

An amount equal to some of the tax offset by the credit previously taken under the investment tax credit may have been "recaptured," if the equipment was disposed of within five years after it was placed in service.[8]

If the credit was recaptured upon a disposition of equipment for which there was a basis reduction, the basis of the equipment for purposes of determining gain or loss was increased immediately prior to disposition by the recapture amount.[9]

---

1. See IRC Sec. 49(a).
2. IRC Sec. 50(d)(1).
3. IRC Sec. 50(d)(5).
4. IRC Sec. 50(b)(1).
5. IRC Sec. 50(b). *Xerox Corp. v. U.S.*, 81-2 USTC ¶9579 (Ct. Cl. 1981).
6. IRC Sec. 50(c)(1).
7. See IRC Sec. 50(d)(5).
8. IRC Sec. 50(a).
9. IRC Sec. 50(c)(2).

DEDUCTIONS

Depreciation

1269. Can the owner of leased equipment take depreciation deductions? How large may the first year deduction be?

In determining the income or loss from the activity, an owner of leased equipment placed in service after 1980 may deduct its cost over a period of years–generally three, five, or seven years depending on the kind of equipment. (See Q 1267 concerning the ownership of leased property.) For property placed in service after 1986, the amount of the deduction is determined by applying a declining balance method to the basis of the property.[1] See Q 1424. Normally, the initial basis of the property is its cost. For property placed in service after 1981 and before 1987, the amount of the deduction is a percentage of the "unadjusted basis," generally, the cost of the property.[2] For an election to expense a portion of the costs of acquiring equipment, see below.

Cost includes the principal amount of debt obligations, whether recourse or not.[3] However, the debt must be bona fide and is not included in basis to the extent the purchase price exceeds the fair market value of the property.[4] Basis for depreciation must be reduced by the portion of the basis that the taxpayer may have elected to treat as an expense (see below). The basis is further reduced by the basis adjustment attributable to the investment tax credit. See Q 1268. The basis for depreciation under the declining balance method is calculated each year as reduced by depreciation deductions allowable in previous years, while the unadjusted basis is generally determined in the first year that a property is placed in service and is not reduced by depreciation deductions.

Depreciation is limited in the year in which equipment is placed in service to the portion of the year in which the equipment is considered to be held under the following *conventions*. Equipment is generally treated as placed in service on the midpoint of the year in which placed in service. However, where 40% of depreciable property, other than residential rental property and nonresidential real property, is placed in service during the last three months of the year, equipment placed in service during any quarter of such year is treated as placed in service on the midpoint of such quarter. Property placed in service and disposed of in the same year is not taken into account under the 40% test and the mid-quarter convention.[5] The IRS has provided some relief from the mid-quarter convention if a taxpayer's third or fourth quarter included September 11, 2001.[6]

The mid-quarter 40% test is made without regard to the length of the taxable year. Thus, if property (with exceptions, as noted in the preceding paragraph) is placed in service in a taxable year of three months or less, the mid-quarter convention applies regardless of when the property was placed in service (i.e., 100% of property has been placed in service in the last three months).[7]

---

1. IRC Sec. 168(b).
2. IRC Sec. 168(d), as in effect before the amendments made by TRA '86.
3. *Crane v. Comm.*, 331 U.S. 1 (1947).
4. Rev. Rul. 69-77, 1969-1 CB 59; *Est. of Franklin v. Comm.*, 76-2 USTC ¶9773 (9th Cir. 1976); *Odend'hal v. Comm.*, 84-2 USTC ¶9963 (4th Cir. 1984); see also *Prussin v. Comm.*, 88-2 USTC ¶9601 (3d Cir. 1988), nonacq. AOD 1991-09.
5. IRC Sec. 168(d).
6. Notice 2001-74, 2001-2 CB 551.
7. Rev. Proc. 89-15, 1989-1 CB 816.

In the case of a short taxable year (i.e., a taxable year that is less than 12 months), the recovery allowance for equipment is determined by multiplying the deduction that would have been allowable if the recovery year were not a short taxable year by a fraction, the numerator of which equals the number of months in the short taxable year and the denominator of which is 12.[1] Proposed regulations provided under IRC Section 168(f)(5) (as in effect prior to TRA '86) that a taxable year of a person placing property in service did not include any month prior to the month in which the person began engaging in a trade or business or holding recovery property for the production of income.[2] Presumably, this principle would continue to apply after TRA '86.

A partner who purchases an interest in a partnership after it has commenced business can deduct depreciation attributable only to the period during which he owns his partnership interest.[3]

In the first year of investment in a partnership, a partner's depreciation deduction is generally prorated because of (1) the partnership's short taxable year and (2) the proration of a partner's interest if he purchases an interest after the partnership commences business. As a result, an investor purchasing a partnership interest late in the year will find his first year depreciation deduction substantially limited.

The inability of a partner to take a full first year depreciation deduction if he invests late in the year has created considerable interest in forming equipment leasing programs as grantor trusts. Since for tax purposes the investor in a grantor trust is generally treated as the owner of his proportionate share of the property contained in the trust (under IRC Sections 671 through 679), it is reasoned that the taxable year of each investor is used to determine whether he can take a full year depreciation deduction on his proportionate share. The taxable year of the investor, for depreciation purposes, does not begin prior to the month the investor begins engaging in a trade or business or holding depreciable or recovery property for the production of income.[4] If the investor engages in such activities for the full year, he is entitled to a full first year depreciation deduction (subject to the conventions discussed above). Otherwise, the investor is limited by a short taxable year and corresponding proration of the first year depreciation deduction. However, if the investor engages in a small amount of such activities prior to investment in the program with the purpose of obtaining disproportionately large depreciation deductions, his taxable year (for purposes of the depreciation deduction) does not begin prior to his investment in the program.[5]

S corporations are treated like partnerships for purposes of determining the first year depreciation deduction. The first year depreciation deduction is pro-rated over the year and the deduction is taken only for depreciation allocable to the part of the year the S corporation has been in business or that a shareholder owns his interest. Ownership through a cotenancy or individual ownership is treated like a grantor trust for this purpose. A full first year depreciation deduction (subject to the conventions discussed above) is available to an investor who has throughout the year engaged in a trade or business or held depreciable or recovery property for the production of income.

---

1. Rev. Proc. 89-15, 1989-1 CB 816.
2. Prop. Treas. Reg. §1.168-2(f)(4).
3. IRC Sec. 706(d).
4. Prop. Treas. Reg. §1.168-2(f)(4) (see above).
5. Prop. Treas. Reg. §1.168-2(f)(4) (see above).

Election to Expense

A limited amount of the cost to acquire equipment can be expensed in the year when the equipment is first placed in service.[1] In the case of partnerships and S corporations, the election to expense a portion of capital costs is made at the partnership or S corporation level.[2] The deduction can apply to several pieces of property used in the active conduct of the trade or business, but the aggregate cost deductible for 2007 cannot exceed $112,000 (as indexed).[3] The $112,000 amount is reduced by one dollar for each dollar of such investment above $450,000 (as indexed).[4] After 2009, the $112,000 amount reverts back to $25,000, and the $450,000 amount reverts back to $200,000.

The amount expensed is limited to the aggregate amount of taxable income derived from the active conduct of any trade or business of the taxpayer. An amount that is not deductible because it exceeds the aggregate income from any trade or business may be carried over and taken in a subsequent year. The amount carried over that may be taken in a subsequent year is the lesser of (1) the amounts disallowed because of the taxable income limitation in all prior taxable years (reduced by any carryover deductions in previous taxable years); or (2) the amount of unused expense allowance for such year. The amount of unused expense allowance is the excess of (1) the maximum cost of property that may be expensed taking into account the dollar and income limitations; over (2) the amount the taxpayer elects to expense.[5] Married individuals filing separately are treated as one taxpayer for purposes of determining the amount that may be expensed and the total amount of investment in such property.[6]

The dollar limit applies to partnerships and S corporations and to their partners and shareholders (to the extent the deduction is allowed – see IRC Sec. 179(d)(8)). A partner or S corporation shareholder will reduce his basis in the partnership or S corporation to reflect his share of the cost of property for which an election to expense has been made whether or not such amount is subject to limitation at either the entity or partner/shareholder level.[7] Also, the partnership or S corporation will reduce its basis in the property by the amount of the deduction allocable to each partner or shareholder without regard to whether such individuals can use all of the deduction allocated to them.[8] Recapture provisions apply if the property ceases to be used predominantly in a trade or business before the end of the property's recovery period.[9] Also, amounts expensed under such an election are treated as depreciation deductions for purpose of recapture on sale or disposition (see Q 1277).

1270. Is property leased to governments and other tax-exempt entities eligible for accelerated cost recovery?

Property leased to certain tax-exempt entities (tax-exempt use property) may not, in general, use the normal recovery periods and percentages.[10]

---

1. IRC Sec. 179.
2. Treas. Reg. §1.179-1(h)(1).
3. IRC Sec. 179(b)(1); Rev. Proc. 2006-53, 2006-48 IRB 996.
4. IRC Sec. 179(b)(2); Rev. Proc. 2006-53, 2006-48 IRB 996.
5. IRC Sec. 179(b)(3); Treas. Reg. §1.179-3.
6. IRC Sec. 179(b)(4).
7. Rev. Rul. 89-7, 1989-1 CB 178.
8. Treas. Reg. §1.179-1(f)(2).
9. IRC Sec. 179(d)(10); Treas. Reg. §1.179-1(e).
10. IRC Secs. 168(g)(1)(B), 168(h).

A tax-exempt entity is:

(1) the United States, any State or political subdivision thereof, or any agency or instrumentality of any of the above,

(2) an organization (other than a farmers' cooperative) that is exempt from normal income tax,

(3) any foreign person or entity, and

(4) certain Indian tribal governments.[1]

The deduction for tax-exempt use property is determined by using a straight line method over the recovery period. The recovery period is the greater of the present class life (if no class life–12 years) or 125% of the lease term.[2] Property is assigned to various class lives for purposes of depreciation in Rev. Proc. 87-56.[3] Options to renew and successive leases may be aggregated with the original lease term for this purpose.[4]

Property is not tax-exempt use property if the tax-exempt entity uses it predominantly in an unrelated trade or business that is subject to income tax.[5] Property is considered used predominantly in an unrelated trade or business subject to income tax if it is used in the unrelated trade or business more than 50% of the time it is used during a taxable year. If only a portion of the property is used in an unrelated trade or business, the remainder may be tax-exempt use property.[6] Property leased to a foreign person or entity is not considered tax-exempt use property if more than 50% of the foreign person or entity's gross income is subject to United States income tax.[7]

Property subject to a short-term lease is not treated as tax-exempt use property. A short-term lease is a lease that is for a term which is less than three years, and (if the leased property has a class life) less than the greater of 1 year or 30% of the property's class life.[8] The Internal Revenue Service may aggregate options to renew and successive leases with the original lease term for this purpose. The lease term is determined by the "realistic contemplation of the parties at the time the property is first put into service."[9]

Informal agreements to extend a lease term are included with the original lease term. Options to renew possessed by the lessor or lessee are included in the original lease term, whether exercised or not. Successive leases entered into at the same time concerning the same or substantially similar property may be treated as one lease. The leases will not be aggregated merely because the lessor and lessee entered into a new lease at fair market rental value at the end of the original lease term.[10]

For leases entered into after April 19, 1995, an additional time during which the lessee may not be the lessee will nevertheless be included in the lease term if the lessee

---

1. IRC Sec. 168(h)(2).
2. IRC Secs. 168(g)(2), 168(g)(3).
3. 1987-2 CB 674 (Rev. Proc. 83-35, 1983-1 CB 745, for property placed in service before 1987).
4. IRC Sec. 168(i)(3)(A).
5. IRC Sec. 168(h)(1)(D).
6. Temp. Treas. Reg. §1.168(j)-1T(A-8).
7. IRC Sec. 168(h)(2)(B).
8. IRC Sec. 168(h)(1)(C).
9. Temp. Treas. Reg. §1.168(j)-1T(A-17), adopting *Hokanson v. Comm.*, 84-1 USTC ¶9217 (9th Cir. 1984).
10. Temp. Treas. Reg. §1.168(j)-1T(A-17).

(or a related person) retains an obligation to pay rent or make a payment in the nature of rent with respect to such period. A payment in the nature of rent is a payment intended to substitute for rent or to pay or supplement the rental payments of another. For example, a payment in the nature of rent includes payments required to be made for such other period if (1) the leased property is not leased, (2) the leased property is leased for terms that do not meet certain conditions, or (3) there is a failure to pay rent. In addition, for leases entered into after April 25, 1996, if property is subject to one or more leases (including subleases) entered into as part of one transaction (or series of related transactions), the lease term includes all periods described in any of such leases.[1] No inference is intended with respect to leases entered into prior to such dates.[2]

For transfers made after April 19, 1995, if tax-exempt use property is transferred (directly or indirectly) in a like-kind exchange under IRC Section 1031 (see Q 1422) among related persons and a principle purpose of the transfer or any related transaction is to avoid or limit the application of the alternative depreciation system for tax-exempt use property, property received in exchange for tax-exempt use property (tainted property) must be depreciated under the alternative depreciation system for tax-exempt use property using the same methods and periods previously used for the transferred tax-exempt property. Generally, this rule applies to the extent the basis of the tainted property does not exceed the basis of the transferred tax-exempt use property.[3] No inference is intended with respect to transfers prior to such date.[4]

Deductions related to tax-exempt use property may be further limited to the amount of income from the property.[5]

1271. Is property used outside the United States eligible for accelerated cost recovery?

The normal recovery periods and methods may not be used for recovery property used predominantly outside the United States.[6] For property placed in service after 1986, a straight line method is used over the present class life of the property (12 years if no present class life).[7] See Q 1424. For property placed in service before 1987, a declining balance switching to a straight line method is used over the present class life of the property (12 years if no present class life), unless an election is made for recovery property to use a straight line method over a different recovery period. The recovery period elected for pre-1987 property used predominantly outside the United States may not be shorter than the present class life.[8] Property is assigned to various class lives for purposes of depreciation in Rev. Proc. 87-56.[9]

Property is considered used predominantly outside the United States if it is physically located outside the United States during more than 50% of the taxable year. If the property is placed in service after the start of the taxable year, the 50% determination is made for the period beginning when first placed in service and ending the last day

1. Treas. Reg. §1.168(i)-2.
2. TD 8667, 1996-1 CB 22.
3. Treas. Reg. §1.168(h)-1.
4. TD 8667, 1996-1 CB 22.
5. See IRC Sec. 470.
6. IRC Sec. 168(g)(1)(A).
7. IRC Sec. 168(g)(2).
8. IRC Sec. 168(f)(2), as in effect prior to amendment by TRA '86.
9. 1987-2 CB 674 (Rev. Proc. 83-35, 1983-1 CB 745, for property placed in service before 1987).

of the taxable year. This restriction applies whether the property is used predominantly outside the United States by the lessor or lessee. The determination is made with respect to the taxable year of the lessor.[1]

There are certain listed exceptions to the restriction on use of normal recovery periods and methods for property used predominantly outside the United States.[2] These include generally: aircraft, rolling stock, vessels, motor vehicles, and containers used partly in the United States for transportation or commerce; property used predominantly in certain possessions of the United States; certain U.S. communication satellites; submarine cable systems linking the United States and other countries; certain property used for exploring, developing, removing, or transporting resources from certain waters or land thereunder; and certain property used to generate energy for use in the United States. These may use normal periods and methods even if used outside the United States for more than 50% of the year.

Interest

1272. Can the owner of leased equipment deduct interest on amounts borrowed to purchase the property?

The owner of leased equipment may generally deduct each year amounts paid for interest on indebtedness incurred to purchase the equipment. The interest may be deducted only over the period to which a prepayment relates, not when prepaid.[3] However, the interest will generally be subject to the passive loss rule (see Q 1275).

Expenses

1273. What expenses can the owner of leased equipment deduct?

The owner of leased equipment may deduct each year "all the ordinary and necessary expenses paid or incurred during the taxable year in carrying on a trade or business…" and all ordinary and necessary expenses paid or incurred during the taxable year (1) for the production and collection of income; (2) for the management, conservation, or maintenance of property held for the production of income; or (3) in connection with the determination, collection, or refund of any tax.[4] However, such expenses will generally be subject to the passive loss rule (see Q 1275).

Routine repair and maintenance expenses are deductible in the year paid or incurred as business expenses or expenses for the production of income, but the cost of improvements must be capitalized (added to the owner's basis in the property) and recovered through cost recovery or depreciation deductions.[5] Repair expenses are those "which neither materially add to the value of the property nor appreciably prolong its life, but keep it in an ordinary, efficient operating condition…"[6] Capital improvements increase the value, prolong the life, or alter the use for which the property is suitable.[7]

---

1. Prop. Treas. Reg. §1.168-2(g)(5).
2. IRC Sec. 168(g)(4).
3. IRC Secs. 461(g)(1), 461(h).
4. IRC Secs. 162(a), 212.
5. IRC Sec. 263(a).
6. Treas. Reg. §1.162-4.
7. Treas. Reg. §1.263(a)-1(a), §1.263(a)-1(b); *Illinois Merchants Trust Co. v. Comm.*, 4 BTA 103 (1926).

Where equipment is leased on a "triple net lease" basis, the lessee pays insurance, taxes, and expenses necessary to maintain the property. Consequently, the lessor will have none of those expenses to deduct.[1]

Start-up expenditures incurred prior to the start of a trade or business must normally be capitalized. However, a partnership, S corporation, grantor trust, or individual owner may elect to deduct (subject to the passive loss rule) up to $5,000 of start-up expenses (reduced by the amount that such expenses exceed $50,000). The remainder of the start-up expenses may be deducted over the 180-month period beginning with the month the trade or business begins. IRC Sec. 195. Syndication costs are not eligible for this amortization.[2] If the business or trade is disposed of before the end of the amortization period, the remaining deferred expenses may be deducted under the loss provisions of IRC Section 165.[3]

A partnership or corporation may elect to deduct (subject to the passive loss rule) up to $5,000 of start-up expenses (reduced by the amount that such expenses exceed $50,000). The remainder of the start-up expenses may be deducted over the 180-month period beginning with the month the corporation or partnership begins business.[4] Syndication costs must be capitalized.[5] If the partnership is liquidated before the end of the amortization period, the remaining deferred expenses are a partnership deduction in its final taxable year under the loss provisions of IRC Section 165.[6] Even if a partnership is abandoned before the end of the amortization period, the remaining deferred expenses are not deductible prior to liquidation.[7]

At Risk Limitation

·1274. Does the "at risk" limitation on losses apply to individual investors in an equipment leasing program? If so, what effect will it have?

Yes, the "at risk" rule will apply unless the investment is in an entity taxed as a C corporation, other than a closely-held corporation (generally, more than 50% control by 5 or fewer owners). The "at risk" rule will not apply to a closely-held corporation's equipment leasing activities if 50% or more of the corporation's gross receipts are attributable to equipment leasing.[8] See Q 1286.

In general, the "at risk" rule limits the deduction an investor may claim for his share of net losses generated by an equipment leasing program to the amount he has at risk in that program. The rule does not prohibit an investor from offsetting his share of the deductions generated by the program against the income he receives from that program. For a detailed explanation of the operation of the at risk limitation, see Q 1288 to Q 1291.

Put as simply as possible, an investor is initially "at risk" to the extent that he is not protected against the loss of money or other property he contributes to the program. For the specifics as to how an investor's "amount at risk" is calculated, see Q 1287.

1. See *James v. Comm.*, 90-1 USTC ¶50,185 (10th Cir. 1990).
2. Sen. Fin. Com. Rpt. on P.L. 96-605 (Misc. Rev. Act of 1980).
3. IRC Sec. 195(b)(2).
4. IRC Secs. 709, 248.
5. Rev. Rul. 85-32, 1985-1 CB 186; Treas. Reg. §1.248-1(b)(3)(i).
6. Treas. Reg. §1.709-1(b)(2).
7. Rev. Rul. 89-11, 1989-1 CB 179.
8. See IRC Secs. 465(a)(1), 465(c)(4).

Passive Loss Rule

1275. Are equipment leasing activities subject to the passive loss rule? If so, what is the effect to an investor in an equipment leasing program?

Yes, rental activities will generally be considered passive activities subject to the passive loss rule. Even if substantial services are provided, so that the equipment leasing activity is not considered a rental activity, the investor, himself, usually will not materially participate in the program. As a result, the investor in such a program will generally be subject to the passive loss rule. See Q 1292 to Q 1299. However, an entity taxed as a C corporation typically is not subject to the passive loss rule (see Q 1292).

In general, the rule limits the amount of the taxpayer's aggregate deductions from all passive activities to the amount of his aggregate income from all passive activities; passive credits can be taken against only tax attributable to passive activities. The rule is applied separately in the case of a publicly traded partnership; aggregation is permitted only within the partnership. The rule is intended to prevent taxpayers from offsetting salaries, interest, dividends, and other positive income with losses from passive activities. The benefit of the disallowed passive losses and credits is generally not lost, but rather is postponed until such time as the taxpayer has additional passive income or disposes of the activity. See Q 1292 to Q 1299.

DEFERRED RENT

1276. When is deferred rental income included in income?

Cash basis taxpayers generally include rental payments in income in the taxable year in which they are actually or constructively received. Leasing programs have sometimes used deferred or stepped rent schedules in order to delay receipt of income until later years of the program, with the effect of increasing loss deductions in early years. However, lessors under certain deferred or stepped payment lease agreements entered into after June 8, 1984 are required to report rental income as it accrues, as well as interest on rent accrued but unpaid.[1] Agreements are subject to this rule if at least one amount allocable to the use of the property during a calendar year is to be paid after the close of the following calendar year, or if there are increases in the amount to be paid as rent under the agreement. This accrual requirement does not apply if the aggregate value of the money and other property received and to be received for use of the property is $250,000 or less.[2] These rules are discussed in further detail in Q 1230.

DISPOSITION OF EQUIPMENT

1277. How is gain or loss on sale of leased equipment treated?

The amount realized on the sale or other disposition of property in excess of adjusted basis is gain; if the amount realized is less than adjusted basis, it is loss.[3] The basis of property is generally its cost reduced by the portion of cost which the taxpayer elects to treat as an expense (see Q 1269) and by the basis adjustment attributable to the investment tax credit (see Q 1268).[4] Also, the basis is reduced each year by the amount

1. IRC Sec. 467(a).
2. IRC Sec. 467(d).
3. IRC Sec. 1001.
4. IRC Secs. 1012, 1016(a).

of the depreciation taken so that the *adjusted* basis in the property reflects accumulated depreciation deductions. If depreciation is not deducted, the basis must nonetheless be reduced by the amount of depreciation allowable.[1] If the investment tax credit is recaptured in connection with property as to which a basis adjustment was required, then the basis is increased by such recaptured amount.[2]

Where leased equipment has been depreciated, gain on the sale of the property must be treated as ordinary income to the extent of all depreciation deductions allowed.[3] The gain in excess of the recaptured ordinary income is "IRC Section 1231" gain; loss is "IRC Section 1231" loss. See Q 1233 for an explanation of the treatment of IRC Section 1231 gains and losses. See Q 1408 if the equipment is sold on the installment method.

ALTERNATIVE MINIMUM TAX

1278. What items does an equipment leasing program generate which require that adjustments be made to or tax preferences added to alternative minimum taxable income?

The investor may have the following adjustments to alternative minimum taxable income (AMTI) or tax preferences in connection with investment in an equipment leasing program which passes losses and deductions through to the investor.

(1) Passive activity losses (determined by taking into account the adjustments to AMTI and tax preferences) are not allowed in calculating AMTI. There is no phase-in of the disallowance of passive activity losses as there is under the regular tax.[4]

(2) Generally, equipment placed in service after 1998 must be depreciated using a 150% declining balance method switching to the straight-line method at a time to maximize the deduction over the regular recovery periods. Equipment placed in service after 1986 and before 1999 must be depreciated using a 150% declining balance method switching to the straight-line method at a time to maximize the deduction over the following periods:[5]

tax-exempt use property subject to a lease	longer of 125% of lease term or period below
personal property with no class life	12 years
all other property	the class life
TRA '86 assigns certain property to recovery periods without regard to their class life, e.g., automobiles and light trucks.	

The adjusted basis of such property is determined using this method.[6]

For property placed in service after 1980 and before 1987, the amount by which the accelerated deduction allowable for the year exceeds the deduction which would

---

1. IRC Sec. 1016(a).
2. IRC Sec. 50(c)(2).
3. IRC Sec. 1245.
4. IRC Sec. 58(b).
5. IRC Sec. 56(a)(1)(A).
6. IRC Sec. 56(a)(6).

have been allowable for the year had the equipment been depreciated using a straight-line method and a half-year convention over the following recovery periods is a tax preference item.[1]

In the case of:	The recovery period is:
3-year property	5 years
5-year property	8 years
10-year property	15 years
15-year public utility property	22 years

If a recovery period which is longer than that indicated in the table above is used, because the recovery property is used outside the United States (see Q 1271) or an election of an alternative recovery period has been made (see Q 1424), no item of tax preference is created.[2]

For equipment placed in service before 1981, the excess of the allowable deduction over the straight-line method using the class life of the equipment is a tax preference item.

Property is assigned to various *class lives* in Rev. Proc. 87-56.[3] These class lives can also be found in IRS Publication 946.

CATTLE

CATTLE FEEDING

1279. What is a cattle feeding program? What is the tax effect of such programs?

Cattle feeding programs involve the purchase of immature cattle that are usually raised and fed under a contract with a feedlot that furnishes the feed and maintenance. The cattle are sold to a packing house when they reach the desired weight. Feeding programs typically last from four to nine months before the animals are marketable. The tax treatment of these programs, which are generally considered high-risk investments, was changed considerably by TRA '86, reducing their popularity to a great extent.

Generally, limited partnerships and S corporations act as flow-through entities, and partners and shareholders report their share of the entity's income, deductions, and credits on their own tax returns (see Q 1190). (Electing large partnerships have somewhat different flow-through rules than regular partnerships (see Q 1191).) However, if a publicly traded partnership is taxed as a corporation, the income, deductions, and credits are reported by the partnership and do not flow through to the partners. Electing 1987 partnerships are subject to both an entity level tax and the flow-through rules. In general, investment in a publicly traded partnership taxed as a corporation will be taxed as an investment in a corporation. See Q 1189 for the treatment of publicly traded partnerships.

---

1. IRC Sec. 57(a)(6).
2. IRC Sec. 57(a)(12), prior to amendment by TRA '86.
3. 1987-2 CB 674 (Rev. Proc. 83-35, 1983-1 CB 745, for property placed in service before 1987).

Expenses Added To Inventory Or Capitalized

In the case of most "tax shelters," certain corporations engaged in farming, and partnerships with such corporations as a partner, those expenses incurred in connection with producing cattle or attributable to cattle acquired for resale must be capitalized or added to the cost of inventory.[1] Generally, including such costs in inventory or capitalizing these costs prevents a current expense deduction and has the effect of reducing income or gain from the sale of the property. An exception applies to costs associated with inventory, so that costs may be expensed if the taxpayer's average annual gross receipts for the preceding three taxable years do not exceed $10,000,000 (as determined under certain aggregation rules).[2]

A "tax shelter" is (1) any enterprise, other than a C corporation, if at any time interests in the enterprise have been offered for sale in an offering required to be registered with any federal or state securities agency, (2) any farming enterprise other than a C corporation that allocates more than 35% of its losses during any period to investors who do not actively take part in the management of the operation, or (3) any enterprise a significant purpose of which is tax avoidance.[3]

The following types of corporations engaged in farming are exempted from the above capitalization rules (if not otherwise deemed to be "tax shelters"): (1) S corporations and (2) corporations meeting certain gross receipts tests. A corporation meets the gross receipts test if its annual gross receipts for each prior tax year (after 1975) do not exceed $1,000,000. A corporation controlled (as defined in the IRC) by one, two, or three families meets the gross receipts test if its annual gross receipts for each prior tax year (after 1985) do not exceed $25,000,000. For purposes of the gross receipts tests, all members of a controlled group of corporations are considered one corporation.[4]

So long as a partnership (provided it is not deemed to be a "tax shelter") does not have a non-exempt corporation as a partner, it will not be subject to the above capitalization rules.[5]

Other Expenses

Generally, corporations engaged in farming (other than those exempted from the capitalization rules, as described above), partnerships with a corporation as a partner, and "tax shelters" are required to use the accrual method of accounting.[6]

The accrual method of accounting precludes current deductions for amounts not yet economically incurred (i.e., it eliminates the overstating of present expenses). Thus, in the case of farming entities required to use the accrual method, the formerly common practice of accelerating deductions into the program's first taxable year is eliminated. This is accomplished by requiring that deductions may not be taken until (1) all events have occurred that establish that the expense has been incurred, and (2) the amount of the liability can be established with reasonable accuracy. No amount is considered to be "incurred" until "economic performance" occurs. For example, if a limited partnership that is treated as a "tax shelter" is obligated to pay for services or

---

1. IRC Sec. 263A(a).
2. IRC Sec. 263A(b)(2).
3. IRC Secs. 461(i)(3), 461(i)(4), 464(c), 6662(d)(2)(C)(ii).
4. IRC Secs. 263A(d)(1), 447(c), 447(d), 447(h).
5. IRC Sec. 263A(d)(1)(A).
6. IRC Secs. 447(a), 448(a).

property, economic performance takes place as the services or property are provided. Similarly, if it is required to pay for use of property, economic performance occurs as the taxpayer uses the property.[1]

Generally, a deduction by accrual basis taxpayers is allowed for certain "recurring items" in the tax year prior to the occurrence of economic performance if the amount and existence of the obligation has been established in the prior year, and economic performance occurs within the shorter of a reasonable period or 8½ months after the close of the taxable year.[2] However, "tax shelters" generally may not use this exception to the economic performance rule.[3]

A special rule applies to the deduction of expenses for feed and similar supplies by "tax shelters," corporations and partnerships required to use the accrual method. A deduction for the taxable year is limited to amounts of feed or supplies actually used or consumed during the taxable year (unless they are on hand at the end of the taxable year because of fire, storm, other casualty, or disease or drought).[4] In the case of cattle feeding programs, feed is a major item of expense.

In the case of taxpayers who are permitted to use the cash method, deductions for feed and supplies are also limited if they are not primarily engaged in farming and they have unconsumed farm supplies at the end of the tax year in excess of 50% of the deductible farming expenses for that year (other than the unconsumed farm supplies). The amount of unconsumed expenses in excess of 50% of deductible farm expenses (other than the unconsumed farm supplies) may not be taken until the taxable year the feed or supplies are used or consumed.[5]

Investors who do not materially participate in the management of a cattle feeding program may also have the deductibility of expenses limited by the effect of the "passive loss" rules, see Q 1292.

BREEDING CATTLE

Generally

1280. What is a cattle breeding program?

Cattle breeding is an intermediate to long-term investment (typically lasting at least five years) made with the primary objective of developing capital assets, (e.g., increasing the herd size). Receiving capital gain treatment upon sale of the herd is a significant objective of cattle breeding programs.

Traditional breeding programs involve the purchase of a herd of breeding cattle (either beef or dairy cattle) that is managed by a firm specializing in breeding. Male offspring (steer calves) are generally sold for ordinary income each year, but female calves (heifers) are usually kept (unless they are unsuitable) in order to expand the herd.

Embryo transplant technology has resulted in a form of breeding program called a "Super Cow" program. These ventures involve the purchase of several prize breeding

---

1. IRC Sec. 461(h).
2. IRC Sec. 461(h)(3).
3. IRC Sec. 461(i)(1).
4. IRC Sec. 464.
5. IRC Sec. 464(f).

cows (each may cost in excess of $150,000) along with a herd of "recipient" cows that have inferior bloodlines. The donor (or "super") cows are artificially inseminated and the resulting embryos are transplanted into the recipient cows. Donor cows are super-ovulated so that they produce more eggs for fertilization than they would normally. A donor cow can thus produce multiple offspring in one year rather than the one that would be produced naturally. Recipient cows usually have little value aside from the embryo they carry. Some programs lease recipient cows from another party until the resulting calves are weaned. Embryo transplant operations are much more expensive to manage than the traditional form of breeding program.

Many programs will use technology without purchasing super cows by combining direct breeding with artificial insemination and the purchase of superior embryos, often leasing recipient cows in order to decrease capital expenditures and increase deductions.

Breeding operations are usually carried on by limited partnerships, but S corporations, joint ventures and direct ownership are also used. Some super cow programs are formed as tenancies-in-common in which an individual investor owns an undivided fractional interest in one or several cows and the investor receives income or is allocated losses based on his fractional interest. Generally, limited partnerships and S corporations act as flow-through entities, and partners and shareholders report their share of the entity's income, deductions, and credits on their own tax returns (see Q 1190). (Electing large partnerships have somewhat different flow-through rules than regular partnerships (see Q 1191).) However, if a publicly traded partnership is taxed as a corporation, the income, deductions, and credits are reported by the partnership and do not flow through to the partners. Electing 1987 partnerships are subject to both an entity level tax and the flow-through rules. In general, investment in a publicly traded partnership taxed as a corporation will be taxed as an investment in a corporation. See Q 1189 for the treatment of publicly traded partnerships.

Deductions

1281. Are breeding cattle depreciable?

Yes. Amounts expended for the purchase of breeding cattle are capital expenditures for which depreciation deductions may be taken.[1] Because most investment entities involved in cattle breeding must capitalize the expenses of breeding and raising cattle (see Q 1282), the depreciation allowance is of significant importance. Accrual basis taxpayers may elect to inventory breeding cattle instead of capitalizing the purchase price and taking depreciation deductions.[2] See Q 1283.

Depreciation deductions cannot be taken for the period before property is first "placed in service," that is, placed in a condition or state of readiness for a specified function in a business or investment.[3] Thus, if the taxpayer acquires immature livestock not yet suitable for breeding, he may not begin to depreciate the cost until they reach maturity.[4]

---

1. Treas. Reg. §1.162-12(a).
2. Treas. Reg. §1.61-4(b).
3. Prop. Treas. Reg. §1.168-2(l)(2).
4. See Farmer's Tax Guide, IRS Pub. 225 (2006), p. 37.

The method of determining the amount of allowable depreciation deduction depends on when the property is placed in service. Cattle placed in service after 1986 are depreciated under a modified form of the Accelerated Cost Recovery System (ACRS).

The post-1986 ACRS deduction is determined by depreciating cattle (1) over a five or seven year period using the 150% declining balance method, changing to the straight line method for the taxable year for which the change in methods yields a larger allowance, or (2) over a five or seven year period using the straight line method. The same method and period must be used for all cattle placed in service during the same year.[1] The initial basis of the property is the basis upon acquisition (usually the cost of the property, see Q 1415), reduced by the amount, if any, elected for amortization or an IRC Section 179 deduction (see Q 1424). Basis is reduced each year by the amount of depreciation allowable (whether or not the deduction is actually taken).[2] Alternatively, depreciation can be calculated by multiplying the unadjusted basis of the property by depreciation rates contained in Rev. Proc. 87-57.[3]

Depreciation is limited in the years when cattle are acquired or disposed of. Cattle are treated as placed in service or disposed of on the midpoint of the year of acquisition or disposition and depreciation may be taken for the half year. However, if more than 40% of the aggregate value of depreciable property (other than residential rental property and nonresidential real property) placed in service for the year is placed in service during the last three months of the year, cattle placed in service during *any* quarter of a year are treated as placed in service on the midpoint of that quarter. Property placed in service and disposed of in the same year is not taken into account under the 40% test and the mid-quarter convention. IRC Sec. 168(d). The IRS has provided some relief from the mid-quarter convention if the taxpayer's third or fourth quarter included September 11, 2001.[4]

Recapture on Sale

On sale or disposition of cattle placed in service after 1980, amounts deducted for depreciation are recaptured as ordinary income, so that gain is ordinary income to the extent of depreciation taken.[5] Amounts expensed under the provisions of IRC Section 179 (discussed in Q 1282 and Q 1424) and the adjustments to basis that resulted from claiming the investment tax credit (see Q 1268) are treated as depreciation deductions.[6] See Q 1424 for a general explanation of depreciation.

1282. What costs of a breeding program must be capitalized? When may a deduction be taken for costs that are expensed?

Expenses Added To Inventory Or Capitalized

In the case of most "tax shelters," certain corporations engaged in farming, and partnerships with a corporation as a partner, those expenses incurred in connection with producing cattle or attributable to cattle acquired for resale must be capitalized or added to the cost of inventory.[7] Generally, including these costs in inventory or capitalizing

1. IRC Secs. 168(b), 168(c), 168(g); Rev. Proc. 87-56, 1987-2 CB 674.
2. IRC Secs. 1012, 1016(a).
3. 1987-2 CB 687.
4. Notice 2001-74, 2001-2 CB 551.
5. IRC Sec. 1245(a).
6. IRC Secs. 1245(a)(2)(c), 50(c)(4).
7. IRC Secs. 263A(a), 263A(d).

these costs prevents a current expense deduction and also has the effect of reducing income or gain from the sale of the property. Therefore, taxpayers affected by these rules would generally not be able to expense the costs of breeding or raising cattle.

Exceptions to certain of the uniform capitalization rules are available to the following entities that are engaged in farming: (1) a sole proprietorship; (2) a partnership that is not a "tax shelter" and that does not have a non-exempt corporation as a partner; (3) an S Corporation engaged in farming that is not deemed to be a "tax shelter;" and (4) any corporation engaged in farming that is not deemed to be a "tax shelter" and that meets certain gross receipts tests. A corporation meets the gross receipts test if its annual gross receipts for each prior tax year (after 1975) do not exceed $1,000,000. A corporation controlled (as defined in the IRC) by one, two, or three families meets the gross receipts test if its annual gross receipts for each prior tax year (after 1985) do not exceed $25,000,000. For purposes of the gross receipts tests, all members of a controlled group of corporations are considered one corporation.[1] The exceptions available to these taxpayers are as follows:

(a)   Any animal produced by the taxpayer that has a preproductive life of two years or less where costs are incurred by the taxpayer *before 1989*.[2] While "preproductive life" is not defined in the IRC, as described here, it appears to mean the period before which the animal is reasonably expected to be sold or disposed of.[3]

(b)   Any animal produced by the taxpayer without regard to the length of its preproductive life, where costs were incurred *after 1988*.[4]

A "tax shelter" is (1) any enterprise, other than a C corporation, if at any time interests in the enterprise have been offered for sale in an offering required to be registered with any federal or state securities agency, or (2) any farming enterprise other than a C corporation that allocates more than 35% of its losses during any period to investors who do not actively take part in the management of the operation, or (3) any enterprise a significant purpose of which is tax avoidance.[5]

For rules treating certain publicly traded partnerships as corporations, see Q 1189.

Other Expenses

Generally, corporations engaged in farming (other than those exempted from the capitalization rules, as described above), partnerships with a corporation as a partner, and "tax shelters" are required to use the accrual method of accounting.[6]

The accrual method of accounting precludes current deductions for amounts not yet economically incurred. Thus, in the case of farming entities required to use the accrual method, the practice of taking a deduction for expenses that are paid for but not yet needed, is eliminated. This is accomplished by requiring that deductions may

---

1. IRC Secs. 447(c), 447(d), 447(h).
2. IRC Sec. 263A(d)(1), prior to amendment by TAMRA '88.
3. See IRC Sec. 447(b), prior to amendments by TAMRA '88 and TRA '86.
4. IRC Sec. 263A(d)(1).
5. IRC Secs. 461(i)(3), 461(i)(4).
6. IRC Secs. 447(a), 448(a).

not be taken until (1) all events have occurred that establish that the expense has been incurred, and (2) the amount of the liability can be established with reasonable accuracy. No amount is considered to be "incurred" until "economic performance" occurs. For example, if a limited partnership that is treated as a "tax shelter" is obligated to pay for services or property, economic performance takes place as the services or property are provided. Similarly, if it is required to pay for use of property, economic performance occurs as the taxpayer uses the property.[1]

Generally, a deduction by accrual basis taxpayers is allowed for certain "recurring items" in the tax year prior to the occurrence of economic performance if the amount and existence of the obligation has been established in the prior year, and economic performance occurs within the shorter of a reasonable period or 8½ months after the close of the taxable year.[2] However, "tax shelters" generally may not use this exception to the economic performance rule.[3]

A special rule applies to the deduction of expenses for feed and similar supplies by "tax shelters," corporations, and partnerships required to use the accrual method. A deduction for the taxable year is limited to amounts of feed or supplies actually used or consumed during the taxable year (except for amounts on hand at the end of the year due to fire, storm, other casualty, or disease or drought).[4]

In the case of taxpayers who are permitted to use the cash method, deductions for feed and supplies are also limited if they are not primarily engaged in farming and they have unconsumed farm supplies at the end of the tax year in excess of 50% of the deductible farming expenses for that year (other than the unconsumed farm supplies). The amount of unconsumed expenses in excess of 50% of deductible farm expenses (other than the unconsumed farm supplies) may not be taken until the taxable year the feed or supplies are used or consumed.[5]

Investors who do not materially participate in the management of a cattle breeding program may also have the deductibility of expenses limited by the effect of the "passive loss" rules, see Q 1292.

For rules treating certain publicly traded partnerships as corporations, see Q 1189.

Election To Expense Or Capitalize Certain Expenses

A limited amount of the cost to acquire cattle (or other depreciable property) can be expensed in the year when the cattle (or property) is first placed in service (even by the tax shelters, corporations and partnerships required to capitalize other expenses).[6] In the case of partnerships and S corporations, the election to expense a portion of capital costs is made at the partnership or S corporation level.[7] The deduction can apply to several pieces of property used in the active conduct of the trade or business, but the aggregate cost deductible for 2007 cannot exceed $112,000 (as indexed).[8] The $112,000 amount

---

1. IRC Sec. 461(h).
2. IRC Sec. 461(h)(3).
3. IRC Sec. 461(i)(1).
4. IRC Sec. 464.
5. IRC Sec. 464(f).
6. IRC Sec. 179(a).
7. Treas. Reg. §1.179-1(h)(1).
8. IRC Sec. 179(b)(1); Rev. Proc. 2006-53, 2006-48 IRB 996.

is reduced by one dollar for each dollar of investment above $450,000 (as indexed).[1] The $112,000 and $450,000 amounts will revert to $25,000 and $200,000, respectively, after 2009. The amount expensed is limited to the aggregate amount of taxable income derived from the active conduct of any trade or business of the taxpayer. An amount that is not deductible because it exceeds the aggregate income from any trade or business may be carried over and taken in a subsequent year. The amount carried over that may be taken in a subsequent year is the lesser of (1) the amounts disallowed because of the taxable income limitation in all prior taxable years (reduced by any carryover deductions in previous taxable years); or (2) the amount of unused expense allowance for the year. The amount of unused expense allowance is the excess of (1) the maximum cost of property that may be expensed taking into account the dollar and income limitations; over (2) the amount the taxpayer elects to expense.[2]

Married individuals filing separately are treated as one taxpayer for purposes of determining the amount that may be expensed and the total amount of investment in the property.[3] The dollar limit applies to partnerships and S corporations and to each partner and shareholder.[4] A partner or S corporation shareholder will reduce his basis in the partnership or S corporation to reflect his share of the cost of property for which an election to expense has been made whether or not the amount is subject to limitation at either the entity or partner/shareholder level.[5] Also, the partnership or S corporation will reduce its basis by the amount of the deduction allocable to each partner or shareholder without regard to whether these individuals can use all of the deduction allocated to them.[6] Recapture provisions apply if the property ceases to be used primarily in a trade or business before the end of the property's recovery period. (For property placed in service before 1987, recapture is required only if the property was converted to nonbusiness use within two years after it was placed in service.)[7] Also, amounts expensed under an election are treated as depreciation deductions for purpose of recapture on sale or disposition (see Q 1283).

Sale Or Disposition Of Cattle

1283. How is gain taxed when breeding cattle are sold?

Gain from a sale or disposition of cattle depreciated under the ACRS method is generally recaptured as ordinary income to the extent of all depreciation deductions previously allowed. Amounts expensed under the provisions of IRC Section 179 (discussed in Q 1282 and Q 1424) and the adjustments to basis that resulted from claiming the investment tax credit (see Q 1268) are treated as depreciation deductions.[8] If there is a loss on sale of the property, no recapture is necessary.[9]

Gain (in excess of amounts recaptured) from sale or disposition of cattle held for breeding purposes (including cattle inventoried by certain accrual basis taxpayers), and which are held for 24 months or more from the date of acquisition, is "IRC Section

---

1. IRC Sec. 179(b)(2); Rev. Proc. 2006-53, 2006-48 IRB 996.
2. IRC Sec. 179(b)(3); Treas. Reg. §1.179-3.
3. IRC Sec. 179(b)(4).
4. IRC Sec. 179(d)(8).
5. Rev. Rul. 89-7, 1989-1 CB 178.
6. Treas. Reg. §1.179-1(f)(2).
7. IRC Sec. 179(d)(10); Treas. Reg. §1.179-1(e).
8. IRC Secs. 1245(a)(2)(c), 50(c)(4).
9. IRC Sec. 1245.

1231" gain, eligible for long-term capital gain treatment.[1] For this purpose, the holding period of an animal born into the herd begins at birth.[2] For a discussion of "IRC Section 1231" gain, see Q 1233. For the treatment of long-term capital gain, see Q 1420.

Gain from the sale of cattle held for sale in the ordinary course of business is ordinary income. Uncertainty often arises as to the treatment of cattle periodically culled from the herd because of their unsuitability for breeding. (However, annual disposition of steer calves and of animals clearly unsuitable for breeding from birth results in ordinary income since these animals are destined for sale.) Whether an animal is held for breeding is determined from all the facts and circumstances. Although the purpose for which an animal is held is ordinarily shown by its actual use, a breeding purpose may be present if an animal is disposed of within a reasonable time after its intended use is prevented or made undesirable by reason of accident, disease, drought, unfitness of the animal for breeding, or similar reasons. An animal is not deemed to be held for breeding merely because it is suitable or merely because it is held for sale to others as a breeding animal. Even if an animal has been bred, it may not be considered to be held for breeding if use of the animal for breeding is negligible or if the animal is bred in order to provide desirable characteristics.[3]

In order for a cash basis taxpayer to determine gain from the sale of cattle born into the herd, the gross sale price is reduced by any expenses of sale (such as sales commissions or freight or hauling from the farm to the commission company). Such animals have a zero basis if the costs of raising them were deducted while the animals were being raised. Gain or loss from the sale of purchased livestock is determined by subtracting the adjusted basis and the sale expenses from the gross sale price.[4]

Accrual basis partnerships, S corporations, corporations and individuals directly engaged in cattle breeding may either capitalize the cost of breeding cattle (and take deductions for depreciation) or value cattle according to an inventory method.[5] Gain from the sale of inventoried breeding cattle held for 24 months or more is eligible for capital gains treatment under IRC Section 1231.[6] Four inventory methods are available for livestock: the cost method, lower of cost or market method, unit-livestock-price method, or farm-price method.[7] (For more information about these methods of valuation, see IRS Publication 538 (Accounting Periods and Methods).) Gain is determined by subtracting the animal's last inventory value (used instead of basis) and sale expenses from the gross sale price.[8] The amount of gain received depends on the inventory method used, as a low valuation method will result in a higher amount of gain.

Alternative Minimum Tax

1284. What adjustments and tax preference items are generated by a cattle breeding program for purposes of the alternative minimum tax?

---

1. IRC Sec. 1231(b)(3); Treas. Reg. §1.1231-2(a).
2. *Greer v. U.S.*, 408 F.2d 631 (6th Cir. 1969).
3. Treas. Reg. §1.1231-2(b)(1).
4. See Farmer's Tax Guide, IRS Pub. 225 (2006), p. 53.
5. Treas. Reg. §1.61-4(b).
6. *U.S. v. Catto*, 66-1 USTC ¶9376 (U.S. 1966).
7. See Farmer's Tax Guide, IRS Pub. 225 (2006), p. 7.
8. *Carter v. Comm.*, 257 F.2d 595 (5th Cir. 1958).

The investor may have the following adjustments to alternative minimum taxable income (AMTI) or tax preferences in connection with investment in a cattle breeding program that passes losses and deductions through to the investor:

(1) Losses from tax shelter farm activities (determined by taking into account the adjustments to AMTI and tax preferences) are not allowed in calculating AMTI, except to the extent the taxpayer is insolvent or upon disposition of the tax shelter farm activity. There is no phase-in of the disallowance of passive activity losses as there is under the regular tax.

"Tax shelter farm activities" are any farm activities involving any enterprise, other than a C corporation, if (1) the farm activity is a passive activity (see Q 1293), or (2) at any time interests in the enterprise have been offered for sale in an offering required to be registered with any federal or state securities agency, or (3) the enterprise allocates more than 35% of its losses during any period to investors who do not actively take part in the management of the operation.[1]

(2) For cattle placed in service before 1999, generally, more accelerated methods of depreciation are available for regular tax purposes than are available for alternative minimum tax purposes. An adjustment to alternative minimum taxable income may be required if property placed in service after 1986 and before 1999 is depreciated differently for alternative minimum tax purposes than it is for regular tax purposes. For example, for regular tax purposes, cattle placed in service after 1986 can be depreciated over five years using the 150% declining balance method, switching to the straight line method at a time to maximize the deduction. For alternative minimum tax purposes, cattle placed in service after 1986 and before 1999 are depreciated over seven years by using the 150% declining balance method, switching to the straight line method at a time to maximize the deduction. If for regular tax purposes the taxpayer depreciates the cattle using a straight line alternative method over five or seven years, for alternative minimum tax purposes the cattle must be depreciated using a straight line method over seven years. For cattle placed in service after 1998, there is no AMTI adjustment for depreciation because cattle are depreciated the same way for regular tax purposes and for purposes of determining AMTI.[2] The adjusted basis of property is determined with respect to the depreciation method used.[3]

For a general discussion of the alternative minimum tax, see Q 1440.

LIMITATION ON LOSS DEDUCTIONS

AT RISK

1285. What is the "at risk" rule with respect to losses?

The "at risk" rule is a group of provisions in the IRC and regulations that limit the current deductibility of "losses" generated by certain tax shelters (and certain other activities) to the amount that the taxpayer actually has "at risk" (i.e., in the economic sense) in the tax shelter. The primary targets of this "at risk" rule are the limited partner and the nonrecourse financing of a limited partner's investment in the shelter (which

1. IRC Sec. 58.
2. IRC Sec. 56(a)(1).
3. IRC Sec. 56(a)(6).

was once common in all tax shelters); however, the rule also applies to certain corporations and general partners in both limited and general partnerships and to non-leverage risk-limiting devices (e.g., guaranteed repurchase agreements) designed to generate tax deductions in excess of the amount for which the investor actually bears a risk of loss in a shelter.[1]

Other at risk provisions of the IRC limit the availability of the investment tax credit with respect to property acquired for purposes of the tax shelters or other activities described in Q 1286.[2]

1286. To what types of investment activities does the "at risk" rule apply?

The "at risk" rule applies to each of the following activities when engaged in by an individual (including partners and S corporation shareholders) as a trade or business or for the production of income:

…holding, producing, or distributing motion picture films or video tapes;

…farming (including raising, shearing, feeding, caring for, training, or management of animals);

…leasing of depreciable personal property (and certain other "IRC Section 1245" property);

…exploring for, or exploiting, oil and gas reserves (see Q 1240 to Q 1263);

…exploring, or exploiting, geothermal deposits;

…holding real property (see Q 1221 for effective date and transitional relief rules);

…all other activities engaged in by a taxpayer in carrying on a trade or business or for the production of income.[3] Apparently, if a publicly traded partnership is taxed as a corporation (see Q 1189), the partnership is not subject to the at risk rules unless it is closely-held (generally, more than 50% control by five or fewer owners).[4]

1287. Under the at risk rule, how is an individual's "amount at risk" determined?

In the most general terms, an individual is "at risk" to the extent he is not protected against the loss of the money or other property he contributes to the activity. If he borrows the money he contributes to the activity, he is "at risk" only to the extent he is not protected against the loss of the borrowed amount (i.e., to the extent he is personally liable for repayment of such amount).[5] A partner's "amount at risk" is not affected by a loan made to the partnership by any other partner.[6] Payment by a purchaser to the

---

1. See Sen. Rep. 94-938, 1976-3 CB (vol. 3) 57, at 83.
2. See IRC Secs. 49(a)(1), 49(a)(2).
3. IRC Secs. 465(c), 464(e); Prop. Treas. Regs. §§1.465-42, 1.465-43, 1.465-44, 1.465-45.
4. See IRC Sec. 465(a).
5. Prop. Treas. Reg. §1.465-6.
6. Prop. Treas. Reg. §1.465-7.

seller for an interest in an activity is treated by the purchaser as a contribution to the activity.[1]

More specifically, an individual has "at risk" in an activity an amount equal to the total of:[2]

1. *The amount of money he has contributed to the activity.* If an individual borrows the money he contributes to an activity (or, in the case of a limited partnership, the money with which he purchases his interest), he is "at risk" only to the extent he is personally liable to repay such amounts, or to the extent he pledges as security property not used in the activity.[3]

In the case of a partnership, amounts required to be contributed under the partnership agreement are not "at risk" until the contribution is actually made. Similarly, a partner's amount at risk does not include the amount of a note that is payable to the partnership and on which the partner is personally liable until such time as the proceeds are applied to the activity.[4]

2. *His tax basis (for determining loss) in any property (other than money) contributed to the activity.* If the individual has borrowed funds to purchase the property he contributes to the activity, he will be "at risk" with respect to such property only to the extent that he would have been "at risk" had he contributed the borrowed funds instead of the purchased property.[5]

3. *Amounts borrowed in the conduct of the activity for use in the activity to the extent the individual is personally liable for repayment.* If an individual is personally liable for amounts borrowed in the conduct of the activity, he is "at risk" to the extent of such amounts regardless of the fact that property used in the activity is also pledged as security for such amounts.[6] The fact that the partnership or other partners are in the chain of liability does not reduce the amount a partner is "at risk" if the partner bears ultimate responsibility.[7] In the case of liabilities on which the individual is initially personally liable (i.e., recourse liabilities), but which after the occurrence of some event or lapse of a period of time will become nonrecourse, the individual is considered "at risk" during the period of recourse liability if (a) the borrowing arrangement was motivated primarily for business reasons and not tax avoidance, and (b) the arrangement is consistent with the normal commercial practice of financing the activity for which the money was borrowed.[8] As to the effect of repayment by the individual of a liability for which he is personally liable, see Prop. Treas. Reg. §1.465-24(b).

4. *Amounts borrowed for use in the activity and for which the individual is not personally liable for repayment, but only to the extent he pledges property that is not used in the activity as security for repayment.* In this case he is "at risk" only to the extent that the amount of the liability does not exceed the fair market value of the pledged property. If the fair market value of the security changes after the loan is made, a redetermination

---

1. Prop. Treas. Reg. §1.465-22(d).
2. IRC Sec. 465(b).
3. Treas. Reg. §1.465-20; Prop. Treas. Regs. §§1.465-6, 1.465-25.
4. Prop. Treas. Reg. §1.465-22(a).
5. See Prop. Treas. Reg. §1.465-23.
6. See Let. Rul. 7927007.
7. *Pritchett v. Comm.*, 87-2 USTC ¶9517 (9th Cir. 1987).
8. Prop. Treas. Reg. §1.465-5. See Rev. Rul. 82-123, 1982-1 CB 82; Rev. Rul. 81-283, 1981-2 CB 115.

of the amount at risk *must* be made using the new fair market value.[1] Property will *not* be treated as security if such property itself is financed (directly or indirectly) by loans secured with property contributed to the activity.[2] As to the effect of repaying the loan or contributing the security to the activity, see Prop. Treas. Reg. §1.465-25.

Notwithstanding the fact that an individual is personally liable (as in (3), above) or has pledged security for borrowed funds (as in (4), above), borrowed amounts cannot (except to the extent provided in future regulations) be considered at risk (1) if they are borrowed from a person who has an interest (other than as a creditor) in the activity, or (2) if they are borrowed from a person who is related to another person (other than the taxpayer) having an interest in the activity.[3]

For purposes of the foregoing rule, a "related" person generally includes the following: members of a family (i.e., an individual and his brothers, sisters, spouse, ancestors, and lineal descendants); a partnership and any partner owning, directly or indirectly, 10% of the capital or profits interests in such partnership; two partnerships in which the same persons own, directly or indirectly, more than 10% of the capital or profits interest; an individual and a corporation in which such individual owns, directly or indirectly, more than 10% in value of the outstanding stock; two corporations that are members of the same controlled group; a grantor and a fiduciary of the same trust; fiduciaries of trusts that have a common grantor; a fiduciary of a trust and the beneficiaries of that trust, or beneficiaries of another trust if both trusts have the same grantor; a fiduciary of a trust and a corporation if more than 10% in value of outstanding stock is owned, directly or indirectly, by the trust or by the grantor of the trust; a person and a tax-exempt organization controlled by such person or family of such person; a corporation and a partnership in which the same person owns a more-than-10% interest (by value of stock in the case of the corporation and by capital or profits interest in the case of the partnership); two or more S corporations if more than 10% of the stock (by value) of each is owned by the same person; an S corporation and a C corporation if more than 10% of the stock (by value) is owned by the same person; and an executor of an estate and a beneficiary of such estate (except in the case of a sale or exchange in satisfaction of a pecuniary bequest).[4]

Amounts borrowed from family members or other persons related to the taxpayer may be considered at risk under certain limited circumstances.[5]

An individual is not considered "at risk" with respect to any amount that is protected against loss through guarantees, stop loss agreements, nonrecourse financing (other than qualified nonrecourse financing of real estate described in (5), below), or other similar arrangements.[6] An investor is *not* at risk with respect to a note that may be satisfied by transferring to the creditor property that is derived from the activity if there is no obligation on the part of the investor-borrower to pay the difference should the value of the property transferred be less than the amount of the note.[7]

---

1. Prop. Treas. Reg. §1.465-25(a).
2. IRC Sec. 465(b)(2).
3. IRC Sec. 465(b)(3).
4. IRC Secs. 465(b)(3)(C), 267(b), 707(b)(1).
5. IRC Sec. 465(b)(3). See General Explanation–TRA '84, pp. 735-736.
6. IRC Sec. 465(b)(4). See S. Rep. 938, 94th Cong., 2d Sess. 49, *reprinted in* 1976-3 CB (vol. 3) 57 at 87. See Rev. Rul. 78-413, 1978-2 CB 167; Rev. Rul. 79-432, 1979-2 CB 289.
7. Rev. Rul. 85-113, 1985-2 CB 150.

5. *Qualified nonrecourse financing with respect to the activity of holding real property.* An investor in real estate (excluding mineral property) is considered at risk with respect to nonrecourse financing if:

(a) no person is personally liable for repayment (except to the extent provided in regulations),

(b) the financing is secured by real property used in the activity,

(c) the financing is borrowed with respect to the activity of holding real property,

(d) the financing is not convertible debt, *and either* (1) the financing is borrowed from a "qualified person" or represents a loan from any federal, state, or local government or instrumentality thereof, or is guaranteed by any federal, state, or local government, *or* (2) the financing is borrowed from a related person upon commercially reasonable terms that are substantially the same terms as loans involving unrelated persons.[1]

A "qualified person" is one who is actively and regularly engaged in the business of lending money and who is *not* (1) related in certain ways to the investor, (2) the one from whom the taxpayer acquired the property (or related to such a person), or (3) a person who receives a fee with respect to the lessor's investment in the real estate (or related to such a person).[2] In the case of a partnership, a partner's share of qualified nonrecourse financing of the partnership is determined on the basis of the partner's share of such liabilities incurred in connection with such financing.[3]

In any case, if a taxpayer engages in a pattern of conduct or utilizes a device that is not within normal business practice or that has the effect of avoiding the "at risk" limitations, his amount at risk may be adjusted to more accurately reflect the amount that is actually at risk. For example, if considering all the facts and circumstances, it appears that an event that results in an increased amount at risk at the close of one year will be accompanied by an event that will decrease the amount at risk after the year ends, these amounts may be disregarded, unless the taxpayer can establish a valid business purpose for the events and establish that the resulting increases and decreases are not a device for avoiding the at risk limitations in the earlier year.[4]

A partner's amount at risk is increased by the amount of his share of undistributed partnership income and his share of any tax-exempt proceeds.[5] It is reduced by distributions of taxable income and by losses deducted.[6] It is also reduced by nondeductible expenses relating to production of tax-exempt income of the activity.[7]

1288. What "losses" will be disallowed by the at risk rule? May disallowed losses be carried over to other years?

"Loss" is given a special meaning for purposes of applying the at risk limitations. "At risk loss" is the excess of the income tax deductions (including deductions normally

---

1. IRC Sec. 465(b)(6).
2. IRC Secs. 465(b)(6)(D)(i), 49(a)(1)(D)(iv).
3. IRC Sec. 465(b)(6)(C).
4. Prop. Treas. Reg. §1.465-4.
5. Prop. Treas. Reg. §1.465-22(c)(1).
6. Prop. Treas. Regs. §§1.465-22(b), 1.465-22(c)(2).
7. Prop. Treas. Reg. §1.465-22(c)(2).

accorded special treatment, such as tax preferences, short-term loss, long-term loss) attributable to the covered activity *over* the income received or accrued during the year from the activity. (Both deductions and income are determined without regard to the at risk provisions at this point.) Thus, otherwise allowable deductions may be taken freely against income generated by the activity regardless of the taxpayer's amount at risk in the activity. The at risk provisions act only to deny a deduction when the taxpayer attempts to use a loss incurred in the covered activity to offset income received by the taxpayer from a separate source.[1]

Losses disallowed because of the at risk rule may be carried forward indefinitely and deducted in future years to the extent that the activity produces net income for that year, or to the extent the taxpayer's amount at risk has been increased by additional contributions, etc. to the activity.[2] However, because "at risk loss" is made up of various deductions (including some normally accorded special tax treatment), the proposed regulations provide ordering rules that allocate the items of deductions between the current and carryover years. Items disallowed in the current tax year will retain their character when treated as deductions in succeeding years.[3]

The proposed regulations provide that when only a portion of "at risk loss" is allowed as a deduction for the tax year, the individual items of deduction making up the "at risk loss" will be allowed in the following order: (1) capital losses are allowed first; (2) all items entering into computation of "IRC Section 1231" property (see Q 1233) come next; (3) deductible items to the extent they are not tax preference items and are not described in (1) or (2) above follow; (4) all items of deduction that are tax preference items not allowed under (1) or (2) above come last. Furthermore, items of deduction described in (4), that are disallowed by reason of the at risk rule must be further subdivided according to the tax year in which they were originally paid or accrued; when such deductions are eventually allowed, those deductions paid or accrued earliest will be allowed first.[4]

1289. May a limited partner aggregate amounts he has "at risk" in different tax shelters in order to determine his allowable deductions?

No. The IRC requires that a limited partner apply the "at risk" limitations separately with respect to each limited partnership interest owned. The IRC also grants the Treasury Department authority to issue regulations requiring aggregation or separation of activities subject to the at risk rule; it is unclear what those regulations might require.[5]

Furthermore, should one of the taxpayer's limited partnerships be engaged in more than one activity covered by the at risk rule (e.g., oil exploration and equipment leasing), the taxpayer is generally required to treat each covered activity as a separate activity for purposes of applying the at risk limitations.[6] However, until otherwise provided, partnerships and S corporations can aggregate activities within each of certain categories for purposes of the at risk rule. The categories within which aggregation is permitted are oil and gas properties, geothermal properties, farms, and films and video tapes.[7]

1. IRC Sec. 465; Prop. Treas. Reg. §1.465-2(a).
2. IRC Sec. 465(a)(2); Prop. Treas. Reg. §1.465-2(b).
3. Prop. Treas. Reg. §1.465-38(b).
4. Prop. Treas. Regs. §§1.465-38(a), 1.465-38(c).
5. IRC Sec. 465(c). See General Explanation–TRA '84, p. 735.
6. IRC Sec. 465(c)(2)(A). See Temp. Treas. Reg. §1.465-1T.
7. Notice 89-39, 1989-1 CB 681.

1290. May an individual's "amount at risk" in an activity be less than zero (i.e., a negative amount)? If so, what are the tax effects of a negative amount at risk?

Although the amount of loss that is allowed as a deduction for the tax year cannot reduce a taxpayer's amount at risk below zero, it is possible to have a negative amount at risk. For example, if a distribution exceeding his amount at risk by $100 is made to the taxpayer, his amount at risk is reduced to a negative $100. (A negative amount at risk may also result when a recourse obligation is changed to nonrecourse, or when a guarantee that relieves the taxpayer of personal liability for a debt goes into effect.)[1]

If a taxpayer's amount at risk falls below zero, he must recognize income to the extent his amount at risk is reduced below zero. An amount equal to the amount included in income is then carried over as a deduction with respect to the activity in the following tax year. In effect, the reduction (by distribution or other event) is treated as preceding the loss deductions previously taken that offset the original amount at risk, and the loss deduction in effect is treated as disallowed and carried over to a subsequent year. However, the amount required to be included in income when the at risk amount falls below zero cannot exceed the aggregate amount of reductions in the amount at risk that have taken place because of losses in prior years, reduced by any amounts included in income in prior years because the amount at risk had fallen below zero.[2]

1291. Does the "at risk" rule affect an individual's tax basis in his tax shelter limited partnership?

No. The at risk rule and the limitations it imposes on the deduction of losses does *not* affect the tax basis of property involved in the covered activity (including the tax basis of a limited interest in a partnership engaged in the covered activity) for purposes of determining gain or loss on disposition, calculating depreciation or depletion, or any other purpose.[3]

PASSIVE LOSS RULE

1292. What is the "passive loss" rule?

Under the passive loss rule, aggregate losses from "passive" activities (see Q 1293) may generally be deducted in a year only to the extent they do not exceed aggregate income from passive activities in that year; credits from passive activities may be taken against tax liability allocated only to passive activities.[4] (Aggregation is not permitted in the case of certain publicly traded partnerships, see below.) The rule generally applies to losses incurred in tax years beginning after 1986, but is phased in with respect to losses of certain previously held interests. The rule is intended to prevent losses from passive activities from offsetting salaries, interest, dividends and income from "active" businesses. It applies to individuals, estates, trusts, closely held C corporations, and personal service corporations.

An *individual* can also deduct a limited amount of losses (and the deduction-equivalent of credits) arising from certain rental real estate activities against nonpassive

---

1. See Prop. Treas. Reg. §1.465-3.
2. IRC Sec. 465(e).
3. Prop. Treas. Reg. §1.465-1(e).
4. IRC Sec. 469.

income. See Q 1299. A *closely held C corporation* (other than a personal service corporation) can deduct its passive activity losses against its net active income (other than its investment, or "portfolio," income) and its passive credits can be applied against its tax liability attributable to its net active income.[1] Generally, a corporation is "closely" held if it has five or fewer shareholders who own more than 50% of the value of the stock.[2] A personal service corporation is a corporation whose principal activity is the performance of personal services and whose services are substantially performed by employee-owners.[3]

An exception to the passive loss restrictions is applied to certain casualty losses resulting from unusual events such as fire, storm, shipwreck, earthquake, etc. Losses from such casualties are generally not subject to the passive loss rule.[4] Likewise, passive activity income does not include reimbursements for such losses if (1) the reimbursement is includable in gross income under Treas. Reg. §1.165-1(d)(2)(iii) as an amount the taxpayer had deducted in a prior taxable year, and (2) the deduction for the loss was not a passive activity deduction. In other words, both the losses and the reimbursement should be taken into account in the calculation of the partnership's gross income, not its passive activity gross income.[5] The exception does not apply to losses that occur regularly in the conduct of the activity, such as theft losses from shoplifting in a retail store, or accident losses sustained in the operation of a rental car business.[6]

Special restrictions apply to *publicly traded partnerships* under the passive loss rule. The rule is applied separately to items attributable to a publicly traded partnership; thus, income, losses, and credits attributable to the partnership may not be aggregated with other income, losses, and credits of the taxpayer/partner for purposes of the passive loss rule.[7] Net passive loss from a publicly traded partnership will be treated as passive, while net passive income from a publicly traded partnership is to be treated as investment income (see Q 1304).[8] Generally, net passive loss from a publicly traded partnership is carried forward until the partner has additional passive income from the partnership or the partner disposes of his partnership interest (see Q 1297). Also, the $25,000 rental real estate exemption (see Q 1299) is available with respect to a publicly traded partnership only in connection with the low-income housing credit (see Q 1227) and the rehabilitation investment credit (see Q 1228). Furthermore, a taxpayer will not be treated as having disposed of his entire interest in an activity of a publicly-traded partnership until he disposes of his entire interest in the partnership. A publicly traded partnership is a partnership that is traded on an established securities market or is readily tradable on a secondary market (or the substantial equivalent thereof).[9] It would seem that if a publicly traded partnership is taxed as a corporation (see Q 1189), the partnership is not a taxpayer subject to the passive loss rule.[10]

Losses and credits disallowed under the passive loss rule may be carried over to offset passive income and the tax attributable to it in later years. See Q 1297. Suspended losses and credits of an activity may also offset the income and tax of that activity when

---

1. IRC Sec. 469(e)(2).
2. IRC Sec. 469(j)(1).
3. IRC Sec. 469(j)(2).
4. Temp. Treas. Reg. §1.469-2T(d)(2), Treas. Reg. §1.469-2(d)(2)(xi).
5. Temp. Treas. Reg. §1.469-2T(c)(7), Treas. Reg. §1.469-2(c)(7)(vi).
6. TD 8290, 1990-1 CB 109.
7. IRC Sec. 469(k)(1).
8. Notice 88-75, 1988-2 CB 386.
9. IRC Sec. 469(k).
10. See IRC Sec. 469(a).

the activity ceases to be passive or there is a change in status of a closely held corporation or personal service corporation. See Q 1298. As to losses allowed upon disposition of an interest in a passive activity, see Q 1297.

The passive loss rule applies to passive losses incurred in tax years beginning after 1986. It does not apply to any loss or credit carried over from a year beginning before 1987.[1] A taxpayer may elect to treat investment interest (see Q 1304) as a passive activity deduction if the interest was carried over from a year prior to 1987 and is attributable to property used in a passive activity after 1986.[2] However, the interest deduction is not treated as being from a pre-enactment interest in a passive activity.[3]

1293. Under the passive loss rule, what is a passive activity?

A passive activity is any activity (see Q 1294 for rules defining an activity) that involves the conduct of a trade or business in which the taxpayer does not "materially participate."[4] The IRC indicates that regulations may define the term "trade or business" to include activities in connection with a trade or business or activities that are engaged in for the production of income under IRC Section 212. The Service is studying this matter.[5] Regulations provide that the Service will treat real property held for the production of income under IRC Section 212 as a trade or business for purposes of the rental real estate with material participation exception (see Q 1299).

The term "passive activity" does not include a working interest in an oil or gas property that the taxpayer holds directly or through an entity that does not limit the liability of the taxpayer with respect to the interest (see Q 1245).[6] It also does not include the activity of trading personal property (e.g., stocks or bonds) on behalf of the owners of interests in the activity.[7]

Whether an activity is passive or not with regard to a partner or an S corporation shareholder is determined at the level of the partner or shareholder not at the level of the entity. Such determination is made with regard to the entity's taxable year (not the partner's or shareholder's taxable year).[8] However, if a publicly traded partnership is taxed as a corporation (see Q 1189), the partnership is the taxpayer, and apparently the partnership is not subject to the passive loss rule.[9] In the case of a limited partnership interest in an electing large partnership, all passive loss limitation activities of the partnership are treated as a single passive activity (see Q 1191).

Rental Activities

Except as provided below, a passive activity includes any rental activity, without regard to whether the taxpayer materially participates in the activity.[10] A rental activity is any activity where payments are principally for the use of tangible property.[11] How-

1. TRA '86 Sec. 501(c)(2).
2. TAMRA '88 Sec. 1005(c)(11).
3. Notice 89-36, 1989-1 CB 677.
4. IRC Sec. 469(c).
5. TD 8175(II)(A), 1988-1 CB 191.
6. IRC Sec. 469(c)(3).
7. Temp. Treas. Reg. §1.469-1T(e)(6).
8. Temp. Treas. Regs. §§1.469-2T(e)(1), 1.469-3T(b)(3).
9. See IRC Sec. 469(a).
10. IRC Sec. 469(c)(2).
11. IRC Sec. 469(j)(8).

ever, there are a number of exceptions to this rule. An activity is not treated as a rental activity if: (1) the average rental period is less than eight days, (2) the average rental period is less than 31 days and substantial personal services are provided, (3) the rental of the property is incidental to the receipt of personal services or to a nonrental activity, (4) the taxpayer makes the property available on a nonexclusive basis during regular business hours, (5) the taxpayer rents property to a passthrough entity engaged in a nonrental activity, in his capacity as an owner of that entity, or (6) the personal use of a residence that is also rented out exceeds the greater of 14 days or 10% of the rental days (see Q 1225).[1]

See Q 1299 for special rules for rental real estate.

"Material Participation" Defined

In general, a taxpayer is considered to *materially participate* in an activity if he is involved in the operations of the activity on a regular, continuous, and substantial basis.[2] The material participation requirement is met by an individual if he satisfies any one of the following five tests: (1) he does substantially all of the work required by the activity, (2) he participates in the activity for more than 500 hours during the year, (3) he participates in the activity for more than 100 hours during the year and meets certain other requirements, (4) he has materially participated in the activity in 5 out of the 10 preceding years (determined without regard to this test), or (5) he has materially participated in the activity, which involves the performance of personal services, in any three preceding years. An individual who is a limited partner is treated as materially participating only if he also owns a general partnership interest, or if he can meet tests (2), (4), or (5).[3]

In determining whether an individual materially participates, the participation of the individual's spouse is considered.[4] Work done in the individual's capacity as an investor is not treated as participation unless the individual is involved in the day-to-day management or operations of the activity. The extent to which an individual participates may be shown by any reasonable means.[5]

A closely held C corporation or a personal service corporation is considered to materially participate in an activity if (a) one or more stockholders who owns more than 50% (by value) of the outstanding stock of the corporation materially participates *or* (b) if the C corporation (other than a personal service corporation) has an active full time manager throughout the year, at least three full-time nonowner employees whose services are directly related to the business of the corporation, and certain deductions of the business exceed 15% of the income for the year.[6]

Whether a trust materially participates in an activity is determined by reference to the persons who conduct the business activity on the trust's behalf, not just whether the trustee materially participates in the activity.[7]

---

1. Temp. Treas. Reg. §1.469-1T(e)(3); IRC Sec. 469(j)(10).
2. IRC Sec. 469(h)(1).
3. Temp. Treas. Reg. §1.469-5T.
4. IRC Sec. 469(h)(5).
5. Temp. Treas. Reg. §1.469-5T(f).
6. IRC Sec. 469(h)(4).
7. *Carter Trust v. Comm.*, 2003-1 USTC ¶50,418 (N.D. Tex. 2003).

Characterization of Income and Expenses

Certain income and expenses of a passive activity are not considered passive activity income or expenses in determining passive activity income and loss: income from interest, dividends, annuities or royalties not derived in the ordinary course of a trade or business; expenses allocable to such income; and gain or loss not derived in the ordinary course of a trade or business that is attributable to the disposition of property either producing such income or held for investment. An interest in a passive activity is not treated as property held for investment. Income from the investment of working capital is not derived in the ordinary course of a trade or business.[1]

Interest deductions attributable to passive activities are subject to limitation under the passive loss rule, not under the investment interest limitation.[2]

In order to prevent taxpayers from defeating the purpose of the passive loss rule by structuring transactions to produce passive income from what are essentially active businesses or portfolio investments, Treasury was given very broad regulatory authority for carrying out the provisions of IRC Section 469. The IRC specifies that regulations may: provide that certain items of gross income will not be taken into account in determining income and loss from an activity, require that net income or gain from a limited partnership or other passive activity not be treated as passive income or loss, and allocate interest expense among activities.[3] In the following instances, part or all of the income from a passive activity may be treated as income that is not from a passive activity: (1) the individual participates in such passive activity for more than 100 hours during the year, (2) less than 30% of the property used in a rental activity is depreciable property, (3) there is net interest income from a passive equity-financed lending activity, (4) rental of property developed by the taxpayer commenced within 12 months of disposition of such property, (5) the taxpayer rents property to a trade or business in which the taxpayer materially participates, and (6) the taxpayer acquires certain royalty interests in intangible property previously developed by a passthrough entity.[4]

If gain is recognized in a taxable year beginning after 1986 with respect to an activity sold or exchanged before 1987, the gain is treated as passive if the activity would have been passive had the passive loss rule been in effect in the year the activity was sold or exchanged and in all succeeding years.[5]

The Service has issued temporary and proposed regulations that provide complex tracing rules allocating interest expense (other than qualified residence interest) on the basis of the use of the proceeds of the underlying debt.[6] (See Q 1301.) Once allocated, interest on proceeds used to purchase a passive activity is taken into account in determining income or loss from the activity. Characterization of interest on proceeds used to purchase a partnership or S corporation interest depends on whether the activity is passive to the partner or shareholder.[7]

Income from discharge of indebtedness is generally characterized as income from a passive activity to the extent that the debt is allocated to passive activity expenditures.[8]

---

1. IRC Sec. 469(e).
2. IRC Sec. 163(d)(4)(D).
3. IRC Sec. 469(l).
4. Temp. Treas. Reg. §1.469-2T(f), Treas. Reg. §1.469-2(f).
5. TRA '86 Sec. 501(c)(4) as amended by TAMRA '88, Sec. 1005(a)(10).
6. Temp. Treas. Reg. §1.163-8T.
7. Ann. 87-4, 1987-3 IRB 17.
8. Rev. Rul. 92-92, 1992-25 CB 103.

Self-Charged Interest

Interest income and deductions in connection with loans between a taxpayer and a "passthrough entity" (a partnership or S corporation) in which the taxpayer owns a direct or indirect interest may be allocated under the following "self-charged interest rules" rather than the rules above. An indirect interest means an interest held through one or more passthrough entities.[1]

Taxpayer loans to the entity. The self-charged interest rules apply for a taxable year if: (1) the borrowing entity has deductions for its taxable year for interest charged by persons who own direct or indirect interests in the borrowing entity at any time during the entity's taxable year; (2) the taxpayer owns a direct or indirect interest in the borrowing entity at any time during the entity's taxable year and the taxpayer has gross income for the taxable year from interest charged to the borrowing entity by either the taxpayer or a passthrough entity through which the taxpayer holds an interest in the borrowing entity; and (3) the taxpayer's share of the borrowing entity's self-charged interest deductions includes passive activity deductions.[2]

If the rules apply, the passive activity gross income and passive activity deductions from that activity are determined under the following rules: (1) the applicable percentage of each item of the taxpayer's income for the taxable year from interest charged to the borrowing entity is treated as passive activity gross income from the activity; and (2) the applicable percentage of each deduction for the taxable year for interest expense that is properly allocable to the taxpayer's income from the interest charged to the borrowing entity is treated as a passive activity deduction from the activity.[3]

Interest expense is properly allocable to the taxpayer's income if it is allocated under Temporary Treasury Regulation Section 1.163-8T to an expenditure that: (1) is properly chargeable to a capital account with respect to the investment producing the interest income; or (2) may reasonably be taken into account as a cost of producing the item of interest income.[4]

The applicable percentage is determined by dividing (1) the taxpayer's share for the taxable year of the borrowing entity's self-charged interest deductions that are treated as passive activity deductions from the activity by (2) the greater of: (a) the taxpayer's share for the taxable year of the borrowing entity's aggregate self-charged interest deductions for all activities (regardless of whether the deductions are treated as passive activity deductions); or (b) the taxpayer's aggregate income for the taxable year from interest charged to the borrowing entity for all activities of the borrowing entity. The applicable percentage is determined separately for each activity.[5]

Entity loans to the taxpayer. Similarly, the self-charged interest rules apply for a taxable year if (1) the lending entity has gross income for the entity taxable year from interest charged by the lending entity to persons who own direct or indirect interests in the lending entity at any time during the entity taxable year; (2) the taxpayer owns a direct or indirect interest in the lending entity at any time during the entity's taxable year and has deductions for the taxable year for interest charged by the lending entity

---

1. Treas. Reg. §1.469-7.
2. Treas. Reg. §1.469-7(c)(1).
3. Treas. Reg. §1.469-7(c)(2).
4. Treas. Reg. §1.469-7(f).
5. Treas. Reg. §1.469-7(c)(3).

to the taxpayer or a passthrough entity through which the taxpayer holds an interest in the lending entity; and (3) the taxpayer's deductions for interest charged by the lending entity include passive activity deductions.[1]

If the rules apply, the passive activity gross income and passive activity deductions from the activity are determined under the following rules: (1) the applicable percentage of the taxpayer's share for the taxable year of each item of the lending entity's self-charged interest income is treated as passive activity gross income from the activity; (2) the "applicable percentage" of the taxpayer's share for the taxable year of each deduction for interest expense that is properly allocable to the lending entity's self-charged interest income is treated as a passive activity deduction from the activity.[2]

Interest expense is properly allocable to the taxpayer's income if it is allocated under Temporary Treasury Regulation Section 1.163-8T to an expenditure that: (1) is properly chargeable to a capital account with respect to the investment producing the interest income; or (2) may reasonably be taken into account as a cost of producing the item of interest income.[3]

The applicable percentage is determined by dividing (1) the taxpayer's deductions for the taxable year for interest charged by the lending entity, to the extent treated as passive activity deductions from the activity, by (2) the greater of: (a) the taxpayer's aggregate deductions for all activities for the taxable year for interest charged by the lending entity (regardless of whether these deductions are treated as passive activity deductions); or (b) the taxpayer's aggregate share for the taxable year of the lending entity's self-charged interest income for all activities of the lending entity. The applicable percentage is determined separately for each activity.[4]

Special rules apply to situations where a loan occurs between identically-owned passthrough entities.[5]

If the taxpayer and the passthrough entity have different taxable years or accounting methods, related interest income and interest deductions may be recognized in different years, possibly with adverse results.[6]

The self-charged interest rules apply to taxable years ending after 1986, unless the passthrough entity makes an election to have the rules not apply. Such an election applies to the taxable year for which the election is made and all subsequent years until the election is revoked. An election can be revoked only with the consent of the IRS.[7]

1294. How is an activity defined for purposes of the passive loss rule?

Regulations allow taxpayers to use a facts-and-circumstances approach to define one or more trade or business activities as a single activity if the activities constitute an appropriate economic unit for purposes of IRC Section 469. (In the case of a limited

1. Treas. Reg. §1.469-7(d)(1).
2. Treas. Reg. §1.469-7(d)(2).
3. Treas. Reg. §1.469-7(f).
4. Treas. Reg. §1.469-7(d)(3).
5. Treas. Reg. §1.469-7(e).
6. See Treas. Reg. §1.469-7(h) (Ex. 4).
7. Treas. Reg. §1.469-11(a)(4); Treas. Reg. §1.469-7(g).

partnership interest in an electing large partnership, all passive loss limitation activities of the partnership are treated as a single passive activity (see Q 1191).) Relevant factors to consider include: (1) similarities and differences in types of businesses; (2) the extent of common control; (3) the extent of common ownership; (4) geographical location; and (5) interdependencies between the activities. There may be more than one reasonable method for grouping activities.[1]

Rental activities may not be grouped with trade or business activities unless either the rental activity is insubstantial in relation to the trade or business activity or vice versa, or ownership interests in the trade and business activity are held in the same proportion as ownership interests in the rental activity.[2] An activity involving the rental of real property and an activity involving the rental of personal property may not be treated as a single activity (unless the personal property is provided in connection with the real property or vice versa).[3] For activities conducted through partnerships, S corporations, or C corporations subject to the passive loss rules, the entity must first group its activities under the above rules. Individual partners and shareholders may then group those activities with others conducted directly by the individual taxpayer or with activities conducted through other partnerships, S corporations, or C corporations subject to the passive loss rules, under the same rules. However, a shareholder or partner may not treat activities grouped by an entity as separate activities.[4]

A taxpayer involved as a limited partner or limited entrepreneur in certain activities (generally, holding, producing, or distributing motion picture films or videotapes; farming; equipment leasing; or exploring for, or exploiting oil and gas resources or geothermal resources) may group that activity with another activity only if the two activities are in the same type of business and the grouping is appropriate under the facts-and-circumstances test above.[5]

Once a taxpayer has grouped individual activities under the rules above, he may not regroup them in subsequent taxable years unless the original grouping was clearly inappropriate or there is a material change in facts and circumstances making the original grouping clearly inappropriate.[6] The IRS may regroup a taxpayer's activities if any of the activities resulting from the taxpayer's grouping is not an appropriate economic unit and a principal purpose of the taxpayer's grouping (or failure to regroup) is to circumvent the underlying purpose of IRC Section 469.[7]

A taxpayer who disposes of substantially all of an activity may treat the disposed interest as a separate activity, but only if the taxpayer can establish with reasonable certainty both (1) the amount of deductions and credits allocable to that part of the activity for that taxable year under IRC Section 469 and (2) the amount of gross income and any other deductions and credits allocable to that part of the activity for the taxable year.[8]

In general, for the first taxable year ending after May 10, 1992, taxpayers that are not in compliance with the activity grouping rules of Treas. Reg. §1.469-4 must regroup

---

1. Treas. Reg. §1.469-4(c).
2. Treas. Reg. §1.469-4(d)(1).
3. Treas. Reg. §1.469-4(d)(2).
4. Treas. Reg. §1.469-4(d)(5).
5. Treas. Reg. §1.469-4(d)(3).
6. Treas. Reg. §1.469-4(e).
7. Treas. Reg. §1.469-4(f).
8. Treas. Reg. §1.469-4(g).

their activities under those rules without regard to how the activities were previously grouped. Further, regrouping is permissible for the first taxable year ending after May 10, 1992 even if the taxpayer is already in compliance with the activity grouping rules of Treas. Reg. §1.469-4.[1]

For special rules relating to rental real estate in which a taxpayer materially participates, see Q 1299.

Taxable Years Ending After August 9, 1989 and Before May 11, 1992

For taxable years ending after August 9, 1989 and before May 11, 1992, regulations define an activity using a building blocks approach based on (1) rules identifying business and rental operations constituting an undertaking, and (2) rules permitting or requiring aggregation or segregation of certain operations or undertakings.[2]

Taxable Years Ending Before August 10, 1989

For taxable years ending before August 10, 1989, a taxpayer's business and rental operations may be organized into activities under any reasonable method (including use of the definition of activity contained in former[3] For additional transitional guidance with regard to reasonable methods prior to the issuance of the temporary regulations, see Notice 88-94.[4]

1295. How do the passive loss rule and other limitations on the use of credits interact with each other?

The IRC seems to provide that credits must be allowable under the limitations that apply to a particular credit (e.g., the general business credit limitation) before the credit enters into the calculation of the amount of credits attributable to passive activities.[5] Then, if the credit is allowable under the passive credit limitation (i.e., passive credits may offset only tax liability attributable to passive activities) or the $25,000 rental real estate exemption (see Q 1299), the credit would become subject to overall limitations that apply to all credits (e.g., credits may not reduce regular tax liability to less than tentative minimum tax liability). This appears to be consistent with explanations contained in committee reports for TRA '86.[6] However, temporary regulations seem to provide that a credit must be allowable under the passive loss rule before the credit is taken into consideration under the limitations that apply to a group of credits (e.g., the general business credit limitation).[7] The reports go on to say that if the credit is otherwise allowable under the passive loss rule (including the $25,000 rental real estate exemption), but is disallowed when aggregated with nonpassive credits because of other limitations (e.g., credits may not reduce regular tax liability to less than tentative minimum tax liability), the passive loss so disallowed becomes a nonpassive credit arising in that year. The treatment of the credit is then determined by the general rules

---

1. Treas. Reg. §1.469-11(a)(1), Treas. Reg. §1.469-11(b)(3)(ii).
2. Former Temp. Treas. Reg. §1.469-4T.
3. Temp. Treas. Reg. §1.469-4T). Former Temp. Treas. Reg. §1.469-4T(p).
4. 1988-2 CB 419.
5. IRC Sec. 469(d)(2).
6. See Sen. Rep. 99-313, 1986-3 CB (vol. 3) 713, 724 and Conf. Rep. 99-841, 1986-3 CB (vol. 4) 137, 143.
7. Temp. Treas. Reg. §1.469-3T.

that apply to the credits, including carryover rules, and not under the passive loss rule. While less than clear, the temporary regulations seem to be in accord.[1]

See Q 1296 concerning the interaction of the limitations on the "at risk" rule, the passive loss rule, and the deductibility of losses in excess of basis with respect to investment in a partnership or S corporation.

1296. How is a passive loss treated if the taxpayer is subject to other limitations on loss deductions?

The determination of whether a loss is disallowed under the passive loss rule is made *after* the application of (1) the limitations on the deductibility of losses in excess of basis with respect to investment in a partnership (see Q 1200) or S corporation (see Q 1218), and (2) the "at risk" rule (see Q 1285 to Q 1291). A passive loss that would not be allowed because of the basis limitations or the at risk rule is suspended and carried forward under the basis and/or at risk provisions, not the passive loss rule. The amount becomes subject to the passive loss rule in subsequent years when it would be otherwise allowable under both the basis and at risk limitations.[2]

According to the Senate Finance Committee Report, TRA '86, amounts at risk are reduced even if deductions that would be allowed under the at risk rule are suspended under the passive loss rule. Similarly, basis is reduced if the deduction would be allowed under the at risk rule but is suspended under the passive loss rule. When a taxpayer's amount at risk or basis has been reduced by a deduction not allowed under the passive loss rule, the amount at risk or basis is not reduced again when the deduction becomes allowable under the passive loss rule.[3]

1297. May disallowed passive losses and credits be carried over and taken in a later year? How are passive losses and credits treated on the disposition of an interest in a passive activity?

A passive loss or credit disallowed under the passive loss rule in one year may be carried over and taken in a later year in which the taxpayer has passive activity income or tax liability.[4] However, if passive losses (or credits) from a publicly traded partnership (see Q 1189) are carried forward, such losses (or credits) may be offset only by passive income (or tax attributable to passive income) from the same partnership.[5] Special rules apply in the case of a rental real estate activity (see Q 1299).

If a passive activity is disposed of in a fully taxable transaction, losses from the activity will receive *ordinary loss treatment*, (i.e., they may generally be used to offset other income of the taxpayer) to the extent that they exceed net income or gain from all passive activities (determined without regard to the losses just discussed) for the year. This treatment applies both to current year losses as well as losses carried over from previous years, with respect to the activity disposed of. The IRS has been given the authority to issue regulations that will take income or gain from previous years into account to prevent the misuse of this rule.[6] However, a taxpayer will not be treated as

---

1. See Temp. Treas. Reg. §1.469-3T.
2. Temp. Treas. Reg. §1.469-2T(d).
3. Sen. Rep. 99-313, 1986-3 CB (vol. 3) 713, 723.
4. IRC Sec. 469(b).
5. IRC Sec. 469(k)(1).
6. IRC Sec. 469(g)(1).

having disposed of his entire interest in an activity of a publicly-traded partnership (see Q 1189) until he disposes of his entire interest in the partnership.[1]

For the purpose of determining gain or loss from a disposition of property, the taxpayer may elect to increase the basis of the property immediately before disposition by an amount equal to the part of any unused credit that reduced the basis of the property for the year the credit arose.[2] If the passive interest disposed of is sold under the installment method (see Q 1408), previously disallowed passive losses are allowed as a deduction in the same proportion as gain recognized for the year bears to gross profit from the sale.[3]

If the disposition of the passive interest is to a related person in an otherwise fully taxable transaction, suspended losses remain with the taxpayer and may continue to offset other passive income of the taxpayer. The taxpayer is considered to have disposed of his interest in a transaction described in the preceding paragraph when the related party later disposes of the passive interest in a taxable transaction to a party unrelated to the taxpayer.[4]

If the disposition is by death, the carried over losses may be deducted only to the extent the losses exceed the step-up in basis (see Q 1415) of the interest in the passive activity.[5] If the disposition is by gift, the losses are not deductible. Instead, the donor's basis just before the transfer is increased by the amount of the disallowed losses allocable to the interest.[6] However, where a donor makes a gift of less than his entire interest, a portion of the carried over losses is allocated to the gift and increases the donor's basis and a portion of the losses continue to be treated as passive losses attributable to the interest that the donor has retained.[7]

If a trust or estate distributes an interest in a passive activity, the basis of such interest immediately before the distribution is increased by the amount of passive losses allocable to the interest, and such losses are never deductible.[8]

The rules relating to the treatment of suspended losses and credits when the activity is disposed of require that losses and credits carried over from year to year be traceable to a particular activity. Thus, where there are losses or credits from two or more activities which, in the aggregate, exceed passive gains from other passive activities, the amount disallowed and carried over must be allocated among the different activities and between capital and ordinary loss. Disallowed passive losses are allocated among activities in proportion to the loss from each activity. The disallowed loss allocated to an activity is then allocated ratably among deductions attributable to the activity. Disallowed credits are allocated ratably among all credits attributable to passive activities.

In identifying the deductions or credits that are disallowed, the taxpayer need account separately only for those items that if separately taken into account by the taxpayer would result in an income tax liability different from that which would result if such deduc-

---

1. IRC Sec. 469(k)(3).
2. IRC Sec. 469(j)(9).
3. IRC Sec. 469(g)(3).
4. IRC Sec. 469(g)(1)(B).
5. IRC Sec. 469(g)(2).
6. IRC Sec. 469(j)(6).
7. Sen. Rep. 99-313, 1986-3 CB (vol. 3) 713, 726.
8. IRC Sec. 469(j)(12).

tion were not taken into account separately. Deductions arising from a rental real estate activity, or in connection with a capital or IRC Section 1231 asset, must be accounted for separately. Credits (other than the low-income housing or rehabilitation credits) arising from a rental real estate activity must also be accounted for separately.[1]

1298. How are suspended passive losses treated when an activity ceases to be passive or if a closely held C corporation or personal service corporation changes status?

If an activity ceases to be passive (e.g., because the taxpayer begins to participate materially), its unused losses (or credits) from prior years continue to be passive, but may be used against the income (and tax liability) of that activity. If there is a change in the status of a closely held C corporation or personal service corporation, its suspended losses from prior years will continue to be treated as if the status of the corporation had not changed.[2]

For an explanation of losses allowed upon disposition of an interest in a former passive activity, see Q 1297.

1299. What amount of passive losses (and the deduction-equivalent of credits) from rental real estate activities may an individual deduct against nonpassive income?

First, it should be noted that certain rental real estate activities may no longer be subject to the passive loss rules. For tax years beginning after 1993, a rental real estate activity of a taxpayer is not automatically considered a rental activity subject to the passive loss rules for a year, but only if during the year (1) more than one-half of the personal services performed by the taxpayer in trades or businesses during the year is in real property trades or businesses in which the taxpayer materially participates, and (2) the taxpayer performs more than 750 hours of service during the year in the real property trades or businesses. See "Rental Real Estate with Material Participation" below. Few investors in real estate syndications will qualify for this exception.

An *individual* can deduct losses (and the deduction-equivalent of credits) attribut-able to all rental real estate activities subject to the passive loss rules in which he has "actively participated" (and has at least a 10% interest in the activity at all times during the year) against as much as $25,000 of nonpassive income.[3] The $25,000 amount is reduced by fifty cents for each dollar by which the individual's adjusted gross income exceeds $100,000.[4] *Adjusted gross income*, for this purpose, does not include social se-curity or railroad retirement benefits, is not reduced by contributions to an IRA, any passive loss or loss from rental real estate with material participation, deductions for student loan interest, deductions for qualified tuition and related expenses (see Q 1314), or deductions for production income, and is not reduced by the exclusions for savings bonds interest used to pay higher education expenses (see Q 1141) or certain adoption assistance programs.[5]

---

1. Temp. Treas. Reg. §1.469-1T(f).
2. IRC Sec. 469(f).
3. IRC Sec. 469(i).
4. IRC Sec. 469(i)(3)(A).
5. IRC Sec. 469(i)(3)(F).

The rules above are applied differently to deductions of amounts equivalent to the low income housing credit (see Q 1227) or the rehabilitation credit (see Q 1228). First, the requirement that the individual own at least a 10% interest in the activity and "actively participate" does not apply to these deductions.[1] Furthermore, with respect to the rehabilitation credit, the $25,000 amount is not phased out until the individual has adjusted gross income of $200,000 instead of $100,000.[2] With respect to property placed in service after 1989, there is no phase-out of the $25,000 rental real estate exemption with respect to the low-income housing tax credit.[3] For property placed in service before 1990, the $25,000 exemption amount for rental real estate with respect to the low-income housing tax credit does not begin to phase out until a taxpayer has income in excess of $200,000.

The $25,000 amount is not available to married individuals who file separately but who did not live apart at all times during the year. For married individuals who file separately and did live apart at all times during the year, the $25,000, $100,000, and $200,000 amounts are cut in half (i.e., $12,500, $50,000, and $100,000).[4] For up to two years after a decedent's death, an *estate* may offset up to $25,000 (subject to the phase-out rule) of nonpassive income with passive losses and credits from a rental real estate activity in which the decedent actively participated before his death. The estate's $25,000 amount is reduced by the rental real estate exemption amount that would be allowable to the surviving spouse calculated as if the spouse were not subject to the phase-out rule.[5]

The $25,000 rental real estate exemption is available with respect to a publicly traded partnership subject to the passive loss rule (see Q 1292) only to the extent that the low-income housing credit and the rehabilitation credit exceed the regular tax liability attributable to income from the partnership.[6]

Before passive losses from a rental real estate activity can be used to offset nonpassive income, they must first be netted against other real estate activities in which the taxpayer actively participates, then against other passive income. Any remaining losses may be applied against up to $25,000 of nonpassive income. If losses are otherwise deductible under the $25,000 rule, but the taxpayer cannot deduct all or part of them in the current year because passive losses exceed the taxpayer's nonpassive income, the excess losses are treated as a net operating loss arising in that year which can be carried back and forward in accordance with the net operating loss rules.[7] With regard to the interaction of the passive loss rule with other limitations on the use of credits or the deductibility of losses, see Q 1295 and Q 1296.

An individual must *actively participate* in the rental real estate activity and have at least a 10% interest in the activity at all times during the year in order to take advantage of the $25,000 exemption amount (unless he is claiming the deduction equivalent of the low income housing or rehabilitation credit, as noted above). Except as provided in regulations, a limited partner is not treated as actively participating with respect to a

---

1. IRC Sec. 469(i)(6)(B).
2. IRC Sec. 469(i)(3)(B).
3. IRC Sec. 469(i)(3)(D).
4. IRC Sec. 469(i)(5).
5. IRC Sec. 469(i)(4).
6. IRC Sec. 469(k).
7. Sen. Rep. 99-313, 1986-3 CB (vol. 3) 713, 722, 736-37.

limited partnership interest.[1] A taxpayer can meet the active participation requirement by making management decisions, such as "approving new tenants, deciding on rental terms, approving capital or repair expenditures, and other similar decisions," and arranging for others to provide services such as repairs. Regular, continuous, and substantial involvement in operations is not required. In determining whether a person actively participates, the participation of his spouse is considered. In determining what is an activity, it may be necessary to consider the degree of business and functional integration among different properties or units of property.[2]

The rule allowing up to $25,000 of rental real estate losses and credit-equivalents to offset nonpassive income does not apply to losses and credits carried over from a year in which the taxpayer did not actively participate. Credits and losses that were disallowed in a prior year, because they exceeded the rental real estate exemption amount in that year, are only deductible under the $25,000 rule if the taxpayer actively participates in the year to which the losses and credits are carried over.[3]

Rental Real Estate with Material Participation

For tax years beginning after 1993, a rental real estate activity of a taxpayer is not automatically considered a rental activity (see Q 1293) subject to the passive loss rules for a year, but only if during the year (1) more than one-half of the personal services performed by the taxpayer in trades or businesses during the year is in real property trades or businesses (see below) in which the taxpayer materially participates (see Q 1293), and (2) the taxpayer performs more than 750 hours of service during the year in such real property trades or businesses (making the taxpayer a qualifying taxpayer). For purposes of (2), personal services performed as an employee are not treated as performed in a real property trade or business unless the employee is a 5% owner. In the case of a closely held C corporation, the requirements are considered met if more than 50% of the gross receipts of the corporation are derived from real property trades or businesses in which the corporation materially participates. With respect to a joint return, these requirements are met only if either spouse separately satisfies the requirements.[4] Work performed by the taxpayer's spouse in a trade or business is treated as work performed by the taxpayer regardless of whether the spouses file a joint return.[5] Personal services does not include work performed in the individual's capacity as an investor.[6]

Any interest in rental real estate, including real property held for the production of income under IRC Section 212, is considered a trade or business for purposes of the rental real estate with material participation exception.[7] However, any rental real estate that the taxpayer grouped with a trade or business activity because the rental real estate was insubstantial in relation to the trade or business activity, or because the ownership interests in each activity were held in the same proportion (see Q 1294) is not an interest in rental real estate for purposes of the rental real estate with material participation exception.[8] A real property trade or business is any real property development, redevelopment, construction, reconstruction, acquisition, conversion, rental, operation, management,

---

1. IRC Sec. 469(i)(6).
2. Sen. Rep. 99-313, 1986-3 CB (vol. 3) 713, 737-38.
3. IRC Sec. 469(i)(1).
4. IRC Sec. 469(c)(7).
5. Treas. Reg. §1.469-9(c)(4).
6. Treas. Reg. §1.469-9(b)(4).
7. Treas. Reg. §1.469-9(b)(1).
8. Treas. Reg. §1.469-9(b)(3).

leasing, or brokerage trade or business.[1] A facts and circumstances approach is used in determining the taxpayer's real property trade or business and, once determined, may not be changed unless the original determination was clearly inappropriate or a material change in circumstances has occurred that makes the earlier determination clearly inappropriate.[2] Each interest of a qualifying taxpayer in rental real estate will be treated as a separate rental real estate activity, unless an election is made to treat all rental real estate as a single activity (see below). A qualifying taxpayer may not group a rental real estate activity with any other activity.[3]

A qualifying taxpayer may elect to treat all interests in rental real estate as a single rental real estate activity and that election is binding for the taxable year in which it is made and for all future years in which the taxpayer is a qualifying taxpayer unless the taxpayer revokes the election because of a material change in circumstances. The fact that an election may prove less advantageous in one year is not in itself a material change in circumstances. Nor is a break in the taxpayer's status as a qualifying taxpayer necessarily a material change in circumstances.[4] If a taxpayer makes this election and at least one rental real estate interest is held by the taxpayer as a limited partnership interest, the combined rental real estate activity will be treated as a limited partnership interest for the purpose of determining material participation (see Q 1293) unless the taxpayer's share of gross rental income from all his limited partnership interests in rental real estate is less than 10% of his share of gross rental income from all interests in rental real estate for the year.[5]

In the absence of an election by a qualifying taxpayer, interests in rental real estate held by a partnership or S corporation passthrough entity are treated as one or more activities as grouped by the passthrough entity (see Q 1294). However, if the election is not made and the qualifying taxpayer holds at least a 50% interest in the capital, profits, or losses, of a passthrough entity, each interest in rental real estate held by the passthrough entity is treated as a separate activity of the qualifying taxpayer, regardless of the way the passthrough entity groups activities. If one passthrough entity owns at least a 50% interest in the capital, profits, or losses of another passthrough entity, each interest in rental real estate held by the lower-tier entity will be a separate interest in rental real estate of the upper-tier entity regardless of the way the lower-tier entity groups activities.[6]

The $25,000 rental real estate exemption of IRC Section 469(i) (discussed above) also applies to the passive losses and credits from rental real estate activities (including prior-year disallowed passive activity losses and credits from rental real estate activities in which the taxpayer materially participates) of a qualifying taxpayer. The $25,000 rental real estate exemption is determined after application of the rental real estate with material participation rules. However, losses allowable under the rental real estate with material participation rules are not taken into account in determining adjusted gross income for purposes of phase-out of the $25,000 rental real estate exemption.[7]

Example. Al owns building X and building Y, both interests in rental real estate. In 1995, Al is a qualifying taxpayer under the rental real estate with material participation rules. Al does not elect

---

1. IRC Sec. 469(c)(7)(C).
2. Treas. Reg. §1.469-9(d).
3. Treas. Reg. §1.469-9(e)(3).
4. Treas. Reg. §1.469-9(g).
5. Treas. Reg. §1.469-9(f).
6. Treas. Reg. §1.469-9(h).
7. Treas. Reg. §1.469-9(j).

to treat X and Y as one activity under the rental real estate with material participation rules. As a result, X and Y are treated as separate activities. Al materially participates in X which has $100,000 of passive losses disallowed from prior years and produces $20,000 of losses in 1995. Al does not materially participate in Y which produces $40,000 of income in 1995. Al also has $50,000 of income from other nonpassive sources in 1995. Al otherwise meets the requirements of the $25,000 rental real estate exemption.

Because X is not a passive activity in 1995, the $20,000 of losses produced by X in 1995 are nonpassive losses that may be used by Al to offset part of the $50,000 of nonpassive income. Accordingly, Al is left with $30,000 ($50,000 - $20,000) of nonpassive income. In addition, Al may use the prior year disallowed passive losses of X to offset any income from X and passive income from other sources. Therefore, Al may offset the $40,000 of passive income from Y with $40,000 of passive losses from X.

Because Al has $60,000 ($100,000 - $40,000) of passive losses remaining from X and meets all of the requirements of the $25,000 rental real estate exemption, Al may offset up to $25,000 of nonpassive income with passive losses from X under the exemption. As a result, Al has $5,000 ($30,000 - $25,000) of nonpassive income remaining and disallowed passive losses from X of $35,000 ($60,000 - $25,000) in 1995.[1]

A taxpayer may have regrouped his activities without regard to the manner in which they were grouped in the preceding taxable years for the first taxable year beginning after December 31, 1993 to the extent necessary or appropriate to take advantage of the rental real estate with material participation exception.[2] See also Q 1294.

HOBBY LOSS RULE

1300. What is the "hobby loss" rule? How does it limit deductions?

The "hobby loss" rule limits a taxpayer's deductions if the Service determines that the taxpayer did not enter into the activity with a profit motive or that he continued in a money-losing venture after the possibility of profit has lost its importance to him. Once it is determined that the activity was not profit-motivated, the amount by which deductions exceed income attributable to the activity (e.g., the amount of loss attributable to the activity) is not deductible.[3] Thus, the taxpayer can deduct amounts that are deductible without regard to any profit motive (such as otherwise allowable interest, certain taxes, and casualty losses) and expenses that are allowable for activities engaged in for profit, to the extent that gross income attributable to the activity exceeds the deductions allowed without regard to profit motive. These deduction limitations apply to an activity continued without a profit motive from the time when the nature of the activity changed.

Whether an activity is engaged in for profit is determined from all relevant facts and circumstances.[4] Some factors that will be considered in determining whether or not the activity is profit-motivated include: (1) whether the activity is conducted in a businesslike manner; (2) the qualifications of the taxpayer or his advisers; (3) the amount of time and effort spent by the taxpayer or whether his agents and employees are competent to carry on the activity (the taxpayer need not personally manage the operation); (4) the potential for appreciation of the venture's assets; (5) the taxpayer's history with similar or dissimilar programs; (6) the taxpayer's success or failure with the

---

1. Treas. Reg. §1.469-9(j)(2).
2. Treas. Reg. §1.469-11(b)(3)(iii).
3. IRC Sec. 183.
4. Treas. Reg. §1.183-2(b).

particular activity; (7) the amount of occasional profits in relation to losses and to the amount of the taxpayer's investment; (8) the taxpayer's financial status, whether he can benefit from losses, and whether his main source of income is from some other activity; (9) elements of personal pleasure or recreation he derives from the activity.

A "reasonable" expectation of profit is not required, as when the probability of loss is much greater than the probability of gain.[1] However, the taxpayer must engage in the activity with a genuine profit motive.[2] All facts and circumstances are taken into consideration, but greater weight is given to objective facts than to the parties' mere statements of their intent.[3]

Deductions permitted by the hobby loss rule are determined and allowed according to the following sequence: (1) amounts allowable under other IRC provisions without regard to whether the activity is profit-motivated (but other IRC provisions limiting the amount of these deductions would apply, such as limitations imposed on deductions for interest payments under IRC Sec. 163(d)); (2) to the extent that the gross income attributable to the activity exceeds deductions allowable under (1) above, amounts that would be allowed if the activity were engaged in for profit and that do not result in basis adjustments; (3) to the extent that the gross income attributable to the activity exceeds deductions allowable under (1) and (2) above, amounts that would be allowed if the activity was engaged in for profit and that result in basis adjustments, such as depreciation, partially worthless bad debts, and the disallowed portion of a casualty loss.[4]

Although IRC Section 183 addresses only the activities of individuals and S corporations, both the Service and Tax Court have taken the position that it also applies to partnerships.[5] The rule is applied at the partnership level and is reflected in the partner's distributive shares.[6]

If the gross income from the activity (determined without regard to profit motive) exceeds deductions for three or more taxable years in a period of five consecutive taxable years, the activity is presumed to be conducted for profit. (The net operating loss deduction is not taken into account as a deduction for this purpose.)[7] However, the Service is not prevented from attempting to rebut the presumption.[8]

The taxpayer may elect to postpone a determination of whether the presumption applies. The election postpones a profit determination until after the close of the fifth taxable year of the activity, so the Service will not try to limit deductions until the end of that year. Generally, the election must be made within three years after the due date (without regard to extensions) of the return for the first year of the activity.[9] However, making the election extends the statutory period for assessment of deficiency until two years after the due date (without extensions) for filing the return for the fifth year.[10]

---

1. *Dreicer v. Comm.*, 78 TC 642 (1982), aff'd. without op. 702 F.2d 1205 (1983).
2. *Fox v. Comm.*, 80 TC 972 (1983).
3. *Engdahl v. Comm.*, 72 TC 659 (1979).
4. IRC Sec. 183(b); Treas. Reg. §1.183-1(b).
5. Rev. Rul. 77-320, 1977-2 CB 78; *Silberman v. Comm.*, TC Memo 1983-782.
6. Rev. Rul. 77-320, above.
7. IRC Sec. 183(d).
8. *Dunn v. Comm.*, 70 TC 715 (1978).
9. Temp. Treas. Reg. §12.9.
10. IRC Sec. 183(e).

If an electing taxpayer dies, the five year presumption period ends, even if profits are realized by the taxpayer's estate in winding up the activity. As the estate is a separate entity from the taxpayer, the estate's profits are not to be taken into consideration with regard to the for profit presumption in connection with the taxpayer's activity in years prior to his death.[1] The two year extension period for the statutory assessment of any deficiency begins to run from the time for filing a return for the year of death if death occurs during the five year period.[2]

---

1. Rev. Rul. 79-204, 1979-2 CB 111.
2. TAM 8718001.

DEDUCTION OF INTEREST AND EXPENSES

INTEREST

Generally

1301. Is interest expense deductible?

To be deductible, interest must be paid or accrued on an "indebtedness" and the indebtedness must be that of the taxpayer. A taxpayer generally cannot deduct the interest he pays on the debt of another.[1] See also Q 1303.

However, certain interest expenses are not deductible: for example, interest paid on a loan used to buy or carry tax-exempt securities (see Q 1306); or interest on debt incurred or continued to buy or carry mutual funds to the extent that exempt-interest dividends are distributed to the shareholder (see Q 1170); and under certain circumstances, the interest on a loan used to buy or carry a life insurance policy or an endowment or annuity contract.[2]

The deduction of some interest expenses is deferred, such as the interest on borrowing incurred or continued to purchase or carry market discount bonds (Q 1308), Treasury bills, or short-term corporate obligations (Q 1307), and certain borrowing between related parties.[3] Cash basis taxpayers must allocate prepaid interest payments to the year or years in which payments represent a charge for the use of borrowed money and may take a deduction only for the amount properly allocable to the specific tax year.[4]

Special rules limit the deduction of personal interest (see Q 1302), qualified residence interest (see Q 1303), investment interest (see Q 1304), student loan interest (see Q 1309) and interest subject to the passive loss rule (see Q 1292, Q 1293). Proposed and temporary regulations provide complex and detailed rules for allocating interest expense for the purpose of applying these limits. See Q 1305 for an explanation of the interest tracing rules.

Personal Interest

1302. What is personal interest? Is it deductible?

Personal interest is generally interest on debt incurred to buy consumer items (other than loans secured by a personal residence, as discussed in Q 1303) such as cars, televisions, etc. Personal interest is any interest *other than* interest allocable to passive activities (Q 1292), trade or business interest, investment interest (Q 1304), qualified residence interest (Q 1303), or interest payable under IRC Section 6601 on any unpaid portion of federal estate tax during the period there is an extension of time for payment in effect with respect to a reversionary or remainder interest.[5] Personal interest is not deductible.[6]

---

1. But see Treas. Reg. §1.163-1(b).
2. IRC Sec. 264.
3. IRC Sec. 267.
4. IRC Sec. 461(g).
5. IRC Sec. 163(h)(2).
6. IRC Sec. 163(h)(1).

Personal interest includes interest on tax deficiencies. See *Robinson v. Comm.*[1] (holding that Temp. Treas. Regs. §§1.163-8T and 1.163-9T(b)(2)(i)(A) are valid; further holding that the interest on the underpayment of the taxpayer's income tax liability was nondeductible personal interest; and also holding that *Redlark v. Comm.*,[2] *rev'd and remanded*, 141 F.3d 936 (9th Cir. 1998) will no longer be followed).[3] It also includes otherwise deductible borrowing to buy personal life insurance.

Interest on *qualified higher education loans* (see Q 1309) is not personal interest.[4]

The allocation of debt to expenditures under temporary regulations is explained in Q 1305.

Qualified Residence Interest

1303. Is interest on debt secured by a taxpayer's residence deductible?

Yes, within limits. "Qualified residence interest" is deductible, subject to the definitions and limitations explained below. "Qualified residence interest" is interest paid or accrued during the taxable year on acquisition indebtedness or home equity indebtedness with respect to a qualified residence of the taxpayer.[5] Generally, it is deductible without regard to the expenditure to which it is allocated under the interest tracing rules. It is not taken into account in determining passive activity income or loss or the amount of investment interest.[6]

Interest paid by a taxpayer on a mortgage upon real estate of which he is the legal or equitable owner may be deducted as interest on indebtedness, even though the taxpayer is not directly liable on the mortgage obligation.[7] The Tax Court has held that a married couple was entitled to deduct amounts they paid on a construction loan taken by the builder as qualified residence interest although they were not personally obligated to repay the loan. The court concluded that the couple had a possessory and an equitable interest in the residence and could therefore deduct the applicable amounts.[8] The Tax Court has also held that married taxpayers could deduct interest they paid on a mortgage as qualified residence interest, even though the taxpayer's brother was the person directly liable on the mortgage obligation. The court found the taxpayers had held the benefits and burdens of ownership and thus were the equitable owners of the home and entitled to deduct qualified residence interest.[9]

The Tax Court denied a deduction for mortgage interest to individuals renting a home under a lease with an option to purchase the property; although the house was their principal residence, they did not have legal or equitable title to the home and the earnest money did not provide ownership status.[10] Similarly, the Tax Court held that

---

1. 119 TC 44 (2002).
2. 106 TC 31 (1996).
3. See also *Alfaro v. Comm.*, TC Memo 2002-309 (following *Robinson*, above), *aff'd*, No. 03-60261 (5th Cir. 2003); *Fitzmaurice v. United States*, 87 AFTR 2d ¶2001-429 (S.D. TX 2001).
4. IRC Sec. 163(h)(2)(F).
5. IRC Sec. 163(h)(3)(A).
6. Temp. Treas. Reg. §1.163-8T(m)(3).
7. Treas. Reg. §1.163-1(b).
8. *Belden v. Comm.*, TC Memo 1995-360.
9. *Uslu v. Comm.*, TC Memo 1997-551.
10. *Blanche v. Comm.*, TC Memo 2001-63, *aff'd*, 2002 U.S. App. LEXIS (5th Cir. 2002).

because a taxpayer had an option agreement and not an agreement for the purchase and sale of property, the taxpayer could not deduct mortgage interest or real property taxes. According to the court, the taxpayer had not acquired sufficient benefits and burdens relating to the property to be deemed the equitable owner of the property.[1] An individual member of a homeowner's association was denied a deduction for interest paid by the association on a common building because the member was not the party primarily responsible for repaying the loan and the member's principal residence was not the specific security for the loan.[2] Assuming that the loan is otherwise a bona fide debt secured by the principal residence, a taxpayer may deduct interest paid on a mortgage loan from his qualified plan even where the amount by which the loan exceeded the $50,000 limit of IRC Section 72(p) is deemed to be a taxable distribution.[3]

New, Temporary Mortgage Insurance Deduction

Premiums paid by a taxpayer during the taxable year for "qualified mortgage insurance" in connection with acquisition indebtedness for the taxpayer's qualified residence will be treated as interest that is qualified residence interest.[4] But the amount otherwise treated as interest must be reduced (but not below zero) by 10% of the amount per each $1,000 or fraction thereof ($500 for married individuals filing separate returns) that the taxpayer's adjusted gross income exceeds $100,000 ($50,000 for married individuals filing separate returns) for the taxable year.[5] This favorable tax treatment does not apply to any mortgage insurance contracts issued *before* January 1, 2007, and does not apply to amounts paid or accrued *after* December 31, 2007 (or property allocable to any period after that date).[6]

"Qualified mortgage insurance" means (1) mortgage insurance provided by the VA, FHA, or Rural Housing Administration, and (2) private mortgage insurance (as defined by Section 2 of the Homeowners Protection Act of 1998).[7] A special rule for prepaid qualified mortgage insurance requires that any amount prepaid by a taxpayer for qualified mortgage insurance, which is properly allocable to any mortgage the payment of which extends to periods that are after the close of the taxable year in which the amount is paid, will be treated as paid in those periods so allocated. No deduction is allowed for the unamortized balance of an account if the mortgage is satisfied before the end of its term. This does not, however, apply to amounts paid for qualified mortgage insurance provided by the VA or the Rural Housing Administration.[8]

Definitions

Acquisition indebtedness: The definition of acquisition indebtedness has three parts: (1) the debt must be incurred to acquire, construct or substantially improve a residence; (2) the residence must be a "qualified residence"; and (3) the debt must be secured by the residence.[9] This definition is subject to the further definitions and limitations discussed below. Although all three parts must occur before the debt is "acquisition indebtedness," they need not occur simultaneously. For example, a taxpayer may incur debt in 2004

---

1. *Jones v. Comm.*, TC Memo 2006-176.
2. Let. Rul 200029018.
3. FSA 200047022.
4. IRC Sec. 163(h)(3)(E)(i), as added by TRHCA 2006.
5. IRC Sec. 163(h)(3)(E)(ii), as added by TRHCA 2006.
6. IRC Secs. 163(h)(3)(E)(iii), 163(h)(3)(E)(iv), as added by TRHCA 2006.
7. IRC Sec. 163(h)(4)(E), as added by TRHCA 2006.
8. IRC Sec. 163(h)(4)(F), as added by TRHCA 2006.
9. IRC Sec. 163(h)(3)(B).

to construct a residence and secure it by the residence. When the residence becomes a qualified residence in 2005, the debt would become "acquisition indebtedness."

Home equity indebtedness: Home equity indebtedness means any indebtedness (1) that is secured by the qualified residence but is not acquisition indebtedness, (2) to the extent that it does not exceed the fair market value of the residence reduced by the amount of acquisition indebtedness. The aggregate amount that may be treated as home equity indebtedness (if incurred after October 13, 1987) is $100,000.[1] Limits with respect to debt incurred on or before October 13, 1987 are discussed below.

Incurred to acquire, construct or substantially improve: There are two ways that the requirement that a debt be "incurred to acquire, construct or substantially improve a residence" can be met. First, if the proceeds of a debt are used, within the meaning of the tracing rules found in Temp. Treas. Reg. §1.163-8T, to acquire, construct or substantially improve the residence, the requirement is met. For example, a conventional, bank-financed consumer purchase of a principal residence will typically qualify under this provision because the loan proceeds will be traceable to the purchase of the residence. Alternatively, there is a 90-day rule (see below) under which debt may qualify. See Q 1305 for an explanation of the interest tracing rules. The limit on the amount of debt that may be treated as "incurred to acquire, construct or substantially improve" a residence is the cost of the residence, including any improvements.

Qualified residence: A qualified residence is the taxpayer's principal residence and *one* other residence that the taxpayer (a) used for personal purposes during the year for more than the greater of 14 days or 10% of the number of days it was rented at a fair rental value, or (b) did not rent during the year.[2] The IRS has ruled that where a principal residence is destroyed and the taxpayer sells the remaining land or reconstructs the dwelling and reoccupies it as the taxpayer's principal residence within a reasonable time period, the property will continue to be treated as a qualified residence for the period between the destruction and the sale or reconstruction and reoccupation of the land.[3]

Secured by: Temporary regulations provide generally that an instrument of debt such as a mortgage, deed of trust or land contract will meet the "secured by" requirement, while a security interest such as a mechanic's lien or judgment lien will not.[4] If indebtedness used to purchase a residence is secured by property other than the residence, the interest incurred on it is not residential interest but is personal interest.[5] Where a taxpayer uses an annuity contract as collateral to obtain or continue a mortgage loan, the allocable amount of interest is nondeductible to the extent the loan is collateralized by the annuity contract.[6] However, where loans from IRC Section 401(a) qualified plans were secured by the debtors' principal residences, the Service determined that the interest (which was otherwise deductible) was qualified residence interest.[7]

The Conference report for the Tax Reform Act of 1986 indicates that the security interest must be one perfected under local law.

---

1. IRC Sec. 163(h)(3)(C).
2. IRC Sec. 163(h)(5)[(4)](A). See, e.g., FSA 200137033.
3. Rev. Rul. 96-32, 1996-1 CB 177.
4. Temp. Treas. Reg. §1.163-10T(o)(1).
5. Let. Ruls. 8742025, 8743063, 8906031.
6. Rev. Rul. 95-53, 1995-2 CB 30.
7. Let. Rul. 8935051.

In the case of housing cooperatives, debt secured by stock held by the taxpayer as a tenant-stockholder is treated as secured by the residence the taxpayer is entitled to occupy as a tenant-stockholder.[1] Even though state or local law (or the cooperative agreement) may restrict the use of such stock as security, the stock may be treated as securing such debt if the taxpayer can satisfy the IRS that the debt was incurred to acquire the stock.[2] Also, if state homestead laws or other debtor protection laws (in effect on August 16, 1986) restrict the rights of secured parties with respect to certain types of residential mortgages, interest on the debt is not treated as nondeductible personal interest, as long as the lender has a perfected security interest and the interest on the debt is otherwise qualified residence interest.[3]

Limitation Amounts

There is a limitation of $1,000,000 on the amount of aggregate debt that may be treated as "acquisition indebtedness," *but* the amount of refinanced debt that may be treated as acquisition indebtedness is limited to the amount of debt being refinanced.[4] The deductibility of interest incurred on "home equity indebtedness" is limited to debt of $100,000, or the amount of equity (that is, the fair market value of the home less the acquisition indebtedness), whichever is less.[5]

The effect of this limitation is that for transactions after 1987, a homeowner who wishes to borrow against the equity in his home can deduct the interest only on $100,000 of such debt *or* on the amount that is equal to his equity, whichever is less. Interest on amounts over this limit do not qualify as "home equity indebtedness."

Indebtedness incurred on or before October 13, 1987 (and limited refinancing of it) that is secured by a qualified residence is considered acquisition indebtedness. This pre-October 14, 1987 indebtedness is not subject to the $1,000,000 aggregate limit, but is included in the aggregate limit as it applies to indebtedness incurred after October 13, 1987.[6]

Qualified residence interest is not subject to the rules that apply to personal interest even if the amounts borrowed are used to buy consumer goods (see Q 1302).[7]

90-day Rules

In order to be *incurred to acquire, construct or substantially improve* a residence, a debt must (a) be traceable under the tracing rules of Temp. Treas. Reg. §1.163-8T to the purchase of a qualified residence, or (b) qualify under one of two 90-day rules.[8]

The 90-day rule with respect to *acquiring* a residence provides that expenditures to acquire the residence within 90 days before or after the date the debt is incurred can be treated as "incurred to acquire" the residence.

The 90-day rule with respect to *constructing* or *substantially improving* a residence is somewhat more complex. A debt incurred *before* the residence or improvement is

---

1. IRC Sec. 163(h)(5)[(4)](B).
2. See Temp. Treas. Reg. §1.163-10T(q)(2).
3. IRC Sec. 163(h)(5)[(4)](C).
4. IRC Sec. 163(h)(3)(B); Notice 88-74, 1988-2 CB 385.
5. IRC Sec. 163(h)(3)(C).
6. IRC Sec. 163(h)(3)(D).
7. TD 8145, 1987-2 CB 47.
8. Notice 88-74, above.

complete may be treated as "incurred to construct or substantially improve" a residence to the extent of expenditures (to construct or improve the residence) made no more than 24 months prior to the date the debt is incurred. If the debt is incurred no later than 90 days *after* the residence is complete, it may be treated as "incurred to construct or substantially improve" a residence to the extent of expenditures (to construct or improve the residence) made during the following period: beginning 24 months before the residence or improvement is complete, and ending on the date the debt is incurred.

Guidelines state that a determination of whether a residence or an improvement is "complete" depends upon all the facts and circumstances.[1]

Date of Loan

The date a debt is "incurred" will be the date the loan proceeds are disbursed to or for the benefit of the taxpayer (typically the loan closing date). There is an exception to this rule, to the effect that taxpayers may (apparently if it is to their advantage) treat debt as incurred on the date that a written application is made to incur the debt. This may be done only to the extent that funds are actually disbursed within a reasonable time, which is described as 30 days. (A "reasonable time" is also provided, in the event the application is rejected, for the taxpayer to reapply for a loan.) This provision does not apply for purposes of determining whether debt is pre-October 13, 1987 indebtedness.[2]

Refinancings

Refinancing of a debt that was incurred to acquire, construct or substantially improve a residence will be treated in the same manner as the first debt, to the extent that the proceeds are used to refinance the first debt. (The tracing rules found in Temporary Treasury Regulation Section 1.163-8T are used to determine how the proceeds are used. See Q 1305.)

If a taxpayer uses part of the loan proceeds to refinance an existing debt and the remaining proceeds for other purposes, the debt may qualify as acquisition indebtedness to the extent of the refinancing. The remaining debt may qualify as home equity indebtedness, up to the applicable limits.

Reimbursements of Interest Overcharges

Taxpayers generally are not permitted a deduction for an interest payment made on a debt for which no liability exists or reasonably appears to exist. However, if a taxpayer in good faith makes an interest payment on an adjustable rate mortgage (ARM), and a portion of the interest is later determined to have been erroneously charged, the taxpayer is permitted under IRC Section 163(a) to deduct the interest overcharge in the year paid. The taxpayer's recovery of the overcharge is includable in the taxpayer's gross income in the year of recovery, but only to the extent that the prior deduction of the overcharge reduced the taxpayer's income tax in a prior tax year. This result is the same whether the lender refunds the overcharge or reduces the outstanding principal on the taxpayer's mortgage by the amount of the overcharge.[3]

---

1. Notice 88-74, above.
2. Notice 88-74, above.
3. Rev. Rul. 92-91, 1992-2 CB 49.

Debt Incident to Divorce

Regulations will provide that a debt incurred to acquire the interest of a spouse or former spouse pursuant to a divorce or legal separation will be treated as debt incurred to acquire a residence (for purposes of the definition of "acquisition indebtedness" in IRC Section 163) without regard to the manner the transaction would otherwise be treated under IRC Section 1041 (regarding transfers incident to divorce).[1]

Prepaid Interest and Points

Cash basis taxpayers must generally allocate prepaid interest payments to the year or years in which payments represent a charge for the use of borrowed money and may take a deduction only for the amount properly allocable to the specific tax year. However, points paid on debt incurred to buy or improve (and secured by) the taxpayer's principal residence are generally excepted from the prepaid interest limitation if payment of points is an established business practice in the area *and* the amount does not exceed the amount generally charged in the area.[2]

The IRS has stated that points paid in connection with the acquisition of a principal residence will generally be deductible by a cash basis taxpayer in the year paid if all of the following requirements are satisfied: (1) the amount is clearly shown on the settlement statement as points charged for the mortgage; (2) the points are computed as a percentage of the principal amount of the debt; (3) the payment of points is an established business practice in the area, and the amount of points paid does not exceed the amount generally charged in that area; (4) the points are paid in connection with the acquisition of a principal residence, and the loan is secured by that residence; (5) the points do not exceed the sum of the funds provided at or before closing by the purchaser, plus any points paid by the seller, and such funds paid by the purchaser may not be borrowed from the lender or mortgage; and (6) the points may not be a substitute for amounts that ordinarily are stated separately on the settlement statement, such as appraisal fees, inspection fees, property taxes, etc.[3]

The fact that a full deduction was available for points in the year they were paid did not mean the taxpayers were required to claim it in that year, according to a private letter ruling. A couple for whom it was more advantageous to take the standard deduction in the year the mortgage was obtained were not precluded from amortizing the points over the life of the loan, starting in the following tax year.[4]

In the event that points are paid by the seller (or charged to the seller) in connection with a loan to the taxpayer, they can still be treated as paid directly by the taxpayer if all the tests above are met, *and* provided that the taxpayer subtracts the amount of any seller-paid points from the purchase price of the home in computing its basis. But such treatment is not available for the following: (a) the amount of points paid on acquisition and allocable to principal in excess of the amount that may be treated as acquisition indebtedness; (b) points paid for loans used to *improve* (as opposed to acquire) a principal residence; (c) points paid for loans used to purchase or improve a residence that is not the taxpayer's principal residence; and (d) points paid on a refinancing loan, home

---

1. Notice 88-74, above. See also Let. Rul. 8928010.
2. IRC Sec. 461(g).
3. See IRS Pub. 530.
4. See Let. Rul. 199905033.

equity loan, or line of credit.[1] "Loan origination fees" include points paid on FHA and VA loans if the points were paid during taxable years beginning after 1990.[2]

Refinancings

Points paid on refinancing a principal residence must generally be amortized over the life of the loan.[3] However, a taxpayer who was able to establish a direct link between acquisition of a residence and the necessity of refinancing to complete that step was permitted to take a current deduction for such points.[4]

In *Hurley v. Comm.*,[5] the Tax Court stated that IRC Section 461(g)(2) provides two instances where a taxpayer may deduct the entire amount of points paid to *refinance* a personal residence: (1) when the taxpayer refinances in order to purchase a new home; or (2) refinances in order to make improvements to the home. Consequently, the court stated, points paid when a taxpayer refinances a personal residence simply or only for the purpose of obtaining a lower payment are not deductible (citing *Kelly v. Comm.*[6]). The court further stated that IRC Section 461(g)(2) applies if a taxpayer pays points to refinance "in connection with" the improvement of his principal residence; and based on the intent of Congress, the Tax Court applies a broad interpretation of the phrase "in connection with." In *Hurley*, the Tax Court upheld the taxpayers' $4,400 deduction for points they paid to refinance their mortgage where the evidence (testimonial and otherwise) demonstrated to the court's satisfaction that the taxpayers had negotiated the refinancing of their personal residence in order to finance their home improvements (e.g., the home improvements started nine days after the refinancing). The court acknowledged that the taxpayers had saved money as a result of the refinancing, but also noted that the refinancing had financially enabled the taxpayers to complete the improvements to their principal residence. The court determined it was immaterial that the cost of the taxpayers' improvements ($18,735) exceeded their savings from the refinancing ($14,400) because the difference was not grossly disproportionate.

If part of the refinancing proceeds are used to improve the taxpayer's principal residence, the portion of points allocable to the improvements may be deducted in the year paid.[7]

The IRS has stated that if a homeowner is refinancing a mortgage for a *second* time, a taxpayer may deduct all the not-yet-deducted points from the first refinancing when that loan is paid off.[8]

Investment Interest

1304. Is interest on amounts borrowed in order to make or hold taxable investments deductible?

Yes, within limits. The Code permits a deduction for interest paid in the year on indebtedness properly allocable to property held for investment (so-called "investment interest.")[9] See Q 1305 for an explanation of the interest tracing regulations.

1. See IRS Pub. 530.
2. Rev. Proc. 92-12A, 1992-1 CB 664, *as modified by* Rev. Proc. 94-27, 1994-1 CB 613.
3. IR-2003-127 (11-3-2003).
4. *Huntsman v. Comm.*, 90-2 USTC ¶50,340 (8th Cir. 1990), *rev'g* 91 TC 917 (1988).
5. TC Summary Opinion 2005-125.
6. TC Memo 1991-605.
7. Rev. Rul. 87-22, 1987-1 CB 146.
8. IR-2003-127 (11-3-03).
9. IRC Sec. 163(d).

However, there is a limit on *otherwise allowable* deductions that may be taken by an individual investor for investment interest.[1] (Interest not deductible for some other reason, such as interest on indebtedness to purchase or carry tax-exempt obligations, is not taken into consideration in determining the amount subject to this limit.) Deductible short sale expenses (Q 1024, Q 1025) are treated as interest subject to the limit.[2]

Generally, the investment interest deduction is limited to the amount of "net investment income" (see below). Any other investment interest expense is considered excess investment interest and is disallowed.[3]

"Net investment income" is investment income *reduced* by the deductible expenses–other than interest–that are directly connected with its production.[4] For purposes of this calculation, the 2% floor on miscellaneous itemized deductions is applied *before* investment income is reduced by investment expenses; thus, only those investment expenses that are allowable as a deduction *after* application of the 2% floor operate to reduce investment income.[5] See Q 1310 for an explanation of the deduction for investment expenses.

"Investment income" means the *sum* of: (1) gross income from property held for investment (other than net gain attributable to dispositions of such property); (2) the *excess*, if any, of (i) "net gain" attributable to the disposition of property held for investment *over* (ii) the "net capital gain" determined by taking into account gains and losses from dispositions of property held for investment; *and* (3) any net capital gain (or, if less, the net gain amount described in (2)), with respect to which a special election is made (see below).[6] In other words, "investment income," for purposes of computing the investment interest deduction, generally does *not* include net capital gain from the disposition of investment property, *unless* the election described below is made.[7]

The Tax Court held that "net gain" for purposes of IRC Section 163(d)(4)(B)(ii) means the excess (if any) of total gains over total losses, including capital loss carryovers, from the disposition of property held for investment. The court further held that "net gain," as that term is used in IRC Section 163(d)(4)(B)(ii), required inclusion of the taxpayers' capital losses and capital loss carryovers for purposes of calculating the IRC Section 163(d)(1) limit on the investment interest expense deduction.[8]

"Investment income" includes "qualified dividend income" (see Q 1420) *only* to the extent the taxpayer *elects* to treat such income as investment income.[9] See also IRC Sec. 1(h)(11)(D)(i) (qualified dividend income does *not* include any amount the taxpayer takes into account as investment income under IRC Section 163(d)(4)(B)).

Special elections are available that allow taxpayers to *elect* in any year to include all or a portion of net capital gain or qualified dividend income attributable to dispositions of property held for investment, as investment income. If the elections are made, any net capital gain or qualified dividend income treated as investment income will be subject to

1. IRC Sec. 163(d).
2. IRC Sec. 163(d)(3)(C).
3. IRC Sec. 163(d)(1).
4. See IRC Sec. 163(d)(4)(A).
5. Conference Agreement for TRA '86 at pp. 153-154.
6. IRC Sec. 163(d)(4)(B).
7. House Committee Report, OBRA '93.
8. *Gorkes v. Comm.*, TC Summary Opinion 2003-160.
9. IRC Sec. 163(d)(4)(B) (flush sentence); see Treas. Reg. §1.163(d)-1(a).

the taxpayer's ordinary income tax rates.[1] The advantage of making the elections is that a taxpayer may increase the amount of his investment income against which investment interest is deducted, thus receiving the full benefit of the deduction.[2]

The elections for net capital gain and qualified dividend income must be made on or before the due date (including extensions) of the income tax return for the taxable year in which the net capital gain is recognized, or the qualified dividend income is received, respectively.[3] (But compare Let. Rul. 200033020, in which a taxpayer was permitted to make a late election to treat capital gains as investment income based on the Service's conclusion that the taxpayer had acted reasonably and in good faith, and that granting the extension would not prejudice the interests of the government.[4]

The elections are made on Form 4952, "Investment Interest Expense Deduction" and may not be revoked for that year, except with IRS permission.[5] See, e.g., Let. Rul. 200146018 (where the Service ruled that the taxpayers' correct status as securities traders would have entitled them to treat such gains as investment income anyway; thus, allowing them to revoke their prior election did not prejudice the interest of the government or cause undue administrative burdens). However, making the election in one year does not bind the taxpayer for any other year.[6]

In an unpublished private letter ruling, the taxpayer (whose former tax return preparer had recently died) prepared his return for Year 1 using commercial software. The return involved significant securities transactions, including net long-term capital gains. The return also reflected investment interest expense, some of which was disallowed due to lack of net investment income. The taxpayer was not aware: that he could have made an election to include in investment income all or part of the net capital gain; the necessity for making the election; nor how it could impact his return or the provisions for amending the return until the taxpayer subsequently sought help from a tax professional in the summer of Year 3. Upon review of Year 1 and Year 2, the tax professional noted the item and explained the situation to the taxpayer. The taxpayer requested consent to revoke the default election made inadvertently when the taxpayer filed the return, and to permit him to make an informed election by filing an amended return. The Service granted the taxpayer an extension of time for making the election, requiring the taxpayer to file a revised Form 4952 and Schedule D and to include a copy of the ruling with an amended return for Year 1. The Service also granted consent to revoke the first election made on the Year 1 return.[7]

The Service privately ruled that: (1) the term "property" (under IRC Section 163(d)(5)(A)(i)) included interest-free loans (which are deemed to yield gross income as a result of interest imputed under IRC Section 7872) to a tax-exempt foundation; (2) any imputed interest income deemed received by the taxpayer on the potential loan from the line of credit to the foundation would be "investment income" (under IRC Section 163(d)(4)(B)(i)); and (3) any interest paid by the taxpayer on the line of credit used to make the potential loan to the foundation would be "investment interest" (under IRC Section 163(d)(3)(A)).[8]

---

1. Treas. Reg. §1.163(d)-1(a).
2. See IRC Sec. 163(d)(4).
3. Treas. Reg. §1.163(d)-1(b).
4. See also Let. Rul. 200303013.
5. Treas. Regs. §§1.163(d)-1(b), 1.163(d)-1(c).
6. See Treas. Reg. §1.163(d)-1(c).
7. Let. Rul. 161402-04, *unpublished* (March 22, 2005).
8. Let. Rul. 200503004.

The IRS has determined that capital loss carryovers that reduce taxable gain for income tax purposes in the year to which carried as a result of the election should also reduce investment income to the same extent for purposes of the investment expense limitation.[1]

Investment interest expense disallowed because of the investment income limitation will be treated as investment interest paid or accrued in the succeeding tax year.[2] The IRS will not limit the carryover of a taxpayer's disallowed investment interest to a succeeding taxable year to the taxpayer's taxable income for the taxable year in which the interest is paid or accrued.[3] Prior to the issuance of Revenue Ruling 95-16, several federal courts had held that no taxable income limitation existed on the amount of disallowed investment interest that could be carried over.[4]

Investment interest expense and investment income and expenses do not include items from a trade or business in which the taxpayer materially participates. The IRS has determined that interest on a loan incurred to purchase stock in a C corporation was investment interest (where the purchaser was not a dealer or trader in stock or securities), even though the purchaser acquired the stock to protect his employment with the C corporation.[5] In a decision citing Revenue Ruling 93-68, the Tax Court held that interest on indebtedness incurred to purchase a taxpayer's share of stock in a family-owned mortuary business was subject to the investment interest limitation, despite the fact that the taxpayer purchased the stock to conduct business full time and the fact that no dividends had been paid on the stock.[6]

The investment interest limitation is coordinated with the passive loss rules (see Q 1292 to Q 1299) created by TRA '86, so that interest and income subject to the passive loss rules are not taken into consideration under the investment interest limitation.[7] Interest expense incurred to purchase an interest in a passive activity is allocated to that passive activity and is not investment interest.[8] (Very generally, a passive activity is any activity that involves the conduct of a trade or business in which the taxpayer does not materially participate and any rental activity.[9]) However, portfolio income of a passive activity and expense (including interest expense) allocable to it is considered investment income and expense, not passive income and expense.[10]

Temporary regulations provide that, for purposes of the investment interest and passive loss rules, interest expense is generally allocated on the basis of the use of the proceeds of the underlying debt (see Q 1305).

Future regulations will clarify the treatment of interest on a debt incurred to purchase a partnership or S corporation interest. IRS guidance generally requires that such interest expense be allocated among all the assets of the entity using any reasonable

---

1. TAM 9549002.
2. IRC Sec. 163(d)(2).
3. Rev. Rul. 95-16, 1995-1 CB 9.
4. See *Sharp v. U.S.*, 94-1 USTC ¶50,001 (Fed.Cir. 1993); *Beyer v. Comm.*, 90-2 USTC ¶50,536 (4th Cir. 1990); *Haas v. U.S.*, 861 F. Supp. 43 (W.D. Mich. 1994); *Richardson v. U.S.*, 94-1 USTC ¶50,111 (W.D. Okla. 1994); *Lenz v. Comm.*, 101 TC 260 (1993); *Flood v. U.S.*, 845 F. Supp. 1367, 94-1 USTC ¶50,259 (D. Alaska 1993).
5. Rev. Rul. 93-68, 1993-2 CB 72.
6. *Russon v. Comm.*, 107 TC 263 (1996).
7. IRC Secs. 163(d), 469.
8. Temp. Treas. Reg. §1.163-8T(a)(4)(B).
9. IRC Sec. 469.
10. IRC Sec. 469(e)(1).

method.[1] Regulations will also clarify the treatment of interest on debt of passthrough entities allocated to distributions to the owners of the entity. If the debt of a passthrough entity is allocable under the interest tracing rules to distributions to owners of the entity, then the interest tracing rules will govern allocation of the owner's share of the entity's interest based on the owner's use of the debt proceeds. An optional allocation rule permits passthrough entities to allocate their interest expense to expenditures during the taxable year other than distributions, if certain requirements are met. The special rules for passthrough entities will not apply to taxpayers who use such entities to avoid or circumvent the interest tracing rules.[2]

1305. How is interest traced to personal, investment, and passive activity expenditures?

Generally, the interest tracing rules allocate debt and the interest on it to expenditures according to the use of the debt proceeds. The deductibility of the interest is generally determined by the expenditure to which it is allocated. The allocation of interest under these rules is unaffected by the use of any asset or property to secure the debt; for example, interest on a debt traced to the purchase of an automobile will be personal interest even though the debt may be secured by shares of stock.[3]

Specific Ordering Rules

The tracing of debt proceeds is accomplished by specific rules that determine the order in which amounts borrowed are used. The allocation of debt under these specific ordering rules depends on the manner in which the debt proceeds are distributed to and held by the borrower. The following alternatives and results are described in regulations:

(1) *Proceeds are deposited in borrower's account that also contains unborrowed funds:* The first expenditures made from the account (with two exceptions) will be treated as made from the debt proceeds to the extent thereof. If proceeds from more than one debt are deposited, the funds will be considered expended in the order in which they were deposited. If they were deposited simultaneously, they will be treated as deposited in the order in which the debts were incurred.[4]

Exceptions to this rule are: (a) any expenditure made from an account within the 30 days before or after the debt proceeds are deposited may be treated as made from the debt proceeds (to the extent thereof); and (b) if an account consists solely of debt proceeds and interest income on those proceeds, any expenditures from the account may be treated as first from the interest income, to the extent thereof at the time of the expenditure.[5]

> *Example*: Gladys purchases a certificate of deposit on May 1 for $3,000. On May 8 she borrows $5,000 and deposits it into her checking account, which also contains $5,000 of unborrowed funds. On May 21 she makes a down payment of $5,000 on a new car. On May 23 she invests $2,000 in stocks. Under rule (1), above, the debt proceeds (and interest thereon) would be traced to the car and characterized as personal interest; however, exception (a) permits Gladys to designate *any* expenditures during the 30 days before or after deposit as coming from the debt proceeds. Thus, Gladys

1. Notice 89-35, 1989-1 CB 675; see also Let. Rul. 9215013.
2. Notice 89-35, above.
3. Temp. Treas. Reg. §1.163-8T(c).
4. Temp. Treas. Reg. §1.163-8T(c)(4)(ii).
5. Notice 89-35, 1989-1 CB 675.

may trace the debt to the purchase of the certificate of deposit and the stock, and thus determine the deductibility of her interest expense under the rules for investment interest.

(2) *Proceeds are disbursed to a third party:* Expenditures directly to a person selling property or providing services to the borrower are treated as expenditures from the debt proceeds.[1]

(3) *No disbursement is made:* If the debt does not involve any cash disbursements (for example, the borrower is assuming a loan, or the seller is financing the purchase) the debt is treated as if the borrower had made an expenditure for the purpose to which the debt relates.[2]

(4) *Proceeds are disbursed to the borrower in cash:* Any expenditure made within 30 days before or after the debt proceeds are received in cash may be treated as made from the debt proceeds. Otherwise, the debt will be treated as used for personal expenditures. If the proceeds are deposited into the borrower's account and an expenditure is made from those proceeds (under the ordering rules described above) in the form of a cash withdrawal, the proceeds will be considered received in cash.[3]

(5) *Proceeds are held in an account:* Debt proceeds are treated as held for investment purposes while held in an account, even if the account does not bear interest. When an expenditure is made, the debt is reallocated as described above. The taxpayer may either reallocate the debt on the date of the expenditure *or* on the first day of the month (or the date of deposit, if later than the first day of the month) so long as all expenditures from the account are treated similarly.[4]

Repayments and Refinancings

When a debt is allocable to more than one type of expenditure, repayments are applied in a manner that maximizes the deductibility of the remaining interest. Thus, for example, if a debt is allocated to personal, investment, and passive activity expenditures, repayment would be applied first against the portion attributable to the personal expenditure.[5] If a debt (including interest on it or borrowing charges other than interest) is repaid with the proceeds of a second debt, the second debt will be allocated to the same expenditures as the repaid debt.[6] If, however, the amount of the second debt exceeds the amount of repayment, the excess will be allocated according to the normal allocation rules described above.

Reallocation of Debt

Debt that is allocated to an expenditure properly chargeable to a capital account with respect to an asset must be reallocated when the asset is sold or the nature of its use changes. For example, debt (and the interest on it) allocated to a computer purchased for business use must be reallocated to a personal expenditure if the computer is converted to personal use.[7]

---

1. Temp. Treas. Reg. §1.163-8T(c)(3)(i).
2. Temp. Treas. Reg. §1.163-8T(c)(3)(ii).
3. Notice 89-35, 1989-1 CB 675.
4. Temp. Treas. Reg. §1.163-8T(c)(4)(i).
5. Temp. Treas. Reg. §1.163-8T(d)(1).
6. Temp. Treas. Reg. §1.163-8T(e).
7. Temp. Treas. Reg. §1.163-8T(j).

Coordination With Other Provisions

Generally, any Internal Revenue Code provision that disallows, defers, or capitalizes an interest expense will be applied without regard to the expenditure to which the debt is allocated under these regulations, except that interest expense allocated to a personal expenditure is not capitalized.[1] For example, an interest expense on debt incurred or continued to purchase or carry tax-exempt obligations is not deductible regardless of the expenditure to which the debt is allocated under the regulations.[2] Interest expense that is not deductible because of a deferral provision is taken into account as allocated, but is deferred to the year in which it becomes deductible. Thus, for example, interest on an amount borrowed by an accrual method taxpayer from a related cash basis taxpayer is deferred even though allocated to a passive activity expenditure. When the expense becomes deductible it will be allocated to the passive activity regardless of how it is allocated when it is no longer deferred.[3]

1306. Is interest on indebtedness incurred to purchase or carry tax-exempt obligations deductible?

No deduction is allowed for interest on indebtedness "incurred or continued to purchase or carry" obligations the *interest* on which is tax-exempt.[4] (Where the obligation offers tax-exempt income other than interest, see Q 1311.) Whether debt was "incurred to purchase or carry" obligations on which interest is tax-exempt depends on the individual taxpayer's purpose for borrowing.[5] Where the necessary purpose to use borrowed funds to *buy or carry* tax-exempt interest obligations is shown, the interest deduction will be denied, even though no tax-exempt interest is currently being received.[6] Furthermore, the deduction is denied even though the taxpayer's motives are not tax avoidance but to realize a taxable profit from sale instead of interest.[7]

The taxpayer's purpose in borrowing requires an examination of all the facts and circumstances involved.[8] Purpose can be established by direct or by circumstantial evidence. According to IRS guidelines, if the loan proceeds can be directly traced to the purchase, there is direct evidence of a purpose to *purchase*. Nonetheless, this evidence is not conclusive, as the IRS acknowledges in pointing out that the deduction is not denied where proceeds of bona fide business borrowing are temporarily invested in tax-exempt interest obligations.[9]

Use of tax-exempt interest obligations as collateral for debt is direct evidence of a purpose to *carry* the obligations.[10] The Tax Court has determined that the use of tax-exempt municipal bonds as collateral did not, of itself, establish the necessary purpose to carry the bonds.[11] However, in a later Tax Court decision, the use of tax-exempt municipal bonds as collateral *did* establish a direct relationship between the carrying of

1. Temp. Treas. Reg. §1.163-8T(m)(2)(ii).
2. Temp. Treas. Reg. §1.163-8T(m)(2)(i).
3. Temp. Treas. Reg. §1.163-8T(m)(6), Ex.(2).
4. IRC Sec. 265(a)(2).
5. Rev. Proc. 72-18, 1972-1 CB 740, *as clarified by* Rev. Proc. 74-8, 1974-1 CB 419, and *as modified by* Rev. Proc. 87-53, 1987-2 CB 669.
6. *Clyde C. Pierce Corp. v. Comm.*, 120 F.2d 206 (5th Cir. 1941); *Illinois Terminal R.R. Co. v. U.S.*, 375 F.2d 1016 (Ct. Cl. 1967).
7. *Denman v. Slayton*, 282 U.S. 514 (1931).
8. *Indian Trail Trading Post, Inc. v. Comm.*, 60 TC 497 (1973), *aff'd per curiam*, 503 F.2d 102 (6th Cir. 1974).
9. Rev. Rul. 55-389, 1955-1 CB 276.
10. *Wisconsin Cheesemen, Inc. v. U.S.*, 388 F.2d 420 (7th Cir. 1968); Rev. Proc. 72-18, above.
11. See *Lang v. Comm.*, TC Memo 1983-318.

the bonds and the borrowing, even though the loan proceeds were used for an investment purpose.[1]

Lacking direct evidence, if the facts and circumstances support a reasonable inference that the purpose of the borrowing was to purchase or carry tax-exempt interest
obligations, the deduction will be denied. However, a deduction will not be denied
merely because the investor also holds such tax-exempt obligations.[2] Generally, the
interest deduction will not be disallowed if borrowing is for a personal purpose (and
the interest would otherwise be deductible). Thus, an individual who holds tax-exempt
municipal bonds and takes out a mortgage to buy a residence is not required to sell his
municipal bonds to finance the purchase.[3]

Similarly, the deduction will not generally be denied if the indebtedness is incurred
or continued in connection with the active conduct of a trade or business (other than
as a dealer in tax-exempt obligations) and the loan is not in excess of business needs.
Nonetheless, if the business need could reasonably have been foreseen when the tax-exempt obligations were bought, a rebuttable presumption arises that there was a purpose
to carry the tax-exempt obligations by means of borrowing.[4]

On the other hand, where there is outstanding indebtedness not directly connected
with personal expenditures and not incurred or continued in connection with the active
conduct of a business, and the individual owns tax-exempt obligations, a purpose to *carry*
the tax-exempt obligations *will* be inferred, but may be rebutted. The inference will
be made even though the debt is ostensibly incurred or continued to purchase or carry
other portfolio investments not connected with the active conduct of trade or business.
Thus, deduction of interest on a margin account by an individual holding tax-exempt
obligations was disallowed, even though only taxable securities were purchased in that
account.[5] (The management of one's personal investments is not considered a trade or
business.[6]) A limited partnership interest is generally considered a passive activity.[7] If
the taxpayer borrows to buy such an interest while holding tax-exempts, it is possible
that the IRS will infer an intent to carry tax-exempt obligations and will disallow the
interest deduction.

According to IRS guidelines, there will generally be a direct connection between
borrowing and purchasing or carrying existing tax-exempt interest obligations if the
debt is incurred to finance new portfolio investments. This presumption can be rebutted,
the IRS says, by showing the taxpayer could not have sold his holdings of tax-exempt
interest obligations. But it cannot be overcome by showing the tax-exempts could have
been sold only with difficulty or at a loss, or that the investor owned other investment
amounts that could have been liquidated, or that an investment adviser recommended
that a prudent investor should maintain a particular percentage of assets in tax-exempt
obligations.[8]

If a fractional part of the indebtedness is *directly* traceable to holding tax-exempt
interest obligations, the same fractional part of interest paid will be disallowed. In any

1. See *Rifkin v. Comm.*, TC Memo 1988-255.
2. *Ball v. Comm.*, 54 TC 1200 (1970).
3. Rev. Proc. 72-18, Sec. 4.02, above.
4. *Wisconsin Cheesemen, Inc. v. U.S.*, above; Rev. Proc. 72-18, Sec. 4.03, above.
5. *McDonough v. Comm.*, 577 F.2d 234 (4th Cir. 1978).
6. *Higgins v. Comm.*, 312 U.S. 212 (1941).
7. Ann. 87-4, 1987-3 IRB 17.
8. Rev. Proc. 72-18, Sec. 4.04, above.

other case, where the interest deduction is to be disallowed, an allocable portion of the interest is disallowed. The portion is determined by multiplying the total interest on the debt by a fraction: the numerator is the average amount during the tax year of the taxpayer's tax-exempt obligations (valued at adjusted basis), and the denominator is the average amount during the tax year of the taxpayer's total assets (valued at adjusted basis) minus the amount of any indebtedness the interest on which is not subject to disallowance under IRC Section 265(a)(2).[1]

If a partnership incurs debt or holds tax-exempt obligations, the partners are treated as incurring or holding their partnership share of each such debt or tax-exempt obligation. The purposes of the partnership in borrowing are attributed to the general partners.[2]

However, if an individual's investment in tax-exempt obligations is insubstantial, the requisite purpose will generally not be inferred in the absence of direct evidence. Investment will generally be considered insubstantial if the average amount of tax-exempt obligations (valued at their adjusted basis) is not more than 2% of the average adjusted basis of his portfolio investments and any assets held in the active conduct of a trade or business.[3]

The IRS has ruled that the interest deduction will be disallowed on a joint return if indebtedness that was incurred by one spouse is allocable to the acquisition of tax-exempt securities by the other.[4]

If the proceeds of a short sale are used (as determined under the foregoing rules) to "purchase or carry" tax-exempt obligations, certain expenses of that short sale (see Q 1024, Q 1025) may not be deducted.[5]

See Q 1304 for the limit on allowable investment interest deductions and Q 1305 for rules relating to the allocation of interest expense for purposes of the limit. See also Q 1311 for limits on the deduction of expenses incurred in producing tax-exempt income other than interest.

1307. Is interest paid on amounts borrowed to purchase or carry Treasury bills or short-term taxable corporate obligations deductible?

Where indebtedness is "incurred or continued" by a cash basis investor to purchase or carry Treasury bills, other short-term taxable government obligations, or taxable corporate short-term obligations (i.e., obligations with a fixed maturity date not more than one year from the date of issue), the current deductibility of interest expenses will be subject to limitation and deferral. However, if the taxpayer is required to or elects to include interest and acquisition discount or original issue discount as it accrues (as discussed in Q 1093, Q 1095), the otherwise allowable deduction of interest will not be limited or deferred except by any limit on deductibility applicable under the interest tracing rules (see Q 1305).[6]

---

1. Rev. Proc. 72-18, Secs. 7.01, 7.02, above. See also *McDonough v. Comm.*, TC Memo 1982-236.
2. Rev. Proc. 72-18, Sec. 4.05, above.
3. Rev. Proc. 72-18, Sec. 3.05, above.
4. Rev. Rul. 79-272, 1979-2 CB 124.
5. IRC Sec. 265(a)(5).
6. IRC Secs. 1281, 1282.

If the taxpayer does not include discount and interest as it accrues, the deductibility of interest expense incurred to purchase or carry the obligation is subject to certain limitations. Such interest will be deductible to the extent of includable interest income from the obligation. Interest expenses in excess of that amount will be deductible only to the extent that the interest expense exceeds the total amount of discount and interest accrued (but not includable) while the taxpayer held the bond during the year.[1] Thus, the excess interest expense that is equal to the discount and interest accruing in the year (but is not currently includable in income) is not currently deductible. The deduction is deferred to a later year when includable interest income on the obligation exceeds interest expense for the year, or to the year of disposition.[2]

In the case of short sales of securities, expenses that are not required to be capitalized (see Q 1024, Q 1025) are treated as interest expenses subject to these limitation and deferral rules if the proceeds of the short sale are used to purchase or carry Treasury bills or other taxable short-term government or corporate obligations.[3]

Whether amounts are borrowed or are loans continued to purchase or carry short-term obligations depends on the taxpayer's purpose for borrowing. In determining the individual's purpose, the IRS will, apparently, apply the same principles applied in determining if indebtedness is incurred or continued to purchase or carry tax-exempt bonds (see Q 1306).

1308. Is interest paid on amounts borrowed to purchase or carry market discount bonds deductible?

Bonds Issued After July 18, 1984, and Bonds Issued Before July 19, 1984 and Acquired After April 30, 1993

If amounts are borrowed or indebtedness is continued in order to purchase or carry a bond issued *after* July 18, 1984 at a market discount, or a bond issued *before* July 19, 1984 and purchased on the market at a discount after April 30, 1993, the interest expense is deductible to the extent that stated interest (or original issue discount) paid or accrued on it is includable in income for the year. (For the income tax treatment of market discount upon disposition of such bonds, see Q 1111 to Q 1114.) If interest expense exceeds that amount, it will be deductible to the extent that it exceeds the market discount allocable to the days on which the bond was held during the tax year. Interest expense that is allocable to the market discount accruing in the year is not currently deductible; the deduction is deferred.[4]

Amounts so disallowed in one year may be deductible in a later year in which includable interest on the obligation is greater than the interest expense for that year. Generally, the taxpayer may elect, on a bond by bond basis, to deduct an amount of previously disallowed interest expense up to the difference.[5]

Any deferred interest expense not previously deducted under that election becomes deductible in the year in which the bond is sold or redeemed. If the bond is disposed of in a transaction in which part or all of the gain is not recognized (e.g., a gift), the

---

1. IRC Sec. 1282(a).
2. IRC Secs. 1282, 1277(b).
3. IRC Secs. 1282(c), 1277(c).
4. IRC Sec. 1277.
5. IRC Sec. 1277(b)(1)(A).

deferred interest is allowed as a deduction at that time only to the extent that gain is recognized. (See, e.g., Q 1112 with respect to gain that is recognized on a gift.) To the extent deferred interest expense is not allowed as a deduction upon the disposition of the bond in such a nonrecognition transaction, the disallowed interest expense will be treated as disallowed interest expense of the transferee of transferred basis property, or the transferor who receives exchanged basis property in the transaction.[1] (Transferred basis property is property having a basis determined in whole or in part by the basis of the transferor.[2] Exchanged basis property is property having a basis determined in whole or in part by other property held at any time by the person for whom the basis is being determined.[3]) Thus, in the case of a market discount bond that is transferred basis property (a gift, for example), the transferee will be entitled to deduct the previously disallowed interest expense as if it were his own.

On the other hand, interest expense allocable to market discount *is* currently deductible, not deferred, if the taxpayer has elected to treat the market discount as current income as it accrues under either the straight line or constant interest rate method.[4] This election is discussed in Q 1110. Unless the interest expense on borrowing is greater than the sum of (1) interest income on the bond that would be includable in gross income in the absence of the election *plus* (2) the amount of market discount accruing over the days the bond was held in the year, the election will merely result in a wash; in other words, the deduction and the included interest will offset each other.

Whether amounts are borrowed or loans continued in order to purchase or carry market discount bonds depends on the taxpayer's purpose for borrowing. In determining the individual's purpose, the IRS will, presumably, apply the same principles applied in determining if indebtedness is incurred or continued to purchase or carry tax-exempt bonds (see Q 1306).

Noncapitalized expenses incurred in short sales of securities are treated as interest expenses subject to the deferred deduction rules if the proceeds of the short sales are used to purchase or carry a market discount bond.[5]

During the time the deduction of interest is deferred because it is on indebtedness incurred or continued to purchase or carry market discount bonds (or is an expense of a short sale the proceeds of which are used to purchase or carry market discount bonds), the interest (or short sale) expense is not counted as interest expense for other purposes (for example, in disallowing interest on amounts borrowed to buy tax-exempt bonds).

Bonds Issued Before July 19, 1984
and Acquired Before May 1, 1993

If a market discount bond was issued before July 19, 1984 and acquired on the market after that date but before May 1, 1993, the taxpayer generally will not be required to treat any part of the gain on disposition that is attributable to market discount as interest income (see Q 1111). However, if deferred interest expense on such a bond is deducted on disposition, an equal amount of any gain on the disposition must be

---

1. IRC Sec. 1277(b)(2).
2. IRC Sec. 7701(a)(43).
3. IRC Sec. 7701(a)(44).
4. IRC Sec. 1278(b).
5. IRC Sec. 1277(c). See General Explanation–TRA '84, p. 98.

treated as interest income.[1] Similarly, if the bond is disposed of in a nonrecognition transaction, an interest-characterization rule will apply at the time gain is recognized and the deferred interest expense is deducted by the transferee.[2]

If amounts are borrowed or indebtedness is continued to purchase or carry bonds that were issued and acquired on or before July 18, 1984 at a market discount, the interest expense paid in the year is not disallowed simply because market discount is not recognized until disposition of the bond. Furthermore, when gain attributable to the market discount is recognized it is treated as capital gain (see Q 1420 for the treatment of capital gain).

Interest on Education Loans

1309. Is student loan interest deductible?

An above-the-line deduction (see Q 1423) is available to middle income taxpayers for interest paid on a "qualified education loan" (i.e., college loans – see below) subject to certain limitations.[3] (*Editor's Note*: The 60-month limit on the student loan interest deduction was *permanently* repealed under PPA 2006.)

The amount of the deduction is limited to a maximum of $2,500.[4] The deduction is phased out ratably for taxpayers with modified adjusted gross income (MAGI–see below) between $100,000 and $130,000 (married filing jointly) or $50,000 and $65,000 (single).[5] The $50,000 and the $100,000 amounts are adjusted for inflation (as rounded to the next lowest multiple of $5,000).[6] In 2007, the indexed levels are: $110,000 - $140,000 (married filing jointly); $55,000 - $70,000 (single). The phaseout is accomplished by reducing the otherwise deductible amount by the ratio that the taxpayerxs MAGI over the applicable limit bears to $15,000 (the deduction cannot be reduced below zero).

> *Example:* In 2007, Mr. and Mrs. Jump paid $900 in interest on a student loan that otherwise qualifies for the deduction under the statutory requirements described below. The Jumps' MAGI in 2007 was $115,000. The ratio that their MAGI in excess of $110,000 [$115,000 - $110,000 = $5,000] bears to $15,000 is one to three; consequently, the amount otherwise deductible is reduced by one-third, to $600 [$900 - (⅓ x 900) = $600].

Modified adjusted gross income is the taxpayer's adjusted gross income as determined *before* the deduction for qualified tuition and related expenses[7] (see Q 1314) and the exclusions for income derived from certain foreign sources or sources within United States possessions,[8] and *after* the inclusion of any taxable Social Security benefits,[9] any deductible IRA contributions,[10] adjustments for passive activity losses or credits[11] (see Q 1292), the exclusion for savings bond interest used for education expenses[12] (see Q 1141), and the exclusion for certain adoption expenses.[13]

---

1. IRC Sec. 1277(d), prior to repeal by OBRA '93.
2. See General Explanation–TRA '84, p. 98.
3. IRC Sec. 221(a).
4. IRC Sec. 221(b)(1); Treas. Reg. §1.221-1(c).
5. IRC Sec. 221(b)(2); Treas. Reg. §1.221-1(d)(1).
6. IRC Sec. 221(f); Treas. Reg. §1.221-1(d)(3).
7. IRC Sec. 222.
8. IRC Secs. 911, 931, 933.
9. IRC Sec. 86.
10. IRC Sec. 219.
11. IRC Sec. 469.
12. IRC Sec. 135.
13. IRC Sec. 137. IRC Sec. 221(b)(2)(C); Treas. Reg. §1.221-1(d)(2).

Eligibility. The individual claiming the deduction must be legally obligated to make the interest payments under the terms of the loan.[1] But if a third party who is not legally obligated to make a payment of interest on a qualified education loan makes an interest payment on behalf of a taxpayer who is legally obligated to make the payment, then the taxpayer is treated as receiving the payment from the third party and, in turn, paying the interest.[2] See, e.g., Treas. Reg. §1.221-1(b)(4)(ii), Example 1 (payment by employer) and Example 2 (payment by parent).

The deduction may not be taken: (1) by an individual who may be claimed as a dependent on another's tax return; (2) if the expense can be claimed as a deduction elsewhere on the return; or (3) by married taxpayers filing separate returns.[3]

A *qualified education loan* is any indebtedness incurred by the taxpayer *solely* to pay "qualified higher education expenses" (see below) that are: (1) incurred on behalf of the taxpayer, his spouse, or a dependent at the time the indebtedness was incurred; (2) paid or incurred within a "reasonable period of time" (see below) before or after the indebtedness was incurred, and (3) attributable to education furnished in an academic period during which the recipient was an "eligible student" (see below).[4]

The determination of whether qualified higher education expenses are paid or incurred within a "reasonable period of time" generally is made based on all the relevant facts and circumstances. However, qualified higher education expenses are treated as paid or incurred within a reasonable period of time before or after the taxpayer incurs the indebtedness if: (1) the expenses are paid with the proceeds of education loans that are part of a federal postsecondary education loan program; or (2) the expenses relate to a particular academic period and the loan proceeds used to pay the expenses are disbursed within a period that begins 90 days prior to the start of the academic period and ends 90 days after the end of that academic period.[5]

The term qualified education loan does not include indebtedness owed to certain related persons. In addition, a loan from a qualified plan – including an IRC Section 403(b) plan or from a life insurance or annuity contract held by such a plan – is not a qualified education loan.[6]

A loan does not have to be issued or guaranteed under a federal postsecondary education loan program to be a qualified education loan.[7]

A qualified education loan includes indebtedness incurred solely to refinance a qualified education loan. A qualified education loan includes a single, consolidated indebtedness incurred solely to refinance two or more qualified education loans of a borrower.[8]

Qualified higher education expenses means the cost of attendance at an "eligible education institution" (see below) reduced by the sum of: (1) the amounts excluded from gross income under IRC Section 127 (employer educational assistance programs), IRC

---

1. Treas. Reg. §1.221-1(b)(1).
2. Treas. Reg. §1.221-1(b)(4)(i).
3. IRC Secs. 221(e), 221(c); Treas. Regs. §§1.221-1(b)(2), 1.221-1(b)(3); 1.221-1(g)(2).
4. IRC Sec. 221(d)(1); Treas. Reg. §1.221-1(e)(3)(i).
5. Treas. Reg. §1.221-1(e)(3)(ii).
6. IRC Sec. 221(d)(1); Treas. Reg. §1.221-1(e)(3)(iii).
7. Treas. Reg. §1.221-1(e)(3)(iv).
8. Treas. Reg. §1.221-1(e)(3)(v).

Section 135 (income from U.S. Savings bonds used to pay for higher education expenses – see Q 1141), IRC Section 529 (distributions from qualified tuition programs – see Q 1414), or IRC Section 530 (distributions from a Coverdell Education Savings Account, formerly known as an Education IRA – see Q 1412) by reason of such expenses; (2) the amount of any excludable scholarship, allowance or payments (other than a gift, bequest, devise or inheritance) received by an individual for expenses attributable to enrollment; *and* (3) certain educational assistance allowances provided to veterans or members of the armed forces.[1]

An *eligible education institution* generally includes any accredited postsecondary institution (i.e., college, university or vocational school) offering an educational program for which it awards a bachelor's degree or a 2-year degree, as well as those that conduct an internship or residency program leading to a degree or certificate awarded by an institute of higher learning, a hospital, or a health care facility that offers postgraduate training. The term also includes those institutions offering at least a 1-year program that trains students for gainful employment in a recognized profession.[2]

An *eligible student* means any student who is enrolled in a degree, certificate or other program leading to a recognized credential at an eligible education institution, and who is carrying at least half of a normal full-time work load in the course of study.[3]

Interest. Amounts paid on an qualified education loan are deductible if the amounts are "interest" for federal income tax purposes. "Interest" includes qualified stated interest and original issue discount, which generally includes "capitalized interest" (i.e., any accrued and unpaid interest on a qualified education loan that, in accordance with the terms of the loan, is added by the lender to the outstanding principal balance of the loan).[4]

The Preamble to the final regulations states: "generally, fees such as loan origination fees or late fees, are interest if the fees represent a charge for the use or forbearance of money. Therefore, if the fees represent compensation to the lender for the cost of specific services performed in connection with the borrower's account, the fees are not interest for federal income tax purposes.[5] Tax Court found that certain fees, including insurance fees, were similar to payments for services rendered and not deductible as interest." Preamble, TD 9125, 68.[6]

In general, a payment is treated first as a payment of interest to the extent of the interest that has accrued and remains unpaid as of the date the payment is due, and second as a payment of principal.[7]

Reporting requirements. Certain reporting requirements must be met by a payee who receives interest totaling $600 or more with respect to a single payor on one or more covered student loans. Generally, the payee must file Form 1098-E (Student Loan Interest Statement) with respect to that interest, and provide the payor with

---

1. IRC Sec. 221(d)(2); Treas. Reg. §1.221-1(e)(2).
2. IRC Secs. 221(d)(2), 25A(f)(2); Treas. Reg. §1.221-1(e)(1).
3. IRC Secs. 221(d)(3), 25A(b)(3).
4. Treas. Reg. §1.221-1(f)(1).
5. See Rev. Rul. 69-188, 1969-1 CB 54, *amplified by*, Rev. Rul. 69-582, 1969-2 CB 29; see also, e.g., *Trivett v. Comm.*, TC Memo 1977-161, *aff'd on other grounds*, 611 F.2d 655 (6th Circ. 1979).
6. Fed. Reg. 25489, 25490 (5-7-2004).
7. Treas. Reg. §1.221(f)(3).

the same information. For the final regulations relating to the information reporting requirements for payments of interest on qualified education loans (including the filing of information returns in an electronic format in lieu of a paper format), see Treas. Regs. §§1.6050S-3, 1.6050S-4; 67 Fed. Reg. 20901 (4-29-2002); 69 Fed. Reg. 7567 (2-18-2004); and 1.6050S-3, 68 Fed. Reg. 25489 (5-7-2004). The Service has provided information for payees/filers who receive payments of interest on qualified education loans to request a waiver of penalties for failure to report payments of loan origination fees and capitalized interest received in 2005 for qualified education loans made on or after September 1, 2004.[1]

Effective dates. The final regulations are effective May 7, 2004. The final regulations apply to periods governed by IRC Section 221, as amended by EGTRRA 2001, which relates to interest paid on qualified educational loans after December 31, 2001.[2]

EXPENSES

1310. What expenses paid in connection with the production of investment income are deductible?

The IRC allows individuals a deduction for *ordinary* and *necessary* expenses paid in the year for the production or collection of income, or paid for the management, conservation or maintenance of property held for the production of income, whether or not, in either case, they are business expenses.[3] Personal management of one's investments is not the conduct of a trade or business.[4] This is so without regard to the amount of time spent managing the investments or to the size of the portfolio.[5]

The deduction applies to expenses in connection with both income and gain from sales. The deduction is taken by a cash method taxpayer in the year the expense is paid. This deduction is limited to expenses related to the production of income that is subject to federal income tax.[6] However, it may be income realized in a prior year or anticipated in a subsequent year (as, for example, defaulted bonds bought with the expectation of gain on resale). The expenses are deductible even if no income is realized in the year.[7] Expenses not for the production of income or the management, conservation or maintenance of property held for the production of income, but paid in connection with activities carried on primarily as a sport or hobby may be limited (see Q 1300).[8] Whether a transaction is carried on primarily for the production of income or for the management, conservation or maintenance of property held for the production of income rather than primarily as a sport or hobby or recreation depends on the facts and circumstances involved (see Q 1300).

To be deductible, expenses must be "reasonable in amount" and "bear a reasonable and proximate relation" to the production or collection of taxable income or the management, conservation or maintenance of property held for the production of income.[9]

---

1. See Notice 2006-5, 2006-4 IRB 248.
2. Treas. Reg. §1.221-1(h).
3. IRC Sec. 212.
4. *Higgins v. Comm.*, 312 U.S. 212 (1941).
5. *Moller v. U.S.*, 83-2 USTC ¶9698 (Fed. Cir. 1983).
6. IRC Sec. 265(a)(1).
7. Treas. Reg. §1.212-1(b).
8. IRC Sec. 183(b)(2); Treas. Regs. §§1.183-1, 1.212-1(c).
9. Treas. Reg. §1.212-1(d); *Bingham's Trust v. Comm.*, 325 U.S. 365 (1945).

Expenses that enter into the determination of income or loss of a passive activity are subject to the limitations of the passive loss rule, and are not deducted as investment expenses. In general, a passive activity is any activity involving the conduct of a trade or business in which the taxpayer does not materially participate and any rental activity.[1] Generally, an individual may deduct aggregate losses for the year from a passive activity only to the extent that they do not exceed aggregate income from passive activities in that year. The passive loss rules are explained in Q 1292 to Q 1299.

Expenses of a passive activity that are allocable to income from interest, dividends, annuities, or royalties not derived in the ordinary course of a trade or business are *not* treated as passive activity expenses, but rather are treated under the general rules applicable to other investment expenses.[2]

Investment expenses are generally treated as "miscellaneous itemized deductions" (which also include certain non-investment expenses–see Q 1428). These expenses are, therefore, deductible from adjusted gross income only to the extent that the aggregate of all miscellaneous itemized deductions for the taxable year exceeds 2% of adjusted gross income.[3] Only those investment expenses that are deductible (i.e., those remaining after the 2% floor has been applied) are considered in the calculation of net investment income. (See Q 1304.) For purposes of this calculation, the 2% floor is applied against all other miscellaneous itemized deductions before it is applied against investment expenses.[4]

The more common expenses, provided they have the required relationship to the production of income (and deductible only to the extent that they exceed the 2% floor) include: (a) rental expense of a safe deposit box used to store taxable securities; (b) subscriptions to investment advisory services; (c) investment counsel fees; (d) custodian's fees; (e) services charged in connection with a dividend reinvestment plan; (f) service, custodian, and guarantee fees charged by the issuer of mortgage-backed securities (Q 1145 and Q 1147);[5] (g) bookkeeping services; (h) office expenses in connection with investment activities, such as rent, water, telephone, stamps, stationery, etc.;[6] (i) premiums paid for indemnity bond required for issuance of new stock certificates to replace certificates mislaid, lost, stolen or destroyed.[7]

The Tax Court denied a deduction for mutual fund shareholders' pro rata share of the annual operating expenses incurred by the mutual funds in which they owned shares. Because publicly offered mutual funds pass through income to shareholders on a net basis (i.e., gross income minus expenses), the Tax Court concluded that the shareholders had already received the benefit of a reduction in income for these costs and, therefore, were not entitled to deduct the operating expenses as investment expenses.[8]

Partners in an investment club partnership formed solely to invest in securities and whose income is derived solely from taxable dividends, interest, and gains from security sales, may deduct their distributive shares of the partnership's reasonable operating expenses incurred in its tax year that are proximately related to the partnership's

1. IRC Sec. 469(c).
2. IRC Sec. 469(e)(1).
3. IRC Sec. 67.
4. Conference Report (TRA '86) at pp. 153-154.
5. See *Loew v. Comm.*, 7 TC 363 (1946).
6. See *Scott v. Comm.*, TC Memo 1979-109.
7. See Rev. Rul. 62-21, 1962-1 CB 37.
8. *Tokh v. Comm.*, TC Memo 2001-45.

investment activities. Operating expenses include postage, stationery, safe deposit box rentals, bank charges, fees for accounting and investment services, rent and utility charges. Investment partnerships are not engaged in business because management of activities with respect to one's own account is not a trade or business.[1]

The Tax Court held that fees withheld from a trust beneficiary's distribution to repay, under a court order, expenses incurred by the trustee and other beneficiaries in dealing with her frivolous objections to the trust's accounting were deductible under IRC Section 212. Citing *Ostrom v. Comm.*,[2] the court reasoned that if the origin and character of the claim arise out of a taxpayer's position as a seeker after profit (which in this case was the motivation underlying her objections to the accounting), then it did not matter that the taxpayer's expenditures were made because of the imposition of a court sanction to compensate the victims of the taxpayer's improper actions.[3]

Expenses may be nondeductible because they are personal in nature, or because they are not ordinary and necessary. Examples of such expenses would include: newspaper and magazine costs, where it is not clear that the publications were used principally for investment activities rather than personal activities;[4] travel to attend shareholders' meetings;[5] fees paid for maintenance of interest paying checking accounts where the fee is charged for the privilege of writing checks instead of maintaining the interest bearing account and the checks written are personal;[6] travel expenses going to watch a broker's ticker tape regularly but not directly related to any particular transactions entered into for profit;[7] maintenance of an art collection where personal pleasure, not investment, was the most important purpose for the collection;[8] and expenses of maintaining a personal residence.[9] An expense not otherwise deductible that is paid in contesting a liability against an individual does not become deductible simply because property held for production of income might have to be used or sold to satisfy the liability.[10]

Expenses may be nondeductible because of other IRC Sections. For example, expenses that are capital in nature are not deductible, such as broker's commissions and fees in connection with acquiring property.[11] They are added to the basis of property. Similarly, selling expenses are offset against selling price used in determining capital gains and losses, not deducted as expenses.[12] A safe purchased to store property used in the production of income was ruled to be a capital expenditure.[13] Expenses to defend, acquire, or perfect title to property are capital in nature.[14] Legal expenses incurred to recover taxable interest and dividends are deductible, but portions allocable to the recovery of a capital asset (e.g., stock) are not deductible, but rather are capitalized.[15] No deduction is allowed for expenses allocable to attending a convention, seminar, or

1. Rev. Rul. 75-523, 1975-2 CB 257.
2. 77 TC 608 (1991).
3. *Di Leonardo v. Comm.*, TC Memo 2000-120.
4. *Tokh v. Comm.*, TC Memo 2001-45.
5. Rev. Rul. 56-511, 1956-2 CB 170.
6. Rev. Rul. 82-59, 1982-1 CB 47.
7. *Walters v. Comm.*, 28 TC Memo 22 (1969).
8. *Wrightsman v. U.S.*, 428 F.2d 1316 (Ct. Cl. 1970).
9. Treas. Reg. §1.212-1(h).
10. Treas. Reg. §1.212-1(m).
11. *Vestal v. U.S.*, 498 F.2d 487 (8th Cir. 1947).
12. *Milner v. Comm.*, 1 TCM 513 (1943).
13. Let. Rul. 8218037.
14. Treas. Reg. §1.212-1(k); *Kelly v. Comm.*, 23 TC 682 (1955), *aff'd*, 228 F.2d 512 (7th Cir. 1956); *Collins v. Comm.*, 54 TC 1656 (1970).
15. Treas. Reg. §1.212-1(k); *Nickell v. Comm.*, 831 F.2d 1265 (6th Cir. 1987).

similar meeting unless the expenses are ordinary and necessary expenses of carrying on a trade or business.[1]

A federal district court has held that payments made to discharge a preexisting lien on property (e.g., stock) are part of the purchase price of the property and, as such, must be capitalized. The court further held that the attorney's fees incurred with discharging the lien should also be included in the purchaser's basis under IRC Section 1012, again as costs of acquiring the stock.[2]

Where purchasers of a hotel incurred legal fees maintaining a lawsuit to recover damages from the seller for misrepresentations that caused the taxpayers to pay an inflated price for the property, the Tax Court held that the litigation arose out of, was incurred in connection with, and was directly related to the acquisition of the property; accordingly, the legal fees were required to be capitalized.[3]

With regard to deduction of loan premiums and amounts equal to cash dividends to cover short sales, see Q 1024 and Q 1025.

Deduction of interest in connection with investments may be limited to the amount of net investment income (Q 1304), or otherwise limited if the purpose of borrowing is to acquire or keep tax-exempt obligations (Q 1306), market discount bonds (Q 1308), or taxable short-term obligations (Q 1307).

1311. Are expenses paid for the production of tax-exempt income deductible?

Any expense that would otherwise be deductible under any Internal Revenue Code section is not deductible if it is allocable to tax-exempt income other than tax-exempt interest.[4] Expenses allocable to tax-exempt interest may be deductible if they are trade or business expenses, taxes, or depreciation, but the same expenses allocable to tax-exempt income other than interest are not deductible.

If an expense is allocable to both nonexempt income and exempt income, a reasonable proportion, determined in the light of all the facts and circumstances, is allocated to each.[5] Legal fees incurred to collect Social Security benefits have been held deductible only to the extent that they were allocable to the portion of benefits that were includable in the taxpayer's gross income.[6] In the absence of evidence showing a more reasonable basis for allocation, the expense has been allocated between taxable and tax-exempt income in the proportion that each bears to the total taxable and nontaxable income in the year.[7]

1312. Are expenses relating to tax questions deductible?

Yes. The IRC permits a deduction for ordinary and necessary expenses paid in the year in connection with the determination, collection or refund of any tax.[8] This

---

1. IRC Sec. 274(h)(7).
2. *Lobato v. United States*, 2002 U.S. Dist. LEXIS (N.D. OK 2002).
3. *Winter v. Comm.*, TC Memo 2002-173.
4. IRC Sec. 265(a)(1).
5. Treas. Reg. §1.265-1(c).
6. Rev. Rul. 87-102, 1987-2 CB 78.
7. *Jamison v. Comm.*, 8 TC 173 (1947); *Ellis v. Comm.*, 6 TCM 662 (1947); *Mallinckrodt v. Comm.*, 2 TC 1128 (1943), *acq.*; Rev. Rul. 59-32, 1959-1 CB 245 *as clarified by* Rev. Rul. 63-27, 1963-1 CB 57.
8. IRC Sec. 212(3).

includes expenses for: the preparation of income tax returns;[1] the cost of tax books used in preparing tax returns;[2] accountant's tax advice;[3] legal fees for obtaining a letter ruling;[4] legal or accounting fees contesting a tax deficiency, whether or not successfully;[5] or claiming a refund;[6] and appraisal fees necessary to establish a charitable deduction.[7] The Tax Court held that miles driven (165.5) by a taxpayer, for the purpose of copying and filing his personal federal income tax return, constituted an ordinary and necessary expense paid by him in connection with the determination of his federal income taxes; accordingly, the mileage was held to be properly deductible as a miscellaneous itemized deduction.[8]

"The requirement that the expenses be 'ordinary and necessary' implies that they must be reasonable in amount and must bear a reasonable and proximate relation" to the determination, collection or refund of taxes.[9]

The expenses may relate to income, estate, gift, property, or any other tax, whether federal, state or municipal.[10]

The burden of proof is on the taxpayer to establish the extent to which expenses are allocable to tax advice rather than to nondeductible personal expenditures (e.g., will preparation, estate planning). In the absence of an itemization or other evidence supporting a claimed deduction, only that portion that the IRS deems reasonably allocable to the tax advice will be deductible.[11]

The deduction may be deferred or disallowed in whole or in part if the taxpayer has tax-exempt income (Q 1311), or if the expense is taken into account in determining income or loss of a passive activity (Q 1292), or is treated as an investment expense (Q 1310).

1313. How are business expenses reported for income tax purposes?

The amount of the deduction for expenses incurred in carrying on a trade or business depends upon whether the individual is an independent contractor or an employee. Independent contractors may deduct all allowable business expenses from gross income (generally on Schedule C) to arrive at adjusted gross income.[12] The business expenses of an employee are deductible from adjusted gross income if he itemizes, but only to the extent that they exceed 2% of adjusted gross income when aggregated with other "miscellaneous itemized deductions" (described in Q 1428).

A full-time life insurance salesperson will not be treated as an "employee" for purposes of IRC Sections 62 and 67 merely because he is a "statutory employee" for

1. *Loew v. Comm.*, 7 TC 363 (1946); Treas. Reg. §1.212-1(l).
2. *Contini v. Comm.*, 76 TC 447 (1981), *acq.* 1981-2 CB 1.
3. *Collins v. Comm.*, 54 TC 1656 (1970).
4. *Kaufmann v. U.S.*, 227 F. Supp. 807 (W.D. Mo. 1963).
5. *Bingham's Trust v. Comm.*, 325 U.S. 365 (1945).
6. *Cammack v. Comm.*, 5 TC 467 (1945); *Williams v. McGowan*, 152 F.2d 570 (2d Cir. 1945).
7. Rev. Rul. 67-461, 1967-2 CB 125.
8. *Stussy v. Comm.*, TC Memo 2003-232.
9. *Bingham's Trust v. Comm.*, above.
10. Treas. Reg. §1.212-1(l).
11. *Wong v. Comm.*, TC Memo 1989-683.
12. IRC Sec. 62(a)(1).

Social Security tax purposes.[1] The IRS has frequently challenged insurance agents' claims of independent contractor status; however, its position has been struck down by at least two circuit courts of appeals, both of which held that the fact that an insurance agent received certain employee benefits did not preclude his being considered an independent contractor based on all the other facts and circumstances of the case.[2] The IRS has instructed its attorneys to discontinue the practice of challenging certain independent contractor status claims of insurance agents who were treated as employees by the companies for whom they worked.[3] However, industrial agents (or "debit agents") are treated as employees for tax purposes.[4] Thus, as in the case of any employee, a debit agent can deduct transportation and away-from-home traveling expenses from adjusted gross income if he itemizes, only to the extent that the aggregate of these and other miscellaneous itemized deductions exceeds 2% of adjusted gross income.[5]

Self-employed taxpayers are permitted a deduction equal to one-half of their self-employment (i.e., Social Security) taxes for the taxable year. This deduction is treated as attributable to a trade or business that does not consist of the performance of services by the taxpayer as an employee; thus it is taken "above-the line."[6]

In a legal memorandum concerning the deductibility of medical insurance costs, the Service ruled as follows: (1) A sole proprietor who purchases health insurance in his individual name has established a plan providing medical care coverage with respect to his trade or business, and therefore may deduct the medical care insurance costs for himself, his spouse, and dependents under IRC Section 162(l), but only to the extent the cost of the insurance does not exceed the earned income derived by the sole proprietor from the specific trade or business with respect to which the insurance was purchased. (2) A self-employed individual may deduct the medical care insurance costs for himself and his spouse and dependents under a health insurance plan established for his trade or business up to the net earnings of the specific trade or business with respect to which the plan is established, but a self-employed individual may not add the net profits from all his trades and businesses for purposes of determining the deduction limit under IRC Section 162(l)(2)(A). However, if a self-employed individual has more than one trade or business, he may deduct the medical care insurance costs of the self-employed individual and his spouse and dependents under each specific health insurance plan established under each specific business up to the net earnings of that specific trade or business.[7] Later, with respect to the same taxpayer, the Service ruled that a self-employed individual cannot deduct the costs of health insurance on Schedule C; instead, the deduction under IRC section 162(l) must be claimed as an adjustment to gross income on the front of Form 1040.[8]

In *Allemeier v. Commissioner*,[9] the Tax Court held that the taxpayer could deduct his expenses ($15,745) incurred in earning a master's degree in business administration to the extent those expenses were substantiated and education-related. The court based its decision on the fact that the taxpayer's MBA did not satisfy a minimum education

1. Rev. Rul. 90-93, 1990-2 CB 33.
2. *Ware v. U.S.*, 67 F.3d 574 (6th Cir. 1995); *Butts v. Comm.*, TC Memo 1993-478, *aff'd*, 49 F.3d 713 (11th Cir. 1995).
3. Notice N(35)000-141 (Doc. 96-31376), *Litigation Strategy for Certain Insurance Agents Claiming Independent Contractor Status* (Dec. 2, 1996).
4. Rev. Rul. 58-175, 1958-1 CB 28.
5. IRC Sec. 67.
6. IRC Sec. 164(f).
7. CCA 200524001.
8. CCA 200623001.
9. TC Memo 2005-207.

requirement of his employer, nor did the MBA qualify the taxpayer to perform a new trade or business.

Expenses for business meals and entertainment must meet one of two tests, as defined in regulations, in order to be deductible. The meal must be: (1) "directly related to" the active conduct of the trade or business, or (2) "associated with" the trade or business. Generally, the deduction for business meal and entertainment expenses is limited to 50% of allowable expenses.[1] The 50% otherwise allowed as a deduction is *then* subject to the 2% floor which applies to miscellaneous itemized deductions.[2] The taxpayer or his employee generally must be present for meal expenses to be deductible, and expenses that are lavish or extravagant may be disallowed. Substantiation is required for lodging expenses and, in the case of expenditures incurred on or after October 1, 1995, for most items of $75.00 or more.[3] An employee must generally provide an "adequate accounting" of reimbursed expenses to his employer.[4]

1314. Are expenses relating to higher education deductible?

Yes, for a *limited* time. For taxable years beginning *after* December 31, 2001 and *before* January 1, 2008, an above-the-line deduction (see Q 1423) is available for "qualified tuition and related expenses" (see below) paid by the taxpayer during the taxable year, subject to certain limitations.[5]

In 2007, a deduction of $4,000 is available for taxpayers with adjusted gross income (see Q 1423) that does not exceed the following limits: single, $65,000; married filing jointly, $130,000. A more limited deduction of $2,000 is available in 2007 for taxpayers with adjusted gross income that falls within the following limits: married filing jointly, $130,001 - $160,000; single, $65,001 - $80,000. Taxpayers with adjusted gross income above these limits will not be entitled to a deduction.[6] (Note that the phaseout limits will *not* be adjusted for inflation.) As a practical matter, this deduction can be used by taxpayers whose income is too high to utilize the Hope Scholarship or Lifetime Learning Credit.

Adjusted gross income (see Q 1423) for this purpose is determined *before* the exclusions for income derived from certain foreign sources or sources within United States possessions and *after* the inclusion of any taxable Social Security benefits, the exclusion for savings bond interest used for education expenses, the exclusion for certain adoption expenses, any deductible IRA contributions, interest on education loans, and adjustments for passive activity losses or credits.[7]

Qualified tuition and related expenses are tuition and fees required for the enrollment or attendance of the taxpayer, the taxpayer's spouse, or any dependent of the taxpayer (for whom he is allowed a dependency exemption) at an "eligible educational institution." Qualified tuition and related expenses do not include nonacademic fees such as room and board, medical expenses, transportation, student activity fees, athletic fees, insurance expenses, personal, living, family or other expenses unrelated to a student's

---

1. IRC Sec. 274(n)(1).
2. Temp. Treas. Reg. §1.67-1T(a)(2).
3. IRC Sec. 274; Treas. Reg. §1.274-5(c)(2)(iii).
4. Treas. Reg. §1.274-5(f)(4).
5. IRC Sec. 222(e), as amended by TRHCA 2006; IRC Sec. 222(a).
6. IRC Secs. 222(b)(2)(A), 222(b)(2)(B).
7. IRC Sec. 222(b)(2)(C).

academic course of instruction. Additionally, qualified tuition and related expenses do not include expenses for a course involving sports, games or hobbies, unless it is part of the student's degree program.[1] For the definition of *eligible educational institution*, see Q 1438.

Limitations

Coordination with other provisions. The deduction for qualified tuition and related expenses is not allowed for any expenses for which there is a deduction available.[2] Taxpayers are not eligible to claim the deduction for qualified higher education expenses and a Hope or Lifetime Learning Credit in the same year with respect to the same student.[3]

The amount of qualified tuition and related expenses is limited by the sum of the amounts paid for the benefit of the student, such as scholarships, education assistance advances, and payments (other than a gift, bequest, devise, or inheritance) received by an individual for educational expenses attributable to enrollment.[4]

The total amount of qualified tuition and related expenses for the deduction must be *reduced* by the amount of such expenses taken into account in determining the following exclusions: (1) interest from U.S. Savings bonds used to pay for higher education expenses;[5] (2) distributions from qualified tuition programs;[6] and (3) distributions from a Coverdell Education Savings Account.[7] For these purposes, the excludable amount under IRC Section 529 does not include that portion of the distribution that represents a return of contributions to the plan.[8]

Eligibility. If the student is claimed as a dependent on another individual's tax return (e.g., parents) he cannot claim the deduction for himself.[9] The deduction is not available to married taxpayers filing separately.[10]

Identification. For the deduction to be permitted, the taxpayer must provide the name and the taxpayer identification (i.e., Social Security) number of the student for whom the credit is claimed.[11]

Timing. A deduction is permitted for any taxable year only to the extent that the qualified tuition and related expenses are connected with enrollment at an institution of higher education during the taxable year.[12] However, this does not apply to expenses paid during a taxable year *if* those expenses are connected with an academic term beginning during the taxable year, *or* during the first three months of the next taxable year.[13]

The Secretary may provide regulations necessary and appropriate to carry out these provisions, including recordkeeping and information reporting regulations.[14]

---

1. IRC Sec. 222(d)(1), 25A(f)(1).
2. IRC Sec. 222(c)(1).
3. IRC Sec. 222(c)(2)(A).
4. IRC Secs. 25A(g)(2), 222(d)(1).
5. IRC Sec. 135.
6. IRC Sec. 529.
7. IRC Sec. 530.
8. IRC Sec. 222(c)(2)(B).
9. IRC Sec. 222(c)(3).
10. IRC Sec. 222(d)(4).
11. IRC Sec. 222(d)(2).
12. IRC Sec. 222(d)(3)(A).
13. IRC Sec. 222(d)(3)(B).
14. IRC Sec. 222(d)(6).

CHARITABLE GIFTS

GENERAL

1315. What general rules apply to charitable deductions?

An individual may deduct certain amounts for charitable contributions. IRC Sec. 170(a). The amount of a contribution of property other than money is generally equal to the fair market value of the property.[1] However, under certain circumstances, the deduction for a gift of property must be reduced; see Q 1323. For guidelines concerning the determination of fair market value, see Q 1316.

The amount that may be deducted in any one year is subject to certain income percentage limits that depend on the type of property, the type of charitable organization to which the gift is made, and whether the contribution is made directly "to" the charity or "for the use of" the charity (see Q 1320). An individual who does not itemize deductions may not take a charitable deduction.

As a general rule, a gift of less than an individual's entire interest in property is not deductible, but certain exceptions are provided (see Q 1327, Q 1329, and Q 1337).

For a charitable contribution to be deductible, the charity must receive some benefit from the donated property.[2] In addition, the donor cannot expect to receive some economic benefit (aside from the tax deduction) from the charity in return for the donation.[3] For instance, if a taxpayer contributes substantially appreciated property, and later reacquires it from the charity under a prearrangement, or if the charity sells the appreciated property and uses the proceeds to purchase other property from the taxpayer under a similar arrangement, the taxpayer recognizes gain on the contribution.[4] However, where there is no arrangement, and no duty on the part of the charity to return the property to the donor, the taxpayer is entitled to a deduction. In addition, if the charity does return the property, the taxpayer receives a new basis in the property (i.e., the price he paid to reacquire it).[5]

In determining whether a payment that is partly in consideration for goods or services (i.e., a quid pro quo contribution) qualifies as a charitable deduction, the IRS has adopted the 2-part test set forth in *United States v. American Bar Endowment*.[6] In order for a charitable contribution to be deductible, a taxpayer must (1) intend to make a payment in excess of the fair market value of the goods or services received, and (2) actually make a payment in an amount that exceeds the fair market value of the goods or services.[7] The deduction amount may not exceed the excess of (1) the amount of any cash paid and the fair market value of the goods or services; *over* (2) the fair market value of the goods or services provided in return.[8]

---

1. Treas. Reg. §1.170A-1(c)(1).
2. See *Winthrop v. Meisels*, 180 F.Supp. 29 (DC NY 1959), *aff'd*, 281 F.2d 694 (2d Cir. 1960).
3. *Stubbs v. U.S.*, 70-2 USTC ¶9468 (9th Cir.), *cert. den.*, 400 U.S. 1009 (1971).
4. *Blake v. Comm.*, 83-1 USTC 86,081.
5. *Sheppard v. U.S.*, 361 F.2d 972 (Ct. Cl. 1966).
6. 477 U.S. 105 (1986).
7. Treas. Reg. §1.170A-1(h)(1).
8. Treas. Reg. §1.170A-1(h)(2).

The Tax Court has held that tuition payments paid by taxpayers to religious day schools for the secular and religious education of their children were not deductible as a charitable contribution, including amounts paid to one of the schools for after-school religious education classes.[1]

Where a company transfers an amount it holds on a taxpayer's behalf to a charity: (1) the payment received by the company from the Internet vendor is a rebate (resulting from prior purchases from the vendor) and, thus, is not includable in the taxpayer's gross income; and (2) the amount transferred is a charitable contribution that is deductible by the taxpayer in the year that the company (acting as the taxpayer's agent) transfers the taxpayer's rebate to charity.[2]

Certain goods or services received in return for a charitable contribution may be disregarded for purposes of determining whether a taxpayer has made a charitable contribution, the amount of any charitable contribution, and whether any goods or services have been provided that must be substantiated or disclosed.[3] These items include goods or services that have an insubstantial value under IRS guidelines, certain annual membership benefits received for a payment of $89 or less, and certain admissions to events.[4]

If an otherwise deductible charitable contribution to a university (or other institution of higher learning) directly or indirectly entitles the donor to purchase tickets for athletic events in a stadium of the institution, the contribution is 80% deductible, to the extent that the contribution is not a payment for the tickets themselves.[5] The Service has determined that the portion of the payment made to a state university's foundation, for which the donor (an S corporation) received the right to purchase tickets for seating in a skybox at athletic events in an athletic stadium of the university, was deductible under IRC Section 170(l). The Service reasoned that the portion of the payment to the foundation for the right to buy the tickets for seating was considered as being paid for the benefit of the university; thus, 80% of such portion was deductible. The Service also stated that the remainder of the payment (consisting of the ticket purchase, the right to use the skybox, the passes to visit the skybox, and the parking privileges) was not deductible.[6]

The IRS determined that contributions made to a university for the purpose of constructing a building providing meeting space for campus organizations qualified for a charitable deduction under IRC Section 170. With the exception of the meeting rooms leased to individual sororities, the facilities in the building would be open to all students. Because the facts indicated that the contributions were indeed gifts to the college, and not gifts to the sororities using the college as a conduit, the Service determined that the requirements of Rev. Rul. 60-37.[7]

Charitable split dollar. Responding to perceived abuses, in 1999 Congress passed legislation that denies a charitable deduction for certain transfers associated with split

---

1. See *Sklar v. Comm.*, 125 TC 281 (2005); see also *Sklar v. Comm.*, No. 00-70753 (9th Cir. 2001), *aff'g*, TC Memo 2000-118.
2. Let. Rul. 200142019. See also Let. Ruls. 200228001, 200230039.
3. Treas. Regs. §§1.170A-1(h), 1.170A-13(f)(8).
4. Treas. Reg. §1.170A-13(f)(8). See also Rev. Proc. 2006-53, 2006-48 IRB 996.
5. IRC Sec. 170(l).
6. See TAM 200004001.
7. 1960-2 CB 73 had been satisfied. Let. Rul. 9829053. See also Let. Ruls. 200003013, 199929050.

dollar insurance arrangements.[1] Charitable split-dollar insurance reporting requirements are set forth in Notice 2000-24.[2] For the split dollar rules, see Treas. Reg. §1.7872-15, TD 9092[3] See also *Roark v. Comm.*[4] (denying charitable income tax deductions where charitable split dollar life insurance policies were involved).

1316. How is fair market value of a gift of property determined?

Where property other than money is donated to charity, it is necessary to determine the property's fair market value.

Fair market value is "the price at which the property would change hands between a willing buyer and a willing seller, neither being under any compulsion to buy or sell and both having reasonable knowledge of relevant facts."[5]

The willing buyer has often been viewed as a retail consumer, not a middleman.[6] However, in the case of unset gemstones, the ultimate consumer is generally a jeweler engaged in incorporating the gems in jewelry. Therefore, the fair market value is based on the price that a jeweler would pay a wholesaler to acquire such stones.[7]

It is often helpful to rely on expert appraisals in determining the fair market value of property.[8] In fact, an appraisal is required for some gifts (see Q 1318). However, it is possible that the IRS or the Tax Court will consider factors in addition to those considered by the taxpayer's appraiser(s) which may reduce the value of the gift and, thus, the charitable deduction. See *Williford v. Comm.*[9] (involving oversized artwork); *Doherty v. Comm.*[10] (involving artwork of questionable quality and authenticity); *Arbini v. Comm.*[11] (involving newspapers; and holding that the appropriate market for purposes of determining the fair market value of the newspapers is the wholesale market). The IRS has warned taxpayers that some promoters are likely to inflate the value of a charitable deduction for gemstones and lithographs, thus subjecting the taxpayer to higher taxes and possible penalties. IR 83-89. Earlier case law has indicated that an auction price may be helpful in determining the value of art.[12]

The burden of proof is on the taxpayer to establish fair market value.[13] Evidence of what an organization is willing to pay for copies of a manuscript is evidence of the value of the original manuscript, but it is not conclusive.[14]

1. See IRC Sec. 170(a)(10); see also Notice 99-36, 1999-26 CB 1284.
2. 2000-1 CB 952.
3. 68 Fed. Reg. 54336 (9-17-2003); Notice 2002-8, 2002-1 CB 398.
4. TC Memo 2004-271; *Addis v. Comm.*, 2004-2 USTC ¶50,291 (9th Cir. 2004), *cert. denied* (No. 04-843, February 22, 2005), *aff'g*, 118 TC 528 (2002); and *Weiner v. Comm.*, TC Memo 2002-153, *cert. denied* (No. 04-838, February 22, 2005).
5. Treas. Reg. §1.170A-1(c); Rev. Rul. 68-69, 1968-1 CB 80.
6. See *Goldman v. Comm.*, 388 F.2d 476 (6th Cir. 1967).
7. *Anselmo v. Comm.*, 80 TC 872 (1983), *aff'd*, 757 F.2d 1208 (11th Cir. 1985).
8. See *Tripp v. Comm.*, 337 F.2d 432 (7th Cir. 1964); *Est. of DeBie v. Comm.*, 56 TC 876 (1971), acq. 1972-2 CB 1 and 1972-2 CB 2.
9. TC Memo 1992-450.
10. TC Memo 1992-98.
11. TC Memo 2001-141.
12. *Mathias v. Comm.*, 50 TC 994 (1968), *acq.* 1969-2 CB xxiv. But see *McGuire v. Comm.*, 44 TC 801 (1965), *acq. in result* 1966-2 CB 6.
13. See *Weil v. Comm.*, TC Memo 1967-78; *Schapiro v. Comm.*, TC Memo 1968-44.
14. *Barringer v. Comm.*, TC Memo 1972-334. See also *Kerner v. Comm.*, TC Memo 1976-12.

The price paid for hospital equipment purchased from a bankruptcy trustee was not determinative of the equipment's fair market value; instead the substantially higher appraisal established the value of the donated equipment.[1]

For property that is transferred to a charity and subject to an option to repurchase, fair market value under IRC Section 170 is the value of the property upon the expiration of the option.[2] See Q 1321 regarding when a deduction is permitted for a charitable contribution.

Guidelines for valuing property generally can be found in Rev. Proc. 66-49[3] (see Q 1318), and Announcement 2001-22.[4] See also *Crocker v. Comm.*[5] (describing the three methods of determining fair market value of commercial real estate: (1) the replacement method, (2) the comparable sales method, and (3) the income capitalization method).

Planning Point: *New limitation on charitable contributions of clothing and household items.* In order to qualify for a charitable contribution deduction under PPA 2006, contributed clothing and household items must be in "good used condition or better." The Treasury Department may issue regulations denying a deduction for items of minimal value. This rule will not apply where the contribution of a single item of clothing or a single household item is valued at more than $500 and a "qualified appraisal" (see Q 1318) is included with the donor's return. The new limitation applies to contributions made after August 17, 2006.[6] *Ted R. Batson, Jr., MBA, CPA, Senior Vice President of Professional Services and Gregory W. Baker, JD, CFP®, CAP, Senior Vice President of Legal Services for Renaissance.*

Intellectual property. The American Jobs Creation Act of 2004 (AJCA 2004) provides strict rules for charitable donations of patents and intellectual property.[7] For the temporary regulations providing guidance for the filing of information returns by donees relating to qualified intellectual property contributions, see Temp. Treas. Reg. §1.6050L-2T, TD 9206[8]; and Announcement 2005-49.[9]

1317. What verification is required to substantiate a deduction for a charitable contribution of a qualified vehicle?

General

AJCA 2004 provides new substantiation requirements for contributions of vehicles for which the claimed value exceeds $500. Under AJCA 2004, no deduction is allowed for a contribution of a "qualified vehicle" (see below) with a claimed value of more than $500 *unless:*

(1)   the taxpayer substantiates the contribution by a "contemporaneous" (see below) written acknowledgement of the contribution by the charity that

---

1. *Herman v. U.S.* and *Brown v. U.S.* (consolidated actions), 99-2 USTC ¶50,889 (E.D. Tenn. 1999).
2. TAM 9828001.
3. 1966-2 CB 1257, as modified by Rev. Proc. 96-15, 1996-2 CB 627.
4. 2001-11 IRB 895.
5. TC Memo 1998-204.
6. See IRC Sec. 170(f)(16), as added by PPA 2006.
7. See IRC Secs. 170(e)(1)(B), 6050L; IRC Sec. 170(m). See also Rev. Rul. 2003-28, 2003-11 IRB 594; Notice 2005-41, 2005-23 IRB 1203; Notice 2004-7, 2004-3 IRB 310; and IRS News Release IR-2003-141 (12-22-2003).
8. 70 Fed. Reg. 29450 (5-23-2005).
9. 2005-29 IRB 119. See also Notice 2005-41, 2005-23 IRB 1203.

meets certain requirements (see below), and includes the acknowledgement with the tax return that includes the deduction; *and*

(2)   if the charity sells the vehicle without any "significant intervening use or material improvement" (see below) of the vehicle by the charity, the amount of the deduction does not exceed the gross proceeds received from the sale ("gross proceeds limitation").[1]

Note that the substantiation rules under IRC Section 170(f)(8)–applicable to contributions of more than $250 (see Q 1318)–do *not* apply to a contribution described above.[2]

The *acknowledgment* must include the following information:

(A)   the name and taxpayer identification number of the donor;

(B)   the vehicle identification number (or similar number);

(C)   in the case of a "qualified vehicle" to which (2), above, applies: (i) a certification that the vehicle was sold in an arm's length transaction between unrelated parties; (ii) the gross proceeds from the sale; *and* (iii) a statement that the deductible amount may not exceed the amount of such gross proceeds;

(D)   in the case of a "qualified vehicle" to which (2), above, does *not* apply: (i) a certification of the intended use or material improvement of the vehicle and the intended duration of such use; *and* (ii) a certification that the vehicle would not be transferred in exchange for money, other property, or services before completion of the use or improvement;

(E)   whether the donee organization provided any goods or services in consideration, in whole or in part, for the qualified vehicle; *and*

(F)   a description and good faith estimate of the value of any goods or services referred to in (E), above, or if such goods or services consist solely of intangible religious benefits, a statement to that effect.[3]

An acknowledgement is considered "contemporaneous" if the charity provides it within 30 days of the sale of the qualified vehicle, *or* in the case of an acknowledgement including a certification as described in (D), above, the contribution of the qualified vehicle.[4]

The term "qualified vehicle" means any motor vehicle manufactured primarily for use on public streets, roads, and highways, boat, or airplane. But the term does not include any property described in IRC Section 1221(a)(1) (i.e., inventory).[5]

A charity is required to provide an acknowledgement containing the required information to the Secretary. The information must be provided at the time and in

---

1. IRC Sec. 170(f)(12)(A).
2. IRC Sec. 170(f)(12)(A)(i).
3. IRC Secs. 170(f)(12)(B).
4. IRC Sec. 170(f)(12)(C).
5. IRC Sec. 170(f)(12)(E).

the manner prescribed by the Secretary.[1] A charity that knowingly furnishes a false or fraudulent acknowledgment, or that knowingly fails to furnish such an acknowledgment in the manner, at the time, and showing the required information (see above), will be subject to a penalty.[2]

The substantiation requirements explained above apply to contributions made after December 31, 2004.[3]

The Secretary will prescribe such regulations or other guidance (see below) as may be necessary to carry out the purposes of these requirements. In addition, the Secretary may prescribe regulations or other guidance that exempt sales of vehicles by the charity that are in direct furtherance of the charity's charitable purposes from the requirements that (1) the donor may not deduct an amount in excess of the gross proceeds from the sale, and (2) the charity certify that the vehicle will not be transferred in exchange for money, other property, or services before completion of a significant use or material improvement by the charity.[4] The Conference Committee conferees intend that such guidance may be appropriate, for example, if an organization directly furthers its charitable purposes by selling automobiles to needy persons at a price significantly below fair market below.[5] The conferees further intend that the Service strictly construe the requirement of "significant use or material improvement."[6]

The Service has released new Form 1098-C (Contributions of Motor Vehicles, Boats, and Airplanes), which is used by charities to report the contribution of qualified vehicles to the IRS. The form may also be used to provide the donor with a contemporaneous written acknowledgement of the contribution.

Interim Guidance on Qualified Vehicle Contributions

The Service has provided interim guidance regarding charitable contributions of qualified vehicles.[7] The guidance is generally effective for contributions made on or after January 1, 2005. The rules stated below apply until regulations become effective.

Deductions Exceeding $500

Disposition or use by charity. If the claimed value of a donated "qualified vehicle" (see above) exceeds $500, the amount of the deduction may be limited depending on the use of the qualified vehicle by the charity:

(1)   If the qualified vehicle is sold by the charity without a significant intervening use or material improvement by the charity, then (except as provided in item (3), below) the deduction claimed by the donor may *not* exceed the gross proceeds received from the sale of the qualified vehicle ("the gross proceeds limitation"). The Service cautions that in no event may the deduction for a donated vehicle exceed the amount otherwise allowable under IRC Section 170(a) (i.e., the fair market value).

---

1. IRC Sec. 170(f)(12)(D).
2. See IRC Sec. 6720.
3. Act Sec. 884(c), AJCA 2004; Act Sec. 403(nn), TTCA 2005.
4. See IRC Sec. 170(f)(12)(F).
5. H.R. Conf. Rep. No. 108-755.
6. H.R. Conf. Rep. No. 108-755.
7. Notice 2005-44, 2005-25 IRB 1287.

(2)   If the charity makes a significant intervening use of or material improvement to a qualified vehicle, the donor is not subject to the gross proceeds limitation. However, the deduction claimed by the donor may not exceed the fair market value of the qualified vehicle.

(3)   According to the Service and the Treasury Department, the gross proceeds limitation in item (1), above, does *not* apply to: (a) a sale occurring on or after January 1, 2005, of a qualified vehicle to a needy individual at a price significantly below fair market value; or (b) a gratuitous transfer to a needy individual, in direct furtherance of a charity's charitable purpose of relieving the poor and distressed or the underprivileged who are in need of a means of transportation (pursuant to IRC Section 170(f)(12(F)).[1] Mere application of the proceeds from the sale of a qualified vehicle to a needy individual to any charitable purpose does not directly further a charity's charitable purpose.[2]

For items (1), (2) and (3), above, the donor must obtain an acknowledgment from the charity that meets the requirements set forth below (see "Contemporaneous written acknowledgment"). Furthermore, with respect to items (2) and (3), above, the donor must also substantiate the fair market value in the manner described below (see "Fair Market Value").[3]

Contemporaneous written acknowledgment. Under the Code, a donor must obtain a contemporaneous written acknowledgment from the charity *and* include the acknowledgment with the tax return on which the deduction is claimed.[4] All acknowledgments must include the name and taxpayer identification number of the donor, the vehicle identification number, and the date of the contribution. Additional information is required depending on the use of the qualified vehicle by the charity, as stated below:

(1)   For a contribution of a qualified vehicle that is sold by the charity without any significant intervening use or material improvement by the charity in a sale, the acknowledgment must also contain: (a) the date the qualified vehicle was sold; (b) a certification that the qualified vehicle was sold in an arm's length transaction between unrelated parties; (c) a statement of the gross proceeds from the sale; and (d) a statement that the deductible amount may not exceed the amount of the gross proceeds. The acknowledgment is considered to be contemporaneous if the charity furnishes the acknowledgment to the donor no later than 30 days after the date of the sale.

(2)   For a contribution of a qualified vehicle for which the charity intends to make a significant intervening use of or material improvement to, the acknowledgment must also contain (a) a certification and detailed description of (i) the intended significant intervening use by the charity and the intended duration of the use, or (ii) the intended material improvement by the charity; *and* (b) a certification that the qualified vehicle will not be sold before completion of the use or improvement. The acknowledgment

---

1. See H.R. Conf. Rep. No. 755, 108th Cong., 2nd Session 750 (2004).
2. Notice 2005-44, above.
3. Notice 2005-44, above.
4. IRC Sec. 170(f)(12).

is considered contemporaneous if the charity furnishes the acknowledgment to the donor within 30 days of the date of the contribution.

(3)   For a contribution of a qualified vehicle that is (a) sold at a price significantly below fair market value or (b) gratuitously transferred to a needy individual, the acknowledgment also must contain a certification that: (i) the charity will sell the qualified vehicle to a needy individual at a price significantly below fair market value (or, if applicable, that the charity gratuitously will transfer the qualified vehicle to a needy individual); *and* (ii) that the sale (or transfer) will be in direct furtherance of the charity's charitable purpose of relieving the poor and distressed or the underprivileged who are in need of a means of transportation. The acknowledgment is considered contemporaneous if the charity furnishes the acknowledgment to the donor no later than 30 days after the date of the contribution.[1]

Fair Market Value

A donor claiming a deduction for the fair market value of a qualified vehicle must be able to substantiate the "fair market value." The Treasury regulations provide that "fair market value" is the price at which the property would change hands between a willing buyer and a willing seller, neither being under any compulsion to buy or sell and each having reasonable knowledge of relevant facts.[2]

A reasonable method of determining the fair market value of a qualified vehicle is by reference to an established used vehicle pricing guide. Many factors must be taken into account when using a used vehicle pricing guide to determine fair market value. A used vehicle pricing guide establishes the fair market value of a particular vehicle *only if* the guide lists a sales price for a vehicle that is: the same make, model, and year; and sold in the same area, in the same condition, with the same or substantially similar options or accessories, and with the same or substantially similar warranties or guarantees as the vehicle in question.[3]

The Service and the Treasury Department intend to issue regulations under IRC Section 170 clarifying that the dealer retail value listed in a used vehicle pricing guide for a particular vehicle is *not* an acceptable measure of fair market value of a similar vehicle. The regulations will clarify that for contributions made after June 3, 2005 and before the date regulations become effective, an acceptable measure of the fair market value of a vehicle is an amount that does not exceed the price listed in a used vehicle pricing guide for a private party sale of a similar vehicle. The regulations limiting the fair market value of a vehicle to an amount that does not exceed the private party sale price will apply to contributions of vehicles made after June 3, 2005. In addition, the Service and the Treasury Department will consider whether other values (e.g., the dealer trade-in value) are appropriate measures of the fair market value of a vehicle (for purposes of IRC Section 170). Any regulations limiting the fair market value of a vehicle to an amount less than the private party sale value will not apply to contributions made prior to the date that regulations to that effect become effective.[4]

---

1. Notice 2005-44, above.
2. Treas. Reg. §1.170A-1(c)(2).
3. See, e.g., Rev. Rul. 2002-67, 2002-47 IRB. 873.
4. Notice 2005-44, above.

Qualified Appraisal

A "qualified appraisal" is required for a deduction in excess of $5,000 for a qualified vehicle if the deduction is not limited to gross proceeds from the sale of the vehicle.[1] For the explanation of what constitutes a "qualified appraisal," see Q 1317 ("Contributions Exceeding $5,000").[2]

Deductions of $500 or Less

Contemporaneous written acknowledgment. A contribution of a qualified vehicle with a claimed value of at least $250 must be substantiated by a contemporaneous written acknowledgment of the contribution by the charity. For a qualified vehicle with a claimed value of at least $250 but not more than $500, the acknowledgment must contain the following information: (1) the amount of cash and a description (but not value) of any property other than cash contributed; (2) whether the charity provided any goods or services in consideration, in whole or in part, for the cash or property contributed; and (3) a description and good faith estimate of the value of any goods or services provided by the charity in consideration for the contribution (or, if such goods or services consist solely of intangible religious benefits, a statement to that effect).[3]

To satisfy the contemporaneous requirement, the acknowledgment must be obtained by the donor on or before the earlier of the date on which the donor files a return for the taxable year in which the contribution was made, *or* the due date (including extensions) of that return.

Sale of qualified vehicle yields gross proceeds of $500 or less. If a donor contributes a qualified vehicle that is subsequently sold (in a sale not described in item (3), above) without any significant intervening use or material improvement by the charity, *and* the sale yields gross proceeds of $500 or less, the donor may be allowed a deduction equal to the *lesser* of: (1) the fair market value of the qualified vehicle on the date of the contribution; *or* (2) $500 (subject to the terms and limitations of IRC Section 170). Under these circumstances, the donor must substantiate the fair market value, and, if the fair market value is $250 or more, must substantiate the contribution with an acknowledgment that meets the requirements of IRC Section 170(f)(8).[4]

Other Guidance

The Service has released a series of questions and answers concerning the new rules for vehicle donations.[5] In addition, the Service has provided information reporting guidance to donee organizations that receive contributions of certain motor vehicles, boats, and airplanes.[6] For additional information on vehicle donations, see Publication 4303, *A Donor's Guide to Car Donations*, and Publication 4302, *A Charity's Guide to Car Donations* (7-2004), at: www.irs.gov/.

The Service has announced its awareness of questionable practices involving charities selling donated vehicles at auction price, but claiming that the sales were to needy individuals at prices significantly below fair market value. By so doing, these charities

---

1. IRC Sec. 170(f)(11)(A)(ii)(I).
2. Notice 2005-44, above.
3. IRC Sec. 170(f)(8).
4. Notice 2005-44, above.
5. See IRS Information Letter INFO 2005-129 (8-3-2005), at: http://www.irs.gov/pub/irs-wd/05-0129.pdf.
6. See Notice 2006-1, 2006-4 IRB 347.

have claimed that the sales trigger an exception to the general rule that the deduction allowed to the donor is limited to the proceeds from the charity's sale. The Service's position is that vehicles sold at auction are not sold at prices significantly below fair market value. Therefore, the Service will not treat vehicles sold at auction as qualifying for the exception for sales to needy individuals at prices below fair market value.[1]

The IRS is also aware of questions that have arisen as to whether the charity must sell the vehicle in 2005 in order for the donor who donated the vehicle in 2005 to receive a deduction for 2005. According to the Service, the charity does not need to sell the vehicle in 2005. A taxpayer can take a charitable contribution deduction only for the year the vehicle is transferred to the charity, even if the vehicle is not sold by the charity until a later year. However, a taxpayer cannot take a charitable contribution deduction of $500 or more for a vehicle donation unless the taxpayer has received a written acknowledgment of the donation from the charity and attached the acknowledgment to the return. If the taxpayer receives the written acknowledgment after filing the tax return for the year of the donation, the taxpayer may, after receiving the acknowledgment, file an amended return for that year and claim the deduction on the amended return. The taxpayer must attach the acknowledgment to the amended return.[2]

1318. What verification is required to substantiate a deduction for a charitable contribution?

The IRC provides that "[a] charitable contribution shall be allowable as a deduction only if verified under regulations prescribed by the Secretary."[3]

Enhanced Recordkeeping Requirement for Contributions of Money

Planning Point: Under PPA 2006, to receive a deduction for a contribution of money (i.e., cash, checks), a donor must retain either a bank record or a written communication from the charity showing the name of the charity and the date and amount of the contribution. This requirement applies to all contributions made in taxable years beginning after August 17, 2006.[4] *Comment*: To comply with this new requirement, a donor may no longer rely on contemporaneous notations of cash contributions, a check register, or other self-created records of cash contributions. Only a canceled check, bank record, or receipt issued by the charity will suffice. *Ted R. Batson, Jr., MBA, CPA, Senior Vice President of Professional Services and Gregory W. Baker, JD, CFP®, CAP, Senior Vice President of Legal Services for Renaissance.*

The IRS has issued guidance on how charitable contributions made by payroll deduction may meet the new requirements of IRC Section 170(f)(17). The Service clarified that unlike IRC Section 170(g)(8), which only applies to contributions of $250 or more (see below), IRC Section 170(f)(17) applies to *any* contribution of a cash, check, or other monetary gift. To substantiate a deduction a taxpayer must maintain either (1) a bank record or (2) a written communication from the donee organization showing the name of the donee organization, as well as the date and amount of the contribution. For a charitable contribution made by payroll deduction, a pay stub, Form W-2, or other employer-furnished document that sets forth the amount withheld for payment to a donee organization, along with a pledge card prepared by or at the direction of the

1. IR-2005-145 (12-22-2005).
2. IR-2005-149 (12-22-2005).
3. IRC Sec. 170(a)(1).
4. See IRC Sec. 170(f)(17), as added by PPA 2006.

donee organization, will be deemed to be a "written communication from the donee organization" that satisfies the requirements of IRC Section 170(f)(17).[1]

Contributions of $250 or More

For contributions of money the taxpayer is generally required to maintain a canceled check, a receipt from the donee organization, or some other reliable written records showing the name of the donee, the amount of the contribution, and the date of the contribution.[2] However, charitable contributions of $250 or more (whether in cash or property) generally must also be substantiated by a contemporaneous written acknowledgment of the contribution supplied by the charitable organization.[3]

The acknowledgment must include the following information: (1) the amount of cash contributed and a description (excluding value) of any property contributed, (2) a statement of whether the charitable organization provided any goods or services in consideration for the contribution, and (3) a description and good faith estimate of the value of any such goods or services, or (4) a statement to the effect that the goods or services provided consisted solely of intangible religious benefits.[4] The acknowledgment will be considered "contemporaneous" if it is obtained by the taxpayer on or before the earlier of (1) the date the taxpayer files his return for the year, or (2) the due date (including extensions) for filing the return.[5] Substantiation is not required if the information is reported on a return filed by the charitable organization.[6] Publication 1771 states that an organization can provide the acknowledgement electronically, such as via an e-mail addressed to the donor.[7]

For contributions of property other than money, the taxpayer is generally required to maintain a receipt from the donee organization showing the name of the donee, the date and location of the contribution, and a description of the property, including the value of it.[8]

Generally, charitable contributions of $250 or more made by an employee through payroll deduction may be substantiated with a combination of two documents: (1) a pay stub, Form W-2, or a document furnished by the taxpayer's employer that sets forth the amount withheld from the taxpayer's wages, *and* (2) a pledge card or document prepared by or at the direction of the donee organization that states that the organization does not provide goods or services as whole or partial consideration for any contributions made by payroll deduction. The amount withheld from each paycheck is treated as a separate contribution. Therefore, the substantiation requirements of IRC Section 170(f)(8) will not apply to such contributions unless the employer deducts $250 or more from a single paycheck for the purpose of payment to a donee organization.[9]

Certain goods or services received by a contributing taxpayer (quid pro quo contributions) may be disregarded for substantiation purposes (see Q 1315).

---

1. See Notice 2006-110, 2006-51 IRB 1127; IR-2006-186 (12-1-2006).
2. Treas. Reg. §1.170A-13(a). See, e.g., *Jennings v. Comm.*, TC Memo 2000-366, *aff'd*, 88 AFTR 2d 2001-5337 (6th Cir. 2001).
3. IRC Sec. 170(f)(8)(A).
4. IRC Sec. 170(f)(8)(B); Treas. Reg. §1.170A-13(f)(2).
5. IRC Sec. 170(f)(8)(C); Treas. Reg. §1.170A-13(f)(3).
6. IRC Sec. 170(f)(8)(D).
7. Pub. 1771, p. 6.
8. Treas. Reg. §1.170A-13(b)(1).
9. Treas. Reg. §1.170A-13(f)(11).

Contributions Exceeding $500

AJCA 2004 provides increased reporting requirements for noncash charitable contributions with a claimed value of more than $500.[1] The rules are effective for contributions made after June 3, 2004.[2]

Under AJCA 2004, a deduction for a contribution of property with a claimed value exceeding $500 will generally be denied to any individual, partnership, or corporation that fails to satisfy the property description *and* appraisal requirements.[3] (However, there are two exceptions to the general rule. Under the first exception, the appraisal requirements, for property valued at more than $5,000 and at more than $500,000 (see below), do not apply to readily valued property, such as cash, publicly traded securities, and any "qualified vehicle" (see Q 1317) for which an acknowledgment is provided. Under the second exception, the general rule does not apply if it is shown that the failure to meet the requirements is due to reasonable cause and not to willful neglect.[4] For purposes of determining the thresholds, property (and all similar items of property) donated to one charity will be treated as one property.[5]

If the claimed value of the donated property exceeds $500, the taxpayer must include with the tax return a *description of the property*.[6] Specifically, the taxpayer must complete and attach to his tax return Form 8283 ("Noncash Charitable Contributions"), which includes a description of the property and an acknowledgment by the organization of the amount and value of the gift. (The property description requirement does not apply to a C corporation that is not a personal service corporation or a closely held C corporation.) In addition, AJCA 2004 requires that a *qualified appraisal* be obtained when the claimed value of the property exceeds $5,000 (see below) or $500,000 (see below).[7]

Under the special rule for pass-through entities (partnerships or S corporations), the above requirements will be applied at the entity level; however, the deduction will be denied at the partner or shareholder level.[8]

The Secretary may prescribe regulations as may be necessary or appropriate to carry out the purposes of the reporting requirements for noncash charitable contributions over $500.[9]

Contributions Exceeding $5,000

In addition to satisfying the requirements described above, the *qualified appraisal* requirement for contributions of property for which a deduction of more than $5,000 is claimed is met if the individual, partnership, or corporation: (1) obtains a qualified appraisal of the property; and (2) attaches to the tax return information regarding the property and the appraisal (as the Secretary may require).[10] According to the regulations, donors who claim a deduction for a charitable gift of property (except publicly traded securities) valued in excess of $5,000 ($10,000 for nonpublicly traded stock) are required

---

1. IRC Sec. 170(f)(11).
2. Act. Sec. 883(b), AJCA 2004.
3. IRC Sec. 170(f)(11)(A)(i).
4. IRC Sec. 170(f)(11)(A)(ii).
5. IRC Sec. 170(f)(11)(F).
6. IRC Sec. 170(f)(11)(B).
7. IRC Secs. 170(f)(11)(C), 170(f)(11)(D).
8. IRC Sec. 170(f)(11)(G).
9. IRC Sec. 170(f)(11)(H).
10. IRC Secs. 170(f)(11)(C), 170(f)(11)(E).

to obtain a qualified appraisal report, attach an appraisal summary (containing the information specified in regulations) to their return for the year in which the deduction is claimed, and maintain records of certain information related to the contribution.[1]

A taxpayer who failed to obtain such an appraisal for a gift of nonpublicly traded stock was denied a deduction, even though the IRS did not dispute the value of the claimed gift.[2] The Tax Court distinguished its holding in *Hewitt* from a 1993 decision in which it had permitted a deduction to a taxpayer who substantially, though not fully, complied with the appraisal requirement. In the earlier ruling, the taxpayer had obtained an appraisal from a qualified appraiser, completed and attached Form 8283, but had failed to include all the information required of an appraisal summary.[3] The Fourth Circuit Court of Appeals concurred in the Tax Court's analysis, stating that "*Bond* does not suggest that a taxpayer who completely fails to observe the appraisal regulations has substantially complied with them." The Fourth Circuit further stated: "[I]n *Bond*, the taxpayers made a good faith effort to comply with the appraisal requirement. In the case at bar, the Hewitts utterly ignored the appraisal requirement." (For more information about the appraisal and summary, see the instructions for Schedule A, Form 1040, and IRS Publication 526, Charitable Contributions.)

A qualified appraiser may not be the taxpayer, a party to the transaction in which the taxpayer acquired the property, the donee, an employee of any of the above, or any other person who might appear not to be totally independent.[4] See e.g., *Davis v. Comm.*[5] (appraisals upheld where appraiser was determined to be financially independent of the donor, and no conspiracy or collusive relationship was established).

In *Wortmann, et al. v. Comm.*,[6] the Tax Court substantially reduced the taxpayers' charitable deduction (from $475,000 to $76,200) after it concluded that the property appraisal was dubious and not well supported by valuation methodology.

The appraiser cannot base his fee on a percentage of the appraisal value, unless the fee is based on a sliding scale that is paid to a generally recognized association regulating appraisers.[7] See Q 1316 concerning obtaining a "Statement of Value" for certain contributions of art.

The "computational period" is weekly during October through December and monthly during January through September. Taxpayers who are exempted from obtaining a qualified appraisal because the securities meet these five requirements must attach a partially completed appraisal summary (section B of Form 8283) to the appropriate returns. The summary must contain the information required by parts I and II of the Form.[8]

If the donor gives similar items of property (such as books, stamps, paintings, etc.) to the same donee during the taxable year, only one appraisal and summary is required. If similar items of property are given during the same taxable year to several donees, and

---

1. Treas. Reg. §1.170A-13(c)(2).
2. *Hewitt v. Comm.*, 109 TC 258 (1997), *aff'd*, 166 F.3d 332 (4th Cir. 1998).
3. See *Bond v. Comm.*, 100 TC 32 (1993).
4. Treas. Reg. §1.170A-13(c)(5)(iv).
5. TC Memo 1999-250.
6. TC Memo 2005-227.
7. Treas. Reg. §1.170A-13(c)(6).
8. Ann. 86-4, 1986-4 IRB 51.

the aggregate value of the donations exceeds $5,000, a separate appraisal and summary must be made for each donation.[1] The appraisal summary is signed and dated by the donee as an acknowledgement of the donation.[2]

Taxpayers making contributions of art appraised at $50,000 or more, may wish to request from the IRS a "Statement of Value" (which appears to be the equivalent of a letter ruling as to the value of a particular transfer that is made at death, by inter vivos gift, or as a charitable contribution).[3] The request must include specified information, including a description of the artwork, the cost, manner and date of acquisition, and a copy of an appraisal (which meets requirements set forth in Section 8 of the revenue procedure). The user fee for obtaining a Statement of Value is $2,500 for up to three items of art.[4]

The regulations state that taxpayers need not obtain a qualified appraisal of securities whose claimed value exceeds $5,000 if the donated property meets the definition of "publicly traded securities." Publicly traded securities are those (1) listed on a stock exchange in which quotations are published on a daily basis or (2) regularly traded in a national or regional over-the-counter market for which published quotations are available.[5]

Securities that do not meet the above requirements may still be considered publicly traded securities if they meet the following five requirements: (1) the issue is regularly traded during the computational period in a market that is reflected by the existence of an interdealer quotation system for the issue; (2) the issuer or its agent computes the issue's average trading price for the computational period; (3) the average price and total volume of the issue during the computational period are published in a newspaper of general circulation throughout the U.S. not later than the last day of the month following the end of the calendar quarter in which the computational period ends; (4) the issuer or its agent keeps books and records that list for each transaction during the computational period involving each issue covered by this procedure the date of the settlement of the transaction, the name and address of the broker or dealer making the market in which the transaction occurred, and the trading price and volume; and (5) the issuer or agent permits the IRS to review the books and records.[6]

Substantiation for contributions of more than $500,000. For property contributions for which a deduction of more than $500,000 is claimed, the individual, partnership, or corporation must attach the qualified appraisal of the property to the tax return for the taxable year.[7]

Subsequent Disposition by Charity

If the charitable donee disposes of "charitable deduction property" that is subject to the above rules within two years after its receipt, the donee must provide an information return to the IRS. "Charitable deduction property" includes any property (other than publicly traded securities) for which a charitable deduction was taken under IRC Sec-

---

1. Treas. Reg. §1.170A-13(c)(4)(iv)(B).
2. Treas. Reg. §1.170A-13(c)(4)(iii).
3. See Rev. Proc. 96-15, 1996-1 CB 627, as modified by Announcement 2001-22, 2001-11 IRB 895 (effective for requests submitted after January 15, 1996).
4. Rev. Proc. 96-15, above, Sec. 7.01(2).
5. Treas. Reg. §1.170A-13(c)(7)(ix)(A).
6. Treas. Reg. §1.170A-13(c)(7)(ix)(B).
7. IRC Secs. 170(f)(11)(D), 170(f)(11)(E).

tion 170 where the claimed value of the property (plus the claimed value of all similar items of property donated by the donor to one or more donees) was in excess of $5,000.[1] The return must show the name, address, and taxpayer identification number of the donor, a description of the property, the date of the contribution, the date of disposition, and the amount received on disposition. A copy of the return must be provided to the donor. Failure to file the return may subject the donee to a penalty.[2] However, final regulations will provide that donee reporting is not required upon disposition of donated property within two years of receipt if the value of the property (as stated in the donor's appraisal summary) was not in excess of $5000 at the time the donee signed the summary. In addition, no reporting will be required if the donee consumes or distributes property without receiving anything in exchange and the consumption or distribution is in furtherance of the donee's charitable purpose (such as the distribution of medical supplies by a tax-exempt relief agency).[3]

1319. What penalty applies if a taxpayer overvalues property donated to charity?

If a taxpayer underpays his tax because of a substantial valuation misstatement of property donated to charity, he may be subject to a penalty of 20% of the underpayment attributable to the misstatement.[4] However, this penalty applies only if the underpayment attributable to the misstatement exceeds $5,000 ($10,000 for a corporation other than an S corporation or a personal holding company).[5] A "substantial valuation misstatement" exists if the value claimed is 150% or more of the amount determined to be correct.[6] If the value claimed is 200% or more of the amount determined to be correct, there is a "gross valuation misstatement," which is subject to a 40% underpayment penalty.[7]

Planning Points: The thresholds for determining that a misstatement has occurred have been lowered as follows: *substantial misstatement* (lowered from 200% to 150% or more of the amount determined to be correct); *gross misstatement* (lowered from 400% to 200% or more of the amount determined to be correct). The Act also repeals the reasonable cause exception for underpayments due to gross valuation misstatements.

In addition, a new penalty will be imposed on appraisers who knowingly prepare an appraisal to be used in connection with a return that results in an underpayment of tax due to a substantial or gross valuation misstatement. The penalty is the *lesser* of: (1) the greater of 10% of the understatement in tax resulting from the valuation misstatement, or $1,000; *or* (2) 125% of the fee received by the appraiser. The penalty may be avoided if the appraiser can demonstrate that the appraised value was "more likely than not" the proper value. The Act also sets new standards for determining that an appraiser is a "qualified appraiser." In general, a "qualified appraiser" is an individual: (1) certified by a professional appraiser organization; (2) that regularly performs appraisals for which he or she is compensated; (3) that can demonstrate verifiable education and experience valuing the type of property appraised; and (4) that has not been prohibited from practicing before the IRS during the 3-year period ending on the date of appraisal.

---

1. IRC Sec. 6050L.
2. IRC Sec. 6721; Treas. Reg. §1.6050L-1. See SCA 200101031.
3. Ann. 86-1, 1986-1 IRB 35.
4. IRC Secs. 6662(a), 6662(b)(3).
5. See IRC Sec. 6662(d).
6. IRC Sec. 6662(e)(1)(A), as amended by PPA 2006.
7. IRC Sec. 6662(h)(2)(A)(i), as amended by PPA 2006.

The provisions modifying the thresholds applicable to valuation misstatements and establishing new standards for qualified appraisers are generally effective for returns filed after August 17, 2006. Where the valuation misstatement arises from an appraisal of a façade easement (see Q 1339), the provisions related to valuation misstatements and qualified appraiser standards are effective for returns filed after July 25, 2006.[1] *Ted R. Batson, Jr., MBA, CPA, Senior Vice President of Professional Services and Gregory W. Baker, JD, CFP®, CAP, Senior Vice President of Legal Services for Renaissance.*

For guidance on the circumstances under which the disclosure on a taxpayer's return with respect to an item or a position is adequate for the purpose of reducing the understatement of income tax under IRC Section 6662(d), see Rev. Proc. 2005-75.[2]

For transitional guidance on the new definition of "qualified appraisal" and "qualified appraiser" (in IRC Section 170(f)(11)) for purposes of substantiating deductions for charitable contributions of property, see Notice 2006-96.[3]

DEDUCTION LIMITS

1320. What are the income percentage limits for deduction of a charitable contribution?

The IRC makes a distinction between gifts "to" a charitable organization and gifts "for the use of" a charitable organization.

50% limit. Generally, an individual is allowed a charitable deduction of up to 50% of his adjusted gross income for any contribution (other than certain property, see Q 1323) *to:* churches; schools; hospitals or medical research organizations; organizations that normally receive a substantial part of their support from federal, state, or local governments or from the general public and that aid any of the above organizations; federal, state, and local governments. Also included in this list is a limited category of private foundations (i.e., private operating foundations and conduit foundations[4] that generally direct their support to public charities. The above organizations are often referred to as "50%-type organizations."[5]

30% limit. The deduction for contributions of most long-term capital gain property to the above organizations, contributions *for the use of* any of the above organizations, as well as contributions (other than long-term capital gain property) *to* or *for the use of* any other types of charitable organizations (i.e., most private foundations) is limited to the lesser of (a) 30% of the taxpayer's adjusted gross income, or (b) 50% of adjusted gross income minus the amount of charitable contributions allowed for contributions to the 50%-type charities.[6]

20% limit. The deduction for contributions of long-term capital gain property to most private foundations (see Q 1324) is limited to the lesser of (a) 20% of the taxpayer's adjusted gross income, or (b) 30% of adjusted gross income minus the amount of charitable contributions allowed for contributions to the 30%-type charities.[7]

1. See IRC Secs. 170(f)(11)(E), 6662(e)(1), 6662(h)(2), 6664(c)(2), as amended by PPA 2006; IRC Sec. 6695A, as added by PPA 2006.
2. 2005-50 IRB 1137.
3. 2006-46 IRB 902.
4. See IRC Sec. 170(b)(1)(E).
5. IRC Sec. 170(b)(1)(A).
6. IRC Secs. 170(b)(1)(B), 170(b)(1)(C).
7. IRC Sec. 170(b)(1)(D).

Deductions denied because of the 50%, 30% or 20% limits may be carried over and deducted over the next five years, retaining their character as 50%, 30% or 20% type deductions.[1]

Gifts are "to" a charitable organization if made directly to the organization. Even though the gift may be intended to be used by the charity, and the charity may use it, if it is given *directly* to the charity, it is a gift to the charity and not "for the use of" the charity, for purposes of the deduction limits. Unreimbursed out-of-pocket expenses incurred on behalf of an organization (e.g., unreimbursed travel expenses of volunteers) are deductible as contributions "to" the organization if they are directly related to performing services for the organization (and, in the case of travel expenses, there is no significant element of personal pleasure, recreation, or vacation in such travel).[2]

"For the use of" applies to indirect contributions to a charitable organization.[3] The term "for the use of" does not refer to a gift of the right to use property. Such a gift would generally be a nondeductible gift of less than the donor's entire interest (see Q 1327).

1321. When is the deduction for charitable contributions taken?

Generally, the deduction for a contribution is taken in the year the gift is made.[4] However, in the case of a contribution of a future interest in tangible personal property only (e.g., stamps, artwork, etc.), the contribution is considered made (and the deduction allowable) only "when all intervening interests in, and rights to the actual possession or enjoyment of, the property have expired" or are held by parties unrelated to the donor.[5]

This rule does not apply to gifts of undivided present interests, or to gifts of future interests in real property or in intangible personal property.[6] The grant of stock options by a company to a charitable trust resulted in a deduction in the year in which the options were exercised.[7] Where real estate was transferred to a charity and subject to an option to repurchase, the IRS determined that fair market value under IRC Section 170 would be the value of the property *upon the expiration of the option*.[8] A fixture that is to be severed from real property is treated as tangible personal property.[9] The deduction for a charitable contribution made by an accrual basis S corporation is properly passed through to shareholders and taken in the year that the contribution is actually paid.[10]

See Q 1327 for an explanation of the deduction for gifts of partial interests, and Q 1328 to Q 1338 for an explanation of gifts through charitable trusts.

1322. Can an individual deduct the fair market value of appreciated real estate or intangible personal property such as stocks or bonds given to a charity?

1. IRC Secs. 170(d)(1), 170(b)(1)(D)(ii); Treas. Reg. §1.170A-10(b).
2. IRC Sec. 170(j); *Rockefeller v. Comm.*, 676 F.2d 35 (2nd Cir. 1982), *aff'g*, 76 TC 178 (1981), *acq. in part*, 1984-2 CB 2; Rev. Rul. 84-61, 1984-1 CB 39. See Rev. Rul. 58-279, 1958-1 CB 145.
3. See Treas. Reg. §1.170A-8(a)(2). See *Davis v. United States*, 495 U.S. 472 (1990).
4. IRC Sec. 170(a)(1).
5. IRC Sec. 170(a)(3). See also Treas. Reg. §1.170A-5.
6. Treas. Regs. §§1.170A-5(a)(2), 1.170A-5(a)(3).
7. Let. Ruls. 200202034, 8849018.
8. TAM 9828001.
9. IRC Sec. 170(a)(3).
10. TAM 200004001. See also Rev. Rul. 2000-43, 2000-2 CB 333.

If an individual makes a charitable contribution to a public charity of real property or intangible personal property, the sale of which would have resulted in long-term capital gain (see below), he is generally entitled to deduct the full fair market value of the property, but the deduction for the gift is limited to the lesser of 30% of adjusted gross income or the unused portion of the 50% limit (see Q 1320).[1] See Q 1323 for the rules that apply to gifts of tangible personal property, and Q 1324 regarding gifts to private foundations.

A deduction denied because it exceeds 30% of the individual's adjusted gross income may be carried over and treated as a contribution of capital gain property in each of the next five years.[2]

> *Example.* In 2005, Mr. Copeland had adjusted gross income of $600,000. He made a charitable contribution of long-term capital gain stock worth $200,000 to his church. His deduction is limited to $180,000 (30% of $600,000). In 2006, Mr. Copeland's adjusted gross income is $700,000. He contributes $100,000 worth of long-term capital gain bonds to the church. He may deduct $120,000 in 2006 ($100,000 plus $20,000 carried over from 2005), since the total does not exceed 30% of his adjusted gross income for 2006 ($210,000).

An individual may elect to take a gift of long-term capital gain property into account at its adjusted basis instead of its fair market value; if he does so, the income percentage limit for the contribution is increased to 50% instead of 30%. However, such an election applies to all such contributions made during the taxable year.[3] The election is generally irrevocable.[4]

If the charitable contribution is of property that, if sold at the time of the contribution, would result in income that would not otherwise qualify for long-term capital gain treatment (e.g., short-term capital gain), the deduction must be reduced by the amount of gain that would not be long-term capital gain.[5] If the entire gain would be income other than long-term capital gain (see above), the allowable deduction would be limited to the taxpayer's adjusted basis in the contributed property.

Special rules apply to charitable contributions of S corporation stock in determining whether gain on the stock would have been long-term capital gain if the stock were sold by the taxpayer.[6]

Donors making charitable contributions of the long-term capital gain portion of futures contracts must mark the contracts to market as of the dates the contracts are transferred to the donee and recognize the accrued long-term capital gains as income.[7] The amount of taxable gain or deductible loss recognized by the transferor at the time of the charitable transfer equals the difference between the fair market value of the futures contract at the time of the transfer and the transferor's tax basis in the futures contract, as adjusted under IRC Section 1256(a)(2), to account for gains and losses already recognized in prior tax years under the mark to market rules.[8]

---

1. See IRC Sec. 170(b)(1)(C); Treas. Reg. §1.170A-8(d)(1).
2. IRC Secs. 170(b)(1)(C); Treas. Reg. §1.170A-10(c).
3. IRC Secs. 170(b)(1)(C)(iii), 170(e)(1).
4. *Woodbury v. Comm.*, 90-1 USTC ¶50,199 (10th Cir. 1990), *aff'g*, TC Memo 1988-272.
5. IRC Sec. 170(e)(1)(A); Treas. Reg. §1.170A-4(a).
6. IRC Sec. 170(e)(1).
7. *Greene v. U.S.*, 79 F.3d 1348 (2nd Cir. 1996).
8. *Greene v. U.S.*, 84 AFTR 2d 99-5415 (2nd Cir. 1999).

Taxpayers who transferred appreciated stock to charitable organizations in the midst of a ongoing tender offer and merger were taxed on the gain on the stock under the "anticipatory assignment of income doctrine" where the charitable gifts occurred after the taxpayers' interests in a corporation had ripened into rights to receive cash.[1] But where taxpayers assigned warrants to four charities after receiving a letter announcing that all issued and outstanding stock of the company would be purchased, the Tax Court held that under Revenue Ruling 78-197,[2] the Service could treat the proceeds of the sales of the warrants by the charities as income to the donors *only if* at the time the assignments took place, the charitable donees were legally bound or could be compelled to sell the warrants.[3]

A taxpayer who donated stock to a supporting organization, where the voting rights had been transferred for a business purposes to a third party many years ago, was permitted to claim a charitable deduction.[4]

1323. May an individual deduct the fair market value of appreciated tangible personal property, such as art, stamps, coins, and gems given to a charitable organization?

The answer depends on whether the use of the gift is *related* to the exempt purpose of the charity to which the property is given. Generally, a contribution of appreciated tangible personal property whose sale would result in long-term capital gain (see below) is deductible at the property's full fair market value up to 30% of the individual's adjusted gross income, *if* the charity makes use of the property in a way that is related to its charitable purpose or function (i.e., it is a "related-use" gift).[5] The limit is generally 20% in the case of private foundations (see Q 1324). However, if the use by the donee exempt organization is unrelated to its charitable purpose or function (or the gift is to a private foundation, see Q 1324) the amount of the charitable contribution taken into account is generally limited to the donor's adjusted basis.[6]

The regulations provide the following example as to the meaning of "unrelated use": "[I]f a painting contributed to an education[al] institution is used by that organization for educational purposes by being placed in its library for display and study by art students, the use is not an unrelated use; but if the painting is sold and the proceeds used by the organization for educational purposes, the use of the property is an unrelated use."[7] In addition, the regulations state that contributions of furnishings used by the charitable organization in its offices and buildings in the course of carrying out its functions will be considered a related use gift.[8]

The IRS determined that a gift of seeds, plants and greenhouses to an IRC Section 501(c)(3) school's plant science curriculum was a related use gift, and that a gift of a violin to a charitable organization whose exempt purpose included loaning instruments to music students was a related use gift.[9] The Service has also determined that

---

1. See *Ferguson v. Commissioner*, 174 F.3d 997 (9th Cir. 1999).
2. 1978-1 CB 83.
3. *Rauenhorst v. Comm.*, 119 TC 157 (2002).
4. Let Rul. 200108012.
5. IRC Sec. 170(b)(1)(C); Treas. Reg. §1.170A-8(d)(1).
6. IRC Sec. 170(e)(1)(B).
7. Treas. Reg. §1.170A-4(b)(3)(i).
8. Treas. Reg. §1.170A-4(b)(3)(i).
9. Let. Ruls. 9131052, 9147049.

contributions of art to a Jewish community center for use in the center's recreational, educational, and social activities were related use gifts.[1]

In the case of contributions of long-term capital gain "related use" property to public charities, an individual may elect to value the gift at its adjusted basis instead of its fair market value. If he does so, the 30% of adjusted gross income limit does not apply; instead, the donor may deduct the amount of his adjusted basis in the gift, up to 50% of adjusted gross income. If the taxpayer makes the election, it applies to all gifts of long-term capital gain property during the year.[2] Such an election is generally irrevocable.[3]

The amount of the deduction for a contribution of tangible personal property must be reduced by the amount of gain that would *not* be long-term capital gain (i.e., gain on a capital asset held for more than one year) if the contributed property had been sold at its fair market value at the time of the contribution.[4] Thus, for example, if the entire gain would be ordinary income, the allowable deduction would be limited to the taxpayer's adjusted basis in the contributed property. It makes no difference, in such a case, whether or not the property is put to a related use.[5] Ordinary income property includes a work of art created by the donor.[6]

Planning Point: Contributions of "related use" tangible personal property that is sold, exchanged, or otherwise disposed of within three years of contribution are now potentially subject to recapture of the deduction claimed. If the charity sells, exchanges, or otherwise disposes of the property during the tax year in which the contribution is made, the donor's deduction is simply limited to the donor's adjusted tax basis in the property. If the charity disposes of the property after the end of the tax year in which the contribution is made and before the last day of the 3-year period starting on the date of the gift, then the donor must include in ordinary income an amount equal to the excess of the deduction claimed over the donor's adjusted tax basis in the property.

Example: Susan contributes a stamp collection to the Hanover Philatelic Museum. The museum expects to put the collection on display. The collection is valued at $300,000 and Susan's adjusted tax basis for the collection is $5,000. Two years after Susan's contribution, the museum sells the collection to a private collector for $400,000. In the year of sale, Susan must include in ordinary income $295,000 ($300,000 minus $5,000).

Hidden Trap: It is possible (perhaps even likely) that the applicable marginal tax rate in the year in which the deduction was claimed will be lower than the applicable marginal tax rate in the year in which the deduction is recaptured. Therefore, the tax liability created from the inclusion of the recapture amount may exceed the tax savings realized from claiming the deduction. It is often the case that a $300,000 deduction has a different relative impact on a taxpayer's tax burden than a $300,000 item of income. For example, the inclusion of an item in income will cause an increase in adjusted gross income (AGI) and a ripple effect through such items as taxation of Social Security benefits (see Q 1410), the loss of the child tax credit (see Q 1437), reduction in personal

---

1. Let. Rul. 9833011.
2. IRC Secs. 170(b)(1)(C)(iii), 170(e)(1).
3. *Woodbury v. Comm.*, 90-1 USTC ¶50,199 (10th Cir. 1990), *aff'g*, TC Memo 1988-272.
4. IRC Sec. 170(e)(1)(A); Treas. Reg. §1.170A-4(a).
5. See IRC Sec. 170(e)(1)(A); Treas. Reg. §1.170A-4(a).
6. Treas. Reg. §1.170A-4(b)(1).

exemptions (see Q 1425), reduction in itemized deductions (see Q 1427), an increase in the 2% floor for miscellaneous itemized deductions (see Q 1428), and an increase in the 7.5% floor for deductible medical expenses (see Q 1429).

Recapture can be avoided if an officer of the charity in a written statement, under penalty of perjury: certifies that the use of the property was a related use and describes how the property was used and how this use furthered its charitable mission; or states the charity's intended use of the property at the time of contribution and certifies that this intended use has become impossible or infeasible to implement.

Example: In the example above, if the Hanover Philatelic Museum prepares a certification that meets the new rules, then Susan will not be required to include any amount in ordinary income as a result of the sale of the collection.

In addition, any person that identifies tangible personal property a related use property and knows that the property is not intended for a related use will be assessed a $10,000 penalty. The deduction recapture rules apply to contributions of "related use" tangible personal property after September 1, 2006. The new $10,000 penalty is effective for identifications made after August 17, 2006. [1] *Ted R. Batson, Jr., MBA, CPA, Senior Vice President of Professional Services and Gregory W. Baker, JD, CFP®, CAP, Senior Vice President of Legal Services for Renaissance.*

1324. May an individual take a deduction for charitable contributions to private foundations?

Yes, subject to certain limits. Most private foundations are family foundations subject to the special contribution limits described below. Certain other private foundations (i.e., conduit foundations and private operating foundations, which operate much like public charities) are treated as 50%-type organizations and subject to the rules for those organizations as explained in Q 1320.[2] The term "private foundations" as used below refers to standard private non-operating (e.g., family) foundations.

The deduction for a gift of long-term capital gain property "to" or "for the use of" a private foundation is subject to an income percentage limit of the lesser of (a) 20% of adjusted gross income, or (b) the unused portion of the 30% limit.[3] A deduction denied because it exceeds 20% of adjusted gross income may be carried over and treated as a 20%-type deduction over the next five years.[4]

Ordinarily, the value that is taken into account for a gift of long-term capital gain property to or for the use of a private foundation is limited to the donor's adjusted basis (i.e., the value of the gift is reduced by the amount that would be long-term capital gain if the property were sold at its fair market value at the time the gift was made).[5] However, if the gift is of publicly traded securities that meet the definition of "qualified appreciated stock" and the contribution is made to a private foundation, the gift will be deductible at its full fair market value.[6]

1. See IRC Secs. 170(e)(1)(B)(i), 6050L(a), as amended by PPA 2006; IRC Secs. 170(e)(7), 6720B, as added by PPA 2006.
2. See IRC Secs. 170(b)(1)(E), 170(b)(1)(A)(vii).
3. See IRC Sec. 170(b)(1)(D)(i).
4. IRC Sec. 170(b)(1)(D)(ii).
5. IRC Sec. 170(e)(1)(B).
6. IRC Sec. 170(e)(1)(B)(ii); IRC Sec. 170(e)(5).

Qualified appreciated stock is generally publicly traded stock that, if sold on the date of contribution at its fair market value, would result in a long-term capital gain.[1] A contribution of stock will not constitute qualified appreciated stock to the extent that it exceeds 10% of the value of all outstanding stock of the corporation; family attribution rules apply in reaching the 10% level, as do prior gifts of stock.[2]

The Service has determined that shares in a mutual fund can constitute qualified appreciated stock.[3] Restricted stock cannot be qualified appreciated stock, despite the availability of market quotations for other stock of the same class, because a restriction on transferability may materially affect the value of the stock.[4] Unlisted stock does not constitute qualified appreciated stock within the meaning of IRC Section 170(e)(5). According to the Service, this is because the legislative history indicates that IRC Section 170(e)(5) is to be applied *only* to situations where price quotations for the contributed stock are readily available on an established securities market.[5] Therefore, it is *not* sufficient merely that market quotations for the stock are readily available (e.g., from established brokerage firms); rather, the market quotations must be readily available on an established securities market.[6]

Private foundation contributions other than long-term capital gain property are subject to an income percentage limit of the lesser of (a) 30% of adjusted gross income, or (b) 50% minus the amounts contributed to 50%-type organizations (see Q 1320).[7] The deduction for a gift of property other than long-term capital gain property (e.g., stock held for one year or less) is limited to the donor's adjusted basis.[8]

Bargain Sales

1325. How is the charitable contribution deduction computed when property is sold to a charity at a reduced price?

If property is sold to a charity for less than its fair market value (a bargain sale), the individual must first determine whether a charitable deduction is allowable under the general rules governing charitable deductions (see Q 1315 and Q 1320). The taxpayer must then determine the amounts of the allowable deduction and gain (if any) that will result from the transaction. To do this he must calculate what percentage of the property's fair market value is being contributed and what percentage is being sold. (The fair market value of the contributed portion is the fair market value of the entire property less the amount realized on the sale.[9] The fair market value of the portion sold is the amount realized on the sale.) The taxpayer's adjusted basis in the property is then allocated to each portion in these proportions.[10]

To determine whether there is an allowable deduction for the contributed portion, and the amount of any such deduction, the value of the contributed portion must be

---

1. See IRC Sec. 170(e)(5).
2. IRC Sec. 170(e)(5)(C). See, e.g., Let. Ruls. 200112022, 200112024, 200112025.
3. Let. Rul. 199925029. See also Let. Rul. 200322005 (American Depositary Receipts (ADRs) constitute qualified appreciated stock).
4. Let. Ruls. 9320016. Cf. Let. Rul. 9825031 and 9746050.
5. See e.g., Let. Rul. 199915053.
6. See e.g., *Todd v. Comm.*, 118 TC 334 (2002).
7. IRC Sec. 170(b)(1)(B).
8. See IRC Sec. 170(e)(1)(A).
9. Treas. Reg. §1.170A-4(c)(3).
10. IRC Sec. 1011(b); Treas. Regs. §§1.170A-4(c)(2)(i), 1.1011-2.

reduced by any gain that would *not* have been long-term capital gain that would have been realized had the contributed portion been sold, taking into account the basis allocated to it.[1] If the sale of the contributed portion by the donor would have resulted in long-term capital gain, (see example 2, below) no reduction is required unless the gift is tangible personal property the use of which will be unrelated to the function of the charity (see Q 1323), or the gift is to a private foundation (see Q 1324).[2]

After any such reduction required by IRC Section 170(e)(1) has been made, the remaining amount of the contribution is the allowable deduction. For the portion of the property that is being sold, the allocated basis is subtracted from the amount realized on the sale to determine the donor/seller's taxable gain on the transaction.

> *Example 1.* Mr. Hagin sells ordinary income property to his church for $4,000, which is the amount of his adjusted basis. The property has a fair market value of $10,000. The contribution portion of the transaction has a value of $6,000 ($10,000 fair market value less $4,000 amount realized) that represents 60% of the value of the property. The amount realized represents 40% of the value of the property ($4,000/$10,000). The adjusted basis ($4,000) is therefore allocated as follows: 40% of it ($1,600) becomes Mr. Hagin's basis in the "sold" portion and 60% of it ($2,400) becomes his basis in the "contributed" portion. The $6,000 "contribution portion" of the transaction has an allocated basis of $2,400. If it were sold, he would recognize $3,600 of ordinary income. The deduction for the $6,000 contribution is therefore reduced by $3,600. Mr. Hagin has a charitable deduction of $2,400. Because Mr. Hagin is receiving $4,000 for the "sold" portion and has an allocated basis in it of $1,600, he recognizes $2,400 of ordinary income with respect to the sale part of the transaction. The church's basis in the property received will be $6,400; this consists of the sum of the bargain sale price ($4,000) and the amount of Mr. Hagin's basis ($2,400) in the gift portion.[3]

> *Example 2.* The facts are the same as in Example 1, except that the property was long-term capital gain stock. Mr. Hagin's allocations of basis are the same as above; therefore, he recognizes $2,400 on the sale portion of the transaction. However the contributed portion is not subject to a reduction; thus, he is permitted a deduction of $6,000. The church's basis in the stock will be $6,400, determined the same way as in Example 1.

A taxpayer who makes charitable contributions of long-term capital gain property may elect to apply the provisions of IRC Section 170(e)(1), with respect to all such contributions, thus using adjusted basis instead of fair market value to determine the value of the gifts. This election will permit the individual to take a higher proportion of his income as charitable deductions than would otherwise be allowed (see Q 1322).

The Code requires, therefore, that if a charitable deduction is permitted under IRC Section 170, the taxpayer must determine whether the bargain sale results in a charitable deduction and, if so, the amount of the deduction. It then requires that the adjusted basis of the property be allocated between the portions contributed and sold, based on their relative proportions of the property's fair market value.[4] Gain is recognized on the sale portion to the extent the amount realized exceeds the allocated basis; however, no loss is recognized if the sale amount is less than the allocated basis of the sold portion.[5] The amount of the deduction for the contributed portion is determined as if property having the allocated basis and allocated fair market value were given. (see Q 1322, Q 1323).

---

1. IRC Sec. 170(e)(1)(A); Treas. Reg. §1.1011-2(a).
2. IRC Sec. 170(e)(1)(B).
3. See Treas. Reg. §1.170A-4(d), Example 5.
4. IRC Secs. 170(e)(2), 1011(b); Treas. Reg. §1.170A-4(c)(2).
5. Treas. Reg. §1.1001-1(e).

The result is essentially two transactions—a sale of property that may result in taxable income, and a deductible contribution of property. In some cases, the application of these rules may result in a taxable gain in excess of the allowed deduction. If the property is subject to a liability, the amount of the liability is treated as an amount realized (see Q 1326).[1]

In a bargain sale, the charitable deduction was properly claimed in the year that the sale was completed, because in that year a sufficient quantity of benefits and burdens of ownership had passed to the charitable organization.[2] Bargain sale treatment was denied to a taxpayer who inflated his valuation to a figure that would enable him to recover his original investment in the boat (in the form of cash plus tax savings from the inflated tax deduction).[3]

PROPERTY SUBJECT TO A LIABILITY

1326. How is the amount of a charitable contribution affected when a taxpayer donates property subject to a mortgage or other debt?

When property subject to a liability is contributed to a charity, the amount of the liability is treated as an amount realized, even if the charity does not assume or pay the debt.[4] The property is considered sold for the amount realized, and the contribution is subject to the bargain sale rules (see Q 1325).

If, in connection with a charitable contribution a liability is assumed by the charity, or if property is donated that is subject to a liability, the amount of the charitable contribution may not include any interest paid (or to be paid) by the donor for any period after the contribution if an interest deduction for the amount is allowable to the donor.[5] If the property is a bond, the contribution must be reduced by the amount of interest paid by the taxpayer on indebtedness incurred to purchase or carry the bond that is attributable to any period before the making of the contribution. However, the amount of such a reduction is limited to the interest or interest equivalent (e.g., bond discount) on the bond that is not includable in the donor's income.[6]

> *Example.* (a) On January 1, 1992, Mr. Capps, an individual using the cash receipts and disbursements method of accounting, purchased for $9,280 a 5½%, $10,000, 20-year Omega Corporation bond, the interest on which was payable semi-annually on June 30 and December 31. The Omega Corporation had issued the bond on January 1, 1992, at a discount of $720 from the principal amount. On December 1, 2002, Mr. Capps donated the bond to a charitable organization, and, in connection with the contribution, the charitable organization assumed an indebtedness of $7,000 that Mr. Capps had incurred to purchase and carry the bond.
>
> (b) During the calendar year 2002, Mr. Capps paid accrued interest of $330 on the indebtedness for the period from January 1, 2002, to December 1, 2002, and an interest deduction of $330 is allowable for such amount. Of the bond discount of $36 a year ($720 divided by 20 years), $33 (11/12 of $36) is includable in Mr. Capps' income. Of the $550 of annual interest receivable on the bond, he will include in income only the June 30, 2002, payment of $275.

---

1. Treas. Reg. §1.1011-2(a)(3).
2. See *Musgrave v. Comm.*, TC Memo 2000-285.
3. *Styron v. Comm.*, TC Summary Opinion 2001-64.
4. Treas. Reg. §1.1001-2; Rev. Rul. 81-163, 1981-1 CB 433. See Let. Rul. 9329017; *Guest v. Comm.*, 77 TC 9 (1981), *acq.* 1982-2 CB 1; *Crane v. Comm.*, 331 U.S. 1 (1947).
5. IRC Sec. 170(f)(5); Treas. Reg. §1.170A-3(a).
6. IRC Sec. 170(f)(5)(B); Treas. Reg. §1.170A-3(c).

(c) The market value of the Omega Corporation bond on December 1, 2002, was $9,902. This value includes $229 of interest receivable that had accrued from July 1 to December 1, 2002.

(d) The amount of the charitable contribution determined without regard to the reduction required by IRC Section 170(f)(5) is $2,902 ($9,902, the value of the property on the date of gift, less $7,000, the amount of the liability assumed by the charitable organization). In determining the amount of the allowable charitable deduction, the value of the gift ($2,902) must be reduced to eliminate from the deduction that portion for which Mr. Capps has been allowed an interest deduction. Although the amount of such interest deduction was $330, the reduction required by this section is limited to $229, since the reduction is not to exceed the amount of interest income on the bond that is not includable in Mr. Capps' income.[1]

PARTIAL INTERESTS

General

1327. Can a deduction be taken for a charitable contribution of less than the donor's entire interest?

Generally, a taxpayer may not deduct a charitable contribution that is not in trust, if it is of less than his entire interest in property. (A deduction of a partial interest will be allowed to the extent a deduction would be allowed if the interest had been transferred in trust.[2] See Q 1328 to Q 1338.) However, a taxpayer may deduct contributions of partial interests if they are made to each of several charities, with the result that the entire interest in the property has been given to charitable organizations. An individual may make a gift of a partial interest in property if that is his entire interest, but not if partial interests were created to avoid the application of the rule prohibiting gifts of less than the individual's entire interest.[3]

Exceptions: A deduction *is* allowed for a contribution of less than the donor's entire interest in property in the following instances:

(a) *Editor's Note:* See Planning Point, below. The taxpayer donates an undivided portion of his entire interest.[4] An undivided portion is a "fraction or percentage of each and every substantial interest or right owned by the donor in such property and must extend over the entire term of the donor's interest in such property and in other property into which such property is converted."[5] See Rev. Rul. 57-293[6] (undivided ¼ ownership and ¼ possession of art object); Rev. Rul. 72-419[7] (undivided 20% *remainder* interest which was the donor's only interest in the property).[8] The *right* to possession of an undivided portion of the taxpayer's entire interest has been held sufficient to constitute a charitable gift, even where the donee did not actually choose to take possession.[9] See also Let. Ruls. 200223013, 200223014 (the gift of a fractional interest in any work of the donors' collection accepted by the donee (subject to the gift and loan agreement) would qualify as a gift of an undivided portion of the donors' entire interest in the work, relying on *Winokur*, above; thus, the undivided fractional interest

---

1. See Treas. Reg. §1.170A-3(d) Example (2).
2. IRC Sec. 170(f)(3)(A); Treas. Reg. §1.170A-7(a).
3. Treas. Reg. §1.170A-7(a)(2)(i).
4. IRC Sec. 170(f)(3)(B)(ii).
5. Treas. Reg. §1.170A-7(b)(1).
6. 1957-2 CB 153.
7. 1972-2 CB 104.
8. See Let. Ruls. 8145055, 8639019.
9. See *Winokur v. Comm.*, 90 TC 733 (1988), *acq.*, 1989-1 CB 1.

would be deductible). The possibility that a charity's undivided fractional interest may be divested upon the occurrence or nonoccurrence of some event has been determined not to defeat an otherwise deductible contribution where the possibility is deemed so remote as to be negligible.[1] A charitable gift of an "overriding royalty interest" or a "net profits interest" in an oil and gas lease did not constitute an undivided portion of the donor's entire interest in an oil and gas lease where the donor owned a working interest under the lease.[2]

(b) The taxpayer donates an irrevocable remainder interest in a personal residence or farm.[3]

(c) The taxpayer makes a qualified conservation contribution (see Q 1339).[4]

The Service privately ruled that a donor's transfer of a policy to a charity, while retaining bare legal title, was not a retention of a substantial interest for purposes of the partial interest rule. Thus, the donor did not violate the partial interest rule, and would be allowed to claim the charitable contribution deduction on the first day following the end of the 30-day cancellation period.[5]

The Service has ruled that a contribution of a patent to a qualified charity will *not* be deductible if: (1) the taxpayer retains any substantial right in the patent; or (2) the taxpayer's contribution of a patent is subject to a conditional reversion, unless the likelihood of the reversion is so remote as to be negligible. On the other hand, a contribution of a patent subject to a license or transfer restriction will be deductible, but the restriction *reduces* what would otherwise be the fair market value of the patent at the time of the contribution and, therefore, *reduces* the amount of the charitable contribution.[6]

Planning Point: An income tax contribution deduction is allowed only for gifts of a fractional interest in tangible personal property if the donor and the donee are the only parties that hold an interest in the property immediately prior to the contribution. Where property is owned by multiple persons, the Secretary of the Treasury may issue regulations permitting an income and gift tax contribution deduction for such a gift if all owners contribute a pro rata share of their interests in the property.

The fair market value used in valuing additional gifts of fractional interests in the same property is the lesser of the fair market value at the date of the first contribution and the fair market value at the date of the additional contribution.

Example: On November 11, 2006, Art C. Lector contributes a 20% interest in a sculpture to the local art museum. Two years later, when the sculpture has tripled in value, Art gives the remaining 80% interest in the sculpture to the museum. Because the sculpture appreciated in value, Art's contribution deduction is based on the sculpture's November 11, 2006 fair market value (the date of his initial fractional gift).

The contribution deduction allowed for income and gift tax is subject to recapture (with interest) if the charity does not receive all of the remaining interest in the prop-

---

1. Let. Rul. 9303007.
2. See Rev. Rul. 88-37, 1988-1 CB 522.
3. IRC Sec. 170(f)(3)(B)(i); Treas. Regs. §§1.170A-7(b)(3), 1.170A-7(b)(4).
4. IRC Sec. 170(f)(3)(B)(iii).
5. Let. Rul. 200209020.
6. Rev. Rul. 2003-28, 2003-1 CB 594.

erty within 10 years of the gift or the date of the donor's death, whichever is earlier. In addition, recapture is triggered if during this period the charity does not take physical possession of the property and use the property in a use related to its exempt purpose. If recapture is triggered, an additional penalty tax of 10% of the recaptured amount is imposed for both income and gift tax.

This provision is effective for contributions made after August 17, 2006.[1] *Ted R. Batson, Jr., MBA, CPA, Senior Vice President of Professional Services and Gregory W. Baker, JD, CFP®, CAP, Senior Vice President of Legal Services for Renaissance.*

Right to Use Property

The right to use property is less than the entire interest in property owned by an individual and is subject to the rules governing a charitable contribution of less than the donor's entire interest.[2] Therefore, generally no deduction will be allowed.

However, in some cases, a deduction has been allowed for the costs of repairing and maintaining property owned by the taxpayer but used by the charity. These deductions have been allowed as contributions "for the use of" the charity.[3] But, the Service has also denied a deduction for maintenance and repair costs in other instances.[4] To be deductible, the costs must be unreimbursed expenses "directly attributable to the performance of … volunteer services."[5]

A deduction was denied to a taxpayer who donated a week's use of his vacation home to a charitable auction. The IRS also noted that the successful bidder would not be permitted a charitable deduction to the extent that valuable consideration is received in return (i.e., the bidder paid fair rental for a week's use of the home).[6]

Tenant-stockholders were allowed to exclude $500,000 of gain from the disposition of their shares of stock in their cooperative apartment which was coordinated with a donation of the same shares to a charitable organization.[7]

Charitable Remainder Trusts

1328. What is a charitable remainder trust? How are charitable remainder trusts used as planning tools?

A charitable remainder trust (CRT) is a trust instrument that provides for specified payments to one or more individuals, with an irrevocable remainder interest in the trust property to be paid to or held for a charity.[8] CRTs are a notable exception to the general rule that an individual may not take a charitable deduction for a gift of less than his entire interest in property.

The IRC requirements for CRTs are specific and detailed (see Q 1329 to Q 1332). The purpose of these requirements is to assure that a charitable contribution is actually

---

1. See IRC Secs. 170(o), as added by PPA 2006.
2. IRC Sec. 170(f)(3)(A).
3. See *Est. of Carroll v. Comm.*, 38 TC 868 (1962); Rev. Rul. 58-279, 1958-1 CB 145.
4. Rev. Rul. 58-279, above; Rev. Rul. 69-239, 1969-1 CB 198.
5. Rev. Rul. 58-279, above.
6. Rev. Rul. 89-51, 1989-1 CB 89.
7. See FSA 200149007.
8. See Treas. Reg. §1.664-1(a)(1)(i).

made and that its present value can be determined with accuracy. To be immediately deductible, the gift must be of real property or intangibles; a gift of a remainder interest in tangible personal property is deductible only when all intervening interests have expired or are held by parties unrelated to the donor.[1]

Although the charitable remainder trust provisions were enacted in 1969, the use of them has grown dramatically since the mid-1980s. With the growth in their popularity came widespread use (and sometimes misuse) of CRTs as a planning vehicle. CRTs are commonly marketed in conjunction with "wealth replacement trusts." A typical plan calls for an individual owning appreciated capital gain property to give the property in trust to a charity, but retain a right to payment for life (and/or the life of a spouse or child). The trust becomes owner of the property; it frequently sells the property and reinvests the proceeds. The proceeds may be invested in tax-exempt securities, which may pass through tax-exempt income to the beneficiaries (see Q 1335).

The CRT/wealth replacement trust combination is designed to provide the donor a charitable deduction for the full fair market value of the gift, (subject to the limits explained in Q 1322), remove the property from his estate, defer or avoid tax to the donor on the capital gain portion of the gift (see Q 1335), and provide either a fixed or variable stream of payments that may be tailored somewhat to meet the needs of the donor. "Wealth replacement" is then accomplished through funding an irrevocable trust with life insurance in an amount equal to or greater than the value of the property given. Ideally, the cost of the premiums is offset in whole or in part by the tax benefit of the charitable deduction, the unused portion of which may be carried over for up to five years (see Q 1320). At the death of the donor (or the last noncharitable beneficiary), the trust property goes to the charity, and the life insurance proceeds to the beneficiaries of the life insurance trust.

Planning Point: The life insurance policy purchased by the trustee of the wealth replacement trust is typically a survivorship policy. This type of policy is used for two reasons: (1) the premiums are generally more affordable, particularly if one of the donors is otherwise uninsurable; and (2) the payment of the life insurance death benefit typically coincides with the timing when the heirs would normally receive the asset being replaced. *Ted R. Batson, Jr., MBA, CPA, Senior Vice President of Professional Services for Renaissance.*

Planning Point: Often the amount of insurance purchased for wealth replacement is equal to the value of the property contributed to the charitable remainder trust. However, this is not a requirement. Depending on the goals of the client, it may be appropriate to purchase less insurance or more insurance. With less insurance, the client's income distributions bear a lesser burden in supporting the premium payments. With more insurance, the client is able to leverage the life insurance to create a greater benefit to the life insurance trust beneficiaries. *Ted R. Batson, Jr., MBA, CPA, Senior Vice President of Professional Services for Renaissance.*

Planning Point: While charitable remainder trusts and wealth replacement trusts are often presented as an integrated plan, it is important to note there is a proper order to funding these trusts. The wealth replacement trust is usually implemented first in order to ensure that there is no gap in asset protection between the delivery of the contribu-

---

1. IRC Sec. 170(a)(3); Treas. Reg. §1.170A-5.

tion to the charitable remainder trust and the purchase of the life insurance contract. One consequence of this order is that the first life insurance premium must be funded out-of-pocket rather than from the income distributions from the charitable remainder trust. *Ted R. Batson, Jr., MBA, CPA, Senior Vice President of Professional Services for Renaissance.*

The CRT must provide for periodic payments within limits set forth in the Code (see Q 1330, Q 1331) and based on the net fair market value of the trust assets. If the trust is a charitable remainder *annuity* trust (CRAT), the fair market value will be determined only once (at the inception of the trust) and the payout amount will be fixed based on that valuation. If the trust is a charitable remainder *unitrust* (CRUT), the fair market value will be determined annually and the payout amount (not the percentage) will vary from year to year as the value of the trust fluctuates. Most CRTs provide for a payout of between 5% and 10%. See Q 1335 regarding the taxation of these payments to the beneficiary.

Obviously, the higher the payout and the greater the number of noncharitable beneficiaries, the lower the value of the remainder interest the charity will ultimately receive. Generally, the value of the remainder interest passing to the charity generally must be at least 10% of the net fair market value of the property placed in the trust.[1] See Q 1330, Q 1331.

Annual valuation (which is required for charitable remainder unitrusts and not permitted for any other charitable trust) increases the flexibility of a CRUT considerably. It permits the donor to make additional contributions to the trust, thus providing a certain degree of control over the amount of the resulting payment stream. Assuming the trust investments perform reasonably well, the variable payments provide a hedge against inflation. In contrast, a charitable remainder *annuity* trust provides a fixed payment amount, and additional contributions to the trust are not permitted.

In the absence of authorization to the contrary, a charitable remainder trust may be forced to invade the corpus of the trust if the performance of its investments is such that income is insufficient to meet the payout requirement. One way to alleviate this problem is through the *net income unitrust*, which limits its payout to the trust's net income, if that amount is less than the percentage payout called for by the trust. Another variation is a *net income with makeup unitrust*, in which a net income unitrust is permitted to make up payments that were called for in earlier years but were not made because trust income was less than the required payment. Both of these instruments are specifically authorized by the IRC.[2] *Flip unitrusts* are permitted under final regulations, but only under very limited and narrow conditions (see Q 1331).[3] However, no other variations from these prescribed payout structures are permitted.

Planning Point: A common use of the flip unitrust is when a charitable remainder trust is funded with unmarketable assets, such as real property, closely held stock, or some other type of asset for which there is not a ready market. A flip unitrust is used so that the trustee will not be compelled to make a payment without sufficient liquidity to make the payment. In a properly structured flip unitrust, the trustee would only be required to pay the net income of the trust to the income beneficiary until the unmarketable

---

1. IRC Sec. 664(d).
2. See IRC Sec. 664(d)(3); Treas. Reg. §1.664-3(a)(1).
3. See Treas. Reg. §1.664-3(a)(1)(i)(c).

property was sold and the trust's assets became liquid. *Ted R. Batson, Jr., MBA, CPA, Senior Vice President of Professional Services for Renaissance.*

The flexibility of the net income with makeup unitrust (sometimes called a "spigot trust") has led to its use as a retirement planning tool. Under a typical arrangement, an investor establishes a net income with makeup unitrust, which then invests the contributed property in growth assets with little or no income, such as zero coupon bonds. Additional contributions are made as often as the donor wishes; inside growth of the trust assets typically occurs tax free (see Q 1336). In addition, the donor receives a charitable deduction for a portion of each contribution, based on the present value of the remainder interest (see Q 1334), assuming the trust otherwise qualifies as a CRUT (see Q 1331). When the donor nears retirement, trust investments are shifted to income producing assets, and the payout increases as the trust "makes up" the payments that were not made in earlier years.

The Service has privately ruled that a taxpayer would not recognize gain or loss as a result of transferring stock from a qualified plan to a charitable remainder unitrust upon his separation from service. Furthermore, the taxpayer would receive an income tax charitable deduction, subject to the income percentage limits, for the contribution of the stock to the CRUT in an amount equal to the fair market value of the stock at the time of the transfer less the value of the taxpayer's remainder unitrust interest.[1]

An individual's choice as to which of these vehicles to use may depend in large part on the degree of flexibility needed. The majority of charitable trusts use the *charitable remainder unitrust* form, because it offers the greatest degree of flexibility with respect to future contributions, the timing and amount of the payment stream, and the degree to which the individual may have an effect on the administration of the trust. However, charitable remainder unitrusts are the most expensive to administer.

Certain other factors may affect the decision as to which trust form is preferable. A donor who prefers fixed payments over variable payments may prefer a charitable remainder annuity trust; the age of the donor may have a significant impact on this preference and on the degree of flexibility needed. If the property being contributed is illiquid, a trust with an inflexible payout arrangement would be ill-advised. A donor who wishes to avoid set-up and administration expenses may prefer to contribute to a *pooled income fund* (see Q 1329, Q 1332), or a donor advised fund (see Q 1333).

The 10% remainder interest value requirement may prevent some formerly acceptable arrangements from being permissible if established after July 28, 1997, particularly in the case of a younger couple (e.g., under 45) utilizing a payout over two lives. See Q 1330, Q 1331.

One final factor that may affect the donor's choice of CRT vehicles is the extent to which he wishes to maintain control over the administration of the trust assets. Provided the trust adheres to strict limitations, the grantor of a charitable remainder unitrust or annuity trust may be able to successfully act as a trustee; the contributor to a pooled income fund may not.[2] Traditionally, advisers recommended against a grantor's acting as trustee of a charitable remainder trust, fearing that the grantor trust rules (see Q 1450) might result in its disqualification. However, the IRS has ruled, as well as indicated in

1. See Let. Ruls. 200215032, 200202078, 200038050, 199919039.
2. IRC Sec. 642(c)(5)(E).

letter rulings, that a CRT that is otherwise properly designed and administered will not be disqualified merely because the grantor acts as a trustee.[1]

Spousal Election Rights and Charitable Remainder Trusts. The IRS and Treasury Department have issued guidance providing a safe harbor procedure to avoid the disqualification of a charitable remainder annuity trust (CRAT) or charitable remainder unitrust (CRUT) if, under applicable state law, the grantor's surviving spouse has a right of election exercisable upon the grantor's death to receive an elective, statutory share of the grantor's estate, and that share could be satisfied in whole or part from assets of the CRAT or CRUT (in violation of IRC Section 664(d)).[2]

The surviving spouse's elective right to receive an elective share of the grantor's estate (if the share could include any assets of a CRAT or CRUT created or funded by the grantor) will be *disregarded* for purposes of determining whether the CRAT or CRUT has met the requirements of IRC Section 664(d) continuously since its creation if all of the following requirements are satisfied:

(1)   *Waiver effective under state law:* The surviving spouse must irrevocably waive the right of election to whatever extent necessary to ensure that no part of the trust (other than the annuity or unitrust interest of which the surviving spouse is the named recipient under the terms of the trust) may be used to satisfy the elective share. A valid waiver of the elective share or elective right will satisfy the requirements in the preceding sentence if the waiver is valid under applicable state law, in writing, and signed and dated by the surviving spouse.

(2)   *Timing of waiver:* For CRATs and CRUTs created by the grantor on or after June 28, 2005, the requirements set forth in item (1), above, must be satisfied on or before the date that is six months after the due date (excluding extensions) for filing Form 5227 (the trust's information return) for the year in which the *later* of the following occurs: (i) the creation of the trust; (ii) the date of the grantor's marriage to the surviving spouse; (iii) the date the grantor first becomes domiciled or resident in a jurisdiction whose law provides a right of election that could be satisfied from the assets of the trust; or (iv) the effective date of applicable state law creating a right of election.

(3)   *Trustee to retain copy:* A copy of the signed waiver must be provided to the trustee of the CRAT or CRUT. The trustee must retain the copy in the official records of the trust as long as the contents may become material in the administration of any internal revenue law.

After the release of Revenue Procedure 2005-24, commentators asserted that the procedure places an undue burden on taxpayers and trustees seeking to comply with the safe harbor rule. The Service and Treasury Department subsequently announced they are reconsidering the approach of Revenue Procedure 2005-24, including the safe harbor rule. Consequently, the Service is extending the June 28, 2005, grandfather date. Thus, until further guidance is published regarding the spousal right of election on a trust's qualification as a CRAT or CRUT, the Service will disregard the existence of

---

1. Rev. Rul. 77-285, 1977-2 CB 213; Let. Ruls. 200029031, 9048050, 8809085.
2. Rev. Proc. 2005-24, 2005-16 IRB 909.

such a right of election—*even without a waiver*—but only if the surviving spouse does not exercise the right of election.[1]

For details as to the requirements for a charitable remainder annuity trust, see Q 1330, for charitable remainder unitrusts see Q 1331, and for pooled income fund requirements, see Q 1332. For the tax treatment of the payments to the noncharitable beneficiary, see Q 1335. To calculate the amount of the deduction for a CRT gift, see Q 1334, and for general limits on all charitable deductions of long-term capital gain property, see Q 1322.

Sample Trusts

The IRS generally does not issue rulings concerning whether a charitable remainder trust that provides for annuity or unitrust payments for one or two measuring lives satisfies the requirements of IRC Section 664.[2] Instead, taxpayers are directed to follow sample forms for charitable remainder trusts. The IRS stated in 1992 that any CRT that "substantially follows" one of the sample forms, that operates in a manner consistent with the terms of the trust instrument, and that is valid under local law will be recognized by the Service as a valid CRT.[3]

In 2003, the Service released updated sample declarations of trusts and alternate provisions that meet the CRAT requirements under IRC Section 664 and Treas. Reg. §1.664-2. The new forms for inter vivos CRATs are: (1) Rev. Proc. 2003-53, 2003-2 CB 230 (one measuring life), *superseding*, Rev. Proc. 89-21, 1989-1 CB 842; (2) Rev. Proc. 2003-54, 2003-2 CB 236 (term of years); (3) Rev. Proc. 2003-55, 2003-2 CB 242 (consecutive interests for two measuring lives), *superseding*, Sec. 4 of Rev. Proc. 90-32, 1990-2 CB 546; and (4) Rev. Proc. 2003-56, 2003-2 CB 249 (concurrent and consecutive interests for two measuring lives), *superseding*, Sec. 5 of Rev. Proc. 90-32, 1990-2 CB 546. The new forms for testamentary CRATs are: (5) Rev. Proc. 2003-57, 2003-2 CB 257 (one measuring life), *superseding*, Sec. 6 of Rev. Proc. 90-32, 1990-2 CB 546; (6) Rev. Proc. 2003-58, 2003-2 CB 262 (term of years); (7) Rev. Proc. 2003-59, 2003-2 CB 268 (consecutive interests for two measuring lives), *superseding*, Sec. 7 of Rev. Proc. 90-32, 1990-2 CB 546; and (8) Rev. Proc. 2003-60, 2003-2 CB 274 (concurrent and consecutive interests for two measuring lives), *superseding*, Sec. 8 of Rev. Proc. 90-32, 1990-2 CB 546.

In 2005, the Service released updated sample forms for CRUTs. The new forms for inter vivos CRUTs are: (1) Rev. Proc. 2005-52, 2005-34 IRB 326 (one measuring life); (2) Rev. Proc. 2005-53, 2005-34 IRB 339 (term of years); (3) Rev. Proc. 2005-54, 2005-34 IRB 353 (consecutive interests for two measuring lives); (4) Rev. Proc. 2005-55, 2005-34 IRB 367 (concurrent and consecutive interests for two measuring lives). The new forms for testamentary CRUTs are: (5) Rev. Proc. 2005-56, 2005-34 IRB 383 (one measuring life); (6) Rev. Proc. 2005-57, 2005-34 IRB 392 (term of years); (7) Rev. Proc. 2005-58, 2005-34 IRB 402 (consecutive interests for two measuring lives); and (8) Rev. Proc. 2005-59, 2005-34 IRB 412 (concurrent and consecutive interests for two measuring lives).

---

1. Rev. Proc. 2006-15, 2006-8 IRB 501.
2. Rev. Proc. 92-3, 1992-1 CB 561, Sec. 4.37.
3. See Rev. Procs. 90-30, 90-31, 90-32 (*but see below*), 90-33, 1990-1 CB 534, 539, 546, 551; Rev. Proc. 89-20, 1989-1 CB 841.

Filing

Split-interest charitable trusts are now required to file each year the form required by the Secretary of the Treasury. Historically this has been Form 1041-A, Trust Accumulation of Charitable Amounts. PPA 2006 eliminates the current exception that exempted such trusts from filing the form if all of the net income of the trust was distributed currently. The exception continues to apply to non-charitable trusts that must file Form 1041-A as a result of claiming a deduction under IRC Sec. 642(c).[1]

Planning Point: This change impacts charitable remainder trusts, charitable lead trusts, and pooled income funds. It remains to be seen whether Treasury will create a new form for split-interest charitable trusts or continue to use Form 1041-A.

In addition, the penalty for failure to file the form (required by new IRC Section 6034(a)) is increased from $10 to $20 for each day the form is late. The maximum penalty that may be imposed is increased from $5,000 to $10,000. However, for certain large trusts with gross income in excess of $250,000, the penalty is $100 per day up to a maximum of $50,000 [2]

Under current law, Form 1041-A is subject to public inspection. PPA 2006 clarifies that information regarding the noncharitable beneficiaries of charitable split-interest trusts is not subject to public inspection.[3]

1329. Can a deduction be taken for a contribution to a charitable remainder trust or a pooled income fund?

Yes. An individual may make an immediately deductible gift in trust to a charity, but keep (or give to another person or persons) the right to receive regular payments from the trust before the charity receives any amount. The IRC narrowly defines the types of charitable trusts, in order to assure that an accurate determination can be made of the value of the contribution. To receive this special treatment, the gift must be to a *charitable remainder annuity trust* (see Q 1330), a *charitable remainder unitrust* (see Q 1331), or a *pooled income fund* (see Q 1332).[4] Any individual beneficiaries must be alive when the trust is created.

To be immediately deductible, the gift must be of real property or intangibles; a gift of a remainder interest in tangible personal property is deductible only when all intervening interests have expired or are held by parties unrelated to the donor.[5] The IRC also permits a deduction for a gift of an income interest, generally referred to as a *charitable lead trust* (see Q 1337).

A gift to a charitable remainder trust (or pooled income fund) may be made during an individual's life or at his death by his will. The right of the noncharitable beneficiary (or beneficiaries) to receive payments may extend for life or for a term of up to 20 years. Obviously, however, the value of the charitable deduction will be inversely proportionate to the length of noncharitable payments. Generally, the value of the remainder interest passing to the charity generally must be at least 10% of the net fair market value of the

1. IRC Sec. 6034, as amended by PPA 2006.
2. IRC Sec. 6652(c)(2)(C), as amended by PPA 2006.
3. IRC Sec. 6104(b), as amended by PPA 2006.
4. IRC Sec. 170(f)(2)(A); Treas. Reg. §1.170A-6(b).
5. IRC Sec. 170(a)(3); Treas. Reg. §1.170A-5.

property placed in the trust.[1] See Q 1334 for an explanation of the actual calculation of the amount of the deduction.

The extent to which the deduction may be used in any given year is subject to the general limitations on charitable deductions (see Q 1322, Q 1323, Q 1324).[2] See Q 1506 and Q 1532 regarding the estate tax charitable deduction for a gift to a charitable remainder trust.

1330. What is a charitable remainder annuity trust?

A charitable remainder annuity trust provides to a noncharitable beneficiary a fixed payment at least annually of not less than 5% nor more than 50% of the initial net fair market value of all property placed in the trust, with an irrevocable remainder interest to be paid to or held for a charity.[3] For example, the trust may provide for concurrent payment of $400 to husband for life and $600 to wife for life, or it may provide for payment of $1000 to husband and wife for their joint lives and then to the survivor for life.[4] Because the payment amount is fixed at the inception of the trust, valuation occurs only once and the payout cannot be limited to the net income of the trust. Furthermore, the donor cannot make additional payments to the trust.[5]

10% remainder interest requirement. Generally, the value of the remainder interest (i.e., the deduction) must equal at least 10% of the initial fair market value of all property placed in the trust.[6] The value of a remainder interest for this purpose is calculated using the IRC Section 7520 interest rate, which is published every month by the IRS. The calculation of the deduction can be made using the current rate or either of the previous two months' rates. For a charitable remainder annuity trust, the charitable deduction increases as the IRC Section 7520 rate increases; therefore, one should choose the highest rate of the three month period for the best deduction. See Q 1334 for an explanation of the calculation of the deduction.

Noncharitable beneficiary. The IRC requires that the trust payout be made to one or more persons (at least one of whom is not a charitable organization and, in the case of individuals, only to an individual who is living at the time of the creation of the trust) for a term of years (not exceeding 20) or for the life or lives of the individual or individuals.[7] All individual beneficiaries must be living at the time of the creation of the trust.[8] The trust may provide that a beneficiary's interest will terminate on the happening of a specified contingency.[9]

IRC Section 664 and regulations thereunder require that to qualify as a charitable remainder trust, a trust must meet the definition of, and function exclusively as, a charitable remainder trust from the time the trust is created. No payments other than those described may be made to anyone other than a qualified charity. Following the termination of all noncharitable payments, the remainder interest is transferred to the charity or retained by the trust for the benefit of the charity.[10]

---

1. IRC Sec. 664(d).
2. Treas. Reg. §1.170A-6(b)(2).
3. IRC Sec. 664(d)(1); Treas. Reg. §1.664-1(a)(1).
4. Treas. Reg. §1.664-2(a)(1).
5. Treas. Reg. §1.664-2(b).
6. IRC Sec. 664(d)(1)(D).
7. IRC Sec. 664(d)(1)(A).
8. Treas. Reg. §1.664-2(a)(3).
9. IRC Sec. 664(f).
10. IRC Sec. 664(d)(1).

In 2002, the Service ruled that distributions from a CRUT to a separate "special needs" trust for the life of a disabled beneficiary, rather than for a term of years, did not preclude the CRUT from qualifying under the Code. A trust may qualify as a CRUT if: (1) the unitrust amounts will be paid for the life of a financially disabled individual to a separate trust that will administer these payments on behalf of that individual; and (2) upon the individual's death, the trust will distribute the remaining assets to the individual's estate, or, after reimbursing the state for any Medicaid benefits provided to the individual, subject to the individual's general power of appointment.[1]

The IRS permitted the grantor of a charitable remainder annuity trust to terminate the trust by assigning his annuity interest to the charitable remainder beneficiary. The IRS determined that the gift would not retroactively disqualify the trust, and that once "completed" the gift would qualify for a charitable contribution deduction under IRC Section 170. However, the Service stipulated that the gift would be "completed" only (1) when (and to the extent that) assets traceable to the assignment are expended or distributed, or (2) when the grantor permanently resigned as officer and director of the charity to which the assignment was being made.[2]

Payout timing. To qualify as a charitable remainder annuity trust, the trust must pay the sum certain to the noncharitable beneficiary at least annually. See, e.g., *Atkinson v. Comm.*[3] (estate tax charitable deduction denied where the trust had not paid the required annuity payments to the grantor during her lifetime).

Under final regulations, the annuity amount may be paid within a reasonable time after the close of the year for which it is due if either of the following occur: (a) the character of the annuity amount in the recipient's hands is income under IRC Section 664(b)(1), (2), or (3); or (b) the trust distributes property (other than cash) that it owned as of the close of the taxable year to pay the annuity amount, and the trustee elects to treat any income generated by the distribution as occurring on the last day of the taxable year for which the amount is due. Additionally, for CRATs that were created before December 10, 1998, the annuity amount may be paid within a reasonable time after the close of the taxable year for which it is due if the percentage used to calculate the annuity amount is 15% or less.[4]

1331. What is a charitable remainder unitrust?

A charitable remainder unitrust provides to a noncharitable beneficiary a variable payment stream based on an annual valuation of the trust assets, with an irrevocable remainder interest to be paid to or held for the benefit of a charity. The payout must be a fixed percentage of not less than 5% nor more than 50% of the net fair market value of the trust assets, and is paid at least annually to the noncharitable beneficiary or beneficiaries.[5] (But see Let. Rul. 200108035, where a split-payout was approved.) Since the trust is valued annually, the donor may make additional contributions to the trust. To qualify as a charitable remainder trust, a trust must meet the definition of, and function exclusively as, a charitable remainder trust from the time the trust is created.[6]

---

1. Rev. Rul. 2002-20, 2002-1 CB 794, *superseding*, Rev. Rul. 76-270, 1976-2 CB 194. See also Let. Rul. 200240012.
2. Let. Rul. 9124031.
3. 115 TC 26 (2000), *aff'd*, 2002-2 USTC ¶60,449 (11th Cir. 2002).
4. Treas. Reg. §1.664-2(a)(1)(i).
5. IRC Sec. 664(d)(2)(A); Treas. Reg. §1.664-1(a)(1).
6. Treas. Reg. §1.664-1(a)(4).

Thus, if a trust does not qualify as a charitable remainder unitrust at its inception, it never will.[1]

The IRS denied both trust and CRUT status to an entity that was proposed to be established by an S corporation essentially to receive its profits and make distributions to its owners. The Service ruled that the proposed entity would not qualify as a trust under Treas. Regs. §§1.301.7701-4(a), 1.301-7701-4(c), or as a valid CRUT.[2]

10% Remainder Interest Requirement

The value of the remainder interest (i.e., the deduction) must equal at least 10% of the net fair market value of the property as of the date it is contributed to the trust.[3] The value of a remainder interest for this purpose is calculated using the IRC Section 7520 interest rate, which is published every month by the IRS. The calculation of the deduction can be made using the current rate or either of the previous two months' rates. See Q 1334 for an explanation of the calculation of the deduction.

If a transfer to an existing charitable remainder unitrust does not meet the 10% remainder interest value requirement, the contribution will be treated as if it were made to a separate trust; thus, the existing CRUT will not become disqualified by a contribution that does not meet this requirement.[4] It appears that the separate trust will be taxed as a complex trust, since it will not meet the requirements for a CRT.

The Service privately ruled that reducing the unitrust payment percentage for additional contributions to ensure that the value of the charity's interest would be no less than 10% of the fair market value of the additional property would not cause the CRUT to be disqualified *if* the total annual unitrust payment percentage for the additional contribution did not fall below 5% annually.[5]

Noncharitable Beneficiary

The IRC requires that the trust payout be made to one or more persons (at least one of whom is not a charitable organization and, in the case of individuals, only to an individual who is living at the time of the creation of the trust) for a term of years (not exceeding 20) or for the life or lives of the individual or individuals.[6] The IRS has determined that where unitrust amounts were payable to a separate trust for the life of the grantor's son rather than to the son himself, this requirement was not met.[7]

Any individual noncharitable beneficiary must be living at the time the trust is established.[8] Of course, the longer the trust has to make unitrust payments, the smaller the value of the remainder interest will be. The trust may provide that the interest of a noncharitable beneficiary will terminate on the happening of a particular contingency.[9]

---

1. See, e.g., Let. Rul. 200122045.
2. Let. Rul. 200203034.
3. IRC Sec. 664(d)(2)(D).
4. See IRC Sec. 664(d)(4).
5. Let. Rul. 200245048.
6. IRC Sec. 664(d)(2)(A).
7. See Let. Ruls. 9710008, 9710009, 9710010, revoking Let. Ruls. 9619042, 9619043, 9619044.
8. IRC Sec. 664(d)(2)(A).
9. IRC Sec. 664(f).

No payments other than those described in IRC Section 664 may be made to anyone other than a qualified charity. A trust will not qualify as a charitable remainder unitrust if it makes payments on a liability of the grantor.[1] Following the termination of all lifetime and term payments, the remainder interest in the trust must be transferred to or for the use of the charity or retained by the trust for such use.[2]

In 2002, the Service ruled that distributions from a CRUT to a separate "special needs" trust for the life of a disabled beneficiary, rather than for a term of years, did not preclude the CRUT from qualifying under the Code. A trust may qualify as a CRUT if: (1) the unitrust amounts will be paid for the life of a financially disabled individual to a separate trust that will administer these payments on behalf of that individual; and (2) upon the individual's death, the trust will distribute the remaining assets to the individual's estate, or, after reimbursing the state for any Medicaid benefits provided to the individual, subject to the individual's general power of appointment.[3]

Timing of Payout

To qualify as a charitable remainder unitrust, the trust must pay its unitrust amount to the noncharitable beneficiary at least annually. Under final regulations, the unitrust amount for fixed percentage CRUTs may be paid within a reasonable time *after* the close of the year for which it is due if either of the following occur: (a) the character of the unitrust amount in the recipient's hands is income under IRC Section 664(b)(1), (2), or (3); or (b) the trust distributes property (other than cash) that it owned as of the close of the taxable year to pay the unitrust amount, and the trustee elects to treat any income generated by the distribution as occurring on the last day of the taxable year for which the amount is due. Additionally, for fixed percentage CRUTs that were created before December 10, 1998, the unitrust amount may be paid within a reasonable time after the close of the taxable year for which it is due if the percentage used to calculate the unitrust amount is 15% or less.[4]

Income Exception CRUTS

A payout that is a fixed percentage of asset value will increase if the trust asset value increases. It is thus possible for a payout of a fixed percentage of trust asset value to exceed trust income; requiring that trust assets themselves be used to make payments. Therefore, to prevent invasion of the trust corpus, the trust instrument may limit the payout to the amount of the trust income, if that amount is less than the amount of the specified percentage; this is commonly referred to as a *net income unitrust*.[5]

The trust may also limit the payout to the amount of trust income if it is less than the stated percentage, but provide for the deficiency to be made up to the extent trust income exceeds the amount of the specified percentage in later years. This is commonly referred to as a *net income with makeup unitrust* (NIMCRUT).[6] Under this last alternative payout method, a trust with low-income, high-growth assets can pay little or no income to a high-bracket beneficiary; if trust assets produce high income at a later time, larger payouts can be made that include make-up amounts, perhaps when the beneficiary's marginal tax bracket is lower or his income need is greater (see Q 1328).

---

1. Let. Rul. 9015049.
2. IRC Secs. 664(d)(2)(C).
3. Rev. Rul. 2002-20, 2002-1 CB 561, *superseding*, Rev. Rul. 76-270, 1976-2 CB 194. See also Let. Rul. 200240012.
4. Treas. Reg. §1.664-2(a)(1)(i).
5. IRC Sec. 664(d)(3)(A).
6. IRC Sec. 664(d)(3)(B).

However, the trust provisions may not restrict the trustee from investing trust assets in a manner that could result in the annual realization of a reasonable amount of income or gain from disposition of trust assets.[1]

The trust instrument must specify which, if any, of the income exception methods will be used for any year; the method of determining the unitrust payout may not be discretionary with the trustee.[2]

Final regulations defining income for trust purposes. The IRS and the Treasury Department recognize that state statutes are in the process of changing traditional concepts of income and principal in response to investment strategies that seek total positive return on trust assets. These statutes are designed to ensure that, when a trust invests in assets that may generate little traditional income (including dividends, interest, and rents), the income and remainder beneficiaries are allocated reasonable amounts of the total return of the trust (including both traditional income and capital appreciation of trust assets) so that both classes of beneficiaries are treated impartially. The final regulations revise the definition of income under IRC Section 643(b) to reflect changes in the definition of trust accounting income under state laws.[3]

Under the final regulations, "trust income" (for purposes of Treas. Reg. §1.664-3(a)(1)(i)(b)) generally means income as defined under IRC Section 643(b) and the applicable regulations. The final regulations provide that trust income may *not* be determined by reference to a fixed percentage of the annual fair market value of the trust property, notwithstanding any contrary provision in applicable state law.[4]

The final regulations also provide as follows:

(1)   Proceeds from the sale or exchange of any assets contributed to the trust by the donor must be allocated to principal, and not to trust income, at least to the extent of the fair market value of those assets on the date of their contribution to the trust.

(2)   Proceeds from the sale or exchange of any assets purchased by the trust must be allocated to principal, and not to trust income, at least to the extent of the trust's purchase price of those assets.

(3)   Except as provided in (1) and (2), above, proceeds from the sale or exchange of any assets (i) contributed to the trust by the donor or (ii) purchased by the trust *may* be allocated to *income*, pursuant to the terms of the governing instrument, *if* not prohibited by applicable local law. A discretionary power to make this allocation may be granted to the trustee under the terms of the governing instrument, but *only* to the extent that the state statute permits the trustee to make adjustments between income and principal to treat beneficiaries impartially.[5]

For the applicability dates of the rules stated in items (1), (2), and 3), above, see Treas. Reg. §1.664-3(a)(1)(i)(b)(4).

1. Treas. Reg. §1.664-1(a)(3).
2. See Treas. Reg. §1.664-3.
3. Preamble, TD 9102, 69 Fed. Reg. 12, 13 (1-2-2004).
4. Treas. Reg. §1.664-3(a)(1)(i)(b)(3).
5. Treas. Reg. §1.664-3(a)(1)(i)(b)(3).

Capital gain NIMCRUT. The IRS has approved in numerous situations a NIM-CRUT provision granting the trustee the power to allocate post-contribution capital gain on assets that produce no income or limited income to trust income. Such a provision coupled with a provision treating a specific amount of any unitrust deficiency as a liability in valuing the trust's assets complied with the requirements for charitable remainder unitrusts.[1]

Self-dealing. The Service has ruled that the purchase of deferred annuity contracts by the independent trustee of a NIMCRUT did not adversely affect the CRUT's tax-exempt status. Moreover, where the donor received no present value from the contract right to receive annuity payments, and did not control the investment decision, the purchase of deferred annuity contracts did not constitute an act of self-dealing.[2] This technical advice memorandum led to modification of an aggressive approach the Service had taken on the issue of self-dealing by NIMCRUTs in its 1997 Exempt Organizations Continuing Professional Education Text (Topic K).[3]

The Service determined that the transfer of a life insurance policy to an income exception CRUT would not disqualify the CRUT.[4]

FLIP Unitrusts

Special requirements apply to a CRUT that is funded with assets that are illiquid. Under the conditions described below, the grantor may employ a net income with makeup provision until the assets are sold, thus preventing an ill-timed sale or an invasion of the trust corpus, then switch (i.e., "flip") to a fixed percentage payout once the assets have been sold. A trust that provides first for the use of a net income with makeup payout, followed by a fixed percentage payout is referred to as a *flip unitrust*.

Final regulations allow the use of flip unitrusts provided all the following conditions are satisfied:

(a) The trust instrument must provide that the one-time change in payout methods (i.e., the flip) is triggered on a specific date, or by a single event whose occurrence is not discretionary with, or within the control of, the trustees or any other persons.[5] Permissible triggering events include marriage, divorce, death, the birth of a child, or the sale of "unmarketable assets" (i.e., assets other than cash, cash equivalents, or assets that can be readily sold or changed for cash equivalents). For example, unmarketable assets would include real property, closely held stock, and unregistered securities for which there is no available exemption permitting public sale.[6]

(b) Following the "flip," only fixed percentage payouts (i.e., no net income makeup amounts) may be provided under the terms of the trust.[7] According to the preamble to the regulations, any makeup amounts remaining due at the time of the change in payout methods are forfeited when the trust converts to the fixed percentage method.[8]

1. See Let. Ruls. 9711013, 9511029, 9511007, 9442017.
2. TAM 9825001.
3. See Internal Revenue Service Exempt Organizations Continuing Professional Education Text for Fiscal Year 1999, Chapter P, 30 Years After the 1969 TRA – Recent Developments Under Chapter 42 (IRC Section 4940 – Investment Income Tax).
4. See Let. Rul. 199915045. See also Let. Rul. 200117016 (stock redemptions did not result in self-dealing).
5. Treas. Reg. §1.664-3(a)(1)(i)(c).
6. Treas. Regs. §§1.664-1(a)(7), 1.664-3(a)(1)(i)(d).
7. Treas. Reg. §1.664-3(a)(1)(i)(c)(3).
8. TD 8791, 63 Fed. Reg. 68188 (12-10-98).

(c) The "flip" may be made *only* from the net income method to the fixed percentage method.[1] A CRUT cannot convert from a fixed percentage method to a net income method without losing its status as a CRT.[2]

(d) The change from the net income with makeup amount method to the fixed percentage payout method must occur at the beginning of the taxable year that immediately follows the taxable year during which the triggering date or event occurs.[3]

The provisions set forth in the final regulations for flip unitrusts are effective for CRUTs created on or after December 10, 1998. Generally, a trust may *not* be amended or reformed to *add* a flip provision.[4] However, prior to June 30, 2000 a trust that contained a flip provision could be amended or reformed to comply with these rules, regardless of whether it was created on or after the effective date of the final regulations.[5] Furthermore, prior to that date a net income unitrust could also be reformed to *add* a provision allowing a conversion to the fixed percentage method provided the triggering event does not occur in a year prior to the year in which the court issues the order reforming the trust.[6] Adding the conversion provisions would not cause the CRUT to lose its tax-exempt status, and would not be considered an act of self-dealing if the trustee *initiated* legal proceedings to reform the trust by June 30, 2000.[7]

Reformation of Trust

A trust must qualify as a charitable remainder unitrust at its inception in order to generate a charitable deduction. The extent to which the provisions of a CRUT may be changed in any way after its inception has been the subject of a variety of ruling requests.

In a position consistent with the final regulations described above, the IRS has prohibited the reformation of a trust to change from a net income with make-up provision to a fixed percentage provision[8] or to remove a net income limitation[9]. However, as noted above, prior to June 30, 2000 the final regulations permitted a unitrust created on or after December 10, 1998 that contained a "flip" provision at its inception to be reformed or amended to comply with the requirements of the final regulations.[10] Furthermore, as stated above, adding the conversion provisions would not cause the CRUT to lose its tax-exempt status, and would not be considered an act of self-dealing if the trustee *initiated* legal proceedings to reform the trust by June 30, 2000.[11]

The Service ruled that reforming a CRUT by converting the trust from a net income method CRUT (NIMCRUT) to a fixed percentage CRUT would not adversely affect the CRUT's qualification status.[12]

---

1. Treas. Reg. §1.664-3(a)(1)(i)(c).
2. TD 8791, 63 Fed. Reg. 68188 (12-10-98).
3. Treas. Reg. §1.664-3(a)(1)(i)(c).
4. Treas. Reg. §1.664-3(a)(1)(i)(f)(2).
5. Treas. Reg. §1.664-3(a)(1)(i)(f)(2).
6. Treas. Reg. § 1.664-3(a)(1)(i)(f)(3).
7. Notice 99-31, 1999-1 CB 1185; Treas. Reg. §1.664-3(a)(1)(i)(f)(3).
8. Let. Rul. 9506015.
9. Let. Rul. 9516040.
10. See Treas. Reg. §1.664-3(a)(1)(i)(f)(2).
11. Notice 99-31, 1999-1 CB 1185; Treas. Reg. §1.664-3(a)(1)(i)(f)(3).
12. Let. Rul. 200002029.

The Service has permitted reformation of a trust instrument with respect to certain characteristics that have little or no impact on its payouts. For instance, the reformation of a unitrust to allow a grantor to change or designate other charitable organizations as the remainder beneficiaries did not affect the trust's qualification as a CRUT.[1] Moreover, an amendment that merely reallocated the unitrust amount between the beneficiaries during their joint lives to comply with the requirements for a CRUT, effective retroactively to the date of the creation of the trust, was permitted under the qualified reformation provisions of IRC Section 2055(e)(3).[2] However, the IRS has determined that a trust would be disqualified by an amendment to change the successive order of the noncharitable lifetime beneficiaries, regardless of the consent of all interested parties.[3]

The IRS has also determined that the division of one CRUT into two CRUTs would not cause the original or resultant trusts to fail to qualify under IRC Section 664.[4]

The Service ruled that the assignment of trust principal to three of four named charitable remainder beneficiaries of the CRUT would not disqualify the trust as a CRUT provided that the named charitable remainder beneficiaries were public charities.[5]

The IRS has privately ruled that the donor/unitrust recipient of a CRUT could donate his entire unitrust interest in an existing CRUT to the charitable remainderman in consideration for a gift annuity that would be payable to him.[6]

The termination of a CRUT and the disposition of the donor/noncharitable beneficiary's interest in the trust resulted in the noncharitable beneficiary having to recognize long-term capital gain on the entire amount realized from the disposition of his unitrust interest in the trust. However, no act of self-dealing resulted from the termination and disposition of the unitrust interest.[7]

The Service determined that the rescission of a CRUT (because of the charity's misrepresentations about the income tax consequences of the trust) would be recognized for federal income tax purposes as of the date the trust was created.[8]

50% Payout Limit

The addition by TRA '97 of a 50% ceiling on CRT payouts (for transfers in trust after June 18, 1997) followed earlier IRS challenges of the use of unreasonably high payouts to essentially convert appreciated assets into cash, thus avoiding a substantial portion of the tax on the gain.[9] In transactions the Service viewed as abusive, appreciated assets were transferred to a short-term charitable remainder unitrust with a high percentage unitrust amount (such as 80%). The Service's response to those transactions was that depending on the facts of each case, it would recast the entire transaction to either characterize the unitrust amount as gross income rather than trust corpus, at-

---

1. Let. Rul. 9517020. See also Let. Ruls. 200002029, 9826021, 9818027.
2. Let. Rul. 9845001.
3. Let. Rul. 9143030.
4. See Let. Ruls. 200301020, 200221042, 200143028, 200140027, 200120016, 200109006, 200045038, 200035014, 9851007, 9851006, 9403030. See also Let. Ruls. 200207026, 200205008 (involving partial terminations).
5. See Let. Rul. 200124010.
6. Let. Rul. 200152018.
7. See Let. Ruls. 200208039, 200127033.
8. Let. Rul. 200219012.
9. See Notice 94-78, 1994-2 CB 555.

tribute gain on the sale of trust property to the donor, or challenge the qualification of the trust as an exempt trust under IRC Section 664(c) if the structure and operation of the trust was inconsistent with the IRC requirement that the trust function exclusively as a charitable remainder trust.[1] For the regulations governing the character of distributions from charitable remainder trusts, see Q 1335.

Grantor Powers

It has been established that the following powers provided by a trust instrument to the grantor did not disqualify a charitable remainder unitrust: (1) the power to terminate all or a portion of the trust early and distribute the trust corpus to any charity, (2) the power to change the charitable remaindermen, (3) the power to limit the type of assets the trust may accept or hold (provided the restriction did not violate Treas. Reg. §1.664-1(a)(3), above), and (4) the power to remove and replace the trustee.[2]

The IRS has determined that a trustee of a charitable remainder unitrust that was funded with an insurance policy on the grantor's life could pay the premiums on that policy without disqualifying the trust under IRC Section 664. The grantor was not treated as the owner of the trust because the premiums were payable only out of trust principal. In addition, all amounts received under the policy were allocable to trust principal.[3]

The Service has ruled that there is nothing in the rule governing the tax-exempt status of CRUTs,[4] or the applicable regulations that prohibits a trust from being a permissible grantor/donor for a CRUT.[5]

The Service has determined that a second contribution to a CRUT, whose governing instrument expressly prohibited any additional contributions after the first contribution, would be ignored for federal income tax purposes and would not disqualify the CRUT provided that the grantors amended their tax returns and reported any capital gains and dividend income generated by the second contribution.[6]

In a case of first impression, a bankruptcy court held that a donor's unitrust interest in a self-settled CRUT, and his powers to (1) remove and replace trustees and (2) amend the trust to protect his tax status were the property of the bankruptcy estate.[7]

Appraisal of Unmarketable Assets

The final regulations provide that if the only trustee is the grantor, a noncharitable beneficiary, or a related or subordinate party to the grantor or the noncharitable beneficiary, a CRUT's "unmarketable assets" (defined above) must be valued by *either* an "independent trustee" or by a "qualified appraisal" from a "qualified appraiser."[8] An "independent" trustee" is a person who is *not* the grantor, the grantor's spouse, a noncharitable beneficiary, or a party who is related or subordinate to the grantor, the grantor's spouse, or the noncharitable beneficiary. However, a *co-trustee* who is an "independent"

---

1. See Notice 94-78, above.
2. Let. Rul. 9138024.
3. Let. Rul. 9227017; see also Let. Rul. 199915045.
4. IRC Section 664.
5. Let. Rul. 9821029.
6. Let. Rul. 200052026.
7. See *Lindquist v. Mack*, 2001-2 USTC (CCH) ¶50,754 (D. Minn. 2001).
8. Treas. Reg. §1.664-1(a)(7). See, e.g., Let. Rul. 200245048.

trustee may value the trust's unmarketable assets.[1] For an explanation of the application of the special valuation rules to CRUTs, see Q 1551.

The Service has ruled that a CRUT was not disqualified even though the grantors were also the sole trustees because the trust instrument provided that the trust could only accept, invest in, and hold assets with an objectively ascertainable market value.[2]

1332. What is a pooled income fund?

A pooled income fund is a trust maintained by the charity into which each donor transfers property and from which each named beneficiary receives an income interest. The amount of the income is determined by the rate of return earned by the trust for the year. The remainder interest ultimately passes to the charity that maintains the fund.[3]

All contributions to a pooled income fund are commingled, and all transfers to it must meet the requirements for an irrevocable remainder interest. The pooled income fund cannot accept or invest in tax-exempt securities, and no donor or beneficiary of an income interest can be a trustee of the fund.[4]

Special rules apply to contributions (if permitted) of depreciable property. A pooled income fund that is not prohibited (either under state law or its governing instrument) from accepting contributions of depreciable property must (1) establish a depreciation reserve fund with respect to any depreciable property held by the trust; and (2) calculate the amount of depreciation additions to the reserve in accordance with generally accepted accounting principles.[5] The purpose of these requirements is to insure that the value of the remainder interest is preserved for the charity.[6]

The amount of the charitable contribution deduction allowable for a donation of property to a pooled income fund is the present value of the remainder interest. The present value of the remainder interest is determined by subtracting the present value of the income interest from the fair market value of the property transferred.[7] The present value of the income interest is based on the highest rate of return earned by the fund for any of the three years immediately preceding the taxable year of the fund during which the contribution is made. If the fund has not been in existence for three years, the highest rate of return is deemed to be the interest rate (rounded to the nearest 2/10ths of 1%) that is 1% less than the highest annual average of the monthly IRC Section 7520 interest rates for the three years preceding the year in which the transfer to the fund is made.[8] The deemed rate of return for transfers to new pooled income funds in 2007 is 4.8%.[9]

Under final regulations, the definition of "income" for pooled income funds is amended to reflect certain state statutory changes to the concepts of income and principal. (See Q 1331 for additional background.) The final regulations provide that the term "income" has the same meaning as it does under IRC Section 643(b) and the

---

1. Treas. Reg. §1.664-1(a)(7).
2. Let. Rul. 200029031.
3. IRC Sec. 642(c)(5).
4. IRC Sec. 642(c)(5); Treas. Reg. §1.642(c)-5(b).
5. Rev. Rul. 92-81, 1992-2 CB 119.
6. Rev. Rul. 90-103, 1990-2 CB 159; Let. Rul. 9334020.
7. Treas. Reg. §1.642(c)-6(a)(2).
8. Treas. Reg. §1.642(c)-6(e).
9. Rev. Rul. 2007-2, 2007-3 IRB ___.

regulations, except that income generally may *not* include any long-term capital gains. However, in conformance with the applicable state statute, income may be defined as or satisfied by a unitrust amount, or pursuant to a trustee's power to adjust between income and principal to fulfill the trustee's duty of impartiality, *if* the state statute: (1) provides for a reasonable apportionment between the income and remainder beneficiaries of the total return of the trust; *and* (2) meets the requirements of Treas. Reg. §1.643(b)-1. In exercising a power to adjust, the trustee must allocate to principal, and *not* to income, the proceeds from the sale or exchange of any assets contributed to the fund by any donor or purchased by the fund at least to the extent of the fair market value of those assets on the date of their contribution to the fund or of the purchase price of those assets purchased by the fund. This definition of income applies for taxable years beginning after January 2, 2004.[1]

A group of pooled income funds will be treated as a single community trust if the funds operate under a common name, have a common governing instrument, prepare common reports, and are under the direction of a common governing board that has the power to modify any restriction on distributions from any of the funds, if in the sole judgment of the governing body, the restriction becomes unnecessary, incapable of fulfillment, or inconsistent with the charitable needs of the community or area served.[2] A pooled income fund is considered maintained by such a trust if, in the instrument of transfer: (1) the donor gives the remainder interest to the community trust with full discretion to choose how the remainder interest will be used to further charitable purposes, or (2) the donor either requests or requires that the community trust place the proceeds of the remainder interest in a fund that is designated to be used for the benefit of specific charitable organizations provided the fund is a component part of the community trust.[3]

Examples of the calculation for the amount of a charitable contribution deduction of property transferred to a pooled income fund are provided below.

Example: In March of 2005, Mr. Duplantis transferred property worth $100,000 to a pooled income fund. Income is to be paid to Mrs. Duplantis (age 70) for life. The highest rate of return earned by the fund for any of the three years immediately preceding 2005 was 7.2%.

The value of the remainder interest payable to charity is calculated as follows:

(1) Find the single life annuity factor for a person age 70 at a 7.2% rate of return – 7.8297 (from Single Life Annuity Factors Table in Appendix C).

(2) Convert the factor in (1) to a remainder factor: 1 - (7.8297 × rate return of 7.2%) = .43626.

(3) Multiply the value of the property transferred to the pooled income fund ($100,000) by the factor in (2) (.43626). The amount of the charitable contribution deduction is $43,626. [The same procedure applies to calculating a remainder interest following a pooled income interest for a term certain. However, Term Certain Annuity Factors are used instead of Single Life Annuity Factors.]

Example: Assume the same facts as in the preceding example except that the highest rate of return earned by the fund for any of the three years immediately preceding 2005 was 7.15%. The 7.15% rate of return falls between interest rates for which factors are given (i.e., annuity factors for 7.0% and 7.2%, but not 7.15%, can be found in Appendix C). A linear interpolation must be made.

---

1. Treas. Reg. §1.642(c)-5(a)(5)(i); TD 9102, 69 Fed. Reg. 12 (1-2-2004).
2. Treas. Reg. §1.170A-9(e)(11)(i).
3. Rev. Rul. 96-38, 1996-2 CB 44; See Treas. Reg. §1.170A-9(e)(11)(ii).

The value of the remainder interest payable to charity is calculated as follows:

(1) Find the single life annuity factor for a person age 70 at a 7.0% rate of return – 7.9348 (from Single Life Annuity Factors Table in Appendix C).

(2) Convert the factor in (1) to a remainder factor: 1 - (7.9348 × rate of return of 7.0%) = .44456.

(3) Find the single life annuity factor for a person age 70 at a 7.2% rate of return – 7.8297 (from Single Life Annuity Factors Table in Appendix C).

(4) Convert the factor in (3) to a remainder factor: 1 - (7.8297 × rate of return of 7.2%) = .43626.

(5) Subtract the factor in (4) from the factor in (2): .44456 - .43626 = .00830.

(6) $\dfrac{7.150\% - 7.000\%}{7.200\% - 7.000\%}$ = $\dfrac{X}{.00830}$

$$X = .00622$$

(7) Subtract X in (6) from the remainder factor at 7.0% from (2): .44456 - .00622 = .43834.

(8) Multiply the value of the property transferred to the charitable remainder unitrust ($100,000) by the interpolated remainder factor in (7) (.43834). The amount of the charitable contribution deduction is $43,834. (The same procedure applies to calculating a remainder interest following a pooled income interest for a term certain. However, Term Certain Annuity Factors are used instead of Single Life Annuity Factors.)

The deduction is subject to the regular percentage limits discussed in Q 1320. See Q 1328 for a comparison of pooled income funds with charitable remainder trusts. See Q 1329 for an overview of certain requirements applicable to all such gifts.

1333. What is a donor advised fund?

Planning Point: *New definition of donor advised fund.* PPA 2006 provides (for the first time) a statutory definition of the term "donor advised fund." A "donor advised fund" is a fund or account: (1) in which the contributions of one or more donors are separately identified; (2) which the sponsoring organization owns and controls; and (3) for which the donor (or the donor's designee), by virtue of the donor's status as a donor, has advisory rights (or reasonably expects to have such rights) with respect to the distribution or investment of amounts held in the fund or account.

Donor advised funds do not include any fund or account that only makes distributions to a single, identified charity or governmental entity. In addition a fund for which a donor (or the donor's designee) advises as to which individuals will receive grants for travel, study, or other similar purposes is not a donor advised fund so long as: (1) the advisory privileges are performed exclusively in the advisor's capacity as a member of a committee whose members are appointed by the sponsoring organization; (2) no combination of donors to the fund (or persons related to donors to the fund) has direct or indirect control of the committee; and (3) all grants are awarded on an objective and nondiscriminatory basis pursuant to a procedure that is approved by the board of the sponsoring organization and is designed to meet the general requirements of IRC Sections 4945(g)(1), 4945(g)(2), or 4945(g)(3).

The sponsoring organization of a donor advised fund must be a charity described in IRC Section 170(c) that is not a governmental unit, nor a private foundation. This section is effective for taxable years beginning after August 17, 2006.[1]

Comment: The definition of a sponsoring organization does not exclude a supporting organization from being a sponsoring organization of a donor advised fund program. In addition, there is no requirement that a sponsoring organization be created or organized in the United States. *Ted R. Batson, Jr., MBA, CPA, Senior Vice President of Professional Services and Gregory W. Baker, JD, CFP®, CAP, Senior Vice President of Legal Services for Renaissance.*

A donor advised fund allows the donor to avoid the expense of starting a private foundation himself. These funds are sponsored by commercial investment or financial companies (e.g., mutual fund companies), and also by community foundations. Donor advised funds differ from pooled income funds in that they do *not* provide for a lifetime income stream to the donor or other beneficiary.

Planning Point: To obtain an income tax charitable deduction for a gift to a donor advised fund, the sponsoring organization must issue a contemporaneous, written acknowledgement that states that organization has exclusive legal control over the assets contributed and conforms to the substantiation requirements of IRC Section 170(f)(8)(C). In addition, the sponsoring organization must not be a non-Type III functionally integrated supporting organization, or described in IRC Sections 170(c)(3), 170(c)(4), or 170(c)(5). This amendment is effective for gifts made after February 13, 2007.[2] *Ted R. Batson, Jr., MBA, CPA, Senior Vice President of Professional Services and Gregory W. Baker, JD, CFP®, CAP, Senior Vice President of Legal Services for Renaissance.*

The Service has provided interim guidance regarding the application of certain requirements enacted under PPA 2006 that affect donor advised funds.[3]

An important factor when analyzing donor advised funds is the amount of control that can be exercised by the donor over the fund's distribution of his contributed funds.[4] A purported donor advised fund did not qualify as a publicly supported charity, but instead as a private foundation, where: (1) the potential donors had personal connections to the trustee; (2) the trust did not intend to employ a professional fundraiser (or similar fundraising program); (3) the trust did not budget any money on fundraising activities; (3) and no written documents explained how the trust would solicit funds from the general public who were unknown to the trustee.[5] The Court of Federal Claims has ruled that a donor advised foundation does not qualify for tax-exempt status under IRC Section 501(c)(3).[6]

In two private letter rulings approving what the recipient of the letter rulings referred to as "donor managed investment accounts," the Service approved an arrangement where: (1) under agreements between donors and the charity, donations would

---

1. See IRC Sec. 4966, as added by PPA 2006.
2. See IRC Sec. 170(f)(18), as added by PPA 2006.
3. See Notice 2006-109, 2006-51 IRB 1121.
4. See, e.g., *National Foundation, Inc. v. U.S.*, 13 Cl. Ct. 486 (1987); *The Fund for Anonymous Gifts v. Internal Revenue Service*, 97-2 USTC ¶50,710 (1997), *vacated, and remanded*, 194 F.3d 173 (D.C. Cir. 1999).
5. *The Fund for Anonymous Gifts v. IRS*, 88 AFTR2d ¶6040 (D.C. Cir. 2001).
6. See *New Dynamics Foundation v. U.S.*, No. 99-197T (Cl. Ct. 2006).

be placed into an account, and each donation would be unconditional and irrevocable; (3) donors would surrender all rights to reclaim ownership, possession, or a beneficial interest in any donation; (4) donors or their investment managers would be permitted to manage the investments in the account for 10 years under a limited power of attorney, subject to certain investment restrictions and limitations; (5) the charity would have the right at any time or for any purpose, and in its sole discretion, to withdraw all of the assets held in the account or to terminate the limited power of attorney and the agreement; and (6) the agreement would terminate automatically in cases of severe loss as determined by the charity in its sole discretion. Approving the arrangement, the Service reasoned that the retention of investment management control by the donors, subject to the restrictions and limitations in the agreements, was not substantial enough to affect the deductibility of the property contributed, and did not constitute the retention of a prohibited partial interest under IRC Section 170(f)(3)(see Q 1327).[1] The Service also concluded that a proposed "on-line" donor advised fund would be able to treat contributions made through the donor advised fund as support received from the general public for purposes of meeting the public support test under IRC Section 170(b)(1)(A)(vi) and IRC Section 509(a)(1) and also citing Treas. Reg. §1.507-2(a)(8).[2] The Service privately ruled that the creation of a donor advised fund by a supporting organization did not adversely affect the tax exempt status of the supporting organization.[3] Transfers by donors to donor advised funds established by a public charity were not subject to material restrictions or conditions and, thus, could be treated as public charities.[4]

1334. How much can be deducted for a gift to a charitable remainder annuity trust or unitrust? When is the deduction taken?

An income tax deduction may be claimed for the charitable gift in the year the funds are irrevocably placed in trust, unless the gift is of tangible personal property. (A gift of a future interest, such as a remainder interest, in tangible personal property is deductible only when all the intervening interests have expired or are held by parties unrelated to the donor.[5]) The fair market value of the gift is the present value of the charity's right to receive the trust assets at the end of the intervening interest.[6]

In general, the amount of the charitable contribution deduction allowable for the transfer of property to a charitable remainder *annuity* trust is equal to the present value of the remainder interest. The present value of the remainder interest is determined by subtracting the present value of the annuity payable to the noncharitable beneficiary (see Appendix C) from the fair market value of the property transferred.[7]

> *Example 1.* In September, Mr. Creflo transferred property worth $100,000 to a charitable remainder annuity trust. The trust is to make biannual payments (at the end of each 6-month period) of $3,000 to Mrs. Creflo (age 60) during her lifetime. Assume the IRC Section 7520 interest rates for September and the two preceding months, July and August, were 6.0%, 5.8%, and 5.6%. Mr. Creflo elected to use the 6.0% rate.
>
> The value of the annuity payable to Mrs. Creflo is calculated as follows:

1. Let. Ruls. 200445024, 200445023.
2. Advanced Letter Ruling 2000ARD 203-3 (8-2-2000), *superseding*, Let. Rul. 200037053.
3. See Let. Rul. 200149005.
4. See Let. Rul. 200150039.
5. IRC Sec. 170(a)(3); Treas. Reg. §1.170A-5.
6. Treas. Regs. §§1.664-2(c), 1.664-4(a).
7. Treas. Reg. §1.664-2(c).

(1) Find the single life annuity factor for a person age 60 at a 6.0% interest rate – 10.8279 (from Single Life Annuity Factors Table in Appendix C).

(2) Find the adjustment factor at a 6.0% interest rate for semi-annual annuity payments at the end of each period – 1.0148 (from Annuity Adjustment Factors Table A in Appendix C).

(3) Multiply the aggregate payments received during a year by the factors in (1) and (2) – $6,000 × 10.8279 × 1.0148 = $65,929.

The amount of the charitable contribution deduction is equal to the value of the property transferred to the charitable remainder annuity trust ($100,000) reduced by the value of the annuity payable to Mrs. Creflo ($65,929) – $34,071.

Example 2. If in Example 1, payments were to be made to Mrs. Creflo at the beginning of each 6-month period (instead of at the end of each period), one payment is added to the value of the annuity payable at the end of each period. The value of the annuity payable at the beginning of each period would be $68,929 ($65,929 + $3,000). The amount of the charitable contribution deduction would be equal to the value of the property transferred to the charitable remainder annuity trust ($100,000) reduced by the value of the annuity payable to Mrs. Creflo ($68,929) – $31,071.

Example 3. If payments in Example 1 were to be made for 20 years rather than for Mrs. Creflo's life, the value of the annuity payable to Mrs. Creflo (at the end of each 6-month period) is calculated as follows:

(1) Find the term certain annuity factor for 20 years at a 6.0% interest rate – 11.4699 (from Term Certain Annuity Factors Table in Appendix C).

(2) Find the adjustment factor at a 6.0% interest rate for semi-annual annuity payments at the end of each period – 1.0148 (from Annuity Adjustment Factors Table A in Appendix C).

(3) Multiply the aggregate payments received during a year by the factors in (1) and (2) – $6,000 × 11.4699 × 1.0148 = $69,838.

The amount of the charitable contribution deduction is equal to the value of the property transferred to the charitable remainder annuity trust ($100,000) reduced by the value of the annuity payable to Mrs. Creflo ($69,838) – $30,162.

Example 4. If payments in Example 2 were to be made for 20 years rather than for Mrs. Creflo's life, the value of the annuity payable to Mrs. Creflo (at the beginning of each period) is calculated as follows:

(1) Find the term certain annuity factor for 20 years at a 6.0% interest rate – 11.4699 (from Term Certain Annuity Factors Table in Appendix C).

(2) Find the adjustment factor at a 6.0% interest rate for a term certain annuity payable at the beginning of each semi-annual period – 1.0448 (from Annuity Adjustment Factors Table B in Appendix C).

(3) Multiply the aggregate payments received during a year by the factors in (1) and (2) – $6,000 × 11.4699 × 1.0448 = $71,903.

The amount of the charitable contribution deduction is equal to the value of the property transferred to the charitable remainder annuity trust ($100,000) reduced by the value of the annuity payable to Mrs. Creflo ($71,903) – $28,097.

In general, the amount of the charitable contribution deduction allowable for the transfer of property to a charitable remainder *unitrust* is equal to the present value of the unitrust remainder interest.[1] If the unitrust payments are made annually at the beginning of each year and the annual payout rate is equal to an adjusted payout rate for which factors are given, the present value of the unitrust remainder interest can be calculated simply by multiplying the value of the property transferred to the charitable remainder unitrust by the appropriate unitrust remainder factor (see Appendix C). If the unitrust payments are made other than annually at the beginning of each year or the annual payout rate falls between adjusted payout rates for which factors are given, the calculation of the deduction for a contribution to a charitable remainder unitrust is more complex.

Example 5. In September, Mr. Creflo transferred property worth $100,000 to a charitable remainder unitrust. The trust is to make annual payments (at the beginning of each year) of 5% of the value of the trust corpus (valued annually) to Mrs. Creflo (age 60) during her lifetime (i.e., a 5% annual payout rate).

The present value of the unitrust remainder interest is calculated as follows: Multiply the value of the property transferred to the charitable remainder unitrust ($100,000) by the single life unitrust remainder factor for a person age 60 at a 5% payout rate (.39034 – from Single Life Unitrust Remainder Factors Table in Appendix C). The amount of the charitable contribution deduction is $39,034.

Example 6. If the unitrust payments in Example 5 were to be made for 20 years (at the beginning of each year) rather than for Mrs. Creflo's life, the present value of the unitrust remainder interest is calculated as follows: Multiply the value of the property transferred to the charitable remainder unitrust ($100,000) by the term certain unitrust remainder factor for 20 years at a 5% payout rate (.358486 – from Term Certain Unitrust Remainder Factors Table in Appendix C). The amount of the charitable contribution deduction is $35,849.

Example 7. Assume the same facts as in Example 5, except that payments are to be made at the end of each year. Assume the valuation table interest rates for September and the two preceding months, July and August, were 6.0%, 5.8%, and 5.6%. Mr. Creflo elected to use the 6.0% rate.

The value of the unitrust remainder payable to charity is calculated as follows:

(1) Find the unitrust payout adjustment factor for annual payments to start 12 months after the valuation date at a 6.0% interest rate: .943396 (from Unitrust Payout Adjustment Factors Table in Appendix C).

(2) Multiply the factor in (1) by the annual payout rate to obtain the adjusted payout rate: .943396 × 5% = 4.717%.

(3) Find the single life unitrust remainder factor for a person age 60 at a 4.6% adjusted payout rate: .41754 (from Single Life Unitrust Remainder Factors Table in Appendix C).

(4) Find the single life unitrust remainder factor for a person age 60 at a 4.8% adjusted payout rate: .40364 (from Single Life Unitrust Remainder Factors Table in Appendix C).

(5) Subtract the factor in (4) from the factor in (3): .41754 - .40364 = .01390.

(6) $\dfrac{4.717\% - 4.600\%}{4.800\% - 4.600\%} = \dfrac{X}{.01390}$

$X = .00813$

(7) Subtract X in (6) from the factor at 4.6% from (3): .41754 - .00813 = .40941.

---

1. Treas. Reg. §1.664-4(a).

(8) Multiply the value of the property transferred to the charitable remainder unitrust ($100,000) by the interpolated unitrust remainder factor in (7) (.40941). The amount of the charitable contribution deduction is $40,941. [The same procedure applies to calculating a unitrust remainder interest following a unitrust interest for a term certain. However, Term Certain Unitrust Remainder Factors are used instead of Single Life Unitrust Remainder Factors.]

The remainder interest generally must equal at least 10% of the fair market value of the property placed in the trust.[1] See Q 1330, Q 1331.

The deduction is subject to the regular percentage limits discussed in Q 1320. If depreciable real property is given to the trust, the calculation is more complex.[2] If appreciated property is given to the trust, it may be necessary to reduce the value of the gift by the amount of capital gain or ordinary income that would be realized if the property were sold at fair market value (see Q 1322). If so, basis must be allocated between the noncharitable and charitable interests in order to determine the amount of gain or income, if any, that would be realized on sale of the part of the property contributed to the charity.[3] Basis is allocated to the present value of the remainder interest in the same proportion that the present value of the gift bears to the fair market value of the property.[4] If property given is subject to a loan, the transfer can result in a gain to the donor under the bargain sale rules (see Q 1325).

1335. How are the payments from a charitable remainder trust to a beneficiary taxed?

Amounts distributed to noncharitable beneficiaries retain the character (ordinary income, capital gain, and other income such as tax-exempt income) they had when received by the trust (even if the trust is not taxed on the income). However, the income of the trust is deemed to be distributed in the following order:

First, distributions are treated as made out of the ordinary income of the trust to the extent it has ordinary income for the tax year plus its ordinary income not distributed for prior years. Ordinary income not distributed is carried over as such until the next year.[5]

Second, distributions in excess of ordinary income are considered to be distributions of net capital gain, to the extent of the trust's net capital gain not previously distributed.[6] (See Q 1420 for a detailed explanation of the calculation of capital gains and losses.)

Third, if distributions exceed both accumulated ordinary income and accumulated net capital gain, the excess is treated as other income, including tax-exempt income, to the extent the trust has other income for the tax year and undistributed other income for prior years.[7]

Finally, to the extent distributions for the year exceed the above amounts, the distribution is deemed a non-taxable return of trust corpus.[8] However, see "Accelerated

---

1. IRC Sec. 664(d).
2. See Treas. Reg. §1.170A-12.
3. IRC Sec. 170(e)(2).
4. Treas. Reg. §1.170A-4(c)(1).
5. IRC Sec. 664(b)(1).
6. IRC Sec. 664(b)(2).
7. IRC Sec. 664(b)(3).
8. IRC Sec. 664(b)(4); Treas. Reg. §1.664-1(d).

Charitable Remainder Trusts," below, regarding the "deemed sale" treatment of certain arrangements viewed by the Service as abusive.

If there are two or more recipients, each is treated as receiving a pro rata portion of each category of income included in the distribution.[1]

The amount of the distribution is includable in income by the recipient for the tax year in which the amount is required to be distributed, even though the amount is not distributed until after the close of the trust's tax year. If the recipient and the trust have different tax years, the amount is includable in the tax year of the recipient in which the trust's tax year (in which the amount is required to be distributed) ends.[2] However, if the trust's distributable net income is less than the percentage payout designated in the trust instrument (as may occur by design in the early years of a *net income with makeup unitrust* – see Q 1328), each beneficiary takes into account only his proportionate share of distributable net income.[3]

Amounts received are taxed under these rules, even if the trust itself paid tax on any of its income. The beneficiaries do not get credit for any taxes paid by the trust.[4] (See Q 1336 regarding taxation of a charitable trust.)

The IRS privately ruled that amounts treated as consent dividends may be included in a trust's income for purposes of IRC Section 664(b)(1), but do not constitute trust income for purposes of IRC Section 664(d)(3)(A).[5] The IRS determined that where income received by a charitable remainder trust from its ownership of a limited partnership interest constituted rental activity income, such income would be treated as income from a rental activity in the hands of the unitrust beneficiaries.[6]

Treatment of Annual Distributions to Recipients

In 2005, the Service released final regulations on the ordering rules of IRC Section 664(b) for characterizing distributions from charitable remainder trusts. The final rules reflect changes made to income tax rates, including the rates applicable to capital gains and certain dividends, by TRA 1997, IRSRRA 1998, and JGTRRA 2003.[7]

Assignment of income to categories and classes. A trust's income, including income includible in gross income and other income, is assigned to one of three *categories* in the year in which it is required to be taken into account by the trust. These categories are: (1) gross income, other than gains and amounts treated as gains from the sale or other disposition of capital assets (the "ordinary income category"); (2) gains and amounts treated as gains from the sale or other disposition of capital assets (the "capital gains category"); and (3) other income.[8]

Items within the ordinary income and capital gains categories are assigned to different *classes* based on the federal income tax rate applicable to each type of income in that category in the year the items are required to be taken into account by the trust.

1. Treas. Reg. §1.664-1(d)(3).
2. Treas. Reg. §1.664-1(d)(4)(i).
3. IRC Sec. 662(a)(1).
4. Treas. Reg. §1.664-1(d)(1)(ii).
5. Let. Rul. 199952035.
6. Let. Rul. 9114025.
7. See TD 9190, 70 Fed. Reg. 12793 (3-16-2005).
8. Treas. Reg. §1.664-1(d)(1)(i)(a).

For example, the ordinary income category may include a class of "qualified dividend income" as defined in IRC Section 1(h)(11) (see Q 1420) and a class of all other ordinary income.

In addition, the capital gains category may include separate *classes* for short-term and long-term capital gains and losses, such as: (1) a short-term capital gain class; (2) a 28% long-term capital gain class (i.e., gains and losses from collectibles and IRC Section 1202 gains); (3) an unrecaptured IRC Section 1250 long-term capital gain class (i.e., long-term gains not treated as ordinary income that would be treated as ordinary income if IRC Section 1250(b)(1) included all depreciation); (4) a qualified 5-year long-term capital gain class (as defined by IRC Section 1(h)(9) prior to amendment by JGTRRA 2003); and (5) an all other long-term capital gain class.[1]

After items are assigned to a class, the tax rates may change so that items in two or more classes would be taxed at the same rate if distributed during a particular year. If the changes to the tax rates are permanent, the undistributed items in those classes are combined into one class. However, if the changes to the tax rates are only temporary (for example, the new rate for one class will "sunset" (i.e., expire) in a future year), the classes are kept separate.[2]

Order of distributions. The categories and classes of income (determined under Treas. Reg. §1.664-1(d)(1)(i)) are used to determine the character of an annuity or unitrust distribution from the trust in the hands of the recipient regardless of whether the trust is exempt from taxation under IRC Section 664(c) for the year of the distribution. The determination of the character of amounts distributed or deemed distributed at any time during the taxable year of the trust must be made as of the end of that taxable year.

The tax rate or rates to be used in computing the recipient's tax on the distribution will be the tax rates that are applicable in the year in which the distribution is required to be made, to the classes of income deemed to make up that distribution, and *not* the tax rates that are applicable to those classes of income in the year the income is received by the trust.[3]

The character of the distribution in the hands of the annuity or unitrust recipient is determined by treating the distributions as being made from each category in the following order:

(1) First, from *ordinary income* to the extent of the sum of the trust's ordinary income for the taxable year and its undistributed ordinary income for prior years;

(2) Second, from *capital gain* to the extent of the trust's capital gains (determined under Treas. Reg. §1.664-1(d)(1)(iv));

(3) Third, from *other income* to the extent of the sum of the trust's other income for the taxable year and its undistributed other income for prior years; and

---

1. Treas. Reg. §1.664-1(d)(1)(i)(b).
2. Treas. Reg. §1.664-1(d)(1)(i)(b).
3. Treas. Reg. §1.664-1(d)(1)(ii)(a).

(4)   Finally, from *trust corpus* (with "corpus" defined for this purpose as the net fair market value of the trust assets minus the total undistributed income (but not loss) in Treas. Regs. §§1.664-1(d)(1)(i)(a)(1)-(3)).[1]

If the trust has different classes of income in the ordinary income category, the distribution from that category is treated as being made from each class, in turn, until exhaustion of the class, beginning with the class subject to the highest federal income tax rate and ending with the class subject to the lowest federal income tax rate.[2]

If the trust has different classes of net gain in the capital gains category, the distribution from that category is treated as being made first from the short-term capital gain class and then from each class of long-term capital gain, in turn, until the exhaustion of the class, beginning with the class subject to the highest federal income tax rate and ending with the class subject to the lowest rate.[3]

If two or more classes within the same category are subject to the same current tax rate, but at least one of those classes will be subject to a different tax rate in a future year (e.g., if the current rate "sunsets," or expires), the order of that class in relation to other classes in the category with the same current tax rate is determined based on the future rate or rates applicable to those classes.[4]

Within each category, if there is more than one type of income in a class, amounts treated as distributed from that class are to be treated as consisting of the same proportion of each type of income as the total of the current and undistributed income of that type bears to the total of the current and undistributed income of all types of income included in that class. For example, if rental income and interest income are subject to the same current and future federal income tax rate and, therefore, are in the same class, a distribution from that class will be treated as consisting of a proportional amount of rental income and interest income.[5]

Treatment of losses. In the ordinary income category, a net ordinary loss for the current year is first used to reduce undistributed ordinary income for prior years that is assigned to the same class as the loss. Any excess loss is then used to reduce the current and undistributed ordinary income from other classes, in turn, beginning with the class subject to the highest federal income tax rate and ending with the class subject to the lowest federal income tax rate. If any of the loss exists after all the current and undistributed ordinary income from all classes has been offset, the excess is carried forward indefinitely to reduce ordinary income for future years.[6]

A net loss in the other income category for the current year is used to reduce undistributed income in this category for prior years. Any excess is carried forward indefinitely to reduce other income for future years.[7]

Netting of capital gains and losses. Capital gains of the trust are determined on a cumulative net basis (under the rules of Treas. Reg. §1.664-1(d)(1)) without regard to

---

1. Treas. Reg. §1.664-1(d)(1)(ii)(a).
2. Treas. Reg. §1.664-1(d)(1)(ii)(b).
3. Treas. Reg. §1.664-1(d)(1)(ii)(b).
4. Treas. Reg. §1.664-1(d)(1)(ii)(b).
5. Treas. Reg. §1.664-1(d)(1)(ii)(b).
6. Treas. Reg. §1.664-1(d)(1)(iii)(a).
7. Treas. Reg. §1.664-1(d)(1)(iii)(b).

the provisions of IRC Section 1212. For each taxable year, current and undistributed gains and losses within each class are netted to determine the net gain or loss for that class. The classes of capital gains and losses are then netted against each other in the following order:

(1) *First*, a net loss from a class of long-term capital gain and loss (beginning with the class subject to the highest federal income tax rate and ending with the class subject to the lowest rate) is used to offset net gain from each other class of long-term capital gain and loss, in turn, until exhaustion of the class, beginning with the class subject to the highest federal income tax rate and ending with the class subject to the lowest rate.

(2) *Second*, either:

(a) a net loss from all the classes of long-term capital gain and loss (beginning with the class subject to the highest federal income tax rate and ending with the class subject to the lowest rate) is used to offset any net gain from the class of short-term capital gain and loss; *or*

(b) a net loss from the class of short-term capital gain and loss is used to offset any net gain from each class of long-term capital gain and loss, in turn, until exhaustion of the class, beginning with the class subject to the highest federal income tax rate and ending with the class subject to the lowest federal income tax rate.

Carryforward of net capital gain. If, at the end of a taxable year, and after the application of Treas. Reg. §1.664-1(d)(1)(iv), a trust has any net loss or net gain that is not treated as distributed under Treas. Reg. §1.664-1(d)(1)(ii)(a)(2), the net gain or loss is carried over to succeeding taxable years and retains its character in succeeding taxable years as gain or loss from its particular class.[1]

For examples illustrating the application of the above rules, see Treas. Reg. §1.664-1(d)(1)(viii). For special transitional rules, see Treas. Reg. §1.664-1(d)(1)(vi).

1336. Is the charitable remainder annuity trust or unitrust subject to income tax?

Ordinarily, the trust is not taxed on its income.[2] Under prior law, the trust lost its tax-exempt status for any year in which it had "unrelated business taxable income." The old rule caused the loss of the CRT's exemption for even one dollar of UBTI. TRHCA 2006 modifies the excise tax on unrelated business taxable income of charitable remainder trusts and changes the loss-of-exemption rule. The new law imposes a 100% excise tax, but leaves the CRT's exempt status intact.[3]

Unrelated business taxable income includes income from debt-financed property.[4] Securities purchased on margin have been held to be debt-financed property.[5] An exempt

---

1. Treas. Reg. 1.664-1(d)(1)(v).
2. IRC Sec. 664(c)(1).
3. IRC Sec. 664(c), as amended by TRHCA 2006.
4. Treas. Reg. §1.664-1(c).
5. *Elliot Knitwear Profit Sharing Plan v. Comm.*, 614 F.2d 347 (3rd Cir. 1980).

trust that is a limited partner may receive unrelated business income to the same extent as if it were a general partner.[1] A charitable remainder trust that received unrelated business taxable income from its investments in three limited partnerships was held to be taxable as a complex trust under IRC Section 664(c) to the full extent of its income.[2]

Planning Point: A common source of unrelated business taxable income encountered by charitable remainder trusts is an investment in a hedge fund, real estate limited partnership, or other form of pass-through entity. These types of investment products typically rely on debt of some form to achieve their investment goals. The prospectus or other offering statement should be carefully reviewed to determine if the entity will be reporting unrelated business taxable income to its investors. *Ted R. Batson, Jr., MBA, CPA, is Senior Vice President of Professional Services for Renaissance.*

Charitable Lead Trusts

1337. Can a deduction be taken for a charitable contribution in trust of a right to payment to the charity?

Yes, if certain requirements are met. A *charitable lead trust* is essentially the reverse of a charitable remainder trust; the donor grants a right to payment to the charity, with the remainder reverting to the donor (or his named beneficiaries). Such trusts are commonly called charitable "lead" trusts because the first or leading interest is in the charitable donee. Even though a gift of such an interest in property is less than the entire interest of the donor, its value will be deductible if the interest is in the form of a "guaranteed annuity interest" or a "unitrust interest."[3]

A *guaranteed annuity interest* is an irrevocable right to receive payment of a determinable amount at least annually. A *unitrust interest* is an irrevocable right to receive payment at least annually of a fixed percentage of the fair market value of the trust assets, determined annually. In either case, payments may be made to the charity for a term of years or over the life of an individual (or lives of more than one individual) living at the date of the transfer to the trust.

Only one (or more) of the following individuals may be used as measuring lives: (1) the donor; (2) the donor's spouse; (3) a lineal ancestor of all the remainder beneficiaries; or (4) the spouse of a lineal ancestor of all the remainder beneficiaries. A trust will satisfy the requirement that all noncharitable remainder beneficiaries be lineal descendants of the individual who is the measuring life (or that individual's spouse) if there is less than a 15% probability that individuals who are not lineal descendants will receive any trust corpus. This probability must be computed at the time property is transferred to the trust taking into account the interests of all primary and contingent remainder beneficiaries who are living at that time. The computation must be based on the current applicable Life Table in Treas. Reg. §20.2031-7.[4]

A guaranteed annuity may be made to continue for the shorter of a term of years or lives in being plus a term of years.[5] The IRS determined that an annuity met the requirements for a "guaranteed annuity" even though neither the term nor the amount

---

1. *Service Bolt & Nut Co. Profit Sharing Trust v. Comm.*, 84-1 USTC ¶9127 (6th Cir. 1983).
2. *Newhall Unitrust v. Comm.*, 104 TC 236 (1995), aff'd, 97-1 USTC ¶50,159 (9th Cir. 1997).
3. IRC Sec. 170(f)(2)(B).
4. Treas. Regs. §§1.170A-6(c)(2)(i)(A), 1.170A-6(c)(2)(ii)(A).
5. Rev. Rul. 85-49, 1985-1 CB 330.

was specifically stated; the term was ascertainable as of the death of the grantor, based on a formula described in the trust instrument.[1] The annuity cannot be for the lesser of a designated amount or a fixed percentage of the fair market value of trust assets, determined annually.[2] After termination of the charity's right to payment, the remainder interest in the property is returned to the donor or his designated beneficiaries.

According to final regulations, an income tax charitable deduction is allowable for a charitable annuity or unitrust interest that is *preceded* by a *noncharitable* annuity or unitrust interest. In other words, the final regulations eliminate the requirement that the charitable interest start no later than the commencement of a noncharitable interest in the form of a guaranteed annuity or unitrust interest. However, the final regulations continue to require that any amounts payable for a private purpose before the expiration of the charitable annuity or unitrust interest must be in the form of a guaranteed annuity or unitrust interest, *or* must be payable from a separate group of assets devoted exclusively to private purposes. The final regulations conform the income tax regulations to the Tax Court's decision in *Estate of Boeshore*.[3]

The IRS determined that the requirements for a charitable lead annuity trust were met even though the trust authorized the trustee, who was the grantor's son, to choose among various charities to receive the annuity interest and apportion the payouts among them.[4]

The Service ruled that so long as a donor was treated as the owner of a guaranteed annuity interest for purposes of the grantor trust rules, the income interest transferred in trust to a private foundation qualified as a "guaranteed annuity interest" under IRC Section 170(f)(2)(B). Even though the present value on the date of the transfer exceeded 60% of the aggregate fair market value of all the amounts in trust, the Service reasoned that this did not prevent the income interest from being a "guaranteed annuity interest" because the trust agreement provided that the acquisition and retention of assets that would give rise to an excise tax if the trustee had acquired the assets was prohibited, in accordance with Treas. Reg. §1.170A-6(c)(2)(i)(D).[5]

The partition of a charitable lead annuity trust into three separate trusts to address differences of opinion among trustees as to the choice of charitable beneficiaries and the investment of trust assets did not cause the original trust, the new trusts, or any of the trusts' beneficiaries to realize income or gain.[6]

The Service has privately ruled that the sale of assets, which were pledged as collateral for a promissory note to the family's charitable lead annuity trust, to a limited liability company would not constitute self-dealing so long as the value of the collateral remained as required under the terms of the note, and would not give rise to tax liability under IRC Section 4941 to the CLATs, related family members, the estate, or the marital trusts.[7]

1. Let. Rul. 9118040.
2. Treas. Reg. §1.170A-6(c)(2)(B).
3. 78 TC 523 (1982), *acq. in result*, 1987-2 CB 1. See Treas. Regs. §§1.170A-6(c)(2)(i)(E), 1.170A-6(c)(2)(ii)(D); TD 9068, 68 Fed. Reg. 40130 (7-7-2003), *revoking*, Rev. Rul. 76-225, 1976-1 CB 281.
4. See Let. Rul. 9748009. See also Let. Ruls 200138018, 200043039, 200030014 (charitable gifts were not incomplete even though one or more family members would serve as directors of the charitable beneficiary of the grantors' CLUTs).
5. Let. Rul. 9810019.
6. Let. Rul. 199930036. See also Let. Rul. 200149016.
7. See Let. Rul. 200124029.

The IRS has requested suggestions regarding the creation of sample forms for charitable lead trusts.[1]

1338. Is the deduction for a gift to a charitable lead trust of a right to payment taken in the year of the gift?

An immediate deduction of the present value of all the annual payments to be made over the period may be taken *if* the trust is structured so that the donor is taxable on the income of the trust each year (under the "grantor trust rules"). If the trust is structured so that he is not taxable on trust income, he will not get an income tax deduction for the gift.[2] The IRS has determined that a donor was to be treated as the owner of a charitable lead trust where the donor retained the power to substitute trust property. The donor was entitled to a current deduction in an amount equal to the present value of the unitrust interest.[3]

In general, the amount of the charitable contribution deduction allowable for the transfer of property to a charitable lead *annuity* trust is equal to the present value of the annuity payable to the charity (see Appendix C).

Example 1. In September, Mr. Creflo (age 60) transferred property worth $100,000 to a charitable lead annuity trust that is a grantor trust. The trust is to make biannual payments (at the end of each 6-month period) of $3,000 to the charity during his lifetime. Assume the IRC Section 7520 interest rates for September and the two preceding months, July and August, were 6.4%, 6.2%, and 6.0%. Mr. Creflo elected to use the 6.0% rate.

The value of the annuity payable to charity is calculated as follows:

(1) Find the single life annuity factor for a person age 60 at a 6.0% interest rate – 10.8279 (from Single Life Annuity Factors Table in Appendix C).

(2) Find the adjustment factor at a 6.0% interest rate for semi-annual annuity payments at the end of each period – 1.0148 (from Annuity Adjustment Factors Table A in Appendix C).

(3) Multiply the aggregate payments received during a year by the factors in (1) and (2) – $6,000 × 10.8279 × 1.0148 = $65,929.

The amount of the charitable contribution deduction is equal to $65,929.

Example 2. If in Example 1, payments were to be made to charity at the beginning of each 6-month period (instead of at the end of each period), one payment is added to the value of the annuity payable at the end of each period. The value of the annuity payable at the beginning of each period would be $68,929 ($65,929 + $3,000). The amount of the charitable contribution deduction would be equal to $68,929.

Example 3. If payments in Example 1 were to be made for 20 years rather than for Mr. Creflo's life, the value of the annuity payable to charity (at the end of each 6-month period) is calculated as follows:

(1) Find the term certain annuity factor for 20 years at a 6.0% interest rate – 11.4699 (from Term Certain Annuity Factors Table in Appendix C).

(2) Find the adjustment factor at a 6.0% interest rate for semi-annual annuity payments at the end of each period – 1.0148 (from Annuity Adjustment Factors Table A in Appendix C).

---

1. See Notice 2003-39, 2003-2 CB 10.
2. Treas. Reg. §1.170A-6(c). See, e.g., Let. Rul. 200108032.
3. Let. Rul. 9247024.

(3) Multiply the aggregate payments received during a year by the factors in (1) and (2) – $6,000 × 11.4699 × 1.0148 = $69,838.

The amount of the charitable contribution deduction is equal to $69,838.

Example 4. If payments in Example 2 were to be made for 20 years rather than for Mr. Creflo's life, the value of the annuity payable to charity (at the beginning of each period) is calculated as follows:

(1) Find the term certain annuity factor for 20 years at a 6.0% interest rate – 11.4699 (from Term Certain Annuity Factors Table in Appendix C).

(2) Find the adjustment factor at a 6.0% interest rate for a term certain annuity payable at the beginning of each semi-annual period – 1.0448 (from Annuity Adjustment Factors Table B in Appendix C).

(3) Multiply the aggregate payments received during a year by the factors in (1) and (2) – $6,000 × 11.4699 × 1.0448 = $71,903.

The amount of the charitable contribution deduction is equal to $71,903.

In general, the amount of the charitable contribution deduction allowable for the transfer of property to a charitable lead *unitrust* is equal to the present value of the unitrust interest. If the unitrust payments are made annually at the beginning of each year and the annual payout rate is equal to an adjusted payout rate for which factors are given, the present value of the unitrust interest can be calculated simply by multiplying the value of the property transferred to the charitable lead unitrust by the appropriate unitrust factor (see Appendix C). If the unitrust payments are made other than annually at the beginning of each year or the annual payout rate falls between adjusted payout rates for which factors are given, the calculation of the deduction for a contribution to a charitable lead unitrust is more complex.

Example 5. In September, Mr. Creflo (age 60) transferred property worth $100,000 to a charitable lead unitrust that is a grantor trust. The trust is to make annual payments (at the beginning of each year) of 5% of the value of the trust corpus (valued annually) to charity during his lifetime (i.e., a 5% annual payout rate).

The value of the unitrust payable to charity is calculated as follows:

(1) Find the single life unitrust remainder factor for a person age 60 at a 5.0% adjusted payout rate: .39034 (from Single Life Unitrust Remainder Factors Table in Appendix C).

(2) Calculate the single life unitrust factor for a person age 60 at a 5.0% adjusted payout rate by subtracting the factor in (1) from one – 1 - .39034 = .60966.

(3) Multiply the value of the property transferred to the charitable lead unitrust ($100,000) by the single life unitrust factor for a person age 60 at a 5% payout rate (.60966) – $100,000 × .60966 = $60,966.

The amount of the charitable contribution deduction is $60,966.

Example 6. If the unitrust payments in Example 5 were to be made for 20 years (at the beginning of each year) rather than for Mr. Creflo's life, the present value of the unitrust remainder interest is calculated as follows:

(1) Find the term certain unitrust remainder factor for 20 years at a 5.0% adjusted payout rate: .358486 (from Term Certain Unitrust Remainder Factors Table in Appendix C).

(2) Calculate the term certain unitrust factor for 20 years at a 5.0% adjusted payout rate by subtracting the factor in (1) from one – 1 - .358486 = .641514.

(3) Multiply the value of the property transferred to the charitable lead unitrust ($100,000) by the term certain unitrust factor for 20 years at a 5% payout rate (.641514) – $100,000 × .641514 = $64,151.

The amount of the charitable contribution deduction is $64,151.

Example 7. Assume the same facts as in Example 5, except that payments are to be made at the end of each year. Assume the valuation table interest rates for September and the two preceding months, July and August, were 6.4%, 6.2%, and 6.0%. Mr. Creflo elected to use the 6.0% rate.

The value of the unitrust payable to charity is calculated as follows:

(1) Find the unitrust payout adjustment factor for annual payments to start 12 months after the valuation date at a 6.0% interest rate: .943396 (from Unitrust Payout Adjustment Factors Table in Appendix C).

(2) Multiply the factor in (1) by the annual payout rate to obtain the adjusted payout rate: .943396 × 5% = 4.717%.

(3) Find the single life unitrust remainder factor for a person age 60 at a 4.6% adjusted payout rate: .41754 (from Single Life Unitrust Remainder Factors Table in Appendix C).

(4) Find the single life unitrust remainder factor for a person age 60 at a 4.8% adjusted payout rate: .40364 (from Single Life Unitrust Remainder Factors Table in Appendix C).

(5) Subtract the factor in (4) from the factor in (3): .41754 - .40364 = .01390.

(6) $\dfrac{4.717\% - 4.600\%}{4.800\% - 4.600\%} = \dfrac{X}{.01390}$

$X = .00813$

(7) Subtract X in (6) from the factor at 4.6% from (3): .41754 - .00813 = .40941.

(8) Subtract the interpolated unitrust remainder factor in (7) from one – 1 - .40941 = .59059.

(9) Multiply the value of the property transferred to the charitable lead unitrust ($100,000) by the interpolated unitrust factor in (8) (.59059). The amount of the charitable contribution deduction is $59,059. [The same procedure applies to calculating a unitrust interest for a term certain. However, Term Certain Unitrust Remainder Factors are used instead of Single Life Unitrust Remainder Factors.]

If the donor of a right to payment ceases to be taxable on the trust income before the termination of the interest, he must "recapture," that is, include in his income, an amount equal to the deduction less the discounted value of all amounts required to be, and which actually were, paid before the time he ceased to be taxable on trust income.[1]

Conservation and Facade Easements

1339. Is a gift of a "conservation easement" or a "facade easement" deductible?

The IRC permits a deduction for a contribution of certain real property interests even though the gift is less than the donor's entire interest if the gift is for the preservation

---

1. Treas. Reg. §1.170A-6(c)(4).

of land for recreation or education, the protection of natural habitats, the preservation of open space, or the preservation of historically important land or buildings.[1]

If a donor contributes for any of these purposes his entire interest in real property (he may retain the right to subsurface oil, gas, or other minerals), a remainder interest in the property, or a restriction on the use of the property (a conservation easement), he may be entitled to a deduction. The contribution must be made to a qualified organization (a governmental unit and certain charities), and the restriction on use of the property must be protected in perpetuity.[2] The Tax Court has held that in order to be protected in perpetuity, the deed of gift used to transfer the easement, once properly recorded as required by state law, must not be subordinate to a mortgage holder's security interest.[3]

A trust may not take a charitable deduction (under IRC Sec. 642(c)) or a distribution deduction (under IRC Sec. 661(a)(2)) with respect to a contribution to charity of trust principal that meets the requirements of a qualified conservation contribution (under IRC Section 170(h)).[4]

Conservation Easements

A conservation easement is a restriction on the owner's use of the property. A popular form is the open space or scenic easement, wherein the owner of land agrees to set the land aside to preserve natural, scenic, historic, scientific and recreational areas, for public enjoyment.[5]

The Tax Court held that taxpayers' contributions of conservation easements (encumbered shoreline) were qualified conservation contributions because: (1) they protected a relatively natural habitat of wildlife and plants (in accordance with Treas. Reg. §1.170A-14(d)(3)); and (2) were exclusively for conservation purposes.[6]

The Tax Court held that a taxpayer did not make a contribution of a qualified conservation easement because the attempted grant did not satisfy the conservation purposes required (under IRC Sec 170(h)(4)(A). Specifically, the deed did not preserve open space, an historically important land area, or a certified historical structure.[7]

The IRS approved a contribution of a conservation easement in which the taxpayer retained limited water rights; the conditions of the use of those rights were sufficiently restricted that the Service determined their exercise would not adversely affect the purposes for which the easement was established.[8] The IRS also determined that the proposed inconsistent use of some of a farm (i.e., construction of eight single-family homes) to be burdened by a conservation easement was not significant enough to cancel the conservation purpose of the easement because the conservation easement would still maintain over 80% of the entire tract in its presently undeveloped state, thereby preserving the habitat.[9]

1. IRC Secs. 170(f)(3)(B)(iii), 170(h).
2. IRC Sec. 170(h)(2); Treas. Regs. §§1.170A-14(a),1.170A-14(b), and 1.170A-14(c).
3. *Satullo v. Comm.*, TC Memo 1993-614, *aff'd without opinion*, 67 F.3d 314 (11th Cir. 1995).
4. Rev. Rul. 2003-123, 2003-2 CB 1200, *amplifying*, Rev. Rul. 68-667, 1968-2 CB 289.
5. IRC Sec. 170(h); Treas. Reg. §1.170A-14(d).
6. *Glass v. Comm.*, 124 TC 258 (2005), *aff'd*, 2007-1 USTC ¶50,111 (6th Cir. 2006).
7. *Turner v. Comm.*, 126 TC No. 16 (2006).
8. Let. Rul. 9736016.
9. Let. Rul. 200208019.

Open space easements have been approved by the Service in several instances.[1] (Although some of these rulings were made under prior law, they remain valid under the current IRC Section.)

The deductible value of the easement is generally determined using a "before and after" approach. That is, the value of the total property owned by the taxpayer (including adjacent property that is not encumbered by the easement) before granting the easement is determined. Then, the value of the property after granting the easement is subtracted to determine the value of the easement.[2] For purposes of determining the value of the property before granting of the easement, the Tax Court determined that the highest and best use of the property had to be taken into account.[3]

General guidelines for valuing property can be found in Rev. Proc. 66-49.[4] If there is a substantial record of sales of easements comparable to the one donated, the fair market value of the donation can be based on the sale prices of the comparable easements. However, where previous sellers of easements to the county had generally intended to make gifts to the county by way of bargain sales, the Tax Court determined that the comparable sales approach was inappropriate in a bargain sale of a conservation easement.[5] Increases in the value of any property owned by the donor or a related person that result from the donation, whether or not the other property is contiguous to the donated property, reduce the amount of the deduction by the amount of the increase in the value of the other property.[6]

The Service privately ruled that an estate could properly claim a deduction for the value of a conservation easement attributable to a 68.8% tenancy in common interest includible in the decedent's gross estate notwithstanding the fact that the co-tenants would claim an income tax deduction for the conservation easement granted with respect to the interests in the property they owned.[7]

The Service determined that a taxpayer's exchange of a conservation easement in real property under IRC Section 1031(a) would qualify as a tax-deferred exchange of like-kind property, provided that the properties would be held for productive use in a trade or business, or for investment.[8]

In a legal memorandum, the Service analyzed the issues regarding the Colorado conservation easement credit, including: (1) to the extent a taxpayer is effectively reimbursed for the transfer of the easement through the use, refund, or transfer of the credit, whether that benefit is a *quid pro quo* that either reduces or eliminates a charitable contribution deduction under IRC Section 170; and (2) whether the benefit of the state conservation easement credit is, in substance, an amount realized from the transfer of the easement under IRS Section 1001, generally resulting in capital gain.[9]

---

1. See Rev. Rul. 74-583, 1974-2 CB 80; Rev. Rul. 75-373, 1975-2 CB 77; Let. Ruls. 200002020, 199952037, 9603018, 8641017, 8313123, 8248069.
2. *Symington v. Comm.*, 87 TC 892 (1986); *Fannon v. Comm.*, TC Memo 1986-572; Rev. Rul. 73-339, 1973-2 CB 68; Rev. Rul. 76-376, 1976-2 CB 53. See also *Thayer v. Comm.*, TC Memo 1977-370.
3. *Schapiro v. Comm.*, TC Memo 1991-128.
4. 1966-2 CB 1257, as modified by Rev. Proc. 96-15, 1996-2 CB 627.
5. See *Browning v. Comm.*, 109 TC 303 (1997).
6. Treas. Reg. §1.170A-14(h)(3).
7. Let. Rul. 200143011.
8. Let. Rul. 200201007. See also Let. Ruls. 200203033, 200203042.
9. CCA 200238041.

Improper deductions for conservation easements. The Service has determined that some taxpayers have been claiming inappropriate contribution deductions for cash payments or easement transfers to charitable organizations in connection with purchases of real property. In some of these questionable cases, the charity purchases the property and places a conservation easement on the property. Then, the charity sells the property subject to the easement to a buyer for a price that is substantially less than the price paid by the charity for the property. As part of the sale, the buyer makes a second payment – designated as a "charitable contribution" – to the charity. The total of the payments from the buyer to the charity fully reimburses the charity for the cost of the property. The Service warned that in appropriate cases, it will treat these transactions in accordance with their substance rather than their form. Accordingly, the Service may treat the total of the buyer's payments to the charity as the purchase price paid by the buy for the property. Taxpayers are advised that the Service intends to disallow all or part of any improper deductions and may impose penalties, and also intends to assess excise taxes (under IRC Section 4958) against any disqualified person who receives an excess benefit from a conservation transaction, and against any organization manager who knowingly participates in the transaction. In appropriate cases, the Service may challenge the tax-exempt status of the organization based on the organization's operation for a substantial nonexempt purpose or impermissible private benefit.[1]

Planning Point: PPA 2006 provides an increased AGI limit for certain qualified conservation contributions. The charitable deduction limitation applicable to qualified conservation contributions has been increased from 30% of AGI to 50% of AGI in the year of the gift. Additionally, a new 15-year carryover period is now permitted for the excess of the fair market value over the charitable deduction limit. In future years, the carryover amount is subject to the same ordering rules that apply to carryforwards of other charitable deductions.

Example: Robert makes a qualified conservation contribution valued at $500,000 in 2006. Robert's AGI in 2006 is $180,000 and his cash gifts to charity total $30,000. Robert's charitable deduction for 2006 consists of the $30,000 of cash gifts *plus* $60,000 of the qualified conservation contribution ($180,000 x 50% *minus* $30,000). Robert may carryover the remaining $440,000 of unused qualified conservation contribution to 2007 through 2021.

Special rules for farmers and ranchers. For farmers and ranchers who derive more than half of their gross income from farming or ranching, the charitable deduction limitation applicable to qualified conservation contributions of property available for use in agriculture or livestock production is increased to 100% of AGI. To be eligible for this special treatment, the gift is required to contain a restriction that the property must remain available for use in agriculture or livestock production. A 15-year carryover period is allowed for excess contributions. Qualified conservation contributions that qualify for the 50% of AGI limit must be used to the extent of the 50% limit before applying qualified conservation contributions of property available for use in agriculture or livestock production.

Special rules for closely-held farming and ranching corporations. For closely-held farming and ranching corporations that derive more than half of their gross income from farming and ranching, the charitable deduction limitation applicable to qualified conservation

---

1. Notice 2004-41, 2004-28 IRB 31. See also IR-2004-86 (6-30-2004).

contributions of property used in agriculture or livestock production has now been increased to 100% of AGI for the year of the gift. Any portion of the contribution that is not deductible during the year of gift may be carried over for 15 years subject to the same limitation of 100% of AGI. There is no enhanced charitable deduction for corporations that do not derive more than half of their gross income from farming or ranching.

Generally, the new qualified conservation contribution provisions apply for contributions made in tax years beginning in 2006 and 2007. The special provisions applicable to qualified conservation contributions of property used for agriculture or livestock production apply to contributions made after August 17, 2006 and before the end of the tax year beginning before January 1, 2008.[1] *Ted R. Batson, Jr., MBA, CPA, Senior Vice President of Professional Services and Gregory W. Baker, JD, CFP®, CAP, Senior Vice President of Legal Services for Renaissance.*

Planning Point: *Qualified conservation contributions and the rehabilitation credit.* A taxpayer who makes a qualified conservation contribution must reduce the amount of the contribution by a portion of any rehabilitation credit (see Q 1228) claimed in the five previous years. This provision applies to any qualified conservation contribution made after August 17, 2006.[2] *Ted R. Batson, Jr., MBA, CPA, Senior Vice President of Professional Services and Gregory W. Baker, JD, CFP®, CAP, Senior Vice President of Legal Services for Renaissance.*

Facade Easements

A variation on the conservation easement is the use of a "facade easement," wherein the grantor agrees not to alter the facade or modify the architectural characteristics of a building.

Planning Point: A taxpayer who owns a building in a registered historic district and wishes to qualify for a deduction for a façade easement must follow new guidelines. In general, gifts made after July 25, 2006 must be evidenced by a written agreement that: (1) includes a restriction which preserves the entire exterior of the building (front, rear, sides, and height); (2) prohibits any change in the exterior of the building that is inconsistent with the historical character of the building; and (3) under penalty of perjury is entered into with a "qualified organization" that has the resources and commitment to manage and enforce the restriction.

A "qualified organization" is: a governmental unit; a charity that meets the public support test of IRC Section 170(b)(1)(A)(vi); a charity that meets the public support test of IRC Section 509(a)(2); or a supporting organization controlled by any one of the three types of charities listed above. In addition, the qualified organization that receives such gifts, must also be organized for the purpose of environmental protection, land conservation, open space preservation, or historic preservation. For contributions made in a taxable year beginning after August 17, 2006, taxpayers claiming this deduction must include with their return: (1) a qualified appraisal of the interest contributed; (2) photographs of the entire exterior of the building; and (3) a description of all restrictions placed on the development of the building. Taxpayers that claim a deduction of more than $10,000 for contributions of façade easements after February 13, 2007, must

---

1. See IRC Secs. 170(b)(1)(E), 170(b)(2), as amended by PPA 2006.
2. See IRC Sec. 170(f)(14), as added by PPA 2006.

include a $500 filing fee with their return. By statute, this fee is earmarked for enforcement of the new rules governing the deductibility of all types of qualified conservation contributions, including façade easements.

Effective August 17, 2006, no deduction is allowed for a qualified conservation contribution of a structure or land unless the structure or land is listed in the National Register of Historic Places.[1] *Ted R. Batson, Jr., MBA, CPA, Senior Vice President of Professional Services and Gregory W. Baker, JD, CFP®, CAP, Senior Vice President of Legal Services for Renaissance.*

The amount of the deduction for the contribution of a facade easement is the full fair market value of the easement at the time of the contribution.[2] The fair market value of the facade donation has been determined by applying the "before and after" approach.[3] A substantial record of sales of easements comparable to the one donated results in valuation of the fair market value of the donation based on the sale prices of the comparable easements.[4] If the donation of a facade easement increases the value of the property it would appear that the donation would be reduced by the amount of such increase.[5]

A taxpayer who claims an investment credit for the rehabilitation of a historic structure may be required to recapture a portion of the credit upon the gift of a facade easement for the rehabilitated building (*Editor's Note*: but see also "Planning Point: Qualified conservation contributions and the rehabilitation credit," above, for the law under PPA 2006).[6]

Partnership Interest

1340. What are the tax consequences of a charitable contribution of a partnership interest?

A partnership interest is a capital asset that, if sold, would be given capital gain or loss treatment except to the extent of the partner's share of certain partnership property that, if sold by the partnership, would produce ordinary gain (i.e., his share of "unrealized receivables" and "substantially appreciated inventory").[7] (See Q 1205. See also Q 1420 regarding the treatment of capital gains and losses.) Thus, if a taxpayer makes a charitable contribution of his partnership interest, and if he has held the interest for long enough to qualify for long-term capital gain treatment (i.e., more than one year, as defined in IRC Section 1222(3); see Q 1322), he may deduct the full fair market value of his interest less the amount of ordinary gain, if any, that would have been realized by the partnership for his share of "unrealized receivables" and "substantially appreciated inventory." (His deduction is subject to the applicable limits. See Q 1322.)

If the partnership interest includes a liability (mortgage, etc.), the amount of the liability is treated as an amount realized on the disposition of the partnership inter-

---

1. See IRC Secs. 170(h)(4)(B), 170(h)(4)(C), as amended by PPA 2006; IRC Secs. 170(f)(13), 170(f)(14), as added by PPA 2006.
2. Let. Rul. 8449025.
3. *Hilborn v. Comm.*, 85 TC 677 (1985); *Nicoladis v. Comm.* TC Memo 1988-163; *Dorsey v. Comm.*, TC Memo 1990-242, aff'd, *Griffin v. Comm.*, 911 F.2d 1124 (5th Cir. 1990).
4. See *Akers v. Comm.*, 799 F.2d 243 (6th Cir. 1986).
5. See Treas. Reg. §1.170A-14(h)(3).
6. Rev. Rul. 89-90, 1989-2 CB 3; *Rome I, Ltd. v. Comm.* 96 TC 697 (1991).
7. IRC Sec. 741.

est.[1] Thus, the contribution is subject to the bargain sale rules, and the transfer will be treated, in part at least, as a sale (see Q 1325).[2] (If the partner's share of partnership liabilities exceeds the fair market value of his partnership interest, he may have taxable income, but no deduction under the bargain sale rules.) In *Goodman v. United States*,[3] the taxpayer contributed her partnership interest to charity, subject to her share of partnership debt. The district court held that the taxpayer recognized gain on the transfer equal to the excess of the amount realized over that portion of the adjusted basis of the partnership interest (at the time of the transfer), allocable to the sale under IRC Section 1011(b).[4]

In order to determine the taxable income and the amount of charitable deduction under the bargain sale rules, the following steps must be taken:

1. *Determine the taxable gain on the sale portion.* Under the bargain sale rules, part of the donor's basis is allocated to the portion sold. The basis allocated to the sold portion is the amount of basis that bears the same ratio to his entire basis as the amount realized bears to the market value of the property. Presumably, the sold portion includes the same proportionate part of his share of unrealized receivables and substantially appreciated inventory as it does basis.

> *Example.* Mr. Savelle owns a 10% interest in a partnership that he has held for three years. The fair market value of his interest is $100,000 and his adjusted basis is $50,000. His share of a mortgage on partnership property is $40,000, and his share of "unrealized receivables" (potential depreciation recapture on the mortgaged property) is $5,000 in which the partnership's basis is zero. He donates his entire interest to charity. He is deemed to have received $40,000, his share of partnership liabilities, on the transfer. In effect there are two transactions–a sale for $40,000 and a contribution of $60,000.

> Of Mr. Savelle's $50,000 basis in his partnership interest, $20,000 is allocated to the sale portion: $40,000 (amount realized)/$100,000 (fair market value) × $50,000 (total adjusted basis). The fair market value of the sold portion is $40,000 (amount realized). Mr. Savelle must recognize a gain of $20,000 ($40,000 realized less $20,000 adjusted basis allocated to the sold portion). Of that gain, $2,000 is allocable to unrealized receivables ($5,000 unrealized receivables × $40,000/$100,000). Because the partnership has no basis in the unrealized receivables, the entire $2,000 would be ordinary income. Mr. Savelle must report a taxable long-term capital gain of $18,000 and a taxable ordinary gain of $2,000.

2. *Determine the charitable contribution deduction.* As a general rule, the fair market value of the portion given to charity is deductible except to the extent the property would have generated ordinary income if sold. Consequently, the allowable deduction for the gift portion must be reduced to the extent the portion of the partnership interest given to the charity would produce ordinary income if sold.

> *Example.* The fair market value of Mr. Savelle's gift to charity is $60,000. Because 60% of the partnership interest was given to the charity ($60,000/$100,000), 60% of Mr. Savelle's share of partnership "unrealized receivables," or $3,000 ($5,000 × 60% = $3,000) is considered included in the gift. The balance of the gift would be long-term capital gain on sale. Because $3,000 would be ordinary income on a sale, Mr. Savelle's contribution is reduced by $3,000, and his charitable contribution deduction is $57,000.

Other special rules may apply under certain circumstances, for example, if the partnership owns property subject to tax credit recapture, if it has made installment sales,

---

1. Treas. Reg. §1.1001-2. See *Crane v. Comm.*, 331 U.S. 1 (1947).
2. Rev. Rul. 75-194, 1975-1 CB 80.
3. 2000-1 USTC 50,162 (D.C. Fl. 1999).
4. Citing Rev. Rul. 75-194 and Treas. Reg. §1.1001-2.

or (as might occur in the case of an oil and gas partnership) if it is receiving income in the form of "production payments." See also Q 1326 with regard to prepaid interest.

CHARITABLE IRA ROLLOVER

1341. What is a charitable IRA rollover or qualified charitable distribution?

For tax years 2006 and 2007, a taxpayer age 70½ or older may make a *qualified charitable distribution* from an IRA that will not be includible in the gross income of the taxpayer.[1]

A qualified charitable distribution is any distribution

1.   not exceeding $100,000 in the aggregate during the taxable year;

Planning Point: Only distributions from a taxpayer's own IRA are includible in determining that a taxpayer has met the $100,000 limit. Therefore, while married taxpayers may make qualified distributions totaling $200,000, each spouse may only make distributions of up to $100,000 from their own IRA. *Ted R. Batson, Jr., MBA, CPA, and Gregory W. Baker, JD, CFP®, CAP, Renaissance Administration, LLC.*

2.   made directly, in a trustee-to-charity transfer;

3.   from a traditional or Roth IRA (distributions from SEPs and SIMPLE IRAs do not qualify);

Planning Point: A participant in a qualified plan, an IRC Section 403(b) tax sheltered annuity, or an eligible IRC Section 457 governmental plan must first perform a rollover to a traditional IRA before taking advantage of a charitable IRA rollover. *Ted R. Batson, Jr., MBA, CPA, and Gregory W. Baker, JD, CFP®, CAP, Renaissance Administration, LLC.*

4.   to a public charity (but not a donor-advised fund or supporting organization);

Planning Point: Rollovers to donor-advised funds, supporting organizations, private foundations, charitable remainder trusts, charitable gift annuities, and pooled income funds are not qualified charitable distributions. *Ted R. Batson, Jr., MBA, CPA, and Gregory W. Baker, JD, CFP®, CAP, Renaissance Administration, LLC.*

5.   that would otherwise qualify as a deductible charitable contribution—not including the percentage of income limits in IRC Section 170(b);

6.   to the extent the distribution would otherwise be includible in gross income.[2]

No charitable income tax deduction is allowed for a qualified charitable distribution.[3]

1. IRC Sec. 408(d)(8).
2. IRC Sec. 408(d)(8).
3. IRC Sec. 408(d)(8)(E).

Planning Point: Rollovers to charities by taxpayers who reside in states that tax IRA distributions and do not have a charitable deduction may not escape tax at the state level. *Ted R. Batson, Jr., MBA, CPA, and Gregory W. Baker, JD, CFP®, CAP, Renaissance Administration, LLC.*

If a qualified charitable distribution is made from any IRA funded with nondeductible contributions, the distribution is treated as coming first from deductible contributions and earnings.[1] This is contrary to the general rule that distributions from an IRA with both deductible and nondeductible are deemed made on a pro-rata basis.[2]

Qualified charitable distributions still count toward a taxpayer's required minimum distributions.[3]

For guidance on qualified charitable contributions (including questions and answers), see Notice 2007-7, 2007-__ IRB ___.

---

1. IRC Sec. 408(d)(8)(D).
2. IRC Secs. 72, 408(d)(1).
3. IRC Sec. 408(d)(8).

PART II

GENERAL
FEDERAL INCOME TAXATION

of
INDIVIDUALS

GENERAL RULES

FILING REQUIREMENTS

1400. Who must file a return?

A return must be filed for taxable year 2007 by every individual whose gross income equals or exceeds the following limits:

(1) Married persons filing jointly–$17,500 (if one spouse is blind *or* elderly–$18,550; if both spouses are blind *or* elderly–$19,600; if both spouses are blind *and* elderly–$21,700).[1] A married taxpayer with gross income of $3,400 or more in 2007 must file a return if he and his spouse are living in different households at the end of the taxable year.

(2) Surviving spouse (see Q 1434)–$14,100 (if elderly *or* blind–$15,150; if elderly *and* blind–$16,200).[2]

(3) Head-of-household (see Q 1435)–$11,250 (if blind *or* elderly–$12,550; if elderly *and* blind–$13,850).

(4) Single persons–$8,750 (if blind *or* elderly–$10,050; if blind *and* elderly–$11,350).

(5) Married filing separately–if neither spouse itemizes, a return must be filed if gross income equals or exceeds $8,750 in 2007 (if blind *or* elderly–$9,800; if blind *and* elderly–$10,850).[3] If either spouse itemizes–$3,400.

(6) Dependents–every individual who may be claimed as a dependent of another must file a return for 2007 if he has unearned income in excess of $850 (plus any additional standard deduction if the individual is blind or elderly) or total gross income that exceeds the sum of any additional standard deduction if the individual is blind or elderly plus the greater of (a) $850 or (b) the lesser of (i) $300 plus earned income, or (ii) $5,350.

---

1. IRC Sec. 63(c).
2. IRC Sec. 63(c).
3. IRC Sec. 63(c).

(7) Taxpayers who are non-resident aliens or who are filing a short year return because of a change in their annual accounting period–$3,400.[1]

Certain parents whose children are required to file a return may be permitted to include the child's income over $1,700 on their own return, thus avoiding the necessity of the child filing a return. See Q 1411.

A taxpayer with self-employment income must file a return if *net* self-employment income is $400 or more. See Q 1442.

1401. Who must pay the estimated tax and what penalties are imposed for underpayment of the tax?

Taxpayers are generally required to pay estimated tax if failure to pay would result in an underpayment (see below) of federal income tax.[2] Taxpayers must include the alternative minimum tax and estimated self-employment tax in their calculation of estimated tax (see Q 1440 and Q 1442, respectively).[3] An underpayment is the amount by which a required installment exceeds the amount, if any, paid on or before the due date of that installment (due dates are April 15, June 15, September 15 and January 15 of the following year).[4] The required amount for each installment is 25% of the *required annual payment.*[5]

Generally, the "required annual payment" is the lower of (a) 90% of the tax shown on the return for the taxable year (or, if no return is filed, 90% of the tax for the year), or (b) 100% of the tax shown on the return for the preceding year (but only if the preceding taxable year consisted of 12 months and a return was filed for that year).[6] However, for an individual whose adjusted gross income for the previous tax year exceeded $150,000 ($75,000 in the case of married individuals filing separately), the required annual payment is the lesser of (a) 90% of the current year's tax, as described above, or (b) the *applicable percentage* of the tax shown on the return for the preceding year. The applicable percentage for tax years beginning 2003 or later is 110%. (Different rules applied for installments due in tax years prior to 2000.)[7]

As an alternative to the required annual payment methods in the preceding paragraph, taxpayers can pay estimated tax by paying a specified percentage of the current year's tax, computed by annualizing the taxable income for the months in the taxable year ending before the month in which the installment falls due. The percentages that apply under the annualization method are: 22.5% (1st quarter), 45% (2nd quarter), 67.5% (3rd quarter), and 90% (4th quarter).[8]

However, regardless of the method used to calculate estimated taxes, there is no interest penalty imposed if: (1) the tax shown on the return for the taxable year (or, if no return is filed, the tax) after reduction for withholdings, is less than $1,000; or (2) the taxpayer owed no tax for the preceding year (a taxable year consisting of 12 months)

---

1. IRC Secs. 6012(a), 63(c), 151; Rev. Proc. 2006-53, 2006-48 IRB 996.
2. IRC Sec. 6654.
3. IRC Sec. 6654(d)(2)(B)(i).
4. IRC Secs. 6654(b), 6654(c).
5. IRC Sec. 6654(d)(1)(A).
6. IRC Sec. 6654(d)(1)(B).
7. IRC Sec. 6654(d)(1)(C).
8. IRC Sec. 6654(d)(2).

and the taxpayer was a U.S. citizen or resident for the entire taxable year.[1] Otherwise, underpayment results in imposition of an interest penalty, compounded daily, at an annual rate that is adjusted quarterly so as to be three percentage points over the short-term applicable federal rate.[2] (See Q 1409).

If the taxpayer elects to apply an overpayment to the succeeding year's estimated taxes, the overpayment is applied to unpaid installments of estimated tax due on or after the date(s) the overpayment arose in the order in which they are required to be paid to avoid an interest penalty for failure to pay estimated income tax with respect to such tax year.[3] For application of the estimated tax to trusts and estates, see Q 1449.

TAX YEAR

1402. What is an individual's "taxable year"?

The basic *period* for computing income tax liability is one year, known as the *taxable year*. The taxable year may be either (a) the calendar year or (b) a fiscal year. A "calendar year" is a period of 12 months ending on December 31. A "fiscal year" is a period of 12 months ending on the last day of a month other than December.[4]

Generally, a taxpayer may decide whether he wishes to use the calendar year or fiscal year in reporting his tax liability. Most individuals report on a calendar year basis. The year used for reporting tax liability must generally correspond to the taxpayer's accounting period.[5] Thus, if the taxpayer keeps books on a fiscal year basis he cannot determine his tax liability on a calendar year basis. But if the taxpayer keeps no books, he must report on a calendar year basis.[6] Once the taxpayer has chosen his tax year, he cannot change without the permission of the Internal Revenue Service.[7] A principal partner cannot change to a taxable year other than that of the partnership unless he establishes, to the satisfaction of the IRS, a business purpose for doing so.[8]

Under certain circumstances, partnerships, S corporations, and personal service corporations are required to use the calendar year for computing income tax liability.[9]

A short period return is required (1) where the taxpayer changes his annual accounting period, and (2) where a taxpayer has been in existence for only part of a taxable year.[10] A short period is treated in the law as a "taxable year."[11]

If the short period return is made because of a change in accounting period, the income during the short period must be annualized, and deductions and exemptions prorated.[12] But income for the short period is not required to be annualized if the taxpayer is not in existence for the entire taxable year.[13]

1. IRC Sec. 6654(e).
2. IRC Sec. 6621(a)(2).
3. Rev. Rul. 99-40, 1999-2 CB 441.
4. IRC Secs. 441(a), 441(b), 441(d), 441(e).
5. IRC Sec. 441(f)(1).
6. IRC Sec. 441(g).
7. IRC Sec. 442.
8. IRC Sec. 706(b)(2).
9. See IRC Secs. 441(i), 706(b), 1378.
10. IRC Sec. 443(a).
11. IRC Sec. 441(b)(3).
12. IRC Secs. 443(b), 443(c).
13. Treas. Reg. §1.443-1(a)(2).

For the final regulations affecting taxpayers who want to adopt an annual accounting period (under IRC Section 441), or who must receive approval to adopt, change, or retain their annual accounting periods (under IRC Section 442), see Treas. Regs. §§1.441-0, 1.441-1, 1.441-2, 1.441-3, 1.441-4; TD 8996.[1]

For the general procedures for establishing a business purpose and obtaining approval to adopt, change, or retain an annual accounting period, see Rev. Proc. 2002-39.[2]

The procedure under which IRC Section 442 allows individuals (e.g., sole proprietors) filing tax returns on a fiscal year basis to obtain automatic approval to change their annual accounting period to a calendar year is set forth in Revenue Procedure 2003-62.[3]

The exclusive procedures for (1) certain partnerships, (2) S corporations, (3) electing S corporations, (4) personal service corporations, and (5) trusts to obtain automatic approval to adopt, change, or retain their annual accounting period are set forth in Revenue Procedure 2006-46.[4]

CALCULATING THE TAX

1403. What are the basic steps in computing an individual's tax liability?

The computation is made up of these basic steps:

...Gross income for the taxable year is determined (see Q 1404 to Q 1422).

...Certain deductions are subtracted from gross income to arrive at adjusted gross income (see Q 1423, Q 1424).

...The deduction for personal and dependency exemptions (taking into consideration any phaseout amount) is determined (see Q 1425, Q 1426).

...Itemized deductions (taking into consideration any limitations thereon) are totaled (see Q 1427 to Q 1429), compared to the *standard deduction* (see Q 1431), and (generally) the greater amount, along with the deduction for exemptions, is deducted from adjusted gross income to arrive at taxable income.

...The proper tax rate is applied to taxable income to determine the tax (see Appendix A).

...The following amounts are subtracted from the tax to determine the net tax payable or overpayment refundable: (1) credits (see Q 1436), and (2) prepayments toward the tax (e.g., tax withheld by an employer or payments made on an estimated tax return).

1.　67 Fed. Reg. 35009 (5-17-2002).
2.　2002-1 CB 1046, *as modified by*, Notice 2002-72, 2002-2 CB 843, *and further modified by*, Rev. Proc. 2003-79, 2003-2 CB 1036.
3.　2003-2 CB 299, *modifying, amplifying, and superseding*, Rev. Proc. 66-50, 1966-2 CB 1260, and *modifying and superseding*, Rev. Proc. 81-40, 1981-2 CB 604. See also Ann. 2003-49, 2003-2 CB 339.
4.　2006-45 IRB 859.

The steps in calculating the alternative minimum tax are explained in Q 1440.

GROSS INCOME

1404. What items are included in gross income? What items are excluded from gross income?

Gross income includes all income (whether derived from labor or capital) *less* those items that are excludable by law. Thus, gross income includes salary, fees, commissions, business profits, interest and dividends, rents, alimony received, and gains from sale of property—but not mere return of capital. IRC Sec. 61(a).

Some of the items that can be *excluded* from gross income and received tax free by an individual taxpayer are: gifts and inheritances;[1] gain (within limits) from the sale of a personal residence (see Q 1239); 50% of gain (within limits) from the sale of certain qualified small business stock held for more than five years (see Q 1019 and Q 1020); interest on many bonds of a state, city or other political subdivision (see Q 1123); Social Security and railroad retirement benefits (within limits—see Q 1410); veterans' benefits (but retirement pay is taxable);[2] Workers' Compensation Act payments (within limits);[3] death proceeds of life insurance and, as to death proceeds of insurance on the life of an insured who died before October 23, 1986, up to $1,000 annually of interest received under a life income or installment option by a surviving spouse;[4] amounts paid or expenses incurred by an employer for qualified adoption expenses in connection with the adoption of a child by an employee if the amounts are furnished pursuant to an adoption assistance program;[5] contributions to a "Medicare Advantage MSA" by the Department of Health and Human Services;[6] exempt-interest dividends from mutual funds (see Q 1162); interest on certain U.S. savings bonds purchased after 1989 and used to pay higher education expenses (within limits—see Q 1141);[7] contributions paid by an employer to Health Savings Accounts;[8] distributions from Health Savings Accounts used to pay qualified medical expenses;[9] and federal subsidies for prescription drug plans.[10]

1405. When does a cash basis taxpayer "receive" income? What is the doctrine of constructive receipt?

As a general rule, taxable income must be computed under the method of accounting regularly used by the taxpayer.[11] There are two commonly accepted methods for recognizing income and expense: (1) the cash basis and (2) the accrual basis.[12]

Under the cash basis, the general rule is that all items that constitute gross income (whether in the form of cash, property or services) are includable for the taxable year in

---

1. IRC Sec. 102.
2. IRC Sec. 104(a)(4).
3. IRC Sec. 104(a)(1).
4. IRC Secs. 101(a), 101(d).
5. IRC Sec. 137.
6. IRC Sec. 138.
7. See IRC Sec. 135.
8. IRC Sec. 106(d).
9. IRC Sec. 223(f)(1).
10. IRC Sec. 139A.
11. IRC Sec. 446(a).
12. IRC Sec. 446(c).

which they are actually or constructively received.[1] Salary checks received in one year but not cashed until a later year are income when received unless substantial restrictions are placed on current negotiation or the issuer is insolvent.[2] A taxpayer who refused to cash a check in which his entire qualified plan balance was erroneously distributed was unsuccessful in deferring the date on which it was deemed received.[3]

As a general rule, expenses are deductible by a cash basis taxpayer for the taxable year in which they are paid.[4]

The doctrine of constructive receipt of income affects only cash basis taxpayers. Under this doctrine, a cash basis taxpayer is required to report income that has been credited to his account or set apart for him in such a way that he may draw on it freely at any time – even though he has not actually received it.[5] Thus, a cash basis taxpayer must report the interest credited to his bank savings account in the year it is credited regardless of whether he withdraws the interest or leaves it on deposit (see Q 1155).

However, the doctrine applies only where the taxpayer's control of the income is unrestricted. Thus, a sum is not constructively received if it is only conditionally credited, or if it is indefinite in amount, or if the payor has no funds, or if it is subject to any other substantial limitation. Also the courts say, generally, that there can be no constructive receipt of an amount that is available only through surrender of a valuable right.[6]

Under the accrual method, income is includable for the taxable year in which the right to receive the income becomes fixed and the amounts receivable become determinable with reasonable accuracy.[7] Expenses are deductible for the taxable year in which the liability for payment becomes definite and the amounts payable become reasonably certain but only to the extent that economic performance with respect to the item has occurred.[8]

For the revised comprehensive procedures by which taxpayers may obtain *automatic* consent to change their method of accounting, see Rev. Proc. 2002-9.[9]

The Tax Court held that a contract for a deed resulted in a completed sale of real property for tax purposes in the year that the contract was executed; therefore, income attributable to that disposition was required to be recognized and reported in the taxable year in which the contract was executed.[10] Controlling shareholders of a privately held company that sold derivative instruments through flow-through entities were required to recognize their pro rata share of the gain in the year that the shares were sold.[11] An investor who experienced losses on foreign currency contracts that required repayment on a future maturity date, but who was unable to post adequate collateral in the year

---

1. IRC Sec. 451(a); Treas. Reg. §1.451-2(a).
2. *Chapman v. Comm.*, TC Memo 1982-307; *Baxter v. Comm.*, 816 F.2d 493 (9th Cir. 1987), *rev'g in part* TC Memo 1985-378.
3. See Let. Rul. 9826036.
4. IRC Sec. 461(a).
5. Treas. Reg. §1.451-2. See, e.g., *Visco v. Comm*, 281 F.3d 101 (3rd Cir. 2002), *aff'g*, TC Memo 2000-77 (employment-related dispute).
6. See *Cohen v. Comm.*, 39 TC 1055 (1963).
7. Treas. Reg. §1.451-1(a).
8. IRC Sec. 461(h).
9. 2002-1 CB 327; *as modified by*, Rev. Proc. 2002-19, 2002-1 CB 696, and Rev. Proc. 2002-54, 2002-2 CB 432.
10. *Keith v. Comm.*, 115 TC 605 (2000).
11. FSA 200111011.

the losses were sustained, was entitled to deduct the losses in the year in which the debt was repaid.[1] Under the constructive receipt doctrine, the mere right of an employee to make an election to cash out future vacation leave under the employer's plan would not result in taxable income for the employee under the cash method of accounting if the employee chose not to make such an election.[2]

1406. What are the tax consequences of a discharge of indebtedness?

Gross income generally includes income from discharge of indebtedness.[3] However, debt discharge is excluded from gross income if the discharge: (1) occurs in a Title 11 bankruptcy case; (2) occurs when the taxpayer is insolvent; (3) the indebtedness discharged is "qualified farm indebtedness";[4] or (4) in the case of a taxpayer other than a C corporation, the indebtedness discharged is "qualified real property business indebtedness".[5]

The Treasury regulations reiterate that the discharge of indebtedness, in whole or in part, generally results in the realization of income. For example, if an individual performs services for a creditor, who in consideration thereof cancels the debt, the debtor realizes income in the amount of the debt as compensation for his services. A taxpayer may realize income by the payment or purchase of his obligations at less than face value. In general, if a shareholder in a corporation that is indebted to him gratuitously forgives the debt, the transaction amounts to a contribution to the capital of the corporation to the extent of the principal of the debt.[6]

1407. What are the income tax consequences of below-market loans?

Editor's Note: The Sarbanes-Oxley Act of 2002 (P.L. 107-204) adopted new securities law provisions intended to deter and punish corporate and accounting fraud and corruption, ensure justice for wrongdoers, and protect the interests of workers and shareholders of publicly-traded corporations. However, it would appear that one provision of the Act indirectly impacts below-market loans made to executives of publicly-traded corporations. See "Securities law restrictions on personal loans," below.

Generally, a below-market loan is any demand loan with an interest rate that is below the applicable federal rate (see below) *or* any term loan in which the amount received by the borrower exceeds the present value of all payments due under the loan. A demand loan is any loan that is payable in full at any time on the demand of the lender, or that has an indefinite maturity. All other loans are generally term loans.[7] The IRC essentially recharacterizes a below-market loan as two transactions: (1) an arm's-length loan requiring payment of interest at the applicable federal rate, and (2) a transfer of funds by the lender to the borrower ("imputed transfer").[8]

---

1. FSA 200106005.
2. Let. Rul. 200130015.
3. IRC Sec. 61(a)(12).
4. Under IRC Section 108(g)(2).
5. Under IRC Section 108(c)(3). IRC Sec. 108(a).
6. Treas. Reg. §1.61-12(a).
7. IRC Secs. 7872(e), 7872(f).
8. Prop. Treas. Reg. §1.7872-1(a).

Gift Loans

A below-market demand or term loan is a gift loan if the foregoing of interest is in the nature of a gift.[1] The lender is deemed to have transferred to the borrower and the borrower is deemed to have transferred to the lender an amount equal to the forgone interest.[2] "Forgone interest" is the *excess of* the amount of interest that would have been payable if it accrued at the applicable federal rate and was payable on the last day of the calendar year *over* any interest actually payable on the loan during such period.[3] In the case of below-market gift loans between natural persons, the transfer is treated, for both the borrower and the lender, as occurring on the last day of the borrower's taxable year.[4] The amount of forgone interest is included in the gross income of the lender; deductibility by the borrower depends on how the interest is classified for tax purposes (i.e., personal, passive, etc.–see Q 1301).

These rules do not apply to any below-market gift loan between individuals on any day the aggregate outstanding amount of *all* loans made directly between them (husband and wife are treated as one person) does not exceed $10,000; however, this de minimis exception will not apply to any gift loan directly attributable to the purchase or carrying of income-producing assets.[5] In addition, a special rule limits the amount of income included in the lender's gross income to the borrower's net investment income for the year if: (1) the aggregate outstanding amount of all loans made directly between *individuals* does not exceed $100,000; (2) the lender has a signed statement from the borrower, stating the amount of borrower's net investment income properly allocable to the loan; (3) the time or amount of investment income cannot be manipulated by the borrower, and (4) tax avoidance is not one of the principal purposes of the interest arrangements.[6] Net investment income equals the excess of investment income over investment expenses, *plus* any amount that would be includable as interest on all deferred payment obligations were the original issue discount rules to apply. Deferred payment obligations include annuities, U.S. savings bonds and short-term obligations. Net investment income will be treated as zero in any year it does not exceed $1,000.[7]

For the gift tax consequences of below-market gift loans, see Q 1518.

Compensation-Related Loans and
Corporation-Shareholder Loans

In the case of demand loans that are compensation-related (e.g., employer to employee, between an independent contractor and the individual for whom the services are provided and, under proposed regulations, between a partnership and a partner in certain circumstances) or corporation-shareholder loans, the same transfer and retransfer of forgone interest is deemed to have occurred as explained in gift loans, above.[8] The lender in a compensation-related loan will have interest income to the extent of the forgone interest and a corresponding deduction for compensation paid (if reasonable). The borrower will have compensation income, but a deduction for the forgone interest will be

---

1. IRC Sec. 7872(f)(3).
2. IRC Sec. 7872(a)(1).
3. IRC Sec. 7872(e)(2).
4. IRC Sec. 7872(a)(2); Prop. Treas. Reg. §1.7872-6(b)(3).
5. IRC Sec. 7872(c)(2); Prop. Treas. Reg. §1.7872-8(b)(3).
6. IRC Sec. 7872(d)(1); Prop. Treas. Regs. §§1.7872-8(c), 1.7872-11(g)(3).
7. IRC Sec. 7872(d)(1)(E).
8. IRC Secs. 7872(c)(1)(B), 7872(c)(1)(C); Prop. Treas. Reg. §1.7872-4(c).

subject to the limitations on interest deductions (see Q 1301). The same consequences result in corporation-shareholder loans except that the forgone interest is treated as a dividend; therefore, there is no deduction available to the lender-corporation.

In the case of below-market term loans that are compensation-related or corporation-shareholder loans, the lender is deemed to have transferred to the borrower and the borrower is deemed to have received a cash payment equal to the *excess of* the amount loaned *over* the present value (determined as of the date of the loan, using a discount rate equal to the applicable federal rate) of all payments required to be made under the terms of the loan.[1] The excess is treated as original issue discount and, generally, treated as transferred on the day the loan was made. The lender can deduct the amount treated as original issue discount as compensation in compensation-related loans and will include such amount as interest income as it accrues over the term of the loan. The borrower will have includable compensation on the day the loan is made, but deductions (if allowed–see Q 1301) for the "imputed" interest can be taken only as such interest accrues over the loan period. With regard to corporation-shareholder loans, the same results occur except that the amount treated as original issue discount is considered a dividend, and there is no deduction available to the lender-corporation.

Compensation-related loans and corporation-shareholder loans, whether demand or term, are not subject to either of the above rules on any day the aggregate outstanding amount of all loans between the parties does not exceed $10,000 and tax avoidance is not one of the principal purposes of the interest arrangements.[2] With respect to term loans that are not gift loans, once the aggregate outstanding amount exceeds $10,000, this de minimis exception no longer applies, even if the outstanding balance is later reduced below $10,000.[3]

In a case of first impression involving below-market loans made to noncontrolling shareholders, the Tax Court held that the below-market loan rules may apply to a loan to a majority *or* a minority shareholder. The court also held that direct *and* indirect loans are subject to these rules.[4]

Securities law restrictions on personal loans. Section 402 of the Sarbanes-Oxley Act of 2002 (P.L. 107-204) amended Section 13 of the Securities and Exchange Act of 1934 (15 USC 78m) to prohibit "issuers" (i.e., publicly-traded companies) from directly or indirectly (1) extending or maintaining credit, or (2) arranging for the extension of credit, or renewing an extension of credit, in the form of a personal loan to or for any director or executive officer (or equivalent) of that issuer. The narrow exceptions to this rule are loans made for the following purposes: home improvement; consumer credit; any extension of credit under an open-end credit plan; a charge card; or any extension of credit by a broker or dealer to buy, trade, or carry securities. To fall within the exception, the loan must also be (1) made or provided in the ordinary course of business of the company, (2) of a type that is generally made available by the company to the public, and (3) made on market terms, or terms that are no more favorable than those offered by the issuer to the general public for such extensions of credit.

Thus, it would appear that a below-market loan made by a publicly-traded company to a director or executive officer for a purpose other than those outlined in

---

1. IRC Sec. 7872(b)(1).
2. IRC Sec. 7872(c)(3).
3. IRC Sec. 7872(f)(10).
4. *Rountree Cotton, Inc. v. Comm.*, 113 TC 422 (1999), *aff'd per curiam*, 87 AFTR 2d ¶2001-718 (10th Cir. 2001).

the exceptions would be prohibited under the new securities law. Extensions of credit maintained by a company on July 30, 2002 are not subject to the prohibition so long as no material modification is made to any term of the loan and the loan is not renewed on or after that date.

Other Loans

In addition to the loans discussed above, below-market loans in which one of the principal purposes is tax avoidance or, to the extent provided for in regulations, in which the interest arrangements have a significant effect on the federal tax liability of either party, will also be subject to the above rules.[1] The Service has determined that the interest arrangements of certain loans *will not* be considered as having a significant effect on the federal tax liability of either party–tax exempt obligations, obligations of the U.S. government, life insurance policy loans, etc.–and, unless one of the principal purposes is tax avoidance, such transactions will not be subject to the below-market loan rules.[2]

Applicable Federal Rate

The applicable federal rate (see Q 1409) for demand loans is the short-term rate in effect during the period for which the forgone interest is being determined, compounded semiannually.[3] In the case of a below-market loan of a fixed principal amount that remains outstanding for the entire calendar year, forgone interest is equal to the *excess of* the "blended annual rate" for that calendar year multiplied by the outstanding principal *over* any interest payable on the loan properly allocable to the calendar year. The blended annual rate is published annually with the AFRs for the month of July.[4] The blended annual rate for the calendar year 2006 is 4.71%.[5]

For term loans, the applicable federal rate is the corresponding federal rate (i.e., short-, mid-, or long-term) in effect on the day the loan was made, compounded semiannually.[6]

The applicable federal rates are determined by the Secretary on a monthly basis.[7] The Secretary may by regulation permit a rate that is lower than the applicable federal rate to be used under certain circumstances.[8]

Reporting Requirements

In any taxable year in which the lender or the borrower either has imputed income or claims a deduction for an amount imputed under IRC Section 7872, he must, (1) attach a statement to his income tax return explaining that it relates to the amount includable in income or deductible by reason of the below-market loan rules; (2) provide the name, address and taxpayer identification number of the other party; and (3) specify the amount includable or deductible and the mathematical assumptions and method used in computing the amounts imputed.[9]

---

1. IRC Sec. 7872(c)(1).
2. Temp. Treas. Reg. §1.7872-5T.
3. IRC Sec. 7872(f)(2)(B).
4. Rev. Rul. 86-17, 1986-1 CB 377.
5. Rev. Rul. 2006-35, 2006-28 IRB 50.
6. IRC Sec. 7872(f)(2)(A).
7. IRC Sec. 1274(d).
8. See IRC Sec. 1274(d)(1)(D).
9. Prop. Treas. Reg. §1.7872-11(g).

For additional IRS guidance on arm's length issues, the timing of interest recognition and the allocation of interest and principal, see *Market Segment Specialization Program (MSSP) Shareholder Loan Audit Techniques Guide*.[1]

1408. What is an installment sale? How is it taxed?

Editor's Note: JGTRRA 2003 reduced capital gain rates for sales or exchanges occurring *on or after* May 6, 2003 and *before* January 1, 2009.[2] For the tax treatment of installment payments, see Q 1420.

An installment sale is a disposition of property (other than marketable securities, certain real property, and "inventory") where at least one payment is to be received by the seller after the close of the taxable year in which the disposition occurs.[3] It is not necessary that there be more than one payment.

Unless the taxpayer *elects out* on or before the due date, including extensions, for filing his federal income tax return for the taxable year in which the disposition occurred, any gain must be reported under this method.[4] An election out is made by reporting all of the gain on the transaction in the year of the sale. A decision by the taxpayer not to elect out is generally irrevocable unless the IRS finds that the taxpayer had good cause for failure to make a timely election.[5] Good cause will not be found if the purpose of a late election out is tax avoidance.[6] However, where a taxpayer intended to use the installment method but failed to do so through his accountant's error, the IRS permitted the taxpayer to revoke his election out of the installment method.[7] Similarly, the IRS has granted permission to revoke an election out where the election was not the result of a conscious choice by the taxpayer.[8] But see *Krause v. Comm.*[9] (holding that an election out will not be revoked when one of the purposes for the revocation is the avoidance of federal income taxes).

Loss cannot be reported on the installment method.[10] Dealers generally are not permitted to use the installment method (with exceptions for farm property and certain timeshares and residential lots).[11] See Q 1017 for the treatment of gain from the sale of publicly traded stock.

Under the installment method, the total payment is divided into (a) return of the seller's investment, (b) profit, and (c) interest income. Generally, where the sale price is over $3,000 and any payment is deferred more than one year, interest must be charged on payments due more than six months after the sale at least at 100% of the "applicable federal rate," compounded semiannually, or it will be imputed at that rate.[12] However, the following are exceptions to this general rule: (1) if less than 100% of the AFR, a rate of no greater than 9%, compounded semiannually, will be imputed

1. This IRS guide can be viewed or downloaded at the following address: http://www.irs.gov/pub/irs-mssp/a8shloan.pdf.
2. IRC Sec. 1(h), as amended by JGTRRA 2003.
3. IRC Sec. 453(b).
4. IRC Secs. 453(a), 453(d); *Bolton v. Comm.*, 92 TC 303 (1989).
5. Temp. Treas. Reg. §15A.453-1(d); Rev. Rul. 90-46, 1990-1 CB 107.
6. Let. Rul. 9230003.
7. Let. Rul. 9218012. See also Let. Rul. 200226039.
8. Let. Ruls. 9419012, 9345027.
9. TC Memo 2000-343
10. See IRC Sec. 453.
11. IRC Secs. 453(b)(2)(A), 453(l)(2).
12. IRC Sec. 483.

in the case of sales of property (other than new IRC Section 38 property) if the stated principal amount of the debt instrument does not exceed $4,800,800 in 2007;[1] (2) if less than 100% of the AFR, a rate of no greater than 6%, compounded semiannually, is imputed on aggregate sales of land during a calendar year between an individual and a member of his family (i.e., brothers, sisters, spouse, ancestors, and lineal descendants) to the extent the aggregate sales do not exceed $500,000 (the general rule of 100% of the AFR, compounded semiannually, applies to the excess);[2] and (3) a rate of 110% of the AFR, compounded semiannually, applies to sales or exchanges of property if, pursuant to a plan, the transferor or any related person leases a portion of the property after the sale or exchange ("sale-leaseback" transactions).[3]

The applicable federal rate (see Q 1409) will be the lowest of the AFRs in effect for any month in the 3-month period ending with the first calendar month in which there is a binding contract in writing.[4]

All interest received by the taxpayer is ordinary income.[5] In some cases, depending on the property and amount involved, the interest (or imputed interest) to be paid over the period of the loan must be reported as "original issue discount" that accrues in daily portions; in other cases the interest is allocated among the payments and that much of each payment is treated as interest includable and deductible according to the accounting method of the buyer and seller.

Once interest is segregated, any depreciation is recaptured and recognized as ordinary income in the year of sale to the extent of gain on the sale.[6] In the case of an installment sale of IRC Section 1250 property (i.e., generally, most real estate subject to the allowance for depreciation under IRC Section 167,[7] regulations state that un-recaptured IRC Section 1250 gain (which is generally taxed at a maximum marginal rate of 25%–see Q 1420) must be taken into account *before* any adjusted net capital gain (taxed at a maximum of 15%/5%–see Q 1420).[8] This means that the allocation of unrecaptured IRC Section 1250 gain is front-loaded, *not* prorated over the life of the installment transaction.

For installment sales of IRC Section 1250 property occurring before May 7, 1997, the amount of unrecaptured IRC Section 1250 gain that is taken into account on payments received after May 6, 1997 under the regulations is determined as follows: amounts received after the sale date but before May 7, 1997 are treated as if unrecaptured IRC Section 1250 gain on payments received before May 7, 1997 had been taken into account before adjusted net capital gain.[9] In other words, the taxpayer is permitted to treat payments after May 6, 1997 as though the regulations had already been applied to earlier payments. Also, if the amount of unrecaptured IRC Section 1250 gain on payments received after May 6, 1997 and before August 24, 1999 would have been less under the Internal Revenue Code than the amount as determined under the regulations, the lesser amount may be used to determine the amount of unrecaptured IRC Section 1250 gain that remains to be taken into account.[10]

---

1. Rev. Rul. 2007-4, 2007-4 IRB ___; IRC Sec. 1274A.
2. IRC Sec. 483(e)(3).
3. IRC Sec. 1274(e).
4. IRC Sec. 1274(d)(2)(B).
5. Treas. Reg. §1.483-1.
6. IRC Sec. 453(i).
7. See IRC Sec. 1250(c).
8. Treas. Reg. §1.453-12(a).
9. Treas. Reg. §1.453-12(b).
10. Treas. Reg. §1.453-12(c).

Once depreciation has been recaptured, any adjusted net capital gain (see Q 1420) is allocated to each payment by determining a profit percentage (ratio of total profit to be realized to total selling price, exclusive of interest and any recaptured depreciation) that is applied to the noninterest portion of each installment.[1] Thus, if the selling price (the principal amount or imputed principal amount) was $10,000 and the total profit to be realized after depreciation has been recaptured is $2,000, 20% ($2,000/$10,000) of each dollar collected (after segregating interest) is gain that must be reported as income for that taxable year. Whether the gain is adjusted net capital gain or ordinary income is determined by the type of asset sold and the length of the holding period.

In determining the ratio, selling price may have to be adjusted for outstanding indebtedness on the property.[2]

Sales Between Related Parties

There are strict rules governing installment reporting of sales between "related" parties. Except as noted below, "related" persons include the following: (1) members of the same family (i.e., brothers, sisters, spouses, ancestors and lineal descendants); (2) an individual and a corporation of which the individual actually or constructively owns more than 50% of the stock; (3) a grantor and a fiduciary of a trust; (4) fiduciaries of two trusts if the same person is the grantor of both; (5) a fiduciary and a beneficiary of the same trust; (6) a fiduciary of a trust and a beneficiary of another trust set up by the same grantor; (7) a fiduciary of a trust and a corporation of which the grantor of the trust actually or constructively owns more than 50% of the stock; (8) a person and an IRC Section 501 tax-exempt organization controlled by the person or members of his family (as described in (1) above); (9) a corporation and a partnership if the same person actually or constructively owns more than 50% of the stock of the corporation, and has more than a 50% interest in the partnership; (10) two S corporations if the same persons actually or constructively own more than 50% of the stock of each; (11) an S corporation and a C corporation, if the same persons actually or constructively own more than 50% of the stock of each; or (12) generally, an executor and a beneficiary of an estate.[3]

For purposes of determining the ownership of stock, an individual is considered to own stock owned by family members (brothers and sisters, spouse, ancestors and lineal descendants), and stock owned by a corporation, partnership, estate, or trust in proportion to the interest in the entity owned by the individual or a family member, or a partner owning stock in the same corporation in which the individual owns stock.[4] A different definition of "related" generally applies to sales made before October 24, 1986. A different definition of "related" also applies in the case of sales of depreciable property, as explained below.[5]

If a related purchaser disposes of the property before the related seller has received the entire selling price, a special "second disposition" rule applies. This rule provides that the amount realized on the second disposition, (to the extent it exceeds payments already received by the related seller) will be treated as though it had been received by the related seller *on the date of the second disposition*. However, this rule generally does not apply if: the second disposition occurs more than two years after the first disposi-

---

1. See IRC Sec. 453(c).
2. Temp. Treas. Reg. §15A.453-1. See, however, *Professional Equities, Inc. v. Comm.*, 89 TC 165 (1987).
3. IRC Secs. 453(f)(1), 318(a), 267(b).
4. IRC Secs. 453(f)(1), 318(a), 267(c).
5. See IRC Sec. 453(g).

tion; the second disposition is an involuntary conversion, the threat of which did not exist at the time of the first disposition; the second disposition occurs after the death of either of the related parties; or neither disposition had as one of its principal purposes the avoidance of income tax.[1] If an installment sale between related parties is canceled or payment is forgiven, the *seller* must recognize gain in an amount equal to the difference between the fair market value of the obligation on the date of cancellation (but in no event less than the face amount of the obligation) and the seller's basis in the obligation.[2] The Service ruled that no disposition occurred on the substitution of new installment notes, without any other changes, because there was no evidence that the rights accruing to the sellers under the installment sale had either disappeared or been materially altered.[3]

A sale of depreciable property between related parties may *not* be reported on the installment method, unless it is shown that avoidance of income tax was not a principal purpose. For purposes of this rule only, "related persons" refers generally to controlled business entities, not natural persons related by family.[4]

Interest Surcharge

Generally, an interest surcharge is applied to installment obligations in which deferred payments for sales during the taxable year exceed $5,000,000. Exceptions to this rule are provided for: (1) property used or produced in the trade or business of farming, (2) timeshares and residential lots, and (3) personal use property.[5]

The amount of the interest surcharge is determined by multiplying the "applicable percentage" of the deferred tax liability by the underpayment rate in effect at the end of the taxable year. The "applicable percentage" is determined by dividing the portion of the aggregate obligations for the year that exceeds $5,000,000 by the aggregate face amount of such obligations that are outstanding at the end of the taxable year. If an obligation remains outstanding in subsequent taxable years, interest must be paid using the same percentage rate as in the year of the sale.[6] In addition, if the installment obligation is pledged as security for a loan, the net proceeds of the loan will be treated as a payment received on the installment obligation (up to the total contract price); however, no additional gain is recognized on subsequent payments of such amounts already treated as received. The date of such constructive payment will be (a) the date the proceeds are received *or* (b) the date the indebtedness is secured, whichever is later.[7]

Planning Point: This interest surcharge on installment sales with deferred payments can be minimized in some cases by splitting the sale between a husband and wife, and. in two taxable years. For example, a $20 million business owned by a couple could be split into two $10 million sales, and the transaction could be completed in two stages: $5 million per spouse in December, followed by $5 million per spouse in January. Structured this way, the sale would not trigger the interest surcharge. *Robert S. Keebler, CPA, MST, Virchow, Krause & Company, LLP, Green Bay, Wisconsin.*

---

1. IRC Sec. 453(e).
2. IRC Sec. 453B(f).
3. FSA 200125073.
4. IRC Sec. 453(g).
5. IRC Sec. 453A(b).
6. IRC Sec. 453A(c).
7. IRC Sec. 453A(d)(1). See Revenue Act of 1987 Conf. Rept., at pages 22-23.

1409. What is the applicable federal rate?

The applicable federal rate (AFR) is used in determining the amount of interest in the case of certain below market loans for both income and gift tax purposes (see Q 1407, Q 1518), in imputing interest on debt instruments given on the sale or exchange of property (see Q 1236, Q 1408), and for determining interest and present values in connection with deferred payments for the use of property or services (see Q 1230).

The applicable federal rates are determined by the Secretary on a monthly basis (and published in a revenue ruling). The rates—short-term, mid-term and long-term—are based on the average market yield on the outstanding marketable obligations of the United States with maturity periods of three years or less, more than three but not more than nine years, and over nine years.[1] The AFRs for each month are published in *TaxFacts News* and Section 57 of the *ASRS*, both National Underwriter publications, as the rates become available. The AFRs can also be found at: www.nationalunderwriter. com/taxfactsfx/.

In the case of any sale or exchange, the applicable federal rate will be the lowest 3-month rate. The lowest 3-month rate is the lowest of the AFRs in effect for any month in the 3-month period ending with the first calendar month in which there is a binding contract in writing.[2]

The Secretary may by regulation permit a rate that is lower than the applicable federal rate to be used under certain circumstances.[3]

To determine the appropriate AFR to apply in the case of below-market loans, see Q 1407 and Q 1518. To determine the appropriate AFR in the case of deferred rent, see Q 1230.

1410. Are Social Security and railroad retirement benefits taxable?

If a taxpayer's modified adjusted gross income plus one-half of the Social Security benefits (including tier I railroad retirement benefits) received during the taxable year *exceeds* certain base amounts, then a portion of the benefits received must be included in gross income and taxed as ordinary income. "Modified adjusted gross income" is a taxpayer's adjusted gross income (disregarding the foreign income, savings bond, adoption assistance program exclusions, the deductions for education loan interest and for qualified tuition and related expenses) *plus* any tax-exempt interest income received or accrued during the taxable year.[4]

A taxpayer whose modified adjusted gross income plus one-half of his Social Security benefits exceed a base amount is required to include in gross income the *lesser* of (a) 50% of the excess of such combined income over the base amount, *or* (b) 50% of the Social Security benefits received during the taxable year.[5] The "base amount" is $32,000 for married taxpayers filing jointly, $25,000 for unmarried taxpayers, and zero ($0) for married taxpayers filing separately who have not lived apart for the entire taxable year.[6]

---

1. IRC Sec. 1274(d)(1).
2. IRC Sec. 1274(d)(2).
3. See IRC Sec. 1274(d)(1)(D).
4. IRC Sec. 86(b)(2).
5. IRC Sec. 86(a)(1).
6. IRC Sec. 86(c)(1).

In a case of first impression, the Tax Court held that for purposes of IRC Section 86(c)(1)(C)(ii), the term "live apart" means living in separate residences. Thus, where the taxpayer lived in the same residence as his spouse for at least 30 days during the tax year in question (even though maintaining separate bedrooms), the Tax Court ruled that he did not "live apart" from his spouse at all times during the year; therefore, the taxpayer's base amount was zero.[1]

In addition to the initial tier of taxation as discussed above, a percentage of Social Security benefits that exceed an adjusted base amount will be includable in a taxpayer's gross income. The "adjusted base amount" is $44,000 for married taxpayers filing jointly, $34,000 for unmarried taxpayers, and zero ($0) for married individuals filing separately who did not live apart for the entire taxable year.[2] If a taxpayer's modified adjusted gross income plus one-half of his Social Security benefits exceed the adjusted base amount, his gross income will include the *lesser* of (a) 85% of the Social Security benefits received during the year, *or* (b) the sum of − (i) 85% of the excess over the adjusted base amount, plus (ii) the smaller of − (A) the amount that is includable under the initial tier of taxation (see above), or (B) $4,500 (single taxpayers) or $6,000 (married taxpayers filing jointly).[3]

> *Example 1.* A married couple files a joint return. During the taxable year, they received $12,000 in Social Security benefits and had a modified adjusted gross income of $35,000 ($28,000 plus $7,000 of tax-exempt interest income). Their modified adjusted gross income plus one-half of their Social Security benefits [$35,000 + (½ of $12,000) = $41,000] is greater than the applicable *base amount* of $32,000 but less than the applicable *adjusted base amount* of $44,000; therefore, $4,500 [the lesser of one-half of their benefits ($6,000) or one-half of the excess of $41,000 over the base amount (½ × ($41,000 - $32,000), or $4,500)] is included in gross income.

> *Example 2.* During the taxable year, a single individual had a modified adjusted gross income of $33,000 and received $8,000 in Social Security benefits. His modified adjusted gross income plus one-half of his Social Security benefits [$33,000 + (½ of $8,000) = $37,000] is greater than the applicable *adjusted base amount* of $34,000. Thus, $6,550 [the lesser of 85% of his benefits ($6,800), or 85% of the excess of $37,000 over the adjusted base amount (85% × ($37,000 - $34,000), or $2,550) plus the lesser of $4,000 (the amount includable under the initial tier of taxation) or $4,500] is included in gross income.

An election is available that permits a taxpayer to treat a lump sum payment of benefits as received in the year to which the benefits are attributable.[4]

Any workers' compensation pay that reduced the amount of Social Security received and any amounts withheld to pay Medicare insurance premiums are included in the figure for Social Security benefits.[5] In *Green v. Comm.*,[6] the taxpayer argued that his Social Security disability benefits were excludable from gross income[7] because they had been paid in lieu of workmens' compensation. The Tax Court determined, however, that Title II of the Social Security Act is *not* in the nature of a workmens' compensation act. Instead, the Act allows for disability payments to individuals regardless of employment. Consequently, the taxpayer's Social Security disability benefits were includable in gross income.

---

1. *McAdams v. Comm.*, 118 TC 373 (2002).
2. IRC Sec. 86(c)(2).
3. IRC Sec. 86(a)(2).
4. IRC Sec. 86(e).
5. Rev. Rul. 84-173, 1984-2 CB 16.
6. TC Memo 2006-39.
7. Under IRC Section 104(a)(1).

In a case of first impression, the Tax Court held that a taxpayer's Social Security disability insurance benefits (payable as a result of the taxpayer's disability due to lung cancer that resulted from exposure to Agent Orange during his Vietnam combat service) were includable in gross income under IRC Section 86 and were not excludable under IRC Section 104(a)(4). The court reasoned that Social Security disability insurance benefits do not take into consideration the nature or cause of the individual's disability. Furthermore, the Social Security Act does not consider whether the disability arose from service in the Armed Forces or was attributable to combat-related injuries. Eligibility for purposes of Social Security disability benefits is determined on the basis of the individual's prior work record, not on the cause of his disability. Moreover, the amount of Social Security disability payments is computed under a formula that does not consider the nature or extent of the injury. Consequently, because the taxpayer's Social Security disability insurance benefits were not paid for personal injury or sickness in military service within the meaning of IRC Section 104(a)(4), the benefits were not eligible for exclusion under IRC Section 104(a)(4).[1]

Tax-exempt interest is included in the calculation made to determine whether Social Security payments are includable in gross income.[2] It has been determined that although this provision may result in indirect taxation of tax-exempt interest, it is not unconstitutional.[3]

Railroad retirement benefits (other than tier I benefits) are taxed like benefits received under a qualified pension or profit sharing plan. For this purpose, the tier II portion of the taxes imposed on employees and employee representatives is treated as an employee contribution, while the tier II portion of the taxes imposed on employers is treated as an employer contribution.[4] Legislation enacted in 2001 provides increased benefits for surviving spouses and adjustments to the tier II tax rates.[5]

1411. How is unearned income of a child treated for federal income tax purposes?

Property Given Under The Uniform Gifts to Minors Act Or The Uniform Transfers To Minors Act

Taxable income derived from custodial property is, ordinarily, taxed to the minor donee. To the extent that the custodian uses custodial income to discharge the legal obligation of any person to support or maintain the minor, such income is taxable to that person.[6] For this purpose, it makes no difference who is the custodian or who is the donor. State laws differ as to what constitutes a parent's obligation to support. A person who may be claimed as a dependent by another may use a standard deduction of $850 in 2007 to offset unearned income (or, if higher, the dependent may take a standard deduction in the amount of the sum of $300 and his *earned* income, up to a total of $5,350 in 2007, as indexed for inflation—see Q 1431). Dependents for whom another taxpayer is allowed a personal exemption cannot take a personal exemption for themselves (see Q

---

1. *Reimels v. Comm.*, 123 TC 245 (2004), *aff'd*, 436 F.3d 344 (2d Cir. 2006); *Haar v. Comm.*, 78 TC 864, 866 (1982), *aff'd*, 709 F.2d 1206 (8th Cir. 1983), *followed*.
2. IRC Sec. 86(b)(2)(B).
3. *Goldin v. Baker*, 809 F.2d 187 (2nd Cir. 1987), *cert. denied*, 484 U.S. 816 (1988).
4. See IRC Sec. 72(r)(1).
5. See Secs. 101 and 204, The Railroad Retirement and Survivors' Improvement Act of 2001.
6. IRC Sec. 61; Rev. Rul. 56-484, 1956-2 CB 23; Rev. Rul. 59-357, 1959-2 CB 212.

1425). The *unearned* income of most children under age 18 (previously age 14) above a threshold amount is taxable to the children at their parents' marginal rate.

Unearned Income of Children under Age 18

Editor's Note: JGTRRA 2003 lowered income tax rates to 25%, 28%, 33%, and 35% for tax years beginning after December 31, 2002. For taxpayers in the 10% and 15% income tax brackets, the tax rate on qualifying dividends and capital gains is reduced from 10% to 5% in 2003 through 2007, and all the way down to 0% in 2008 through 2010. For the sunset (i.e., expiration) dates of these provisions, see Q 1432.

Children under the age of 18 (previously age 14) must pay tax on their unearned income above a certain amount at their parents' marginal rate.[1] The tax applies to all unearned income, regardless of when the assets producing the income were transferred to the child.

The so-called "kiddie tax" applies to children who have not attained the age of 18 (previously age 14) before the close of the taxable year, who have at least one parent alive at the close of the taxable year, and who have over $1,700 (in 2007) of unearned income.[2] The tax is the greater of (A) the tax the child would pay at his own tax rate (i.e., in the absence of IRC Sec. 1(g)), or (B) the sum of (1) the tax he would pay on net unearned income at the parent's top rate, plus (2) the tax he would pay on all other income (other than "net unearned income") at his own rate.[3]

The tax applies only to "net unearned income." "Net unearned income" is defined as adjusted gross income that is not attributable to earned income, and that exceeds (1) the $850 standard deduction for a dependent child, *plus* (2) the greater of $850 or (if the child itemizes) the amount of allowable itemized deductions that are directly connected with the production of his unearned income.[4]

"Earned income," essentially, means all compensation for personal services actually rendered.[5] A child is therefore taxed at his own rate on reasonable compensation for services.

Regulations specify that "unearned income" includes any Social Security or pension payments received by the child, income resulting from a gift under the Uniform Gift to Minors Act, and interest on both earned and unearned income.[6] In the case of a trust, distributable net income that is includable in the child's net income can trigger the tax; however, most accumulation distributions received by a child from a trust will not be included in the child's gross income because of the minority exception under IRC Section 665(b).[7] Generally, the tax on accumulation distributions does not apply to domestic trusts (see Q 1449). The source of the assets that produce unearned income need not be the child's parents.[8] The application of the "kiddie tax" to funds provided to a child by sources other than the child's parents was held constitutional.[9]

---

1. IRC Sec. 1(g).
2. IRC Sec. 1(g)(2), as amended by TIPRA 2005.
3. IRC Sec. 1(g)(1).
4. IRC Sec. 1(g)(4); Rev. Proc. 2006-53, 2006-48 IRB 996.
5. IRC Secs. 911(d)(2), 1(g)(4)(A)(i).
6. Temp. Treas. Reg. §1.1(i)-1T, A-8, A-9, A-15.
7. Temp. Treas. Reg. §1.1(i)-1T, A-16.
8. Temp. Treas. Reg. §1.1(i)-1T, A-8.
9. See *Butler v. U.S.*, 798 F. Supp. 574 (E.D. Mo. 1992).

Example: Cole is a child who is under 18 years of age at the end of the taxable year beginning on January 1, 2007. Both of Cole's parents are alive at the end of the taxable year. During 2007, Cole receives $2,400 in interest from his bank account and $1,700 from a paper route. Some of the interest earned by Cole from the bank account is attributable to Cole's paper route earnings that were deposited in the account. The balance of the account is attributable to cash gifts from Cole's parents and grandparents and interest earned prior to 2007. Some cash gifts were received by Cole prior to 2007. Cole has no itemized deductions and is eligible to be claimed as a dependent on his parent's return. Therefore, for the taxable year 2007, Cole's standard deduction is $2,000, the amount of Cole's earned income, plus $300. Of this standard deduction amount, $850 is allocated against unearned income, and $1,150 is allocated against earned income. Cole's taxable unearned income is $1,550, of which $850 is taxed without regard to section 1(g). The remaining taxable unearned income of $700 is net unearned income and is taxed under section 1(g). The fact that some of Cole's unearned income is attributable to interest on principal created by earned income and gifts from persons other than Cole's parents or that some of the unearned income is attributable to property transferred to Cole prior to 2007, will not affect the tax treatment of this income under section 1(g).

The parent whose taxable income is taken into account is (a) in the case of parents who are not married, the custodial parent of the child (determined by using the support test for the dependency exemption) and (b) in the case of married individuals filing separately, the individual with the greater taxable income.[1] If the custodial parent files a joint return with a spouse who is not a parent of the child, the total joint income is applicable in determining the child's rate. "Child," for purposes of the kiddie tax, includes children who are adopted, related by the half-blood, or from a prior marriage of either spouse.[2]

If there is an adjustment to the parent's tax, the child's resulting liability must also be recomputed. In the event of an underpayment, interest, but not penalties, will be assessed against the child.[3]

In the event that a child does not have access to needed information contained in the tax return of a parent, he (or his legal representative) may, by written request to the IRS, obtain such information from the parent's tax return as is needed to file an accurate return.[4] The IRS has stated that where the necessary parental information cannot be obtained before the due date of the child's return, no penalties will be assessed with respect to any reasonable estimate of the parent's taxable income or filing status, or of the net investment income of the siblings.[5]

Certain parents may elect to include their child's unearned income over $1,700 on their own return, thus avoiding the necessity of the child filing a return. The election is available to parents whose child has gross income of more than $850 and less than $8,500 (in 2007), all of which is from interest and dividends.[6]

The election will not be available if there has been backup withholding under the child's Social Security number or if estimated tax payments have been made in the name and Social Security number of the child. If the election is made, any gross income of the child in excess of $1,700 in 2007 is included in the parent's gross income for the taxable year. (However, the inclusion of the child's income will increase the parent's adjusted gross income for purposes of certain other calculations, such as the 2% floor on

1. Temp. Treas. Reg. §1.1(i)-1T, A-11, A-12.
2. Temp. Treas. Reg. §1.1(i)-1T, A-13, A-14.
3. Temp. Treas. Reg. §1.1(i)-1T, A-17, A-19.
4. Temp. Treas. Reg. §1.1(i)-1T, A-22.
5. Ann. 88-70, 1988-16 IRB 37.
6. IRC Sec. 1(g)(7); Rev. Proc. 2006-53, above.

miscellaneous itemized deductions and the limitation on medical expenses.) Any interest that is an item of tax preference of the child (e.g., private activity bonds) will be treated as a tax preference of the parent. For each child to whom the election applies, there is also a tax of 10% of the lesser of $850 or the excess of the gross income of such child over $850. If the election is made, the child will be treated as having no gross income for the year.[1] The threshold and ceiling amounts for the availability of this election, the amount used in computing the child's alternative minimum tax, and a threshold amount used in computing the amount of tax are indexed for inflation.

For treatment of the unearned income of minor children under the alternative minimum tax, see Q 1440.

1412. What is an Education Savings Account?

Education IRAs were renamed Coverdell Education Savings Accounts (ESAs) in 2001.[2] An ESA means a trust or custodial account created exclusively for the purpose of paying the "qualified education expenses" of the designated beneficiary of the trust, and that is designated as an ESA at the time it is created.[3] The designated beneficiary of an ESA must be a life-in-being as of the time the account is established.[4] ESAs are exempt from taxation (except for unrelated business income tax, if applicable).[5] Distributions from ESAs for "qualified education expenses" are not includable in income and contributions to ESAs are not deductible.[6]

Annual contributions may be made up until the due date (excluding extensions) for filing the tax return for the calendar year for which such contributions were intended.[7]

Contributions must be made in cash and must be made on or before the date on which the beneficiary attains age 18 unless the beneficiary is a special needs beneficiary. A special needs beneficiary is to be defined in Treasury regulations; however, according to the Conference Report, a special needs beneficiary will include an individual who because of a physical, mental, or emotional condition (including learning disabilities) requires additional time to complete his or her education.[8]

In general, aggregate contributions to an ESA on behalf of a beneficiary (except in the case of rollover contributions) cannot exceed $2,000.[9] The maximum contribution amount is phased-out for certain high-income contributors. The maximum contribution for single filers is reduced by the amount that bears the same ratio to such maximum amount as the contributor's *modified adjusted gross income* (MAGI) in excess of $95,000 bears to $15,000.[10] For joint filers, the maximum contribution is reduced by the amount that bears the same ratio to such maximum amount as the contributor's *modified adjusted gross income* (MAGI) in excess of $190,000 bears to $30,000.[11] For this purpose, MAGI

1. IRC Sec. 1(g)(7)(B).
2. P.L. 107-22 (7-26-2001).
3. IRC Secs. 530(b), 530(g).
4. IRC Sec. 530(b)(1).
5. IRC Sec. 530(a).
6. IRC Sec. 530(d).
7. IRC Sec. 530(b)(5).
8. IRC Sec. 530(b)(1).
9. IRC Sec. 530(b)(1)(A)(iii).
10. IRC Sec. 530(c)(1).
11. IRC Sec. 530(c)(1).

is adjusted gross income without regard to the exclusions for income derived from certain foreign sources or sources within United States possessions.[1] For taxable years beginning after 2001, contributions to an ESA are not limited due to contributions made to a qualified state tuition program in the same year.

Contributions in excess of the maximum annual contribution (as reduced for high-income contributors) that are not returned before the first day of the sixth month of the taxable year following the taxable year in which the contribution was made are subject to the 6% excess contribution excise tax under Code section 4973(a).[2] Note that any excess contributions from previous taxable years, to the extent not corrected, will continue to be taxed as excess contributions in subsequent taxable years.[3]

A distribution from an ESA is subject to income tax using the IRC Section 72(b) exclusion ratio for investment in the contract.[4] However, distributions from an ESA are excludable from income tax if the distributions received during the year are used solely for the "qualified education expenses" of the designated beneficiary.[5]

Qualified education expenses include both "qualified *higher* education expenses" and "qualified *elementary* and *secondary* education expenses."[6] Qualified higher education expenses include tuition, fees, costs for books, supplies, and equipment required for the enrollment or attendance of the student at any "eligible educational institution," and amounts contributed to a qualified tuition program.[7] Room and board (up to a certain amount) is also included if the student is enrolled at least half-time.[8] An "eligible educational institution" is any college, university, vocational school, or other postsecondary educational institution described in section 481 of the Higher Education Act of 1965.[9] Thus, virtually all accredited public, nonprofit, and proprietary postsecondary institutions are considered eligible educational institutions.[10]

Qualified education expenses must be reduced by any scholarships received by the individual, any educational assistance provided to the individual, or any payment for such expenses (other than a gift, devise, bequest, or inheritance) that is excludable from gross income. These expenses must also be reduced by the amount of any such expenses that were taken into account in determining the Hope Scholarship Credit or the Lifetime Learning Credit.[11] (Note that for taxable years beginning before 2002 these education credits could not be claimed in a taxable year in which distributions from an ESA were excluded from income.[12])

Qualified elementary and secondary education expenses include tuition, fees, and costs for academic tutoring, special needs services, books, supplies, and other equipment that are incurred in connection with the enrollment or attendance of the designated beneficiary at any public, private, or religious school that provides elementary or secondary

---

1. IRC Sec. 530(c)(2).
2. IRC Sec. 4973(e)(2).
3. IRC Sec. 4973(e).
4. IRC Sec. 530(d)(1).
5. IRC Sec. 530(d)(2)(A).
6. IRC Sec. 530(b)(2).
7. IRC Secs. 529(e)(3), 530(b)(2).
8. IRC Sec. 530(b)(2).
9. See IRC Sec. 529(e)(5).
10. Notice 97-60, 1997-2 CB 310, at 16 (Sec. 3, A16).
11. IRC Sec. 530(d)(2)(C).
12. IRC Sec. 25A(e)(2), prior to amendment by EGTRRA 2001.

education (K through 12) as determined under state law. Also included are expenses for room and board, uniforms, transportation, supplementary items and services (including extended day programs) that are required or provided by such schools, and any computer technology or certain related equipment used by the beneficiary and the beneficiary's family during any of the years the beneficiary is in school.[1]

If a designated beneficiary receives distributions from both an ESA and a qualified tuition program and the aggregate distributions exceed the "qualified education expenses" of the designated beneficiary, then the expenses must be allocated among such distributions for purposes of determining the amount excludable under each.[2] Any "qualified education expenses" taken into account for purposes of this exclusion may not be taken into account for purposes of any other deductions, credits, or exclusions.[3]

Where distributions from the ESA exceed the "qualified education expenses" of the designated beneficiary for the year, the amount includable is determined by: (1) calculating the amount subject to tax under IRC Section 72(b) (without regard to the following proration); (2) multiplying the amount in (1) by the ratio of "qualified education expenses" to total distributions; and (3) subtracting the amount in (2) from the amount in (1).[4]

If a distribution from an ESA is includable in the income of the recipient, the amount includable in income will be subject to an additional 10% penalty tax unless the distribution is (1) made after the death of the beneficiary of the ESA, (2) attributable to the disability of such beneficiary (within the meaning of IRC Section 72(m)(7)), (3) made in an amount equal to a scholarship, allowance, or other payment under IRC Section 25A(g)(2), or (4) includable in income because expenses were reduced by the amount claimed as a Hope Scholarship Credit or a Lifetime Learning Credit.[5] The penalty tax also does not apply to any distribution of an excess contribution and the earnings thereon if such contribution and earnings are distributed before the first day of the sixth month of the taxable year following the taxable year in which the contribution was made.[6] However, the earnings are includable in the contributor's income for the taxable year in which such excess contribution was made.

No part of the assets of the ESA can be used to purchase life insurance.[7] Nor can the assets of the ESA be commingled with other property except in a common trust fund or common investment fund.[8] If the beneficiary engages in a prohibited transaction, the account loses its status as an ESA and will be treated as distributing all of its assets. If the beneficiary pledges the account as security for a loan, the amount so pledged will be treated as a distribution from the account.[9]

An amount may be rolled over from one ESA to another ESA, without being treated as a distribution (and without being subject to taxation) *only* if the beneficiary of the recipient ESA is the same as the beneficiary of the original ESA, or a member of such beneficiary's family. The new beneficiary must be under age 30 as of the date of such

1. IRC Sec. 530(b)(4).
2. IRC Sec. 530(d)(2)(C)(ii).
3. IRC Sec. 530(d)(2)(D).
4. IRC Sec. 530(d)(2)(B).
5. IRC Sec. 530(d)(4).
6. IRC Sec. 530(d)(4)(C).
7. IRC Sec. 530(b)(1)(C).
8. IRC Sec. 530(b)(1)(D).
9. IRC Sec. 530(e).

distribution or change, except in the case of a special needs beneficiary.[1] The rollover contribution must be made no later than 60 days after the date of the distribution from the original ESA. However, no more than one rollover may be made from an ESA during any 12-month period.[2] Similarly, the beneficiary of an ESA may be changed without taxation or penalty if the new beneficiary is a member of the family of the previous ESA beneficiary and has not attained age 30 or is a special needs beneficiary.[3] Transfer of an individual's interest in an ESA can be made from one spouse to another pursuant to a divorce (or upon the death of a spouse) without changing the character of the ESA.[4] Likewise, non-spouse survivors who acquire an original beneficiary's interest in an ESA upon the death of the beneficiary will be treated as the original beneficiary of the ESA as long as the new beneficiary is a family member of the original beneficiary.[5]

Upon the death of the beneficiary of the ESA, any balance to the credit of the beneficiary must be distributed to his estate within 30 days. The balance remaining in an ESA must also be distributed within 30 days after a beneficiary, other than a special needs beneficiary, reaches age 30.[6] Any balance remaining in the ESA is deemed distributed within 30 days after such events.[7] The earnings on any distribution under this provision are includable in the beneficiary's gross income.[8]

Under Section 225 of BAPCPA 2005, funds placed in an "education individual retirement account" (as defined in IRC Section 530(b)(1)) no later than 365 days before the date of the filing of the bankruptcy petition may be excluded from the bankruptcy estate if certain conditions are met.[9]

For guidance regarding certain reporting requirements and transition rules applicable to Coverdell ESAs, see Notice 2003-53.[10] See Q 1503 for the estate tax treatment and Q 1527 for the gift tax treatment of ESAs.

1413. What is a qualified tuition program?

Editor's note regarding PPA 2006: The qualified tuition program provisions that were scheduled to expire by reason of the EGTRRA sunset provision included: (1) the provision that makes qualified withdrawals from qualified tuition accounts fully exempt from income tax; (2) the repeal of a pre-EGTRRA requirement that there be more than a de minimis penalty imposed on amounts not used for educational purposes, and the imposition of the 10% additional tax on distributions not used for qualified higher education purposes; (3) the provision permitting certain private educational institutions to establish prepaid tuition programs that qualify under IRC Section 529 if they receive a ruling or determination to that effect from the IRS, and if the assets are held in a trust created or organized for the exclusive benefit of designated beneficiaries; (4) certain provisions permitting rollovers from one account to another account; (5) certain rules regarding the treatment of room and board as qualifying expenses; (6) certain rules regarding coordination with Hope Scholarship and Lifetime Learning Credit provi-

---

1. IRC Sec. 530(b)(1).
2. IRC Sec. 530(d)(5).
3. IRC Secs. 530(b)(1), 530(d)(6).
4. IRC Sec. 530(d)(7).
5. IRC Sec. 530(d)(7).
6. IRC Sec. 530(b)(1)(E).
7. IRC Sec. 530(d)(8).
8. IRC Sec. 530(d)(1).
9. 11 USC 541(b), as amended by BAPCPA 2005.
10. 2003-33 IRB 362.

sions; (7) the provision that treats first cousins as members of the family for purposes of the rollover and change in beneficiary rules; and (8) certain provisions regarding the education expenses of special needs beneficiaries. All of the above provisions have been made permanent.[1] The Act also provides that the Secretary shall prescribe such regulations as may be necessary or appropriate to prevent abuse of 529 plans.[2]

A qualified tuition program is a program established and maintained by a state (or agency or instrumentality thereof) *or* by one or more "eligible educational institutions" (see below) that meet certain requirements (see below) *and* under which a person may buy tuition credits or certificates on behalf of a *designated beneficiary* (see below) that entitle the beneficiary to a waiver or payment of *qualified higher education expenses* (see below) of the beneficiary. These plans are often collectively referred to as "529 plans." In the case of a state-sponsored qualified tuition program, a person may make contributions to an account established to fund the qualified higher education expenses of a designated beneficiary.[3] Qualified tuition programs sponsored by "eligible educational institutions" (i.e., private colleges and universities) are *not* permitted to offer savings plans; these institutions may sponsor only pre-paid tuition programs.[4]

To be treated as a qualified tuition program, a state program or privately sponsored program must:

(1)   mandate that contributions and purchases be made in cash only;

(2)   maintain a separate accounting for each designated beneficiary;

(3)   provide that no designated beneficiary or contributor may directly or indirectly direct the investment of contributions or earnings (but see below);

(4)   not allow any interest in the program or portion thereof to be used as security for a loan; *and*

(5)   provide *adequate safeguards* (see below) to prevent contributions on behalf of a designated beneficiary in excess of those necessary to provide for the beneficiary's qualified higher education expenses.[5]

(The former requirement that a qualified state tuition program impose a "more than de minimis penalty" on any refund of earnings not used for certain purposes has been repealed.[6] See "Penalties," in Q 1414.)

With respect to item (3), above, the IRS announced a special rule stating that state-sponsored qualified tuition savings plans may permit parents to change the investment strategy (1) once each calendar year, and (2) whenever the beneficiary designation is changed. According to the IRS, final regulations are expected to provide that in order to qualify under this special rule, the state-sponsored qualified tuition program savings plan must: (1) allow participants to select among only broad-based investment strate-

---

1. Sec. 1304(a), PPA 2006.
2. IRC Sec. 529(f), as added by PPA 2006.
3. IRC Sec. 529(b)(1); Prop. Treas. Reg. §1.529-2(b).
4. IRC Sec. 529(b)(1)(A).
5. IRC Sec. 529(b).
6. IRC Sec. 529(b)(3).

gies designed exclusively by the program; and (2) establish procedures and maintain appropriate records to prevent a change in investment options from occurring more frequently than once per calendar year, or upon a change in the designated beneficiary of the account. According to the IRS, qualified tuition programs and their participants may rely on the 2001 guidance pending the issuance of final regulations under IRC Section 529.[1]

A program established and maintained by one or more "eligible educational institutions" must satisfy two requirements to be treated as a qualified tuition program: (1) the program must have received a ruling or determination that it meets the applicable requirements for a qualified tuition program; *and* (2) the program must provide that assets are held in a "qualified trust."[2] "Eligible educational institution" means an accredited *post-secondary* college or university that offers credit towards a bachelor's degree, associate's degree, graduate-level degree, professional degree, or other recognized post-secondary credential *and* that is eligible to participate in federal student financial aid programs.[3] For these purposes, *qualified trust* is defined as a domestic trust for the exclusive benefit of designated beneficiaries that meets the requirements set forth in the IRA rules, (i.e., a trust maintained by a bank, or other person who demonstrates that it will administer the trust in accordance with the requirements, and where the trust assets will not be commingled with other property, except in a common trust fund or common investment fund).[4]

The term *qualified higher education expenses* means (1) tuition, fees, books, supplies, and equipment required for a designated beneficiary's enrollment or attendance at an eligible educational institution (including certain vocational schools), and (2) expenses for special needs services incurred in connection with enrollment or attendance of a special needs beneficiary.[5] Qualified higher education expenses also include reasonable costs for room and board, within limits. Generally, they may not exceed: (1) the allowance for room and board that was included in the cost of attendance in effect on the date that EGTRRA 2001 was enacted as determined by the school for a particular academic period, or *if greater* (2) the actual invoice amount the student residing in housing owned and operated by the private college or university is charged by such institution for room and board costs for a particular academic period.[6]

A safe harbor provides the definition of what constitutes *adequate safeguards* to prevent contributions in excess of those necessary to meet the beneficiary's qualified higher education expenses. The safe harbor is satisfied if all contributions to the account are prohibited once the account balance reaches a specified limit that is applicable to all accounts of beneficiaries with the same expected year of enrollment.[7] The total of all contributions may not exceed the amount established by actuarial estimates as necessary to pay tuition, required fees, and room and board expenses of the beneficiary for five years of undergraduate enrollment at the highest cost institution allowed by the program.[8]

---

1. Notice 2001-55, 2001-39 IRB 299.
2. IRC Secs. 529(b)(1), 529(e)(5).
3. See Prop. Treas. Reg. §1.529-1(c).
4. IRC Sec. 529(b)(1).
5. IRC Sec. 529(e)(3)(A).
6. IRC Sec. 529(e)(3)(B).
7. Prop. Treas. Reg. §1.529-2(i)(2).
8. Prop. Treas. Reg. §1.529-2(h)(2).

Coordination rules. A taxpayer may claim a Hope Scholarship or Lifetime Learning Credit *and* exclude distributions from a qualified tuition program on behalf of the same student in the same taxable year *if* the distribution is not used to pay the same educational expenses for which the credit was claimed.[1] See Q 1438. An individual is required to *reduce* his total qualified higher education expenses by certain scholarships *and* by the amount of expenses taken into account in determining the Hope or Lifetime Learning credit allowable to the taxpayer (or any other person).[2]

A contribution to a qualified tuition program can be made in the same taxable year as a contribution to a Coverdell Education Savings Account for the benefit of the same designated beneficiary without incurring an excise tax. (See Q 1412.)[3] If the aggregate distributions from a qualified tuition program exceed the total amount of qualified higher education expenses taken into account *after* reduction for the Hope and Lifetime Learning credits, then the expenses must be allocated between the Coverdell Education Savings Account distributions and the qualified tuition program distributions for purposes of determining the amount of the exclusion.[4]

The total amount of qualified tuition and related expenses for the deduction for qualified tuition and related expenses is *reduced* by the amount of such expenses taken into account in determining the exclusion for distributions from qualified tuition programs. For these purposes, the excludable amount under IRC Section 529 does not include that portion of the distribution that represents a return of contributions to the plan.[5]

Reporting. Each officer or employee having control over a qualified tuition program must report to the IRS and to designated beneficiaries with respect to contributions, distributions, and other matters that the IRS may require. The reports must be filed and furnished to the above individuals in the time and manner determined by the IRS.[6] In 2001, the IRS released guidance regarding certain recordkeeping, reporting, and other requirements applicable to qualified tuition programs in light of the amendments to IRC Section 529 under EGTRRA 2001.[7] Qualified tuition programs and their participants may rely on Notice 2001-81 pending the issuance of final regulations under IRC Section 529. (Note that reporting was not required for calendar years before 1999.[8])

As a general rule, a qualified tuition program is exempt from federal income tax, except the tax on unrelated business income of charitable organizations imposed by IRC Section 511.[9]

Under Section 225 of BAPCPA 2005, funds used to purchase a tuition credit or certificate or contributed to an account under a QTP no later than 365 days before the date of the filing of the bankruptcy petition may be excluded from the bankruptcy estate if certain conditions are met.[10]

---

1. See IRC Sec. 529(c)(3)(B)(v).
2. IRC Sec. 529(c)(3)(B)(v).
3. IRC Sec. 4973(e).
4. IRC Sec. 529(c)(3)(B)(vi).
5. IRC Sec. 222(c)(2)(B).
6. IRC Sec. 529(d); Prop. Treas. Reg. §1.529-4.
7. See Notice 2001-81, 2001-52 IRB 617.
8. Notice 97-52, 1997-2 CB 306.
9. IRC Sec. 529(a).
10. 11 USC 541(b), as amended by BAPCPA 2005.

IRC Section 529 generally took effect for taxable years ending after August 20, 1996; special transitional rules applied for earlier programs. See Q 1414 for the tax treatment of distributions from qualified tuition programs. See Q 1504 for the estate tax treatment and Q 1528 for the gift tax treatment of qualified tuition programs.

1414. How are distributions from a qualified tuition program taxed?

Editor's Note: The tax-free treatment for qualified distributions from 529 plans (i.e., withdrawals used to pay qualified higher education expenses) under EGTRRA 2001 has been made permanent. In other words, this tax break will *not* end on December 31, 2010, as originally scheduled under EGTRRA 2001.[1] For the impact of PPA 2006 on other qualified tuition program provisions that were scheduled to expire, see the *Editor's Note* in Q 1413.

Distributions from *state* qualified tuition programs are fully excludable from gross income *if* the distributions are used to pay "qualified higher education expenses" (see Q 1413) of the designated beneficiary.[2] (For the general rule governing nonqualified distributions, see below.) Beginning in 2004, distributions from pre-paid tuition programs sponsored by *private* colleges and universities are also fully excludable from gross income to the extent those distributions are used to pay qualified higher education expenses of the designated beneficiary.[3]

In the case of excess cash distributions, the amount otherwise includable in gross income must be reduced by a proportion that is equal to the ratio of expenses to distributions.[4] In-kind distributions are not includable in gross income so long as they provide a benefit to the distributee which, if paid for by the distributee himself, would constitute payment of a qualified higher education expense.[5]

Nonqualified distributions (i.e., distributions that *not* used to pay "qualified higher education expenses") are includable in the gross income of the distributee under the rules of IRC Section 72 to the extent they are not excludable under some other Code provision.[6] Distributions are treated as representing a pro rata share of the principal (i.e., contributions) and accumulated earnings in the account.[7] For purposes of applying IRC Section 72, the Code provides that (1) all qualified tuition programs of which an individual is a designated beneficiary must generally be treated as one program, (2) all distributions during a taxable year must be treated as one distribution, and the value of the contract, income on the contract, and (3) investment in the contract must be computed as of the close of the calendar year in which the taxable year begins.[8]

The IRS announced in 2001 that the final regulations are expected to provide that only those accounts maintained by a qualified tuition program and having the same account owner and the same designated beneficiary must be aggregated for purposes of computing the earnings portion of any distribution.[9] The IRS also stated that the final regulations are expected to revise the time for determining the earnings portion

---

1. See Sec. 1304, PPA 2006.
2. IRC Sec. 529(c)(3)(B).
3. IRC Sec. 529(c)(3)(B).
4. IRC Sec. 529(c)(3)(B).
5. IRC Sec. 529(c)(3)(B).
6. IRC Sec. 529(c)(3)(A).
7. IRC Sec. 72(e)(9).
8. IRC Sec. 529(c)(3)(D).
9. Notice 2001-81, 2001-2 CB 617.

of any distribution from a qualified tuition account. Specifically, for distributions made after 2002 such programs will be required to determine the earnings portion of each distribution *as of the date of the distribution*. A different effective date applies to direct transfers between qualified tuition programs.[1]

Penalties on nonqualified distributions. For taxable years beginning before 2002, a qualified *state* tuition program was required to impose a "more than de minimis penalty" on any refund of earnings not used for qualified higher education expenses of the beneficiary.[2] See Prop. Treas. Reg. §1.529-2 for the safe harbor definition of "more than de minimis." For taxable years beginning after 2001, the state-imposed penalty is repealed.[3]

In place of that penalty, a 10% additional tax will be imposed on nonqualified distributions in the same manner as the 10% additional tax is imposed on certain distributions from Coverdell Education Savings Accounts (see Q 1412).[4] However, the 10% additional tax will not apply to any payment or distribution in any taxable year before 2004 that is includable in gross income, but used for qualified higher education expenses of the designated beneficiary.[5] According to the Conference Committee Report, this means that the earnings portion of a distribution from a qualified tuition program of a private institution that is made in 2003, and that is used for qualified higher education expenses, is *not* subject to the additional tax even though the earnings portion is includable in gross income.[6] The 10% additional tax also does not apply if the payment or distribution is (1) made to a beneficiary on or after the death of the designated beneficiary, or (2) attributable to the disability of the designated beneficiary.[7]

The IRS has announced that with respect to any distributions made *after* 2001, a qualified tuition program will no longer be required to verify how distributions are used or to collect any penalty, but the program must continue to verify whether the distribution is used for qualified higher education expenses of the beneficiary and to collect a "more than de minimis penalty" on nonqualified distributions made *before* 2002.[8]

Rollovers. Any portion of a distribution that is transferred within 60 days to the credit of a "new designated beneficiary" (see below) who is a "member of the family" (see below) of the designated beneficiary, is not includable in the gross income of the distributee. (In other words, a distribution generally can be "rolled over" within 60 days from one family member to another.)[9] A change in designated beneficiaries with respect to an interest in the same qualified tuition program will not be treated as a distribution provided that the new beneficiary is a member of the family of the old beneficiary.[10] A transfer of credits (or other amounts) for the benefit of the *same* designated beneficiary from one qualified tuition program to another is not considered a distribution; however, only one transfer within a 12-month period can receive such rollover treatment.[11] According to the Conference Committee Report, a program-to-program transfer on

---

1. See Notice 2001-81, 2001-2 CB 617.
2. IRC Sec. 529(b)(3), prior to amendment by EGTRRA 2001.
3. IRC Sec. 529(b)(3).
4. IRC Secs. 529(c)(6), 530(d)(4).
5. IRC Sec. 529(c)(6).
6. H.R. Conf. Rep. No. 107-84.
7. IRC Sec. 530(d)(4)(B).
8. Notice 2001-81, above.
9. See Prop. Treas. Regs. §§1.529-3(a) and (b); Prop. Treas. Reg. §1.529-1(c).
10. IRC Sec. 529(c)(3)(C).
11. IRC Sec. 529(c)(3)(C)(iii).

behalf of the same beneficiary is intended to allow a transfer between a prepaid tuition program and a savings program maintained by the same state, *or* a transfer between a state-sponsored plan and a prepaid private tuition program.[1]

Generally, *member of the family* means an individual's (1) spouse, (2) child or his descendant, (3) stepchild, (4) sibling or step sibling, (5) parents and their ancestors, (6) stepparents, (7) nieces or nephews, (8) aunts and uncles, or (9) in-laws, (10) the spouse of any of the individuals in (2) through (9), and (11) any first cousin of the designated beneficiary.[2] (However, for any contracts issued before August 20, 1996, IRC Section 529(c)(3)(C) will not require that a distribution be transferred to a member of the family or that a change in beneficiaries may be made only to a member of the family.[3]) A *designated beneficiary* is (1) the individual designated at the beginning of participation in the qualified tuition program as the beneficiary of amounts paid (or to be paid) to the program; (2) in the case of a rollover of a distribution or change in beneficiaries within a family (as described above), the new beneficiary; and (3) in the case of an interest in a qualified tuition program that is purchased by a state or local government (or its agency or instrumentality) or certain tax-exempt 501(c)(3) organizations as part of a scholarship program, the individual receiving the interest as a scholarship.[4]

1415. What is "tax basis"?

"Tax basis" is the method the Internal Revenue Code employs to keep a continuous total of an individual's "investment" in a particular item of property so that when the property is sold, or otherwise transferred or disposed of, an accurate assessment of the individual's gain or loss can be made for tax purposes.[5]

When an individual acquires an item of property, he is considered to have also acquired an initial tax basis in that property that, depending on the manner of acquisition, may be (1) its cost, (2) its fair market value as of a specified date, or (3) a substituted tax basis. (Basis is a "substituted basis" when it is determined in whole or in part by reference to the property's basis in the hands of a prior individual, or by reference to other property held at some time by the person for whom the basis is determined.[6] See below as to which of these applies to a given manner of acquisition.) However, during the period of time the individual owns the property his tax basis does not necessarily remain fixed at its initial basis. Instead, it is adjusted during the period of ownership to reflect certain real or artificial additions to, and returns of, the initial "investment." (For example, tax basis is increased for such things as improvements; it is reduced for such things as allowable depreciation or depletion.) When adjusted in this manner, an individual's tax basis at a particular time is often referred to as his "adjusted tax basis."[7]

Property Acquired by Purchase or Exchange

With respect to property purchased or acquired in a taxable exchange on or after March 1, 1913, a taxpayer's basis is cost (the cash he paid for the property or the fair market value of the property he gave for it).[8] If the property was acquired by purchase

---

1. H.R. Conf. Rep. No. 107-84 (EGTRRA 2001).
2. IRC Sec. 529(e)(2); IRC Sec. 152(a).
3. TRA '97, Sec. 211(f)(6).
4. IRC Sec. 529(e)(1).
5. IRC Sec. 1011(a).
6. IRC Sec. 7701(a)(42).
7. IRC Sec. 1016.
8. IRC Sec. 1012.

before March 1, 1913, basis for determining gain is cost, or fair market value as of March 1, 1913, whichever is greater; for determining loss, the basis is cost.

Special rules apply to stock exchanges made pursuant to a plan of corporate reorganization.[1] For the final regulations under IRC Section 358 providing guidance regarding the determination of the basis of stock or securities received in exchange for, or with respect to, stock or securities in certain transactions, see Q 1017. For the rules applicable to stock received in a demutualization, see Q 1017. The Service and the Treasury Department have withdrawn the proposed regulations relating to redemptions of stock in which the redemption proceeds are treated as a dividend distribution.[2]

Property Acquired From a Decedent

Decedent Dying in Year Other Than 2010

Stepped up basis. As a general rule, the basis of property that has been acquired from a decedent is the fair market value of the property at the date of the decedent's death (i.e., the basis is "stepped up" or "stepped down," as the case may be, to the fair market value). This rule applies generally to all property includable in the decedent's gross estate for federal estate tax purposes (whether or not an estate tax return is required to be filed). It applies also to the survivor's one-half of community property where at least one-half of the value of the property was included in the decedent's gross estate. As an exception, however, the rule does not apply to "income in respect of a decedent" (see Q 1430); normally the basis of such income is zero.[3] As another exception, the rule does not apply to appreciated property acquired by the decedent by gift within one year of his death where the one receiving the property from the decedent is the donor or the donor's spouse; in such case the basis of the property in the hands of the donor (or spouse) is the adjusted basis of the property in the hands of the decedent immediately before his death.[4] If an estate tax return is filed and the executor elects the alternative valuation (see Q 1536), the basis is the fair market value on the alternative valuation date instead of its value on the date of death.[5]

If property in the estate of a decedent is transferred to an heir, legatee, devisee, or beneficiary in a transaction that constitutes a sale or exchange, the basis of the property in the hands of the heir, legatee, devisee, or beneficiary is the fair market value on the date of the transfer (not on the date of decedent's death). Likewise, the executor or administrator of the estate will recognize a gain or loss on the transaction. For example, if the executor of the will, to satisfy a bequest of $10,000, transfers to the heir stock worth $10,000, which had a value of $9,000 on the decedent's date of death, the estate recognizes a $1,000 gain, and the basis of the stock to the heir is $10,000.[6]

Jointly held property. Note that the "stepped up" basis rule applies only to property includable in the decedent's gross estate for federal estate tax purposes.[7] Thus, one acquiring property from a decedent who held the property jointly with another (or others) under the general rule of estate tax includability (i.e., the entire value of the property is includable in the estate of the first joint owner to die except to the extent

1. See IRC Sec. 354.
2. See 71 Fed. Reg. 20044 (4-19-2006).
3. IRC Sec. 1014(c).
4. IRC Sec. 1014(e).
5. IRC Sec. 1014(a).
6. Treas. Reg. §1.1014-4(a)(3).
7. IRC Sec. 1014(b)(9).

the surviving joint owner(s) can prove contribution to the cost—see Q 1501) receives a stepped up basis in the property in accordance with that rule. By contrast, one who acquires property from a decedent spouse who with the surviving spouse had a *qualified joint interest* in the property (see Q 1501) receives a stepped up basis equal to one-half the value of that interest.

Community property. The stepped up basis rule applies in the case of community property both to the decedent's one-half interest and to the surviving spouse's one-half interest.[1]

Qualified terminable interest property. Upon the death of the donee spouse or surviving spouse, qualified terminable interest property (see Q 1506) is considered as "acquired from or to have passed from the decedent" for purposes of receiving a new basis at death.[2]

Decedent Dying in 2010

Modified carryover basis. In 2010, along with repeal of the estate tax for one year, a modified carryover basis regime (with limited step-up in basis) replaces the step-up in basis for property acquired from a decedent. That is, the basis of the person acquiring property from a decedent dying in 2010 will generally be equal to the lesser of (1) the adjusted basis of the decedent (i.e., carried over to recipient from decedent), or (2) the fair market value of the property at the date of the decedent's death. However, step-up in basis is retained for up to $1,300,000 of property acquired from a decedent. In the case of certain transfers to a spouse, step-up in basis will be available for an additional $3,000,000 of property acquired from a decedent. In the case of a decedent nonresident who is not a United States citizen, step-up in basis will be available for only $60,000 of property acquired from the decedent.[3]

Property Acquired by Gift

If the property was acquired by gift after 1920, the basis for determining gain is generally the same as in the hands of the donor. However, in the case of property acquired by gift after September 1, 1958 and before 1977, this basis may be increased by the amount of any gift tax paid, but total basis may not exceed the fair market value of the property at the time of gift. In the case of property received by gift after 1976, the donee takes the donor's basis plus a *part* of the gift tax paid. The added fraction is the amount of the gift tax paid that is attributable to appreciation in the value of the gift over the donor's basis. The amount of attributable gift tax bears the same ratio to the amount of gift tax paid as net appreciation bears to the value of the gift.[4]

For the purpose of determining loss, the basis of property acquired by gift after 1920 is the foregoing substituted basis, or the fair market value of the property at the time of gift, whichever is lower.[5] As to property acquired by gift before 1921, basis is the fair market value of the property at time of acquisition.[6]

---

1. IRC Sec. 1014(b)(6).
2. IRC Sec. 1014(b)(10).
3. IRC Secs. 1014(f), 1022.
4. IRC Sec. 1015.
5. IRC Sec. 1015(a).
6. IRC Sec. 1015(c).

Property Acquired in a Generation-Skipping Transfer

Generally, in the case of property received in a generation-skipping transfer (see Q 1510), the transferee takes the adjusted basis of the property immediately before the transfer plus a *part* of the generation-skipping transfer (GST) tax paid. The added fraction is the amount of the GST tax paid that is attributable to appreciation in the value of the transferred property over its previous adjusted basis. The amount of attributable GST tax bears the same ratio to the amount of GST tax paid as net appreciation bears to the value of the property transferred. Nevertheless, basis is not to be increased above fair market value. When property is acquired by gift in a generation-skipping transfer, the basis of the property is increased by the gift tax basis adjustment (see above) before the generation-skipping transfer tax basis adjustment is made.[1]

However, where property is transferred in a taxable termination (see Q 1510) that occurs at the same time and as a result of the death of an individual, the basis of such property is increased (or decreased) to fair market value, except that any increase (or decrease) in basis is limited by multiplying such increase (or decrease) by the inclusion ratio used in allocating the generation-skipping tax exemption (see Q 1511).[2]

Property Acquired From a Spouse or Incident to Divorce

Where property is transferred between spouses, or former spouses incident to a divorce, after July 18, 1984 pursuant to an instrument in effect after that date, the transferee's basis in the property is generally the adjusted basis of the property in the hands of the transferor immediately before the transfer and no gain or loss is recognized at the time of transfer (unless, under certain circumstances, the property is transferred in trust).[3] These rules may apply to transfers made after 1983 if both parties elect.[4] See Q 1447 regarding transfers incident to divorce.

1416. What is a "capital asset"?

For tax purposes, a "capital asset" is any property that, in the hands of the taxpayer, is not: (1) property (including inventory and stock in trade) held primarily for sale to customers; (2) real or depreciable property used in his trade or business; (3) copyrights and literary, musical, or artistic compositions (or similar properties) created by the taxpayer, or merely owned by him, if his tax basis in the property is determined (other than by reason of IRC Section 1022, which governs the basis determination of inherited property) by reference to the creator's tax basis; (4) letters, memoranda, and similar properties produced by or for the taxpayer, or merely owned by him, if his tax basis is determined by reference to the tax basis of such producer or recipient; (5) accounts or notes receivable acquired in his trade or business for services rendered or sales of property described in (1), above; (6) certain publications of the United States government; (7) any commodities derivative financial instrument held by a commodities derivatives dealer; (8) any hedging instrument that is clearly identified as such by the required time; and (9) supplies of a type regularly used or consumed by the taxpayer in the ordinary course of his trade or business.[5]

---

1. IRC Sec. 2654(a)(1).
2. IRC Sec. 2654(a)(2).
3. IRC Secs. 453B(g), 1041; Temp. Treas. Reg. §1.1041-1T, A-1.
4. Temp. Treas. Reg. §1.1041-1T, A-16.
5. IRC Sec. 1221; Treas. Reg. §1.1221-1.

Generally, any property held as an investment is a capital asset, except that rental real estate is generally not a capital asset because it is treated as a trade or business asset (see Q 1220).[1]

1417. When is capital gain or loss short-term? When is it long-term? How is an individual's "holding period" calculated?

Generally, a capital gain or loss is long-term if the property giving rise to the gain or loss was owned *for more than one year*; it is short-term if the property was owned for *one year or less*.[2] For an explanation of the tax treatment of capital gains and losses, see Q 1420.

To determine how long a taxpayer has owned property (i.e., his "holding period"), begin counting on the day *after* the property is acquired; the same date in each successive month is the first day of a new month. The date on which the property is disposed of is included (i.e., counted) in the holding period.[3] If property is acquired on the last day of the month, the holding period begins on the first day of the following month. Therefore, if it is sold prior to the first day of the 13th month following the acquisition, the gain or loss will be short-term.[4] According to IRS Pub. 544 (Nov. 1982), if property is acquired *near* the end of the month and the holding period begins on a date that does not occur in every month (e.g., the 29th, 30th, or 31st), the last day of each month that lacks that date is considered to begin a new month; however, later editions of Pub. 544 have omitted this statement.

> *Example 1.* Mrs. Copeland bought a capital asset on January 1, 2007. She would begin counting on January 2, 2007. The 2nd day of each successive month would begin a new month. If Mrs. Copeland sold the asset on January 1, 2008, her holding period would not be more than one year. To have a long-term capital gain or loss she would have to sell the asset on or after January 2, 2008.

> *Example 2.* Mrs. Brim bought a capital asset on January 30, 2007. She would begin counting on January 31, 2007. Since February does not have 31 days, Mrs. Brim will start a new month on February 28. In months that have only 30 days, the 30th will begin a new month.

Special rules apply in the case of gains or losses on regulated futures contracts, single stock futures (see Q 1073), nonequity option contracts, and foreign currency contracts (see Q 1076). Furthermore, the short sale rules (see Q 1022) and tax straddle rules (see Q 1077 to Q 1084) may require a tolling or recalculation of an individual's holding period.

Tacking of Holding Periods

In some cases, the IRC allows a taxpayer to add another individual's holding period in the same property, or the taxpayer's holding period in other property, to the taxpayer's holding period. This is referred to as "tacking" of holding periods.[5]

For an explanation of how the holding period is determined for stock received by a policyholder or annuity holder in a demutualization transaction, see SCA 200131028.

---

1. See IRS Pub. 544.
2. IRC Sec. 1222.
3. Rev. Rul. 70-598, 1970-2 CB 168.
4. Rev. Rul. 66-7, 1966-1 CB 188.
5. IRC Sec. 1223(2).

Where applicable, tacking of holding periods is discussed in the appropriate answer.

1418. How are securities that are sold or transferred identified for tax purposes?

When an individual sells or otherwise transfers securities (i.e., stocks, bonds, mutual fund shares, etc.) from holdings that were purchased or acquired on different dates or at different prices (or tax bases), he must generally be able to identify the lot from which the transferred securities originated in order to determine his tax basis and holding period. If he is unable to adequately identify the lot, he will usually be deemed to have transferred the securities in the order in which they were acquired, by a "first-in, first-out" (FIFO) method.[1] However, in cases involving mutual fund shares he may be permitted to use an "average basis" method to determine his tax basis and holding period in the securities transferred (see Q 1171).

Generally, identification is determined by the certificate delivered to the buyer or other transferee. The security represented by the certificate is deemed to be the security sold or transferred. This is true even if the taxpayer intended to sell securities from another lot, or instructed his broker to sell securities from another lot.[2]

There are several exceptions to the general rule of adequate identification. One occurs when the securities are left in the custody of a broker or other agent. If the seller specifies to the broker which securities to sell or transfer, and if the broker or agent sends a written confirmation of the specified securities within a reasonable time, then the specified securities are the securities sold or transferred, even though different certificates are delivered to the buyer or other transferee.[3] If the securities held are United States securities (Treasury bonds, notes, etc.) recorded by a book-entry on the books of a Federal Reserve Bank, then identification is made when the taxpayer notifies the Reserve Bank (or the person through whom the taxpayer is selling the securities) of the lot number (assigned by the *taxpayer*) of the securities to be sold or transferred, and when the Reserve Bank (or the person through whom the taxpayer sells the securities) provides the taxpayer with a written advice of transaction, specifying the amount and description of securities sold or transferred.[4]

Another exception arises when the taxpayer holds a single certificate representing securities from different lots. If the taxpayer sells part of the securities represented by the certificate through a broker, adequate identification is made if the taxpayer specifies to the broker which securities to sell, and if the broker sends a written confirmation of the specified securities within a reasonable time. If the taxpayer sells the securities himself, then there is adequate identification if he keeps a written record identifying the particular securities he intended to sell.[5]

A third exception occurs when the securities are held by a trustee, or by an executor or administrator of an estate. An adequate identification is made if the trustee, executor, or administrator specifies in writing in the books or records of the trust or estate the securities to be sold, transferred or distributed. (In the case of a distribution, the trustee,

1. Treas. Reg. §1.1012-1(c)(1).
2. Treas. Reg. §1.1012-1(c)(2).
3. Treas. Reg. §1.1012-1(c)(3)(i).
4. Treas. Reg. §1.1012-1(c)(7); Rev. Rul. 71-21, 1971-1 CB 221.
5. Treas. Reg. §1.1012-1(c)(3)(ii).

executor, or administrator must also give the distributee a written document specify-ing the particular securities distributed.) In such a case, the specified securities are the securities sold, transferred or distributed, even though certificates from a different lot are delivered to the purchaser, transferee or distributee.[1]

1419. How is a loss realized on a sale between related persons treated for income tax purposes?

If an individual sells property at a loss to a related person (as defined below), that loss may *not* be deducted or used to offset capital gains for income tax purposes.[2] It makes no difference that the sale was a bona fide, arm's-length transaction.[3] Neither does it matter that the sale was made indirectly through an unrelated middleman.[4] The loss on the sale of stock will be disallowed even though the sale and purchase are made separately on a stock exchange and the stock certificates received are not the certificates sold.[5] However, these rules will not apply to any loss of the distributing corporation (or the distributee) in the case of a distribution in complete liquidation.[6]

A loss realized on the exchange of properties between related persons will also be disallowed under these rules.[7] Whether loss is realized in transfers between spouses during marriage or incident to divorce is explained in Q 1447.

For this purpose, persons are related if they are: (1) members of the same fam-ily (i.e., brothers, sisters, spouses, ancestors and lineal descendants; but not if they are in-laws;[8] (2) an individual and a corporation of which the individual actually or con-structively owns more than 50% of the stock; (3) a grantor and a fiduciary of a trust; (4) fiduciaries of two trusts if the same person is the grantor of both; (5) a fiduciary and a beneficiary of the same trust; (6) a fiduciary of a trust and a beneficiary of another trust set up by the same grantor; (7) a fiduciary of a trust and a corporation of which the trust or the grantor of the trust actually or constructively owns more than 50% of the stock; (8) a person and an IRC Section 501 tax-exempt organization controlled by the person or members of his family (as described in (1) above); (9) a corporation and a partnership if the same person actually or constructively owns more than 50% of the stock of the corporation, and has more than a 50% interest in the partnership; (10) two S corporations if the same persons actually or constructively own more than 50% of the stock of each; (11) an S corporation and a C corporation, if the same persons actually or constructively own more than 50% of the stock of each; or (12) generally, an executor and a beneficiary of an estate.[9] Special rules apply for purposes of determining constructive ownership of stock.[10] The relationship between a grantor and fiduciary did not prevent recognition of loss on a sale of stock between them where the fiduciary purchased the stock in his individual capacity and where the sale was unrelated to the grantor-fiduciary relationship.[11]

---

1. Treas. Reg. §1.1012-1(c)(4).
2. IRC Sec. 267(a); Treas. Reg. §1.267(a)-1.
3. Treas. Reg. §1.267(a)-1(c).
4. See *Hassen v. Comm.*, 599 F.2d 305 (9th Cir. 1979).
5. *McWilliams v. Comm.*, 331 U.S. 694 (1947).
6. IRC Sec. 267(a)(1).
7. IRC Sec. 267(a)(1).
8. See Let. Rul. 9017008.
9. IRC Sec. 267(b).
10. See IRC Sec. 267(c).
11. Let. Rul. 9017008.

Generally, loss will be disallowed on a sale between a partnership and a partner who owns more than a 50% interest, or between two partnerships if the same persons own more than a 50% interest in each.[1] Furthermore, with respect to transactions between two partnerships having one or more common partners *or* in which one or more of the partners in each partnership are related (as defined above), a portion of the loss will be disallowed according to the relative interests of the partners.[2] If the transaction is between a partnership and an individual who is related to one of the partners (as defined above), any deductions for losses will be denied with respect to the related partner's distributive share, but not with respect to the relative shares of each unrelated partner.[3] Loss on a sale or exchange (other than of inventory) between two corporations that are members of the same controlled group (using a 50% test instead of 80%) is generally not denied but is deferred until the property is transferred outside the controlled group.[4]

If the related person to whom property was originally sold (or exchanged), sells or exchanges the same property (or property whose tax basis is determined by reference to such property) at a gain, the gain will be recognized only to the extent it exceeds the loss originally denied by reason of the related parties rules.[5]

Special rules apply to installment sales between related parties (see Q 1408) and to the deduction of losses (see Q 1285 to Q 1300).

In a case of first impression, the Tax Court held that IRC Section 382(l)(3)(A)(i)—which provides that an "individual" and all members of his family described in IRC Section 318(a)(1) (i.e., his spouse, children, grandchildren, and parents) are treated as one individual for purposes of applying IRC Section 382 (which limits the amount of pre-change losses that a loss corporation may use to offset taxable income in the taxable years or periods following an ownership change)—applies solely from the perspective of individuals who are shareholders (as determined under applicable attribution rules) of the loss corporation. The court further held that siblings are not treated as one individual under IRC Section 382(l)(3)(A)(i).[6] Accordingly, in *Garber*, the sale of shares by one brother to the other brother resulted in an ownership change with respect to the closely held corporation within the meaning of IRC Section 382(g).

1420. How is an individual taxed on capital gains and losses?

Adjusted net capital gain is generally subject to a maximum rate of 15%. (See "Reduction in Capital Gain Rates," below.) However, detailed rules as to the exact calculation of the capital gains tax result in some exceptions.[7]

"Adjusted net capital gain" is *net capital gain* reduced (but not below zero) by the sum of: (1) *unrecaptured IRC Section 1250 gain*; and (2) *28% rate gain* (both defined below); *plus* (3) "qualified dividend income" (as defined in IRC Section 1(h)(11)(B); see "New Lower Rates for Qualified Dividend Income").[8]

---

1. IRC Sec. 707(b).
2. Temp. Treas. Reg. §1.267(a)-2T(c), A-2.
3. Treas. Reg. §1.267(b)-1(b).
4. IRC Sec. 267(f).
5. IRC Sec. 267(d); Treas. Reg. §1.267(d)-1.
6. *Garber Industries Holding Co., Inc., v. Comm.*, 124 TC 1 (2005); *aff'd*, 2006-1 USTC ¶50,109 (5th Cir. 2006).
7. IRC Sec. 1(h).
8. IRC Sec. 1(h)(3).

Gain is determined by subtracting the adjusted basis of the asset sold or exchanged from the amount realized. Loss is determined by subtracting the amount realized from the adjusted basis of the asset sold or exchanged. See Q 1415. The amount realized includes both money and the fair market value of any property received. IRC Sec. 1001. Gains and losses from the sale or exchange of capital assets are either short-term or long-term. Generally, in order for gain or loss to be long-term, the asset must have been held for more than one year. See Q 1417.

Generally, taxpayers may elect to treat a portion of net capital gain as investment income.[1] If the election is made, any net capital gain included in investment income will be subject to the taxpayer's marginal income tax rate. The election must be made on or before the due date (including extensions) of the income tax return for the taxable year in which the net capital gain is recognized. The election is to be made on Form 4952, "Investment Interest Expense Deduction."[2] See Q 1304.

Net capital gain is the excess of net long term capital gain for the taxable year over net short term capital loss for such year.[3] However, net capital gain for any taxable year is reduced (but not below zero) by any amount the taxpayer takes into account under the investment income exception to the investment interest deduction.[4] See Q 1304.

The Code provides that for a taxpayer with a net capital gain for any taxable year, the tax will not exceed the *sum* of the following five items:

(A) the tax computed at regular rates (without regard to the rules for capital gain) on the *greater* of (i) taxable income reduced by the net capital gain, or (ii) the *lesser* of (I) the amount of taxable income taxed at a rate below 25% (See Appendix B), *or* (II) taxable income reduced by the adjusted net capital gain;

(B) 5% (0% in the case of taxable years beginning after 2007) of so much of the taxpayer's adjusted net capital gain (or, if less, taxable income) as does not exceed the *excess* (if any) of (i) the amount of taxable income that would (without regard to this paragraph) be taxed at a rate below 25% (see Appendix B) *over* (ii) the taxable income reduced by the adjusted net capital gain;

(C) 15% of the taxpayer's adjusted net capital gain (or, if less, taxable income) in *excess* of the amount on which a tax is determined under (B) above;

(D) 25% of the *excess* (if any) of (i) the unrecaptured IRC Section 1250 gain (or, if less, the net capital gain (determined without regard to qualified dividend income)), *over* (ii) the *excess* (if any) of (I) the sum of the amount on which tax is determined under (A) above, *plus* the net capital gain, *over* (II) taxable income; *and*

(E) 28% of the amount of taxable income in excess of the sum of the amounts on which tax is determined under (A) through (D) above.[5]

It is important to note that as a result of this complex formula, generally, the maximum capital gains rate on adjusted net capital gain will be 15% to the extent an individual is taxed at the 25% or higher marginal rates (see Q 1432), and 5% (0% in 2008 through 2010) to the extent the individual is taxed at the 15% or 10% rates.[6]

---

1. See IRC Secs. 163(d)(4)(B), 1(h)(2).
2. Treas. Reg. §1.163(d)-1.
3. IRC Sec. 1222(11).
4. IRC Secs. 163(d)(4)(B)(iii), 1(h)(2).
5. IRC Secs. 1(h)(1)(D); 1(h)(1)(A), 1(h)(1)(B), IRC Secs. 1(h)(1)(C), 1(h)(1)(E).
6. IRC Sec. 1(h).

IRC Section 1250 provides for the recapture of gain on certain property on which accelerated depreciation has been used. "Unrecaptured IRC Section 1250 gain" means the *excess*, if any, of: (i) that amount of long-term capital gain (not otherwise treated as ordinary income) that would be treated as ordinary income if IRC Section 1250(b)(1) included all depreciation and the applicable percentage under IRC Section 1250(a) were 100%; *over* (ii) the excess, if any of (a) the sum of collectibles loss, net short-term capital loss and long-term capital loss carryovers, *over* (b) the sum of collectibles gain and IRC Section 1202 gain. However, at no time may the amount of unrecaptured IRC Section 1250 gain that is attributable to sales, exchanges and conversions described in IRC Section 1231(a)(3)(A) for any taxable year exceed the net IRC Section 1231 gain, as defined in IRC Section 1231(c)(3) for such year.[1]

"28% rate gain" means the *excess*, if any, of (A) the *sum* of collectibles gain and IRC Section 1202 gain (i.e., gain on certain small businesses), *over* (B) the *sum* of (i) collectibles loss, (ii) net short-term capital loss, and (iii) long-term capital loss carried over under IRC Section 1212(b)(1)(B) (i.e., the excess of net long-term capital loss over net short-term capital gain, carried over to the succeeding taxable year).[2]

"Collectibles gain or loss" is gain or loss on the sale or exchange of a collectible that is a capital asset held for more than one year, but only to the extent such gain is taken into account in computing gross income and such loss is taken into account in computing taxable income.[3] Examples of collectibles include artwork, gems and coins.[4] For additional details, see Q 1185 and Q 1186.

"IRC Section 1202 gain" means the *excess* of (A) the gain that would be excluded from gross income under IRC Section 1202 but for the percentage limitation in IRC Section 1202(a) *over* (B) the gain excluded from gross income under IRC Section 1202 (i.e., 50% exclusion for certain qualified small business stock).[5] See Q 1019 and Q 1020 for details. (JGTRRA 2003 provides that for alternative minimum tax purposes, an amount equal to 7% of the amount excluded from gross income for the taxable year under IRC Section 1202 will be treated as a preference item.[6] See Q 1020.)

The foregoing rules essentially establish four groups of capital assets (based upon pre-existing tax rates): (1) short-term capital assets, with no special tax rate; (2) 28% capital assets, generally consisting of collectibles gain or loss, and IRC Section 1202 gain; (3) 25% capital assets, consisting of assets that generate unrecaptured IRC Section 1250 gain; and (4) 15%/5% (0% in the case of taxable years beginning after 2007 for taxpayers in the 15%/10% ordinary income tax brackets) capital assets, consisting of all other long-term capital assets. Within each group, gains and losses are netted. The effect of this process is generally that if there is a net loss from (1), it is applied to reduce any net gain from (2), (3), or (4), in that order. If there is a net loss from (2) it is applied to reduce any net gain from (3) or (4), in that order. If there is a net loss from (4), it is applied to reduce any net gain from (2) or (3), in that order.[7]

---

1. IRC Sec. 1(h)(6).
2. IRC Sec. 1(h)(4).
3. IRC Sec. 1(h)(5).
4. See IRC Sec. 408(m)(2).
5. IRC Sec. 1(h)(7).
6. IRC Sec. 57(a)(7).
7. IRC Sec. 1(h)(1); Notice 97-59, 1997-2 CB 309.

After all of the netting above, if there are net losses, up to $3,000 ($1,500 in the case of married individuals filing separately) of losses can be deducted against ordinary income.[1] Apparently, any deducted loss would be treated as reducing net loss from (1), (2), or (4), in that order. Any remaining net losses could be carried over to other taxable years, retaining its group classifications. If there are net gains, such gains would generally be taxed as described above.

Generally, to the extent a capital loss described above exceeds the $3,000 limit ($1,500 in the case of married individuals filing separately), it may be carried over to other taxable years, but always retaining its character as long-term or short-term. However, special rules apply in determining the carryover amount from years in which a taxpayer has no taxable income.[2]

Collectibles gain and IRC Section 1250 gains under IRC Section 1(h) are subject to special rules when an interest in a pass-through entity (i.e., partnership, S corporation, or trust) is sold or exchanged. Regulations finalized in 2000 provide rules for dividing the holding period of an interest in a partnership.[3]

The Service has classified "basis-shifting transactions" (i.e., certain redemptions of stock in transactions not subject to U.S. tax in which the basis of the redeemed stock is purported to shift to a U.S. taxpayer) as "listed transactions," meaning that they are viewed by the Service as "tax avoidance transactions" (i.e., tax shelters).[4] For the tax shelter rules applicable to investors (including individuals), see Q 1335 ("Accelerated Charitable Remainder Trusts").

Special rules apply in the case of wash sales (see Q 1030), short sales (see Q 1022), and IRC Section 1256 contracts (see Q 1076).

Reduction in Capital Gain Rates for Individuals

Long-term capital gains incurred on or after May 6, 2003 are subject to lower tax rates. For taxpayers in the 25% tax bracket and higher (28%, 33% and 35% in 2007), the rate on long-term capital gains is reduced from 20% to 15% in 2003 through 2010. For taxpayers in the 15% and 10% brackets, the rate on long-term capital gains is reduced from 10% to 5% in 2003 through 2007, and all the way down to 0% in 2008 through 2010. The lower capital gain rates are effective for taxable years ending on or after May 6, 2003 and beginning before January 1, 2011. On December 31, 2010, the lower rates on long-term capital gains will "sunset" (expire), after which time the prior capital gain rates (20%, 10%) will, once again, be effective.[5] For the treatment of long-term capital gains incurred prior to May 6, 2003, see the "Transitional rules," below.

Collectibles gain, IRC Section 1202 gain (i.e., qualified small business stock), and unrecaptured IRC Section 1250 gain continue to be taxed at their current tax rates (i.e., 28% for collectibles gain and IRC Section 1202 gain, and 25% for unrecaptured IRC Section 1250 gain).[6]

---

1. IRC Sec. 1211(b).
2. IRC Secs. 1211(b), 1212(b).
3. See TD 8902, 2000-2 CB 323.
4. See Notice 2004-67, 2004-41 IRB 600. See also FSAs 200202057, 200201012.
5. IRC Sec. 1(h)(1); Sec. 102, TIPRA 2005, *amending*, Sec. 303, JGTRRA 2003.
6. IRC Sec. 1(h).

Repeal of qualified 5-year gain. For tax years beginning after December 31, 2000, if certain requirements were met, the maximum rates on "qualified 5-year gain" could be reduced to 8% and 18% (in place of 10% and 20% respectively). Furthermore, a non-corporate taxpayer in the 25% bracket (or higher) who held a capital asset on January 1, 2001 could elect to treat the asset as if it had been sold and repurchased for its fair market value on January 1, 2001 (or on January 2, 2001 in the case of publicly traded stock). If a noncorporate taxpayer made this election, the holding period for the elected assets began after December 31, 2000, thereby making the asset eligible for the 18% rate if it was later sold after having been held by the taxpayer for more than five years from the date of the deemed sale and deemed reacquisition.[1] Under JGTRRA 2003, the 5-year holding period requirement, and the 18% and 8% tax rates for qualified 5-year gain are repealed. When the 15%/5% rates for capital gains "sunset" (expire), the 5-year holding period requirement and 18% and 8% rates will, once again, be effective.[2]

Transitional rules. In the case of a taxable year that *includes* May 6, 2003, the amount of tax determined under (B) above, will generally be equal to the *sum* of:

(A)　5% of the *lesser* of: (i) the net capital gain determined by taking into account only gain or loss taken into account for the portion of the taxable year on or after May 6, 2003 (determined without regard to collectibles gain or loss and IRC Section 1202 gain); *or* (ii) the amount on which a tax is determined under (B), above (without regard to this subsection);

(B)　8% of the *lesser* of: (i) the qualified 5-year gain (as that term was defined on May 27, 2003 under IRC Section 1(h)(9)) taken into account for the portion of the taxable year before May 6, 2003; *or* (ii) the *excess* (if any) of (I) the amount on which a tax is determined under (B), above (without regard to this subsection), *over* (II) the amount on which a tax is determined under (A), above; *plus*

(C)　10% of the *excess* (if any) of: (i) the amount on which a tax is determined under (B), above (without regard to this subsection), *over* (ii) the sum of the amounts on which a tax is determined under (A) and (B), above.[3]

In the case of a taxable year that includes May 6, 2003, the amount of tax determined under (C), above, will generally be equal to the *sum* of:

(A)　15% of the *lesser* of: (i) the *excess* (if any) of the amount of net capital gain determined under subparagraph (A)(i) of paragraph (1) of this subsection, *over* the amount on which a tax is determined under subparagraph (A) of paragraph (1) of this subsection; *or* (ii) the amount on which a tax is determined under (C), above (without regard to this subsection); *plus*

(B)　20% of the *excess* (if any) of: (i) the amount on which a tax is determined under (C), above (without regard to this subsection); *over* (ii) the amount on which a tax is determined under subparagraph (A), of this paragraph.[4]

1.　IRC Secs. 1(h)(2), 1(h)(9), prior to amendment by JGTRRA 2003; Sec. 414(a) of JCWAA 2002, and Sec. 314(c) of the Community Renewal Tax Relief Act of 2000, amending Sec. 311(e) of TRA '97.
2.　IRC Secs. 1(h)(2), 1(h)(9), as repealed by JGTRRA 2003; Act Sec. 107, JGTRRA 2003.
3.　Act. Sec. 301(c)(1), JGTRRA 2003.
4.　Act Sec. 301(c)(2), JGTRRA 2003.

With respect to any pass-through entity (e.g., a mutual fund), the determination of when gains and losses are properly taken into account will be made at the entity level.[1]

Dividends that are "qualified dividend income" (see below) will be treated as gain properly taken into account for the portion of the taxable year on or after May 6, 2003.[2]

Lower Rates for Qualified Dividend Income

Under prior law, dividends were treated as ordinary income and, thus, were subject to ordinary income tax rates. Under JGTRRA 2003, "qualified dividend income" (see below) is treated as "net capital gain" (see below) and is, therefore, subject to new lower tax rates. For taxpayers in the 25% income tax bracket and higher), the maximum rate on qualified dividends paid by corporations to individuals is 15% in 2003 through 2010. For taxpayers in the 15% and 10% income tax brackets, the tax rate on qualified dividend income is reduced to 5% in 2003 through 2007, and all the way down to 0% in 2008 through 2010. The preferential treatment of qualified dividends as net capital gains will "sunset" (expire) on December 31, 2010, after which time the prior treatment of dividends will, once again, be effective.[3] In other words, dividends will once again be taxed at ordinary income tax rates.

Qualified dividend income. Certain dividends are taxed as "net capital gain" for purposes of the reduction in the tax rates on dividends. "Net capital gain" for this purpose means net capital gain *increased* by "qualified dividend income" (without regard to this paragraph).[4] "Qualified dividend income" means dividends received during the taxable year from domestic corporations and "qualified foreign corporations" (defined below).[5]

The term qualified dividend income does *not* include the following:

(1)   dividends paid by tax-exempt corporations;

(2)   any amount allowed as a deduction under IRC Section 591 (relating to the deduction for dividends paid by mutual savings banks, etc.);

(3)   dividends paid on certain employer securities as described in IRC Section 404(k);

(4)   any dividend on a share (or shares) of stock that the shareholder has not held for more than 60 days during the *121-day* period beginning 60 days before the ex-dividend date (as measured under IRC Section 246(c)). For preferred stock, the holding period is more than 90 days during the *181-day* period beginning 90 days before the ex-dividend date *if* the dividends are attributable to a period exceeding 366 days (note, however, that if the preferred dividends are attributable to a period totalling less than 367 days, the holding period stated in the preceding sentence applies).[6]

---

1. Act Sec. 301(c)(4), JGTRRA 2003.
2. Act Sec. 301(c)(5), JGTRRA 2003.
3. IRC Sec. 1(h)(1); Sec. 102, TIPRA 2005, *amending*, Sec. 303, JGTRRA 2003.
4. IRC Sec. 1(h)(11)(A).
5. IRC Sec. 1(h)(11)(B).
6. IRC Sec. 1(h)(11)(B).

Special rules. Qualified dividend income does *not* include any amount that the taxpayer takes into account as investment income under IRC Section 163(d)(4)(B).[1] If an individual, trust, or estate receives qualified dividend income from one or more dividends that are "extraordinary dividends" (within the meaning of IRC Section 1059(c)), any loss on the sale or exchange of such share(s) of stock will, to the extent of such dividends, be treated as long-term capital loss.[2]

A dividend received from a mutual fund or REIT is subject to the limitations under IRC Sections 854 and 857.[3] For the treatment of mutual fund dividends and REIT dividends under JGTRRA 2003, see Q 1162 and Q 1179, respectively.

Pass-through entities. In the case of partnerships, S corporations, common trust funds, trusts, and estates, the rule that qualified dividends are taxable as capital gains applies to taxable years ending after December 31, 2002, except that dividends received by the entity prior to January 1, 2003 are *not* treated as qualified dividend income.[4]

Qualified foreign corporations. The term "qualified foreign corporation" means a foreign corporation incorporated in a possession of the United States, or a corporation that is eligible for benefits of a comprehensive income tax treaty with the United States. If a foreign corporation does not satisfy either of these requirements, it will nevertheless be treated as such with respect to any dividends paid by that corporation *if* its stock (or ADRs with respect to such stock) is readily tradable on an established securities market in the United States.[5]

Common stock (or an ADR in respect of such stock) is considered "readily tradable on an established securities market in the United States" if it is listed on a national securities exchange that is registered under Section 6 of the Securities Exchange Act of 1934 (15 USC 78(f)), or on the NASDAQ Stock Market. As stated in the Securities and Exchange Commission's Annual Report for 2002, registered national exchanges include (as of September 30, 2002) the American Stock Exchange (AMEX), Boston Stock Exchange, Cincinnati Stock Exchange, Chicago Stock Exchange, New York Stock Exchange (NYSE), Philadelphia Stock Exchange, and the Pacific Stock Exchange.[6]

In order to meet the "treaty test," the foreign corporation must be eligible for benefits of a comprehensive income tax treaty with the United States that the Treasury Secretary determines is satisfactory for these purposes, and the treaty must also provide for the exchange of tax information. For the current list of tax treaties meeting these requirements, see Notice 2003-69.[7]

The term "qualified foreign corporation" does *not* include any foreign corporation *if,* for the taxable year of the corporation in which the dividend was paid (or the preceding taxable year), the corporation is a passive foreign investment company (as defined in section 1297).[8]

---

1. IRC Sec. 1(h)(11)(D)(i). See also Temp. Treas. Reg. 1.163(d)-1T.
2. IRC Sec. 1(h)(11)(D).
3. IRC Sec. 1(h)(11)(D)(iii).
4. Act Sec. 402(a)(6) of WFTRA 2004, amending Act Sec. 302(f) of JGTRRA 2003.
5. IRC Sec. 1(h)(11)(C).
6. Notice 2003-71, 2003-43 IRB 922.
7. 2003-42 IRB 851.
8. IRC Sec. 1(h)(11)(C)(iii).

Special rules apply in determining a taxpayer's foreign tax credit limitation under IRC Section 904 in the case of qualified dividend income. For these purposes, rules similar to the rules of IRC Section 904(b)(2)(B) (concerning adjustments to the foreign tax credit limitation to reflect any capital gain rate differential) will apply to any qualified dividend income.[1]

For information reporting and other guidance on foreign stock dividends, see Notice 2006-3;[2] Notice 2004-71;[3] and Notice 2003-79.[4]

Reporting Requirements under JGTRRA 2003

New boxes have been added to Form 1099-DIV to allow for the reporting of qualified dividends (Box 1b) and post-May 5, 2003 capital gain distributions (Box 2b). Likewise, new boxes have also been added to Form 1099-B for reporting post-May 5, 2003 profits or losses from regulated futures or currency contracts.[5] Payments made in lieu of dividends ("substitute payments") are *not* eligible for the lower rates applicable to qualified dividends.[6] For the information reporting requirements for such payments, see Notice 2003-67;[7] Announcement 2003-75;[8] Treas. Reg. §1.6045-2(a)(3)(i); TD 9103.[9]

1421. How are gains and losses treated for "traders in securities"?

In general, investors' losses are classified as capital losses, may be used to offset capital gains, and can only offset up to $3,000 of ordinary income each year (see Q 1420). On the other hand, a "trader in securities" (see below) may elect to recognize gain or loss on any security held in connection with a trade or business at the close of any taxable year as if the security were sold at its fair market value at year-end.[10] Consequently, gains or losses with respect to such securities—whether deemed sold at year-end under the mark-to-market method of accounting (see Q 1075, Q 1076), or actually sold during the taxable year—are treated as ordinary income or loss.[11] Therefore, if a taxpayer is in business as a trader in securities and makes a mark-to-market election (under IRC Section 475(f)(1)) with respect to sales of securities held in connection with his business, the taxpayer's net loss from that business will be an ordinary loss that is fully deductible.[12]

How does an individual investor achieve "trader" status? The Tax Court stated in *Chen* that:

"In order to qualify as a trader (as opposed to an investor) [the taxpayer's] purchases and sales of securities *** must have constituted a trade or business. 'In determining whether a taxpayer who manages his own investments is a trader, and thus engaged in a trade or business, relevant considerations are the taxpayer's

1. See IRC Sec. 1(h)(11)(C)(iv).
2. 2006-3 IRB 306.
3. 2004-45 IRB 793
4. 2003-50 IRB 1206.
5. See Announcement 2003-55, 2003-38 IRB 597.
6. H.R. Rep. No. 108-94, 108th Cong., 1st Sess. 31 n. 36 (2003).
7. 2003-40 IRB 752.
8. 2003-49 IRB 1195.
9. 68 Fed. Reg. 74847 (12-29-2003).
10. See IRC Sec. 475(f)(1)(A)(i); *Chen v. Comm.*, TC Memo 2004-132.
11. See IRC Secs. 475(d)(3)(A), 475(f)(1)(D); *Chen v. Comm.*, TC Memo 2004-132.
12. See IRC Section 165(c)(1); *Chen v. Comm.*, TC Memo 2004-132.

investment intent, the nature of the income to be derived from the activity, and the frequency, extent, and regularity of the taxpayer's securities transactions.'[1] In general, investors purchase and hold securities 'for capital appreciation and income' whereas traders buy and sell 'with reasonable frequency in an endeavor to catch the swings in the daily market movements and profit thereby on a short-term basis.'[2] For a taxpayer to be considered a trader, the taxpayer's trading activity must be 'substantial,' and it must be 'frequent, regular, and continuous to be considered part of a trade or business. * * * Sporadic trading does not constitute a trade or business.'[3] ('We accept the fact that to be engaged in a trade or business, the taxpayer must be involved in the activity with continuity and regularity * * *. A sporadic activity * * * does not qualify.').'[4]

In *Chen*, the taxpayer effected 323 transactions involving the purchase of securities, most of which he held for less than one month. Approximately 94% of Chen's transactions occurred during February, March, and April, with no transactions occurring in six of the other nine months. Chen attempted to retroactively elect mark-to-market accounting as a trader so that he could treat his losses as fully deductible ordinary losses incurred in a trade or business. But the Tax Court held that Chen was not a trader in securities eligible to make a mark-to-market election because Chen did not meet the second requirement for trader status— frequent, regular, and continuous trading. In the court's view, Chen's purchases and sales of securities were only frequent, regular, and continuous during the months of February, March, and April. The court also noted that Chen maintained a full-time job as a computer chip engineer. According to the court, in cases in where taxpayers have been held to be "traders in securities," the number and frequency [of trades] indicated that they were engaged in market transactions almost daily for a substantial and continuous period, generally exceeding a single taxable year. Furthermore, those activities constituted the taxpayers' sole or primary income-producing activity." The Tax Court concluded that because Chen's daily trading activities covered only a portion of a single year, and securities trading was not the sole or even primary activity in which Chen engaged for the production of income, Chen was not eligible for trader status.[5]

For the circumstances in which a late Section 475(f) election will be allowed, see *Vines v. Comm.*[6]

Traders are allowed to fully deduct their expenses as business expenses. See Q 1313. Conversely, investors' expenses are classified as miscellaneous itemized deductions and are subject to the 2%-of-adjusted gross income (AGI) threshold. See Q 1428. The expenses of investors are also subjected to additional limitations. See Q 1304 – investment interest expense; Q 1310 – expenses paid in connection with the production of investment income; and Q 1312 – expenses relating to tax questions.

1422. What is a "like-kind" exchange? How is it taxed?

1. *Moller v. U.S.*, 721 F.2d 810, 813 (Fed. Cir. 1983).
2. *Liang v. Comm.*, 23 TC 1040, 1043 (1955).
3. *Boatner v. Commissioner*, TC Memo. 1997-379, *aff'd*, 164 F.3d 629 (9th Cir. 1998); see also *Commissioner v. Groetzinger*, 480 U.S. 23, 35 (1987).
4. *Chen v. Comm.*, TC Memo 2004-132.
5. *Chen v. Comm.*, TC Memo 2004-132.
6. 126 TC No. 15 (2006).

In a like-kind exchange, a taxpayer exchanges property he holds as an investment or for productive use in a trade or business for other property of the same nature or character (but not necessarily of an equivalent grade or quality) that will be held either as an investment or for productive use in a trade or business. The property exchanged must be tangible; stocks, bonds, notes, other securities or evidences of indebtedness, and partnership interests are *not* eligible for like-kind exchange treatment. An exchange of properties that are of different kinds or classes is not a "like-kind" exchange.[1]

A special rule applies to any partnership that has elected under IRC Section 761(a) to be excluded from the application of subchapter K. An interest in such a partnership generally is treated as an interest in each of the assets of the partnership, not as an interest in the partnership.[2]

In order to qualify as a like-kind exchange, the transaction must also meet the following requirements: (1) the taxpayer must identify the property to be received in the exchange within 45 days after he transfers the property he relinquishes in the exchange, *and* (2) he must receive the like-kind property within 180 days after the date of his transfer or, if earlier, before the due date of his tax return for the tax year (not including extensions).[3] The Service has privately ruled that it is not authorized under IRC Section 6503(b) to suspend the 180-day replacement period under IRC Section 1031(a)(3) where a taxpayer's assets are within court custody.[4]

For the final regulations replacing the use of the Standard Industrial Classification (SIC) system with the North American Industry Classification System (NAIC) for determining what properties are of a like class for purposes of IRC Section 1031, see Treas. Reg. §1.1031(a)-2; TD 9202.[5]

The IRS has provided safe harbors for programs involving ongoing exchanges of tangible personal property using a single intermediary (i.e., "LKE programs" or "like-kind exchange programs").[6]

According to the IRS, the like-kind standard has traditionally been interpreted more narrowly in the case of exchanges of personal property as compared to exchanges of real property.[7]

The Service has ruled that depreciable tangible personal properties were of a like class, even if they did not belong to the same general asset class.[8] The Service has also ruled that transfers of relinquished leased vehicles, followed by the acquisition of replacement leased vehicles through a qualified intermediary, were deferred exchanges qualifying for nonrecognition of gain or loss under IRC Section 1031.[9]

In technical advice, the Service ruled that the exchange of intangible property by a domestic entity for the intangible property of a foreign entity does not qualify as a like-kind exchange to the extent that the exchange is of property used predominantly

---

1. IRC Sec. 1031; Treas. Reg. §1.1031(a)-1.
2. IRC Sec. 1031(a)(2).
3. IRC Sec. 1031(a)(3).
4. Let. Rul. 200211016.
5. 70 Fed. Reg. 28818 (5-19-2005).
6. See Rev. Proc. 2003-39, 2003-22 IRB 971.
7. See, e.g., *California Federal Life Insurance Co. v. Comm.*, 680 F.2d 85, 87 (9th Cir. 1982).
8. Let. Rul. 200327029.
9. Let. Ruls. 200241013, 200240049.

within the United States for property used predominantly outside the United States. According to the Service—and contrary to the taxpayer's argument—IRC Section 1031(h)(2)(A) clearly provides that personal property used predominantly within the United States and personal property used predominantly outside the United States are not property of like-kind. The statute does not make a distinction between tangible and intangible personal property.[1]

Gain on an exchange of property that fails to qualify for nonrecognition treatment under the like-kind exchange rules may be reportable under the installment method.[2] The Tax Court found that a transaction qualified as an installment sale and not a like-kind exchange where the payment for a transfer of real property was not received until the year after the property's conveyance.[3]

See Q 1238 for an explanation of regulations and safe harbors governing deferred exchanges, and for the procedures governing reverse exchanges.

Receipt of "boot". If the taxpayer receives only like-kind property in the exchange, no taxable gain or loss is reported on his income tax return as a result of the exchange regardless of his tax basis in and value of the respective properties.[4] However, if in addition to like-kind property, the taxpayer receives cash or other property that is different in kind or class from the property he transferred (i.e., non-like-kind property–often referred to as "boot"), any gain he realizes in the exchange will be taxable to the extent of the sum of the amount of cash and the fair market value of the nonlike-kind property received; any loss realized in such an exchange may *not* be taken into account in calculating the taxpayer's income tax.[5]

If the taxpayer receives only like-kind property, but transfers cash or other non-like-kind property as part of the exchange, regulations indicate that the nonrecognition rules apply to the like-kind properties, but not to the "boot."[6]

Assumption of Liabilities. If, in an exchange, one party assumes a liability of the other party or receives property subject to a liability, he will be deemed to have transferred "boot" in an amount equal to the liability. The party who transfers the property subject to the liability or whose liability is assumed will be deemed to have received the "boot." If each party to an exchange either assumes a liability of the other party or acquires property subject to a liability, the amounts of such liabilities will be offset and only the difference will be treated as "boot" given and received by the applicable parties.[7] Generally, liabilities that qualify to offset or reduce any taxable boot received are those to which the property received was subject to prior to the exchange and that then are assumed as part of the exchange.[8]

The Service ruled that if a partnership enters into an exchange that qualifies as a deferred like-kind exchange, in which property subject to a liability is transferred in one taxable year of the partnership, and property subject to a liability is received in the

1. See TAM 200602034.
2. Treas. Reg. §1.1031(k)-1(j)(2).
3. *Christensen v. Comm.*, TC Memo 1996-254.
4. IRC Sec. 1031(a).
5. IRC Secs. 1031(b), 1031(c); Treas. Reg. §1.1031(b)-1.
6. Treas. Regs. §§1.1031(a)-1(a)(2), 1.1031(d)-1(e). See *Allegheny County Auto Mart*, TC Memo, 1953-140, *aff'd per curiam*, 208 F.2d 693 (3rd Cir. 1953); *W.H. Hartman Co. v. Comm.*, 20 BTA 302 (1930).
7. Treas. Reg. §1.1031(d)-2. See Rev. Rul. 59-229, 1959-2 CB 180.
8. See Treas. Reg. §1.1031(d)-2, Ex. 2.

following taxable year of the partnership, the liabilities must be netted for purpose of IRC Section 752. Any net decrease in a partner's share of partnership liability must be taken into account for purposes of IRC Section 752(b) in the first taxable year of the partnership, and any net increase in a partner's share of partnership liability must be taken into account for purposes of IRC Section 752(a) in the second year of the partnership.[1]

Basis. The tax basis of like-kind property received in a tax-free (or partially tax-free) like-kind exchange is generally equal to the adjusted tax basis of the like-kind property given. There are, however, two exceptions. First, if an individual transfers cash or non-like-kind property or assumes a liability of the other party to the exchange (i.e., the transferee) that exceeds the liabilities (if any) assumed by the transferee, the individual's tax basis in the like-kind property received is equal to his adjusted tax basis in the property given *increased by* the *sum of* (1) the amount of cash and the fair market value of non-like-kind property given and (2) the net liability assumed. Second, if liabilities assumed by the transferee exceed the liabilities (if any) assumed by the individual (transferor) and no other cash or boot is transferred by the individual, the individual's tax basis in the like-kind property he receives is equal to his adjusted tax basis in the like-kind property given *decreased by* the net amount of liabilities assumed by the transferee.[2]

The tax basis of any nonlike-kind property received in a like-kind exchange is the fair market value of the nonlike-kind property on the date of the exchange.[3]

Related Party Exchanges. If a like-kind exchange that results in nonrecognition of gain or loss occurs between related parties, followed by a disposition of either property within two years of the date of the last transfer that was part of the like-kind exchange, then the original transaction will not qualify for nonrecognition treatment.[4] For purposes of this rule, the term "disposition" does not include dispositions resulting from the death of the taxpayer or (if earlier) the related person. The 2-year disposition rule also will not apply to involuntary conversions, so long as the exchange occurred before the threat or imminence of the conversion. An exception is also provided where it can be established that neither the exchange nor the subsequent disposition had as its principal purpose the avoidance of income tax.[5]

"Related persons," for purposes of this rule, include the following: (1) members of the same family (i.e., brothers, sisters, spouses, ancestors and lineal descendants); (2) an individual and a corporation of which the individual actually or constructively owns more than 50% of the stock; (3) a grantor and a fiduciary of a trust; (4) fiduciaries of two trusts if the same person is the grantor of both; (5) a fiduciary and a beneficiary of the same trust; (6) a fiduciary of a trust and a beneficiary of another trust set up by the same grantor; (7) a fiduciary of a trust and a corporation of which the grantor of the trust actually or constructively owns more than 50% of the stock; (8) a person and an IRC Section 501 tax-exempt organization controlled by the person or members of his family (as described in (1) above); (9) a corporation and a partnership if the same person actually or constructively owns more than 50% of the stock of the corporation, and has more than a 50% interest in the partnership; (10) two S corporations if the same persons actually or constructively own more than 50% of the stock of each; (11)

1. Rev. Rul. 2003-56, 2003-23 IRB 985.
2. IRC Sec. 1031(d), Treas. Reg. §1.1031(d)-2.
3. Treas. Reg. §1.1031(d)-1(c).
4. IRC Sec. 1031(f)(1).
5. IRC Sec. 1031(f)(2).

an S corporation and a C corporation, if the same persons actually or constructively own more than 50% of the stock of each; (12) a person and a partnership of which the person actually or constructively owns more than 50% of the capital interest or profits interest; (13) two partnerships if the same persons actually or constructively own more than 50% of the capital interest or profits interest of each; or (14) generally, an executor and a beneficiary of an estate.[1]

Any transaction, or series of transactions, structured to avoid the related party rules for like-kind exchanges will not qualify for nonrecognition treatment.[2] The Service has ruled that a taxpayer who transfers relinquished property to a qualified intermediary for replacement property formerly owned by a related party is *not* entitled to nonrecognition treatment under IRC Section 1031(a) if, as part of the transaction, the related party receives cash or other non-like-kind property for the replacement property.[3] If the risk of holding any property is substantially diminished by a short sale, by the holding of a put option, or by another person holding a right to acquire the property, then the running of the 2-year period will be suspended during the period that the option or other right is held.[4]

Recapture. In a like-kind exchange where boot is given or received, the recapture provisions applicable to certain depreciable property apply (see Q 1424). If property for which an investment credit was taken is exchanged before the investment credit recapture period ends, a percentage will be recaptured (see Q 1268).[5]

For the rules coordinating like-kind exchange tax treatment with the exclusion of gain on the sale of a personal residence, see Q 1239.

Adjusted Gross Income

1423. How is adjusted gross income determined?

Adjusted gross income is determined by subtracting the following deductions from gross income: (a) expenses directly incurred in carrying on a trade, business or profession (not as an employee – see Q 1313); (b) the deduction allowed for contributions made by a self-employed individual to a qualified pension, annuity, or profit sharing plan, or a simplified employee pension or SIMPLE IRA plan; (c) certain reimbursed expenses of an employee in connection with his employment, provided the reimbursement is included in gross income (if the employee accounts to his employer and reimbursement does not exceed expenses, reporting is not required); (d) deductions related to property held for the production of rents and royalties (within limits); (e) deductions for depreciation and depletion by a life tenant, an income beneficiary of property held in trust, or an heir, legatee or devisee of an estate; (f) deductions for losses from the sale or exchange of property (see Q 1420); (g) the deduction allowed for amounts paid in cash by an eligible individual to a traditional individual retirement account (IRA), or individual retirement annuity; (h) the deduction allowed for amounts forfeited as penalties because of premature withdrawal of funds from time savings accounts (see Q 1160); (i) alimony payments made to the taxpayer's spouse (see Q 1448); (j) certain reforestation expenses; (k) certain jury duty pay remitted to the taxpayer's employer; (l)

---

1. IRC Secs. 1031(f)(3), 267(b), 707(b)(1).
2. IRC Sec. 1031(f)(4).
3. Rev. Rul. 2002-83, 2002-49 IRB 927.
4. IRC Sec. 1031(g).
5. IRC Sec. 50(a)(1).

moving expenses permitted by IRC Sec. 217; (m) the deduction for Archer Medical Savings Accounts under IRC Section 220(i) (*Editor's Note*: the deduction is extended through 2007 under TRHCA 2006); (n) the deduction for interest on education loans; (o) the deduction for qualified tuition and related expenses (*Editor's Note*: the deduction is extended through 2007 under TRHCA 2006); (p) the deduction for contributions (within limits) to Health Savings Accounts; (q) the deduction for attorneys' fees involving discrimination suits; and (r) the deduction for certain expenses of elementary and secondary school teachers up to $250 (*Editor's Note*: the deduction is extended through 2007 under TRHCA 2006).

1424. What is the deduction for depreciation?

Depreciation is a deduction that permits recovery, over a period of time, of capital invested in tangible property used in a trade or business or held for the production of income.[1] It is a deduction taken in arriving at adjusted gross income.[2] Only property that has a limited useful life may be depreciated. Land does not have a limited life and, therefore, cannot be depreciated. However, the improvements on land can be depreciated. Inventory and stock in trade are not depreciable.[3] A taxpayer who purchases a term interest in property cannot amortize or depreciate the cost of the property during any period in which the remainder interest is held by a related person. This rule is effective for interests created or acquired after July 27, 1989, in taxable years ending after such date.[4] (However, life tenants and beneficiaries of estates and trusts may be allowed the regular depreciation deduction if the property is depreciable property.[5]

The method used to determine the rate of depreciation depends on when the property was placed into service. Property is "placed into service" when it is first placed in a condition or state of readiness and availability for a specifically assigned function for use in a trade or business, for the production of income, or in a tax-exempt or personal activity.[6]

Property "Placed in Service" After 1986

Generally, the Accelerated Cost Recovery System (ACRS) was modified for property placed in service after 1986. An election could be made to apply the post-1986 ACRS to property that was placed in service between July 31, 1986 and January 1, 1987 (unless such property would have been subject to the anti-churning rules if it had been placed in service after 1986).[7] If real property is acquired before 1987 and converted from personal use to a depreciable use after 1986, the post-1986 ACRS is to be used.[8]

The post-1986 ACRS deduction is calculated by applying to the basis of the property either (1) a declining balance method that switches to the straight line method at a time which maximizes the deduction or (2) a straight line method.[9] The initial basis in the property is the basis of the property upon acquisition (usually the cost of the property, see Q 1415), reduced by the amount, if any, elected for amortization or an

---

1. IRC Secs. 167(a), 168(a).
2. IRC Secs. 62(a)(1), 62(a)(4).
3. Treas. Reg. §1.167(a)-2.
4. IRC Sec. 167(e).
5. See IRC Sec. 167(d).)
6. Prop. Treas. Reg. §1.168-2(l)(2).
7. TRA '86, Sec. 203(a)(1)(B), as amended by TAMRA '88, Sec. 1002(c)(1).
8. TAMRA '88, Sec. 1002(c)(3).
9. IRC Sec. 168(b).

IRC Section 179 deduction (see "Election to Expense," below), and further reduced by any basis reduction required in connection with taking the investment tax credit (see Q 1268).[1] The basis of the property is reduced each year by the amount of the depreciation allowable.[2] Optional depreciation tables set out in Revenue Procedure 87-57 may be used in place of the methods above.[3] Because land cannot be depreciated, the cost basis of improved land must be allocated between the land and improvements.[4] The ACRS deduction is limited in the case of certain automobiles and other "listed property" placed in service after June 18, 1984. See "Limitations," below.

In general, for certain property acquired after September 11, 2001, and before January 1, 2005, a depreciation "bonus" of 30% may be taken in the year the property is placed in service.[5] For certain property acquired after May 5, 2003, and before January 1, 2005, 50% bonus depreciation may be taken.[6] The IRS has provided procedures on how to claim the bonus depreciation.[7] For eligible property, taxpayers may elect 50% bonus depreciation, 30% bonus depreciation, or no bonus depreciation.

For property used both in an individual's trade or business (or for the production of income) and in a personal or tax-exempt activity during a taxable year, depreciation is allocated to all uses of the property, and only the portion attributable to the trade or business or production of income use is deductible.[8]

The classification of property by recovery period and depreciation method is as follows:[9]

3 years 200% DB*	class life of 4 years or less, certain horses, qualified rent-to-own property
5 years 200% DB*	class life of more than 4 but less than 10 (e.g., heavy trucks, buses, offshore drilling equipment, most computer and data handling equipment, cattle, helicopters and non-commercial aircraft, automobiles and light trucks)
7 years 200% DB*	class life of 10 or more but less than 16 (e.g., most office furnishings, most agricultural machinery and equipment, theme park structures, most railroad machinery, equipment and track, commercial aircraft), motorsports entertainment complexes, Alaska natural gas pipelines, property without a class life and not otherwise classified under TRA '86
10 years 200% DB*	class life of 16 or more but less than 20 (e.g., vessels, barges and similar water transportation equipment, petroleum refining equipment)
15 years 150% DB*	class life of 20 or more but less than 25 (e.g., industrial steam and electric generation/distribution systems, cement manufacturing equipment, commercial water transportation equipment (freight or passenger), nuclear power production plants)

1. IRC Sec. 50(c)(1); Treas. Reg. §1.179-1(f)(1).
2. IRC Sec. 1016(a)(2).
3. Rev. Proc. 87-57, 1987-2 CB 687.
4. See Treas. Reg. §1.167(a)-5.
5. IRC Sec. 168(k)(1).
6. IRC Sec. 168(k)(4).
7. Rev. Proc. 2003-50, 2003-29 IRB 119.
8. Prop. Treas. Reg. §1.168-2(d)(2)(ii).
9. IRC Secs. 168(c), 168(e), Rev. Proc. 87-57, above.

20 years 150% DB*	class life of 25 or more (e.g., certain farm buildings, railroad structures and improvements, telephone central office buildings, gas utility production plants and distribution facilities), but excluding real property with class life of 27.5 years or more
27.5 years straight line	residential rental property
39 years straight line	nonresidential real property (class life of 27.5 years or more)
50 years straight line	railroad grading or tunnel bore

* Declining balance method switching to the straight line method at a time to maximize the deduction. Substitute 150% DB for 200% DB if 3-, 5-, 7-, or 10-year property is used in a farming business. An election can be made to use the straight line method instead of the declining balance method. Also, with respect to 3-, 5-, 7-, and 10-year property, an election can be made to use 150% DB.

Property is assigned to various *class lives* in Rev. Proc. 87-56.[1] These class lives can also be found in IRS Publication 946. The Tax Reform Act of 1986 assigned certain property to recovery periods without regard to their class life (e.g., automobiles and light trucks). Also, intangible property that is depreciable is subject to special recovery periods. If computer software is depreciable, the deduction is calculated using a straight line method over 36 months.[2] Computer software acquired after August 10, 1993 is generally depreciable if it (a) is a program designed to cause a computer to perform a desired function, (but generally not a database) and (b) either (1) is readily available for purchase by the general public, is subject to a nonexclusive license, and has not been substantially modified, or (2) is not acquired in a transaction involving the acquisition of assets constituting a trade or business.[3] Certain mortgage servicing rights may be depreciated over 108 months using the straight line method.[4]

Certain rights that are not acquired in a transaction involving the acquisition of a trade or business are subject to special rules for depreciation. Depreciation deductions for (1) rights to receive tangible property or services under a contract or a government grant; (2) interests in patents or copyrights; or (3) certain contracts of fixed duration or amount, are to be defined in the regulations.[5] Regulations generally require the amortization of the right to receive property under a contract or government grant by multiplying the basis of the right by a fraction. The numerator of the fraction is the amount of property or services received during the taxable year and the denominator is the total amount to be received under the contract or government grant. For a patent or copyright, the deduction is generally equal to the amount paid during a taxable year if the purchase price is paid on an annual basis as either a fixed amount per use or a fixed percentage of revenue from the patent or copyright, otherwise it is depreciated either ratably over its useful life or by using the income forecast method. The basis of a right to an unspecified amount over a fixed duration of less than 15 years is amortized ratably over the period of the right.[6]

In the years in which property is acquired or disposed of, depreciation is limited to the portion of the year in which the property is considered to be held under the

---

1. 1987-2 CB 674.
2. IRC Sec. 167(f)(1).
3. IRC Secs. 167(f)(1), 197(e)(3)(B).
4. IRC Sec. 167(f)(3).
5. IRC Sec. 167(f)(2).
6. Treas. Reg. §1.167(a)-14(c).

following *conventions*: Residential rental property, nonresidential real property, and railroad grading or tunnel bore are treated as placed in service (or disposed of) on the mid-point of the month in which placed in service (or disposed of). Property, other than such real property, is generally treated as placed in service (or disposed of) on the mid-point of the year in which placed in service. However, the mid-quarter convention (instead of the mid-year convention) applies to depreciable property placed in service during the taxable year if the aggregate bases of property placed in service during the last three months of the taxable year exceeds 40% of the aggregate bases of property placed in service (or disposed of) during the taxable year ("the 40% test"). "Aggregate bases" is defined as the sum of the depreciable bases of all items of depreciable property taken into account in applying the 40% test. For taxable years ending after January 30, 1991, property not taken into account in applying the test include the following: (1) real property subject to the mid-month convention (described above), and (2) property placed in service and disposed of in the same taxable year. Conversely, property that would be taken into account in applying the 40% test includes: (1) listed property (discussed under "Limitations," below) placed in service during the taxable year, and (2) property placed in service, disposed of, subsequently reacquired, and again placed in service in the same taxable year (but only the basis of the property on the later of the dates that the property is placed in service is considered).[1] The IRS has provided some relief from the mid-quarter convention if a taxpayer's third or fourth quarter included September 11, 2001.[2]

Regardless of whether the mid-year convention or the mid-quarter convention applies, no depreciation deduction is available for property placed in service and disposed of in the same year.[3]

Property subject to the mid-month convention is treated as placed in service (or disposed of) on the mid-point of the month without regard to whether the taxpayer has a short taxable year (i.e., a taxable year that is less than 12 months). The mid-quarter 40% test is also made without regard to the length of the taxable year. Thus, if property (with exceptions, as noted in the preceding paragraph) is placed in service in a taxable year of three months or less, the mid-quarter convention applies regardless of when such property was placed in service (i.e., 100% of property has been placed in service in the last three months).[4]

In the case of a short taxable year and with respect to property to which the mid-year or mid-quarter convention applies, the recovery allowance is determined by multiplying the deduction that would have been allowable if the recovery year were not a short taxable year by a fraction, the numerator of which equals the number of months in the short taxable year and the denominator of which is 12.[5] Proposed regulations provided under IRC Section 168(f)(5) (as in effect prior to TRA '86) that a taxable year of a person placing property in service did not include any month prior to the month in which the person began engaging in a trade or business or holding recovery property for the production of income.[6] Presumably, this principle would continue to apply after TRA '86.

---

1. IRC Sec. 168(d); Treas. Reg. §1.168(d)-1.
2. Notice 2001-74, 2001-2 CB 551.
3. Temp. Treas. Reg. §1.168(d)-1T(b)(3)(ii).
4. Rev. Proc. 89-15, 1989-1 CB 816.
5. Rev. Proc. 89-15, 1989-1 CB 816.
6. Prop. Treas. Reg. §1.168-2(f)(4).

Alternative Depreciation System

An *alternative depreciation system* is provided for (1) tangible property used predominately outside the United States, (2) tax-exempt use property, (3) tax-exempt bond financed property, (4) certain imported property covered by an executive order regarding countries engaging in unfair trade practices, and (5) property for which an election is made. The election may be made with respect to each property in the case of nonresidential real property and residential rental property. For all other property, the election is made with respect to all property placed in service within a recovery class during a taxable year.[1]

The alternative depreciation is determined using the straight line method and the applicable convention, above, over the following periods:[2]

tax-exempt use property subject to a lease	longer of 125% of lease term or period below
residential rental property and nonresidential real property	40 years
personal property with no class life	12 years
railroad grading or tunnel bore	50 years
all other property	the class life

TRA '86 assigns certain property to recovery periods without regard to their class life, e.g., automobiles and light trucks.

General Asset Accounts

Assets that are subject to either the general depreciation system of IRC Section 168(a) or the alternative depreciation system of IRC Section 168(g) may be grouped in one or more general asset accounts. The assets in a particular general asset account are generally depreciable as a single asset. Such an account must include only assets that have the same class, depreciation method, recovery period, convention, and that are placed in service in the same tax year. An asset may not be included in a general asset account if the asset is used in a personal activity at any time before the end of the tax year in which it was placed in service.[3]

Upon disposition of an asset from a general asset account, the asset is treated as having an adjusted basis of zero, and the total amount realized on the disposition is generally recognized as ordinary income. However, the ordinary income treatment is limited to the unadjusted basis of the account less amounts previously recognized as ordinary income. The character of the amounts in excess of such ordinary income is determined under other applicable provisions of the IRC (other than IRC Sections 1245 and 1250). Because the basis of the property is considered to be zero, no loss is recognized on such a disposition. Generally, the basis in the account is recoverable only through depreciation, unless the taxpayer disposes of all the assets in the account.[4]

---

1. IRC Sec. 168(g).
2. IRC Sec. 168(g)(2)(C).
3. Treas. Reg. §1.168(i)-1(c).
4. Treas. Reg. §1.168(i)-1(e).

Anti-churning Rules

"Anti-churning rules" require the use of the pre-1981 depreciation methods for property placed in service after 1980 (including property placed in service after 1986) if the property or substituted property was used, owned, or leased by certain persons before 1981. In the case of personal property, ACRS may not be used if: the investor or a party related to him owned or used the property in 1980; the property is leased to anyone who owned or used the property in 1980; or the property is acquired from its 1980 owner but the person actually using the property does not change. In the case of real property, ACRS may not be used if a related party owned the property in 1980, the property is leased back to its 1980 owner or to a party related to its 1980 owner, or the property is acquired for property of the individual or related party owned in 1980 in certain like kind exchanges, rollovers of low-income housing, involuntary conversions or repossessions.[1]

Additional "anti-churning" rules require the use of pre-1987 depreciation methods for property placed in service after 1986 if (1) the property or substituted property was used, owned, or leased by certain individuals before 1987 *and* (2) use of the post-1986 ACRS would result in a larger depreciation deduction than could be taken under preexisting law. Rules similar to those in the previous paragraph are to be applied to determine whether property is considered as property used, owned, or leased before 1987, substituting 1986 for 1980 and 1987 for 1981.[2]

The "anti-churning" rules do not apply with respect to property receiving a new basis under IRC Section 1014(a) when the property is acquired from a decedent (see Q 1415).[3] The share of community property received by a surviving spouse at the other spouse's death will not qualify for this exception to the anti-churning rules if the property was placed into service by both spouses prior to the decedent spouse's death (i.e., the general placed in service rules would apply).[4]

Unit of Production Method

Instead of using ACRS, a property owner may elect to use the unit of production method of depreciation (if appropriate) or any other method not expressed in a term of years.[5] For example, under the unit of production method, the depreciation deduction for a machine that, it is estimated, will produce 1,000,000 shoes (units) before wearing out, and that produces 250,000 units in the first year, would be:

$$\frac{250,000}{1,000,000} \text{ x basis.}$$

Election to Expense

A taxpayer may elect to treat the cost of certain qualifying property as an expense in the year the property is placed in service.[6] To qualify, property must be eligible for depreciation or certain amortization provisions, it must be personal property (or fall

---

1. IRC Secs. 168(f)(5)(A), 168(e)(4) (prior to amendment by TRA '86).
2. IRC Sec. 168(f)(5)(B).
3. IRC Secs. 168(f)(5), 168(e)(4)(H) (prior to amendment by TRA '86).
4. *Est. of Gasser v. Comm.*, 93 TC 236 (1989).
5. IRC Sec. 168(f)(1).
6. IRC Sec. 179.

within certain other categories described in IRC Section 1245(a)(3), such as property used for manufacturing or as a storage facility), and must have been acquired by purchase (from an unrelated person) for use in the active conduct of a trade or business. This property does not include any air conditioning or heating units or any ineligible property described in IRC Section 50(b) (certain property used outside the U.S., for lodging, by tax-exempt organizations, or by governments or foreign persons or entities). This election is not available to a trust or estate, nor can it be used for property held for the production of income.[1]

The aggregate cost that can be expensed when making this election is $112,000 (as indexed) in 2007. This amount is reduced by one dollar for each dollar of the cost of the above described property placed in service during the taxable year that exceeds $450,000 (as indexed). The $112,000 and $450,000 amounts are indexed for inflation through 2009. After 2009, the $112,000 amount is reduced to $25,000, and the $450,000 amount is reduced to $200,000.[2] The amount expensed is limited to the aggregate amount of income derived from the active conduct of any trade or business of the taxpayer. An amount that is not deductible because it exceeds the aggregate taxable income from any trade or business may be carried over and taken in a subsequent year. The amount that may be carried over and taken in a subsequent year is the lesser of (1) the amounts disallowed because of the taxable income limitation in all prior taxable years (reduced by any carryover deductions in previous taxable years); or (2) the amount of unused expense allowance for such year. The amount of unused expense allowance is the excess of (1) the maximum cost of property that may be expensed taking into account the dollar and income limitations; over (2) the amount the taxpayer elects to expense.[3] Married individuals filing separately are treated as one taxpayer for purposes of determining the amount that may be expensed and the total amount of investment in such property.[4] No General Business Credit is allowed for any amount expensed under IRC Section 179.[5]

Deductions permitted pursuant to a valid election to expense costs are not prorated if the taxpayer has a short tax year.[6]

Limitations

For any *passenger automobile* placed in service during taxable years after June 18, 1984, the amount of the depreciation deduction, including any amount elected as an expense (see above), cannot exceed the monetary limitations as set forth under the applicable heading in the exhibit, below. Note that once the unadjusted basis of an automobile is recovered, depreciation is no longer deductible. For certain automobiles acquired after September 11, 2001, and before January 1, 2005, the first year depreciation limitation is increased by $4,600. For certain automobiles purchased after May 5, 2003 and before January 1, 2005, the first year depreciation limit is increased by $7,650.[7]

---

1. IRC Secs. 179(d)(1), 179(d)(4).
2. IRC Sec. 179(b), as amended by TIPRA 2005; Rev. Proc. 2006-53, 2006-48 IRB 996.
3. IRC Sec. 179(b)(3); Treas. Reg. §1.179-3.
4. IRC Sec. 179(b)(4).
5. IRC Sec. 179(d)(9).
6. Treas. Reg. §1.179-1(c)(1).
7. See IRC Secs. 168(k)(2)(F), IRC Sec. 168(k)(4)(D).

Property Placed in Service	First Year	Second Year	Third Year	Succeeding Years
6-19-84 through 4-2-85	$4,000	$6,000	$6,000	$6,000
4-3-85 through 1986	$3,200	$4,800	$4,800	$4,800
1987 and 1988	$2,560	$4,100	$2,450	$1,475
1989 and 1990	$2,660	$4,200	$2,550	$1,475
1991	$2,660	$4,300	$2,550	$1,575
1992	$2,760	$4,400	$2,650	$1,575
1993	$2,860	$4,600	$2,750	$1,675
1994	$2,960	$4,700	$2,850	$1,675
1995 and 1996	$3,060	$4,900	$2,950	$1,775
1997	$3,160	$5,000	$3,050	$1,775
1998	$3,160	$5,000	$2,950	$1,775
1999	$3,060	$5,000	$2,950	$1,775
2000, 2001, 2002, and 2003	$3,060	$4,900	$2,950	$1,775
2004	$2,960	$4,800	$2,850	$1,675
2005	$2,960	$4,700	$2,850	$1,675
2006	$2,960	$4,800	$2,850	$1,775

[Rev. Proc. 2006-18, 2006-12 IRB 645; Rev. Proc. 2005-13, 2005-12 IRB 759; Rev. Proc. 2004-20, 2004-13 IRB 642; Rev. Proc. 2003-75, 2003-2 CB 1018; Rev. Proc. 2002-14, 2002-1 CB 450; Rev. Proc. 2001-19, 2001-1 CB 732; Rev. Proc. 2000-18, 2000-1 CB 722; Rev. Proc. 99-14, 1999-1 CB 413; Rev. Proc. 98-30, 1998-2 CB 930; Rev. Proc. 97-20, 1997-1 CB 647; Rev. Proc. 96-25, 1996-1 CB 681; Rev. Proc. 95-9, 1995-1 CB 498; Rev. Proc. 94-53, 1994-2 CB 712; Rev. Proc. 93-35, 1993-2 CB 472; Rev. Proc. 92-43, 1992-1 CB 873; Rev. Proc. 91-30, 1991-1 CB 563; Rev. Proc. 90-22, 1990-1 CB 504; Rev. Proc. 89-64, 1989-2 CB 783; IRC Sec. 280F(a).]

The dollar limitations are determined in the year the automobile is placed in service and are subject to an inflation adjustment (rounded to the nearest multiple of $100) for the calendar year in which the automobile is placed in service.[1] Taxpayers who lease passenger automobiles and are allowed a deduction for the lease are required to reduce the deduction if the fair market value of the automobile is greater than a certain amount. For lease terms beginning in 2006, the amount is $15,200. This reduction is accomplished by including in gross income an amount determined from tables promulgated by the IRS. The amount to be added to income is dependent on the fair market value of the automobile at the time the lease term begins. The higher the value of the automobile, the more that is added to income.[2] "Passenger automobiles" do not include ambulances, hearses, trucks, vans or other vehicles used by a taxpayer in a trade or business of transporting persons or property for compensation or hire.[3]

The amount of the depreciation deductions is also limited for "listed property" placed in service (or leased) after June 18, 1984 (generally) if the business use of the property does not exceed 50% of its total use during the taxable year.[4] "Listed property" includes any passenger automobile or other property used for transportation (generally, unless used in transportation business); any property of a type used for entertainment, recreation or amusement; any computer (except computers used exclusively at a regular business establishment or at a dwelling unit that meets the home office requirement); any cellular telephone (or similar equipment); or other property specified by the regulations.[5] In the case of passenger automobiles, this personal use limitation is applied after the passenger automobile limitation, above.[6]

---

1. IRC Sec. 280F(d)(7).
2. See Treas. Reg. §1.280F-7; Rev. Proc. 2006-18, 2006-12 IRB 645.
3. IRC Sec. 280F(d)(5)(B).
4. IRC Sec. 280F(b).
5. IRC Sec. 280F(d)(4).
6. IRC Sec. 280F(a)(2).

If the business use of the listed property does not exceed 50%, depreciation under the regular pre-1987 ACRS and post-1986 ACRS is not allowed. For such property placed in service after 1986, the amount of the depreciation deduction is limited to that amount determined using the alternative depreciation system (see above).[1] For such property placed in service after June 18, 1984 and before 1987, the amount of the recovery is generally limited to that amount determined using the straight line method over the following earnings and profit lives:[2]

In the case of:	The applicable recovery period is:
3-year property	5 years
5-year property	12 years
10-year property	25 years
15-year public utility property	35 years
19-year real prop. and low income housing	40 years

The more-than-50% business use requirement must be met solely by use of the listed property in a trade or business, without regard to the percentage of any use in another income producing activity. However, the percentage of use in any other income producing activity is added to the business use when determining the unadjusted basis of the property subject to depreciation (the unadjusted basis is the same as the initial basis, described above). If the listed property meets the more-than-50% business use requirement in the year it is placed in service and ceases to do so in a subsequent year, then any "excess depreciation" will be recaptured and included in gross income in the year it ceases to meet the requirement. "Excess depreciation" is the *excess*, if any, of the depreciation allowable while the property met the business use requirement *over* the depreciation that would have been allowable if the property had not met the requirement for the taxable year it was placed in service.[3] This excess depreciation recapture is distinct from the depreciation recapture that occurs on early disposition; see "Recapture," below.

Depreciable Intangible Assets

Generally, taxpayers are permitted a depreciation deduction for certain intangible property. The depreciation deduction is allowable for certain computer software, business interests and rights, and mortgage servicing rights.[4] The deduction generally is allowable for depreciable intangible property acquired after August 10, 1993, unless the taxpayer elects to take the deduction for such intangible property acquired after July 25, 1991. If the taxpayer chooses, he may also elect to forgo taking the depreciation deduction and, instead, amortize such intangible property if the property was acquired by the taxpayer pursuant to a written contract in effect on August 10, 1993 and at all times up to the date of acquisition.[5]

Intangible property for which the depreciation deduction is allowable includes (1) any computer program designed to cause a computer to perform a desired function (but it generally does not include any data base), (2) a right under a contract or granted by a government entity that entitles the taxpayer to receive tangible property or services,

---

1. IRC Sec. 280F(b)(1).
2. IRC Secs. 280F(b)(2), 312(k), both as in effect prior to amendment by TRA '86.
3. IRC Sec. 280F(b)(2).
4. IRC Sec. 167(f).
5. OBRA '93, Sec. 13261(g).

(3) a right under a contract or granted by a government agency if such right has a fixed duration of less than 15 years, or if such right is fixed as to amount and would otherwise be recoverable under a method similar to a unit-of-production method, (4) any interest in a patent or copyright, and (5) any right to service indebtedness that is secured by residential real property. Generally, if any of the intangible property described above was acquired by the taxpayer upon the acquisition of a trade or business, the depreciation deduction will not be allowable.[1]

Effect on Basis

Each year, an individual's basis is reduced by the amount of the depreciation deduction taken so that his adjusted basis in the property reflects accumulated depreciation deductions. If depreciation is not deducted, his basis must nonetheless be reduced by the amount of depreciation allowable, but the deduction may not be taken in a subsequent year.[2]

Recapture

Upon disposition of property, the seller often realizes more than his basis after it has been reduced for depreciation. Legislative policy is that on certain dispositions of depreciated property the seller realizes a gain that is, at least in part, attributable to depreciation. To prevent a double benefit, the IRC requires that some of the gain that would otherwise generally be capital gain, must be treated as ordinary income. In effect, it requires the seller to "recapture" some of the ordinary income earlier offset by the depreciation.[3] In addition, if depreciated property ceases to be used predominantly in a trade or business before the end of its recovery period, the owner must recapture in the tax year of cessation any benefit derived from expensing such property.[4] This provision is effective for property placed in service in tax years ending after January 25, 1993.[5]

EXEMPTIONS AND DEDUCTIONS FROM ADJUSTED GROSS INCOME

1425. What personal exemptions is an individual entitled to deduct in calculating his taxable income?

Taxpayers generally are permitted to deduct the following personal exemption amounts: (1) For taxable years beginning in 2007, $3,400 for husband and wife each on a joint return ($6,800 for both); (2) $3,400 for a taxpayer filing a single or separate return; (3) $3,400 for the spouse of a taxpayer filing a separate return, provided the spouse has *no gross* income and is not claimed as the dependent of another taxpayer.[6] The personal exemption amount is adjusted annually for inflation.[7] Generally, the exemption will not be allowed unless the Social Security number of the individual for whom the personal exemption is being claimed is provided.[8]

The personal exemptions of certain upper income taxpayers are phased out over defined income levels. The dollar amount of personal and dependency exemptions of

1. IRC Secs. 167(f), 197(e)(4), 197(e)(6).
2. IRC Sec. 1016(a)(2).
3. IRC Secs. 1245, 1250.
4. Treas. Reg. §1.179-1(e)(1).
5. Treas. Reg. §1.179-6.
6. Rev. Proc. 2006-53, 2006-48 IRB 996.
7. IRC Sec. 151.
8. IRC Sec. 151(e).

taxpayers with adjusted gross income above certain levels is reduced by an "applicable percentage" in the amount of two percentage points for every $2,500 (or fraction thereof; $1,250 in the case of a married individual filing separately) by which the taxpayer's adjusted gross income exceeds the following threshold amounts in 2007: Married filing jointly (and surviving spouses): $234,600; Head of household: $195,500; Single: $156,400; Married filing separately: $117,300. The phaseout is completed at the following income levels: Married filing jointly (and surviving spouses): $357,100; Head of household: $318,000; Single: $278,900; Married filing separately: $178,550. These amounts are adjusted annually for inflation.[1]

Editor's Note Beginning in 2006, the phaseout is gradually reduced each year until it is completely repealed in 2010. The amended phaseout amount is calculated by multiplying the otherwise applicable phaseout amount by the "applicable fraction." The applicable fraction for each year is as follows: 66.6% (⅔) in 2006 and 2007; 33.3% (⅓) in 2008 and 2009; and 0% in 2010.[2]

A child or other dependent (i.e., an individual who may be claimed as a dependent by another taxpayer) who files his own return cannot claim a personal exemption for himself.[3]

1426. What conditions must be met to entitle the taxpayer to a dependency exemption?

A taxpayer may claim the dependency exemption for each dependent with respect to whom the following tests are met.[4] The term "dependent" means a "qualifying child" (see below) or a "qualifying relative" (see below).[5]

Dependents may not claim a personal exemption for themselves in addition to the exemption claimed by the taxpayer who supports them.[6] The dependent, if married, must not file a joint return with his or her spouse.[7] In addition, the term "dependent" does not include an individual who is not a citizen or resident of the United States (*or* a resident of Canada or Mexico). However, a legally adopted child who does not satisfy the residency or citizenship requirements may nevertheless qualify as a dependent if certain requirements are met.[8]

The taxpayer may claim the exemption even though the dependent files a return. The taxpayer must include the Social Security number of any dependent claimed on his return.[9]

Qualifying child. The term "qualifying child" means an individual who:

(1)   is the taxpayer's "child" (see below) or a descendant of such a child, *or* the taxpayer's brother, sister, stepbrother, stepsister or a descendant of any such relative;

---

1. IRC Secs. 151(d)(3), 151(d)(4); Rev. Proc. 2006-53, above.
2. IRC Secs. 151(d)(3)(E), 151(d)(3)(F).
3. IRC Sec. 151(d)(2).
4. IRC Secs. 151, 152.
5. IRC Sec. 152(a).
6. IRC Sec. 152(b)(1).
7. IRC Sec. 152(b)(2).
8. IRC Sec. 152(b)(3).
9. See, e.g., *Miller v. Comm.*, 114 TC 184 (2000).

(2)   has the same principal place of abode as the taxpayer for more than one-half of the taxable year;

(3)   has not attained the age of 19 as of the close of the calendar year in which the taxable year begins, *or* is a student who has not attained the age of 24 as of the close of the calendar year; *and*

(4)   has *not* provided over one-half of the individual's own support for the calendar year in which the taxpayer's taxable year begins.[1]

The term "child" means an individual who is: (1) a son, daughter, stepson, or stepdaughter of the taxpayer; or (2) an "eligible foster child" of the taxpayer.[2] An "eligible foster child" means an individual who is placed with the taxpayer by an authorized placement agency or by judgment decree, or other order of any court of competent jurisdiction.[3] Any adopted children of the taxpayer are treated the same as natural born children.[4]

Qualifying relative. The term "qualifying relative" means an individual:

(1)   who is the taxpayer's:

         (i) child or a descendant of a child,

         (ii) brother, sister, stepbrother, or stepsister,

         (iii) father or mother or an ancestor of either, or stepfather or stepmother,

         (iv) son or daughter of a brother or sister of the taxpayer,

         (v) brother or sister of the father or mother of the taxpayer,

         (vi) son-in-law, daughter-in-law, father-in-law, mother-in-law, brother-in-law, or sister-in-law, or

         (vii) an individual (other than a spouse) who, for the taxable year of the taxpayer, has the same principal place of abode as the taxpayer and is a member of the taxpayer's household;

(2)   whose gross income for the calendar year in which the taxable year begins is less than the exemption amount (see below);

(3)   for whom the taxpayer provides over one-half of the individual's support for the calendar year in which the taxable year begins; *and*

(4)   who is not a qualifying child of the taxpayer or of any other taxpayer for any taxable year beginning in the calendar year in which the taxable year begins.

---

1. IRC Sec. 152(c). See also FS-2205-7 (Jan. 2005).
2. IRC Sec. 152(f)(1).
3. IRC Sec. 152(f)(1)(C).
4. IRC Sec. 152(f)(1)(B).

The amount of the personal exemption ($3,400 in 2007) is adjusted annually for inflation. The exemption is subject to phaseout for certain upper income taxpayers. For details, see Q 1425.

Special rule for divorced parents. In the case of divorced parents who between them provide more than one-half of a child's support for the calendar year, and have custody of the child for more than one-half of the calendar year, the custodial parent (i.e., the one having custody for the greater portion of the year) is generally allowed the dependency exemption. However, the noncustodial parent can claim the exemption if the custodial parent signs a written declaration (i.e., Form 8332, or a statement conforming to the substance of Form 8332) agreeing not to claim the child as a dependent, *and* the noncustodial parent attaches the declaration to his tax return for the calendar year. The noncustodial parent can also claim the exemption if a divorce decree or separation agreement executed before 1985 expressly provides such and he provides at least $600 for the support of the child during the calendar year.[1] The Tax Court held that the special support rule under IRC Section 152(e) applies to parents who have never been married as well as divorced parents.[2]

The Service has clarified that a custodial parent may revoke the release of the dependency exemption and, therefore, claim the dependency exemption himself, but only if the noncustodial parent agrees and does not claim the child.[3]

In *Miller v. Comm.*,[4] the Tax Court denied the dependency exemption to the noncustodial parent where the custodial parent had not signed a release of the claim to the exemption; the court order, giving the noncustodial parent the right to claim the exemption, was held not to be a valid substitute.

In *Boltinghouse v. Comm.*,[5] the Tax Court held that there is no requirement in IRC Section 152(e) or the regulations that a spouse's waiver of his claim to a dependency exemption deduction be incorporated into a divorce decree to be effective. The court stated that such a requirement would make Form 8332 itself ineffective on its own. The court also recognized that under the applicable state law (Delaware), the separation agreement created binding contractual obligations that did not cease upon the entry of a divorce decree (regardless of whether the agreement was merged or incorporated into the decree).

In *Omans v. Comm.*,[6] the Tax Court determined that the custodial parent's certified signature on the settlement agreement signified her sworn agreement to the settlement agreement's contents, including her former spouse's entitlement to the dependency exemption.

A state appeals court held that federal law does not preempt a state family law court in its discretion from alternating the dependency exemption between the parents, even though one parent may have custody during the calendar year for less than half the year.[7]

---

1. IRC Secs. 152(e).
2. *King v. Comm.*, 121 TC 245 (2003).
3. Legal Memorandum 200007031.
4. 114 TC 184 (2000).
5. TC Memo 2003-134.
6. TC Summary Opinion 2005-110.
7. *Rios v. Pulido*, 2002 Cal. App. LEXIS 4412 (2nd App. Dist. 2002).

Life insurance premiums on a child's life are not included in determining the cost of his support.[1]

The Tax Court held that a dependent's self-employment loss did not reduce her earned income for purposes of determining her standard deduction under IRC Section 63(c)(5)(B).[2]

Deductions

1427. What itemized deductions may be taken by an individual taxpayer?

Itemized deductions are subtracted *from* adjusted gross income in arriving at taxable income; they may be claimed in addition to deductions *for* adjusted gross income (see Q 1423). Itemized deductions are also referred to as "below-the-line" deductions.

In 2007, the aggregate of most itemized deductions is reduced dollar-for-dollar by the lesser of (1) 3% of the amount of the individual's adjusted gross income that exceeds $156,400 ($78,200 in the case of a married taxpayer filing separately) or (2) 80% of the amount of such itemized deductions otherwise allowable for the taxable year.[3] The threshold income amounts at which the limit is imposed are adjusted annually for inflation.[4]

For taxable years beginning after 2005 and before 2010, the limitation on itemized deductions is gradually reduced until it is completely repealed in 2010. The amended limitation amount is calculated by multiplying the otherwise applicable limitation amount by the "applicable fraction." The "application fraction" for each year is as follows: 66.6% (⅔) in 2006 and 2007; 33.3% (⅓) in 2008 and 2009; and 0% in 2010.[5]

The limitation on itemized deductions is not applicable to medical expenses deductible under IRC Section 213, investment interest deductible under IRC Section 163(d), or certain casualty loss deductions.[6] The limitation also is not applicable to estates and trusts.[7] For purposes of certain other calculations, such as the limits on deduction of charitable contributions or the 2% floor on miscellaneous itemized deductions, the limitations on each separate category of deductions are applied *before* the overall ceiling on itemized deductions is applied.[8] The deduction limitation is not taken into account in the calculation of the alternative minimum tax.[9]

Among the itemized deductions taxpayers may be able to claim are the following:

...Interest, within limits (see Q 1301 to Q 1308).

---

1. *Kittle v. Comm.*, TC Memo 1975-150; *Vance v. Comm.*, 36 TC 547 (1961).
2. *Briggs v. Comm.*, TC Summary 2004-22.
3. IRC Sec. 68(a).
4. IRC Sec. 68(b); Rev. Proc. 2006-53, 2006-48 IRB 996.
5. IRC Sec. 68(f).
6. IRC Sec. 68(c).
7. IRC Sec. 68(e).
8. IRC Sec. 68(d).
9. IRC Sec. 56(b)(1)(F).

...Personal expenses for the production or collection of taxable income, within limits (see Q 1310), or in conjunction with the determination, collection or refund of any tax (but some of these expenses may be considered "miscellaneous itemized deductions" (see Q 1312). Deduction of expenses paid in connection with tax-exempt income may be disallowed (see Q 1311). Certain business expenses and expenses for the production of rents and royalties are deductible *in arriving at* adjusted gross income (see Q 1423).

...Personal taxes of the following types: state, local and foreign real property taxes; state and local personal property taxes; state, local and foreign income, war profits, and excess profits taxes; and the generation-skipping tax imposed on income distributions. If taxes other than these are incurred in connection with the acquisition or disposition of property, they must be treated as part of the cost of such property or as a reduction in the amount realized on the disposition.[1]

Sales tax deduction option extended through 2007. Under AJCA 2004, taxpayers may elect to deduct state and local general sales taxes instead of state and local income taxes when they itemize deductions.[2] Initially, this option was only available for tax years 2004 and 2005, but it was extended, and is now available for tax years 2006 and 2007 as well.[3]

The itemized deduction may be based on *actual* sales taxes, or on the optional sales tax *tables* published by the IRS.[4] In general, a taxpayer can deduct actual state and local general sales taxes paid if the tax rate was the same as the general sales tax rate. If the tax rate is more than the general sales tax rate, sales taxes on motor vehicles are deductible as general sales taxes, but the tax is deductible only up to the amount of tax that would have been imposed at the general sales tax rate. Sales taxes on food, clothing, medical supplies, and motor vehicles are deductible as a general sales tax even if the tax rate was less than the general sales tax rate.[5] The Service reminds taxpayer that actual receipts showing general sales taxes paid must be kept to use the actual expense method.[6]

Using the optional state sales tax tables, taxpayers use their income level and number of exemptions to find the sales tax amount for their state.[7] Taxpayers may add an amount for *local* sales taxes if appropriate. In addition, taxpayers may add to the table amount any sales taxes paid on: (1) a motor vehicle, but only up to the amount of tax paid at the general sales tax rate; and (2) an aircraft, boat, home, or home building materials if the tax rate is the same as the general sales tax rate.[8]

The Service comments that although the sales tax deduction mainly benefits taxpayers with a state or local sales tax but no income tax (i.e., Alaska, Florida, South Dakota, Texas, Washington, and Wyoming), it may also give a larger deduction to any taxpayer who paid more in sales taxes than income taxes. For example, an individual may have bought a new car, thus boosting the sales tax total, or claimed tax credits, thus

---

1. IRC Sec. 164(a).
2. IRC Sec. 164(b)(5)(A).
3. IRC Sec. 164(b)(5)(I), as amended by TRHCA 2006.
4. See IRC Sec. 164(b)(5)(H).
5. See IRC Secs. 164(b)(5)(C), 164(b)(5)(D), 164(b)(5)(F). See also Pub. 600, State and Local General Sales Taxes (2006); FS-2006-9 (Jan. 2006).
6. Pub. 600.
7. See Publication 600, State and Local General Sales Taxes, pp. 2 - 4 (2006).
8. See Pub. 600, State and Local General Sales Taxes (2006); see also FS-2006-9 (Jan. 2006).

lowering the state income tax paid.[1] For additional guidance on claiming the sales tax deduction, see Notice 2005-31.[2]

...Uncompensated personal casualty and theft losses. But these are deductible only to the extent that the aggregate amount of uncompensated losses in excess of $100 (for each casualty or theft) exceeds 10% of adjusted gross income.[3] The taxpayer must file a timely insurance claim for damage to property that is not business or investment property or else the deduction is disallowed to the extent that insurance would have provided compensation.[4] Uncompensated casualty and theft losses in connection with a taxpayer's business or in connection with the production of income are deductible in full (see Q 1233).

Stock losses. The IRS has announced that it intends to disallow deductions under IRC Section 165(a) for theft losses relating to declines in value of publicly traded stock when the decline is attributable to corporate misconduct. If the stock is sold or exchanged or becomes wholly worthless, any resulting loss will be treated as a capital loss. Furthermore, the Service may also impose penalties under IRC Section 6662 in such cases.[5]

...Contributions to charitable organizations, within certain limitations (see Q 1315, Q 1340).

...Unreimbursed medical and dental expenses and expenses for the purchase of prescribed drugs or insulin incurred by the taxpayer for himself and his spouse and dependents, to the extent that such expenses exceed 7.5% of his adjusted gross income (see Q 1429).

...Expenses of an employee connected with his employment. Generally, such expenses are "miscellaneous itemized deductions" (see Q 1428).

...Federal estate taxes and generation-skipping transfer taxes paid on "income in respect of a decedent" (see Q 1430).

Generally, certain moving expenses permitted under IRC Section 217 are deductible directly from gross income (see Q 1423).

Many of these deductions are disallowed in calculating the alternative minimum tax (see Q 1440).

In chief counsel advice, the Service has determined that deductions for expenses paid or incurred in connection with the administration of an individual's estate in bankruptcy, which would have not been incurred if the property were not held by the bankrupt estate, are treated as allowable in arriving at adjusted gross income.[6]

1428. What are miscellaneous itemized deductions? What limits apply?

1. FS-2006-9 (Jan. 2006).
2. 2005-14 IRB 830.
3. IRC Sec. 165(h).
4. IRC Sec. 165(h)(4)(E).
5. Notice 2004-27, 2004-1 CB 782; Treasury Release JS-1263 (3-25-2004).
6. CCA 200630016.

"Miscellaneous itemized deductions" are deductions *from* adjusted gross income ("itemized deductions") *other than* the deductions for (1) interest, (2) taxes, (3) non-business casualty losses and gambling losses, (4) charitable contributions, (5) medical and dental expenses, (6) impairment-related work expenses for handicapped employees, (7) estate taxes on income in respect of a decedent, (8) certain short sale expenses (see Q 1024, Q 1025), (9) certain adjustments under the IRC claim of right provisions, (10) unrecovered investment in an annuity contract, (11) amortizable bond premium (see Q 1120, Q 1126), and (12) certain expenses of cooperative housing corporations.[1]

"Miscellaneous itemized deductions" are allowed only to the extent that the aggregate of all such deductions for the taxable year exceeds 2% of adjusted gross income.[2] For tax years beginning before 2010, miscellaneous itemized deductions are also subject to the reduction for certain upper income taxpayers (see Q 1427).

Miscellaneous itemized deductions generally include unreimbursed employee business expenses, such as professional society dues or job hunting expenses, and expenses for the production of income, such as investment advisory fees or the cost for storage of taxable securities in a safe deposit box.[3]

Expenses that relate to both a trade or business activity and a production of income or tax preparation activity (see Q 1310, Q 1312) must be allocated between the activities on a reasonable basis.[4]

Certain legal expenses from employment-related litigation may be deductible.[5] In *Biehl v. Comm.*,[6] the Ninth Circuit Court of Appeals affirmed the Tax Court's holding that attorneys' fees paid in connection with employment related litigation must be treated as a miscellaneous itemized deduction, and *not* as an above-the-line deduction. The Ninth Circuit stated that simply because a lawsuit arises of out the taxpayer's former employment, that determination is not sufficient to qualify the taxpayer's attorneys' fees for an above-the-line deduction under IRC Section 62(a)(2)(A). Concurring in the Tax Court's analysis, the Ninth Circuit reiterated that the proper inquiry in deciding whether an expense has a "business connection" is what the expenditure was "in connection with" and not simply whether the expenditure arose from, or had its origins in, the taxpayer's trade or business. According to the appeals court, whereas IRC Section 62(a)(1) only requires that the expense be attributable to a trade or business, the language in IRC Section 62(a)(2)(A) is much more definite. The court concluded that for a reimbursable expense to qualify for an above-the-line deduction, not only must it be attributable to a trade or business, it must also have been incurred during the course of "performance of services as an employee."[7]

The IRC prohibits the indirect deduction, through pass-through entities, of amounts (i.e., miscellaneous itemized deductions) that would not be directly deductible by individuals.[8] However, publicly offered mutual funds are not subject to this rule, and "pass-through entity," for this purpose, does not include estates, trusts (except for grantor

1. IRC Sec. 67(b).
2. IRC Sec. 67(a).
3. Temp. Treas. Reg. §1.67-1T(a)(1).
4. Temp. Treas. Reg. §1.67-1T(c).
5. See, e.g., *Kenseth v. Comm.*, 88 AFTR 2d 2001-5153; *Brenner v. Comm.*, TC Memo 2001-127; *Reynolds v. Comm.*, 296 F.3d 608 (7th Cir. 2002).
6. No. 02-72723 (9th Cir. 2003).
7. *Biehl*, above, *aff'g*, 118 TC 467 (2002).
8. IRC Sec. 67(c)(1); Temp. Treas. Reg. §1.67-2T.

trusts and certain common trust funds) cooperatives or real estate investment trusts.[1] Affected pass-through entities (including partnerships, S corporations, nonpublicly-offered mutual funds and REMICs) must generally allocate to each investor his respective share of such expenses; the investor must then take the items into account for purposes of determining his taxable income and deductible expenses, if any.[2] See Q 1148, Q 1162, Q 1176, Q 1189, and Q 1218 regarding REMICs, mutual funds, exchange-traded funds, publicly traded limited partnerships, and S corporations, respectively.

1429. What are the limits on the medical expense deduction?

A taxpayer who itemizes deductions can deduct unreimbursed expenses for "medical care" (the term "medical care" includes dental care) and expenses for *prescribed* drugs or insulin for himself, his spouse and his dependents, to the extent that such expenses exceed 7.5% of his adjusted gross income. (On a joint return, the 7.5% floor is based on the combined adjusted gross income of husband and wife.) The taxpayer first determines his net unreimbursed expenses by subtracting all reimbursements received during the year from total expenses for medical care paid during the year. He must then subtract 7.5% of his adjusted gross income from net unreimbursed medical expenses; only the balance, if any, is deductible.[3] The deduction for medical expenses is not subject to the reduction in itemized deductions for certain upper income taxpayers. (See Q 1427.)

"Medical care" is defined as amounts paid: (a) for the diagnosis, cure, mitigation, treatment, or prevention of disease, or for the purpose of affecting any structure or function of the body; (b) for transportation primarily for and essential to such medical care; (c) for qualified long-term services; or (d) for insurance covering such care or for any qualified long-term care insurance contract.[4]

The term "medical care" does not include cosmetic surgery or other similar procedures unless necessary to correct a deformity resulting from a congenital abnormality, a personal injury resulting from accident or trauma, or a disfiguring disease.[5] But see *Al-Murshidi v. Comm.*[6] (the surgical removal of excess skin from a formerly obese individual was not "cosmetic surgery" for purposes of IRC Section 213(d)(9)(A) because the procedures meaningfully promoted the proper function of the individual's body and treated her disease; thus, the costs of the surgical procedures were deductible despite the "cosmetic surgery" classification given to the procedures by the surgeon).

A taxpayer can deduct the medical expenses he pays for a dependent (within the specified limits) even though he is not entitled to a dependency exemption. The fact that the dependent's income exceeds $3,400 (in 2007) for the year is immaterial so long as the taxpayer has furnished over one-half of his support. A child of parents who are divorced (or in some situations, separated) *and* who between them provide more than one-half of the child's support for the calendar year and have custody of the child for more than one-half of the calendar year will be treated as a dependent of both parents for purposes of this deduction.[7] But in the case of a multiple support agreement, only the person designated to take the dependency exemption may deduct the dependent's

---

1. IRC Sec. 67(c); Temp. Treas. Reg. §1.67-2T(g)(2).
2. Temp. Treas. Reg. §1.67-2T(a).
3. IRC Sec. 213.
4. IRC Sec. 213(d)(1).
5. IRC Sec. 213(d)(9); see, e.g., Let. Rul. 200344010.
6. TC Summary Opinion 2001-185.
7. IRC Sec. 213(d)(5).

medical expenses, and then only to the extent that he actually paid the expenses.[1] See Q 1426.

Deductible medical expenses include amounts paid for lodging, up to $50 per individual per night, while away from home *primarily for and essential to* medical care if such care is provided by a physician in a licensed hospital (or similar medical care facility) and there is no element of personal pleasure, recreation or vacation in the travel away from home. No deduction is allowed if the lodgings are "lavish or extravagant."[2] A mother was permitted to deduct lodging expenses incurred when her child was receiving medical care away from home and her presence was essential to such care.[3] A parent's costs of attending a medical conference (i.e., registration fee, transportation costs) to obtain information about a chronic disease affecting the parent's child were deductible so long as the costs were primarily for and essential to the medical care of the dependent. However, the costs of meals and lodging incurred by the parent while attending the conference were not deductible.[4] The Service privately ruled that taxpayers could deduct special education tuition for their children as a medical care expense where the children attended a school primarily to receive medical care in the form of special education and in those years each child had been diagnosed as having a medical condition that handicapped the child's ability to learn.[5]

Generally, medical expenses are deductible only in the year they are paid, regardless of when the expenses were incurred. (But see *Zipkin v. U.S.*,[6] holding that expenses incurred by a taxpayer to build a home to meet his wife's special health needs were properly deducted in the year the home became habitable, even though the costs had been paid in earlier years.) Costs paid by parents to modify a van used to transport their handicapped child were deductible in the year those costs were paid; however, the court held that depreciation was not a deductible medical expense.[7] However, medical expenses of a decedent paid out of his estate within one year from date of death are considered paid by the decedent at the time the expenses were incurred.[8] A decedent's medical expenses cannot be taken as an income tax deduction unless a statement is filed waiving the right to deduct them for estate tax purposes. Amounts not deductible under IRC Section 213 may not be treated as deductible medical expenses for estate tax purposes. Thus, expenses that do not exceed the 7.5% floor are not deductible.[9]

The Social Security hospital tax that an individual pays as an employee or self-employed person cannot be deducted as a medical expense.[10] But a 65-year-old who has signed up for the supplementary medical plan under Medicare can treat his monthly premiums as amounts paid for insurance covering medical care. See Q 154.[11] A new voluntary prescription drug insurance program, Medicare Part D, went into effect on January 1, 2006. According to the Service, an individual taxpayer can include in medical expenses the premiums paid for Medicare Part D insurance.[12]

1. Treas. Reg. §1.213-1(a)(3)(i).
2. IRC Sec. 213(d)(2).
3. Let. Rul. 8516025.
4. Rev. Rul. 2000-24, 2000-19 IRB 963.
5. See Let. Rul. 200521003.
6. 2000-2 USTC ¶50,863 (D. Minn. 2000).
7. *Henderson v. Comm.*, TC Memo 2000-321.
8. IRC Sec. 213(c).
9. Rev. Rul. 77-357, 1977-2 CB 328.
10. See IRC Sec. 213(d).
11. Rev. Rul. 66-216, 1966-2 CB 100.
12. See Pub. 502, Medical and Dental Expenses (2006).

The unreimbursed portion of an entrance fee for life care in a residential retirement facility that is allocable to future medical care is also deductible as a medical expense in the year paid (but, if the resident leaves the facility and receives a refund, the refund is includable in gross income to the extent it is attributable to the deduction previously allowed).[1] Either the percentage method or the actuarial method may be used to calculate the portions of monthly service fees (paid for lifetime residence in a continuing care retirement community) allocable to medical care.[2]

Amounts paid by an individual for medicines and drugs, which can be purchased without a doctor's prescription, are not deductible.[3] However, amounts paid by an individual for equipment (e.g., crutches), supplies (e.g., bandages), or diagnostic devices (e.g., blood sugar test kits) may qualify as amounts paid for medical care and may be deductible under IRC Section 213. (In this ruling, the IRS determined that the crutches were used to mitigate the effect of the taxpayer's injured leg and the blood sugar test kits were used to monitor and assist in treating the taxpayer's diabetes; accordingly, the costs were amounts paid for medical care and were deductible.)[4]

The costs of nutritional supplements, vitamins, herbal supplements, and "natural medicines" cannot be included in medical expenses unless they are recommended by a doctor as treatment for a specific medical condition diagnosed by a doctor.[5] Certain expenses for smoking cessation programs and products are deductible as a medical expense.[6]

Amounts paid by individuals for breast reconstruction surgery following a mastectomy for cancer, and for vision correction surgery are medical care expenses and are deductible. But amounts paid by individuals to whiten teeth discolored as a result of age are not medical care expenses and are not deductible.[7]

Costs paid by individuals for participation in a weight-loss program as treatment for a specific disease or diseases (e.g., obesity, hypertension, or heart disease) diagnosed by a physician are deductible as medical expenses; however, costs of diet food are not deductible.[8] According to Publication 502 (2006), this includes fees paid by a taxpayer for membership in a weight reduction group and attendance at periodic meetings. Membership dues for a gym, health club, or spa cannot be included in medical expenses, but separate fees charged for weight loss activities can be included as medical expenses. In informational guidance, the IRS has also stated that taxpayers may deduct exercise expenses, including the cost of equipment to use in the home, if required to treat an illness (including obesity) diagnosed by a physician. For an exercise expense to be deductible, the taxpayer must establish the purpose of the expense is to treat a disease rather than to promote general health, and that the taxpayer would not have paid the expense but for this purpose.[9]

1. Rev. Rul. 76-481, 1976-2 CB 82, *as clarified by* Rev. Rul. 93-72, 1993-2 CB 77; Let. Rul. 8641037.
2. *Baker v. Comm.*, 122 TC 143 (2004).
3. Rev. Rul. 2003-58, 2003-22 IRB 959.
4. Rev. Rul. 2003-58, above; see also IRS Information Letter INFO-2003-169 (6-13-2003).
5. Pub. 502, Medical and Dental Expenses (2006).
6. See Rev. Rul. 99-28, 1999-25 IRB 6.
7. Rev. Rul. 2003-57, 2003-22 IRB 959.
8. Rev. Rul. 2002-19, 2002-16 IRB 778.
9. Information Letter INFO 2003-0202.

Expenses for childbirth classes were deductible as a medical expense to the extent that the class prepared the taxpayer for an active role in the process of childbirth.[1] Egg donor fees and expenses relating to obtaining a willing egg donor count as medical care expenses that are deductible.[2]

The Service has clarified that no deduction is allowed for the cost of drugs imported from Canada.[3]

1430. What is income in respect of a decedent and how is it taxed? Is the recipient entitled to an income tax deduction for estate and generation-skipping transfer taxes paid on this income?

"Income in respect of a decedent" (IRD) refers to those amounts to which a decedent was entitled as gross income, but that were not includable in his taxable income for the year of his death.[4] It can include, for example: renewal commissions of a sales representative; payment for services rendered before death or under a deferred compensation agreement; and, proceeds from sales on the installment method (see Q 1408). Generally, if stock is acquired in an S corporation from a decedent, the pro rata share of any income of the corporation that would have been IRD if that item had been acquired directly from the decedent is IRD.[5]

The IRS has determined that a distribution from a qualified plan of the balance as of the employee's death is IRD.[6] The Service has also privately ruled that a distribution from a 403(b) tax sheltered annuity is IRD.[7] The Service also concluded that a death benefit paid to beneficiaries from a deferred variable annuity would be IRD to the extent that the death benefit exceeded the owner's investment in the contract.[8] In addition, the Service has determined that distributions from a decedent's individual retirement account were IRD, including those parts of the distributions used to satisfy the decedent's estate tax obligation, since the individual retirement account was found to have automatically vested in the beneficiaries.[9] However, a rollover of funds from a decedent's IRA to a marital trust and then to the surviving spouse's IRA was not IRD where the surviving spouse was the sole trustee and sole beneficiary of the trust.[10] Gain realized upon the cancellation at death of a note payable to a decedent has been held to be IRD to the decedent's estate.[11]

The unreported increase in value reflected in the redemption value of savings bonds as of the date of a decedent's death constitutes income in respect of a decedent.[12] See Q 1142. If savings bonds on which the increases in value have not been reported are inherited, or the subject of a bequest, the reporting of such amounts may be delayed until the bonds are redeemed or disposed of by the legatee, or reach maturity, whichever

---

1. Let. Rul. 8919009.
2. Let. Rul. 200318017; see also Information Letter INFO 2005-0102 (3-29-2005).
3. See Information Letter INFO 2005-0011 (3-14-2005); see also Pub. 502 (2006).
4. IRC Sec. 691(a).
5. IRC Sec. 1367(b).
6. Rev. Rul. 69-297, 1969-1 CB 131; Rev. Rul. 75-125, 1975-1 CB 254.
7. Let. Rul. 9031046.
8. Let. Rul. 200041018.
9. Let. Rul. 9132021. See Rev. Rul. 92-47, 1992-1 CB 198. See also Let. Rul. 200336020.
10. Let. Rul. 200023030.
11. *Est. of Frane v. Comm.*, 998 F.2d 567 (8th Cir. 1993).
12. See Rev. Rul. 64-104, 1964-1 CB 223.

is first.[1] However, to the extent savings bonds are distributed by an estate or trust to satisfy *pecuniary* obligations or legacies, the estate or trust is required to recognize the unreported incremental increase in the redemption price of Series E bonds as income in respect of a decedent.[2]

The Service determined that in the case of a taxpayer who dies before a short sale of stock is closed, any income that may result from the closing of the short sale is not IRD, and the basis of any stock held on the date of the taxpayer's death will be stepped up.[3] The Court of Appeals for the Tenth Circuit has held that an alimony arrearage paid to the estate of a former spouse was IRD and thus, taxable to the recipient beneficiaries as ordinary income.[4]

Generally IRD must be included in the gross income of the recipient; however, a deduction is normally permitted for estate and generation-skipping transfer taxes paid on the income. The amount of the total deduction is determined by computing the federal estate tax (or generation-skipping transfer tax) with the net IRD included and then recomputing the tax with the net IRD excluded. The difference in the two results is the amount of the income tax deduction. However, if two or more persons receive IRD of the same decedent, each recipient is entitled to only a proportional share of the income tax deduction. Similarly, if the IRD is received over more than one taxable year, only a proportional part of the deduction is allowable each year. Where the income would have been ordinary income in the hands of the decedent, the deduction is an itemized deduction.[5] The recipient does not receive a stepped up basis (see Q 1415).[6] A beneficiary was allowed to claim a deduction for IRD attributable to annuity payments that had been received even though the estate tax had not yet been paid.[7]

In technical advice, the stated that the value of a decedent's IRA should not be discounted for estate tax purposes to reflect income taxes that will be payable by the beneficiaries upon receipt of distributions from the IRAs or for lack of marketability. The Service reasoned that the deduction is a statutory remedy for the adverse income tax impact and makes any valuation discount inappropriate if the deduction applies.[8] Courts have likewise denied discounts for lack of marketability.[9] The Service also determined that a deduction claimed on a decedent's estate tax return – which represented income taxes paid by the estate on the estate's income tax return, which in turn were triggered by the amount distributed to the estate from the decedent's IRAs – was not allowable as a deduction under IRC Section 2053. According to the Service, even if the estate had not claimed the IRD deduction, the income taxes paid on the distributions from the IRAs would still not be deductible under IRC Section 2053 because any additional benefit beyond what Congress had intended would be unwarranted.[10]

The Service has ruled that if the owner-annuitant of a deferred annuity contract dies *before* the annuity starting date, and the beneficiary receives a death benefit under

---

1. See Let. Ruls. 9845026, 9507008, 9024016.
2. Let. Rul. 9507008.
3. Let. Rul. 9436017. See IRC Sec. 1014.
4. *Kitch v. Comm.*, 97-1 USTC ¶50,124 (10th Cir. 1996).
5. IRC Sec. 691(c); Rev. Rul. 78-203, 1978-1 CB 199.
6. IRC Sec. 1014(c).
7. FSA 200011023.
8. TAM 200247001; see also TAM 200303010.
9. See *Est. of Smith v. U.S.*, 300 F.Supp.2d 474 (S.D. TX 2004), *appeal docketed*, No. 04-20194 (5th Cir. 2004); *Est. of Robinson v. Comm.*, 69 TC 227 (1977).
10. Let. Rul. 200444021.

the annuity contract, the amount received by the beneficiary in a lump sum in excess of the owner-annuitant's investment in the contract is includible in the beneficiary's gross income as IRD. If the death benefit is instead received in the form of a series of periodic payments, the amounts received are likewise includible in the beneficiary's gross income in an amount determined under IRC Section 72 as IRD.[1] See, e.g., Let. Rul. 200537019 (where the Service ruled that the amount equal to the excess of the contract's value over the decedent's basis, which would be received by the estate as the named beneficiary of the contract upon surrender of the contract, would constitute IRD includible by the estate in its gross income; however, the estate would be entitled to a deduction for the amounts of IRD paid to charities in the taxable year, or for the remaining amounts of IRD that would be set aside for charitable purposes).

The Tax Court determined that because a signed withdrawal request from the decedent constituted an effective exercise of the decedent's right to a lump-sum distribution during his lifetime, the lump-sum distribution from TIAA-CREF was therefore income to the decedent and properly includable in the decedent's income. Accordingly, the court held, the lump sum payment received by the decedent's son was not a death benefits payment and, thus, was not includable in the son's gross income as IRD.[2]

In *Estate of Kahn*,[3] the Tax Court held that in computing the gross estate value, the value of the assets held in the IRAs is not reduced by the anticipated income tax liability following the distribution of IRAs, in part because IRC Section 691(c) addresses the potential double tax issue. The Tax Court further held that a discount for lack of marketability is not warranted because the assets in the IRAs are publicly traded securities. Payment of the tax upon distribution is not a prerequisite to making the assets in the IRA marketable; consequently there is no basis for the discount. In technical advice the Service has also determined that a discount for lack of marketability is not available to an estate where the deduction for IRD is available to mitigate the potential income tax liability triggered by the IRD assets.[4]

STANDARD DEDUCTION

1431. What is the standard deduction?

There are two ways that taxable income may be calculated: taxpayers may subtract from adjusted gross income (see Q 1423) the sum of their personal exemptions and the standard deduction. Alternatively, taxpayers can deduct from adjusted gross income their allowable personal exemptions (see Q 1425, Q 1426) and the total of their itemized deductions (see Q 1427).[5]

In the case of individuals, the standard deduction for taxable years beginning in 2007 is $10,700 for married individuals filing jointly and surviving spouses; $7,850 for heads of households, $5,350 for single individuals and married individuals filing separately.[6] The standard deduction is adjusted annually for inflation.[7]

---

1. Rev. Rul. 2005-30, 2005-20 IRB 1015.
2. *Eberly v. Comm.*, TC Summary Op. 2006-45.
3. 125 TC 227 (2005).
4. TAM 200247001; see also TAM 200303010.
5. IRC Sec. 63.
6. IRC Sec. 63(c); Rev. Proc. 2006-53, 2006-48 IRB 996.
7. IRC Sec. 63(c)(4).

Individuals who do not itemize and who are elderly (age 65 or older) or blind are entitled to increase their standard deduction. For taxable years beginning in 2007, individuals who are married or are surviving spouses are each entitled to an additional deduction of $1,050 if they are elderly and an additional $1,050 deduction if they are blind. The extra standard deduction is $1,300 for unmarried elderly taxpayers and $1,300 for unmarried blind taxpayers.[1] The additional amounts for elderly and blind individuals are indexed for inflation.[2]

The following taxpayers are ineligible for the standard deduction and thus must itemize their deductions or take a standard deduction of zero dollars: (1) married taxpayers filing separately, if either spouse itemizes (see e.g., Legal Memorandum 200030023), (2) non-resident aliens, (3) taxpayers filing a short year return because of a change in their annual accounting period, and (4) estates or trusts, common trust funds, or partnerships.[3]

For taxable years beginning in 2007, the standard deduction for an individual who *may* be claimed as a dependent by another taxpayer is the greater of $850 or the sum of $300 and the dependent's earned income (but the standard deduction so calculated cannot exceed the regular standard deduction amount above).[4] These dollar amounts are adjusted for inflation.[5]

"Marriage penalty" relief. EGTRRA 2001 increased the basic standard deduction for a married couple filing a joint return, providing for a phase-in of the increase until the basic standard deduction for a married couple filing jointly equaled twice the basic standard deduction for an unmarried individual filing a single return by 2009. JGTRRA 2003 accelerated the phase-in, providing that the basic standard deduction for a married couple filing a joint return equaled twice the standard deduction for an unmarried individual filing a single return for 2003 and 2004, then reverting to the lower, gradually increasing standard deduction amounts provided for under EGTRRA for 2005 through 2009. However, under WFTRA 2004 the standard deduction for married individuals filing jointly (and surviving spouses) is twice the amount (200%) of the standard deduction for unmarried individuals filing single returns for tax years beginning *after* December 31, 2003.[6] The larger standard deduction for married individuals filing jointly will "sunset" (expire) for taxable years beginning after December 31, 2010, at which time the standard deduction in effect prior to the enactment of EGTRRA 2001 will become effective (i.e., the standard deduction for married individuals filing jointly will, once again, be 167% of the standard deduction for single individuals).[7]

RATES

1432. What are the federal income tax rates for individuals?

EGTRRA 2001 reduced income tax rates above 15% for individuals, trusts and estates. EGTRRA 2001 also provided for subsequent rate reductions to occur in 2004

---

1. IRC Sec. 63(f); Rev. Proc. 2006-53, above.
2. IRC Sec. 63(c)(4).
3. IRC Sec. 63(c)(6).
4. IRC Sec. 63(c)(5); Rev. Proc. 2006-53, above.
5. IRC Sec. 63(c)(4).
6. IRC Sec. 63(c), as amended by WFTRA 2004.
7. Act Sec. 107, JGTRRA 2003.

and 2006.[1] JGTRRA 2003 accelerated the reductions that were scheduled to occur in 2004 and 2006. Thus, for 2003 and thereafter, the income tax rates above 15% are lowered to 25%, 28%, 33% and 35% (down from 27%, 30%, 35%, and 38.6%).[2] This provision is effective for taxable years beginning after December 31, 2002.

The income brackets to which each rate applies depend upon whether a separate return, joint return, head-of-household return, or single return is filed. (For an explanation of which taxpayers may file jointly or as a head-of-household, see Q 1434 and Q 1435.) Children under the age of 18 (previously age 14) are generally taxed on unearned income at their parent's marginal rate (see Q 1411).[3] The income brackets are indexed annually for inflation.[4] Separate tax rates may apply to capital gains (see Q 1420).

Larger 10% tax bracket effective through 2010. EGTRRA created a new 10% bracket that applied to the first $12,000 of taxable income for married individuals filing jointly, $6,000 for single individuals, and $10,000 for heads of households. EGTRRA 2001 also provided a scheduled increase, beginning in 2008, under which the $6,000 level would have increased to $7,000, and the $12,000 level would have increased to $14,000 (with those levels to be adjusted annually for inflation for taxable years beginning after December 31, 2008).

JGTRRA 2003 accelerated the scheduled increases to 2003 and 2004. Consequently, in 2004 the taxable income levels (as indexed) were: $14,300 for married individuals filing jointly; $7,150 for single individuals and married individuals filing separately; and $10,200 for heads of households.[5] (See Income Tax Tables, Appendix B.)

For 2005 through 2010, the 10% brackets were scheduled to revert to the levels provided under EGTRRA 2001. Thus, in 2005 through 2007 the income levels would have dropped to $12,000 for married individuals filing jointly, $6,000 for single individuals, and $10,000 for heads of households. Not until 2008 would the income levels for the 10% brackets have once again increased to $14,000 for married individuals filing jointly and $7,000 for single individuals (with annual adjustments for inflation beginning after December 31, 2008).

WFTRA 2004 extends the expanded 10% brackets through 2010 at the 2003 levels. Thus, the size of the 10% bracket through 2010 is $14,000 for married individuals and $7,000 for single individuals (with annual indexing from 2003).[6] In 2007, the indexed 10% brackets are $15,650 (married filing jointly), $7,825 (single and married filing separately), and $11,200 (head of household).[7]

The 10% tax bracket will "sunset" (expire) for tax years beginning after December 31, 2010, at which time the 10% tax bracket will be eliminated and the portion of the income that was taxed in the 10% bracket will once again be subject to taxation in the 15% bracket.[8]

---

1. IRC Secs. 1(i)(1), 1(i)(2), prior to amendment by JGTRRA 2003.
2. IRC Sec. 1(i)(2), as amended by JGTRRA 2003.
3. IRC Sec. 1(g), as amended by TIPRA 2005.
4. IRC Sec. 1(f).
5. Rev. Proc. 2003-85, 2003-49 IRB 1184.
6. IRC Sec. 1(i)(1)(B).
7. Rev. Proc. 2006-53, 2006-48 IRB 996.
8. IRC Sec. 1(i)(1); Act Sec. 105, WFTRA 2004; Act Sec. 107, JGTRRA 2003.

"Marriage penalty" relief. EGTRRA 2001 increased the size of the 15% bracket for married couples filing joint returns to twice the size of the corresponding bracket for unmarried individuals filing single returns, phasing in the increase over four years, beginning in 2005. JGTRRA 2003 accelerated those increases, making the size of the 15% bracket for married individuals filing jointly equal to twice the size of the corresponding bracket for unmarried individuals filing single returns for taxable years beginning in 2003 and 2004. For taxable years beginning after 2004, the applicable percentages were scheduled to revert to those provided under EGTRRA 2001.

Under WFTRA 2004, the 15% bracket for married individuals filing jointly is twice the size (200%) of the corresponding bracket for unmarried individuals filing single returns for tax years beginning *after December 31, 2003*.[1] The larger 15% bracket for married individuals filing jointly will "sunset" (expire) for taxable years beginning after December 31, 2010, at which time the tax bracket that was in effect prior to the enactment of EGTRRA 2001 will become effective (i.e., the 15% bracket for single individuals will, once again, be 160% of the 15% bracket for married individuals filing jointly).[2]

1433. How are taxes indexed?

The individual rate brackets, basic standard deduction, and personal exemption amounts are adjusted annually for inflation.[3] Indexing also applies to the additional standard deduction for the blind and elderly, the adoption credit, the exclusion for employer-provided adoption assistance, and the threshold income levels for: phaseout of personal exemptions; phaseout of the savings bond interest exclusion; phaseout of the deduction for interest on a qualified education loan; phaseout of the adoption credit; phaseout of the exclusion for employer-provided adoption assistance; and the ceiling on itemized deductions.[4] The Hope Scholarship and Lifetime Learning Credits are also indexed for inflation, as are the threshold income levels for their phaseout.[5]

Indexing provides the benefit of preventing tax rate increases that result purely from inflation, as taxpayers' escalating income levels push them into higher tax brackets. It also ensures that the income levels at which certain tax benefits are eliminated remain at inflation-adjusted levels so that the provisions continue to benefit those taxpayers for whom they were intended.

The indexing factor (referred to in the IRC as the cost-of-living adjustment) is the percentage by which the Consumer Price Index (CPI) for the *prior* calendar year exceeds the CPI for a year designated as a reference point in each respective IRC Section. In all cases, the CPI is the average Consumer Price Index as of the close of the 12-month period ending on August 31 of the calendar year.[6] Thus, for example, in calculating the new tax rate schedules, the minimum and maximum dollar amounts for each rate bracket (except as described below) are increased by the applicable cost-of-living adjustment. The rates (percentages) themselves are not adjusted. This method of increase explained above, however, does not apply to the phaseout of the marriage penalty in the 15% bracket (see Q 1432).[7]

1. IRC Sec. 1(f)(8), as amended by WFTRA 2004.
2. Sec. 105, WFTRA 2004; Sec. 107, JGTRRA 2003.
3. IRC Secs. 1(f), 63(c)(4), 151(d)(4).
4. IRC Secs. 63(c)(4), 23(h), 137(f), 151(d)(4)(B), 135(b)(2)(B), 221(g), and 68(b)(2).
5. IRC Sec. 25A(h).
6. IRC Secs. 1(f)(3), 1(f)(4).
7. IRC Sec. 1(f)(2).

The Secretary of the Treasury has until December 15 of each calendar year to publish new tax rate schedules (for joint returns, separate returns, single returns, head of household returns, and for returns by estates and trusts) that will be effective for taxable years beginning in the subsequent calendar year.[1] See Q 1432 and the tax tables in Appendix A of this book.

1434. Who may file a joint return?

A husband and wife. Gross income and deductions of both spouses are included; however, a joint return may be filed even though one spouse has no income. A widow or widower *who has a dependent child* may file as a "surviving spouse" and calculate his tax using joint return tax rates for two years after the taxable year in which the spouse died. However, no personal exemption is allowed for the deceased spouse except in the year of death.[2]

1435. Who may use head-of-household rates?

An individual who meets the four requirements below:

1. He must be (a) unmarried, or legally separated from his spouse under a decree of divorce or of separate maintenance, or (c) married, living apart from his spouse during the last six months of the taxable year, and maintain as his home a household that constitutes the principal place of abode for a "qualifying child" (as defined in IRC Sec. 152(c); see Q 1426) with respect to whom the individual is entitled to claim a deduction, and with respect to whom the taxpayer furnishes over one-half the cost of maintaining such household during the taxable year.[3]

2. He must maintain as his home a household in which one or more of the following persons lives: (a) a qualifying child (if that individual is unmarried, it is not necessary that he have less than $3,400 (in 2007) of income or that the head-of-household furnish more than one-half his support; if the qualifying child is married, he must qualify as a dependent of the taxpayer claiming head-of-household status or would qualify except for the waiver of the exemption by the custodial parent (see Q 1426)), *or* (b) any other person for whom the taxpayer can claim a dependency exemption except a cousin or unrelated person living in the household.[4] An exception to this rule is made with respect to a taxpayer's dependent mother or father: so long as he maintains the household in which the dependent parent lives, it need not be his home.[5]

3. He must contribute over one-half the cost of maintaining the home.[6]

4. He must not be a nonresident alien.[7]

CREDITS

1436. What credits may be taken against the tax?

---

1. IRC Sec. 1(f)(1).
2. IRC Secs. 1(a), 2(a), 6013(a). See IRC Sec. 151(b).
3. IRC Secs. 2(b)(1), 2(c), 7703(b).
4. IRC Sec. 2(b)(1); Treas. Reg. §1.2-2(b).
5. IRC Sec. 2(b)(1).
6. IRC Sec. 2(b)(1).
7. IRC Secs. 2(b), 2(d).

After rates have been applied to compute the tax, certain payments and credits may be subtracted from the tax to arrive at the amount of tax payable. *Refundable credits* are recoverable regardless of the amount of the taxpayer's tax liability for the taxable year. The refundable credits include:

...Taxes withheld from salaries and wages.[1]

...Overpayments of tax.[2]

...The excess of Social Security withheld (two or more employers).[3]

...The earned income credit.[4]

...The 65% health care tax credit for uninsured workers displaced by trade competition.[5]

The *nonrefundable credits* are as follows:

...The personal credits—which consist of the child and dependent care credit[6]; the credit for the elderly and the permanently and totally disabled[7]; the qualified adoption credit[8]; the nonrefundable portion of the child tax credit[9]; the Hope Scholarship and Lifetime Learning credits[10] (see Q 1438); the credit for elective deferrals and IRA contributions (the "saver's credit"[11]);

...The nonbusiness energy property credit[12]; and the residential energy efficient property credit[13].

...Other nonbusiness credits.[14]

...The general business credit (see Q 1262) is the sum of the following credits determined for the taxable year: (1) the investment credit determined under IRC Section 46 (see Q 1268) (including the rehabilitation credit; see Q 1228); (2) the work opportunity credit (see Note, below) determined under IRC Section 51(a); (3) the alcohol fuels credit determined under IRC Section 40(a); (4) the research credit (see *Note*, below) determined under IRC Section 41(a); (5) the low-income housing credit (see Q 1227) determined under IRC Section 42(a); (6) the enhanced oil recovery credit (see Q 1262) under IRC Section 43(a); (7) in the case of an eligible small business, the disabled access credit determined under IRC Section 44(a); (8) the renewable electricity production credit under IRC Section 45(a) (extended through 2008 under TRHCA 2006); (9) the empowerment zone employment credit determined under IRC Section

---

1. IRC Sec. 31(a).
2. IRC Sec. 35.
3. Treas. Reg. §1.31-2.
4. IRC Sec. 32.
5. IRC Sec. 35, as amended by the Trade Act of 2002.
6. IRC Sec. 21.
7. IRC Sec. 22.
8. IRC Sec. 23.
9. See IRC Sec. 24.
10. IRC Sec. 25A.
11. IRC Sec. 25B, which became permanent under Section 812 of PPA 2006.
12. IRC Sec. 25C.
13. IRC Sec. 25D.
14. See e.g., IRC Secs. 53, 901.

1396(a); (10) the Indian employment credit (see *Note*, below) as determined under IRC Section 45A(a); (11) the employer social security credit determined under IRC Section 45B(a); (12) the orphan drug credit determined under IRC Section 45C(a); (13) the new markets tax credit determined under IRC Section 45D(a); (14) in the case of an eligible employer (as defined in IRC Section 45E(c)); the small employer pension plan startup cost credit determined under IRC Section 45E(a); (15) the employer-provided child care credit determined under IRC Section 45F(a); (16) the railroad track maintenance credit determined under IRC Section 45G(a); (17) the biodiesel fuels credit determined under IRC Section 40A(a); (18) the low sulfur diesel fuel production credit determined under IRC Section 45H(a); (19) the marginal oil and gas well production credit determined under IRC Section 45I(a); (20) for tax years beginning after September 20, 2005, the distilled spirits credit determined under IRC Section 5011(a); (21) for tax year beginning after August 8, 2005, the advanced nuclear power facility production credit determined under IRC Section 45J(a); (22) for property placed in service after December 31, 2005, the nonconventional source production credit determined under IRC Section 45K(a); (23) the energy efficient home credit determined under IRC Section 45L(a); (24) the energy efficient appliance credit determined under IRC Section 45M(a); (25) the portion of the alternative motor vehicle credit to which IRC Section 30B(g)(1) applies; and (26) the portion of the alternative fuel vehicle refueling property credit to which IRC Section 30C(d)(1) applies.[1] *Editor's Note*: Under TRHCA 2006, the work opportunity credit, Indian employment credit, and research credit were extended through the end of 2007.

ETIA 2005 provides an alternative motor vehicle credit for qualified fuel cell vehicles, advanced lean-burn technology vehicles, qualified hybrid vehicles; and qualified alternative fuel vehicles.[2] (This credit replaced the prior deduction for qualified clean-fuel vehicle property, which expired on December 31, 2005.[3]) The portion of the credit attributable to vehicles of a character subject to an allowance for depreciation is treated as a portion of the general business credit; the remainder of the credit is a personal credit allowable to the extent of the excess of the regular tax (reduced by certain other credits) over the alternative minimum tax for the taxable year.[4]

For tax years beginning in 2006, all of the nonrefundable personal credits are available for offset against the regular income tax and the alternative minimum tax.[5] Beginning January 1, 2007, the only nonrefundable personal credits available for offset against the regular income tax and the alternative minimum tax are the (1) nonrefundable adoption credit, (2) nonrefundable child tax credit, and the saver's credit (see above). A credit may also be allowed for prior years' alternative minimum tax liability (see Q 1431).

1437. Who qualifies for the child tax credit?

A child tax credit is available for each "qualifying child" (defined below) of eligible taxpayers who meet certain income requirements. The child tax credit is $1,000 through 2010.[6] The increased child tax credit will "sunset" (expire) for tax years beginning after December 31, 2010, at which time the child tax credit will return to its pre-EGTRRA level (i.e., $500).[7]

1. IRC Sec. 38(b).
2. IRC Sec. 30B.
3. See Sec. 1348, ETIA 2005; IRC Sec. 179A.
4. See IRC Sec. 30B(g).
5. IRC Sec. 26(a), as amended by TIPRA 2005.
6. IRC Sec. 24(a).
7. Sec. 105, WFTRA 2004; Sec. 107, JGTRRA 2003; IRC Sec. 6429.

The term *qualifying child* means a "qualifying child" of the taxpayer (as defined under IRC Section 152(c) – see below) who has not attained the age of 17.[1]

"Qualifying child" means, with respect to any taxpayer for any taxable year, an individual:

(1)   who is the taxpayer's "child" (see below) or a descendant of such a child, *or* the taxpayer's brother, sister, stepbrother, or stepsister or a descendant of any such relative;

(2)   who has the same principal place of abode as the taxpayer for more than one-half of the taxable year; *and*

(3)   who has *not* provided over one-half of such individual's own support for the calendar year in which the taxpayer's taxable year begins.[2]

Additionally, a qualifying child must be either a citizen or a resident of the United States.[3]

The term "child" means an individual who is: (1) a son, daughter, stepson, or step-daughter of the taxpayer; or (2) an "eligible foster child" of the taxpayer.[4] An "eligible foster child" means an individual who is placed with the taxpayer by an authorized placement agency or by judgment decree, or other order of any court of competent jurisdiction.[5] Any adopted children of the taxpayer are treated the same as natural born children.[6]

The amount of the credit is reduced for taxpayers whose modified adjusted gross income (MAGI) exceeds certain levels. A taxpayer's MAGI is his adjusted gross income without regard to the exclusions for income derived from certain foreign sources or sources within United States possessions. The credit amount is reduced by $50 for every $1000 or fraction thereof, by which the taxpayer's MAGI exceeds the following threshold amounts: $110,000 for married taxpayers filing jointly, $75,000 for unmarried individuals, and $55,000 for married taxpayers filing separately.[7]

The child tax credit is refundable to the extent of 15% of the taxpayer's earned income in excess of $10,000 (as indexed–see below).[8] For example, if the taxpayer's earned income is $16,000, the excess amount would be $6,000 ($16,000 - $10,000 = $6,000), and the taxpayer's refundable credit for one qualifying child would be $900 ($6,000 x 15% = $900). For families with three or more qualifying children, the credit is refundable to the extent that the taxpayer's Social Security taxes exceed the taxpayer's earned income credit *if* that amount is greater than the refundable credit based on the taxpayer's earned income in excess of $10,000 (as indexed–see below).[9] The $10,000 amount is indexed for inflation ($11,750 in 2007).[10] (Prior to 2001, the child tax credit was refundable only for individuals with three or more qualifying children.[11])

---

1. IRC Sec. 24(c)(1).
2. IRC Sec. 152(c).
3. IRC Sec. 24(c)(2).
4. IRC Sec. 152(f)(1).
5. IRC Sec. 152(f)(1)(C).
6. IRC Sec. 152(f)(1)(B).
7. IRC Sec. 24(b)(2).
8. IRC Sec. 24(d)(1)(B)(i).
9. IRC Sec. 24(d)(1).
10. IRC Sec. 24(d)(3); Rev. Proc. 2006-53, 2006-48 IRB 996.
11. IRC Sec. 24(d), prior to amendment by EGTRRA 2001.

The nonrefundable child tax credit can be claimed against the individual's regular income tax *and* alternative minimum tax (see Q 1436). The nonrefundable child tax credit cannot exceed the excess of (i) the sum of the taxpayer's regular tax plus the alternative minimum tax over (ii) the sum of the taxpayer's nonrefundable personal credits (other than the child tax credit, adoption credit, and saver's credit) and the foreign tax credit for the taxable year.[1] For tax years beginning after 2001, the refundable child tax credit is not required to be reduced by the amount of the taxpayer's alternative minimum tax.[2] The nonrefundable credit must be reduced by the amount of the refundable credit.[3]

Some additional restrictions applying to the child tax credit include: (1) an individual's tax return must identify the name and taxpayer identification number (Social Security number) of the child for whom the credit is claimed; and (2) the credit may be claimed only for a full taxable year, unless the taxable year is cut short by the death of the taxpayer.[4] For purposes of applying a uniform method of determining when a child attains a specific age, the Service has ruled that a child attains a given age on the anniversary of the date that the child was born (e.g., a child born on January 1, 1987, attains the age of 17 on January 1, 2004).[5] The IRS stated that it would apply Revenue Ruling 2003-72 retroactively and would notify those taxpayers entitled to a refund for 2002 as a result of Revenue Ruling 2003-72.[6]

The supplemental child tax credit, which was available before 2002 to certain lower income taxpayers, has been repealed IRC Sec. 32(n), repealed by EGTRRA 2001.

1438. What are the Hope Scholarship and Lifetime Learning Credits?

The Hope Scholarship Credit and the Lifetime Learning Credit are available to certain eligible taxpayers who pay qualified tuition and related expenses.[7]

Hope Scholarship Credit

The Hope Scholarship Credit provides a credit for each *eligible student* equal to the sum of: (1) 100% of qualified tuition and related expenses up to $1,100; plus (2) 50% of qualified tuition and related expenses in excess of $1,100, up to the applicable limit. The applicable limit is two times the $1,100 amount.[8] The amounts used to calculate the credit are adjusted for inflation and rounded to the next lowest multiple of $100.[9] The maximum credit for 2007 is $1,650 ($1,100 + (50% × $1,100).

The Hope Scholarship Credit is available only for the first two years of postsecondary education, and can be used in only two taxable years.[10] To qualify for the credit, the student must carry at least half of a full-time academic workload for an academic period during the taxable year.[11]

---

1. IRC Sec. 24(b)(3).
2. IRC Sec. 24(d).
3. IRC Sec. 24(d)(1).
4. IRC Secs. 24(e), 24(f).
5. Rev. Rul. 2003-72, 2003-2 CB 346.
6. IRS Information Letter INFO-2003-0215 (8-29-2003).
7. IRC Sec. 25A.
8. IRC Secs. 25A(b)(1), 25A(b)(4); Treas. Reg. §1.25A-3(a).
9. IRC Sec. 25A(h)(1).
10. Treas. Reg. §1.25A-3(c).
11. IRC Sec. 25A(b)(2); Treas. Reg. §1.25A-3(d)(ii).

An *eligible student* generally means a student who: (1) for at least one academic period beginning in the calendar year, is enrolled at least half-time in a program leading to a degree, certificate, or other recognized educational credential and is enrolled in one of the first two years of postsecondary education, and (2) is free of any conviction for federal or state felony offenses consisting of the possession of a controlled substance.[1]

Qualified tuition and related expenses are tuition and fees required for the enrollment or attendance of the taxpayer, the taxpayer's spouse, or any dependent of the taxpayer (for whom he is allowed a dependency exemption) at an "eligible education institution."[2] Qualified tuition and related expenses do not include nonacademic fees such as room and board, medical expenses (including required student health fees), transportation, student activity fees, athletic fees, insurance expenses, and similar personal, living or family expenses unrelated to a student's academic course of instruction.[3] Additionally, qualified tuition and related expenses do not include expenses for a course involving sports, games or hobbies, unless it is part of the student's degree program.[4]

An *eligible educational institution* generally means a postsecondary educational institution that: (a) provides an educational program for which it awards a bachelor's degree, or a 2-year program that would be accepted for credit towards a bachelor's degree; (b) has at least a one year program that trains students for gainful employment in a recognized profession; (c) participates in a federal financial aid program under Title IV of the Higher Education Act of 1965 or is certified by the Department of Education as eligible to participate in such a program; or (d) meets requirements for certain postsecondary vocational, proprietary institutions of higher learning and certain institutions outside the United States. In any event, the institution must also be accredited or have been granted pre-accreditation status.[5]

An *academic period* means a quarter, semester, trimester or other period of study (such as summer school session) as reasonably determined by an eligible educational institution.[6]

Lifetime Learning Credit

The Lifetime Learning Credit is available in an amount equal to 20% of "qualified tuition and related expenses" (defined above) paid by the taxpayer during the taxable year for any course of instruction at an "eligible educational institution" (defined above) taken to acquire or improve the job skills of the taxpayer, his spouse or dependents. The Lifetime Learning Credit is a per taxpayer credit and the maximum credit available does not vary with the number of students in the family. The maximum amount of the credit in 2006 is $2,000 (20% of up to $10,000 of qualified tuition and related expenses).[7]

Qualified tuition and related expenses, for the purposes of the Lifetime Learning Credit, include expenses for graduate as well as undergraduate courses. The Lifetime Learning Credit applies regardless of whether the individual is enrolled on a full-time,

1. IRC Sec. 25A(b)(3); Notice 97-60, 1997-2 CB 310 (Sec. 1, A3); Treas. Reg. §1.25A-3(d)(1).
2. Treas. Reg. §1.25A-2(d)(1).
3. Treas. Reg. §1.25A-2(d)(3).
4. IRC Sec. 25A(f)(1); Treas. Reg. §1.25A-2(d)(5).
5. See IRC Sec. 25A(f)(2); Section 481, Higher Education Act of 1965; Treas. Reg. §1.25A-2(b).
6. Treas. Reg. §1.25A-2(c).
7. IRC Sec. 25A(c); Treas. Reg. §1.25A-4(a).

half-time, or less than half-time basis. Additionally, the Lifetime Learning Credit is available for an unlimited number of taxable years.[1]

Where taxpayers had pre-paid their child's tuition in November 2001 for the academic period that began during the first three months of the following taxable year (i.e., the spring semester of 2002), the prepayment amount was properly includable in the calculation of the taxpayers' Lifetime Learning Credit for the 2001 taxable year, not the 2002 taxable year.[2]

Limitations and Phaseouts

The Code sets forth special rules coordinating the interaction of these credits. The Lifetime Learning Credit is not available with respect to a student for whom an election is made to take the Hope Scholarship Credit during the same taxable year.[3] However, the taxpayer may use the Hope Scholarship Credit for one student and the Lifetime Learning Credit for other students in the same taxable year.

Both credits are subject to the same phaseout rules based on the taxpayer's modified adjusted gross income (MAGI). MAGI is the taxpayer's adjusted gross income without regard to the exclusions for income derived from certain foreign sources or sources within United States possessions. The maximum credit in each case is reduced by the credit multiplied by a ratio. For single taxpayers, the ratio equals the excess of (i) the taxpayers' MAGI over $40,000 to (ii) $10,000. For married taxpayers filing jointly, the ratio equals (a) the excess of the taxpayer's MAGI over $80,000 to (b) $20,000.[4] The $40,000 and $80,000 amounts are adjusted for inflation and rounded to the next lowest multiple of $1,000.[5] For 2007, the threshold amounts are $47,000 for single taxpayers and $94,000 for married taxpayers filing jointly.[6]

The amount of qualified tuition and related expenses for both credits is limited by the sum of the amounts paid for the benefit of the student, such as scholarships, education assistance advances, and payments (other than a gift, bequest, devise, or inheritance) received by an individual for educational expenses attributable to enrollment.[7] The IRS has determined that qualified tuition and related expenses paid with distributions of educational benefits from a trust could be used to compute Hope Scholarship and Lifetime Learning Credits if the distributions were included in the taxable income of the beneficiaries.[8]

Neither credit is allowed unless a taxpayer elects to claim it on a timely filed (including extensions) federal income tax return for the taxable year in which the credit is claimed. The election is made by completing and attaching Form 8863, Education Credits (Hope and Lifetime Learning Credits), to the return.[9] Neither credit is allowed unless the taxpayer provides the name and the taxpayer identification (i.e., Social Security) number of the student for whom the credit is claimed.[10]

1. Treas. Regs. §§1.25A-4(b), 1.25A-4(c).
2. *Patel v. Comm.*, TC Summary Opinion 2006-40.
3. IRC Sec. 25A(c)(2)(A); Treas. Reg. §1.25A-1(b).
4. IRC Sec. 25A(d); Treas. Reg. §1.25A-1(c).
5. IRC Sec. 25A(h)(2); Treas. Reg. §1.25A-1(c)(3).
6. Rev. Proc. 2006-53, 2006-48 IRB 996.
7. IRC Sec. 25A(g)(2); Treas. Reg. §1.25A-5(c).
8. Let. Rul. 9839037.
9. Treas. Reg. §1.25A-1(d).
10. Treas. Reg. §1.25A-1(e).

If the student is claimed as a dependent on another individual's tax return (e.g., parents) he cannot claim either credit for himself, even if he paid the expenses himself.[1] (The Service has privately ruled that a student was entitled to claim a Hope Scholarship Credit on his own return even though his parents were eligible to claim him as a dependent, but chose not to do so.[2]) However, if another individual is eligible to claim the student as a dependent, but does not do so, only the student may claim the Hope or Lifetime Learning Credit for his own qualified tuition and related expenses.[3] Both credits are unavailable to married taxpayers filing separately.[4] Neither of these credits is allowed for any expenses for which there is a deduction available.[5] Taxpayers are not eligible to claim a Hope or Lifetime Learning Credit and the deduction for qualified higher education expenses in the same year with respect to the same student.[6]

A taxpayer may claim a Hope Scholarship or Lifetime Learning Credit *and* exclude distributions from a qualified tuition program on behalf of the same student in the same taxable year *if* the distribution is not used to pay the same educational expenses for which the credit was claimed.[7] See Q 1413.

A taxpayer can claim a Hope Scholarship or Lifetime Learning Credit *and* exclude distributions from a Coverdell Education Savings Account (ESA – see Q 1412) on behalf of the same student in the same taxable year *if* the distribution is *not* used to pay the same educational expenses for which the credit was claimed.[8] A taxpayer may elect *not* to have the Hope Scholarship or Lifetime Learning Credit apply with respect to the qualified higher education expenses of an individual for any taxable year.[9]

Reporting. For the reporting requirements for higher education tuition and related expenses, see IRC Sec. 6050S, as amended by P.L. 107-131 (1-16-2002). For the reporting requirements for qualified tuition and related expenses, see Treas. Reg. §1.6050S-1; TD 9029.[10]

1439. What energy credits may be taken against the tax?

Credit for Nonbusiness Energy Property

An individual taxpayer may claim as a credit an amount equal to *the sum of:* (1) 10% of the amount paid or incurred by the taxpayer for "qualified energy efficiency improvements" (see below) installed during the taxable year; *and* (2) the amount of the "residential energy property expenditures" (see below) paid or incurred by the taxpayer during the taxable year.[11]

Qualified energy efficiency improvements means any energy efficient "building envelope component" (see below) that meets certain energy conservation criteria, if: (1) the component is installed in or on a dwelling located in the United States that is owned

---

1. IRC Sec. 25A(g)(3); Treas. Reg. §1.25A-1(f)(1).
2. Let. Rul. 200236001.
3. Treas. Reg. §1.25A-1(f)(1).
4. IRC Sec. 25A(g)(6); Treas. Reg. §1.25A-1(g).
5. IRC Sec. 25A(g)(5); Treas. Reg. §1.25A-5(d).
6. IRC Sec. 222(c)(2)(A).
7. See IRC Sec. 529(c)(3)(B)(v).
8. See IRC Sec. 530(d)(2)(C).
9. IRC Sec. 25A(e).
10. 67 Fed. Reg. 77678 (12-19-02). See also Notice 2006-72, 2006-36 IRB 363.
11. IRC Sec. 25C(a).

and used by the taxpayer as his principal residence; (2) original use of the component commences with the taxpayer; *and* (3) the component reasonably can be expected to remain in use for at least five years.[1] The term "building envelope component" means: (1) any insulation material or system specifically and primarily deigned to reduce the heat loss or gain of a dwelling when installed in or on the dwelling; (2) exterior windows, including skylights; (3) exterior doors; and (4) metal roofs if the roof has appropriate coatings specifically and primarily designed to reduce the hear gain of the dwelling.[2]

In recent guidance, the Service clarified that a component will be treated as reasonably expected to remain in use for at least five years if the manufacturer offers, at no extra charge, at least a two-year warranty providing for repair or replacement of the component in the event of a defect in materials or workmanship. However, if the manufacturer does not offer such a warranty, all relevant facts and circumstances are taken into account in determining whether the component reasonably can be expected to remain in use for at least five years. The Service also confirmed that a taxpayer may rely on a manufacturer's certification that a building envelope component is an "eligible building envelope component." A taxpayer is not required to attach the certification to the tax return on which the credit is claimed, but should retain the certification statement as part of his records. In addition, the Service stated that a credit is allowed *only* for amounts paid or incurred to purchase the components, *not* for the onsite preparation, assembly, or original installation of the components.[3]

Residential energy property expenditures means expenditures made by the taxpayer for "qualified energy property" that is: (1) installed on or in connection with a dwelling unit located in the United States and owned and used by the taxpayer as the taxpayer's principal residence; *and* (2) originally placed in service by the taxpayer.[4] The term "qualified energy property" means: (1) "energy-efficient building property" (see below); (2) a qualified natural gas, propane, oil furnace or hot water boiler; or (3) an advanced main air circulating fan. All of the types of property listed in the preceding sentence must meet certain performance and quality standards.[5] "Energy efficient building property" means: (1) electric heat pump water heaters; (2) electric heat pumps; (3) geothermal heat pumps; (4) central air conditioners; and (5) natural gas, propane, or oil water heaters.[6]

The Service has confirmed that a taxpayer may rely on a manufacturer's certification that a product is "qualified energy property." A taxpayer is not required to attach the certification to the tax return on which the credit is claimed, but should retain the certification statement as part of his records. In addition, the Service stated that a credit is allowed for amounts paid or incurred to purchase qualified energy property *and* for expenditures for labor costs allocable to the onsite preparation, assembly, or original installation of the property.[7]

The lifetime limitation with respect to any taxpayer for any taxable year is $500.[8] An additional limit of $200 applies to windows.[9] Other limits are as follows: advanced

---

1. IRC Sec. 25C(c)(1).
2. IRC Sec. 25C(c)(2).
3. Notice 2006-26, 2006-11 IRB 622.
4. IRC Sec. 25C(d)(1).
5. IRC Sec. 25C(d)(2).
6. IRC Sec. 25C(d)(3).
7. Notice 2006-26, 2006-11 IRB 622.
8. IRC Sec. 25C(b)(1).
9. IRC Sec. 25C(b)(2).

main air circulating fans – $50; qualified natural gas, propane, oil furnace or hot water boilers – $150; and energy-efficient building property – $300.[1]

The credit is available for property placed in service after December 31, 2005 and before January 1, 2008.[2]

The Service has issued guidance regarding the credit for nonbusiness energy property.[3]

Residential Energy Efficient Property Credit

An individual taxpayer may claim as a credit an amount equal to *the sum of* 30% of the following expenditures made by the taxpayer during the taxable year: (1) "qualified photovoltaic property" (see below); (2) "qualified solar water heating property" (see below); *and* (3) "qualified fuel cell property" (see below).[4] Solar water heating property must be certified in order for the credit to be claimed.[5]

"Qualified solar water heating property expenditure" means an expenditure for property to heat water for use in a dwelling unit located in the United States and used as a residence by the taxpayer if at least half of the energy used by such property for such purpose is derived from the sun. The term "qualified photovoltaic property expenditure" means an expenditure for property that uses solar energy to generate electricity for use in a dwelling unit located in the United States and used as a residence by the taxpayer. "Qualified fuel cell property expenditure" means an expenditure for qualified fuel cell property (as defined in IRC Section 48(c)(1)) installed on or in connection with a dwelling unit located in the United States and used as a principal residence by the taxpayer.[6]

A special rule provides that expenditures allocable to a swimming pool, hot tub, or any other energy storage medium that has a function other than the function of storage cannot be taken into account for these purposes.[7]

The maximum credit allowed for any taxable year cannot exceed $2,000 with respect to any qualified photovoltaic property expenditures or qualified solar water heating property expenditures, and $500 with respect to each half kilowatt of capacity of qualified fuel cell property (as defined in section 48(c)(1)) for which qualified fuel cell property expenditures are made.[8] The unused portion of the credit can be carried forward to the succeeding taxable year.[9]

The credit is available for property placed in service after December 31, 2005 and before January 1, 2009.[10]

---

1. IRC Sec. 25C(b)(3).
2. See Sec. 1333, Energy Policy Act of 2005; IRC Sec. 25C(g).
3. See Notice 2006-71, 2006-34 IRB 316; Notice 2006-53, 2006-25 IRB 1180; Notice 2006-26, 2006-11 IRB 622.
4. IRC Sec. 25D(a).
5. IRC Sec. 25D(b)(2).
6. IRC Sec. 25D(d).
7. IRC Sec. 25D(d)(3).
8. IRC Sec. 25D(b).
9. See IRC Sec. 25D(c).
10. See Sec. 1333, Energy Policy Act of 2005; IRC Sec. 25D(g), as amended by TRHCA 2006.

Alternative Motor Vehicle Credit

The alternative motor vehicle credit is equal to the *sum* of: (A) the new qualified fuel cell motor vehicle credit; (B) the new advanced lean burn technology motor vehicle credit; (C) the new qualified hybrid vehicle credit; and (D) the new qualified alternative motor vehicle credit.[1] (This credit replaces the prior deduction for qualified clean-fuel vehicle property, which sunsets on December 31, 2005.[2])

(A) The new qualified fuel cell motor vehicle credit is based on the weight of the vehicle, and ranges from $8,000 (8,500 pound maximum) to $40,000 (26,000 pound maximum).[3] The amount determined above with respect to a passenger automobile or light truck is *increased* if the vehicle achieves certain fuel efficiencies (based on the 2002 model year city fuel economy), ranging from $1,000 to $4,000.[4] The credit for passenger automobiles and light trucks can be as much as $12,000.

The term "new qualified fuel cell motor vehicle" means a motor vehicle: (1) propelled by power derived from one or more fuel cells that convert chemical energy directly into electricity by combining oxygen with hydrogen fuel that is stored on board the vehicle in any form and may or may not require reformation prior to use; (2) that, in the case of a passenger vehicle or light truck, has received a certificate that the vehicle meets certain emission levels; (3) the original use of which begins with the taxpayer; (4) that is acquired for use or lease by the taxpayer and not for resale; and (5) that is made by a manufacturer.[5]

(B) The amount of the new advanced lean burn technology motor vehicle credit is based on fuel economy, and ranges from $400 to $2,400. The amount of the credit is *increased* by the conservation credit (based on lifetime fuel savings), and ranges from $250 to $1,000.[6] The credit for passenger automobiles and light trucks can be as much as $3,400.

The term "advanced lean burn technology motor vehicle" means a passenger automobile or light truck: (1) with an internal combustion engine that (i) is designed to operate primarily using more air than is necessary for complete combustion of the fuel, (ii) incorporates direct injection, (iii) achieves at least 125% of the 2002 model year city fuel economy, and (iv) for 2004 and later model vehicles, has received a certificate that the vehicle meets or exceeds certain emission standards; (2) the original use of which begins with the taxpayer; (3) is acquired for use or lease by the taxpayer and not for resale; and (4) is made by a manufacturer.[7]

(C) The new qualified hybrid motor vehicle credit amount is determined as follows: (1) If the new qualified hybrid motor vehicle is a passenger automobile or light truck weighing no more than 8,500 pounds, the credit amount is the sum of the fuel economy amount and the conservation credit (see (B), above).[8] (2) For other motor vehicles, the credit amount is equal to the applicable percentage of the "qualified incremental hybrid cost" (i.e., the excess of the manufacturer's suggested retail price for such vehicle over

---

1. IRC Sec. 30B(a).
2. See Sec. 1348, ETIA 2005; IRC Sec. 179A.
3. IRC Sec. 30B(b)(1).
4. IRC Sec. 30B(b)(2).
5. IRC Sec. 30B(b)(3).
6. IRC Sec. 30B(c)(2).
7. IRC Sec. 30B(c)(3).
8. IRC Sec. 30B(d)(2)(A).

the price for a comparable gas or diesel powered vehicle) of the vehicle as certified.[1] The credit for passenger automobiles and light trucks can be as much as $3,400.

A "new qualified hybrid motor vehicle" means a motor vehicle that: (1) draws propulsion energy from onboard sources of stored energy that are both (i) an internal combustion or heat engine using consumable fuel, and (ii) a rechargeable energy storage system; (2) has been certified as meeting specified emission standards; (3) has maximum available power meeting certain percentages based on weight; (4) the original use of which begins with the taxpayer; (5) is acquired for use or lease by the taxpayer; and (6) is made by a manufacturer.[2]

(D) The new qualified alternative fuel motor vehicle credit is an amount equal to the applicable percentage of the incremental cost of any new qualified alternative fuel motor vehicle.[3] The "applicable percentage" is 50%, plus 30% if the vehicle has been certified as meeting certain emission standards.[4] The "incremental cost" (i.e., the excess of the manufacturer's suggested retail price for the vehicle over the price for a gas or diesel powered vehicle of the same model) cannot exceed between $4,000 to $32,000 based on the weight of the vehicle.[5]

"New qualified alternative fuel motor vehicle" means any motor vehicle: (1) that is only capable of operating on an alternative fuel; (2) the original use begins with the taxpayer; (3) is acquired by the taxpayer for use or lease but not for resale; and (4) is made by a manufacturer.[6] "Alternative fuel" means compressed natural gas, liquefied natural gas, liquefied petroleum gas, hydrogen, and any liquid at least 85% of the volume of which consists of methanol.[7]

Certifications and Limitations

Certifications. The tax credit for hybrid vehicles may be as much as $3,400 for those who purchase the most fuel-efficient vehicles. (For the guidance used by manufacturers in certifying credit amounts, see Notice 2006-9.[8]) The Service cautions that even though a manufacturer has certified a vehicle, taxpayers must meet the following requirements to qualify for the credit:

(1) The vehicle must be placed in service after December 31, 2005, and purchased on or before December 31, 2010.

(2) The original use of the vehicle must begin with the taxpayer claiming the credit.

(a) The credit may only be claimed by the original owner of a new, qualifying, hybrid vehicle and does not apply to a used hybrid vehicle.

(3) The vehicle must be acquired for use or lease by the taxpayer claiming the credit.

---

1. IRC Sec. 30B(d)(2)(B).
2. IRC Sec. 30B(d)(3).
3. IRC Sec. 30B(e)(1).
4. IRC Sec. 30B(e)(2).
5. IRC Sec. 30B(e)(3).
6. IRC Sec. 30B(e)(4)(A).
7. IRC Sec. 30B(e)(4)(B).
8. 2006-6 IRB 413.

(a) The credit is only available to the original purchaser of a qualifying hybrid vehicle. If a qualifying vehicle is leased to a consumer, the leasing company may claim the credit.

(b) For qualifying vehicles used by a tax-exempt entity, the person who sold the qualifying vehicle to the person or entity using the vehicle is eligible to claim the credit, but only if the seller clearly discloses in a document to the tax-exempt entity the amount of credit.

(4)   The vehicle must be used predominantly within the United States.

Limitations. There is a limit on the number of new qualified hybrid and advanced lean burn technology vehicles eligible for the credit. The phaseout period begins with the second calendar quarter following the calendar quarter that includes the first date on which the number of qualified vehicles manufactured by the manufacturer is at least 60,000.[1] The Service publishes notices (http://www.irs.gov/newsroom/index.html) providing the adjusted credit amount based on the actual number of vehicles sold for the applicable quarter.

Effective dates. The credits are in effect as follows: new qualified fuel cell motor vehicle credit (2006 – 2014); (B) new advanced lean burn technology motor vehicle credit (2006 – 2010); (C) new qualified hybrid vehicle credit (2006 – 2010); and (D) new qualified alternative fuel motor vehicle credit (2006 – 2010).

ALTERNATIVE MINIMUM TAX

1440. How is the alternative minimum tax calculated?

Generally

In addition to the tax calculated under the normal rates, it is sometimes necessary for a taxpayer to pay the *alternative minimum tax (AMT)*. The AMT is calculated by first determining the alternative minimum taxable income (AMTI), reducing this amount by the allowable exemption to determine taxable excess, and then applying a two-tier tax rate schedule to the amount of the taxable excess. The two-tier rate schedule applies a 26% rate to taxable excess that does not exceed $175,000 ($87,500 for married taxpayers filing separately), and a 28% rate to taxable excess over that amount. The resulting amount is the taxpayer's tentative minimum tax. The preferential tax rates on certain capital gains held for more than twelve months and certain dividends are also used when determining the taxpayer's tentative minimum tax (see Q 1420).[2]

If the tentative minimum tax reduced by the AMT foreign tax credit exceeds the regularly calculated tax (with adjustments) for the tax year, the excess is the AMT. Regularly calculated tax for AMT purposes excludes certain taxes including: (1) the alternative minimum tax; (2) the tax on benefits paid from a qualified retirement plan in excess of the plan formula to a 5% owner; (3) the 10% penalty tax for certain premature distributions from annuity contracts; (4) the 10% additional tax on certain early distributions from qualified retirement plans; (5) the 10% additional tax for certain taxable distributions from modified endowment contracts; (6) taxes relating to the recapture of

---

1. IRC Sec. 30B(f).
2. IRC Secs. 55(a), 55(b).

the federal subsidy from use of qualified mortgage bonds and mortgage credit certificates; (7) the additional tax on certain distributions from education IRAs; and (8) the 15% additional tax on medical savings account distributions not used for qualified medical expenses. Regularly calculated tax is reduced by the foreign tax credit, the Puerto Rico and possession tax credit, and the Puerto Rico economic activity credit.[1]

The American Jobs Creation Act of 2004 repealed the 90-percent limit on the AMT foreign tax credit for tax years beginning after 2004.[2] For tax years beginning before 2005, the AMT foreign tax credit is limited to the excess of the tentative minimum tax (determined without regard to such credit) over 10% of the tentative minimum tax (determined without regard to the AMT foreign tax credit, the AMT net operating loss deduction, and the tax preference exception for certain intangible drilling costs of independent producers).[3]

For tax years from 2000 through 2006, certain nonrefundable personal credits (see Q 1436) may be used to reduce the sum of a taxpayer's regular tax liability and AMT liability.[4]

For tax years beginning after 2006, certain nonrefundable personal credits (except for the adoption expenses credit, the child tax credit, and the credit for elective deferrals and IRA contributions) may not reduce a taxpayer's regular tax liability to less than the taxpayer's tentative minimum tax.[5]

Alternative Minimum Taxable Income

Alternative minimum taxable income is taxable income, with adjustments made in the way certain items are treated for AMT purposes, and increased by any items of tax preference.[6]

Except as otherwise provided below, the provisions that apply in determining the regular taxable income of a taxpayer also generally apply in determining the AMTI of the taxpayer.[7] In addition, references to a noncorporate taxpayer's adjusted gross income (AGI) or modified AGI in determining the amount of items of income, exclusion, or deduction must be treated as references to the taxpayer's AGI or modified AGI as determined for regular tax purposes.[8]

Exemption

Exemption amounts of $62,550 (in 2006; $45,000 after 2006) on a joint return (or for a surviving spouse), $42,500 (in 2006; $33,750 after 2006) on a single return, $31,275 (in 2006; $22,500 after 2006) on a married filing separate return, and $22,500 on an estate or trust return, are available in calculating the taxable excess. These exemption amounts are reduced by 25% of the amount by which the AMTI exceeds $150,000 on a joint return, $112,500 on a single return and $75,000 on a separate return or in the

---

1. IRC Secs. 55(c)(1), 26(b).
2. AJCA 2004, Sec. 421.
3. IRC Sec. 59(a)(2), prior to repeal by AJCA 2004.
4. IRC Sec. 26(a), as amended by TIPRA 2005.
5. IRC Sec. 26(a), as amended by TIPRA 2005.
6. IRC Sec. 55(b)(2).
7. Treas. Reg. §1.55-1(a).
8. Treas. Reg. §1.55-1(b).

case of an estate or trust.[1] In 2006, a married individual filing a separate return must increase AMTI by the lesser of (a) 25% of the excess of the AMTI over $200,100, or (b) $31,275. After 2006, a married individual filing a separate return must increase AMTI by the lesser of (a) 25% of the excess of the AMTI over $165,000, or (b) $22,500.[2] For children subject to the "kiddie tax" (Q 1411) the exemption is the lesser of the above amounts or the child's earned income plus $6,300 (as indexed for 2007).[3]

Adjustments

In general, the following adjustments are made to taxable income in computing alternative minimum taxable income: (1) generally, property must be depreciated using a less accelerated method or the straight line method over a period which is longer than that used for regular tax purposes, except that a longer period is not required for property placed in service after 1998; (2) the AMT net operating loss is deductible only up to 90% of AMTI determined without regard to such net operating loss; (3) no deduction is allowed for miscellaneous itemized deductions; (4) generally, no deduction is allowed for state and local taxes unless attributable to a trade or business, or property held for the production of income (recovery of state tax disallowed for AMT purposes in a previous year is not added to AMTI in the year recovered); (5) medical expenses are allowed as a deduction only to the extent such expenses exceed 10% of adjusted gross income; (6) interest on indebtedness secured by a primary or second residence is generally deductible (within dollar limitations) if incurred in acquiring, constructing, or substantially improving the residence; however, the amount of refinanced indebtedness with regard to which interest is deductible is limited to the amount of indebtedness immediately prior to refinancing; (7) no standard deduction is allowed; (8) no deduction for personal exemptions is allowed; (9) the limitation on itemized deductions for upper-income taxpayers does not apply; (10) the taxpayer will include any amount realized due to a transfer of stock pursuant to the exercise of an incentive stock option; (11) AMTI is determined using losses from any tax shelter farm activity (determined by taking into account the AMTI adjustments and tax preferences) only to the extent that the taxpayer is insolvent or when the tax shelter farm activity is disposed of; and (12) passive activity losses (determined by taking into account the adjustments to AMTI and tax preferences) are not allowed in determining AMTI except to the extent that the taxpayer is insolvent.[4]

Preference Items

Items of tax preference which must be added to AMTI include: (1) the excess of depletion over the adjusted basis of property (except in the case of certain independent producers and royalty owners); (2) the excess of intangible drilling costs expensed (other than drilling costs of a nonproductive well) over the amount allowable for the year if the intangible drilling costs had been amortized over a 10 year period to the extent the excess is greater than 65% of the net income from oil, gas, and geothermal properties (with an exception for certain independent producers); (3) tax-exempt interest on specified private activity bonds (but reduced by any deduction not allowed in computing the regular tax if the deduction would have been allowable if the tax-exempt interest were includable in gross income); (4) accelerated depreciation or amortization on certain

---

1. IRC Sec. 55(d), as amended by TIPRA 2005.
2. See IRC Sec. 55(d), as amended by TIPRA 2005.
3. IRC Sec. 59(j); Rev. Proc. 2006-53, 2006-48 IRB 996.
4. IRC Secs. 56, 58.

property placed in service before 1987; and (5) seven percent of the amount excluded under IRC Section 1202 (gain on sales of certain small business stock).[1]

Credit for Prior Year Minimum Tax Liability

A taxpayer subject to the AMT in one year may be allowed a minimum tax credit against regular tax liability in subsequent years. The credit is equal to the total of the adjusted minimum taxes imposed in prior years reduced by the amount of minimum tax credits allowable in prior years. However, the amount of the credit cannot be greater than the excess of the taxpayer's regular tax liability (reduced by certain credits such as certain business related credits and certain investment credits) over the tentative minimum tax. The adjusted net minimum tax for any year is the AMT for that year reduced by the amount that would be the AMT if: (1) the only adjustments were those concerning the limitations on certain deductions (such as state taxes, certain itemized deductions, the standard deduction and personal exemptions); (2) the only preferences were those dealing with depletion, tax exempt interest, and small business stock; and (3) the limit on the foreign minimum tax credit did not apply. The adjusted net minimum tax is increased by the amount of any nonconventional fuel source credit and qualified electric vehicles credit that was not allowed for that year due to the AMT. For tax years after 2006 and before 2013, if an individual has minimum tax credits that have not been usable for three years, those long-term unused credits may be treated as a refundable credit.[2]

SOCIAL SECURITY TAXES

1441. What are the Social Security tax rates for 2007?

The rates for 2007, as adjusted by an automatic cost-of-living increase in the earnings base, are:

Self-employment tax: 15.30% (12.40% OASDI and 2.90% hospital insurance). In 2007, the OASDI tax is imposed on up to $97,500 of self-employment income for a maximum tax of $12,090. The hospital insurance tax is imposed on all of a taxpayer's self-employment income. However, an above-the-line deduction is permitted for one-half of self-employment taxes paid by an individual and attributable to a trade or business carried on by the individual (not as an employee) (see Q 1313.[3]

FICA tax (on employer and employee, each): 7.65% (6.20% OASDI and 1.45% hospital insurance). In 2007, the OASDI tax is imposed on up to $97,500 of wages for a maximum tax of $6,045 for the employer and $6,045 for the employee, or $12,090 for employer and employee together. The hospital insurance tax is imposed on all of a taxpayer's wages.[4]

Back wages paid as the result of a settlement agreement are subject to FICA and FUTA taxes in the year the wages are actually paid, not in the year the wages were earned or should have been paid.[5]

---

1. IRC Sec. 57(a).
2. IRC Sec. 53, as amended by TRHCA 2006.
3. IRC Sec. 164(f).
4. IRC Secs. 3101(b), 3121(u).
5. *U.S. v. Cleveland Indians Baseball Co.*, 87 AFTR2d ¶2001-798 (U.S. 2001). See also *The Phillies v. U.S.* 87 AFTR2d 2001-983 (E.D. PA. 2001).

1442. Who must pay the self-employment tax?

An individual whose net earnings from self-employment are $400 or more for the taxable year must pay the self-employment tax.[1] In 2007, such an individual must file a Schedule SE and pay Social Security taxes on up to $97,500 of self-employment income. (The hospital insurance tax is imposed on all of a taxpayer's self-employment income.) However, an above-the-line deduction is permitted for one-half of the self-employment tax paid by an individual and attributable to a trade or business carried on by the individual (not as an employee).[2] If the individual also works in covered employment as an *employee*, his self-employment income (subject to the self-employment tax) is only the difference, if any, between his "wages" as an employee and the maximum Social Security earnings base.

COMMUNITY PROPERTY

1443. How can community property law affect the federal income tax treatment of investment income?

Community property law applies in determining whether property and the income it produces is community property or separate property if (1) in the case of income from personal property the spouses or either of them is domiciled in a community property state; or (2) in the case of income from real property the property is located in a community property state, regardless of the spouses' domicile(s).[3]

In the states of Arizona, California, Nevada, New Mexico, and Washington, income from separate property is separate property of the spouse who owns the property. In the states of Idaho, Louisiana, and Texas, income from separate property is community property. (In Wisconsin, under the Marital Property Act, income from individual (separate) property is marital (community) property. For federal income tax purposes, the IRS has recognized that spouses' rights under the Wisconsin Marital Property Act are community property rights.[4]) In May, 1998 Alaska adopted a wholly consensual community property statute, which allows married couples to select which assets are community property and which assets are to be held in some other form of ownership. Both resident and non-resident married couples may classify property as community property by transferring it to a community property trust which has been established under the provisions of the statute.[5]

In all community property states, the income from community property is, of course, community property. And in all states, spouses can have community property converted to separate property by partitioning or by making gifts or sales of their community interests in property. For federal income tax purposes, the distinctions between separate property and community property are important when the spouses file separate returns.

The rules in all community property states for determining whether property is separate or community are quite similar. In general, separate property is property owned

---

1. IRC Sec. 6017.
2. IRC Sec. 164(f).
3. *Poe v. Seaborn*, 282 US 101 (1930); Boris I. Bittker, *Federal Taxation of Income, Estates and Gifts* (Boston: Warren, Gorham & Lamont, Inc., 2nd Ed., 1991) vol. 3, ¶76.2.
4. Rev. Rul. 87-13, 1987-1 CB 20.
5. Notice 98-53, 1998-2 CB 640.

by a spouse before marriage and brought into the marriage as such, property acquired by a spouse by gift, will or inheritance during marriage, and property exchanged for separate property or bought with separate funds during marriage. Once property is identified as separate property, it remains separate property as long as it can be traced. All other property is community property (i.e., property owned one-half by each spouse). Earnings of the spouses while domiciled in a community property state are community property. Property acquired during marriage with community funds is presumed to be community property even if title to the property is taken in the name of one spouse only. The presumption can be rebutted only by clear and convincing evidence that the spouses intended the property to be the separate property of the spouse who has title.

The Tax Court held that a married couple's marriage contract had the effect of stopping the application of Louisiana's community property laws for federal income tax purposes, noting that shortly before marrying the couple "filed for registry" (in the parish where both of them resided) a marriage contract stating that "the intended husband and wife shall be separate in property."[1]

In general, if property is bought partly with community funds and partly with separate funds, the property is partly community and partly separate in proportion to the source of the funds. If the property is bought with separate and community funds that have been so commingled that it is not known what part is separate and what part is community, the whole will probably be considered community, and consequently the property purchased will likewise be community. But see Q 1446 for a different effect of commingling when spouses move to a noncommunity property state.

The IRS may disallow the benefits of any community property law to any taxpayer who acts as if he or she were solely entitled to certain income and failed to notify his or her spouse before the due date (including extensions) for filing the return for the taxable year in which the income was derived of the nature and amount of such income.[2] In Service Center Advice, the Service stated that taxpayers domiciled in community property states have an undivided one-half interest in the entire community so that their filing status must be married filing jointly or, if married filing separately, their returns must each reflect one-half of the total community income and expenses. The Service must establish facts and evidence to demonstrate that IRC Section 66(b) applies (i.e., it may disregard community property laws where the spouse is not notified of community income).[3]

A California appeals court held that a spouse's early retirement benefit must be characterized as community property where (1) the benefit is payable pursuant to a contract entered into during the marriage, and (2) the years of qualifying employment occurred before the parties' separation.[4]

The Tax Court held that in a community property jurisdiction, the spouse of a distributee who did not receive a distribution from an IRA should not be treated as a distributee (under IRC Section 408(d)) despite whatever his or her community property interest in the IRA may have been under state law. Thus, under these circumstances, distributions are taxable to the distributee and the penalty tax (under IRC Section 72(t))

---

1. *Downing v. Comm.*, TC Memo 2003-347.
2. IRC Sec. 66(b).
3. SCA 200030022.
4. *Drapeau v. Drapeau*, (Cal. Ct. App. No. A090032, October 30, 2001).

applies to the distributee spouse, only.[1] The Tax Court also held that the taxpayer's gross income from his continued employment—which he received in lieu of retirement benefits—did *not* include the amount of payments to which his former spouse was entitled under California community property law on the basis of the pension earned by the taxpayer.[2]

For guidance on the classification for federal tax purposes of a qualified entity that is owned by a husband and wife as community property under the laws of a state, foreign country, or possession of the United States, see Rev. Rul. 2002-69.[3]

For more information, see IRS Publication 555, "Federal Tax Information on Community Property."

1444. How is community income reported if spouses are living apart from one another?

Special rules apply in reporting certain community income of two individuals who are married to one another at any time during the calendar year, if all the following conditions exist:

(1) The spouses live apart all year.

(2) The spouses do not file a joint return with each other for a tax year beginning or ending within the calendar year.

(3) Either or both spouses have earned income for the calendar year that is community income.

(4) The spouses have not transferred, directly or indirectly, any of their earned income between themselves before the end of the year.

If all these conditions exist, the spouses must report their community income as explained below.[4]

Earned income. Earned income that is not trade or business or partnership income is treated as the income of the spouse who performed the personal services.

Trade or business income. Trade or business income and deductions attributable to such trade or business are treated as the gross income and deductions of the husband unless the wife exercises substantially all of the management and control of such trade or business, in which case all of such gross income and deductions are treated as the gross income and deductions of the wife.

Partnership income or loss. A partner's distributive share of partnership income or loss from a trade or business carried on by a partnership is the income or loss of the partner, and no part of it is his spouse's.

---

1. See *Morris v. Comm.*, TC Memo 2002-17, *Bunney v. Comm.*, 114 TC 259 (2000).
2. *Dunkin v. Comm.*, 124 TC 180 (2005).
3. 2002-2 CB 760.
4. IRC Secs. 66(a), 879(a).

Income from separate property. Community income derived from a spouse's separate property (see Q 1443) is treated as that spouse's income.

All other community income. All other community income, such as dividends, interest, rents, royalties, or gains, is treated as provided in the applicable community property law.[1]

If an individual subject to the foregoing special rules (1) does not include in gross income an item of community income properly includable under the above rules in the other spouse's gross income, and (2) establishes that he or she did not know of, and had no reason to know of, such item of community income, and the IRS determines that under the facts and circumstances it would be inequitable to include such item of community income in that individual's income, then the income item will be includable in the other spouse's gross income (rather than in the individual's gross income).[2] The Service has released guidance for taxpayers seeking equitable innocent spouse relief under IRC Section 66(c).[3]

The Tax court held that it has authority to review the Service's determination that a spouse is not entitled to equitable relief under IRC Section 66(c).[4] The Tax Court also held that unlike IRC Section 6015(e) (which provides for equitable relief from liability for the understatement of tax), IRC Section 66 does not provide for jurisdiction permitting a taxpayer to file a "stand alone" petition in response to a denial of a request for relief made pursuant to IRC Sec. 66(c).[5]

For the treatment of community income in general, see Treas. Reg. §1.66-1. For the treatment of community income where spouses live apart, see Treas. Reg. §1.66-2. With respect to the denial of benefits of community property law where the spouse is not notified, see Treas. Reg. §1.66-3. For the rules governing the request for relief from the operation of community property law, see Treas. Reg. §1.66-4.

1445. How does community property law affect the federal income tax treatment of dividends received from corporate stock?

If local law characterizes the income as community income (see Q 1443), the dividends are treated as having been received one-half by each spouse. This rule has been held to apply to dividend income received by a spouse as marital property under the Wisconsin Marital Property Act.[6] If the dividends are characterized as separate property and the spouses file separate returns, each spouse reports his or her own separate income.[7]

1446. If spouses move from a community property state to a common law state, will their community property rights in the property they take with them be recognized and protected by the law of their new domicile?

---

1. IRC Sec. 66(a).
2. IRC Sec. 66(c).
3. See Rev. Proc. 2003-61, 2003-2 CB 296, *superseding,* Rev. Proc. 2000-15, 2000-1 CB 447.
4. *Beck v. Comm.,* TC Memo 2001-198; *revised acq.,* AOD CC-2002-05 (12-9-2002).
5. *Bernal v. Comm.,* 120 TC 102 (2003).
6. Rev. Rul. 87-13, 1987-1 CB 20.
7. IRS Pub. 555.

Yes.[1] Thus, if the spouses report their incomes separately, the income from the community property or from property into which the community property is traceable is reported by the spouses as belonging one-half to each.[2] If income is community income, the deductions applicable to it must be taken one-half from each spouse's portion if they file separately.[3] But if community property is commingled with one spouse's separate property so that the original community property cannot be traced, the income from the property must be reported as that spouse's separate income, if the spouses file separately.[4]

DIVORCE

PROPERTY SETTLEMENT

1447. Do transfers of property between spouses, or between former spouses incident to a divorce, result in taxable gains and losses?

Property transferred between spouses or former spouses incident to a divorce generally will not result in recognition of gain or loss (unless the transfer is by trust, under certain circumstances, or pursuant to an instrument in effect on or before July 18, 1984, and the spouses or former spouses have not elected otherwise).[5] The property transferred will be treated as if it were acquired by gift, and the transferor's basis in the property will be carried over to the transferee, whether the fair market value of the property is more or less than the transferor's basis.[6] Ordinarily, if the fair market value of property transferred as a gift is less than the donor's basis, the fair market value is the donee's basis for determining loss (see Q 1415).

This nonrecognition rule means that the transfer of property between divorcing spouses in exchange for the release of marital claims generally will not result in a gain or loss to the transferor spouse. A transfer is considered made "incident to a divorce" if it is made within one year after the date the marriage ceases, or if the transfer is related to the cessation of the marriage.[7] A transfer is related to the cessation of a marriage if: (1) the transfer is pursuant to a divorce or separation instrument; and (2) the transfer occurs not more than six years after the date on which the marriage ceases.

Transfers not meeting the above two requirements are presumed *not* to be related to the cessation of a marriage, but taxpayers may overcome this presumption by showing that the transfer was made to effect the division of property owned by the former spouses at the time of the cessation of the marriage. Taxpayers may show this by establishing certain factors, such as legal impediments, hampered an earlier transfer of the property, provided that the transfer occurs promptly after any cause for the delay is resolved.[8] For example, a transfer of a business interest between former spouses that did not occur within six years of their divorce was considered incident to divorce since there existed a legal dispute between the former spouses concerning the value of the property and

1. *Johnson v. Comm.*, 7 BTA 820 (1927).
2. *Phillips v. Comm.*, 9 BTA 153 (1927).
3. *Stewart v. Comm.*, 95 F.2d 821 (5th Cir. 1938).
4. *Johnson v. Comm.*, 1 TC 1041 (1943), appeal dismissed, 139 F.2d 491 (8th Cir. 1943).
5. IRC Sec. 1041. See IRS Pub. 504, *Tax Information for Divorced or Separated Individuals*.
6. IRC Sec. 1041(b).
7. IRC Sec. 1041(c).
8. Temp. Treas. Reg. §1.1041-1T(b).

the terms of payment.[1] See also *Young v. Comm.*,[2] in which a transfer within four years of the divorce was considered to have been made "incident to divorce," thus making all gain on the transaction taxable to the transferee spouse.[3]

While the nonrecognition rule shields from recognition gain that would ordinarily be recognized on a sale or exchange of property, it does not shield from recognition interest income that is ordinarily recognized upon the assignment of that property to another taxpayer. Where a husband transferred Series E and EE bonds to his wife pursuant to a divorce settlement, the IRS determined that he must include as income the unrecognized interest accrued from the date of original issuance to the date of transfer. This income does not constitute gain, for purposes of the nonrecognition rule, but rather is interest income subject to the general rule that deferred, accrued interest on United States savings bonds be included as income in the year of transfer. The wife's basis in the bonds became the amount of the husband's basis *plus* the amount of deferred, accrued interest recognized by him upon transfer.[4]

The Tax Court held that the nonrecognition provided in IRC Section 1041 does not apply to interest income received by a spouse through monthly installment payments made on a promissory note executed to effect a division of marital property. The court reasoned that the principal and interest potions of an installment payment constitute two distinct items that give rise to separate federal income tax consequences. Thus, the portions of the monthly installment payments that were allocated to principal under the terms of the separation agreement were not taxable to the payee spouse, but the portions allocated to interest were taxable to her.[5]

Where property is transferred by trust, either between spouses, or between former spouses incident to divorce, gain will be recognized by the transferor to the extent that the sum of the liabilities assumed by the transferee plus the amount of liabilities to which the property is subject exceeds the total of the adjusted basis of all the property transferred. The transferee's basis will be adjusted to reflect the amount of gain recognized by the transferor.[6]

In addition, the transfer of an installment obligation generally will not trigger gain, and transfer of investment credit property will not result in recapture if the property continues to be used in a trade or business.[7] However, where installment obligations are transferred in trust, gain will be recognized by the transferor to the extent that the obligation's fair market value at the time of transfer exceeds its basis.[8]

The transfer of an interest in an individual retirement account or an individual retirement annuity to a spouse pursuant to a divorce or separation instrument will not be considered a taxable event. The individual retirement account will be treated as owned by the transferee at the time of transfer, and the transfer does not result in taxable gain or loss.[9] However, the statutory requirements for this nonrecognition treatment must be

---

1. Let. Rul. 9235026.
2. 113 TC 152 (1999), *aff'd*, 2001 U.S. App. Lexis 2365 (4th Cir. 2001).
3. Let. Rul. 200233022.
4. Rev. Rul. 87-112, 1987-2 CB 207.
5. *Yankwich v. Comm.*, TC Memo 2002-37.
6. IRC Sec. 1041(e).
7. IRC Secs. 50(a)(5)(B), 453(h); Temp. Treas. Reg. §1.1041-1T(d), A-13. See IRS Pub. 537.
8. IRC Secs. 50(a)(5)(B), 453B(g).
9. IRC Sec. 408(d)(6).

strictly observed.[1] The Service privately ruled that a husband's payment of a lump-sum in exchange for his ex-wife's community property interest in a nonqualified deferred compensation plan payable to the husband by his employer constituted nontaxable transfers between former spouses related to the cessation of their marriage. Furthermore, the assignment of income doctrine did not cause the wife to be taxed when her former husband received payment of that deferred compensation from his employer.[2]

The IRS has determined that the division of one charitable remainder unitrust (CRUT – see Q 1331) into two CRUTs to effectuate a property settlement in a divorce proceeding does not cause the original or resultant trusts to fail to qualify under IRC Section 664.[3]

The Service has ruled that when nonstatutory stock options and nonqualified deferred compensation are transferred incident to divorce, the nonstatutory stock options will be taxed at the time that the receiving spouse exercises the options, and the deferred compensation will be taxed when paid (or made available) to the receiving spouse.[4] In addition, the Service has ruled that the transfer of interests in nonstatutory stock options and nonqualified deferred compensation from the employee spouse to the nonemployee spouse incident to divorce does not result in a payment of wages for FICA and FUTA tax purposes. The nonstatutory stock options are subject to FICA and FUTA taxes at the time of exercise by the nonemployee spouse to the same extent as if the options had been retained and exercised by the employee spouse. The nonqualified deferred compensation also remains subject to FICA and FUTA taxes to the same extent as if the rights to the compensation had been retained by the employee spouse. To the extent FICA and FUTA taxation apply, the wages are those of the employee spouse. The employee portion of the FICA taxes is deducted from the wages as, and when, the wages are taken into account for FICA tax purposes. The employee portion of the FICA taxes is deducted from the payment to the nonemployee spouse. The revenue ruling also contains reporting requirements with respect to such transferred interests.[5]

Stock redemptions. If a corporation redeems stock owned by a wife, and the wife's receipt of property with respect to the stock is treated, under applicable tax law, as a constructive distribution to the husband (i.e., where the nonredeeming shareholder has a primary and unconditional obligation to purchase the redeeming shareholder's stock), the final regulations treat the redemption as (1) a transfer of the stock by the wife to the husband, followed by (2) a transfer of the stock by the husband to the redeeming corporation.[6] Nonrecognition treatment would apply to the deemed transfer of stock by the wife to the husband (assuming IRC Section 1041 requirements are otherwise satisfied), so that no gain or loss would be included on account of that portion of the transaction. However, nonrecognition treatment would *not* apply to the deemed transfer of stock from the husband to the redeeming corporation.[7]

The receipt of any property by the wife from the redeeming corporation with respect to the stock would be recharacterized as (1) a transfer of such property to the

---

1. See, e.g., *Jones v. Comm.*, TC Memo 2000-219.
2. Let. Rul. 200442003.
3. See, e.g., Let. Ruls. 200301020, 200221042, 200143028, 200120016, 200109006, 200045038, 200035014, 9851007, 9851006, 9403030.
4. Rev. Rul. 2002-22, 2002-1 CB 849.
5. Rev. Proc. 2004-60, 2004-24 IRB 1051, *modifying*, Notice 2002-31, 2002-1 CB 908. See also Let. Rul. 200646003.
6. Treas. Reg. §1.1041-2(a)(2).
7. Treas. Reg. §1.1041-2(b)(2).

husband by the redeeming corporation in exchange for the stock, in a transaction to which nonrecognition treatment would *not* apply, followed by (2) a transfer by the husband to the wife in a transaction, to which nonrecognition treatment would apply (assuming the requirements of IRC Section 1041 are otherwise satisfied).[1] For details of the rules applicable to constructive transfers between spouses and former spouses, see Treas. Reg. §1.1041-2; TD 9035.[2]

A divided Tax Court held that a stock redemption incident to divorce qualified for nonrecognition treatment where the ex-wife was considered to have transferred property to a third party on behalf of her ex-husband. The court further held that the primary and unconditional obligation standard is not an appropriate standard to apply in a case involving a corporate redemption in a divorce setting.[3] See also *Craven v. U.S.*[4] (stock redemption incident to divorce qualified for nonrecognition treatment). But see FSA 200222008 (where the Service ruled that based on the language in the settlement agreement, the redemption should be treated as a complete termination of the wife's interest; thus, the wife was taxable on the stock redemption. The Service reasoned that the intent of IRC Section 1041 and the parties involved was best served by respecting the form of the redemption transaction.) For the tax treatment of stock options transferred incident to a divorce, generally, see FSA 200005006.

Where a husband transferred his 25% interest in real property to his former wife, in consideration for a settlement agreement that provided to her a credit against the $500,000 equalizing money judgment that he owed to her, and the former wife then sold her undivided 50% interest in the same property to an unrelated third party, the Tax Court held as follows: (1) The first transaction, which occurred within one year after the date of the divorce, took place incident to divorce and, therefore, qualified for nonrecognition treatment under IRC Section 1041(a)(2). (2) The second transaction did *not* fall within IRC Section 1041(a)(2) because it was not a transfer to, or on behalf of, the taxpayer's former husband and incident to divorce. The Tax Court reasoned that the wife's sale of the property to the unrelated third party did not satisfy any legal obligation or liability that the taxpayer's former husband owed to her (or anyone else). Accordingly, the Tax Court concluded that the wife would have to recognize gain resulting from the sale in her interest in the property.[5]

Transfers occurring before July 19, 1984 were subject to substantially different rules, which sometimes resulted in a taxable gain to the transferor spouse. For application of the gift tax to property settlements, see Q 1518.

1448. Are alimony payments included in the gross income of the recipient? May the payor spouse take a deduction for these payments?

Alimony and separate maintenance payments generally are taxable to the recipient and deductible from gross income by the payor (even if the payor does not itemize).[6] Payments of arrearages from prior years are taxed to a cash basis taxpayer in the year

---

1. Treas. Regs. §§1.1041-2(a)(2), 1.1041-2(b)(2).
2. 67 Fed. Reg. 1534 (1-13-2003).
3. *Read v. Comm.*, 114 TC 14 (2000), *aff'd per curiam, Mulberry Motor Parts, Inc. v. Comm.*, 88 AFTR2d ¶2001-5385 (11th Cir. 2001).
4. 215 F.3d 1201 (11th Cir. 2000).
5. *Walker v. Comm.*, TC Memo 2003-335; compare *Read, Craven*, above.
6. IRC Secs. 71(a), 215(a).

of receipt.[1] Furthermore, the Tenth Circuit Court of Appeals has held that an alimony arrearage paid to the estate of a former spouse was taxable as income in respect of a decedent (see Q 1430).[2]

A payment received by (or on behalf of) a recipient spouse pursuant to a divorce or separation instrument executed after 1984 is an alimony or separate maintenance payment if: (1) the payment is made in cash; (2) the divorce or separation instrument does not designate the payment as *not* includable or deductible as alimony;[3] (3) there is no liability to make the payments after the death of the recipient,[4] where the Tax Court held that "substitute" payments – i.e., post-death payments that would begin as a result of the death of the taxpayer's ex-wife, and would substitute for a continuation of the payments that terminated on her death, and that otherwise qualified as alimony – were not deductible alimony payments); and (4) if the individuals are legally separated under a decree of divorce or separate maintenance, the spouses are not members of the same household at the time the payment is made.[5]

A divorce or separation instrument includes any decree of divorce or separate maintenance or a written instrument incident to such, a written separation agreement, or other decree requiring spousal support or maintenance payments.[6] The failure of the divorce or separation instrument to provide for termination of payments at the death of the recipient will not disqualify payments from alimony treatment.[7] However, if both the divorce or separation instrument and state law fail to unambiguously provide for the termination of payments upon death, such payments may be disqualified from receiving alimony treatment.[8]

It has been held that an attorney's letter detailing a settlement agreement constituted a separation instrument for purposes of determining whether payments made thereunder were alimony.[9] However, a list of expenses by the former wife, negotiation letters between attorneys, notations on the husband's check to his former wife indicating support, and the fact that the husband actually provided support did not constitute a written separation agreement for purposes of IRC Sections 71(b)(2) and 215.[10] A husband's payments to his wife during the couple's separation under a later invalidated separation agreement and subsequent payments made pursuant to a circuit court's orders were held to be alimony or separate maintenance payments.[11]

The deduction for alimony paid is limited to the amount required under the divorce or separation instrument.[12] Payments made voluntarily by a husband to his spouse, which were not mandated by a qualifying divorce decree or separation instrument, were not

1. *Coleman v. Comm.*, TC Memo 1988-442.
2. *Kitch v. Comm.*, 97-1 USTC ¶50,124 (10th Cir. 1996).
3. See *Richardson v. Comm.*, 125 F.3d 551 (7th Cir. 1997), *aff'g* T.C. Memo 1995-554; see also Let. Rul. 200141036).
4. See, e.g., *Okerson v. Comm.*, 123 TC 258 (2004).
5. IRC Sec. 71(b).
6. IRC Sec. 71(b)(2).
7. See IRC Sec. 71(b)(1)(D); TRA '86 Conf. Rept. at page 849.
8. *Hoover v. Comm.*, 97-1 USTC ¶50,111 (6th Cir. 1996); *Ribera v. Comm.*, TC Memo 1997-38. See *Mukherjee v. Comm.*, TC Memo 2004-98; *Lovejoy v. Comm*, 293 F.3d 1208 (10th Cir. 2002), *aff'g, Miller v. Comm.*, TC Memo 1999-273; *Thomas D. Berry v. Comm*, 2002 U.S. App. LEXIS 10785 (10th Cir. 2002), *aff'g*, TC Memo 2000-373; *Fithian v. United States*, 2002-2 USTC ¶50,629 (9th Cir. 2002). But see *Kean v. Comm.*, 2005-1 USTC ¶50,397 (3rd Cir. 2005), *aff'g*, TC Memo 2003-163; *Michael K. Berry v. Comm.*, TC Memo 2005-91.
9. *Azenaro v. Comm.*, TC Memo 1989-224.
10. *Ewell v. Comm.*, TC Memo 1996-253.
11. *Richardson v. Comm.*, 125 F.3d 551 (7th Cir. 1997), *aff'g*, TC Memo 1995-554.
12. *Ritchie v. Comm.*, TC Memo 1989-426.

deductible to the husband.[1] Where the husband made his initial payment too early because he wanted to "get it over with," and because it was convenient for him to schedule his alimony payments on or immediately after his paydays, the Tax Court concluded that the husband's premature payment was voluntary because it fell outside the scope of the qualified divorce instrument. Accordingly, the payment was not deductible by the husband as alimony.[2]

According to the General Explanation of TRA '84, where a beneficial interest in a trust is transferred or created incident to a divorce or separation, the payments by the trust will be treated the same as payments to a trust beneficiary under IRC Section 682, disregarding that the payments may qualify as alimony. Thus, instead of including payments entirely as ordinary income, the transferee, as beneficiary, may be entitled to the flow-through of tax-exempt income.

The Tax Court held that interest income, which arose from annual payments made to the taxpayer by her former husband under their divorce settlement, was taxable to the wife. The court further held that because the wife was not able to differentiate between the costs incurred in connection with the divorce, and the amounts paid to obtain the interest income, the taxpayer was therefore not entitled to deduct the interest income under IRC Section 212 (i.e., as an ordinary and necessary expense paid or incurred for the production or collection of income).[3]

The Tax Court held that a contract for deed is a third-party debt instrument; consequently, the taxpayer could not deduct the value of the contract for deed transferred to his former spouse as alimony because it did not constitute a cash payment.[4]

In deciding whether the transfer of ownership of an annuity contract itself constituted alimony, the Service determined that because IRC Section 71 and the Treasury regulations make it clear that in order to constitute alimony a payment must be in cash, the transfer of ownership of the annuity contract to the taxpayer in this instance did not constitute alimony includable in the taxpayer's gross income.[5]

For the types of payments that can constitute alimony payments, see *Mozley v. Comm.*[6] (military retirement payments); *Zinsmeister v. Comm.*[7] (payments on first mortgage, real estate taxes, and miscellaneous expenses); *Marten v. Comm.*[8] (life insurance premiums paid on former wife's life insurance policy insuring the couple's paraplegic child); but cf. *Thomas D. Berry v. Comm.*[9] (former wife's attorney's fees not deductible). Alimony can include rental payments paid to a former spouse. *Israel v. Comm.*[10] Lump sum payments made by a husband to his former wife under a consent judgment were not deductible under IRC Section 215(a) except to the extent the lump sum constituted past due alimony.[11]

---

1. *Meyer v. Comm.* TC Memo 2003-12. See also *Ali v. Comm.*, TC Memo 2004-284.
2. See *Ray v. Comm.*, TC Summary Opinion 2006-110.
3. *Cipriano v. Comm.*, No. 02-1055 (3rd Cir. 2003), *aff'g*, TC Memo 2001-157.
4. *Lofstrom v. Comm.*, 125 TC 271 (2005).
5. Let. Rul. 200536014.
6. TC Memo 2001-125.
7. TC Memo 2000-364, *aff'd per curiam*, 88 AFTR2d ¶2001-5479 (8th Cir. 2001).
8. TC Memo 1999-340, *on motion for reconsideration, holding reaffirmed in* TC Memo 2000-185; *aff'd per curiam, Comm. v. Lane*, 2002 U.S. App. LEXIS 8367 (9th Cir. 2002).
9. 2002 U.S. App. LEXIS 10785 (10th Cir. 2002), *aff'g*, TC Memo 2000-373.
10. TC Memo 1995-500. See Temp. Treas. Reg. §1.71-1T(b), A-6.
11. *Barrett v. U.S.*, 96-1 USTC ¶50,084 (5th Cir. 1996).

Recapture. Alimony recapture rules generally require recapture in the third post-separation year of "excess" payments (i.e., disproportionately large payments made in either the first or second years–or both–that are deemed to represent nondeductible property settlements previously deducted as alimony). The first post-separation year is the first calendar year in which alimony or separate maintenance payments are made; the second and third years are the next two calendar years thereafter.

The amount recaptured is included in the income of the payor spouse and deducted from the gross income of the recipient. The amount recaptured is determined by first comparing the alimony payments made for the second and third post-separation years. If payments during the second year exceed the payments during the third year by more than $15,000, the excess is "recaptured." Next, the payments during the first year are compared with the average of the payments made during the second year (as reduced by any recaptured excess) and the payments made during the third year. If the payments made during the first year exceed the average of the amounts paid during the second (as reduced) and third years by more than $15,000, the excess is also recaptured.[1]

There are limited exceptions to the recapture rule: if payments cease because of the marriage of the recipient or the death of either spouse before the close of the third separation year, or to the extent payments required over at least a 3-year period are tied to a fixed portion of income from a business or property or compensation, the payments will not come within these rules. Furthermore, payments under temporary support orders do not come within the recapture rules.[2]

Payments made under instruments executed before 1985 are taxed under different rules, (i.e., IRC Section 71 prior to TRA '84, unless the instrument is modified after 1984). Depending on the date of modification after 1984, either the TRA '84 rules and a 3-year recapture period will apply, or the recapture rules for instruments executed after 1986 (described above) will apply.

Child support. Any portion of an alimony payment specified in the divorce or separation instrument as payable for child support is not treated as alimony.[3] In *Freyre v. U.S.*,[4] the appeals court held that because the divorce court order did not specifically designate or fix the disputed monthly payments as child support, as required in the statute[5] and the treasury regulations,[6] the payments had to be considered as alimony and, thus, were deductible by the taxpayer.[7]

Even portions not specified as child support may be treated as child support to the extent that the amount of the alimony payment provided for in the divorce or separation instrument is to be reduced on the occurrence of a contingency relating to a child or at a time clearly associated with such a contingency (e.g., the year a child would turn 18 years old).[8] If the divorce or separation instrument provides for alimony and child support payments, any payment of less than the amount specified in the instrument will be applied first as child support, to the extent of the amount specified in the instrument.[9]

---

1. IRC Sec. 71(f).
2. IRC Sec. 71(f)(5); Temp. Treas. Reg. §1.71-1T(d), A-25.
3. IRC Sec. 71(c)(1).
4. No. 04-5580 (6th Cir. 2005).
5. IRC Sec. 71(c)(1).
6. Treas. Reg. §1.71-1(e).
7. See also *Preston v. Comm.*, 209 F.3d 1281 (11th Cir. 2000).
8. IRC Sec. 71(c)(2). See Let. Rul. 9251033.
9. IRC Sec. 71(c)(3).

The Tax Court determined that an agreement between former spouses, absent a court modification of their divorce decree, would not alter the tax consequences of this provision.[1] A parent was required to include in his gross income the portion of a distribution from his pension plan that was used to satisfy a back child support obligation.[2]

The Service has privately ruled that interest paid on past due child support is taxable income to the recipient parent. According to the Service, interest income is not excludable income in the same manner as amounts designated for child support are excludible. The Service reasoned that for child support to be excludable from gross income, the decree, instrument or agreement must specifically designate the sum as child support; interest that is assessed later does not come under an amount specifically designated as child support.[3]

When a payor spouse claims alimony payments as a deduction, he is required to furnish the recipient spouse's Social Security number on his tax return for each taxable year the payments are made.[4] Alimony paid by a U.S. citizen spouse to a foreign spouse is deductible by the payor spouse even though the recipient is not taxable on the income under a treaty; however, the penalty for failing to include the recipient's Taxpayer Identification Number (TIN) on the payor's tax return may still apply.[5]

TRUSTS AND ESTATES

1449. How is the federal income tax computed for trusts and estates?

Taxable income is computed by subtracting the following from gross income: allowable deductions; amounts distributable to beneficiaries; and the exemption. Estates are allowed a $600 exemption. For trusts that are required to distribute all their income currently, the exemption is $300; for all other trusts, $100. Certain trusts that benefit disabled persons may use the personal exemptions available to individuals.[6] A standard deduction is not available.[7] Rates are determined from a table for estates and trusts (see Appendix A).

For estates of decedents dying after August 5, 1997, an election may be made to treat a *qualified revocable trust* as part of the decedent's estate for income tax purposes. The election must be made by both the executor of the estate and the trustee of the qualified revocable trust. A qualified revocable trust is a trust that was treated as a grantor trust during the life of the decedent due to his power to revoke the trust (see Q 1450). If such an election is made, the trust will be treated as part of the decedent's estate for tax years ending after the date of the decedent's death and before the date that is two years after his death (if no estate tax return is required) or the date that is six months after the final determination of estate tax liability (if an estate tax return is required).[8]

---

1. *Blair v. Comm.*, TC Memo 1988-581.
2. *Stahl v. Comm.*, TC Memo 2001-22.
3. Let. Rul. 200444026.
4. Temp. Treas. Reg. §1.215-1T, A-1.
5. CCA 200251004.
6. IRC Sec. 642(b).
7. IRC Sec. 63(c)(6).
8. IRC Sec. 645.

Generally, income that is accumulated by a trust is taxable to the trust, and income that is distributable to beneficiaries is taxable to the beneficiaries.[1] A beneficiary who may be claimed as a dependent by another taxpayer may not use a personal exemption, and his standard deduction may not exceed the greater of (1) $500 ($850 as indexed for 2007); or (2) $250 ($300 as indexed for 2007) plus earned income.[2] The amount of trust income which can be offset by the basic standard deduction will be reduced if the beneficiary has other income (see Q 1425, Q 1431). Also, trust income taxable to a beneficiary under 18 years of age may be taxed at his parents' marginal tax rate (see Q 1411).[3]

Deductions available to an estate or trust are generally subject to the 2% floor on miscellaneous itemized deductions.[4] However, deductions for costs incurred in connection with the administration of an estate or trust that would not have been incurred if the property were not held by the estate or trust are fully deductible from gross income.[5]

It has been held that trust advisory fees incurred by a trust, due to the co-trustees' inexperience with large sums of money and their need to fulfill fiduciary duties imposed by state law, were fees incurred as a result of property being held in trust and, thus, were not subject to the 2% floor for miscellaneous itemized deductions.[6] However, other courts have held that payments for private investment advice *are* subject to the 2% floor for miscellaneous itemized deductions.[7]

For distributions in taxable years beginning after August 5, 1997, the throwback rule for accumulation distributions from trusts in IRC Sections 665-667 has been eliminated for domestic trusts, except for domestic trusts that were once foreign trusts, and except in the case of trusts created before March 1, 1984, which would be aggregated with other trusts under the multiple trust rules.[8] Generally, for those trusts subject to the throwback rule, if a trust distributes income which it has accumulated after 1968, all of the income is taxed to the beneficiary upon distribution. The amounts distributed are treated as if they had been distributed in the preceding years in which the income was accumulated, but are includable in the income of the beneficiary for the current year. The "throwback" method of computing the tax in effect averages the tax attributable to the distribution over three of the five preceding taxable years of the beneficiary, excluding the year with the highest and the year with the lowest taxable income.[9]

Excess taxes paid by the trust may not be refunded, but the beneficiary may take a credit to offset any taxes (other than the alternative minimum tax) paid by the trust. However, a beneficiary who receives accumulation distributions from more than two trusts may not take such an offset for taxes paid by the third and any additional trusts. But if distributions to a beneficiary from a trust total less than $1,000 for the year, this penalty will not apply to distributions from that trust.[10]

---

1. IRC Secs. 641(a), 652(a).
2. IRC Secs. 151(d)(2), 63(c)(5); Rev. Proc. 2006-53, 2006-48 CB 996.
3. IRC Secs. 651-652, 661-663.
4. IRC Sec. 67(a).
5. IRC Sec. 67(e).
6. *O'Neill Irrevocable Trust v. Comm.*, 93-1 USTC ¶50,332 (6th Cir. 1993), *nonacq.*, 1994-2 CB 1, *rev'g* 98 TC 227 (1992).
7. *Scott v. U.S.*, 2003-1 USTC ¶50,428 (4th Cir. 2003); *Mellon Bank v. U.S.*, 2001-2 USTC ¶50,621 (Fed. Cir. 2001) *Rudkin Testamentary Trust v. Comm.*, 2006-2 USTC ¶50,569 (2d Cir. 2006).
8. IRC Sec. 665(c).
9. IRC Secs. 666-667.
10. IRC Secs. 666-667.

Distributions of income accumulated by a trust before the beneficiary is born or before he attains age 21 are not considered accumulation distributions and thus are not generally subject to the throwback rules.[1]

Estates are required to file estimated tax for taxable years ending two years or more after the date of the decedent's death.[2] Trusts generally are required to pay estimated tax (see Q 1401). However, there are two exceptions to this rule: (1) with respect to any taxable year ending before the date that is two years after the decedent's death, trusts owned by the decedent (under the grantor trust rules) and to which the residue of the decedent's estate will pass under his will need not file estimated tax (if no will is admitted to probate, this rule will apply to a trust which is primarily responsible for paying taxes, debts and administration expenses); and (2) charitable trusts (as defined in IRC Section 511) and private foundations are not required to file estimated tax.[3] A trustee may elect to treat any portion of a payment of estimated tax made by the trust for any taxable year as a payment made by a beneficiary of the trust. Any amount so treated is treated as paid or credited to the beneficiary on the last day of the taxable year.[4]

1450. What is a grantor trust? How is a grantor trust taxed?

A grantor who retains certain interests in a trust he creates may be treated as the "owner" of all or part of the trust and thus taxed on the income of the trust in proportion to his ownership. There are five categories of interests for which the IRC gives detailed limits as to the amount of control the grantor may have without being taxed on the trust income. These categories are: reversionary interests, power to control beneficial enjoyment, administrative powers, power to revoke, and income for benefit of grantor.[5] With respect to any taxable year ending within two years after a grantor/decedent's death, any trust, all of which was treated under these grantor trust rules as owned by the decedent, is not required to file an estimated tax return (see Q 1449).[6]

Reversionary Interests

Generally, a grantor will be treated as the owner of any portion of a trust in which he has a reversionary interest in either the corpus or the income, if, as of the date of inception of that portion of the trust, the value of such interest exceeds 5% of the value of the trust.[7] There is an exception to this rule where the reversionary interest will take effect at the death before age 21 of a beneficiary who is a lineal descendant of the grantor.[8] For transfers in trust made prior to March 2, 1986, the reversionary interest was not limited to a certain percentage, and so long as it took effect *after* 10 years it did not result in taxation of the grantor.[9] Using a 7% valuation table, the value of the reversionary interest of a term trust falls below 5% if the trust runs more than about 44 years. The value of a reversion will depend on the interest rate and the valuation tables required to be used (see App. C).

---

1. IRC Sec. 665(b).
2. IRC Sec. 6654(l).
3. IRC Sec. 6654(l).
4. IRC Sec. 643(g).
5. IRC Secs. 673-677.
6. IRC Sec. 6654(l)(2)(B).
7. IRC Sec. 673(a).
8. IRC Sec. 673(b).
9. IRC Sec. 673(a), prior to amendment by TRA '86.

Power to Control Beneficial Enjoyment

If the grantor has any power of disposition over the beneficial enjoyment of any portion of the trust, and such power is exercisable without the approval of an adverse party, he will be treated (i.e., taxed) as the owner of that portion.[1] A grantor may do any of the following without such action resulting in his being treated as the owner of that portion of the trust: (1) reserve the power to dispose of the trust corpus by will, (2) allocate corpus or income among charitable beneficiaries (so long as it is irrevocably payable to the charities), (3) withhold income temporarily (provided the accumulated income must ultimately be paid to or for the benefit of the beneficiary), (4) allocate receipts and disbursements between corpus and income, and (5) distribute corpus by a "reasonably definite standard."[2] An example of a "reasonably definite standard" is found in Treasury Regulation §1.674(b)-1(b)(5): "for the education, support, maintenance and health of the beneficiary; for his reasonable support and comfort; or to enable him to maintain his accustomed standard of living; or to meet an emergency." A grantor also may retain the power to withhold income during the disability or minority of a beneficiary.[3] However, if *any person* has the power to add or change beneficiaries, other than providing for the addition of after-born or after-adopted children, the grantor will be treated as the owner.[4]

IRC Section 674(c) allows powers, solely exercisable by a trustee or trustees (none of whom is the grantor, and no more than half of whom are related or subordinate parties who are subservient to the wishes of the grantor), to distribute, apportion, or accumulate income to or for beneficiaries or pay out trust corpus to or for a beneficiary without the grantor being considered the owner of the trust. A related or subordinate party is a person who is not an adverse party and who is the grantor's spouse if living with the grantor; the grantor's father, mother, issue, brother or sister; an employee of the grantor; or a corporation or employee of a corporation if the grantor and the trust have significant voting control of the corporation.[5] An adverse party is any person having a substantial beneficial interest in a trust which would be adversely affected by the exercise or nonexercise of the power the person possesses respecting the trust.[6]

The grantor will also not be considered the owner of the trust due to a power solely exercisable by a trustee or trustees, none of whom are the grantor or the grantor's spouse living with the grantor, to distribute, apportion, or accumulate income to or for a beneficiary as long as the power is limited to a reasonably definite external standard set forth in the trust instrument.[7] Regulations treat a reasonably definite external standard as synonymous with a reasonably definite standard, described above.[8]

Income for Benefit of Grantor

If the trust income is (or, in the discretion of the grantor or a nonadverse party, or both, may be) distributed or held for the benefit of the grantor or his spouse, he will be treated as the owner of it.[9] This provision applies to the use of trust income for the

---

1. IRC Sec. 674(a).
2. IRC Sec. 674(b).
3. IRC Sec. 674(b)(7).
4. IRC Sec. 674(c).
5. IRC Sec. 672(c).
6. IRC Sec. 672(a).
7. IRC Sec. 674(d).
8. Treas. Reg. §1.674(d)-1.
9. IRC Sec. 677(a).

payment of premiums for insurance on the life of the grantor or his spouse, although taxation does not result from the mere power of the trustee to purchase life insurance. This provision is also invoked any time trust income is used *for the benefit of the grantor*, to discharge a legal obligation. Thus, when trust income is used to discharge the grantor's legal support obligations, it is taxable income to the grantor.[1] State laws vary as to what constitutes a parent's obligation to support; however, such a determination may be based in part on the background, values and goals of the parents, as well as the children.[2]

The mere power of the trustee to use trust income to discharge a legal obligation of the grantor will not result in taxable income to the grantor. Under IRC Section 677(b), there must be an actual distribution of trust income for the grantor's benefit in order for the grantor to be taxable on the amounts expended.

Other Grantor Powers

A grantor's power to revoke the trust will result in his being treated as owner of it. This may happen by operation of law in states requiring that the trust instrument explicitly state that the trust is irrevocable. Such a power will also be inferred where the grantor's powers are so extensive as to be substantially equivalent to a power of revocation, such as a power to invade the corpus.[3]

Certain administrative powers retained by the grantor will result in his being treated as owner of the trust; these include the power to deal with trust funds for less than full and adequate consideration, the power to borrow without adequate interest or security, or borrowing from the trust without completely repaying principal and interest before the beginning of the taxable year.[4]

---

1. IRC Sec. 677(b).
2. *Stone v. Comm.*, TC Memo 1987-454; *Braun v. Comm.*, TC Memo 1984-285.
3. IRC Sec. 676.
4. IRC Sec. 675.

PART III

FEDERAL TRANSFER TAX

on

INVESTMENTS

Including General Estate, Gift, and Generation-Skipping Transfer Taxation of Individuals

ESTATE TAX

GENERAL

1500. Starting Point – What is the federal estate tax?

The federal estate tax is an excise tax on the right to transfer property at death.[1] EGTRRA 2001 repeals the estate tax for one year in 2010. Technically, EGTRRA 2001 repeals the estate tax for decedents dying after 2009. However, EGTRRA 2001 sunsets (or expires) after 2010.[2]

The estate tax is measured by the value of the property or property interests transferred. The estate tax is an extension of the gift tax, which is an excise tax on the right to transfer property during life (see Q 1517). In fact, in general, both kinds of transfers are taxed according to the same rate schedule and a unified credit applies to both. As is explained at Q 1517, the gift tax is cumulative and the tax rates are progressive. Thus, while taxable lifetime gifts may cause gifts made in subsequent years to be taxed at higher rates, all lifetime taxable gifts (if substantial enough) tend to push the taxable estate into higher tax brackets. That is, the cumulative effect follows through to the last taxable transfer a person makes–at death. This effect is seen clearly when the steps in the computation of the estate tax are followed.

An estate tax return, if required, must generally be filed within nine months after the decedent's death. A six month extension for filing is available. Tax is generally due within nine months after the decedent's death, but certain extensions for payment may be available. See Q 1508.

The Federal Estate Tax Worksheet, below, shows the steps for calculating the estate tax. Calculation starts with determining what is includable in the decedent's gross estate (see Q 1501). In general, the gross estate includes property owned by the decedent at death, as well as property in which the decedent retained or held certain strings such as a retained income interest, a reversionary interest, a right to change beneficial interests, jointly owned property, a general power of appointment, certain interests in annuities or life insurance, and certain transfers within three years of death. A limited exclusion is available from the gross estate for conservation easements (Q 1505).

---

1. IRC Sec. 2001.
2. IRC Sec. 2210; EGTRRA 2001 Sec. 901.

Federal Estate Tax Worksheet

1	Year of Death		
2	Gross Estate (before exclusions)		$ Q 1501
3	- Conservation Easement Exclusion		($ Q 1505)
4	Gross Estate		$ Q 1501
5	- Funeral and Administration Expenses Deduction	$ Q 1506	
6	- Debts and Taxes Deduction	$ Q 1506	
7	- Losses Deduction	$ Q 1506	
8	- Subtotal: 5 to 7		($)
9	Adjusted Gross Estate		$
10	- Marital Deduction	$ Q 1506	
11	- Charitable Deduction	$ Q 1506	
12	- Other Deductions	$ Q 1506	
13	- Subtotal: 10 to 12		($)
14	Taxable Estate		$
15	+ Adjusted Taxable Gifts		$
16	Computation Base		$
17	Tax on Computation Base		$ Appendix B
18	- Gift Tax on Adjusted Taxable Gifts		($ Appendix B)
19	Tentative Tax		$ Appendix B
20	- Unified Credit	$ Q 1507	
21	- State Death Tax Credit	$ Q 1507	
22	- Pre-1977 Gift Tax Credit	$ Q 1507	
23	- Previously Taxed Property Credit	$ Q 1507	
24	- Foreign Death Tax Credit	$ Q 1507	
25	- Total Credits		$ Q 1507)
26	Federal Estate Tax		$

Property includable in the gross estate is generally valued at fair market value on the date of death (Q 1535). An election may be available to use an alternative valuation date six months after death (Q 1536).

Certain deductions (Q 1506) are available against the gross estate. Deductions for funeral and administration expenses, debts and taxes, and losses are subtracted from the gross estate to produce an adjusted gross estate. The adjusted gross estate is used to determine qualification for a few tax benefits, such as estate tax deferral under IRC Section 6166 (see Q 1508).

Unlimited marital and charitable deductions are available for certain transfers to surviving spouses and charities. A deduction for state death taxes is also available. The taxable estate equals the gross estate reduced by all deductions.

Tax is imposed on the taxable estate. Tax rates (Appendix B) are generally progressive and tax is based on cumulative taxable transfers during lifetime and at death. To implement this, tax is calculated on the sum of the taxable estate and adjusted taxable gifts (the computation base), and the gift tax that would have been payable on adjusted taxable gifts (using the tax rates in effect at decedent's death) is then subtracted out. Adjusted taxable gifts are taxable gifts (the balance after subtracting allowable exclusions and deductions) made by the decedent after 1976 other than gifts includable in the decedent's gross estate.

Planning Point: A gift made after August 5, 1997, cannot be revalued, if the gift was adequately disclosed on a gift tax return and the gift tax statute of limitations (generally, three years) has passed.[1] Consider filing gift tax returns even for annual exclusion gifts.

The tentative tax is then reduced by credits (Q 1507) to produce estate tax payable. The unified credit is generally the most important credit available.

GROSS ESTATE

1501. What items are includable in a decedent's gross estate for federal estate tax purposes?

The items that comprise the gross estate are described in IRC Sections 2033-2046 and the regulations thereunder. Gratuitous transfers of federal, state, and municipal obligations are discussed in Q 1523. See Q 1505 for an exclusion from the gross estate.

IRC Section 2033

Property in Which the Decedent Had an Interest

"The gross estate of a decedent who was a citizen or resident of the United States at the time of his death includes under IRC Section 2033 the value of all property, whether real or personal, tangible or intangible, and wherever situated, beneficially owned by the decedent at the time of his death ...[see Q 1523]. Real property is included whether it came into the possession and control of the executor or administrator or passed directly to heirs or devisees .... Notes or other claims held by the decedent are likewise included even though they are cancelled by the decedent's will. Interest and rents accrued at the date of the decedent's death constitute a part of the gross estate. Similarly, dividends which are payable to the decedent or his estate by reason of the fact that on or before the date of the decedent's death he was a stockholder of record (but which have not been collected at death) constitute a part of the gross estate."[2]

Interest accrued, for example, on certificates of deposit owned at death and payable after death but forfeitable in the event of surrender during the owner's life[3] is includable in the decedent's estate under IRC Section 2033. The result is not changed by the fact that the decedent owned the CDs as a joint tenant when he died.[4]

Note that it is only property "beneficially owned" by the decedent that is includable under IRC Section 2033. Thus, IRC Section 2033 does not reach property held by the decedent in trust for others. On the other hand, the decedent's beneficial interest in property held by another as trustee is includable under IRC Section 2033 unless the decedent's death terminates his interest.

IRC Section 2033 does not embrace interests which terminate on the decedent's death, such as his life interest in a trust. (But such termination may be subject to the

---

1. IRC Sec. 2001(f).
2. Treas. Reg. §20.2033-1.
3. See Federal Reserve Banking Regulation Section 217.4.
4. *Jeschke v. U.S.*, 87-1 USTC ¶13,713 (10th Cir. 1987).

tax on generation-skipping transfers—see Q 1510.) Similarly, if a decedent sells property in exchange for notes which provide that his death will extinguish the balance owing at that time, such balance will not be includable in the decedent's estate under IRC Section 2033 if the sale was for an adequate and full consideration and the cancellation provision was part of the bargained for consideration.[1]

Among the items includable in a decedent's gross estate are his rights to future income: for example, his right to payments under an individual deferred compensation agreement or partnership income continuation plan. Such rights—called "income in respect of a decedent"—are included at their present (commuted) value. Since the income is also subject to income tax in the hands of the person who receives it (decedent's estate or beneficiary), the recipient is allowed an income tax deduction for the estate tax paid on the income right (see Q 1430).

The decedent's interest in any business he owns at his death, whether as a proprietor, a partner or a shareholder in a corporation, is likewise includable under IRC Section 2033.

Local property law (state law) determines the nature and extent of decedent's ownership rights in property at the time of his death. Under community property law, for instance, property acquired by a husband or wife during marriage by purchase with community funds is generally considered to be owned one-half by each spouse. Consequently, upon the death of the spouse who dies first, only one-half of the community property is includable in his gross estate. Ten states—Alaska, Arizona, California, Idaho, Louisiana, Nevada, New Mexico, Texas, Washington, and Wisconsin—operate under some form of community property system.

The value of social security survivor benefits, either lump sum or monthly annuity, is not includable in the decedent's estate under IRC Section 2033.[2]

IRC Section 2034

Dower and Curtesy Interests and Their Statutory Substitutes

IRC Section 2034 specifically includes in the gross estate the interest of the decedent's surviving spouse "existing at the time of the decedent's death as dower or curtesy, or by virtue of a statute creating an estate in lieu of dower or curtesy."

At one time, certain courts held that dower and curtesy interests were not subject to death taxes because they were not received by transfer from the decedent. IRC Section 2034 was enacted to make sure that these marital interests would not escape the federal estate tax. The full value of the property without deduction of the surviving spouse's interest is includable in the gross estate.

IRC Section 2035

Gifts within Three Years of Death

Subject to two kinds of exceptions, gifts made within three years of death are not brought back into the donor's gross estate under the bringback rule of IRC Section 2035 (see below). *However*, gift tax paid by the decedent or his estate on any gifts made by

---

1. *Est. of Moss v. Comm.*, 74 TC 1239 (1980), acq. in result, 1981-1 CB 2.
2. Rev. Rul. 55-87, 1955-1 CB 112; Rev. Rul. 67-277, 1967-2 CB 322; Rev. Rul. 81-182, 1981-2 CB 179.

the decedent or his spouse within three years of the decedent's death is includable in the gross estate in any case, regardless of whether the value of the gift itself is includable under IRC Section 2035 or any other IRC section.[1] Gift tax paid by decedent's spouse on a split-gift within three years of decedent's death was included in decedent's estate where the decedent had funneled money to his spouse who then transferred the money to a life insurance trust (and to the IRS to pay gift tax); the transfers were treated as collapsed into one transaction under the step-transaction doctrine.[2]

The first kind of exception applies (1) where a donor gratuitously transfers property within three years of death but retains an interest in that property described in IRC Section 2036 (transfer with a retained life estate), 2037 (transfer taking effect at death with reversionary interest retained), 2038 (transfer with power retained to revoke or amend), or 2042 (incidents of ownership in insurance on life of donor), or (2) where a donor transfers property subject to such a retained interest more than three years before death, but relinquishes that interest within three years of death. The bringback rule applies to these transfers whether or not a gift tax return was required to be filed.[3] The entire value of the property transferred under this exception is includable in the decedent's gross estate, including the value of the property, if any, transferred by the decedent's consenting spouse (i.e., a split gift–see Q 1530). If the consenting spouse dies within three years of the gift and the entire value of the gift was includable in the donor spouse's estate under IRC Section 2035, the consenting spouse's portion of the gift is not an adjusted taxable gift and is not includable in the consenting spouse's gross estate.[4] The gift tax paid by the donor spouse or his estate is includable in the donor spouse's estate, and the gift tax paid by the consenting spouse or her estate is includable in the consenting spouse's estate.[5] However, gift tax paid by decedent's spouse on a gift split between the spouses within three years of decedent's death was included in decedent's estate where the spouse did not have sufficient assets to pay the spouse's share of the gift tax and the decedent transferred assets to the spouse to pay the taxes.[6]

A transfer from a revocable trust is treated as made directly by the grantor.[7] Such a transfer will generally be subject to the three-year bringback rule only with respect to gift tax paid within three years of death and for the limited purpose of the second exception below.

The second kind of exception retains the three-year bringback rule of IRC Section 2035 for the purposes of (a) determining the estate's qualification for (1) IRC Section 303 stock redemptions (redemption of stock held by a decedent at death in an amount not in excess of death taxes and settlement costs under special income tax rules that treat the redemption as a capital transaction rather than as a dividend), and (2) current use valuation for qualified real property (see Q 1535), and (b) determining property subject to estate tax liens.[8] With respect to the IRC Section 6166 extension of the time to pay estate tax (see Q 1508), the requirement that the decedent's interest in a closely held business must exceed 35% of the adjusted gross estate is met by an estate only if the estate meets the requirement both with and without the application of the bringback

---

1. IRC Sec. 2035(b); Rev. Rul. 81-229, 1981-2 CB 176; Rev. Rul. 82-198, 1982-2 CB 206.
2. *Brown v. U.S.*, 2003-1 USTC ¶60,462 (9th Cir. 2003).
3. IRC Sec. 2035(a).
4. IRC Sec. 2001(e); Rev. Rul. 82-198, 1982-2 CB 206.
5. IRC Sec. 2035(b); Rev. Rul. 82-198, above.
6. TAM 9729005.
7. IRC Sec. 2035(e).
8. IRC Sec. 2035(c)(1).

rule.[1] An exception to this second exception is that any gifts (other than a transfer with respect to a life insurance policy) not required to be reported on a gift tax return filed by the decedent for the year the gift was made are not includable in the gross estate. Gifts up to the limit of the gift tax annual exclusion and qualified transfers (see Q 1530), but not split gifts, do not require the filing of a return. Another exception to the second exception is a gift which qualifies for the gift tax marital deduction (see Q 1531).[2]

The Bringback Rule

The bringback rule of IRC Section 2035, referred to above, operates as follows: In general, gifts made by the decedent (in trust or otherwise) which are caught by the three-year rule, are includable in the decedent's estate. Also includable is the amount of any gift tax paid by the decedent or his estate on any gifts made by the decedent or his spouse within three years prior to decedent's death; the gift tax is includable regardless of whether the value of the gift itself is includable under IRC Section 2035 or any other IRC section.[3] Where the decedent made a "net gift" (i.e., a gift made on the condition that the donee pay the gift tax—see Q 1525), the amount includable in the gross estate is the total value of the property transferred.[4]

IRC Section 2036

Gifts with Life Interest Retained

IRC Section 2036 is one of the three sections (2036, 2037, 2038) dealing with incomplete lifetime transfers. This section brings into the gross estate lifetime gifts of property where the donor has retained the use of the property or the income from the property for life. Included are transfers made directly to a donee and transfers made to an irrevocable trust for designated beneficiaries.

Specifically, IRC Section 2036 requires to be included in an individual's gross estate any property which he gratuitously transfers during his lifetime if he retains "for his life or for any period not ascertainable without reference to his death or for any period which does not in fact end before his death," either:

"(1) the possession or enjoyment of, or the right to income from, the property, or

"(2) the right, either alone or in conjunction with any person, to designate the persons who shall possess or enjoy the property or the income therefrom."

The cases are not in agreement on whether the decedent's retention of possession or enjoyment of, or the right to income from, property must be evidenced by an agreement, or by a prearrangement, or merely by circumstantial evidence.[5]

Excepted from the scope of IRC Section 2036 is a transfer of property by way of "a bona fide sale for an adequate and full consideration in money or money's worth."[6] Courts have had to wrestle with the interpretation of this exception in "widow's elec-

---

1. IRC Sec. 2035(c)(2).
2. IRC Sec. 2035(c)(3).
3. IRC Sec. 2035(b); Rev. Rul. 81-229, 1981-2 CB 176; Rev. Rul. 82-198, 1982-2 CB 206.
4. Let. Rul. 8317010.
5. See *Lee v. U.S.*, 86-1 USTC ¶13,649 (W.D. Ky. 1985).
6. IRC Sec. 2036(a).

tion" cases. Typically, a married decedent leaves certain property (and/or certain community property) in trust for his children, with all income to the surviving spouse for her lifetime, on the condition that the surviving spouse transfer certain of her property (or community property share) to the trust. The surviving spouse thus has her choice between what has been provided for her in the will and her statutory (intestate) share (or community property share). If the widow elects to take under the will, and transfers the agreed-upon property to the trust in exchange for a life income from all the trust assets, what has she transferred for purposes of IRC Section 2036? Has she transferred the entire property, or has she transferred only a remainder interest? If she is considered to have transferred the entire property, and the value of property transferred exceeds the value of the life income interest she receives in return, then she has not made a "bona fide sale for an adequate and full consideration" and the entire value of the property she transferred is includable in her gross estate under IRC Section 2036. If, however, she is considered to have transferred only a remainder interest, and that interest is of less value than the value of her life income from trust assets in excess of the value of the property she actually transferred, then she will have received adequate and full consideration for the transfer, and none of the property she actually transferred will be includable in her estate under IRC Section 2036. Case law appears to support the former interpretation.[1]

IRC Section 2037

Gifts Taking Effect at Death

IRC Section 2037 requires inclusion in the gross estate of any interest in property transferred by the decedent if both of the following conditions are met:

(1) Possession or enjoyment of the property can, through ownership of the transferred interest, be obtained only by surviving the decedent, and

(2) The decedent has retained a reversionary interest in the property which, immediately before his death, exceeded 5% of the value of the property.

An example would be a transfer to an irrevocable living trust under the following terms: income to grantor's wife for her life; property to revert to grantor if living at wife's death, and if not, property to their daughter.

Assuming that the grantor predeceases his wife and daughter, the value of the daughter's interest—the value of the property less the wife's life interest—is includable in the grantor's gross estate. Obviously, the daughter had to survive her grantor father in order to receive the property. And in all probability the grantor's reversionary interest, valued immediately before his death, exceeded 5% of the value of the property.

The term "reversionary interest" means any possibility that the *property* may return to the donor or to his estate, and any possibility that the property may become subject to a power of disposition by him. The term does not, however, include a possibility that the income alone may return to the donor or his estate. Thus, retention of a secondary life estate would not constitute a reversionary interest (although it would cause inclusion under IRC Section 2036). Also, the term "reversionary interest" does not include a mere expectancy by the decedent that upon the death of the transferee

---

1. *Gradow v. U.S.*, 90-1 USTC ¶60,010 (9th Cir. 1990).

he (or his estate) may reacquire the property under the will of the transferee or under state inheritance laws.[1]

IRC Section 2038

Gifts with Power Retained to Revoke or Amend

IRC Section 2038 brings into a decedent's gross estate property that he has gratuitously transferred if immediately before his death he possessed the power to alter, amend, revoke, or terminate the transfer.

The language of the section refers to transfers "by trust or otherwise" but generally the section applies to transfers in trust. The most obvious example of the applicability of IRC Section 2038 is, of course, the revocable living trust. Where the grantor of a trust retains until his death the power to revoke the trust, the full value of the trust corpus is includable in his gross estate.

It makes no difference whether the decedent could exercise the power alone or only in conjunction with another person.

It also makes no difference in what capacity the decedent could exercise the power—whether as grantor, trustee, or co-trustee.

IRC Section 2038 is not limited to transfers where the decedent *retained* the power to alter, amend, revoke, or terminate at the time of transfer, except with respect to transfers made on or before June 22, 1936. With respect to transfers made after that date, possession of such a power at death will cause inclusion in the gross estate regardless of when or from what source the decedent acquired the power. Thus, IRC Section 2038 would reach a case in which the decedent, who had not originally retained the power, subsequently succeeded to it by being appointed a trustee.

IRC Section 2038 also reaches transfers to an *irrevocable* trust if the settlor possesses at his death the power to alter or amend the trust.[2] However, the provision in a trust instrument for the inclusion of all the settlor's after-born and after-adopted children as additional beneficiaries is not the retention of a power to change the beneficial interests of the trust within the meaning of IRC Section 2038.[3]

The regulations also make it clear that the mere discretionary power reserved to the grantor to accumulate or distribute trust income for a single beneficiary is sufficient to bring the trust property into the grantor's estate under IRC Section 2038.[4]

However, if the grantor's power to affect the beneficial enjoyment of the transferred property is limited by an ascertainable objective and external standard, the power will not fall within IRC Section 2038. The Internal Revenue Service acquiesces in the ascertainable standard doctrine established by the cases.[5] For information on the ascertainable standard doctrine, see Stephens, Maxfield, Lind & Calfee, Federal Estate

---

1. Treas. Reg. §20.2037-1(c)(2).
2. *Marshall v. U.S.*, 338 F. Supp. 1321 (D. Md. 1972).
3. Rev. Rul. 80-255, 1980-2 CB 272.
4. Treas. Reg. §20.2038-1(a).
5. 1947-2 CB 2; Rev. Rul. 73-143, 1973-1 CB 407.

and Gift Taxation (Boston: Warren, Gorham & Lamont, 7th ed.), ¶4.10[5], and the cases cited therein.

If a grantor creates an irrevocable trust under which the trustee is given the power to distribute income and principal unlimited by an ascertainable standard, the value of the trust property will be includable in the grantor's estate under IRC Section 2038 (and also under IRC Section 2036) if (1) the grantor names himself as trustee or retains at his death the power to do so, or (2) the grantor retains at his death the power to remove the trustee without cause and replace him with another.[1] However, a later revenue ruling modified Rev. Rul. 79-353 to provide that the above-described estate tax holding will not be applied to a transfer or to an addition to a trust, made before October 29, 1979, the date of publication of the revenue ruling, if the trust was irrevocable on October 28, 1979.[2] However, for purposes of IRC Section 2036 or IRC Section 2038, the Service will no longer include trust property in a decedent grantor's estate where the grantor retains the right to replace the trustee but can replace the trustee with only an independent corporate trustee.[3]

IRC Section 2039

Annuities

IRC Section 2039 deals with annuities or other payments receivable by any beneficiary under any form of contract or agreement by reason of surviving the decedent. Subsections (a) and (b) of that section state the circumstances under which such an annuity or payment is includable in the decedent's gross estate. Thus, IRC Section 2039 applies to death and survivor benefits under annuity contracts and under optional settlements of living proceeds from life insurance policies and endowment contracts.

Exclusions under various provisions of IRC Section 2039 may apply to employee annuities which are part of qualified pension and profit sharing plans; to employee annuities payable under nonqualified deferred compensation plans, including death benefit only plans; to certain tax sheltered annuity plans; and to individual retirement savings plans. See *Tax Facts on Insurance & Employee Benefits*, published annually by The National Underwriter Company, for information on these exclusions.

IRC Section 2040

Joint Interests

IRC Section 2040 deals with all classes of property held jointly with right of survivorship. This includes, for example, jointly held real estate, jointly held bonds, and joint bank accounts. IRC Section 2040 does not deal with other forms of co-ownership in which property interests pass at death other than automatically to surviving co-owners. Thus, tenancies in common and community property interests are includable under IRC Section 2033, not under IRC Section 2040.

The general rule of IRC Section 2040 requires that the entire value of the jointly owned property must be included in the gross estate of the joint owner who dies first, except such part as can be shown to have originally belonged to the survivor and never to have been acquired from the decedent "for less than an adequate and

---

1. Treas. Reg. §20.2038-1(a)(3); Rev. Rul. 79-353, 1979-2 CB 325.
2. Rev. Rul. 81-51, 1981-1 CB 458.
3. Rev. Rul. 95-58, 1995-2 CB 191; *Est. of Wall v. Comm.*, 101 TC 300 (1993).

full consideration in money or money's worth."[1] Thus, the rule is as follows: if the decedent furnished the entire purchase price, the entire property is includable; if the decedent furnished a part only of the purchase price, only a corresponding proportion of the property is includable; if the decedent furnished no part of the purchase price, no part of the property is includable.[2] *But see below for special rule applicable to spouses who own property jointly.*

Where the joint owners are related (not spouses) and the survivor paid part of the purchase price, he must be able to prove that the funds did not come to him by way of gift from the decedent. In other words, the purchase price will be traced to its original source; and the burden of proof is not on the IRS but on the survivor. It is often a difficult matter to prove the extent of contribution of the survivor to the joint ownership. If the assets of the joint owners became inextricably commingled prior to acquisition of the jointly owned property, proof may be impossible and the property will be wholly includable in the decedent's gross estate.

But while money or property acquired by the surviving joint owner by gift from the decedent and contributed to the purchase price of the jointly held property is traced to the decedent for purposes of IRC Section 2040, *income* from property so acquired which is contributed to the purchase price is treated as the survivor's own contribution for purposes of IRC Section 2040.[3] Further, IRS has ruled that where the survivor's contribution to the purchase price of jointly held property was traced to proceeds from the sale of property acquired by the survivor with money received from the decedent by gift, the sale proceeds attributable to appreciation in value of the property during the period the survivor owned the property were treated as the survivor's own contribution for purposes of IRC Section 2040. Also, consistent with the above-cited regulation, the Service ruled that sale proceeds attributable to income from the property received by the survivor and reinvested were treated as the survivor's individual contribution.[4]

Rev. Rul. 79-372 is also consistent with earlier case law, as noted in the ruling. However, the regulations call for a different result when the survivor's contribution was of property received by gift from the decedent (rather than of proceeds from the sale of such property), which property had appreciated in value during the period held by the survivor. In this situation the regulations require that the portion of the purchase price attributable to such appreciation be traced to the decedent for purposes of IRC Section 2040.[5]

Where the property was acquired by the decedent and the other joint owner by devise, bequest, or inheritance, or by gift from a third party, the decedent's fractional share of the property is included in his gross estate. For example, if the decedent's father has conveyed the property by gift to the decedent and his wife in joint tenancy or tenancy by the entirety, one-half of the property will be includable in the gross estate of whichever spouse dies first.[6]

---

1. IRC Sec. 2040(a).
2. Treas. Reg. §20.2040-1(c).
3. Treas. Reg. §20.2040-1(c)(5).
4. Rev. Rul. 79-372, 1979-2 CB 330.
5. Treas. Reg. §20.2040-1(c)(4).
6. IRC Sec. 2040(a).

Spouses Who Own Property Jointly:
Qualified Joint Interests

Effective for estates of decedents dying after 1981, in the case of joint interests created after 1976, notwithstanding the provisions of IRC Section 2040 explained above (subsection (a)), only one-half the value of a *qualified joint interest* is included in a decedent's gross estate under IRC Section 2040. [The rule for inclusion in a decedent's estate for spousal jointly owned property is still based upon consideration furnished if the joint interest was created prior to 1977.[1]] A *qualified joint interest* means any interest in property held by the decedent and the decedent's spouse as (a) tenants by the entirety; or (b) joint tenants with right of survivorship, but only if the decedent and the spouse of the decedent are the only joint tenants.[2] However, with respect to decedents dying after November 10, 1988, if the decedent's spouse is not a United States citizen, interests in property held by the decedent and the decedent's spouse are not treated as a *qualified joint interest* (apparently unless the transfer to the surviving spouse is in a qualified domestic trust, see Q 1506).[3] For purposes of applying the consideration furnished test (see above) where the *qualified joint interest* rule does not apply because the decedent's spouse is not a United States citizen, consideration furnished by the decedent to the decedent's spouse before July 14, 1988 is generally treated as consideration furnished by the decedent's spouse.[4]

IRC Section 2041

Powers of Appointment

IRC Section 2041 governs the includability in the decedent's gross estate of property subject to his power of appointment. For estate tax purposes, a "power of appointment" is a power which has been given to the decedent by another person, as distinguished from a power *retained* by him over property which he formerly owned. A power of appointment enables the holder thereof to dispose of property he does not own.

Example. Husband's will provides that part of his estate is to be placed in trust. The will gives his wife all the trust income for her life and also the power to designate who shall receive the trust principal after her death. If the wife fails to exercise her power, the trust principal is to go to their daughter. Actually she exercises her power by executing a will in which she leaves the trust principal to their son.

In this example, the husband is the *donor* of the power; the wife is the *donee* of the power; their son is the *appointee* of the power; and the daughter, had the wife failed to exercise her power, would have been the *taker in default of appointment*.

Of course, powers of appointment can be created otherwise than by a testamentary trust. They can also be created, for example, by the terms of a living trust, or by the terms of a life insurance beneficiary arrangement.

The law provides two sets of rules for gift and estate taxation of powers of appointment. The first set of rules deals with powers created before October 22, 1942, sometimes called "pre-1942" powers. The second set of rules governs powers created after October 21, 1942, sometimes called "post-1942" powers.

---

1. *Gallenstein v. U.S.*, 92-2 USTC ¶60,114 (6th Cir. 1992); *Patten v. U.S.*, 97-2 USTC ¶60,279 (4th Cir. 1997); *Anderson v. U.S.*, 96-2 USTC ¶60,235 (D.C. Md. 1996); *Hahn v. Comm.*, 110 TC 140 (1998), acq. 2001-42 IRB iii.
2. IRC Sec. 2040(b).
3. IRC Sec. 2056(d).
4. OBRA '89, Sec. 7815(d)(16).

A power of appointment created by will is considered as created on the date of the testator's death. A power created by an inter vivos instrument is considered created on the date the instrument takes effect.[1] Thus, in the case of a living trust, the power is created when the trust takes effect, even though the trust is revocable. Likewise, in the case of life insurance, the power is created when the beneficiary designation is made, even though the designation is revocable.

Regardless of when the power is created, however, it is not taxable in any event unless it is a "general" power of appointment.

General Power of Appointment

The IRC defines a general power of appointment as a power which is exercisable in favor of the decedent, his estate, his creditors, or the creditors of his estate. Here the "decedent" is, of course, the donee—that is, the holder of the power.

A power exercisable in favor of either the holder or his estate is a general power of appointment; it need not be exercisable in favor of both. Thus, if the holder can withdraw all or part of the principal for any purpose, he has a general power of appointment exercisable in favor of himself. Or, if he can will the property to anyone he wishes, including his own estate, he has a general power of appointment exercisable in favor of his estate.

However, a power to "consume, invade, or appropriate" the principal for the holder's own benefit is not a general power of appointment if it is limited by an "ascertainable standard" relating to the holder's "health, education, support, or maintenance." According to the regulations: "A power is limited by such a standard if the extent of the holder's duty to exercise and not to exercise the power is reasonably measurable in terms of his needs for health, education, or support (or any combination of them). As used in this subparagraph, the words 'support' and 'maintenance' are synonymous and their meaning is not limited to the bare necessities of life. A power to use property for the comfort, welfare, or happiness of the holder of the power is not limited by the requisite standard. Examples of powers which are limited by the requisite standard are powers exercisable for the holder's 'support,' 'support in reasonable comfort,' 'maintenance in health and reasonable comfort,' 'support in his accustomed manner of living,' 'education, including college and professional education,' 'health,' and 'medical, dental, hospital and nursing expenses and expenses of invalidism.' In determining whether a power is limited by an ascertainable standard, it is immaterial whether the beneficiary is required to exhaust his other income before the power can be exercised."[2]

A pre-1942 power is not considered to be a "general" power of appointment if it is exercisable only in conjunction with another person. And a post-1942 power is not considered to be a "general" power of appointment if it is exercisable only in conjunction with the donor of the power or only in conjunction with someone who has a substantial interest in the property which is adverse to the holder's interest.[3] It has been held that a trustee does not have a substantial and adverse interest simply because the trust is a taker in default of exercise of the power, so long as the trustee himself is not a beneficiary of the trust.[4]

---

1. Treas. Reg. §20.2041-1(e).
2. Treas. Reg. §20.2041-1(c)(2).
3. *Est. of Maxant*, TC Memo 1980-414; Rev. Rul. 82-156, 1982-2 CB 206.
4. *Miller v. U.S.*, 387 F.2d 866 (3rd Cir. 1968); *Est. of Towle v. Comm.*, 54 TC 368 (1970).

In the past, a number of letter rulings have determined that a beneficiary who has the power to remove a trustee will be treated as holding any powers held by the trustee for purpose of determining whether the beneficiary holds a general power of appointment. Let. Ruls. 8916032, 9113026 (does not apply to transfers in trust before October 29, 1979, if trust was irrevocable on October 28, 1979). However, for purposes of IRC Section 2036 or IRC Section 2038, the Service will no longer include trust property in a decedent grantor's estate where the grantor retains the right to replace the trustee but can replace the trustee with only an independent corporate trustee.[1] More recently, the power to remove a trustee and replace the trustee with as independent corporate trustee was not treated as the retention of powers held by the trustee for purposes of IRC Section 2041.[2] Hopefully, this represents an extension by the Service of its new policy with regard to trustee removal under IRC Section 2036 and IRC Section 2038 to IRC Section 2041. Similarly, a beneficiary's right to veto a replacement trustee and to petition a court for appointment of an independent replacement trustee was not treated as a general power of appointment.[3]

Any power of appointment which is not a general power is called a "special" or "limited" power. A special power of appointment is not taxable in the holder's estate regardless of when it was created.

Post-1942 Power: Generally

The *mere possession* at death of a post-1942 general power of appointment will cause the property to be included in the holder's gross estate. Thus:

If the decedent had a general power of appointment which he could have exercised by will in favor of his estate, the property subject to the power is taxable in his estate whether or not he exercised the power; or

If, immediately before his death, the decedent had a general power of appointment which he could have exercised in his own favor during his lifetime, the property subject to the power is taxable in his estate.

But even though the decedent does not still possess the power at the time of his death, if he has had such a power and has exercised or released it or allowed it to lapse during his lifetime, the property which was subject to the power may, under some circumstances, be included in his gross estate.

Thus, if the decedent once possessed a general power of appointment and has exercised or released it in such a way that had the property been his own it would have been included in his gross estate under one of the IRC Sections 2035 through 2038, then the property that was subject to the power is includable in his gross estate.

Post-1942 Power: Non-Cumulative
Annual Withdrawal Rights

In many situations, an insured or the grantor of a trust will wish to give his beneficiary not only all the income from the fund, but also a right to withdraw some limited amount of principal each year. If the beneficiary does not exercise his right of withdrawal in any year, the right expires or "lapses" at the end of the year. Where it

---

1. Rev. Rul. 95-58, 1995-2 CB 191; *Est. of Wall v. Comm.*, 101 TC 300 (1993).
2. Let. Rul. 9607008.
3. Let. Rul. 9741009.

cannot be carried forward to subsequent years, it is characterized as a "non-cumulative" withdrawal right.

Where the beneficiary permits such a right to lapse, gift and estate taxes may result by reason of the lapse. In other words, by not withdrawing the amount she could have withdrawn the beneficiary has made a gift to those persons designated to receive the principal.

However, in framing the powers of appointment tax law, Congress recognized that modest annual withdrawal rights are socially desirable and that their use, within limits, should not be discouraged. Therefore, an exemption is granted in an amount equal to whichever is greater: $5,000 or 5% of the value of the fund as of the date of the lapse of the power.

Consequently, where a non-cumulative power of withdrawal is permitted to lapse, only the excess over and above the $5,000 or 5% of the fund will be subject to gift and estate taxes. This excess is treated as a transfer with life income retained. But the entire amount which could have been withdrawn in the year of death, but was not withdrawn, is includable in the gross estate since this power has not lapsed at the time of death.

Pre-1942 Power

Prior to 1942, property subject to a general power of appointment was taxable in the donee's estate only if the power was *exercised*. Thus, the property is includable in the holder's gross estate only if (1) he has exercised the power by will at his death, or (2) he has exercised the power during life in such a way that had the property been owned by him it would have been includable under one of the IRC Sections 2035-2038.

IRC Section 2042

Life Insurance Proceeds

IRC Section 2042 deals specifically with the includability of life insurance proceeds in the gross estate of the *insured*. The proceeds are includable in the insured's gross estate under IRC Section 2042 if they are:

(1) Receivable by or for the benefit of insured's estate; or

(2) Receivable by a beneficiary other than the insured's estate *and* the insured possessed at his death any of the incidents of ownership in the policy (whether exercisable by the insured alone or only in conjunction with another person). For more information on this subject, see *Tax Facts on Insurance & Employee Benefits*, published annually by The National Underwriter Company.

IRC Section 2043

Transfers for Insufficient Consideration

If any one of the transfers described in IRC Sections 2035 through 2038 and 2041 is made for consideration in money or money's worth, but the consideration is not adequate and full, the excess of the fair market value of the property transferred over the consideration received is the amount includable in the gross estate.[1] There is a split of

---

1. IRC Sec. 2043(a).

authority over whether adequate and full consideration is measured by reference to what would otherwise be included in the estate or using time value of money discounts.[1]

In general, for purposes of the estate tax, a relinquishment or promised relinquishment of dower or curtesy, or of a statutory substitute therefor, or of other marital rights in the decedent's property or estate, is not considered consideration "in money or money's worth." However, an exception is made for the limited purpose of allowing a deduction from the gross estate in the case of a transfer which meets the following conditions: Where a husband and wife enter into a written agreement relative to their marital and property rights and divorce occurs within the three-year period beginning on the date one year before the agreement is entered into, any transfer of property or interests in property made pursuant to the agreement to either spouse in settlement of his or her marital or property rights is deemed to be a transfer made for a full and adequate consideration in money or money's worth. The deduction allowed is for the value of the property transferred as a claim against the estate (see Q 1506).

IRC Section 2044

Marital Deduction Property in Which
Decedent Had a Qualifying Income Interest

A marital deduction is allowed for transfers of "qualified terminable interests" if the decedent's executor (or donor) so elects and the spouse receives a "qualifying income interest" in the property for life. (See Q 1506, Q 1531.) If the property subject to the qualifying income interest is not disposed of prior to the death of the surviving spouse, the fair market value of the property determined as of the date of the spouse's death (or alternate valuation date, if so elected) is included in the spouse's gross estate pursuant to IRC Section 2044.

IRC Section 2046

Disclaimers

It is possible for a person who is (or would be) the transferee of an interest in property to refuse to accept the interest and thus prevent any part of the value of the property from being included in his gross estate at his death. However, with respect to transfers creating an interest in the person disclaiming made after December 31, 1976, the refusal must take the form of a *qualified disclaimer*.[2]

A *qualified disclaimer* means an irrevocable and unqualified refusal to accept an interest in property. The refusal must satisfy four conditions. First, the refusal must be in writing. Second, the written refusal must be received by the transferor of the interest, his legal representative, or the holder of the legal title to the property not later than nine months after the day on which the transfer creating the interest is made. However, if later, the period for making the disclaimer will not expire in any case until nine months after the day on which the person making the disclaimer attains age 21. Third, the person must not have accepted the interest or any of its benefits before making the disclaimer.

1. *Gradow v. U.S.*, 90-1 USTC ¶60,010 (Fed. Cir. 1990); *Pittman v. U.S.*, 95-1 USTC ¶60,186 (E.D.N.C. 1994); *Parker v. U.S.*, 95-1 USTC ¶60,199 (N.D. Ga. 1995); *Est. of D'Ambrosio v. Comm.*, 96-2 USTC ¶60,252 (3rd Cir. 1996), rev'g 105 TC 252 (1995); *Wheeler v. Comm.*, 97-2 USTC ¶60,278 (5th Cir. 1997), rev'g 96-1 USTC ¶60,226 (W.D. Tex. 1996); *Est. of Magnin v. Comm.*, 99-2 USTC ¶60,347 (9th Cir. 1999), rev'g TC Memo 1996-25.
2. IRC Secs. 2046, 2518(a).

Fourth, the interest must pass to a person other than the person making the disclaimer as a result of the refusal to accept the property.[1]

A power with respect to property[2] is treated as an interest in such property.[3] The exercise of a power of appointment to any extent by the donee of the power is an acceptance of its benefits.[4]

A written transfer of the transferor's (disclaimant's) entire interest in property to the person or persons who would otherwise have received the property if an effective disclaimer had been made will be treated as a valid disclaimer for federal estate and gift tax purposes provided the transfer is timely made and the transferor has not accepted any of the interest or any of its benefits.[5]

IRC Section 2701

Recapture of Qualified Payments

Additional estate tax may be due with respect to certain transfers of interests in corporations or partnerships to reflect cumulative but unpaid distributions on retained interests (see Q 1550).[6]

IRC Section 2704

Deemed Transfer of Lapsing Right

There may be a deemed transfer at death upon the lapse of certain voting or liquidation rights in a corporation or partnership (see Q 1553).[7]

1502. In whose estate is property held in custodianship under the Uniform Gifts to Minors Act or the Uniform Transfers to Minors Act includable for federal estate tax purposes?

The value of property transferred under the Uniform Act is includable in the gross estate of the *donor* if the donor dies while serving as custodian. (But see the discussion of gifts made within three years of death at Q 1501.) In all other circumstances, custodial property is includable only in the gross estate of the donee.[8] If H and W make identical gifts under the Uniform Act, each naming the other as custodian, for federal estate tax purposes each will be deemed to have transferred the property over which he held custodianship rights at death even though the property actually transferred by him was in the custody of the other.[9] Custodial property is not included in the estate of a custodian who consented to a split gift of the property by her spouse.[10]

---

1. IRC Sec. 2518(b).
2. See IRC Section 2041, Powers of Appointment, above.
3. IRC Sec. 2518(c)(2).
4. Treas. Reg. §25.2518-2(d)(1)(i); Let. Rul. 8142008.
5. IRC Sec. 2518(c)(3), as added by ERTA '81, and effective for transfers creating an interest in the person disclaiming made after 1981.
6. IRC Sec. 2701.
7. IRC Sec. 2704.
8. Rev. Rul. 57-366, 1957-2 CB 618; Treas. Reg. §20.2038-1(a); Rev. Rul. 59-357, 1959-2 CB 212; Rev. Rul. 70-348, 1970-2 CB 193; *Est. of Prudowsky*, 55 TC 890 (1971), aff'd per curiam, 465 F.2d 62 (7th Cir. 1972); *Stuit v. Comm.*, 452 F.2d 190 (7th Cir. 1971).
9. *Exchange Bank & Trust Co. of Fla. v. U.S.*, 82-2 USTC ¶13,505 (Fed. Cir. 1982).
10. Rev. Rul. 74-556, 1974-2 CB 300.

Where the donor dies while serving as custodian, the value of the custodial property is includable in his estate under IRC Section 2038(a)(1), as a transfer with the power retained to alter, amend, revoke or terminate. This result is reached because of the custodian's power, under section 4 of the Uniform Act, to withhold enjoyment of the custodial property until the donee reaches majority. To avoid this result, the donor should name someone other than himself as custodian, and should not accept appointment as successor custodian.

The IRS has ruled that the power given the donee's parent (under section 4(c) of the Gifts to Minors Act) or interested person (under section 14(b) of the Transfers to Minors Act) to petition the court to order the custodian to expend funds for the minor's support, maintenance, or education is not a general power of appointment; therefore, the custodial property is not includable in the parent's or interested person's gross estate under IRC Section 2041.[1]

1503. Is an education savings account includable in an individual's gross estate?

Upon the distribution of an education savings account on account of the death of the beneficiary, the amount of the education savings account is includable in the estate of the beneficiary, not the contributor. However, where a donor elects to have contributions prorated over a five year period for gift tax purposes (see Q 1527) and dies during such period, the gross estate of the donor includes prorated contributions allocated to periods after the donor's death.[2]

See Q 1527 for the gift tax treatment and Q 1412 for the income tax treatment of education savings accounts.

1504. Is a qualified tuition program includable in an individual's gross estate?

No interest in a qualified tuition program is includable in the estate of any individual for purposes of the estate tax, with two exceptions: (1) a distribution to the estate of the beneficiary upon the beneficiary's death; and (2) if such a donor dies before the end of a five-year gift tax proration period (see Q 1528), the gross estate of the donor will include the portion of contributions allocable to periods after the death of the donor.[3]

See Q 1528 for the gift tax treatment and Q 1413 for the income tax treatment of qualified tuition programs.

EXCLUSION

1505. What estate tax exclusion is available for a qualified conservation easement?

An estate tax exclusion is provided for qualified conservation easements.[4] An irrevocable election must be made by the executor if the exclusion is to apply. The exclusion

---

1. Rev. Rul. 77-460, 1977-2 CB 323.
2. IRC Secs. 530(d)(3), 529(c)(4).
3. IRC Sec. 529(c)(4).
4. IRC Sec. 2031(c).

is available for the lesser of (1) the applicable percentage of the value of land subject to the qualified conservation easement, reduced by the amount of any charitable deduction for the easement under IRC Section 2055(f), or (2) the exclusion limitation.[1] The applicable percentage is equal to 40% reduced (but not below zero) by two percentage points for every percentage point (or fraction thereof) by which the value of the conservation easement is less than 30% of the value of the land (determined without regard to the easement and reduced by any development right).[2] After 2001, the exclusion limitation is $500,000. See Appendix B for limitations in other years.[3]

The land subject to the conservation easement must be located in the United States or its possessions (for decedents dying in 2001 to 2009).[4] For decedents dying before 2000 or after 2010, the land subject to the conservation easement must generally on the date of the decedent's death be located (1) within 25 miles of a metropolitan area, (2) within 25 miles of part of the National Wilderness Preservation System, or (3) within 10 miles of an Urban National Forest.

The land subject to the conservation easement must be owned by decedent or members of decedent's family at all times during the three year period ending at decedent's death.[5]

The exclusion is not available to the extent that the land is subject to acquisition indebtedness or retained development rights (excludes certain farming uses).[6] Nor is the exclusion available if the easement is granted after the death of the decedent and anyone receives an income tax deduction with regard to granting of the easement.[7]

DEDUCTIONS

1506. What deductions are allowed from the gross estate in arriving at the taxable estate for federal estate tax purposes?

The following deductions are allowed from the gross estate in arriving at the taxable estate (see Q 1500):

(1) To the extent allowable by the law, (a) funeral expenses, (b) administration expenses, (c) claims against the estate, and (d) unpaid mortgages on or other indebtedness against property included at its full value in the gross estate;

(2) casualty and theft losses incurred during settlement of the estate and not compensated for by insurance or otherwise;

(3) the marital deduction;

(4) the charitable bequests deduction;

---

1. IRC Secs. 2031(c)(1), 2031(c)(6).
2. IRC Sec. 2031(c)(2).
3. IRC Sec. 2031(c)(3).
4. IRC Sec. 2031(c)(8)(A)(i), as amended by EGTRRA 2001.
5. IRC Sec. 2031(c)(8)(A)(ii).
6. IRC Secs. 2031(c)(4), 2031(c)(5).
7. IRC Sec. 2031(c)(9).

(5) the qualified family-owned business interest deduction; and

(6) state death taxes.[1]

IRC Section 2053

Expenses, Indebtedness, Taxes

Most of the claims, expenses, and charges payable by the estate under local law are allowable deductions from the gross estate. These include: (1) funeral expenses; (2) administration expenses; (3) certain taxes; (4) indebtedness and claims against the estate.

Funeral expenses are generally allowable, although the regulations limit the expenditure for a tombstone, monument, mausoleum, or burial lot to a reasonable amount.

Administration expenses include chiefly fees or commissions of executors and attorneys, and miscellaneous costs incurred in connection with the preservation and settlement of the estate, including determination and contest of death taxes. Expenditures not essential to the proper settlement of the estate, but incurred for the individual benefit of the heirs, legatees, or devisees, may not be taken as deductions.[2] Expenses for selling property of the estate are deductible if the sale is necessary in order to pay the decedent's debts, expenses of administration, or taxes, to preserve the estate, or to effect distribution. The phrase "expenses for selling property" includes brokerage fees and other expenses attending the sale, such as the fees of an auctioneer if it is reasonably necessary to employ one.[3]

A large estate may have a large block of stock in a single corporation that the executor determines must be sold to meet estate settlement costs and death taxes. Often, it is found that the best method of sale in these circumstances is to register the securities with the SEC for public sale by means of a secondary offering through an underwriter. The agreement between the executor and the underwriter may be either of two kinds: "Under a 'firm commitment' agreement the underwriter agrees to purchase a specific amount of stock for a fixed price at a certain time. In contrast, under a 'best efforts' agreement the underwriter sells the stock for the stockholder as an agent and only agrees to use its best efforts in obtaining sales."[4] Under a firm commitment agreement, the executor undertakes to pay all registration and incidental selling expenses plus an "underwriting discount" paid to the underwriter. The underwriting discount amounts to the difference between the amount realized on sale of the shares to the public and the amount paid by the underwriter for the shares. The Internal Revenue Service has taken the position that "underwriting fees" (by which the Service clearly means to include the "underwriting discount") are not considered in determining the blockage discount to be accorded in valuing the stock for federal estate tax purposes (see Q 1537), but instead are deductible under IRC Section 2053 as administration expenses (assuming the sale was necessary to administer the estate).[5] Whether the courts will go along with the Service is another matter. The Tax Court has taken the position that expenses of a secondary offering should not be allowed to reduce the value of the stock and at the

1. IRC Secs. 2053-2058, as amended by EGTRRA 2001.
2. Treas. Reg. §20.2053-3(a); *Est. of Posen v. Comm.*, 75 TC 355 (1980).
3. Treas. Reg. §20.2053-3(d)(2).
4. *Est. of Jenner v. Comm.*, 577 F.2d 1100, footnote 3 (7th Cir. 1978).
5. Rev. Rul. 83-30, 1983-1 CB 722.

same time be allowed as IRC Section 2053 expenses.[1] As for the underwriting discount, the Tax Court has disallowed it as an IRC Section 2053 expense, viewing the transaction between the underwriter and the estate as simply a sale of stock from the estate to the underwriter.[2] The U.S. Court of Appeals for the Ninth Circuit has allowed the underwriting discount as an IRC Section 2053 expense when it has been allowed as an administration expense by the probate court and without regard to whether it has been considered in valuing the stock.[3] The Seventh Circuit appears generally in accord with the Ninth Circuit.[4] For a discussion of these cases and others, see *Rifkind v. U.S.*[5]

IRC Section 642(g) says that amounts allowable under IRC Section 2053 or 2054 as a deduction in computing the taxable estate shall not be allowed as a deduction (or as an offset against the sales price of property in determining gain or loss) in computing the taxable income of the estate unless the executor files a statement that the amounts have not been allowed as deductions under IRC Section 2053 or 2054 and waives the right to claim such deductions in the future. It has been held that where an estate necessarily incurred expenses in selling securities for the purpose of obtaining funds with which to pay estate settlement costs and taxes and used such expenses as offsets against the selling price of the securities in computing estate income taxes, and where the IRS did not require the above-described statement and waiver, the estate was free to claim the selling expenses as an estate tax deduction under IRC Section 2053.[6]

IRC Section 265(1), says that no deduction will be allowed for federal income tax purposes for expenses for production of income (see Q 1311) allocable to tax exempt income. Assume, for example, that during a taxable year an estate receives $200,000 of income, $25,000 of which is tax exempt because it is interest on municipal bonds. Assume, also, that in the same period the estate disbursed $50,000 for attorneys' fees and $30,000 for miscellaneous administration expenses, neither amount attributable to either the taxable or the tax exempt income. By virtue of the above-described limitation of IRC Section 265(1), the executor is allowed to deduct on the estate's federal income tax return no more than $70,000 of the $80,000 in fees and expenses, the portion allocable to includable income:

$$\frac{\$200,000 - 25,000}{\$200,000} \times 80,000 = \$70,000$$

Assume that as a condition of allowance of the income tax deduction, the IRS required of the executor the statement and waiver described in the preceding paragraph. Would the waiver preclude the executor from claiming a deduction on the estate tax return under IRC Section 2053, for the $10,000 balance of fees and expenses he was not allowed to deduct on the income tax return? No, says the IRS, he is not so precluded.[7]

As a general rule, claims against the estate which are founded on a promise or agreement are not deductible unless they were contracted for an adequate consideration in money or money's worth. An exception is made for enforceable pledges to qualified

1. *Est. of Joslyn v. Comm.*, 57 TC 722 (1972), rev'd 500 F.2d 382 (9th Cir. 1974).
2. *Est. of Joslyn v. Comm.*, above, 63 TC 478 (1975), on remand from the Ninth Circuit.
3. *Est. of Joslyn v. Comm.*, above, 566 F.2d 677 (9th Cir. 1977), rev'g 63 TC 478 (1975).
4. *Est. of Jenner v. Comm.*, 577 F.2d 1100 (7th Cir. 1978), rev'g TC Memo 1977-54.
5. 84-2 USTC ¶13,577 (Cl. Ct. 1984).
6. *Smith v. U.S.*, 26 AFTR 2d ¶147,513 (E.D. Mo. 1970).
7. Rev. Rul. 59-32, 1959-1 CB 245; Rev. Rul. 63-27, 1963-1 CB 57, clarifying Rev. Rul. 59-32.

charitable organizations. Such pledges are deductible even though not contracted for an adequate consideration in money or money's worth. A release of dower or other marital rights generally is not deemed an adequate consideration; but a claim for alimony is fully deductible if founded on a divorce decree.

A payment in settlement of a will contest is not deductible from the gross estate. A claim to share in the estate is to be distinguished from a claim against the estate.[1]

Unpaid mortgages are deductible provided the property subject to the mortgage is included at its full value in the gross estate.

Property taxes accrued prior to decedent's death, and taxes on income received during the decedent's life are deductible. The property taxes, however, must be enforceable obligations (a lien upon the property) at the time of death. Ordinarily, state and foreign death taxes are not deductible, but may be taken as a credit against the tax (see Q 1507). As an exception, however, the executor may elect to deduct any state or foreign taxes paid on bequests which qualify as charitable deductions under the federal estate tax law. If deducted, they cannot, of course, be taken as a credit against the tax. An estate tax deduction is not allowed for death taxes paid to a city even though a credit is not allowed for such taxes (see Q 1507).[2]

In community property states, the extent to which administration expenses and claims are deductible depends upon their treatment under state law. If they are expenses or debts of the entire community, only one-half of them is deductible.

A deduction is allowed for expenses and debts attributable to non-probate property includable in the gross estate. They are deductible even though they exceed the property in the gross estate which under local law is subject to the claims against the estate. However, to the extent that they exceed such property they are not deductible unless actually paid before the due date for filing the estate tax return.

IRC Section 2054

Casualty and Theft Losses

Losses incurred during the period of administration from fire, storm, or other casualty, or from theft, are deductible to the extent not compensated by insurance or otherwise.

IRC Section 2055

Charitable Bequests Deduction

An estate tax deduction is allowed for the full amount of bequests to charity (but not in excess of the value of the transferred property required to be included in the gross estate). The deduction is not subject to percentage limitations such as are applicable to the charitable deduction under the income tax.

---

1. *Est. of Moore v. Comm.*, TC Memo 1987-587.
2. TAM 9422002.

Specifically, IRC Section 2055 provides a deduction for bequests:

(1) to or for the use of the United States, any state, territory, any political subdivision thereof, or the District of Columbia, for exclusively public purposes;

(2) to or for the use of corporations organized and operated exclusively for religious, charitable, scientific, literary, or educational purposes, or to foster amateur sports competition, and the prevention of cruelty to children or animals (and which meet certain other conditions);

(3) to trustees, or fraternal societies, orders or associations operating under the lodge system, but only if the bequests are to be used exclusively for religious, charitable, scientific, literary, or educational purposes, or for the prevention of cruelty to children or animals (and if certain other conditions are met); and

(4) to or for the use of any veterans' organization incorporated by Act of Congress or to any of its components, so long as no part of the net earnings inures to the benefit of any private shareholder or individual.[1]

If any death taxes are, either by the terms of the will, by the law of the jurisdiction under which the estate is administered, or by the law of the jurisdiction imposing the particular tax, payable in whole or in part out of the bequests otherwise deductible as charitable contributions, then the amount deductible is the amount of such bequests reduced by the amount of such taxes.[2] Prior to the issuance of regulations discussed below, in a similar situation, it was held that the marital deduction (see "IRC Section 2056, Marital Deduction," below) was reduced where administration expenses were paid from the marital share principal, but not where administration expenses were paid from income from the marital share.[3]

Regulations, effective for estates of decedents dying after December 3, 1999, now provide rules for reducing the charitable share by administration expenses depending on the type of expense: transmission expenses or management expenses.[4]

Transmission expenses are defined as expenses that would not have been incurred but for the decedent's death. Transmission expenses are also defined as any administration expense that is not a management expense. Transmission expenses paid from the charitable share reduce the charitable share.

Management expenses are defined as expenses related to investment, preservation, and maintenance of the assets during a reasonable period of estate administration. Management expenses attributable to the charitable share do not reduce the charitable share except to the extent that the expense is deducted under IRC Section 2053 as an administration expense. Management expenses which are paid by the charitable share but which are not attributable to the charitable share reduce the charitable share.

In *U.S. Trust Co. (Chisholm Est.) v. U.S.*,[5] the executors satisfied a charitable bequest by making the distribution out of estate income. The estate claimed and was

---

1. IRC Sec. 2055(a).
2. IRC Sec. 2055(c).
3. *Comm. v. Est. of Hubert*, 97-1 USTC ¶60,261 (U.S. 1997).
4. Treas. Reg. §20.2055-3.
5. 86-2 USTC ¶13,698 (5th Cir. 1986), rev'g and remanding 85-2 USTC ¶13,642 (S.D. Miss. 1985).

allowed an estate tax deduction under IRC Section 2055 for the bequest. The estate could not claim an income tax charitable contributions deduction because the will did not specify that the bequest be paid out of estate income.[1] The estate claimed but was not allowed an income tax distribution deduction under IRC Sec. 661(a)(2) for the same distribution.

Property which is transferred to the charity by the exercise or nonexercise of a general power of appointment is considered transferred by the donee of the power rather than by the donor of the power. Or, to paraphrase, property includable in the decedent's gross estate under IRC Section 2041 (see Q 1501) received by a charity is considered a bequest of such decedent.[2]

An estate tax charitable deduction was denied for the transfer of a residuary interest in the estate to charity where the amount of the charitable deduction was not ascertainable at the time of death because of discretionary powers given to personal representatives to distribute the estate to other potential beneficiaries.[3] Also, in TAM 9327006, an estate tax charitable deduction was denied where a trustee was given discretion to select donees from among various charities, and not all of the charities were on the IRS list of charities for which a charitable deduction is permitted.

Where an interest in property (other than a remainder interest in a personal residence or farm or an undivided portion of the decedent's entire interest in property) passes from the decedent to a charity and an interest in the same property passes (for less than adequate and full consideration in money or money's worth) from the decedent to a non-charity, no estate tax charitable contributions deduction is allowed for the interest going to the charity unless—

(a) in the case of a remainder interest, such interest is in a trust which is a *charitable remainder annuity trust* (see Q 1330) or a *charitable remainder unitrust* (see Q 1331) or a *pooled income fund* (see Q 1332), or

(b) in the case of any other interest, such interest is in the form of a guaranteed annuity or is a fixed percentage distributed yearly of the fair market value of the property (to be determined yearly).[4]

If the decedent has created a qualified charitable remainder trust in which his surviving spouse is the only noncharitable beneficiary other than certain ESOP remainder beneficiaries (see "IRC Section 2056, Marital Deduction," below), the estate will receive a charitable contributions deduction for the value of the remainder interest. However, if the property in the trust is "qualified terminable interest property" and the surviving spouse's interest is a "qualifying income interest for life" (see "IRC Section 2056, Marital Deduction," below), the charitable contributions deduction may be taken by the surviving spouse's estate upon her death, the decedent's estate having taken a marital deduction (assuming the executor's election) for the entire value of the property.[5]

Where a decedent left shares of stock to a charity but specified in his will that dividends from the stock during administration of the estate be paid to an individual,

---

1. IRC Sec. 642(c).
2. IRC Sec. 2055(b).
3. *Est. of Marine v. Comm.*, 93-1 USTC ¶60,131 (4th Cir. 1993).
4. IRC Sec. 2055(e)(2).
5. Treas. Reg. §20.2044-1(b).

it was held that the estate tax charitable contributions deduction was not allowable.[1] However, in Let. Rul. 8506089, a decedent left the residue of his estate to a charity on the condition that the charity take on the obligation to pay an annuity equal to 7% of the value of the estate assets going to the charity to his brother for his lifetime. The Service ruled that because the annuity was payable out of the general assets of the charity rather than out of the assets in the decedent's estate going to the charity, the bequest was not a split interest gift in the same property; accordingly, a charitable contributions deduction was allowed equal to the amount by which the value of the property transferred by the decedent to the charity exceeded the present value of the annuity payable to the decedent's brother.

In *Oetting v. U.S.*,[2] a trust receiving assets from the residue of an estate provided that the assets would be used first to provide life incomes of $100 per month for the lifetimes of three elderly ladies and the remainder paid to four qualified charities. Since the total assets received by the trust greatly exceeded expectations, the trustees petitioned the probate court for permission to buy annuities for the income beneficiaries with a fraction of the trust assets and to pay the balance immediately to the charities. The court so decreed, the trustees bought the annuities for $23,000 and paid the balance, $558,000, to the charities. The court allowed the estate a charitable contributions deduction for the amount paid to the charities, reasoning that since the amount going to the charities was certain, it was not a split interest in the same property for purposes of IRC Section 2055.

In general, a trust can be reformed to qualify for the estate tax charitable deduction if:

(1) the difference in actuarial value of the qualified trust at time of death and its value at time of reformation is no greater than 5% of its value at time of reformation;

(2) the term of the trust is the same before and after reformation (however, if the term of years for a trust exceeds 20 years, the term can be shortened to 20 years);

(3) any changes are effective as of date of death;

(4) the charitable deduction would have been allowable at death if not for the split-interest rules (which generally require use of annuity, unitrust, and pooled income interests); and

(5) any payment to a noncharitable beneficiary before the remainder vests in possession must have been an annuity or unitrust interest (the lower of income or the unitrust amount, with make-up provisions, is permitted). This fifth provision does not apply if judicial proceedings are started to qualify the interests for the estate tax charitable deduction no later than 90 days after (a) the due date (including extensions) for filing the estate tax return, or (b) if no estate tax return is required, the due date (including extensions) for filing the income tax return for the first taxable year of the trust for which such a return must be filed.[3]

A reformation done solely to obtain a charitable deduction (in contrast to a reformation done pursuant to a will contest) must meet the requirements of IRC Section

---

1. Rev. Rul. 83-45, 1983-1 CB 233.
2. 83-2 USTC ¶13,533 (8th Cir. 1983).
3. IRC Sec. 2055(e)(3).

2055(e)(3).[1] The amount of a charitable deduction taken with respect to property transferred to charity pursuant to a will contest cannot exceed the actuarial value of what the charity could have received under a will or through intestate succession.[2]

IRC Section 2056

Marital Deduction

The estate tax marital deduction is a deduction allowed from the gross estate for interests in property (including community property) which pass from the decedent to his (or her) surviving spouse and which are included in determining the value of the gross estate; the deduction is limited only by the value of such qualifying interests.[3] In general, a marital deduction is not available if the surviving spouse is not a United States citizen unless property passes to the surviving spouse in a qualified domestic trust (QDOT) (see below).

The deduction is limited to the *net* value of qualifying property interests passing to the surviving spouse. Thus, the value of such interests must be reduced by federal and state death taxes payable out of those interests, by encumbrances on those interests, and by any obligation imposed by the decedent upon the surviving spouse with respect to the passing of such interests.[4] Prior to the issuance of regulations discussed below, the marital deduction was reduced where administration expenses were paid from the marital share principal, but not where administration expenses were paid from income from the marital share.[5]

Regulations, effective for estates of decedents dying after December 3, 1999, provide rules for reducing the marital share by administration expenses depending on the type of expense: transmission expenses or management expenses.[6]

Transmission expenses are defined as expenses that would not have been incurred but for the decedent's death. Transmission expenses are also defined as any administration expense that is not a management expense. Transmission expenses paid from the marital share reduce the marital share.

Management expenses are defined as expenses related to investment, preservation, and maintenance of the assets during a reasonable period of estate administration. Management expenses attributable to the marital share do not reduce the marital share except to the extent that the expense is deducted under IRC Section 2053 as an administration expense. Management expenses which are paid by the marital share but which are not attributable to the marital share reduce the marital share.

To qualify for the marital deduction, the property interest must be includable in decedent's gross estate, and must "pass from" the decedent to his surviving spouse.[7] (A duty of consistency may require that property be includable in the surviving spouse's estate if a marital deduction was claimed in the first spouse's estate even if the marital

---

1. *Est. of Burdick v. Comm.*, 92 USTC ¶60,122 (9th Cir. 1992).
2. *Terre Haute First Nat'l Bank v. U.S.*, 91-1 USTC ¶60,070 (S.D. Ind. 1991).
3. IRC Sec. 2056(a).
4. IRC Sec. 2056(b)(4); *Adee v. U.S.*, 83-2 USTC ¶13,534 (D. Kan. 1983).
5. *Comm. v. Est. of Hubert*, 97-1 USTC ¶60,261 (U.S. 1997).
6. Treas. Reg. §20-2056(b)-4.
7. IRC Sec. 2056(a).

deduction was improperly claimed in the first spouse's estate.[1] It may come to her in any of the following ways: (a) by will; (b) under state inheritance laws; (c) by dower or curtesy (or statute in lieu of dower or curtesy); (d) by lifetime gift (made in such way as to cause inclusion in the gross estate–see Q 1501); (e) by right of survivorship in jointly owned property; (f) by power of appointment; (g) as proceeds of insurance on decedent's life; (h) as survivor's interest in an annuity.[2]

Certain "terminable interests" in property do not qualify for the marital deduction. The purpose of this rule is to insure inclusion in the surviving spouse's estate of any property remaining in her estate at her death which escaped the initial tax in the predeceased spouse's estate.

A "terminable interest" in property is an interest which will terminate or fail on the lapse of time or on the occurrence or the failure to occur of some contingency. Life estates, terms for years, annuities, patents, and copyrights are therefore terminable interests.[3] Some terminable interests are deductible and some are nondeductible under the marital deduction law. In general, a "terminable interest" is nondeductible if (1) another interest in the same property passes (for less than an adequate consideration) from the decedent to someone other than his spouse or his spouse's estate *and* (2) the other person may possess or enjoy any part of the property after the spouse's interest ends.[4]

Generally speaking, therefore, a terminable interest is *deductible* if *no* interest in the property passes to someone other than the surviving spouse or her estate which may be possessed or enjoyed after the spouse's interest ends. So if the decedent transfers all his interest in a straight life annuity, for instance, the interest will ordinarily qualify. There are two exceptions to this rule, however: Even though no one else takes an interest in the same property, a terminable interest will not qualify if (1) the decedent has *directed* his executor or trustee to acquire a terminable interest for his surviving spouse; or (2) an interest passing to the surviving spouse may be satisfied out of a group of assets which includes a nondeductible interest.[5]

Where spouses own property as joint tenants with right of survivorship or as tenants by the entirety, upon the death of one spouse, the surviving spouse succeeds to absolute ownership of the entire property. This succession occurs by virtue of the form of ownership, not by virtue of any will provision or intestate succession laws. Such succession qualifies for the marital deduction, but only, of course, to the extent the interest to which the surviving spouse succeeds was includable in the decedent's gross estate. (See Q 1501.)

A terminable interest passing to decedent's spouse may be a deductible interest even though an interest in the property may be enjoyed by someone else after her interest ends: (1) if the interest is terminable only because of a survivorship clause; (2) if the interest is the right to income for life with general power of appointment over the property producing the income; (3) if the interest consists of life insurance or annuity proceeds held by the insurer under an agreement that gives the spouse a life income interest in

---

1. *Est. of Letts v. Comm.*, 2000-1 USTC ¶60,374 (11th Cir. 2000); TAM 200407018.)
2. IRC Sec. 2056(c).
3. IRC Sec. 2056(b); Treas. Reg. §20.2056(b)-1(b).
4. IRC Sec. 2056(b)(1).
5. IRC Secs. 2056(b)(1)(C), 2056(b)(2).

the proceeds plus a general power of appointment over the proceeds; (4) if the interest is a "qualifying income interest for life" in "qualified terminable interest property."

A survivorship clause will preserve the marital deduction if (1) the only condition under which the surviving spouse's interest will terminate is the death of the surviving spouse within six months after decedent's death, or her death as a result of a common disaster, and (2) the condition does not occur.[1]

"Qualified terminable interest property" (QTIP) means property (1) which passes from the decedent, (2) in which the surviving spouse has a "qualifying income interest for life," and (3) as to which the executor makes an irrevocable election on the federal estate tax return to have the marital deduction apply. The surviving spouse has a "qualifying income interest for life" if (a) the surviving spouse is entitled to all the income from the property, payable annually or at more frequent intervals, and (b) no person has a power to appoint any part of the property to any person other than the surviving spouse unless the power is exercisable only at or after the death of the surviving spouse.[2] Apparently, the last requirement is violated even if it is the surviving spouse who is given the lifetime power to appoint to someone other than the surviving spouse.[3]

An income interest does not fail to qualify as a qualifying income interest for life merely because the income accumulated by the trust between the last date of distribution and the surviving spouse's death is not required to be either distributed to such spouse's estate or subject to a general power of appointment exercisable by such spouse.[4] However, any income from the property from the date the QTIP interest is created to the death of the spouse with the QTIP interest which has not been distributed before such spouse's death is included in such spouse's estate under IRC Section 2044 to the extent it is not included in the estate under any other IRC provision.[5]

In Technical Advice Memorandum 9139001, the marital deduction was denied because (1) a son's right to purchase stock in a QTIP trust at book value was treated as the power to withdraw property from the trust (i.e., as a power to appoint property to someone other than the spouse), and (2) the spouse and the trustee lacked the right to make the closely held stock, in which the son held all voting rights, income productive. Similarly, a marital deduction was denied where the trustee could sell stock in a QTIP trust to a son at book value.[6] While Technical Advice Memorandum 9113009 had provided that a QTIP marital deduction would be denied if the non-QTIP portion of the estate were not funded with an amount equal to the face value of loans guaranteed by the decedent, it was withdrawn by Technical Advice Memorandum 9409018 which provided instead that the marital deduction would not be reduced by the entire unpaid balance of the guaranteed loans unless at the time of death it would appear that a default after the marital deduction were funded would be likely, that marital deduction property would be used to pay the entire unpaid balance of such loans, and that subrogation rights held by the marital portion would appear to be worthless. According to Technical Advice Memorandum 9206001, a QTIP marital deduction was not available where the spouse was given an income interest in only certain types of property held in a trust and the trustee could change the mix of assets in the trust.

1. IRC Sec. 2056(b)(3).
2. IRC Sec. 2056(b)(7).
3. TAM 200234017.
4. Treas. Reg. §20.2056(b)-7(d)(4).
5. Treas. Reg. §20.2044-1(d)(2).
6. *Est. of Rinaldi v. U.S.*, 97-2 USTC ¶60,281 (Ct. Cl. 1997).

The IRS has conceded the validity of the contingent QTIP marital deduction (i.e., where the surviving spouse's qualifying income interest is contingent upon the QTIP election being made), if the QTIP election is made.[1]

The term "property" includes an interest in property, and a specific portion of property is treated as separate property.[2] However, a specific portion must be determined on a fractional or percentage basis.[3] The term "property" also contemplates income-producing property; the deduction will thus be disallowed as to nonincome-producing property if under local law the spouse has no power to convert the property to income-producing property or to compel such conversion.[4]

A survivor annuity in which only the surviving spouse has a right to receive payments during such spouse's life is treated as a qualifying income interest for life unless otherwise elected on the decedent spouse's estate tax return.[5]

There are five kinds of trusts that will qualify for the marital deduction: (1) the "qualified terminable interest property trust," (2) the "life estate with power of appointment trust," (3) the "estate trust," (4) the "special rule charitable remainder trust," and (5) the "qualified domestic trust." The first two and the fourth are specific exceptions to the nondeductible terminable interest rule; the third does not come under the rule; the fifth is the only form permitted if the surviving spouse is not a United States citizen.

If qualified terminable interest property, as defined above, passes to the surviving spouse in trust, the trust is called a qualified terminable interest property trust (or QTIP trust). The surviving spouse must have a qualifying interest for life in the trust property; neither the trustee nor anyone else must have the power to appoint any part of the trust property to anyone other than the surviving spouse during her lifetime; and the decedent's executor must make the election to have the trust qualify for the marital deduction.

An *estate trust* is a trust in which the property interest transferred from the decedent passes only to the surviving spouse (and the estate of the surviving spouse) and to no other person.

A *life estate with power of appointment trust* is a trust in which the property interest transferred from the decedent passes not only to the surviving spouse but to someone else (for less than an adequate consideration) who may possess or enjoy any part of the property after the spouse's interest ends. If such a trust is to avoid failing to qualify for the marital deduction by reason of being a nondeductible terminable interest, it must meet the requirements of IRC Section 2056(b)(5). In general, the surviving spouse must be given an income interest for life and the power to appoint the property to the surviving spouse or the surviving spouse's estate.

If the surviving spouse is the only noncharitable beneficiary (other than certain ESOP remainder beneficiaries) of a "qualified charitable remainder trust" created by the decedent, the spouse's interest is not considered a nondeductible terminable inter-

---

1. Treas. Regs. §§20-2056(b)-7(d)(3), 20-2056(b)-7(h)(Ex. 6).
2. IRC Sec. 2056(b)(7).
3. IRC Sec. 2056(b)(10).
4. Let. Ruls. 8304040, 8339018, 8745003.
5. IRC Sec. 2056(b)(7)(C).

est and the value of such interest will qualify for the marital deduction. A "qualified charitable remainder trust" means a charitable remainder annuity trust (see Q 1330) or a charitable remainder unitrust (see Q 1331).[1]

In general, a marital deduction is not available for a transfer to a surviving spouse who is not a United States citizen unless the transfer is to a *qualified domestic trust (QDOT)* for which the executor has made an election.[2] A QDOT must qualify for the marital deduction under (1), (2), (3), or (4), as well as meet the following requirements. At least one trustee of the QDOT must be a United States citizen or a domestic corporation and no distribution (other than a distribution of income) may be made from the trust unless that trustee has the right to withhold any additional gift or estate tax imposed on the trust. Additional gift tax is due on any distribution while the surviving spouse is still alive (other than a distribution to the surviving spouse of income or on account of hardship). Additional estate tax is due on any property remaining in the QDOT at the death of the surviving spouse (or at the time the trust ceases to qualify as a QDOT, if earlier). The additional gift or estate tax is calculated as if any property subject to the tax had been included in the taxable estate of the first spouse to die.[3]

Regulations add additional requirements in order to ensure the collection of the deferred estate tax. If the fair market value (as finally determined for estate tax purposes, see Q 1535, but determined without regard to any indebtedness with respect to the assets) of the assets passing to the QDOT exceeds $2,000,000, then the QDOT must provide that either (1) at least one U.S. trustee is a bank,[4] (2) at least one trustee is a U.S. branch of a foreign bank and another trustee is a U.S. trustee, or (3) the U.S. trustee furnish a bond or security or a line of credit equal to 65% of the fair market value of the QDOT corpus. The line of credit must be issued by (1) a U.S. bank, (2) a U.S. branch of a foreign bank, or (3) a foreign bank and confirmed by a U.S. bank.[5]

A QDOT with assets of less than $2,000,000 must either (a) meet one of the requirements for a trust exceeding $2,000,000, or (b) provide that (1) no more than 35% of the fair market value (determined annually on last day of trust's taxable year) of assets consists of real property located outside the U.S., and (2) all other QDOT assets be physically located within the U.S. at all times during the trust term. All QDOTs for the benefit of a surviving spouse are aggregated for purposes of the $2,000,000 threshold. A QDOT owning more than 20% of the voting stock or value in a corporation with 15 or fewer shareholders (or 20% of the capital interest in a partnership with 15 or fewer partners) is deemed to own a pro rata share of the assets of the corporation (or the pro rata share of the greater of the QDOT's interest in the capital or profits of the partnership) for purposes of the 35% foreign real property limitation. All interests in the corporation (or partnership) held by or for the benefit of the surviving spouse or the surviving spouse's family (includes brothers, sisters, ancestors, and lineal descendants) are treated as one person for purpose of determining the number of shareholders (or partners) and whether a 20% or more interest exists. However, the attribution rules do not apply in determining the QDOT's pro rata share of the corporation's (or partnership's) assets. Interests in other entities (such as another trust) are treated similarly to corporations (and partnerships).[6]

---

1. IRC Sec. 2056(b)(8).
2. IRC Sec. 2056(d).
3. IRC Sec. 2056A.
4. As defined in IRC Section 581.
5. Treas. Reg. §20.2056A-2T(d)(1)(i).
6. Treas. Reg. §20.2056A-2T(d)(1)(ii).

For purposes of the $2,000,000 QDOT threshold and the amount of a bond or letter of credit required, up to $600,000 in value attributable to the surviving spouse's personal residence and related furnishings held by the QDOT may be excluded. However, the personal residence exclusion does not apply for purposes of determining whether 35% of the fair market value of assets consists of real property located outside the U.S. A personal residence is either the principal residence of the surviving spouse or one other residence of the surviving spouse. A personal residence must be available for use by the surviving spouse at all times and may not be rented to another party. Related furnishings include furniture and commonly used items within the value associated with normal household use; rare artwork, valuable antiques, and automobiles are not included. If a residence ceases to be used as the surviving spouse's personal residence or a residence is sold, the personal residence exclusion ceases to apply with regard to that residence. However, if part or all of the amount of the adjusted sales price of the residence is reinvested in a new personal residence within 12 months of the date of sale, the exclusion continues to the extent the adjusted sales price is reinvested in the new residence. Also, if a residence ceases to be used as the surviving spouse's personal residence or a residence is sold, the exclusion can be allocated to another personal residence of the surviving spouse that is held by a QDOT of the surviving spouse. In this instance, the exclusion can be up to $600,000 (less the amount previously allocated to a personal residence that continues to qualify for the exclusion).[1]

IRC Section 2057

Qualified Family-Owned Business Interests Deduction

For decedents dying before 2005 or after 2010, an estate tax deduction is available for up to $675,000 of qualified family-owned business interests.[2] If the deduction is taken, the unified credit equivalent (see Q 1507) is changed to equal the lesser of (1) the regular unified credit equivalent, or (2) $1,300,000 minus the amount of the qualified family-owned business deduction. The deduction is not available for decedents dying in 2004 to 2010.[3] However, the unified credit is increased substantially for 2004 to 2009 (see Appendix B) and the estate tax is repealed in 2010 (see Q 1500).

In order to qualify for the family-owned business deduction, at least 50% of the value of the adjusted gross estate must consist of the sum of (1) family-owned business interests included in the estate and (2) certain gifts of family-owned business interests.[4] Gifts of family-owned business interests include family-owned business interests that decedent gave to members of decedent's family if the members of decedent's family retained such interests until decedent's death.[5] The family-owned business interest is not reduced by an IRC Section 303 redemption for purposes of making the initial determination of qualifying for the family-owned business deduction.[6]

For this purpose, the adjusted gross estate means the gross estate reduced by the estate tax deductions for claims against the estate and debts under IRC Sections 2053(a)(3) and 2053(a)(4), and increased by certain gifts. These gifts include (to the extent not otherwise includable in the estate): (1) family-owned business interests that decedent

---

1. Treas. Reg. §20.2056A-2T(d)(1)(iv).
2. IRC Sec. 2057.
3. IRC Secs. 2057(j), 2210, as added by EGTRRA 2001.
4. IRC Sec. 2057(b)(1)(C).
5. IRC Sec. 2057(b)(3).
6. Rev. Rul. 2003-61, 2003-24 IRB 1015.

gave to members of decedent's family if the members of decedent's family retained such interests until decedent's death; (2) gifts to spouse within 10 years of decedent's death (excluding those under (1)); and (3) gifts within three years of death (excluding annual exclusion gifts to family members and those under (1) or (2)).[1]

Family-owned means that either (1) 50% of the business must be owned by decedent and members of decedent's family; or (2) 30% of the business must be owned by decedent and members of decedent's family and (a) 70% of the business is owned by two families, or (b) 90% of the business is owned by three families.[2]

However, family-owned business interests do not include (1) a business whose principal place of business is not in the United States; (2) any entity whose stock or debt is readily traded on an established securities or secondary market; (3) an entity, other than a bank or building and loan association, if more than 35% of the adjusted gross income of the entity for the year which includes the date of decedent's death is personal holding company income; and (4) the portion of the business which consists of (a) cash or marketable securities in excess of reasonably expected day-to-day working capital needs, and (b) assets held for the production of personal holding company income or foreign personal holding company income.[3]

Personal holding company income generally includes dividends, interest, royalties, annuities, rents, personal property use by a shareholder, and personal service contracts.[4] However, personal holding company income does not include income from a net cash lease of property to another family member who uses the property in a way which would not cause income from the property to be treated as personal holding company income if the lessor had engaged directly in the activity of the lessee.[5]

Similar to the requirements for special use valuation, (1) for at least five of the eight years ending on decedent's death, the business interests must have been owned by decedent or members of decedent's family, and decedent or members of decedent's family must have materially participated in the business,[6] and (2) for 10 years after decedent's death (or until the earlier death of the qualified heir), such business interests must be owned by qualified heirs, and qualified heirs must materially participate in the business.[7] Qualified heirs include members of decedent's family, as well as any employee who has been an active employee of the business for at least 10 years before the decedent's death.[8]

Additional tax, plus interest thereon, is due if the ownership or material participation requirements are not met after decedent's death.[9] The additional tax is equal to the following percentage of the tax savings attributable to use of the family-owned business deduction, depending on when the failure to meet the requirements occurs.

---

1. IRC Sec. 2057(c).
2. IRC Sec. 2057(e)(1).
3. IRC Sec. 2057(e)(2).
4. IRC Sec. 543(a).
5. IRC Sec. 2057(e)(2).
6. IRC Sec. 2057(b)(1)(D).
7. IRC Sec. 2057(f)(1).
8. IRC Sec. 2057(j)(1).
9. IRC Sec. 2057(f).

	Recapture
Year	Percentage
1-6	100
7	80
8	60
9	40
10	20

For this purpose, an IRC Section 303 redemption is not treated as a disposition of the family-owned business interest.[1]

IRC Section 2058

State Death Tax Deduction

A deduction is available for federal estate tax purposes for estate, inheritance, legacy, or succession taxes (i.e., death taxes) paid to any state or the District of Columbia with respect to the estate of the decedent.[2] The deduction is available from 2005 to 2009, and the estate tax is repealed for one year in 2010. A credit for state death taxes (see Q 1507) is available before 2005 and after 2010.

The deduction is available only for state death taxes actually paid and claimed as a deduction before the later of (1) 4 years after the filing of the federal estate tax return; (2) 60 days after a decision of the Tax Court with respect to a timely filed petition for redetermination of a deficiency; or (3) with respect to a timely filed claim for refund or credit of the federal estate tax, the later of (a) 60 days of the mailing of a notice of disallowance by the IRS, (b) 60 days after the decision of any court of competent jurisdiction on such claim, or (c) 2 years after the taxpayer files a notice of waiver of disallowance.

CREDITS

1507. What credits are allowed against the federal estate tax?

After the tax is computed (see Q 1500), such of the following credits as may be applicable may be taken against the tax to determine the tax actually payable:

...Unified credit[3]

...Credit for state death taxes[4]

...Credit for gift tax[5]

...Credit for estate tax on prior transfers[6]

...Foreign death tax credit[7]

---

1. Rev. Rul. 2003-61, 2003-24 IRB 1015.
2. IRC Sec. 2058, as added by EGTRRA 2001.
3. IRC Sec. 2010.
4. IRC Sec. 2011.
5. IRC Sec. 2012.
6. IRC Sec. 2013.
7. IRC Sec. 2014.

IRC Section 2010

Unified Credit

The unified credit is a dollar amount allocated to each taxpayer that can be applied against the gift tax and the estate tax. The estate tax unified credit is equal to $780,800 in 2007 which translates into a tentative tax base (or unified credit exemption equivalent or applicable exclusion amount) of $2,000,000 in 2007.[1] See Appendix B for amounts in other years (and gift tax amounts).

The credit is reduced directly by 20% of the amount of lifetime gift tax exemption the decedent elected to use on any gifts made after September 8, 1976 (this $30,000 exemption was repealed by the Tax Reform Act of 1976 as to gifts made after 1976). The 20% reduction is made even though the value of the property to which the exemption applied is brought back into the estate for estate tax purposes. The reduction is not a deprivation of property under the due process clause of the U. S. Constitution.[2]

The credit is also reduced (but indirectly) by the amount of unified credit applied against any gift tax imposed on the decedent's post-1976 gifts. The indirect reduction is accomplished by adding to the taxable estate the amount of all taxable gifts made by the decedent after 1976, other than gifts includable in the gross estate, and then applying the estate tax rates to the sum (see Q 1500).

IRC Section 2011

Credit for State Death Taxes

For decedents dying before 2005 or after 2010, a credit is allowed against the federal estate tax for state death taxes—inheritance, legacy, estate and succession taxes—paid to any state of the United States or the District of Columbia with respect to property included in the gross estate (but see phaseout of credit, below).[3] The federal estate tax credit for state death taxes paid was not available where the property subject to state death taxes was not includable in the federal gross estate.[4] The credit is limited to the amount of state death taxes actually paid and does not include, for instance, the amount of any discount allowed by the state for prompt payment.

The credit is limited to specified percentages of the "adjusted taxable estate" in excess of $40,000 (see Appendix B). The "adjusted taxable estate" is the taxable estate reduced by $60,000. The maximum amount for which a credit can be taken was reduced by 25% in 2002, 50% in 2003, and 75% in 2004.[5] (See IRC Sec. 2011(b), Appendix B.) The credit is replaced by a deduction for state death taxes (see Q 1506) in 2005 to 2009.[6]

All states collect at least the maximum credit. Some states have enacted estate taxes exactly equal to the maximum credit. Some states refer to the maximum credit as it existed prior to the current phaseout by EGTRRA 2001. States that impose an inheritance tax have also an "additional estate tax" which is designed to absorb the difference between the inheritance tax and the maximum credit should the inheritance

---

1. IRC Sec. 2010, as amended by EGTRRA 2001.
2. *U.S. v. Hemme*, 86-1 USTC ¶13,671 (U.S. 1986); *Est. of Allgood v. Comm.*, TC Memo 1986-455.
3. IRC Sec. 2011.
4. *Est. of Owen v. Comm.*, 104 TC 498 (1995).
5. IRC Sec. 2011(b)(2), as added by EGTRRA 2001.
6. IRC Sec. 2011(g), as added by EGTRRA 2001.

tax be less than the maximum credit. In most cases, however, the basic inheritance tax will exceed the maximum amount allowable as a credit.

IRC Section 2012

Credit for Gift Tax

A credit is allowed for federal gift tax paid on property transferred by the decedent during life but included in the gross estate, *but only as to gifts made on or before December 31, 1976*.[1] The credit cannot exceed an amount which bears the same ratio to the estate tax imposed (after deducting the unified credit and the credit for state death taxes) as the value of the gift(s) (at time of gift or at time of death, whichever is lower) bears to the value of the gross estate minus charitable and marital deductions allowed.[2] In the case of (pre-1977) "split gifts" made by the decedent and his consenting spouse (see Q 1530), the gift taxes paid with respect to both halves of the gift are eligible for the credit.[3]

The gift tax credit cannot be taken with respect to gifts made after December 31, 1976. However, in the computation of the estate tax, an adjustment is made for federal gift tax paid on post-1976 gifts not included in the donor-decedent's gross estate (see Q 1500).

IRC Section 2013

Credit for Estate Tax on Prior Transfers

Under IRC Section 2013, the federal estate tax otherwise payable by a decedent's estate is credited with all or a part of the amount of federal estate tax paid with respect to the transfer of property to the decedent (the transferee) by a person (the transferor) who died within 10 years before, or within two years after, the decedent's death. The credit is designed, of course, to alleviate the impact of repeated estate taxation where successive deaths of the transferor and transferee occur within a relatively short time of each other.

The full amount of the credit is available if the transferor died within two years of the death of the decedent (either before or after). If the transferor predeceased the decedent by more than two years, the credit allowed is the following percentage of the full credit:

(1)   80%, if transferor died within the 3rd or 4th years preceding decedent's death;

(2)   60%, if transferor died within the 5th or 6th years preceding decedent's death;

(3)   40%, if transferor died within the 7th or 8th years preceding decedent's death;

(4)   20%, if transferor died within the 9th or 10th years preceding decedent's death;

---

1. IRC Sec. 2012(e).
2. IRC Sec. 2012(a).
3. IRC Sec. 2012(c).

No credit is allowable if the transferee predeceased the transferor by more than 2 years.[1]

The credit (before percentage reductions, if applicable) is the portion of the *transferor's* federal estate tax attributable to the value of the property transferred, *but limited to* the portion of the *transferee's* federal estate tax attributable to the value of the property transferred.[2]

When there are two or more transferor estates, the credit is computed separately for each transferor estate. But the *limitation* is computed concurrently, i.e., by aggregating the value of the property received from the transferor estates.[3] And each transfer meeting the requirements of IRC Section 2013 must be taken into account in computing the credit; no waiver of the credit with respect to any transfer that meets the requirements of IRC Section 2013 is permitted.[4] Also, the limitation must be apportioned among the transferors so that the credit and the limitation are computed separately for each transferor. Thus, as to each transferor, the potential credit will be the lesser of the estate tax attributable to the transferred property in the transferor's estate or that portion of the estate tax attributable to the transferred property in the decedent's estate. The lesser of the credit or the limitation is then multiplied by the applicable percentage (determined by when the transferor's death occurred relative to the time of the transferee's death, as described above) to determine the allowable credit.[5]

The prior transfer is not required to be traced into the decedent's gross estate. The credit is available even though the property was given away, consumed, or destroyed by the decedent during his life. Further, the term "property" includes any beneficial interest in property, including a general power of appointment (see Q 1501).[6] The term includes also a life estate in property.[7]

The credit may be allowed against the present decedent's estate even though the prior decedent from whom he received the property was his spouse. However, the credit is allowed only with respect to property for which no marital deduction was allowed in the prior decedent's estate.[8]

IRC Section 2014

Foreign Death Tax Credit

A foreign death tax credit is provided for United States citizens and residents. The credit applies to property which is subject to both federal and foreign death taxes.[9] However, if there is a treaty with the foreign country levying a tax for which a credit is allowable, the executor may elect whether to rely on the IRC credit provisions or the treaty provisions.

---

1. IRC Sec. 2013(a).
2. IRC Secs. 2013(b), 2013(c)(1).
3. IRC Sec. 2013(c)(2).
4. Rev. Rul. 73-47, 1973-1 CB 397.
5. Treas. Reg. §20.2013-6, Example (2); *Est. of Meyer v. Comm.*, 83 TC 350 (1984), aff'd 86-1 USTC ¶13,650 (2nd Cir. 1985).
6. IRC Sec. 2013(e).
7. Rev. Rul. 59-9, 1959-1 CB 232.
8. IRC Sec. 2013(d)(3).
9. IRC Sec. 2014.

FILING AND PAYMENT

1508. What are the requirements for filing the federal estate tax return and paying the tax?

Except for extensions of time granted under conditions to be explained, a federal estate tax return (Form 706), if required, must be filed, and the tax paid, by the executor within nine months after the decedent's death.[1]

If it is impossible or impracticable for the executor to file a reasonably complete return within nine months from the date of death, the district director or the director of a service center may, upon a showing of good and sufficient cause, grant a reasonable extension of time for filing the return. Unless the executor is abroad, the extension cannot exceed six months.[2] An automatic six month extension for the Form 706 is available to anyone who applies for the extension.[3]

The tax is due nine months after decedent's death, whether or not an extension of time for filing the return has been granted.[4] However, an extension of time for payment of any part of the tax shown on the return, not to exceed 12 months, may be granted by the district director or the director of a service center, at the request of the executor, if an examination of all the facts and circumstances discloses that such request is based upon reasonable cause.[5] In addition, the Service has been given authority to enter into written agreements to pay taxes in installments when the Service determines that such an agreement will facilitate the payment of taxes.[6] Interest must be paid on any extension (see "Extension of Time for Payment," below).

The executor cannot escape responsibility for timely filing of an estate tax return or timely payment of the tax by delegating the responsibility to his attorney or accountant. Ignorance of the necessity to file a return or of the due date of the return is no excuse; the executor is required to exercise reasonable care in ascertaining these requirements.[7] However, the penalty for late filing[8] does not apply to an executor who by reason of his age, health, and lack of experience is incapable of meeting the criteria of ordinary business care and prudence required by the regulations.[9]

Minimum Return Requirements

Whether or not a return is required depends on the size of the gross estate (see Q 1501), and possibly also on what kinds of gifts were made by the decedent during life. Generally, a return must be filed if the gross estate of a decedent who is a U.S. citizen or resident exceeds the estate tax unified credit equivalent ($2,000,000 in 2007). However, the $2,000,000 (in 2007) amount is reduced by the amount of *taxable* gifts (the value of the property given after subtracting allowable exclusions and deductions—see Q 1517) made by the decedent after December 31, 1976, except gifts includable in the

---

1. IRC Secs. 6018(a), 6075(a), 6151(a).
2. IRC Sec. 6081(a); Treas. Reg. §20.6081-1(a).
3. Treas. Reg. §20.6081-1.
4. IRC Sec. 6151(a).
5. IRC Sec. 6161(a)(1).
6. IRC Sec. 6159.
7. *U.S. v. Boyle*, 105 SCt 687 (1985); *U.S. v. Blumberg*, 86-1 USTC ¶13,658 (C.D. Cal. 1985).
8. IRC Sec. 6151(a)(1).
9. *U.S. v. Boyle* (concurring opinion), above; *Brown v. U.S.*, 86-1 USTC ¶13,656 (M.D. Tenn. 1985).

gross estate. Also, if the decedent made any gifts after September 8, 1976 and before January 1, 1977, the above amounts are further reduced by any amount allowed as a specific gift tax exemption (see Q 1533) with respect to such gifts.[1] See Appendix B for amounts in other years.

Extension of Time for Payment:

Reasonable Cause (10-year maximum)

The IRS may, for "reasonable cause," extend the time for payment of any part of the estate tax for a reasonable period not in excess of 10 years from the date the tax is due under the general rule (nine months after decedent's death). This "reasonable cause" extension also applies to any part of any installment payment of the tax (and deficiency, if any, added to such installment) where an extension has been granted under the "closely held business interest" provisions (see below).[2] Interest is compounded daily and charged on these reasonable cause extensions at an annual rate adjusted quarterly so as to be three percentage points over the short-term federal rate.[3] The underpayment rate for the last quarter of 2006 is 8%.[4]

Extension of Time for Payment:

Closely Held Business Interest

Under IRC Section 6166, if the decedent's interest in a closely held business exceeds 35% of the *adjusted gross estate*, the portion of the federal estate tax (including the generation-skipping transfer tax if it is imposed on a direct skip transfer occurring as a result of decedent's death) attributable to that interest may be paid in annual installments (maximum of 10), and the executor may elect to delay the beginning of the installment payments up to five years.[5] The *adjusted gross estate* is the gross estate less deductions allowable under IRC Section 2053 and IRC Section 2054 (see Q 1506).[6] In the case of a gift within three years of death (see Q 1501), the requirement that the value of the business interest exceed 35% of the gross estate is met by the estate only if the estate meets the requirement both with and without the application of the bringback rule.[7]

For decedents dying prior to 1998, a special 4% interest rate applies to the portion of tax on which payment is deferred under IRC Section 6166. However, if such portion exceeds $345,800, reduced by the amount of unified credit allowable against the tax, the excess amount will bear interest at the regular underpayment rate (see above).[8] In 1997, the maximum amount of deferred tax eligible for the 4% interest rate was $153,000.

For decedents dying after 1997, a special 2% interest rate applies to the portion of tax on which payment is deferred under IRC Section 6166. However, if such portion exceeds the amount of tax which would be calculated on the sum of $1,000,000 as indexed ($1,250,000 in 2007) plus the unified credit equivalent, reduced by the amount of the unified credit (see "IRC Section 2010, Unified Credit," in Q 1507) allowable

---

1. IRC Sec. 6018(a).
2. IRC Sec. 6161(a)(2).
3. IRC Secs. 6601(a), 6621(a)(2).
4. Rev. Rul. 2006-49, 2006-40 IRB 584.
5. IRC Sec. 6166(a).
6. IRC Sec. 6166(b)(6).
7. IRC Sec. 2035(c)(2).
8. IRC Sec. 6601(j), prior to amendment by TRA '97.

against the tax, the excess amount will bear interest at 45% of the regular underpayment rate (see above). The $1,000,000 amount is adjusted for inflation, rounded down to the next lowest multiple of $10,000, after 1998.[1] No deduction is permitted for estate or income tax purposes for the interest payable on such deferred tax.[2] In 2006, the maximum amount of deferred tax eligible for the 2% interest rate is $562,500. See Appendix B for amounts in other years.

If an election to defer taxes was made for a decedent dying before 1998, an irrevocable election could be made before 1999 to apply the lower interest rates (and the corresponding interest deduction disallowance) to payments due after the election was made (however, the 2% portion is equal to the amount which would be the 4% portion were it not for this election).[3]

For purposes of determining whether an estate qualifies for an IRC Section 6166 extension, the term "interest in a closely held business" means–

(A) an interest as a proprietor in a trade or business carried on as a proprietorship;

(B) an interest as a partner in a partnership carrying on a trade or business, if–

(i) 20% or more of the total capital interest in such partnership is included in determining the gross estate of the decedent, or

(ii) such partnership had 45 (15 for decedents dying before 2002 or after 2010) or fewer partners; or

(C) stock in a corporation carrying on a trade or business if–

(i) 20% or more in value of the voting stock of such corporation is included in determining the gross estate of the decedent, or

(ii) such corporation had 45 (15 for decedents dying before 2002 or after 2010) or fewer shareholders.[4]

For purposes of applying the foregoing rules, community property or property the income from which is community property and property held by a husband and wife as joint tenants, tenants by the entirety, or tenants in common is treated as though the property were owned by one shareholder or one partner, as the case may be. Also, property owned, directly or indirectly, by or for a corporation, partnership, estate, or trust is considered as being owned proportionately by or for its shareholders, partners, or beneficiaries. For purposes of the preceding sentence, a person is treated as a beneficiary of any trust only if he has a present interest in the trust. All stock and partnership interests owned by the decedent and his family are treated as owned by the decedent. The decedent's family for this purpose includes only his spouse, his ancestors, his lineal descendants, and his brothers and sisters.[5] As to any capital interest in a partnership or any nonreadily-tradable stock (i.e., stock for which at the time of decedent's death there

---

1. IRC Sec. 6601(j).
2. IRC Secs. 163(k), 2053(c)(1)(D).
3. TRA '97, Sec. 503(d)(2).
4. IRC Sec. 6166(b)(1).
5. IRC Sec. 6166(b)(2).

was no market on a stock exchange or in an over-the-counter market) attributable to the decedent under the rules described in this paragraph, the value of such interest does not qualify for the five-year deferral or the special 2% or 4% interest rates.[1]

The term "interest in a closely held business" means (with regard to a stockholder interest) "stock in a corporation carrying on a trade or business." "Business," for purposes of IRC Section 6166, according to the IRS, refers to a business such as manufacturing, mercantile or service enterprise, as distinguished from management of investment assets.[2] According to the IRS, the level of activity is the factor that distinguishes an "active business" from mere passive ownership and management of income producing assets. In several rulings since 1961, the Service has tried to make the distinction in various fact situations:

Rev. Rul. 61-55:[3] The ownership, exploration, development, and operation of oil and gas properties is a "trade or business" within the meaning of IRC Section 6166, but the mere ownership of royalty interests in oil properties is not.

Rev. Rul. 75-366:[4] Farms operated by tenant farmers under agreements that the decedent would pay 40% of the expenses and receive 40% of the crops, and in which the decedent had actively participated in the important management decisions, constitute an interest in a closely held business for purposes of IRC Section 6166.

Rev. Rul. 75-367:[5] A decedent's ownership of an electing small business corporation engaged in home construction on the decedent's land, a sole proprietorship that developed the land and sold the homes, and a business office and warehouse shared with the corporation, constitute an interest in a closely held business for purposes of IRC Section 6166.

Let. Rul. 8524037: Commercial rental property as to which the decedent maintained a business office, hired a janitor/maintenance man, plumber, carpenter, electrician, contracted out larger jobs, ordered and supervised work done by employees, qualifies as an interest in a closely held business for purposes of IRC Section 6166.

Let. Rul. 8529026: Commercial warehouse, as to which the decedent owned the land on which it stood and negotiated leases with the tenants; carried out routine inspections of the property to determine necessary maintenance; carried out all maintenance and repair work; hired others to carry out additional maintenance; dealt with bankruptcy proceedings of two tenants and with subsequent lawsuits over a sublease; negotiated with tenants, attorneys, architects, and contractors with respect to modifications to the warehouse to suit tenants' needs; maintained an office in his home from which he performed all bookkeeping, paid monthly expenses, and maintained all correspondence concerning the warehouse; decedent's sons helped him with all aspects of the warehouse business. Held that the decedent's activity was not sufficient to qualify as an interest in a closely held business for purposes of IRC Section 6166.

TAM 8601005: Interest in a general partnership leasing ranchland on a net-lease basis to a limited partnership actively engaged in ranching and in which the decedent

---

1. IRC Sec. 6166(b)(7).
2. Let. Ruls. 8352086, 8451014, 8524037, 8529026, 8942018, 9621007.
3. 1961-1 CB 713.
4. 1975-2 CB 472.
5. 1975-2 CB 472.

was a limited partner. The Service said the land was not held simply as a passive income producing investment, but rather was used as an integral part of the trade or business of ranching. Accordingly, it was held that the decedent's interest in the general partnership was an interest in the business enterprise and not simply a passive investment.

Revenue Ruling 2006-34,[1] provides that, for purposes of determining whether a decedent's interest in real estate is an interest in an asset used in an active trade or business, the Service will consider all facts and circumstances, including the activities of agents and employees, the activities of management companies or other third parties, and the decedent's ownership interest in any management company or other third party. The Service will consider the following nonexclusive list of factors (no single factor is dispositive):

- The amount of time the decedent devoted to the trade or business.

- Whether an office was maintained from which the activities of the decedent were conducted or coordinated, and whether the decedent maintained regular business hours for that purpose.

- The extent to which the decedent was actively involved in finding new tenants and negotiating and executing leases.

- The extent to which the decedent provided landscaping, grounds care, or other services beyond the mere furnishing of leased premises.

- The extent to which the decedent personally made, arranged for, performed, or supervised repairs and maintenance to the property.

- The extent to which the decedent handled tenant repair requests and complaints.

For purpose of this list of factors, the term decedent generally includes agents and employees of the decedent, partnership, LLC, or corporation.

For purposes of IRC Section 6166, at the executor's election, the portion of the stock of any holding company which represents direct ownership (or indirect ownership through one or more other holding companies) by such company in a "business company" (i.e., a corporation carrying on a trade or business) is deemed to be stock in such business company. However, as to such holding company stock, the five-year delay and the 2% or 4% interest provisions (see above) will not apply.[2]

The value included in the computations necessary to determine if the estate qualifies for an IRC Section 6166 extension is the value determined for purposes of the estate tax.[3] Thus, in the case of a farm or other business as to which the executor elected special use valuation (see Q 1535), the special use valuation is treated as the value of the property as to which it applies, for purposes of IRC Section 6166.[4]

Also, for purposes of such valuation, the value of passive assets held by the business is not includable. In general, the term "passive asset" includes any stock held in another

1. 2006-26 IRB 1172.
2. IRC Sec. 6166(b)(8).
3. IRC Sec. 6166(b)(4).
4. House Report No. 94-1380, pages 32-33.

corporation. However, holding company stock included in the executor's election, explained just above, is not considered a passive asset. Also, if a corporation owns 20% or more in value of the voting stock of another corporation, or such other corporation has 45 (15 for decedents dying before 2002 or after 2010) or fewer stockholders, and 80% or more of the value of the assets of each such corporation is attributable to active assets, then such corporations are treated as one corporation. In other words, if the foregoing conditions are met, then for purposes of the passive asset rule, the corporation is not considered to hold stock in another corporation.[1]

For purposes of IRC Section 6166, interests in two or more closely held businesses, with respect to each of which there is included in determining the value of the decedent's gross estate 20% or more of the total value of each such business, are treated as an interest in a single closely held business. For purposes of this 20% requirement, an interest in a closely held business which represents the surviving spouse's interest in property held by the decedent and the surviving spouse as community property or as joint tenants, tenants by the entirety, or tenants in common is treated as having been included in determining the value of the decedent's gross estate.[2] However, an interest so attributed will not qualify for the 5-year deferral or the special 2% or 4% interest rates.[3]

In general, if any payment of principal or interest is not paid when due, the whole of the unpaid portion of the tax payable in installments must be paid upon notice and demand from the district director. However, if the full amount of the delinquent payment (principal and all accrued interest) is paid within six months of the original due date, the remaining tax balance is not accelerated. Rather, the payment loses eligibility for the special interest rates (see above) and a penalty is imposed, equal to 5% per month based on the amount of the payment.[4]

The IRC Section 6166 election terminates and the whole of the unpaid portion of the tax payable in installments becomes due and is payable upon notice and demand from the district director if (1) any portion of the business interest is distributed, sold, exchanged, or otherwise disposed of, or money and other property attributable to such an interest is withdrawn from the business, and (2) the aggregate of such distributions, sales, exchanges, or other dispositions and withdrawals equals or exceeds 50% of the value of such interest.[5] A sale of business assets by the estate to satisfy unpaid mortgages encumbering the business property is not considered a disposition for purposes of the IRC Section 6166 election; however, to the extent proceeds from such a sale exceed the amount used to satisfy the mortgages, the transaction is considered a disposition.[6] Distributions in redemption of stock under IRC Sec. 303 (distributions in redemption of stock held by a decedent at death in an amount not in excess of death taxes and settlement costs under special income tax rules that treat the redemption as a capital transaction rather than as a dividend), are not counted as withdrawals or as disposals of decedent's interest in the business if an amount equal to any such distribution is paid in estate tax on or before the due date of the first installment of tax due after the distribution, or, if earlier, within one year after the distribution. However, an IRC Section 303 redemption does reduce the value of the business (as of the applicable valuation date) by the amount

---

1. IRC Sec. 6166(b)(9).
2. IRC Sec. 6166(c).
3. IRC Sec. 6166(b)(7).
4. IRC Sec. 6166(g)(3).
5. IRC Sec. 6166(g)(1)(A).
6. Let. Rul. 8441029.

redeemed, for purposes of determining whether other withdrawals, distributions, sales, exchanges, or disposals meet the applicable 50% test.[1]

Reversionary or Remainder Interest

If the gross estate includes a reversionary or remainder interest, the executor may elect to postpone payment of the portion of the tax attributable to that interest until six months after termination of the precedent interest in the property. Notice of the election to exercise postponement, together with supporting documents and information, must be filed with the District Director before the due date for payment of the tax. The IRS may, for "reasonable cause," extend payment of the tax postponed because of the reversionary or remainder interest for up to an additional three years beyond the postponement period referred to above.[2]

GENERATION-SKIPPING TRANSFER TAX

1509. Starting Point – What is the federal generation-skipping transfer tax?

The federal generation-skipping transfer (GST) tax is a tax on the right to transfer property to a skip person (a person two or more generations (see Q 1512) younger than the transferor).[3] The GST tax is repealed for one year in 2010. Technically, EGTRRA 2001 repeals the GST tax for transfers after 2009. However, EGTRRA 2001 sunsets (or expires) after 2010.[4]

Depending on the transfer, a generation-skipping transfer is reported on either a gift tax return or an estate tax return. The person required to file the return (Q 1515) and pay the tax (Q 1516) also depends on the type of transfer.

Generation-skipping transfers (Q 1510) include direct skips, taxable terminations, and taxable distributions. Taxable terminations and taxable distributions apply to certain terminations of interests in trusts or distributions from trusts. A husband and wife can elect to have all generation-skipping transfers made by either spouse during the year treated as made one-half by each spouse (Q 1513).

Value is generally the value of the taxable amount at the time of the transfer (Q 1511).

A couple of exclusions are available from GST tax. A $12,000 (in 2007) annual exclusion is available for certain present interest gifts on a per donor/donee basis. An unlimited exclusion is available for qualified transfers for educational and medical purposes. See Q 1511.

A $2,000,000 (in 2007) GST exemption is available to each transferor. Great flexibility is available to allocate or not allocate GST exemption to transfers. An inclusion ratio is derived from allocations of GST exemption to, in effect, determine the amount subject to GST tax. See Q 1511.

---

1. IRC Sec. 6166(g)(1)(B).
2. IRC Sec. 6163.
3. IRC Sec. 2601.
4. IRC Sec. 2664; EGTRRA 2001 Sec. 901.

Tax is imposed on generation-skipping transfers. The tax rate (Appendix B) is a flat rate equal to the top estate tax rate. Tax is equal to the tax rate times the inclusion ratio times the GST (Q 1511).

1510. What is a generation-skipping transfer (GST) on which a generation-skipping transfer tax (GST tax) is imposed?

In general, it is a transfer to a person two or more generations younger than the transferor (called a "skip person"; see Q 1512 regarding generation assignments), and can take any one of three forms: (1) a taxable distribution, (2) a taxable termination, and (3) a direct skip. A trust is also a skip person if the trust can benefit only persons two or more generations younger than the transferor.[1] The GST tax is repealed for one year in 2010.[2]

Transferor

A "transferor," in the case of any property subject to the federal estate tax, is the decedent. In the case of any property subject to the federal gift tax, the transferor is the donor.[3] Thus, to the extent that a lapse of a general power of appointment (including a right of withdrawal) is subject to gift or estate tax, the powerholder becomes the transferor with respect to such lapsed amount.[4] Thus, a *Crummey* powerholder should not be treated as a transferor with respect to the lapse of a withdrawal power if the amount lapsing in any year is no greater than (1) $5,000, or (2) 5% of the assets out of which exercise of the power could be satisfied.[5]

If there is a generation-skipping transfer of any property and immediately after such transfer such property is held in trust, a different rule (the "multiple skip" rule) applies to subsequent transfers from such trust. In such case, the trust is treated as if the transferor (for purposes of subsequent transfers) were assigned to the first generation above the highest generation of any person having an "interest" (see below) in such trust immediately after such transfer.[6] If no person holds an interest immediately after the GST, then the transferor is assigned to the first generation above the highest generation of any person in existence at the time of the GST who may subsequently hold an interest in the trust.[7]

For the effect of making a "reverse QTIP election," see Q 1511.

Direct Skip

A direct skip is a transfer subject to federal gift or estate tax to a skip person. However, with respect to transfers before 1998, such a transfer was not a direct skip if the transfer was to a grandchild of the transferor or of the transferor's spouse or former spouse, and the grandchild's parent who was the lineal descendant of the transferor or his spouse or former spouse was dead at the time of the transfer. In other words, a person could be stepped-up in generations because a parent who had been in the line of descent predeceased such person. This rule could be reapplied to lineal descendants

---

1. IRC Secs. 2611(a), 2613.
2. IRC Sec. 2664; EGTRRA 2001 Sec. 901.
3. IRC Sec. 2652(a)(1).
4. Treas. Reg. §26.2652-1(a).
5. Let. Rul. 9541029.
6. IRC Sec. 2653(a).
7. Treas. Reg. §26.2653-1.

below that of a grandchild. Persons assigned to a generation under this rule were also assigned to such generation when such persons received transfers from the portion of a trust attributable to property to which the step-up in generation rule applied.[1] For purposes of this predeceased child rule, a living descendant who died no later than 90 days after a transferor was treated as predeceasing the transferor if treated as predeceased under the governing instrument or state law.[2] For a more expansive predeceased parent rule after 1997, see Q 1512.

In some circumstances, whether a step-up in generation was available could depend on whether a QTIP or a reverse QTIP marital election was made for GSTT purposes (see Q 1511). If the parent of a grandchild-distributee died after the transfer by a grandparent to a generation-skipping trust but before the distribution from the trust to the grandchild and a reverse QTIP election had been made, the distribution was a taxable termination and the "step-up in generation" rule was not available. However, if the reverse QTIP election had not been made, the distribution was eligible for the "step-up in generation" exception from treatment as a direct skip and was not subject to GSTT.[3]

Also, for purposes of the GST tax, the term "direct skip" did not include any transfer before January 1, 1990, from a transferor to a grandchild of the transferor to the extent that the aggregate transfers from such transferor to such grandchild did not exceed $2 million. This $2 million exemption was available with respect to a transfer in trust only if (1) during the life of such individual no portion of the trust corpus or income could be distributed to or for the benefit of any other person, (2) the trust would be included in such individual's estate if such individual were to die before the trust terminated, and (3) all of the income of the trust had to be distributed at least annually to the grandchild once he reached 21. Requirement (3) applied only to transfers after June 10, 1987. However, the Committee Report indicated that this requirement was not satisfied by a *Crummey* demand power.[4]

The $2 million per grandchild exemption applied to transfers to grandchildren only; the step-up in generation rule for a predeceased parent did not apply. A transfer which would have been a direct skip were it not for the $2 million exemption was likewise exempted from being treated as a taxable termination or taxable distribution. However, the rules which apply to the taxation of multiple skips will apply to subsequent transfers from such trust.

Taxable Termination

A taxable termination occurs when an "interest in property" (see below) held in trust (or some arrangement having substantially the same effect as a trust) for a skip person is terminated by an individual's death, lapse of time, release of a power, or otherwise, unless either (1) a non-skip person has an interest in the trust immediately after such termination, or (2) at no time after the termination may a distribution be made from the trust to a skip person, other than a distribution the probability of which occurring is so remote as to be negligible (i.e., less than a 5% actuarial probability). If upon the termination of an interest in a trust by reason of the death of a lineal descendant of the transferor, a portion of the trust is distributed to skip persons (or to trusts for such

---

1. IRC Sec. 2612(c)(2), prior to amendment by TRA '97.
2. Treas. Reg. §26.2612-1(a)(2)(i).
3. Rev. Rul. 92-26, 1992-2 CB 314.
4. TRA '86, Sec. 1433(b)(3), as amended by TAMRA '88, Sec. 1014(h)(3).

persons), such partial termination is treated as taxable. If a transfer subject to estate or gift tax occurs at the time of the termination, the transfer is not a taxable termination (but it may be a direct skip).[1]

Taxable Distribution

A taxable distribution is any distribution from a trust to a skip person (other than a taxable termination or a direct skip).[2]

Generation-Skipping Transfer Exceptions

However, the following are not considered generation-skipping transfers:

(1) Any transfer which, if made during life by an individual, would be a "qualified transfer" (see Q 1530); and

(2) Any transfer to the extent (a) the property transferred was subject to a prior GST tax, (b) the transferee in the prior transfer was in the same generation as the current transferee or a younger generation, and (c) the transfers do not have the effect of avoiding the GST tax.[3]

Interest in Property

A person has an "interest in property" held in trust if (at the time the determination is made) such person—

(1) has a present right to receive income or corpus from the trust (Ex: a life income interest);

(2) is a permissible current recipient of income or corpus from the trust (Ex: a beneficiary entitled to distribution of income or corpus, but only in the discretion of the trustee) and is not a charitable organization (specifically, one described in IRC Section 2055(a)); or

(3) is such a charitable organization and the trust is a charitable remainder annuity trust (see Q 1330), a charitable remainder unitrust (see Q 1331), or a pooled income fund (see Q 1332).

In determining whether a person has an interest in a trust, the fact that income or corpus may be used to satisfy a support obligation is disregarded if such use is discretionary or made pursuant to the Uniform Gifts to Minors Act (or similar state statute). In other words, a parent is not treated as having an interest in a trust merely because the parent acts as guardian for a child. However, a parent would be treated as having an interest in the trust if support obligations are mandatory.[4]

An interest may be disregarded if it is used *primarily* to postpone or avoid the generation-skipping tax.[5] The regulations provide that an interest is disregarded if *a*

---

1. IRC Sec. 2612(a); Treas. Reg. §26.2612-1(b).
2. IRC Sec. 2612(b).
3. IRC Sec. 2611(b).
4. IRC Sec. 2652(c)(3).
5. IRC Sec. 2652(c)(2).

significant purpose for the creation of the interest is the postponement or avoidance of the generation-skipping tax.[1]

Effective Date and Transitional Rules

The rules explained here and in the succeeding questions apply generally to any generation-skipping transfer (GST) made after October 22, 1986. Also, any lifetime transfer after September 25, 1985, and on or before October 22, 1986, is treated as if made on October 23, 1986. These rules will not, however, apply to the following:

(1) Any GST under a trust that was irrevocable on September 25, 1985, but only to the extent that such transfer is not made out of corpus (or income attributable to such corpus) added to the trust after September 25, 1985;

(2) Any GST under a will or revocable trust executed before October 22, 1986, if the decedent died before January 1, 1987; and

(3) Any GST–

(a) under a trust to the extent such trust consists of property included in the gross estate of a decedent (other than property transferred by the decedent during his life after October 22, 1986), or reinvestments thereof, or

(b) which is a direct skip that occurs by reason of the death of any decedent;

but only if such decedent was, on October 22, 1986, under a mental disability to change the disposition of his property and did not regain his competence to dispose of such property before the date of his death.[2] It appears that Congress does not intend for the third grandfathering rule to apply with respect to property transferred after August 3, 1990 to an incompetent person, or to a trust of such a person.[3]

1511. How is the amount of tax on a GST determined? What is the GST exemption and how is it applied in determining the GST tax?

The amount of tax is the "taxable amount" (based on the kind of GST involved–see Q 1510) multiplied by the "applicable rate."[4] The applicable rate of tax applied to the taxable amount is itself a product. It is a product of the maximum federal estate tax rate in effect at the time of the GST (45% in 2007, see Appendix B) and the "inclusion ratio" with respect to the transfer.[5] The inclusion ratio, in turn, depends on allocations of the "GST exemption."[6] The GST tax is repealed for one year in 2010.[7]

Taxable Amount

In the case of a taxable distribution, the taxable amount is the value of the property received by the transferee reduced by any expense incurred by the transferee with respect to the GST tax imposed on the distribution. If any portion of the GST tax

---

1. Treas. Reg. §26.2612-1(e)(2)(ii).
2. TRA '86, Sec. 1433(a), (b), as amended by TAMRA '88, Sec. 1014(h)(2).
3. OBRA '90, Sec. 11703(c)(3).
4. IRC Sec. 2602.
5. IRC Sec. 2641.
6. IRC Sec. 2642.
7. IRC Sec. 2664; EGTRRA 2001 Sec. 901.

with respect to a taxable distribution is paid out of the trust, the taxable distribution is increased by such an amount.[1]

In the case of a taxable termination, the taxable amount is the value of all property with respect to which the taxable termination has occurred, reduced by the expenses, similar to those allowed as a deduction under IRC Section 2053 in determining the taxable estate for estate tax purposes (see Q 1506, the first heading), with respect to which the taxable termination has occurred.[2]

In the case of a direct skip, the taxable amount is the value of the property received by the transferee.[3] Where a life estate was given to a skip person and a remainder interest was given to a non-skip person, the value of the entire property (and not just the actuarial value of the life estate) was subject to GST tax.[4]

GST Exemption

For purposes of determining the inclusion ratio, every individual is allowed a GST exemption of $2,000,000 (in 2007, see Appendix B) which may be allocated irrevocably by him (or his executor) to any property with respect to which he is the transferor. In 2004 to 2009, the GST exemption is equal to the estate tax unified credit equivalent (applicable exclusion amount) rather than to $1 million as indexed (see Appendix B). [The $1,000,000 amount is adjusted for inflation, rounded down to the next lowest multiple of $10,000, after 1998 and before 2004 (and after 2010). Any indexing increase in the GST exemption is available for all generation-skipping transfers occurring in the year of the increase and subsequent years in which the GST exemption is equal to $1 million as indexed up to the year of the decedent's death.][5] The GST tax is repealed for one year in 2010. In general, an individual or the individual's executor may allocate the GST exemption at any time from the date of the transfer until the time for filing the individual's federal estate tax return (including extensions actually granted), regardless of whether a return is required (see Q 1508).[6]

The GST exemption is automatically allocated to lifetime direct skips unless otherwise elected on a timely filed federal gift tax return (see Q 1534).[7]

In addition, any unused GST exemption is automatically allocated to indirect skips to a GST trust, effective 2001 to 2009.[8] An indirect skip is a transfer (other than a direct skip) subject to gift tax to a GST trust. A transferor can elect to have the automatic allocation not apply to (1) an indirect skip, or (2) to any or all transfers made by the individual to a particular trust. The transferor can also elect to treat a trust as a GST trust with respect to any or all transfers made by the individual to the trust. Nevertheless, an allocation still cannot be made until the end of any estate tax inclusion period (see below).

A GST trust is a trust that could have a generation-skipping transfer with respect to the transferor unless:

---

1. IRC Sec. 2621.
2. IRC Sec. 2622.
3. IRC Sec. 2623.
4. TAM 9105006.
5. IRC. Sec. 2631, as amended by EGTRRA 2001.
6. IRC Sec. 2632.
7. IRC Sec. 2632(b).
8. IRC Sec. 2632(c), as added by EGTRRA 2001.

1.   The trust provides that more than 25% of the trust corpus must be distributed to, or may be withdrawn by, one or more individuals who are non-skip persons, either (a) before the individual's 46th birthday, (b) on or before a date prior to such birthday, or (c) an event that may reasonably be expected to occur before such birthday.

2.   The trust provides that more than 25% of the trust corpus must be distributed to, or may be withdrawn by, one or more individuals who are non-skip persons and who are living on the date of death of an individual identified in the trust (by name or class) who is more than 10 years older than such individuals.

3.   The trust provides that, if one or more individuals who are non-skip persons die before a date or event described in (1) or (2), more than 25% of the trust corpus must either (a) be distributed to the estate(s) of one or more of such individuals, or (b) be subject to a general power of appointment exercisable by one or more of such individuals.

4.   Any portion of the trust would be included in the gross estate of a non-skip person (other than the transferor) if such person died immediately after the transfer.

5.   The trust is a charitable lead annuity trust (CLAT), charitable remainder annuity trust (CRAT), charitable remainder unitrust (CRUT), or a charitable lead unitrust (CLUT) with a non-skip remainder person.

For purposes of these GST trust rules, the value of transferred property is not treated as includable in the gross estate of a non-skip person nor subject to a power of withdrawal if the withdrawal right does not exceed the amount of the gift tax annual exclusion with respect to the transfer. It is also assumed that a power of appointment held by a non-skip person will not be exercised.

Regulations generally permit elections to allocate or not allocate GST exemption to individual transfers or to all current or future transfers to a trust, or any combination of these. An election with regard to all transfers to a trust can later be revoked with respect to future transfers to the trust. The regulations also permit elections with regard to individual transfers to a trust even where an election is in place with regard to all transfers to a trust.[1]

Planning Point: It probably makes sense for grantors to make elections to allocate or not allocate GST exemption with respect to all transfers to a particular trust. GST exemption can be allocated to trusts benefiting skip persons; while allocations are not made to trusts benefiting non-skip persons. If need be, the election could be changed later, for future transfers.

A retroactive allocation of the GST exemption can be made when certain non-skip beneficiaries of a trust predecease the transferor, effective 2001 to 2009. The non-skip beneficiary must (1) have an interest or a future interest (for this purpose, a future interest means the trust may permit income or corpus to be paid to such person on a date or dates in the future) in the trust to which any transfer has been made, (2) be a lineal

---

1. Treas. Reg. §26.2632-1.

descendant of a grandparent of the transferor or of a grandparent of the transferor's spouse or former spouse, (3) be assigned to a generation lower than that of the transferor, and (4) predecease the transferor. In such a case, an allocation of the transferor's unused GST exemption (determined immediately before the non-skip person's death) can be made to any previous transfer or transfers to the trust (value of transfer is its gift tax value at the time of the transfer) on a chronological order. The allocation is made by the transferor on the gift tax return for the year of the non-skip person's death. The allocation is treated as effective immediately before the non-skip person's death.[1]

> *Example.* Grandparent creates a trust for the primary benefit of Child, with Grandchild as contingent remainder beneficiary. Grandparent doesn't expect Grandchild will receive anything, or that the trust will be generation-skipping; so he doesn't allocate GST exemption to the trust. (Or, perhaps, allocation of the GST exemption was simply overlooked.) Child dies unexpectedly before Grandparent. There is a GST taxable termination at Child's death. Grandparent can make a retroactive allocation of GST exemption to the trust to reduce or eliminate the GST tax on the taxable termination.

With regard to lifetime transfers other than a direct skip, an allocation is made on the federal gift tax return. An allocation can use a formula (e.g., the amount necessary to produce an inclusion ratio of zero). An allocation on a timely filed gift tax return is generally effective as of the date of the transfer. An allocation on an untimely filed gift tax return is generally effective as of the date the return is filed and is deemed to precede any taxable event occurring on such date. (For certain retroactive allocations, see above.) An allocation of the GST exemption is irrevocable after the due date. However, an allocation of GST exemption to a trust (other than a charitable lead annuity trust, see below) is void to the extent the amount allocated exceeds the amount needed to produce an inclusion ratio of zero (see below).[2]

An executor can make an allocation of the transferor's unused GST exemption on the transferor's federal estate tax return. An allocation with respect to property included in the transferor's estate is effective as of the date of death. A late allocation of the GST with respect to a lifetime transfer can be made by the executor on the estate tax return and is effective as of the date the allocation is filed. A decedent's unused GST exemption is automatically and irrevocably allocated on the due date for the federal estate tax return to the extent not otherwise allocated by the executor. The automatic allocation is made to nonexempt property: first to direct skips occurring at death, and then to trusts with potential taxable distributions or taxable terminations.[3]

Inclusion Ratio

In general, the inclusion ratio with respect to any property transferred in a GST is the excess of one minus (a) the "applicable fraction" for the trust from which the transfer is made, or (b) in the case of a direct skip, the applicable fraction determined for the skip.[4]

The "applicable fraction" is a fraction (a) the numerator of which is the amount of the GST exemption allocated to the trust (or to the property transferred, if a direct skip), and (b) the denominator of which is the value of the property transferred reduced by (i) the sum of any federal estate or state death tax actually recovered from the trust attributable to such property, (ii) any federal gift tax or estate tax charitable deduction

---

1. IRC Sec. 2632(d), as added by EGTRRA 2001.
2. Treas. Reg. §26.2632-1(b).
3. IRC Sec. 2632(e), as redesignated by EGTRRA 2001, Treas. Reg. §26.2632-1(d).
4. IRC Sec. 2642(a)(1).

allowed with respect to such property, and (iii) with respect to a direct skip, the portion that is a nontaxable gift (see below). The fraction should be rounded to the nearest one-thousandth, with five rounded up (i.e., .2345 is rounded to .235). If the denominator of the applicable fraction is zero, the inclusion ratio is zero.[1]

> *Example.* In the year 2007, G transfers irrevocably in trust for his grandchildren $6 million and allocates all his $2,000,000 GST exemption to the transfer. The applicable fraction is 2,000,000/6,000,000, or .333. The inclusion ratio is 1 minus .333, or .667. The maximum estate tax rate, 45%, is applied against the inclusion ratio, .667. The resulting percentage, 30.0%, is applied against the value of the property transferred, $6,000,000, to produce a GST tax of $1,800,000. The tax is paid by G, the transferor, because this is a direct skip (other than a direct skip from a trust) (see Q 1510).

> *Example.* Same facts as in preceding example, except that for federal gift tax purposes G's wife consented to a split gift of the $6 million (see Q 1513). Thus, for GST tax purposes as well, the gift is considered split between the spouses. If they both elect to have their respective GST exemptions allocated to the transfer, the applicable fraction for each is 2,000,000/3,000,000, or .667. The inclusion ratio is 1 minus .667, or .333. The maximum estate tax rate, 45%, is applied against the inclusion ratio, .333. The resulting percentage, 15.0%, is applied against the value of the property transferred, $3,000,000, to produce a GST tax of $450,000 for each, or a total GST tax of $900,000 on the $6 million transfer. The tax is paid ½ each by G and G's wife, the transferors, because each gift is a direct skip (other than a direct skip from a trust) (see Q 1510).

> *Example.* In 2007, G transfers $100,000 to a trust and allocates $100,000 GST exemption to the trust. The trust has an inclusion ratio of zero, and taxable distributions and taxable terminations can be made free of GST tax.

> *Example.* In 2007, G transfers $100,000 to a trust and allocates no GST exemption to the trust. If all the trust beneficiaries are grandchildren of G, G has made a direct skip fully subject to GST tax. The GST tax is $45,000 ($100,000 transfer × 45% GST tax rate in 2007) and is payable by G. If the trust beneficiaries are children and grandchildren of G, the trust has an inclusion ratio of one, and GST transfers are fully subject to tax at the GST tax rate at the time of any later transfer.

If there is more than one transfer in trust the applicable fraction must be recomputed at the time of each transfer. Thus, if property is transferred to a preexisting trust, the "recomputed applicable fraction" is determined as follows: The numerator of such fraction is the sum of (1) the amount of the GST exemption allocated to the property involved in such transfer and (2) the nontax portion of the trust immediately before the transfer. (The nontax portion of the trust is the value of the trust immediately before the transfer multiplied by the applicable fraction in effect before such transfer.) The denominator of such fraction is the value of the trust immediately after the transfer reduced by (i) the sum of any federal estate or state death tax actually recovered from the trust attributable to such property, (ii) any federal gift tax or estate tax charitable deduction allowed with respect to such property, and (iii) with respect to a direct skip, the portion that is a nontaxable gift (see below).[2]

> *Example.* In the year 1995, G transfers irrevocably in trust for his children and grandchildren $4 million and allocates all his $1 million GST exemption to the transfer. The applicable fraction is 1,000,000/4,000,000, or .250. The inclusion ratio is 1 minus .250, or .750.

> In 2001, the trust makes a taxable distribution to the grandchildren of $100,000. The maximum estate tax rate, 55% in 2001, is applied against the inclusion ratio, .750. The resulting percentage, 41.3%, is multiplied by the $100,000 transfer, resulting in a GST tax of $41,300. GST taxes in this example are paid by the grandchildren, the transferees, because the transfers are taxable distributions (see Q 1516).

---

1. IRC Sec. 2642(a)(2), Treas. Reg. §26.2642-1.
2. IRC Sec. 2642(d)(2), Treas. Reg. §26.2642-4.

In 2007, the trust makes a taxable distribution to the grandchildren of $100,000. The maximum estate tax rate, 45% in 2007, is applied against the inclusion ratio, .750. The resulting percentage, 33.75%, is multiplied by the $100,000 transfer, resulting in a GST tax of $33,750.

Later in 2007, when the trust property has grown to $6 million, G transfers an additional $3 million to the trust. An additional $1,000,000 of GST exemption is available to G in 2007 ($2,000,000 GST exemption in 2007 minus $1,000,000 exemption already used). The numerator of the recomputed fraction is the value of the nontax portion of the trust immediately before the transfer, or $1.5 million (value of the trust, $6 million, multiplied by the applicable fraction of .250), plus $1,000,000 additional exemption, or $2,500,000. The denominator of the recomputed fraction is $9 million (the sum of the transferred property, $3 million, and the value of all the property in the trust immediately before the transfer, $6 million). The applicable fraction is 2,500,000/9,000,000, or .278. The inclusion ratio is 1 minus .278, or .722.

Later in 2007, the trust makes a taxable distribution to the grandchildren of $100,000. The maximum estate tax rate, 45% in 2007, is applied against the inclusion ratio, .722. The resulting percentage, 32.49%, is multiplied by the $100,000 transfer, resulting in a GST tax of $32,490.

Planning Point: Trusts are usually created with an inclusion ratio of either one (GST transfers, if any, with respect to trust are fully taxable) or zero (fully exempt from GST tax). A trust has an inclusion ratio of zero if GST exemption is allocated to any transfer to the trust that is not a nontaxable gift (an allocation of GST exemption is not needed for a direct skip nontaxable gift (see below); it has an inclusion ratio of zero). For information on severing a trust to create separate trusts with inclusion ratios of zero and one, see "Separate Trusts," below.

Valuation

"Value" of the property is its value at the time of the transfer. In the case of a direct skip of property that is included in the transferor's gross estate, the value of the property is its estate tax value. In the case of a taxable termination with respect to a trust occurring at the same time as and as a result of the death of an individual, an election may be made to value at the alternate valuation date (see Q 1536). In any case, the value of the property may be reduced by any consideration given by the transferee.[1]

For purposes of determining the GST inclusion ratio, certain other valuation rules may apply in some instances. For purposes of determining the denominator of the applicable fraction (see above), the value of property transferred during life is its fair market value as of the effective date of the GST exemption allocation (see above). However, with respect to late allocations of the GST exemption to a trust, the transferor may elect (solely for purpose of determining the fair market value of trust assets) to treat the allocation as made on the first day of the month in which the allocation is made. This election is not effective with respect to a life insurance policy, or a trust holding a life insurance policy, if the insured individual has died. For purposes of determining the denominator of the applicable fraction, the value of property included in the decedent's gross estate is its value for estate tax purposes. However, special use valuation (see Q 1535) is not available unless the recapture agreement under IRC Section 2032A specifically refers to the GST tax. There are special rules in the regulations concerning the allocation of post-death appreciation or depreciation with respect to pecuniary payments and residuary payments made after a pecuniary payment.[2]

---

1. IRC Sec. 2624.
2. IRC Sec. 2642(b)(2)(A), Treas. Reg. §26.2642-2.

Charitable Lead Annuity Trusts

With respect to property transferred after October 13, 1987, the GST tax exemption inclusion ratio for any charitable lead annuity trust (see Q 1337) is to be determined by dividing the amount of exemption allocated to the trust by the value of the property in the trust following the charitable term. For this purpose, the exemption allocated to the trust is increased by interest determined at the interest rate used in determining the amount of the estate or gift tax charitable deduction with respect to such a trust over the charitable term. With respect to a late allocation of the GST exemption (see above), interest accrues only from the date of the late allocation. The amount of GST exemption allocated to the trust is not reduced even though it is determined at a later time that a lesser amount of GST exemption would have produced a zero inclusion ratio.[1]

Estate Tax Inclusion Period (ETIP)

With respect to inter vivos transfers subject at some point in time to the GST tax, the allocation of any portion of the GST tax exemption to such a transfer is postponed until the earlier of (a) the expiration of the period (not to extend beyond the transferor's death) during which the property being transferred would be included in the transferor's estate (other than by reason of the gifts within three years of death rule of IRC Section 2035) if he died, or (b) the GST. For purposes of determining the inclusion ratio with respect to such exemption, the value of such property is: (a) its estate tax value if it is included in the transferor's estate (other than by reason of the three year rule of IRC Section 2035), or (b) its value determined at the end of the ETIP. However, if the allocation of the exemption under the second valuation method is not made on a timely filed gift tax return for the year in which the ETIP ends, determination of value is postponed until such allocation is filed.[2]

> *Example.* Grantor sets up an irrevocable trust: income retained for 10 years, then life estate for children, followed by remainder to grandchildren. The valuation of property for purpose of the inclusion rule is delayed until the earlier of the expiration of the 10-year period or the transferor's death. If the grantor were to die during such time the property would be included in the grantor's estate under IRC Section 2036(a) (see Q 1501). However, if the grantor survived the 10-year period and failed to make an allocation of the exemption on a timely filed gift tax return, the determination of value is postponed until the earlier of the time an allocation is filed or death.

Except as provided in regulations, for purpose of the GST tax exemption allocation rules, any reference to an individual or a transferor is generally treated as including the spouse of such individual or transferor.[3] Thus, an ETIP includes the period during which, if death occurred, the property being transferred would be included in the estate (other than by reason of the gifts within three years of death rule of IRC Section 2035) of the transferor or the spouse of the transferor. The property is not considered as includable in the estate of the transferor or the spouse of the transferor if the possibility of inclusion is so remote as to be negligible (i.e., less than a 5% actuarial probability). The property is not considered as includable in the estate of the spouse of the transferor by reason of a withdrawal power limited to the greater of $5,000 or 5% of the trust corpus if the withdrawal power terminates no later than 60 days after the transfer to trust. Apparently, the ETIP rules do not apply if a reverse QTIP election (see below) is made. The ETIP terminates on the earlier of (1) the death of the transferor; (2) the time at which no portion would be includable in the transferor's estate (other than by

---

1. IRC Sec. 2642(e), Treas. Reg. §26.2642-3.
2. IRC Sec. 2642(f).
3. IRC Sec. 2642(f)(4).

reason of IRC Section 2035) or, in the case of the spouse who consents to a split-gift, the time at which no portion would be includable in the other spouse's estate; (3) the time of the GST (but only with respect to property involved in the GST); or (4) in the case of an ETIP arising because of an interest or power held by the transferor's spouse, at the earlier of (a) the death of the spouse, or (b) the time at which no portion would be includable in the spouse's estate (other than by reason of IRC Section 2035).[1]

> *Example.* Grantor sets up an irrevocable trust: income retained for the shorter of nine years or life, remainder to grandchild. Grantor and spouse elect to split the gift. If spouse dies during trust term, spouse's executor can allocate GST exemption to spouse's deemed one-half of the trust. However, the allocation is not effective until the earlier of the expiration of grantor's income interest or grantor's death.

The regulations provide that the election out of automatic allocation of GST exemption for either a direct skip or an indirect skip can be made at any time up until the due date for filing the gift tax return for the year the ETIP ends. If the transfer subject to an ETIP occurred in an earlier year, the election must specify the particular transfer. An affirmative allocation of GST exemption cannot be revoked after the due date for filing the gift tax return for the year the affirmative election is made (or after the allocation is made in the case of a late allocation), even where actual allocation is not effective until the end of an ETIP.[2]

Separate Trusts

In general, portions of a trust are not to be treated as separate trusts. However, portions attributable to different transferors, substantially separate and independent shares of different beneficiaries of a trust, and trusts treated as separate trusts under state law are to be treated as separate trusts for GST tax purposes.[3] However, treatment of a single trust as separate shares for purposes of the GST tax does not permit treatment as separate trusts for purposes of filing or payment of tax, or for purposes of any other tax. Additions to, or distributions from, such a trust are allocated pro-rata among all shares unless expressly provided otherwise. In general, a separate share is not treated as such unless it exists at all times from and after creation of the trust.

Trusts created from a qualified severance are treated as separate trusts for GST tax purposes, effective for 2001 to 2009. A qualified severance means the division of a single trust into two or more trusts under the trust document or state law if (1) the single trust is divided on a fractional basis, and (2) in the aggregate, the terms of the new trusts provide for the same succession of interests of beneficiaries as are provided in the original trust. In the case of a trust with a GST inclusion ratio of greater than zero and less than one (i.e., the trust is partially protected from the GST by allocations of the GST exemption), a severance is a qualified severance only if the single trust is divided into two trusts, one of which receives a fractional amount equal to the GST applicable fraction multiplied by the single trust's assets. The trust receiving the fractional amount receives an inclusion ratio of zero (i.e., it is not subject to GST tax), and the other trust receives an inclusion ratio of one (i.e., it is fully subject to GST tax).[4]

Otherwise, severance of a trust included in the taxable estate (or created in the transferor's will) into single shares will be recognized for GST purposes if (1) the trusts

---

1. Treas. Reg. §26.2632-1(c).
2. Treas. Reg. §26.2632-1.
3. IRC Sec. 2654(b).
4. IRC Sec. 2642(a), as added by EGTRRA 2001.

are severed pursuant to the governing instrument or state law, (2) such severance occurs (or a reformation proceeding is begun and is indicated on the estate tax return) prior to the date for filing the estate tax return (including extensions actually granted), and (3) the trusts are funded using (a) fractional interests or (b) pecuniary amounts for which appropriate adjustments are made.[1]

Proposed regulations provide that a severance must be done on a fractional or percentage basis; a severance based on a specific pecuniary amount is not permitted. The terms of the new trusts must provide in the aggregate for the same succession of beneficiaries. With respect to trusts from which discretionary distributions may be made on a non pro rata basis, this requirement can be satisfied even if each permissible beneficiary might be a beneficiary of only one of the separate trusts, but only if no beneficial interest is shifted to a lower generation and the time for vesting of any beneficial interest is not extended. The separate trusts must be funded with property from the severed trust with either a pro rata portion of each asset or on a non pro rata basis. If funded on a non pro rata basis, the separate trusts must be funded by applying the appropriate severance fraction or percentage to the fair market value of all the property on the date of funding.[2]

Planning Point: The advantage of having portions or shares of a trust treated as separate trusts is that the transferor can decide whether or not to allocate a portion of his GST tax exemption to each separate trust and the trustee can make distributions from the separate trusts in a way which minimizes GST tax.

Nontaxable Gifts

In the case of any direct skip which is a nontaxable gift, the inclusion ratio is zero. For this purpose, a nontaxable gift means any transfer of property to the extent the transfer is not treated as a taxable gift by reason of the gift tax annual exclusion (taking into account the split gift provision for married couples—see Q 1530) or the "qualified transfer" exclusion (see Q 1530). In other words, there is no GST tax imposed on direct skip gifts that come within the gift tax annual exclusion or that are "qualified transfers." However, with respect to transfers after March 31, 1988, a nontaxable gift which is a direct skip to a trust for the benefit of an individual has an inclusion ratio of zero only if (1) during the life of such individual no portion of the trust corpus or income may be distributed to or for the benefit of any other person, and (2) the trust would be included in such individual's estate if the trust did not terminate before such individual died.[3]

Reverse QTIP Election

A qualified terminable interest property (QTIP) election can be made to qualify property for the estate tax (see Q 1506) and gift tax (see Q 1531) marital deductions. A reverse QTIP election may be made for such property under the GST tax. The effect of making the reverse QTIP election is to have the decedent or the donor treated as the transferor (see Q 1510) for GST tax purposes. However, if a reverse QTIP election is made for property in a trust, the election must be made for all of the property in the trust. However, the Committee Report states that if the executor indicates on the federal estate tax return that separate trusts will be created, such trusts will be treated as separate trusts. In other words, separate trusts can be created so that the QTIP

---

1. Treas. Reg. §26.2654-1.
2. Prop. Treas. Reg. §26.2642-6.
3. IRC Sec. 2642(c).

and reverse QTIP election can be made for different amounts, and thus minimize all transfer taxes.[1] See "Separate Trusts," above regarding the creation of separate shares from a single trust.

> *Example.* In 2007, decedent (who has made $500,000 of taxable gifts protected by the unified credit) with a $4,000,000 estate leaves $1,500,000 in a credit shelter trust and $2,500,000 to his surviving spouse in a QTIP trust, reducing his estate tax to zero. (Assume each trust would be subject to GST tax to the extent that the $2,000,000 exemption is not allocated to such trust.) The executor allocates $1,500,000 of the decedent's $2,000,000 GST tax exemption to the credit shelter trust and makes a reverse QTIP election as to $500,000 of the QTIP property so that the decedent's full $2,000,000 exemption can be used. The surviving spouse's $2,000,000 exemption amount may then be used to protect the remaining $2,000,000 of property, and the entire $4,000,000 has escaped GST tax (assuming separate QTIP trusts of $2,000,000 and $500,000 are created).

Basis Adjustment

Where the basis of property subject to the GST tax is increased (or decreased) to fair market value because property transferred in a taxable termination occurs at the same time and as a result of the death of an individual, any increase (or decrease) in basis is limited by multiplying such increase (or decrease) by the inclusion ratio used in allocating the GST exemption.[2]

1512. How are individuals assigned to generations for purposes of the GST tax?

An individual (and his spouse or former spouse) who is a lineal descendant of a grandparent of the transferor (or the transferor's spouse) is assigned to that generation which results from comparing the number of generations between the grandparent and such individual with the number of generations between the grandparent and the transferor (or the transferor's spouse). A relationship by legal adoption is treated as a relationship by blood, and a relationship by the half-blood is treated as a relationship of the whole blood.[3]

A person who could be assigned to more than one generation is assigned to the youngest generation. However, regulations provide that adopted individuals will be treated as one generation younger than the adoptive parent where: (1) a transfer is made to the adopted individual from the adoptive parent, the spouse or former spouse of the adoptive parent, or a lineal descendant of a grandparent of the adoptive parent; (2) the adopted individual is a descendant of the adoptive parent (or the spouse or former spouse of the adoptive parent); (3) the adopted individual is under age 18 at the time of adoption; and (4) the adoption is not primarily for the purpose of avoiding GST tax.[4]

However, with respect to terminations, distributions, and transfers occurring after 1997, where an individual's parent is dead at the time of a transfer subject to gift or estate tax upon which the individual's interest is established or derived, such individual will be treated as being one generation below the lower of (1) the transferor's generation or (2) the generation of the youngest living ancestor of the individual who is also a descendant of the parents of the transferor or the transferor's spouse. This predeceased parent rule applies to collateral relatives (e.g., nieces and nephews) only if there are no living lineal

---

1. IRC Sec. 2652(a)(3). See Let. Ruls. 9133016, 9002014.
2. IRC Sec. 2654(a)(2).
3. IRC Secs. 2651(a), 2651(b), 2651(c).
4. Treas. Reg. §26.2651-2.

descendants of the transferor at the time of the transfer.[1] For a narrower predeceased parent rule that applied to direct skips before 1998, see Q 1510.

Regulations make clear that if the generation-skipping property is subject to gift tax or estate tax on more than one occasion, the time for determining application of the predeceased parent rule is on the first of such occasions. In the case of a qualified terminable interest property (QTIP) marital deduction election, the time for determining application of the predeceased parent rule can essentially wait until the surviving spouse dies or makes a gift of the QTIP property. However, where a reverse QTIP election is made, application of the predeceased parent rule is made at the time of the first spouse's death. Also, at times property may be transferred to a trust before the predeceased parent rule is applicable. Later, the predeceased parent rule applies to additional property transferred to the trust. The additional property is treated as being held in a separate trust for GST tax purposes. Each portion has, in effect, a separate transferor.[2]

An individual who cannot be assigned to a generation under the foregoing rules is assigned to a generation on the basis of his date of birth. An individual born not more than 12½ years after the date of birth of the transferor is assigned to the transferor's generation. An individual born more than 12½ years but not more than 37½ years after the date of birth of the transferor is assigned to the first generation younger than the transferor. There are similar rules for a new generation every 25 years.[3]

1513. Can married couples make a split gift for purposes of the GST tax?

Yes. If a split gift is made for gift tax purposes (see Q 1530), such gift will be so treated for purposes of the GST tax.[4] Split gifts allow spouses to, in effect, utilize each other's annual exclusions and exemptions (see Q 1511). One memorandum permitted a taxpayer to elect after his spouse's death to split gifts with his spouse and thus take advantage of his spouse's GST tax exemption where the gifts were made by the taxpayer shortly before the spouse's death.[5]

1514. What credits are allowed against the GST tax?

For decedents dying before 2005 or after 2010, if a GST (other than a direct skip) occurs at the same time as and as a result of the death of an individual, a credit against the GST tax imposed is allowed in an amount equal to the GST tax actually paid to any state in respect to any property included in the GST, but the amount cannot exceed 5% of the GST tax.[6] The credit is eliminated for 2005 to 2010.[7]

1515. What are the return requirements with respect to the GST tax?

---

1. IRC Sec. 2651(e).
2. Treas. Reg. §26.2651-1.
3. IRC Sec. 2651(d).
4. IRC Sec. 2652(a)(2).
5. TAM 9404023.
6. IRC Sec. 2604.
7. IRC Secs. 2604(c), 2664, as added by EGTRRA 2001.

The person required to file the return is the person liable for paying the tax (see Q 1516). In the case of a direct skip (other than from a trust), the return must be filed on or before the due date for the gift or estate tax return with respect to the transfer. In all other cases, the return must be filed on or before the 15th day of the 4th month after the close of the taxable year of the person required to make the return.[1]

1516. Who is liable for paying the GST tax?

In the case of a taxable distribution, the tax is paid by the transferee. In the case of a taxable termination or a direct skip from a trust, the tax is paid by the trustee. In the case of a direct skip (other than a direct skip from a trust), the tax is paid by the transferor. Unless the governing instrument of transfer otherwise directs, the GST tax is charged to the property constituting the transfer.[2]

GIFT TAX

GENERAL

1517. Starting Point – What is the federal gift tax?

The federal gift tax is an excise tax on the right to transfer property during life.[3] The gift tax is a cumulative tax and the tax rates are progressive. Gifts made in prior years are taken into account in computing the tax on gifts made in the current year, with the result that later gifts are usually taxed in a higher bracket than earlier gifts (a drop in tax rates could obviate this result). Moreover, the tax is a *unified* tax; the same tax that is imposed on taxable gifts is imposed on taxable estates. However, the estate tax is repealed for one year in 2010 (see Q 1500), while the gift tax is not.

A gift tax return, if required, must generally be filed by April 15 of the following year. A six month extension for filing is available. Tax is generally due by April 15, but certain extensions for payment may be available. See Q 1534.

The Federal Gift Tax Worksheet, below, shows the steps for calculating the gift tax. Calculation starts with determining what a gift for gift tax purposes is (see Q 1518). In general, gifts include gratuitous transfers of all kinds. A husband and wife can elect to have all gifts made by either spouse during the year treated as made one-half by each spouse (Q 1529). A qualified disclaimer is not treated as a gift (Q 1520).

Gifts are generally valued at fair market value on the date of the gift (Q 1535). Special rules apply for a wide variety of investments and to net gifts (Q 1525), and Chapter 14 special valuation rules apply to transfers to family members of certain interests in corporations, partnerships, or trusts (Q 1549).

A couple of exclusions are available from gifts. A $12,000 (in 2007) annual exclusion is available for present interest gifts on a per donor/donee basis. An unlimited exclusion is available for qualified transfers for educational and medical purposes. See Q 1530.

---

1. IRC Sec. 2662.
2. IRC Sec. 2603.
3. IRC Sec. 2501.

A couple of deductions are also available. Unlimited marital (Q 1531) and charitable (Q 1532) deductions are available for certain transfers to the donor's spouse and to charities.

Taxable gifts equals gifts made during the year reduced by all exclusions and deductions.

Tax is imposed on taxable gifts. Tax rates (Appendix B) are generally progressive and tax is based on cumulative taxable transfers during lifetime. To implement this, tax is calculated on total taxable gifts, the sum of the taxable gifts made during the year (current taxable gifts) and prior taxable gifts, and the gift tax that would have been payable on prior taxable gifts (using the current tax rates) is then subtracted out.

Planning Point: A gift made after August 5, 1997, cannot be revalued, if the gift was adequately disclosed on a gift tax return and the gift tax statute of limitations (generally, three years) has passed.[1] Consider filing gift tax returns even for annual exclusion gifts.

The tentative tax is then reduced by the unified credit (Q 1533) to produce gift tax payable.

Federal Gift Tax Worksheet

Current Year		
Current Gifts		Q 1518
- Annual Exclusions	Q 1530	
- Qualified Transfers Exclusion	Q 1530	
- Marital Deduction	Q 1531	
- Charitable Deduction	Q 1532	
- Total Reductions		
Current Taxable Gifts		
+ Prior Taxable Gifts		
Total Taxable Gifts		
Tax on Total Taxable Gifts		Appendix B
- Tax on Prior Taxable Gifts		Appendix B
Tentative Tax		Appendix B
- Unified Credit		Q 1533
Federal Gift Tax		

1518. What kinds of transfers are subject to the federal gift tax?

The gift tax applies to a transfer by way of gift whether the transfer is in trust or otherwise, whether the gift is direct or indirect, and whether the property is real or personal, tangible or intangible. For example, a taxable transfer may be effected by the creation of a trust; the forgiving of a debt (see Q 1522); the assignment of a judgment; the transfer of cash, certificates of deposit, federal, state, municipal, or corporate bonds, or stocks.[2]

---

1. IRC Sec. 6501(c)(9).
2. Treas. Reg. §25.2511-1(a).

All transactions whereby property or property rights or interests are gratuitously passed or conferred upon another, regardless of the means or device employed, constitute gifts subject to tax.[1] Donative intent on the part of the transferor is not an essential element in the application of the gift tax to the transfer. The application of the tax is based on the objective facts of the transfer and the circumstances under which it is made, rather than on the subjective motives of the donor.[2] Generally, if property is transferred gratuitously or for an inadequate consideration, a gift (of the full value of the property transferred or the portion in excess of the consideration given) will be considered a gift.[3]

Shareholders of nonparticipating preferred stock in profitable family held corporations have been held to have made gifts to the common stockholders (typically descendants of the preferred shareholder) by waiving payment of dividends or simply by failing to exercise conversion rights or other options available to a preferred stockholder to preserve his position.[4] The Tax Court has held that the failure to convert noncumulative preferred stock to cumulative preferred stock did not give rise to a gift, but that thereafter a gift was made each time a dividend would have accumulated. However, the failure to exercise a put option at par plus accumulated dividends plus interest was not treated as a gift of foregone interest.[5]

A transaction involving the nonexercise by a son of an option under a cross-purchase buy-sell agreement followed by the sale of the same stock by the father to a third party when the fair market value of the stock was substantially higher than the option price was treated as a gift from the son to the father.[6] Also, a father indirectly made a gift to his son to the extent that the fair market value of stock exceeded its redemption price when the father failed to exercise his right under a buy-sell agreement to have a corporation redeem all of the available shares held by his brother-in-law's estate and the stock passed to the son.[7]

With respect to a trust, the grantor/income beneficiary may be treated as making additional gifts of remainder interests in each year that the grantor fails to exercise his right to make nonproductive or underproductive property normally productive.[8] A mother made gifts to her children to the extent that the children were paid excessive trustee fees from the marital deduction trust of which the mother was a beneficiary.[9] However, a grantor of a trust does not make a gift to trust beneficiaries by paying the income tax on trust income taxable to the grantor under the grantor trust rules (see Q 1450).[10]

Letter Ruling 9113009 (withdrawn without comment by TAM 9409018) had ruled that a parent who guaranteed loans to his children made a gift to his children because, without the guarantees, the children could not have obtained the loans or, at the very least, would have paid a higher interest rate.

---

1. Treas. Reg. §25.2511-1(c).
2. Treas. Reg. §25.2511-1(g)(1).
3. *Hollingsworth v. Comm.*, 86 TC 91 (1986).
4. TAMs 8723007, 8726005.
5. *Snyder v. Comm.*, 93 TC 529 (1989).
6. Let. Rul. 9117035.
7. TAM 9315005.
8. Let. Rul. 8945006.
9. TAM 200014004.
10. Rev. Rul. 2004-64, 2004-27 IRB 7.

The gift tax is imposed only on completed gifts (see Q 1519).

Where spouses enter into joint and mutual wills, the surviving spouse may be treated as making a gift of a remainder interest at the other spouse's death.[1]

The transfer of a qualifying income interest for life in qualified terminable interest property for which a marital deduction was allowed (see Q 1506, Q 1531) will be treated as a transfer of such property for gift tax purposes.[2] If a QTIP trust is severed into Trust A and Trust B and the spouse renounces her interest in Trust A, such renunciation will not cause the spouse to be treated as transferring Trust B under IRC Section 2519.[3]

The spouse is entitled to collect from the donee the gift tax on the transfer of a QTIP interest. The amount treated as a transfer for gift tax purposes is reduced by the amount of the gift tax the spouse is entitled to recover from the donee. Thus, the transfer is treated as a net gift (see Q 1525). The failure of a spouse to exercise the right to recover gift tax from the donee is treated as a transfer of the unrecovered amount to the donee when the right to recover is no longer enforceable. If a written waiver of the right of recovery is executed before the right becomes unenforceable, the transfer of the unrecovered gift tax is treated as made on the later of (1) the date of the waiver, or (2) the date the tax is paid by the transferor. Any delay in exercise of the right of recovery is treated as an interest-free loan (see Q 1521) for gift tax purposes.[4]

Where a surviving spouse acquires a remainder interest in QTIP marital deduction property in connection with a transfer of property or cash to the holder of the remainder interest, the surviving spouse makes a gift to the remainder person under both IRC Section 2519 (disposition of QTIP interest) and IRC Sections 2511 and 2512 (transfers and valuation of gifts). The amount of the gift is equal to the greater of (1) the value of the remainder interest, or (2) the value of the property or cash transferred to the holder of the remainder interest.[5] On the other hand, children would be treated as making a gift if the children transfer their remainder interest in a QTIP marital deduction trust to the surviving spouse.[6]

Any subsequent transfer by the donor spouse of an interest in such property is not treated as a transfer for gift tax purposes, unless the transfer occurs after the donee spouse is treated as having transferred such property under IRC Section 2519 or after such property is includable in the donee spouse's estate under IRC Section 2044 (see Q 1501).[7] Also, if property for which a QTIP marital deduction was taken is includable in the estate of the spouse who was given the QTIP interest and the estate of such spouse fails to recover from the person receiving the property any estate tax attributable to the QTIP interest being included in such spouse's estate, such failure is treated as a transfer for gift tax purposes unless (1) such spouse's will waives the right to recovery, or (2) the beneficiaries cannot compel recovery of the taxes (e.g., where the executor is given discretion to waive the right of recovery in such spouse's will).[8]

1. *Grimes v. Comm.*, 88-2 USTC ¶13,774 (7th Cir. 1988).
2. IRC Sec. 2519.
3. Let. Ruls. 200116006, 200122036.
4. Treas. Regs. §§25.2207A-1(b), 25.2519-1(c)(4).
5. Rev. Rul. 98-8, 1998-1 CB 541.
6. Let. Rul. 199908033.
7. IRC Sec. 2523(f)(5).
8. Treas. Reg. §20.2207A-1(a).

The gift tax is not applicable to a transfer for a full and adequate consideration in money or money's worth, or to ordinary business transactions (i.e., transactions which are bona fide, at arm's length, and free from any donative intent). A consideration not reducible to a value in money or money's worth, as love and affection, promise of marriage, etc., is wholly disregarded, and the entire value of the property transferred constitutes the amount of the gift. Similarly, a relinquishment or promised relinquishment of dower or curtesy, or of a statutory estate created in lieu of dower or curtesy, or of other marital rights in the spouse's property or estate, is not considered to any extent a consideration "in money or money's worth."[1]

Transfers of property or interest in property made under the terms of a written agreement between spouses in settlement of their marital or property rights are deemed to be for an adequate and full consideration in money or money's worth and, therefore, exempt from the gift tax (whether or not such agreement is approved by a divorce decree), if the spouses obtain a final decree of divorce from each other within the three-year period beginning on the date one year before the agreement is entered into.[2]

For recapture rules applicable where distributions are not timely made in connection with the transfer of an interest in a corporation or partnership which is subject to the Chapter 14 valuation rules, see Q 1550. For deemed transfers upon the lapse of certain voting or liquidation rights in a corporation or partnership, see Q 1553.

A gift may be made of foregone interest with respect to interest-free and bargain rate loans (see Q 1521).

COMPLETE GIFT

1519. When does a complete gift take place for purposes of the federal gift tax?

The gift is complete when the donor has so parted with dominion and control over the property or interest in property he is giving as to leave in him no power to change its disposition whether for his own benefit or for the benefit of another.[3] In general, a transfer of an interest in a revocable trust is incomplete until the interest becomes irrevocable. However, if the interest becomes irrevocable at the grantor's death, it will generally be subject to estate tax (see Q 1501) rather than to gift tax.

If a donor delivers a properly endorsed stock certificate to the donee or the donee's agent, the gift is completed for gift tax purposes on the date of delivery. If the donor delivers the certificate to his bank or broker as his agent, or to the issuing corporation or its transfer agent, for transfer into the name of the donee, the gift is completed on the date the stock is transferred on the books of the corporation.[4]

A transfer of a nonstatutory stock option which was not traded on an established market would be treated as a gift to a family member on the later of (1) the transfer or (2) the time when the donee's right to exercise the option is no longer conditioned on the performance of services by the transferor.[5]

---

1. Treas. Reg. §25.2512-8.
2. IRC Sec. 2516.
3. Treas. Reg. §25.2511-2(b).
4. Treas. Reg. §25.2511-2(h); Rev. Rul. 54-554, 1954-2 CB 317; Rev. Rul. 54-135, 1954-1 CB 205.
5. Rev. Rul. 98-21, 1998-1 CB 975.

The gratuitous transfer by the maker of a legally binding promissory note is a completed gift (the transfer of a legally unenforceable promissory note is an incomplete gift); if the note is unpaid at the donor's death, the gift is not treated as an adjusted taxable gift in computing the tentative estate tax (see Q 1500), and no deduction is allowable from the gross estate for the promisee's claim with respect to the note (see Q 1506).[1]

In the case of a gift by check, when is the gift complete, when the check is delivered, or when the check is cashed? In the litigation to date, the courts initially appeared to make a distinction between gifts to charitable donees and gifts to noncharitable donees. In the former case it has been held that at least where there is timely presentment and payment, payment of the check by the bank relates back to the date of delivery for purposes of determining completeness of the gift.[2] In the latter case, the courts have shown less of a willingness to apply the "relation back" doctrine. In *Est. of Dillingham v. Comm.*,[3] the noncharitable donees did not cash the checks until 35 days after their delivery, the donor's death having intervened. The court said that this delay cast doubt as to whether the checks were unconditionally delivered. Since the estate failed to prove unconditional delivery, the court declined to extend the relation back doctrine to the case before it. It then turned to local law to determine whether the decedent had parted with dominion and control upon delivery of the checks. It determined that under applicable local law (Oklahoma), the donor did not part with dominion and control until the checks were cashed. However, in *Est. of Gagliardi v. Comm.*,[4] checks written by a brokerage firm and charged against the decedent's account prior to decedent's death were treated as completed gifts to the noncharitable donees even though some checks were cashed after decedent's death. Also, in *Est. of Metzger v. Comm.*,[5] the relation-back doctrine was applied to gifts made by check to noncharitable beneficiaries where the taxpayer was able to establish: (1) the donor's intent to make gifts, (2) unconditional delivery of the checks, (3) presentment of the check during the year for which a gift tax annual exclusion was sought and within a reasonable time after issuance, and (4) that there were sufficient funds to pay the checks at all relevant times. In *W. H. Braum Family Partnership v. Comm.*,[6] the relation-back doctrine was not applied where the taxpayer could not establish either (2) or (4). In response to *Metzger*, the Service has issued a revenue ruling providing that a gift by check to a noncharitable beneficiary will be considered complete on the earlier of (1) when the donor has so parted with dominion and control under state law such that the donor can no longer change its disposition, or (2) when the donee deposits the check, cashes the check against available funds, or presents the check for payment if the following conditions are met: (a) the check must be paid by the drawee bank when first presented for payment to the drawee bank; (b) the donor must be alive when the check is paid by the drawee bank; (c) the donor must have intended a gift; (d) delivery of the check by the donor must have been unconditional; (e) the check must be deposited, cashed or presented in the calendar year for which the completed gift tax treatment is sought; and (f) the check must be deposited, cashed or presented within a reasonable time of issuance.[7]

---

1. Rev. Rul. 84-25, 1984-1 CB 191.
2. *Est. of Spiegel v. Comm.*, 12 TC 524 (1942).
3. 90-1 USTC ¶60,021 (10th Cir. 1990).
4. 89 TC 1207 (1987).
5. 94-2 USTC ¶60,179 (4th Cir. 1994), aff'g 100 TC 204 (1993).
6. TC Memo 1993-434.
7. Rev. Rul. 96-56, 1996-2 CB 161.

DISCLAIMERS

1520. If a person refuses to accept an interest in property (a disclaimer), is he considered to have made a gift of the interest for federal gift tax purposes?

Not if he makes a *qualified disclaimer*. A "qualified disclaimer" means an irrevocable and unqualified refusal to accept an interest in property created in the person disclaiming by a taxable transfer made after 1976. With respect to inter vivos transfers, for the purpose of determining when a timely disclaimer is made (see condition (3) below), a taxable transfer occurs when there is a completed gift for federal gift tax purposes regardless of whether a gift tax is imposed on the completed gift. Thus, gifts qualifying for the gift tax annual exclusion are regarded as taxable transfers for this purpose.[1] Furthermore, a disclaimer of a remainder interest in a trust created prior to the enactment of the federal gift tax was subject to the gift tax where the disclaimer was not timely and the disclaimer occurred after enactment of the gift tax.[2] In order to effectively disclaim property for transfer tax purposes, a disclaimer of property received from a decedent at death should generally be made within nine months of death rather than within nine months of the probate of the decedent's will.[3]

In general, the disclaimer must satisfy these conditions: (1) the disclaimer must be irrevocable and unqualified; (2) the disclaimer must be in writing; (3) the writing must be delivered to the transferor of the interest, his legal representative, the holder of the legal title to the property, or the person in possession of the property, not later than nine months after the later of (a) the day on which the transfer creating the interest is made, or (b) the day on which the disclaimant reaches age 21; (4) the disclaimant must not have accepted the interest disclaimed or any of its benefits; and (5) the interest disclaimed must pass either to the spouse of the decedent or to a person other than the disclaimant without any direction on the part of the person making the disclaimer.[4] A person cannot disclaim a remainder interest in property while retaining a life estate or income interest in the same property.[5]

If a person makes a qualified disclaimer, for purposes of the federal estate, gift, and generation-skipping transfer tax provisions, the disclaimed interest in property is treated as if it had never been transferred to the person making the qualified disclaimer. Instead it is considered as passing directly from the transferor of the property to the person entitled to receive the property as a result of the disclaimer. Accordingly, a person making a qualified disclaimer is not treated as making a gift. Similarly, the value of a decedent's gross estate for purposes of the federal estate tax does not include the value of property with respect to which the decedent or his executor has made a qualified disclaimer.[6]

In the case of a joint tenancy with rights of survivorship or a tenancy by the entirety, the interest which the donee receives upon creation of the joint interest can be disclaimed within nine months of the creation of the interest and the survivorship interest received

---

1. Treas. Reg. §25.2518-2(c)(3).
2. *U.S. v. Irvine*, 94-1 USTC ¶60,163 (U.S. 1994).
3. *Est. of Fleming v. Comm.*, 92-2 USTC ¶60,113 (7th Cir. 1992).
4. IRC Sec. 2518(b); Treas. Reg. §25.2518-2(a).
5. *Walshire v. Comm.*, 2002-1 USTC ¶60,439 (8th Cir. 2002).
6. Treas. Reg. §25.2518-1(b).

upon the death of the first joint tenant to die (deemed to be a one-half interest in the property) can be disclaimed within nine months of the death of the first joint tenant to die, *without regard to* (1) whether either joint tenant can sever unilaterally under local law, (2) the portion of the property attributable to consideration furnished by the disclaimant, or (3) the portion of the property includable in the decedent's gross estate under IRC Section 2040. However, in the case of a creation of a joint tenancy between spouses or tenancy by the entirety created after July 13, 1988 where the *donee spouse is not a U.S. citizen*, a surviving spouse can make a disclaimer within nine months of the death of the first spouse to die of any portion of the joint interest that is includable in the decedent's estate under IRC Section 2040. Also, in the case of a transfer to a *joint bank, brokerage, or other investment account* (e.g., mutual fund account) where the transferor can unilaterally withdraw amounts contributed by the transferor, the surviving joint tenant may disclaim amounts contributed by the first joint tenant to die within nine months of the death of the first joint tenant to die.[1]

For purposes of a qualified disclaimer, the mere act of making a surviving spouse's statutory election is not to be treated as an acceptance of an interest in the disclaimed property or any of its benefits. However, the disclaimer of a portion of the property subject to the statutory election must be made within nine months of the decedent spouse's death, rather than within nine months of the surviving spouse's statutory election.[2]

A power with respect to property is treated as an interest in such property.[3] The exercise of a power of appointment to any extent by the donee of the power is an acceptance of its benefits.[4]

A beneficiary who is under 21 years of age has until nine months after his 21st birthday in which to make a qualified disclaimer of his interest in property. Any actions taken with regard to an interest in property by a beneficiary or a custodian prior to the beneficiary's 21st birthday will not be an acceptance by the beneficiary of the interest.[5] This rule holds true even as to custodianship gifts in states which provide that custodianship ends when the donee reaches an age below 21.[6]

INTEREST-FREE AND BARGAIN RATE LOANS

1521. Are gifts made of foregone interest with respect to interest-free and bargain rate loans?

An interest-free or low-interest loan within a family or in any other circumstances where the foregone interest is in the nature of a gift results in a gift subject to the federal gift tax. IRC Section 7872 applies in the case of term loans made after June 6, 1984 and demand loans outstanding after that date.

In general, IRC Section 7872 recharacterizes a below-market loan (an interest-free or low-interest loan) as an arm's length transaction in which the lender (1) made a loan to the borrower in exchange for a note requiring the payment of interest at a statutory

---

1. Treas. Reg. §25.2518-2(c)(4).
2. Rev. Rul. 90-45, 1990-1 CB 176.
3. IRC Sec. 2518(c)(2).
4. Treas. Reg. §25.2518-2(d)(1); Let. Rul. 8142008.
5. Treas. Reg. §25.2518-2(d)(3).
6. Treas. Reg. §25.2518-2(d)(4), Example 11.

rate, and (2) made a gift, distributed a dividend, made a contribution to capital, paid compensation, or made another payment to the borrower which, in turn, is used by the borrower to pay the interest. The difference between the statutory rate of interest and the rate (if any) actually charged by the lender, the "foregone interest," is thus either a gift to the borrower or income to him, depending on the circumstances. The income tax aspects of below-market loans are discussed in Q 1407. The gift tax aspects of such loans are discussed here.

First, some definitions: The term "gift loan" means any below-market loan where the foregoing of interest is in the nature of a gift. The term "demand loan" means any loan which is payable in full at any time on the demand of the lender. The term "term loan" means any loan which is not a demand loan. The term "applicable federal rate" means: in the case of a demand loan or a term loan of up to three years, the federal short-term rate; in the case of a term loan over three years but not over nine years, the federal mid-term rate; in the case of a term loan over nine years, the federal long-term rate. In the case of a term loan the applicable rate is compounded semiannually. These rates are reset monthly.[1] The "present value" of any payment is determined (a) as of the date of the loan, and (b) by using a discount rate equal to the applicable federal rate.[2] The term "below-market loan" means any loan if (a) in the case of a demand loan, interest is payable on the loan at a rate less than the applicable federal rate, or (b) in the case of a term loan, the amount loaned exceeds the present value of all payments due under the loan. The term "foregone interest" means, with respect to any period during which the loan is outstanding, the excess of (a) the amount of interest that would have been payable on the loan for the period if the interest accrued on the loan at the applicable federal rate and were payable annually on the last day of the appropriate calendar year, over (b) any interest payable on the loan properly allocable to the period.

In the case of a demand gift loan, the foregone interest is treated as transferred from the lender to the borrower and retransferred by the borrower to the lender as interest on the last day of each calendar year the loan is outstanding. In the case of a term gift loan, the lender is treated as having transferred on the date the loan was made, and the borrower is treated as having received on such date, cash in an amount equal to the excess of (a) the amount loaned over (b) the present value of all payments which are required to be made under the terms of the loan. The provisions do not apply in the case of a gift loan between individuals (a husband and wife are treated as one person) that at no time exceeds $10,000 in the aggregate amount outstanding on *all* loans, whether below-market or not. The $10,000 de minimis exception does not apply, however, to loans attributable to acquisition of income-producing assets.

IRC Section 7872 does not apply to life insurance policy loans.[3] Neither does IRC Section 7872 apply to loans to a charitable organization if at no time during the taxable year the aggregate outstanding amount of loans by the lender to that organization does not exceed $250,000.[4]

The Tax Court has held that IRC Section 483 and safe harbor interest rates contained therein do not apply for gift tax purposes. Consequently, the value of a promissory note given in exchange for real property was discounted to reflect time value of money concepts under IRC Section 7282 (without benefit of IRC Section 483).[5]

1. IRC Sec. 1274(d).
2. See Prop. Treas. Reg. §1.7872-14.
3. Prop. Treas. Reg. §1.7872-5(b)(4).
4. Temp. Treas. Reg. §1.7872-5T(b)(9).
5. *Frazee v. Comm.*, 98 TC 554 (1992).

Prior to enactment of IRC Section 7872, the Supreme Court held that, in the case of an interest-free demand loan made within a family, a gift subject to federal gift tax is made of the value of the use of the money lent.[1] The court did not decide how to value such a gift, but implicit in the decision was the assumption that low-interest or interest-free loans within a family context have, since the first federal gift tax statute was enacted in 1924, resulted in gifts. Rev. Proc. 85-46[2] provided guidance in valuing and reporting gift demand loans not covered by IRC Section 7872.

FORGIVENESS OF DEBT

1522. If an individual transfers property or an interest in property to children or grandchildren or to an irrevocable trust for same, and takes back noninterest-bearing term notes covering the value of the property transferred, which notes the transferor intends to forgive as they come due, what are the gift implications?

If the transferor's receipt of the noninterest-bearing notes is characterized as a "term gift loan," the lender/transferor will be treated as having transferred on the date of the receipt, and the borrower/transferee will be treated as having received on such date, cash in an amount equal to the excess of (a) the amount loaned over (b) the present value of all payments required to be made under the terms of the loan (see Q 1518).[3] If the receipt of the notes is not so characterized, then the discussion in the following paragraph, relating to transactions occurring before June 7, 1984, is pertinent.

The IRS takes the position that such a transfer is a gift of the entire value of the property or interest given at the time of the transfer and is not a sale. If the transfer is of a remainder interest in property, it is a future interest gift that does not qualify for the gift tax annual exclusion (see Q 1530). The Service distinguishes between an intent to forgive the notes and donative intent (see Q 1518) with respect to transfer of the property: "A finding of an intent to forgive the note relates to whether the transaction was in reality a bona fide sale or a disguised gift."[4] The Tax Court, however, makes a distinction based on the nature of the notes given, holding that if the notes are secured by valid vendor's liens, the transaction is to be treated as a sale; a gift occurs on each date a note is due and forgiven, the value of the gift being the amount due on the note.[5]

INCOME TAX EXEMPT OBLIGATIONS

1523. Are gratuitous transfers by individuals of federal, state, and municipal obligations subject to federal transfer taxation?

Yes. It is provided by statute that gratuitous transfers of obligations that are exempt from federal income tax are not exempt from federal estate tax, gift tax, or generation-skipping transfer tax, as the case may be, at least as to estates of decedents dying, gifts made, and transfers made on or after June 19, 1984. In the case of any provision of law enacted after July 18, 1984, such provision is not treated as exempting the transfer of

---

1. *Dickman v. Comm.*, 104 S. Ct. 1086 (1984).
2. 1985-2 CB 507.
3. IRC Secs. 7872(b)(1), 7872(d)(2).
4. Rev. Rul. 77-299, 1977-2 CB 343; *Deal*, 29 TC 730 (1958).
5. *Haygood v. Comm.*, 42 TC 936 (1964), nonacq. 1977-2 CB 2; *Est. of Kelley v. Comm.*, 63 TC 321 (1974), nonacq. 1977-2 CB 2.

property from such transfer taxes unless it refers to the appropriate IRC provisions.[1] Also, the removal of transfer tax exemption applies in the case of any transfer of property (or interest in property) if at any time there was filed an estate or gift tax return showing such transfer as subject to federal estate or gift tax.[2] Congress also added that no inference was to be drawn that transfers of such obligations occurring before such time were exempt from transfer taxation.

In *U.S. v. Wells Fargo*,[3] the United States Supreme Court determined that "tax-exempt" bonds have always been subject to transfer taxes unless specifically provided otherwise by statute (even before enactment of TRA '84, Sec. 641). This determination was based on the longstanding principle that tax exemption cannot be inferred. The differing language concerning project notes issued pursuant to Housing Acts, providing at one time for exemption from all taxation and at another for exemption from all taxation except surtax, estate, inheritance, and gift taxes, could be explained by the need to address a surtax in 1937, and not by a Congressional intent to exempt the project notes from estate taxation, the court concluded. The project notes were not exempt from transfer taxes, the court ruled, and included the notes in the decedent's estate.

JOINT OWNERSHIP

1524. What are the federal gift tax implications of taking title to investment property in joint names?

There may be a gift for federal gift tax purposes either at the time title is taken in joint names or at a later time when one of the joint owners reduces some or all of the property to his own possession. Consider the following examples:

"If A creates a joint bank account for himself and B (or a similar type of ownership by which A can regain the entire fund without B's consent), there is a gift to B when B draws upon the account for his own benefit, to the extent of the amount drawn without any obligation to account for a part of the proceeds to A. Similarly, if A purchases a United States savings bond, registered as payable to 'A or B,' there is a gift to B when B surrenders the bond for cash without any obligation to account for a part of the proceeds to A."[4] Likewise, "where A, with his separate funds, creates a joint brokerage account for himself and B, and the securities purchased on behalf of the account are registered in the name of a nominee of the firm, A has not made a gift to B, for federal gift tax purposes, unless and until B draws upon the account for his own benefit without any obligation to account to A. If B makes a withdrawal under such circumstances, the value of the gift by A would be the sum of money or the value of the property actually withdrawn from the account by B."[5]

"If A with his own funds purchases property and has the title conveyed to himself and B as joint owners, with rights of survivorship (other than a joint ownership described in [the foregoing paragraph]) but which rights may be defeated by either party severing his interest, there is a gift to B in the amount of half the value of the property."[6]

---

1. TRA '84, Sec. 641.
2. TRA '84, Sec. 641(b)(2).
3. 88-1 USTC ¶13,759 (U.S. 1988).
4. Treas. Reg. §25.2511-1(h)(4).
5. Rev. Rul. 69-148, 1969-1 CB 226.
6. Treas. Reg. §25.2511-1(h)(5).

Where A purchases and registers U.S. Treasury notes in the names of A or B or survivor, in a jurisdiction in which this registration creates a joint tenancy, there is a completed gift of the survivorship rights in the notes and an undivided one-half interest in the interest payments and redemption rights pertaining to the notes; in a jurisdiction in which a joint tenancy is not created by such registration, there is a gift of the survivorship rights in the interest payments and in the notes at maturity.[1] Computation of the value of the gifts in both situations is set forth in Rev. Rul. 78-215.

In the above examples, if A and B are husband and wife, any gift will be offset by the marital deduction to the extent available (see Q 1531).[2]

NET GIFTS

1525. What are the federal gift tax results if the donee agrees to pay the gift tax?

If a gift is made subject to the express or implied condition that the donee pay the gift tax, the donor may deduct the amount of tax from the gift in determining the value of the gift. In such a transaction, the donor receives consideration for the transfer in the amount of the gift tax paid by the donee; thus, to the extent of the tax paid, the donee does not receive a gift.[3] Similarly, if the donor makes a gift in trust subject to an agreement that the trustee pay the gift tax, the value of the property transferred is reduced for gift tax purposes by the amount of the tax.[4]

The computation of the tax requires the use of an algebraic formula, since the amount of the tax is dependent on the value of the gift which in turn is dependent on the amount of the tax. The formula is

$$\frac{\text{Tentative Tax}}{1 \text{ plus Rate of Tax}} = \text{True Tax}.$$

Examples illustrating the use of this formula, with the algebraic method, to determine the tax in a net gift situation are contained in IRS Publication 904 (Rev. May 1985). Three of the examples show the effect of a state gift tax upon the computation.

Although the donee pays the tax, it is the *donor's* unified credit that is used in computing the gift tax, not the donee's.[5]

UNIFORM GIFTS TO MINORS ACT

1526. How is a gift of property under the Uniform Gifts to Minors Act or under the Uniform Transfers to Minors Act treated for federal gift tax purposes?

Any transfer of property to a minor under either Uniform Act constitutes a complete gift for federal gift tax purposes to the extent of the full fair market value of the

---

1. Rev. Rul. 78-215, 1978-1 CB 298.
2. Treas. Reg. §25.2523(d)-1.
3. Rev. Rul. 75-72, 1975-1 CB 310; *Diedrich v. Comm.*, 102 S. Ct. 2414 (1982).
4. *Lingo*, 13 TCM 436 (1959); *Harrison*, 17 TC 1350 (1952), acq. 1952-2 CB 2.
5. Let. Rul. 7842068.

property transferred. Generally, such a gift qualifies for the gift tax annual exclusion (see Q 1530).[1] The allowance of the exclusion is not affected by the amendment of a state's Uniform Act lowering the age of majority and thus requiring that property be distributed to the donee at age 18.[2] These rulings base the allowance of the exclusion on the assumption that gifts under the Uniform Act come within the purview of IRC Section 2503(c). Gifts to minors under IRC Section 2503(c) must pass to the donee on his attaining age 21. If a state statute varies from the Uniform Act by providing that under certain conditions custodianship may be extended past the donee's age 21, gifts made under those conditions would not qualify for the exclusion. For tables of state laws concerning the Uniform Acts, see Appendix D.

EDUCATION SAVINGS ACCOUNT

1527. When is a gift made with respect to an education savings account?

Contributions to an education savings account are treated as completed gifts to the beneficiary of a present interest in property which can qualify for the gift tax and generation-skipping transfer (GST) tax annual exclusion. If contributions for a year exceed the gift tax annual exclusion, the donor can elect to prorate the gifts over a five year period beginning with such year. A contribution to an education savings account does not qualify for the gift tax or GST tax exclusion for qualified transfers for educational purposes.[3] Distributions from an education savings account are not treated as taxable gifts. Also, if the designated beneficiary of the education savings account is changed, or if funds in education savings account are rolled over to a new beneficiary, such a transfer is subject to the gift tax or GST tax only if the new beneficiary is a generation below the old beneficiary. Transfers within the same generation do not trigger a gift tax liability.[4]

See Q 1503 for the estate tax treatment and Q 1412 for the income tax treatment of education savings accounts.

QUALIFIED TUITION PROGRAM

1528. When is a gift made with respect to a qualified tuition program?

For gift tax and generation-skipping transfer (GST) tax purposes, a contribution to a qualified tuition program on behalf of a designated beneficiary is not treated as a qualified transfer for purposes of the gift tax and GST tax exclusion for educational expenses, but is treated as a completed gift of a present interest to the beneficiary which qualifies for the annual exclusion (see Q 1530). If a donor makes contributions to a qualified tuition program in excess of the gift tax annual exclusion, the donor may elect to take the donation into account ratably over a five-year period.[5] Distributions from a qualified tuition program are not treated as taxable gifts. Also, if the designated beneficiary of a qualified tuition program is changed, or if funds in a qualified tuition

1. Rev. Rul. 56-86, 1956-1 CB 449; Rev. Rul. 59-357, 1959-2 CB 212.
2. Rev. Rul. 73-287, 1973-2 CB 321.
3. IRC Secs. 530(d)(3), 529(c)(2).
4. IRC Secs. 530(d)(3), 529(c)(5).
5. IRC Sec. 529(c)(2).

program are rolled over to the account of a new beneficiary, such a transfer is subject to the gift tax or generation-skipping transfer tax only if the new beneficiary is a generation below the old beneficiary.[1]

See Q 1504 for the estate tax treatment and Q 1413 for the income tax treatment of qualified tuition programs.

SPLIT GIFTS

1529. When is the "split-gift" provision available?

When a husband or wife makes a gift to a *third* person, it may be treated as having been made one-half by each if the other spouse consents to the gift.[2]

Planning Point: The split-gift provision enables a spouse who owns most of the property to take advantage of the other spouse's annual exclusions (see Q 1530) and unified credit (see Q 1533). Thus, a spouse, with the other spouse's consent, can give up to $24,000 (2 × $12,000 annual exclusion in 2007, see Appendix B) a year to each donee free of gift tax, and, in addition, will have both their unified credits to apply against gift tax imposed on gifts in excess of the annual exclusion. Moreover, by splitting the gifts between husband and wife, they will fall in lower gift tax brackets.

Where spouses elect to use the "split-gift" provision, the consent applies to all gifts made by either spouse to third persons during the calendar year.[3] A technical advice memorandum permitted a taxpayer to elect after his spouse's death to split gifts with his spouse where the gifts were made by the taxpayer shortly before the spouse's death.[4]

EXCLUSIONS

1530. What gift tax exclusions are available to a donor?

The Annual Exclusion

The gift tax annual exclusion is an exclusion of $10,000 as indexed ($12,000 in 2007, see Appendix B) per calendar year per donee applied to gifts of a present interest in property. The $10,000 amount is adjusted for inflation, rounded down to the next lowest multiple of $1,000, after 1998.[5] The exclusion is not cumulative; that is, an exclusion unused in one year cannot be carried over and used in a future year. A gift of a present interest is one in which the donee has the right to immediate possession, use, and enjoyment of the property.

The exclusion does not apply to gifts of a future interest in property, i.e., the right to use and enjoy the property only in the future. For example, if G transfers income producing property in trust, the terms of which provide that the income from the trust property will be paid to A for his lifetime and upon A's death the trust property will be paid to B free of trust, A's life income interest would be a present interest gift and B's remainder interest would be a future interest gift. G would be allowed to exclude from

---

1. IRC Sec. 529(d)(5)(B).
2. IRC Sec. 2513; Treas. Reg. §25.2513-1.
3. IRC Sec. 2513(a)(2).
4. TAM 9404023.
5. IRC Sec. 2503(b).

the value of gifts reported on his gift tax return the value of A's life income interest up to $12,000 (in 2006, assuming G made no other present interest gifts to A during the calendar year), but he would not be able to exclude any of the value of B's remainder interest. If the trustee were given discretion to withhold payments of income to A and add such amounts to the trust corpus, A's income interest would not be a present interest, and G would not be allowed to claim any exclusion.

A gift of property to a trust which directs the trustee to distribute the trust income annually to the beneficiary is a present interest gift of an income interest qualifying for the annual exclusion. However, a gift of property to a trust which directs the trustee to distribute from the trust annually a certain dollar amount to the beneficiary is a gift of a future interest not qualifying for the exclusion.[1]

A gift of property in trust will qualify for the gift tax annual exclusion if the trust terms (1) provide that the trust beneficiary (or beneficiaries) be given timely written notice (notice given within 10 days after the transfer has been held timely) that the beneficiary has a reasonable period (45 days has been held reasonable) within which to demand immediate withdrawal (usually the trust specifies that the withdrawal right is limited to the amount of the exclusion), and (2) give the trustee the power to convert property in the trust to cash to the extent necessary to meet withdrawal demands. Such trusts are popularly known as Crummey trusts, after the name of a leading case that upheld them.[2]

The IRS has ruled with respect to Crummey trusts that the annual exclusion could not be applied to trust contributions on behalf of trust beneficiaries who had withdrawal rights as to the contributions (except to the extent they exercised their withdrawal rights) but who had either no other interest in the trust (a naked power) or only remote contingent interests in the remainder.[3] However, the Tax Court has rejected the IRS's argument that a power holder must hold rights other than the withdrawal right to obtain the annual exclusion. The withdrawal right (assuming there is no agreement to not exercise the right) is sufficient to obtain the annual exclusion.[4] (Language in *Cristofani* appears to support use of naked powers although case did not involve naked powers). In an Action On Decision, the Service stated that, applying the substance over form doctrine, the annual exclusions should not be allowed where the withdrawal rights are not in substance what they purport to be in form. If the facts and circumstances show an understanding that the power is not meant to be exercised or that exercise would result in undesirable consequences, then creation of the withdrawal right is not a bona fide gift of a present interest and an annual exclusion should not be allowed.[5] In TAM 9628004, annual exclusions were not allowed where transfers to trust were made so late in the first year that *Crummey* withdrawal powerholders had no opportunity to exercise their rights, most powerholders had either no other interest in the trust or discretionary income or remote contingent remainder interests, and withdrawal powers were never exercised in any year. However, annual exclusions were allowed where the IRS was unable to prove that there was an understanding between the donor and the beneficiaries

---

1. *Est. of Kolker v. Comm.*, 80 TC 1082 (1983).
2. *Crummey v. Comm.*, 397 F.2d 82 (9th Cir. 1968); Rev. Rul. 73-405, 1973-2 CB 321; Rev. Rul. 81-7, 1981-1 CB 474; Rev. Rul. 83-108, 1983-2 CB 167; Let. Ruls. 8022048, 8134135, 8118051, 8134135, 8445004, 9625031.
3. TAMs 9141008, 9045002, 8727003.
4. *Est. of Cristofani v. Comm.*, 97 TC 74 (1991), acq. in result, 1996-2 CB 1.
5. AOD 1996-010.

that the withdrawal rights should not be exercised.[1] In TAM 9731004, annual exclusions were denied where eight trusts were created for eight primary beneficiaries, but *Crummey* withdrawal powers were given to 16 or 17 persons who never exercised their powers and most powerholders held either a remote contingent interest or no interest other than the withdrawal power in the trusts in which the powerholder was not the primary beneficiary.

The annual exclusion was not allowed where the beneficiaries waived their right to receive notice of contributions to trust with respect to which their withdrawal rights could be exercised. Furthermore, the annual exclusion was not allowed because the grantor set up a trust which provided that notice was to be given to the trustee as to whether a beneficiary could exercise a withdrawal power with respect to a transfer to trust and the grantor never notified the trustee that the withdrawal powers could be exercised with respect to any of the transfers to trust.[2]

Substance over form analysis may be applied to deny annual exclusions where indirect transfers are used in an attempt to obtain inappropriate annual exclusions for gifts to intermediate recipients.[3] For example, suppose A transfers $12,000 to each of B, C, and D in 2007. By arrangement, B, C, and D each immediately transfer $12,000 to E. The annual exclusion for A's indirect transfers to E is limited to $12,000 and A has made taxable gifts of $24,000 to E.

An outright gift of a bond, note (though bearing no interest until maturity), or other obligation which is to be discharged by payments in the future is a gift of a present interest.[4] Normally, a direct gift of shares of corporate stock is a present interest gift. However, if the gift is made subject to a stock transfer restriction agreement under which the donee is prohibited for a period of time from selling or pledging the stock, it has been held that the gift is one of a future interest which does not qualify for the gift tax annual exclusion.[5]

It has been held that the gift of a portion of the donor's interest in real property, if under the terms of the transfer the donee receives the present unrestricted right to the immediate use, possession, and enjoyment of an ascertainable interest in the property, qualifies for the gift tax annual exclusion.[6]

If a donor transfers a specified portion of real property subject to an "adjustment clause" (i.e., under terms that provide that if the IRS subsequently determines that the value of the specified portion exceeds the amount of the annual exclusion, the portion of property given will be reduced accordingly, or the donee will compensate the donor for the excess), the adjustment clause will be disregarded for federal tax purposes.[7]

A gift of property to a minor, whether in trust or otherwise, is not considered a gift of a future interest in property if the terms of the transfer satisfy all the following conditions:

---

1. *Est. of Kohlsaat v. Comm.*, TC Memo 1997-212; *Est. of Holland v. Comm.*, TC Memo 1997-302.
2. TAM 9532001.
3. *Heyen v. U.S.*, 91-2 USTC ¶60,085 (10th Cir. 1991).
4. Treas. Reg. §25.2503-3.
5. Rev. Rul. 76-360, 1976-2 CB 298.
6. Rev. Rul. 83-180, 1983-2 CB 169.
7. Rev. Rul. 86-41, 1986-1 CB 300.

(1) Both the property itself and its income may be expended by or for the benefit of the donee before he attains the age of 21 years;

(2) Any portion of the property and its income not disposed of under (1) will pass to the donee when he attains the age of 21 years; and

(3) Any portion of the property and its income not disposed of under (1) will be payable either to the estate of the donee or as he may appoint under a general power of appointment if he dies before attaining the age of 21 years.[1]

A gift to a minor under the Uniform Gifts to Minors Act or under the Uniform Transfers to Minors Act generally is a gift of a present interest and qualifies for the annual exclusion.[2] Most states in recent years have adopted the later Uniform Transfers to Minors Act, which allows for any kind of property, real or personal, tangible or intangible, to be transferred under the Act. Other states have amended their Uniform Gifts to Minors Act to provide for gifts of various kinds of property ranging from real estate to partnership interests and other tangible and intangible interests in property. Originally, the Uniform Act provided for gifts of only money or securities. The allowance of the exclusion is not affected by the amendment of a state's Uniform Act lowering the age of majority and thus requiring that property be distributed to the donee at age 18.[3] The revenue rulings cited in this paragraph base the allowance of the exclusion on the assumption that gifts under the Uniform Act come within the purview of IRC Section 2503(c). Gifts to minors under IRC Section 2503(c) must pass to the donee on his attaining age 21. If a state statute varies from the Uniform Act by providing that under certain conditions custodianship may be extended past the donee's age 21, gifts made under those conditions would not qualify for the exclusion. For a state-by-state summary of the types of property which can be given under, and the adult age for purposes of, the Uniform Act, see Appendix D.

A gift of property to a corporation generally represents a gift of a future interest in the property to the individual shareholders to the extent of their proportionate interests in the corporation.[4] Also a gift for the benefit of a corporation is a gift of a future interest in the property to its shareholders and does not qualify for the annual exclusion.[5] However, gifts made to individual partnership capital accounts have been treated as gifts of a present interest which qualify for the annual exclusion where the partners were free to make immediate withdrawals of the gifts from their capital accounts.[6] However, annual exclusions were denied for gifts of limited partnership interests where (1) the general partner could retain income for any reason whatsoever, (2) limited partnership interests could not be transferred or assigned without the permission of a supermajority of other partners, and (3) limited partnership interests generally could not withdraw from the partnership or receive a return of capital contributions for many years into the future.[7] Similarly, annual exclusions were denied for gifts of business interests where the beneficiaries were not free to withdraw from the business entity, could not sell their

---

1. IRC Sec. 2503(c); Treas. Reg. §25.2503-4(a).
2. Rev. Rul. 59-357, 1959-2 CB 212; Rev. Rul. 73-287, 1973-2 CB 321.
3. Rev. Rul. 73-287, 1973-2 CB 321.
4. Treas. Reg. §25.2511-1(h)(1); Rev. Rul. 71-443, 1971-2 CB 337; *Stinson v. U.S.*, 2000-1 USTC ¶60,377 (7th Cir. 2000); *Hollingsworth v. Comm.*, 86 TC 91 (1986).
5. Let. Rul. 9114023.
6. *Wooley v. U.S.*, 90-1 USTC ¶60,013 (S.D. Ind. 1990).
7. TAM 9751003.

interests, and could not control whether any income would be distributed (and no immediate income was expected).[1]

A donor's gratuitous payment of the monthly amount due on the mortgage on a house owned in joint tenancy by others has been held a present interest gift to the joint tenants in proportion to their ownership interests.[2]

By means of the "split gift" provision (see Q 1529), a married couple can effectively use each other's annual exclusions. Thus, if, in 2007, A makes a $24,000 gift of securities to his child, C, and A's wife, B, joins in making the gift (by signifying her consent on the gift tax return), the gift would be considered as having been made one-half by each, the exclusion is effectively doubled, and no gift tax would have to be paid (assuming neither A nor B made any other gifts to C during the calendar year).[3] However, say A and B join in making the same gift to F, child of A's brother D and wife E, while at the same time D and E make similar gifts to C and F, the scheme does not effectively again double the exclusion.[4]

If the spouse of the donor is not a United States citizen, the annual exclusion for a transfer from the donor spouse to the non-citizen spouse is increased from $10,000 (as indexed) to $100,000 as indexed ($125,000 in 2007, see Appendix B) (provided the transfer would otherwise qualify for the marital deduction if the donee spouse were a United States citizen). The $100,000 amount is adjusted for inflation, as is the $10,000 amount (see above).[5] However, the marital deduction is not available for a transfer to a spouse who is not a United States citizen (see Q 1531).

Exclusion for "Qualified Transfers"

A "qualified transfer" is not considered a gift for gift tax purposes. A "qualified transfer" means any amount paid on behalf of an individual–

(A) as tuition to an educational organization[6] for the education or training of such individual, or

(B) to any person who provides medical care[7] with respect to such individual as payment for such medical care.[8] A technical advice memorandum treated tuition payments for future years as qualified transfers where the payments were nonrefundable.[9]

DEDUCTIONS

1531. What is the gift tax marital deduction?

It is a deduction for the entire value of gifts made between spouses.[10] The deduction does not apply, however, to a gift of a "nondeductible terminable interest" in property.[11]

---

1. *Hackl v. Comm.*, 2003-2 USTC ¶60,465 (7th Cir. 2003), aff'g 118 TC 279 (2002).
2. Rev. Rul. 82-98, 1982-1 CB 141.
3. IRC Sec. 2513; Treas. Reg. §25.2513-1.
4. TAM 8717003; *Sather v. Comm.*, 2001-1 USTC ¶60,409 (8th Cir. 2001); *Schuler v. Comm.*, 2002-1 USTC ¶60,432 (8th Cir. 2002).
5. IRC Sec. 2523(i).
6. Described in IRC Section 170(b)(1)(A)(ii).
7. As defined in IRC Section 213(d).
8. IRC Sec. 2503(e); Rev. Rul. 82-98, 1982-1 CB 141.
9. Let. Rul. 299602002; TAM 199941013.
10. IRC Sec. 2523(a).
11. IRC Sec. 2523(b); Treas. Regs. §§25.2523(a)-1(b)(2), 25.2523(b)-1.

A "terminable interest" in property is an interest which will terminate or fail on the lapse of time or on the occurrence or failure to occur of some contingency. Life estates, terms for years, annuities, patents, and copyrights are therefore terminable interests. However, a bond, note, or similar contractual obligation, the discharge of which would not have the effect of an annuity or term for years, is not a terminable interest.[1]

In general, if a donor transfers a terminable interest in property to the donee spouse, the marital deduction is disallowed with respect to the transfer if the donor spouse also (1) transferred an interest in the same property to another donee, *or* (2) retained an interest in the same property in himself, *or* (3) retained a power to appoint an interest in the same property, *and* (4) gave the other donee, himself, or the possible appointee the right to possess or enjoy any part of the property after the termination or failure of the interest transferred to the donee spouse.[2] *However*, a terminable interest in property qualifies for the marital deduction if the donee spouse is given (1) a right to the income from the property for life and a general power of appointment over the principal; or (2) a "qualifying income interest for life" in property transferred by the donor spouse as to which the donor must make an election (on or before the date, including extensions, for filing a gift tax return with respect to the year in which the transfer was made–see Q 1534) to have the marital deduction apply. The donee spouse has a "qualifying income interest for life" if (1) the donee spouse is entitled to all the income from the property, payable annually or at more frequent intervals, and (2) no person has a power to appoint any part of the property to any person other than the donee spouse during the donee spouse's lifetime.[3] Also, the interest of a donee spouse in a joint and survivor annuity in which only the donor and donee spouses have a right to receive payments during such spouses' joint lifetimes is treated as a "qualifying income interest for life" unless the donor spouse irrevocably elects otherwise within the time allowed for filing a gift tax return.[4] In the two exceptions to the nondeductible terminable interest rule explained above, income producing property is contemplated. If a gift of nonincome producing property in a form to comply with either of the two exceptions is proposed, Treasury Regulation Section 25.2523(e)-1(f) should be read carefully. A marital deduction has been disallowed for a transfer to an irrevocable trust where state law provided that the interest given the spouse would be revoked upon divorce and the grantor had not provided in the trust instrument that the trust would not be revoked upon divorce.[5]

If the spouse of the donor is not a United States citizen, the marital deduction is not available for a transfer to such a spouse. However, in such a case, the annual exclusion (see Q 1530) for the transfer from the donor spouse to the non-citizen spouse is increased from $10,000 (as indexed) to $100,000 as indexed ($125,000 in 2007, see Appendix B) (provided the transfer would otherwise qualify for the marital deduction if the donee spouse were a United States citizen). The $100,000 amount is adjusted for inflation, as is the $10,000 amount (see Q 1530).[6]

1532. Is a gift tax deduction allowed for gifts to charity?

Yes. In general, a deduction is allowed for the entire value of gifts to qualified charitable organizations.[7]

---

1. Treas. Reg. §25.2523(b)-1(a)(3).
2. Treas. Reg. §25.2523(b)-1(a)(2).
3. IRC Secs. 2523(e), 2523(f).
4. IRC Sec. 2523(f)(6).
5. TAM 9127005.
6. IRC Sec. 2523(i).
7. IRC Secs. 2522(a), 2522(b).

Where a donor makes a gift of an interest in property (other than a remainder interest in a personal residence or farm or an undivided portion of the donor's entire interest in property or certain gifts of property interests exclusively for conservation purposes) to a qualified charity, and an interest in the same property is retained by the donor or is given to a donee not a charity, no charitable deduction is allowed for the interest given the charity unless—

(1) in the case of a remainder interest, such interest is in a trust which is a *charitable remainder annuity trust* (see Q 1330) or a *charitable remainder unitrust* (see Q 1331) or a pooled income fund (see Q 1332), or

(2) in the case of any other interest (such as an interest in the income from a short term trust), such interest is in the form of a guaranteed annuity or is a fixed percentage distributed yearly of the fair market value of the property (to be determined yearly).[1]

A charitable contribution deduction is allowable for a gift to charity of a legal remainder interest in the donor's personal residence even though the interest conveyed to charity is in the form of a tenancy in common with an individual.[2]

If an individual creates a qualified charitable remainder trust in which his spouse is the only non-charitable beneficiary other than certain ESOP remainder beneficiaries, the grantor will receive a charitable contributions deduction for the value of the remainder interest.[3]

UNIFIED CREDIT

1533. What is the gift tax unified credit?

It is a dollar amount ($345,800 in 2007) that is credited against the gift tax computed as shown in Q 1517 (see Appendix B for amounts in other years).[4] (For application of the unified credit to the federal estate tax, see Q 1507.)

The amount of unified credit allowed against the tax on gifts made in any calendar year cannot exceed the dollar amount of credit applicable to the period in which the gifts were made, reduced by the sum of the amounts of unified credit allowed the donor against gifts made in all prior calendar periods, and reduced further by the rule explained in the next paragraph (but in no event can the allowable credit exceed the amount of the tax).

The unified credit was enacted by the Tax Reform Act of 1976. Under prior law, separate exemptions were provided for estate and gift taxes. The gift tax specific exemption was $30,000 for each donor (or $60,000 if the donor's spouse joined in making the gift). The exemption was not applied automatically, as in the case of the unified credit, but had to be elected by the donor, and once used was gone. The law provides that as to gifts made after September 8, 1976, and before January 1, 1977, if the donor elected to apply any of his lifetime exemption to such gifts, his unified credit is reduced by

---

1. IRC Sec. 2522(c); Rev. Rul. 77-275, 1977-2 CB 346.
2. Rev. Rul. 87-37, 1987-1 CB 295, revoking Rev. Rul. 76-544, 1976-2 CB 288.
3. IRC Sec. 2522(c)(2).
4. IRC Sec. 2505, as amended by EGTRRA 2001.

an amount equal to 20% of the amount allowed as a specific exemption.[1] (The unified credit is not reduced by any amount allowed as a specific exemption for gifts made prior to September 9, 1976.)

By means of the "split gift" provision (see Q 1529), a married couple can effectively use each other's unified credit.

FILING AND PAYMENT

1534. What are the requirements for filing the gift tax return and paying the tax?

A donor need not file a gift tax return if the only gifts he makes during the calendar year are covered by the annual exclusion (Q 1530) or the marital deduction (Q 1531), or are gifts to charity of the donor's entire interest in the property transferred where the donor does not (and has not) transferred any interest in the property to a noncharitable beneficiary. (Amounts paid on behalf of an individual as tuition to an educational organization or to a person providing medical care for him are not considered gifts for gift tax purposes.[2] However, in the case of a split gift (where the donor's spouse joins in making a gift to a third party), a gift tax return must be filed even though the amount of the gift comes within the spouses' annual exclusions.

The return (Form 709) is due on or before April 15 following close of the calendar year for which the return is made; however, if the donor is given an extension of time for filing his income tax return, the same extension applies to filing the gift tax return. Where a gift is made during the calendar year in which the donor dies, the time for filing the gift tax return is not later than the time (including extensions) for filing the estate tax return.[3] However, should the time for filing the estate tax return fall later than the 15th day of April following the close of the calendar year, the time for filing the gift tax return is on or before the 15th day of April following the close of the calendar year, unless an extension (not extending beyond the time for filing the estate tax return) was granted for filing the gift tax return. If no estate tax return is required to be filed, the time for filing the gift tax return is on or before the 15th day of April following the close of the calendar year, unless an extension was given for filing the gift tax return.[4]

The penalty for failure to file timely a federal tax return is 5% of the tax for each month the return is past due, up to a maximum of 25%. The penalty can be avoided only if "it is shown that such failure is due to reasonable cause and not due to willful neglect."[5] The regulations say that "reasonable cause" means that the taxpayer filing a late return must show that he "exercised ordinary business care and prudence and was nevertheless unable to file the return within the prescribed time."[6] In *U.S. v. Boyle*,[7] the Supreme Court held that a taxpayer's reliance on an agent who says he will file the appropriate tax return does not avoid the penalty tax for failure to make a timely filing. However, the court was careful to distinguish the case where the taxpayer relies on his tax advisor to determine whether a return should be filed at all. In *Est. of Buring v.*

1. IRC Sec. 2505(c).
2. IRC Sec. 2503(e).) IRC Sec. 6019.
3. IRC Sec. 6075.
4. IRC Sec. 6075; Treas. Reg. §25.6075-1(b)(2).
5. IRC Sec. 6651(a)(1).
6. Treas. Reg. §301.6651-1(c)(1).
7. 105 S. Ct. 687 (1985).

Comm.,[1] the estate avoided the penalty tax because the court found that the decedent had relied upon her accountant's advice in failing to file gift tax returns for substantial advances of cash the decedent made to her son, even though the accountant apparently had not actually advised her that it was not necessary to file gift tax returns.

The gift tax is payable by the donor on the date the gift tax return is due to be filed (April 15). An extension of time given to file the return does not act as an extension of time to pay the tax.[2] If the donor does not pay the tax when it is due, the donee is liable for the tax to the extent of the value of the gift.[3] If an extension of time for payment of the tax is granted, interest compounded daily is charged at an annual rate adjusted quarterly so as to be three percentage points over the short term federal rate.[4] The underpayment rate for the last quarter of 2006 is 8%.[5]

VALUATION

GENERAL

1535. Starting Point – How is investment property valued for federal transfer tax purposes?

"Fair market value" is the measure, defined as "the price at which the property would change hands between a willing buyer and a willing seller, neither being under any compulsion to buy or to sell and both having reasonable knowledge of relevant facts." In the case of the estate tax, fair market value is determined as of the date of the decedent's death, except that if the executor elects the alternate valuation method, fair market value is determined in accordance with the rules explained at Q 1536. In the case of the gift tax, fair market value is determined as of the date of the gift. Property is not to be valued at the value at which it is assessed for local tax purposes unless that value represents the fair market value as of the applicable valuation date. All relevant facts and elements of value as of the applicable valuation date are to be considered in every case.[6]

In the case of any taxable gift which is a direct skip within the meaning of the generation-skipping transfer tax (GST tax) (see Q 1510 et seq.), the amount of such gift is increased by the amount of the GST tax imposed on the transfer.[7] See Q 1511 for special GST tax valuation rules.

Special rules apply to the valuation of particular kinds of investment property, such as stocks and bonds (Q 1537), notes (Q 1539), mutual fund shares (Q 1542), certain kinds of business interests (Q 1544). See Q 1546 on the valuation of real estate. The principle of blockage discounting, applied in the valuation of a sizeable block of shares of corporate stock (see Q 1537), can also be applied in valuing art work.[8] Special rules also apply where, under certain conditions spelled out in IRC Section 2032A, an executor

---

1. TC Memo 1985-610.
2. IRC Secs. 2502(c), 6151(a).
3. IRC Sec. 6324(b); *Comm. v. Chase Manhattan Bank*, 259 F.2d 231 (5th Cir. 1958).
4. IRC Secs. 6601(a), 6621(a)(2).
5. Rev. Rul. 2006-49, 2006-40 IRB 584.
6. Treas. Regs. §§20.2031-1(b), 25.2512-1.
7. IRC Sec. 2515.
8. *Calder v. Comm.*, 85 TC 713 (1985).

may elect to value, for federal estate tax purposes, real property (called "qualified real property") devoted to farming or other trade or business (called "qualified use") by the decedent or a member of the decedent's family on the date of the decedent's death, on the basis of its actual use rather than by taking into account the "highest and best" use to which the property could be put. See also Q 1316.

Property includable in a surviving spouse's estate as qualified terminable interest property (see Q 1506) under IRC Section 2044 (see Q 1501) is not aggregated with other property includable in the estate for estate tax valuation purposes.[1] However, property included in the gross estate because of a general power of appointment under IRC Section 2041 (see Q 1501) should be aggregated with property owned outright by the powerholder for estate tax valuation purposes.[2]

With respect to gift and estate tax returns, 20% of an underpayment attributable to a substantial gift or estate tax valuation understatement is added to tax. There is a substantial gift or estate tax valuation understatement if (1) the value claimed was 50% or less of the correct amount, and (2) the underpayment exceeds $5,000. If the value claimed was 25% or less of the correct amount (and the underpayment exceeds $5,000), 40% of an underpayment attributable to such a gross gift or estate tax valuation understatement is added to tax.[3] The 20% or 40% penalty is not imposed with respect to any portion of the underpayment for which it is shown that there was reasonable cause and the taxpayer acted in good faith.[4]

A gift which is disclosed on a gift tax return in a manner adequate to apprise the Service of the nature of the item may not be revalued after the statute of limitations (generally, three years after the return is filed) has expired.[5]

See Q 1549 for Chapter 14 special valuation rules.

1536. How does the executor's election of the alternate valuation method affect the valuation of property for federal estate tax purposes?

The law permits the executor to elect an alternate valuation method if the election will decrease the value of the gross estate and the sum of the amount of the federal estate tax and generation-skipping transfer tax payable by reason of the decedent's death with respect to the property includable in the decedent's gross estate.[6] If the alternate valuation method is elected, the property will be valued under the following rules:

Any property distributed, sold, exchanged or otherwise disposed of within six months after decedent's death is valued as of the date of such distribution, sale, exchange or other disposition. The phrase "distributed, sold, exchanged, or otherwise disposed of" comprehends all possible ways by which property ceases to form a part of the gross estate. For example, money on hand at the date of the decedent's death which is thereafter used in the payment of funeral expenses, or which is thereafter invested, falls within the term "otherwise disposed of." The term also includes the surrender of a

---

1. *Est. of Bonner v. U.S.*, 96-2 USTC ¶60,237 (5th Cir. 1996), rev'g an unpublished decision (S.D. Tex.); *Est. of Mellinger v. Comm.*, 112 TC 26 (1999), acq. AOD 1999-006.
2. FSA 200119013; *Est. of Fontana v. Comm.*, 118 TC 318 (2002).
3. IRC Sec. 6662.
4. IRC Sec. 6664(c)(1).
5. IRC Sec. 6501(c)(9).
6. IRC Sec. 2032; Treas. Reg. §20.2032-1(b)(1).

stock certificate for corporate assets in complete or partial liquidation of a corporation pursuant to IRC Section 331. The term does not, however, extend to transactions which are mere changes in form. Thus, it does not include a transfer of assets to a corporation controlled by the transferor in exchange for its stock in a transaction with respect to which no gain or loss would be recognized for income tax purposes under IRC Section 351. Nor does it include an exchange of stock or securities in a corporation for stock or securities in the same corporation or another corporation in a transaction, such as a merger, recapitalization, reorganization or other transaction described in IRC Section 368(a) or IRC Section 355, with respect to which no gain or loss is recognizable for income tax purposes under IRC Section 354 or IRC Section 355.[1]

In *Est. of Smith v. Comm.*,[2] the decedent's stock in X corporation was exchanged for stock and warrants in Y corporation pursuant to a plan of merger. The court held that the warrants were received in exchange for the estate's stock in X and were to be valued as of the date of the merger. The Commissioner conceded, surprisingly, that the transaction should not be treated as an "exchange" with respect to the receipt of *stock* in Y, and that even though the value of the Y stock had declined substantially between the decedent's date of death and the alternate valuation date, the stock should be valued as of the alternate valuation date. The court's decision, however, was limited to the controverted issue as to the proper valuation date of the warrants. Apparently, the IRS soon changed its mind. In Rev. Rul. 77-221,[3] on substantially similar facts, the Service concluded that the exchange of X stock for Y stock and warrants constitutes an "exchange" and held that the X stock given in exchange was to be valued as of the date of the exchange.

If the property is listed stock and is sold in an arm's length transaction, the stock is valued at the actual selling price.[4] An exercise of stock rights is a "disposition" thereof; their value is equal to the excess, if any, of the fair market value of the stock acquired by such rights at the time the rights are exercised over the subscription price.[5]

Any property not distributed, sold, exchanged or otherwise disposed of within six months after decedent's death is valued as of the date six months after death. When shares of stock in the estate are sold at a discount between the date of death and the alternate valuation date, such sales and the number of shares sold cannot be taken into account in determining whether the shares remaining in the estate at the alternate valuation date are eligible for "blockage" valuation (see Q 1537).[6]

Any property interest whose value is affected by mere lapse of time is valued as of the date of decedent's death. But an adjustment is made for any change in value during the six-month period (or during the period between death and distribution, sale or exchange) which is not due to mere lapse of time.[7] The phrase "affected by mere lapse of time" has no reference to obligations for the payment of money, whether or not interest bearing, the value of which changes with the passage of time.[8]

---

1. Treas. Reg. §20.2032-1(c)(1).
2. 63 TC 722 (1975).
3. 1977-1 CB 271.
4. Rev. Rul. 70-512, 1970-2 CB 192; *Est. of Van Horne v. Comm.*, 83-2 USTC ¶13,548 (9th Cir. 1983), aff'g 78 TC 728 (1982).
5. Rev. Rul. 58-576, 1958-2 CB 256.
6. *Est. of Van Horne v. Comm.*, 83-2 USTC ¶13,548 (9th Cir. 1983), aff'g 78 TC 728 (1982).
7. IRC Sec. 2032(a).
8. Treas. Reg. §20.2032-1(f).

If the alternate valuation method is elected, it must be applied to all the property included in the gross estate, and cannot be applied to only a portion of the property.[1]

The election to value property using the alternate valuation method must be made no later than one year after the due date (including extensions) for filing the estate tax return. The election is irrevocable, unless it is revoked no later than the due date (including extensions) for filing the estate tax return. If use of the alternate valuation method would not result in a decrease in both the value of the gross estate and the amount of estate tax and generation-skipping transfer tax on a filed return, a protective election can be made to use the alternate valuation method if it is later determined that such a decrease would occur. A request for an extension of time to make the election or protective election may be made if the estate tax return was filed no later than one year after the due date (including extensions) for filing the estate tax return but an election or protective election was not made on the return.[2]

Property earned or accrued (whether received or not) after the date of the decedent's death and during the alternate valuation period with respect to property included in the gross estate is excluded in valuing the gross estate under the alternate valuation method, and is referred to as "excluded property."[3]

Thus, as to *interest-bearing obligations* included in the gross estate ("included property"), interest accrued after the date of death and before the subsequent valuation date constitutes "excluded property." However, any part payment of principal made between the date of death and the subsequent valuation date, or any advance payment of interest for a period after the subsequent valuation date made during the alternate valuation period which has the effect of reducing the value of the principal obligation as of the subsequent valuation date, will be included in the gross estate, and valued as of the date of such payment.[4]

The same principles applicable to interest-bearing obligations also apply to *leased realty or personalty* which is included in the gross estate and with respect to which an obligation to pay rent has been reserved. Both the realty or personalty itself and the rents accrued to the date of death constitute "included property," and each is to be separately valued as of the applicable valuation date. Any rent accrued after the date of death and before the subsequent valuation date is "excluded property." Similarly, the principle applicable with respect to interest paid in advance is equally applicable with respect to advance payments of rent.[5]

Assets sold continue as included property, "even though they change in form."[6] Where royalty and working interests in oil and gas property were included property, the proceeds from the sale of oil and gas extracted from this property between the date of the decedent's death and the alternate valuation date were held to be included property (merely the translation of the decedent's interest in the in-place reserves the decedent owned at the time of her death into cash). As for the portion of proceeds to

1. Treas. Reg. §20.2032-1(b)(2).
2. IRC Sec. 2032(d); Treas. Reg. §20.2032-1(b).
3. Treas. Reg. §20.2032-1(d).
4. Treas. Reg. §20.2032-1(d)(1).
5. Treas. Reg. §20.2032-1(d)(2).
6. Treas. Reg. §20.2032-1(d).

be included in the gross estate, the appropriate value was held to be the in-place value of the oil and gas on the date of its severance.[1]

In the case of *noninterest-bearing obligations sold at a discount*, such as savings bonds, the principal obligation and the discount amortized to the date of death are property interests existing at the date of death and constitute "included property." The obligation itself is to be valued at the subsequent valuation date without regard to any further increase in value due to amortized discount. The additional discount amortized after death and during the alternate valuation period is the equivalent of interest accruing during that period and is, therefore, not to be included in the gross estate under the alternate valuation method.[2]

Shares of stock in a corporation and dividends declared to stockholders of record on or before the date of the decedent's death and not collected at the date of death constitute "included property" of the estate. On the other hand, ordinary dividends out of earnings and profits (whether in cash, shares of the corporation, or other property) declared to stockholders of record after the date of the decedent's death are "excluded property" and are not to be valued under the alternate valuation method. If, however, dividends are declared to stockholders of record after the date of the decedent's death with the effect that the shares of stock at the subsequent valuation date do not reasonably represent the same "included property" of the gross estate as existed at the date of the decedent's death, the dividends are "included property," except to the extent that they are out of earnings of the corporation after the date of the decedent's death. For example, if a corporation makes a distribution in partial liquidation to stockholders of record during the alternate valuation period which is not accompanied by a surrender of a stock certificate for cancellation, the amount of the distribution received on stock included in the gross estate is itself "included property," except to the extent that the distribution was out of earnings and profits since the date of the decedent's death. Similarly, if a corporation, in which the decedent owned a substantial interest and which possessed at the date of the decedent's death accumulated earnings and profits equal to its paid-in capital, distributed all of its accumulated earnings and profits as a cash dividend to shareholders of record during the alternate valuation period, the amount of the dividends received on stock includable in the gross estate will be included in the gross estate under the alternate valuation method. Likewise, a stock dividend distributed under such circumstances is "included property."[3] "Included property" also includes the following: (a) nontaxable stock rights and proceeds from the sale of such rights occurring after decedent's death but before the alternate valuation date, where the rights are issued subsequent to the decedent's death in respect of stock owned by the decedent at death; (b) a nontaxable stock dividend received subsequent to decedent's death but before the alternate valuation date; (c) payments on the principal of mortgages received between the date of death and the alternate valuation date.[4] But where an estate owned mutual fund shares, and between the date of the decedent's death and the alternate valuation date capital gains dividends attributable solely to gains on stocks held by the companies at decedent's death were declared and paid, it was held that the dividends were not "included property."[5]

---

1. *Est. of Johnston v. U.S.*, 86-1 USTC ¶13,655 (5th Cir. 1986) , rev'g and remanding 84-2 USTC ¶13,591 (N.D. Tex. 1984), cert. den. 6-23-86.
2. Treas. Reg. §20.2032-1(d)(3).
3. Treas. Reg. §20.2032-1(d)(4).
4. Rev. Rul. 58-576, 1958-2 CB 625.
5. Rev. Rul. 76-234, 1976-1 CB 271.

In the determination of the value of a decedent's gross estate, dividends declared before death, on stock includable in the gross estate, payable to stockholders of record after the date of the decedent's death, must be considered in making an adjustment in the ex-dividend quotation of the stock at the date of the decedent's death. Such dividends may not be included in the gross estate under the alternate method of valuing the gross estate either as a separate asset or as an adjustment of the ex-dividend quoted value of the stock as of the alternate valuation date or as of some intermediate date.

Under the alternate method of valuing the gross estate, stock includable in the gross estate and selling ex-dividend is to be valued at its ex-dividend quoted selling price as of the alternate valuation date or at any intermediate valuation date, increased by the amount of dividends declared on the stock during the alternate valuation period payable to stockholders of record subsequent to the alternate valuation date or such intermediate date. No part of the value so determined is deemed to be excluded property in determining the value of the gross estate.[1]

1537. How are stocks and bonds listed on an exchange or in an over-the-counter market valued for federal transfer tax purposes?

In general, their value is the fair market value per share or bond on the applicable valuation date (see Q 1535). If there is a market for stocks or bonds, on a stock exchange, in an over-the-counter market, or otherwise, the mean between the highest and lowest quoted selling prices on the valuation date is the fair market value per share or bond. (Listed securities and Treasury bonds must be reported and valued in dollar fractions smaller than eighths or thirty-seconds, respectively, if the mean selling price on the applicable valuation date results in a smaller fraction.[2])

Restricted securities (sometimes referred to as "unregistered securities," "investment letter stock," "control stock," or "private placement stock") are securities that cannot lawfully be distributed to the general public until a registration statement relating to the corporation underlying the securities has been filed and made effective by the SEC. Information and guidance in the valuation of these securities is contained in Rev. Rul. 77-287.[3]

If there were no sales on the valuation date but there were sales on dates within a reasonable period both before and after the valuation date, the fair market value is determined by taking a weighted average of the means between the highest and lowest sales on the nearest date before and the nearest date after the valuation date. The average is to be weighted inversely by the respective numbers of trading days between the selling dates and the valuation date. If the stocks or bonds are listed on more than one exchange, the records of the exchange where the stocks or bonds are principally dealt in should be employed if such records are available in a generally available listing or publication of general circulation. In the event that such records are not so available and such stocks or bonds are listed on a composite listing of combined exchanges in a generally available listing or publication of general circulation, the records of such combined exchanges should be employed.[4]

---

1. Rev. Rul. 60-124, 1960-1 CB 368.
2. Rev. Rul. 68-272, 1968-1 CB 394.
3. 1977-2 CB 319. For recent cases dealing with the valuation of restricted securities, see *Est. of Stratton v. Comm.*, TC Memo 1982-744; *Est. of Sullivan v. Comm.*, TC Memo 1983-185; *Est. of Gilford v. Comm.*, 88 TC 38 (1987).
4. Treas. Regs. §§20.2031-2(a), 20.2031-2(b)(1), 25.2512-2(a), 25.2512-2(b)(1).

If it is established with respect to bonds for which there is a market on a stock exchange, that the highest and lowest selling prices are not available for the valuation date in a generally available listing or publication of general circulation but that closing selling prices are so available, the fair market value per bond is the mean between the quoted closing selling price on the valuation date and the quoted closing selling price on the trading day before the valuation date. If there were no sales on the trading day before the valuation date but there were sales on a date within a reasonable period before the valuation date, the fair market value is determined by taking a weighted average of the quoted closing selling price on the valuation date and the quoted closing selling price on the nearest date before the valuation date. The closing selling price for the valuation date is to be weighted by the number of trading days between the previous selling date and the valuation dates. If there were no sales within a reasonable period before the valuation date but there were sales on the valuation date, the fair market value is the closing selling price on such valuation date. If there were no sales on the valuation date but there were sales on dates within a reasonable period both before and after the valuation date, the fair market value is determined by taking a weighted average of the quoted closing selling prices on the nearest date before and the nearest date after the valuation date. The average is to be weighted inversely by the respective numbers of trading days between the selling dates and the valuation date. If the bonds are listed on more than one exchange, the records of the exchange where the bonds are principally dealt in should be employed.[1]

If the above measures are inapplicable because actual sales are not available during a reasonable period beginning before and ending after the valuation date, the fair market value may be determined by taking the mean between the bona fide bid and asked prices on the valuation date, or if none, by taking a weighted average of the means between the bona fide bid and asked prices on the nearest trading date before and the nearest trading date after the valuation date, if both such nearest dates are within a reasonable period. The average is to be determined in the manner described above.[2]

If the foregoing measures are inapplicable because no actual sale prices or bona fide bid and asked prices are available on a date within a reasonable period before the valuation date, but such prices are available on a date within a reasonable period after the valuation date, or vice versa, then the mean between the highest and lowest available sale prices or bid and asked prices may be taken as the value.[3]

If it is established that the value of any bond or share of stock determined on the basis of selling or bid and asked prices as provided above does not reflect the fair market value thereof, then some reasonable modification of that basis or other relevant facts and elements of value are considered in determining the fair market value.

To quote the Tax Court: "In general, property is valued as of the valuation date on the basis of market conditions and facts available on that date *without regard to hindsight.*–The rule that has been developed, and which we accept, is that subsequent events are not considered in fixing fair market value, except to the extent that they were reasonably foreseeable at the date of valuation."[4]

---

1. Treas. Regs. §§20.2031-2(b)(2); 25.2512-2(b)(2).
2. Treas. Regs. §§20.2031-2(c); 25.2512-2(c).
3. Treas. Regs. §§20.2031-2(d); 25.2512-2(d).
4. *Est. of Gilford v. Comm.*, 88 TC 38 (1987).

Where sales at or near the date of death or gift are few or of a sporadic nature, such sales alone may not indicate fair market value. In certain exceptional cases, the size of the block of stock to be valued in relation to the number of shares changing hands in sales may be relevant in determining whether selling prices reflect the fair market value of the block of stock to be valued. If the executor or donor can show that the block of stock to be valued is so large in relation to the actual sales on the existing market that it could not be liquidated in a reasonable time without depressing the market, the price at which the block could be sold as such outside the usual market, as through an underwriter, may be a more accurate indication of value than market quotations.[1] "[W]here a security is actively traded on the market and the block in question represents, let's say, less than three months' average market trading, any blockage claim should be given careful examination before a discount is approved."[2] The IRS has held that in the estate tax setting underwriting fees, necessarily incurred in marketing a large block of stock, are deductible as an administration expense under IRC Section 2053(a)(2), and are not considered in determining the blockage discount to be accorded in valuing the stock under IRC Section 2031 (see Q 1506). Where a blockage discount is allowed, says the Service, the relevant valuation figure is the price that the public would pay to the underwriter for the stock, not the price the underwriter would pay to the estate.[3] For a recent discussion of the blockage discount issue, see *Est. of Sawade v. Comm.*[4]

If actual sale prices and bona fide bid and asked prices are lacking, then the fair market value is to be determined by taking the following factors into consideration:

(1) In the case of corporate or other bonds, the soundness of the security, the interest yield, the date of maturity, and other relevant factors; and

(2) In the case of shares of stock, the company's net worth, prospective earning power and dividend-paying capacity, and other relevant factors.

Some of the "other relevant factors" referred to in (1) and (2) above are: the good will of the business; the economic outlook in the particular industry; the company's position in the industry and its management; the degree of control of the business represented by the block of stock to be valued; and the values of securities of corporations engaged in the same or similar lines of business which are listed on a stock exchange. However, the weight to be accorded such comparisons or any other evidentiary factors considered in the determination of a value depends upon the facts of each case.[5] In addition to the relevant factors described above, consideration is also given to nonoperating assets, including proceeds of life insurance policies payable to or for the benefit of the company, to the extent such nonoperating assets have not been taken into account in the determination of net worth, prospective earning power and dividend-earning capacity.[6]

Another person may hold an option or a contract to purchase securities owned by a decedent at the time of his death. The effect, if any, that is given to the option or contract price in determining the value of the securities for estate tax purposes depends upon the circumstances of the particular case. Little weight will be accorded a price contained

---

1. Treas. Regs. §§20.2031-2(e); 25.2512-2(e).
2. *IRS Valuation Guide for Income, Estate and Gift Taxes*, page 194 (published by Commerce Clearing House on May 11, 1982).
3. Rev. Rul. 83-30, 1983-1 CB 224.
4. TC Memo 1984-626, aff'd 86-2 USTC ¶13,672 (8th Cir. 1986).
5. See, e.g., *Est. of Cook v. U.S.*, 86-2 USTC ¶13,678 (W.D. Mo. 1986).
6. Treas. Regs. §§20.2031-2(f); 25.2512-2(f).

in an option or contract under which the decedent is free to dispose of the underlying securities at any price he chooses during his lifetime. Such is the effect, for example, of an agreement on the part of a shareholder to purchase whatever shares of stock the decedent may own at the time of his death. Even if the decedent is not free to dispose of the underlying securities at other than the option or contract price, such price will be disregarded in determining the value of the securities unless it is determined under the circumstances of the particular case that the agreement represents a bona fide business arrangement and not a device to pass the decedent's shares to the natural objects of his bounty for less than an adequate and full consideration in money or money's worth.[1] For a recent case applying this regulation, see *Dorn v. U.S.*[2] In any event, an option or a contract to purchase securities which fails to meet the Chapter 14 valuation rules test for such options or agreements (see Q 1552) will be disregarded.[3]

In any case where a dividend is declared on a share of stock before the decedent's death but payable to stockholders of record on a date after his death and the stock is selling "ex-dividend" on the date of the decedent's death, the amount of the dividend is added to the ex-dividend quotation in determining the fair market value of the stock as of the date of the decedent's death.[4]

1538. What effect does it have on valuation of shares of stock for federal transfer tax purposes if they are pledged as security?

The full value of securities pledged to secure an indebtedness of the decedent is included in the gross estate. If the decedent had a trading account with a broker, all securities belonging to the decedent and held by the broker at the date of death must be included at their fair market value as of the applicable valuation date. Securities purchased on margin for the decedent's account and held by a broker must also be returned at their fair market value as of the applicable valuation date. The amount of the decedent's indebtedness to a broker or other person with whom securities were pledged is allowed as a deduction from the gross estate.[5] The deduction is taken under IRC Sec. 2053.

If the shares of stock are pledged to secure a debt that was not the decedent's debt at his death, their value includable in the gross estate is reduced to reflect the encumbrance. The amount of the reduction depends upon such factors as the decedent's right to receive dividends, the size of the debt, and the outlook for timely repayment of the debt.[6]

1539. How are notes, mortgages, and mortgage participation certificates valued for federal transfer tax purposes?

The fair market value of notes, secured or unsecured, is presumed to be the amount of unpaid principal, plus interest accrued to the date of death or gift, unless the executor or the donor establishes that the value is lower or that the notes are worthless. If not returned at face value, plus accrued interest, satisfactory evidence must be submitted that the note is worth less than the unpaid amount (because of the interest rate, date of maturity, or other cause), or that the note is uncollectible, either

---

1. Treas. Reg. §20.2031-2(h).
2. 87-2 USTC ¶13,732 (3rd Cir. 1987), reversing 86-2 USTC ¶13,701 (W.D. Pa. 1986).
3. IRC Sec. 2703.
4. Treas. Reg. §20.2031-2(i); Rev. Rul. 54-399, 1954-2 CB 279.
5. Treas. Reg. §20.2031-2(g).
6. *Est. of Hall v. Comm.*, TC Memo 1983-355.

in whole or in part (by reason of the insolvency of the party or parties liable, or for other cause), and that any property pledged or mortgaged as security is insufficient to satisfy the obligation.[1]

Mortgages and mortgage participation certificates come within the scope of the above regulation. The presumption that their face value is their true value governs unless the representative of the estate submits convincing evidence to the contrary.

If it is contended that the actual value of mortgages or mortgage participation certificates is less than their face value, pertinent factors to be taken into consideration in fixing the correct value include the valuation of real estate and any collateral covered by the mortgages, arrears in taxes and interest, gross and net rentals, foreclosure proceedings, assignment of rents, prior liens or encumbrances, present interest yield, over-the-counter sales, bid and asked quotations, and etc. The existence of an over-the-counter market for such securities and the quotations and opinions of value furnished by brokers and real estate appraisers cannot be accepted as conclusive evidence of the value of such securities. Such sales and bid and asked quotations are merely items to be considered with other evidence in fixing values.

In valuing unit mortgages, consideration will be given first to the value of the property securing the mortgages, applying the same factors as are used in fixing the valuation of real estate owned in fee. Where the mortgage is amply secured, the value will be determined to be its face value plus accrued interest to the date of death. Where the security is insufficient, the mortgage will be valued upon the basis of the fair market value of the property less back taxes, estimated foreclosure expenses, and, where justified, the expense of rehabilitation. If the mortgage is not affected by moratorium laws, the mortgagee's recourse against the mortgagor personally will be taken into consideration. The valuation of such assets is a question of fact and the burden of proof is upon the estate to overcome the presumption that the face value is the true value where a lower value is sought to be established.[2]

1540. How are Series E/EE and H/HH United States Savings Bonds valued for federal transfer tax purposes?

Apparently, they are valued at their redemption value on the applicable valuation date. In Rev. Rul. 55-278,[3] A, in 1948, bought Series E bonds with his own funds and had them registered in the names of A and B in the alternative as co-owners. In 1953, A had the bonds reissued in the name of B alone in order to effect a gift to him of A's co-ownership therein. The IRS held that the value of the gift made by A to B in 1953 was the redemption value of the bonds at the time they were reissued. Said the Service, "since Series E United States savings bonds are generally nonnegotiable and nontransferable, they are nonmarketable and, accordingly, have no particular 'market' value. Although ownership therein is transferable by death and by reissue in certain cases ..., their only definitely indicated or ascertainable value is the amount at which they are redeemable by the United States Treasury." Presumably, the same would be true of Series H/HH bonds, since they are likewise nonnegotiable and nontransferable.

---

1. Treas. Regs. §§20.2031-4; 25.2512-4.
2. Rev. Rul. 67-276, 1967-2 CB 321.
3. 1955-1 CB 471.

1541. How is a non-negotiable savings certificate issued without discount by a Federal Reserve member bank valued for federal estate tax purposes when death occurs between interest periods?

Federal regulations provide that a time deposit, or the portion thereof requested, must be paid before maturity without a forfeiture of interest, where requested, upon the death of any owner of the time deposit funds.[1] Accordingly, the savings certificate is valued at the principal amount plus unpaid interest attributable to the period between the last interest payment date preceding death and the date of death.[2]

1542. How are mutual fund shares valued for federal transfer tax purposes?

The fair market value of a share in an open-end investment company (commonly known as a "mutual fund") is the public redemption price of a share. In the absence of an affirmative showing of the public redemption price in effect at the time of death or gift, the last public redemption price quoted by the company for the date of death or gift shall be presumed to be the applicable public redemption price. If the estate tax alternate valuation method under IRC Section 2032 is elected, the last public redemption price quoted by the company for the alternate valuation date is the applicable redemption price. If there is no public redemption price quoted by the company for the applicable valuation date (e.g., the valuation date is a Saturday, Sunday, or holiday), the fair market value of the mutual fund share is the last public redemption price quoted by the company for the first day preceding the applicable valuation date for which there is a quotation. In any case where a dividend is declared on a share in an open-end investment company before the decedent's death but payable to shareholders of record on a date after his death and the share is quoted "ex-dividend" on the date of the decedent's death, the amount of the dividend is added to the ex-dividend quotation in determining the fair market value of the share as of the date of the decedent's death. As used in this paragraph, the term "open-end investment company" includes only a company which on the applicable valuation date was engaged in offering its shares to the public in the capacity of an open-end investment company.[3] Participating agreement shares in mutual funds are valued at the liquidation value and not at the public offering price on the date of death (following *Cartwright*).[4]

1543. How are United States silver coins valued for federal estate tax purposes?

If they have a fair market value which exceeds their face value, they are valued at their fair market value.[5] The ruling says that the same conclusion would apply to paper currency owned by the decedent and having a fair market value in excess of its face value.

1544. How are business interests valued for federal transfer tax purposes?

---

1. 12 CFR §217.4(d)(9)(i).
2. Rev. Rul. 79-340, 1979-2 CB 320.
3. Treas. Regs. §§20.2031-8(b); 25.2512-6(b); *U.S. v. Cartwright*, 411 U.S. 546 (1973).
4. *Est. of Sparling v. Comm.*, 60 TC 330 (1973).
5. Rev. Rul. 78-360, 1978-2 CB 228.

The fair market value of any interest in a business, whether a partnership or a proprietorship, is the net amount which a willing purchaser, whether an individual or a corporation, would pay for the interest to a willing seller, neither being under any compulsion to buy or to sell and both having reasonable knowledge of the relevant facts. The net value is determined on the basis of all relevant factors including—

(1) A fair appraisal as of the applicable valuation date of all the assets of the business, tangible and intangible, including good will;

(2) The demonstrated earning capacity of the business; and

(3) The other factors set forth in the regulations[1] relating to the valuation of corporate stock, to the extent applicable (see Q 1545).

Special attention should be given to determining an adequate value of the good will of the business. Complete financial and other data upon which the valuation is based should be submitted with the return, including copies of reports of examinations of the business made by accountants, engineers, or any technical experts as of or near the applicable valuation date.[2]

For additional special valuation rules contained in IRC Chapter 14, see Q 1549 to Q 1553.

Approach of the Courts

Historically, in valuation cases, the courts have tended to strike a compromise between the values asserted by the contending parties. However, in recent years, particularly in the Tax Court, the values found have tended to lean toward the party presenting the more meritorious case. Credit must be given for this shift to former Chief Judge of the Tax Court, Theodore Tannenwald. After years of experience, Judge Tannenwald found that the "compromise the difference" approach of the courts merely encouraged the parties to assert extreme values. In a 1980 valuation decision, *Buffalo Tool & Die Mfg. Co., Inc. v. Comm.*,[3] Judge Tannenwald took the occasion to admonish the parties thus:

"We are convinced that the valuation issue is capable of resolution by the parties themselves through an agreement which will reflect a compromise Solomon-like adjustment, thereby saving the expenditure of time, effort, and money by the parties and the court—a process not likely to produce a better result. Indeed, each of the parties should keep in mind that, in the final analysis, the court may find the evidence of valuation by one of the parties sufficiently more convincing than that of the other party, so that the final result will produce a significant financial defeat for one or the other, rather than a middle-of-the-road compromise which we suspect each of the parties expects the court to reach." (At page 452).

The new approach is reflected in a number of recent valuation decisions.[4]

---

1. See Treas. Regs. §§20.2031-2(f), 20.2031-2(h), 25.2512-2(f).
2. Treas. Regs. §§20.2031-3, 25.2512-3.
3. 74 TC 441.
4. *Est. of McGill v. Comm.*, TC Memo 1984-292 (voting trust certificates); *Est. of Gallo v. Comm.*, TC Memo 1985-363 (closely held stock); *Est. of Gillet v. Comm.*, TC Memo 1985-394 (closely held stock); *Est. of Rubish v. Comm.*, TC memo 1985-406 (ranch); *Est. of Watts v. Comm.*, TC Memo 1985-595 (partnership interest).

Effect of Buy-Sell Agreement

For purchase agreements entered into after October 8, 1990, or substantially modified after such date, the value of a closely held business interest is to be determined without regard to any purchase agreement exercisable at less than fair market value (determined without regard to such purchase agreement) unless the purchase agreement (1) is a bona fide business arrangement, (2) is not a device to transfer the property to members of the decedent's family for less than full or adequate consideration in money or money's worth, and (3) has terms comparable to those entered into by persons in an arm's length transaction.[1] See Q 1552.

Assuming the requirements of IRC Section 2703 are met, or that IRC Section 2703 does not apply, it is possible that the *estate tax* value of a business interest (including closely held stock) may be controlled by the price or formula contained in a business purchase (buy-sell) agreement. The Internal Revenue Service officially takes the position that the facts of each case must be examined to determine whether the agreement price will be accepted for estate tax purposes.[2] Case law has established, however, that if the following conditions are met, the agreement price will hold for estate tax purposes, even though the fair market value of the business interest may be substantially more at the valuation date than the agreement price:

(1) The estate must be obligated to sell at death (under either a mandatory purchase agreement or an option held by the designated purchaser).

(2) The agreement must prohibit the owner from disposing of his interest during his lifetime at a price higher than the contract or option price.

(3) The price must be fixed by the terms of the agreement or the agreement must contain a formula or method for determining the price.

(4) The agreement must be an arm's length business transaction and not a gift. Thus, the purchase price must be fair and adequate at the time the agreement is made, particularly if the parties are closely related.[3]

In a number of cases, the price set in the agreement was held to control the estate tax value of the business interest.[4]

Unlike the situation with respect to the estate tax, it is not possible, by following certain rules, to draft a business buy-sell agreement in such a way that it will fix the value of a business interest for gift tax purposes. However, an agreement restricting lifetime sale will be considered with all other pertinent factors, and may tend to lower the value of the business interest.[5]

---

1. IRC Sec. 2703.
2. Treas. Regs. §§20.2031-2(h), 20.2031-3; Rev. Rul. 59-60, 1959-1 CB 237.
3. *Slocum v. U.S.*, 256 F. Supp. 753 (S.D.N.Y. 1966).
4. *Brodrick v. Gore,* 224 F.2d 892 (10th Cir. 1955); *May v. McGowan,* 194 F.2d 396 (2nd Cir. 1952); *Comm. v. Child's Estate,* 147 F.2d 368 (2nd Cir. 1952);. *Comm. v. Bensel,* 100 F.2d 639 (3rd Cir. 1939); *Lomb v. Sugden,* 82 F.2d 166 (2nd Cir. 1936); *Wilson v. Bowers,* 57 F.2d 682 (2nd Cir. 1932); *Mandel v. Sturr,* 266 F.2d 321 (2nd Cir. 1959); *Fiorito v. Comm.,* 33 TC 440, acq. 1960-1 CB 4; *Est. of Littick,* 31 TC 181, acq. in result, 1984-2 CB 1; *Est. of Weil,* 22 TC 1267, acq. 1955-2 CB 10; *Est. of Salt,* 17 TC 92, acq. 1952-1 CB 4; *Est. of Maddock,* 16 TC 324, acq. 1951-2 CB 3. See also Treas. Regs. §§20.2031-2(h), 20.2031-3.
5. *Est. of James v. Comm.,* 148 F.2d 236 (2nd Cir. 1945); *Kline v. Comm.,* 130 F.2d 742 (3rd Cir. 1942); *Krauss v. U.S.,* 140 F.2d 510 (5th Cir. 1944); *Comm. v. McCann,* 146 F.2d 385 (2nd Cir. 1944); *Spitzer v. Comm.,* 153 F.2d 967 (8th Cir. 1946); Rev. Rul. 189, 1953-2 CB 294.

1545. How are shares of stock in closely held corporations valued for federal transfer tax purposes?

IRC Section 2031(b) deals with the valuation, for estate tax purposes, of unlisted stock and securities. It says: "In the case of stock and securities of a corporation the value of which, by reason of their not being listed on an exchange and by reason of the absence of sales thereof, cannot be determined with reference to bid and asked prices or with reference to sales prices, the value thereof shall be determined by taking into consideration, in addition to all other factors, the value of stock or securities of corporations engaged in the same or a similar line of business which are listed on an exchange."

Rev. Rul. 59-60,[1] contains a broad discussion of factors which the IRS believes should be considered in valuing shares of stock in closely held corporations or in corporations where market quotations are either lacking or too scarce to be recognized. The Service says that in these cases, "all available financial data, as well as all relevant factors affecting the fair market value, should be considered. The following factors, although not all-inclusive, are fundamental and require careful analysis in each case:

"(a) The nature of the business and the history of the enterprise from its inception.

"(b) The economic outlook in general and the condition and outlook of the specific industry in particular.

"(c) The book value of the stock and the financial condition of the business.

"(d) The earning capacity of the company.

"(e) The dividend-paying capacity.

"(f) Whether or not the enterprise has good-will or other intangible value.

"(g) Sales of the stock and the size of the block of stock to be valued.

"(h) The market price of stocks of corporations engaged in the same or a similar line of business having their stocks actively traded in a free and open market, either on an exchange or over-the-counter."[2]

If a block of stock represents a controlling interest in a corporation, a "control premium" generally adds to the value of the stock. If, however, the shares constitute a minority ownership interest, a "minority discount" is often applied to the value. See, e.g., *Martin v. Comm.*,[3] which deals with discounts to be applied to shares of stock representing a minority interest in a holding company that in turn held minority interests in seven operating companies. A premium may also attach for swing vote attributes where one block of stock may exercise control by joining with another block of stock.[4] One memorandum valued stock included in the gross estate at a premium as a controlling interest, while applying a minority discount to the marital deduction (see Q 1506)

1. 1959-1 CB 237.
2. Sec. 4.01.
3. TC Memo 1985-424.
4. TAM 9436005.

portion which passed to the surviving spouse.[1] Just because an interest being valued is a minority interest does not mean that a minority discount is available.[2] However, one case valued stock with voting rights at no more than stock without voting rights.[3]

If a donor transfers shares in a corporation to each of the donor's children, the Service will no longer consider family control when valuing the gift under IRC Section 2512. Thus, a minority discount will not be disallowed solely because a transferred interest would be part of a controlling interest if such interest were aggregated with interests held by family members.[4] Indeed, a minority discount was recently allowed even when the person to whom the interest was transferred was already a controlling shareholder.[5]

The Tax Court has determined that an estate would not be allowed a minority discount where the decedent transferred a small amount of stock immediately prior to death for the sole purpose of reducing her interest from a controlling interest to a minority interest for valuation purposes.[6] Also, a partnership or LLC may be included in the gross estate under IRC Section 2036 without benefit of discounts if a decedent puts everything he owns in the partnership or LLC and retains complete control over the income of the partnership or LLC.[7]

For a recent case discussing the valuation of voting trust certificates representing the decedent's beneficial interest in stock of a closely held corporation, see *Est. of McGill v. Comm.*[8]

In general, when valuing an operating company that sells goods and services, primary consideration is given to earnings, and when valuing a company that merely holds investments, primary consideration is given to asset values. However, if a company is not easily characterized as one or the other, appropriate weight should be given to both earnings and assets.[9]

For the effect of a buy-sell agreement on the valuation of closely held stock, see Q 1544.

For additional special valuation rules contained in IRC Chapter 14, see Q 1549 to Q 1553.

1546. How is real estate valued for federal transfer tax purposes?

There are three basic approaches appraisers use in arriving at the fair market value of real estate: (1) the market data, or comparable sales approach, (2) the capitalization of income approach, and (3) the reproduction cost less depreciation approach.[10]

1. TAM 9403005.
2. *Godley v. Comm.*, 2002-1 USTC ¶60,436 (4th Cir. 2002) (partnerships held housing projects subject to long-term government contracts).
3. *Est. of Simplot v. Comm.*, 2001-1 USTC ¶60,405 (9th Cir. 2001).
4. Rev. Rul. 93-12, 1993-1 CB 202, revoking Rev. Rul. 81-253, 1981-2 CB 187.
5. TAM 9432001.
6. *Est. of Murphy v. Comm.*, TC Memo 1990-472.
7. *Est. of Strangi v. Comm.*, TC Memo 2003-145; *Kimbell v. U.S.*, 2003-1 USTC 60,455 (N.D. Tex. 2003).
8. TC Memo 1984-292.
9. *Martin v. Comm.*, TC Memo 1985-424.
10. *IRS Valuation Guide*, pages 18-19.

(1) *Market data.* An arm's length sale of the property in question on the valuation date would of course determine its fair market value. Lacking such a circumstance, the next best indication of value would be the price for which a reasonably comparable piece of property was sold on or near the valuation date. This approach is particularly useful in the valuation of unimproved real estate.[1]

(2) *Capitalization of income.* The projected net income from the property, either before or after depreciation, interest and income taxes, from the highest and best use of the property is estimated and then capitalized at a rate which represents a fair return on the particular investment at the particular time, considering the risks involved. This approach is particularly useful in the appraisal of business properties.

(3) *Reproduction cost.* This approach requires an estimate of the cost of replacing a structure, an estimate of the depreciation and obsolescence that has taken place in the existing structure, and an appraisal of the land involved. Use of this method is extremely limited for ordinary federal tax valuation purposes.

An undivided fractional interest in property is normally determined to be a proportionate part of the value of the whole property. If any discount is allowed, the taxpayer must produce evidence that partial interests in real property in the locality sell for less than their proportionate shares of the whole.[2]

1547. How are mineral properties valued for federal transfer tax purposes?

Treasury Regulation Section 1.611-2(d) provides, for income tax purposes, as follows:

"(d) Determination of fair market value of mineral properties, and improvements, if any. – (1) If the fair market value of the mineral property and improvements at a specified date is to be determined for the purpose of ascertaining the basis [see Q 1415], such value must be determined, subject to approval or revision by the district director, by the owner of such property and improvements in the light of the conditions and circumstances known at that date, regardless of later discoveries or developments or subsequent improvements in methods of extraction and treatment of the mineral product. The district director will give due weight and consideration to any and all factors and evidence having a bearing on the market value, such as cost, actual sales and transfers of similar properties and improvements, bona fide offers, market value of stocks or shares, royalties and rentals, valuation for local or State taxation, partnership accountings, records of litigation in which the value of the property and improvements was in question, the amount at which the property and improvements may have been inventoried or appraised in probate or similar proceedings, and disinterested appraisals by approved methods.

"(2) If the fair market value must be ascertained as of a certain date, analytical appraisal methods of valuation, such as the present value method will not be used:

(i) If the value of a mineral property and improvements, if any, can be determined upon the basis of cost or comparative values and replacement value of equipment, or

---

1. See Rev. Proc. 79-24, 1979-1 CB 565.
2. *Est. of Iacono,* TC Memo 1980-520.

(ii) If the fair market value can reasonably be determined by any other method."

Lambert v. U.S.,[1] concerned the federal estate tax valuation of an estate's one-half interest in a coal mining business operated as a partnership. The parties agreed that the Treasury Regulations on cost depletion provided guidance as to the valuation of coal properties. Citing Treas. Reg. §1.611-2(d)(2), above, the court found that the estate's witness had properly determined the value of the intangible assets, including the coal reserves and good will, upon the basis of comparative values, and that for that reason, the analytical methods applied by the government and its witness were not appropriate. Accordingly, the court found that the estate had met its burden of showing that the government's valuation of $3,772,326 for the coal company was excessive and that the fair market value, as determined by the estate, was $2,126,000.

Treasury Regulation Section 1.611-2(e) provides, for income tax purposes, as follows:

"(e) Determination of the fair market value of mineral property by the present value method. – (1) To determine the fair market value of a mineral property and improvements by the present value method, the essential factors must be determined for each mineral deposit. The essential factors in determining the fair market value of mineral deposits are:

(i) The total quantity of mineral in terms of the principal or customary unit (or units) paid for in the product marketed,

(ii) The quantity of mineral expected to be recovered during each operating period,

(iii) The average quality or grade of the mineral reserves,

(iv) The allocation of the total expected profit to the several processes or operations necessary for the preparation of the mineral for market,

(v) The probable operating life of the deposit in years,

(vi) The development cost,

(vii) The operating cost,

(viii) The total expected profit,

(ix) The rate at which this profit will be obtained, and

(x) The rate of interest commensurate with the risk for the particular deposit.

"(2) If the mineral deposit has been sufficiently developed, the valuation factors specified in subparagraph (1) of this paragraph may be determined from past operating experience. In the application of factors derived from past experience, full allowance should be made for probable future variations in the rate of exhaustion, quality or grade of the mineral, percentage of recovery, cost of development, production, interest rate,

---

1. 85-2 USTC ¶13,637 (W.D. Va. 1985).

and selling price of the product marketed during the expected operating life of the mineral deposit. Mineral deposits for which these factors cannot be determined with reasonable accuracy from past operating experience may also be valued by the present value method; but the factors must be deduced from concurrent evidence, such as the general type of the deposit, the characteristics of the district in which it occurs, the habit of the mineral deposits, the intensity of mineralization, the oil-gas ratio, the rate at which additional mineral has been disclosed by exploitation, the stage of the operating life of the deposit, and any other evidence tending to establish a reasonable estimate of the required factors.

"(3) Mineral deposits of different grades, locations, and probable dates of extraction should be valued separately. The mineral content of a deposit shall be determined in accordance with paragraph (c) of this section. In estimating the average grade of the developed and prospective mineral, account should be taken of probable increases or decreases as indicated by the operating history. The rate of exhaustion of a mineral deposit should be determined with due regard to the limitations imposed by plant capacity, by the character of the deposit, by the ability to market the mineral product, by labor conditions, and by the operating program in force or reasonably to be expected for future operations. The operating life of a mineral deposit is that number of years necessary for the exhaustion of both the developed and prospective mineral content at the rate determined as above. The operating life of oil and gas wells is also influenced by the natural decline in pressure and flow, and by voluntary or enforced curtailment of production. The operating cost includes all current expense of producing, preparing, and marketing the mineral product sold (due consideration being given to taxes) exclusive of allowable capital additions, as described in §§1.612-2 and 1.612-4 [see Q 1248 through Q 1251], and deductions for depreciation and depletion [see Q 1252 through Q 1261], but including cost of repairs. This cost of repairs is not to be confused with the depreciation deduction by which the cost of improvements is returned to the taxpayer free from tax. In general, no estimates of these factors will be approved by the district director which are not supported by the operating experience of the property or which are derived from different and arbitrarily selected periods.

"(4) The value of each mineral deposit is measured by the expected gross income (the number of units of mineral recoverable in marketable form multiplied by the estimated market price per unit) less the estimated operating cost, reduced to a present value as of the date for which the valuation is made at the rate of interest commensurate with the risk for the operating life, and further reduced by the value at that date of the improvements and of the capital additions, if any, necessary to realize the profits. The degree of risk is generally lowest in cases where the factors of valuation are fully supported by the operating record of the mineral enterprise before the date for which the valuation is made. On the other hand, higher risks ordinarily attach to appraisals on any other basis."

1548. How is timber valued for federal transfer tax purposes?

The estate tax regulations offer little guidance in the selection of an appropriate method for valuing timber property. However, Treas. Reg. §1.611-3(f), covering the depletion allowance deduction for income tax purposes, contains the following useful information:

"(f) *Determination of fair market value of timber property.* (1) If the fair market value of the property at a specified date is the basis for depletion deductions, such value shall be determined, subject to approval or revision by the district director upon audit, by the owner of the property in the light of the most reliable and accurate information available with reference to the condition of the property as it existed at that date, regardless of all subsequent changes, such as changes in surrounding circumstances, and methods of exploitation, in degree of utilization, etc. Such factors as the following will be given due consideration:

(i) Character and quality of the timber as determined by species, age, size, condition, etc.;

(ii) The quantity of timber per acre, the total quantity under consideration, and the location of the timber in question with reference to other timber;

(iii) Accessibility of the timber (location with reference to distance from a common carrier, the topography and other features of the ground upon which the timber stands and over which it must be transported in process of exploitation, the probable cost of exploitation and the climate and the state of industrial development of the locality); and

(iv) The freight rates by common carrier to important markets.

"(2) The timber in each particular case will be valued on its own merits and not on the basis of general averages for regions; however, the value placed upon it, taking into consideration such factors as those mentioned in this paragraph, will be consistent with that of other similar timber in the region. The district director will give weight and consideration to any and all facts and evidence having a bearing on the market value, such as cost, actual sales and transfers of similar properties, the margin between the cost of production and the price realized for timber products, market value of stock or shares, royalties and rentals, valuation for local or State taxation, partnership accountings, records of litigation in which the value of the property has been involved, the amount at which the property may have been inventoried or appraised in probate or similar proceedings, disinterested appraisals by approved methods, and other factors."

In a case involving estate tax valuation of undivided minority interests in timberland, the Tax Court, quoting from paragraph (2) of the foregoing regulation, added that where available the use of comparative sales is the method of valuation most preferred by that court and by the Ninth Circuit (to which appeal lay).

In that case, the government's appraisers based their valuation on 24 sales of "stumpage" believed by them to be the most comparable because of their similar characteristics and their proximity in time to the valuation date and in location to the subject property. In addition, the appraisers used seven other transactions involving timber and land in the same general vicinity. The prices of the sales considered comparable were adjusted by the appraisers for differences in timber, quality, accessibility and other logging costs, volume, species mix, and time of sale. The government's appraisers concluded that the total value of the timber on the land in which decedent had an undivided interest was $29,500,000 at the date of her death. With one exception, the government's appraisers used the same sales as comparables to determine that the value of the underlying land supporting the timber at decedent's death was $9,500,000.

The executor, however, contended that the sales upon which the government's appraisers relied involved timber that was not comparable to the timber in which the decedent had an undivided interest. He also contended that the sales used as comparables by the government's appraisers were not properly adjusted to bring them into comparability. With respect to the government's land valuation, the executor contended that the appraisal failed to adjust for acreage in the subject land that was barren, or to adjust adequately for differences in steepness of terrain.

The court examined the points of difference between the parties, found merit in several of the executor's contentions, and concluded that the government's valuation should be reduced by 20%, i.e., to $31,200,000.

Finally was the issue of a minority discount to be applied to the decedent's undivided aliquot portion of the $31,200,000 valuation. The government contended that no minority discount should be allowed. The executor contended that a discount of at least 60% was warranted. On this issue the estate's witnesses were persuasive. The court was convinced from their testimony of the disabilities associated with a minority undivided interest in timber property, including lack of marketability, lack of management, lack of general control, lack of liquidity, and potential partitionment expenses, that a minority discount of 60% was reasonable, and the court so held.[1] See also *Harwood v. Comm.*,[2] which concerned valuation of a minority interest in a limited partnership engaged in the timber business.

CHAPTER 14 SPECIAL VALUATION RULES

1549. What are the Chapter 14 special valuation rules?

Special valuation rules are contained in IRC Chapter 14. Chapter 14 generally focuses on establishing the value of various interests transferred to family members at the time of the transfer when the transferor retains certain interests in the property being transferred. Special rules apply to certain transfers of interests in corporations and partnerships (see Q 1550), to certain transfers of interests in trusts and even remainder and joint purchase transactions (see Q 1551), to certain agreements, options, rights or restrictions exercisable at less than fair market value (see Q 1552), and to various lapsing rights and restrictions (see Q 1553).

1550. What special valuation rules apply to the transfer of an interest in a corporation or partnership under Chapter 14?

As a general rule, the value of a transferred residual interest is equal to the value of the transferor's entire interest prior to the transfer reduced by the value of the interest retained by the transferor. For the purpose of determining whether a transfer of an interest in a corporation or partnership to (or for the benefit of) a "member of the transferor's family" is a gift (and the value of the transfer), the value of any "applicable retained interest" that is held by the transferor or an "applicable family member" immediately after the transfer is treated as being zero unless the applicable retained interest is a "distribution right" which consists of the right to receive a "qualified payment."[3] Where an applicable retained interest consists of a distribution right which consists of the right to receive a qualified payment and there are one or more liquidation, put, call, or conversion rights with respect to such interest, the value of all such rights is to

1. *Est. of Sels v. Comm.*, TC Memo 1986-501.
2. 82 TC 239 (1980), aff'd per order (9th Cir. March 18, 1986).
3. IRC Secs. 2701(a)(1), 2701(a)(3)(A).

be determined by assuming that each such liquidation, put, call, or conversion right is exercised in a manner which results in the lowest value.[1] IRC Section 2701 does not apply to distribution rights with respect to qualified payments where there is no liquidation, put, call, or conversion right with respect to the distribution right.[2] If the transfer subject to these rules is of a junior equity interest in a corporation or partnership, the transfer must be assigned a minimum value under the "junior equity rule."[3]

These rules do not apply if for either the transferred interest or the applicable retained interest market quotations are readily available (as of the date of transfer) on an established securities market. Also, the rules do not apply if the applicable retained interest is of the same class as the transferred interest, or if the applicable retained interest is proportionally the same as the transferred interest (disregarding nonlapsing differences with respect to voting in the case of a corporation, or with respect to management and limitations on liability in the case of a partnership).[4] An exception from the rules is also provided for a transfer of a vertical slice of interests in an entity (defined as a proportionate reduction of each class of equity interest held by the transferor and applicable family members in the aggregate).[5]

Definitions and Rules

Transfers

The rules apply to transfers with respect to new, as well as existing, entities.[6] Transfers may be either direct or indirect. Furthermore, except as provided in regulations, a contribution to capital, a redemption, a recapitalization, or other change in capital structure of a corporation or partnership is treated as a transfer if the taxpayer or an applicable family member receives an applicable retained interest in the transaction, or as provided under regulations, holds such an interest immediately after the transfer.[7] Any termination of an interest is also treated as a transfer.[8]

Applicable Retained Interests

An "applicable retained interest" is any interest in an entity with respect to which there is (1) a distribution right and the transferor and applicable family members control the entity immediately before the transfer, or (2) a liquidation, put, call, or conversion right.[9] (Regulations or rulings may provide that any applicable retained interest be treated as two or more interests.[10]) A "distribution right" is any right to a distribution from a corporation with respect to its stock, or from a partnership with respect to a partner's interest in the partnership, other than (1) a distribution with respect to any interest if such right is junior to the rights of the transferred interest, (2) any right to receive a guaranteed payment of a fixed amount from a partnership under IRC Section 707(c), or (3) a liquidation, put, call, or conversion right.[11]

---

1. IRC Sec. 2701(a)(3)(B).
2. IRC Sec. 2701(a)(3)(C).
3. IRC Sec. 2701(a)(4).
4. IRC Sec. 2701(a)(2).
5. Treas. Reg. §25.2701-1(c)(4).
6. Treas. Reg. §25.2701-1(b)(2)(i).
7. IRC Sec. 2701(e)(5).
8. IRC Sec. 2701(d)(5).
9. IRC Sec. 2701(b).
10.IRC Sec. 2701(e)(7); Treas. Reg. §25.2701-7.
11.IRC Sec. 2701(c)(1).

For these purposes, a liquidation, put, call, or conversion right is treated as a distribution right rather than as a liquidation, put, call, or conversion right if (1) it must be exercised at a specific time and at a specific amount, or (2) the liquidation, put, call, or conversion right: (a) can be converted into a fixed amount or fixed percentage of the same class of shares of stock as the transferred shares; (b) is nonlapsing; (c) is subject to proportionate adjustments for splits, combinations, reclassifications, and similar changes in the capital stock; and (d) is subject to adjustments for accumulated but unpaid distributions. (Similar rules are to apply to liquidation, put, call, or conversion rights in a partnership.) Where a liquidation, put, call, or conversion right is treated as exercised in a manner which produces the lowest value in the general rule above, such a right is treated as a distribution right which must be exercised at a specific time and at a specific amount.[1]

Regulations provide that applicable retained interests consist of (1) extraordinary payment rights, and (2) distribution rights held in a controlled entity.[2] The term "extraordinary payment rights" is used to refer to liquidation, put, call, or conversion rights, the exercise or nonexercise of which affects the value of the transferred interests.[3] The following are treated as neither extraordinary payment rights nor distribution rights: (1) mandatory fixed payment rights; (2) liquidation participation rights (other than ones in which the transferor, members of the transferor's family, and applicable family members have the ability to compel liquidation); and (3) non-lapsing conversion rights subject to proportionate adjustments for changes in equity and to adjustments to take account of accumulated but unpaid qualified payments.[4]

Qualified Payments

A "qualified payment" means any dividend payable on a periodic basis at a fixed rate (including rates tied to specific market rates) on any cumulative preferred stock (or comparable payment with respect to a partnership). With respect to the transferor, an otherwise qualified payment is to be treated as such unless the transferor elects otherwise. With respect to applicable family members, an otherwise qualified payment is not to be treated as such unless the applicable family member so elects. A transferor or an applicable family member can make an irrevocable election to treat any distribution right (which is otherwise not a qualified payment) as a qualified payment, payable at such times and in such amounts as provided in the election (such times and amounts not to be inconsistent with any underlying legal instruments creating such rights).[5] The value assigned a right for which an election is made cannot exceed fair market (determined without regard to IRC Section 2701).[6]

Attribution

A "member of the transferor's family" includes the transferor's spouse, lineal descendants of the transferor or transferor's spouse, and the spouse of any such descendant.[7] An "applicable family member" with respect to a transferor includes the transferor's spouse, an ancestor of the transferor or transferor's spouse, and the spouse of any such ancestor.[8] An individual is treated as holding interests held indirectly through a corporation,

---

1. IRC Sec. 2701(c)(2).
2. Treas. Reg. §25.2701-2(b)(1).
3. Treas. Reg. §25.2701-2(b)(2).
4. Treas. Reg. §25.2701-2(b)(4).
5. IRC Sec. 2701(c)(3).
6. Treas. Reg. §25.2701-2(c)(2).
7. IRC Sec. 2701(e)(1).
8. IRC Sec. 2701(e)(2).

partnership, trust, or other entity.[1] In the case of a corporation, "control" means 50% ownership (by vote or value) of the stock. In the case of a partnership, "control" means 50% ownership of the capital or profits interests, or in the case of a limited partnership, the ownership of any interest as a general partner.[2] When determining control, an individual is treated as holding any interest held by an applicable family member (see above), including (for this purpose) any lineal descendant of any parent of the transferor or the transferor's spouse.[3]

Minimum Value/Junior Equity Rule

If the transfer subject to these rules is of a junior equity interest in a corporation or partnership, the value of the transferred interest cannot be less than the amount which would be determined if the total value of all junior equity interests in the entity were equal to 10% of the sum of (1) the total value of the equity interests in the entity, and (2) the total amount of debt owed the transferor or an applicable family member by the entity.[4] For this purpose, indebtedness does not include (1) short term indebtedness incurred for the current conduct of trade or business, (2) indebtedness owed to a third party solely because it is guaranteed by the transferor or an applicable family member, and (3) amounts set aside for qualified deferred compensation to the extent such amounts are not available to the entity. While a properly structured lease is not treated as indebtedness, arrearages with respect to a lease are indebtedness.[5]

Valuation Method

For purposes of IRC Section 2701, the amount of a gift is determined as follows: (1) determine the fair market value of all family-held equity interests in the entity (treat as if held by one individual); (2) subtract out the sum of (a) the fair market value of all family-held senior equity interests in the entity other than applicable retained interests (treat as if held by one individual) and (b) the value of applicable retained interests as valued under IRC Section 2701; (3) allocate the remaining value among the transferred interests and other family-held subordinate interests; (4) reduce the value allocated to the transferred interests to adjust for a minority or similar discount or for consideration received for the transferred interest.[6]

Recapture

If "qualified payments" are valued under these rules, additional estate or gift tax may be due at the time of a later taxable event to reflect cumulative but unpaid distributions. The amount of an increase in estate or gift tax is equal to the excess (if any) of (1) the value of the qualified payments as if each payment had been timely made during the period beginning with the transfer subject to these rules and ending with the taxable event and each payment were reinvested at the (capitalization or discount) interest rate used to value the applicable retained transfer at the time of the transfer, over (2) the value of the qualified payments actually made adjusted to reflect reinvestment as in (1). For this purpose, any payment made within four years of its due date is treated as made on its due date.[7] The due date is the date specified in the governing interest as the date on which the payment is to be made (or if no date is specified, the last day of each calendar

---

1. IRC Sec. 2701(e)(3).
2. IRC Sec. 2701(b)(2).
3. IRC Sec. 2701(b)(2)(C).
4. IRC Sec. 2701(a)(4).
5. Treas. Reg. §25.2701-3.
6. Treas. Reg. §25.2701-3(b).
7. IRC Sec. 2701(d).

year).[1] A transfer of a debt obligation bearing compound interest at a rate not less than the appropriate IRC Section 7520 discount rate from the due date of the payment and with a term of no more than four years is treated as payment.[2]

Regulations limit the amount of the increase in gift or estate tax attributable to recapture in order to prevent double inclusion of the same transfer in the transfer tax system. The mitigation provisions include reduction of the amount recaptured by the sum of (1) the portion of the fair market value of the qualified payment interest which is attributable to cumulative but unpaid distributions; (2) to the extent held by the individual at the time of a taxable event, the fair market value of any equity interest received by the individual in lieu of qualified payments; and (3) the amount by which the individual's aggregate taxable gifts were increased to reflect failure of the individual to enforce his rights to qualified payments.[3]

As an overall limitation, the amount of any increase in tax due to cumulative but unpaid distributions will not exceed the applicable percentage of the excess (if any) of (1) the value (determined as of the date of the taxable event) of all equity interests in the entity which are junior to the applicable retained interest, over (2) the value of such interests (determined as of the date of the earlier transfer subject to these rules). The numerator of the applicable percentage is equal to the number of shares in the corporation held (as of the date of the taxable event) by the transferor which are applicable retained interests of the same class. The denominator of the applicable percentage is equal to the total number of shares in the corporation (as of the date of the taxable event) which are of the same class as the shares used in the numerator. (A similar rule applies to partnerships.)[4] The applicable percentage equals the largest ownership percentage interest in any preferred interest held by the interest holder.[5] The appreciation limitation does not apply if the interest holder elects to treat the late payment of a qualified payment as a taxable event (see below).[6]

For purposes of an increase in tax due to cumulative but unpaid distributions, a "taxable event" includes (1) the death of the transferor if the applicable retained interest is included in the transferor's estate, (2) the transfer of an applicable retained interest, and (3) at the election of the taxpayer, the payment of a qualified payment which is made after its four-year grace period.[7] Also, a termination of a qualified payment interest is treated as a taxable event. Thus, a taxable event occurs with respect to an individual indirectly holding a qualified payment interest held by a trust on the earlier of (1) the termination of the individual's interest in the trust, or (2) the termination of the trust's interest in the qualified payment interest. However, if the value of the qualified payment interest would be included in the individual's federal gross estate if the individual were to die immediately after the termination, the taxable transfer does not occur until the earlier of (1) the time the interest would no longer be includable in the individual's estate (other than by reason of the gifts within three years of death rule of IRC Section 2035), or (2) such individual's death.[8]

---

1. Treas. Reg. §25.2701-4(c)(2).
2. Treas. Reg. §25.2701-4(c)(5).
3. Treas. Reg. §25.2701-4(c)(1).
4. IRC Sec. 2701(d)(2)(B).
5. Treas. Reg. §25.2701-4(c)(6)(iii).
6. Treas. Reg. §25.2701-4(d)(2).
7. IRC Sec. 2701(d)(3)(A).
8. Treas. Regs. §§25.2701-4(b)(1), 25.2701-4(b)(2).

A "taxable event" does not include an applicable retained interest includable in the transferor's estate and passing under the marital deduction. Nor does a "taxable event" include a lifetime gift to a spouse which does not result in a taxable gift because the marital deduction is taken, or the spouse pays consideration for the transfer. However, such a spouse is thereafter treated in the same manner as the transferor.[1]

An applicable family member is treated the same as the transferor with respect to any applicable retained interest retained by such family member. Also, if the transferor transfers an applicable retained interest to an applicable family member (other than the transferor's spouse), the applicable family member is treated the same as the transferor with respect to distributions accumulating after the time of the taxable event. In the case of a transfer of an applicable retained interest from an applicable family member to the transferor, IRC Section 2701 continues to apply as long as the transferor holds the interest.[2]

Adjustment to Mitigate Double Taxation

As provided in regulations, if there is a later transfer or inclusion in the gross estate of property which was subject to IRC Section 2701, adjustments are to be made for gift, estate, and generation-skipping transfer tax purposes to reflect any increase in valuation of a prior taxable gift or any recapture under IRC Section 2701.[3]

IRC Section 2701 interests transferred after May 4, 1994. An individual (the initial transferor) who has previously made a transfer subject to IRC Section 2701 (the initial transfer) may be permitted a reduction in his taxable gifts for gift tax purposes or adjusted taxable gifts for estate tax purposes. If the holder of the IRC Section 2701 interest (i.e., the applicable retained interest, see above) transfers the interest to an individual other than the initial transferor or an applicable family member of the initial transferor in a transfer subject to estate or gift tax during the lifetime of the initial transferor, then the initial transferor can reduce the amount upon which his tentative tax is calculated for gift tax purposes in the year of the transfer. The amount of the reduction is generally equal to the lesser of (1) the amount by which the initial transferor's taxable gifts were increased by reason of IRC Section 2701, or (2) the amount by which the value of the IRC Section 2701 interest at the time of the subsequent transfer exceeds its value at the time of the initial transfer (the duplicated amount). Any unused reduction can be carried over and applied in succeeding years; any reduction remaining at death can be applied in the initial transferor's estate. The amount upon which the initial transferor's tentative tax is calculated for estate tax purposes may also be reduced (generally occurs if the IRC Section 2701 interest is retained until the initial transferor's death or if there is a carryover of any unused reduction). If the holder of the IRC Section 2701 interest transfers the interest to an individual other than the initial transferor or an applicable family member of the initial transferor in an exchange for consideration during the lifetime of the initial transferor, then the reduction is taken by the initial transferor's estate and calculated as if the value of the consideration were included in the estate at its value at the time of the exchange. Property received in a nonrecognition exchange for an IRC Section 2701 interest is thereafter treated as the IRC Section 2701 interest for adjustment purposes. Reductions are calculated separately for each class of IRC Section 2701 interests. If spouses elected to treat the initial transfer as a split gift (see Q 1530), then (1) each spouse may be entitled to reductions if there is a transfer of the

---

1. IRC Sec. 2701(d)(3)(B).
2. IRC Sec. 2701(d)(4).
3. IRC Sec. 2701(e)(6).

IRC Section 2701 interest during their joint lives; and (2) if there is a transfer of the IRC Section 2701 interest at or after the death of either spouse, then (a) the donor spouse's estate may be entitled to reductions; and (b) the consenting spouse's aggregate sum of taxable gifts and gift tax payable on prior gifts are reduced to eliminate any remaining effect of IRC Section 2701 if the consenting spouse survives the donor spouse. In any event, no reduction is available to the extent that double taxation has otherwise been avoided.[1]

IRC Section 2701 interests transferred before May 5, 1994. The initial transferor can use the final regulations (see above), the proposed regulations (see below), or any other reasonable interpretation of the statute.[2]

A person who has previously made a transfer subject to IRC Section 2701 is permitted a reduction in his adjusted taxable gifts for estate tax purposes. Whether a person is a transferor is determined without regard to the split-gift provisions for spouses (see Q 1530). If any portion of the transferor's IRC Section 2701 interest is transferred to the transferor's spouse in a nontaxable event (e.g., the marital deduction), any reduction in adjusted taxable gifts is taken by such spouse rather than the transferor.[3]

The amount of the reduction is equal to the lesser of (1) the amount by which the transferor's taxable gifts were increased by reason of IRC Section 2701, or (2) the amount of the excess estate tax value of such interest multiplied by a fraction. The excess estate tax value equals the estate value of the IRC Section 2701 interest reduced by the value of such interest under IRC Section 2701 at the time of the transfer. In the case of an IRC Section 2701 interest transferred during life, the estate tax value equals the sum of (1) the increase in taxable gifts resulting from the transfer of the IRC Section 2701 interest, and (2) consideration received in exchange for the transfer. The numerator of the fraction above equals the value allocated under step 3 of the "Valuation Method" (see heading above); the numerator of the fraction equals the value allocated under step 2 of the "Valuation Method."[4] However, no reduction is available to the extent that double taxation has otherwise been avoided.[5]

Miscellaneous

These provisions apply to transfers after October 8, 1990. However, with respect to property transferred before October 9, 1990, any failure to exercise a right of conversion, to pay dividends, or to exercise other rights to be specified in regulations, is not to be treated as a subsequent transfer.[6]

With respect to gifts made after October 8, 1990, the gift tax statute of limitations on a transfer subject to these provisions does not run unless the transaction is disclosed on a gift tax return in a manner adequate to apprise the IRS of the nature of the retained and transferred interests.[7]

---

1. Treas. Reg. §25.2701-5.
2. Treas. Reg. §25.2701-5(h).
3. Prop. Treas. Reg. §25.2701-5(a).
4. Prop. Treas. Reg. §25.2701-5(b).
5. Prop. Treas. Reg. §25.2701-5(c).
6. OBRA '90, Sec. 11602(e)(1).
7. IRC Sec. 6501(c)(9); OBRA '90, Sec. 11602(e)(2).

Effect on Corporate and Partnership Transactions

Recapitalizations and Transfers of Stock

If a parent recapitalizes a corporation into common and preferred stock and gives the common stock to his children, the value of the common stock is determined by subtracting from the value of the entire corporation the value of the preferred stock as determined under IRC Section 2701. If the parent treats the preferred stock's right to dividends as qualified payments, the right to such payments is assigned a present value. However, the value assigned to the common stock must be at least equal to the value determined under the junior equity rule above. If the parent does not receive the preferred dividends within four years of their due dates, the parent may be treated as making additional transfers of the accumulated, but undistributed dividends, at the time of a subsequent transfer of the preferred stock. On the other hand, if the parent does not treat the right to dividends as qualified payments, such a right is assigned a value of zero.

Similarly, if a parent owns 80% of a corporation and a child owns 20% of the same corporation and the parent's common stock is exchanged for preferred stock, the value of what the parent has transferred and what the parent has retained are determined under IRC Section 2701.

Even if the child pays consideration for the common stock, whether the parent has made a transfer (and the value of such transfer) is determined under IRC Section 2701.

If a parent and a child each contributes to the start up of a new business and the parent receives preferred stock while the child receives common stock, the parent is treated as if he received common stock and preferred stock and then exchanged the common stock for the balance of the preferred stock. The value of what the parent has transferred and what the parent has retained are determined under IRC Section 2701.

However, a gift or a sale of stock to a child is not subject to IRC Section 2701 if the stock is of the same class as that retained by the parent. Also, a gift or a sale of stock to a child is not subject to IRC Section 2701 if the stock is proportionately the same as that retained by the parent (e.g., retained stock is entitled to $2 of dividends for every $1 of dividends paid to transferred stock), without regard to nonlapsing voting rights (i.e., parent can retain control with nonlapsing voting right).

If applicable family members receive or retain applicable retained interests at the time of a gift or a sale of stock to a child, the transaction may be subject to IRC Section 2701 even though the parent is willing to terminate his equity relationship with the corporation.

IRC Section 2701 could be avoided by selling the common stock to a nonfamily member, such as a valuable employee. Proceeds of the sale could then be distributed to the children.

Of course, IRC Section 2701 does not apply if either the transferred interest (common stock) or retained interest (preferred stock) is publicly traded. Also, with regard to retained distribution rights, IRC Section 2701 does not apply if the transferor and applicable family members do not control the corporation immediately before the transfer. However, with regard to liquidation, put, call, or conversion rights (other than those treated as distribution rights, see above), IRC Section 2701 can apply even if the transferor and applicable family members do not control the corporation.

If the typical recapitalization is reversed (i.e., the parent retains the common stock and transfers the preferred stock), IRC Section 2701 should not apply (assuming no retention of applicable retained interests by parent or applicable family members).

Partnership Freezes

The traditional partnership freeze worked similarly to the traditional estate freeze recapitalization. It too is caught by the IRC Section 2701 special valuation rules. Most of the techniques employed to reduce the effect of, or to avoid, the valuation rules with respect to a recapitalization will also work with a partnership. Examination of the partnership agreement will be required to determine which partners hold which rights. Note that in the case of a limited partnership, "control" includes the holding of any interest as a general partner. Also, any right to receive a guaranteed payment of a fixed amount from a partnership under IRC Section 707(c) is not treated as a distribution right.

Other Changes in Capital Structure

Other changes in capital structure may also be caught by the IRC Section 2701 special valuation rules. Except as provided in regulations, a contribution to capital, a redemption, a recapitalization, or other change in capital structure of a corporation or partnership is treated as a transfer if the taxpayer or an applicable family member receives an applicable retained interest in the transaction, or as provided under regulations, holds such an interest immediately after the transfer.

Nonequity Interests

The IRC Section 2701 special valuation rules apply only to equity interests. Thus, none of the following should be treated as a retained interest for purposes of IRC Section 2701: an installment sale of an interest in a corporation or partnership, an exchange of an interest in a corporation or partnership for a private annuity, an employment contract or deferred compensation, or debt owed by a corporation or partnership to a transferor or applicable family member.[1] However, the total amount of debt owed the transferor or an applicable family member by the entity is a factor in the junior equity rule above.

1551. What special valuation rules apply to the transfer of an interest in trust, or to certain remainder or joint purchase transactions, under Chapter 14?

As a general rule, the value of a transferred remainder interest is equal to the value of the transferor's entire interest prior to the transfer reduced by the value of the interest retained by the transferor. For the purpose of determining whether a transfer of an interest in a trust to (or for the benefit of) a member of the transferor's family is a gift (and the value of the transfer), the value of any interest retained by the transferor or an applicable family member is treated as being zero unless the retained interest is a qualified interest. This rule does not apply to an incomplete gift (a transfer that would not be treated as a gift whether or not consideration was received), to a transfer to a trust if the only property to be held by the trust is a residence to be used as a personal residence by persons holding term interests in the trust, or to the extent that regula-

---

1. See TAM 9436006.

tions provide that a transfer is not inconsistent with IRC Section 2702.[1] Also, IRC Section 2702 does not apply to (1) certain charitable remainder trusts, (2) a pooled income fund, (3) a charitable lead trust in which the only interest in the trust other than the remainder interest or a qualified annuity or unitrust interest is the charitable lead interest, (4) the assignment of a remainder interest if the only interest retained by the transferor or an applicable family member is as a permissible recipient of income in the sole discretion of an independent trustee, and (5) a transfer in trust to a spouse for full and adequate consideration in connection with a divorce if any remaining interests in the trust are retained by the other spouse.[2] For transfers to a trust made after May 17, 1997, regulations exempt charitable remainder unitrusts (CRUTs) from IRC Section 2702 only if the trust provides for simple unitrust payments, or in the case of a CRUT with a lesser of trust income or the unitrust amount provision, the grantor and/or the grantor's spouse (who is a citizen of the U.S.) are the only noncharitable beneficiaries.[3] Modified rules apply to certain qualified tangible property.

For these purposes, a transfer in trust does not include (1) the exercise, release, or lapse of a power of appointment over trust property that would not be a transfer for gift tax purposes, or (2) the exercise of a qualified disclaimer. An interest in trust includes a power with respect to a trust which would cause any portion of the transfer to be incomplete for gift tax purposes.[4]

Retained Interests

Retained is defined as the same person holds an interest both before and after the transfer in trust. Thus, a transfer of an income interest for life in trust to an applicable family member in conjunction with the transfer of a remainder interest in trust to a member of the transferor's family is not subject to IRC Section 2702. However, with respect to the creation of a term interest (e.g., a joint purchase creating a term and remainder interest), any interest held by the transferor immediately after the transfer is treated as held both before and after the transfer.[5] A negotiable note received in exchange for publicly traded stock sold to a trust was not treated as a retained interest in a trust.[6]

Qualified Interests

A "qualified interest" is an annuity or unitrust interest, or, if all other interests in the trust are annuity or unitrust interests, a noncontingent remainder interest. A *qualified annuity interest* means a right to receive fixed amounts (or a fixed fraction or percentage of the property transferred to the trust) not less frequently than annually. A *qualified unitrust interest* means a right to receive amounts which are payable not less frequently than annually and are a fixed percentage of the fair market value of the property in the trust (determined annually).[7] A qualified annuity interest can provide for an annuity amount (or fixed fraction or percentage) which increases by not more than 120% of the stated dollar amount (or fixed fraction or percentage) payable in the preceding year.[8] A

---

1. IRC Sec. 2702(a).
2. Treas. Reg. §25.2702-1(c).
3. Treas. Reg. §25.2702-1(c)(3).
4. Treas. Reg. §25.2702-2(a).
5. Treas. Reg. §25.2702-2(a)(3).
6. TAM 9436006.
7. IRC Sec. 2702(b).
8. Treas. Reg. §25.2702-3(b)(1)(ii).

qualified unitrust interest can provide for a unitrust percentage which increases by not more than 120% of the fixed percentage payable in the preceding year.[1]

The retention of a power to revoke a qualified annuity or unitrust interest of the transferor's spouse is treated as retention of the qualified annuity or unitrust interest.[2] Contingent annuity interests retained by the grantor or given to the grantor's spouse were not qualified interests.[3] Regulations treat an interest with the following characteristics as a qualified interest retained by the grantor: an annuity or unitrust interest that is (1) given to the spouse of the grantor; and (2) contingent only on (a) the spouse surviving, or (b) that the grantor does not revoke the spouse's interest.[4] The grantor makes an additional gift to the remainder person when the spouse's interest is revoked or the grantor survives the trust term without having revoked the interest.

A right to receive each year the *lesser of* an annuity interest or a unitrust interest is not treated as a qualified interest. The right to receive each year the *greater of* an annuity interest or a unitrust interest is treated as a qualified interest. However, the qualified interest is valued at the greater of the two interests.[5] A right of withdrawal, whether or not cumulative, is not a qualified annuity or unitrust interest.[6]

A qualified annuity or unitrust interest may permit the payment of income in excess of the annuity or unitrust amount to the transferor or applicable family member with the retained annuity or unitrust interest. However, the annuity or unitrust interest is valued without regard to the right to excess income (which is not a qualified annuity or unitrust interest).[7] Also, a qualified annuity interest may permit the payment of an amount sufficient to reimburse the grantor for any income tax due on income in excess of the annuity amount; the annuity interest is valued without regard to such reimbursement right.[8] Distributions from the trust cannot be made to anyone other than the transferor or applicable family member who holds the qualified annuity or unitrust interest.[9]

The term of the annuity or unitrust interest must be for the life of the transferor or applicable family member, for a specified term of years, or for the shorter of the two periods.[10] There is a split of authority as to whether valuation may be based on two lives, or just one life.[11] Regulations permit certain revocable spousal interests (see above), but value the retained grantor and spouse's interests separately as for a single life.[12]

An example in the regulations had provided that where a grantor retained the right to annuity payments for 10 years and the payments continued to his estate if he died during the 10-year term, the annuity was valued as for 10 years or until the grantor's prior death (i.e., as a temporary annuity).[13] The Tax Court ruled that the example was

1. Treas. Reg. §25.2702-3(c)(1)(ii).
2. Treas. Reg. §25.2702-2(a)(5).
3. TAMs 9707001, 9717008, 9741001; *Cook v. Comm.*, 2001-2 USTC ¶60,422 (7th Cir. 2001), aff'g 115 TC 15 (2000).
4. Treas. Reg. §25.2702-3(d)(2).
5. Treas. Reg. §25.2702-3(d)(1).
6. Treas. Regs. §§25.2702-3(b)(1)(i), 25.2702-3(c)(1)(i).
7. Treas. Regs. §§25.2702-3(b)(1)(iii), 25.2702-3(c)(1)(iii).
8. Let. Ruls. 9441031, 9345035.
9. Treas. Reg. §25.2702-3(d)(2).
10. Treas. Reg. §25.2702-3(d)(3).
11. *Schott v. Comm.*, 2003-1 USTC 60,457 (9th Cir. 2003), rev'g TC Memo 2001-110; *Cook v. Comm.*, 2001-2 USTC ¶60,422 (7th Cir. 2001), aff'g 115 TC 15 (2000).
12. Reg. §25.2702-3(e)(Ex. 8).
13. Treas. Reg. §25.2702-3(e)(Ex. 5).

invalid, that the annuity should be valued as for 10 years (i.e., as a term annuity).[1] The IRS has changed the regulations so as to follow *Walton*.[2] Note that if the trust property reverted to grantor's estate if the grantor died during the 10-year term, the annuity is valued as for 10 years or until the grantor's prior death.[3] These results should apply likewise to unitrust payments.

The IRS will not issue rulings or determination letters on whether annuity interests are qualified interests under IRC Section 2702 where (1) the amount of the annuity payable annually is more than 50% of the initial fair market value of the property transferred to trust, or (2) the value of the remainder interest is less than 10% of the initial fair market value of the property transferred to trust. For purposes of the 10% test, the value of the remainder interest is determined under IRC Section 7520 without regard to the possibility that the grantor might die during the trust term, or that the trust property might revert to the grantor or the grantor's estate.[4]

Commutation (generally, an actuarially based acceleration or substitution of benefits) of a qualified annuity or unitrust interest is not permitted.[5] Additional contributions are not permitted with qualified annuity interests.[6]

The use of notes, other debt instruments, options or similar financial arrangements in satisfaction of the annuity or unitrust requirements under IRC Section 2702 is prohibited.[7]

A remainder (or reversion) interest is treated as a *qualified remainder interest* if: (1) all interests in the trust (other than non-contingent remainder interests) are either qualified annuity interests or qualified unitrust interests (thus, an excess income provision is not permitted for this purpose); (2) each remainder interest is entitled to all or a fractional share of the trust property when all or a fractional share of the trust terminates (a transferor's right to receive the original value of the trust property, or a fractional share, would not qualify); and (3) the remainder is payable to the beneficiary or the beneficiary's estate in all events (i.e., it is non-contingent).[8]

A qualified interest is to be valued using the valuation tables prescribed by IRC Section 7520.[9] For valuation rules for certain qualified tangible property, see below.

Qualified Tangible Property

If the nonexercise of rights under a term interest in tangible property would not have a substantial effect on the valuation of the remainder interest, the interest is valued at the amount for which it could be sold to an unrelated third person (i.e., market value is used instead of the valuation tables or zero valuation).[10] *Qualified tangible property* is tangible property (1) for which a depreciation or depletion allowance would not be allowable if the property were used in a trade or business or held for the production

---

1. *Walton v. Comm.*, 115 TC 589 (2000).
2. Treas. Reg. §25.2702-3(e)(Ex. 5).
3. Treas. Reg. §25.2702-3(e)(Ex. 1).
4. Rev. Proc. 2006-3, Sec. 4.50, 2006-1 IRB 122.
5. Treas. Reg. §25.2702-3(d)(4).
6. Treas. Reg. §25.2702-3(b)(4).
7. Treas. Reg. §25.2702-3.
8. Treas. Reg. §25.2702-3(f).
9. IRC Sec. 2702(a)(2)(B).
10. IRC Sec. 2702(c)(4).

of income, and (2) as to which the nonexercise of any rights under the term interest would not affect the value of the property passing to the remainderperson. A de minimis exception is provided at the time of the transfer to trust for improvements to the property which would be depreciable provided such improvements do not exceed 5% of the fair market value of the entire property.[1]

Term interests in qualified tangible property are valued using actual sales or rentals that are comparable both as to the nature and character of the property and the duration of the term interest. Little weight is given appraisals in the absence of comparables. Tables used in valuing annuity, unitrust, estate, and remainder interests under IRC Section 7520 are not evidence of what a willing buyer would pay a willing seller for an interest in qualified tangible property.[2] If the taxpayer cannot establish the value of the term interest, the interest is valued at zero.[3]

If, during the term, the term interest is converted into property other than qualified tangible property, the conversion is treated as a transfer of the unexpired portion of the term interest (valued as of the time of the original transfer) unless the trust is converted to a qualified annuity interest (see above).[4] If an addition or improvement is made to qualified tangible property such that the property would no longer be treated as qualified tangible property, the property is subject to the conversion rule above. If the addition or improvement would not change the nature of the qualified tangible property, the addition or improvement is treated as an additional transfer subject to IRC Section 2702.[5]

Personal Residences

IRC Section 2702 does not apply to the transfer of an interest in a personal residence trust or a qualified personal residence trust.[6] However, a person is limited to holding a term interest in only two such trusts.[7] A personal residence trust or a qualified personal residence trust which does not meet the requirements in the regulations may be modified (by judicial modification or otherwise, so long as the modification is effective under state law), if the reformation commences within 90 days of the due date (including extensions) for filing the gift tax return and is completed within a reasonable time after commencement. In the case of a trust created before 1997, the reformation must commence within 90 days after December 23, 1997, and be completed within a reasonable time after commencement.[8]

A *personal residence* is defined as either (1) the principal residence of the term holder, (2) a residence of the term holder which the term holder uses for personal use during the year for a number of days which exceeds the greater of 14 days or 10% of the days during the year that the residence is rented at fair market value, or (3) an undivided fractional interest in either (1) or (2). A personal residence includes appurtenant residential structures and a reasonable amount of land (taking into account the residence's size and location). Personal property, such as household furnishings, is not included in

---

1. Treas. Reg. §25.2702-2(c)(2).
2. Treas. Reg. §25.2702-2(c)(3).
3. Treas. Reg. §25.2702-2(c)(1).
4. Treas. Reg. §25.2702-2(c)(4).
5. Treas. Reg. §25.2702-2(c)(5).
6. IRC Sec. 2702(a)(3)(A)(ii); Treas. Reg. §25.2702-5(a).
7. Treas. Reg. §25.2702-5(a).
8. Treas. Reg. §25.2702-5(a)(2).

a personal residence. A personal residence is treated as such as long as it is not occupied by any other person (other than the spouse or a dependent) and is available at all times for use by the term holder as a personal residence. A personal residence can be rented out if the rental use is secondary to the primary use as a personal residence (but see above). Use of the residence as transient lodging is not permitted if substantial services are provided (e.g., a hotel or a bread and breakfast). Spouses may hold interests in the same personal residence or qualified personal residence trust.[1]

A *personal residence trust* is a trust which is prohibited for the entire term of the trust from holding any property other than one residence to be used as the personal residence of the term holder(s). A personal residence trust cannot permit the personal residence to be sold, transferred, or put to any other use. Expenses of the trust can be paid by the term holder. A personal residence trust can hold proceeds payable as a result of damage to, or destruction or involuntary conversion of, the personal residence for reinvestment in a personal residence within two years of receipt of such proceeds.[2] Also, with respect to trusts created after May 16, 1996, a personal residence trust must be prohibited from selling or transferring, directly or indirectly, the residence to the grantor, the grantor's spouse, or an entity controlled by the grantor or the grantor's spouse, at any time after the original term interest during which the trust is a grantor trust. A distribution upon or after the expiration of the original duration of the trust term to another grantor trust of the grantor or the grantor's spouse pursuant to the trust terms will not be treated as a sale or transfer to the grantor or grantor's spouse if the second trust prohibits sale or transfer of the property to the grantor, the grantor's spouse, or an entity controlled by the grantor or the grantor's spouse. This prohibition against a transfer to the grantor or the grantor's spouse does not apply to a transfer pursuant to the trust document or a power retained by the grantor in the event the grantor dies prior to the expiration of the original duration of the trust term. Nor does this prohibition apply to a distribution (for no consideration) of the residence to the grantor's spouse pursuant to the trust document at the expiration of the original duration of the trust term.[3]

A *qualified personal residence trust* is generally prohibited for the entire term of the trust from holding any property other than one residence to be used as the personal residence of the term holder(s), but certain exceptions are available. Thus, a qualified personal residence trust is permitted to hold cash in a separate account, but not in excess of the amount needed (1) for payment of trust expenses (including mortgage payments) currently due or expected within the next six months, (2) for improvements to the residence to be paid within the next six months, and (3) for purchase of a personal residence either (a) within three months of the creation of the trust, or (b) within the next three months pursuant to a previously entered into contract to purchase. Improvements to the personal residence which meet the personal residence requirements are permitted.[4]

Generally, sales proceeds (including income thereon) may be held in a qualified personal residence trust in a separate account until the earlier of (1) two years from the date of sale, (2) termination of the term holder's interest, or (3) purchase of a new residence. Insurance proceeds (including, for this purpose, certain amounts received upon an involuntary conversion) paid to a qualified personal residence trust for damage or destruction to the personal residence may also be held in the trust in a separate account

---

1. Treas. Regs. §§25.2702-5(b), 25.2702-5(c)(2).
2. Treas. Reg. §25.2702-5(b).
3. Treas. Regs. §§25.2702-5(b)(1), 25.2702-7.
4. Treas. Reg. §25.2702-5(c)(5).

for a similar period of time.[1] However, with respect to trusts created after May 16, 1996, a qualified personal residence trust must be prohibited from selling or transferring, directly or indirectly, the residence to the grantor, the grantor's spouse, or an entity controlled by the grantor or the grantor's spouse, during the original trust term and at any time after the original term interest during which the trust is a grantor trust. A distribution upon or after the expiration of the original duration of the trust term to another grantor trust of the grantor or the grantor's spouse pursuant to the trust terms will not be treated as a sale or transfer to the grantor or grantor's spouse if the second trust prohibits sale or transfer of the property to the grantor, the grantor's spouse, or an entity controlled by the grantor or the grantor's spouse. This prohibition against a transfer to the grantor or the grantor's spouse does not apply to a transfer pursuant to the trust document or a power retained by the grantor in the event the grantor dies prior to the expiration of the original duration of the trust term. Nor does this prohibition apply to a distribution (for no consideration) of the residence to the grantor's spouse pursuant to the trust document at the expiration of the original duration of the trust term.[2]

Cash held by a qualified personal residence trust in excess of the amounts permitted above must be distributed to the term holder at least quarterly. Furthermore, upon termination of the term holder's interest, any cash held by a qualified personal residence trust for payment of trust expenses must be distributed to the term holder within 30 days.[3]

The qualified personal residence trust must provide that any trust income be distributed at least annually to the term holder.[4] Distributions from a qualified personal residence trust cannot be made to anyone other than the term holder during any term interest.[5] Commutation (generally, an actuarially based acceleration or substitution of benefits) of a qualified personal residence trust is not permitted.[6]

A qualified personal residence trust ceases to be a qualified personal residence trust if the residence ceases to be used or held for use as the personal residence of the term holder. A residence is held by the trust for use as the personal residence of the term holder so long as the residence is not occupied by any other person (other than the spouse or a dependent of the term holder) and is available at all times for use by the term holder. A sale of a personal residence is not treated as a cessation of use as a personal residence if the personal residence is replaced by another within two years of the sale. The trust must provide that if damage to or destruction of the residence renders it unusable as a residence, the trust ceases to be a qualified personal residence trust unless the residence is repaired or replaced within two years.[7]

A qualified personal residence trust must provide that within 30 days of ceasing to be a qualified personal residence trust with respect to any assets, either (1) the assets must be distributed to the term holder; (2) the assets must be put into a separate share of the trust for the balance of the term holder's interest as a qualified annuity interest; or (3) the trustee may elect either (1) or (2). The amount of such an annuity must be no less than the amount determined by dividing the lesser of the original value of all

1. Treas. Regs. §§25.2702-5(c)(5)(ii), 25.2702-5(c)(7).
2. Treas. Regs. §§25.2702-5(c)(9), 25.2702-7.
3. Treas. Reg. §25.2702-5(c)(5)(ii)(A)(2).
4. Treas. Reg. §25.2702-5(c)(3).
5. Treas. Reg. §25.2702-5(c)(4).
6. Treas. Reg. §25.2702-5(c)(6).
7. Treas. Reg. §25.2702-5(c)(7).

interests retained by the term holder or the value of all the trust assets by an annuity valuation factor reflecting the valuation table rate on the date of the original transfer and the original term of the term holder's interest. If only a portion of the trust continues as a qualified personal residence trust, then the annuity determined in the preceding sentence is reduced in proportion to the ratio that assets which still qualify as a personal residence trust bear to total trust assets.[1]

Remainder Interest Transactions and Joint Purchases

The transfer of an interest in property with respect to which there are one or more term interests (e.g., transfer of a remainder interest) is to be treated as a transfer of an interest in trust.[2] A leasehold interest in property is not treated as a term interest provided a good faith effort is made to set the lease at a fair rental value.[3] If a person acquires a term interest in property in a joint purchase (or series of related transactions) with members of his family, then such person is treated as though he acquired the entire property and then transferred the interests acquired by the other persons in the transaction to such persons in return for consideration furnished by such persons.[4] For this purpose, the amount considered transferred by such individual is not to exceed the amount which such individual furnished for such property.[5] Special rules apply to "qualified tangible property" (see above).

Attribution

A "member of the family" with respect to an individual includes such individual's spouse, any ancestor or lineal descendant of such individual or such individual's spouse, any brother or sister of the individual, and any spouse of the above.[6] An "applicable family member" with respect to a transferor includes the transferor's spouse, an ancestor of the transferor or transferor's spouse, and the spouse of any such ancestor.[7]

Adjustment to Mitigate Double Taxation

A gift tax and estate tax adjustment is provided to mitigate the double taxation of retained interests previously valued under IRC Section 2702. In the case of a transfer by gift of a retained interest previously valued under IRC Section 2702 using the zero valuation rule or the qualified tangible property rule, a reduction in aggregate taxable gifts is available in calculating gift tax. If a retained interest previously valued under IRC Section 2702 using the zero valuation rule or using the qualified tangible property rule is later included in the gross estate, a reduction in adjusted taxable gifts is available in calculating estate tax. The amount of the reduction in aggregate taxable gifts or adjusted taxable gifts is equal to the lesser of (1) the increase in the taxable gifts resulting from the retained interest being initially valued under the zero valuation rule or the qualified tangible property rule, or (2) the increase in taxable gifts or gross estate resulting from the subsequent transfer of the interest. For purposes of (2), the annual exclusion is applied first to transfers other than the transfer valued under the zero valuation rule or the qualified tangible property rule. One-half of the amount of reduction may be assigned to a consenting spouse if gifts are split under IRC Section 2513.[8]

1. Treas. Reg. §25.2702-5(c)(8).
2. IRC Sec. 2702(c)(1).
3. Treas. Reg. §25.2702-4(b).
4. IRC Sec. 2702(c)(2).
5. Treas. Reg. §25.2702-4(c).
6. IRC Sec. 2702(e).
7. IRC Secs. 2702(a)(1), 2701(e)(2).
8. Treas. Reg. §25.2702-6.

Miscellaneous

These provisions apply to transfers after October 8, 1990. However, with respect to property transferred before October 9, 1990, any failure to exercise a right of conversion, to pay dividends, or to exercise other rights to be specified in regulations, is not to be treated as a subsequent transfer.[1]

With respect to gifts made after October 8, 1990, the gift tax statute of limitations on a transfer subject to these provisions does not run unless the transaction is disclosed on a gift tax return in a manner adequate to apprise the IRS of the nature of the retained and transferred interests.[2]

Effect on Trust, Remainder Interest, and Joint Purchase Transactions

GRITs, GRATs, and GRUTs

Generally, a grantor retained income trust (GRIT) should no longer be used unless the only property to be held by the trust is a residence to be used as a personal residence by persons holding term interests in the trust. Under IRC Section 2702, the grantor is treated as though he transferred the entire property to the remainderperson at the time of the creation of the GRIT since his retained income interest is valued at zero (except with respect to the personal residence exception or unless the remainderperson is not a member of the transferor's family).[3]

Instead, grantor retained annuity trusts (GRATs) and grantor retained unitrusts (GRUTs) can be used to leverage gifts. The retained annuity or unitrust interest is valued using the government valuation tables provided under IRC Section 7520. Notes, other debt instruments, options or similar financial arrangements cannot be used in satisfaction of the annuity or unitrust requirements. The value of the transferred remainder interest is equal to the value of the entire property reduced by the value of the retained interest. A reversion or general power of appointment retained by the grantor which is contingent upon the grantor dying during the trust term will no longer reduce the value of the transferred property. However, the value of the retained interest is reduced by such a contingency.

Charitable Trusts

Transfers to charitable remainder annuity trusts (CRATs), certain charitable remainder unitrusts (CRUTs), and pooled income funds are not subject to IRC Section 2702. Also, IRC Section 2702 does not apply to a charitable lead trust in which the only interest in the trust other than the remainder interest or a qualified annuity or unitrust interest is the charitable lead interest. For transfers to a trust made after May 17, 1997, regulations exempt CRUTs from IRC Section 2702 only if the trust provides for simple unitrust payments, or in the case of a CRUT with a lesser of trust income or the unitrust amount provision, the grantor and/or the grantor's spouse (who is a citizen of the U.S.) are the only noncharitable beneficiaries.[4]

---

1. OBRA '90, Sec. 11602(e)(1).
2. IRC Sec. 6501(c)(9); OBRA '90, Sec. 11602(e)(2).
3. See Let. Rul. 9109033.
4. Treas. Reg. §25.2702-1(c)(3).

Irrevocable Life Insurance Trusts

Irrevocable life insurance trusts should not be affected by IRC Section 2702. Generally, the full value of transfers to an irrevocable life insurance trust are already treated as gifts (except to the extent that annual exclusions are available).

Other Trusts

If a term interest (whether for life or term of years) is given to the transferor's spouse, an ancestor of the transferor or transferor's spouse, or the spouse of any such ancestor, and a remainder interest is given to any member of the transferor's family, IRC Section 2702 should not apply because the grantor has not retained a term interest.

Remainder Interest Transaction (RIT)

In general, if a person retains a term interest (whether for life or term of years) in property and sells or give a remainder interest in the property to another family member, the value of the transferred property will be equal to the full value of the property unless the transferor retained an annuity or unitrust interest in the property (i.e., the value of a retained income interest is valued at zero).

However, if the nonexercise of rights under a term interest in tangible property would not have a substantial effect on the valuation of the remainder interest, the interest is valued at the amount for which it could be sold to an unrelated third person (i.e., market value is used instead of the valuation tables or zero valuation). The Senate Committee Report to OBRA '90 gives a painting, or undeveloped real estate, as examples of such tangible property. Depletable property is given as an example of property which would not qualify for this special rule. See "Qualified Tangible Property," above.

Split Purchases (Splits)

If a person acquires a term interest in property in a joint purchase (or series of related transactions) with members of his family, then such person is treated as though he acquired the entire property and then transferred the interests acquired by the other persons in the transaction to such persons in return for consideration furnished by such persons. Thus, if a father and son purchase rental property and the father receives an interest for life and the son receives a remainder interest, the father is treated as though he sold the remainder interest to his son for the consideration furnished by the son. The transaction is then essentially treated as a sale of a remainder interest (see above).

1552. What special valuation rules apply to certain agreements, options, rights, or restrictions exercisable at less than fair market value under Chapter 14?

For estate, gift, and generation-skipping transfer tax purposes, the value of any property is to be determined without regard to any restriction on the right to sell or use such property, or any option, agreement, or other right to acquire or use the property at less than fair market value (determined without regard to such an option, agreement, or right). However, the previous sentence is not to apply if the option, agreement, right, or restriction (1) is a bona fide business arrangement, (2) is not a device to transfer the property to members of the decedent's family for less than full and adequate consideration in money or money's worth, and (3) has terms comparable to those entered into by persons in an arm's length transaction.[1] The three prongs of the test must be inde-

---

1. IRC Sec. 2703.

pendently satisfied.[1] All three prongs of the test are considered met if more than 50% of the value of the property subject to the right or restriction is owned by persons who are not members of the transferor's family or natural objects of the transferor's bounty. The property owned by such other persons must be subject to the right or restriction to the same extent as the property owned by the transferor.[2]

To determine whether a buy-sell agreement or other restrictive agreement has terms comparable to those entered into by persons in an arm's length transaction, the following factors are to be considered: "the expected term of the agreement, the current fair market value of the property, anticipated changes in value during the term of the agreement, and the adequacy of any consideration given in exchange for the rights granted."[3] The terms of a buy-sell agreement or other restrictive agreement must be comparable to those used as a general practice by unrelated persons under negotiated agreements in the same business. Isolated comparables do not meet this requirement. More than one recognized method may be acceptable. Where comparables are difficult to find because the business is unique, comparables from similar businesses may be used.[4]

In the case of a partnership (or LLC) created on a decedent's deathbed, the IRS has stated that the partnership was the agreement for purposes of IRC Section 2703, and the partnership should be ignored because the partnership was not a valid business arrangement and the partnership was a device to transfer the underlying property to the family members for less than adequate consideration. Even if the partnership was not ignored, the Service stated that it would ignore the restrictions on use of the property contained in the partnership's agreement; such restrictions also would fail IRC Section 2703.[5] A couple of courts have rejected the idea that the partnership can be ignored for purposes of IRC Section 2703.[6]

For more information on valuing a closely held business interest, see Q 1544, Q 1545.

Effective Date and Transition Rules

This provision applies to agreements, options, rights, or restrictions entered into or granted after October 8, 1990, and agreements, options, rights, or restrictions substantially modified after October 8, 1990.[7] Any discretionary modification of an agreement that results in other than a de minimis change in the quality, value, or timing of the agreement is a substantial modification. Generally, a modification required by the agreement is not considered a substantial modification. However, if the agreement requires periodic modification, the failure to update the agreement is treated as a substantial modification unless the updating would not have resulted in a substantial modification. The addition of a family member as a party to a right or restriction is treated as a substantial modification unless (1) the addition is mandatory under the terms of the right or restriction or (2) the added family member is in a generation (using the generation-skipping transfer tax definitions of generations) no lower than the lowest

1. Treas. Reg. §25.2703-1(b)(2).
2. Treas. Reg. §25.2703-1(b)(3).
3. Treas. Reg. §25.2703-1(b)(4)(i).
4. Treas. Reg. §25.2703-1(b)(4)(ii).
5. TAMs 9723009, 9725002, 9730004, 9735003, 9736004, 9842003.
6. *Est. of Strangi v. Comm.*, 2002 USTC ¶60,441 (5th Cir. 2002), aff'g 115 TC 478 (2000); *Church v. U.S.*, 2000-1 USTC ¶60,369 (W.D. Tex. 2000).
7. OBRA '90, Sec. 11602(e)(1)((A)(ii).

generation of any individuals already party to the right or restriction. The modification of a capitalization rate in a manner that bears a fixed relationship to a specified market rate is not treated as a substantial modification. Furthermore, a modification that results in an option price that more closely approximates fair market value is not treated as a substantial modification.[1]

Effect on Options and Buy-sell Agreements

In order to help fix values for estate, gift, and generation-skipping transfer tax purposes, newly executed or substantially modified options and buy-sell agreements exercisable at less than fair market value between persons who are the natural objects of each other's bounty will generally have to meet all three of IRC Section 2703's requirements. Otherwise, such agreement will be disregarded in valuing the property. Old options and buy-sell agreements which are not substantially modified after October 8, 1990 are not affected by IRC Section 2703. IRC Section 2703's provisions apply to agreements involving either business or nonbusiness property.

1553. What special valuation rules apply to certain lapsing rights and restrictions under Chapter 14?

In general, IRC Section 2704(a) provides that the lapse of certain voting or liquidation rights in a family owned business results in a taxable transfer by the holder of the lapsing right. IRC Section 2704(b) provides generally that certain restrictions on liquidating a family owned business are ignored in valuing a transferred interest. These provisions apply to restrictions or rights (or limitations on rights) created after October 8, 1990.[2]

For more information on valuing a closely held business interest, see Q 1544, Q 1545.

Lapse of Certain Rights

For estate, gift, and generation-skipping transfer tax purposes, if there is a lapse of a voting or liquidation right in a corporation or partnership and the individual holding such right (the "holder") immediately before the lapse and members of the holder's family control the entity (both before and after the lapse), then the holder is treated as making a transfer. The value of the transfer is equal to the amount (if any) by which the value of all interests in the entity held by the holder immediately prior to the lapse (determined as if all voting and liquidation rights were nonlapsing) exceeds the sum of (1) the value of such interests immediately after the lapse (determined as if held by one individual), and (2) in the case of a lapse during the holder's life, any consideration in money or money's worth received by the holder with respect to such lapse.[3]

A *voting right* is defined as a right to vote with respect to *any* matter of the entity. Also, with respect to a partnership, the right of a general partner to participate in partnership management is treated as a voting right. A *liquidation right* is the right to compel (including by aggregate voting power) the entity to acquire *all or a portion* of

---

1. Treas. Reg. §25.2703-1(c).
2. OBRA '90, Sec. 11602(e)(1)(A)(iii).
3. IRC Sec. 2704(a); Treas. Regs. §§25.2704-1(a), 25.2704-1(d).

the holder's equity interest in the entity.[1] A lapse of a voting or liquidation right occurs when a presently exercisable right is restricted or eliminated.[2]

The transfer of an interest which results in the lapse of a liquidation right is not subject to IRC Section 2704(a) if the rights with respect to the transferred interest are not restricted or eliminated. However, a transfer that results in the elimination of the transferor's right to compel the entity to acquire an interest of the transferor which is subordinate to the transferred interest is treated as a lapse of a liquidation right with respect to the subordinate interest. The lapse rule does not apply to the lapse of a liquidation right with respect to (1) a transfer that was previously valued in the hands of the holder as a transfer of an interest in a corporation or partnership under IRC Section 2701 (see Q 1550), or (2) the lapse of a liquidation right to the extent that immediately after the lapse the holder (or the holder's estate) and members of the holder's family cannot liquidate an interest that the holder could have liquidated prior to the lapse. Whether an interest can be liquidated immediately after the lapse is determined under state law or, if the governing instruments are less restrictive than the state law which would apply in the absence of such instruments, the governing instruments. For this purpose, any applicable restriction under IRC Section 2704(b) (see below) is disregarded.[3]

If a lapsed right may be restored only upon the occurrence of a future event not within the control of the holder or the holder's family, the lapse is deemed to occur at the time the lapse becomes permanent with respect to the holder (e.g., upon the transfer of the interest).[4]

For attribution rules, see below.

Transfers Subject to Applicable Restrictions

If there is a transfer of an interest in a corporation or partnership to (or for the benefit of) a member of the transferor's family and the transferor and members of transferor's family control the entity (immediately before the transfer), any applicable restriction is to be disregarded in valuing the transferred interest for estate, gift, or generation-skipping transfer tax purposes.[5] If an applicable restriction is disregarded under this rule, the rights of the transferor are valued under the state law that would apply but for the limitation (which is treated as if it did not exist).[6]

"Applicable restriction" means any restriction which effectively limits the ability of the corporation or partnership to liquidate if either (1) the restriction lapses (in whole or in part) after the transfer, or (2) the transferor or any member of the transferor's family, acting alone or collectively, can remove the restriction (in whole or in part) after the transfer.[7] Applicable restriction treatment was avoided where the consent of all parties was required and a charity (a nonfamily member) had become a partner.[8]

---

1. Treas. Reg. §25.2704-1(a)(2).
2. Treas. Regs. §§25.2704-1(b), 25.2704-1(c)(1).
3. Treas. Reg. §25.2704-1(c).
4. Treas. Reg. §25.2704-1(a)(3).
5. IRC Sec. 2704(b)(1).
6. Treas. Reg. §25.2704-2(c).
7. IRC Sec. 2704(b)(2).
8. *Kerr v. Comm.*, 2002-1 USTC ¶60,440 (5th Cir. 2002).

However, any restriction imposed or required by any federal or state law is not treated as an applicable restriction.[1] Thus, the definition of an applicable restriction has been limited to a restriction which is more restrictive than the limitations which would apply under state law if there were no restriction. Also, whether there is the ability to remove a restriction is determined under the state law which would apply in the absence of the restrictive provision in the governing instruments.[2]

An applicable restriction does not include any commercially reasonable restriction which arises as part of any financing by the corporation or partnership with a person who is not related to the transferor or transferee, or a member of the family of either.[3] Regulations provide that an applicable restriction does not include any commercially reasonable restriction which arises as a result of any unrelated person providing capital in the form of debt or equity to the corporation or partnership for the entity's trade or business operations. For this purpose, the regulations apply the relationship rules of IRC Section 267(b), except that the term "fiduciary of a trust" under the relationship rules is modified to generally exclude banks, trust companies, and building and loan associations.[4]

Furthermore, an applicable restriction does not include an option, right to use property, or other agreement subject to IRC Section 2703 (see Q 1552).[5]

With respect to a partnership (or LLC) created on a decedent's deathbed, the IRS has disregarded restrictions where the partnership provided that a partner could not liquidate his interest, while state law provided a less restrictive provision.[6] A few cases that have held that partnership liquidation provisions were no more restrictive than state law and should not be ignored under IRC Section 2704(b).[7]

Attribution

The following attribution rules or definitions generally apply for purposes of the rules which apply to certain lapsing rights and applicable restrictions under IRC Section 2704.

In the case of a corporation, "control" means 50% ownership (by vote or value) of the stock. In the case of a partnership, "control" means 50% ownership of the capital or profits interests, or in the case of a limited partnership, the ownership of any interest as a general partner.[8]

A "member of the family" with respect to an individual includes such individual's spouse, any ancestor or lineal descendant of such individual or such individual's spouse, any brother or sister of the individual, and any spouse of the above.[9]

An individual is treated as holding interests held indirectly through a corporation, partnership, trust, or other entity.[10] Thus, transfers may be either direct or indirect.

---

1. IRC Sec. 2704(b)(3)(B).
2. Treas. Reg. §25.2704-2(b).
3. IRC Sec. 2704(b)(3)(A).
4. Treas. Reg. §25.2704-2(b).
5. Treas. Reg. §25.2704-2(b).
6. TAMs 9723009, 9725002, 9730004, 9735003, 9736004, 9842003.
7. *Kerr v. Comm.*, 113 TC 449 (1999); *Knight v. Comm.*, 115 TC 506 (2000).
8. IRC Secs. 2704(c)(1), 2701(b)(2).
9. IRC Sec. 2704(c)(2).
10. IRC Secs. 2704(c)(3), 2701(e)(3).

APPENDIX A

INCOME TAX TABLES

Individuals, Estates and Trusts

(Tax Years Beginning in 2007)

Col. 1 Taxable Income	Separate Return Tax on Col. 1	Separate Return Rate on Excess	Joint Return Tax on Col. 1	Joint Return Rate on Excess	Single Return Tax on Col. 1	Single Return Rate on Excess	Head of Household Tax on Col. 1	Head of Household Rate on Excess	Trusts and Estates Tax on Col. 1	Trusts and Estates Rate on Excess
$	$	%	$	%	$	%	$	%	$	%
0	0	10.0	0	10.0	0	10.0	0	10.0	0	15.0
2,150	215	10.0	215	10.0	215	10.0	215	10.0	323	25.0
5,000	500	10.0	500	10.0	500	10.0	500	10.0	1,035	28.0
7,650	765	10.0	765	10.0	765	10.0	· 765	10.0	1,777	33.0
7,825	783	15.0	783	10.0	783	15.0	783	10.0	1,835	33.0
10,450	1,176	15.0	1,045	10.0	1,176	15.0	1,045	10.0	2,701	35.0
11,200	1,289	15.0	1,120	10.0	1,289	15.0	1,120	15.0	2,964	35.0
15,650	1,956	15.0	1,565	15.0	1,956	15.0	1,788	15.0	4,521	35.0
31,850	4,386	25.0	3,995	15.0	4,386	25.0	4,218	15.0	10,191	35.0
42,650	7,086	25.0	5,615	15.0	7,086	25.0	5,838	25.0	13,971	35.0
63,700	12,349	25.0	8,773	25.0	12,349	25.0	11,100	25.0	21,339	35.0
64,250	12,486	28.0	8,910	25.0	12,486	25.0	11,238	25.0	21,531	35.0
77,100	16,084	28.0	12,123	25.0	15,699	28.0	14,450	25.0	26,029	35.0
97,925	21,915	33.0	17,329	25.0	21,530	28.0	19,656	25.0	33,317	35.0
110,100	25,933	33.0	20,373	25.0	24,939	28.0	22,700	28.0	37,579	35.0
128,500	32,005	33.0	24,973	28.0	30,091	28.0	27,852	28.0	44,019	35.0
160,850	42,681	33.0	34,031	28.0	39,149	33.0	36,910	28.0	55,341	35.0
174,850	47,301	35.0	37,951	28.0	43,769	33.0	40,830	28.0	60,241	35.0
178,350	48,526	35.0	38,931	28.0	44,924	33.0	41,810	33.0	61,466	35.0
195,850	54,651	35.0	43,831	33.0	50,699	33.0	47,585	33.0	67,591	35.0
349,700	108,498	35.0	94,601	35.0	101,469	35.0	98,356	35.0	121,439	35.0

Corporations†

(Tax Years Beginning in 2007)

Col. 1 Taxable Income	Tax on Col. 1	Rate on Excess
-0-	-0-	15%
$ 50,000	7,500	25%
$ 75,000	13,750	34%
$ 100,000	22,250	39% *
$ 335,000	113,900	34%
$10,000,000	3,400,000	35%
$15,000,000	5,150,000	38% **
$18,333,333	6,416,667	35%

†   Personal Service Corporations are taxed at a flat rate of 35%.

*   A 5% surtax is imposed on income above $100,000 until the benefit of the 15 and 25% tax rates has been canceled. Thus, taxable income from $100,001 to $335,000 is taxed at the rate of 39%.

**   Corporations with taxable income over $15,000,000 are subject to an additional tax of the lesser of 3% of the excess over $15,000,000 or $100,000. Thus, taxable income exceeding $18,333,333 is taxed at 35%. See Ann. 93-133, 1993-32 IRB 12.

Individuals, Estates and Trusts
(Tax Years Beginning in 2006)

Col. 1 Taxable Income $	Separate Return Tax on Col. 1 $	Separate Return Rate on Excess %	Joint Return Tax on Col. 1 $	Joint Return Rate on Excess %	Single Return Tax on Col. 1 $	Single Return Rate on Excess %	Head of Household Tax on Col. 1 $	Head of Household Rate on Excess %	Trusts and Estates Tax on Col. 1 $	Trusts and Estates Rate on Excess %
0	0	10.0	0	10.0	0	10.0	0	10.0	0	15.0
2,050	205	10.0	205	10.0	205	10.0	205	10.0	308	25.0
4,850	485	10.0	485	10.0	485	10.0	485	10.0	1,008	28.0
7,400	740	10.0	740	10.0	740	10.0	740	10.0	1,722	33.0
7,550	755	15.0	755	10.0	755	15.0	755	10.0	1,771	33.0
10,050	1,130	15.0	1,005	10.0	1,130	15.0	1,005	10.0	2,596	35.0
10,750	1,235	15.0	1,075	10.0	1,235	15.0	1,075	15.0	2,841	35.0
15,100	1,888	15.0	1,510	15.0	1,888	15.0	1,728	15.0	4,364	35.0
30,650	4,220	25.0	3,843	15.0	4,220	25.0	4,060	15.0	9,806	35.0
41,050	6,820	25.0	5,403	15.0	6,820	25.0	5,620	25.0	13,446	35.0
61,300	11,883	25.0	8,440	25.0	11,883	25.0	10,683	25.0	20,534	35.0
61,850	12,020	28.0	8,578	25.0	12,020	25.0	10,820	25.0	20,726	35.0
74,200	15,478	28.0	11,665	25.0	15,108	28.0	13,908	25.0	25,049	35.0
94,225	21,085	33.0	16,671	25.0	20,715	28.0	18,914	25.0	32,057	35.0
106,000	24,971	33.0	19,615	25.0	24,012	28.0	21,858	28.0	36,179	35.0
123,700	30,812	33.0	24,040	28.0	28,968	28.0	26,814	28.0	42,374	35.0
154,800	41,075	33.0	32,748	28.0	37,676	33.0	35,522	28.0	53,259	35.0
168,275	45,522	35.0	36,521	28.0	42,122	33.0	39,295	28.0	57,975	35.0
171,650	46,703	35.0	37,466	28.0	43,236	33.0	40,240	33.0	59,156	35.0
188,450	52,583	35.0	42,170	33.0	48,780	33.0	45,784	33.0	65,036	35.0
336,550	104,418	35.0	91,043	35.0	97,653	35.0	94,657	35.0	116,871	35.0

Corporations†
(Tax Years Beginning in 2006)

Col. 1 Taxable Income	Tax on Col. 1	Rate on Excess
-0-	-0-	15%
$ 50,000	7,500	25%
$ 75,000	13,750	34%
$ 100,000	22,250	39% *
$ 335,000	113,900	34%
$10,000,000	3,400,000	35%
$15,000,000	5,150,000	38% **
$18,333,333	6,416,667	35%

†   Personal Service Corporations are taxed at a flat rate of 35%.

*   A 5% surtax is imposed on income above $100,000 until the benefit of the 15 and 25% tax rates has been canceled. Thus, taxable income from $100,001 to $335,000 is taxed at the rate of 39%.

**   Corporations with taxable income over $15,000,000 are subject to an additional tax of the lesser of 3% of the excess over $15,000,000 or $100,000. Thus, taxable income exceeding $18,333,333 is taxed at 35%. See Ann. 93-133, 1993-32 IRB 12.

APPENDIX B

Transfer Tax Tables

2007-2009 Gift and Estate Tax Table

Taxable Gift/Estate		Tax on	Rate on
From	To	Col. 1	Excess
$ 0	$ 10,000	$ 0	18%
10,000	20,000	1,800	20%
20,000	40,000	3,800	22%
40,000	60,000	8,200	24%
60,000	80,000	13,000	26%
80,000	10,0000	18,200	28%
100,000	150,000	23,800	30%
150,000	250,000	38,800	32%
250,000	500,000	70,800	34%
500,000	750,000	155,800	37%
750,000	1,000,000	248,300	39%
1,000,000	1,250,000	345,800	41%
1,250,000	1,500,000	448,300	43%
1,500,000	....	555,800	45%

2010 Gift Tax Only Table

Taxable Gift/Estate		Tax on	Rate on
From	To	Col. 1	Excess
$ 0	$ 10,000	$ 0	18%
10,000	20,000	1,800	20%
20,000	40,000	3,800	22%
40,000	60,000	8,200	24%
60,000	80,000	13,000	26%
80,000	10,0000	18,200	28%
100,000	150,000	23,800	30%
150,000	250,000	38,800	32%
250,000	500,000	70,800	34%
500,000	....	155,800	35%

2011 Gift and Estate Tax Table

Taxable Gift		Tax on	Rate on
From	To	Col. 1	Excess
$ 0	$ 10,000	$ 0	18%
10,000	20,000	1,800	20%
20,000	40,000	3,800	22%
40,000	60,000	8,200	24%
60,000	80,000	13,000	26%
80,000	10,0000	18,200	28%
100,000	150,000	23,800	30%
150,000	250,000	38,800	32%
250,000	500,000	70,800	34%
500,000	750,000	155,800	37%
750,000	1,000,000	248,300	39%
1,000,000	1,250,000	345,800	41%
1,250,000	1,500,000	448,300	43%
1,500,000	2,000,000	555,800	45%
2,000,000	2,500,000	780,800	49%
2,500,000	3,000,000	1,025,800	53%
3,000,000	10,000,000	1,290,800	55%
10,000,000	17,184,000	5,140,800	60%
17,184,000	....	9,451,200	55%

2006 Gift and Estate Tax Table

Taxable Gift/Estate		Tax on	Rate on
From	**To**	**Col. 1**	**Excess**
$ 0	$ 10,000	$ 0	18%
10,000	20,000	1,800	20%
20,000	40,000	3,800	22%
40,000	60,000	8,200	24%
60,000	80,000	13,000	26%
80,000	10,0000	18,200	28%
100,000	150,000	23,800	30%
150,000	250,000	38,800	32%
250,000	500,000	70,800	34%
500,000	750,000	155,800	37%
750,000	1,000,000	248,300	39%
1,000,000	1,250,000	345,800	41%
1,250,000	1,500,000	448,300	43%
1,500,000	2,000,000	555,800	45%
2,000,000	....	780,800	46%

IRC Secs. 2001(c), 2502(a), 2210, as amended by EGTRRA 2001. See Q 1529.

Estate Tax Unified Credit

Year	Exclusion Equivalent	Unified Credit
2000-2001	675,000	220,550
2002-2003	$1,000,000	$345,800
2004-2005	$1,500,000	$555,800
2006-2008	$2,000,000	$780,800
2009	$3,500,000	$1,455,800
2010	NA	NA
2011	$1,000,000	$345,800

IRC Sec. 2010(c), as amended by EGTRRA 2001. See Q 1507.

Gift Tax Unified Credit

Year	Exclusion Equivalent	Unified Credit
1977 (1-1 to 6-30)	$ 30,000	$ 6,000
1977 (7-1 to 12-31)	120,667	30,000
1978	134,000	34,000
1979	147,333	38,000
1980	161,563	42,500
1981	175,625	47,000
1982	225,000	62,800
1983	275,000	79,300
1984	325,000	96,300
1985	400,000	121,800
1986	500,000	155,800
1987-1997	600,000	192,800
1998	625,000	202,050
1999	650,000	211,300
2000-2001	675,000	220,550
2002-2009	1,000,000	345,800
2010	1,000,000	330,800
2011-	1,000,000	345,800

IRC Secs. 2505(a), 2010(c), as amended by EGTRRA 2001. See Q 1533.

Maximum State Death Tax Credit (SDTC)

Adjusted Taxable Estate		Credit on Col. 1	Rate on Excess
From	To		
$ 40,000	$ 90,000	$ 0	.8%
90,000	140,000	400	1.6%
140,000	240,000	1,200	2.4%
240,000	440,000	3,600	3.2%
440,000	640,000	10,000	4.0%
640,000	840,000	18,000	4.8%
840,000	1,040,000	27,600	5.6%
1,040,000	1,540,000	38,800	6.4%
1,540,000	2,040,000	70,800	7.2%
2,040,000	2,540,000	106,800	8.0%
2,540,000	3,040,000	146,800	8.8%
3,040,000	3,540,000	190,800	9.6%
3,540,000	4,040,000	238,800	10.4%
4,040,000	5,040,000	290,800	11.2%
5,040,000	6,040,000	402,800	12.0%
6,040,000	7,040,000	522,800	12.8%
7,040,000	8,040,000	650,800	13.6%
8,040,000	9,040,000	786,800	14.4%
9,040,000	10,040,000	930,800	15.2%
10,040,000		1,082,800	16.0%

For this purpose, the term "adjusted taxable estate" means the taxable estate reduced by $60,000.

Reduction in Maximum SDTC

Year	Multiply Maximum SDTC Above By
2002	75%
2003	50%
2004	25%
2005-2009	0% *
2010	NA
2011-	100%

*deduction for state death taxes paid replaces credit

IRC Secs. 2011(b), 2011(g), 2058, as amended by EGTRRA 2001. See Q 1507 and Q 1506.

Qualified Family-Owned Business Deduction

Year	Deduction Limitation
1998-2003	$675,000
2004-2010	NA
2011-	$675,000

IRC Secs. 2057(a)(2), 2057(j), as amended by EGTRRA 2001. See Q 1506.

Estate Tax Deferral: Closely Held Business

Year	4% Interest Limitation
1997	$153,000

Year	$1,000,000 Indexed
1998	$1,000,000
1999	$1,010,000
2000	$1,030,000
2001	$1,060,000
2002	$1,100,000
2003	$1,120,000
2004	$1,140,000
2005	$1,170,000
2006	$1,200,000
2007	$1,250,000

Year	2% Interest Limitation
1998	$410,000
1999	$416,500
2000	$427,500
2001	$441,000
2002	$484,000
2003	$493,800
2004	$532,200
2005	$539,900
2006	$552,000
2007	$562,500
2008-2009	$562,500 *
2010	NA
2011-	$557,500 *

*Based upon $1,250,000 as indexed for 2007. May increase.

IRC Secs. 6166, 6601(j). Calculations reflect EGTRRA 2001 changes. See Q 1509.

Special Use Valuation Limitation

Year	Limitation
1997-1998	$750,000
1999	$760,000
2000	$770,000
2001	$800,000
2002	$820,000
2003	$840,000
2004	$850,000
2005	$870,000
2006	$900,000
2007	$940,000

IRC Sec. 2032A(a). See Q 1535.

Qualified Conservation Easement Exclusion

Year	Exclusion Limitation
1998	$100,000
1999	$200,000
2000	$300,000
2001	$400,000
2002-2009	$500,000
2010	NA
2011-	$500,000

IRC Sec. 2031(c)(3). See Q 1505.

Gift (and GST) Tax Annual Exclusion

Year	Annual Exclusion
1997-2001	$10,000
2002-2005	$11,000
2006-2007	$12,000

IRC Sec. 2503(b). See Q 1511 and Q 1530.

Gift Tax Annual Exclusion
(Donee Spouse not U.S. Citizen)

Year	Annual Exclusion
1997-1998	$100,000
1999	$101,000
2000	$103,000
2001	$106,000
2002	$110,000
2003	$112,000
2004	$114,000
2005	$117,000
2006	$120,000
2007	$125,000

IRC Sec. 2523(i). See Q 1530.

Generation-Skipping Transfer Tax Table

Year	Tax Rate
2001	55%
2002	50%
2003	49%
2004	48%
2005	47%
2006	46%
2007-2009	45%
2010	NA
2011-	55%

IRC Secs. 2641, 2001(c), 2664, as amended by EGTRRA 2001. See Q 1511.

Generation-Skipping Transfer Tax Exemption

Year	GST Exemption
1997-1998	$1,000,000
1999	$1,010,000
2000	$1,030,000
2001	$1,060,000
2002	$1,100,000
2003	$1,120,000
2004-2005	$1,500,000
2006-2008	$2,000,000
2009	$3,500,000
2010	NA
2011-	$1,120,000*

*Plus increases for indexing for inflation after 2003.

IRC Secs. 2631, 2010(c), as amended by EGTRRA 2001. See Q 1511.

Indexed Amounts Source

Year	Rev. Proc.
1999	98-61, 1998-2 CB 811
2000	99-42, 1999-46 IRB 568
2001	2001-13, 2001-3 IRB 337
2002	2001-59, 2001-52 IRB 623
2003	2002-70, 2002-46 IRB 845
2004	2003-85, 2003-49 IRB 1184
2005	2004-71, 2004-50 IRB 970
2006	2005-70, 2005-47 IRB 979
2007	2006-53, 2006-48 IRB 996

APPENDIX C

VALUATION TABLES

The value of an annuity, a unitrust interest, an estate (income or use interest) for life or term of years, or a remainder or a reversionary interest is valued for most income, estate, gift, and generation-skipping transfer tax purposes using the following valuation tables and the current IRC Section 7520 interest rate for the month in which the valuation date occurs. If a charitable deduction is involved, the taxpayer can use the interest rate for either of the two preceding months or the current month.

The Section 7520 interest rate for each month is published in a revenue ruling. The Section 7520 interest rate for each month is also published in *Tax Facts News*, a National Underwriter publication, as the rate becomes available. It can also be found at www.TaxFactsOnline.com/.

Selected single life and term certain annuity tables and single life and term certain unitrust remainder tables are provided here. [IRS Publications 1457 and 1458 contain extensive valuation tables.] For purposes of these tables, round the age of any person whose life is used to measure an interest to the age of such person on his birthday nearest the valuation date.

Both the single life and term certain annuity tables provide factors for annuity interests which can be converted into an income factor or a remainder factor following an income interest. An annuity factor is converted into an income factor by multiplying the annuity factor by the interest rate. An income factor is converted into a remainder factor following an income interest by subtracting the income factor from 1.

The value of an income interest or a remainder interest following an income interest is equal to the principal amount multiplied by the appropriate income or remainder factor. See Q 1332 for examples of the calculation of a remainder interest in the context of charitable pooled income funds.

The value of an annuity payable *at the end of each period* is equal to the aggregate payment received during the year multiplied by the annuity factor multiplied by the appropriate Table A annuity adjustment factor. The value of an annuity payable *at the beginning of each period during the life of a person* is equal to the sum of the value of an annuity payable at the end of each period plus the amount of one additional payment. The value of an annuity payable *at the beginning of each period during a term certain* is equal to the aggregate payment received during the year multiplied by the annuity factor multiplied by the appropriate Table B annuity adjustment factor.

The value of a remainder interest following an annuity interest is equal to the value of the annuity subtracted from the value of the property transferred out of which (or in return for which) the annuity is payable.

See Q 1338 for examples illustrating the calculation of the value of annuity interests and remainder interests following an annuity interest in the context of charitable lead annuity trusts, and Q 1334 for examples in the context of charitable remainder annuity trusts.

Both the single life and term certain unitrust remainder tables provide factors for unitrust remainder interests which can be converted into a unitrust factor. A unitrust remainder factor is converted into a unitrust factor by subtracting the unitrust remainder factor from 1.

In general, the value of a unitrust or a unitrust remainder interest is equal to the principal amount multiplied by the appropriate unitrust or unitrust remainder factor. However, see Q 1338 for examples illustrating the calculation of unitrust and unitrust remainder interests in the context of charitable lead unitrusts, and Q 1334 for examples in the context of charitable remainder unitrusts.

ANNUITY ADJUSTMENT FACTORS TABLE A*

FREQUENCY OF PAYMENTS

INTEREST RATE	ANNUALLY	SEMI ANNUALLY	QUARTERLY	MONTHLY	WEEKLY
3.0%	1.0000	1.0074	1.0112	1.0137	1.0146
3.2%	1.0000	1.0079	1.0119	1.0146	1.0156
3.4%	1.0000	1.0084	1.0127	1.0155	1.0166
3.6%	1.0000	1.0089	1.0134	1.0164	1.0175
3.8%	1.0000	1.0094	1.0141	1.0173	1.0185
4.0%	1.0000	1.0099	1.0149	1.0182	1.0195
4.2%	1.0000	1.0104	1.0156	1.0191	1.0205
4.4%	1.0000	1.0109	1.0164	1.0200	1.0214
4.6%	1.0000	1.0114	1.0171	1.0209	1.0224
4.8%	1.0000	1.0119	1.0178	1.0218	1.0234
5.0%	1.0000	1.0123	1.0186	1.0227	1.0243
5.2%	1.0000	1.0128	1.0193	1.0236	1.0253
5.4%	1.0000	1.0133	1.0200	1.0245	1.0262
5.6%	1.0000	1.0138	1.0208	1.0254	1.0272
5.8%	1.0000	1.0143	1.0215	1.0263	1.0282
6.0%	1.0000	1.0148	1.0222	1.0272	1.0291
6.2%	1.0000	1.0153	1.0230	1.0281	1.0301
6.4%	1.0000	1.0158	1.0237	1.0290	1.0311
6.6%	1.0000	1.0162	1.0244	1.0299	1.0320
6.8%	1.0000	1.0167	1.0252	1.0308	1.0330
7.0%	1.0000	1.0172	1.0259	1.0317	1.0339
7.2%	1.0000	1.0177	1.0266	1.0326	1.0349
7.4%	1.0000	1.0182	1.0273	1.0335	1.0358
7.6%	1.0000	1.0187	1.0281	1.0344	1.0368
7.8%	1.0000	1.0191	1.0288	1.0353	1.0378
8.0%	1.0000	1.0196	1.0295	1.0362	1.0387
8.2%	1.0000	1.0201	1.0302	1.0370	1.0397
8.4%	1.0000	1.0206	1.0310	1.0379	1.0406
8.6%	1.0000	1.0211	1.0317	1.0388	1.0416
8.8%	1.0000	1.0215	1.0324	1.0397	1.0425
9.0%	1.0000	1.0220	1.0331	1.0406	1.0435
9.2%	1.0000	1.0225	1.0339	1.0415	1.0444
9.4%	1.0000	1.0230	1.0346	1.0424	1.0454
9.6%	1.0000	1.0235	1.0353	1.0433	1.0463
9.8%	1.0000	1.0239	1.0360	1.0442	1.0473
10.0%	1.0000	1.0244	1.0368	1.0450	1.0482
10.2%	1.0000	1.0249	1.0375	1.0459	1.0492
10.4%	1.0000	1.0254	1.0382	1.0468	1.0501
10.6%	1.0000	1.0258	1.0389	1.0477	1.0511
10.8%	1.0000	1.0263	1.0396	1.0486	1.0520

*For use in calculating the value of an annuity payable at the end of each period or, if the term of the annuity is determined with respect to one or more lives, an annuity payable at the beginning of each period.

ANNUITY ADJUSTMENT FACTORS TABLE B*

FREQUENCY OF PAYMENTS

INTEREST RATE	ANNUALLY	SEMI ANNUALLY	QUARTERLY	MONTHLY	WEEKLY
3.0%	1.0300	1.0224	1.0187	1.0162	1.0152
3.2%	1.0320	1.0239	1.0199	1.0172	1.0162
3.4%	1.0340	1.0254	1.0212	1.0183	1.0172
3.6%	1.0360	1.0269	1.0224	1.0194	1.0182
3.8%	1.0380	1.0284	1.0236	1.0205	1.0192
4.0%	1.0400	1.0299	1.0249	1.0215	1.0203
4.2%	1.0420	1.0314	1.0261	1.0226	1.0213
4.4%	1.0440	1.0329	1.0274	1.0237	1.0223
4.6%	1.0460	1.0344	1.0286	1.0247	1.0233
4.8%	1.0480	1.0359	1.0298	1.0258	1.0243
5.0%	1.0500	1.0373	1.0311	1.0269	1.0253
5.2%	1.0520	1.0388	1.0323	1.0279	1.0263
5.4%	1.0540	1.0403	1.0335	1.0290	1.0273
5.6%	1.0560	1.0418	1.0348	1.0301	1.0283
5.8%	1.0580	1.0433	1.0360	1.0311	1.0293
6.0%	1.0600	1.0448	1.0372	1.0322	1.0303
6.2%	1.0620	1.0463	1.0385	1.0333	1.0313
6.4%	1.0640	1.0478	1.0397	1.0343	1.0323
6.6%	1.0660	1.0492	1.0409	1.0354	1.0333
6.8%	1.0680	1.0507	1.0422	1.0365	1.0343
7.0%	1.0700	1.0522	1.0434	1.0375	1.0353
7.2%	1.0720	1.0537	1.0446	1.0386	1.0363
7.4%	1.0740	1.0552	1.0458	1.0396	1.0373
7.6%	1.0760	1.0567	1.0471	1.0407	1.0383
7.8%	1.0780	1.0581	1.0483	1.0418	1.0393
8.0%	1.0800	1.0596	1.0495	1.0428	1.0403
8.2%	1.0820	1.0611	1.0507	1.0439	1.0413
8.4%	1.0840	1.0626	1.0520	1.0449	1.0422
8.6%	1.0860	1.0641	1.0532	1.0460	1.0432
8.8%	1.0880	1.0655	1.0544	1.0471	1.0442
9.0%	1.0900	1.0670	1.0556	1.0481	1.0452
9.2%	1.0920	1.0685	1.0569	1.0492	1.0462
9.4%	1.0940	1.0700	1.0581	1.0502	1.0472
9.6%	1.0960	1.0715	1.0593	1.0513	1.0482
9.8%	1.0980	1.0729	1.0605	1.0523	1.0492
10.0%	1.1000	1.0744	1.0618	1.0534	1.0502
10.2%	1.1020	1.0759	1.0630	1.0544	1.0512
10.4%	1.1040	1.0774	1.0642	1.0555	1.0521
10.6%	1.1060	1.0788	1.0654	1.0565	1.0531
10.8%	1.1080	1.0803	1.0666	1.0576	1.0541

*For use in calculating the value of a term certain annuity payable at the beginning of each period.

TERM CERTAIN ANNUITY FACTORS

INTEREST RATE

YEARS	3.0%	3.2%	3.4%	3.6%	3.8%	4.0%	4.2%	4.4%	4.6%
1	0.9709	0.9690	0.9671	0.9653	0.9634	0.9615	0.9597	0.9579	0.9560
2	1.9135	1.9079	1.9024	1.8970	1.8915	1.8861	1.8807	1.8753	1.8700
3	2.8286	2.8178	2.8070	2.7963	2.7857	2.7751	2.7646	2.7542	2.7438
4	3.7171	3.6994	3.6818	3.6644	3.6471	3.6299	3.6129	3.5959	3.5791
5	4.5797	4.5537	4.5279	4.5023	4.4769	4.4518	4.4269	4.4022	4.3778
6	5.4172	5.3815	5.3461	5.3111	5.2764	5.2421	5.2082	5.1746	5.1413
7	6.2303	6.1836	6.1374	6.0918	6.0467	6.0021	5.9579	5.9143	5.8712
8	7.0197	6.9608	6.9027	6.8454	6.7887	6.7327	6.6775	6.6229	6.5690
9	7.7861	7.7140	7.6429	7.5727	7.5036	7.4353	7.3680	7.3016	7.2362
10	8.5302	8.4438	8.3587	8.2748	8.1923	8.1109	8.0307	7.9518	7.8740
11	9.2526	9.1510	9.0510	8.9526	8.8557	8.7605	8.6667	8.5745	8.4837
12	9.9540	9.8362	9.7205	9.6067	9.4949	9.3851	9.2771	9.1710	9.0666
13	10.6350	10.5002	10.3679	10.2381	10.1107	9.9856	9.8629	9.7423	9.6239
14	11.2961	11.1436	10.9941	10.8476	10.7040	10.5631	10.4250	10.2896	10.1567
15	11.9379	11.7671	11.5998	11.4359	11.2755	11.1184	10.9645	10.8138	10.6661
16	12.5611	12.3712	12.1854	12.0038	11.8261	11.6523	11.4822	11.3159	11.1530
17	13.1661	12.9566	12.7519	12.5519	12.3566	12.1657	11.9791	11.7968	11.6186
18	13.7535	13.5238	13.2997	13.0810	12.8676	12.6593	12.4560	12.2575	12.0637
19	14.3238	14.0735	13.8295	13.5917	13.3599	13.1339	12.9136	12.6987	12.4892
20	14.8775	14.6061	14.3419	14.0847	13.8342	13.5903	13.3528	13.1214	12.8960

INTEREST RATE

YEARS	4.8%	5.0%	5.2%	5.4%	5.6%	5.8%	6.0%	6.2%	6.4%
1	0.9542	0.9524	0.9506	0.9488	0.9470	0.9452	0.9434	0.9416	0.9398
2	1.8647	1.8594	1.8542	1.8489	1.8437	1.8385	1.8334	1.8283	1.8232
3	2.7335	2.7232	2.7131	2.7030	2.6929	2.6829	2.6730	2.6632	2.6534
4	3.5625	3.5460	3.5295	3.5132	3.4971	3.4810	3.4651	3.4493	3.4336
5	4.3535	4.3295	4.3056	4.2820	4.2586	4.2354	4.2124	4.1895	4.1669
6	5.1083	5.0757	5.0434	5.0114	4.9797	4.9484	4.9173	4.8866	4.8561
7	5.8285	5.7864	5.7447	5.7034	5.6626	5.6223	5.5824	5.5429	5.5039
8	6.5158	6.4632	6.4113	6.3600	6.3093	6.2592	6.2098	6.1609	6.1127
9	7.1716	7.1078	7.0449	6.9829	6.9217	6.8613	6.8017	6.7429	6.6848
10	7.7973	7.7217	7.6473	7.5739	7.5016	7.4303	7.3601	7.2908	7.2226
11	8.3944	8.3064	8.2199	8.1346	8.0508	7.9682	7.8869	7.8068	7.7280
12	8.9641	8.8633	8.7641	8.6666	8.5708	8.4765	8.3838	8.2927	8.2030
13	9.5077	9.3936	9.2815	9.1714	9.0633	8.9570	8.8527	8.7502	8.6494
14	10.0264	9.8986	9.7733	9.6503	9.5296	9.4112	9.2950	9.1809	9.0690
15	10.5214	10.3797	10.2408	10.1046	9.9712	9.8404	9.7122	9.5866	9.4634
16	10.9937	10.8378	10.6851	10.5357	10.3894	10.2462	10.1059	9.9685	9.8340
17	11.4444	11.2741	11.1075	10.9447	10.7854	10.6296	10.4773	10.3282	10.1823
18	11.8744	11.6896	11.5091	11.3327	11.1604	10.9921	10.8276	10.6668	10.5097
19	12.2847	12.0853	11.8907	11.7009	11.5156	11.3347	11.1581	10.9857	10.8174
20	12.6763	12.4622	12.2536	12.0502	11.8519	11.6585	11.4699	11.2860	11.1066

TERM CERTAIN ANNUITY FACTORS

INTEREST RATE

YEARS	6.6%	6.8%	7.0%	7.2%	7.4%	7.6%	7.8%	8.0%	8.2%
1	0.9381	0.9363	0.9346	0.9328	0.9311	0.9294	0.9276	0.9259	0.9242
2	1.8181	1.8130	1.8080	1.8030	1.7980	1.7931	1.7882	1.7833	1.7784
3	2.6436	2.6339	2.6243	2.6148	2.6053	2.5958	2.5864	2.5771	2.5678
4	3.4180	3.4026	3.3872	3.3720	3.3568	3.3418	3.3269	3.3121	3.2974
5	4.1445	4.1222	4.1002	4.0783	4.0567	4.0352	4.0138	3.9927	3.9718
6	4.8260	4.7961	4.7665	4.7373	4.7082	4.6795	4.6511	4.6229	4.5950
7	5.4653	5.4271	5.3893	5.3519	5.3149	5.2784	5.2422	5.2064	5.1709
8	6.0650	6.0179	5.9713	5.9253	5.8798	5.8349	5.7905	5.7466	5.7033
9	6.6276	6.5710	6.5152	6.4602	6.4058	6.3521	6.2992	6.2469	6.1953
10	7.1553	7.0890	7.0236	6.9591	6.8955	6.8328	6.7710	6.7101	6.6500
11	7.6504	7.5739	7.4987	7.4245	7.3515	7.2796	7.2088	7.1390	7.0702
12	8.1148	8.0280	7.9427	7.8587	7.7761	7.6948	7.6148	7.5361	7.4586
13	8.5505	8.4532	8.3577	8.2637	8.1714	8.0807	7.9915	7.9038	7.8176
14	8.9592	8.8513	8.7455	8.6415	8.5395	8.4393	8.3409	8.2442	8.1493
15	9.3426	9.2241	9.1079	8.9940	8.8822	8.7726	8.6650	8.5595	8.4559
16	9.7022	9.5731	9.4466	9.3227	9.2013	9.0823	8.9657	8.8514	8.7393
17	10.0396	9.8999	9.7632	9.6294	9.4984	9.3702	9.2446	9.1216	9.0012
18	10.3561	10.2059	10.0591	9.9155	9.7751	9.6377	9.5033	9.3719	9.2433
19	10.6530	10.4924	10.3356	10.1824	10.0327	9.8863	9.7434	9.6036	9.4670
20	10.9315	10.7607	10.5940	10.4313	10.2725	10.1174	9.9660	9.8181	9.6737

INTEREST RATE

YEARS	8.4%	8.6%	8.8%	9.0%	9.2%	9.4%	9.6%	9.8%	10.0%
1	0.9225	0.9208	0.9191	0.9174	0.9158	0.9141	0.9124	0.9107	0.9091
2	1.7735	1.7687	1.7639	1.7591	1.7544	1.7496	1.7449	1.7402	1.7355
3	2.5586	2.5494	2.5403	2.5313	2.5223	2.5134	2.5045	2.4956	2.4869
4	3.2829	3.2684	3.2540	3.2397	3.2255	3.2115	3.1975	3.1836	3.1699
5	3.9510	3.9304	3.9099	3.8897	3.8696	3.8496	3.8298	3.8102	3.7908
6	4.5673	4.5399	4.5128	4.4859	4.4593	4.4329	4.4068	4.3809	4.3553
7	5.1359	5.1012	5.0669	5.0330	4.9994	4.9661	4.9332	4.9006	4.8684
8	5.6604	5.6181	5.5762	5.5348	5.4939	5.4535	5.4135	5.3740	5.3349
9	6.1443	6.0940	6.0443	5.9952	5.9468	5.8990	5.8517	5.8051	5.7590
10	6.5907	6.5322	6.4745	6.4177	6.3615	6.3062	6.2516	6.1977	6.1446
11	7.0025	6.9357	6.8700	6.8052	6.7413	6.6784	6.6164	6.5553	6.4951
12	7.3824	7.3073	7.2334	7.1607	7.0891	7.0187	6.9493	6.8810	6.8137
13	7.7328	7.6495	7.5675	7.4869	7.4076	7.3297	7.2530	7.1776	7.1034
14	8.0561	7.9645	7.8745	7.7862	7.6993	7.6140	7.5301	7.4477	7.3667
15	8.3543	8.2546	8.1567	8.0607	7.9664	7.8738	7.7829	7.6937	7.6061
16	8.6295	8.5217	8.4161	8.3126	8.2110	8.1114	8.0136	7.9178	7.8237
17	8.8833	8.7677	8.6545	8.5436	8.4350	8.3285	8.2241	8.1218	8.0216
18	9.1174	8.9942	8.8736	8.7556	8.6401	8.5269	8.4162	8.3077	8.2014
19	9.3334	9.2028	9.0750	8.9501	8.8279	8.7084	8.5914	8.4769	8.3649
20	9.5327	9.3948	9.2602	9.1285	8.9999	8.8742	8.7513	8.6311	8.5136

SINGLE LIFE ANNUITY FACTORS
(For valuation dates occurring after April 30, 1999)

AGE	INTEREST RATE								
	3.0%	3.2%	3.4%	3.6%	3.8%	4.0%	4.2%	4.4%	4.6%
35	23.0151	22.2347	21.4960	20.7963	20.1331	19.5040	18.9067	18.3393	17.7998
36	22.7471	21.9863	21.2657	20.5826	19.9347	19.3196	18.7352	18.1796	17.6510
37	22.4728	21.7317	21.0293	20.3629	19.7303	19.1293	18.5579	18.0143	17.4968
38	22.1916	21.4704	20.7862	20.1366	19.5195	18.9327	18.3745	17.8431	17.3368
39	21.9039	21.2026	20.5366	19.9039	19.3023	18.7300	18.1851	17.6659	17.1710
40	21.6092	20.9277	20.2801	19.6643	19.0784	18.5206	17.9891	17.4824	16.9990
41	21.3071	20.6455	20.0163	19.4176	18.8474	18.3042	17.7862	17.2921	16.8204
42	20.9978	20.3561	19.7454	19.1637	18.6094	18.0809	17.5766	17.0951	16.6351
43	20.6815	20.0597	19.4674	18.9029	18.3645	17.8507	17.3601	16.8914	16.4434
44	20.3583	19.7564	19.1825	18.6351	18.1127	17.6137	17.1369	16.6811	16.2450
45	20.0293	19.4471	18.8916	18.3613	17.8548	17.3707	16.9078	16.4648	16.0408
46	19.6943	19.1317	18.5945	18.0813	17.5907	17.1215	16.6724	16.2425	15.8306
47	19.3543	18.8112	18.2922	17.7960	17.3212	16.8668	16.4316	16.0147	15.6149
48	19.0090	18.4852	17.9843	17.5050	17.0460	16.6064	16.1851	15.7811	15.3935
49	18.6586	18.1541	17.6711	17.2085	16.7653	16.3405	15.9330	15.5419	15.1665
50	18.3029	17.8173	17.3521	16.9063	16.4787	16.0685	15.6748	15.2968	14.9336
51	17.9422	17.4754	17.0279	16.5986	16.1866	15.7910	15.4110	15.0459	14.6949
52	17.5776	17.1294	16.6992	16.2863	15.8897	15.5087	15.1424	14.7901	14.4512
53	17.2094	16.7794	16.3665	15.9697	15.5884	15.2217	14.8690	14.5295	14.2026
54	16.8378	16.4258	16.0299	15.6491	15.2829	14.9304	14.5911	14.2643	13.9494
55	16.4630	16.0687	15.6894	15.3245	14.9731	14.6347	14.3087	13.9945	13.6915
56	16.0851	15.7082	15.3454	14.9959	14.6593	14.3348	14.0219	13.7202	13.4290
57	15.7044	15.3446	14.9979	14.6638	14.3416	14.0308	13.7310	13.4415	13.1621
58	15.3221	14.9790	14.6482	14.3290	14.0211	13.7238	13.4368	13.1595	12.8915
59	14.9392	14.6124	14.2970	13.9926	13.6986	13.4146	13.1402	12.8748	12.6183
60	14.5560	14.2452	13.9449	13.6549	13.3746	13.1036	12.8415	12.5879	12.3426
61	14.1723	13.8770	13.5916	13.3156	13.0487	12.7904	12.5404	12.2985	12.0641
62	13.7872	13.5071	13.2361	12.9739	12.7201	12.4743	12.2363	12.0057	11.7822
63	13.4007	13.1354	12.8785	12.6298	12.3888	12.1553	11.9290	11.7095	11.4967
64	13.0136	12.7626	12.5195	12.2839	12.0555	11.8339	11.6191	11.4106	11.2082
65	12.6260	12.3890	12.1593	11.9364	11.7202	11.5104	11.3067	11.1090	10.9169
66	12.2375	12.0141	11.7974	11.5870	11.3827	11.1843	10.9916	10.8043	10.6223
67	11.8474	11.6373	11.4332	11.2349	11.0422	10.8550	10.6729	10.4959	10.3238
68	11.4565	11.2592	11.0673	10.8808	10.6995	10.5231	10.3515	10.1845	10.0219
69	11.0660	10.8809	10.7010	10.5259	10.3555	10.1896	10.0281	9.8709	9.7177
70	10.6773	10.5041	10.3356	10.1715	10.0117	9.8560	9.7043	9.5565	9.4124
71	10.2919	10.1302	9.9726	9.8191	9.6695	9.5236	9.3814	9.2427	9.1074
72	9.9107	9.7599	9.6128	9.4695	9.3296	9.1932	9.0601	8.9302	8.8034
73	9.5343	9.3939	9.2570	9.1233	8.9928	8.8655	8.7411	8.6197	8.5011
74	9.1617	9.0313	8.9040	8.7796	8.6581	8.5395	8.4235	8.3102	8.1995
75	8.7918	8.6709	8.5528	8.4374	8.3245	8.2142	8.1064	8.0009	7.8977
76	8.4237	8.3120	8.2027	8.0958	7.9912	7.8889	7.7888	7.6909	7.5950
77	8.0577	7.9546	7.8537	7.7550	7.6583	7.5637	7.4711	7.3803	7.2915
78	7.6944	7.5996	7.5067	7.4157	7.3266	7.2393	7.1538	7.0700	6.9878
79	7.3357	7.2487	7.1634	7.0798	6.9978	6.9175	6.8387	6.7614	6.6857
80	6.9842	6.9045	6.8263	6.7496	6.6744	6.6006	6.5282	6.4572	6.3875
81	6.6420	6.5691	6.4976	6.4274	6.3585	6.2908	6.2245	6.1593	6.0952
82	6.3101	6.2436	6.1782	6.1141	6.0511	5.9892	5.9284	5.8687	5.8100
83	5.9884	5.9278	5.8683	5.8098	5.7523	5.6958	5.6402	5.5856	5.5319
84	5.6748	5.6197	5.5656	5.5123	5.4600	5.4085	5.3578	5.3080	5.2590

SINGLE LIFE ANNUITY FACTORS
(For valuation dates occurring after April 30, 1999)

INTEREST RATE

AGE	4.8%	5.0%	5.2%	5.4%	5.6%	5.8%	6.0%	6.2%	6.4%
35	17.2865	16.7978	16.3321	15.8882	15.4645	15.0601	14.6737	14.3042	13.9508
36	17.1478	16.6683	16.2113	15.7752	15.3589	14.9612	14.5810	14.2174	13.8693
37	17.0038	16.5338	16.0855	15.6575	15.2486	14.8578	14.4841	14.1264	13.7839
38	16.8542	16.3938	15.9543	15.5345	15.1333	14.7496	14.3824	14.0308	13.6940
39	16.6989	16.2483	15.8178	15.4065	15.0130	14.6365	14.2761	13.9307	13.5997
40	16.5376	16.0968	15.6756	15.2727	14.8872	14.5182	14.1646	13.8256	13.5005
41	16.3697	15.9391	15.5272	15.1330	14.7556	14.3941	14.0475	13.7151	13.3962
42	16.1955	15.7750	15.3726	14.9873	14.6182	14.2643	13.9249	13.5993	13.2866
43	16.0148	15.6046	15.2119	14.8356	14.4748	14.1288	13.7967	13.4779	13.1716
44	15.8277	15.4279	15.0449	14.6777	14.3255	13.9874	13.6628	13.3510	13.0512
45	15.6347	15.2455	14.8723	14.5144	14.1707	13.8408	13.5237	13.2190	12.9259
46	15.4358	15.0572	14.6940	14.3453	14.0104	13.6886	13.3792	13.0817	12.7954
47	15.2315	14.8636	14.5103	14.1710	13.8449	13.5314	13.2298	12.9396	12.6601
48	15.0215	14.6643	14.3211	13.9913	13.6741	13.3689	13.0751	12.7923	12.5198
49	14.8060	14.4595	14.1264	13.8061	13.4978	13.2010	12.9152	12.6399	12.3744
50	14.5845	14.2488	13.9258	13.6150	13.3158	13.0275	12.7497	12.4819	12.2236
51	14.3572	14.0323	13.7196	13.4184	13.1281	12.8484	12.5787	12.3185	12.0674
52	14.1250	13.8109	13.5083	13.2167	12.9355	12.6644	12.4027	12.1502	11.9064
53	13.8878	13.5844	13.2920	13.0100	12.7380	12.4754	12.2219	11.9771	11.7405
54	13.6459	13.3533	13.0710	12.7986	12.5356	12.2817	12.0363	11.7992	11.5700
55	13.3993	13.1173	12.8451	12.5823	12.3284	12.0830	11.8459	11.6165	11.3947
56	13.1480	12.8766	12.6144	12.3611	12.1163	11.8796	11.6505	11.4290	11.2145
57	12.8921	12.6313	12.3791	12.1353	11.8995	11.6713	11.4505	11.2366	11.0295
58	12.6325	12.3821	12.1399	11.9055	11.6787	11.4590	11.2463	11.0402	10.8404
59	12.3701	12.1300	11.8976	11.6725	11.4545	11.2433	11.0387	10.8403	10.6479
60	12.1051	11.8751	11.6524	11.4365	11.2273	11.0246	10.8279	10.6371	10.4520
61	11.8371	11.6172	11.4040	11.1973	10.9968	10.8023	10.6136	10.4304	10.2526
62	11.5655	11.3555	11.1517	10.9540	10.7622	10.5759	10.3951	10.2195	10.0488
63	11.2903	11.0899	10.8955	10.7067	10.5234	10.3453	10.1723	10.0041	9.8407
64	11.0118	10.8211	10.6358	10.4558	10.2809	10.1109	9.9456	9.7849	9.6285
65	10.7303	10.5490	10.3728	10.2014	10.0348	9.8728	9.7151	9.5617	9.4124
66	10.4454	10.2733	10.1059	9.9431	9.7847	9.6305	9.4804	9.3342	9.1918
67	10.1563	9.9933	9.8347	9.6802	9.5299	9.3834	9.2407	9.1017	8.9663
68	9.8637	9.7096	9.5595	9.4133	9.2709	9.1320	8.9967	8.8648	8.7361
69	9.5685	9.4231	9.2813	9.1432	9.0085	8.8771	8.7490	8.6240	8.5020
70	9.2720	9.1350	9.0014	8.8711	8.7440	8.6199	8.4988	8.3806	8.2652
71	8.9754	8.8466	8.7210	8.5983	8.4785	8.3615	8.2473	8.1357	8.0267
72	8.6796	8.5587	8.4407	8.3254	8.2128	8.1027	7.9951	7.8900	7.7872
73	8.3852	8.2719	8.1613	8.0531	7.9474	7.8440	7.7429	7.6440	7.5473
74	8.0912	7.9853	7.8818	7.7806	7.6815	7.5846	7.4898	7.3970	7.3061
75	7.7968	7.6980	7.6014	7.5068	7.4142	7.3236	7.2349	7.1480	7.0628
76	7.5011	7.4093	7.3193	7.2312	7.1449	7.0603	6.9775	6.8963	6.8167
77	7.2044	7.1192	7.0356	6.9537	6.8735	6.7948	6.7177	6.6421	6.5679
78	6.9073	6.8283	6.7510	6.6751	6.6006	6.5276	6.4560	6.3858	6.3168
79	6.6114	6.5385	6.4670	6.3968	6.3280	6.2604	6.1941	6.1290	6.0650
80	6.3191	6.2519	6.1860	6.1213	6.0577	5.9953	5.9340	5.8738	5.8147
81	6.0324	5.9706	5.9100	5.8504	5.7918	5.7343	5.6778	5.6222	5.5676
82	5.7524	5.6957	5.6400	5.5852	5.5314	5.4785	5.4265	5.3753	5.3250
83	5.4791	5.4272	5.3762	5.3259	5.2765	5.2280	5.1801	5.1331	5.0868
84	5.2108	5.1633	5.1166	5.0707	5.0255	4.9810	4.9372	4.8940	4.8516

SINGLE LIFE ANNUITY FACTORS
(For valuation dates occurring after April 30, 1999)

INTEREST RATE

AGE	6.6%	6.8%	7.0%	7.2%	7.4%	7.6%	7.8%	8.0%	8.2%
35	13.6125	13.2885	12.9779	12.6800	12.3942	12.1198	11.8561	11.6027	11.3589
36	13.5360	13.2166	12.9103	12.6164	12.3343	12.0633	11.8029	11.5524	11.3114
37	13.4556	13.1410	12.8391	12.5493	12.2711	12.0036	11.7465	11.4992	11.2611
38	13.3710	13.0613	12.7640	12.4785	12.2041	11.9404	11.6868	11.4426	11.2076
39	13.2822	12.9774	12.6848	12.4037	12.1335	11.8736	11.6235	11.3827	11.1508
40	13.1886	12.8890	12.6013	12.3247	12.0587	11.8028	11.5564	11.3191	11.0904
41	13.0899	12.7957	12.5130	12.2411	11.9794	11.7276	11.4851	11.2514	11.0261
42	12.9862	12.6975	12.4198	12.1527	11.8956	11.6480	11.4094	11.1794	10.9576
43	12.8772	12.5942	12.3218	12.0596	11.8071	11.5639	11.3294	11.1033	10.8851
44	12.7630	12.4857	12.2187	11.9616	11.7139	11.4751	11.2448	11.0227	10.8082
45	12.6439	12.3724	12.1110	11.8591	11.6163	11.3821	11.1561	10.9380	10.7274
46	12.5198	12.2543	11.9985	11.7519	11.5140	11.2845	11.0630	10.8491	10.6425
47	12.3910	12.1316	11.8815	11.6403	11.4075	11.1829	10.9659	10.7563	10.5537
48	12.2572	12.0040	11.7597	11.5240	11.2965	11.0767	10.8644	10.6591	10.4607
49	12.1184	11.8715	11.6332	11.4031	11.1808	10.9660	10.7584	10.5577	10.3634
50	11.9743	11.7338	11.5014	11.2770	11.0601	10.8505	10.6477	10.4515	10.2616
51	11.8249	11.5908	11.3646	11.1460	10.9345	10.7301	10.5322	10.3407	10.1552
52	11.6708	11.4432	11.2231	11.0103	10.8045	10.6052	10.4123	10.2256	10.0446
53	11.5119	11.2908	11.0770	10.8701	10.6698	10.4759	10.2881	10.1061	9.9298
54	11.3483	11.1339	10.9263	10.7254	10.5308	10.3422	10.1595	9.9824	9.8107
55	11.1800	10.9722	10.7709	10.5760	10.3871	10.2040	10.0265	9.8543	9.6873
56	11.0068	10.8056	10.6108	10.4219	10.2387	10.0611	9.8889	9.7217	9.5594
57	10.8289	10.6344	10.4459	10.2631	10.0858	9.9137	9.7467	9.5845	9.4270
58	10.6468	10.4591	10.2769	10.1002	9.9287	9.7622	9.6005	9.4434	9.2907
59	10.4613	10.2802	10.1044	9.9338	9.7681	9.6071	9.4507	9.2987	9.1510
60	10.2724	10.0979	9.9286	9.7640	9.6041	9.4487	9.2977	9.1507	9.0079
61	10.0798	9.9120	9.7490	9.5905	9.4365	9.2866	9.1409	8.9991	8.8611
62	9.8830	9.7218	9.5651	9.4127	9.2644	9.1202	8.9798	8.8431	8.7100
63	9.6817	9.5271	9.3767	9.2303	9.0879	8.9492	8.8141	8.6826	8.5544
64	9.4764	9.3283	9.1842	9.0438	8.9072	8.7740	8.6443	8.5179	8.3947
65	9.2670	9.1254	8.9875	8.8532	8.7223	8.5947	8.4703	8.3490	8.2307
66	9.0532	8.9180	8.7863	8.6579	8.5327	8.4107	8.2916	8.1754	8.0621
67	8.8342	8.7054	8.5799	8.4574	8.3380	8.2214	8.1076	7.9965	7.8881
68	8.6106	8.4881	8.3687	8.2521	8.1383	8.0271	7.9186	7.8126	7.7091
69	8.3830	8.2668	8.1533	8.0425	7.9343	7.8286	7.7253	7.6243	7.5256
70	8.1525	8.0424	7.9348	7.8297	7.7270	7.6266	7.5285	7.4325	7.3386
71	7.9202	7.8161	7.7143	7.6148	7.5175	7.4223	7.3292	7.2381	7.1490
72	7.6867	7.5884	7.4923	7.3982	7.3062	7.2162	7.1280	7.0418	6.9573
73	7.4526	7.3600	7.2694	7.1807	7.0938	7.0088	6.9255	6.8439	6.7640
74	7.2172	7.1301	7.0448	6.9613	6.8795	6.7993	6.7208	6.6438	6.5684
75	6.9795	6.8978	6.8177	6.7393	6.6624	6.5871	6.5132	6.4407	6.3697
76	6.7388	6.6623	6.5874	6.5139	6.4418	6.3712	6.3018	6.2338	6.1670
77	6.4952	6.4238	6.3539	6.2852	6.2178	6.1517	6.0868	6.0231	5.9606
78	6.2492	6.1828	6.1176	6.0536	5.9908	5.9291	5.8686	5.8091	5.7506
79	6.0023	5.9406	5.8801	5.8206	5.7622	5.7048	5.6484	5.5930	5.5385
80	5.7566	5.6995	5.6433	5.5882	5.5340	5.4807	5.4283	5.3768	5.3262
81	5.5139	5.4611	5.4092	5.3582	5.3080	5.2587	5.2101	5.1624	5.1154
82	5.2754	5.2268	5.1788	5.1317	5.0853	5.0397	4.9948	4.9506	4.9071
83	5.0413	4.9964	4.9523	4.9089	4.8661	4.8240	4.7825	4.7417	4.7015
84	4.8097	4.7686	4.7280	4.6881	4.6487	4.6100	4.5718	4.5342	4.4971

UNITRUST PAYOUT ADJUSTMENT FACTORS

Number of Months That Valuation Date Precedes First Payout		Factors For Payout At The End Of Each			

Interest Rate	At Least	But Less Than	Annual Period	Semiannual Period	Quarterly Period	Monthly Period
2.8%	..	1	1.000000	.993144	.989727	.987454
	1	2	.997701	.990861	.987452	.985184
	2	3	.995408	.988583	.985182	
	3	4	.993120	.986311	.982918	
	4	5	.990837	.984044		
	5	6	.988560	.981782		
	6	7	.986287	.979525		
	7	8	.984020			
	8	9	.981758			
	9	10	.979502			
	10	11	.977250			
	11	12	.975004			
	12	.	.972763			

Interest Rate	At Least	But Less Than	Annual Period	Semiannual Period	Quarterly Period	Monthly Period
3.0%	..	1	1.000000	.992665	.989010	.986579
	1	2	.997540	.990222	.986577	.984152
	2	3	.995086	.987786	.984150	
	3	4	.992638	.985356	.981729	
	4	5	.990195	.982932		
	5	6	.987759	.980514		
	6	7	.985329	.978102		
	7	8	.982905			
	8	9	.980487			
	9	10	.978075			
	10	11	.975669			
	11	12	.973268			
	12	.	.970874			

Interest Rate	At Least	But Less Than	Annual Period	Semiannual Period	Quarterly Period	Monthly Period
3.2%	..	1	1.000000	.992187	.988296	.985707
	1	2	.997379	.989586	.985705	.983123
	2	3	.994764	.986992	.983121	
	3	4	.992156	.984405	.980544	
	4	5	.989555	.981824		
	5	6	.986961	.979250		
	6	7	.984374	.976683		
	7	8	.981794			
	8	9	.979220			
	9	10	.976653			
	10	11	.974093			
	11	12	.971539			
	12	.	.968992			

UNITRUST PAYOUT ADJUSTMENT FACTORS

| Number of Months That Valuation Date Precedes First Payout | | | Factors For Payout At The End Of Each | | | |

Interest Rate	At Least	But Less Than	Annual Period	Semiannual Period	Quarterly Period	Monthly Period
3.4%	..	1	1.000000	.991711	.987583	.984838
	1	2	.997218	.988951	.984836	.982098
	2	3	.994443	.986200	.982095	
	3	4	.991676	.983456	.979363	
	4	5	.988917	.980720		
	5	6	.986165	.977991		
	6	7	.983422	.975270		
	7	8	.980685			
	8	9	.977957			
	9	10	.975236			
	10	11	.972522			
	11	12	.969816			
	12	.	.967118			

Interest Rate	At Least	But Less Than	Annual Period	Semiannual Period	Quarterly Period	Monthly Period
3.6%	..	1	1.000000	.991236	.986873	.983972
	1	2	.997057	.988319	.983969	.981076
	2	3	.994123	.985410	.981073	
	3	4	.991197	.982510	.978186	
	4	5	.988280	.979619		
	5	6	.985372	.976736		
	6	7	.982472	.973861		
	7	8	.979581			
	8	9	.976698			
	9	10	.973823			
	10	11	.970957			
	11	12	.968100			
	12	.	.965251			

Interest Rate	At Least	But Less Than	Annual Period	Semiannual Period	Quarterly Period	Monthly Period
3.8%	..	1	1.000000	.990762	.986165	.983108
	1	2	.996897	.987688	.983105	.980057
	2	3	.993803	.984623	.980054	
	3	4	.990719	.981568	.977013	
	4	5	.987645	.978522		
	5	6	.984580	.975485		
	6	7	.981525	.972458		
	7	8	.978479			
	8	9	.975443			
	9	10	.972416			
	10	11	.969398			
	11	12	.966390			
	12	.	.963391			

UNITRUST PAYOUT ADJUSTMENT FACTORS

Interest Rate	Number of Months That Valuation Date Precedes First Payout		Factors For Payout At The End Of Each			
	At Least	But Less Than	Annual Period	Semiannual Period	Quarterly Period	Monthly Period
4.0%	..	1	1.000000	.990290	.985459	.982247
	1	2	.996737	.987059	.982244	.979042
	2	3	.993485	.983838	.979038	
	3	4	.990243	.980628	.975844	
	4	5	.987011	.977428		
	5	6	.983791	.974239		
	6	7	.980581	.971060		
	7	8	.977381			
	8	9	.974192			
	9	10	.971013			
	10	11	.967844			
	11	12	.964686			
	12	.	.961538			

Interest Rate	At Least	But Less Than	Annual Period	Semiannual Period	Quarterly Period	Monthly Period
4.2%	..	1	1.000000	.989820	.984755	.981389
	1	2	.996577	.986432	.981385	.978030
	2	3	.993166	.983056	.978026	
	3	4	.989767	.979691	.974679	
	4	5	.986380	.976338		
	5	6	.983004	.972996		
	6	7	.979639	.969666		
	7	8	.976286			
	8	9	.972945			
	9	10	.969615			
	10	11	.966296			
	11	12	.962989			
	12	.	.959693			

Interest Rate	At Least	But Less Than	Annual Period	Semiannual Period	Quarterly Period	Monthly Period
4.4%	..	1	1.000000	.989350	.984054	.980533
	1	2	.996418	.985806	.980529	.977021
	2	3	.992849	.982275	.977017	
	3	4	.989293	.978757	.973517	
	4	5	.985749	.975251		
	5	6	.982219	.971758		
	6	7	.978700	.968277		
	7	8	.975195			
	8	9	.971702			
	9	10	.968221			
	10	11	.964753			
	11	12	.961298			
	12	.	.957854			

2007 Tax Facts on Investments

UNITRUST PAYOUT ADJUSTMENT FACTORS

Interest Rate	Number of Months That Valuation Date Precedes First Payout		Factors For Payout At The End Of Each			
	At Least	But Less Than	Annual Period	Semiannual Period	Quarterly Period	Monthly Period
4.6%	..	1	1.000000	.988882	.983354	.979680
	1	2	.996259	.985183	.979676	.976015
	2	3	.992532	.981498	.976011	
	3	4	.988820	.977826	.972360	
	4	5	.985121	.974168		
	5	6	.981436	.970524		
	6	7	.977764	.966894		
	7	8	.974107			
	8	9	.970463			
	9	10	.966832			
	10	11	.963216			
	11	12	.959613			
	12	.	.956023			

Interest Rate	At Least	But Less Than	Annual Period	Semiannual Period	Quarterly Period	Monthly Period
4.8%	..	1	1.000000	.988415	.982657	.978830
	1	2	.996101	.984561	.978825	.975013
	2	3	.992217	.980722	.975008	
	3	4	.988348	.976898	.971206	
	4	5	.984494	.973089		
	5	6	.980655	.969294		
	6	7	.976831	.965515		
	7	8	.973022			
	8	9	.969228			
	9	10	.965448			
	10	11	.961684			
	11	12	.957934			
	12	.	.954199			

Interest Rate	At Least	But Less Than	Annual Period	Semiannual Period	Quarterly Period	Monthly Period
5.0%	..	1	1.000000	.987950	.981961	.977982
	1	2	.995942	.983941	.977977	.974014
	2	3	.991901	.979949	.974009	
	3	4	.987877	.975973	.970057	
	4	5	.983868	.972013		
	5	6	.979876	.968069		
	6	7	.975900	.964141		
	7	8	.971940			
	8	9	.967997			
	9	10	.964069			
	10	11	.960157			
	11	12	.956261			
	12	.	.952381			

UNITRUST PAYOUT ADJUSTMENT FACTORS

	Number of Months That Valuation Date Precedes First Payout		Factors For Payout At The End Of Each			

Interest Rate	At Least	But Less Than	Annual Period	Semiannual Period	Quarterly Period	Monthly Period
5.2%	..	1	1.000000	.987486	.981268	.977137
	1	2	.995784	.983323	.977132	.973018
	2	3	.991587	.979178	.973012	
	3	4	.987407	.975050	.968911	
	4	5	.983244	.970940		
	5	6	.979099	.966847		
	6	7	.974972	.962771		
	7	8	.970862			
	8	9	.966769			
	9	10	.962694			
	10	11	.958636			
	11	12	.954594			
	12	.	.950570			

Interest Rate	At Least	But Less Than	Annual Period	Semiannual Period	Quarterly Period	Monthly Period
5.4%	..	1	1.000000	.987023	.980577	.976295
	1	2	.995627	.982707	.976289	.972026
	2	3	.991273	.978409	.972019	
	3	4	.986938	.974131	.967769	
	4	5	.982622	.969871		
	5	6	.978325	.965629		
	6	7	.974047	.961407		
	7	8	.969787			
	8	9	.965546			
	9	10	.961323			
	10	11	.957119			
	11	12	.952934			
	12	.	.948767			

Interest Rate	At Least	But Less Than	Annual Period	Semiannual Period	Quarterly Period	Monthly Period
5.6%	..	1	1.000000	.986562	.979888	.975455
	1	2	.995470	.982092	.975449	.971036
	2	3	.990960	.977643	.971029	
	3	4	.986470	.973214	.966630	
	4	5	.982001	.968805		
	5	6	.977552	.964416		
	6	7	.973124	.960047		
	7	8	.968715			
	8	9	.964326			
	9	10	.959958			
	10	11	.955609			
	11	12	.951279			
	12	.	.946970			

UNITRUST PAYOUT ADJUSTMENT FACTORS

	Number of Months That Valuation Date Precedes First Payout		Factors For Payout At The End Of Each			

Interest Rate	At Least	But Less Than	Annual Period	Semiannual Period	Quarterly Period	Monthly Period
5.8%	..	1	1.000000	.986102	.979201	.974618
	1	2	.995313	.981479	.974611	.970050
	2	3	.990647	.976879	.970043	
	3	4	.986004	.972300	.965496	
	4	5	.981382	.967742		
	5	6	.976782	.963206		
	6	7	.972204	.958691		
	7	8	.967646			
	8	9	.963111			
	9	10	.958596			
	10	11	.954103			
	11	12	.949631			
	12	.	.945180			

Interest Rate	At Least	But Less Than	Annual Period	Semiannual Period	Quarterly Period	Monthly Period
6.0%	..	1	1.000000	.985643	.978516	.973784
	1	2	.995156	.980868	.973776	.969067
	2	3	.990336	.976117	.969059	
	3	4	.985538	.971389	.964365	
	4	5	.980764	.966684		
	5	6	.976014	.962001		
	6	7	.971286	.957341		
	7	8	.966581			
	8	9	.961899			
	9	10	.957239			
	10	11	.952603			
	11	12	.947988			
	12	.	.943396			

Interest Rate	At Least	But Less Than	Annual Period	Semiannual Period	Quarterly Period	Monthly Period
6.2%	..	1	1.000000	.985185	.977833	.972952
	1	2	.995000	.980259	.972944	.968087
	2	3	.990024	.975358	.968079	
	3	4	.985074	.970481	.963238	
	4	5	.980148	.965628		
	5	6	.975247	.960799		
	6	7	.970371	.955995		
	7	8	.965519			
	8	9	.960691			
	9	10	.955887			
	10	11	.951107			
	11	12	.946352			
	12	.	.941620			

UNITRUST PAYOUT ADJUSTMENT FACTORS

| | Number of Months That Valuation Date Precedes First Payout | | Factors For Payout At The End Of Each | | | |

Interest Rate	At Least	But Less Than	Annual Period	Semiannual Period	Quarterly Period	Monthly Period
6.4%	..	1	1.000000	.984729	.977152	.972122
	1	2	.994844	.979652	.972114	.967110
	2	3	.989714	.974600	.967101	
	3	4	.984611	.969575	.962115	
	4	5	.979534	.964576		
	5	6	.974483	.959602		
	6	7	.969458	.954654		
	7	8	.964460			
	8	9	.959487			
	9	10	.954539			
	10	11	.949617			
	11	12	.944721			
	12	.	.939850			

Interest Rate	At Least	But Less Than	Annual Period	Semiannual Period	Quarterly Period	Monthly Period
6.6%	..	1	1.000000	.984274	.976473	.971295
	1	2	.994688	.979046	.971286	.966136
	2	3	.989404	.973845	.966127	
	3	4	.984149	.968672	.960995	
	4	5	.978921	.963527		
	5	6	.973721	.958408		
	6	7	.968549	.953318		
	7	8	.963404			
	8	9	.958286			
	9	10	.953196			
	10	11	.948132			
	11	12	.943096			
	12	.	.938086			

Interest Rate	At Least	But Less Than	Annual Period	Semiannual Period	Quarterly Period	Monthly Period
6.8%	..	1	1.000000	.983821	.975796	.970471
	1	2	.994533	.978442	.970461	.965165
	2	3	.989095	.973092	.965156	
	3	4	.983688	.967772	.959879	
	4	5	.978309	.962481		
	5	6	.972961	.957219		
	6	7	.967641	.951985		
	7	8	.962351			
	8	9	.957089			
	9	10	.951857			
	10	11	.946653			
	11	12	.941477			
	12	.	.936330			

UNITRUST PAYOUT ADJUSTMENT FACTORS

Number of Months That Valuation Date Precedes First Payout

Factors For Payout At The End Of Each

Interest Rate	At Least	But Less Than	Annual Period	Semiannual Period	Quarterly Period	Monthly Period
7.0%	..	1	1.000000	.983368	.975121	.969649
	1	2	.994378	.977839	.969639	.964198
	2	3	.988787	.972342	.964187	
	3	4	.983228	.966875	.958766	
	4	5	.977700	.961439		
	5	6	.972203	.956033		
	6	7	.966736	.950658		
	7	8	.961301			
	8	9	.955896			
	9	10	.950522			
	10	11	.945178			
	11	12	.939864			
	12	.	.934579			

Interest Rate	At Least	But Less Than	Annual Period	Semiannual Period	Quarterly Period	Monthly Period
7.2%	..	1	1.000000	.982917	.974449	.968830
	1	2	.994223	.977239	.968819	.963233
	2	3	.988479	.971593	.963222	
	3	4	.982769	.965980	.957658	
	4	5	.977091	.960400		
	5	6	.971446	.954851		
	6	7	.965834	.949335		
	7	8	.960255			
	8	9	.954707			
	9	10	.949192			
	10	11	.943708			
	11	12	.938256			
	12	.	.932836			

Interest Rate	At Least	But Less Than	Annual Period	Semiannual Period	Quarterly Period	Monthly Period
7.4%	..	1	1.000000	.982467	.973778	.968013
	1	2	.994069	.976640	.968002	.962271
	2	3	.988172	.970847	.962260	
	3	4	.982311	.965088	.956552	
	4	5	.976484	.959364		
	5	6	.970692	.953673		
	6	7	.964935	.948017		
	7	8	.959211			
	8	9	.953521			
	9	10	.947866			
	10	11	.942243			
	11	12	.936654			
	12	.	.931099			

UNITRUST PAYOUT ADJUSTMENT FACTORS

Number of Months That Valuation Date Precedes First Payout

Factors For Payout At The End Of Each

Interest Rate	At Least	But Less Than	Annual Period	Semiannual Period	Quarterly Period	Monthly Period
7.6%	..	1	1.000000	.982019	.973109	.967199
	1	2	.993914	.976042	.967187	.961313
	2	3	.987866	.970103	.961301	
	3	4	.981854	.964199	.955451	
	4	5	.975879	.958331		
	5	6	.969940	.952499		
	6	7	.964037	.946703		
	7	8	.958171			
	8	9	.952340			
	9	10	.946544			
	10	11	.940784			
	11	12	.935058			
	12	.	.929368			

Interest Rate	At Least	But Less Than	Annual Period	Semiannual Period	Quarterly Period	Monthly Period
7.8%	..	1	1.000000	.981571	.972442	.966387
	1	2	.993761	.975447	.966374	.960357
	2	3	.987560	.969361	.960345	
	3	4	.981398	.963312	.954353	
	4	5	.975275	.957302		
	5	6	.969190	.951329		
	6	7	.963143	.945393		
	7	8	.957133			
	8	9	.951161			
	9	10	.945227			
	10	11	.939329			
	11	12	.933468			
	12	.	.927644			

Interest Rate	At Least	But Less Than	Annual Period	Semiannual Period	Quarterly Period	Monthly Period
8.0%	..	1	1.000000	.981125	.971777	.965578
	1	2	.993607	.974853	.965564	.959405
	2	3	.987255	.968621	.959392	
	3	4	.980944	.962429	.953258	
	4	5	.974673	.956276		
	5	6	.968442	.950162		
	6	7	.962250	.944088		
	7	8	.956099			
	8	9	.949987			
	9	10	.943913			
	10	11	.937879			
	11	12	.931883			
	12	.	.925926			

UNITRUST PAYOUT ADJUSTMENT FACTORS

	Number of Months That Valuation Date Precedes First Payout		Factors For Payout At The End Of Each			
Interest Rate	At Least	But Less Than	Annual Period	Semiannual Period	Quarterly Period	Monthly Period
8.2%	..	1	1.000000	.980680	.971114	.964771
	1	2	.993454	.974261	.964757	.958455
	2	3	.986951	.967883	.958441	
	3	4	.980490	.961547	.952167	
	4	5	.974072	.955253		
	5	6	.967695	.949000		
	6	7	.961361	.942788		
	7	8	.955068			
	8	9	.948816			
	9	10	.942605			
	10	11	.936434			
	11	12	.930304			
	12	.	.924214			

Interest Rate	At Least	But Less Than	Annual Period	Semiannual Period	Quarterly Period	Monthly Period
8.4%	..	1	1.000000	.980237	.970453	.963966
	1	2	.993301	.973670	.963952	.957509
	2	3	.986647	.967148	.957494	
	3	4	.980037	.960669	.951080	
	4	5	.973472	.954233		
	5	6	.966951	.947841		
	6	7	.960474	.941491		
	7	8	.954039			
	8	9	.947648			
	9	10	.941300			
	10	11	.934994			
	11	12	.928731			
	12	.	.922509			

Interest Rate	At Least	But Less Than	Annual Period	Semiannual Period	Quarterly Period	Monthly Period
8.6%	..	1	1.000000	.979794	.969794	.963164
	1	2	.993148	.973081	.963149	.956565
	2	3	.986344	.966414	.956550	
	3	4	.979586	.959793	.949996	
	4	5	.972874	.953217		
	5	6	.966209	.946686		
	6	7	.959589	.940200		
	7	8	.953014			
	8	9	.946484			
	9	10	.940000			
	10	11	.933559			
	11	12	.927163			
	12	.	.920810			

UNITRUST PAYOUT ADJUSTMENT FACTORS

| Number of Months That Valuation Date Precedes First Payout | | | Factors For Payout At The End Of Each | | | |

Interest Rate	At Least	But Less Than	Annual Period	Semiannual Period	Quarterly Period	Monthly Period
8.8%	..	1	1.000000	.979353	.969136	.962365
	1	2	.992996	.972494	.962349	.955624
	2	3	.986041	.965683	.955609	
	3	4	.979135	.958919	.948916	
	4	5	.972278	.952203		
	5	6	.965468	.945534		
	6	7	.958706	.938912		
	7	8	.951992			
	8	9	.945324			
	9	10	.938703			
	10	11	.932129			
	11	12	.925600			
	12	.	.919118			

Interest Rate	At Least	But Less Than	Annual Period	Semiannual Period	Quarterly Period	Monthly Period
9.0%	..	1	1.000000	.978913	.968481	.961567
	1	2	.992844	.971908	.961551	.954686
	2	3	.985740	.964954	.954670	
	3	4	.978686	.958049	.947839	
	4	5	.971683	.951193		
	5	6	.964730	.944387		
	6	7	.957826	.937629		
	7	8	.950972			
	8	9	.944167			
	9	10	.937411			
	10	11	.930703			
	11	12	.924043			
	12	.	.917431			

Interest Rate	At Least	But Less Than	Annual Period	Semiannual Period	Quarterly Period	Monthly Period
9.2%	..	1	1.000000	.978474	.967827	.960772
	1	2	.992693	.971324	.960755	.953751
	2	3	.985439	.964226	.953734	
	3	4	.978238	.957180	.946765	
	4	5	.971089	.950186		
	5	6	.963993	.943243		
	6	7	.956949	.936350		
	7	8	.949956			
	8	9	.943014			
	9	10	.936123			
	10	11	.929283			
	11	12	.922492			
	12	.	.915751			

TERM CERTAIN UNITRUST REMAINDER FACTORS

ADJUSTED PAYOUT RATE

YEARS	4.0%	4.2%	4.4%	4.6%	4.8%	5.0%	5.2%	5.4%	5.6%
1	.960000	.958000	.956000	.954000	.952000	.950000	.948000	.946000	.944000
2	.921600	.917764	.913936	.910116	.906304	.902500	.898704	.894916	.891136
3	.884736	.879218	.873723	.868251	.862801	.857375	.851971	.846591	.841232
4	.849347	.842291	.835279	.828311	.821387	.814506	.807669	.800875	.794123
5	.815373	.806915	.798527	.790209	.781960	.773781	.765670	.757627	.749652
6	.782758	.773024	.763392	.753859	.744426	.735092	.725855	.716716	.707672
7	.751447	.740557	.729802	.719182	.708694	.698337	.688111	.678013	.668042
8	.721390	.709454	.697691	.686099	.674677	.663420	.652329	.641400	.630632
9	.692534	.679657	.666993	.654539	.642292	.630249	.618408	.606765	.595317
10	.664833	.651111	.637645	.624430	.611462	.598737	.586251	.573999	.561979
11	.638239	.623764	.609589	.595706	.582112	.568800	.555766	.543003	.530508
12	.612710	.597566	.582767	.568304	.554170	.540360	.526866	.513681	.500800
13	.588201	.572469	.557125	.542162	.527570	.513342	.499469	.485942	.472755
14	.564673	.548425	.532611	.517222	.502247	.487675	.473496	.459701	.446280
15	.542086	.525391	.509177	.493430	.478139	.463291	.448875	.434878	.421289
16	.520403	.503325	.486773	.470732	.455188	.440127	.425533	.411394	.397697
17	.499587	.482185	.465355	.449079	.433339	.418120	.403405	.389179	.375426
18	.479603	.461933	.444879	.428421	.412539	.397214	.382428	.368163	.354402
19	.460419	.442532	.425304	.408714	.392737	.377354	.362542	.348282	.334555
20	.442002	.423946	.406591	.389913	.373886	.358486	.343690	.329475	.315820

ADJUSTED PAYOUT RATE

YEARS	5.8%	6.0%	6.2%	6.4%	6.6%	6.8%	7.0%	7.2%	7.4%
1	.942000	.940000	.938000	.936000	.934000	.932000	.930000	.928000	.926000
2	.887364	.883600	.879844	.876096	.872356	.868624	.864900	.861184	.857476
3	.835897	.830584	.825294	.820026	.814781	.809558	.804357	.799179	.794023
4	.787415	.780749	.774125	.767544	.761005	.754508	.748052	.741638	.735265
5	.741745	.733904	.726130	.718421	.710779	.703201	.695688	.688240	.680855
6	.698724	.689870	.681110	.672442	.663867	.655383	.646990	.638687	.630472
7	.658198	.648478	.638881	.629406	.620052	.610817	.601701	.592701	.583817
8	.620022	.609569	.599270	.589124	.579129	.569282	.559582	.550027	.540615
9	.584061	.572995	.562115	.551420	.540906	.530571	.520411	.510425	.500609
10	.550185	.538615	.527264	.516129	.505206	.494492	.483982	.473674	.463564
11	.518275	.506298	.494574	.483097	.471863	.460866	.450104	.439570	.429260
12	.488215	.475920	.463910	.452179	.440720	.429527	.418596	.407921	.397495
13	.459898	.447365	.435148	.423239	.411632	.400320	.389295	.378550	.368081
14	.433224	.420523	.408169	.396152	.384465	.373098	.362044	.351295	.340843
15	.408097	.395292	.382862	.370798	.359090	.347727	.336701	.326002	.315620
16	.384427	.371574	.359125	.347067	.335390	.324082	.313132	.302529	.292264
17	.362131	.349280	.336859	.324855	.313254	.302044	.291213	.280747	.270637
18	.341127	.328323	.315974	.304064	.292579	.281505	.270828	.260534	.250610
19	.321342	.308624	.296383	.284604	.273269	.262363	.251870	.241775	.232065
20	.302704	.290106	.278008	.266389	.255233	.244522	.234239	.224367	.214892

TERM CERTAIN UNITRUST REMAINDER FACTORS

ADJUSTED PAYOUT RATE

YEARS	7.6%	7.8%	8.0%	8.2%	8.4%	8.6%	8.8%	9.0%	9.2%
1	.924000	.922000	.920000	.918000	.916000	.914000	.912000	.910000	.908000
2	.853776	.850084	.846400	.842724	.839056	.835396	.831744	.828100	.824464
3	.788889	.783777	.778688	.773621	.768575	.763552	.758551	.753571	.748613
4	.728933	.722643	.716393	.710184	.704015	.697886	.691798	.685750	.679741
5	.673535	.666277	.659082	.651949	.644878	.637868	.630920	.624032	.617205
6	.622346	.614307	.606355	.598489	.590708	.583012	.575399	.567869	.560422
7	.575048	.566391	.557847	.549413	.541089	.532873	.524764	.516761	.508863
8	.531344	.522213	.513219	.504361	.495637	.487046	.478585	.470253	.462048
9	.490962	.481480	.472161	.463003	.454004	.445160	.436469	.427930	.419539
10	.453649	.443925	.434388	.425037	.415867	.406876	.398060	.389416	.380942
11	.419171	.409298	.399637	.390184	.380934	.371885	.363031	.354369	.345895
12	.387314	.377373	.367666	.358189	.348936	.339902	.331084	.322475	.314073
13	.357879	.347938	.338253	.328817	.319625	.310671	.301949	.293453	.285178
14	.330680	.320799	.311193	.301854	.292777	.283953	.275377	.267042	.258942
15	.305548	.295777	.286297	.277102	.268184	.259533	.251144	.243008	.235119
16	.282326	.272706	.263394	.254380	.245656	.237213	.229043	.221137	.213488
17	.260870	.251435	.242322	.233521	.225021	.216813	.208887	.201235	.193847
18	.241044	.231823	.222936	.214372	.206119	.198167	.190505	.183124	.176013
19	.222724	.213741	.205101	.196794	.188805	.181125	.173741	.166643	.159820
20	.205797	.197069	.188693	.180657	.172946	.165548	.158452	.151645	.145117

ADJUSTED PAYOUT RATE

YEARS	9.4%	9.6%	9.8%	10.0%	10.2%	10.4%	10.6%	10.8%	11.0%
1	.906000	.904000	.902000	.900000	.898000	.896000	.894000	.892000	.890000
2	.820836	.817216	.813604	.810000	.806404	.802816	.799236	.795664	.792100
3	.743677	.738763	.733871	.729000	.724151	.719323	.714517	.709732	.704969
4	.673772	.667842	.661951	.656100	.650287	.644514	.638778	.633081	.627422
5	.610437	.603729	.597080	.590490	.583958	.577484	.571068	.564708	.558406
6	.553056	.545771	.538566	.531441	.524394	.517426	.510535	.503720	.496981
7	.501069	.493377	.485787	.478297	.470906	.463613	.456418	.449318	.442313
8	.453968	.446013	.438180	.430467	.422874	.415398	.408038	.400792	.393659
9	.411295	.403196	.395238	.387420	.379741	.372196	.364786	.357506	.350356
10	.372634	.364489	.356505	.348678	.341007	.333488	.326118	.318896	.311817
11	.337606	.329498	.321567	.313811	.306224	.298805	.291550	.284455	.277517
12	.305871	.297866	.290054	.282430	.274989	.267729	.260646	.253734	.246990
13	.277119	.269271	.261628	.254187	.246941	.239886	.233017	.226331	.219821
14	.251070	.243421	.235989	.228768	.221753	.214937	.208317	.201887	.195641
15	.227469	.220053	.212862	.205891	.199134	.192584	.186236	.180083	.174121
16	.206087	.198928	.192001	.185302	.178822	.172555	.166495	.160634	.154967
17	.186715	.179830	.173185	.166772	.160582	.154609	.148846	.143286	.137921
18	.169164	.162567	.156213	.150095	.144203	.138530	.133069	.127811	.122750
19	.153262	.146960	.140904	.135085	.129494	.124123	.118963	.114007	.109247
20	.138856	.132852	.127096	.121577	.116286	.111214	.106353	.101694	.097230

TERM CERTAIN UNITRUST REMAINDER FACTORS

ADJUSTED PAYOUT RATE

YEARS	11.2%	11.4%	11.6%	11.8%	12.0%	12.2%	12.4%	12.6%	12.8%
1	.888000	.886000	.884000	.882000	.880000	.878000	.876000	.874000	.872000
2	.788544	.784996	.781456	.777924	.774400	.770884	.767376	.763876	.760384
3	.700227	.695506	.690807	.686129	.681472	.676836	.672221	.667628	.663055
4	.621802	.616219	.610673	.605166	.599695	.594262	.588866	.583507	.578184
5	.552160	.545970	.539835	.533756	.527732	.521762	.515847	.509985	.504176
6	.490318	.483729	.477214	.470773	.464404	.458107	.451882	.445727	.439642
7	.435402	.428584	.421858	.415222	.408676	.402218	.395848	.389565	.383368
8	.386637	.379726	.372922	.366226	.359635	.353147	.346763	.340480	.334297
9	.343334	.336437	.329663	.323011	.316478	.310063	.303764	.297579	.291507
10	.304881	.298083	.291422	.284896	.278501	.272236	.266098	.260084	.254194
11	.270734	.264102	.257617	.251278	.245081	.239023	.233102	.227314	.221657
12	.240412	.233994	.227734	.221627	.215671	.209862	.204197	.198672	.193285
13	.213486	.207319	.201317	.195475	.189791	.184259	.178877	.173640	.168544
14	.189575	.183684	.177964	.172409	.167016	.161779	.156696	.151761	.146971
15	.168343	.162744	.157320	.152065	.146974	.142042	.137266	.132639	.128158
16	.149488	.144191	.139071	.134121	.129337	.124713	.120245	.115927	.111754
17	.132746	.127754	.122939	:118295	.113817	.109498	.105334	.101320	.097450
18	.117878	.113190	.108678	.104336	.100159	.096139	.092273	.088554	.084976
19	.104676	.100286	.096071	.092024	.088140	.084410	.080831	.077396	.074099
20	.092952	.088853	.084927	.081166	.077563	.074112	.070808	.067644	.064614

ADJUSTED PAYOUT RATE

YEARS	13.0%	13.2%	13.4%	13.6%	13.8%	14.0%	14.2%	14.4%	14.6%
1	.870000	.868000	.866000	.864000	.862000	.860000	.858000	.856000	.854000
2	.756900	.753424	.749956	.746496	.743044	.739600	.736164	.732736	.729316
3	.658503	.653972	.649462	.644973	.640504	.636056	.631629	.627222	.622836
4	.572898	.567648	.562434	.557256	.552114	.547008	.541937	.536902	.531902
5	.498421	.492718	.487068	.481469	.475923	.470427	.464982	.459588	.454244
6	.433626	.427679	.421801	.415990	.410245	.404567	.398955	.393407	.387925
7	.377255	.371226	.365279	.359415	.353631	.347928	.342303	.336757	.331288
8	.328212	.322224	.316332	.310535	.304830	.299218	.293696	.288264	.282920
9	.285544	.279690	.273944	.268302	.262764	.257327	.251991	.246754	.241613
10	.248423	.242771	.237235	.231813	.226502	.221302	.216209	.211221	.206338
11	.216128	.210725	.205446	.200286	.195245	.190319	.185507	.180805	.176212
12	.188032	.182910	.177916	.173047	.168301	.163675	.159165	.154769	.150485
13	.163588	.158766	.154075	.149513	.145076	.140760	.136564	.132483	.128515
14	.142321	.137809	.133429	.129179	.125055	.121054	.117172	.113405	.109751
15	.123819	.119618	.115550	.111611	.107798	.104106	.100533	.097075	.093728
16	.107723	.103828	.100066	.096432	.092922	.089531	.086257	.083096	.080043
17	.093719	.090123	.086657	.083317	.080098	.076997	.074009	.071130	.068357
18	.081535	.078227	.075045	.071986	.069045	.066217	.063500	.060887	.058377
19	.070936	.067901	.064989	.062196	.059517	.056947	.054483	.052120	.049854
20	.061714	.058938	.056280	.053737	.051303	.048974	.046746	.044614	.042575

TERM CERTAIN UNITRUST REMAINDER FACTORS

ADJUSTED PAYOUT RATE

YEARS	14.8%	15.0%	15.2%	15.4%	15.6%	15.8%	16.0%	16.2%	16.4%
1	.852000	.850000	.848000	.846000	.844000	.842000	.840000	.838000	.836000
2	.725904	.722500	.719104	.715716	.712336	.708964	.705600	.702244	.698896
3	.618470	.614125	.609800	.605496	.601212	.596948	.592704	.588480	.584277
4	.526937	.522006	.517111	.512249	.507423	.502630	.497871	.493147	.488456
5	.448950	.443705	.438510	.433363	.428265	.423214	.418212	.413257	.408349
6	.382505	.377149	.371856	.366625	.361455	.356347	.351298	.346309	.341380
7	.325895	.320577	.315334	.310165	.305068	.300044	.295090	.290207	.285393
8	.277662	.272491	.267403	.262399	.257478	.252637	.247876	.243194	.238589
9	.236568	.231617	.226758	.221990	.217311	.212720	.208216	.203796	.199460
10	.201556	.196874	.192291	.187803	.183411	.179110	.174901	.170781	.166749
11	.171726	.167343	.163063	.158882	.154799	.150811	.146917	.143115	.139402
12	.146310	.142242	.138277	.134414	.130650	.126983	.123410	.119930	.116540
13	.124656	.120905	.117259	.113714	.110269	.106920	.103665	.100501	.097428
14	.106207	.102770	.099436	.096202	.093067	.090026	.087078	.084220	.081449
15	.090489	.087354	.084321	.081387	.078548	.075802	.073146	.070577	.068092
16	.077096	.074251	.071505	.068853	.066295	.063825	.061442	.059143	.056925
17	.065686	.063113	.060636	.058250	.055953	.053741	.051612	.049562	.047589
18	.055965	.053646	.051419	.049280	.047224	.045250	.043354	.041533	.039784
19	.047682	.045599	.043603	.041690	.039857	.038100	.036417	.034805	.033260
20	.040625	.038760	.036976	.035270	.033639	.032081	.030590	.029166	.027805

ADJUSTED PAYOUT RATE

YEARS	16.6%	16.8%	17.0%	17.2%	17.4%	17.6%	17.8%	18.0%	18.2%
1	.834000	.832000	.830000	.828000	.826000	.824000	.822000	.820000	.818000
2	.695556	.692224	.688900	.685584	.682276	.678976	.675684	.672400	.669124
3	.580094	.575930	.571787	.567664	.563560	.559476	.555412	.551368	.547343
4	.483798	.479174	.474583	.470025	.465501	.461008	.456549	.452122	.447727
5	.403488	.398673	.393904	.389181	.384503	.379871	.375283	.370740	.366241
6	.336509	.331696	.326940	.322242	.317600	.313014	.308483	.304007	.299585
7	.280648	.275971	.271361	.266816	.262337	.257923	.253573	.249285	.245060
8	.234061	.229608	.225229	.220924	.216691	.212529	.208437	.204414	.200459
9	.195207	.191034	.186940	.182925	.178987	.175124	.171335	.167620	.163976
10	.162802	.158940	.155160	.151462	.147843	.144302	.140837	.137448	.134132
11	.135777	.132238	.128783	.125410	.122118	.118905	.115768	.112707	.109720
12	.113238	.110022	.106890	.103840	.100870	.097978	.095162	.092420	.089751
13	.094441	.091538	.088719	.085979	.083318	.080733	.078223	.075784	.073416
14	.078763	.076160	.073637	.071191	.068821	.066524	.064299	.062143	.060055
15	.065689	.063365	.061118	.058946	.056846	.054816	.052854	.050957	.049125
16	.054784	.052720	.050728	.048807	.046955	.045168	.043446	.041785	.040184
17	.045690	.043863	.042104	.040412	.038785	.037219	.035713	.034264	.032870
18	.038106	.036494	.034947	.033462	.032036	.030668	.029356	.028096	.026888
19	.031780	.030363	.029006	.027706	.026462	.025271	.024130	.023039	.021994
20	.026505	.025262	.024075	.022941	.021858	.020823	.019835	.018892	.017991

TERM CERTAIN UNITRUST REMAINDER FACTORS

ADJUSTED PAYOUT RATE

YEARS	18.4%	18.6%	18.8%	19.0%	19.2%	19.4%	19.6%	19.8%	20.0%
1	.816000	.814000	.812000	.810000	.808000	.806000	.804000	.802000	.800000
2	.665856	.662596	.659344	.656100	.652864	.649636	.646416	.643204	.640000
3	.543338	.539353	.535387	.531441	.527514	.523607	.519718	.515850	.512000
4	.443364	.439033	.434735	.430467	.426231	.422027	.417854	.413711	.409600
5	.361785	.357373	.353004	.348678	.344395	.340154	.335954	.331797	.327680
6	.295217	.290902	.286640	.282430	.278271	.274164	.270107	.266101	.262144
7	.240897	.236794	.232751	.228768	.224843	.220976	.217166	.213413	.209715
8	.196572	.192750	.188994	.185302	.181673	.178107	.174602	.171157	.167772
9	.160403	.156899	.153463	.150095	.146792	.143554	.140380	.137268	.134218
10	.130889	.127716	.124612	.121577	.118608	.115705	.112865	.110089	.107374
11	.106805	.103961	.101185	.098477	.095835	.093258	.090744	.088291	.085899
12	.087153	.084624	.082162	.079766	.077435	.075166	.072958	.070810	.068719
13	.071117	.068884	.066716	.064611	.062567	.060584	.058658	.056789	.054976
14	.058031	.056071	.054173	.052335	.050554	.048830	.047161	.045545	.043980
15	.047354	.045642	.043989	.042391	.040848	.039357	.037918	.036527	.035184
16	.038640	.037153	.035719	.034337	.033005	.031722	.030486	.029295	.028147
17	.031531	.030242	.029004	.027813	.026668	.025568	.024511	.023494	.022518
18	.025729	.024617	.023551	.022528	.021548	.020608	.019706	.018843	.018014
19	.020995	.020038	.019123	.018248	.017411	.016610	.015844	.015112	.014412
20	.017132	.016311	.015528	.014781	.014068	.013388	.012739	.012120	.011529

ADJUSTED PAYOUT RATE

YEARS	20.2%	20.4%	20.6%	20.8%	21.0%	21.2%	21.4%	21.6%	21.8%
1	.798000	.796000	.794000	.792000	.790000	.788000	.786000	.784000	.782000
2	.636804	.633616	.630436	.627264	.624100	.620944	.617796	.614656	.611524
3	.508170	.504358	.500566	.496793	.493039	.489304	.485588	.481890	.478212
4	.405519	.401469	.397450	.393460	.389501	.385571	.381672	.377802	.373962
5	.323604	.319570	.315575	.311620	.307706	.303830	.299994	.296197	.292438
6	.258236	.254377	.250567	.246803	.243087	.239418	.235795	.232218	.228687
7	.206073	.202484	.198950	.195468	.192039	.188662	.185335	.182059	.178833
8	.164446	.161178	.157966	.154811	.151711	.148665	.145673	.142734	.139847
9	.131228	.128297	.125425	.122610	.119852	.117148	.114499	.111904	.109361
10	.104720	.102125	.099588	.097107	.094683	.092313	.089996	.087733	.085520
11	.083566	.081291	.079073	.076909	.074799	.072743	.070737	.068782	.066877
12	.066686	.064708	.062784	.060912	.059092	.057321	.055599	.053925	.052298
13	.053215	.051507	.049850	.048242	.046682	.045169	.043701	.042277	.040897
14	.042466	.041000	.039581	.038208	.036879	.035593	.034349	.033146	.031981
15	.033888	.032636	.031427	.030261	.029134	.028047	.026998	.025986	.025009
16	.027042	.025978	.024953	.023966	.023016	.022101	.021221	.020373	.019557
17	.021580	.020679	.019813	.018981	.018183	.017416	.016680	.015973	.015294
18	.017221	.016460	.015731	.015033	.014364	.013724	.013110	.012522	.011960
19	.013742	.013102	.012491	.011906	.011348	.010814	.010305	.009818	.009353
20	.010966	.010429	.009918	.009430	.008965	.008522	.008099	.007697	.007314

TERM CERTAIN UNITRUST REMAINDER FACTORS

ADJUSTED PAYOUT RATE

YEARS	22.0%	22.2%	22.4%	22.6%	22.8%	23.0%	23.2%	23.4%	23.6%
1	.780000	.778000	.776000	.774000	.772000	.770000	.768000	.766000	.764000
2	.608400	.605284	.602176	.599076	.595984	.592900	.589824	.586756	.583696
3	.474552	.470911	.467289	.463685	.460100	.456533	.452985	.449455	.445944
4	.370151	.366369	.362616	.358892	.355197	.351530	.347892	.344283	.340701
5	.288717	.285035	.281390	.277782	.274212	.270678	.267181	.263720	.260296
6	.225200	.221757	.218359	.215004	.211692	.208422	.205195	.202010	.198866
7	.175656	.172527	.169446	.166413	.163426	.160485	.157590	.154740	.151933
8	.137011	.134226	.131490	.128804	.126165	.123574	.121029	.118531	.116077
9	.106869	.104428	.102036	.099694	.097399	.095152	.092950	.090794	.088683
10	.083358	.081245	.079180	.077163	.075192	.073267	.071386	.069548	.067754
11	.065019	.063209	.061444	.059724	.058048	.056415	.054824	.053274	.051764
12	.050715	.049176	.047680	.046227	.044813	.043440	.042105	.040808	.039548
13	.039558	.038259	.037000	.035779	.034596	.033449	.032337	.031259	.030214
14	.030855	.029766	.028712	.027693	.026708	.025756	.024835	.023944	.023084
15	.024067	.023158	.022281	.021435	.020619	.019832	.019073	.018341	.017636
16	.018772	.018017	.017290	.016590	.015918	.015270	.014648	.014049	.013474
17	.014642	.014017	.013417	.012841	.012288	.011758	.011250	.010762	.010294
18	.011421	.010905	.010411	.009939	.009487	.009054	.008640	.008244	.007865
19	.008908	.008484	.008079	.007693	.007324	.006971	.006635	.006315	.006009
20	.006949	.006601	.006270	.005954	.005654	.005368	.005096	.004837	.004591

ADJUSTED PAYOUT RATE

YEARS	23.8%	24.0%	24.2%	24.4%	24.6%	24.8%	25.0%	25.2%	25.4%
1	.762000	.760000	.758000	.756000	.754000	.752000	.750000	.748000	.746000
2	.580644	.577600	.574564	.571536	.568516	.565504	.562500	.559504	.556516
3	.442451	.438976	.435520	.432081	.428661	.425259	.421875	.418509	.415161
4	.337147	.333622	.330124	.326653	.323210	.319795	.316406	.313045	.309710
5	.256906	.253553	.250234	.246950	.243701	.240486	.237305	.234157	.231044
6	.195763	.192700	.189677	.186694	.183750	.180845	.177979	.175150	.172359
7	.149171	.146452	.143775	.141141	.138548	.135996	.133484	.131012	.128580
8	.113668	.111303	.108982	.106702	.104465	.102269	.100113	.097997	.095920
9	.086615	.084591	.082608	.080667	.078767	.076906	.075085	.073302	.071557
10	.066001	.064289	.062617	.060984	.059390	.057833	.056314	.054830	.053381
11	.050293	.048860	.047464	.046104	.044780	.043491	.042235	.041013	.039822
12	.038323	.037133	.035977	.034855	.033764	.032705	.031676	.030677	.029707
13	.029202	.028221	.027271	.026350	.025458	.024594	.023757	.022947	.022162
14	.022252	.021448	.020671	.019921	.019195	.018495	.017818	.017164	.016533
15	.016956	.016301	.015669	.015060	.014473	.013908	.013363	.012839	.012333
16	.012921	.012388	.011877	.011385	.010913	.010459	.010023	.009603	.009201
17	.009845	.009415	.009003	.008607	.008228	.007865	.007517	.007183	.006864
18	.007502	.007156	.006824	.006507	.006204	.005915	.005638	.005373	.005120
19	.005717	.005438	.005173	.004919	.004678	.004448	.004228	.004019	.003820
20	.004356	.004133	.003921	.003719	.003527	.003345	.003171	.003006	.002850

SINGLE LIFE UNITRUST REMAINDER FACTORS

(For valuation dates occurring after April 30, 1999)

ADJUSTED PAYOUT RATE

AGE	4.0%	4.2%	4.4%	4.6%	4.8%	5.0%	5.2%	5.4%	5.6%	5.8%
35	.20816	.19405	.18107	.16910	.15808	.14791	.13853	.12987	.12187	.11448
36	.21540	.20109	.18791	.17574	.16451	.15414	.14455	.13569	.12749	.11990
37	.22287	.20838	.19500	.18263	.17120	.16062	.15083	.14177	.13337	.12558
38	.23060	.21593	.20236	.18979	.17816	.16739	.15739	.14813	.13953	.13154
39	.23858	.22374	.20998	.19723	.18540	.17442	.16423	.15477	.14597	.13779
40	.24684	.23183	.21789	.20496	.19294	.18177	.17138	.16172	.15272	.14434
41	.25538	.24021	.22611	.21299	.20079	.18943	.17885	.16899	.15980	.15123
42	.26421	.24889	.23463	.22134	.20896	.19741	.18665	.17660	.16721	.15845
43	.27332	.25786	.24344	.23000	.21744	.20572	.19477	.18453	.17496	.16601
44	.28271	.26712	.25257	.23896	.22625	.21435	.20322	.19281	.18305	.17391
45	.29235	.27665	.26196	.24821	.23534	.22328	.21198	.20139	.19145	.18213
46	.30225	.28644	.27163	.25774	.24472	.23251	.22105	.21028	.20018	.19068
47	.31238	.29647	.28155	.26754	.25438	.24201	.23040	.21947	.20919	.19952
48	.32275	.30676	.29173	.27760	.26431	.25181	.24004	.22896	.21852	.20868
49	.33335	.31729	.30217	.28794	.27453	.26190	.24999	.23876	.22817	.21817
50	.34419	.32808	.31289	.29856	.28505	.27229	.26026	.24889	.23814	.22799
51	.35528	.33912	.32387	.30946	.29585	.28299	.27083	.25933	.24845	.23815
52	.36657	.35038	.33507	.32060	.30691	.29395	.28168	.27005	.25904	.24861
53	.37805	.36185	.34651	.33198	.31821	.30517	.29280	.28106	.26993	.25937
54	.38972	.37352	.35815	.34358	.32976	.31664	.30418	.29234	.28110	.27042
55	.40157	.38539	.37002	.35542	.34155	.32836	.31583	.30390	.29256	.28177
56	.41361	.39746	.38209	.36748	.35358	.34034	.32774	.31574	.30431	.29342
57	.42582	.40971	.39437	.37976	.36584	.35257	.33992	.32785	.31634	.30536
58	.43817	.42212	.40682	.39222	.37829	.36500	.35231	.34019	.32862	.31756
59	.45061	.43464	.41939	.40482	.39090	.37759	.36488	.35272	.34109	.32996
60	.46314	.44726	.43207	.41754	.40364	.39034	.37761	.36542	.35375	.34257
61	.47577	.45999	.44488	.43041	.41655	.40326	.39053	.37833	.36662	.35540
62	.48852	.47286	.45785	.44345	.42964	.41639	.40367	.39146	.37974	.36848
63	.50141	.48589	.47098	.45667	.44293	.42972	.41703	.40484	.39311	.38184
64	.51440	.49903	.48426	.47005	.45638	.44324	.43060	.41843	.40671	.39544
65	.52749	.51229	.49766	.48357	.47001	.45694	.44435	.43223	.42054	.40927
66	.54069	.52568	.51121	.49726	.48381	.47084	.45833	.44626	.43461	.42337
67	.55404	.53924	.52495	.51115	.49784	.48498	.47256	.46056	.44898	.43778
68	.56751	.55293	.53883	.52521	.51205	.49932	.48701	.47511	.46360	.45246
69	.58105	.56671	.55283	.53940	.52640	.51382	.50165	.48985	.47844	.46738
70	.59461	.58052	.56687	.55365	.54084	.52843	.51639	.50473	.49342	.48245
71	.60813	.59431	.58091	.56791	.55529	.54306	.53118	.51966	.50847	.49761
72	.62158	.60804	.59490	.58213	.56973	.55768	.54598	.53461	.52357	.51283
73	.63493	.62168	.60881	.59629	.58411	.57227	.56076	.54955	.53866	.52806
74	.64822	.63528	.62268	.61042	.59848	.58686	.57555	.56453	.55380	.54335
75	.66149	.64887	.63657	.62458	.61290	.60151	.59041	.57959	.56904	.55875
76	.67478	.66249	.65049	.63880	.62739	.61625	.60538	.59478	.58443	.57432
77	.68807	.67612	.66446	.65307	.64194	.63108	.62046	.61009	.59995	.59005
78	.70134	.68975	.67843	.66736	.65654	.64596	.63561	.62548	.61558	.60590
79	.71451	.70330	.69233	.68160	.67109	.66081	.65074	.64088	.63123	.62178
80	.72749	.71666	.70605	.69566	.68548	.67550	.66573	.65615	.64676	.63755
81	.74019	.72975	.71950	.70946	.69961	.68994	.68047	.67117	.66205	.65310
82	.75256	.74250	.73263	.72293	.71342	.70407	.69490	.68589	.67705	.66837
83	.76461	.75493	.74542	.73608	.72690	.71788	.70902	.70031	.69175	.68333
84	.77641	.76712	.75798	.74900	.74016	.73147	.72292	.71451	.70624	.69810

SINGLE LIFE UNITRUST REMAINDER FACTORS
(For valuation dates occurring after April 30, 1999)

ADJUSTED PAYOUT RATE

AGE	6.0%	6.2%	6.4%	6.6%	6.8%	7.0%	7.2%	7.4%	7.6%	7.8%
35	.10764	.10131	.09545	.09002	.08498	.08030	.07596	.07193	.06818	.06469
36	.11287	.10635	.10031	.09470	.08949	.08465	.08015	.07596	.07206	.06842
37	.11835	.11165	.10542	.09963	.09424	.08923	.08457	.08022	.07617	.07238
38	.12412	.11722	.11081	.10484	.09927	.09409	.08926	.08475	.08054	.07661
39	.13017	.12308	.11648	.11032	.10458	.09922	.09422	.08955	.08518	.08109
40	.13653	.12925	.12246	.11612	.11020	.10466	.09949	.09465	.09011	.08587
41	.14322	.13575	.12877	.12225	.11614	.11043	.10508	.10007	.09537	.09097
42	.15025	.14259	.13542	.12871	.12243	.11654	.11101	.10583	.10097	.09640
43	.15762	.14977	.14242	.13552	.12905	.12298	.11729	.11193	.10690	.10217
44	.16534	.15731	.14976	.14269	.13604	.12979	.12391	.11838	.11318	.10828
45	.17338	.16516	.15743	.15017	.14334	.13691	.13086	.12516	.11979	.11472
46	.18174	.17334	.16544	.15800	.15099	.14438	.13816	.13228	.12674	.12150
47	.19041	.18184	.17375	.16613	.15895	.15217	.14576	.13972	.13400	.12860
48	.19941	.19066	.18240	.17461	.16724	.16029	.15371	.14749	.14161	.13604
49	.20873	.19981	.19138	.18342	.17588	.16875	.16201	.15562	.14956	.14383
50	.21839	.20931	.20072	.19259	.18489	.17759	.17067	.16412	.15790	.15199
51	.22840	.21917	.21041	.20212	.19426	.18679	.17971	.17299	.16660	.16054
52	.23872	.22933	.22043	.21198	.20395	.19633	.18909	.18220	.17566	.16943
53	.24934	.23981	.23076	.22216	.21399	.20621	.19881	.19176	.18506	.17867
54	.26026	.25060	.24141	.23267	.22434	.21642	.20886	.20166	.19480	.18826
55	.27149	.26171	.25239	.24351	.23504	.22697	.21927	.21192	.20491	.19821
56	.28303	.27313	.26369	.25468	.24608	.23787	.23003	.22254	.21538	.20854
57	.29488	.28487	.27531	.26618	.25746	.24912	.24114	.23351	.22621	.21923
58	.30699	.29688	.28722	.27798	.26914	.26067	.25257	.24481	.23738	.23025
59	.31932	.30913	.29937	.29002	.28107	.27249	.26427	.25639	.24882	.24157
60	.33186	.32159	.31175	.30231	.29325	.28457	.27623	.26823	.26055	.25317
61	.34463	.33429	.32437	.31485	.30571	.29692	.28848	.28037	.27257	.26507
62	.35767	.34728	.33730	.32770	.31847	.30960	.30106	.29285	.28495	.27734
63	.37100	.36057	.35053	.34087	.33157	.32262	.31400	.30569	.29769	.28998
64	.38458	.37412	.36404	.35433	.34498	.33596	.32726	.31887	.31078	.30298
65	.39841	.38794	.37783	.36809	.35868	.34961	.34085	.33239	.32422	.31633
66	.41252	.40205	.39193	.38216	.37272	.36361	.35479	.34628	.33804	.33008
67	.42696	.41650	.40639	.39661	.38715	.37800	.36915	.36059	.35230	.34428
68	.44169	.43126	.42116	.41139	.40193	.39277	.38390	.37530	.36697	.35890
69	.45666	.44628	.43622	.42648	.41703	.40787	.39898	.39037	.38201	.37391
70	.47181	.46150	.45149	.44178	.43236	.42321	.41433	.40571	.39735	.38922
71	.48707	.47683	.46689	.45723	.44785	.43873	.42987	.42126	.41290	.40476
72	.50239	.49225	.48238	.47279	.46346	.45439	.44556	.43697	.42862	.42048
73	.51774	.50770	.49793	.48841	.47915	.47013	.46135	.45280	.44447	.43635
74	.53316	.52324	.51358	.50416	.49498	.48603	.47731	.46880	.46051	.45242
75	.54872	.53894	.52939	.52008	.51100	.50214	.49349	.48505	.47681	.46877
76	.56446	.55483	.54543	.53624	.52728	.51852	.50996	.50160	.49344	.48546
77	.58037	.57091	.56167	.55263	.54380	.53516	.52671	.51845	.51038	.50247
78	.59643	.58716	.57809	.56922	.56053	.55203	.54372	.53557	.52760	.51980
79	.61253	.60346	.59459	.58590	.57738	.56904	.56086	.55286	.54501	.53732
80	.62853	.61969	.61102	.60252	.59419	.58601	.57800	.57014	.56243	.55487
81	.64433	.63571	.62726	.61897	.61082	.60283	.59499	.58729	.57974	.57232
82	.65984	.65146	.64324	.63515	.62722	.61942	.61176	.60423	.59683	.58957
83	.67506	.66693	.65893	.65108	.64335	.63575	.62828	.62093	.61371	.60660
84	.69010	.68222	.67447	.66684	.65934	.65195	.64468	.63753	.63049	.62356

SINGLE LIFE UNITRUST REMAINDER FACTORS
(For valuation dates occurring after April 30, 1999)

ADJUSTED PAYOUT RATE

AGE	8.0%	8.2%	8.4%	8.6%	8.8%	9.0%	9.2%	9.4%	9.6%	9.8%
35	.06144	.05841	.05558	.05295	.05048	.04818	.04603	.04401	.04212	.04035
36	.06503	.06187	.05892	.05616	.05358	.05116	.04890	.04678	.04480	.04293
37	.06885	.06555	.06247	.05958	.05688	.05435	.05198	.04975	.04766	.04570
38	.07293	.06949	.06627	.06325	.06043	.05777	.05528	.05295	.05075	.04868
39	.07726	.07368	.07032	.06717	.06421	.06143	.05882	.05637	.05406	.05189
40	.08189	.07816	.07465	.07137	.06827	.06537	.06263	.06006	.05764	.05535
41	.08683	.08295	.07930	.07587	.07264	.06960	.06674	.06405	.06150	.05910
42	.09210	.08807	.08427	.08069	.07733	.07415	.07116	.06833	.06567	.06315
43	.09771	.09352	.08957	.08585	.08233	.07902	.07589	.07294	.07014	.06750
44	.10367	.09932	.09521	.09134	.08768	.08423	.08096	.07787	.07495	.07218
45	.10994	.10543	.10117	.09715	.09334	.08974	.08634	.08311	.08005	.07716
46	.11656	.11189	.10747	.10329	.09933	.09559	.09204	.08867	.08548	.08245
47	.12349	.11866	.11408	.10974	.10564	.10174	.09805	.09454	.09121	.08805
48	.13077	.12577	.12103	.11654	.11228	.10823	.10439	.10074	.09727	.09397
49	.13839	.13323	.12833	.12368	.11926	.11506	.11107	.10728	.10366	.10022
50	.14639	.14107	.13601	.13120	.12663	.12228	.11813	.11419	.11043	.10685
51	.15477	.14928	.14407	.13910	.13437	.12987	.12558	.12149	.11758	.11386
52	.16350	.15785	.15248	.14735	.14247	.13781	.13337	.12913	.12508	.12122
53	.17258	.16678	.16124	.15597	.15093	.14612	.14153	.13714	.13294	.12893
54	.18201	.17606	.17037	.16493	.15974	.15478	.15004	.14550	.14116	.13700
55	.19182	.18570	.17986	.17428	.16893	.16382	.15893	.15424	.14976	.14546
56	.20199	.19573	.18974	.18400	.17851	.17325	.16821	.16338	.15875	.15430
57	.21254	.20613	.20000	.19412	.18848	.18307	.17789	.17291	.16814	.16355
58	.22343	.21688	.21060	.20458	.19880	.19325	.18792	.18280	.17788	.17316
59	.23461	.22793	.22151	.21535	.20943	.20374	.19827	.19301	.18795	.18309
60	.24608	.23927	.23272	.22642	.22036	.21454	.20893	.20354	.19834	.19334
61	.25786	.25092	.24425	.23782	.23163	.22567	.21993	.21440	.20907	.20393
62	.27001	.26295	.25616	.24961	.24329	.23721	.23134	.22568	.22021	.21494
63	.28255	.27538	.26847	.26180	.25537	.24916	.24316	.23738	.23179	.22639
64	.29545	.28817	.28116	.27438	.26783	.26150	.25539	.24949	.24377	.23825
65	.30871	.30134	.29423	.28735	.28069	.27426	.26803	.26201	.25618	.25054
66	.32238	.31493	.30772	.30075	.29399	.28746	.28113	.27500	.26906	.26331
67	.33651	.32899	.32170	.31464	.30780	.30118	.29475	.28852	.28248	.27663
68	.35108	.34349	.33614	.32901	.32209	.31538	.30887	.30256	.29643	.29047
69	.36604	.35841	.35100	.34381	.33683	.33005	.32346	.31707	.31085	.30481
70	.38132	.37366	.36620	.35896	.35193	.34509	.33844	.33197	.32568	.31957
71	.39685	.38916	.38167	.37440	.36732	.36043	.35372	.34720	.34084	.33466
72	.41257	.40486	.39736	.39006	.38295	.37602	.36927	.36270	.35629	.35005
73	.42844	.42074	.41323	.40591	.39878	.39182	.38504	.37843	.37198	.36568
74	.44454	.43685	.42934	.42202	.41488	.40791	.40110	.39446	.38798	.38165
75	.46092	.45326	.44577	.43846	.43132	.42435	.41754	.41088	.40438	.39802
76	.47766	.47004	.46259	.45530	.44818	.44122	.43442	.42776	.42125	.41488
77	.49475	.48718	.47979	.47255	.46547	.45853	.45175	.44511	.43861	.43225
78	.51216	.50467	.49735	.49017	.48314	.47626	.46951	.46290	.45643	.45008
79	.52978	.52239	.51515	.50806	.50110	.49427	.48759	.48102	.47459	.46828
80	.54745	.54018	.53304	.52603	.51916	.51242	.50580	.49930	.49292	.48666
81	.56503	.55788	.55085	.54396	.53718	.53053	.52399	.51757	.51126	.50507
82	.58242	.57540	.56851	.56173	.55506	.54851	.54207	.53574	.52951	.52339
83	.59962	.59274	.58598	.57933	.57279	.56635	.56001	.55378	.54765	.54161
84	.61674	.61002	.60341	.59690	.59049	.58418	.57796	.57184	.56582	.55988

SINGLE LIFE UNITRUST REMAINDER FACTORS
(For valuation dates occurring after April 30, 1999)

ADJUSTED PAYOUT RATE

AGE	10.0%	10.2%	10.4%	10.6%	10.8%	11.0%	11.2%	11.4%	11.6%	11.8%
35	.03869	.03713	.03567	.03429	.03299	.03177	.03061	.02953	.02850	.02753
36	.04118	.03953	.03798	.03653	.03515	.03386	.03263	.03148	.03039	.02936
37	.04385	.04211	.04048	.03894	.03748	.03611	.03481	.03359	.03243	.03134
38	.04674	.04490	.04318	.04155	.04001	.03856	.03719	.03589	.03466	.03350
39	.04984	.04791	.04609	.04437	.04274	.04120	.03975	.03837	.03707	.03583
40	.05320	.05116	.04924	.04742	.04571	.04408	.04254	.04108	.03970	.03839
41	.05683	.05469	.05267	.05075	.04894	.04722	.04559	.04405	.04258	.04119
42	.06077	.05851	.05638	.05436	.05245	.05063	.04891	.04728	.04573	.04425
43	.06500	.06263	.06039	.05827	.05625	.05433	.05252	.05079	.04915	.04759
44	.06956	.06707	.06472	.06248	.06035	.05834	.05642	.05459	.05286	.05121
45	.07441	.07180	.06933	.06698	.06474	.06262	.06059	.05867	.05684	.05509
46	.07958	.07685	.07425	.07178	.06943	.06720	.06507	.06304	.06110	.05926
47	.08504	.08218	.07946	.07687	.07440	.07205	.06981	.06768	.06564	.06369
48	.09083	.08784	.08499	.08228	.07969	.07722	.07487	.07262	.07047	.06842
49	.09695	.09382	.09085	.08801	.08530	.08271	.08024	.07788	.07562	.07346
50	.10344	.10018	.09707	.09410	.09127	.08856	.08597	.08349	.08112	.07885
51	.11031	.10691	.10367	.10057	.09761	.09477	.09206	.08946	.08697	.08459
52	.11752	.11399	.11061	.10738	.10429	.10132	.09849	.09577	.09316	.09066
53	.12509	.12142	.11791	.11454	.11132	.10823	.10526	.10242	.09969	.09707
54	.13302	.12921	.12556	.12206	.11870	.11548	.11239	.10942	.10657	.10383
55	.14134	.13738	.13359	.12995	.12646	.12311	.11989	.11679	.11382	.11096
56	.15004	.14595	.14202	.13824	.13462	.13113	.12778	.12456	.12146	.11847
57	.15914	.15491	.15084	.14693	.14317	.13955	.13607	.13272	.12949	.12638
58	.16861	.16424	.16004	.15599	.15209	.14834	.14473	.14125	.13789	.13465
59	.17840	.17390	.16955	.16537	.16134	.15746	.15371	.15010	.14662	.14325
60	.18851	.18387	.17939	.17507	.17091	.16689	.16302	.15927	.15566	.15217
61	.19898	.19420	.18958	.18513	.18084	.17669	.17268	.16881	.16506	.16145
62	.20985	.20494	.20020	.19561	.19119	.18691	.18277	.17877	.17490	.17115
63	.22117	.21613	.21126	.20654	.20199	.19758	.19331	.18918	.18518	.18131
64	.23291	.22774	.22274	.21791	.21322	.20869	.20429	.20004	.19592	.19192
65	.24508	.23979	.23467	.22971	.22490	.22025	.21573	.21135	.20710	.20299
66	.25774	.25233	.24709	.24202	.23709	.23231	.22767	.22318	.21881	.21457
67	.27095	.26543	.26009	.25489	.24985	.24496	.24021	.23560	.23111	.22676
68	.28469	.27908	.27363	.26833	.26319	.25819	.25332	.24860	.24400	.23954
69	.29894	.29324	.28769	.28230	.27705	.27195	.26699	.26216	.25746	.25288
70	.31362	.30783	.30219	.29671	.29137	.28618	.28112	.27619	.27139	.26672
71	.32864	.32277	.31706	.31150	.30608	.30079	.29564	.29063	.28573	.28096
72	.34396	.33803	.33225	.32661	.32112	.31575	.31052	.30542	.30044	.29559
73	.35955	.35356	.34772	.34201	.33645	.33101	.32571	.32053	.31547	.31053
74	.37547	.36943	.36354	.35778	.35215	.34666	.34129	.33604	.33091	.32590
75	.39181	.38574	.37980	.37400	.36833	.36278	.35735	.35205	.34686	.34178
76	.40865	.40256	.39660	.39076	.38505	.37947	.37400	.36864	.36340	.35827
77	.42601	.41991	.41394	.40808	.40235	.39674	.39124	.38585	.38056	.37539
78	.44386	.43777	.43180	.42594	.42020	.41457	.40906	.40365	.39834	.39314
79	.46209	.45602	.45007	.44422	.43849	.43287	.42735	.42193	.41661	.41139
80	.48052	.47449	.46856	.46275	.45704	.45143	.44592	.44051	.43519	.42997
81	.49898	.49300	.48712	.48134	.47566	.47008	.46460	.45921	.45391	.44870
82	.51737	.51145	.50563	.49990	.49427	.48873	.48328	.47792	.47265	.46746
83	.53567	.52983	.52407	.51841	.51284	.50735	.50195	.49663	.49139	.48624
84	.55403	.54828	.54261	.53702	.53151	.52609	.52075	.51549	.51030	.50519

SINGLE LIFE UNITRUST REMAINDER FACTORS

(For valuation dates occurring after April 30, 1999)

ADJUSTED PAYOUT RATE

AGE	12.0%	12.2%	12.4%	12.6%	12.8%	13.0%	13.2%	13.4%	13.6%	13.8%
35	.02661	.02574	.02492	.02414	.02340	.02270	.02203	.02140	.02080	.02022
36	.02838	.02746	.02658	.02575	.02496	.02422	.02350	.02283	.02218	.02157
37	.03030	.02932	.02838	.02750	.02666	.02586	.02510	.02438	.02369	.02303
38	.03239	.03135	.03035	.02941	.02851	.02766	.02685	.02608	.02534	.02464
39	.03466	.03355	.03249	.03149	.03053	.02962	.02876	.02793	.02715	.02640
40	.03714	.03596	.03484	.03377	.03275	.03178	.03086	.02998	.02914	.02833
41	.03987	.03861	.03742	.03628	.03520	.03416	.03318	.03224	.03134	.03048
42	.04285	.04152	.04025	.03903	.03788	.03678	.03573	.03473	.03377	.03285
43	.04610	.04468	.04333	.04205	.04082	.03965	.03853	.03746	.03644	.03546
44	.04963	.04813	.04670	.04533	.04403	.04278	.04159	.04045	.03936	.03832
45	.05342	.05183	.05032	.04887	.04748	.04616	.04489	.04368	.04252	.04141
46	.05750	.05582	.05421	.05267	.05121	.04980	.04846	.04717	.04593	.04475
47	.06183	.06006	.05836	.05673	.05518	.05369	.05226	.05089	.04958	.04832
48	.06646	.06459	.06279	.06107	.05943	.05785	.05634	.05488	.05349	.05216
49	.07140	.06942	.06752	.06571	.06397	.06230	.06070	.05916	.05768	.05626
50	.07667	.07459	.07259	.07068	.06884	.06708	.06538	.06376	.06219	.06069
51	.08231	.08012	.07801	.07599	.07406	.07220	.07041	.06869	.06703	.06544
52	.08826	.08596	.08375	.08163	.07959	.07763	.07574	.07392	.07218	.07049
53	.09456	.09214	.08982	.08759	.08544	.08338	.08139	.07948	.07763	.07586
54	.10120	.09867	.09623	.09389	.09164	.08946	.08737	.08536	.08342	.08154
55	.10820	.10556	.10301	.10055	.09819	.09591	.09371	.09159	.08955	.08757
56	.11560	.11283	.11016	.10759	.10511	.10272	.10042	.09819	.09605	.09397
57	.12338	.12050	.11771	.11502	.11243	.10993	.10751	.10518	.10293	.10075
58	.13153	.12852	.12562	.12281	.12011	.11749	.11496	.11252	.11016	.10787
59	.14001	.13687	.13385	.13092	.12810	.12537	.12273	.12017	.11770	.11531
60	.14880	.14554	.14240	.13935	.13641	.13356	.13080	.12813	.12555	.12305
61	.15795	.15457	.15130	.14813	.14507	.14210	.13923	.13644	.13375	.13113
62	.16753	.16402	.16063	.15734	.15415	.15107	.14808	.14518	.14237	.13964
63	.17757	.17393	.17042	.16700	.16370	.16049	.15738	.15437	.15144	.14860
64	.18805	.18429	.18065	.17712	.17369	.17036	.16714	.16400	.16096	.15800
65	.19899	.19511	.19135	.18769	.18415	.18070	.17735	.17410	.17094	.16787
66	.21045	.20645	.20257	.19880	.19513	.19157	.18810	.18473	.18146	.17827
67	.22252	.21841	.21441	.21052	.20673	.20305	.19947	.19599	.19259	.18929
68	.23519	.23096	.22685	.22284	.21895	.21515	.21146	.20786	.20436	.20094
69	.24843	.24409	.23987	.23575	.23175	.22784	.22404	.22033	.21672	.21320
70	.26216	.25772	.25339	.24918	.24507	.24106	.23715	.23333	.22961	.22598
71	.27631	.27178	.26735	.26304	.25882	.25471	.25070	.24679	.24296	.23923
72	.29084	.28622	.28170	.27729	.27298	.26877	.26467	.26065	.25673	.25290
73	.30571	.30100	.29639	.29189	.28749	.28320	.27899	.27489	.27087	.26694
74	.32100	.31621	.31152	.30694	.30246	.29807	.29378	.28959	.28548	.28146
75	.33681	.33195	.32719	.32253	.31797	.31351	.30914	.30486	.30067	.29657
76	.35324	.34832	.34350	.33877	.33415	.32961	.32517	.32082	.31656	.31238
77	.37032	.36535	.36047	.35570	.35101	.34642	.34192	.33750	.33317	.32892
78	.38803	.38302	.37811	.37329	.36856	.36392	.35937	.35490	.35051	.34621
79	.40627	.40124	.39630	.39145	.38669	.38201	.37742	.37291	.36848	.36413
80	.42484	.41980	.41485	.40998	.40520	.40050	.39588	.39134	.38688	.38249
81	.44357	.43854	.43358	.42871	.42392	.41921	.41457	.41001	.40553	.40112
82	.46235	.45733	.45238	.44752	.44273	.43802	.43338	.42881	.42431	.41989
83	.48116	.47616	.47123	.46638	.46161	.45690	.45227	.44770	.44320	.43877
84	.50015	.49519	.49030	.48548	.48073	.47604	.47143	.46688	.46239	.45797

SINGLE LIFE UNITRUST REMAINDER FACTORS
(For valuation dates occurring after April 30, 1999)

ADJUSTED PAYOUT RATE

AGE	14.0%	14.2%	14.4%	14.6%	14.8%	15.0%	15.2%	15.4%	15.6%	15.8%
35	.01967	.01915	.01866	.01818	.01773	.01729	.01688	.01648	.01610	.01573
36	.02098	.02043	.01989	.01938	.01890	.01843	.01799	.01756	.01715	.01676
37	.02241	.02181	.02124	.02069	.02017	.01967	.01920	.01874	.01830	.01788
38	.02397	.02333	.02272	.02214	.02158	.02105	.02053	.02004	.01957	.01912
39	.02568	.02500	.02434	.02372	.02312	.02254	.02200	.02147	.02096	.02048
40	.02757	.02684	.02614	.02546	.02482	.02421	.02362	.02305	.02251	.02199
41	.02966	.02888	.02813	.02741	.02672	.02606	.02543	.02482	.02424	.02368
42	.03198	.03114	.03034	.02957	.02883	.02812	.02744	.02679	.02617	.02557
43	.03453	.03363	.03277	.03195	.03116	.03040	.02967	.02897	.02830	.02766
44	.03732	.03637	.03545	.03457	.03372	.03291	.03213	.03138	.03066	.02997
45	.04034	.03932	.03834	.03740	.03650	.03563	.03480	.03399	.03322	.03248
46	.04362	.04253	.04148	.04048	.03951	.03859	.03769	.03684	.03601	.03521
47	.04711	.04595	.04484	.04377	.04274	.04175	.04080	.03988	.03899	.03814
48	.05087	.04964	.04845	.04731	.04621	.04516	.04414	.04316	.04222	.04130
49	.05490	.05359	.05233	.05111	.04995	.04882	.04774	.04669	.04568	.04471
50	.05924	.05785	.05651	.05522	.05398	.05278	.05163	.05051	.04944	.04840
51	.06391	.06244	.06101	.05964	.05832	.05705	.05582	.05464	.05349	.05239
52	.06887	.06731	.06581	.06435	.06295	.06160	.06030	.05904	.05782	.05664
53	.07415	.07249	.07090	.06936	.06788	.06645	.06506	.06373	.06243	.06118
54	.07974	.07799	.07631	.07468	.07311	.07160	.07013	.06871	.06734	.06601
55	.08567	.08383	.08206	.08034	.07868	.07708	.07552	.07402	.07257	.07116
56	.09197	.09003	.08816	.08635	.08460	.08291	.08127	.07968	.07814	.07665
57	.09864	.09661	.09464	.09273	.09089	.08910	.08737	.08570	.08408	.08250
58	.10567	.10353	.10146	.09946	.09751	.09563	.09381	.09205	.09033	.08867
59	.11299	.11075	.10858	.10648	.10444	.10246	.10055	.09869	.09688	.09513
60	.12063	.11828	.11600	.11380	.11166	.10958	.10757	.10561	.10371	.10187
61	.12860	.12614	.12376	.12145	.11921	.11703	.11492	.11286	.11087	.10893
62	.13699	.13443	.13194	.12952	.12717	.12489	.12267	.12052	.11843	.11639
63	.14584	.14316	.14056	.13804	.13558	.13319	.13087	.12862	.12643	.12429
64	.15513	.15234	.14963	.14699	.14443	.14193	.13951	.13715	.13485	.13262
65	.16488	.16198	.15916	.15641	.15374	.15113	.14860	.14614	.14373	.14140
66	.17517	.17215	.16921	.16635	.16357	.16086	.15822	.15565	.15314	.15070
67	.18608	.18295	.17990	.17693	.17403	.17121	.16847	.16579	.16317	.16062
68	.19762	.19437	.19121	.18813	.18513	.18220	.17935	.17656	.17384	.17119
69	.20976	.20641	.20314	.19995	.19684	.19381	.19084	.18795	.18513	.18237
70	.22244	.21898	.21561	.21232	.20910	.20596	.20289	.19989	.19696	.19410
71	.23559	.23203	.22855	.22515	.22183	.21859	.21542	.21232	.20929	.20632
72	.24915	.24549	.24192	.23842	.23500	.23165	.22838	.22518	.22205	.21899
73	.26310	.25935	.25567	.25208	.24856	.24511	.24175	.23845	.23522	.23206
74	.27753	.27368	.26991	.26622	.26261	.25907	.25561	.25222	.24889	.24563
75	.29255	.28862	.28476	.28098	.27728	.27365	.27009	.26661	.26319	.25984
76	.30828	.30426	.30032	.29646	.29268	.28896	.28532	.28175	.27825	.27481
77	.32475	.32067	.31666	.31272	.30886	.30507	.30135	.29769	.29411	.29059
78	.34198	.33783	.33376	.32976	.32583	.32197	.31818	.31445	.31080	.30720
79	.35985	.35565	.35153	.34747	.34348	.33957	.33571	.33193	.32821	.32455
80	.37818	.37394	.36977	.36567	.36163	.35767	.35377	.34993	.34615	.34244
81	.39678	.39250	.38830	.38417	.38010	.37609	.37215	.36827	.36445	.36068
82	.41553	.41124	.40701	.40285	.39875	.39471	.39074	.38682	.38297	.37917
83	.43441	.43011	.42587	.42169	.41757	.41352	.40952	.40558	.40169	.39786
84	.45361	.44930	.44506	.44088	.43676	.43269	.42868	.42473	.42082	.41698

2007 Tax Facts on Investments

SINGLE LIFE UNITRUST REMAINDER FACTORS

(For valuation dates occurring after April 30, 1999)

ADJUSTED PAYOUT RATE

AGE	16.0%	16.2%	16.4%	16.6%	16.8%	17.0%	17.2%	17.4%	17.6%	17.8%
35	.01538	.01505	.01472	.01441	.01412	.01383	.01355	.01329	.01303	.01278
36	.01639	.01603	.01568	.01535	.01503	.01472	.01442	.01414	.01386	.01359
37	.01748	.01709	.01672	.01636	.01602	.01569	.01537	.01506	.01476	.01448
38	.01869	.01827	.01787	.01749	.01712	.01676	.01642	.01609	.01577	.01546
39	.02001	.01957	.01914	.01872	.01832	.01794	.01757	.01722	.01687	.01654
40	.02149	.02101	.02055	.02010	.01967	.01926	.01886	.01848	.01811	.01775
41	.02314	.02263	.02213	.02165	.02119	.02074	.02031	.01990	.01950	.01912
42	.02499	.02443	.02390	.02338	.02288	.02240	.02194	.02150	.02107	.02065
43	.02703	.02644	.02586	.02531	.02477	.02426	.02376	.02328	.02281	.02237
44	.02930	.02866	.02804	.02744	.02687	.02631	.02578	.02526	.02476	.02428
45	.03176	.03107	.03041	.02977	.02915	.02855	.02798	.02742	.02688	.02636
46	.03445	.03371	.03299	.03230	.03164	.03100	.03038	.02978	.02920	.02864
47	.03732	.03653	.03576	.03503	.03431	.03362	.03296	.03232	.03169	.03109
48	.04043	.03958	.03876	.03797	.03720	.03647	.03575	.03506	.03439	.03375
49	.04377	.04286	.04199	.04114	.04032	.03953	.03877	.03802	.03731	.03661
50	.04740	.04643	.04549	.04459	.04371	.04287	.04205	.04125	.04048	.03974
51	.05132	.05028	.04928	.04832	.04738	.04648	.04560	.04475	.04393	.04313
52	.05550	.05440	.05334	.05231	.05131	.05034	.04941	.04850	.04762	.04677
53	.05997	.05880	.05767	.05657	.05551	.05448	.05348	.05251	.05157	.05066
54	.06473	.06348	.06228	.06111	.05998	.05888	.05782	.05679	.05579	.05481
55	.06980	.06848	.06720	.06596	.06476	.06359	.06246	.06136	.06030	.05926
56	.07521	.07381	.07246	.07114	.06987	.06863	.06742	.06626	.06512	.06402
57	.08098	.07950	.07806	.07667	.07531	.07400	.07273	.07149	.07028	.06911
58	.08706	.08550	.08398	.08251	.08108	.07969	.07834	.07702	.07574	.07450
59	.09343	.09178	.09018	.08862	.08711	.08564	.08421	.08282	.08147	.08015
60	.10008	.09834	.09665	.09501	.09342	.09186	.09035	.08888	.08745	.08606
61	.10705	.10522	.10344	.10171	.10003	.09839	.09680	.09524	.09373	.09226
62	.11442	.11249	.11062	.10880	.10703	.10530	.10362	.10198	.10039	.09883
63	.12222	.12020	.11823	.11631	.11445	.11263	.11086	.10914	.10746	.10582
64	.13044	.12832	.12626	.12425	.12229	.12038	.11852	.11670	.11494	.11321
65	.13912	.13690	.13473	.13263	.13057	.12857	.12661	.12470	.12284	.12103
66	.14831	.14599	.14373	.14152	.13937	.13726	.13521	.13321	.13126	.12935
67	.15814	.15571	.15335	.15104	.14878	.14658	.14443	.14234	.14029	.13828
68	.16860	.16607	.16360	.16119	.15883	.15653	.15429	.15209	.14995	.14785
69	.17967	.17704	.17447	.17196	.16951	.16711	.16476	.16247	.16023	.15803
70	.19131	.18857	.18590	.18329	.18074	.17824	.17579	.17340	.17106	.16878
71	.20343	.20059	.19782	.19511	.19245	.18986	.18732	.18483	.18239	.18001
72	.21599	.21306	.21019	.20738	.20462	.20193	.19929	.19671	.19417	.19169
73	.22896	.22593	.22296	.22005	.21720	.21441	.21168	.20899	.20637	.20379
74	.24244	.23931	.23625	.23324	.23030	.22741	.22458	.22180	.21908	.21641
75	.25656	.25334	.25018	.24708	.24404	.24106	.23813	.23526	.23245	.22968
76	.27144	.26813	.26488	.26169	.25856	.25549	.25247	.24951	.24660	.24375
77	.28714	.28374	.28041	.27714	.27392	.27077	.26766	.26462	.26162	.25868
78	.30367	.30020	.29680	.29345	.29015	.28692	.28374	.28061	.27753	.27451
79	.32095	.31742	.31394	.31052	.30716	.30385	.30059	.29739	.29424	.29115
80	.33878	.33519	.33165	.32817	.32474	.32137	.31805	.31479	.31157	.30840
81	.35698	.35334	.34975	.34621	.34273	.33930	.33593	.33260	.32932	.32610
82	.37542	.37174	.36810	.36452	.36099	.35752	.35409	.35071	.34738	.34410
83	.39409	.39037	.38670	.38308	.37951	.37599	.37252	.36910	.36573	.36240
84	.41318	.40943	.40574	.40209	.39850	.39495	.39144	.38799	.38458	.38121

SINGLE LIFE UNITRUST REMAINDER FACTORS
(For valuation dates occurring after April 30, 1999)

ADJUSTED PAYOUT RATE

AGE	18.0%	18.2%	18.4%	18.6%	18.8%	19.0%	19.2%	19.4%	19.6%	19.8%
35	.01254	.01231	.01209	.01187	.01167	.01147	.01127	.01108	.01090	.01072
36	.01334	.01309	.01285	.01262	.01240	.01218	.01197	.01177	.01157	.01138
37	.01420	.01394	.01368	.01343	.01319	.01296	.01274	.01252	.01231	.01210
38	.01517	.01488	.01460	.01434	.01408	.01383	.01358	.01335	.01312	.01290
39	.01622	.01591	.01562	.01533	.01505	.01478	.01452	.01427	.01402	.01378
40	.01741	.01707	.01675	.01644	.01614	.01585	.01557	.01529	.01503	.01477
41	.01875	.01839	.01804	.01770	.01738	.01706	.01676	.01646	.01618	.01590
42	.02025	.01986	.01949	.01912	.01877	.01843	.01810	.01779	.01748	.01718
43	.02193	.02151	.02111	.02072	.02034	.01997	.01962	.01927	.01894	.01861
44	.02381	.02336	.02292	.02250	.02209	.02169	.02131	.02094	.02058	.02023
45	.02586	.02537	.02490	.02444	.02400	.02357	.02316	.02276	.02237	.02199
46	.02810	.02758	.02707	.02658	.02610	.02564	.02519	.02476	.02433	.02392
47	.03051	.02994	.02940	.02887	.02835	.02786	.02737	.02690	.02645	.02601
48	.03312	.03251	.03192	.03135	.03080	.03026	.02974	.02924	.02875	.02827
49	.03594	.03529	.03466	.03404	.03345	.03287	.03231	.03177	.03124	.03072
50	.03902	.03832	.03764	.03698	.03634	.03572	.03512	.03453	.03396	.03341
51	.04236	.04161	.04088	.04017	.03949	.03882	.03817	.03755	.03693	.03634
52	.04594	.04514	.04436	.04360	.04286	.04215	.04146	.04078	.04012	.03949
53	.04977	.04892	.04808	.04727	.04648	.04572	.04498	.04425	.04355	.04286
54	.05387	.05295	.05206	.05120	.05035	.04954	.04874	.04796	.04721	.04648
55	.05825	.05728	.05632	.05540	.05450	.05363	.05278	.05195	.05114	.05036
56	.06295	.06191	.06090	.05991	.05895	.05802	.05711	.05623	.05537	.05453
57	.06797	.06687	.06579	.06474	.06372	.06273	.06176	.06082	.05990	.05900
58	.07329	.07212	.07098	.06986	.06878	.06772	.06669	.06569	.06471	.06376
59	.07887	.07763	.07641	.07523	.07408	.07296	.07186	.07080	.06976	.06875
60	.08471	.08339	.08210	.08085	.07963	.07844	.07727	.07614	.07504	.07396
61	.09083	.08943	.08807	.08674	.08545	.08419	.08296	.08176	.08059	.07944
62	.09732	.09584	.09441	.09300	.09163	.09030	.08900	.08772	.08648	.08527
63	.10422	.10266	.10114	.09966	.09821	.09680	.09542	.09408	.09276	.09148
64	.11153	.10988	.10828	.10672	.10519	.10370	.10224	.10082	.09943	.09807
65	.11926	.11752	.11584	.11419	.11257	.11100	.10946	.10796	.10649	.10505
66	.12748	.12566	.12389	.12215	.12045	.11879	.11717	.11559	.11403	.11252
67	.13633	.13442	.13255	.13072	.12894	.12719	.12548	.12381	.12218	.12058
68	.14580	.14379	.14183	.13992	.13804	.13621	.13441	.13265	.13093	.12925
69	.15589	.15379	.15174	.14973	.14776	.14584	.14395	.14211	.14030	.13853
70	.16654	.16434	.16220	.16010	.15804	.15602	.15405	.15211	.15022	.14836
71	.17767	.17539	.17315	.17095	.16880	.16670	.16463	.16261	.16062	.15868
72	.18926	.18688	.18455	.18226	.18002	.17782	.17567	.17355	.17148	.16944
73	.20127	.19879	.19636	.19398	.19165	.18936	.18711	.18490	.18274	.18062
74	.21379	.21122	.20870	.20622	.20380	.20141	.19907	.19678	.19452	.19231
75	.22697	.22430	.22169	.21912	.21660	.21413	.21170	.20931	.20696	.20466
76	.24095	.23819	.23549	.23283	.23022	.22765	.22513	.22265	.22022	.21782
77	.25579	.25295	.25016	.24741	.24471	.24206	.23945	.23688	.23436	.23188
78	.27154	.26861	.26574	.26291	.26013	.25739	.25470	.25205	.24944	.24688
79	.28810	.28510	.28215	.27924	.27638	.27357	.27080	.26807	.26538	.26274
80	.30529	.30222	.29919	.29622	.29329	.29040	.28756	.28476	.28200	.27928
81	.32292	.31979	.31670	.31366	.31066	.30771	.30480	.30193	.29910	.29632
82	.34087	.33768	.33454	.33144	.32838	.32537	.32240	.31947	.31658	.31373
83	.35912	.35588	.35269	.34954	.34643	.34336	.34034	.33735	.33440	.33150
84	.37789	.37461	.37137	.36818	.36503	.36191	.35884	.35581	.35281	.34985

SINGLE LIFE UNITRUST REMAINDER FACTORS
(For valuation dates occurring after April 30, 1999)

ADJUSTED PAYOUT RATE

AGE	20.0%	20.2%	20.4%	20.6%	20.8%	21.0%	21.2%	21.4%	21.6%	21.8%
35	.01055	.01038	.01022	.01007	.00991	.00977	.00962	.00948	.00935	.00922
36	.01120	.01102	.01085	.01068	.01052	.01036	.01020	.01005	.00991	.00977
37	.01190	.01171	.01153	.01135	.01117	.01100	.01083	.01067	.01052	.01036
38	.01269	.01248	.01228	.01209	.01190	.01172	.01154	.01136	.01120	.01103
39	.01355	.01333	.01311	.01290	.01270	.01250	.01231	.01212	.01194	.01176
40	.01453	.01428	.01405	.01382	.01360	.01339	.01318	.01298	.01278	.01259
41	.01563	.01537	.01512	.01487	.01464	.01440	.01418	.01396	.01375	.01354
42	.01689	.01660	.01633	.01607	.01581	.01556	.01531	.01508	.01484	.01462
43	.01830	.01799	.01770	.01741	.01713	.01686	.01659	.01634	.01609	.01584
44	.01989	.01955	.01923	.01892	.01862	.01833	.01804	.01776	.01749	.01723
45	.02162	.02126	.02092	.02058	.02025	.01993	.01962	.01932	.01903	.01874
46	.02353	.02314	.02277	.02240	.02205	.02170	.02137	.02104	.02072	.02041
47	.02558	.02516	.02476	.02436	.02398	.02361	.02324	.02289	.02255	.02221
48	.02781	.02736	.02692	.02649	.02608	.02568	.02529	.02490	.02453	.02417
49	.03022	.02974	.02927	.02881	.02836	.02793	.02750	.02709	.02669	.02630
50	.03287	.03235	.03184	.03135	.03086	.03039	.02994	.02949	.02906	.02864
51	.03576	.03520	.03465	.03412	.03360	.03309	.03260	.03212	.03165	.03120
52	.03886	.03826	.03767	.03710	.03654	.03599	.03546	.03495	.03444	.03395
53	.04220	.04155	.04091	.04030	.03970	.03911	.03854	.03799	.03744	.03692
54	.04576	.04507	.04439	.04373	.04308	.04246	.04184	.04125	.04066	.04009
55	.04959	.04885	.04812	.04741	.04672	.04605	.04539	.04475	.04413	.04352
56	.05371	.05291	.05214	.05138	.05064	.04992	.04922	.04853	.04786	.04721
57	.05813	.05728	.05645	.05564	.05485	.05408	.05333	.05260	.05188	.05118
58	.06283	.06192	.06104	.06017	.05933	.05851	.05771	.05692	.05616	.05541
59	.06776	.06679	.06585	.06493	.06403	.06316	.06230	.06146	.06065	.05985
60	.07291	.07188	.07088	.06991	.06895	.06802	.06710	.06621	.06534	.06449
61	.07833	.07724	.07617	.07513	.07412	.07312	.07215	.07121	.07028	.06937
62	.08409	.08293	.08180	.08070	.07962	.07856	.07753	.07652	.07554	.07457
63	.09022	.08900	.08780	.08663	.08548	.08436	.08327	.08220	.08115	.08012
64	.09674	.09544	.09417	.09293	.09172	.09053	.08937	.08823	.08712	.08603
65	.10365	.10228	.10093	.09962	.09833	.09707	.09584	.09464	.09346	.09230
66	.11103	.10958	.10816	.10677	.10541	.10408	.10277	.10150	.10025	.09902
67	.11901	.11748	.11598	.11451	.11307	.11166	.11028	.10893	.10761	.10631
68	.12760	.12599	.12440	.12285	.12134	.11985	.11839	.11696	.11556	.11419
69	.13680	.13510	.13343	.13180	.13020	.12864	.12710	.12559	.12412	.12267
70	.14654	.14476	.14301	.14129	.13961	.13797	.13635	.13476	.13321	.13168
71	.15677	.15490	.15307	.15127	.14950	.14777	.14607	.14441	.14277	.14117
72	.16745	.16549	.16357	.16169	.15984	.15802	.15624	.15449	.15277	.15109
73	.17853	.17649	.17448	.17251	.17057	.16867	.16681	.16497	.16317	.16140
74	.19014	.18800	.18591	.18385	.18182	.17984	.17788	.17597	.17408	.17223
75	.20240	.20017	.19799	.19584	.19373	.19165	.18962	.18761	.18564	.18370
76	.21547	.21316	.21088	.20865	.20645	.20429	.20216	.20007	.19801	.19599
77	.22944	.22704	.22468	.22236	.22007	.21782	.21561	.21343	.21129	.20918
78	.24435	.24187	.23942	.23702	.23465	.23232	.23002	.22776	.22553	.22334
79	.26013	.25757	.25505	.25256	.25011	.24770	.24532	.24298	.24067	.23840
80	.27660	.27396	.27136	.26880	.26628	.26379	.26134	.25892	.25654	.25419
81	.29357	.29086	.28819	.28556	.28297	.28041	.27788	.27539	.27294	.27052
82	.31092	.30815	.30541	.30272	.30005	.29743	.29484	.29228	.28976	.28727
83	.32863	.32580	.32300	.32024	.31752	.31483	.31218	.30956	.30697	.30442
84	.34693	.34405	.34120	.33839	.33561	.33287	.33016	.32748	.32484	.32222

SINGLE LIFE UNITRUST REMAINDER FACTORS
(For valuation dates occurring after April 30, 1999)

ADJUSTED PAYOUT RATE

AGE	22.0%	22.2%	22.4%	22.6%	22.8%	23.0%	23.2%	23.4%	23.6%	23.8%
35	.00909	.00896	.00884	.00872	.00860	.00849	.00838	.00827	.00817	.00807
36	.00963	.00949	.00936	.00924	.00911	.00899	.00887	.00876	.00865	.00854
37	.01022	.01007	.00993	.00979	.00966	.00953	.00941	.00928	.00916	.00904
38	.01087	.01072	.01057	.01042	.01028	.01014	.01000	.00987	.00974	.00961
39	.01159	.01142	.01126	.01110	.01095	.01080	.01065	.01051	.01037	.01023
40	.01241	.01222	.01205	.01188	.01171	.01155	.01139	.01123	.01108	.01093
41	.01334	.01314	.01295	.01277	.01258	.01241	.01224	.01207	.01190	.01174
42	.01440	.01419	.01398	.01378	.01358	.01339	.01321	.01302	.01285	.01267
43	.01561	.01538	.01515	.01493	.01472	.01451	.01431	.01411	.01392	.01373
44	.01697	.01672	.01648	.01624	.01601	.01578	.01556	.01535	.01514	.01493
45	.01846	.01819	.01793	.01767	.01742	.01718	.01694	.01670	.01648	.01626
46	.02011	.01982	.01953	.01925	.01898	.01872	.01846	.01820	.01796	.01772
47	.02188	.02157	.02126	.02095	.02066	.02037	.02009	.01982	.01955	.01929
48	.02382	.02347	.02314	.02281	.02249	.02218	.02188	.02158	.02129	.02101
49	.02591	.02554	.02518	.02483	.02448	.02414	.02381	.02349	.02318	.02287
50	.02822	.02782	.02743	.02705	.02667	.02631	.02595	.02560	.02526	.02493
51	.03075	.03032	.02989	.02948	.02908	.02868	.02830	.02792	.02755	.02719
52	.03347	.03300	.03255	.03210	.03166	.03124	.03082	.03042	.03002	.02963
53	.03640	.03589	.03540	.03492	.03445	.03399	.03355	.03311	.03268	.03226
54	.03954	.03900	.03847	.03795	.03745	.03695	.03647	.03600	.03554	.03508
55	.04292	.04234	.04177	.04121	.04067	.04014	.03962	.03911	.03862	.03813
56	.04657	.04594	.04533	.04474	.04415	.04358	.04302	.04248	.04195	.04142
57	.05049	.04983	.04917	.04853	.04791	.04730	.04670	.04611	.04554	.04498
58	.05468	.05396	.05326	.05258	.05191	.05125	.05061	.04999	.04937	.04877
59	.05907	.05830	.05756	.05683	.05611	.05541	.05473	.05406	.05340	.05276
60	.06366	.06284	.06205	.06127	.06050	.05976	.05903	.05831	.05761	.05692
61	.06848	.06762	.06677	.06594	.06512	.06433	.06355	.06278	.06203	.06130
62	.07363	.07270	.07180	.07091	.07005	.06920	.06837	.06755	.06675	.06597
63	.07912	.07814	.07718	.07623	.07531	.07441	.07352	.07265	.07180	.07097
64	.08496	.08392	.08289	.08189	.08091	.07995	.07900	.07808	.07717	.07629
65	.09117	.09006	.08897	.08791	.08686	.08584	.08484	.08386	.08289	.08195
66	.09782	.09664	.09549	.09436	.09325	.09216	.09110	.09005	.08903	.08802
67	.10504	.10379	.10257	.10137	.10019	.09904	.09791	.09680	.09571	.09464
68	.11285	.11153	.11023	.10896	.10772	.10650	.10530	.10412	.10296	.10183
69	.12125	.11985	.11848	.11714	.11582	.11453	.11326	.11202	.11079	.10959
70	.13018	.12871	.12727	.12585	.12446	.12309	.12175	.12044	.11914	.11787
71	.13959	.13804	.13652	.13503	.13356	.13212	.13071	.12932	.12795	.12661
72	.14943	.14780	.14621	.14463	.14309	.14158	.14009	.13862	.13718	.13577
73	.15966	.15796	.15628	.15463	.15301	.15141	.14984	.14830	.14679	.14530
74	.17040	.16861	.16685	.16512	.16342	.16174	.16010	.15848	.15689	.15532
75	.18179	.17992	.17807	.17626	.17447	.17272	.17099	.16929	.16762	.16597
76	.19400	.19204	.19011	.18821	.18634	.18450	.18269	.18091	.17916	.17743
77	.20710	.20506	.20305	.20107	.19912	.19719	.19530	.19344	.19160	.18979
78	.22118	.21905	.21696	.21490	.21286	.21086	.20889	.20694	.20503	.20314
79	.23616	.23396	.23178	.22964	.22753	.22544	.22339	.22137	.21937	.21741
80	.25187	.24959	.24734	.24512	.24293	.24077	.23864	.23654	.23447	.23243
81	.26813	.26578	.26345	.26116	.25890	.25667	.25446	.25229	.25015	.24803
82	.28481	.28239	.28000	.27763	.27530	.27300	.27073	.26849	.26627	.26409
83	.30190	.29941	.29695	.29453	.29213	.28976	.28742	.28511	.28283	.28058
84	.31964	.31710	.31458	.31209	.30963	.30720	.30480	.30243	.30009	.29777

APPENDIX D

REFERENCE 1

Kinds of Property That Can Be Given Under the Uniform Gifts To Minors Act and the Uniform Transfers To Minors Act In the Various States

Note: Under the official texts of the original (1956) and revised (1966) versions of the Uniform Gifts to Minors Act, gifts of securities and money can be made. Both the 1956 Act and the 1966 Act define a "security" as "includ(ing) any note, stock, treasury stock, bond, debenture, evidence of indebtedness, [certificate of interest or participation in an oil, gas or mining title or lease or in payments out of production under such a title or lease,] collateral trust certificate, transferable share, voting trust certificate or, in general, any interest or instrument commonly known as a security, or any certificate of interest or participation in, any temporary or interim certificate, receipt or certificate of deposit for, or any warrant or right to subscribe to or purchase, any of the foregoing. The term does not include a security of which the donor is the issuer." (The bracketed text in the definition of a "security" is material characterized by the drafters of the 1956 and 1966 Acts as optional.) A few states have modified the foregoing definition of a "security"; those modifications have *not* been included in this table.

The 1966 Act adds that gifts of certain life insurance policies and annuity contracts can be made. That Act defines a "life insurance policy or annuity contract" as "a life insurance policy or annuity contract issued by an insurance company [authorized to do business in this state] on the life of a minor to whom a gift of the policy or contract is made in the manner prescribed in this act or on the life of a member of the minor's family." (It appears that the drafters of the 1966 Act considered the bracketed text to be recommended yet optional.) The 1966 Act defines a "member" of the "minor's family" as "any of the minor's parents, grandparents, brothers, sisters, uncles and aunts, whether of the whole blood or the half blood, or by or through legal adoption." Again, variations in the definitions adopted by particular states have *not* been included in this table.

It is important to note that both the 1956 and 1966 Acts have been withdrawn from recommendation for enactment by the National Conference of Commissioners on Uniform State Laws. Only Vermont has not adopted a version of the Uniform Transfers to Minors Act.

It seems that the Uniform Transfers To Minors Act (1983) was intended to permit the transfer in custodianship of any kind of interest in any kind of property. However, the text of that Act does not clearly accomplish that purpose. Most states that have adopted a version of the 1983 Act have failed to remove the ambiguities presented by that Act's text. For each of these states, the table tries to present a reasonable conclusion about the kind of property that the subject state intended to make eligible for transfer in custodianship. Some of the states that have carried over the textual ambiguities of the 1983 Act have adopted clarifying comments that help one interpret their statutes. The entry for each of these states carries a dagger ("†"), indicating that the conclusion presented draws insight from the state's comments. However, research has found no evidence of the adoption of clarifying comments in the vast majority of states that have carried over the textual ambiguities of the 1983 Act. The entry for each of these states bears an asterisk ("*").

It appears, based on comments to the 1983 Act, that the 1956 and 1966 Acts did not contemplate the transfer of equitable property interests but that the 1983 Act did intend to allow the transfer of equitable interests in property. Some statutes seem to contemplate the eligibility of equitable interests while also including language that seems to limit the eligible property interests to legal interests. In such cases, this table indicates that at least legal interests in property are eligible and alerts the reader that the eligibility of equitable interests is unclear.

This table is designed to reflect the provisions relevant to current transactions. Statutory citations are to the complete texts of the various statutes.

Alabama. Any kind of interest in any kind of property.† *See* Ala. Code 35-5A-1 through 35-5A-24.

Alaska. Any kind of interest in any kind of property.* *See* Alaska Stat. 13.46.010 through 13.46.999.

Arizona. Any kind of interest in any kind of property.* *See* Ariz. Rev. Stat. Ann. 14-7651 through 14-7671.

Arkansas. Any kind of interest in any kind of property.* *See* Ark. Code Ann. 9-26-201 through 9-26-227.

California. Any kind of interest in any kind of property.† *See* Cal. Prob. Code 3900 through 3925.

Colorado. Any kind of interest in any kind of property.* *See* Colo. Rev. Stat. 11-50-101 through 11-50-126.

Connecticut. Any kind of interest in any kind of property.* *See* Gen. Stats. Ann. 45a-557 through 45a-560b.

Delaware. Any kind of interest in any kind of property.* *See* Del. Code Ann., tit. 12, 4501 through 4523.

District of Columbia. Any kind of interest in any kind of property.* *See* D.C. Code Ann. 21-301 through 21-324.

Florida. Any kind of interest in any kind of property.* *See* Fla. Stat. Ann. 710.101 through 710.126.

Georgia. Any kind of interest in any kind of property.* *See* Ga. Code Ann. 44-5-110 through 44-5-134.

Hawaii. Any kind of interest in any kind of property.* *See* Haw. Rev. Stat. 553A-1 through 553A-24.

Idaho. Any kind of interest in any kind of property.* *See* Idaho Code 68-801 through 68-825.

Illinois. Any kind of interest in any kind of property.* *See* 760 ILCS 20/1 through 20/24.

Indiana. Any kind of interest in any kind of property.* *See* Ind. Code Ann. 30-2-8.5-1 through 30-2-8.5-40 .

Iowa. Any kind of interest in any kind of property, except tangible personal property subject to registration of ownership with a state or federal agency.* *See* Iowa Code Ann. 565B.1 through 565B.25.

Kansas. Any kind of interest in any kind of property.* *See* Kan. Stat. Ann. 38-1701 through 38-1726.

Kentucky. Any kind of interest in any kind of property.* *See* Ky. Rev. Stat. Ann. 385.012 through 385.252.

Louisiana. Any kind of interest in any kind of property.* *See* La. Rev. Stat. Ann. 9:751 through 9:773.

Maine. Any kind of interest in any kind of property.* *See* Me. Rev. Stat. Ann. 33, 1651 through 1674.

Maryland. Any kind of interest in any kind of property.* *See* Md. Est. & Trusts Code Ann. 13-301 through 13-324.

Massachusetts. Any kind of interest in any kind of property.* *See* Mass. Ann. Laws ch. 201A, 1 through 24.

Michigan. Any kind of interest in any kind of property.* *See* Mich. Comp. Laws Ann. 554.521 through 554.552.

Minnesota. Any kind of interest in any kind of property.* *See* Minn. Stat. Ann. 527.21 through 527.44.

Mississippi. Any kind of interest in any kind of property.* *See* Miss. Code Ann. 91-20-1 through 91-20-49.

Missouri. Any present or future interest in property, real or personal, tangible or intangible, legal or equitable. *See* Mo. Ann. Stat. 404.005 through 404.094.

Montana. Any kind of interest in any kind of property.† *See* Mont. Code Ann. 72-26-501 through 72-26-803.

Nebraska. Any kind of interest in any kind of property.* *See* Neb. Rev. Stat. 43-2701 through 43-2724.

Nevada. At least any kind of legal interest in any kind of property; eligibility of equitable interests is unclear.* *See* Nev. Rev. Stat. Ann. 167.010 through 167.100.

New Hampshire. Any kind of interest in any kind of property.* *See* N.H. Rev. Stat. Ann. 463-A:1 through 463-A:26.

New Jersey. Any kind of interest in any kind of property.* *See* N.J. Stat. Ann. 46:38A-1 through 46:38A-57.

New Mexico. Any kind of interest in any kind of property.* *See* N.M. Stat. Ann. 46-7-11 to 46-7-34.

New York. Any kind of interest in any kind of property.* *See* N.Y. Est. Powers & Trusts Law 7-6.1 through 7-6.26.

North Carolina. Any kind of interest in any kind of property.* *See* N.C. Gen. Stat. 33A-1 through 33A-24.

North Dakota. Any kind of interest in any kind of property.* *See* N.D. Cent. Code 47-24.1-01 through 47-24.1-22.

Ohio. At least legal interests in any kind of property; eligibility of equitable interests is unclear. *See* Oh. Rev. Code Ann. 5814.01 through 5814.09.

Oklahoma. Any kind of interest in any kind of property.* *See* Okla. Stat. Ann. tit. 58, 1201 through 1225.

Oregon. Any kind of interest in any kind of property.* *See* Or. Rev. Stat. 126.805 through 126.886.

Pennsylvania. Any kind of interest in any kind of property.* *See* 20 Pa. Cons. Stat. Ann. 5301 through 5321.

Rhode Island. Any kind of interest in any kind of property.* *See* R.I. Gen. Laws 18-7-1 through 18-7-26.

South Carolina. At least legal interests in any kind of property; eligibility of equitable interests is unclear. While the statute does not specifically list proceeds of life insurance policies or of annuity contracts as eligible property, it does allow custodians to be named as beneficiaries on at least certain policies and contracts whether or not ownership of such policies or contracts is given. *See* S.C. Code Ann. 20-7-140 through 20-7-240.

South Dakota. Any kind of interest in any kind of property.* *See* S.D. Codified Laws Ann. 55-10A-1 to 55-10A-26.

Tennessee. Any kind of interest in any kind of property.* *See* Tenn. Code Ann. 35-7-201 through 35-7-226.

Texas. Any kind of interest in any kind of property.* *See* Tex. Prop. Code Ann. 141.001 through 141.025.

Utah. Any kind of interest in any kind of property.* *See* Utah Code Ann. 75-5a-101 through 75-5a-123.

Vermont. At least securities and money. Statute appears intended to also include certain life insurance policies and certain annuity contracts. *See* Vt. Stat. Ann. tit. 14, 3201 through 3209.

Virginia. Any kind of interest in any kind of property.* *See* Va. Code Ann. 31-37 through 31-59.

Washington. Any kind of interest in any kind of property.* *See* Wash. Rev. Code Ann. 11.114.010 through 11.114.904.

West Virginia. Any kind of interest in any kind of property.* *See* W.Va. Code 36-7-1 through 36-7-24.

Wisconsin. Any kind of interest in any kind of property.* *See* Wis. Stat. Ann. 54.854 through 54.898.

Wyoming. Any kind of interest in any kind of property.* *See* Wyo. Stat. Ann. 34-13-114 through 34-13-137.

REFERENCE 2

Donee's Age at Which Custodianship Established Under the Uniform Gifts To Minors Act (UGMA) or the Uniform Transfers To Minors Act (UTMA) Ends

Note: This table is designed to reflect provisions relevant to custodianships entered into today.

Alabama. 21 or earlier death for transfers by irrevocable lifetime gift, transfers by irrevocable exercise of a power of appointment, or transfers authorized in a will or trust. Age of majority (generally 19) or earlier death for other transfers. *See* Ala. Code §§35-5A-21, 26-1-1.

Alaska. Generally 21 or earlier death for transfers by irrevocable lifetime gift, transfers by irrevocable exercise of a power of appointment, or transfers authorized in a will or trust; however, age may be changed to any age from 18 through 25 — but in the case of a transfer by irrevocable gift, the use of an amended age may be made subject to the minor's right to compel, during the six-month period beginning on the minor's 21st birthday, immediate distribution. 18 or earlier death for other transfers. *See* Alaska Stat. §§13.46.190, 13.46.195. Special rules apply to stock held under the Alaska Native Claims Settlement Act. See Alaska Stat. §13.46.085(e).

Arizona. 21 or earlier death for transfers by irrevocable lifetime gift, transfers by irrevocable exercise of a power of appointment, or transfers authorized in a will or trust. 18 or earlier death for other transfers. *See* Ariz. Rev. Stat. Ann. §14-7670.

Arkansas. Generally 21 or earlier death for transfers by irrevocable lifetime gift, transfers by irrevocable exercise of a power of appointment, or transfers authorized in a will or trust; however, for any such transfer, the applicable age may be lowered to any age between 18 and 21. 18 or earlier death for other transfers. *See* Ark. Code Ann. §9-26-220.

California. Generally 18 or earlier death. However, termination may be delayed for custodianships established by a revocable nomination of a custodian (not later than age 25), an irrevocable lifetime gift (not later than age 21), an irrevocable exercise of a power of appointment (not later than age 25), a transfer authorized in a will or trust (not later than age 25), or any other transfer (not later than age 25 or earlier termination). *See* Cal. Prob. Code §§3920, 3920.5.

Colorado. 21 or earlier death. *See* Colo. Rev. Stat. §11-50-121.

Connecticut. 21 or earlier death. *See* Conn. Gen. Stats. Ann. §45a-559e.

Delaware. 21 or earlier death for transfers by irrevocable lifetime gift, transfers by irrevocable exercise of a power of appointment, or transfers authorized in a will or trust. 18 or earlier death for other transfers. *See* Del. Code Ann., tit. 12, §4520.

District of Columbia. 18 or earlier death. *See* D.C. Code Ann. §21-320.

Florida. 21 or earlier death for transfers by irrevocable lifetime gift, transfers by irrevocable exercise of a power of appointment, or transfers authorized in a will or trust. 18 or earlier death for other transfers. *See* Fla. Stat. Ann. §710.123.

Georgia. 21 or earlier death for transfers by irrevocable lifetime gift, transfers by irrevocable exercise of a power of appointment, or transfers authorized in a will or trust. Age of majority (generally 18) or earlier death for other transfers. *See* Ga. Code Ann. §§44-5-130, 39-1-1(a).

Hawaii. 21 or earlier death for transfers by irrevocable lifetime gift, transfers by irrevocable exercise of a power of appointment, or transfers authorized in a will or trust. 18 or earlier death for other transfers. *See* Haw. Rev. Stat. §553A-20.

Idaho. 21 or earlier death for transfers by irrevocable lifetime gift, transfers by irrevocable exercise of a power of appointment, or transfers authorized in a will or trust. 18 or earlier death for other transfers. *See* Idaho Code §68-820.

Illinois. 21 or earlier death for transfers by irrevocable lifetime gift, transfers by irrevocable exercise of a power of appointment, or transfers authorized in a will, trust, or other governing instrument. Age of majority (generally 18) or earlier death for other transfers. *See* 760 ILCS 20/21, 755 ILCS 5/11-1.

Indiana. 21 or earlier death. *See* Ind. Code Ann. §30-2-8.5-35.

Iowa. 21 or earlier death. *See* Iowa Code Ann. §565B.20.

Kansas. 21 or earlier death for transfers by irrevocable lifetime gift, transfers by irrevocable exercise of a power of appointment, or transfers authorized in a will or trust. 18 or earlier death for other transfers. *See* Kan. Stat. Ann. §38-1721.

Kentucky. 18 or earlier death. *See* Ky. Rev. Stat. Ann. §385.202.

Louisiana. 18, earlier judicial emancipation, or earlier death. *See* La. Rev. Stat. Ann. §9:770.

Maine. Generally 18 or earlier death for transfers by irrevocable lifetime gift, transfers by irrevocable exercise of a power of appointment, or transfers authorized in a will or trust; however, for any such transfer, the custodianship may be extended to a later age but not beyond 21. Age of majority (generally 18) or earlier death for other transfers. *See* Me. Rev. Stat. Ann. 33, §1671; 1, §§72, 73.

Maryland. 21 or earlier death for transfers by irrevocable lifetime gift, transfers by irrevocable exercise of a power of appointment, transfers authorized in a will or trust, transfers by a personal representative or trustee in the absence of a will or under a will or trust that does not authorize such a transfer, or transfers by a conservator. 18 or earlier death for other transfers. *See* Md. Est. & Trusts Code Ann. §13-320.

Massachusetts. 21 or earlier death for transfers pursuant to a revocable nomination of a custodian to receive property upon the occurrence of a future event, transfers by irrevocable lifetime gift, transfers by irrevocable exercise of a power of appointment, or transfers authorized in a will or trust. Age of majority (generally 18) or earlier death for other transfers. *See* Mass. Ann. Laws ch. 201A, §20; ch. 4, §7; ch. 231, §85P.

Michigan. 18 or earlier death. *See* Mich. Comp. Laws Ann. §554.546.

Minnesota. 21 or earlier death for transfers by irrevocable lifetime gift, transfers by irrevocable exercise of a power of appointment, or transfers authorized in a will or trust. 18 or earlier death for other transfers. *See* Minn. Stat. Ann. §527.40.

Mississippi. 21 or earlier death for transfers by irrevocable lifetime gifts, transfers by irrevocable exercise of a power of appointment, or transfers authorized in a will or trust. 18 or earlier death for other transfers. *See* Miss. Code Ann. §91-20-41.

Missouri. 21 or earlier death, except that for custodial property created by a transfer from a person other than a donor custodianship ends on the minor's attaining the age of 18 and requesting the property (or earlier death). *See* Mo. Ann. Stat. §404.051(5)(1).

Montana. 21 or earlier death for transfers by irrevocable lifetime gift, transfers by irrevocable exercise of a power of appointment, or transfers authorized in a will or trust. 18 or earlier death for other transfers. *See* Mont. Code Ann. §72-26-803.

Nebraska. 21 or earlier death for transfers by irrevocable lifetime gift, transfers by irrevocable exercise of a power of appointment, or transfers authorized in a will or trust. Age of majority (generally 19) or earlier death for other transfers. *See* Neb. Rev. Stat. §43-2721, §43-2101.

Nevada. Generally 18 or earlier death. However, for a transfer by irrevocable lifetime gift, the custodianship can be extended to an age not later than the age of 21 (or earlier death); for a transfer by irrevocable exercise of a power of appointment, for a transfer authorized in a will or trust, or for a future transfer pursuant to a revocable nomination of custodian, the custodianship can be extended to an age not later than the age of 25 (or earlier death). *See* Nev. Rev. Stat. Ann. §§167.034, 167.095.

New Hampshire. 21 or earlier death for transfers by irrevocable lifetime gift, transfers by irrevocable exercise of a power of appointment, or transfers authorized in a will or trust. 18 or earlier death for other transfers. *See* N.H. Rev. Stat. Ann. §463-A:20.

New Jersey. Generally 21 or earlier death for transfers by irrevocable lifetime gift, transfers by irrevocable exercise of a power of appointment, or transfers authorized in a will or trust; however, for any such transfer, the transferor (at the time of the transfer) (it is not clear whether this includes personal representatives or trustees making transfers authorized in wills or trusts) or the governing will or trust may direct that the custodianship end at an earlier age "after the minor attains the age of 18 years"; furthermore, a custodian may in his discretion terminate a custodianship any time after the minor reaches 18, but this power may not be exercised prior to a termination age fixed by the transferor — it is not clear whether this prohibition extends to termination ages fixed by governing wills or trusts. Age of majority (generally 18) or earlier death for other transfers. *See* N.J. Stat. Ann. §§46:38A-52, 46:38A-31, 9:17B-1, 9:17B-3.

New Mexico. 21 or earlier death for transfers by irrevocable lifetime gift, transfers by irrevocable exercise of a power of appointment, or transfers authorized in a will or trust. Age of majority (generally 18) or earlier death for other transfers. *See* N.M. Stat. Ann. §§46-7-31, 28-6-1.

New York. 21, or earlier death for transfers by irrevocable gift, by irrevocable exercise of a power of appointment or transfers authorized in a will or trust. 18 or earlier death for other transfers. *See* N.Y. Est. Powers & Trusts Law §§7-6.20.

North Carolina. Generally 21 or earlier death for transfers by irrevocable lifetime gift, transfers by irrevocable exercise of a power of appointment, or transfers authorized in a will or trust; however, for any such transfer, the custodianship may be shortened and may terminate after the age of 18 and before the age of 21. 18 or earlier death for other transfers. *See* N.C. Gen. Stat. §33A-20.

North Dakota. 21 or earlier death for transfers by irrevocable lifetime gift, transfers by irrevocable exercise of a power of appointment, or transfers authorized in a will or trust. 18 or earlier death for other transfers. *See* N.D. Cent. Code §47-24.1-20.

Ohio. Generally 21 or earlier death. However, if the donor or the transferor specifies an earlier age between 18 and 21 for the custodianship to end, the custodianship ends at that age or the minor's earlier death. *See* Oh. Rev. Code Ann. §5814.04(D).

Oklahoma. Generally 18 or earlier death for transfers by irrevocable lifetime gift, transfers by irrevocable exercise of a power of appointment, or transfers authorized in a will or trust; however, for any such transfer, the custodianship may be lengthened so that it terminates. Age of majority (generally 18) or earlier death for other transfers. *See* Okla. Stat. Ann. tit. 58, 1221; tit. 15, §13; tit. 10, §91.

Oregon. 21 or earlier death for transfers by irrevocable lifetime gift, transfers by irrevocable exercise of a power of appointment, or transfers authorized in a will or trust. 18 or earlier death for other transfers. *See* Or. Rev. Stat. §126.869.

Pennsylvania. 21 or earlier death for transfers by irrevocable lifetime gift, transfers by irrevocable exercise of a power of appointment, or transfers authorized in a will or trust. Age of majority (generally 21) or earlier death for other transfers. *See* 20 Pa. Cons. Stat. Ann. §5320; 1 Pa. Cons. Stat. Ann. §1991.

Rhode Island. 18 or earlier death. *See* R.I. Gen. Laws §18-7-21.

South Carolina. 18 or earlier death. *See* S.C. Code Ann. §20-7-180(4).

South Dakota. 18 or earlier death. *See* S.D. Codified Laws §55-10A-22.

Tennessee. Generally 21 or earlier death. Custodianship can be extended to a later age up to age 25, but extending custodianship beyond age 21 requires declaration that deferral of termination will cause the transfer to be a gift of a future interest, if the gift is an inter vivos gift, which may have adverse federal and state gift tax consequences. *See* Tenn. Code Ann. §35-7-221.

Texas. 21 or earlier death for transfers by irrevocable lifetime gift, transfers by irrevocable exercise of a power of appointment, or transfers authorized in a will or trust. Age of majority (generally 18) or earlier death for other tranfers. *See* Tex. Prop. Code Ann. §141.021; Tex. CP&R Code §129.001.

Utah. 21 or earlier death for transfers by irrevocable lifetime gift, transfers by irrevocable exercise of a power of appointment, or transfers authorized in a will or trust. Age of majority (generally 18) or earlier death for other transfers. *See* Utah Code Ann. §§75-5a-121, 15-2-1.

Vermont. Age of majority (generally 18) or earlier death. *See* Vt. Stat. Ann. tit. 14, §3204(d); tit. 1, §173.

Virginia. Generally 18 or earlier death. However, for transfers by irrevocable lifetime gift, transfers by irrevocable exercise of a power of appointment, or transfers authorized in a will or trust may be extended to end at age 21 or earlier death. *See* Va. Code Ann. §31-56.

Washington. 21 or earlier death for transfers by irrevocable lifetime gift, transfers by irrevocable exercise of a power of appointment, or transfers authorized in a will or trust. 18 or earlier death for other transfers. *See* Wash. Rev. Code Ann. §11.114.200.

West Virginia. 21 or earlier death for transfers by irrevocable lifetime gift, transfers by irrevocable exercise of a power of appointment, or transfers authorized in a will or trust. Age of majority (generally 18) or earlier death for other transfers. *See* W.Va. Code §§36-7-20, 2-3-1.

Wisconsin. 21 or earlier death for transfers by irrevocable lifetime gift, transfers by irrevocable exercise of a power of appointment, or transfers authorized in a will or trust. 18 or earlier death for other transfers. *See* Wis. Stat. Ann. §54.892.

Wyoming. 21 or earlier death for transfers by irrevocable lifetime gift, transfers by irrevocable exercise of a power of appointment, or transfers authorized in a will or trust. Age of majority (generally 18) or earlier death for other transfers. *See* Wyo. Stat. Ann. §§34-13-133, 14-1-101(a), 8-1-102(a)(i) and 8-1-102(a)(iii).

APPENDIX E

CITATIONS IN STATUTES AUTHORIZING DURABLE POWER OF ATTORNEY

State	Citation	State	Citation
Ala.	Code of Ala. (1975) §26-1-2	Mont.	MCA 72-5-501, 72-5-502
Alas.	AS §13.26.332	Nebr.	RSN (1943) §30-2664 to -2672
Ariz.	ARS §§14-5501, -5504, -5505		
Ark.	AC 1987 §§28-68-101 to 28-68-203	Nev.	NRS 111.460
		N.H.	RSA 506:6
Cal.	Probate Code §§4000-4034	N.J.	NJSA 46:2B-8.1 to 8.13
Colo.	CRS §15-14-501	N.M.	NMS (1978) §§45-5-501, -505
Conn.	CGSA §45a-562	N.Y.	Gen. Obl. Law §§5-1501, -1505, -1506
Del.	DCA, Title 12, §§4901-4905		
D.C.	DCC §§21-2081 to -2085	N.C.	GS §32A-8 to -14
Fla.	FSA §709.08	N.D.	CC §30.1-30-01 to -06
Ga.	Ga Code §10-6-36	Ohio	RC §1337.09
Haw.	HRS §551D-1	Okla.	58 OSA §§1071 to 1077
Idaho	IC §§15-5-501 to -507	Ore.	ORS 127.005
Ill.	755 ILCS 45/2-1 et seq	Pa.	20 Pa. CSA §§5604 to 5606
Ind.	IC 30-5-4-2, 30-5-10-3	R.I.	GL §34-22-6.1
Iowa	ICA §§633B.1, 633B.2	S.C.	CLSC 1976, §62-5-501 to -505
Kan.	KS §58-652		
Ky.	KRS 386.093	S.D.	SDCL, §59-7-2.1
La.	LSA-CC Art. 2985 to 3034	Tenn.	TCA, §§34-6-101 to -111
Me.	18-A MRSA §§5-501, 5-502		
		Tex.	Prob. Code §§481 to 506
Md.	MCA (E&T) §§13-601, 13-602	Utah	UCA, §75-5-501, -502
		Vt.	VSA, T. 14, §§3507 to 3508
Mass.	MGLA c. 201B, §§1-7	Va.	Code of Va. §11-9.1 to -9.5
Mich.	MCLA 700.5501, .5504	Wash.	RCWA 11.94.010
Minn.	MSA §523.07, -.08	W.Va.	WVC §§39-4-1 to 39-4-7
Miss.	MC (1972) §§87-3-101 to -113	Wisc.	WSA §243.07
Mo.	VAMS §§404.700 to .735	Wyo.	WSA §3-5-101

APPENDIX F

Age of Majority* in the Various States

State	Age	Citation	State	Age	Citation
Ala.	19	Code of Ala. §26-1-1	Nebr.	19	RSN §43-2101
			Nev.	18	NRS §129.010
Alas.	18	AS §25.20.010	N.H.	18	RSA §§21:44, 21-B:1
Ariz.	18	ARS §1-215(19)	N.J.	18	NJSA §§9:17B-1, -3
Ark.	18	AC 1987, §9-25-101	N.M.	18	NMS (1978) §28-6-1
Cal.	18	Family Code §6500	N.Y.	18	E.g., CPLR §105(j);
Colo.	21†	CRS 2-4-401(6)			Gen. Obl. Law
Conn.	18	CGSA §1-1d			§§1-202, 3-101(1)
Del.	18	DCA, Title 1, §701	N.C.	18	GS §§48A-1, -2
D.C.	18	DCC §46-101	N.D.	18	CC §§14-10-01, -02
Fla.	18	FSA §743.07	Ohio	18	RC §3109.01
Ga.	18	Ga. Code §39-1-1(a)	Okla.	18	15 OSA §13††;
Haw.	18	HRS §577-1			10 OSA §91
Idaho	18	IC §32-101	Ore.	18	ORS §109.510
Ill.	18	755 ILCS 5/11-1	Pa.	21†	1 Pa.CSA §1991
Ind.	18	IC §§1-1-4-5(1), (8)	R.I.	18	GL §15-12-1
Iowa	18	ICA §599.1	S.C.	18	S.C. Const. Art. 17,
Kan.	18	KS §38-101			§14; CLSC 1976
Ky.	18	KRS §2.015			§15-1-320
La.	18	LSA-CC Art. 29	S.D.	18	SDCL §26-1-1
Me.	18	1 MRSA §§72, 73	Tenn.	18	TCS §§1-3-105(1),
Md.	18	MCA (1957) Art. 1, §24			-113(a)
			Tex.	18	VTCA, CP&R Code
Mass.	18	MGLA c.4, §7; c.231, §85p			§129.001
			Utah	18	UCA, §15-2-1
Mich.	18	MCL §722.52	Vt.	18	VSA, T. 1 §173
Minn.	18	MSA §§645.45(3), (14); 645.451	Va.	18	Code of Va. §1-13.42
			Wash.	18†	RCWA §26.28.010
Miss.	21	MC (1972) §1-3-27	W.Va.	18	WVC §2-3-1
Mo.	18††	VAMS §431.055	Wisc.	18	WSA §§990.01(3), (20)
Mont.	18	Mont. Const. Art. II, §14; MCA §41-1-101	Wyo.	18	WSA §§8-1-102(a)(i), (iii), 14-1-101(a)

* Except where noted, this table sets forth the generally applicable age of majority for each state (and the District of Columbia, which is considered to be a state for this table). It is common for states to establish a generally applicable age of majority and to also provide different ages of competence or different "adult" ages or different ages of majority applicable for specific purposes. This table does not try to comprehensively list those special purpose ages. For example, this table does not reflect that many states provide a reduced minimum age of competence to contract for certain types of insurance. Also by way of example, the listed ages may not necessarily be the adult ages for purposes of (1) support obligations or (2) the custodial transfer acts adopted by the various states. Furthermore, some states provide procedures whereby a minor may have the disabilities of minority removed before reaching the age of majority. This table does not identify the availability of such procedures. Finally, certain events, like marriage, could have the effect of conferring majority upon one who would otherwise be a minor. This table does not try to list such accelerating events.

† At least Colorado and Pennsylvania provide a special, general age of competence to contract, sue, and be sued: 18. See CRS §13-22-101 (also age of general competence to manage estate and to make health care decisions for self and issue); 23 Pa.C.S.A. §5101.

†† Age 18 for general competency to contract.

APPENDIX G

AFTER-TAX EQUIVALENTS
OF TAX-EXEMPT YIELDS

Bracket	10%	15%	20%	25%	26%	28%	30%	33%	34%	35%	38%	39%
4.00	4.44	4.71	5.00	5.33	5.41	5.56	5.71	5.97	6.06	6.15	6.45	6.56
4.10	4.56	4.82	5.13	5.47	5.54	5.69	5.86	6.12	6.21	6.31	6.61	6.72
4.20	4.67	4.94	5.25	5.60	5.68	5.83	6.00	6.27	6.36	6.46	6.77	6.89
4.30	4.78	5.06	5.38	5.73	5.81	5.97	6.14	6.42	6.52	6.62	6.94	7.05
4.40	4.89	5.18	5.50	5.87	5.95	6.11	6.29	6.57	6.67	6.77	7.10	7.21
4.50	5.00	5.29	5.63	6.00	6.08	6.25	6.43	6.72	6.82	6.92	7.26	7.38
4.60	5.11	5.41	5.75	6.13	6.22	6.39	6.57	6.87	6.97	7.08	7.42	7.54
4.70	5.22	5.53	5.88	6.27	6.35	6.53	6.71	7.01	7.12	7.23	7.58	7.70
4.80	5.33	5.65	6.00	6.40	6.49	6.67	6.86	7.16	7.27	7.38	7.74	7.87
4.90	5.44	5.76	6.13	6.53	6.62	6.81	7.00	7.31	7.42	7.54	7.90	8.03
5.00	5.56	5.88	6.25	6.67	6.76	6.94	7.14	7.46	7.58	7.69	8.06	8.20
5.10	5.67	6.00	6.37	6.80	6.89	7.08	7.29	7.61	7.73	7.85	8.23	8.36
5.20	5.78	6.12	6.50	6.93	7.03	7.22	7.43	7.76	7.88	8.00	8.39	8.52
5.30	5.89	6.24	6.62	7.07	7.16	7.36	7.57	7.91	8.03	8.15	8.55	8.69
5.40	6.00	6.35	6.75	7.20	7.30	7.50	7.71	8.06	8.18	8.31	8.71	8.85
5.50	6.11	6.47	6.87	7.33	7.43	7.64	7.86	8.21	8.33	8.46	8.87	9.02
5.60	6.22	6.59	7.00	7.47	7.57	7.78	8.00	8.36	8.48	8.62	9.03	9.18
5.70	6.33	6.71	7.12	7.60	7.70	7.92	8.14	8.51	8.64	8.77	9.19	9.34
5.80	6.44	6.82	7.25	7.73	7.84	8.06	8.29	8.66	8.79	8.92	9.35	9.51
5.90	6.56	6.94	7.37	7.87	7.97	8.19	8.43	8.81	8.94	9.08	9.52	9.67
6.00	6.67	7.06	7.50	8.00	8.11	8.33	8.57	8.96	9.09	9.23	9.68	9.84
6.10	6.78	7.18	7.62	8.13	8.24	8.47	8.71	9.10	9.24	9.38	9.84	10.00
6.20	6.89	7.29	7.75	8.27	8.38	8.61	8.86	9.25	9.39	9.54	10.00	10.16
6.30	7.00	7.41	7.87	8.40	8.51	8.75	9.00	9.40	9.55	9.69	10.16	10.33
6.40	7.11	7.53	8.00	8.53	8.65	8.89	9.14	9.55	9.70	9.85	10.32	10.49
6.50	7.22	7.65	8.12	8.67	8.78	9.03	9.29	9.70	9.85	10.00	10.48	10.66
6.60	7.33	7.76	8.25	8.80	8.92	9.17	9.43	9.85	10.00	10.15	10.65	10.82
6.70	7.44	7.88	8.37	8.93	9.05	9.31	9.57	10.00	10.15	10.31	10.81	10.98
6.80	7.56	8.00	8.50	9.07	9.19	9.44	9.71	10.15	10.30	10.46	10.97	11.15
6.90	7.67	8.12	8.62	9.20	9.32	9.58	9.86	10.30	10.45	10.62	11.13	11.31
7.00	7.78	8.24	8.75	9.33	9.46	9.72	10.00	10.45	10.61	10.77	11.29	11.48
7.10	7.89	8.35	8.87	9.47	9.59	9.86	10.14	10.60	10.76	10.92	11.45	11.64
7.20	8.00	8.47	9.00	9.60	9.73	10.00	10.29	10.75	10.91	11.08	11.61	11.80
7.30	8.11	8.59	9.12	9.73	9.86	10.14	10.43	10.90	11.06	11.23	11.77	11.97
7.40	8.22	8.71	9.25	9.87	10.00	10.28	10.57	11.04	11.21	11.38	11.94	12.13
7.50	8.33	8.82	9.37	10.00	10.14	10.42	10.71	11.19	11.36	11.54	12.10	12.30
7.60	8.44	8.94	9.50	10.13	10.27	10.56	10.86	11.34	11.52	11.69	12.26	12.46
7.70	8.56	9.06	9.62	10.27	10.41	10.69	11.00	11.49	11.67	11.85	12.42	12.62
7.80	8.67	9.18	9.75	10.40	10.54	10.83	11.14	11.64	11.82	12.00	12.58	12.79
7.90	8.78	9.29	9.87	10.53	10.68	10.97	11.29	11.79	11.97	12.15	12.74	12.95
8.00	8.89	9.41	10.00	10.67	10.81	11.11	11.43	11.94	12.12	12.31	12.90	13.11
8.10	9.00	9.53	10.13	10.80	10.95	11.25	11.57	12.09	12.27	12.46	13.06	13.28
8.20	9.11	9.65	10.25	10.93	11.08	11.39	11.71	12.24	12.42	12.62	13.23	13.44
8.30	9.22	9.76	10.38	11.07	11.22	11.53	11.86	12.39	12.58	12.77	13.39	13.61
8.40	9.33	9.88	10.50	11.20	11.35	11.67	12.00	12.54	12.73	12.92	13.55	13.77
8.50	9.44	10.00	10.63	11.33	11.49	11.81	12.14	12.69	12.88	13.08	13.71	13.93
8.60	9.56	10.12	10.75	11.47	11.62	11.94	12.29	12.84	13.03	13.23	13.87	14.10
8.70	9.67	10.24	10.88	11.60	11.76	12.08	12.43	12.99	13.18	13.38	14.03	14.26
8.80	9.78	10.35	11.00	11.73	11.89	12.22	12.57	13.13	13.33	13.54	14.19	14.43
8.90	9.89	10.47	11.13	11.87	12.03	12.36	12.71	13.28	13.48	13.69	14.35	14.59
9.00	10.00	10.59	11.25	12.00	12.16	12.50	12.86	13.43	13.64	13.85	14.52	14.75
9.10	10.11	10.71	11.38	12.13	12.30	12.64	13.00	13.58	13.79	14.00	14.68	14.92
9.20	10.22	10.82	11.50	12.27	12.43	12.78	13.14	13.73	13.94	14.15	14.84	15.08
9.30	10.33	10.94	11.63	12.40	12.57	12.92	13.29	13.88	14.09	14.31	15.00	15.25
9.40	10.44	11.06	11.75	12.53	12.70	13.06	13.43	14.03	14.24	14.46	15.16	15.41
9.50	10.56	11.18	11.88	12.67	12.84	13.19	13.57	14.18	14.39	14.62	15.32	15.57
9.60	10.67	11.29	12.00	12.80	12.97	13.33	13.71	14.33	14.55	14.77	15.48	15.74
9.70	10.78	11.41	12.13	12.93	13.11	13.47	13.86	14.48	14.70	14.92	15.65	15.90
9.80	10.89	11.53	12.25	13.07	13.24	13.61	14.00	14.63	14.85	15.08	15.81	16.07
9.90	11.00	11.65	12.38	13.20	13.38	13.75	14.14	14.78	15.00	15.23	15.97	16.23
10.00	11.11	11.76	12.50	13.33	13.51	13.89	14.29	14.93	15.15	15.38	16.13	16.39
10.10	11.22	11.88	12.63	13.47	13.65	14.03	14.43	15.07	15.30	15.54	16.29	16.56
10.20	11.33	12.00	12.75	13.60	13.78	14.17	14.57	15.22	15.45	15.69	16.45	16.72
10.30	11.44	12.12	12.88	13.73	13.92	14.31	14.71	15.37	15.61	15.85	16.61	16.89
10.40	11.56	12.24	13.00	13.87	14.05	14.44	14.86	15.52	15.76	16.00	16.77	17.05
10.50	11.67	12.35	13.13	14.00	14.19	14.58	15.00	15.67	15.91	16.15	16.94	17.21
10.60	11.78	12.47	13.25	14.13	14.32	14.72	15.14	15.82	16.06	16.31	17.10	17.38
10.70	11.89	12.59	13.38	14.27	14.46	14.86	15.29	15.97	16.21	16.46	17.26	17.54
10.80	12.00	12.71	13.50	14.40	14.59	15.00	15.43	16.12	16.36	16.62	17.42	17.70
10.90	12.11	12.82	13.63	14.53	14.73	15.14	15.57	16.27	16.52	16.77	17.58	17.87
11.00	12.22	12.94	13.75	14.67	14.86	15.28	15.71	16.42	16.67	16.92	17.74	18.03

TAX EXEMPT YIELDS

TABLE OF CASES

Case	Q	Case	Q
Addis v. Comm.	1315	Brauer v. Comm.	1238
Adee v. U.S.	1506	Braun v. Comm.	1450
Akers v. Comm.	1339	Brenner v. Comm.	1428
Al-Murshidi v. Comm.	1429	Briggs v. Comm.	1426
Alexander v. Comm.	1228	Brodrick v. Gore	1544
Alfaro v. Comm.	1302	Brountas v. Comm.	1194
Ali v. Comm.	1448	Brown v. Comm.	1194
Allegheny County Auto Mart	1422	Brown v. U.S.	1316, 1501, 1508
Allemeier v. Comm.	1313	Browning v. Comm.	1339
Allen v. Comm.	1220	Bryant v. Comm.	1128
Allgood, Est. of v. Comm.	1507	Buchholz v. Comm.	1225
American Bar Endowment, U.S. v.	1315	Buffalo Tool & Die Mfg. Co., Inc. v. Comm.	1544
Anderson v. Helvering	1253	Bunn, Willcuts v.	1125
Anderson v. U.S.	1501	Bunney v. Comm.	1443
Anselmo v. Comm.	1316	Burdick, Est. of v. Comm.	1506
Apkin v. Comm.	1139	Buring, Est. of v. Comm.	1534
Arbini v. Comm.	1316	Butler v. U.S.	1411
Atkinson v. Comm.	1330	Butts v. Comm.	1313
Avery v. Comm.	1002	Byers v. Comm.	1225
Azenaro v. Comm.	1448	Calder v. Comm.	1535
Baker v. Comm.	1429	California Fed. Life Ins. Co. v. Comm.	1188, 1422
Baker, Goldin v.	1123, 1410	Cammack v. Comm.	1312
Baker, South Carolina v.	1151	Campbell, Fleming v.	1237
Ball v. Comm.	1306	Carlton v. U.S.	1238
Bankline Oil Co., Helvering v.	1253	Carroll, Est. of v. Comm.	1327
Barker v. Comm.	1238	Carter v. Comm.	1283
Barker v. U.S.	1237	Carter Trust v. Comm.	1293
Barnhill v. Comm.	1120	Cartwright	1542
Barrett v. U.S.	1448	Cartwright, U.S. v.	1542
Barringer v. Comm.	1316	Catto, U.S. v.	1283
Bauer v. U.S.	1220	Chapman v. Comm.	1405
Baxter v. Comm.	1405	Chase Manhattan Bank, Comm. v.	1534
Beall v. Comm.	1239	Chen v. Comm.	1421
Beck v. Comm.	1444	Child's Estate, Comm. v.	1544
Belden v. Comm.	1303	Christensen v. Comm.	1422
Belz Investment Co. v. Comm.	1267	Church v. U.S.	1552
Bensel, Comm. v.	1544	Cipriano v. Comm.	1448
Bernal v. Comm.	1444	Cleveland Indians Baseball Co., U.S. v.	1441
Bernard v. Comm.	1237	Clyde C. Pierce Corp. v. Comm.	1306
Beyer v. Comm.	1304	Cohen v. Comm.	1405
Biehl v. Comm.	1428	Coleman v. Comm.	1267, 1448
Biggs v. Comm.	1238	Collins v. Comm.	1310, 1312
Bingham	1022	Contini v. Comm.	1312
Bingham's Trust v. Comm.	1310, 1312	Cook v. Comm.	1551
Black v. Comm.	1237	Cook, Est. of v. U.S.	1537
Blair v. Comm.	1448	Cordner v. U.S.	1003, 1188
Blake v. Comm.	1315	Coupe v. Comm.	1238
Blanche v. Comm.	1303	Crane v. Comm.	1204, 1232, 1269, 1326, 1340
Block v. Comm.	1194	Craven v. U.S.	1447
Blumberg, U.S. v.	1508	Crichton, Comm. v.	1237
Boatner v. Comm.	1421	Crigler v. Comm.	1032
Boehm v. Comm.	1032	Cristofani, Est. of v. Comm.	1530
Boeshore, Est. of	1337	Crocker v. Comm.	1316
Bolker v. Comm.	1237	Crummey v. Comm.	1530
Boltinghouse v. Comm.	1426	Davis v. Comm.	1318
Bolton v. Comm.	1225, 1408	Davis v. Dept. of Revenue	1123
Bond v. Comm.	1318	Davis v. U.S.	1320
Bonner, Est. of v. U.S.	1535	Davis, Dept. of Revenue v.	1123
Bowers, Wilson v.	1544	De Cou v. Comm.	1231
Boyle, U.S. v.	1508, 1534	Deal	1522
Brandenburger v. U.S.	1224	DeBie, Est. of v. Comm.	1316
Brannen v. Comm.	1190		

Case	Q	Case	Q
DeLoss v. Comm.	1032	Garcia v. Comm.	1238
Denman v. Slayton	1306	Gasser, Est. of v. Comm.	1424
Deputy v. duPont	1155	Gates Rubber Co. v. Comm.	1248
Di Leonardo v. Comm.	1310	Georgeff v. United States	1032
Diagonal Spreads.	1070	Gibson Products Co.–Kell Blvd. v. U.S.	1194
Dickman v. Comm.	1521	Gilford, Est. of v. Comm.	1537
Diedrich v. Comm.	1525	Gillet, Est. of v. Comm.	1544
Dillingham, Est. of v. Comm.	1519	Glass v. Comm.	1339
District Bond Co. v. Comm.	1128	Godley v. Comm.	1545
Doherty v. Comm.	1316	Godwin, In re	1239
Dolese v. Comm.	1195	Goldin v. Baker	1123, 1410
Dorn v. U.S.	1537	Goldman v. Comm.	1316
Dorsey v. Comm.	1339	Goodman v. U.S.	1340
Downing v. Comm.	1443	Gore, Brodrick v.	1544
Drapeau v. Drapeau	1443	Gorkes v. Comm.	1304
Dreicer v. Comm.	1300	Gradow v. U.S.	1501
Dunbar v. Comm.	1032	Gray, First Ky. Co. v.	1133
Dunkin v. Comm.	1443	Green v. Comm.	1410
Dunn v. Comm.	1300	Greene v. U.S.	1322
DuPont v. Comm.	1022	Greer v. U.S.	1283
duPont, Deputy v.	1155	Grier v. U.S.	1220
D'Ambrosio, Est. of v. Comm.	1501	Griffin v. Comm.	1339
Earl, Lucas v.	1006	Grimes v. Comm.	1518
Eberly v. Comm.	1430	Groetzinger, Comm. v.	1421
Elliot Knitwear Profit Sharing Plan		Guest v. Comm.	1210, 1326
v. Comm.	1336	Guinan v. U.S.	1239
Ellis v. Comm.	1311	Gummer v. U.S.	1239
Engdahl v. Comm.	1300	Haar v. Comm.	1410
Engle, Comm. v.	1258, 1259	Haas v. U.S.	1304
Estroff, Est. of v. Comm.	1029	Hackl v. Comm.	1530
Everett v. Comm.	1237	Hager v. Comm.	1194
Ewell v. Comm.	1448	Hahn v. Comm.	1501
Exchange Bank & Trust Co. of Fla.		Hall, Est. of v. Comm.	1538
v. U.S.	1502	Hamilton v. U.S.	1197
Exxon v. U.S.	1248	Hanlin v. Comm.	1031
Fackler v. Comm.	1220	Harbor Bancorp & Subsidiaries v. Comm.	1123
Fannon v. Comm.	1339	Harrison	1525
Ferguson v. Comm.	1322	Hart v. Comm.	1025
Fiorito v. Comm.	1544	Harwood v. Comm.	1548
First Ky. Co. v. Gray	1133	Hassen v. Comm.	1419
Fisher v. Comm.	1133	Hawkins v. Comm.	1196
Fisher v. U.S.	1017	Haygood v. Comm.	1522
Fithian v. U.S.	1448	Heiss v. Comm.	1032
Fitzmaurice v. U.S.	1302	Helvering v. Bankline Oil Co.	1253
Fleming v. Campbell	1237	Helvering, Anderson v.	1253
Fleming, Est. of v. Comm.	1520	Helvering, Rand v.	1032
Flood v. U.S.	1304	Hemme, U.S. v.	1507
Fontana, Est. of v. Comm.	1535	Henderson v. Comm.	1429
Fox v. Comm.	1300	Herman v. U.S.	1316
Frane, Est. of v. Comm.	1430	Hewitt v. Comm.	1318
Frank Lyon Co. v. U.S.	1267	Heyen v. U.S.	1530
Franklin, Est. of v. Comm.	1267, 1269	Higgins v. Comm.	1306, 1310
Frazee v. Comm.	1521	Hilborn v. Comm.	1339
Freyre v. U.S.	1448	Hill, U.S. v.	1263
Fund for Anonymous Gifts, The v. IRS	1333	Hilton v. Comm.	1267
Gaffney v. Comm.	1116	Hokanson v. Comm.	1270
Gagliardi, Est. of v. Comm.	1519	Holland, Est. of v. Comm.	1530
Gajewski v. Comm.	1155	Hollingsworth v. Comm.	1518, 1530
Gallenstein v. U.S.	1501	Hood v. Comm.	1137
Gallo, Est. of v. Comm.	1544	Hoover v. Comm.	1448
Garber Industries Holding Co., Inc.		Hubert, Est. of, Comm. v.	1506
v. Comm.	1419	Huntsman v. Comm.	1303

Case	Q	Case	Q
Hurley v. Comm.	1303	Letts, Est. of v. Comm.	1506
Iacono, Est. of	1546	Levine, Est. of v. Comm.	1210
Illinois Dept. of Revenue,		Levy v. Comm.	1251
Rockford Life Ins. v.	1146	Liang v. Comm.	1421
Illinois Merchants Trust Co.		Lieb v. Comm.	1121
v. Comm.	1220, 1273	Lindquist v. Mack	1331
Illinois Terminal R.R. Co. v. U.S.	1306	Lingo	1525
Indian Trail Trading Post, Inc. v. Comm.	1306	Lipke v. Comm.	1196
IRS, Fund for Anonymous Gifts, The v.	1333	Littick, Est. of	1544
Irvine, U.S. v.	1520	Lobato v. U.S.	1310
Israel v. Comm.	1448	Lockhart Leasing Co. v. U.S.	1267
Jaglom v. Comm.	1133	Loew v. Comm.	1310, 1312
James v. Comm.	1273	Lofstrom v. Comm.	1448
James, Est. of v. Comm.	1544	Lomb v. Sugden	1544
Jamison v. Comm.	1311	Louisiana Land and Exploration Co.	
Jefferson Lake Sulphur Co. v. Lambert	1252	v. Comm.	1256
Jenner, Est. of v. Comm.	1506	Lovejoy v. Comm.	1448
Jennings v. Comm.	1318	LTV Corp. v. Comm.	1267
Jeschke v. U.S.	1501	Lucas v. Earl	1006
Johnson v. Comm.	1210, 1446	M&W Gear Co. v. Comm.	1267
Johnston, Est. of v. U.S.	1536	Mack, Lindquist v.	1331
Jolley v. Comm.	1251	Maddock, Est. of	1544
Jones v. Comm.	1303, 1447	Madorin v. Comm.	1205, 1211
Joslin v. U.S.	1188	Magneson v. Comm.	1237
Joslyn, Est. of v. Comm.	1506	Magnin, Est. of v. Comm.	1501
Kahn, Est. of	1430	Mallinckrodt v. Comm.	1311
Kaufmann v. U.S.	1312	Mandel v. Sturr	1544
Kean v. Comm.	1448	Marine, Est. of v. Comm.	1506
Keeler v. Comm.	1079	Marshall v. U.S.	1501
Keith v. Comm.	1405	Marten v. Comm.	1448
Keller v. Comm.	1251	Martin v. Comm.	1267, 1545
Kelley, Est. of v. Comm.	1522	Mathias v. Comm.	1316
Kelly v. Comm.	1303, 1310	Maxant, Est. of	1501
Kenseth v. Comm.	1428	May v. McGowan	1544
Kerner v. Comm.	1316	McAdams v. Comm.	1410
Kerr v. Comm.	1553	McCann, Comm. v.	1544
Kidder v. Comm.	1031	McDonough v. Comm.	1306
Kimbell v. U.S.	1545	McGill, Est. of v. Comm.	1544, 1545
King v. Comm.	1426	McGowan, May v.	1544
Kirby Petroleum Co. v. Comm.	1253	McGowan, Williams v.	1312
Kitch v. Comm.	1430, 1448	McGuire v. Comm.	1316
Kittle v. Comm.	1426	McKinney v. Comm.	1225
Klarkowski v. Comm.	1237	McWilliams v. Comm.	1419
Kline v. Comm.	1544	Meisels, Winthrop v.	1315
Knight v. Comm.	1553	Mellinger, Est. of v. Comm.	1535
Kohlsaat, Est. of v. Comm.	1530	Mellon Bank v. U.S.	1449
Kolker, Est. of v. Comm.	1530	Metzger, Est. of v. Comm.	1519
Krause v. Comm.	1246, 1408	Meyer v. Comm.	1448
Krauss v. U.S.	1544	Meyer, Est. of v. Comm.	1507
L.A. Thompson Scenic Ry. Co.		Michael K. Berry v. Comm.	1448
v. Comm.	1099, 1102	Middleton v. Comm.	1232
Lagreide v. Comm.	1220	Midland-Ross Corp., U.S. v.	1100, 1103
Lambert v. U.S.	1547	Miller v. Comm.	1426, 1448
Lambert, Jefferson Lake Sulphur Co. v.	1252	Miller v. U.S.	1248, 1501
Landers v. Comm.	1139	Milner v. Comm.	1310
Lane, Comm. v.	1448	Moller v. U.S.	1310, 1421
Lang v. Comm.	1306	Moody v. Comm.	1076
Lary v. Comm.	1188	Moore, Est. of v. Comm.	1506
Laureys v. Comm.	1070, 1071	Morris v. Comm.	1443
Lavery v. Comm.	1099, 1102	Morton v. Comm.	1032
Lee v. U.S.	1501	Moss, Est. of v. Comm.	1501
Lenz v. Comm.	1304	Mozley v. Comm.	1448

Case	Q	Case	Q
Mukherjee v. Comm.	1448	Richardson v. Comm.	1196, 1448
Mulberry Motor Parts, Inc. v. Comm.	1447	Richardson v. U.S.	1304
Murphy, Est. of v. Comm.	1545	Rickaby v. Comm.	1133
Musgrave v. Comm.	1325	Rifkin v. Comm.	1306
Narver v. Comm.	1194	Rifkind v. U.S.	1506
National Foundation, Inc. v. U.S.	1333	Rinaldi, Est. of v. U.S.	1506
NationsBank v. Variable Annuity		Rios v. Pulido	1426
Life Ins. Co.	1154	Ritchie v. Comm.	1448
New Dynamics Foundation v. U.S.	1333	Roark v. Comm.	1315
Newhall Unitrust v. Comm.	1336	Roberts v. U.S.	1076, 1083
Nickell v. Comm.	1310	Robinson v. Comm.	1302
Nicoladis v. Comm.	1339	Robinson, Est. of v. Comm.	1430
Noll v. Comm.	1133	Rockefeller v. Comm.	1320
Northwest Acceptance Corp. v. Comm.	1267	Rockford Life Ins. v. Illinois Dept.	
Obland v. U.S.	1099, 1102	of Revenue	1146
Oden v. Comm.	1193	Rome I, Ltd. v. Comm.	1339
Odend'hal v. Comm.	1269	Rountree Cotton, Inc. v. Comm.	1407
Oesterreich v. Comm.	1267	Royster v. Comm.	1156
Oetting v. U.S.	1506	Rubish, Est. of v. Comm.	1544
Okerson v. Comm.	1448	Rudkin Testamentary Trust v. Comm.	1449
Omans v. Comm.	1426	Russon v. Comm.	1304
Ostrom v. Comm.	1310	Rutland v. Comm.	1238
Owen, Est. of v. Comm.	1507	Salt, Est. of	1544
O'Neill Irrevocable Trust v. Comm.	1449	Sather v. Comm.	1530
Pacific Affiliate, Inc. v. Comm.	1127	Satullo v. Comm.	1339
Paradiso v. Comm.	1171	Sawade, Est. of v. Comm.	1537
Paragon Jewel Coal Co., Inc. v. Comm.	1252	Schapiro v. Comm.	1316, 1339
Parker v. U.S.	1501	Schott v. Comm.	1551
Patel v. Comm.	1438	Schuler v. Comm.	1530
Patten v. U.S.	1501	Scott v. Comm.	1310
Pauley v. U.S.	1251	Scott v. U.S.	1449
Phillies, The v. U.S.	1441	Seaborn, Poe v.	1443
Phillips v. Comm.	1446	Sels, Est. of v. Comm.	1548
Pittman v. U.S.	1501	Service Bolt & Nut Co. Profit Sharing	
Podell v. Comm.	1190	Trust v. Comm.	1336
Poe v. Seaborn	1443	Sharp v. Comm.	1304
Popa, In re	1239	Shattuck v. Comm.	1133
Posen, Est. of v. Comm.	1506	Sheppard v. U.S.	1315
Potts v. Comm.	1258	Silberman v. Comm.	1300
Preston v. Comm.	1448	Simplot, Est. of v. Comm.	1545
Pritchett v. Comm.	1287	Sklar v. Comm.	1315
Professional Equities, Inc. v. Comm.	1408	Slayton, Denman v.	1306
Provost v. U.S.	1021	Slocum v. U.S.	1544
Prudowsky, Est. of	1502	Smith v. U.S.	1506
Prussin v. Comm.	1269	Smith, Est. of v. Comm.	1536
Pulido, Rios v.	1426	Smith, Est. of v. U.S.	1430
Puscas v. Comm.	1249	Snyder v. Comm.	1518
R.O. Holton & Co. v. Comm.	1133	South Carolina v. Baker	1151
Rand v. Helvering	1032	Sparling, Est. of v. Comm.	1542
Raphan v. U.S.	1194	Spiegel, Est. of v. Comm.	1519
Rauenhorst v. Comm.	1322	Spitzer v. Comm.	1544
Ray v. Comm.	1448	Stahl v. Comm.	1448
Read v. Comm.	1447	Standard Oil Co. (Ind.) v. Comm.	1248
Redlark v. Comm.	1302	Starker v. U.S.	1237, 1238
Regals Realty Co. v. Comm.	1237	Starr v. Comm.	1121
Reimels v. Comm.	1410	Starr, Est. of v. Comm.	1267
Rendall v. Comm.	1032	Steffen, In re	1032
Resser v. Comm.	1070, 1071	Stewart v. Comm.	1446
Reynolds v. Comm.	1428	Stewart, U.S. v.	1125
Ribera v. Comm.	1448	Stinson v. U.S.	1530
Rice's Toyota World, Inc. v. Comm.	1267	Stone v. Comm.	1450

Case	Q
Stonehill v. Comm.	1190
Stradlings Building Materials, Inc. v. Comm.	1251
Stranahan, Est. of v. Comm.	1006
Strangi, Est. of v. Comm.	1545, 1552
Stratton, Est. of v. Comm.	1537
Stubbs v. U.S.	1315
Stuit v. Comm.	1502
Sturr, Mandel v.	1544
Stussy v. Comm.	1312
Styron v. Comm.	1325
Sugden, Lomb v.	1544
Sullivan, Est. of v. Comm.	1537
Sun Co., Inc. v. Comm.	1248
Sun Oil Co. v. Comm.	1267
Symington v. Comm.	1339
Taylor v. Comm.	1239
Terre Haute First Nat'l Bank v. U.S.	1506
Texaco, Inc. v. U.S.	1248
Thayer v. Comm.	1339
Thomas, Est. of	1267
Thomas D. Berry v. Comm.	1448
Tobey v. Comm.	1133
Todd v. Comm.	1324
Tokh v. Comm.	1310
Towle, Est. of v. Comm.	1501
Tripp v. Comm.	1316
Trivett v. Comm.	1309
Truman v. U.S.	1190
Tufts, Comm. v.	1204, 1232
Turner v. Comm.	1339
U.S. Trust Co. (Chisholm Est.) v. U.S.	1506
Union Nat'l Bank of Troy v. U.S.	1220
Uslu v. Comm.	1303
Van Brunt v. Comm.	1006
Van Horne, Est. of v. Comm.	1536
Vance v. Comm.	1426
Variable Annuity Life Ins. Co., NationsBank v.	1154
Vestal v. U.S.	1310
Vines v. Comm.	1421
Visco v. Comm.	1405

Case	Q
Von Muff v. Comm.	1238
W. H. Braum Family Partnership v. Comm.	1519
W.D. Haden Co. v. Comm.	1238
W.H. Hartman Co. v. Comm.	1422
Walker v. Comm.	1447
Wall, Est. of v. Comm.	1501
Walshire v. Comm.	1520
Walters v. Comm.	1310
Walton v. Comm.	1551
Ware v. U.S.	1313
Watts, Est. of v. Comm.	1544
Weil v. Comm.	1316
Weil, Est. of	1544
Weiner v. Comm.	1315
Wells Fargo, U.S. v.	1523
Western Fed. Sav. & Loan Ass'n v. Comm.	1009
Wheeler v. Comm.	1501
Wildman v. Comm.	1194
Willcuts v. Bunn	1125
Williams v. Comm.	1218
Williams v. McGowan	1312
Williams v. U.S.	1196
Williford v. Comm.	1316
Wilson v. Bowers	1544
Winokur v. Comm.	1327
Winter v. Comm.	1310
Winthrop v. Meisels	1315
Wisconsin Cheesemen, Inc. v. U.S.	1306
Wong v. Comm.	1312
Woodbury v. Comm.	1322, 1323
Woodward Est. v. Comm.	1120
Wooley v. U.S.	1530
Wortmann, et al. v. Comm.	1318
Wrightsman v. U.S.	1310
Xerox Corp. v. U.S.	1268
Yankwich v. Comm.	1447
Yarbro v. Comm.	1232
Young v. Comm.	1032, 1447
Zinsmeister v. Comm.	1448
Zipkin v. U.S.	1429

NUMERICAL FINDING LIST

Revenue Ruling	Q		Q
154	1021	67-277	1501
189	1544	67-461	1312
54-65	1171	68-61	1139
54-135	1519	68-69	1316
54-251	1137	68-145	1142
54-399	1537	68-272	1537
54-554	1519	68-667	1339
55-87	1501	69-15	1012
55-278	1139, 1540	69-77	1269
55-389	1306	69-135	1105
55-540	1267	69-148	1524
55-655	1139	69-188	1309
55-749	1237	69-202	1009, 1012
56-86	1526	69-223	1194
56-211	1002	69-239	1327
56-406	1029, 1033	69-263	1099, 1102, 1125
56-452	1029	69-297	1430
56-484	1411	69-582	1309
56-511	1310	70-231	1030
56-602	1029	70-348	1502
56-653	1010	70-414	1248
57-49	1125	70-512	1536
57-244	1238	70-521	1003
57-293	1327	70-544	1146
57-366	1502	70-545	1146
57-421	1163, 1167	70-598	1417
58-2	1139	70-627	1015
58-175	1313	71-21	1418
58-210	1031	71-252	1251
58-211	1031	71-316	1029
58-234	1047, 1049, 1060, 1061	71-350	1010
58-275	1136	71-443	1530
58-279	1320, 1327	71-520	1029
58-435	1139	71-521	1049, 1058, 1059
58-536	1137	71-579	1251
58-576	1536	72-134	1129
59-9	1507	72-135	1194
59-32	1311, 1506	72-151	1237
59-60	1544, 1545	72-199	1017
59-229	1422	72-265	1105
59-357	1411, 1502, 1526, 1530	72-312	1104
59-418	1029	72-350	1194
60-17	1127	72-410	1164
60-37	1315	72-419	1327
60-124	1536	72-478	1021
60-177	1001, 1025	72-515	1237
60-195	1031	72-521	1024, 1025
60-210	1111, 1125	72-575	1129
60-284	1133	72-587	1125, 1128
61-55	1508	73-47	1507
62-21	1310	73-112	1125, 1134
62-127	1121	73-143	1501
63-27	1311, 1506	73-211	1251
64-89	1143	73-220	1155
64-104	1142, 1430	73-221	1155
64-302	1139	73-287	1526, 1530
64-324	1005	73-329	1029
66-7	1417	73-339	1339
66-216	1429	73-405	1530
67-276	1539	73-476	1237

	Q		Q
73-524	1028	78-413	1287
74-40	1204	79-42	1015
74-169	1146	79-73	1258
74-172	1128	79-143	1184, 1185, 1187
74-501	1011	79-204	1300
74-556	1502	79-272	1306
74-562	1002	79-300	1226
74-583	1339	79-340	1541
75-20	1160	79-353	1501
75-21	1160	79-372	1501
75-72	1525	79-409	1142
75-112	1134	79-432	1287
75-125	1430	80-61	1157
75-194	1210, 1340	80-71	1251
75-291	1237, 1238	80-143	1125
75-292	1237	80-157	1155
75-366	1508	80-235	1193, 1194
75-367	1508	80-255	1501
75-373	1339	80-292	1003
75-523	1310	80-342	1248
75-548	1015	81-7	1530
76-53	1015, 1016	81-51	1501
76-78	1129	81-63	1125
76-97	1156	81-148	1158
76-214	1184	81-153	1199
76-225	1337	81-163	1326
76-234	1536	81-182	1501
76-249	1188	81-229	1501
76-270	1330, 1331	81-253	1545
76-301	1237	81-266	1258
76-360	1530	81-283	1287
76-376	1339	82-10	1121, 1127
76-481	1429	82-27	1160
76-544	1532	82-59	1159, 1310
77-17	1032	82-96	1184
77-137	1206	82-98	1530
77-149	1015	82-123	1287
77-201	1029, 1031	82-156	1501
77-221	1536	82-163	1170
77-275	1532	82-166	1184
77-285	1328	82-198	1501
77-287	1537	83-30	1506, 1537
77-297	1238	83-42	1009
77-299	1522	83-45	1506
77-320	1300	83-108	1530
77-332	1206	83-151	1194
77-337	1237	83-180	1530
77-357	1429	84-10	1146
77-402	1211	84-14	1256
77-460	1502	84-25	1519
78-5	1101	84-61	1320
78-13	1248	84-118	1194
78-72	1237	84-121	1237
78-181	1065	84-128	1263
78-182	1047, 1049, 1050, 1051, 1052,	84-131	1190
	1053, 1054, 1055, 1056,	84-142	1255
	1057, 1058, 1059, 1060,	84-173	1410
	1062, 1063, 1064, 1066	85-32	1199, 1273
78-197	1322	85-49	1337
78-203	1430	85-87	1029
78-215	1524	85-113	1287
78-360	1543	86-17	1407
78-375	1015, 1016	86-41	1530

738

	Q		Q
86-138	1190	2002-69	1443
87-13	1443, 1445	2002-83	1238, 1422
87-22	1303	2003-7	1074, 1088
87-37	1532	2003-28	1316, 1327
87-102	1311	2003-56	1422
87-112	1139, 1447	2003-57	1429
87-115	1216	2003-58	1429
87-116	1123	2003-61	1506
88-10	1248	2003-72	1437
88-31	1078	2003-123	1339
88-37	1327	2004-15	1088
88-77	1194	2004-64	1518
89-7	1269, 1282	2005-30	1430
89-11	1273	2005-31	1162
89-51	1225, 1327	2005-68	1148
89-56	1248	2005-76	1236
89-90	1228, 1339	2006-34	1508
89-108	1205	2006-35	1407
90-34	1238	2006-49	1508, 1534
90-40	1220	2006-58	1148
90-45	1520	2007-2	1332
90-46	1408	2007-4	1408
90-93	1313		
90-103	1332	**Revenue Procedures**	**Q**
91-38	1227	66-49	1316, 1339
92-25	1258	66-50	1402
92-26	1510	72-18	1306
92-37	1257	74-8	1306
92-47	1430	75-21	1267
92-61	1227	79-24	1546
92-79	1227	81-40	1402
92-81	1332	83-35	1270, 1271, 1278
92-91	1303	85-46	1521
92-92	1293	87-53	1306
93-12	1545	87-56	1270, 1271, 1278, 1281, 1424
93-68	1304	87-57	1281, 1424
93-72	1429	89-15	1269, 1424
93-84	1094, 1096, 1103, 1111, 1125	89-20	1328
94-42	1129	89-21	1328
94-57	1227	89-46	1140
94-63	1068	89-64	1424
95-16	1304	90-22	1424
95-53	1170, 1303	90-32	1328
95-58	1501	91-7	1227
95-70	1125	91-30	1424
96-32	1303	92-3	1328
96-38	1332	92-12	1303
96-56	1519	92-43	1424
98-8	1518	92-67	1110
98-21	1519	92-101	1189
99-28	1429	93-35	1424
99-40	1401	94-27	1303
2000-12	1116	94-53	1424
2000-24	1429	94-57	1227
2000-43	1321	95-9	1424
2001-57	1239	95-27	1231
2002-19	1429	95-28	1227
2002-20	1330, 1331	96-15	1316, 1318, 1339
2002-22	1447	96-25	1424
2002-42	1106	97-20	1424
2002-44	1022	98-30	1424
2002-66	1078	98-48	1020
2002-67	1317	99-14	1424

	Q		Q
99-40	1162	8022048	1530
99-49	1110	8051033	1158
2000-15	1444	8118051	1530
2000-18	1424	8134135	1530
2000-30	1157	8141028	1248
2000-37	1238	8142008	1501, 1520
2001-12	1148, 1150	8145055	1327
2001-19	1424	8218037	1310
2001-21	1100, 1111, 1116, 1120	8248069	1339
2001-28	1267	8304040	1506
2002-9	1110, 1139, 1140, 1405	8313123	1339
2002-14	1424	8317010	1501
2002-19	1405	8339018	1506
2002-39	1402	8345067	1159
2002-50	1039	8350008	1220
2002-54	1405	8352086	1508
2003-39	1422	8404012	1194
2003-50	1424	8406006	1248
2003-53	1328	8413001	1183
2003-54	1328	8423008	1159
2003-55	1328	8429039	1237
2003-56	1328	8441012	1229
2003-57	1328	8441029	1508
2003-58	1328	8443054	1237
2003-59	1328	8444071	1040
2003-60	1328	8445004	1530
2003-61	1444	8445010	1237
2003-62	1402	8449025	1339
2003-75	1424	8451014	1508
2003-79	1402	8506089	1506
2003-85	1432	8516025	1429
2004-20	1424	8519009	1228
2004-30	1148	8524037	1508
2004-51	1238	8529026	1508
2004-60	1447	8541003	1125
2005-13	1424	8542034	1218
2005-14	1239	8601005	1508
2005-24	1328	8602006	1136
2005-52	1328	8636003	1194
2005-53	1328	8639019	1327
2005-54	1328	8641017	1339
2005-55	1328	8641037	1429
2005-56	1328	8717003	1530
2005-57	1328	8718001	1300
2005-58	1328	8723007	1518
2005-59	1328	8723073	1256
2005-70	1315	8726005	1518
2005-75	1319	8727003	1530
2006-3	1551	8728004	1248
2006-15	1328	8742025	1303
2006-18	1424	8743063	1303
2006-46	1402	8745003	1506
2006-53	1141, 1269, 1282, 1400, 1411,	8809085	1328
	1424, 1425, 1427, 1431, 1432,	8844062	1227
	1437, 1438, 1440, 1449	8849018	1321
		8906031	1303
Letter Rulings & TAMs	Q	8916032	1501
7834002	1248	8919009	1429
7837004	1248	8928010	1303
7842068	1525	8935013	1218
7924101	1248	8935051	1303
7927007	1287	8942018	1508
7928066	1015	8945006	1518

	Q		Q
8951072	1229	9441031	1551
9002014	1511	9442017	1331
9009053	1139	9506015	1331
9015049	1331	9507008	1430
9017008	1419	9511007	1331
9024016	1142, 1430	9511029	1331
9031046	1430	9514005	1218
9032016	1041	9516040	1331
9045002	1530	9517020	1331
9048050	1328	9525002	1237
9105006	1511	9532001	1530
9109026	1036	9534024	1218
9109033	1551	9541029	1510
9113009	1506, 1518	9543011	1237
9113026	1501	9548012	1218
9114023	1530	9549002	1304
9114025	1335	9603018	1339
9117035	1518	9607008	1501
9118040	1337	9610016	1218
9124031	1330	9611009	1218
9127005	1531	9619042	1331
9131052	1323	9619043	1331
9132021	1430	9619044	1331
9133016	1511	9621007	1508
9138024	1331	9625031	1530
9139001	1506	9628004	1530
9141008	1530	9707001	1551
9141018	1238	9710008	1331
9143030	1331	9710009	1331
9143053	1237	9710010	1331
9145019	1228	9711013	1331
9147049	1323	9717008	1551
9206001	1506	9723009	1552, 1553
9215013	1304	9725002	1552, 1553
9215049	1237	9729005	1501
9218012	1408	9730004	1552, 1553
9227017	1331	9731004	1530
9230003	1408	9735003	1552, 1553
9235026	1447	9736004	1552, 1553
9247024	1338	9736016	1339
9251033	1448	9741001	1551
9303007	1327	9741009	1501
9308021	1039	9748009	1337
9315005	1518	9751003	1530
9319005	1028	9801030	1040
9320016	1324	9807026	1171
9327006	1506	9809025	1040
9329017	1326	9810019	1337
9334020	1332	9810024	1040
9345027	1408	9818027	1331
9345035	1551	9821029	1331
9403005	1545	9825001	1331
9403030	1331, 1447	9825031	1324
9404023	1513, 1529	9826021	1331
9409018	1506, 1518	9826036	1405
9419012	1408	9828001	1316, 1321
9422002	1506	9829053	1315
9431025	1237	9833011	1323
9432001	1545	9837003	1218
9436005	1545	9839037	1438
9436006	1550, 1551	9842003	1552, 1553
9436017	1430	9845001	1331
9439007	1238	9845026	1430

	Q		Q
9849002	1040	200152018	1331
9851006	1331, 1447	200201007	1339
9851007	1331, 1447	200202034	1321
199905033	1303	200202078	1328
199908033	1518	200203033	1339
199915045	1331	200203034	1331
199915053	1324	200203042	1339
199919039	1328	200205008	1331
199920030	1148	200207005	1040
199920031	1162	200207026	1331
199925029	1324	200208019	1339
199925044	1078, 1079	200208039	1331
199929050	1315	200209020	1327
199930036	1337	200211016	1422
199941013	1530	200215032	1328
199941016	1171	200219012	1331
199952035	1335	200221042	1331, 1447
199952037	1339	200223013	1327
200002020	1339	200223014	1327
200002029	1331	200226039	1408
200003013	1315	200228001	1315
200004001	1315, 1321	200230039	1315
200007033	1040	200233022	1447
200014004	1518	200234017	1506
200018021	1239	200236001	1438
200023030	1430	200240012	1330, 1331
200025046	1171	200240049	1422
200029031	1328, 1331	200241013	1422
200032001	1148	200245048	1331
200033020	1304	200247001	1430
200035014	1331, 1447	200301020	1331, 1447
200037053	1333	200303010	1142, 1430
200038050	1328	200303013	1304
200041018	1430	200318017	1429
200045038	1331, 1447	200322005	1324
200052026	1331	200327029	1422
200104005	1239	200336020	1430
200108032	1338	200344010	1429
200108035	1331	200348020	1009, 1179
200109006	1331, 1447	200407018	1506
200112022	1324	200442003	1447
200112024	1324	200444021	1430
200112025	1324	200444026	1448
200116006	1518	200445023	1333
200117016	1331	200445024	1333
200120016	1331, 1447	200503004	1304
200122001	1009, 1179	200521003	1429
200122036	1518	200536014	1448
200122045	1331	200537019	1430
200124010	1331	200602034	1422
200124029	1337	200604004	1020
200127033	1331	200604033	1074, 1088
200130015	1405	200630004	1239
200139007	1130	200646003	1447
200140027	1331	299602002	1530
200141036	1448		
200142019	1315	**Miscellaneous**	**Q**
200143011	1339	GCM 37359	1248
200143028	1331, 1447	GCM 39036	1031
200146018	1304	GCM 39085	1248
200149005	1333	GCM 39126	1220
200149016	1337	GCM 39309	1128
200150039	1333	GCM 39482	1015

	Q		*Q*
GCM 39619	1248	Notice 2001-74	1269, 1281, 1424
Ann. 84-127	1263	Notice 2001-81	1413, 1414
Ann. 85-91	1079	Notice 2002-8	1315
Ann. 86-1	1318	Notice 2002-31	1447
Ann. 86-4	1318	Notice 2002-47	1037
Ann. 87-4	1293, 1306	Notice 2002-72	1402
Ann. 88-70	1411	Notice 2003-39	1337
Ann. 96-121	1149, 1150	Notice 2003-53	1412
Ann. 2003-49	1402	Notice 2003-67	1420
Ann. 2006-31	1017	Notice 2003-69	1420
Ann. 2006-68	1148	Notice 2003-71	1420
Ann. 2006-91	1017	Notice 2003-79	1420
Notice 87-15	1228	Notice 2004-7	1316
Notice 87-41	1148	Notice 2004-27	1427
Notice 87-67	1148	Notice 2004-39	1162
Notice 88-74	1303	Notice 2004-41	1339
Notice 88-75	1189, 1292	Notice 2004-67	1420
Notice 88-80	1227	Notice 2004-71	1420
Notice 88-91	1227	Notice 2005-31	1427
Notice 88-94	1294	Notice 2005-41	1316
Notice 88-114	1130	Notice 2005-44	1317
Notice 89-35	1304, 1305	Notice 2006-1	1317
Notice 89-36	1292	Notice 2006-3	1420
Notice 89-39	1246, 1289	Notice 2006-5	1309
Notice 90-7	1141	Notice 2006-9	1439
Notice 90-21	1231	Notice 2006-26	1439
Notice 93-11	1148	Notice 2006-29	1178
Notice 94-78	1331	Notice 2006-30	1178
Notice 94-84	1125	Notice 2006-53	1439
Notice 96-51	1107, 1108	Notice 2006-61	1258
Notice 97-52	1413	Notice 2006-62	1262
Notice 97-59	1420	Notice 2006-71	1439
Notice 97-60	1412, 1438	Notice 2006-72	1438
Notice 98-53	1443	Notice 2006-93	1123
Notice 99-31	1331	Notice 2006-96	1319
Notice 99-36	1315	Notice 2006-97	1148
Notice 2000-24	1315	Notice 2006-99	1151
Notice 2001-55	1413	Notice 2006-109	1333
Notice 2001-72	1037	Notice 2006-110	1318
Notice 2001-73	1037	Notice 2007-7	1341

TABLE OF IRC SECTIONS CITED

IRC Sec.	Q	IRC Sec.	Q
1	1191	24(f)	1437
1(a)	1434	25A	1436, 1438
1(e)	1218	25A(b)(1)	1438
1(f)	1432, 1433	25A(b)(2)	1438
1(f)(1)	1433	25A(b)(3)	1309, 1438
1(f)(2)	1433	25A(b)(4)	1438
1(f)(3)	1433	25A(c)	1438
1(f)(4)	1433	25A(c)(2)(A)	1438
1(f)(8)	1432	25A(d)	1438
1(g)	1411, 1432	25A(e)	1438
1(g)(1)	1411	25A(e)(2)	1412
1(g)(2)	1411	25A(f)(1)	1314, 1438
1(g)(4)	1411	25A(f)(2)	1309, 1438
1(g)(4)(A)(i)	1411	25A(g)(2)	1314, 1412, 1438
1(g)(7)	1411	25A(g)(3)	1438
1(g)(7)(B)	1411	25A(g)(5)	1438
1(h)	1162, 1186, 1187, 1408, 1420	25A(g)(6)	1438
1(h)(1)	1420	25A(h)	1433
1(h)(1)(C)	1420	25A(h)(1)	1438
1(h)(1)(D)	1420	25A(h)(2)	1438
1(h)(1)(E)	1420	25B	1436
1(h)(2)	1239, 1420	25C	1436
1(h)(3)	1420	25C(a)	1439
1(h)(4)	1420	25C(b)(1)	1439
1(h)(5)	1420	25C(b)(2)	1439
1(h)(6)	1420	25C(b)(3)	1439
1(h)(7)	1020, 1420	25C(c)(1)	1439
1(h)(9)	1239, 1335, 1420	25C(c)(2)	1439
1(h)(11)	1002, 1155, 1335	25C(d)(1)	1439
1(h)(11)(A)	1420	25C(d)(2)	1439
1(h)(11)(B)	1162, 1420	25C(d)(3)	1439
1(h)(11)(C)	1420	25C(g)	1439
1(h)(11)(C)(iii)	1420	25D	1436
1(h)(11)(C)(iv)	1420	25D(a)	1439
1(h)(11)(D)	1420	25D(b)	1439
1(h)(11)(D)(i)	1304, 1420	25D(b)(2)	1439
1(h)(11)(D)(iii)	1420	25D(c)	1439
1(i)(1)	1432	25D(d)	1439
1(i)(1)(B)	1432	25D(d)(3)	1439
1(i)(2)	1432	25D(g)	1439
2(a)	1434	26(a)	1436, 1440
2(b)	1435	26(b)	1262, 1440
2(b)(1)	1435	30B	1436
2(c)	1435	30B(a)	1439
2(d)	1435	30B(b)(1)	1439
21	1436	30B(b)(2)	1439
22	1436	30B(b)(3)	1439
23	1436	30B(c)(2)	1439
23(h)	1433	30B(c)(3)	1439
24	1436	30B(d)(2)(A)	1439
24(a)	1437	30B(d)(2)(B)	1439
24(b)(2)	1437	30B(d)(3)	1439
24(b)(3)	1437	30B(e)(1)	1439
24(c)(1)	1437	30B(e)(2)	1439
24(c)(2)	1437	30B(e)(3)	1439
24(d)	1437	30B(e)(4)(A)	1439
24(d)(1)	1437	30B(e)(4)(B)	1439
24(d)(1)(B)(i)	1437	30B(f)	1439
24(d)(3)	1437	30B(g)	1436
24(e)	1437	30B(g)(1)	1436

IRC Sec.	Q	IRC Sec.	Q
30C(d)(1)	1436	43(a)	1436
31(a)	1436	43(b)	1262
32	1436	43(c)(1)	1262
32(n)	1437	43(c)(2)	1262
35	1436	43(d)	1262
38	1228, 1408	44(a)	1436
38(b)	1262, 1436	45(a)	1436
38(b)(5)	1227	45A(a)	1436
38(c)	1262	45B(a)	1436
38(c)(1)	1262	45C(a)	1436
38(c)(5)	1262	45D(a)	1436
38(d)	1262	45E(a)	1436
39(a)	1262	45E(c)	1436
39(d)	1262	45F(a)	1436
40(a)	1436	45G(a)	1436
40A(a)	1436	45H(a)	1436
41(a)	1436	45I(a)	1436
42	1226, 1227	45J(a)	1436
42(a)	1436	45K(a)	1436
42(b)	1227	45K(d)(2)(C)	1262
42(b)(1)	1227	45L(a)	1436
42(b)(2)	1227	45M(a)	1436
42(c)	1227	46	1268, 1436
42(d)	1227	47(a)	1228
42(d)(1)	1227	47(a)(2)	1228
42(d)(2)(A)	1227	47(c)	1228
42(d)(2)(B)	1227	47(c)(1)(A)(ii)	1228
42(d)(2)(B)(iv)	1227	47(c)(1)(A)(iii)	1228
42(d)(2)(C)	1227	47(c)(1)(B)	1228
42(d)(2)(D)	1227	47(c)(1)(C)	1228
42(d)(2)(D)(ii)(V)	1227	47(c)(1)(C)(i)	1228
42(d)(3)	1227	47(c)(1)(C)(ii)	1228
42(d)(5)(A)	1227	47(c)(2)(A)	1228
42(d)(5)(C)	1227	47(c)(2)(B)	1228
42(d)(7)	1227	47(c)(2)(B)(i)	1228
42(e)	1227	47(c)(2)(B)(iv)	1228
42(e)(3)	1227	47(c)(2)(B)(vi)	1229
42(f)(1)	1227	47(c)(2)(C)	1228
42(f)(2)	1227	47(c)(3)	1228
42(f)(3)	1227	48	1268
42(f)(5)	1227	48(c)(1)	1439
42(g)(1)	1227	48(q)	1228
42(g)(2)	1227	48A)	1268
42(g)(2)(B)	1227	49(a)	1268
42(g)(2)(D)	1227	49(a)(1)	1227, 1228, 1285
42(g)(2)(D)(ii)	1227	49(a)(1)(D)(iv)	1287
42(g)(2)(E)	1227	49(a)(2)	1227, 1228, 1285
42(g)(3)(A)	1227	49(c)	1268
42(g)(3)(B)	1227	50(a)	1268
42(g)(5)	1227	50(a)(1)	1422
42(h)	1227	50(a)(1)(A)	1228
42(h)(1)	1227	50(a)(1)(B)	1228
42(h)(1)(E)	1227	50(a)(5)(B)	1447
42(h)(4)	1227	50(b)	1268, 1424
42(h)(4)(B)	1227	50(b)(1)	1268
42(h)(6)	1227	50(b)(2)	1228
42(j)	1227	50(c)	1229
42(j)(4)(F)	1227	50(c)(1)	1228, 1268, 1424
42(j)(5)	1227	50(c)(2)	1228, 1268, 1277
42(j)(6)	1227	50(c)(4)	1228, 1281, 1283
42(k)	1227	50(d)(1)	1268
42(l)	1227	50(d)(5)	1229, 1268
43	1262	51(a)	1436

IRC Sec.	Q	IRC Sec.	Q
52(a)	1150	68(b)	1427
52(b)	1150	68(c)	1427
53	1436, 1440	68(d)	1427
55(a)	1440	68(e)	1427
55(b)	1440	68(f)	1427
55(b)(2)	1440	71	1448
55(c)(1)	1440	71(a)	1448
55(d)	1440	71(b)	1448
56	1440	71(b)(1)(D)	1448
56(a)(1)	1226, 1284	71(b)(2)	1448
56(a)(1)(A)	1278	71(c)(1)	1448
56(a)(6)	1278, 1284	71(c)(2)	1448
56(b)(1)(F)	1427	71(c)(3)	1448
56(b)(3)	1037, 1039	71(f)	1448
57(a)	1440	71(f)(5)	1448
57(a)(1)	1263	72	1341, 1414, 1430
57(a)(2)	1263	72(b)	1412
57(a)(2)(B)	1263	72(e)(9)	1414
57(a)(2)(E)	1263	72(m)(7)	1412
57(a)(5)	1123	72(p)	1303
57(a)(5)(A)	1124	72(r)(1)	1410
57(a)(5)(B)	1124, 1169	72(t)	1443
57(a)(5)(C)	1124	83	1037, 1041
57(a)(6)	1278	83(a)	1037
57(a)(7)	1020, 1420	83(b)	1037
57(a)(12)	1278	86	1141, 1309, 1410
58	1284, 1440	86(a)(1)	1410
58(b)	1278	86(a)(2)	1410
59(a)(2)	1440	86(b)(2)	1410
59(d)	1169, 1180	86(b)(2)(B)	1123, 1410
59(e)	1251	86(c)(1)	1410
59(e)(5)	1251	86(c)(1)(C)(ii)	1410
59(e)(6)	1251, 1263	86(c)(2)	1410
59(j)	1440	86(e)	1410
61	1002, 1411	101(a)	1404
61(a)	1404	101(d)	1404
61(a)(12)	1406	102	1404
62	1313	103(a)	1123, 1130
62(a)(1)	1313, 1424, 1428	103(b)	1151, 1152
62(a)(2)(A)	1428	104(a)(1)	1404, 1410
62(a)(4)	1424	104(a)(4)	1404, 1410
62(a)(9)	1160	106(d)	1404
63	1431	108(a)	1406
63(c)	1400, 1431	108(c)(3)	1406
63(c)(4)	1431, 1433	108(d)(7)(A)	1218
63(c)(5)	1431, 1449	108(g)(2)	1406
63(c)(5)(B)	1426	119	1225
63(c)(6)	1431, 1449	121	1239
63(f)	1431	121(a)	1239
64	1223, 1224	121(b)	1239
66	1444	121(b)(2)(A)	1239
66(a)	1444	121(b)(2)(B)	1239
66(b)	1443	121(b)(3)	1239
66(c)	1444	121(c)(1)	1239
67	1310, 1313	121(c)(2)	1239
67(a)	1428, 1449	121(d)(2)	1239
67(b)	1428	121(d)(3)	1239
67(b)(8)	1024	121(d)(4)	1239
67(b)(11)	1120	121(d)(5)	1239
67(c)	1148, 1162, 1428	121(d)(7)	1239
67(c)(1)	1428	121(d)(8)	1239
67(e)	1449	121(d)(9)(A)	1239
68(a)	1427	121(d)(9)(B)	1239

IRC Sec.	Q	IRC Sec.	Q
121(d)(9)(C)	1239	163(e)(5)	1150
121(d)(9)(D)	1239	163(f)	1151
121(d)(10)	1239	163(f)(2)(A)(ii)	1151
121(f)	1239	163(f)(2)(C)	1151
127	1309	163(f)(3)	1151
135	1141, 1144, 1309, 1314, 1404	163(h)(1)	1302
135(a)	1141	163(h)(2)	1302
135(b)(1)	1141	163(h)(2)(F)	1302
135(b)(2)(B)	1433	163(h)(3)(A)	1303
135(c)	1141	163(h)(3)(B)	1303
135(c)(1)	1141	163(h)(3)(C)	1303
135(c)(2)(C)	1141	163(h)(3)(D)	1303
135(c)(4)	1141	163(h)(3)(E)(i)	1303
135(d)	1141	163(h)(3)(E)(ii)	1303
135(d)(2)	1141	163(h)(3)(E)(iii)	1303
137	1141, 1309, 1404	163(h)(3)(E)(iv)	1303
137(f)	1433	163(h)(4)(E)	1303
138	1404	163(h)(4)(F)	1303
139A	1404	163(h)(5)	1303
142(d)(4)(B)	1227	163(i)(1)(B)	1150
149	1151, 1152	163(k)	1508
149(a)(3)	1151	164	1223
149(b)	1130	164(a)	1220, 1427
149(b)(1)	1130	164(b)(5)(A)	1427
149(b)(2)(B)	1130	164(b)(5)(C)	1427
151	1400, 1425, 1426	164(b)(5)(D)	1427
151(b)	1434	164(b)(5)(F)	1427
151(d)(2)	1425, 1449	164(b)(5)(H)	1427
151(d)(3)	1425	164(b)(5)(I)	1427
151(d)(3)(E)	1425	164(c)	1220
151(d)(3)(F)	1425	164(d)	1220
151(d)(4)	1425, 1433	164(f)	1313, 1441, 1442
151(d)(4)(B)	1433	165	1233, 1273
151(e)	1425	165(a)	1032, 1116, 1427
152	1426	165(b)	1032
152(a)	1414, 1426	165(c)(1)	1421
152(b)(1)	1426	165(f)	1032
152(b)(2)	1426	165(g)	1032
152(b)(3)	1426	165(g)(1)	1032
152(c)	1426, 1435, 1437	165(h)	1239, 1427
152(e)	1426	165(h)(4)(E)	1427
152(f)(1)	1426, 1437	165(j)	1151, 1152
152(f)(1)(B)	1426, 1437	165(j)(1)	1152
152(f)(1)(C)	1426, 1437	165(j)(3)	1152
162	1223	167	1220, 1408
162(a)	1220, 1273	167(a)	1424
162(l)	1313	167(d)	1424
162(l)(2)(A)	1313	167(e)	1424
163	1223, 1303	167(f)	1424
163(a)	1303	167(f)(1)	1424
163(d)	1024, 1170, 1300, 1304, 1427	167(f)(2)	1424
163(d)(1)	1304	167(f)(3)	1424
163(d)(2)	1304	168	1220
163(d)(3)(A)	1304	168(a)	1424
163(d)(3)(C)	1025, 1304	168(b)	1269, 1281, 1424
163(d)(4)	1162, 1304	168(b)(3)(B)	1226
163(d)(4)(A)	1304	168(c)	1226, 1281, 1424
163(d)(4)(B)	1170, 1304, 1420	168(d)	1269, 1281, 1424
163(d)(4)(B)(i)	1304	168(e)	1424
163(d)(4)(B)(ii)	1304	168(e)(4)	1424
163(d)(4)(B)(iii)	1420	168(e)(4)(H)	1424
163(d)(4)(D)	1293	168(f)(1)	1424
163(d)(5)(A)(i)	1304	168(f)(2)	1271

IRC Sec.	Q	IRC Sec.	Q
168(f)(5)	1269, 1424	170(f)(8)(C)	1318, 1333
168(f)(5)(A)	1424	170(f)(8)(D)	1318
168(f)(5)(B)	1424	170(f)(11)	1318, 1319
168(g)	1281, 1424	170(f)(11)(A)(i)	1318
168(g)(1)(A)	1271	170(f)(11)(A)(ii)	1318
168(g)(1)(B)	1270	170(f)(11)(A)(ii)(I)	1317
168(g)(2)	1270, 1271	170(f)(11)(B)	1318
168(g)(2)(C)	1424	170(f)(11)(C)	1318
168(g)(3)	1270	170(f)(11)(D)	1318
168(g)(4)	1271	170(f)(11)(E)	1318, 1319
168(h)	1270	170(f)(11)(F)	1318
168(h)(1)(C)	1270	170(f)(11)(G)	1318
168(h)(1)(D)	1270	170(f)(11)(H)	1318
168(h)(2)	1270	170(f)(12)	1317
168(h)(2)(B)	1270	170(f)(12)(A)	1317
168(i)(3)(A)	1270	170(f)(12)(A)(i)	1317
168(k)(1)	1424	170(f)(12)(B)	1317
168(k)(2)(F)	1424	170(f)(12)(C)	1317
168(k)(4)	1424	170(f)(12)(D)	1317
168(k)(4)(D)	1424	170(f)(12)(E)	1317
170	1315, 1316, 1317, 1318,	170(f)(12)(F)	1317
	1321, 1325, 1330, 1339	170(f)(13)	1339
170(a)	1315, 1317	170(f)(14)	1339
170(a)(1)	1318, 1321	170(f)(16)	1316
170(a)(3)	1321, 1328, 1329, 1334	170(f)(17)	1318
170(a)(10)	1315	170(f)(18)	1333
170(b)	1341	170(g)(8)	1318
170(b)(1)(A)	1320	170(h)	1339
170(b)(1)(A)(ii)	1530	170(h)(2)	1339
170(b)(1)(A)(vi)	1333, 1339	170(h)(4)(B)	1339
170(b)(1)(A)(vii)	1324	170(h)(4)(C)	1339
170(b)(1)(B)	1320, 1324	170(j)	1320
170(b)(1)(C)	1320, 1322, 1323	170(l)	1315
170(b)(1)(C)(iii)	1322, 1323	170(m)	1316
170(b)(1)(D)	1320	170(o)	1327
170(b)(1)(D)(i)	1324	171	1120, 1121, 1122, 1126, 1127
170(b)(1)(D)(ii)	1320, 1324	171(a)	1120
170(b)(1)(E)	1320, 1324, 1339	171(b)	1121
170(b)(2)	1339	171(b)(1)	1122, 1127
170(c)	1333	171(b)(2)	1121
170(c)(3)	1333	171(b)(3)	1121, 1127
170(d)(1)	1320	171(b)(4)	1121, 1127
170(e)(1)	1322, 1323, 1325	171(b)(4)(B)	1121
170(e)(1)(A)	1322, 1323, 1324, 1325	171(c)(2)	1120
170(e)(1)(B)	1316, 1323, 1324, 1325	171(d)	1120
170(e)(1)(B)(i)	1323	171(e)	1120
170(e)(1)(B)(ii)	1324	172(b)(2)	1148
170(e)(2)	1325, 1334	172(d)(2)	1020
170(e)(5)	1324	179	1269, 1281, 1283, 1424
170(e)(5)(C)	1324	179(a)	1282
170(e)(7)	1323	179(b)	1424
170(f)(2)(A)	1329	179(b)(1)	1269, 1282
170(f)(2)(B)	1337	179(b)(2)	1269, 1282
170(f)(3)	1333	179(b)(3)	1269, 1282, 1424
170(f)(3)(A)	1327	179(b)(4)	1269, 1282, 1424
170(f)(3)(B)(i)	1327	179(d)(1)	1424
170(f)(3)(B)(ii)	1327	179(d)(2)	1227
170(f)(3)(B)(iii)	1327, 1339	179(d)(4)	1424
170(f)(5)	1326	179(d)(8)	1269, 1282
170(f)(5)(B)	1326	179(d)(9)	1424
170(f)(8)	1317, 1318	179(d)(10)	1269, 1282
170(f)(8)(A)	1318	179A	1436, 1439
170(f)(8)(B)	1318	183	1226, 1227, 1300

IRC Sec.	Q	IRC Sec.	Q
183(b)	1225, 1300	263(g)(2)	1079
183(b)(2)	1310	263(g)(4)(A)	1079
183(d)	1225, 1300	263(h)	1025, 1079
183(e)	1225, 1300	263(h)(1)	1025
195	1220, 1273	263(h)(4)	1025
195(b)(2)	1273	263(h)(5)	1025
196(a)	1262	263(i)	1249
196(b)	1262	263A	1220, 1223, 1226
196(c)	1262	263A(a)	1279, 1282
197(e)(3)(B)	1424	263A(b)(2)	1279
197(e)(4)	1424	263A(d)	1282
197(e)(6)	1424	263A(d)(1)	1279, 1282
212	1148, 1220, 1223, 1273,	263A(d)(1)(A)	1279
	1293, 1299, 1310, 1448	263A(f)	1220
212(3)	1312	264	1301
213	1427, 1429	265(1)	1506
213(c)	1429	265(a)(1)	1310, 1311
213(d)	1429, 1530	265(a)(2)	1024, 1178, 1306
213(d)(1)	1429	265(a)(4)	1170
213(d)(2)	1429	265(a)(5)	1024, 1025, 1306
213(d)(5)	1429	267	1039, 1301
213(d)(9)	1429	267(a)	1096, 1419
213(d)(9)(A)	1429	267(a)(1)	1419
215(a)	1448	267(a)(2)	1220
217	1423, 1427	267(b)	1088, 1150, 1189, 1287,
219	1309		1408, 1419, 1422, 1553
220(i)	1423	267(c)	1234, 1408, 1419
221	1309	267(c)(4)	1189
221(a)	1309	267(d)	1419
221(b)(1)	1309	267(e)	1220
221(b)(2)	1309	267(f)	1419
221(b)(2)(C)	1309	274	1313
221(c)	1309	274(h)(7)	1310
221(d)(1)	1309	274(n)(1)	1313
221(d)(2)	1309	275	1168
221(d)(3)	1309	280A	1225
221(e)	1309	280A(b)	1225
221(f)	1309	280A(d)(2)	1225
221(g)	1433	280A(d)(3)	1225
222	1309	280A(e)	1225
222(a)	1314	280A(f)(1)	1239
222(b)(2)(A)	1314	280A(g)	1225
222(b)(2)(B)	1314	280B	1231
222(b)(2)(C)	1314	280F(a)	1424
222(c)(1)	1314	280F(a)(2)	1424
222(c)(2)(A)	1314, 1438	280F(b)	1424
222(c)(2)(B)	1314, 1413	280F(b)(1)	1424
222(c)(3)	1314	280F(b)(2)	1424
222(d)(1)	1314	280F(d)(4)	1424
222(d)(2)	1314	280F(d)(5)(B)	1424
222(d)(3)(A)	1314	280F(d)(7)	1424
222(d)(3)(B)	1314	301	1009, 1179
222(d)(4)	1314	301(a)	1003
222(d)(6)	1314	301(b)	1003, 1163
222(e)	1314	301(c)	1002, 1014, 1167
223(f)(1)	1404	301(d)	1003
246(c)	1171, 1420	302	1012, 1218
246(c)(4)	1088	303	1218, 1501, 1506, 1508
248	1273	305	1009, 1171, 1179
263(a)	1220, 1273	305(a)	1008, 1009, 1013
263(c)	1249, 1251	305(b)	1009
263(g)	1078, 1079, 1080, 1086	305(d)	1008
263(g)(1)	1079	305(e)(1)	1007

IRC Sec.	Q	IRC Sec.	Q
305(e)(2)	1007	443(b)	1402
305(e)(3)	1007	443(c)	1402
305(e)(4)	1007	446	1121
305(e)(5)	1007	446(a)	1405
305(e)(6)	1007	446(c)	1405
307	1010	447(a)	1279, 1282
311(b)	1218	447(b)	1282
312(k)	1424	447(c)	1279, 1282
312(m)	1151	447(d)	1279, 1282
316	1014	447(h)	1279, 1282
316(a)	1001	448(a)	1279, 1282
317(a)	1001, 1003, 1004	448(a)(2)	1190
318(a)	1408	448(a)(3)	1190
318(a)(1)	1419	448(b)(3)	1190
331	1536	448(d)(3)	1190
351	1536	451(a)	1405
354	1017, 1415, 1536	453	1238, 1408
355	1536	453(a)	1408
358	1017, 1415	453(b)	1408
368(a)	1536	453(b)(2)(A)	1220, 1408
381	1218	453(b)(2)(B)	1205
382	1419	453(c)	1408
382(g)	1419	453(d)	1408
382(l)(3)(A)(i)	1419	453(e)	1408
401(a)	1303	453(f)	1088
403(b)	1309, 1341	453(f)(1)	1408
404(k)	1420	453(g)	1234, 1408
408(d)	1443	453(h)	1447
408(d)(1)	1341	453(i)	1408
408(d)(6)	1447	453(k)	1094, 1096, 1103, 1111, 1125
408(d)(8)	1341	453(l)(1)(B)	1220
408(d)(8)(D)	1341	453(l)(2)	1408
408(d)(8)(E)	1341	453A(b)	1408
408(m)(2)	1420	453A(c)	1408
421(a)	1037, 1038	453A(d)(1)	1408
421(b)	1039	453B(f)	1408
421(c)(1)	1037	453B(g)	1415, 1447
422	1041	454	1139
422(a)	1037	454(a)	1139
422(a)(1)	1039	454(b)	1093, 1132
422(b)	1036	457	1341
422(c)(2)	1039	461	1251
422(c)(3)	1037	461(a)	1405
422(c)(4)(A)	1036	461(g)	1301, 1303
422(c)(5)	1036	461(g)(1)	1220, 1272
422(c)(6)	1037	461(g)(2)	1303
422(d)	1036	461(h)	1251, 1272, 1279, 1282, 1405
424(c)	1037	461(h)(3)	1279, 1282
424(c)(4)	1037	461(i)	1251
424(h)	1040	461(i)(1)	1279, 1282
424(h)(1)	1040	461(i)(2)	1251
424(h)(3)	1040	461(i)(3)	1279, 1282
441	1402	461(i)(4)	1279, 1282
441(a)	1402	464	1279, 1282
441(b)	1402	464(c)	1279
441(b)(3)	1402	464(e)	1286
441(d)	1402	464(f)	1279, 1282
441(e)	1402	465	1200, 1246, 1288
441(f)(1)	1402	465(a)	1286
441(g)	1402	465(a)(1)	1274
441(i)	1402	465(a)(2)	1288
442	1402	465(b)	1246, 1287
443(a)	1402	465(b)(2)	1287

IRC Sec.	Q	IRC Sec.	Q
465(b)(3)	1287	469(k)(1)	1292, 1297
465(b)(3)(C)	1287	469(k)(3)	1297
465(b)(4)	1071, 1287	469(l)	1293
465(b)(6)	1287	470	1270
465(b)(6)(C)	1287	475(d)(3)(A)	1421
465(b)(6)(D)(i)	1287	475(f)(1)	1421
465(c)	1221, 1286, 1289	475(f)(1)(A)(i)	1421
465(c)(2)(A)	1246, 1289	475(f)(1)(D)	1421
465(c)(4)	1274	482	1195
465(e)	1290	483	1408, 1521
467(a)	1230, 1276	483(a)	1236
467(b)	1230	483(b)	1236
467(b)(1)	1230	483(d)(2)	1236
467(b)(5)	1230	483(e)	1236
467(c)	1230	483(e)(3)	1408
467(d)	1230, 1276	501	1408, 1419, 1422
467(e)(1)	1230	501(c)(3)	1323, 1333
467(e)(2)	1230	509(a)(1)	1333
467(e)(3)	1230	509(a)(2)	1339
467(e)(4)	1230	511	1413, 1449
469	1191, 1200, 1222, 1223, 1247,	529	1141, 1309, 1314, 1413
	1292, 1293, 1294, 1304, 1309	529(a)	1413
469(a)	1247, 1262, 1292, 1293	529(b)	1413
469(b)	1297	529(b)(1)	1413
469(c)	1223, 1293, 1310	529(b)(1)(A)	1413
469(c)(1)	1247	529(b)(3)	1413, 1414
469(c)(2)	1222, 1293	529(c)(2)	1527, 1528
469(c)(3)	1247, 1293	529(c)(3)(A)	1414
469(c)(4)	1247	529(c)(3)(B)	1414
469(c)(7)	1222, 1299	529(c)(3)(B)(v)	1413, 1438
469(c)(7)(C)	1299	529(c)(3)(B)(vi)	1413
469(d)(2)	1262, 1295	529(c)(3)(C)	1414
469(e)	1293	529(c)(3)(C)(iii)	1414
469(e)(1)	1304, 1310	529(c)(3)(D)	1414
469(e)(2)	1292	529(c)(4)	1503, 1504
469(f)	1298	529(c)(5)	1527
469(g)(1)	1297	529(c)(6)	1414
469(g)(1)(B)	1297	529(d)	1413
469(g)(2)	1297	529(d)(5)(B)	1528
469(g)(3)	1297	529(e)(1)	1414
469(h)(1)	1293	529(e)(2)	1414
469(h)(4)	1293	529(e)(3)	1412
469(h)(5)	1293	529(e)(3)(A)	1413
469(i)	1225, 1299	529(e)(3)(B)	1413
469(i)(1)	1299	529(e)(5)	1412, 1413
469(i)(3)(A)	1299	529(f)	1413
469(i)(3)(B)	1227, 1228, 1299	530	1309, 1314
469(i)(3)(D)	1227, 1299	530(a)	1412
469(i)(3)(F)	1299	530(b)	1412
469(i)(4)	1299	530(b)(1)	1412
469(i)(5)	1299	530(b)(1)(A)(iii)	1412
469(i)(6)	1299	530(b)(1)(C)	1412
469(i)(6)(B)	1299	530(b)(1)(D)	1412
469(i)(6)(B)(i)	1227	530(b)(1)(E)	1412
469(i)(6)(B)(ii)	1228	530(b)(2)	1412
469(j)(1)	1292	530(b)(4)	1412
469(j)(2)	1292	530(b)(5)	1412
469(j)(6)	1297	530(c)(1)	1412
469(j)(8)	1293	530(c)(2)	1412
469(j)(9)	1297	530(d)	1412
469(j)(10)	1222, 1225, 1293	530(d)(1)	1412
469(j)(12)	1297	530(d)(2)(A)	1412
469(k)	1227, 1228, 1292, 1299	530(d)(2)(B)	1412

IRC Sec.	Q	IRC Sec.	Q
530(d)(2)(C)	1412, 1438	664(b)(1)	1330, 1331, 1335
530(d)(2)(C)(ii)	1412	664(b)(2)	1335
530(d)(2)(D)	1412	664(b)(3)	1335
530(d)(3)	1503, 1527	664(b)(4)	1335
530(d)(4)	1412, 1414	664(c)	1331, 1335, 1336
530(d)(4)(B)	1414	664(c)(1)	1336
530(d)(4)(C)	1412	664(d)	1328, 1329, 1334
530(d)(5)	1412	664(d)(1)	1330
530(d)(6)	1412	664(d)(1)(A)	1330
530(d)(7)	1412	664(d)(1)(D)	1330
530(d)(8)	1412	664(d)(2)(A)	1331
530(e)	1412	664(d)(2)(C)	1331
530(g)	1412	664(d)(2)(D)	1331
543(a)	1506	664(d)(3)	1328
581	1506	664(d)(3)(A)	1331, 1335
591	1155, 1420	664(d)(3)(B)	1331
611	1255	664(d)(4)	1331
612	1257	664(f)	1330, 1331
613	1255	665	1449
613(a)	1255, 1258	665(b)	1411, 1449
613(b)	1256, 1258	665(c)	1449
613(b)(7)	1256	666	1449
613(e)	1258	671	1178, 1269
613A	1255	672(a)	1450
613A(b)	1256	672(c)	1450
613A(b)(1)	1258	673	1450
613A(b)(2)	1258	673(a)	1450
613A(c)	1256	673(b)	1450
613A(c)(1)	1258	674(a)	1450
613A(c)(2)	1258	674(b)	1450
613A(c)(3)	1258	674(b)(7)	1450
613A(c)(4)	1258	674(c)	1450
613A(c)(6)(C)	1258	674(d)	1450
613A(c)(6)(D)	1258	675	1450
613A(c)(6)(H)	1258	676	1450
613A(c)(7)	1258	677(a)	1450
613A(c)(7)(D)	1254, 1260	677(b)	1450
613A(c)(8)(C)	1258	682	1448
613A(c)(9)	1256	691(a)	1430
613A(c)(9)(A)	1256	691(c)	1430
613A(d)	1256	701	1190
613A(d)(1)	1258	702(a)	1190
613A(d)(2)	1256	702(b)	1190
613A(d)(3)	1256	703	1190
613A(d)(4)	1256	704	1196
613A(d)(5)	1259	704(a)	1195
614(a)	1255	704(b)	1195, 1217
641(a)	1449	704(c)	1194, 1195
641(c)	1218	704(d)	1200, 1245
642(b)	1449	705	1193
642(c)	1328, 1339, 1506	705(a)	1193, 1194
642(c)(5)	1332	705(a)(1)	1193
642(c)(5)(E)	1328	705(a)(1)(C)	1260
642(g)	1506	705(a)(2)	1193
643(b)	1331, 1332	705(a)(3)	1193, 1260
643(g)	1449	706(a)	1192, 1251
645	1449	706(b)	1402
651	1449	706(b)(2)	1402
652(a)	1449	706(c)	1203, 1209
661(a)(2)	1339, 1506	706(c)(2)(A)	1213
662(a)(1)	1335	706(c)(2)(B)	1203, 1209
664	1328, 1330, 1331, 1447	706(d)	1196, 1269
664(b)	1335	706(d)(2)	1196

IRC Sec.	Q	IRC Sec.	Q
706(d)(2)(D)	1196	854(b)(5)	1162
706(d)(3)	1196	855	1166
707(b)	1088, 1150, 1419	857(a)	1179
707(b)(1)	1189, 1287, 1422	857(b)(3)(A)	1179
707(c)	1550	857(b)(3)(B)	1179
709	1273	857(b)(3)(C)	1179
709(a)	1199	857(b)(3)(D)	1179
709(b)	1198	857(b)(3)(D)(iii)	1179
721(a)	1243	857(b)(7)	1181
722	1193	857(b)(8)	1179
731(a)	1201	857(c)	1179
731(a)(2)	1201	858(b)	1179
732	1189	860A	1147
733	1201	860B	1147, 1148
736	1208	860B(c)	1148
736(b)	1208	860C	1147
741	1205, 1340	860C(a)	1148
742	1212	860C(b)	1148
743	1216	860C(c)	1148
751	1205, 1210	860C(d)	1148
751(c)	1205	860C(e)	1148
751(d)	1205	860C(e)(2)	1148
751(f)	1205	860D	1147
752	1194, 1422	860D(a)	1148
752(a)	1193, 1422	860E	1148
752(b)	1193, 1197, 1201, 1422	860E(a)	1148
752(d)	1204	860E(a)(1)	1150
761(a)	1237, 1422	860E(a)(3)(A)	1148
771	1191	860E(e)(6)(A)	1148
772	1191	860F(a)(1)	1147
772(a)	1191	860F(d)	1148
772(a)(10)	1191	860F(d)(1)	1150
772(c)(2)	1250, 1251, 1254, 1263	860G	1148
772(f)	1250, 1251, 1254, 1263	860G(a)	1148
773	1191	860G(a)(1)	1148
773(c)	1191	860G(a)(2)	1148
774	1191	860G(a)(3)	1148
775	1191	860G(a)(7)	1148
776	1191	860H	1148, 1149, 1150
776(a)(2)	1258	860H(a)	1149
776(a)(3)	1260	860H(b)	1150
776(b)	1250, 1251, 1254, 1263	860H(c)	1150
851(a)	1189	860H(c)(2)	1150
852(b)(3)	1162	860I	1148, 1149, 1150
852(b)(3)(A)	1165	860I(a)	1150
852(b)(3)(B)	1162	860I(a)(1)	1150
852(b)(3)(C)	1162	860I(a)(2)	1150
852(b)(3)(D)	1165	860I(b)	1150
852(b)(3)(D)(iii)	1165	860I(c)	1150
852(b)(4)	1171	860I(d)	1150
852(b)(4)(B)	1171	860I(d)(1)(A)	1150
852(b)(4)(C)	1171	860I(d)(1)(B)	1150
852(b)(4)(D)	1171	860I(d)(2)	1150
852(b)(4)(E)	1171	860I(e)	1150
852(b)(5)	1162	860J	1148, 1149, 1150
852(b)(7)	1166	860J(a)	1150
852(f)	1171	860J(b)	1150
853	1168	860J(c)	1150
853(b)	1168	860K	1148, 1149, 1150
853(c)	1168	860K(a)	1150
854	1162, 1420	860K(c)	1150
854(b)(1)	1162	860L	1148, 1149, 1150
854(b)(2)	1162	860L(a)	1149

IRC Sec.	Q	IRC Sec.	Q
860L(a)(1)	1149, 1150	1031(f)(2)	1422
860L(a)(1)(D)	1149	1031(f)(3)	1422
860L(a)(2)	1149, 1150	1031(f)(4)	1422
860L(a)(C)	1150	1031(g)	1422
860L(b)(1)	1150	1031(h)(2)(A)	1422
860L(b)(1)(B)(ii)	1150	1033	1228, 1233, 1239
860L(b)(2)	1150	1036	1017
860L(c)	1149	1037(a)	1139
860L(d)	1150	1041	1094, 1096, 1103, 1111, 1136,
860L(e)	1149		1234, 1303, 1415, 1447
860L(e)(2)	1150	1041(a)(2)	1447
860L(e)(3)	1150	1041(b)	1447
860L(e)(3)(D)	1150	1041(c)	1019, 1447
860L(f)(1)	1150	1041(e)	1447
860L(g)	1150	1044	1018
871(k)	1162	1044(a)	1018
879(a)	1444	1044(a)(2)	1018
901	1436	1044(b)(1)	1018
904	1420	1044(b)(2)	1018
904(b)(2)(B)	1420	1044(c)(1)	1018
911	1309	1044(c)(3)	1018
911(d)(2)	1411	1044(c)(4)	1018
931	1309	1044(d)	1018
933	1309	1045	1020
936	1019, 1218	1045(a)	1020
1001	1017, 1125, 1171, 1181,	1045(b)(3)	1020
	1184, 1186, 1187, 1232,	1045(b)(4)	1020
	1233, 1277, 1420	1045(b)(5)	1020
1001(a)	1100, 1103	1059(c)	1420
1011(a)	1415	1091	1031, 1076, 1096
1011(b)	1325, 1340	1091(a)	1029, 1031, 1045, 1049
1012	1277, 1281, 1310, 1415	1091(b)	1030
1014	1430	1091(c)	1030
1014(a)	1216, 1415, 1424	1091(d)	1030, 1172
1014(b)(6)	1415	1091(e)	1022, 1029, 1073
1014(b)(9)	1415	1091(f)	1031
1014(b)(10)	1415	1092	1078, 1079, 1080, 1081, 1083
1014(c)	1415, 1430	1092(a)(1)	1079
1014(e)	1415	1092(a)(1)(B)	1079
1014(f)	1415	1092(a)(2)	1084
1015	1212, 1415	1092(a)(2)(A)	1084
1015(a)	1415	1092(a)(2)(A)(ii)	1082
1015(c)	1415	1092(a)(2)(B)	1082, 1084
1016	1415	1092(b)	1073, 1078
1016(a)	1277, 1281	1092(b)(1)	1079
1016(a)(2)	1424	1092(b)(2)	1082, 1083, 1084
1016(a)(5)	1100, 1120, 1126	1092(c)	1071, 1077, 1078, 1085
1022	1415, 1416	1092(c)(2)(B)	1071
1031	1184, 1187, 1237, 1238,	1092(c)(3)	1077
	1239, 1270, 1422	1092(c)(4)	1078
1031(a)	1017, 1237, 1238,	1092(c)(4)(A)(ii)	1078
	1239, 1339, 1422	1092(c)(4)(B)	1078
1031(a)(1)	1171	1092(c)(4)(C)	1078
1031(a)(2)	1237, 1422	1092(c)(4)(D)	1078
1031(a)(2)(B)	1171	1092(c)(4)(E)	1078
1031(a)(2)(D)	1205	1092(c)(4)(G)	1078
1031(a)(3)	1238, 1422	1092(c)(4)(H)	1078
1031(b)	1237, 1238, 1239, 1422	1092(d)(3)(A)	1078
1031(c)	1422	1092(d)(3)(B)(i)(II)	1073, 1078
1031(d)	1422	1092(d)(3)(B)(ii)	1078
1031(f)	1237	1092(d)(4)	1077
1031(f)(1)	1422	1092(f)	1078

IRC Sec.	Q	IRC Sec.	Q
1201(a)	1165, 1179	1233(h)(1)	1022, 1032, 1049,
1202	1017, 1018, 1019, 1020,		1057, 1060, 1062
	1335, 1420, 1440	1233(h)(2)	1022
1202(a)	1420	1234	1033, 1035
1202(a)(2)	1020	1234(a)	1035, 1048, 1050,
1202(b)	1020		1051, 1055, 1056
1202(b)(3)(B)	1020	1234(a)(2)	1035, 1052, 1057
1202(c)(1)	1019	1234(a)(3)(C)	1059
1202(c)(2)(B)	1019	1234(b)	1065, 1066
1202(c)(3)(A)	1019	1234(b)(1)	1062
1202(c)(3)(B)	1019	1234(c)(2)(B)	1043
1202(d)	1019	1234A(2)	1076
1202(e)(1)	1019	1234B	1073
1202(e)(3)	1019	1234B(a)	1073
1202(e)(4)	1019	1234B(b)	1021, 1022, 1073
1202(f)	1019	1234B(c)	1072
1202(g)	1020	1234B(d)	1021, 1072, 1073
1202(j)	1020	1237(a)	1224
1202(j)(1)	1020	1237(b)(3)	1224
1202(j)(2)	1020	1239(a)	1234
1211(b)	1420	1239(c)(2)	1234
1212	1335	1239(d)	1234
1212(b)	1420	1243	1032
1212(b)(1)(B)	1420	1244	1032
1212(c)	1076, 1083	1245	1228, 1277, 1283, 1286, 1424
1221	1017, 1094, 1183, 1416	1245(a)	1281
1221(a)	1223	1245(a)(2)(c)	1281, 1283
1221(a)(1)	1224, 1317	1245(a)(3)	1424
1222	1017, 1076, 1094, 1171, 1417	1245(a)(5)	1235
1222(3)	1078, 1340	1245(a)(5)(C)	1235
1222(11)	1420	1250	1226, 1335, 1408, 1420, 1424
1223	1017, 1171	1250(a)	1235, 1420
1223(2)	1101, 1417	1250(b)(1)	1235, 1335, 1420
1223(4)	1030	1250(c)	1408
1223(5)	1010, 1035	1254	1251, 1261
1223(15)	1020	1256	1072
1223(16)	1073	1256	1068, 1069, 1071, 1072, 1073,
1227	1079		1074, 1076, 1079, 1080,
1231	1189, 1190, 1200, 1205, 1218,		1081, 1082, 1083, 1420
	1219, 1223, 1224, 1233,	1256(a)	1076, 1080
	1235, 1240, 1245, 1277,	1256(a)(2)	1076, 1322
	1283, 1288, 1297, 1420	1256(a)(3)	1076
1231(a)	1233	1256(a)(4)	1080
1231(a)(1)	1233	1256(b)	1048, 1072, 1074, 1076
1231(a)(2)	1233	1256(b)(5)	1073
1231(a)(3)	1233	1256(c)	1076
1231(a)(3)(A)	1420	1256(c)(2)	1080
1231(b)	1233	1256(d)	1081
1231(b)(3)	1283	1256(e)	1076, 1093, 1095
1231(c)	1233	1256(f)	1076
1231(c)(3)	1420	1256(g)	1048, 1074
1233	1022, 1054, 1059, 1073, 1089	1256(g)(3)	1068
1233(b)	1021, 1049, 1054, 1055,	1256(g)(5)	1044
	1056, 1058, 1073, 1078	1256(g)(6)	1046, 1067, 1068, 1073
1233(b)(1)	1022	1256(g)(6)(B)	1046
1233(b)(2)	1022	1256(g)(7)	1068
1233(c)	1059	1258	1086, 1105
1233(d)	1022, 1078	1258(a)	1022, 1086
1233(e)(2)(D)	1021, 1023, 1073	1258(b)	1086
1233(e)(2)(E)	1021, 1073	1258(c)	1079, 1080, 1081,
1233(f)	1022, 1026		1083, 1084, 1085
1233(f)(3)	1023	1258(c)(2)	1063, 1066

IRC Sec.	Q	IRC Sec.	Q
1258(c)(2)(B)	1078	1271(a)(3)(E)	1094
1258(d)(1)	1078, 1085	1271(a)(4)	1095, 1096
1258(d)(2)	1086	1271(b)	1099
1258(d)(3)	1086	1271(c)	1100, 1103, 1117, 1119
1258(d)(3)(B)	1086	1271(c)(2)	1100, 1117, 1119
1258(d)(4)	1086	1272	1155
1258(d)(5)	1086	1272(a)	1102, 1116
1259	1020, 1021, 1022, 1023, 1028,	1272(a)(1)	1116
	1049, 1050, 1051, 1052, 1053,	1272(a)(2)	1093, 1095
	1054, 1055, 1056, 1057, 1058,	1272(a)(2)(C)	1155
	1065, 1066, 1069, 1071, 1073,	1272(a)(6)	1116, 1148, 1150
	1074, 1078, 1082, 1083,	1272(a)(6)(C)	1120
	1084, 1087, 1088, 1089	1272(b)	1102, 1118
1259(a)	1022, 1054, 1074	1272(b)(1)	1118
1259(a)(1)	1089	1272(b)(2)	1118
1259(a)(2)(A)	1089	1272(b)(4)	1118
1259(a)(2)(B)	1089	1272(d)	1099, 1100, 1118
1259(b)(1)	1022, 1054, 1087	1272(d)(2)	1103, 1116, 1118
1259(b)(2)(A)	1087	1273	1150
1259(b)(2)(B)	1068, 1069, 1074,	1273(a)	1096, 1099, 1116
	1076, 1080, 1087	1273(a)(3)	1102, 1117
1259(b)(2)(C)	1087	1273(b)	1150
1259(b)(3)	1087, 1089	1273(b)(3)	1116
1259(c)	1089	1274(b)	1236
1259(c)(1)	1089	1274(b)(3)(B)	1236
1259(c)(1)(A)	1022, 1054, 1088	1274(c)(2)	1236
1259(c)(1)(C)	1074, 1076, 1080	1274(c)(3)	1236
1259(c)(1)(D)	1022, 1087, 1088	1274(c)(4)	1236
1259(c)(1)(E)	1068, 1069, 1071,	1274(d)	1086, 1407, 1521
	1080, 1088, 1089	1274(d)(1)	1409
1259(c)(2)	1088	1274(d)(1)(D)	1407, 1409
1259(c)(3)	1022, 1088	1274(d)(2)	1409
1259(c)(3)(B)	1088	1274(d)(2)(B)	1408
1259(c)(4)	1088	1274(e)	1236, 1408
1259(d)(1)	1088	1274A(b)	1236
1259(d)(2)	1088	1274A(c)	1236
1259(e)(1)	1054, 1088	1274A(d)(2)	1236
1259(e)(2)	1087	1275(a)(1)	1149
1259(e)(3)	1054, 1088	1275(b)	1236
1260	1048, 1049, 1050, 1051,	1276	1100, 1111, 1112
	1052, 1053, 1065, 1066,	1276(a)	1125
	1074, 1090, 1091	1276(a)(3)	1102, 1110
1260(a)	1091	1276(b)	1110
1260(a)(1)	1091	1276(b)(2)	1110, 1111
1260(a)(2)	1091	1276(b)(3)	1102, 1110
1260(b)(1)	1091	1276(c)	1113, 1114
1260(b)(2)	1091	1276(d)(2)	1100
1260(b)(4)	1091	1277	1024, 1025, 1112, 1308
1260(c)(1)	1090	1277(a)	1115
1260(c)(2)	1090	1277(b)	1307
1260(d)(1)	1090	1277(b)(1)(A)	1308
1260(d)(2)	1090	1277(b)(2)	1113, 1308
1260(d)(3)	1090	1277(b)(2)(B)	1113
1260(d)(4)	1090	1277(c)	1307, 1308
1260(e)	1091	1277(d)	1111, 1113, 1308
1260(f)	1091	1278	1111, 1148
1260(g)	1090	1278(a)(1)	1109, 1125
1271	1132	1278(a)(1)(B)(i)	1096
1271(a)	1103	1278(a)(1)(C)	1113, 1115
1271(a)(2)	1103	1278(a)(1)(D)	1109
1271(a)(2)(B)	1100, 1117	1278(a)(2)	1109
1271(a)(3)	1094, 1132	1278(a)(2)(B)	1109
1271(a)(3)(A)	1096	1278(a)(2)(C)	1109

IRC Sec.	Q	IRC Sec.	Q
1278(b)	1102, 1110, 1111, 1112, 1113, 1114, 1308	1371(d)	1218
		1374	1218
1278(b)(3)	1110	1375(a)	1218
1278(b)(4)	1100, 1110	1375(b)(3)	1218
1281	1307	1375(b)(4)	1218
1281(a)	1093, 1095	1377(a)	1218
1281(a)(2)	1093, 1095	1378	1402
1281(b)	1093, 1095	1396(a)	1436
1281(b)(1)(F)	1095	1402(a)(13)	1202
1282	1024, 1025, 1079, 1307	2001	1500
1282(a)	1097, 1307	2001(e)	1501
1282(b)	1095	2001(f)	1500
1282(b)(2)	1093	2010	1507, 1508
1282(c)	1096, 1097, 1115, 1307	2011	1507
1283	1024, 1025	2011(b)	1507
1283(a)	1093	2011(b)(2)	1507
1283(b)(1)	1093	2011(g)	1507
1283(b)(2)	1093	2012	1507
1283(c)	1093, 1095, 1155	2012(a)	1507
1283(c)(2)	1095	2012(c)	1507
1283(d)	1093, 1094, 1095	2012(e)	1507
1286	1136	2013	1507
1286(a)	1137	2013(a)	1507
1286(c)	1137	2013(b)	1507
1286(d)	1138	2013(c)(1)	1507
1286(d)(1)(A)(ii)	1138	2013(c)(2)	1507
1286(d)(1)(C)	1138	2013(d)(3)	1507
1286(d)(2)	1138	2013(e)	1507
1286(e)(2)	1135, 1149	2014	1507
1286(e)(5)	1135	2031	1537
1287	1152	2031(b)	1545
1287(a)	1152	2031(c)	1505
1288(a)(2)	1125	2031(c)(1)	1505
1288(b)	1125	2031(c)(2)	1505
1288(b)(1)	1125	2031(c)(3)	1505
1361	1218	2031(c)(4)	1505
1361(b)(3)	1218	2031(c)(5)	1505
1361(c)(1)	1218	2031(c)(6)	1505
1361(c)(2)	1218	2031(c)(8)(A)(i)	1505
1361(c)(2)(B)(v)	1218	2031(c)(8)(A)(ii)	1505
1361(d)	1218	2031(c)(9)	1505
1361(e)	1218	2032	1028, 1536, 1542
1362	1218	2032(a)	1536
1362(d)(3)	1218	2032(d)	1536
1363	1218	2032A	1511, 1535
1363(a)	1218	2033	1501
1363(b)	1218	2034	1501
1363(d)	1218	2035	1501, 1511, 1550
1366(a)	1218	2035(a)	1501
1366(a)(1)	1218	2035(b)	1501
1366(b)	1218	2035(c)(1)	1501
1366(d)(1)	1218	2035(c)(2)	1501, 1508
1366(d)(2)	1218	2035(c)(3)	1501
1366(f)(3)	1218	2035(e)	1501
1367(a)(1)	1218	2036	1501, 1545
1367(a)(2)	1218	2036(a)	1501, 1511
1367(a)(2)(A)	1218	2037	1501
1367(b)	1430	2038	1501
1368(b)	1218	2038(a)(1)	1502
1368(c)	1218	2039	1501
1368(e)(3)	1218	2040	1501, 1520
1371(a)	1218	2040(a)	1501
1371(c)	1218	2040(b)	1501

IRC Sec.	Q	IRC Sec.	Q
2041	1501, 1502, 1506, 1535	2518(c)(3)	1501
2042	1501	2519	1518
2043	1501	2522(a)	1532
2043(a)	1501	2522(b)	1532
2044	1501, 1506, 1518, 1535	2522(c)	1532
2046	1501	2522(c)(2)	1532
2053	1430, 1506, 1508, 1511, 1538	2523(a)	1531
2053(a)(2)	1537	2523(b)	1531
2053(a)(3)	1506	2523(e)	1531
2053(c)(1)(D)	1508	2523(f)	1531
2054	1506, 1508	2523(f)(5)	1518
2055	1506	2523(f)(6)	1531
2055(a)	1506, 1510	2523(i)	1530, 1531
2055(b)	1506	2601	1509
2055(c)	1506	2602	1511
2055(e)(2)	1506	2603	1516
2055(e)(3)	1331, 1506	2604	1514
2055(f)	1505	2604(c)	1514
2056	1506	2611(a)	1510
2056(a)	1506	2611(b)	1510
2056(b)	1506	2612(a)	1510
2056(b)(1)	1506	2612(b)	1510
2056(b)(1)(C)	1506	2612(c)(2)	1510
2056(b)(2)	1506	2613	1510
2056(b)(3)	1506	2621	1511
2056(b)(4)	1506	2622	1511
2056(b)(5)	1506	2623	1511
2056(b)(7)	1506	2624	1511
2056(b)(7)(C)	1506	2632	1511
2056(b)(8)	1506	2632(b)	1511
2056(b)(10)	1506	2632(c)	1511
2056(c)	1506	2632(d)	1511
2056(d)	1501, 1506	2632(e)	1511
2056A	1506	2641	1511
2057	1506	2642	1511
2057(b)(1)(C)	1506	2642(a)	1511
2057(b)(1)(D)	1506	2642(a)(1)	1511
2057(b)(3)	1506	2642(a)(2)	1511
2057(c)	1506	2642(b)(2)(A)	1511
2057(e)(1)	1506	2642(c)	1511
2057(e)(2)	1506	2642(d)(2)	1511
2057(f)	1506	2642(e)	1511
2057(f)(1)	1506	2642(f)	1511
2057(j)	1506	2642(f)(4)	1511
2057(j)(1)	1506	2651(a)	1512
2058	1506	2651(b)	1512
2210	1500, 1506	2651(c)	1512
2501	1517	2651(d)	1512
2502(c)	1534	2651(e)	1512
2503(b)	1530	2652(a)(1)	1510
2503(c)	1526, 1530	2652(a)(2)	1513
2503(e)	1530, 1534	2652(a)(3)	1511
2505	1533	2652(c)(2)	1510
2505(c)	1533	2652(c)(3)	1510
2511	1518	2653(a)	1510
2512	1545	2654(a)(1)	1415
2513	1529, 1530, 1551	2654(a)(2)	1415, 1511
2513(a)(2)	1529	2654(b)	1511
2515	1535	2662	1515
2516	1518	2664	1509, 1510, 1511, 1514
2518(a)	1501	2701	1501, 1550, 1553
2518(b)	1501, 1520	2701(a)(1)	1550
2518(c)(2)	1501, 1520	2701(a)(2)	1550

IRC Sec.	Q	IRC Sec.	Q
2701(a)(3)(A)	1550	6034(a)	1328
2701(a)(3)(B)	1550	6049(b)	1123
2701(a)(3)(C)	1550	6050L	1316, 1318
2701(a)(4)	1550	6050L(a)	1323
2701(b)	1550	6050S	1438
2701(b)(2)	1550, 1553	6075	1534
2701(b)(2)(C)	1550	6075(a)	1508
2701(c)(1)	1550	6081(a)	1508
2701(c)(2)	1550	6104(b)	1328
2701(c)(3)	1550	6151(a)	1508, 1534
2701(d)	1550	6151(a)(1)	1508
2701(d)(2)(B)	1550	6159	1508
2701(d)(3)(A)	1550	6161(a)(1)	1508
2701(d)(3)(B)	1550	6161(a)(2)	1508
2701(d)(4)	1550	6163	1508
2701(d)(5)	1550	6166	1500, 1501, 1508
2701(e)(1)	1550	6166(a)	1508
2701(e)(2)	1550, 1551	6166(b)(1)	1508
2701(e)(3)	1550, 1553	6166(b)(2)	1508
2701(e)(5)	1550	6166(b)(4)	1508
2701(e)(6)	1550	6166(b)(6)	1508
2701(e)(7)	1550	6166(b)(7)	1508
2702	1551	6166(b)(8)	1508
2702(a)	1551	6166(b)(9)	1508
2702(a)(1)	1551	6166(c)	1508
2702(a)(2)(B)	1551	6166(g)(1)(A)	1508
2702(a)(3)(A)(ii)	1551	6166(g)(1)(B)	1508
2702(b)	1551	6166(g)(3)	1508
2702(c)(1)	1551	6324(b)	1534
2702(c)(2)	1551	6429	1437
2702(c)(4)	1551	6501(c)(9)	1517, 1535, 1550, 1551
2702(e)	1551	6503(b)	1422
2703	1537, 1544, 1552, 1553	6511(d)	1032
2704	1501, 1553	6511(d)(1)	1032
2704(a)	1553	6601	1302
2704(b)	1553	6601(a)	1508, 1534
2704(b)(1)	1553	6601(j)	1508
2704(b)(2)	1553	6621	1227
2704(b)(3)(A)	1553	6621(a)(2)	1401, 1508, 1534
2704(b)(3)(B)	1553	6621(b)	1086
2704(c)(1)	1553	6651(a)(1)	1534
2704(c)(2)	1553	6652(c)(2)(C)	1328
2704(c)(3)	1553	6654	1401
3101(b)	1441	6654(b)	1401
3121(u)	1441	6654(c)	1401
4701	1151	6654(d)(1)(A)	1401
4701(b)	1151	6654(d)(1)(B)	1401
4940	1331	6654(d)(1)(C)	1401
4941	1337	6654(d)(2)	1401
4945(g)(1)	1333	6654(d)(2)(B)(i)	1401
4958	1339	6654(e)	1401
4966	1333	6654(l)	1449
4973(e)	1412, 1413	6654(l)(2)(B)	1450
4973(e)(2)	1412	6655(g)(4)	1218
5011(a)	1436	6662	1427, 1535
6012(a)	1400	6662(a)	1319
6012(d)	1123, 1162	6662(b)(3)	1319
6013(a)	1434	6662(d)	1319
6015(e)	1444	6662(d)(2)(C)(ii)	1236, 1279
6017	1442	6662(e)(1)	1319
6018(a)	1508	6662(e)(1)(A)	1319
6019	1534	6662(h)(2)	1319
6034	1328	6662(h)(2)(A)(i)	1319

IRC Sec.	Q	IRC Sec.	Q
6664(c)(1)	1535	7704(c)(3)	1189
6664(c)(2)	1319	7704(d)(1)	1189
6695A	1319	7704(e)	1189
6720	1317	7704(f)	1189
6720B	1323	7704(g)	1189
6721	1318	7872	1304, 1407, 1521
7282	1521	7872(a)(1)	1407
7519	1190, 1218	7872(a)(2)	1407
7520	1330, 1331, 1332, 1334,	7872(b)(1)	1407, 1522
	1338, 1550, 1551	7872(c)(1)	1407
7701(a)(30)	1151	7872(c)(1)(B)	1407
7701(a)(42)	1415	7872(c)(1)(C)	1407
7701(a)(43)	1121, 1308	7872(c)(2)	1407
7701(a)(44)	1308	7872(c)(3)	1407
7701(g)	1232	7872(d)(1)	1407
7701(h)(1)	1267	7872(d)(1)(E)	1407
7701(h)(2)	1267	7872(d)(2)	1522
7701(h)(3)	1267	7872(e)	1407
7701(i)(1)	1147	7872(e)(2)	1407
7701(i)(2)	1147	7872(f)	1407
7703(b)	1435	7872(f)(2)(A)	1407
7704	1240	7872(f)(2)(B)	1407
7704(b)	1189	7872(f)(3)	1407
7704(c)(1)	1189	7872(f)(10)	1407

A

ACRS
cattle, breeding...1281
equipment leasing 1269, 1270, 1271
exceptions to
intangible property.....................................1424
property used outside U.S. 1271
recovery system 1424
tax-exempt use property...............................1270
AFR (see "Applicable federal rate")
Accrual method 1405
Adjusted gross income 1423
Adjusted tax basis 1415
Age of majority, by state...........................App. F
Alimony...1448
Alternate valuation, decedent's estate..........1536
Alternative minimum tax 1440
Amortization
bond premium (see "Premium, bond")
construction period interest
and taxes..1220, 1226
rehabilitation expenditures.................1226, 1228
Annual exclusion
generation-skipping transfer tax 1511
gift tax 1530
Applicable federal rate
deferred rent...1230
defined...1409
low interest loans 1407
seller financed loans......................................1236
Applicable imputed income amount
conversion transactions................................1086
Appreciated financial position
defined...1087
Arbitrage operations...........................1026, 1027
"At risk" limitation on losses 1285-1291
adjustments to "amount at risk"....................1287
aggregation of activities................................1289
"amount at risk" defined 1287
borrowed amounts...1287
carryover of disallowed "losses" 1288
cash contributions to covered
activity..1287
covered activities 1286
definition 1285
equipment leasing 1274
"losses" disallowed by limitation..................1288
multiple activities of one taxpayer................1289
negative "amount at risk"..............................1290
nonrecourse financing...................................1287
oil and gas investments.............1245, 1246, 1286
passive loss rule, coordination
with..1296
real estate 1220
tax basis in partnership interest
not affected by...1291
Automobile donations..................................1317

B

Bank deposits (see "Financial institutions")
Basis (see also specific investment property)
generally..1415
Below market loans
corporation-stockholder 1407
employer-employee.......................................1407
family members 1407
gift loans...1407, 1518
gift tax on 1518
seller financing...1236
Blockage discount..1537
Bonds
call privilege
effect on premium
amortization 1120, 1126
premium paid on call of tax
exempt bond..1126
conversion transactions (see "Conversion
Transactions")
convertible
basis of stock after conversion...................1105
conversion...1105
original issue discount...............................1106
premium..1122
sale of stock acquired on conversion
of market discount bond........................1114
corporate
interest...1102
donor, inclusion of accrued in
income....................................1104, 1112
original issue discount (see
"original issue discount",
below)
coupons separated from bond
(see "stripped", below)
defaulted..1133
"flat"...1133
gift of
corporate bond 1104
EE bonds...1139
market discount bond.................................1112
Ginnie Maes...1145
inflation-indexed
(see "Inflation-indexed bonds")
intention to call defined.....................1116, 1119
effect on original issue
discount 1103, 1116, 1119
market discount
borrowing to buy or carry,
interest deduction..........................1115, 1308
convertible bonds, sale of stock................1114
defined..1109
gift
donor, inclusion of accrued
discount in income 1112
sale of bond received as gift...................1113

Q

Bonds (cont'd)

market discount (cont'd)

    sale 1111

    short sales, proceeds used to

        buy or carry 1024, 1025, 1115

    tax straddle, bond part of 1077-1084, 1111

    when taxed 1110

municipal

    alternative minimum tax

        preference 1124, 1440

    guaranteed by U.S. 1130

    insured interest 1129

    interest 1123, 1132

    interest expense incurred to buy

        or carry, deduction 1131, 1306, 1311

    market discount 1111, 1125

    original issue discount 1125

    registration requirement 1151

    sale or redemption 1125

    substantial user 1124

    tax preference item 1124

    unregistered, effect of 1152

original issue discount

    corporate bonds

        issued after July 1, 1982 .... 1102, 1116

        issued before May 28, 1969,

           and after 1954 .... 1102, 1103, 1119

        issued before 1955 1103

        issued May 28, 1969-

           July 1, 1982 .... 1102, 1103, 1118

        retirement 1103

        sale 1103

    municipal bonds 1125

    Treasury bonds

        issued after July 1, 1982 1116

        issued before 1955 1100

        issued on or before July 1, 1982 1117

premium (see "Premium, bond")

registration requirement 1151, 1152

sale

    between interest dates 1100, 1103

    corporate bonds, of 1103

    market discount bonds 1111, 1113

    short-term obligations 1096

    tax-exempt 1125

    wash sale 1030

Savings, U.S.

    E/EE bonds 1139-1142

        child, owned by 1140

        decedent, owned by 1142

        education expenses, exclusion 1141

        exclusion of interest 1141

        interest 1139-1142

        original issue discount 1116

        sale 1142

        valuation 1540

        when interest reported 1139

    H/HH bonds, interest 1143

Q

Bonds (cont'd)

Savings, U.S. (cont'd)

    I bonds 1139, 1141, 1144

    Patriot Bonds 1139

short-term

    borrowing to buy or carry,

        deduction 1097, 1307

    current inclusion of acquisition

        discount 1095

    current inclusion of original issue

        discount 1095

    sale or redemption 1096

    short sales, proceeds used to buy

        or carry 1024, 1025

stripped bonds 1135-1138

    borrowing to buy or carry,

        deduction 1137, 1307, 1308

    taxable, sale or purchase 1137

    tax-exempt, sale or purchase 1138

    tax straddle, part of 1077-1084, 1103

tax-exempt (see "Municipal")

Treasury

    defined 1092, 1098

    holding period 1101

    interest 1099, 1100

    original issue discount (see

        "original issue discount"

        above)

    premium 1099

    redemption 1100

    sale 1100

    tax straddle, part of 1077-1084, 1100

Treasury inflation-protection

    securities 1107, 1108

valuation 1537, 1540

wash sales 1030

worthless 1032

zero coupon bonds 1134

Borrowing, deduction of interest

    (see "Interest expense deduction")

Business expenses, deduction 1313

Business interests, valuation of 1544

Butterfly spreads 1070

C

Call option (see "Options")

Call premium, municipal bond 1128

Call privilege (see "Bonds")

Capital asset, defined 1416

Capital gains and losses 1417, 1420

Car donations 1317

Cash basis method 1405

Cattle breeding

    alternative minimum tax 1284

    capital gains and losses 1280, 1283

    deductions

        depreciation 1281

        expenses 1282

Q

Cattle breeding (cont'd)
  deductions (cont'd)
    feed and supplies.......................................1282
  dispositions
    gain/loss on sale 1283
  forms of investment 1280
  investment credit recapture 1281
  sale 1283
  tax preference items 1284
Cattle feeding
  deductions
    accrual method 1279
    cash method 1279
  feed and supplies..1279
  gain/loss 1279
  sale 1279
  tax shelter...1279
Certificates of deposit 1154, 1155, 1158, 1160
Certified historic structures (see "Real estate")
Chapter 14 special valuation
  rules 1549-1553
Charitable contributions deduction
  acknowledgment required..............................1318
  appraisal required...1318
  appreciated property
    intangible...1322, 1324
    qualified appreciated stock.........................1324
    tangible..1323
  automobile donations 1317
  bargain sales..1325
  boat donations 1317
  conservation easements.................................1339
  donor advised funds 1333
  estate tax...1506
  facade easements...1339
  fair market value 1316
  flip unitrusts 1328, 1331
  generally..1315
  gift funds 1332
  gift tax 1532
  income interests 1337
  income "lead" trust 1337, 1338
  income tax deduction 1315
  intellectual property 1316
  liability, property subject to 1326
  limits on deduction......................................1315
  overvaluation, penalty for 1319
  partial interests 1327
  partnership interest
    contribution of..1340
  patents 1316
  penalty for overvaluation 1319
  percentage limits 1320
  pooled income fund......................................1329
  private foundations.............................1320, 1324
  qualified appreciated stock............................1324
  real estate, contribution of...................1322, 1324
  remainder interests 1329

Q

Charitable contributions deduction (cont'd)
  remainder trusts (see "Charitable
    Trusts")
  right to use property 1327
  stock, gifts of.....................................1322, 1324
  substantiation requirement..................1317, 1318
  tangible personal property.............................1323
  time of deduction 1321
  "to" or "for the use of"
    distinguished 1320
  valuation..1316
  verification 1318
Charitable trusts 1328-1336
  beneficiaries, taxation of
    payments to 1335
  calculation of deduction for
    gift to...1334
  charitable remainder annuity trust,
    (CRAT) defined..1330
  charitable remainder unitrust,
    (CRUT) defined 1331
  donor advised fund......................................1333
  flip unitrusts 1328, 1331
  generally..1328
  limitations on deduction...............................1329
    stock options, grant of..............................1321
  pooled income funds 1332
  special needs trust, CRT................................1331
  taxation of charitable trusts...........................1336
Child tax credit...1437
Children, custodial gifts
  and property
  (see "Uniform Gifts/Transfers to
  Minors Acts")
Children, unearned income of........................1411
Closed-end mutual funds..............................1175
Coins (see also, "Collectibles")
  as collectible...1185
  numismatic vs. bullion-type............................1185
  precious metal, as investment in 1166
  valuation...1543
    bullion, acquired in taxable
      transaction..1182
    estate tax..1543
    numismatic...1188
Collectibles
  coins and currencies as property...................1188
  definition 1185
  exchanges 1187
  sales of 1186
  transactions using "rare" coins.......................1188
Community property
  dividends from corporate stock,
    income taxation of....................................1445
  income taxation of investment
    income, effect on.....................................1443
  move from community property state
    to common law state 1446

Q

Community property (cont'd)
spouses living apart, reporting of
community income.......................................1444
stock redemptions, ...1443
income taxation of
Community trust...1332
Construction period interest and taxes
(see "Real estate")
Constructive receipt.....................................1405
Constructive sale of appreciated
financial position 1087-1089
closed transactions.......................................1088
definitions..1088
forward contract as...............................1074, 1088
future contract as...................................1074, 1088
identified straddles 1084
mixed straddles 1083
multiple positions..1088
nonequity option 1068, 1069, 1087
option purchase as...............................1050-1057,
1065-1067, 1087
purchase of put..........................1049, 1054, 1088
put option treatment as short sale.................1049
regulated futures contracts........1074, 1076, 1087
Section 1256 contracts..............1080, 1088-1089
short sale as 1022, 1087-1089
spread transaction as 1071
stock, application to sale of................1017, 1087
tax treatment of...1089
transition rules...1089
Conversion transactions
generally...1085
taxation of 1086
Convertible bonds (see "Bonds")
Corporation, S..1218
Coverdell Education Savings Account
(see "Education Savings Account")
Credit union deposits
(see "Financial institutions")
Credits against tax
alternative minimum tax 1440
child tax credit..1437
energy credits..1439
alternative motor vehicles credit................1439
nonbusiness energy property credit...........1439
residential energy efficient property
credit...1439
equipment leasing (see "Equipment
leasing")
estate tax..1507
general business credit 1262
gift tax 1533
Hope Scholarship Credit...............................1438
income tax, generally.....................................1436
Lifetime Learning Credit 1438
oil and gas (see "Oil and gas")
real estate (see "Real estate")
retirement savings credit..............................1436

Custodial gifts and property
(see "Uniform Gifts/Transfers to
Minors Acts")

D

Deductions
above the line...1423
below the line 1427
cattle
breeding (see "Cattle breeding")
feeding (see "Cattle feeding")
charitable
contributions.................1315-1340, 1506, 1532
education loan interest..................................1309
equipment leasing (see "Equipment
leasing")
estate tax...1506
expenses
business...1313
interest (see "Interest expenses
deduction")
management of property...........................1310
personal 1310
production of taxable income...................1310
production of tax-exempt
income...1311
tax advice...1312
gift tax 1531, 1532
higher education expenses 1314
income in respect of a decedent...................1430
itemized, generally..1427
medical expenses..1429
miscellaneous itemized 1428
oil and gas (see "Oil and gas")
real estate (see "Real estate")
sales tax...1427
standard deduction 1431
Deferred rent
equipment leasing..1276
real estate 1230
Demutualization 1417
Depreciation
alternative minimum tax...............................1440
cattle, breeding...1281
equipment leasing.....................1269-1271, 1277
generally 1424
real estate 1220
recapture..1235
Discharge of indebtedness 1406
Disclaimers..1520
Dividend reinvestment plans..............1015-1016
Dividends
assignment, gift, or sale of 1006
bonds and notes, payment in 1004
cash dividends..1002
credit union deposits
(see "Financial institutions")
dividend reinvestment plans 1015, 1016

Q

Dividends (cont'd)
extraordinary dividends 1025
fractional shares
cash or scrip in lieu of................................1012
generally 1001
includable in income, when 1002
mutual funds (see also
"Mutual funds")......................................1164
property, paid in...1003
qualified dividends.......... 1002, 1162, 1179, 1420
real estate investment (see "Real estate
investment trusts")
reinvestment plan 1015, 1016
return of capital 1014
savings and loan deposits
(see "Financial institutions")
short sale, reimbursement of..............1001, 1024
stock dividends
generally 1008
tax basis of stock received 1010
taxation of..1009
stock held in street name 1005
stock rights, payment in
rights of another corporation.....................1003
rights of distributing
corporation 1008, 1009
tax basis 1011
stripped preferred stock 1007
valuation, estate tax.......................................1537
warrants (see "Dividends, stock rights"
and "Stock, warrants")

Divorce
alimony..1448
property settlements 1447
stock redemptions..1447
transfers of property incident to 1415

Donor advised funds 1333

Durable power of attorney ....App. E

E

E/EE bonds (see "Bonds", "Savings,
U.S.")

Education savings account
estate tax...1503
gift tax 1527
income tax 1412

Elections
alternate valuation 1536
bond premium, amortization 1120
capital gain, net
investment income,
treated as......................................1162, 1420
child's income, inclusion on
parent's return...1411
electing large partnerships 1191
electing 1987 partnerships...........................1189

Q

Elections (cont'd)
interest on U.S. Savings bonds,
method of reporting...................................1139
installment sales..1408
investment income
net capital gain treated as..........................1420
low income housing, acceleration
of credit...1227
marital deduction (QDOT)..........................1506
marital deduction (QTIP) 1506, 1531
marital deduction (reverse QTIP) 1511
qualified conservation easement
exclusion..1505
qualified family-owned business
deduction...1506
qualified payments, valuation and
treatment of...1550
small business stock
rollover of gain into specialized
small business investment
companies 1018

Enhanced oil recovery credit....................1262

Equipment leasing
alternative minimum tax................................1278
at risk limitation 1274
credits (see "investment
tax credit")
deductions 1269-1275
depreciation 1269-1271
expenses...1273
interest...1272
deferred rent 1276
depreciation 1269-1271
alternative minimum tax............................1278
first year deduction 1269
property used outside the U.S...................1271
recapture 1277
tax-exempt use property 1270
dispositions..1268, 1277
expenses...1273
gain/loss on sale 1277
generally 1264, 1266
investment tax credit......................................1268
lease characterization.....................................1267
limited use property..1267
motor vehicle operating lease 1267
passive loss rule...1275
recapture 1268, 1277
depreciation 1277
investment tax credit...................................1268
sale of equipment...............................1268, 1277
gain/loss..1277
recapture of depreciation 1277
recapture of investment tax
credit..1268
stepped rental payments.................................1276
tax preference items..1278
wrap lease 1265

Q

Estate tax, federal
Chapter 14 special valuation
  rules 1549-1553
computation of tax..1500
credits 1507
custodial property 1502
deductions 1506
exclusions...1505
filing return..1508
general 1500
gross estate...1501
indexed amounts...............................App. B
marital deduction...1506
payment of tax 1508
repeal 1500
return 1508
tables ....App. B
tax rates...App. B
taxable estate..1500
unified credit...1507
Uniform Gifts/Transfers
  to Minors Acts,
    property transferred under 1502
valuation of property (see main entry)
what it is 1500
Estimated tax...1401
Exchange-traded funds 1176
Exchanges (see also type of property
  involved)
like-kind exchange.....................1237, 1238, 1422
Exclusions
estate tax...1505
gift tax 1530
income tax 1404
small business stock, qualified, gain
  from sale of...1019
Exemptions
dependency, requirements for 1426
generation-skipping transfer tax...................1511
personal and dependency,
  amount of...1425
Expenses, deduction (see "Deductions")

F

Fair market value...1535
FASITs
defined..1149
high-yield interest................................1149, 1150
ownership interest................................1149, 1150
regular interest.....................................1149, 1150
repeal 1149, 1150
taxation of interest in...................................1150
Federal estate tax
(see "Estate tax, federal")
Federal gift tax (see "Gift tax, federal")
Federal income tax, generally
(see "Income taxation")

Q

Federal rate, applicable
(see "Applicable federal rate")
Financial asset securitization
investment trust (FASIT)
(see "FASITs,"repeal of)
Financial institutions
certificates of deposit 1154, 1155, 1158, 1160
constructive receipt of interest.....................1155
deposits, forms of...1154
dividends on deposits.....................................1155
gifts received in connection with
  opening account...1157
interest, taxation of..1155
joint savings accounts 1156
minimum deposit, borrowing of...................1158
NOW accounts
  as savings deposit.......................................1154
  check writing fees..1159
original issue discount....................................1155
penalty, early withdrawal 1160
"Flat", bonds traded...1133
"Folios"...1161
Futures
conversion transactions (see
  "Conversion Transactions")
forward contracts..1074
generally 1074
marking-to-market
  generally 1075
  tax rule..1076
regulated futures contracts
  definition..1074
  taxation of..1076
Section 1256 contracts........................1076, 1077
straddles (see "Straddles")
variations margins..1075

G

Gain on sale
capital gain...1420
1231 gain...1233, 1277
Generation-skipping transfer tax
annual exclusion...1511
basis adjustment 1511
charitable lead annuity trust 1511
credit for state GST tax 1514
direct skip...1510
estate tax inclusion period (ETIP)................1511
exemption..1511
generally...1510-1516
generation assignments 1512
generation-skipping transfers.........................1510
inclusion ratio...1511
indexed amounts 1511
nontaxable gifts...1511
payment of 1516
predeceased parent rule......................1510, 1512

2007 Tax Facts on Investments

Q

Generation-skipping transfer tax (cont'd)
repeal..1510
returns, filing of...............................1515
reverse QTIP election 1511
separate trusts...................................1511
split gifts...1513
tables ....App. B
tax rates ....App. B
taxable amount..................................1511
taxable distribution............................1510
taxable termination............................1510
transferor...1510
valuation..1511
Gifts to minors
(see "Uniform Gifts/Transfers to
Minors Acts")
Gift tax, federal
annual exclusion 1530
Chapter 14 special valuation
rules 1549-1553
charitable contributions deduction 1532
completed gift, when 1519
computation of tax............................1517
custodianship gifts.............................1526
disclaimers 1520
donee pays gift tax 1525
exclusions...1530
filing return.......................................1534
gifts subject to tax
custodianship gifts.......................1526
forgiveness of debt 1522
generally 1518
government obligations 1523
joint ownership............................1524
Uniform Gifts/Transfers to Minors
Acts, gifts under......................1526
indexed amounts.........................App. B
marital deduction..............................1531
payment of tax 1534
qualified transfers..............................1530
return...1534
split-gifts 1529
tables ....App. B
tax rates..App. B
unified credit.....................................1533
Uniform Gifts/Transfers to Minors
Acts, gifts under..........................1526
valuation (see main entry)
what it is 1517
"Ginnie Mae" 1145, 1146
Gold (see "Precious metals")

H

H/HH bonds 1143, 1540
Head of household 1435
Hedge Funds 1177
Hobby loss rule.................................1300

Holding period
capital gains & losses 1417
incentive stock options 1037
demutualizations,
stock received in......................1417
Hope Scholarship Credit 1438

I

I bonds 1139, 1141, 1144
Identification of stock and securities..........1418
Imputed interest
below market loans 1407
no interest loans................................1407
seller financing..................................1236
Incentive stock options
defined...1036
disqualifying dispositions...................1039
extension of 1040
FICA/FUTA taxes..............................1037
holding period requirement 1037
charitable trust, early transfer to 1039
modification of 1040
qualifying transfer....................1037, 1038
requirements for 1036
stock appreciation right
granted with 1041
Income in respect of a decedent...............1430
Income taxation (see also specific
investment)
adjusted gross income 1423
alimony..1448
alternative minimum tax....................1440
applicable federal rate 1409
basis 1415
below market loans 1407
business expenses, deduction 1313
cancellation of debt (see "discharge of
indebtedness")
capital assets, definition 1416
capital gains and losses
holding period 1417
taxation of...................................1420
charitable contribution
deductions........................1315-1339
child, unearned income......................1411
community property 1444-1446
constructive receipt...........................1405
corporations, S...................................1218
credits 1436
custodial property 1411
deductions 1427-1431
dependency exemption 1425, 1426
depreciation, generally.......................1424
discharge of indebtedness 1406
divorce 1447, 1448
estates 1449
estimated tax......................................1401

Income taxation (cont'd)
exclusions
generally 1404
qualified tuition program
distributions...............................1413
savings bonds.................................1141
small business stock, sale of 1019
exemptions, amount of personal
and dependency................................1425
exemptions, requirements for
dependency 1426
expenses, deduction for
business..1313
higher education...............................1314
investment................................ 1310-1312
taxes, determination of.......................1312
filing requirements 1400
head of household 1435
holding period 1417
includable income 1404
income in respect of a decedent................1430
identification of stocks and
securities 1418
indexing.......................................1433
installment sales 1408
interest deduction........................ 1301-1308
interest-free loans............................1407
investment credit (see "Real estate",
"Equipment Leasing")
investment interest 1304
joint returns, who may file 1434
kiddie tax.....................................1411
like-kind exchanges
general rules..................................1422
real estate 1237, 1238
limited partnerships.................... 1190-1217
losses on related party sales 1419
medical expense deduction 1429
miscellaneous itemized deductions..............1428
mortgage interest deduction....................1303
points, deduction of...........................1303
railroad retirement benefits,
taxation of 1410
rates, individual..............................1432
related party sales............................1419
residence
gain on sale, exclusion of.....................1239
interest deduction 1303
returns, who must file.........................1400
self employment tax............................1442
short-term vs. long-term.......................1417
Social Security benefits, taxation of..........1410
Social Security tax rates......................1441
standard deduction 1431
tax, calculation of............................1403
tax preference items 1440
tax rates, individual..........................1432
taxable year 1402

Income taxation (cont'd)
trusts.....................................1449, 1450
Uniform Gifts/Transfers to
Minors Acts, income from
custodial property.............................1411
Inflation-indexed bonds
coupon discount bond method 1108
definition 1108
discount bond method...........................1108
Series I savings bonds.........................1144
Treasury Inflation-Protection
Securities 1107
Installment sales.........................1408
**Interest, equivalent tax-exempt
yield** ....App. G
Interest expense deduction
allocation of interest expense.................1305
categories, generally 1301
construction period............................1220
interest overcharge,
reimbursement of...............................1303
investment interest 1304
market discount bonds 1308
municipal bonds 1306
mutual funds...................................1170
partners.......................................1190
personal interest 1302
points...1304
prepaid..1304
qualified education loan interest 1309
qualified residence interest...................1304
related parties................................1220
self-charged interest 1293
short term obligations 1307
tracing rules..................................1305
Interest free loans..............1407, 1518, 1522
Investment credit (see "Real estate,"
"Equipment Leasing," "Cattle
breeding")
Investment interest........................1304

J

Joint ownership of property.............1501, 1524
Joint returns, who may file....................1434

K

Kiddie tax....................................1411

L

Lifetime learning credit......................1438
Like-kind exchange (see also type of
property involved)
generally......................................1422
real property.............................1237, 1238

Q

Limited partnerships

adjustment of partnership basis.....................1216
allocation of income, loss
  death, year of...1216
  "flip-flop"..1197
  gift, year of..1209
  nonrecourse deductions..............................1195
  retroactive 1196
  sale, year of...1203
  special 1195
anti-abuse rule...1217
basis
  decedent's estate or successor....................1215
  donee's 1212
  partner's 1193, 1194
  partnership's, adjustment of.......................1216
  purchaser's 1207
cash distribution to partner............................1201
cash liquidation of interest.............................1208
charitable gift of interest 1340
death of partner 1213, 1214
electing large partnerships 1191
electing 1987 partnerships 1189
gift of partnership
  interest....................................1209, 1210, 1340
grantor trust as holder of
  interest..1211
hedge funds, see "Hedge Funds"
income, reporting of
  decedent's estate or successor, by 1213
  donor of interest, by 1209
  generally...1190, 1191,
                            1192, 1196
  purchaser of interest, by.............................1206
  seller of interest, by....................................1203
liabilities of partnership
  basis of partners, included in 1194
  charitable gift, realized on..........................1210
  death, not realized on 1214
  decrease or increase, effect of....................1201
  gift, realized on 1210
  sale, realized on..1204
losses, limitation on deduction......................1200
note, contribution to.......................................1193
organization expenses, deduction 1198
publicly traded partnerships..........................1189
sale of partnership interest 1203-1206
self-employment tax on limited
  partner 1202
syndication expenses, deduction....................1199
tiered partnerships
  allocation to partners.................................1196
unrealized receivables.........................1205, 1337

Loans

below market (interest free)...........................1407
qualified education,
  deduction of interest...................................1309
seller financing; imputed interest..................1236

Q

Losses

capital..1420
hobby...1300
partnership...1200
passive.. 1292-1299
related party sales..1419
Low-income housing (see "Real estate")

M

Majority, age of, by state ....App. F
Marital deduction
estate tax..1506
gift tax..1531
Mark-to-market rules........................1075, 1076
Market discount, (see "Bonds")
Mid-term gain...1420
Minors, gifts/transfers to
(see "Uniform Gifts/Transfers to
Minors Acts")
Miscellaneous itemized deductions...............1428
Money market mutual funds..............1173, 1174
Mortgage backed securities.................1145, 1146
Mortgage participation certificates 1539
Mortgage pool, taxable 1147
Mortgages
interest deduction 1220, 1303
liability realized 1232
participation certificates, mortgage..............1539
points, deduction of.......................................1303
REITs 1179, 1180, 1181
REMICs 1147, 1148
securities, mortgage backed...............1145, 1146
Taxable Mortgage Pools................................1147
Municipal bonds (see "Bonds")
Mutual funds
alternative capital gains rate,
  corporate 1165
alternative minimum tax 1169
basis
  average basis methods...............................1171
  wash sales..1172
capital gains, undistributed 1165
closed-end funds 1175
defined...1161
dividends
  automatic reinvestment.............................1164
  exclusion from income..............................1162
  generally..1162
  prior year, declared for.............................1166
  qualified dividends 1162
  stock or securities issued in.......................1163
exchange-traded funds 1176
"Folios"...1161
foreign tax credit..1168
hedge funds, see "Hedge Funds"

Q

Mutual funds (cont'd)
interest
deduction of, loan used to
purchase shares 1170
exclusion from income...............................1162
miscellaneous itemized deductions,
passthrough 1162
money market funds.......................................1170
periodic payment plan
(see "Unit trusts")
reinvestment right, effect on basis 1171
return of capital..1167
sale, exchange, or redemption........................1171
tax-managed funds...1174
undistributed capital gains 1165
valuation, estate and gift tax 1542
wash sales...1172

N

Notes, Treasury..................................... 1098-1101
Notes, valuation of.......................................1539
NOW accounts (see "Financial
institutions")

O

Obligations (see "Bonds")
short term corporate 1103, 1116, 1118
Oil and gas
at risk limitation 1245, 1246, 1285-1291
credits, generally..1244
deductions, generally 1244
depletion.. 1252-1261
calculation, generally 1255
cost method
calculation..1257
eligibility...1255
definition 1252
eligibility, generally 1253
independent producers and
royalty owners..1256
limited partnership
calculation of allowance 1254
percentage method
advance royalties.....................................1259
calculation...1258
depletable oil/gas quantity 1258
effect on basis..1260
eligibility..1256
lease bonuses...1259
"proven" properties...................................1256
recapture..1261
tax preference item...................................1263
enhanced oil recovery credit 1262
forms of investment 1240, 1241

Q

Oil and gas (cont'd)
intangible drilling and development
costs... 1248-1251
amortization of...1251
deduction by partner 1251
definition 1248
election to deduct or
capitalize 1249-1251
effect on partners........................... 1250-1251
who makes election.................................1249
nonproductive wells 1249
partner's deduction.......................................1251
partner's election to amortize.....................1251
partnership's election 1249
prepaid costs...1251
recapture...1251
recovery through depletion or
depreciation..1250
tax preference item...........................1263, 1440
taxation of, generally 1249
limitations on deductions of losses 1245
limited partnership (see also
main entry)
as form of investment......................1240, 1241
calculation of depletion
allowance 1254
passive loss rule 1247
purchase of interest, taxation of...................1243
tax preference items 1263
types of drilling programs............................1242
valuation..1547
Options
butterfly spreads...1070
calls
capital asset 1048
closing sales of listed call 1051
definition 1047
exercise of...1053, 1063
lapse of..1052, 1062
purchase of...1049
sale of unlisted call......................................1050
cash settlement options 1043
Chapter 14 special valuation rule..................1552
classification...1044
combination of positions as possible
constructive sale under
Section 1259.............. 1050-1057, 1065-1067,
1087-1089
commissions paid to purchase put
or call 1049
commissions paid to sell put or call..............1061
conversion transaction, as part of.................1049
equity options...................................... 1046-1067
generally...1042
incentive stock options (see "Incentive
Stock Options")
listed vs. unlisted...1044
nonequity options...............................1068, 1069

2007 Tax Facts on Investments

Q

Options (cont'd)

premium paid to purchase put
  or call 1049

premium received for writing put
  or call 1060

put

  capital asset 1048
  closing purchase of listed put.....................1066
  closing sale of listed put.............................1056
  conversion transaction, as part of..............1049
  definition 1047
  exercise of......................................1058, 1064
  lapse of...1057, 1062
  married puts 1059
  premium, treatment of................................1060
  purchase, as short sale.....................1049, 1054
  purchase, generally 1049
  repurchase of unlisted put 1065
  sale of unlisted put 1055
  underlying stock, effect on.........................1054

qualified covered call options 1078
spread transactions.............................. 1070-1071
straddles (see "Straddles")
wash sales...1045

Original issue discount

certificates of deposit 1155
convertible bonds (see "Bonds")
corporate bonds (see "Bonds"
  "original issue discount")
municipal bonds (see "Bonds"
  "municipal")
Savings, U.S. (see "Bonds" "Savings,
  "U.S.")
Treasury bills (see "Treasury bills")
Treasury notes and bonds
  (see "Bonds" "Treasury")

P

Partnerships (see "Limited partnerships")

Passive loss rule

"active participation" 1299
activity, defined 1294
"at risk"...1296
carryovers...1297
credit limitations 1292, 1295, 1297, 1299
dispositions 1297
electing large partnerships 1191
former passive activities 1298
general...1292
limitations on loss deductions,
  coordination with other 1296
low-income housing credit...........................1299
"material participation".................................1293
passive activity, defined 1293
publicly traded partnerships.............1292, 1299
rehabilitation tax credit 1299
rental real estate 1299

Q

Platinum (see "Precious metals")

Points, deduction of on refinancing 1303

Pooled income funds

charitable deductions 1329
community trusts...1332
defined...1332

Powers of appointment 1501

Precious metals

bullion vs. numismatic coins............... 1184, 1185
conversion transactions (see
  "Conversion Transactions")
exchange of...1184
investment in..1182
sale of..1183
valuation of (silver coins) 1543

Premium, bond

amortization 1120
  acquisition premium, original issue
    discount bond............................... 1116, 1118
basis, reduction for municipal
  bonds..1125
convertible bond..1122
corporate bonds................................... 1102, 1103
deduction
  taxable bonds 1120
  tax-exempt bonds 1126
gift, acquired as......................... 1100, 1103, 1117
paid on call before maturity 1128
taxable bonds
  determination of amount
    amortized...1121
  election to amortize....................................1120
tax-exempts
  amortization required 1126
  determination of amount
    amortized...1127
Treasury bonds and notes...................1099, 1100

**Premium paid on call of municipal
bond**..1128

Profit motive 1300

Publicly traded partnerships 1189

Put options (see "Options")

Q

Qualified dividends 1002, 1162, 1179, 1420
Qualified higher education expenses 1314
Qualified tuition programs
estate tax...1504
gift tax 1528
income tax..1413
  general..1413, 1414

R

Rates

estate tax..App. B
generation-skipping transfer ....App. B

Q

Rates (cont'd)
gift tax .... App. B
income tax, individuals 1432
income tax, trusts and estates................... App. A
Social Security 1441
Real estate
at risk limitation 1221
capital gains and losses 1233
casualty and theft losses 1233
certified historic structures
demolition 1231
investment credit....................................1228
lessee 1229
rehabs 1228
construction period interest and
low income housing 1226, 1227
taxes 1220
deductions
depreciation...................................1220, 1424
expenses 1220
improvements...1220
interest..1220
repairs and maintenance..............................1220
taxes 1220
depreciation....................................1220, 1424
ACRS 1424
recapture..1235
development/subdivision 1224
dispositions 1220
gain/loss on sale 1233
exchanges
fourth party intermediary 1238
general rules 1422
non-simultaneous 1238
option, effect of...1237
qualifying property....................................1237
qualifying transactions..............................1238
three party exchanges................................1238
gain/loss 1220-1224, 1233-1234
installment sale..1408
investment credit...............................1228, 1229
basis reduction 1228
lessee's qualification 1229
recapture..1228
involuntary conversion................................1233
like-kind exchanges (see "exchanges", above)
low-income housing.........................1226, 1227
mortgages
interest deduction.............................1220, 1303
liability realized 1233
participation certificates,
mortgage 1539
points, deduction of...................................1303
REITs 1179, 1180, 1181
REMICs 1147, 1148
securities, mortgage backed............. 1145, 1146
Taxable Mortgage Pools..........................1147
points, deduction of.....................................1303

Real estate (cont'd)
principal residence
gain on sale, exclusion of..........................1239
recapture...1220, 1235
recovery property 1235, 1424
rehabilitation expenditures
certified historic structures................1228
low income housing 1226
old buildings...1228
REITs 1179, 1180, 1181
alternative minimum tax 1180
dividends... 1179, 1180
shares, disposal of 1181
related persons 1233, 1234, 1419
definition 1234
effect of divorce 1234
expenses payable to..................................1220
installment sales between..........................1234
sale of property to 1234, 1419
REMICs 1147, 1148
Taxable Mortgage Pool 1147
rent, stepped or deferred 1230
residence
gain on sale, exclusion of..........................1239
sale 1232-1236
gain/loss 1233
mortgage liability realized 1233
related person, to.......................................1234
sale, exchange, redemption 1181
"start-up" expenses 1220
tax credits 1227, 1228
investment..1228
low-income housing.................................1227
recapture...1228
rehabs 1228
tax shelter 1219
Taxable Mortgage Pool 1147
taxes 1220
trade or business..1220
gains/losses...1233
vacant land 1223, 1224
dealer..1224
deductions 1223
development/subdivision 1224
vacation homes...1225
valuation of (estate and gift tax) 1546
alternative minimum tax 1180
beneficiary, taxation of...............................1179
dividends..1181
Real estate investment trusts
(REITs) 1179, 1180, 1181
alternative minimum tax 1180
dividends... 1179, 1180
qualified dividends 1179
shares, disposal of 1181
Real estate mortgage investment
conduits (REMICs) 1147, 1148
Taxable Mortgage Pool 1147

Q

Recapture
cattle, breeding....................................1281, 1283
Ch. 14 special valuation rules 1550
equipment leasing 1268, 1277
oil and gas 1251, 1261
real estate 1220, 1235
Registration requirement for
bonds...1151, 1152
Regulated futures (see "Futures")
Regulated investment companies
(see "Mutual funds")
Related party
Ch. 14 special valuation rules 1549-1553
depreciable property, gain or loss 1234
expenses payable to...1220
installment sales 1408
like-kind exchanges 1237, 1422
real estate (see "Real estate")
sale to
effect on passive loss.................................1297
gain on...1234
loss on 1234, 1419
REMICs
defined..1147
taxable mortgage pool.....................................1147
taxation of interest in 1148
Residence
gain on sale, exclusion of..............................1239
interest deduction 1303
personal residence trust.................................1551
prepaid points, deduction 1303
qualified personal residence trust.................1551
Rollover
specialized small business investment
company stock, rollover of gain into 1018

S

S Corporation...1218
Sale-leaseback
seller financed 1236
Sales tax deduction...1427
Savings and loan deposits
(see "Financial institutions")
Savings bonds (see "Bonds")
Savings certificates, estate tax
valuation of 1541
"Section 1231"
cattle, breeding...1283
equipment leasing 1277
real estate 1233
"Section 1202" gain............................1020, 1420
"Section 1256" contracts 1076, 1077
Securities futures contract..................1072, 1073
Self-employment tax 1442
Series EE Savings Bonds (see "Bonds")
Short sales of stock (see "Stock")
Silver (see "Precious metals")

Q

Small business stock
exclusion for gain from sale of 1020
rollover of gain...1018
Section 1202 stock 1019, 1020
short sales..1022
Social Security
tax rates 1441
taxation of benefits...1410
Specialized small business investment
company
rollover of gain from sale of
stock into..1018
Split gifts
generation-skipping transfer tax 1513
gift tax 1529
Spouses
community property...........................1443-1446
divorce...1447, 1448
joint return..1400
losses on sales between..................................1419
transfers incident to divorce.........................1447
Spread transactions..............................1070-1071
Stamps (see "Collectibles")
Standard deduction...1431
"Stepped" rent
equipment..1276
real estate 1230
Stock
arbitrage operations...........................1026, 1027
bond conversion, acquired on 1105
closely held corporation,
valuation of 1545
constructive sale of 1087-1089
conversion transactions...................... 1085-1086
distributions with respect to..........................1001
dividends (see "Dividends")
exchange or sale..1017
"Folios"...1161
identification of...1418
incentive stock options (see "Incentive
Stock Options")
options, puts and calls (see "Options")
puts and calls (see "Options")
qualified covered call writing.......................1078
qualified dividends (see "Dividends")
qualified small business stock
exclusion for gain from sale of 1019
return of capital...1014
sale or exchange..1017
short sales
arbitrage operations...........................1026, 1027
as appreciated financial position 1087
as constructive sale 1088, 1089
completed by estate......................................1028
completed by trust..1028
conversion transactions...............................1022
defined..1021
generally...1021

Q

Stock (cont'd)

short sales (cont'd)

holding period, effect on 1022

premium, deduction of................................1024

proceeds used to buy or carry market
discount bonds 1024

proceeds used to buy or carry short
term obligations 1024

proceeds used to buy or carry tax
exempt obligations 1024

purchase of put as.......................................1049

qualified small business stock....................1022

reimbursement of dividends..............1001, 1024

Section 1259 consequences..............1022, 1089

short against the box 1021

substantially identical property..................1022

taxation of 1022, 1024, 1027

worthlessness, effect of..............................1032

specialized small business
investment company 1018

splits...1013

straddles (see "Straddles")

stripped preferred stock.................................1007

substantially identical....................................1023

valuation (estate and gift tax)........................1537

warrants

acquisition 1033

generally..1033

sale, exercise, or lapse...............................1035

tax basis...1034

wash sales

generally..1029

options...1045

short sales..1022

substantially identical stock and
securities 1031

taxation of 1030

worthless stock and securities........................1032

Straddles

"applicable" straddles, definition of...............1085

conversion transactions (see
"Conversion Transactions")

definition 1077

generally..1077

"identified" straddles.....................................1084

loss deferral rule..1079

mixed straddles 1081

property subject to...1077

qualified covered calls...................................1078

"Section 1256" contracts...........1076, 1077, 1080

short sale rules...1079

stock..1078

taxation

"applicable" straddles 1086

generally..1079

"identified" straddles.................................1084

mixed straddles 1081-1083

"Section 1256" contracts...........................1080

Q

Straddles (cont'd)

wash sale rules 1079

Substantially identical property 1023, 1031

T

Taxable mortgage pool...................................1147

Taxable year..1402

Tax-exempt bonds (see "Bonds"
"municipal")

Tax-exempt equivalent interest.................App. G

Tax preference items 1440

Tax rates

estate tax...App. B

generation-skipping transfer ....App. B

gift tax ....App. B

income tax, individuals 1432

income tax, trusts and estates....................App. A

Social Security 1441

Transfers to minors
(see "Uniform Gifts/Transfers to
Minors Acts")

Treasury bills

acquisition discount 1168

mandatory inclusion currently 1168

borrowing to buy or carry,
deduction..1168, 1307

capital asset, as..1094

defined 1092

gain or loss 1094

maturity 1094

original issue discount......................1093, 1094

sale 1094

when interest taxed 1093

Treasury inflation-protection securities

defined 1107

taxation of 1108

Treasury notes and bonds (see "Bonds")

Trusts

Chapter 14 special valuation rules 1551

charitable lead trusts 1337-1338

charitable remainder trusts.................1328-1336

annuity trusts 1330

beneficiaries, taxation of
payments to 1335

calculation of deduction for
gift to...1334

flip unitrusts 1331

generally...1328

limitations on deduction.............................1329

pooled income funds 1332

special needs trust, CRT..............................1331

taxation of charitable trusts........................1336

unitrusts..1331

grantor trusts 1450

income tax...1449

income tax rates for.....................................App. A

personal residence trust................................1551